How to use your Connected Casebook

Step 1: Go to **www.CasebookConnect.com** and redeem your access code to get started.

Access Code:

Step 2: Go to your **BOOKSHELF** and select your Connected Casebook to start reading, highlighting, and taking notes in the margins of your e-book.

Step 3: Select the **STUDY** tab in your toolbar to access a variety of practice materials designed to help you master the course material. These materials may include explanations, videos, multiple-choice questions, flashcards, short answer, essays, and issue spotting.

Step 4: Select the **OUTLINE** tab in your toolbar to access chapter outlines that automatically incorporate your highlights and annotations from the e-book. Use the My Notes area for copying, pasting, and editing your book notes or creating new notes.

Step 5: If your professor has enrolled your class, you can select the **CLASS INSIGHTS** tab and compare your own study center results against the average of your classmates.

Is this a used casebook? Access code already scratched off?

You can purchase the Digital Version and still access all of the powerful tools listed above.
Please visit CasebookConnect.com and select Catalog to learn more.

Your Connected Quizzing Access Code
Improve your learning outcomes through formative assessments with powerful reporting.
CasebookConnect.com/CQ

PLEASE NOTE: ... code can only be used once. This access code will expire one year after the discontinuation of the ... must be redeemed before then. CCH reserves the right to discontinue this program at any time for any ... details, please see the Casebook Connect End User Agreement.

PIN: 9111149721 GBsOr2   18854

Scratch off with care.

Please note, after redeeming your access code, you will also be required to enter a **Class Code** provided by your professor.

10073145-0001

Business Organizations

Business Organizations

Second Edition

Theresa A. Gabaldon
Lyle T. Alverson Professor of Law
The George Washington University Law School

Christopher L. Sagers
James A. Thomas Distinguished Professor of Law
Cleveland State University, Cleveland-Marshall College of Law

Wolters Kluwer

Printed in the United States of America.

1 2 3 4 5 6 7 8 9 0

ISBN 978-1-4548-9659-3

Library of Congress Cataloging-in-Publication Data

Names: Gabaldon, Theresa A., 1954- author. | Sagers, Christopher L., 1970-
   author
Title: Business organizations / Theresa A. Gabaldon, Lyle T. Alverson
   Professor of Law, The George Washington University Law School; Christopher
   L. Sagers, James A. Thomas Distinguished Professor of Law, Cleveland State
   University, Cleveland-Marshall College of Law.
Description: Second edition. | New York : Wolters Kluwer, [2018] | Series:
   Aspen casebook series
Identifiers: LCCN 2018025096 | ISBN 9781454896593
Subjects: LCSH: Business enterprises—Law and legislation—United States. |
   Corporation law—United States. | LCGFT: Casebooks (Law)
Classification: LCC KF1355 .G33 2018 | DDC 346.73/065—dc23
LC record available at https://lccn.loc.gov/2018025096

About Wolters Kluwer Legal & Regulatory Solutions U.S.

Wolters Kluwer Legal & Regulatory Solutions U.S. delivers expert content and solutions in the areas of law, corporate compliance, health compliance, reimbursement, and legal education. Its practical solutions help customers successfully navigate the demands of a changing environment to drive their daily activities, enhance decision quality and inspire confident outcomes.

Serving customers worldwide, its legal and regulatory solutions portfolio includes products under the Aspen Publishers, CCH Incorporated, Kluwer Law International, ftwilliam.com and MediRegs names. They are regarded as exceptional and trusted resources for general legal and practice-specific knowledge, compliance and risk management, dynamic workflow solutions, and expert commentary.

To Bob and Will, with thanks.

T.A.G.

To Donut, Juice, Mango, and Hop-Along. Omnia Fieri Possunt.

C.L.S.

Summary of Contents

Contents

11 The Limited Liability Company, Its Special Attributes, and Other Modern Alternatives 303

31 Trading by Insiders: Rule 10b-5   989

32 Trading by Insiders: Short-Swing Trading Under §16(b)   1017

Preface

Introduction

We wrote this book for two primary reasons. First, we think that the leading casebooks at present tend to give too little attention to unincorporated entities and the problems of small business, and that these topics generally should be addressed from a more transactional and problem-focused point of view. As unincorporated entity forms have proliferated, practical exigency requires more grasp of them and of the transactional problems they pose. Those problems can be just as theoretically challenging as those posed by the largest corporation—more so, really—and those lawyers who will represent Fortune 500 companies are as likely to negotiate a joint venture as to give advice on corporate governance. We made the cuts needed to bring in this material, but we made them with a constant focus on preserving traditional coverage and exhaustive analytical rigor. We tightly edited cases and present only one case on many topics, accompanied by explanations and problems to allow discussion of nuances. We tried hard to select interesting cases within the mainstream of those usually taught.

Second, we desire to make learning about business organizations accessible to students in new ways. Because many come to the course with little business background, we put our material in context with liberal doses of exposition. We also thought we could present the material with more variety and visual appeal. Aside from aesthetic improvements, we have added new pedagogical elements in sidebars, flow charts, and test-yourself features. We believe they enhance the overall learning experience at no cost in analytical rigor or coverage.

In sum, this book features:

— Significantly expanded coverage of **agency** and **unincorporated entities**, as well as detailed, problem-focused treatment of **special transactional problems in small and start-up businesses**;
— **Design elements** intended to create visual appeal;
— **Learning aids** such as **flow charts** and **self-testing** devices and special cross-referencing aids to emphasize **connections** among related topics;
— An **expository approach** providing clear context for the traditional case material that also appears;
— Easy to digest sidebar content intended to develop student **numeracy** in **tax, accounting**, and other relevant concepts;
— An interspersed series of exercises on **ethics for business lawyers**; and
— A **glossary** of terms.

The book is accompanied by an **online supplement**, which includes a full complement of edited codes to support the readings in the casebook, sets of transactional problems that can be assigned by the professor, and a module that constitutes roughly a "business concepts for lawyers" study guide. The study guide covers tax, accounting, financial, and economic topics keyed directly to the book, includes some supplementary reading assignments, and contains a variety of sample documents to show students the actual materials that lawyers work with every day.

Because different teachers organize their courses differently, we have endeavored to make individual parts of the book and supplement free standing. We tried to keep the chapters short and modular, and through the use of sidebar explanations or otherwise, the chapters or major sections of chapters in the book should stand alone, facilitating teaching in almost any order. This approach leads to reinforcement of major concepts, as students will encounter them, in different formats and levels of detail, in more than one place. For instance, we emphasize that one of the strongest links between the types of business forms is the law of agency and make sure agency issues are raised with respect to each type of business entity, so that coverage of each can stand alone.

Key to Sidebars

Many of the sidebars in this book are stand-alones to help with understanding a particular case (providing a time-line of events or a diagram of a complicated transaction). But some others are thematically linked with each other, and they have consistent headings. They are:

Room to Argue—indicating an area in which there has been significant academic controversy or conflict among jurisdictions, typically with a key to further reading in the online supplement.

Dear Prof.—providing clarification when an assumption is made in the text about what students already know.

Time out for PR—raising questions of professional ethics related to the chapter materials and providing relatively complete coverage of the problems encountered by business planners and counselors.

Doing the Numbers—introducing useful mathematical and accounting concepts to be emphasized as users desire.

Connections—referring readers to related material elsewhere in the text.

More to the Story—either noting when the text is generalizing but significant exceptions may exist, or providing cultural context that may have affected judicial reasoning.

JD/BMA—explaining significant business terms and concepts.

This May Help—flow charts, diagrams, checklists, tables and other learning aids.

Other Features

Two other features of the book are worth specific mention. First, there are a series of questions interspersed throughout each chapter, beginning in chapter two. These ***Think About This*** questions may be assigned for in-class discussion or simply to help students think things through before coming to class. At the end of each chapter, you also will find a series of ***Test Yourself*** questions that students are encouraged to use on their own. The answers to the ***Test Yourself*** questions, with complete explanations, are in the online supplement.

Editorial Notes

Citations of authority and references of various sorts, along with footnotes, have been omitted from the readings in the book, except where they serve some specific purpose, and the footnotes that have been included have been renumbered consecutively in each chapter. These deletions, the modification of some headings, the correction of typographical errors, and a few miscellaneous deletions and revisions of a minor nature have not been indicated, but other editorial changes in the readings have been.

We very much appreciate hearing from users of this book and encourage you to contact either one of us at the email addresses below with questions or comments.

Good luck and try to have fun!

Best,

Theresa Gabaldon
tgabaldon@law.gwu.edu
Christopher Sagers
c.sagers@csuohio.edu

Acknowledgments

We thank our editors, Richard Mixter and Kathy Langone, as well as their very devoted team members John Devins, Anton Yakovlev, Adele Hutchinson, Renee Cote, Joe Stern, and all the other men and women at Wolters Kluwer and The Froebe Group. We also acknowledge and thank a variety of other folks who assisted in the preparation of this manuscript, including Theresa Gabaldon's executive assistant, Ms. Toni Foncette, and research assistants, Xiaoyang (Winnie) Ma, Timothy Pramiromaruto, Tyler Mann, Faiza Kaukab, Austin Rettew, David Coard, and Hilary Kabak.

Last, but not least, we thank our spouses, Robert Palmer and Annie Wu, our children, Will Palmer, Jonah Sagers, and Jude Sagers, and our dogs, Theo and Max.

Theo

Max

We would like to thank the following copyright holders for granting permission to reprint their materials:

500 Fifth Avenue, photograph. Courtesy of Gryffindor / Wikimedia Commons.

1915 Dodge Brothers Motor Co. Touring Car, photograph. Courtesy of Douglas Wilkinson / Wikimedia Commons.

Blackwell, Thomas F., The Revolution Is Here: The Promise of a Unified Business Entity Code, 24 Journal of Corporation Law 333. Copyright © 2008 Thomas F. Blackwell. Reprinted by permission.

Divorce cake, photograph. Copyright` Frosted Art Bakery, www.frostedart. com. Reprinted by permission.

Hotel Bristol, photograph. Copyright` Museum of the City of New York. Reprinted by permission.

Lovenheim, Peter, *Portrait of a Burger as a Young Calf: The Story of One Man, Two Cows, and the Feeding of a Nation*, New York: Penguin Random House, 2013, front cover. Reprinted by permission.

Minor Myers, *The Decisions of Corporate Special Litigation Committees: An Empirical Investigation*, 84 Ind. L.J. 1309, 1311 (2009).

Nassau Hall, Princeton University, photograph. Courtesy of Smallbones / Wikimedia Commons.

Rich Uncle Pennybags, illustration. Monopoly® & Copyright© 2015 Hasbro, Inc. Used with permission.

Robert T. Smith, photograph. Courtesy of Brad Smith. Used with permission.

Self-Operating Napkin, illustration. Artwork Copyright © and TM Rube Goldberg, Inc. All Rights Reserved. Rube Goldberg® is a registered trademark of Rube Goldberg, Inc. All materials used with permission. rubegoldberg.com.

Springsteen, Bruce, "When You're Alone." Copyright© 1987 Bruce Springsteen (Global Music Rights). Reprinted by permission. International copyright secured. All rights reserved.

Business Organizations

Part 1

Introduction and Overview

1

Introduction: Welcome to the Law of Business Organizations!

This book is about the body of (primarily) state law that governs "business organizations." It is about those legally recognized forms of association that people may create for the purpose of engaging in business and earning profit. They exist to govern the rights and responsibilities of people within them and their relations with the rest of the world.

Chapter Outline

A. Introduction: What We Study in This Book

- Corporate law
- The law of unincorporated entities
- Agency law

1. Why Do We Have Business Entities?: Scale Economies, Other People's Money, and the Fundamental Problem of Business Organization
   - Division of labor
   - Diversification of risk
   - Agency cost

2. The Development of American Business Organization Law
   - The move to general incorporation statutes
   - The preeminence of Delaware
   - The late twentieth-century development of new forms of business and relaxed limitations on old ones

B. A Note on Statutes and Model Codes, and the Role of Statutory Law in Business Organizations

- The Revised Model Business Corporations Act
- The Delaware General Corporation Law
- The American Law Institute Principles of Corporate Governance
- The Revised Uniform Partnership Act and Other Model Unincorporated Entity Codes
- The Restatement (Third) of Agency
- The American Bar Association Model Rules of Professional Conduct

Test Yourself

A. Introduction: What We Study in This Book

When a client first consults a lawyer about starting a business, many choices must be made. One of the most important of them is the subject that makes up most of this book: what form of business entity to create. This chapter initiates discussion of business entities under American law and how they came to be. It also introduces the main sources of authority that will be used throughout the course.

Very roughly speaking, we can break the law of business organizations into three parts: the law of corporations, the law of unincorporated entities, and the law of agency. A "corporation," at the risk of being unduly cute, is an entity formed under a state corporation statute. Corporations have certain special attributes and have a special place, and they are important enough that we often treat them as their own category. They are probably the type of entity you think about when you hear the words "business organization," and most people have some idea that they involve directors, officers, and shareholders.

Unincorporated entities are all the other entity forms that the law makes available to private entrepreneurs, like the general partnership, the limited partnership, and the limited liability company. (It turns out that quite a large number of entity forms fall into this category in American law, more than a dozen depending on how one counts. Only a few of them are now commonly used, however, and those are the ones we cover in this book.) A key part of understanding the law in this book is knowing how corporations and the several unincorporated forms relate and differ, and how lawyers use their strengths and attributes to meet the needs of different clients.

And finally, the common law of agency is a set of general purpose rules that govern relationships among people working within any of these firms—or simply one person working for another. The doing of business almost always means doing things *through* other people, deploying them in one way or another to perform tasks. All such relationships, whether in the executive suite of the largest corporation or the stockroom of a mom-and-pop store, are governed to some degree by the law of agency. Though mentioned last, it is not necessarily least. Agency law is a basic building block in understanding the other two bodies of law with which we deal.

1. Why Do We Have Business Entities?: Scale Economies, Other People's Money, and the Fundamental Problem of Business Organization

Maybe the most basic question we might ask is why people do business together, in groups, and what difference it makes. On the surface these questions might seem obvious, even silly. But indeed they are not. It is not actually obvious why business arrangements have evolved in the particular ways that they have. Things could have gone differently, but they did not.

People form businesses for all kinds of reasons, ranging from the desire for personal fulfillment and independence, to the pursuit of fame and lucre, to the brute practical need to keep body and soul together. Business organizations come in all shapes and sizes, and have all different sorts of problems and needs, and no two of them are entirely alike. One thing that unites them all, however, is a common set of problems about how to structure relationships among their owners, investors, and workers, and how to arrange their relationships with the rest of the world. Our society's solution has been the law of business organizations. This body of law permits two or more people to create business entities that have juridical "personhood," or legal identity separate from their owners, in order to establish those legal relationships. Thus arises what really is a fairly small set of rules—the law of corporations, unincorporated entities, and agency—that governs the internal structure of every business in the United States.

But why do business in *groups*? Indeed, there are reasons not to. One important lesson we'll learn in this course is that business organizations (especially the small ones and *especially* the small, family-owned ones) are fraught with conflicts among their members. They face disagreements over the direction of the business, petty

The Kapauku of New Guinea have money, the institution of credit, interest, sales, and capital—but no form of common ownership. "'Two people cannot work together because they have two different minds' was the reason given by informants in answer to a question about why there is always only one owner of a thing. . . . 'If we were both owners, we would quarrel too much, we would steal from each other in order to obtain most from the field. My children and wives would probably go hungry—oh, it would be bad.'"

Leopold Pospisil, Kapauku Papuans and Their Law 78-79 (1964).

jealousies, personality conflicts, conflicting connivances of greed, and outright fraud and wrongdoing. So we might wonder why one person would ever associate with another in the earning of his or her daily keep. First of all, on the painfully obvious level, the doing of business usually just requires help. Most businesses involve more work than one person could handle and the bringing to bear of more skills than one person could have. Obviously, too, one person might just not have enough money to get a particular business started, and will either have to borrow it or will have to get others to come into the business, adding their financial resources as well as their talents and effort. And some businesses, of course, need a *lot* of money. Apple Inc., for example, is currently capitalized at an amount many times larger than the net wealth of the wealthiest person in the world.

Dear Prof.: What does "capitalization" mean?

This is a good opportunity to point out that this book includes a glossary, and also a lot of boxes like this one to elaborate on technical or auxiliary points. As for the word "capitalization," it has more than one meaning. The first is a technical one used in accounting, to describe a way of recording certain expenditures of money. The second, which is the one intended above, refers to a way of thinking of the value of a company. Specifically, the "capitalization" of a corporation is the sum of its stock, long-term debt, and retained earnings (money that it has earned and has not used or distributed). Many people may also use the term simply to mean the amount of money the owners of a company currently have invested in it.

But there are more interesting reasons that people do business together. First, sometimes spreading some particular kind of work among a group of people will allow them to do the overall task *better*, and not just because they can invest more total effort. Breaking down a task into sub-tasks and assigning them to different people sometimes allows them to complete the individual sub-tasks better and more efficiently. Take an example: When Henry Ford first set out to produce automobiles, he did not ask each individual worker to start from scratch and make a whole car on his own. That would have been absurd, as it likely would have been impossible and in any case it would have taken *forever*. Instead, he broke the making of cars down into hundreds or thousands of individual tasks and assigned particular workers each to perform some particular task, over and over. It turns out that this same trick works for all kinds of tasks, not just production-line projects. The idea, known since the time of the pioneering economist Adam Smith as the "division of labor" (see the "JD/MBA" sidebar that follows), is of huge significance in modern affairs. Among other things, its advantages seem partly to explain why businesses keep getting bigger and bigger, and why quite a number of products and services have for a long time been produced only on a mass scale.

JD/MBA: The Division of Labor

A founder of modern economic theory, the eighteenth-century Scotsman Adam Smith, thought this idea was so important that he said so on the very first page of his most important book. To explain why, he gave the famous example of his visit to a pin factory. One person working alone, he observed, could maybe make one or a few pins in a day. But in a pin factory,

> [o]ne man draws out the wire, another straights it, a third cuts it, a fourth points it, a fifth grinds it at the top for receiving the head; to make the head requires two

> or three distinct operations; to put it on, is a peculiar business, to whiten the pins is another; it is even a trade by itself to put them into the paper; and the important business of making a pin is, in this manner, divided into about eighteen distinct operations. . . . I have seen a small manufactory of this kind where ten men only were employed. . . . But though they were . . . but indifferently accommodated with the necessary machinery, they could, when they exerted themselves, make among them about twelve pounds of pins in a day. There are in a pound upwards of four thousand pins of a middling size. Those ten persons, therefore, could make among them upwards of forty-eight thousand pins in a day.
>
> ADAM SMITH, THE WEALTH OF NATIONS 3 (Mod. Lib. 2000) (1776); *see also* EMILE DURKHEIM, THE DIVISION OF LABOR IN SOCIETY (George Simpson trans., Free Press 1984) (1893).

There is one other reason that a particular entrepreneur might want to involve other people in a business, rather than trying to do it all alone: *diversification of risk.* All businesses face risks, all of them suffer bad times occasionally, and all face at least some risk of financial failure. Even if a given entrepreneur has enough personal money to start up a given business, if he or she finances it entirely individually and the business fails, then the entrepreneur bears 100 percent of the loss. If, instead, he or she can manage to put up only a part of the capital and can share the risk with others, then the firm's failure will not hit any one person so hard. It also frees up some of the entrepreneur's own assets for investment elsewhere, and assuming only some of the investments (whether in his or her own business or otherwise) lose money, then the more diversity of investment the better. Admittedly, involving other people in your business divides the pie into smaller pieces, but it also provides protection and allows you to take advantage of other opportunities.

Incidentally, a related problem is that if an entrepreneur is in it alone, and especially if the profits of the business are tied to the entrepreneur's actual performance of work, then the business (and probably the owner and any dependents who subsist on his or her income) can only earn money when the owner is in the office or the shop, working. This can leave very little personal time for the entrepreneur. There will be no such thing as a paid vacation, for example. It can also cause tremendous trouble if she is injured or otherwise becomes unable to work, and it can make planning for retirement daunting. For all these reasons, small businesses generally and especially one-person businesses can be very tough rows to hoe. While hiring help can ease these difficulties, having employees also poses all sorts of problems, both legal and practical, and the change from one-person operation to a firm with workers can be a change in fundamental character. In fact, the initial hiring of employees is often one of the first really big humps to get over in the life of a growing young business.

In any event, the point is that for all of these reasons the doing of business normally means the doing of at least some things *through other people.* And therein, it turns out, lie some really significant problems. Addressing them is what the law of business organizations is all about.

Peter Jakob Horemans,
Sleeping Kitchen Maid

A first problem is that involving even one other person in your business, however necessary and positive it may be, introduces a basic problem reflecting simple human nature. Understanding it will go a long way to explaining why we have business *law*, and why the law has devised most of the rules we will study in this book. Say that one person (call her "Boss") hires another (call him "Employee") to do something. It is natural that the personal best interests of the two people will not be identical. Boss will hope that Employee will exert great efforts and take very great care that the work he does is everything Boss is hoping for, and will want in exchange only the agreed-upon compensation. Employee, as you might guess, probably won't feel quite like that. Probably many or most people would really rather do less work for the same money, if they can. Some people will try to do as little as possible for the money that they will earn—the bare minimum they can do without getting fired. But it gets worse. Some people in Employee's shoes will see motive and opportunity for deliberate wrongdoing. Depending on the nature of the job, Employee might have access to money or other property of the business, might learn its trade secrets and sell them or otherwise exploit them, or might be able to steal away Boss's clients and start a competing business on his own.

Lawyers and economists often call this collection of problems—this range of self-serving motivations that tend to result in agents not quite performing as well as their bosses hope—the problem of "agency cost." The assistance of another person to accomplish any purpose is likely to result in a performance that is somehow less or different than the hiring person's expectation, and the difference is a "cost" to him or her.

One special manifestation of this problem of agency cost is inherent in multi-member businesses, and it plays a big role in business organization law. This is because such businesses often give some person or group control over resources put in by other investors. The risk is that the managers will either misuse that control or take the business in directions not in the investors' best interests. Sometimes this is so because they have a smaller personal stake in the company's bottom line than do the investors. For example, corporate officers receive salaries for their work but may have no personal share in the company's profits. When that is the case the officer may not work as hard or take as many risks as would maximize the firm's earnings, which is often the investors' only goal. But in a range of other situations different investors in the same business simply will have conflicting interests in its operations. Business organization law mainly deals with this problem by way of one of the most important concepts we'll learn about in this book: the body of rules known as "fiduciary duties." Put simply, a "fiduciary" is a person who has a special obligation to protect the interests of some other person, who is that fiduciary's beneficiary. Corporate officers are always fiduciaries of their corporations, partners and other managers of unincorporated entities are usually fiduciaries of their firms, and agents are fiduciaries of the principals who hire them. All these persons must therefore (subject to some possibility of contractual limitation) act with a legally imposed devotion, honesty, and selflessness they might not otherwise be inclined to feel.

Business organization law also governs some aspects of the relations of the business's members with the rest of the world. Specifically, it helps to resolve otherwise highly contentious problems of who is responsible for what. For example, say four people start a business and the business is unable to cover its own financial obligations. The question arises how those obligations should be apportioned among the four owners. Should they share them equally? If that seems fair, then what if one of them may have already invested more in the business or worked harder for it, or may have received a greater share of its revenues in the past? Would equal sharing seem fair in that case? These sorts of problems would be quite fraught if they had to be worked out from scratch every time one came up, and so the law of business organizations provides off-the-shelf answers to smooth the way and to help investors know what to expect up front. It may be somewhat surprising to learn, but under modern law when most types of businesses have liabilities in excess of their assets, the difference is shifted to third parties entirely. That is, the corporate form and most forms of unincorporated business entities permit the owners of the business to claim "limited liability." This means that they may lose the amount they have voluntarily invested (initially or by reinvestment of earnings), but no more.

Room to Argue

People writing about agency cost often are concerned with the agent's "incentive to shirk" and don't say too much about the reciprocal problem of the employer's incentive to exploit. The law of business organizations primarily, but not necessarily appropriately, leaves most of the concerns of employees to other fields of law. You can read more about this in the online Supplement.

Attempts to align the interests of managers with those of owners sometimes lead to profit-sharing compensation arrangements that prompt managers to focus on short-term returns rather than long-term growth. These, too, are discussed in the online Supplement.

 Dear Prof.: What about nonprofits?

We've excluded a familiar class of organizations from the entities described here—so-called nonprofit corporations, which really are more properly called "tax exempt" corporations. Those entities have largely the same management structure and other attributes as do profit-making corporations. However, they also have certain important differences, including the fact that they do not have shareholders. They also are subject to certain special rules, most notably those set out in the Internal Revenue Code, that distinguish them from profit-making corporations. They are outside the scope of this book.

2. The Development of American Business Organization Law

The use of the legal fiction of the business entity is very ancient. Our "corporation" concept finds roots in the laws of Rome and Greece prior to the time of Christ. Business entity ideas also surface in the legal systems of other cultures, including Judaic, Islamic, and Asian systems, at times long ago. There is apparently something elemental about certain basic problems of all businesses—policy conflicts, personality conflicts, and conflicting motivations of self-interest—that lend themselves to legal resolution through recognition of business entities.

Likewise, as long as there has been Western law in North America there have been business entity concepts here, and entrepreneurs have used them to organize their endeavors. The earliest business forms in the American colonies—the general partnership and the statutory corporation—were received from England along with the rest of the English legal system. The general partnership in principle is very simple. Two or more persons simply agree to join their forces and, normally, their resources, to produce some product or service to be sold for a hoped-for profit. The partnership is therefore literally just a creature of contract created by the parties, though the law has long imposed certain rules on their relations with one another and with other persons. The corporation, by contrast, has always been more rigorously controlled by law. The law has always required most corporations to be organized according to a specific internal, hierarchical management structure and to have a class of owners, known as the company's "shareholders" or "stockholders," who have very specifically defined rights. Corporate law thus has always imposed certain relationships among the owners themselves and between them and the outside world.

 Dear Prof.: So are you saying "stockholder" and "shareholder" are synonyms? How about "stock" and "shares"?

Yes, and pretty much. "Stockholder" and "shareholder" are synonyms. "Stock" and "shares" may be used interchangeably to refer to a specific owner's holding in a corporation. You also will hear people say, however, that a corporation's "stock" is represented by (or divided into) individual "shares." You would not turn that statement around.

The early forms, however, were in some respects quite different than the business forms we now know. The partnership has not changed that much in general outline, but modern partnerships are often considerably more complex and much larger than those of the early American years, and partnership law has evolved to accommodate their more modern needs. The corporation has changed much more. In this respect, it is important to understand that during the country's early years there was considerable popular hostility toward business organizations, reflecting anxiety over accumulations of capital and a more general fear of concentrated power. Such fears were a defining character of American politics at least since the time of Andrew Jackson, and they continue to echo today. However one may feel about it generally, in the case of business organizations that fear was not entirely paranoid, and to some extent reflected the habit of early American government of granting special privileges to business entrepreneurs. While that solicitude was defended as necessary to spur the growth of new business and public improvements, it was perceived by much of the populace as government aid to aristocracy.

More to the Story: Other Legal Considerations

From the archives of the Supreme Court Historical Society

As one example of the granting of special benefits to corporations in the early years of the Republic, consider the Massachusetts corporation at issue in the famous old constitutional law dispute known as the "Charles River Bridge case," Proprietors of the Charles River Bridge v. Proprietors of the Warren Bridge, 36 (11 Pet.) U.S. 420 (1837). Plaintiffs were entrepreneurs who secured a special statutory charter for a company that would build and operate one of the first bridges in the city of Boston. They believed they had been granted an exclusive right to operate it, during quite a long period. Their lawsuit challenging the state's decision to charter a competing bridge, and the Supreme Court's rejection of their claims, would establish seminal rules of constitutional law and American political economy. *See generally* STANLEY I. KUTLER, PRIVILEGE AND CREATIVE DESTRUCTION: THE CHARLES RIVER BRIDGE CASE (1973).

The most striking difference between early and more modern entity law is that initially there was no such thing as what we now call "general" incorporation. That is, for the most part there was no way for businesspeople just to start a corporation, pursuant to the terms of some generic state corporation statute, by filing paperwork in the appropriate government office (as it is done today). Rather, every time an entrepreneur desired to incorporate a business he would have to ask his state legislature for a special charter. Other restrictions were also common, and for the most part they reflected the same popular suspicion of accumulations of capital. Notably, corporations were normally given definite life spans—a corporation would cease to exist after the expiration of a period of time specified in its charter. Limitations were also frequent on the kinds of business in which a corporation could engage (for example, if it were incorporated to operate a turnpike, it could not also operate a grist mill), the sorts of powers it might exercise (for example, corporations were frequently prohibited from owning stock in other corporations), and the total amount of capital it could own. Moreover, the restrictions contained in early corporate law were mandatory, whereas most states now have broadly permissive "enabling" or "default" statutes, under which the basic statutory rules can be modified by the founders of the corporation. Finally, and probably quite importantly, during the first half or so of the nineteenth century, investors in both partnerships and corporations usually had unlimited personal liability. Any time the assets of the business were insufficient to cover its obligations, creditors could execute their claims directly against the personal assets of the company's owners.

More to the Story: The Early History of Limited Liability

Some statutory corporations of this period provided limited liability for shareholders, but only if the legislature explicitly so provided in the corporation's incorporating statute. Entrepreneurs also had access to a somewhat more exotic form known as the "limited partnership," a French import that first appeared in the United States in the 1820s. That form provided limited liability to its "limited partners" (although not to its "general partners"). However, the limited partners were not permitted to have any involvement in the management of the business's affairs—they were to act solely as passive investors. The form was of use, therefore, only where some group of investors was willing to invest money but truly wanted no other involvement in the business's management.

The limited partnership still has some significance in American law, and it is discussed in this book in Chapter 10.

In any case, the real action in the development of modern entity law did not get going until fairly late in the nineteenth century. One thing to bear in mind is that at that time the U.S. economy had a huge amount of energy and possibility. Granted, times were often financially difficult in this period, and the country suffered several recessions and a period of the 1890s that in Europe is still known as the "Great Depression." But this was also a period in which some of the more significant economic developments of American history began to occur: large-scale commercialization of steam-powered machines, the industrialization of manufacturing, long-distance communications and transportation, and the development of the seemingly limitless resources of the undeveloped West. Exploitation of new possibilities called for new kinds of companies and, in particular, bigger ones. The doing of business in a newly industrialized manufacturing economy called for production on a much larger scale, so that by the late nineteenth century it was necessary for entrepreneurs to employ much larger work forces and attract capital from much larger pools of investors. But the restrictiveness of traditional entity law made such things hard to do, creating much pressure for more flexibility.

The seeds of change had already been planted for some time, but it took them a long while to grow. New York experimented with a "general" incorporation statute in 1811—that is, a statute under which a person could create a corporation without specific legislative authorization, simply by filing paperwork with the appropriate government officials. Connecticut followed suit in 1837. But these statutes had comparatively little effect, and indeed in several states that experimented with general incorporation, resort was still more frequently had to special incorporation. For one thing, early general incorporation statutes were usually quite limited. New York's 1811 statute, for example, was open to only a few kinds of businesses, and statutes in other states limited the duration or powers of generally incorporated businesses. For another thing, many businesspeople of the time preferred specific incorporation because they could secure (sometimes by unsavory means) special benefits in their charters.

Economic pressures of the post–Civil War era, however, put the need for change front and center. At this point arises an important and apparently inevitable theme in the history of business law. Government efforts to control business *conduct* through state business organization laws usually fail. The mounting pressure for corporate forms that would permit large accumulations of capital, with flexible powers and management structure, would inevitably find a release somewhere. It would result either in some government capitulation to business desires or, if government attempted to hold its ground and control business behavior through restrictive corporate governance rules, then through the creative efforts of businesspeople and their attorneys. For better or worse, in other words, when it comes to the law of business organizations business usually gets what it wants. For what it may be worth, this appears not to have had all that much to do with actual corruption or undue business influence in policymaking (as we might think after the experience of these jaded latter years). Rather, the tool of business organization law has just been no match for the ingenuity of corporate planners and their lawyers.

So change arose and it did so generally along the lines desired by business. An excellent example is that the early corporation law—including many of the early general incorporation statutes—set limits on the amount of capital any one corporation could hold. This was a problem for many businesses, which found that they could be more profitable by expanding the scale of their operations, but could not do so without investing larger amounts in those operations than permitted by statutory capital limits. State statutes also often tried to prevent businesses from evading these limits through the simple expedient of the "subsidiary." The states did this by prohibiting corporations from owning shares in other corporations. But the way out of that was simple for businesspeople, and at the

Room to Argue: Normative or Descriptive?

Since the 1980s, the school of law and economics has had much to say about the field of business organizations. One of the claims is that the law and economics method of analysis is both normative (explaining what the law should be) and descriptive (providing an explanation for what already has come to pass). You can read more about this and how it relates to the evolution of business law in the online Supplement.

More to the Story: The Delaware Court of Chancery

Delaware has retained the historic distinction between law and equity, and retains two separate court systems: the Superior Court, which has unlimited, statewide civil and criminal jurisdiction, but only in matters of "law"; and the Court of Chancery, which has equity jurisdiction. The Court of Chancery is given jurisdiction over most corporate affairs, in part because many corporate matters involve the equitable problem of fiduciary duty or involve injunctive remedies, and in part because many specific corporate matters have been assigned to the Court by statute.

Map of U.S. with Delaware Highlighted

time apparently was perfectly legal: Entrepreneurs would establish a number of corporations capitalized up to the legal limit, and then would transfer all of their shares into one trust. At common law trustees had always been empowered to use corporate shares granted to the trust (including by using the shares' power to vote in corporate governance matters). So in the case of this new corporate trust device, the "trustee" of the trust became the managerial head of a large family of corporations, which for all practical purposes could act like one big company. This was the structure, for example, of the original Standard Oil, the behemoth monopoly assembled by John D. Rockefeller in Cleveland in the late 1800s.

Another good example, and surely one of the more peculiar developments in U.S. corporate law, is the rise of Delaware as our leading corporate-law state. Today Delaware remains the state of choice for incorporation by a very large number of America's large companies, and the ongoing development of corporate law in Delaware's Court of Chancery has influence far and wide throughout the country. But Delaware's rise was a historical accident. Up until the turn of the twentieth century Delaware had been a comparative non-entity in corporate law, living in the shadow of its neighbor New Jersey. New Jersey was one of the first states to adopt an "enabling" statute, in 1875, and it quickly reaped the rewards of its permissiveness. Many corporations relocated there to take advantage of its law, and accordingly paid that state their taxes. But in 1911 Woodrow Wilson, formerly President of Princeton University and a nationally recognized leader in Progressive politics, became New Jersey's governor. Almost immediately, he spearheaded a stricter corporation law, removing many of the state's permissive enabling provisions. The result, for better or worse, was simply that most corporations that could afford to do so moved their place of incorporation to nearby Delaware, which had a very permissive corporation statute much like New Jersey's had been. New Jersey relented some time thereafter and reinstated a more permissive enabling statute, but by that time most large corporations had settled into cozy harmony with the government of Delaware.

The newly permissive legal environment of the turn of the twentieth century had the result that was apparently desired by businesspeople, and was likely inevitable. A world of very large businesses arose in short order, basically with government's blessing. Indeed, in the space of only about ten years, beginning in the 1890s—a period now known as "the Great Merger Movement"—there arose the largest consolidation of business in Western history.

By no means, by the way, is any of this to argue that public policy should just leave corporations alone or stop trying to control their wrongdoing through legal rules, though that surely is a view taken by persons of certain political persuasions. Conversely, it does not prove in itself that there has been anything nefarious or regrettable in the development of business law, though some others might draw that conclusion. Indeed, one might just as well rewrite the story so that instead of saying the law developed "in the direction desired by business," it developed "as required by practical economic circumstances." We offer no position one way or the other. The idea is only that when government grapples with business behavior through the tool of business *organization* law, as imposed by state governments—the body of law covered in this book—business usually wins.

In any event, in sum, the general theme of the development of our business law has been away from the restrictive and suspicious tradition of the early nineteenth century to an open, highly deferential, and enabling model that has left businesses with broad freedom to tailor their organizational structures as they see fit. All U.S. states now permit general incorporation, and their business entity statutes are mostly, basically, enabling statutes. As a practical matter, having enabling statutes means that the state does not restrict the lines of business, powers, or life span of entities formed under them, and most such statutes also permit broad flexibility in arranging the structure of their management and ownership. Indeed, one chief development of the twentieth century has been to give broad structural freedom to corporations with just a few owners, often called "closely held" or "privately held" companies. In particular, both Delaware and a very influential model statute, the American Bar Association's Model Business Corporation Act, permit closely held corporations to do away with their boards of directors altogether and otherwise manage their affairs with much less formality than had traditionally been required in corporations. Another fairly extraordinary development in the late twentieth century was a virtual land-rush by state legislatures to recognize forms of unincorporated entities that would confer extraordinary flexibility, limited liability, and favorable tax treatment on their owners. In effect, what had been a traditional link between passive investment and the protection of limited liability was severed.

B. A Note on Statutes and Model Codes, and the Role of Statutory Law in Business Organizations

Take note of the following key fact: Every important form of business organization in the United States, except for the sole proprietorship—the one-person, wholly-owned outfit that is not really a business entity so much as the lack of one—is governed by a statute. Moreover, every business organization statute is a state statute. Every state has a corporation statute, a general partnership statute, a limited partnership statute, and so on. Therefore, a fair bit of this book is devoted to analyzing particular statutes.

A minor problem is that all these state statutes vary in their particulars. Obviously we cannot study all the individual variations among all the states, or even among a few of them. Therefore, we will focus on certain codes that happen to be influential or that represent national trends. The codes we use are as follows.

The Revised Model Business Corporation Act.

The Committee on Corporate Laws of the American Bar Association's Section of Business Law first issued the Model Act in 1950 and has revised it several times since. The latest major overhaul was in December 2016. It incorporates all of the substantive changes made since the prior major revision in 1984. Hereinafter the 2016 statute will be referred to as the "Model Act" or MBCA. By far the main source for statutory law we will study will be the Model Act.

The 1984 version of the Model Act, with amendments, has been adopted in some part in a majority of the states, and for the most part the Model Act is fairly representative of the law elsewhere.

The Delaware General Corporation Law.

As mentioned, the state of Delaware has a special place in corporate law, in some part because its corporation statute was influential during the twentieth century on the development of statute law in other states, as well as in the Model Act itself. The Model Act thus is representative of national trends and also incorporates many Delaware innovations. We will therefore only focus on a limited number of Delaware provisions, all of which will be clearly identified in the text. We sometimes focus on specific Delaware provisions when the Delaware case law interpreting those provisions is itself influential.

The American Law Institute Principles of Corporate Governance.

This model code is simply an alternative model corporation statute, which happens to have been adopted by the American Law Institute, the organization that produces the familiar Restatements of Law. In terms of adoption by the states, the ALI *Principles* have been much less successful than the Model Act. However, certain provisions have had important influence, and we will therefore study a few of them.

The Revised Uniform Partnership Act and Other Model Unincorporated Entity Codes.

The National Conference of Commissioners on Uniform State Laws has produced a series of model codes to govern unincorporated entities, and in this book we examine several. The most successful was the Uniform Partnership Act (UPA), promulgated in 1914 and quickly adopted in every state except Louisiana. The UPA was substantially revised in 1997 by the Revised Uniform Partnership Act (RUPA), and while RUPA's adoption has been more grad-

---

Connections: Federal Securities Law

There is a body of federal law that affects the operations of corporations and some other entities—federal securities law—that is also sometimes thought of as a corporate governance law. However, the basic organizing law for all business entities—the law that governs the basic internal affairs and governance of businesses—is exclusively state law.

We discuss a small slice of federal securities law in Part 7.

ual, as of this writing it has become the law of all but ten states. We focus on RUPA rather than UPA, though UPA is still in force in some places, because UPA features more than a few antiquated terms and concepts, as well as some areas of confusion that have been clarified by RUPA. We will also devote time to the Uniform Limited Liability Company Act (ULLCA), adopted in 1996 and substantially revised in 2006, which (in the 18 states in which it has been adopted) authorizes a different type of entity that can startlingly resemble a RUPA partnership. Finally, we also will briefly deal with various iterations of the Uniform Limited Partnership Act (ULPA), most recently substantially revised in 2001. The uniform codes relating to unincorporated entities all underwent harmonization in 2011 and 2013; this book reflects the resulting amendments.

Room to Argue: Corporation Codes and Politics

One might have expected corporation codes no longer to be such political things, given their evident preoccupation with bureaucratic process and red tape. But indeed they still court controversy. While it plays no very overt role in this book, we feel obliged to acknowledge the persisting debate, and to acknowledge that some latter-day controversy has involved differences among the very codes we have chosen to use—the Delaware Code, the MBCA, and the ALI *Principles*.

Debate mainly surrounds the power and autonomy of corporate managers: how much they should have, how much shareholders should retain, and what power shareholders should have to discipline their management through litigation. Corporation codes that are thought of as more "conservative" tend to maximize managers' autonomy and render shareholders relatively passive. As things now stand, the more conservative codes constrain managers almost exclusively through risk of liability under very broad, tort-like "fiduciary" duties enforced through shareholder derivative suits, but they then make those suits hard to bring. Codes thought of as more "liberal" also rely on fiduciary litigation, but make the cases easier to bring, and sometimes also constrain managers with stricter black-letter conduct rules. For example, they have sometimes preserved the older, black-letter rules, like one that made the managers' personal dealings with their corporation automatically voidable, and one that gave shareholders first-refusal rights over issuances of new stock, to prevent dilution of their shares.

Probably the hottest modern controversy surrounded the 1984 revision to the MBCA. Before then, the MBCA was seen as generally middle-of-the-road and moderately pro-shareholder, as it included some black-letter restraints on managers and generally tough fiduciary rules. But the ABA Committee apparently feared that, due to the hostile takeover activity of the 1980s and the fiduciary litigation it engendered, along with a general increase in class litigation at that time, managers were facing too much liability risk. And so after the 1984 revision the MBCA came to be known as a fairly conservative, pro-management code. Critics claim the change was driven by large-firm defense lawyers who had come to control the ABA Committee, and argue that the changes were poorly suited to the many jurisdictions where the MBCA has actually been adopted—states that are almost entirely non-commercial ones, where most corporations are small and closely held. (California, Massachusetts, New York, Texas, and above all, Delaware, each have their own codes, and so the MBCA has no influence there. Delaware's code, in particular, the law governing many publicly traded U.S. corporations, is said by many to already be among the most pro-management.)

We do our best to stay above this fray, though at times we will raise policy issues that are important to understanding the legal rules. For the most part we pick and choose pieces of code to study only because we think they are representative or because they capture something important.

The Restatement (Third) of Agency. "Agency" is a body of common law rules governing situations in which one person (an "agent") does something on behalf of and subject to the control of another person (known as the agent's "principal"). Agency rules are ubiquitous in the law of business entities and, in many regards, the laws of corporations and other business entities could be thought of as just specialized applications of agency law.

In this book we explore agency through study of the Restatement (Third) of Agency.

The American Bar Association Model Rules of Professional Conduct. Finally, as explored a bit in the accompanying "Time Out for PR" below, and in other places in this book, we consider rules from the American Bar Association's Model Rules of Professional Conduct. The Model Rules are not themselves the law, but either they or their predecessor, the ABA's Code of Professional Responsibility, have been adopted in some part in 49 states (California is the exception), plus the District of Columbia and the Virgin Islands. Although there are state-by-state variations in a number of areas, most of them do not relate to the rules we'll read. There is a notable exception, however, with respect to the duty to reveal risks of financial injury to third parties.

    ## Time Out for PR: The Organization as Client

Business lawyers confront a special ethical problem. They always must ask a question that ordinarily is simpler or not even relevant for lawyers representing natural persons. They must ask themselves, "Who is my client?" While a business entity is a "person" for most legal purposes, and can be an attorney's "client," the entity itself cannot act except through its owners or employees. Those persons—through whom the business will engage and communicate with its lawyer—will often have direct personal interests in the company's welfare, and will likely take the lawyer's advice as important in their own lives. Moreover, situations are common in which their personal interests are at odds with one another or at odds with the best interests of the business. Worse yet, especially where those persons are not themselves attorneys, there can be misunderstandings as to whether the business's lawyer represents them as well, and owes them fiduciary duties and the obligation of confidentiality.

This "organization as client" problem implicates one ethical rule in particular. ABA Model Rule of Professional Conduct (MRPC) §1.13 provides that, while representation of both a business and its constituents is *permitted*, *id.* §1.13(g), the organization alone is presumed to be the client so long as the lawyer was "retained by" the organization. Whether the lawyer was "retained by" the organization in any given case, as opposed to the individuals acting on its behalf, is not actually governed by rules of legal ethics. *See id.* at Preamble and Scope §[17]. It is rather a fact-bound question under the common law of agency.* The lawyer should take care, though, that the firm's constituents understand that the lawyer does not represent them, since the attorney-client relationship can be formed inadvertently where circumstances could cause them to believe one exists. Moreover, the lawyer must "explain the identity of the client when the lawyer knows or reasonably should know that the organization's interests are adverse to those of the constituents with whom the lawyer is dealing." *Id.* §1.13(f). In such cases, the lawyer should also advise them to consider independent representation. *Id.* §1.13 cmt. [10]. Rule 1.13 imposes a few other special, sometimes tricky little rules. Importantly, lawyers for organizations sometimes have whistleblower duties. Where the lawyer knows that someone associated with the organization intends to break the law, in a way related to the representation and likely to cause the firm substantial injury, the lawyer must notify appropriate officials within the organization. *Id.* §1.13(b). If that notification fails and serious injury to the firm is imminent, the lawyer may alert outside authorities. *Id.* §1.13(c).

---

* With whom an agency relationship is formed, including an attorney-client relationship, is a question covered at length in this book. The matter is fact-specific and often hard to predict, and basically boils down to the following question: For whose benefit and subject to whose control would a reasonable observer, given all the circumstances and judging from the parties' outward manifestations, think that the lawyer agreed to work? See Chapter 3.

Test Yourself

1. The reasons for involving more than one person in ownership or operation of a business entity do *not* include:

    a. The ability to shift risks to third persons.
    b. The ability to diversify risks.
    c. The ability to achieve economies of scale.
    d. All of the above are reasons to involve more than one person.

2. "Agency cost" means:

    a. The commission that is paid an agent for obtaining a contract.
    b. The pay due to one's employees.
    c. The costs to the principal associated with an agent's motive to serve him- or herself.
    d. Profit-sharing or other arrangements to align an agent's motives with those of his or her principal.

3. "Limited liability" means:

    a. That an investor cannot lose his or her investment.
    b. That an investor cannot lose more than his or her investment.
    c. That an investor can lose his or her investment and may be responsible for a designated percentage or amount in excess of his or her investment.
    d. That an investor must refrain from active management in order to limit his or her risk of loss to the amount of his or her investment.

4. Which of the following would *not* be resolved as a matter of the law of business organizations?

    a. The obligations of corporate officers to the corporation.
    b. The obligations of partners to one another.
    c. The obligations of the corporation to avoid violating various laws of general applicability.
    d. The obligations agents owe principals.

5. A lawyer representing an entity such as a corporation:

    a. Also represents its owners.
    b. Also represents its managers.
    c. Both answer a and answer b.
    d. Neither answer a nor answer b.

2

The Law of Business Organizations Generally, the Choice-of-Entity Problem, and the Basic Problems of the Business Counselor

The major objective of this chapter is to introduce a theme that will be with us throughout the book: the choice-of-entity problem. A basic role of the business lawyer is to advise clients as to what form of entity their business should adopt—should it incorporate, or should it be a partnership, a limited liability company, a limited partnership, or something else?

Chapter Outline

A. The Choice-of-Entity Problem and the Client's Basic Concerns

- Considerations in the choice-of-entity mix
1. Limited Liability
2. Tax

Test Yourself

A. The Choice-of-Entity Problem and the Client's Basic Concerns

To some clients' surprise, the choice of entity can have dramatic practical consequences. If the form of business is chosen poorly, the non-lawyer client may find unexpectedly that he or she is personally responsible for the debts of a business or owes fiduciary duties to another person or faces other undesired consequences.

Because no two situations are exactly alike, no list of the relevant concerns could really be complete. Moreover, while some forms will be better than others for any given business, the choice-of-entity problem really has no right answer. But as a preliminary matter, the following list of factors gives a flavor of the considerations that go into this decision.

1. Limited Liability

Some forms of business entity provide limited liability to some or all of their investors, while other forms do not. "Limited" liability means that the owner of a business cannot be held personally responsible for the obligations of a business.

This is true, for example, of shareholders in a corporation. Imagine that in a given corporation each share is sold for $10. Bob purchases 50 shares directly from the corporation, at a price of $500. If the corporation becomes insolvent, so that its assets are worth less than its total obligations to outside creditors, Bob will face no loss greater than his initial $500. He will have no way to get his $500 back, but the corporation's creditors will be unable to execute their claims against his personal assets, like his home, his car, or his bank account. Limited liability is an important feature for attracting capital from passive investors, who wish to share in a firm's profits but are not willing to put their own personal assets on the line for it.

2. Tax

While it is less true now, tax treatment was traditionally one of the most important concerns in the choice of entity. The problem was made more acute by the fact that the corporation—the only form subject to the so-called double tax—was traditionally the only business entity that provided limited liability for all of its investors. Indeed, the history of business entity law in the twentieth century was largely the story of business planners' struggle to devise an entity that would combine the pass-through taxation of partnerships with the limited liability of corporations. That struggle finally ended in the 1980s, with the introduction of the limited liability partnership (LLP) and the limited liability company (LLC), both of which eventually would provide easy access to both limited liability and desirable tax treatment for most businesses. It is still quite important, though, to get a few key tax concepts under our belts. These are covered in Section B of this chapter.

3. Governance and Internal Conflict

Sooner or later, businesses with more than one owner probably will face disagreements over managerial decisions. It is not uncommon for disagreements to divide managers so severely as to leave the business deadlocked and unable to move forward. Therefore, it is important to understand the ways in which the different entity forms apportion decision-making responsibility and the ways they can be used to anticipate future management problems. For example, the default rules for corporations contemplate the following. The company's owners, known as the "shareholders," are given certain voting rights, with which they elect members of the company's board of directors. The board then acts as the company's primary policymaking body. Day-to-day affairs are managed by one or more corporate officers who are appointed by and serve at the board's direction. The officers usually are employees and are responsible for hiring and monitoring the corporation's other employees. Thus, it often is the case that

> ### Room to Argue: Limited Liability May Not Be an Unmitigated Good
>
> Limited liability permits investors to capture gains while shifting the risk of losses to third parties. The pros and cons of this phenomenon are explored in the online Supplement. It is good to remember, though, that limited liability limits the shareholder's liabilities only for those acts that are not his or her personal acts. *See, e.g.*, Hoagland v. Sandburg, Phoenix & Von Gontard, P.C., 385 F.3d 737, 742 (7th Cir. 2004) ("limited liability [does not] shield the personal assets of investors who cause the corporation to commit a tort or other unlawful act").

one person or a small group—the chief executive officer and other high-ranking officers—makes most important decisions, subject to broad, abstract policy-making by the board. This structure works well in many cases, especially in larger endeavors, where central managers control the investments of many passive investors. It is less well suited for other businesses, as where some group of founding members each desire an equal say in important decisions and would have trouble deciding who should act as chief executive. In contrast to the corporation, general partnerships are known for a much more flexible management structure. By statutory default rules, all partners automatically share equally in all management decisions, but partnership statutes normally allow the partners to vary this rule by agreement. This means that if the founders of the business agree that one or more of the partners should have a lead role in managerial decisions, that can easily be accomplished by agreement. Other types of entities also generally invite more flexible arrangements than do corporations.

Apportioning management rights can be an important issue in serving clients' needs and can be among the most important tools in avoiding conflicts during the life of the business.

 Time Out for PR: Conflicts and Confidences

Talk of internal conflict is a good point at which to consider the difficulty an attorney may experience in navigating the ethical rules governing conflict of interest. Perhaps some of the edge may be taken off if everyone agrees— and frequently is reminded—that the attorney represents only the entity and not any of the individual constituents. There is more about this possibility in the online Supplement, but the starting points are ABA Model Rules 1.7 and 1.13. Rule 1.7 permits representation of clients with concurrent conflicts, if the lawyer reasonably believes competent and diligent representation of both is feasible and each gives informed, written consent. Rule 1.13(g) requires an entity's lawyer to make it clear to constituents just whom the lawyer represents, but Rule 1.13(h) permits simultaneous representation of an organization and its constituents, subject to Rule 1.7.

In any event, imagine that you are a lawyer who, believing Rule 1.7 to be satisfied, has agreed to represent Bill, Ted, Harold, and Kumar in setting up and operating a partnership. One day Bill and Ted approach you and tell you they want to figure out how to circumvent Harold and Kumar's participation in management. Assuming the plan does not constitute crime or fraud, Model Rule 1.6 prohibits disclosure of a client's confidences without informed consent. Model Rule 1.4 simultaneously requires that a client be kept reasonably informed. What does this suggest you should do—or perhaps already have done? Is it realistic?

4. Returns, Liquidity, and Exit

Owners in any business can earn a return on their investments either by sharing in the business's profits or by selling their ownership shares and cashing out appreciation in their value. But the mechanics can vary quite a bit depending on the entity form chosen. For example, shareholders in corporations normally do not participate directly in the firm's profits except through the payment of dividends, which are in the discretion of the company's board of directors, subject to the satisfaction of certain statutory tests. In partnerships, by contrast, partners have broad freedom to modify default statutory rules to provide themselves with periodic profit distributions.

Likewise, different business forms can vary greatly in the degree of liquidity they provide their investors. This fact can be of crucial significance. Shareholders of an exchange-listed corporation, for example, usually have highly liquid investments. Any time they are dissatisfied with their company they can simply sell their stock on the highly active public securities exchanges. Likewise, partners in general partnerships will sometimes have quite liquid investments, though for a completely different reason. On the one hand, partnership interests are normally very difficult to sell, because a partner usually cannot transfer an actual membership in the firm, with its attendant managerial rights, without the unanimous consent of the other partners. (By contrast, a partner generally can sell his or her right to participate in the firm's profits, but it is difficult to do so at a good price, because the purchaser is entitled to no managerial rights.) On the other hand, partners normally have a right to withdraw at will, and withdrawal triggers a statutory process that can effectively force the firm to cash out the departing partner (although the partners are free to agree to their own buyout terms). Some other firms entail illiquid investments, however, at least under statutory default rules.

 Dear Prof.: What makes an investment "liquid" or not?

"Liquidity" is the ease with which an asset can be converted to something that you can spend. Cash, obviously enough, is the most liquid of all assets. Some other investments are pretty liquid as well. Even though you can't spend them as cash, you can easily find someone who will pay you fair value for them. A good example is the stock of a corporation listed on the New York Stock Exchange. In that very large, very active market, it is almost always the case that for any listed security, any owner of a stock can execute a sale and extract the full, fair market value of the asset, instantaneously.

Investors care a lot about liquidity. For example, you might invest your money by just putting it in an interest-bearing bank account. That investment is in effect perfectly liquid—you can withdraw it at any time and in most banks it is backed by uniquely reliable federal deposit insurance. But the interest paid on demand deposits these days is extremely low. So you might try instead something like a "certificate of deposit," in which you put money on deposit in the bank at a higher rate of interest, but agree that you won't withdraw it for specific period, often six months or a year. That's a trade-off. You'd still be making a very low-risk investment and would get a better return, but you would also give up a fair bit of liquidity.

As might already be clear, liquidity is central to the problem of exit. Once you've joined a firm, you can't very well get out unless you have some way to get your money back. And liquidity and returns together can pose a crucial governance problem. Imagine that one member of a firm is dissatisfied in some way, but the ownership shares are very hard to sell at a fair price. If a majority of the other members are not inclined to go along with whatever changes might satisfy that dissenter, they are in a good position to exert extreme pressure. They can make whatever decisions they like, including decisions that restrict the dissenter's ability to share in the firm's profits or otherwise benefit from her investment (so long as those decisions don't require unanimous vote). The dissenter will have very little ability to "vote with her feet" by selling her investment and leaving.

Connections: The Basic Capital Structure—Choice of Debt vs. Equity

A fascinating topic to which we'll return is the basic choice between funding a business with debt and funding it with equity. That is, the proprietors can either borrow money from a bank or other lenders, or they can sell ownership interests in the business.

Indeed, almost all businesses do some of both. The two avenues have different pros and cons, from the perspectives of both the business and the investors.

We explore these points in more depth in several places, including the online Supplement.

5. Capital Structure

Another central problem is how a business will acquire the capital that it needs to operate.

Different forms of business entity accommodate this need differently. Usually, a business's founders will put up at least some of the money needed to get the business going, but they usually also will need funds from others and they will desire as well to spread some of the risk of their venture. Of course, any business can borrow money, either from a bank or from individual private lenders. But different kinds of businesses attract equity investment in different ways. (For our purposes for now, "equity" simply means an ownership interest.) The corporation, for example, permits investors to purchase ownership interests—shares of stock—that do not expose them to personal liability and do not involve them directly in management of the company. The general partnership, by contrast, has no means by which to attract equity investment without these attributes. Every equity investor in a general partnership is a general partner, with some rights to participate in management, ownership rights in the business's profits and property, and unlimited personal liability.

6. Red Tape

Although seldom dispositive, an issue that sometimes matters, especially for very small businesses, is the cost and complexity of the bureaucratic rules that state laws impose on different forms of business entity. A first set of hurdles has to do with creation—that is, establishing the entity's legal existence. Creation can be blindingly simple in some businesses. Sole proprietors can simply start doing business and general partnerships can actually be formed by accident, without the partners subjectively intending to do it or knowing they have. Other forms of businesses, however, require more care in their formation and indeed cannot come into existence without formal filings.

Some entity forms may also entail ongoing bookkeeping and compliance costs. Corporations, for example, generally are required to hold at least one shareholder meeting per year. They also really should hold board meetings with proper written minutes, keep a stock transfer ledger, keep formal books of account, and keep the company's money strictly separate from that of the management and shareholders. Even a corporation with a single shareholder who runs the business should comply with these and other formalities. Although there sometimes are shortcuts, you have to know what they are and it is important to dot the i's and cross the t's when taking them.

The point, of course, is that compliance with these requirements can strike clients as tedious and time-consuming busy-work, which they then may fail to do. If, instead, they hire a lawyer to do it, costs can mount quickly. As we will learn, different entities have different requirements. A starting point, however, is to note that as far as entities involving more than one individual are concerned, corporations generally are thought of as having the most requirements, whereas general partnerships usually have the fewest.

JD/MBA: Paid Help

Professionals can be hired to assist in locating sources of capital. Sometimes these professionals are known as "investment bankers," "underwriters," or "business brokers."

Connections: Bureaucratic Formalities and "Piercing the Corporate Veil"

As we will learn in Chapter 16, courts sometimes use their equitable power to disregard the existence of a limited liability entity and hold the owners personally liable for debts the business is unable to pay. In the case of a corporation, this is known as "piercing the corporate veil." One factor taken into account is whether the owners themselves have disregarded the separate existence of the entity. One common piece of evidence that they've done so is failure to follow the bureaucratic niceties described in the text. Thus, even very small businesses are well advised to observe the ordinary formalities, even when they sometimes might seem silly—as when a corporation's only two shareholders are required to hold a meeting at which they will elect themselves to be the company's only directors and then hold a meeting of the board to appoint themselves as the only officers.

■ **Think about this:**

(A) Liquidity is a basic difference between the closely held corporation and the general partnership. Imagine that Alan, Barb, and Chuck want to start a business, investing roughly equal amounts of initial capital and sharing control among them equally. They could set up their business as a general partnership or they could incorporate it, give themselves equal numbers of shares, and appoint themselves to be the directors. The business would

in most respects be very similar either way. But one big difference is that if they incorporate their firm—which would be much too small to be listed on a securities exchange or have any other very ready market for its shares—their investments will likely be much less liquid. Can you explain why?

(B) If it is true that the power of unilateral dissolution *can* make general partnership ownership a fairly liquid investment, what are the circumstances that make it liquid or not?

B. A Beginner's Guide to the Taxation of Entities

As no doubt you know, whole classes and indeed entire advanced law degrees are offered on individual income tax, corporate tax, and partnership tax, and the little overview that follows isn't even enough to make you dangerous. But it probably will be helpful in thinking about the basic choice-of-entity problem and in understanding some of the other choices this book will discuss.

In General. Many businesses, like most individuals, must pay federal and state taxes. The manner in which a particular business will be taxed—and, as a practical matter, how much it will be taxed—depends to some extent on which form of entity the business chooses. Generally speaking, corporations are subject to "double taxation," under which the corporation must first pay federal income tax on any profits it has earned, and then individual investors (shareholders) must pay income tax on any distributions of profits they receive (normally known as "dividends"). This is a result of the fact that for most legal purposes a corporation is considered a "person" independent from its owners. The government accordingly treats the corporation and its owners as separate taxpayers. Most other business entities, however, enjoy "pass-through" taxation, under which the entity itself pays no income tax and the profits it earns are taxed only when they are distributed to investors.

"Check the Box" Tax Treatment. As we've mentioned before, much of the modern history of American business entity law was tied up in a struggle to achieve both limited liability and pass-through taxation in the same entity. The story is long and involved, but in the end, the traditional struggle ended with the limited liability company (LLC), which became widely available during the 1980s and 1990s, and with the so-called check-the-box tax rules of 1997. The LLC was designed by state legislatures (1) to provide limited liability and (2) to "look like" a partnership for federal income tax purposes. The Treasury Department acquiesced initially by agreeing that LLCs should be taxed as partnerships, wherever their statutory attributes under a given state's law made them "look enough like" a general partnership. Over a period of ten years, the Department's position softened even further, and in 1997 the Department issued its "check-the-box" regulations. In practical effect, any entity *except* a corporation can simply elect not to be taxed. The basic principles are these:

(i) An entity will be taxed as a corporation if it is created under a statute that "describes or refers to the entity as incorporated or as a corporation, body corporate, or body politic" or as "a joint-stock company or joint stock association."

(ii) An entity that is not so classified and has at least two members can elect to be classified for tax purposes either as a corporation or as a partnership by making an election at the time it files its first tax return. If the entity does not formally elect to be taxed as a corporation it will be taxed as a partnership. This means that the entity calculates and reports its income, but does not pay taxes on it. Instead, the income is allocated and taxed directly to the owners.

(iii) An entity that has only one member may elect to be taxed as a corporation or it will be treated as a "nothing," i.e., as though it has no separate existence from its owner.

(iv) If an entity elects to change its classification, it may not change its classification back within five years without permission from the Treasury Department. The conversion of an entity that is currently taxable as a corporation to a partnership is itself a taxable event, treated as though the corporation dissolved and reconstituted itself as a partnership. The conversion in the opposite direction will usually be tax free.

> ### Doing the Numbers: Two-Tier Taxation vs. Pass-Through Taxation
>
> First, (unrealistically) assume that all tax rates, both corporate and individual, are 10 percent.
>
> Second, assume that Yvette and Zander are the equal co-owners of a corporation that earns $10. The corporation will be required to pay $1 of tax. Whenever it distributes the remaining $9 to the shareholders, they will pay $.90, for a total tax burden of $1.90.
>
> Third, assume instead that Yvette and Zander are equal partners in a partnership that earns $10. The partners will together pay a total of $1 of tax. The partnership pays no income tax at all.
>
> There is more on this subject in the online Supplement.

Other Tax Law Assumptions. While we can hardly explore tax law issues in the depth they really deserve, there are a handful of other tax rules that will be very helpful for us to grasp. Accordingly, we will rely for the rest of the book on the following list of simplifying assumptions about the tax treatment of business entities. Needless to say, while these are all accurate rough statements of the law, they are generalizations. In practice the issues are more complex.

(i) *Only Profits Are Taxed.* Generally speaking, taxpayers are responsible for paying tax only on their "income," which means the amount of money they earn minus the expenses they incur in making it. Therefore, businesspeople and business firms that pay tax must pay it only on their profits. Profits equal revenue (the total amount of money the firm brings in) minus all the expenses that the firm incurred in order to earn that revenue (e.g., the salaries of its employees, rent, interest on borrowed money, and so on).

(ii) Pass-Through Taxation. Most business entities are taxed as "pass-through" entities, meaning that the entity itself need not pay any taxes on profits that it earns. Rather, the owners of the business must pay individual income tax on their shares of the firm's profits. The paradigm example is the general partnership. A law firm, for example, pays no taxes itself, but rather its partners each must include their share of the firm's annual profits in their own "income" when filing their own federal income tax returns.

(iii) Double Taxation. Unlike other business entities, the default rule for corporations is that they are subject to "double taxation." This means that the corporation itself must pay income tax on all its profits, and then its shareholders must pay individual income tax on any distributions they receive from the company of those same profits (normally called "dividends"). Corporations that pay double taxation are known as "C Corporations" because their tax treatment is governed by Subchapter C of the Internal Revenue Code. They are to be distinguished from "S Corporations," governed by Subchapter S of the Code, which enjoy pass-through taxation but are subject to limitations on their organization and size. (For a bit more on the S Corp, see the "More to the Story" box at the end of this chapter.)

(iv) Salaries and Interest Are Deductible Business Expenses. As noted above, only "income" is taxed. Business expenses are deducted from revenue to determine income. As also noted, but worth repeating, these deductions include (1) the cost of employees' salaries, and (2) any interest paid on borrowed funds.

(v) Dividends Are Not Deductible Business Expenses. Unlike salaries, interest on debt, and other expenses of doing business, dividends paid to shareholders or other distributions to the owners of an entity *because they are owners* are not deductible by the business entity. If, however, an owner also is an employee, then salary or other compensation paid to that owner *as an employee* would be deductible.

More to the Story: Tax Law Variables

Obviously, there are many aspects of the federal tax scheme beyond the scope of a course on business organizations. One of these is the subject of taxation rates (typically imposed as a percent of taxable income) imposed on corporations and individuals, since these rates vary widely and change frequently. For instance, after the 2017 Tax Cuts and Jobs Act, the corporate tax rate was a flat 21 percent, while the individual rate varied from 0 to 37 percent. Moreover, the rate imposed on dividends received by individuals varied from 0 to 20 percent. To complicate matters, owners of many pass-through businesses may deduct 20 percent of the income passed through before calculating their own taxable income. (For better or worse, that new rule does not benefit law firms whose owners make more than a certain amount.) These nuances can greatly impact business planning.

■ **Think about this:**

(C) Suppose you are counseling a client who has asked you to help in structuring a corporation that does not, because some of the owners are non-resident aliens, qualify for Subchapter S treatment. All of the owners expect to participate in management. What would you suggest to them about paying themselves salaries vis-à-vis making distributions as dividends?

 What does it look like?

Check the online Supplement for the following:

■ An excerpt from the actual instructions for "checking the box" and
■ An excerpt from the actual instructions for making the Subchapter S election

C. Introduction to the Forms of Business Entity

Persons forming a business may choose from a surprising variety of business organization forms—a dozen or more, depending on how one counts. Understanding how these forms differ and how their differences can be used to suit clients' objectives is among the most important services a lawyer can provide to business clients, especially small ones.

Room to Argue: Do We Really Need So Many Options?

A point of confusion when one first studies the law of business organizations is why so many different entity forms are available, especially when (as we shall see) so many of them seem so similar. It will seem to you that there must be some reason, some difference among forms that you're missing that explains why we have them all.

But that's not really the case. While the availability of so many forms has allowed business lawyers to pull off some fancy tricks and wriggle through loopholes here and there, there really is no good reason to have so many forms. State legislatures adopt new business entity statutes over time for various reasons of politics and convenience, and don't bother to repeal the old ones.

In fact, as we shall see in Chapter 11, there has been substantial effort to simplify the law, including by just eliminating some of the less-used entity forms, though for reasons of inertia and lack of political will, it is doubtful this will happen soon.

Before we proceed to a brief summary of the most important entity forms, let's pause to recall two very significant facts:

(a) Every important entity form in the United States, except for one, is governed by a statute. The exception is the sole proprietorship.

(b) Every important entity form in the United States, except for two, requires the filing of some document with a state agency for its creation. The exceptions are the sole proprietorship and the general partnership.

These two facts will have some significance for the summary to follow, and will be with us throughout the book. In any event, while the range of theoretically possible choices is wide, only a handful of the available business entity forms are widely used. They are as follows:

1. The Sole Proprietorship

The sole proprietorship is the simplest and also by far the most common business form in the United States. In such a business, one person owns all the business's assets, owns all of the profits derived from its operations, and has unilateral management authority. The legal identity of the business and the owner, in other words, are the same. Therefore, there is no business entity to form, and no bureaucratic formalities of any kind are required to bring it into existence. A person simply begins selling a product or service and, poof, a sole proprietorship is born.

The chief legal disadvantage of doing business in this way is that the owner will face full personal liability for all of the business's obligations. The owner also takes all the risk of the business—as the only equity owner, there is no one else with whom to share the loss if things go south. On the upside, the sole proprietor has unilateral control and faces no challengers for power, and also enjoys pass-through taxation.

More to the Story: Other Formalities

While no formalities are required to *create* a sole proprietorship, the proprietor may face compliance requirements under state law. For example, in some states a business operating under a trade name, regardless of how it is organized, must make a filing under the state's "fictitious name" statute. In addition, some types of business require certain training and/or licensing.

2. The General Partnership

The general partnership is an ancient business form. A partnership is created when two or more persons agree to act as co-owners of a business for profit. As with the sole proprietorship, no formalities of any kind are required to create a partnership—the entity comes into existence as soon as the parties so agree. A surprising fact, however, is that the law recognizes there to be such an agreement as soon as the parties make *objective* manifestations of its existence. That is, as soon as a reasonable third party would take their words and actions to indicate an intent to form a partnership, there is one, regardless of what their actual intent might be. Thus, even if they don't subjectively intend to create a partnership, they might do it anyway. This can be quite a significant event, because all partners in a general partnership have full personal liability for the debts of the business, they all have equal claims on its profits, they have equal management powers, and they are each one another's fiduciaries. Incidentally, this is a result of the second key generalization with which we began this summary: The general partnership is the only multi-member entity that can be created without a government filing, and so it is also the only such entity that can be created by accident.

 Dear Prof.: What's a "fiduciary"?

A "fiduciary" is someone who is legally charged with the obligation to act on behalf of another rather than on his or her own behalf. The status carries with it a range of duties described at length elsewhere in this book.

The partnership does provide one significant advantage to the business owners, however: the availability of pass-through taxation. Traditionally, this was a chief reason that many small businesses chose it rather than the corporate form, despite the desirability of limited liability. Moreover, partnership can be good for some businesses. Its default rules of equal management and profit sharing make sense for many small firms and professional practices, in which several people of equal talent or seniority desire to work in parity with one another. Its management and profit-sharing structures are also very flexible and can be suited to the peculiar needs of the individual business.

Partnership law was once exclusively common law, but it has been codified in all states since the early twentieth century. A Uniform Partnership Act was promulgated in 1914, and that statute was the law of all states except Louisiana for many years. A Revised Uniform Partnership Act was promulgated in 1997. It was last amended in 2013 and has been adopted, with variations, in a large majority of states. An important theme throughout partnership law is that, although all partnerships are governed by statute, the statutory law is highly flexible and most provisions of partnership statutes can be modified by agreement of the partners, at least as they affect the partners' rights among themselves. For this reason, partnership statutes are often said to be "default" statutes. They set out the rules that will govern a given partnership unless the partners modify them by agreement.

One other important consequence flows from the fact that partnerships can come into existence by accident. Circumstances are common in which, once problems arise, like disputes over rights to profits or major governance decisions, the parties will dispute whether their relationship is a partnership or something else, and that issue can have outcome-determinative consequences.

> ■ **Think about this:**
>
> *(D)* Why do you suppose that when determining whether two or more people have formed a partnership, we don't care about their subjective intent and consider only objective evidence of it? We only ask what reasonable persons would infer the parties' intent to be, judging from their words and actions. In thinking about your answer, consider these two specific questions: If we relied on subjective intent, what would be the risk? Separately, by asking only about objective manifestations of intent, whose interests are we protecting? Third parties? Or the partners themselves? Or is it actually both?

3. The Limited Partnership

The limited partnership (LP) is another old form of business, this one arising in Europe in the Middle Ages and imported into U.S. law in the 1820s. At that time, there was no ready means by which entrepreneurs could attract funds from passive investors, since the only forms available were the general partnership and the corporation, and the idea of corporate-shareholder limited liability had not yet developed. The LP is in most respects simply a general partnership, with one difference. It has a class of partners known as "limited partners" who generally act only as passive investors. They invest money in exchange for partnership interests, which entitle them to a share in the firm's profits, but they enjoy limited liability for the firm's debts. The catch is that the limited partner may not be personally involved in management of the company's affairs, and if a limited partner is found to have been so involved he or she may be held to have full personal liability.

The LP can be formed only by filing an appropriate form with the Secretary of State (or equivalent). Failure to do so properly can result in unlimited liability for all members. However, as with the general partnership, the firm need have no written partnership agreement, and if it has one it generally need not be filed with the government.

LP interests will often be as illiquid as general partnership interests, although limited partnership interests are sometimes publicly traded just like shares of corporate stock. When that is the case, of course, they can be highly liquid. Provided that they are not publicly held (more about this exception elsewhere), LPs are taxed in the same way as general partnerships. That is, they may "check the box" to elect pass-through taxation, meaning that the business itself does not pay taxes on its profits, but the general and limited partners do pay taxes on their shares of the profits.

> ■ **Think about this:**
>
> *(E)* There is a reason that failure to file the appropriate form with the Secretary of State results in unlimited liability exposure for a new

firm's members. If one attempts to form an LP but messes up the paperwork, and then just starts doing business, one has actually formed a different type of business entity. In fact, this same result follows if one attempts to create any business entity that requires a filing for its creation, but fails to file or files improperly. Can you see which kind of entity is actually created?

4. The Limited Liability Company

The limited liability company is a relative newcomer to the law of business organizations. Again, it was the culmination of a decades-long effort by corporate planners to combine the best advantage of the corporation—limited liability—with the best advantage of the general partnership—pass-through taxation. The LLC, which came into being when state governments and the Treasury Department finally acquiesced, thus provides both features, as well as highly flexible governance and financial rules.

Like LPs, LLCs are created only upon the filing of appropriate paperwork with the Secretary of State. The filing typically is known as the company's "articles of association." In most states, this document can be a fairly simple matter, identifying only the company and its members, asserting LLC status, and complying with certain other statutorily required items. LLCs can and frequently do also devise substantial, complicated internal management agreements to govern management and profit sharing, but they are not required to do so.

5. The Corporation

Like the LP and the LLC, a corporation can be formed only by making a filing with the Secretary of State. In the case of a corporation, this filing is known as the "articles of incorporation" or, in some states, the "certificate of incorporation" or "charter." The document to be filed often is more substantial than is the case with unincorporated entities.

Moreover, corporations are normally required by statute to establish a specified management structure. First, a for-profit corporation must be owned by one or more shareholders. Shareholders enjoy full limited liability. However, they also lack any right of direct involvement in the company's management, and participate only through their power to vote at shareholder meetings. Second, a corporation must have a board of directors, elected by the shareholders. The board sets general policy and must make major decisions on behalf the company, including deciding what officers the corporation will have, and what their duties will be. Finally, the company's day-to-day affairs are administered by the company's officers. These generally include a chief executive officer (sometimes also called the "president,"

> **More to the Story: LLPs and LLLPs**
>
> Although this text outlines only the most common forms of doing business, there are two others we'll also spend time on in later chapters: the limited liability partnership (LLP) and the limited liability limited partnership (LLLP). We're sorry for the confusingly similar names. Don't hate the player, hate the game.

Connections: Flexibility Comes Even to the Corporation

While it is true that corporations generally must follow a much stricter, more or less mandatory, off-the-shelf management structure, most states have provided small corporations with flexibility to modify it. For instance, the Model Business Corporations Act (MBCA) permits a corporation to do away with its board and be managed directly by its shareholders if the shareholders unanimously agree. *See* MBCA §7.32. In Delaware, the same effect can be achieved by agreement of a majority of the shareholders.

though many companies have both a CEO as well as a second-in-command officer known as the president), a treasurer, and a secretary. Larger corporations typically have many more officers, including a general counsel (the company's top in-house lawyer), a chief financial officer (who is usually both the company's top in-house accountant and its money manager), and any number of vice presidents or other operating officers.

Shareholders can enjoy a return on their investment either by receiving distributions of profit (often called "dividends") or by selling shares to capture appreciation in their value. Unlike most unincorporated entity investments, corporate stock can be highly liquid if the company's shares are publicly traded. However, in companies that are not publicly traded, shares of stock can be just as illiquid as limited partnership or LLC memberships, and for largely the same reasons.

Very roughly speaking, the advantages of operating a business in corporate form include:

(i) Limited liability of shareholders;
(ii) Centralized, off-the-shelf management, which has the advantages that it is well suited for management of large passive investments, and that it is well understood in the business, financial, and legal communities; and
(iii) Flexibility in capital financing options.

The disadvantages of the corporate form include:

(i) Expense and trouble of formation and maintenance;
(ii) Required initial and continuing formalities; and
(iii) Double taxation.

■ **Think about this:**

(F) In the "Connections" box above, we saw that in Model Act jurisdictions, corporations can do away with their boards of directors and adopt other flexible management rules, by unanimous shareholder agreement. The ability to do so ceases at least as soon as the shares of the company are publicly traded. Do you see why?

(G) Some small corporations that are otherwise subject to double taxation can avoid all or most of the double tax by simply employing their shareholders as employees and paying them salaries rather than dividends. (This can't be done incautiously, because paying salaries for

work not actually done or paying unreasonably high salaries will trigger action by the Internal Revenue Service and can result in penalties and, in cases of gross, deliberate abuse, criminal prosecution.) Can you explain to yourself why doing so avoids double taxation?

More to the Story: The Peculiar Prominence of the "S Corp" and the "Edwards-Gingrich Loophole"

When we say "corporation" in ordinary lawyer talk, we typically mean the "C Corporation" or "C Corp," so named because it is taxed under Subchapter C of the Internal Revenue Code. The C Corp is the entity subject to double taxation. There is another sort of corporation in America, taxed under Subchapter S of the Code and so known as the "S Corporation" or "S Corp." First permitted by the Code in 1958, an S Corp is just like any other state-law corporation, except that it makes an election to be taxed under Subchapter S and must comply with a number of restrictions imposed in the Code. (The limitations have varied over time, and at present require that an S Corp have only one class of stock, no more than 100 shareholders, no non-human shareholders, and no non-resident alien shareholders.) So long as it complies, its shareholders enjoy the usual limited liability of corporations *and* pass-through taxation.

In its day—before the arrival of the LLC—the S Corp was a welcome alternative, but only for businesses that could live with its restrictions (which were even tighter back then, originally permitting no more than ten shareholders). One might have thought that once LLCs and the check-the-box rules came along, demand would end for an entity that could only grant desirable liability and tax treatment with strings attached. One thus might have expected that by the late 1980s, the S Corp would begin a quick fade into irrelevance. But it did not, young friend, nosiree. It is estimated that as recently as 2016, not only did S Corps still outnumber LLCs, they outnumbered C Corps by as much as *three to one*. And C Corps are still common, after all, as they are all but required for use by publicly traded firms, numbering nearly 2 million. That trend is expected to persist well into the future. *See* 1 LARRY E. RIBSTEIN & ROBERT R. KEATINGE, RIBSTEIN AND KEATINGE ON LIMITED LIABILITY COMPANIES §2.1 (2017).

How could this be?

The answer apparently lies in a tax avoidance maneuver made famous by Senator and personal injury lawyer John Edwards. Though by no means did he invent it nor was he the only person to use it, it became controversial when he was discovered—during his 2004 vice-presidential campaign, no less—to have used it to avoid about $600,000 in payroll taxes. In a nice touch of bipartisan equanimity, it was also found in 2010 to have been used by former House Speaker Newt Gingrich. For that reason the trick is now often called the "Edwards-Gingrich Loophole."

The trick is that in businesses whose owners would ordinarily be paid high wages, it actually saves on the tax bill to organize as an S Corp, pay relatively low wages, and pay the remainder as dividends. Both the dividends and the income are taxable to the shareholders as income, but because the firm is an S Corp they are not double taxed. By keeping wages low, the business economizes on "payroll" taxes. (Payroll taxes include Social Security and Medicare taxes, and they are calculated as a percentage of the wages that a business pays its employees. While the Social Security tax is capped so that it has to be paid only up to a certain wage, the Medicare tax has no maximum and must be paid as a percentage of every employee's entire salary.) So, in Senator Edwards's case, during the period in question his personal injury practice—organized as an S Corp—earned him a total of about $25 million, but only about $1.2 million was paid to him as salary. As a result, he paid about $30,000 in Medicare taxes instead of more than $600,000. Speaker Gingrich owned two S Corps that paid him about $400,000 in salary but distributed profit of about $2.4 million, allowing him to avoid $69,000 in Medicare taxes.

The maneuver is legal, so long as salaries paid to owners are reasonable in light of the services they perform, and it is very common. But abuse of it is also common, and the cost to the federal fisc is very large. The Treasury estimates that the amounts lost to the government through use of the Edwards-Gingrich loophole are approximately $25 billion per year.

Test Yourself

1. Alan, a hair stylist, has become at long last fed up with the despotic management of the salon where he works, and he has decided to strike out on his own. He plans to set up a salon in a back room in his home. He will be the only worker in the business, and he will fund its expenses entirely from his own savings. He has come to you for choice-of-entity advice, and he would like to know specifically whether he should incorporate, form an LLC, or take other formal action.

   a. First of all, if Alan takes no legal action, and just starts up his business, in what form of business will he be operating?
   b. What are the pros and cons for Alan of incorporating? Is there an argument to be made that he should not take legal action as to choice of entity?
   c. Consider the possibility that Alan might be best advised to save the money he would pay you to incorporate his business or form some other entity, and spend it on something else, specifically. What might that other thing be?

2. Consider Robin, a woodworker, who, like Alan, decided to start her own small business making furniture from scratch. Initially she was the only worker and funded the business with her own savings. She chose to remain a sole proprietor. But after a few years of successful operation, Robin is ready to take the big step of hiring her first employee. Assuming you don't disagree with her initial decision to remain in sole proprietorship, how does this new addition affect her choice-of-entity concerns?

3. Which of the following characteristics do limited liability companies (LLCs) share with corporations?

   a. Limited liability for all owners.
   b. Strong, centralized management.
   c. Free choice with respect to whether federal taxation is two-tier or pass-through.
   d. All of the above are characteristics shared by LLCs and corporations.

4. Which of the following characteristics do limited partnerships (LPs) share with general partnerships?

   a. Unlimited liability for the general partners.
   b. The risk of inadvertent formation.
   c. Participatory management.
   d. All of the above are characteristics shared by LPs and general partnerships.

5. True or False? With careful planning, a corporation may be able to avoid the burden of two-tier taxation.

6. True or False? An interest in a general partnership usually is more liquid than an interest in a corporation.

7. True or False? Unlike the other primary forms of doing business, sole proprietorships cannot have employees.

Part 2

Agency

3

Introduction to Agency Law

This chapter develops understanding of the agency relationship as the foundation of the various forms of enterprise. It defines the relationship and explores some recurrent issues and themes.

Chapter Outline

A. Introducing Agency Law and Its Role in Business Organizations

1. History and Goals of Agency Law
   - Common law origins
   - Fundamental for all but the simplest forms of business

2. Three Important Generalizations Running Throughout Agency Law
   - Virtually every question is fact-specific
   - Fact questions are determined objectively
   - Parties' intentions are determined from all objective manifestations

B. Forming the Relationship

1. The Basic Test
   - Mutual manifestation of intent
   - Agent acts on principal's behalf
   - Agent is subject to principal's control

2. Applying the Basic Test
   - Corporate directors are not agents
   - Buyers and suppliers pose fact-specific issues
   - Public policy may influence outcomes in unclear cases

C. Specific Issues Surrounding Formation: Capacity, the Varieties of Agency, and the Power of Attorney

1. Capacity
   - Capacity is required on the part of both parties

2. Co-agents, Sub-agents, and Co-principals
   - Co-agents are different from sub-agents
   - An agent may have co-principals

3. Employees and Non-Employee Agents
   - Agents are either employees or independent contractors

4. The Power of Attorney and the Need for a Writing Generally
   - Writings generally are not required to create an agency relationship

Test Yourself

A. Introducing Agency Law and Its Role in Business Organizations

"Agency," simply stated, is a special legal relationship in which one person can make legally binding commitments on behalf of another. Here's one user-friendly definition, from the Restatement (Third) of Agency: "[Agency is a] consensual relationship[] in which one person . . . acts as a representative of or otherwise acts on behalf of another person with power to affect the legal rights and duties of the other person." Restatement (Third) of Agency *Introduction.*

 Dear Prof.: Didn't you say this was a class in business law?

A variety of relationships can be "agencies" even if they may not seem obviously business-like. The attorney-client relationship, for example, is always an agency, and so are many of the grants of health-care or financial decision-making authority commonly given among family members or friends.

But agency is also fundamentally interwoven throughout the law of business organizations, and that law really can't be understood without it. Above all else, the doing of business means doing things *through other people.*

1. History and Goals of Agency Law

Despite its ancient origins and pervasive nature, an interesting fact is that lawyers and academics have begun to question whether agency should really be thought of as an independent body of law. Agency or agency-like ideas are discussed in many other law school courses, and agency is taught as a freestanding course much less often than it once was. This is probably mainly because agency in our system is a common law doctrine, and one that developed during a period of a few centuries in which most of our law was judge-made. During the twentieth century that situation changed rapidly, and there now exist thousands of federal and state statutes that in one way or another modify legal rules in specific situations that might have been governed by agency case law. But there also seems to remain a persistent instinct, within bench, bar, and academy, that agency understood as an independent body of common law rules deserves its own recognition. As the Director of the American Law Institute noted in introducing an early draft of the Restatement (Third) ("Third Restatement" or "Re(3)"), recent U.S. Supreme Court case law relies on the Restatement (Second) as leading authority in federal matters, and the Third Restatement was written "in a period when [the] subject hit the front pages as corporate scandals—Enron in particular—focused on the legal relationships among principals, agents, and affected third parties."

Some Roman Guy

In any case, agency concepts in some very general sense—in which one person can represent another in legally binding fashion—are very ancient, with shadowy manifestations appearing centuries or millennia ago in Greek, Roman, Jewish, Islamic, and other law.[1] While the history has been the subject of much debate, it seems to be taken for granted that agency ideas of some kind are necessary to any but the most primitive notion of the doing of business. It seems not coincidental that the first kernels of contemporary agency law arose during the Middle Ages, along with the rapidly increasing commercial activity that followed the rise of European capitalism. The two things seem connected.

In Europe, agency concepts arose at roughly the same time throughout the continent, and they did so in different legal systems that drew authority from different sources. In fact, in some ancient systems, agency concepts were actually long disfavored, and yet they arose anyway. For example, legal thinkers in ancient Rome conceptualized contracts as uniquely personal relationships, and so they had a hard time conceiving how they could be made by one person but be binding on another. But over time the Roman law found ways to permit legally binding representation in various ways, while avoiding the theoretically problematic matter of calling it agency as such. For example, it came to permit the male head of household of Roman citizen families to make binding contracts through any member of his family, including slaves and other servants. This turns out to be an example of a phenomenon observed in a famous law review article of many years ago, by the eminent legal philosopher Roscoe Pound. As he said, there sometimes comes to be a "distinction between law in the books and law in action"—some way in which the arid, theoretical law in the minds of judges and lawyers simply has not kept pace with changing society. Time and again the law has handled such a problem by adopting some new legal fiction, and Pound said that fictions "show where and how legal theory has yielded to

---

1. The picture above isn't really just some Roman guy, of course. That's the Emperor Justinian of the Byzantine Empire of the sixth century A.D., whose Corpus Iuris Civilis codified existing Roman law. That document included a sophisticated early codification of agency law. See J. Inst. 3.26.

the pressure of lay ideas and lay conduct." Roscoe Pound, *Law in Books and Law in Action*, 44 Am. L. Rev. 12, 14-15 (1910). Fictions reflect the tension between the law's longing for theoretical integrity, on the one hand, and the momentum by which reality proceeds in its own directions, on the other. And so it was that even though Roman legal theory could not conceive of legally binding representation through agents, it achieved the same result by allowing the *pater familias* to act through his household servants—presumably because commercial realities had come to demand it.

But the point here is not philosophical. These historical developments—the fact that agency arose in coincidence with capitalism, that it could arise in similar ways at the same time in different and unrelated legal systems, and that in some systems it arose inexorably despite theoretical tensions—show that, in commercial society, legally binding representation through subordinates has been naturally occurring and fundamental.

2. Three Important Generalizations Running Throughout Agency Law

Before we move on to the substantive rules of agency law, it will be useful to set out a few handy, very big-picture generalizations about the law of agency.

First, virtually every important question in agency law is a fact-specific question as to which there will often be no obviously correct answer. Agency, in other words, is full of questions that ultimately are for the trier of fact. Thus, a word of caution to both lawyer and law student is that there frequently will be no "right" answer to agency questions.

Second, virtually all of these many fact questions are to be determined objectively. That is, the actual, subjective intent of the persons involved in any given scenario normally doesn't matter. What matters is how the facts would appear to a reasonable observer.

Finally, these many important objective determinations usually depend on the "objective manifestations" of one or more people who are involved in some particular situation. An objective manifestation is any outward evidence, observable by other persons, that indicates one's intentions. For example, the agency relationship itself is created when the principal and agent give their objective manifestation of assent to its existence—when they write words, speak words, or engage in conduct that would indicate to a reasonable observer that they intend to create it. What's important is that "objective manifestations" need not be spoken words, and they almost never need to be in writing. They can include taking certain actions (for example, performing tasks as

Connections: Business Entities, Objective Manifestations, and the Need to Protect Reasonable Expectations

Questions like those in the "three important generalizations" will come to seem familiar once we study other business entities. We shall see that the law of partnerships, for example, also relies extensively on "objective manifestations," and it also is characterized by frequent disputes over formation and authority that are to be resolved objectively. And we shall see that corporations and other unincorporated entities raise them too, since authority, vicarious tort liability, and many other issues in those contexts are literally just questions of agency law.

if the agency agreement had been assented to), remaining silent under certain circumstances (for example, failing to deny the existence of an agency relationship or to disclaim that a particular contract was properly authorized), accepting benefits under a contract, granting a person a particular job title, printing up business cards and professional stationery for a person, and so on.

■   **Think about this:**

(A)   It is important to ask why these generalizations run throughout agency law. In particular, ask yourself what underlying policy reason explains the almost uniform insistence on *objective* evidence of intent, and the almost complete disregard for the parties' actual, subjective desires. Above all, people can create agencies by *accident*—two people might find themselves in a principal-agent relationship, with all the legal consequences it imposes on them and third parties, even though one or even both of them never intended it. So ask yourself, whom exactly does the law protect with results like that?

(B)   Whether or not an agency has actually been formed seems like a pretty basic sort of problem, so basic indeed that it is the topic of the very first section of the Restatement (Third). So you might not expect it to be a particularly uncertain one. And yet, the question of formation is very frequently and hotly disputed in litigation. Who would have an incentive to dispute whether an agency had been formed? Note that the answer can vary from case to case.

(C)   Another common dispute will be over whether a given relationship creates an agency or creates some other business entity. For example, one party in a case might claim that a relationship between two people was an agency, while the other claims it was actually a partnership. Why would they do that?

B. Forming the Relationship

   What does it look like?

Check the online Supplement for the following items that are relevant to this section:
■ An agency agreement
■ A simple power of attorney

1. The Basic Test

Agency is necessarily a mutual relationship. There must be some evidence that both principal and agent want it. This is so because its creation has legal consequences for both parties. That being the case, it might seem surprising that the question whether or not an agency relationship was created is often litigated. In theory, the relation is created only when both parties intend it. For that reason, one might think it strange that if the parties intended to create the relationship they would ever deny it. But in fact they frequently do. First, recall that because the "intent" relevant to creation of the relationship is judged objectively, the relationship can be created accidentally. Second, one or more parties will frequently have a strong incentive to deny its existence, regardless of what they actually intended. In lawsuits between principal and agent, the agent may have an incentive to deny the relationship to avoid fiduciary duties, or the principal may have that incentive to avoid any implied duty to pay the agent compensation (which is presumed under Re(3) §8.13; see comment d). In lawsuits by third parties, the principal will have an incentive to deny the relationship to avoid vicarious liability for contracts or torts committed by the agent.

Re(3) §1.01, which defines "agency," contains the test to be applied by the trier of fact to determine whether an agency relation has been formed. It provides in full as follows:

> Agency is the fiduciary relationship that arises when one person (a "principal") manifests assent to another person (an "agent") that the agent shall act on the principal's behalf and subject to the principal's control, and the agent manifests assent or otherwise consents so to act.

Note that even though it is not quite stated in these terms, §1.01 sets out what is really a three-part test. The test is fundamental to the entire law of agency, and you should work out the meaning of each of its parts. As we shall see, one of the more mysterious aspects of agency law is the distinction between agency relationships and other kinds of relationships, and the distinction is made by way of this test. Anyway, seen in this way the test contains the following elements:

1. mutual manifestation of assent,
2. that the agent will act on the principal's behalf, and
3. subject to the principal's control.

Each element has roughly term-of-art status. That is, each has a specific and fairly well-defined doctrinal meaning. Element one is really quite straightforward, if only you remember that "manifestation of assent" can mean lots of things besides just spoken or written words. Element two is harder to capture. In particular, it might seem strange that an agent must be one who acts only "on the principal's behalf" when in fact agents are normally paid for their work, sometimes exorbitantly. But what is intended is that the only benefit the agent may seek is the agreed-upon or implied compensation, and will not seek to benefit at the principal's expense. It is this element that most distinguishes agency from garden variety, arm's-length contract relationships, where it is the norm that parties try to get the best of each other. Finally, element three can also seem a bit counterintuitive, since in many common agency relationships the agent enjoys substantial latitude to decide how to undertake the principal's business. But in all of those relationships, the agent has only as much latitude as the parties agree to when the relationship is first created. Each of these elements is elaborated further in the comments following Re(3) §1.01.

Importantly, an agency relationship is not itself a contract. *See* Re(3) §1.01, comment d. In and of itself, the relationship is not subject to rules of contract law, and there is no requirement that the parties exchange any consideration. A principal and an agent can *also* have a contract, and they frequently do. They can agree to virtually anything concerning the nature of the relationship, the tasks to be performed, the principal's role, the compensation to be paid, and so on, and the fact of having adopted a contract can have real consequences. For example, a principal normally remains free to direct the agent in virtually any way he or she likes, so long as the commands do not violate some other law. But if the parties also agree by contract that the principal will not unreasonably interfere with the conduct of the agent's duties, the principal's interference may breach the contract and the agent may be entitled to damages. (Some agency rules probably cannot be modified by contract, as a matter of public policy. For example, a principal cannot disclaim vicarious liability for torts or contracts, and while the parties can modify the agent's fiduciary duties it is unlikely they could extinguish them entirely.) Parties frequently find it important to adopt a contract, because the default rules of the common law of agency might sometimes frustrate the goals of one or both of them. But whether there is a contract or not, the agency relationship itself and the rules applying to it exist independently. This fact reflects the different policy goals of agency law and contract law. For the most part, the consequences of the terms of a contract arrangement attach because the parties desire it. The consequences of an agency relationship attach, whether the parties intend it or not, *because public policy says so.* Can you see why? Think about the particular legal consequences that follow once a relationship between two people is an agency, and ask why society would decide to impose them in some cases, *in spite of the parties' subjective intentions.*

More to the Story: Agency and Pay

Perhaps a bit surprisingly, an agency can be "gratuitous," meaning the agent receives no pay, but even when it is gratuitous the agent owes all the same fiduciary duties and can bind the principal to all the same contracts and torts. However, much more commonly there will be an exchange of consideration that would be sufficient to support a contract. The agent will perform a task, and in exchange the principal will pay some compensation. Indeed, as mentioned, the principal normally must pay compensation, a duty implied in the absence of contrary agreement. *See* Re(3) §8.13, comment d. But gratuitous agencies can exist so long as the parties so agree.

 ### Time Out for PR

Every lawyer who serves a client is an agent and the client is the lawyer's principal. Think about it: (1) Both parties agree that the attorney-client relationship will exist, (2) the client sets out the goals of the relationship, and (3) the client retains at least some authority to direct the attorney's work on his or her behalf—at least insofar as the client may terminate the relationship at any time. As a result, the attorney is subject to strict obligations, including one not to secretly seek benefits in excess of the agreed-upon compensation or at the client's expense.

In thinking about this conclusion, consider also American Bar Association Model Rule of Professional Conduct 1.2(a), which provides that, subject to certain limitations, a lawyer shall abide by a client's decisions concerning the objectives of representation and consult with the client as to the means by which they are to be pursued, and Rule 1.16(a)(3), which calls (subject to a tribunal's approval if the matter is before a court) for a lawyer's withdrawal in the event of discharge.

2. Applying the Basic Test

In getting the knack for distinguishing agency relationships from other kinds of relationships, it helps to consider practical examples. The former Restatement (Second) set out a helpful set of provisions that considered common business relationships and explained whether or not they constituted agency relationships. *See* Restatement (Second) of Agency §§14A-14O. It will be useful to consider some of these (and they also show up in the case to follow, *A. Gay Jenson Farms*). First, the Restatement pointed out that members of a corporation's board of directors are not "agents" of anyone. Re(2) §14C. Consider why this is so. By statute, most corporations must have boards of directors. The directors are elected, usually annually, at a meeting of all the company's shareholders, by vote of the shareholders. Anyone may serve as a director; they need not own any shares or have any other relation to the company, though often they do own shares and frequently directors also happen to be employed by the company as corporate officers. They are not required by law to be paid for their board membership, though they often are. Upon their election, directors are entrusted, by statute, with all of the corporation's managerial power and with the duty to hire and supervise its officers. They serve for fixed terms and can only be removed (by another vote of the shareholders) with some difficulty. On the basis of this description, you should be able to figure out why directors are not "agents" under the §1.01 test. Do you see which of the three elements is most obviously missing?

Two other provisions are particularly interesting. Under §14J, which was entitled "Agent or Buyer,"

> [o]ne who receives goods from another for resale to a third person is not thereby the other's agent in the transaction: whether he is an agent for this purpose or is himself a buyer depends upon whether the parties agree that his duty is to act primarily for the benefit of the one delivering the goods to him or is to act primarily for his own benefit.

Likewise, §14K, entitled "Agent or Supplier," provided that

> [o]ne who contracts to acquire property from a third person and convey it to another is the agent of the other party only if it is agreed that he is to act primarily for the benefit of the other and not for himself.

The interesting thing about these two provisions is that they both describe common commercial relationships that look like simple contract situations. In each case, some good is being bought and sold, and the person who might or might not be an agent appears to be serving in the role of middleman. But the Restatement suggests that the significant consequences of vicarious liability and fiduciary duty might attach, and there is no way of knowing for sure until a trier of fact has had a chance to sift through the facts.

> ■ **Think about this:**
>
> *(D)* Read both §14J and §14K carefully, and try to imagine hypothetical scenarios that might be governed by them. Imagine such a scenario and ask yourself whether, as trier of fact, you would describe the middleman as an agent or not. Then, ask yourself what aspect of the scenario you would have to change in order to change that person's legal status.

The case set out below is an excellent illustration of these rules at play.

A. GAY JENSON FARMS CO. V. CARGILL, INC.

Supreme Court of Minnesota
309 N.W.2d 285 (1981)

Peterson, J.

[A group of farmers sued defendants Cargill, Inc. ("Cargill") and Warren Grain & Seed Co. ("Warren") on Warren's unfulfilled promise to buy their grain. Warren, a family business, ran a grain elevator in a small Minnesota town. By the time of this action it had gone insolvent under the direction of owners Lloyd and Gary Hill. Cargill is a multinational agricultural products company that acquired grain through Warren and many other small businesses like it.]

[Beginning in 1964, Cargill helped keep the struggling Warren afloat through an agreement under] which . . . Cargill would loan money for working capital to Warren on "open account" financing up to a stated limit, which was originally set as $175,000. . . . Under this contract, Warren would receive funds and pay its expenses by issuing drafts drawn on Cargill through Minneapolis banks. The drafts were imprinted with both Warren's and Cargill's names. Proceeds from Warren's sales would be deposited with Cargill and credited to its account. In return for this financing, Warren appointed Cargill as its grain agent for transaction with the Commodity Credit Corporation. Cargill was also given a right of first refusal to purchase market grain sold by Warren to the terminal market.

A new contract was negotiated in 1967, extending Warren's credit line to $300,000 and incorporating the

> **More to the Story: Other Factors**
>
> Cargill, Inc., is the largest privately held company in the United States in terms of revenue. If it were publicly held, it would be ninth, just ahead of Ford Motors.

provisions of the original contract. It was also stated in the contract that Warren would provide Cargill with annual financial statements and that either Cargill would keep the books for Warren or an audit would be conducted by an independent firm. Cargill was given the right of access to Warren's books for inspection.

In addition, the agreement provided that Warren was not to make capital improvements or repairs in excess of $5,000 without Cargill's prior consent. Further, it was not to become liable as guarantor on another's indebtedness, or encumber its assets except with Cargill's permission. Consent by Cargill was required before Warren would be allowed to declare a dividend or sell and purchase stock.

Officials from Cargill's regional office made a brief visit to Warren shortly after the agreement was executed. They examined the annual statement and the accounts receivable, expenses, inventory, seed, machinery and other financial matters. Warren was informed that it would be reminded periodically to make the improvements recommended by Cargill.[2] At approximately this time, a memo was given to the Cargill official in charge of the Warren account, Erhart Becker, which stated in part: "This organization (Warren) needs very strong paternal guidance." . . .

During this period, Cargill continued to review Warren's operations and expenses and recommend that certain actions should be taken.[3] Warren purchased from Cargill various business forms printed by Cargill and received sample forms from Cargill which Warren used to develop its own business forms.

Cargill wrote to its regional office in 1970 expressing its concern that the pattern of increased use of funds allowed to develop at Warren was similar to that involved in two other cases in which Cargill experienced severe losses. Cargill did not refuse to honor drafts or call the loan, however. A new security agreement which increased the credit line to $750,000 was executed in 1972, and a subsequent agreement which raised the limit to $1,250,000 was entered into in 1976.

Warren was at that time shipping Cargill 90% of . . . [the] grain [it purchased from farmers]. When Cargill's facilities were full, Warren shipped its grain to other companies. Approximately 25% of Warren's total sales was seed grain which was sold directly by Warren to its customers.

As Warren's indebtedness continued to be in excess of its credit line, Cargill began to contact Warren daily regarding its financial affairs. Cargill headquar-

---

2. Cargill headquarters suggested that the regional office check Warren monthly. Also, it was requested that Warren be given an explanation for the relatively large withdrawals from undistributed earnings made by the Hills, since Cargill hoped that Warren's profits would be used to decrease its debt balance. Cargill asked for written requests for withdrawals from undistributed earnings in the future.

3. Between 1967 and 1973, Cargill suggested that Warren take a number of steps, including: (1) a reduction of seed grain and cash grain inventories; (2) improved collection of accounts receivable; (3) reduction or elimination of its wholesale seed business and its specialty grain operation; (4) marketing fertilizer and steel bins on consignment; (5) a reduction in withdrawals made by officers; (6) a suggestion that Warren's bookkeeper not issue her own salary checks; and (7) cooperation with Cargill in implementing the recommendations. These ideas were apparently never implemented, however.

ters informed its regional office in 1973 that, since Cargill money was being used, Warren should realize that Cargill had the right to make some critical decisions regarding the use of the funds. Cargill headquarters also told Warren that a regional manager would be working with Warren on a day-to-day basis as well as in monthly planning meetings. In 1975, Cargill's regional office began to keep a daily debit position on Warren. A bank account was opened in Warren's name on which Warren could draw checks in 1976. The account was to be funded by drafts drawn on Cargill by the local bank.

In early 1977, it became evident that Warren had serious financial problems. Several farmers, who had heard that Warren's checks were not being paid, inquired or had their agents inquire at Cargill regarding Warren's status and were initially told that there would be no problem with payment. In April 1977, an audit of Warren revealed that Warren was $4 million in debt. After Cargill was informed that Warren's financial statements had been deliberately falsified, Warren's request for additional financing was refused. In the final days of Warren's operation, Cargill sent an official to supervise the elevator, including disbursement of funds and income generated by the elevator. . . .

The jury found that Cargill's conduct between 1973 and 1977 had made it Warren's principal. . . . It was concluded that Cargill was jointly liable with Warren for plaintiffs' losses, and judgment was entered for plaintiffs. . . .

1. The major issue in this case is whether Cargill, by its course of dealing with Warren, became liable as a principal on contracts made by Warren with plaintiffs. Cargill contends that no agency relationship was established with Warren, notwithstanding its financing of Warren's operation and its purchase of the majority of Warren's grain. However, we conclude that Cargill, by its control and influence over Warren, became a principal with liability for the transactions entered into by its agent Warren.

Agency is the fiduciary relationship that results from the manifestation of consent by one person to another that the other shall act on his behalf and subject to his control, and consent by the other so to act. . . . In order to create an agency there must be an agreement, but not necessarily a contract between the parties. . . . An agreement may result in the creation of an agency relationship although the parties did not call it an agency and did not intend the legal consequences of the relation to follow. The existence of the agency may be proved by circumstantial evidence which shows a course of dealing between the two parties. . . . When an agency relationship is to be proven

Doing the Numbers: A Deal for Cargill

Ten percent of the grain sold by Warren was bringing in 25 percent of the gross amount it was receiving (known as "total sales" or just "sales"). What does that tell you about the price Cargill was paying for the other 90 percent?

Assume Warren sold 1,000,000 units for a total of $1,000,000. This means that Cargill paid 75 percent, or $750,000, for 90 percent, or 900,000, of the units. $750,000/900,000 = 83 cents per unit.

The other purchasers paid $250,000 for 100,000 units, or $2.50 per unit.

JD/MBA: Debits and Credits

A debit is a financial bookkeeping entry that (among other things) increases an asset. Money someone owes you is an asset, so as the amount of debt increases, debit entries are made.

A credit has the opposite effect, so as a debt is repaid, the debtor's account is "credited."

by circumstantial evidence, the principal must be shown to have consented to the agency since one cannot be the agent of another except by consent of the latter. . . .

Cargill contends that the prerequisites of an agency relationship did not exist because Cargill never consented to the agency, Warren did not act on behalf of Cargill, and Cargill did not exercise control over Warren. We hold that all three elements of agency could be found in the particular circumstances of this case. By directing Warren to implement its recommendations, Cargill manifested its consent that Warren would be its agent. Warren acted on Cargill's behalf in procuring grain for Cargill as the part of its normal operations which were totally financed by Cargill. . . . Further, an agency relationship was established by Cargill's interference with the internal affairs of Warren, which constituted de facto control of the elevator.

A creditor who assumes control of his debtor's business may become liable as principal for the acts of the debtor in connection with the business. Restatement (Second) of Agency §140 (1958). It is noted in comment a to section 140 that:

> A security holder who merely exercises a veto power over the business acts of his debtor by preventing purchases or sales above specified amounts does not thereby become a principal. However, if he takes over the management of the debtor's business either in person or through an agent, and directs what contracts may or may not be made, he becomes a principal, liable as a principal for the obligations incurred thereafter in the normal course of business by the debtor who has now become his general agent. The point at which the creditor becomes a principal is that at which he assumes de facto control over the conduct of his debtor, whatever the terms of the formal contract with his debtor may be.

A number of factors indicate Cargill's control over Warren, including the following:

(1) Cargill's constant recommendations to Warren by telephone;
(2) Cargill's right of first refusal on grain;
(3) Warren's inability to enter into mortgages, to purchase stock or to pay dividends without Cargill's approval;
(4) Cargill's right of entry onto Warren's premises to carry on periodic checks and audits;
(5) Cargill's correspondence and criticism regarding Warren's finances, officers salaries and inventory;
(6) Cargill's determination that Warren needed "strong paternal guidance";
(7) Provision of drafts and forms to Warren upon which Cargill's name was imprinted;
(8) Financing of all Warren's purchases of grain and operating expenses; and
(9) Cargill's power to discontinue the financing of Warren's operations.

We recognize that some of these elements, as Cargill contends, are found in an ordinary debtor-creditor relationship. However, these factors cannot be considered in isolation, but, rather, they must be viewed in light of all the circumstances surrounding Cargill's aggressive financing of Warren.

It is also Cargill's position that the relationship between Cargill and Warren was that of buyer-supplier rather than principal-agent. Restatement (Second) of Agency §14K (1958) compares an agent with a supplier as follows:

> One who contracts to acquire property from a third person and convey it to another is the agent of the other only if it is agreed that he is to act primarily for the benefit of the other and not for himself.

Factors indicating that one is a supplier, rather than an agent, are:

> (1) That he is to receive a fixed price for the property irrespective of price paid by him. This is the most important. (2) That he acts in his own name and receives the title to the property which he thereafter is to transfer. (3) That he has an independent business in buying and selling similar property.

Restatement (Second) of Agency §14K, Comment a (1958).

Under the Restatement approach, it must be shown that the supplier has an independent business before it can be concluded that he is not an agent. The record establishes that all portions of Warren's operation were financed by Cargill and that Warren sold almost all of its market grain to Cargill. Thus, the relationship which existed between the parties was not merely that of buyer and supplier.

Cargill furnished substantially all funds received by the elevator. Cargill . . . ha[d] a right of entry on Warren's premises, and it . . . required maintenance of insurance against hazards of operation. Warren's activities . . . formed a substantial part of Cargill's business that was developed in that area. In addition, Cargill did not think of Warren as an operator who was free to become Cargill's competitor, but rather conceded that it believed that Warren owed a duty of loyalty to Cargill. The decisions made by Warren were not independent of Cargill's interest or its control.

Further, we are not persuaded by the fact that Warren was not one of the "line" elevators that Cargill operated in its own name. The Warren operation, like the line elevator, was financially dependent on Cargill's continual infusion of capital. The arrangement with Warren presented a convenient alternative to the establishment of a line elevator. Cargill became, in essence, the owner of the operation without the accompanying legal indicia.

The amici curiae assert that, if the jury verdict is upheld, firms and banks which have provided business loans to county elevators will decline to make further loans. The decision in this case should give no cause for such concern. We deal here with a business enterprise markedly different from an ordinary bank financing, since Cargill was an active participant in Warren's operations rather than simply a financier. Cargill's course of dealing with Warren was, by its own admission, a paternalistic relationship in which Cargill made the key economic decisions and kept Warren in existence.

Although considerable interest was paid by Warren on the loan, the reason for Cargill's financing of Warren was not to make money as a lender but, rather, to establish a source of market grain for its business. As one Cargill manager noted, "We were staying in there because we wanted the grain." For this reason, Cargill was willing to extend the credit line far beyond the amount originally allocated to Warren. It is noteworthy that Cargill was receiving significant amounts of grain and that, notwithstanding the risk that was recognized by Cargill, the operation was considered profitable. . . .

Affirmed.

JD/MBA: The Make-or-Buy Decision and Its Legal Consequences

In an important sense, the issue posed in *Cargill* and in the problem below is a basic one for business transactional lawyers, and it goes to what may be the most basic problem of business organization: whether a firm should provide some good or service for itself, in-house, or whether it should hire someone else to do it. This is frequently called the *make-or-buy decision.*

All businesses need various inputs and services to make their product or provide their service or do whatever else it is that they do to earn money. And that can mean raw materials, labor, assembled components, warehousing and logistics, and all kinds of other goods and services. For example, most businesses face the problem that Burger Daddy National confronts—how best to get their product from the place where they make it to the place where customers will buy it. And that then poses a basic problem in choosing organizational forms. Should a firm buy the inputs and the downstream distributional services it needs, through contract, or should it produce those things in-house? And if the latter, should it produce them through internal operating divisions, or through separately organized subsidiaries?

This issue is explored in more depth in the online Supplement. It also is related to the attempted outsourcing of labor, which is addressed in Chapter 4.

■ Think about this:

(E) Wilma has set up a new business entity, which she's incorporated, to operate a restaurant in her town of Springfield. It's called Burger Daddy of Springfield, Inc. (BDSI), but it is not a freestanding, self-contained entity. It is a franchise, doing business under license from a national umbrella operation called Burger Daddy National, Inc. ("National"). National does not itself own any restaurants or indeed much in the way of any physical assets. Its main asset is the nationally known name "Burger Daddy," along with other trademarked logos and marketing materials, which it promotes through national advertising campaigns. It licenses these trademarks to tens of thousands of separately organized franchisees nationwide, and they

in turn own and operate the physical restaurants where the burgers are sold. National's licensing agreements are long, complex, and heavily lawyered documents. On the one hand, they set a number of specific rules that franchisees must follow in their operation of their restaurants, to prevent misuse of the trademark, and to maintain quality standards in the food products, cleanliness of stores, and customer service. But on the other hand, they disclaim the creation of any legal relationship between National and the franchisees other than arm's-length contract.

First, what is the basic tension that National's licensing contracts try to navigate with restrictions on franchisees, on the one hand, but disclaimers of agency or partnership, on the other? Here's a harder, more open-ended question: Why sell burgers through franchisees—as most fast-food businesses do? Why doesn't National just own the restaurants directly? What are the pros and cons?

(F) Suppose that you represent a small bank that is considering making a loan to a struggling operator of a local grain elevator. The prospective lender believes the elevator is important to the local economy, but is concerned with some of the business judgments the operator recently has made. What steps can the lender take to protect itself (other than forgo the loan)? What must it avoid?

The next case may hit a little closer to home.

GORTON V. DOTY

Supreme Court of Idaho
69 P.2d 136 (1937)

HOLDEN, J.

In September, 1935, an action was commenced by R.S. Gorton, father of Richard Gorton, to recover expenses incurred by the father for hospitalization, physicians', surgeons', and nurses' fees, and another by the son, by his father as guardian *ad litem*, to recover damages for injuries sustained as a result of an accident. . . . [T]he jury returned a verdict in favor of the father for $870 and another in favor of the son for $5,000. . . . The cases come here upon an appeal from each judgment and order denying a new trial. . . .

It appears that in September, 1934, Richard Gorton, a minor, was a junior in the Soda Springs High School and a member of the football team; that his high school team and the Paris High School team were scheduled to play a game of football at Paris on the 21st. Appellant was teaching at the Soda Springs High School and Russell Garst was coaching the Soda Springs team. On the day the game was played, the Soda Springs High School team was transported to and from Paris in privately owned automobiles. One of the automobiles used for that purpose was owned by appellant. Her car was driven by Mr. Garst, the coach of the Soda Springs High School team.

One of the most difficult questions, if not the most difficult, presented by the record, is, Was the coach, Russell Garst, the agent of appellant while and in driving her car from Soda Springs to Paris, and in returning to the point where the accident occurred?

Briefly stated, the facts bearing upon that question are as follows: That appellant knew the Soda Springs High School football team and the Paris High School football team were to play a game of football at Paris September 21, 1934; that she volunteered her car for use in transporting some of the members of the Soda Springs team to and from the game; that she asked the coach, Russell Garst, the day before the game, if he had all the cars necessary for the trip to Paris the next day; that he said he needed one more; that she told him he might use her car if he drove it; that she was not promised compensation for the use of her car and did not receive any; that the school district paid for the gasoline used on the trip to and from the game; that she testified she loaned the car to Mr. Garst; that she had not employed Mr. Garst at any time and that she had not at any time "directed his work or his services, or what he was doing." . . .

Specifically, "agency" is the relationship which results from the manifestation of consent by one person to another that the other shall act on his behalf and subject to his control, and consent by the other so to act. (Restatement Agency, sec. 1, p. 7[.)] . . .

To enable the Soda Springs football team to play football at Paris, it had to be transported to Paris. Automobiles were to be used and another car was needed. At that juncture, appellant volunteered the use of her car. For what purpose? Necessarily for the purpose of furnishing additional transportation. Appellant, of course, could have driven the car herself, but instead of doing that, she designated the driver (Russell Garst) and, in doing so, made it a condition precedent that the person she designated should drive her car. That appellant thereby at least consented that Russell Garst should act for her and in her behalf, in driving her car to and from the football game, is clear from her act in volunteering the use of her car upon the express condition that he should drive it, and, further, that Mr. Garst consented to so act for appellant is equally clear by his act in driving the car. It is not essential to the existence of authority that there be a contract between principal and agent or that the agent promise to act as such (Restatement Agency, secs. 15, 16, pp. 50-54), nor is it essential to the relationship of principal and agent that they, or either, receive compensation (Restatement Agency, sec. 16, p. 53).

Furthermore, this court held in Willi v. Schaefer Hitchcock Co., 25 P.2d 167, in harmony with the clear weight of authority, that the fact of ownership alone (conceded here), regardless of the presence or absence of the owner in the car at the time of the accident, establishes a *prima facie* case against the owner for the reason that the presumption arises that the driver is the agent of the owner. And we further held that where the facts are such that the trial court is in doubt as to whether the driver of an automobile is the agent of the owner, it is proper to submit the question to the jury. . . .

While it appears that appellant first testified that she permitted Russell Garst to use her car and also that she loaned it to him, it further appears that when she was immediately afterward asked to state the conversation she had with the coach about the matter, she stated that she asked him if he had all the cars necessary for the trip to Paris the next day, that he said he needed one more, that she said he might use her car if he drove it, and, finally, she said that that was the extent of it. It is clear, then, that appellant intended, in relating the conversation she had with the coach, to state, the circumstances fully, because, after having testified to the conversation, she concluded by saying, "That was the extent of it." Thus she gave the jury to understand that those were the circumstances, and all of the circumstances, under which Russell Garst drove her car to the football game. If the appellant fully and correctly related the conversation she had with the coach and the circumstances under which he drove her car, as she unquestionably undertook to, and did, do, it follows that, as a matter of fact, she did not say anything whatever to him about loaning her car and he said nothing whatever to her about borrowing it.

We therefore conclude the evidence sufficiently supports the finding of the jury that the relationship of principal and agent existed between appellant and Russell Garst....

During the course of the closing argument of counsel for respondent, an objection was made by counsel for appellant to certain remarks addressed to the jury. Thereupon the trial court ordered a brief recess and took up such objection in chambers with counsel for the respective parties, whereupon the following proceedings took place outside of the presence of the jury.

> **Mr. GLENNON:**   What I said, your Honor, was in response to counsel's repeated charges that the plaintiff was attempting to mulch (mulct) the defendant in damages, and I stated to the jury in substance, "That you have a right to draw on your experience as business men in determining the facts in this case, and that you know from your experience as business men that prudent automobile owners usually protect themselves against just such contingencies as are involved in this case."

Following that statement by [Mr.] Glennon, counsel for appellant agreed it was substantially correct. Upon returning to the courtroom, the trial judge denied appellant's motion for a mistrial and then instructed the reporter to read the above quoted remarks to the jury, after which the court instructed the jury to disregard the remarks....

Funk & Wagnalls New Standard Dictionary defines the word mulct: "1. To sentence to a pecuniary penalty or forfeiture as a punishment; fine; hence, to fine unjustly, as, to *mulct* the prisoner in $100. 2. To punish." Appellant had testified during the trial that she volunteered the use of her car. To charge, then, that respondent was attempting to "mulct"

More to the Story: The Role of Insurance

The court here considers the objection of defense counsel to statements made by plaintiff's counsel in closing argument. The objection is based on the general rule that the jury is not supposed to know whether the defendant carried liability insurance.

More to the Story: Never Assume the Absence of a Statute

Every state now has a statute addressing owner liability in the event of an auto accident. In some states, the owner is liable if the driver had the owner's express or implied consent. In others, there is a presumption that the driver was acting as the owner's agent.

her in damages carried the inference that respondent was attempting to punish her in damages for having volunteered the use of her car for the commendable purpose of supplying additional transportation for the hometown football team.

And it will be noted that Mr. Glennon stated, and the record shows no denial, that the above-quoted remarks were made by him only in response to *repeated* charges by appellant's counsel that respondent was attempting to *mulct* appellant in damages. There is no evidence whatever in the record justifying such charges. They were made during the course of the argument of counsel for appellant, and were as fully and clearly outside the record as the remarks of counsel for respondent. It was a case of meeting improper argument with improper argument. The remarks complained of were provoked by the conduct of counsel for appellant. Hence, we conclude that appellant has no just cause for complaint. Having reached that conclusion, we find it unnecessary to review the cases cited by counsel for the respective parties. . . .

■ **Think about this:**

(G) Can the outcome in this case possibly be correct? Is there anything to commend it from a policy standpoint?

(H) What could Ms. Doty have done to protect herself, other than to refrain from offering to let other people use her car?

(I) Suppose Ms. Doty purchases a car for the use of Don, her teen-age son. Don is on his way to school when he crashes the car, injuring a third party. Is Ms. Doty liable?

(J) Suppose Ms. Doty purchases a car for the use of Don, her teen-age son. Unbeknown to her, Don allows a friend to drive the car. The friend crashes the car, injuring a third party. Is Ms. Doty liable?

C. Specific Issues Surrounding Formation: Capacity, the Varieties of Agency, and the Power of Attorney

1. Capacity

The agency relationship cannot be created unless both the would-be parties to it have legally sufficient "capacity." The relevant rules appear in Re(3) §§3.04-3.05.

An individual person has capacity to act as principal if he or she would have had capacity at the time of the agent's action to undertake it personally. Re(3) §3.04(1). Whether a non-individual person, like a corporation, has capacity depends on the law governing the organization's existence. Knowing whether capacity exists in any given scenario will be a case-by-case matter, but generally speaking the would-be principal will lack capacity unless under its governing law it is in existence at the time of the agent's action, it would be authorized to undertake the action itself, and nothing has occurred to disempower it. *See* Re(3) §3.04(2) & Re(3) §3.04, comment d.

One special capacity issue deserves mention. Often-times, when some new business is just getting started, the entrepreneurs involved in it (known as "promoters") will take various steps on its behalf. They might do so before they have done all the paperwork or made the appropriate filings or whatever else that is necessary for the business to exist. This sometimes can put them in an awkward legal position. If they intend that the business will be formed as some sort of limited liability entity, and they will be merely its owners and therefore free of personal liability for its obligations, then they will naturally prefer that any transactions they undertake on its behalf bind only the business. But §3.04 makes clear that the entity itself can-not be bound if it does not yet exist, and another provision, Re(3) §6.04, states that the promoters *themselves* are liable on the contract, so long as they knew or reasonably should have known that the entity did not yet exist.

> **Connections**
>
> Contracts made on behalf of companies not yet in existence (and thus lacking principals that have capacity) are often called "pre-incorporation" or "promoter's" contracts. The trouble they cause is a frequent, often serious problem in the lives of small and start-up businesses.
>
> These contracts are dealt with at greater length in Chapter 13.

The capacity of a person to act as an *agent* is different. In effect, any person, human or otherwise, can act as an agent. *See* Re(3) §3.05. The only real qualifi-cations are that (1) some human agents will be subject to limitations imposed by law other than agency, as in the case of attorneys (who must be licensed); and (2) organization agents can act only if their governing law says so (e.g., corporations as a matter of law cannot take any legally effective actions at all until documents evincing their existence are accepted for filing by the Secretary of State). *See* Re(3) §3.05, comment b. However, as made clear in §3.05, comment d, even an agent who is able to act in a given circumstance, and therefore capable of taking action binding on the principal, might evade *personal* liability for those actions for lack of legal capacity to bind him*self*. For example, a minor has capacity to act as agent, but lacks full capacity as a matter of contract law to bind him- or herself to contracts. The minor might be able to bind his or her principal to a contract that purports to bind the agent as well, but because contracts made by minors are voidable at the minor's instance, the minor agent can escape liability.

■ **Think about this:**

(K) Singing sensation Twilah Tween had just turned 13 when she agreed to representation by a prominent Hollywood talent agent named Roger. Over the years of their work together Roger secured her a number of highly desirable deals, including a major recording contract presented to her as a seventeenth birthday surprise. It was for a five-year term and initially she gladly acquiesced to it. When she was just a week shy of her next birthday, however, she decided she'd had enough of the deal. She announced then that she would no longer be bound by it.

> Can she do that, and why or why not?
>
> *(L)*   Suzanne and Rachel, inseparable friends since childhood, are slogging through the fourth and most challenging week so far of a new adventure: opening "Sweet Temptations," their new pastry shop. With a thrilling sense of accomplishment, Suzanne inked her name on the lease for their new space, a retail storefront from which they will sell their wares. Only later that day did she learn that Rachel still had not filed the company's articles of incorporation, which under their state's law is a prerequisite for the corporation to come into existence.
>
>   Among Sweet Temptations, Suzanne, and Rachel, who can be bound by the lease?

2. Co-agents, Sub-agents, and Co-principals

Next, the Restatement (Third) distinguishes among a few different types of agency relationships:

- ☐ **Co-agency:** "Co-agents" are agents of the same principal. They may be appointed by the principal or by another agent authorized to do so. They may be superiors or subordinates of one another, and a superior may direct his or her subordinate co-agent, so long as authority to do so is conferred by the principal. However, co-agents are not agents of one another, so they owe one another no fiduciary duties, and they can create liability only for their common principal, not for one another. *See* Re(3) §1.04(1) & comment a.

- ☐ **Sub-agency:** A "sub-agent" also has the same principal as some other agent, but the relationship between them is quite different than that between co-agents. A sub-agent *is also the agent* of that other agent. So, the sub-agent owes fiduciary duties and can create vicarious liabilities both for the ultimate principal and for that other agent. *See* Re(3) §§1.04(8), 3.15. In sub-agencies, the ultimate principal's interests and instructions are paramount, so that, for example, the sub-agent must obey the principal when his instructions differ from the appointing agent's instructions. *See id.* at comment d.

- ☐ **Agent for Co-principals:** One agent can represent two or more principals in the same matter. This "agency for co-principals" is legally simple, but poses one serious real-world problem—the likelihood that the agent will face conflicting interests. The agent will owe the same fiduciary duties to each principal in equal measure, and if serving one would compromise the agent's ability to serve another with equal zeal, the agent likely faces an impermissible conflict of interest. *See* Re(3) §3.16 & comment b.

Connections: Fiduciary Duty

Many of the special problems raised by these varying agency relationships concern the agent's fiduciary duties, which may vary depending on the agent's particular relationships to other agents or principals in the scenario.

Fiduciary duties are dealt with at greater length in Chapter 12. It is worth noting now, however, that although all agents are fiduciaries, not all fiduciaries are agents.

Time Out for PR

It should be obvious that an attorney representing more than one client is an agent for co-principals. The terms under which such a representation are permissible are governed by American Bar Association Model Rule of Professional Conduct 1.7—but the common law also applies.

Model Rule 1.7, in essence, permits concurrent representations where the attorney reasonably believes he or she can provide competent, diligent representation to all affected clients *and* the clients give informed, written consent.

■ Think about this:

(M) Let's say that a fellow named Jim has been hired by a despotic and self-aggrandizing boss, Wilma. Jim will manage Wilma's new business, Burger Daddy, Inc., and though she won't have an active day-to-day role in managing the joint, Wilma is CEO and sole shareholder of the incorporated business. Jim can't do all the necessary work himself, so he would like to hire some subordinate workers to staff the cashiers, manage the inventory, and so on. Among others, he hires Samantha to work as his assistant. He gives her basic training in the tasks around the store and instructs her as to such matters as hours of work and store policies.

For each of the following pairs of persons, determine whether there is an agency relationship and, if so, what sort of relationship it is:

(i) Burger Daddy, Inc., and Wilma
(ii) Burger Daddy, Inc., and Jim
(iii) Wilma and Jim
(iv) Wilma and Samantha
(v) Jim and Samantha

(N) PrinceCo is an insurance company that has hired Alan, a lawyer who is a partner in a law firm. PrinceCo hired Alan to defend it in a lawsuit against one of its insureds, who indisputably caused an auto accident in which a third party was injured. In serious dispute, however, is the extent of plaintiff's injuries, and Alan suspects that if he could perform some private surveillance of plaintiff he would discover that plaintiff in fact is able to engage in lots of daily physical activity that plaintiff claims are now prevented by his injuries. So Alan calls his client and asks permission to engage Stan to perform the surveillance. Stan is a private investigator, who is not Alan's employee but whom Alan keeps on retainer for just such work.

What's the relationship between Alan and Stan?

(O) In Problem M, Wilma owns the restaurant, but it is organized as a corporation. In all likelihood, Wilma took steps to make clear that Jim (and all the other employees) are only agents of the company, and not her agents directly. Can you see why?

Connections and JD/MBA: Outsourcing Risk and Hassle and the Brave New World of the Sharing/On-demand/Gig Economy

For decades, many merchandisers have preferred to contract with independent contractors to obtain security guard and delivery services rather than to use their own employees. Outsourcing a variety of tasks is becoming increasingly popular for a variety of reasons in addition to avoiding *respondeat superior* liability. The independent contractor/employee distinction and its further implications are addressed more fully in Chapter 4.

3. Employees and Non-Employee Agents

As has been hinted already, some agents are known as "employees." Their principals (unsurprisingly) are known as "employers." (Older terms that have fallen out of popularity, for obvious reasons, are "servant" and "master.") Employees are always agents, and all employees fall within a certain special class of agency. The only real significance this distinction has throughout the entire law of agency is in the area of vicarious tort liability—the body of rules that determine when a principal can be held responsible for the agent's tort. (You may remember something about this from Torts class under the label "*respondeat superior*.") For that reason, the official definition of the term appears in Re(3) §7.07(3)(a), which governs an employer-principal's vicarious tort liability. Under that provision, an "employee" is

an agent whose principal controls or has the right to control the *manner and means* of the agent's performance of work. . . .

(Emphasis added.) Section 7.07(3)(b) then states that a principal can still be liable for the torts of a gratuitous agent, implying that an employee agent can still be an "employee" even if unpaid, so long as the principal has some control over "the manner and means of the . . . work. . . ."

While, for agency law purposes, the employee/non-employee distinction is only of real relevance in the case of vicarious tort liability, in that area the distinction has a huge practical significance. To simplify a bit, it will usually be the case that an employer *is* responsible for culpable injuries caused by employees while they were doing their jobs. A principal usually will *not* be responsible for the torts of non-employee agents. Agents who are not employees are "independent contractors." This can be confusing, since it also is possible to be an independent contractor who is not an agent at all.

 Dear Prof.: I know that employers have to withhold some taxes from the salaries they pay "employees." Can I make the employee/non-employee distinction just by asking whether the principal is withholding taxes from the payments to the agent?

No. On the one hand, it is true that some tax withholding obligations depend on whether a given agent is an "employee," under the common law test that is described in the text. But on the other hand, the determination is actually to be made by the principal—at least until the principal is audited. It is somewhat difficult to apply, and not everyone gets it right. So the fact that a given principal is withholding or not is not a sure guide to whether the agent is an employee. By the way, some people believe that they can avoid withholding if the parties enter an agreement stipulating that the one providing services is an independent contractor. Sorry, but no. It's the actual relationship, not what it's called, that matters.

This may help . . .

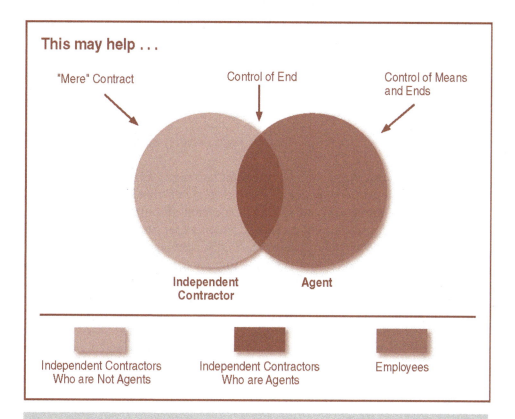

"Mere" Contract

Control of End

Control of Means and Ends

Independent Contractor

Agent

Independent Contractors Who are Not Agents

Independent Contractors Who are Agents

Employees

■ **Think about this:**

(P) Agency law distinguishes employees from non-employees for a simple policy reason. Can you see what it is?

(Q) Consider the usual relationship between a client and a lawyer who works at a law firm, rather than "in house." Is it an employer/employee relationship?

4. The Power of Attorney and the Need for a Writing Generally

Generally speaking, the creation of agency relationships requires no writing whatsoever. The only exception is that many states maintain so-called equal dignity statutes, under which any contract that itself must be in writing can be executed by an agent only if the agent is authorized to do so in a writing that would comply with the relevant statute. *See* Re(3) §3.02.

That said, parties do often commit details of their relationships to writing, and one such writing about which one often hears is the "power of attorney." There is no good reason to focus on this unimportant phrase except to dispel the intuition that it is more important than it really is. The document can be very simple, and there are basically no formal requirements except for the fact that by definition it will be in writing. Under Re(3) §1.04(7) a power of attorney is simply "an instrument that states an agent's authority."

Test Yourself

Assume Applicability of the Restatement (Third) of Agency

1. Bob runs an auto shop. State and federal law require him to dispose of used motor oil properly, which in Bob's case meant that he had to haul it himself to the dump and pay to have it recycled. Recently, Bob was contacted by Phillip, who has begun a new business serving local auto shops by collecting and recycling used oil. Phillip convinces Bob that he can dispose of Bob's used oil more cheaply than he can do it himself, because Phillip can take advantage of volume discounts with recycling companies. Bob agrees to the service and agrees to pay Phillip on a monthly basis to pick up all the used oil he collects.

   The relationship between Bob and Phillip is most likely:

   a. Principal and agent in which Bob is principal.
   b. Contract in which fiduciary duties apply.
   c. Principal and agent in which Phillip is employee.
   d. None of the above.

2. The distinction between "independent contractor agent" and "employee" is most relevant to:

   a. Vicarious contract liability.
   b. Agent's entitlement to compensation.
   c. Both vicarious tort and vicarious contract liability.
   d. *Respondeat superior.*

3. John, an artist, asks his artist friend Tina to take some of his paintings to an art fair with her, and to sell them for him. The fact that John and Tina never discussed whether John would pay her for this service proves that:

   a. Their relationship is not an agency.
   b. Their relationship may be an agency, but if so it is "at will."

c. Their relationship may be an agency, but it is an independent contractor relationship.

d. If anything, that artists are cheap.

4. Fill in the blanks: An employer is liable for the _____ of an employee, as well as for the employee's _____. A principal is liable only for the _____ of an independent contractor, and not for the independent contractor's _____.

5. Fill in the blanks: The _____ has the power to affect the legal relations of the _____.

6. Fill in the blanks: Formation of an agency relationship requires _____ manifestation of assent that the agent act on the principal's _____ and subject to the principal's _____.

7. True or False? Co-agents represent co-principals.

8. True or False? Sub-agency necessarily involves two agents and two principals.

4

The Consequences of Agency and Attempts to Avoid Them

This chapter considers two foundational agency law doctrines, one concerning "authority," and the other vicarious tort liability. Together they largely comprise the system that mediates the constant tension among principals, agents, and third parties over the scope of an agent's power to act on the principal's behalf. They can be thought of as comprising the consequences, from the principal's perspective, of doing business through the work of agents. As for authority, it is the power of the agent to alter the principal's legal rights and obligations. Its most important function is to determine when contracts made by the agent can bind the principal, but it is relevant to some other matters as well. This chapter also deals with the fundamental rules affecting the liabilities of both principal and agent for torts committed by the agent.

In a final section, this chapter addresses a specific, pervasive, real-world problem that also concerns the consequences of agency: the efforts of principals to enjoy the benefits of employing agents while avoiding the consequences. The benefits mainly consist of control—the boss who employs workers gets to tell them how to do their work. But the consequences include the risk of vicarious liability for torts and contracts those workers undertake while doing their duty. As it happens, other consequences can attach as well, especially when the agents are "employee" agents, and many principals might like to avoid these as well. They include federal and state employment law protections, anti-discrimination rules, the federal right to bargain collectively, workplace safety and employee benefits regulation, and so on. The maneuver by which principals try to avoid these responsibilities is to contract with individual workers on terms that retain as much control over the execution of the work as possible, while making the workers look as much as possible like third-party independent contractors.

It so happens that this problem has become very visible in what is coming to be known as the "new economy," and much of what we discuss in that final section will consider new-economy applications. But, as we shall see, what some firms seem to be shooting for in "gig" or "sharing economy" contexts is something people have been doing for a long time.

Chapter Outline

A. Management Powers: The Concept of "Authority" and the Principal's Liability for the Agent's Contracts

1. Authority
   - Actual authority is created by manifestations from the principal to the agent
   - Apparent authority is created by manifestations from the principal to a third party

2. Restatement Contract Rules
   - In general, all authorized contracts bind the principal
   - There are three types of principal: fully disclosed, partially disclosed, and undisclosed
   - The type of principal affects the liability of the agent
   - An estoppel to deny authority requires detrimental reliance "caused" by the putative principal

3. Examples in Application

B. The Principal's Liability for the Agent's Torts

   - The agent is always liable for the agent's own torts

1. Direct Liability
   - Intended conduct or its consequences
   - Authorized through unintended conduct
   - Negligence in hiring or supervising

2. *Respondeat Superior*
   - Principals are liable for the torts of employees acting within the scope of employment

C. Termination of Authority

1. Actual Authority
   - Unilateral termination always is possible, but may give rise to contract damages
   - Notice is required

2. Appearances and the Problem of "Lingering" Authority
   - Apparent authority must be terminated the same way it is created

D. Agency, Employer Evasions, and the "New Economy"

1. Means of Evading Agency Consequences
   - Deliberate outsourcing, sharing, on-demand, and gig arrangements

2. Examples in Application
   - The basic problem of characterization
   - Dual employment

Test Yourself

A. Management Powers: The Concept of "Authority" and the Principal's Liability for the Agent's Contracts

1. Authority

As we have said, doing business means doing things through other people. Indeed, the very reason agents are hired is so that they may conduct a principal's affairs. But that then sets up some tension among principals, agents, and the third parties with whom they do business. On the one hand, doing the principal's business effectively requires third parties to have confidence in the agent's promises. But on the other hand, principals ordinarily also desire that there be some limit to their agents' power to bind them. Agents will normally do

at least some of their work outside the principal's direct supervision, and if their power to bind were unlimited they could cause their principals havoc.

To deal with this tension, the law has devised the concept of "authority"—the legal power of an agent to act on behalf of a principal. For the most part, we think of an agent's authority as a power to make *contracts*, and that probably is the area of its most frequent and important application. But strictly speaking authority is the power to do anything on the principal's behalf. Non-trivial legal consequences can follow from an agent's authority to make representations on behalf of a principal, to receive or give notice for the principal, file court documents and perform other bureaucratic actions, and so on.

Moreover, to deal with the various policy problems that arise in disputes over an agent's authority, the law has devised two different *kinds* of authority. First, "actual authority" is authority that a principal manifestly gives by written words, spoken words, or conduct indicating *to the agent* the principal's intent to create that authority. Restatement (Third) of Agency ("Re(3)") §2.01. "Apparent authority," on the other hand, is not based on what the principal manifests to the agent. It is authority that would be reasonable for a third party to believe an agent holds, based on words or conduct of the principal manifested *to the third party*. Re(3) §2.03. It is possible for an agent to hold apparent authority to do something even when the principal has explicitly instructed the agent not to do it—indeed, that will be the primary case in which apparent authority matters.

| ACTUAL Authority | P → A |
| APPARENT Authority | P → 3P |

See if you can figure out the key and only difference between actual and apparent authority, as described in Re(3) §§2.01 and 2.03. Why does the law draw this distinction? Note that from the third party's perspective, it doesn't matter what authority an agent holds. A contract made with either kind is just as enforceable. But what will be the consequence for the agent if he or she made a contract only with apparent authority, especially if the contract is in some way undesirable to the principal?

Once it is determined that an agent has authority of some nature, the question becomes whether the agent used it to take some action that binds the principal. Now, again, an agent's authority may be used to accomplish many legally binding effects; probably the most important and most often used is the power to bind the principal to contracts. Authority also can sometimes have an effect on vicarious tort liability and on the consequences of notice and notification.

More to the Story: Outmoded "Authority" Terminology Still Floating Around

"Actual" and "apparent" authority are the only two authority concepts used in the Restatement (Third), and the only two we shall use here, but confusion can be caused by the fact that prior Restatements and the courts have often used other words to describe authority. Most important, the Restatement (Second) used the terms "actual" and "apparent," but also used a concept called "inherent" authority. *See* Re(2) §8A. Inherent power was not derived from any manifestation of the principal to anyone, but arose as a matter of policy. It was to be recognized only in narrow circumstances in which it seemed too logically difficult to explain vicarious liability on any action of a principal, but where the courts nevertheless believed that principals ought to be liable *somehow*. The Restatement (Third) has done away with the term, and indeed it seemed fairly unnecessary. In most cases where vicarious liability would have been supported by inherent authority, it could also be based on apparent authority or estoppel.

---

2. Restatement Contract Rules

The Restatement contract rules operate by determining who is to be considered a "party" to a contract made by an agent under any particular circumstance. For the most part, these rules are quite straightforward.

In General. First of all, these rules break down into three basic groups. First are the basic rules of contract liability—the basic system by which you know whether any particular contract binds the principal, the agent, or both. These appear in §§6.01-6.04. Second, §§6.07 and 6.09 deal with remedies issues. Finally, §§6.10-6.11 deal with the effect of representations an agent might make during the course of negotiating with a third party, which can be an important part of the ultimate contract, and can also get both the agent and the principal in trouble.

Next, though it is never explicitly stated in so many words, observe that the basic rules of liability fundamentally boil down to a matter of *interpretation*. Among those several terms in a contract between an agent and third party will normally be some concerning who are the parties to it. Knowing whether the contract is enforceable and against whom turns out to be mainly a matter of figuring out just how the court should understand the intent of the parties. In other words, while §§6.01-6.04 set out a series of rules, they all basically provide that the ultimate issues of liability must be determined through interpretation of the parties' intent.

The Principal's Degree of Disclosure. Re(3) §1.04(2), part of the Restatement's general definitions section, distinguishes three different kinds of principals on the degree to which a third party knows their identity. Sections 6.01-6.03 then set out very subtly differing rules to govern the effect of contracts made by an agent for each type of principal. Their general thrust is that the degree of disclosure makes a difference for the agent, but not for either the principal or the third party, both of which usually are bound.

Connections: Secret Principals and the Great Ore Strike

SEC v. Texas Gulf Sulfur Co., 401 F.2d 833 (2d Cir. 1968), is among the best-known cases in the law of federal securities regulation, and it appears elsewhere in this book.

Defendant Texas Gulf Sulfur (TGS) had found early indications of what would eventually prove to be a massive mineral strike in the Canadian wilderness, beneath land it did not own. Only further testing could show how big the strike would be and where the veins of ore would stretch. A firm in those circumstances might ultimately need to buy up quite a bit of land or mineral rights, perhaps held in small parcels by numerous individuals.

Imagine how differently it might go if TGS's realty purchase agents told sellers for whom they were buying, as opposed to buying as if on their own account.

Note that the Restatement rules contemplate that an agent might contract on behalf of an "undisclosed" principal, defined in Re(3) §1.04(2)(b) as one of whose existence the third party is unaware. That is to say, the third party will do business with the agent, believing the agent is acting on his or her own personal behalf, with no one else involved. The agent, though knowing better, will keep the secret, ordinarily on the principal's orders. And yet this is perfectly permissible, so far as agency law is concerned, with one exception. Section 6.11(4) says that if the agent falsely denies the principal's existence, and either principal or agent had "notice" (meaning, under the Restatement, that they were aware of facts that would have led a reasonable person to infer) that the third party would not have dealt with the principal, then the contract is voidable at the third party's instance. But notice that §6.11(4) does not say the contract is voidable just because, had the principal been disclosed, the third party might have demanded different *terms.* See in particular §6.11 comment d, illustration 10.

 Time Out for PR: Non-disclosure

Read American Bar Association Model Rule of Professional Conduct 8.4(c), which appears below. Would it be permissible for a lawyer to act as an agent on behalf of an undisclosed principal?

Rule 8.4 Misconduct
It is professional misconduct for a lawyer to: . . . (c) engage in conduct involving dishonesty, fraud, deceit or misrepresentation . . . .

This may help . . .

After you read the relevant Re(3) provisions, fill in the table below with "yes" or "no."

Type of Principal	Principal Liable?	Third Party Liable?	Agent Liable?
Fully Disclosed			
Partially Disclosed			
Undisclosed			

◼ **Think about this:**

(A) When would principals want to conceal not only their identities, but their very existence? When would it be an advantage to the principal that the third party actually thinks the agent is contracting on his or her own behalf, and doesn't know the principal even exists?

(B) Can an agent for an undisclosed principal act with apparent authority?

(C) If a person is concerned about the people with whom he or she is dealing, and doesn't want to be misled into contracting with a person secretly representing someone else, what can he or she do? Re(3) §6.03 seems to imply that those contracts are enforceable absent a problem with the agent's authority, and even Re(3) §6.11(4) gives relief only if the party would really have refused to do the deal entirely with a specific principal because of its identity. But there may be hope: *See* Re(3) §6.03, comment d.

Estoppel. Finally, let's consider the problem of vicarious contract liability by estoppel, which arises under Re(3) §2.05. As we shall see, a person may sometimes take on liability even in the absence of any agency relationship at all. We shall study one of these doctrines here and a few more later on.

RE(3) §2.05 ESTOPPEL TO DENY EXISTENCE OF AGENCY RELATIONSHIP

A person who has not made a manifestation that an actor has authority as an agent and who is not otherwise liable as a party to a transaction purportedly done by the actor on that person's account is subject to liability to a third party who justifiably is induced to make a detrimental change in position because the transaction is believed to be on the person's account, if
    (1) the person intentionally or carelessly caused such belief, or
    (2) having notice of such belief and that it might induce others to change their positions, the person did not take reasonable steps to notify them of the facts.

Section 2.05, which calls on us to draw a rather maddening distinction, contemplates that there will be situations in which a person does *not* manifest assent to the creation of agency or authority on the part of another, but nevertheless *does* take some action by which she causes detrimental reliance by some third party. The distinction is maddening because one can "cause" such reliance in two ways, both of which sound suspiciously like manifestations of assent to the creation of an agency relationship or manifestations that would create apparent authority. Under subsections (1) and (2), a person may be estopped where another changes position detrimentally because he believed he was entering into a transaction for the purported principal's behalf, and the purported principal caused that belief "intentionally or carelessly" or failed to take reasonable steps to correct it once he became aware of it.

Connections: Partnership and Agency by Estoppel

Partnership liabilities can be created by estoppel as well. See Chapter 8. But we shall see that the rule governing partnership by estoppel is quite different and more complex, and we will spend some time asking why.

The comments and illustrations to §2.05 are more illuminating, and make clear that situations in which estoppel really matters (cases in which there might be evidence supporting an estoppel theory but none supporting an apparent authority theory) will be fairly uncommon. Consider illustration 2 (which is based on an actual and highly entertaining case):

> P owns a large retail furniture store, known as "P's Furniture Emporium." P, who is often absent from the premises, does not otherwise maintain surveillance over the store's sales force. T, a prospective customer, enters the store and is approached by A, whose demeanor and attire lend A the appearance of a salesperson. After examining floor samples, T purchases several items of furniture for cash, giving the cash to A. A gives T a receipt written on a standard-looking form, with "P's Furniture Emporium" printed at the top. A explains to T that the items purchased are not presently in inventory but will be delivered to T's home within two weeks. A is an imposter who is not an employee or other agent of P. A does not remit any of the cash paid by T to P. No furniture is delivered to T. T's change of position is justified by T's belief that A is what A purports to be, a salesperson with authority to sell from P's inventory. Whether P may deny A's authority is a question for the trier of fact.

The theory of liability suggested in §2.05(1) seems fairly hard to imagine, and, as the comments corroborate, true estoppel cases will most commonly involve the theory in §2.05(2).

Incidentally, note that, as comment d makes clear, the third party will be entitled to a measure of damages based only on a reliance interest, and not expectation damages.

 Dear Prof.: So estoppel requires a change of position on the part of the third party but apparent authority does not? And with apparent authority you can get expectation damages, not just reliance? Right?

Right!

■ **Think about this:**

(D) What facts would be important to a trier of fact asked to resolve the case described in illustration 2 to §2.05?

(E) The following scenario is based on illustration 1 to §2.05: Pauline has two co-agents, Natasha and Boris. Pauline discovers that Boris, acting without any authority, told Dora that Natasha has authority to sell Pauline's business vehicle. This is completely untrue. Pauline could inform Dora that Natasha lacks authority but fails to do so before Dora signs a contract with Natasha and makes a substantial down payment on the car, which Natasha promptly pockets. Does Pauline have to either sell her car or give Dora the amount of her down payment?

3. Examples in Application

The following two cases provide illustrations of agency authority principles in action.

NEWBERRY V. BARTH, INC.

Supreme Court of Iowa
252 N.W.2d 711 (1977)

REYNOLDSON, Justice.

Plaintiff Donald E. Newberry sued defendants Barth, Incorporated and Florence Barth for specific performance of a November 7, 1968 contract to sell a large apartment complex. [The building had been owned personally by Florence and her husband before his death. They formed Barth, Incorporated to purchase the building, a deal they financed with a loan guaranteed by the Federal Housing Administration. As a condition of the guarantee, the FHA became the holder of the company's preferred stock and, as such, was protected by several restrictions in Barth, Inc.'s charter, including that the building could not be sold without FHA approval. The charter was publicly available in the offices of the county recorder and the Iowa Secretary of State. Florence later executed a contract to sell the building to plaintiff. At the time she was the majority surviving holder of the company's common stock and drew a salary from the corporation as its secretary-treasurer and building manager.]

. . . The November 7, 1968 real estate contract . . . designated . . . Florence Barth [as seller] . . . . The purchaser, plaintiff Newberry, thought Florence Barth owned the property, but admitted in the brief time they spent together (when she helped show the real estate) she had never said so.

In defense against the action, defendants assert Florence Barth had no authority to bind the corporation and therefore the latter cannot be compelled to perform the contract . . . . Trial court found both [Florence and Barth, Inc.] were bound by the sales transaction and ordered both to specifically perform the contract . . . .

A recorded deed gave Newberry constructive notice that Barth, Incorporated owned the apartment complex. Florence Barth was thus an agent for a disclosed principal.

We have concluded Mrs. Barth had no actual authority to sell this property. Actual authority includes both express and implied authority.

Express authority is that specifically mentioned by the principal in setting out the extent of the agent's duties. The proof here fails to show express authority. Moreover, the articles specifically prohibited conveyance of real estate without prior consent of the preferred stockholders.

Implied authority of a corporate officer or agent includes all such incidental authority as is necessary, usual and proper to effectuate the main authority expressly conferred. But although a general or managing officer will be presumed, in absence of proof to the contrary, to have authority to contract in the

Connections: The Authority of Officers

As noted in the case, corporate titles frequently do imply to third parties—and, absent instructions to the contrary, to the holders themselves—that the holders have the authority to engage in acts of a particular type. Exactly what might be covered is a question of fact. There is more on this subject in Chapter 17 of this book.

usual course of corporate business, this implied authority ordinarily does not extend to contracts for the sale of the fixed assets of the corporation.

We next consider whether Mrs. Barth had apparent authority to sell this real estate, examining the conduct of the principal to third persons, as opposed to express and implied (actual) authority in which the manifestations of the principal to the agent are controlling. We have already noted the most significant manifestation, the recorded articles of incorporation which restricted the right to sell real estate. However, the "apparent authority" doctrine takes precedence over the "notice" doctrine. Mere want of authority in fact will not relieve a corporation from the burden of a contract made in reasonable reliance upon such appearance of authority.

In this case the only action taken by the corporation was to install Mrs. Barth as apartment manager. By so doing, it clothed her with authority to perform the usual and necessary actions of an apartment manager. However, the corporation did nothing to indicate to third persons, and specifically the plaintiff, that Mrs. Barth had authority to sell the real estate. Plaintiff was unaware of the existence of the corporate defendant.

It is clear Florence Barth had no apparent authority to bind Barth, Incorporated to this contract . . . . It is generally held no officer or agent of a corporation, by virtue of his office alone, has any authority to sell or make a contract for the sale of the corporation's real estate. Barth, Incorporated cannot be held liable under agency law for the sales contract executed by Florence Barth . . . .

 Dear Prof.: Wait a minute. Ms. Barth owned the corporation, so why wouldn't that give her authority to sell its property?

There are a few reasons. First, shareholders are not automatically agents of the corporation they "own." Second, in the usual case, a shareholder's "ownership" is actually pretty limited, giving only a few rights that notably do *not* include the ability to make management decisions. Third, in the *Newberry* case there was a second class of stock ("preferred" stock, which typically has at least some rights that are superior to those associated with "common" stock) the owners of which were specifically given the decision whether the corporation should sell its property.

Yes, but how was Newberry supposed to know all that?

Good question. Courts generally assume that reasonable people understand the law and how it operates—even though it's pretty clear that they don't.

■ Think about this:

(F) Suppose that *Newberry* did not involve the sale of real property but rather the sale of valuable research and development in progress. How, if at all, would that have affected the court's analysis? Do you think it would have affected the outcome?

(G) Would it make sense to argue that since Ms. Barth was the corporation's agent, what she knew about what she was doing should be charged to the corporation? Might an argument then be made for liability under Re(3) §2.05?

It's always good to keep in mind the following question when considering similar cases that come out differently: What does the second case add to your understanding that the first one did not?

ESSCO GEOMETRIC V. HARVARD INDUSTRIES

United States Court of Appeals for the Eighth Circuit
46 F.3d 718 (8th Cir. 1995)

BRIGHT, Senior Circuit Judge.

In this breach of contracts action, Essco Geometrics, Inc., d/b/a Diversified Foam Products (Diversified), a materials supplier, sought damages from Harvard Industries, Inc. (Harvard), a manufacturer of office chairs, for Harvard's failure to honor . . . a written contract for materials . . . . Harvard produces . . . chairs, and . . . . [f]or over thirty years, Diversified supplied a large portion of [the foam that Harvard used to make them] . . . . To determine which companies would supply its foam, Harvard would issue bid requests to several potential suppliers, detailing Harvard's needs for a particular chair contract. The bids submitted did not contractually bind either party, but usually determined which two companies would have Harvard's business, what prices the suppliers would charge, and approximately the quantity sellers would deliver.

> Harvard Industries began as a Massachusetts brewery in 1930 — three years before the end of Prohibition. It wins a dubious distinction award for being the only large firm to have gone into bankruptcy four times.

JD/MBA and Connections: Internal Controls

For accounting and management purposes, it is customary for large organizations to have "internal controls" in place. They can be as simple as requiring two signatures on checks above a certain amount or having approval processes for major contracts, or they can be much more elaborate. They're great when they work. Publicly held entities are, as a matter of federal law, required to have annual audits of the effectiveness of these controls. This is discussed in Chapter 28 of this book.

. . . For over twenty years, Frank Best served as Harvard's purchasing manager. [Best nurtured a close relationship with Edsel Safron, Diversified's president.] . . . In July 1988, Frank Best retired, and Michael Gray, the former purchasing agent, became the new purchasing manager for Harvard. JoAnn Ceresia became Harvard's new purchasing agent under Gray and became responsible for issuing purchase orders as Harvard's day-to-day needs demanded. In September 1988, Ed Kruske became Harvard's new president.

With this new management in place, Harvard began a program to cut costs and improve quality . . . [, as a part of which] Kruske . . . issued two internal memoranda. The first . . . directed that all purchase orders (production and non-production) be initialed by Kruske prior to being sent out to a vendor. The second . . . stipulated that all requisitions of fifty dollars or more have both the departmental manager's approval and Kruske's approval, unless an emergency arose. Michael Gray received both of these directives, but Harvard never notified anyone outside of the company that it had instituted these internal operating procedures.

At the same time that Harvard was implementing these reforms, it began requesting bids for [the supply of foam for a major] contract [to produce chairs it had been awarded by the U.S. General Services Administration (GSA), which purchases goods on behalf of the federal government. Under one earlier GSA contract, Gray and Ceresia decided to make bidding to supply foam for the GSA chairs open to both Diversified and two of Diversified's competitors, Dalco and American Excelsior. Under that prior contract, because Ceresia wanted to diminish Harvard's dependence on Diversified, American Excelsior became Harvard's prior supplier of foam. Moreover, when the new GSA contract was awarded, Ceresia, without Gray's knowledge, decided to exclude Diversified from even bidding to supply foam. Thereafter, Safron persuaded Gray to let Diversified bid, and both because its bid was the cheapest and because American Excelsior's foam turned out to have quality problems, Gray orally promised Safron to give Diversified all of Harvard's foam business on the GSA contract. Gray advised Kruske of Diversified's benefits, but Kruske did not actually become aware of his oral agreement with Diversified until May 1990.]

Pursuant to this oral agreement and mindful of Kruske's admonition that Harvard would only honor written contracts, . . . Safron wrote and delivered a letter to Gray on January 9, 1990 [memorializing the oral agreement] . . . . Both Safron and Gray signified approval by each signing at the bottom of the letter. Both Safron and Gray testified at trial that they understood the letter to represent an exclusive multi-million dollar contract between Harvard and Diversified for all of Harvard's foam needs for all of its chairs for a two-year period.

Later Gray issued Diversified several purchase orders covering parts for the GSA contract . . . [using] standardized forms that circulated throughout Harvard's various departments . . . . Diversified . . . delivered [the] parts, and got paid . . . . Safron [later became] concerned by the receipt of what he believed was an abnormally low number of purchase orders. [Gray explained that Ceresia had been misdirecting orders to Excelsior. After again explaining Diversified's price and quality advantages to Kruske, Gray directed Ceresia to issue all future purchase orders to Diversified.]

Kruske within days thereafter[,] [having first learned of Gray's exclusive supply agreement with Diversified,] put a hold on Gray's purchase orders to Diversified. Soon thereafter, American Excelsior submitted a new bid, unsolicited by Gray, that offered marginally lower prices than Diversified's on the 1990-1992 GSA contract. Three weeks later, Kruske decided to make American Excelsior Harvard's new principal supplier. This lawsuit followed . . . .

III. DISCUSSION

A. Submissibility on Actual or Apparent Authority

. . . Harvard claims that Diversified failed to present sufficient evidence to support its theory that Gray had either actual or apparent authority to bind Harvard to an exclusive, non-cancelable requirements contract. [The question for the court is whether the district court erred in denying Harvard's motion for judgment as a matter of law, and submitting the case to a jury, which then awarded Diversified significant damages.] . . .

1. Actual Authority

. . . [F]or an agent to have actual authority, he must establish that the principal has empowered him, either expressly or impliedly, to act on the principal's behalf. The principal can expressly confer authority by telling his agent what to do or by knowingly acquiescing to the agent's actions. Implied authority flows from express authority, and "encompasses the power to act in ways reasonably necessary to accomplish the purpose for which express authority was granted." Missouri case law suggests that custom and the relations of the parties establish the parameters of implied actual authority. Thus, evidence that an agent historically engaged in related conduct, without limitation, would be enough to support a jury question on the issue of actual authority . . . .

a. Gray's Implied Authority

As an initial matter, both sides agree that no job description outlined the nature of Gray's responsibilities, let alone the scope of his authority. Despite the lack of express authority, however, other documentary evidence and testimonial evidence supports Diversified's claim. First, Gray's own testimony bore on his authority to bind Harvard to the January 9th agreement, and under Missouri law, this testimony alone is enough to make a submissible case. On direct examination, Gray testified as follows:

> **Q.** And did you perceive and were you acting, signing this in your—as part of your job as a purchasing manager of Harvard?
> **A.** Yes . . . .
> **Q.** Did you believe Ed Kruske was in favor of your decision to go with Diversified as of January 1990?
> **A.** Yes . . . .
> **Q.** Did you have any doubt in your mind at all about your authority to sign that document?
> **A.** No . . . .

Second, Gray's October 1989 performance evaluation establishes Harvard's express intention that Gray continue to take a more active role in managing his department and work on further reducing costs. Given the express nature of this evaluation, made only three months before Gray signed the January 9th letter, it would appear that Gray's negotiations with Diversified and the ultimate signing of the agreement furthered the company's objectives. Although not as explicit as a job description, the performance evaluation established enough express authority that a reasonable jury could conclude that Gray acted pursuant to it. See [Barton v. Snellson, 735 S.W.2d 160, 162 (Mo. Ct. App. 1987)] (defining implied actual authority as those "powers incidental and necessary to carry out the express authority") . . . .

A third evidentiary basis for Gray's actual authority is the custom and practice at Harvard and within the industry. Gray testified that he had observed for over fifteen or sixteen years Frank Best, Harvard's former purchasing manager, negotiate with vendors and ultimately select vendors who Best believed would benefit Harvard. Others similarly testified that purchasing managers within the industry customarily made unsupervised decisions as to who would be their company's suppliers.

Although an exclusive, non-cancelable requirements contract differs materially from a standard purchase order, the practical reality of Harvard's (and the rest of the industry's) GSA contracts suggests that when Harvard ultimately selects a vendor for its GSA contracts, that vendor will enjoy between 60% and 70% of Harvard's foam needs for the duration of the one or two year contract . . . .

b. Harvard's Express Limitations

. . . Harvard asserts that it had in fact explicitly limited . . . . [Gray's authority, by way of Kruske's] two internal Harvard memoranda, issued months before January 9th . . . . [In light of them,] Harvard contends that no one could reasonably believe that Gray had acted within the scope of his authority . . . . According to Gray's own testimony, [however,] Kruske's directives were a mere formality. Kruske never refused to sign-off on a requisition or purchase order and the directives themselves did not explicitly limit Gray's authority to negotiate and enter into contracts . . . .

. . . [Moreover,] Marc Treppler, Harvard's former quality control manager, testified that Kruske would not give clear directions and would let his managers make decisions. Michael Gray testified that Kruske "could be led pretty easily." . . .

In sum, the evidence regarding the limitations Harvard placed on Gray's authority and inferences therefrom are conflicting. Reasonable jurors could disagree in their interpretations of the nature of those limitations. Thus, the district court did not err in submitting the issue of Diversified's actual authority claim to the jury.

2. Apparent Authority

Under Missouri law, apparent authority is created by the conduct of the principal which causes a third person reasonably to believe that the purported agent has the authority to act for the principal, and to reasonably and in good faith rely on the authority held out by the principal . . . .

There are essentially three ways to establish apparent authority. One way is by the principal expressly and directly telling a third person that a second person has authority to act on the principal's behalf. Missouri courts have also recognized two other methods of creating apparent authority—by prior acts and by position. As explained in [Earl v. St. Louis Univ., 875 S.W.2d 234, 238 (Mo. Ct. App. 1994)]:

> If a principal allows an agent to occupy a position which, according to the ordinary habits of people in the locality, trade or profession, carries a particular kind of authority, then anyone dealing with the agent is justified in inferring that the agent has such an authority. The principal may also create the appearance of authority by "prior acts." By allowing an agent to carry out prior similar transactions, a principal creates the appearance that the agent is authorized to carry out such acts subsequently.

. . . For over twenty years, Harvard had allowed its purchasing manager, Frank Best, to solicit bids from vendors, negotiate with vendors, and ultimately select vendors for Harvard's governmental and commercial contracts. For most of those years, Diversified provided a substantial amount of Harvard's foam needs . . . . [N]o one ever advised Diversified that Harvard had instituted new internal operating procedures [in 1992] or that the purchasing manager would have less authority to negotiate on behalf of the company . . . .

While Harvard's previous purchasing managers never before had entered an exclusive, non-cancelable requirements contract, and Diversified knew that Harvard had never before entered such a contract, several of Harvard's foam suppliers intimated that the industry custom presumed, without question, that the purchasing manager possessed the authority to bind the company . . . . [1]

---

1. Harvard principally argues that Diversified should have been more suspicious of Gray's authority to negotiate such an agreement. Given the uniqueness of a long-range, exclusive and non-cancelable requirements contract, ... Diversified should have done more to investigate whether, in fact, Gray had the authority to sign the January 9th agreement.

Missouri law, however, imposes no duty on a third party to investigate a purported agent's authority if "'a person of ordinary prudence, conversant with business usages and the nature of the particular business'" could reasonably believe that the agent had such authority . . . .

> ■ **Think about this:**
>
> *(H)* Assume that you are counseling Mr. Kruske as to how to effectuate his control policy. What would you recommend?

B. The Principal's Liability for the Agent's Torts

Room to Argue: Dram-Shop and Other Statutory Liability

Statutes in some states impose liability on the owners of establishments serving alcohol for the damage caused by patrons who were served while obviously intoxicated. Is this a matter of direct or vicarious liability? Does it matter? Moreover, is it good or bad social policy? If good, would it be even better to impose it on the human beings who control a juridical owner?

We now turn to a fundamentally different problem. As a matter of social policy, there is a whole separate realm of conduct by which an agent may bind his principal. Tort liability is something neither the principal nor the agent wants, but assigning it appropriately is a fundamental policy objective of agency law.

Two key distinctions run through the relevant rules. First, the rules distinguish between employment relationships and non-employee agency relationships. In and of itself, the distinction has virtually no other relevance in the law of agency, but in this one context the distinction is very significant. Second, while we are familiar with the concept of vicarious liability—under which the principal can be responsible for the agent's torts—sometimes the principal can take on *direct* liability for torts of the agent. That is, the principal can be liable not only in some derivative sense as a matter of agency law policy, but also because of the principal's own culpability in failing to properly supervise the agent or take care in hiring.

1. Direct Liability

As stated in Re(3) §7.03(1), and elaborated in §7.05, there are three ways in which a principal can take on direct liability for torts caused by an agent. None of these ideas is complicated, and the underlying policy is simple common sense. It might be worth observing that these rules are not technically rules of agency law, but of tort law. In each case, the theoretical basis for the principal's liability is that the principal has personally committed a tort either by acting negligently or intentionally.

As for the theories of direct liability in §7.03(1)(a), under which the principal can be liable for an agent's torts committed with actual authority or that are ratified by the principal, the idea is straightforward. In those cases, the principal has literally committed an intentional tort. For example, if I hire a bodyguard, and I direct him to assault a third party, the bodyguard would be acting with actual authority, and it is clear that I myself have committed an intentional act for which the victim is entitled to recover. (Note that under §7.03(1)(a) a principal can "ratify" a tort. This is a somewhat peculiar notion, or so it might seem. Ratification implies a deliberate desire to make some act binding, but no one would knowingly make himself party to tort liability he could otherwise avoid. And yet ratifications of torts occur and are well recognized. This will be explored further in Chapter 5A.)

Section 7.03 also contemplates cases in which a principal can be directly liable without intentionally committing a tort. First, §7.03(1)(b) says the principal can be liable for injuries caused by the agent if the principal "is negligent in selecting, supervising, or otherwise controlling the agent . . . ." Critically, this is not a vicarious theory of liability, it is a direct theory—that is, a plaintiff must show that in failing to "select, supervise, or control" with adequate care, the principal breached a duty that the principal personally owed to the plaintiff. This calls for a brief detour to substantive tort law. The reason a principal can sometimes have direct liability on such a theory is the same reason that anybody is ever liable for any unintentional tort, and it is perhaps the single most fundamental rule of our tort law: Under any and all circumstances, all of us "ordinarily ha[ve] a duty to exercise reasonable care when the actor's conduct creates a risk of physical harm." Restatement (Third) of Torts §7(a). And wherever a principal "may hire an [agent] to carry out an activity that creates a risk of physical harm[,] . . . its initiation by the actor—albeit through a decision to use an independent contractor—constitutes conduct creating a risk of harm." *Id.* §55, comment c. Thus, the duty is triggered where the principal engages an agent in a task posing a risk of physical harm. However, the principal "owes no duty as to the manner in which the work is performed" except insofar as the principal "retains control over . . . part of the work," in which case the principal must take reasonable care, *id.* §56 (emphasis added).

Accordingly, where an agent is engaged in a task that might cause physical harm, the principal must merely select an agent "who possesses the knowledge, skill, experience, equipment, and personal characteristics that a reasonable person would realize a contractor should have to perform the work without creating unreasonable risk of injury." *Id.* §55, comment e. Moreover, "the hirer's negligence might include giving orders or directions to the contractor without exercising reasonable care; failing to exercise reasonable care to discover dangerous conditions on the land and to eliminate or ameliorate those that are known or should have been discovered by the exercise of reasonable care; failing to use reasonable care as to artificial conditions and activities on the land that pose a risk of physical harm to those off the land; and failing to exercise reasonable care with respect to any part of the work over which the actor has retained control." *Id.*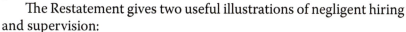

The Restatement gives two useful illustrations of negligent hiring and supervision:

> 1. Telephone Company lays underground cable in parts of a city. Telephone Company hires Martin as the independent contractor to perform the digging necessary for laying the cable. When the job starts, Martin has no previous digging or construction experience and only several hours of practice using a trenching machine. Telephone Company does not inquire into Martin's experience in using trenching machines or working around gas pipes. During the course of the digging, Martin negligently strikes and damages a gas line, causing an explosion that seriously injures Anthony. Telephone Company is subject to liability to Anthony under this Section for failing to use reasonable care in selecting a competent contractor.

2. Tonya hires Blue Moon Movers, a local moving company, to transport furniture and packages from her old office to her new office. Tonya is a chemist, and some of her packages contain chemical mixtures that are combustible at temperatures over 100 degrees Fahrenheit. Tonya does not advise Blue Moon Movers that several boxes contain chemicals combustible at high temperatures. The move occurs on a summer day, and the temperature inside the truck exceeds 100 degrees. An explosion results, causing a collision that injures Darren, another driver. Tonya is subject to liability to Darren under this Section for failing to warn Blue Moon about the chemicals or to take other precautions as to the chemicals.

Finally, Re(3) §7.03(1)(c) says that a principal can be liable where "the principal delegates performance of a duty to use care to protect other persons or their property to an agent who fails to perform the duty." Comments in the Restatement make clear that this rule was meant to include those duties that courts often refer to as "non-delegable" duties, which for reasons of public policy the courts say that principals cannot avoid merely by delegating the work to non-employee agents. The most important of these are duties surrounding so-called intrinsically dangerous activities, such as the use of pesticides or poisons, explosives, fireworks, strong acids, or work involving high-voltage electric lines. *See* Re(3) §7.06, comment a; Dan B. Dobbs, The Law of Torts §337 (2000).

2. Respondeat Superior

The following cases examine the circumstances in which the doctrine of *respondeat superior* will hold a principal liable for the torts of an employee. To be clear, the doctrine does *not* apply to the torts of agents who are not employees—also known as "independent contractors." Re(3) §7.07(3)(a) provides that an "employee" is "an agent whose principal controls or has the right to control the *manner and means* of the agent's performance of work . . . . "

LOURIM V. SWENSEN

Supreme Court of Oregon
977 P.2d 1157 (1999)

GILLETTE, Justice.
    This case arises out of allegations by plaintiff that he was sexually abused by his Boy Scout leader, Swensen, approximately 30 years earlier, when plaintiff was a minor . . . . As against the Boy Scouts, the complaint alleges that the Boy Scout organizations are vicariously liable for Swensen's tortious conduct under the doctrine of *respondeat superior* and that the Boy Scouts are directly liable to plaintiff for negligently failing to have implemented a screening program to prevent child abusers from becoming Boy Scout leaders.
    . . . Plaintiff and his family became close to Swensen, and Swensen was a frequent guest in their home . . . . Swensen gained the opportunity to socialize

with plaintiff and to spend time alone with him and together with other boys in remote places. Swensen also used his position of trust to gain the opportunity to [assault plaintiff sexually].

. . . [A]n employee's conduct was within the scope of employment [if]: (1) the conduct . . . occurred substantially within the time and space limits authorized by the employment; (2) the employee . . . [was] motivated, at least partially, by a purpose to serve the employer; and (3) the act . . . [was] of a kind that the employee was hired to perform. [The court later refers to these as the *Chesterman* requirements, after Chesterman v. Barmon, 305 Or. 439, 442, 753 P.2d 404 (1988).] Applying that framework in this case, the Court of Appeals held that the complaint failed to state a claim, because

> "[t]here simply are no allegations of fact that satisfy all three of the elements of vicarious liability. In particular, there are no facts from which it reasonably could be concluded that Swensen's sexual assaults were acts 'of a kind [an] employee was hired to perform.'"

In Fearing v. Bucher, 328 Or. 367, 977 P.2d 1163 (1999), we addressed whether a complaint against the Archdiocese of Portland in Oregon (Archdiocese) for vicarious liability for a priest's acts of child abuse was sufficient to state a claim . . . . In that case, we held that, in the intentional tort context, it usually is inappropriate for the court to base its decision . . . on whether the intentional tort itself was committed in furtherance of any interest of the employer or involved the kind of activity that the employee was hired to perform. We held that the proper focus rather was whether the complaint contained sufficient allegations of employee conduct that arguably resulted in the acts that led to plaintiff's injury. We concluded that a jury reasonably could infer that the priest's conduct in cultivating a trust relationship with the plaintiff was motivated, at least in part, by a desire to further the interests of the Archdiocese, that that conduct was of a kind that the priest was hired to perform, and that that conduct led to the sexual assaults . . . .

The same is true in the present case. Accepting the allegations in the complaint as true and drawing all reasonable inferences in the plaintiff's favor, a jury reasonably could infer that the sexual assaults were merely the culmination of a progressive series of actions that involved the ordinary and authorized duties of a Boy Scout leader. Additionally, a jury could infer that, in cultivating a relationship with plaintiff and his family, Swensen, at least initially, was motivated by a desire to fulfill his duties as troop leader and that, over time, his motives became mixed. A jury also reasonably could infer that Swensen's performance of his duties as troop leader with respect to plaintiff and his family was a necessary precursor to the sexual abuse and that the assaults were a direct outgrowth of and were engendered by conduct that was within the scope of Swensen's employment. Finally, a jury could infer that Swensen's contact with plaintiff was the direct result of the relationship sponsored and encouraged by the Boy Scouts, which invested Swensen with authority to decide how to supervise minor boys under his care. Based on the foregoing, we conclude, as we did in *Fearing*, that the amended complaint contains allegations sufficient to satisfy all three *Chesterman* requirements. The Court of Appeals erred in concluding otherwise.

. . . [The court also addresses the Boy Scouts' argument that Swensen was not an "employee" for purposes of *respondeat superior*.] It is well established that one can be a servant even though the service is performed gratuitously. The relevant inquiry in determining whether a master-servant relationship exists for respondeat superior purposes is whether the master has the right to control the actions of the servant . . . .

The complaint alleges that, "[a]t all relevant times, Swensen was a volunteer Boy Scout leader, duly authorized by the Boy Scouts and the Cascade Pacific Council to act in that capacity" and that, "[a]s part of his volunteer duties with the Boy Scouts and the Cascade Pacific Council, Swensen was directed to fulfill the role of troop leader or assistant troop leader to [plaintiff's] troop. . . . A jury reasonably could infer from th[at] allegation . . . that the Boy Scouts directed his activities and, thus, that the Boy Scouts had the right to control Swensen's activities as troop leader or assistant troop leader . . . . It is sufficient, we believe, that the complaint allege that Swensen did certain acts while acting as a Boy Scout leader and that the plaintiff was injured while Swensen was acting in that capacity. The connection between the two fairly may be inferred. Other inferences might be drawn instead, but that is a matter for the trier of fact . . . .

■ **Think about this:**

(I) What's the point of all this? Why hold the Boy Scouts responsible for this conduct, which all agree is a horror that no one within the Scouts could have condoned? Is it just retributive, or is some other goal aimed at with vicarious liability?

(J) Suppose that your Business Associations professor is having a bad day and hurls a book at one of your classmates, causing him or her a significant amount of injury. Was your professor acting within the scope of employment? For that matter, are you quite sure that he or she is an employee at all?

The *Jackson* case, immediately below, is not included just for prurient interest. Again, ask yourself how this case adds to the knowledge you gained from the last one.

JACKSON V. RIGHTER

Supreme Court of Utah
891 P.2d 1387 (1995)

STEWART, Associate Chief Justice: . . . .

[Plaintiff's spouse worked at Novell, a computer software firm, as a secretary. Defendant Grover P. Righter was her immediate supervisor. Their relationship became sexual, and included encounters both on Novell's premises during business hours and at hotels and other places off site.] . . . . Mrs. Jackson [later] . . . began a [sexual] relationship with defendant Clay Wilkes, who was employed at that time as an engineering manager in Novell's Sandy[,] [Utah] office . . . . In August 1991, Mr. Righter became Vice President of Univel[,] [another software firm,] and moved to the Sandy office. Mrs. Jackson transferred with him and remained under his direct-line supervision. In December 1991, Mr. Wilkes also became employed by Univel as a technical lead and worked in the same department with Mrs. Jackson at the Sandy office but never supervised her.

　　. . . [T]he Jacksons subsequently divorced. [Plaintiff sues Righter and Wilkes for alienation of his wife's affection, and sues Novell and Univel both as vicariously liable for their employees' torts and as directly liable for negligently supervising and retaining them. The matter is on appeal from the trial court's grant of summary judgment for Novell and Univel.] . . .

A. VICARIOUS LIABILITY OF NOVELL AND UNIVEL

. . . An employer may be vicariously liable under the doctrine of respondeat superior for the harmful actions of an employee if those actions are committed within the scope of the employee's employment. To be considered within the scope of employment, an employee's conduct must (1) "be of the general kind the employee is employed to perform"; (2) "occur within the hours of the employee's work and the ordinary spatial boundaries of the employment"; and (3) "be motivated, at least in part, by the purpose of serving the employer's interest." Birkner [v. Salt Lake County, 771 P.2d 1053, 1056-1057 (Utah 1989)]. Whether an employee's conduct falls within the scope of employment is ordinarily a question of fact. However, where the employee's conduct is so clearly outside the scope of employment that reasonable minds cannot differ, the issue may properly be decided as a matter of law. For example, [J.H. by D.H. v. West Valley City, 840 P.2d 115, 122 (Utah 1992)] held that a police officer's sexual molestations of a youth under his supervision was clearly outside the scope of employment, as a matter of law, because his acts were not of the kind and nature he was employed to perform.

> **(No) More to the Story: The Scope of Employment Test**
>
> The three-element statement in this paragraph very closely mirrors the statement in *Lourim v. Swensen* and is frequently repeated, with minor variations, throughout the case law of many jurisdictions.

　　In this case, Mr. Righter's romantic involvement with Mrs. Jackson was so clearly outside the scope of his employment that reasonable minds could not differ. Applying the *Birkner* criteria, we note, as Novell and Univel concede, that most of Mr. Righter's alleged tortious conduct occurred within the hours and spatial boundaries of his employment. However, Mr. Righter's conduct was not of the general type he was employed to perform, and neither was it intended to serve, nor did it serve, Novell's or Univel's purpose. Mr. Righter was not hired to perform acts of a sexual nature on, or make romantic overtures toward, an employee under his supervision. Plaintiff argues that many of Mr. Righter's alleged tortious acts were part of the conduct he was hired to perform in connection with his authority to promote, evaluate, train, and give raises to Mrs. Jackson. For example, plaintiff asserts that the first time Mr. Righter expressed his attraction for Mrs. Jackson was while he held her hand during a formal employee evaluation in his office. Plaintiff's argument is without merit. Mr. Righter was not authorized to use his supervisory position to engage in a romantic relationship with his subordinates. His romantic advances were not a part of his duties but amounted to an abandonment of the supervisory and managerial responsibilities he was hired to perform.

In addition, while Mr. Righter used his company duties as a springboard for pursuing his relationship with Mrs. Jackson, he was not motivated by the purpose of serving Novell's or Univel's interests. An employee's conduct is usually not in the scope of employment where the employee's motivation for the activity is personal, even though some transaction of business or performance of duty may also occur. Mr. Righter admits that his motives were entirely personal and were in no way directed at the accomplishment of Novell's or Univel's interests . . . .

B. NEGLIGENT SUPERVISION

Plaintiff claims that Novell and Univel were negligent in supervising and retaining Mr. Righter and Mr. Wilkes and that their negligence caused the alienation of Mrs. Jackson's affections. To recover for negligence, a plaintiff must show that the defendant owed the plaintiff a duty, the defendant breached the duty, the breach was a proximate cause of the plaintiff's injuries, and there was in fact injury. Plaintiff has failed to allege facts establishing a duty on the part of Novell or Univel to protect him from his claimed injury.

In the context of a claim for negligent supervision or retention, a duty may arise when an employer could reasonably be expected, consistent with the practical realities of an employer-employee relationship, to appreciate the threat to a plaintiff of its employee's actions and to act to minimize or protect against that threat. Plaintiff asserts that Mr. Righter's and Mr. Wilkes' acts which allegedly alienated Mrs. Jackson's affections were foreseeable because Novell and Univel knew that spousal affections could be alienated by romantic relations among employees and knew or should have known of Mr. Righter's and Mr. Wilkes' relationships with Mrs. Jackson. We disagree. The inquiry is not whether Novell or Univel could foresee that any marital relation may be damaged by any romantic relationship between two employees. A general knowledge that marital relations could foreseeably be damaged is not sufficient to impute to an employer a duty to protect its employees' spouses from a work-place romance. Rather, the inquiry is whether Novell or Univel could reasonably be expected to foresee the threat of alienation of Mrs. Jackson's affections by Mr. Righter's or Mr. Wilkes' acts.

Nothing plaintiff alleges shows that Novell or Univel could reasonably be expected to foresee this threat. Plaintiff claims that Novell knew Mr. Righter promoted Mrs. Jackson, authorized her to record unworked overtime hours, and required her, as his administrative assistant, to spend a great deal of time in his office and accompany him on business trips. However, nothing in these acts would give Novell reason to foresee that the acts would alienate Mrs. Jackson's affections toward plaintiff.

Nor, as plaintiff claims, would a knowledge of Mrs. Jackson's romantic relationships with Mr. Righter or Mr. Wilkes give Novell or Univel reason to know that they should act to minimize or prevent plaintiff's injury. Unlike the foreseeability of a physical injury caused by an employee who has demonstrated violent or deviant propensities, a romantic relationship between employees may or may not give rise to a cause of action by an employee's spouse. Recovery for the alienation of affections depends upon the determination of the controlling cause of the injury and necessarily involves an analysis of the quality of the marriage relationship. The tort will not lie when the personalities or inadequacies of the spouses, not the acts of third persons, caused the breakdown of the bonds that are essential to the consortium interests protected by law. Romantic relationships between employees may only be incidental to, or result from, the primary causes of marital discord and loss of affections. Thus, an employer's awareness of a romantic relationship between two of its employees does not give the employer sufficient knowledge to anticipate a claim for alienation of affections against an employee under its supervision.

Policy considerations also preclude our imposition of a duty upon employers to police the private conduct of their employees for the protection of employees' spouses. The cause of action for alienation of affections provides a remedy when a third person is at fault for the destruction of a marital relation . . . .

In addition, employers have no duty to determine the marital status of their employees. It would be unreasonable to impose upon employers a duty to monitor romantic relationships among their employees to protect marital relations of which they may not even be aware. Indeed, absent some indication of harassment or intimidation, an employer who attempted, merely upon the basis of its knowledge of a romantic relationship, to police the personal conduct of its employees may expose itself to liability for interfering with private relationships.

Plaintiff has also failed to allege facts establishing that any act or omission on the part of Novell or Univel was the proximate cause of his injury. Nothing indicates that more rules or different supervision would have prevented Mr. Righter's or Mr. Wilkes' acts. First, Mr. Righter acknowledged that romantic relationships between supervisors and subordinates were improper and violated the employment rules of Novell and Univel. It is unreasonable to assume that different rules would have affected Mr. Righter's conduct. In addition, despite Novell's advice to Mrs. Jackson that she should distance herself from Mr. Righter and pursue a different career path at Novell, she chose to transfer to Univel, remain under Mr. Righter's supervision, and work in the same department with Mr. Wilkes. Finally, Mr. Wilkes and Mrs. Jackson continued their sexual relationship after taking a leave of absence and finally terminating their employment with Univel. Nothing plaintiff alleges indicates that different actions by Univel would have prevented that relationship . . . .

■ **Think about this:**

(K) As mentioned above, *Lourim v. Swensen* and *Jackson v. Righter* both contain very similar statements of a three-element test for "scope of employment" that is repeated frequently by the courts of many jurisdictions. But it contains two elements that seem at first glance impossible. To paraphrase, the conduct must be both (a) of the general kind for which the employee was hired, and (b) motivated in some sense to serve the employer's interests. But how can that be? The challenged conduct will almost always be, essentially by definition, conduct no employer could want or condone, particularly in the many cases, like *Lourim*, of horrific harms and malevolent wrongdoing. And yet *Lourim* held that, at least in some sense relevant to the policy goals of agency law and vicarious liability, Swensen caused his harm through conduct for which the Boy Scouts employed him and that was motivated for the Scouts' benefit. What gives?

(L) A separate question worth asking, though it's a lot more obvious, is what policy drives the third element: that the conduct occurred during the physical space and time in which the employee is expected to work. What policy goal is served by making employers responsible for conduct only within those boundaries? There might be more than one answer, and to think about it, consider all the policy reasons for which the court balked at vicarious liability in *Jackson*.

(M) Suppose that it were Mrs. Jackson, rather than Mr. Jackson, who was the plaintiff. Suppose further that she alleges the relationships she had with Messrs. Righter and Wilkes had been coerced. Would you expect the same result with respect to the employers' vicarious liability?

In the next case, the injury to the plaintiffs' decedent technically came at the hands of someone other than the principal's employee. As you read it, think about why it might still make sense to impose liability on Revco.

WHITE V. REVCO DISCOUNT DRUG CENTERS, INC.

Supreme Court of Tennessee
33 S.W.3d 713 (2000)

BARKER, J.

[Plaintiffs sued Revco, the national chain of drug stores, for the wrongful death of their decedent at the hands of Boone, an off-duty police officer working in a Revco store as its security guard. After the decedent, one Woodfin, caused a disturbance in the store, Boone issued him a misdemeanor citation (as off-duty police officers may do under Tennessee law), and warned him not to enter the store again. Upon learning that Woodfin had not reported for booking as the citation ordered, Boone's Revco manager directed him to serve Woodfin an arrest warrant at his apartment. Boone took along four or five uniformed police department colleagues. During the attempted arrest, the Revco manager summoned Boone back to the store to issue another citation to a shoplifter. Boone then returned to the apartment to complete the arrest, and during the attempt one of his uniformed colleagues fatally shot Woodfin. The Tennessee Supreme Court here reverses the dismissal of plaintiffs' suit for failure to state a claim.]

[The court began by explaining that, unlike some other jurisdictions, Tennessee would treat an off-duty policeman working as a security guard just as it would treat other employees. The court also found inherent in agency law a policy that generally the employer], rather than the innocent injured plaintiff, should bear [the risks] . . . because [the employer] is better able to absorb [them], and to distribute them, through prices, rates or liability insurance, to the public, and so to shift them to society, to the community at large . . . .

[The court also noted that in addition to torts committed in the scope of employment,] a principal may be held liable for an agent's tortious act, even if that act occurs outside of the scope of the agency, if the act was commanded or directed by the principal. As [we have] stated the rule:

> A master is liable for the tort of his servant where the tortious act is done in obedience to his express orders or directions, even though the service is not within the line of the servant's usual duties, and provided the injury to the third person occurs as the natural, direct, and proximate result of the directed or authorized act . . . .

[Thus,] private employers may be held vicariously liable for the acts of an off-duty police officer employed as a private security guard under any of the following circumstances: (1) the action taken by the off-duty officer occurred within the scope of private employment; [or] (2) the action taken by the off-duty officer occurred outside of the regular scope of employment, if the action giving rise to the tort was taken in obedience to orders or directions of the employer and the harm proximately resulted from the order or direction . . . .

After carefully examining the material allegations of the original and amended complaints, we conclude that the plaintiffs have in fact made sufficient allegations under [both] agency theories, which, if proven, would give rise to vicarious liability on the part of Revco.

First, we find that the plaintiffs have made sufficient allegations to assert a cause of action against Revco based on a tort committed by Boone while acting within the course and scope of his employment with Revco . . . . The amended complaint . . . alleges that Revco employed Boone especially to take advantage of Boone's ability to make arrests and issue citations. F[urther], as evidence of Revco's control over Boone during the relevant period of time, the complaint sets forth the fact that Boone was summoned back to Revco to issue a citation to a shoplifter even while he was attempting to enforce the city's bench warrant. Accordingly, when viewed in a light most favorable to the plaintiffs, we find that the plaintiffs have adequately stated a cause of action against Revco based on the torts of its security guard committed within the scope of his private employment . . . .

Second, we also conclude that the plaintiffs have made sufficient allegations to assert a cause of action based on a tort committed by Boone while in obedience to the orders or directions of Revco. First, the complaint alleges that . . . the Revco manager directed Boone to [follow up on] Woodfin's previous citation for disorderly conduct. The complaint further alleges that upon learning that a bench warrant had been issued for Woodfin's arrest, the Revco Manager directed Boone "to serve the bench warrant to prevent Woodfin from ever returning to Revco and to punish Woodfin for disregarding Revco's no trespass order." If these facts are taken as true, . . . Revco would then be liable for the harm proximately resulting from Boone's actions taken in obedience to its directions, irrespective of whether Boone's actions were within the scope of his employment. Accordingly, we hold that the plaintiffs' complaint has stated a cause of action against Revco for Boone's actions taken in obedience to directions issued by Revco . . . .

■   **Think about this:**

(N) Is it necessary to rely on vicarious liability in order to find Revco liable?

(O) Would it have made any difference in this case if Boone had been an independent contractor rather than an employee? Would that even be possible, given the facts as stated?

C. Termination of Authority

    What does it look like?

Check the online Supplement for the following item relevant to this section:

■   A legal notice of termination of authority

Termination of an agent's authority is normally quite a simple affair, though it can pose one slightly nasty practical problem for principals. That problem, a recurrent one in agency contexts, is the problem of "lingering authority."

1. Actual Authority

The termination of *actual* authority is straightforward and does not ordinarily cause any real difficulties. The means of termination are all set out in the list in Re(3) §3.06, and they are elaborated in §§3.07-3.10. Maybe the most fundamental of these rules is one stated toward the end of the list: Under §§3.06(5) and 3.10, and in the absence of other agreement, either the principal or the agent may unilaterally cancel any grant of authority at any time. Since under those provisions the termination is caused merely by "manifestation" of one or the other,

the termination is to be judged objectively. Under these circumstances—where there is no contrary agreement—the termination in and of itself does not give rise to liability for either party as a matter of agency law. Where there is a contrary agreement, however, unilateral termination by either party would constitute a breach. It also is conceivable that termination by the agent might breach the agent's fiduciary duty under certain circumstances (for example, the agent might thereby become unable to complete a project for the principal under circumstances that cause the principal unnecessary harm). Still, as pointed out in the comments to §3.10, even where the parties agree by contract that authority will last for some specified time, they each remain free to terminate it unilaterally, for the basic reason that agency is always a relationship of mutual consent. In any event, note that under §3.10 one party's termination by unilateral manifestation does not take effect until the other party has notice of it. (As to the meaning of "notice," see Re(3) §5.01(3) and comment c, which are discussed in Chapter 5B.)

Another important doctrinal detail concerning deliberate terminations appears in §3.09, comment c. Some courts hold that both parties are subject to an implied contractual covenant of "good faith," such that they may not use their right of termination in such a way as to selfishly defeat the interests of the other. An example given in comment c is that a court may sometimes hold that a principal's termination of the agent's authority might be done to avoid commissions that are already earned. For example, assume that a real estate agent for the seller of a commercial building has been authorized to execute a contract for its sale on behalf of the principal, but is entitled to a commission only once the final sale contract is closed. The principal might allow the agent to do all the work of finding a buyer and negotiating the contract, but then terminate the agent's authority at the last minute and argue that the principal is entitled to execute the final contract himself, avoiding the duty to compensate the agent. In such a case, a court might hold that the principal in so acting breached the implied contractual covenant of good faith and fair dealing.

A rule closely related to unilateral termination is stated in §3.09. The parties may by contract agree that actual authority will terminate at some specified time or in connection with some particular circumstance, like the accomplishment of some particular transaction. Section 3.09 also provides that even in the absence of such an agreement, actual authority can terminate if circumstances arise rendering it no longer reasonable for the agent to believe that actual authority continues. For example, the price of a good or investment may have gone up so much that the agent cannot reasonably believe the principal would still want the agent to purchase it.

The other circumstances that terminate actual authority are simple enough, though they present several small technical curlicues. Death, at least, is fairly straightforward. If either party is an individual and that person dies, then all actual authority is terminated, though in the case of the principal's death it terminates only when the agent has notice of the death. What may be slightly more confusing is that the principal's death terminates actual authority as against a third party only when *that* person has notice of the death.

■   **Think about this:**

(P)   In each of this long list of cases of termination by other than mutual agreement, the law requires notice of the event causing termination, for policy reasons. Do you see why? Give some thought to the situation of the traveling agent, who may have authority to bind the principal to contracts without prior approval, and might be traveling on business and not be easily reachable.

A similar rule applies to juridical entities. If either party is a juridical person and it ceases to exist, then actual authority is terminated, though again there is a special curlicue. Corporations, partnerships, LLCs, and other such entities are required by their own governing statutes to go through a process of "winding up" their affairs once a decision has been made (or an event has occurred) that will terminate them. During this period, the entity continues to exist as a legal matter, and its officers (or partners or members or whatever, as the case may be) will continue to have some power to bind the entity to contracts. However, they have authority only for contracts that are somehow related to the process of winding up. In other words, the Restatement observes that in the case of juridical persons the process by which the entity will be dissolved in itself will have an effect on the authority of its agents, but that effect will be stated in other law. Once the firm finally does go out of existence, the situation becomes simple—at that point, actual authority is at an end.

 Dear Prof.: I gather from the context that a "juridical person" is an entity like a corporation, partnership, etc. I assume that when this entity goes out of existence it becomes a non-existent principal. Doesn't this mean all authority ends, not just actual authority?

We were actually trying to skirt this for the moment. The analysis is a bit complicated in the partnership scenario where, although the partnership may cease to exist, the partners may still be liable on the basis of apparent authority. There is more about this in Chapter 8.

Loss of capacity, in the absence of contrary agreement, terminates actual authority on a transaction-specific basis. Where the principal loses capacity to do some particular act, then any authority an agent may have had to do that act is terminated. Presumably, if the agent also has authority to do acts as to which the principal still has sufficient capacity, then that part of the agent's authority is not terminated. Now, note an important sub-rule in §3.08(2). The principal and agent may agree in writing that the agent has no authority *until* the principal loses capacity. The obvious practical application of this power will be to provide for the principal's care and affairs if the principal becomes medically or mentally incapacitated. Anyway, by contrast, an *agent's* loss of capacity is a bit of a non-issue; to see why, review what we learned about the capacity to act as agent, as stated in Re(3) §3.05.

Finally, one other important rule is buried in the comments following §3.09. Under comment d to that section, in the absence of other agreement, actual authority simply expires after the duration of a "reasonable period of time."

2. Appearances and the Problem of "Lingering" Authority

In addition to termination of actual authority, the nasty practical problem mentioned above occurs when *apparent* authority is terminated. Recall the different means by which actual and apparent authority are created. The latter depends entirely on the objective reasonableness and subjective actuality of a third party's belief about what a principal has said or done. The sum total of the law governing termination of apparent authority appears in Re(3) §3.11(2): "Apparent authority ends when it is no longer reasonable for the third party with whom an agent deals to believe that the agent continues to act with actual authority." As §3.11(1) makes clear, the mere termination of actual authority in itself has no effect on apparent authority, even if the termination is caused by the principal's explicit directive and even if it arises because the principal has fired the agent. In practice this can cause the problem of "lingering authority," under which a disgruntled or devious agent can continue binding the principal to contracts.

■ **Think about this:**

(Q) Put yourself in the principal's shoes. What on earth are you supposed to do to protect yourself from a maverick terminated agent bent on wreaking havoc with the apparent authority you've given him? Do concerns with libel and/or slander play any role?

D. Agency, Employer Evasions, and the "New Economy"

As a final problem in this chapter concerning the consequences of agency, we will consider an emerging trend in employment relations and an emerging policy conflict working its way through the courts even now. Employers for at least a few decades have been searching for cost-savings and organizational flexibility by redesigning what had been traditional, agency-based relationships of employer and employee. But in doing it they have caused a fair bit of controversy, and workers have challenged them in court.

1. Means of Evading Agency Consequences

FedEx and UPS, the familiar package delivery services, might seem from the outside to be more or less indistinguishable. But on the inside they are very different indeed. UPS is organized in the way one might expect—the company employs its drivers as its own employees. FedEx, by contrast, does not. It denominates its drivers as "owner-operators," and requires them to own their own trucks and sell their delivery services to FedEx as third-party independent contractors. That is so even though they wear FedEx uniforms and their trucks bear FedEx logos, and, as we shall see in a very interesting case excerpt below, they perform their work according to meticulous FedEx rules and oversight. The consequences of this different treatment are stark. UPS drivers earn substantially more money—perhaps as much as double, on average—and enjoy a suite of benefits that FedEx drivers lack, and all because UPS drivers are "employees." Because they are employees protected by federal and state laws, UPS must pay them overtime and provide certain other benefits, and they have used their federal labor-law rights to bargain collectively. They are also protected by all the other federal and state laws that protect "employees," including non-discrimination rules, workers' compensation, and unemployment insurance. *See generally* Lydia DePillis, *How FedEx Is Trying to Save the Business Model That Saved It Millions*, Wash. Post, Oct. 23, 2014.

As we shall see later in this chapter, FedEx is not the only firm to have stretched traditional employment relations along these lines, and the idea is not especially new. FedEx itself initiated its "owner-operator" model in 1985. Likewise, insurance companies and realty firms have long worked through independent agents and brokers, and "temp" agencies have existed for decades in order to satisfy businesses' temporary staffing needs. In recent years, however, some temp agencies have become gigantic. Any given worker (who is an employee of the staffing company) may be deployed wherever demand manifests, although many in fact are assigned to work at a given "user" organization for years. On-demand arrangements of this kind permit the employing firms to outsource their recruiting and human resource functions, and to avoid the employment benefits they give their other workers. And more generally, since at least the 1980s or so all kinds of firms have sought to "outsource" various functions, to exploit cost-savings and (at least aspirationally) organize themselves more efficiently.

New or not, however, the evolution of traditional employment relations seems poised to take on new dimensions in our "new" economy. For one thing, the "sharing economy" has arisen to allow the owners of various assets to share them with other persons for a price. Prominent among them are Airbnb and VRBO-type rental arrangements, and ride-sharing services like Uber and Lyft. Those arrangements entail the sale of services that until recently were performed by employees working for the owners of hotels and taxi fleets. Even more to the point, the "gig economy" simply provides online logistics to connect individual, self-employed service providers with consumers, for one-off service assignments.

> The derivation of the term "gig" is a matter of hot dispute.

Hundreds or thousands of gig-economy platforms now exist, for the sale of everything from limousine trips, to career-coach consulting, to restaurant delivery, to house cleaning, to odd jobs. There is even a platform, an early gig-economy pioneer created by Amazon known as the "Mechanical Turk," through which buyers can hire workers to perform virtually any service of any kind.

How one feels about all this is a fairly ideological affair. On the one hand, loosening traditional relationships and finding organizational flexibility could pose all kinds of benefits for business, consumers, and even workers. In particular, defenders of the gig and sharing economies believe they are nothing short of revolutionary, with immense benefits for consumers and society. But on the other hand, the erosion of longstanding, traditional employment norms has unquestionably had at least short-term impacts on at least some workers that are stark. Critics argue that the effects will be more than just transitional. Critics say the trend will just redistribute wealth upward, further batter a long-suffering middle class, and shift more and more of society's risks to the working poor.

And indeed, this tension has found its way into the courtroom, in ways relevant to this course. In the materials to follow, we will consider some of the most important litigation in which workers have challenged attempts to evade employment protections by characterizing them as independent contractors. While this struggle is probably far from over, the workers so far have won fairly significant success.

As a refresher, recall that the issue in these cases is fundamentally to determine whether the relationships at issue are agencies, and in particular whether they are employer-employee agencies. According to the Restatement of Agency (Third) ("Re(3)") §7.07(3)(a), an "employee" is "an agent whose principal controls or has the right to control the manner and means of the agent's performance of work. . . ." And again, the consequences of finding that the workers in fact are "employees" are various and substantial. As a matter of agency law, employees can subject their employers to binding contracts and the broad tort exposure of *respondeat superior.* As a consequence of other federal and state laws, employers must comply with a wide and elaborate range of protections.

2. Examples in Application

(a) The Basic Question of Characterization

Between 2003 and 2009, cases challenging FedEx's "owner-operator" model were filed in approximately 40 states and consolidated before a single federal district court. The excerpt below is from an appellate decision reversing the district court's decision that the drivers were merely independent contractors. We set out this particular excerpt to explain the FedEx business model.

ALEXANDER V. FEDEX GROUND PACKAGE SYSTEM, INC.

United States Court of Appeals for the Ninth Circuit
765 F.3d 981 (2014)

FLETCHER, Circuit Judge:

. . .

FedEx characterizes its drivers as independent contractors. FedEx's Operating Agreement ("OA") governs its relationship with the drivers. The OA's "Background Statement" provides:

[T]his Agreement will set forth the mutual business objectives of the two parties . . . but the manner and means of reaching these results are within the discretion of the [driver], and no officer or employee of FedEx . . . shall have the authority to impose any term or condition on [the driver] . . . which is contrary to this understanding.

A provision of the OA titled "Discretion of Contractor to Determine Method and Means of Meeting Business Objectives," states:

[N]o officer, agent or employee of FedEx . . . shall have the authority to direct [the driver] as to the manner or means employed. . . . For example, no officer, agent or employee of FedEx . . . shall have the authority to prescribe hours of work, whether or when the [driver] is to take breaks, what route the [driver] is to follow, or other details of performance.

FedEx's relationship with its drivers also is governed by various policies and procedures prescribed by FedEx.

1. JOB REQUIREMENTS

The OA requires FedEx drivers to pick up and deliver packages within their assigned "Primary Service Area[s]." Drivers must deliver packages every day that FedEx is open for business, and must deliver every package they are assigned each day. They must deliver each package within a specific window of time negotiated between FedEx and its customers. After each delivery, drivers must use an electronic scanner to send data about the delivery to FedEx. FedEx does not require drivers to follow specific delivery routes. However, FedEx tells its managers to design and recommend to its drivers routes that will "reduce travel time" and "minimize expenses and maximize earnings and service."

FedEx does not expressly dictate working hours, but it structures drivers' workloads to ensure that they work between 9.5 and 11 hours every working day. If a driver's manager determines that the driver has more work than he or she "can reasonably be expected to handle" in a 9.5 to 11-hour day, the manager may reassign part of the driver's workload to other drivers. Drivers are compensated according to a somewhat complex formula that includes per day and per-stop components. Drivers are expected to arrive at their delivery terminals each morning, and they are not supposed to leave the terminal until all of their packages are available for pick-up. FedEx instructs managers to make sure that drivers properly fill out their paperwork and prepare their packages for delivery. Each terminal sets a time by which all drivers must return at the end of the day.

If drivers want their trucks loaded by FedEx's package-handlers, they must leave their trucks at the terminal overnight.

The OA gives FedEx the authority to "reconfigure" a driver's service area upon five days' written notice. Drivers have the right to propose a plan to avoid reconfiguration, "using means satisfactory to FedEx." FedEx "may, in its sole discretion," reject a plan that does not "provide reasonable means to continue" the driver's service area. Should a driver's service area be reconfigured in such a way that the driver gains customers, FedEx may reduce that driver's pay to compensate other drivers who lost customers in the reconfiguration.

FedEx trains its drivers on how best to perform their job and to interact with customers. The OA provides that, during the first 30 days of the contract term, FedEx "shall . . . familiarize [drivers] with various quality service procedures developed by FedEx." The OA requires drivers to conduct themselves "with integrity and honesty, in a professional manner, and with proper decorum at all times." They must "[f]oster the professional image and good reputation of FedEx."

A driver's managers may conduct up to four ride-along performance evaluations each year, "to verify that [the driver] is meeting the standards of customer service" required by the OA. Managers are supposed to observe and record small details about each step of a delivery, including whether a driver uses a "dolly or cart" to move packages, demonstrates a "sense of urgency," and "[p]laces [his or her] keys on [the] pinky finger of [his or her] non-writing hand" after locking the delivery vehicle. After finishing a ride-along evaluation, managers are supposed to give immediate feedback to drivers about the quality of their work. FedEx contends in this litigation that this feedback constitutes mere recommendations that drivers are free either to follow or disregard.

Drivers must follow FedEx's "Safe Driving Standards." These standards prohibit many illegal acts, such as "[d]riving while under the influence of alcohol or drugs" and "[u]sing a motor vehicle in the commission of a felony." They also forbid some legal conduct, including "[d]riving a motor vehicle in a speed exhibition, contest or drag race" and "[c]arrying passengers not authorized by FedEx."

The OA allows drivers to operate more than one vehicle and route, but only "with the consent of FedEx" and only if "consistent with the capacity of the [driver's] terminal." Drivers may also hire third parties to help perform their work. Third-party helpers must be "qualified pursuant to applicable federal, state and municipal safety standards and [FedEx's] Safe Driving Standards." They must be "fully trained" and must "conform fully" with the OA. Drivers "in good standing" under the OA may assign their rights and obligations to replacement drivers, but any such replacement must be "acceptable to FedEx."

Drivers enter into the OA for an initial term of one, two, or three years. At the end of the initial term, the OA provides for automatic renewal for successive one-year terms if neither party provides notice of their intent not to renew. The OA may be terminated (1) by the parties' mutual agreement; (2) for cause, including a breach of any provision of the OA; (3) if FedEx stops doing business or reduces operations in all or part of the driver's service area; or (4) upon thirty days' written notice by the driver. The OA requires drivers to submit claims for wrongful termination to arbitration.

2. EQUIPMENT AND APPEARANCE REQUIREMENTS

FedEx requires its drivers to provide their own vehicles. Vehicles must not only meet "all applicable federal, state and municipal laws and regulations," but also must be specifically approved by FedEx. The OA allows FedEx to dictate the "identifying colors, logos, numbers, marks and insignia" of the vehicles. All vehicles must be painted "FedEx white," a specific shade of Sherwin-Williams paint, or its equivalent. They must be marked with the FedEx logo, and "maintained in a clean and presentable fashion free of body damage and extraneous markings." FedEx requires vehicles to have specific dimensions, and all vehicles must also contain shelves with specific dimensions. FedEx requires that a "typical package van" have two [shelves] per side, full length of the body. They should be 24″ (−1″, + 3″) deep with a 1″ to 2″ pitch and a front lip not to exceed 2″ height. Top shelf to bottom of roof or roof bow should be 24″ minimum. The lower shelf lip to the bottom of the top shelf should be 24″ (± 3/4″). Aluminum is the preferred material, however marine grade plywood is acceptable. Managers may refuse to let drivers work if their vehicles do not meet these requirements.

Drivers must provide maintenance at their own expense and must "bear all costs and expenses incidental to operation" of the vehicle. Drivers authorize FedEx to pay for vehicle licensing, taxes, and fees, and to deduct these costs from the drivers' pay. The OA gives FedEx such exclusive possession, use, and control of the [vehicle as] required by . . . applicable regulations, but [FedEx] shall have no right or authority . . . to operate the [vehicle] for any purpose (except for incidental yard movement and positioning) unless the [vehicle] is driven either by [the driver] or by an operator engaged by [the driver].

The OA requires that while vehicles are "in the service of FedEx," they must be used "exclusively for the carriage of the goods of FedEx . . . and for no other purpose." Drivers may use their vehicles "for other commercial or personal purposes when [they are] not in the service of FedEx," but only if all "identifying numbers, marks, logos and insignia" are removed or covered up.

FedEx offers a "Business Support Package," which provides drivers with uniforms, scanners, and other necessary equipment. FedEx deducts the cost of the equipment from drivers' pay. Purchase of the package is ostensibly optional, but more than 99 percent of drivers purchase it. The scanners that drivers must use to send delivery information to FedEx are not readily available from any other source.

The OA requires drivers to comply with personal-appearance standards and wear a FedEx uniform "maintained in good condition." The required uniform includes a uniform shirt with the FedEx logo, uniform pants or shorts, dark shoes and socks, and, if the driver chooses to wear a jacket or cap, a uniform jacket and cap with the FedEx logo. Drivers must keep their "personal appearance consistent with reasonable standards of good order as . . . promulgated from time to time by FedEx." Drivers must be "clean shaven, hair neat and trimmed, free of body odor." Managers may refuse to let drivers work if they are improperly dressed or groomed.

> ■ **Think about this:**
>
> **(R)** If the matter had gone to a jury and you were on that jury, would you say that FedEx controls the "manner and means" of the work the FedEx drivers perform?
>
> **(S)** Are FedEx drivers in the relationship described in the excerpt necessarily agents at all?
>
> **(T)** Do you think FedEx drivers *should* be treated as employees? Who wins and who loses if they are?
>
> **(U)** Aside from the benefit to FedEx of avoiding collective bargaining and employment-law protections and so on, do you see how else FedEx might benefit by structuring its relations with drivers as "owner-operators"?

Other litigation has involved new-economy firms, and in particular a fair bit of it has involved the ride-sharing firm Uber. The following case is only one small part of the story. As you will see, California courts apply a presumption that an employment relationship exists if services are provided. This presumption is unusual. The court's analysis of the various factors that generally are used to establish employment is not.

O'CONNOR V. UBER TECHNOLOGIES, INC.

United States District Court for the Northern District of California
82 F. Supp. 3d 1133 (2015)

CHEN, District Judge:

Plaintiffs filed this putative class action on behalf of themselves and other similarly situated individuals who drive for Defendant Uber Technologies, Inc. Plaintiffs claim that they are employees of Uber, as opposed to its independent contractors, and thus are eligible for various statutory protections for employees codified in the California Labor Code, such as a requirement that an employer pass on the entire amount of any gratuity "that is paid, given to, or left for an employee by a patron." Cal. Lab. Code §351.

Pending before the Court is Uber's motion for summary judgment that Plaintiffs are independent contractors as a matter of law. As is discussed below, the Court first concludes that Plaintiffs are Uber's presumptive employees because they "perform services" for the benefit of Uber. The Court next holds that whether an individual should ultimately be classified as an employee or an independent contractor under California law presents a mixed question of law and fact that must typically be resolved by a jury. Finally, because a number of facts material to the employee/independent contractor determination in this case remain in dispute, the Court denies Uber's summary judgment motion.

I. BACKGROUND

In a nutshell, Uber provides a service whereby individuals in need of vehicular transportation can log in to the Uber software application on their smartphone, request a ride, be paired via the Uber application with an available driver, be picked up by the available driver, and ultimately be driven to their final destination. Uber receives a credit card payment from the rider at the end of the ride, a significant portion of which it then remits to the driver who transported the passenger. . . .

Named plaintiffs . . . drive principally for Uber's "uberX" service. uberX drivers transport passengers in their own personal vehicles, which are typically hybrids or other "mid-range" cars. . . . Before becoming "partners" with Uber, Plaintiffs and other aspiring drivers must first complete Uber's application process. Applicants are required to upload their driver's license information, as well as information about their vehicle's registration and insurance. Applicants must also pass a background check conducted by a third party. Would-be drivers are further required to pass a "city knowledge test" and attend an interview with an Uber employee. Interviewees are instructed to "[b]ring your car, dress professionally and be prepared to stay for 1 hour."

Once a prospective driver successfully completes the application and interview stages, the driver must sign contracts with Uber or one of Uber's subsidiaries (Raiser LLC). Those contracts explicitly provide that the relationship between the transportation providers and Uber/Raiser "is solely that of independent contracting parties." The parties "expressly agree that this Agreement is not an employment agreement or employment relationship." The relevant contracts further provide that drivers will be paid a "fee" (*i.e.*, fare) upon the successful completion of each ride. . . . Because Uber receives the rider's payment of the entire fare, the relevant contracts provide that Uber will automatically deduct its own "fee per ride" from the fare before it remits the remainder to the driver. . . .

II. DISCUSSION . . .

A. Applicable Legal Standards . . .

2. California's Test of Employment

The parties agree that determining whether Plaintiffs are employees or independent contractors is an analysis that proceeds in two stages. "First, under California law, once a plaintiff comes forward with evidence that he provided services for an employer, the employee has established a prima facie case that the relationship was one of employer/employee." Narayan v. EGL, Inc., 616 F.3d 895, 900 (9th Cir. 2010). . . . If the putative employee establishes a prima facie case (*i.e.*, shows they provided services to the putative employer), the burden then shifts to the employer to prove, if it can, that the "presumed employee was an independent contractor." *Id.* at 901.

For the purpose of determining whether an employer can rebut a prima facie showing of employment, the Supreme Court's seminal opinion in *Borello* "enumerated a number of indicia of an employment relationship." *Narayan*, 616 F.3d at 901. The "most significant consideration" is the putative employer's "right to control work details." S.G. Borello & Sons, Inc. v. Dep't of Indus. Relations (Borello), 48 Cal. 3d 341, 350 (1989). This right of control need not extend to every possible detail of the work. Rather, the relevant question is whether the entity retains "all necessary control" over the worker's performance. *Id.* at 357.

The Supreme Court has further emphasized that the pertinent question is "not how much control a hirer *exercises*, but how much control the hirer retains the *right* to exercise." Ayala v. Antelope Valley Newspapers Inc., 59 Cal. 4th 522, 533 (2014) (emphases in the original). When evaluating the extent of that control, the Supreme Court has stressed that an employer's "right to discharge at will, without cause" is "strong evidence in support of an employment relationship." *Borello*, 48 Cal. 3d at 350. This is because the "power of the principal to terminate the services of the agent [without cause] gives him the means of controlling the agent's activities." *Ayala*, 59 Cal. 4th at 531.

The putative employer's right to control work details is not the only relevant factor, however, and the control test cannot be "applied rigidly and in isolation." *Borello*, 48 Cal. 3d at 350. Thus, the Supreme Court has also embraced a number of "secondary indicia" that are relevant to the employee/independent contractor determination. *Id.* These additional factors include:

> (a) whether the one performing services is engaged in a distinct occupation or business; (b) the kind of occupation, with reference to whether, in the locality, the work is usually done under the direction of the principal or by a specialist without supervision; (c) the skill required in the particular occupation; (d) whether the principal or the worker supplies the instrumentalities, tools, and the place of work for the person doing the work; (e) the length of time for which the services are to be performed; (f) the method of payment, whether by the time or by the job; (g) whether or not the work is a part of the regular business of the principal; and (h) whether or not the parties believe they are creating the relationship of employer-employee.

Id. at 351. *Borello* also "approvingly cited" five additional factors (some overlapping or closely related to those outlined immediately above) for evaluating a potential employment relationship. 616 F.3d at 900. These additional factors include:

> (1) the alleged employee's opportunity for profit or loss depending on his managerial skill; (2) the alleged employee's investment in equipment or materials required for his task, or his employment of helpers; (3) whether the service rendered requires a special skill; (4) the degree of permanence of the working relationship; and (5) whether the service rendered is an integral part of the alleged employer's business.

Borello, 48 Cal. 3d at 355. While the Supreme Court explained that all thirteen of the above "secondary indicia" are helpful in determining a hiree's employment status, it noted that "the individual factors cannot be applied mechanically as separate tests; they are intertwined and their weight depends on particular combinations." *Id.* at 351. . . .

B. The Plaintiffs Are Uber's Presumptive Employees Because They Provide a Service to Uber

If Plaintiffs can establish that they provide a service to Uber, then a rebuttable presumption arises that they are Uber's employees. *See Narayan*, 616 F.3d at 900. Uber argues that the presumption of employment does not apply here because Plaintiffs provide it no service. The central premise of this argument is Uber's contention that it is not a "transportation company," but instead is a pure "technology company" that merely generates "leads" for its transportation providers through its software. Using this semantic framing, Uber argues that Plaintiffs are simply its customers who buy dispatches that may or may not result in actual rides. In fact, Uber notes that its terms of service with riders specifically state that Uber is under no obligation to actually provide riders with rides at all. Thus, Uber passes itself off as merely a technological intermediary between potential riders and potential drivers. This argument is fatally flawed in numerous respects.

First, Uber's self-definition as a mere "technology company" focuses exclusively on the mechanics of its platform (*i.e.*, the use of internet enabled smartphones and software applications) rather than on the substance of what Uber actually *does* (*i.e.*, enable customers to book and receive rides). This is an unduly narrow frame. Uber engineered a software method to connect drivers with passengers, but this is merely one instrumentality used in the context of its larger business. Uber does not simply sell software; it sells rides. Uber is no more a "technology company" than Yellow Cab is a "technology company" because it uses CB radios to dispatch taxi cabs, John Deere is a "technology company" because it uses computers and robots to manufacture lawn mowers, or Domino Sugar is a "technology company" because it uses modern irrigation techniques to grow its sugar cane. . . .

Even more fundamentally, it is obvious drivers perform a service for Uber because Uber simply would not be a viable business entity without its drivers . . . . Uber's revenues do not depend on the distribution of its software, but on the generation of rides by its drivers. As noted above, Uber bills its riders directly for the entire amount of the fare charged—a fare amount that is set by Uber without any input from the drivers. Uber then pays its drivers eighty percent of the fare it charges the rider, while keeping the remaining twenty percent of the fare as its own "service fee." Put simply, the contracts confirm that Uber *only* makes money if its drivers actually transport passengers.

Furthermore, Uber not only depends on drivers' provision of transportation services to obtain revenue, it exercises significant control over the amount of any revenue it earns: Uber sets the fares it charges riders unilaterally. The record also shows that Uber claims a "proprietary interest" in its riders, which further demonstrates that Uber acts as more than a mere passive intermediary between riders and drivers. For instance, Uber prohibits its drivers from answering rider queries about booking future rides outside the Uber app, or otherwise "soliciting" rides from Uber riders. *See, e.g.*, Handbook at 7 (providing that actively soliciting business from a current Uber client is categorized as a "Zero Tolerance" event that "may result in immediate suspension from the Uber network." . . .

This Court holds, as a matter of law, that Uber's drivers render service to Uber, and thus are Uber's presumptive employees. . . .

D. Uber Is Not Entitled to Summary Judgment Because Material Facts Remain in Dispute and a Reasonable Inference of an Employment Relationship May Be Drawn

Because the ultimate determination of the Plaintiffs' employment status presents a mixed question of law and fact, Uber may only obtain summary judgment if all facts and evidentiary inferences material to the employee/independent contractor determination are undisputed, and a reasonable jury viewing those undisputed facts and inferences could reach but one conclusion—that Uber's drivers are independent contractors as a matter of law.

As noted above, the "principal test of an employment relationship is whether the person to whom service is rendered has the right to control the manner and means of accomplishing the result desired." *Ayala*, 59 Cal. 4th at 531 (quoting *Borello*, 48 Cal. 3d at 350). "Perhaps the strongest evidence of the right to control" is whether Uber can fire its transportation providers at will. *Id.* This critical fact appears to be in dispute. Uber claims that it is only permitted to terminate drivers "with notice or upon the other party's material breach" of the governing contracts. Plaintiffs, however, point out that the actual contracts seem to allow Uber to fire its drivers for any reason and at any time. *See, e.g.*, Addendum at 4 ("Uber will have the right, at all times and at Uber's sole discretion, to reclaim, prohibit, suspend, limit or otherwise restrict the Transportation Company and/or the Driver from accessing or using the Driver App. . . ."). To the extent this important factor in the employee/independent contractor test is in dispute, summary judgment is unwarranted.

Uber further claims that the right to control element is not met because drivers can work as much or as little as they like, as long as they give at least one ride every 180 days (if on the uberX platform) or every 30 days (if on the Uber-Black platform). According to Uber, drivers never have to accept any "leads" generated by Uber (*i.e.*, they can turn down as many rides as they want without penalty), and they can completely control *how* to give any rides they do accept. These contentions are very much in dispute. For instance, while Uber argues that drivers never actually have to accept ride requests when logged in to the Uber application, Plaintiffs provided an Uber Driver Handbook that expressly states: "We expect on-duty drivers to accept all [ride] requests." Handbook at 1. The Handbook goes on to state that "[w]e consider a dispatch that is not accepted to be a rejection," and we "will follow-up with all drivers that are rejecting trips." *Id.* The Handbook further notes that Uber considers "[r]ejecting too many trips" to be a performance issue that could lead to possible termination from the Uber platform. *Id.* at 8. . . .

It is also hotly disputed whether Uber has the right to significantly control the "manner and means" of Plaintiffs' transportation services. Plaintiffs cite numerous documents, written in the language of command, that instruct drivers to, amongst other things: "make sure you are dressed professionally"; send the client a text message when 1-2 minutes from the pickup location ("This is VERY IMPORTANT"); "make sure the radio is off or on soft jazz or NPR"; and "make sure to open the door for your client." As Uber emphasizes, "it is the small details that make for an excellent trip," and Plaintiffs have presented evidence (when viewed in the light most favorable to them) that Uber seeks to control these details right down to whether drivers "have an umbrella in [their] car for clients to be dry until they get in your car or after they get out." . . .

Uber responds that it merely provides its drivers with "suggestions," but does not actually require its drivers to dress professionally or listen to soft jazz or NPR. But the documents discussed above (and others in the record) are not obviously written as mere suggestions, and . . . [i]ndeed, there is evidence of drivers being admonished (or terminated) by Uber for failing to comply with its "suggestions." . . .

Nor can this Court at this juncture credit the argument that Uber has no ability to ensure that any driver actually complies with its "suggestions" or otherwise actively monitor its drivers' performance. In fact, there is evidence suggesting that Uber monitors its drivers to ensure compliance with Uber's many quality control "suggestions." Most notably, Uber requests passengers to give drivers a star rating, on a scale of 1-5, after each completed trip based on the driver's performance. Uber also provides a space for riders to provide written comments or feedback on drivers. Uber documents make it clear that Uber uses these ratings and feedback to monitor drivers and to discipline or terminate them. . . .

Finally, Uber makes much of the fact that Uber has no control over its drivers' hours or whether its drivers even "report" for work more than once in the relevant period. This is a significant point, and . . . might weigh heavily in favor of a finding of independent contractor status. However, . . . freedom to choose one's days and hours of work . . . does not in itself preclude a finding of an employment relationship. The more relevant inquiry is how much control Uber has over its drivers *while they are on duty* for Uber. . . . The fact that some drivers are only on-duty irregularly says little about the level of control Uber can exercise over them when they *do* report to work. . . .

Because the Court concludes that a number of material facts relevant to the "primary" *Borello* analysis are in dispute, thus precluding summary judgment, the Court need not examine in detail each of *Borello*'s numerous secondary factors. The Court nonetheless notes that a reasonable jury could find that numerous secondary factors cut in favor of finding an employment relationship. For instance, a jury could conclude that driving a car (as opposed to, *e.g.*, a truck or bus) does not require a special skill, particularly if no special driver's license is required. . . . A jury could also find, for the reasons previously discussed, that drivers perform a regular and integral part of Uber's business.

To be sure, a number of secondary factors (*e.g.*, drivers use their own vehicle, may employ other drivers to drive on their behalf, and signed an agreement stating no employment relationship is created), do support an independent contractor classification. But even as to these factors, their significance is ambiguous. For instance, the fact that the drivers provide their own vehicles and thus invest significant capital is a substantial factor favoring an independent contractor relationship as Uber properly contends, but this fact alone is not dispositive. . . . Moreover, this *Borello* factor is qualified by the fact that Uber supplies the critical tool of the business—smart phone with the Uber application. . . . In the aggregate, the secondary factors do not clearly cut in one direction. . . .

III. CONCLUSION

The application of the traditional test of employment—a test which evolved under an economic model very different from the new "sharing economy"—to Uber's business model creates significant challenges. Arguably, many of the factors in that test appear outmoded in this context. Other factors, which might arguably be reflective of the current economic realities (such as the proportion of revenues generated and shared by the respective parties, their relative bargaining power, and the range of alternatives available to each), are not expressly encompassed by the *Borello* test. It may be that the legislature or appellate courts may eventually refine or revise that test in the context of the new economy. It is conceivable that the legislature would enact rules particular to the new so-called "sharing economy." Until then, this Court is tasked with applying the traditional multifactor test of *Borello* and its progeny to the facts at hand. For the reasons stated above, apart from the preliminary finding that Uber drivers are presumptive employees, the *Borello* test does not yield an unambiguous result. The matter cannot on this record be decided as a matter of law. Uber's motion for summary judgment is therefore denied.

■ **Think about this:**

(V) One of the disputes in this case was whether Uber had a statutory obligation to pass on gratuities to its drivers. Why do you suppose the statute did not extend to independent contractors as well as employees?

(b) Joint Employment

In the next decision, the National Labor Relations Board applied traditional common law standards to determine when an employee may have more than one employer. A conclusion that joint employment exists could have ramifications well beyond the duty to bargain that was at stake in *Browning-Ferris*. Although the arrangement described may seem to be a bit extreme, in fact it is quite typical of the relationship between staffing and using companies.

BROWNING-FERRIS INDUSTRIES OF CALIFORNIA, INC., D/B/A BFI NEWBY ISLAND RECYCLERY

National Labor Relations Board
362 NLRB No. 186 (2015)

CHAIRMAN PEARCE and MEMBERS MISCIMARRA, HIROZAWA, JOHNSON, and McFERRAN:

In this case, we consider whether the Board should adhere to its current standard for assessing joint-employer status under the National Labor Relations Act or whether that standard should be revised to better effectuate the purposes of the Act, in the current economic landscape.

The issue in this case is whether BFI Newby Island Recyclery (BFI), and Leadpoint Business Services (Leadpoint) are joint employers of the sorters, screen cleaners, and housekeepers whom the Union petitioned to represent. The Regional Director issued a Decision and Direction of Election finding that Leadpoint is the sole employer of the petitioned-for employees. The Union filed a timely request for review of that decision, contending that (a) the Regional Director ignored significant evidence and reached the incorrect conclusion under current Board precedent; and (b) in the alternative, the Board should reconsider its standard for evaluating joint-employer relationships. . . .

The current standard, as reflected in Board decisions such as TLI[, Inc., 271 NLRB 798 (1984)] and Laerco [Transportation, 269 NLRB 324 (1984)], is ostensibly based on a decision of the United States Court of Appeals for the Third Circuit, NLRB v. Browning-Ferris Industries of Pennsylvania, Inc., 691 F.2d 1117 (3d Cir. 1982), which endorsed the Board's then-longstanding standard. But, as we will explain, the Board, without explanation, has since imposed additional requirements for finding joint-employer status, which have no clear basis in the Third Circuit's decision, in the common law, or in the text or policies of the Act. [These additional requirements are (1) that a joint employer must not only possess the authority to control employees' terms and conditions of employment, but also must exercise that authority; and (2) that the joint employer's control must be direct and immediate.] The Board has never articulated how these additional requirements are compelled by the Act or by the common-law definition of the employment relationship. They appear inconsistent with prior caselaw that has not been expressly overruled.

Moreover, these additional requirements — which serve to significantly and unjustifiably narrow the circumstances where a joint-employment relationship can be found — leave the Board's joint-employment jurisprudence increasingly out of step with changing economic circumstances, particularly the recent dramatic growth in contingent employment relationships. This disconnect potentially undermines the core protections of the Act for the employees impacted by these economic changes. . . .

Today, we restate the Board's joint-employer standard to reaffirm the standard articulated by the Third Circuit in [the] *Browning-Ferris* decision. Under this standard, the Board may find that two or more statutory employers are joint employers of the same statutory employees if they "share or codetermine those matters governing the essential terms and conditions of employment." In determining whether a putative joint employer meets this standard, the initial inquiry is whether there is a common-law employment relationship with the employees in question. If this common-law employment relationship exists, the inquiry then turns to whether the putative joint employer possesses sufficient control over employees' essential terms and conditions of employment to permit meaningful collective bargaining. . . .

I. FACTS

A. Overview

BFI owns and operates the Newby Island recycling facility, which receives approximately 1,200 tons per day of mixed materials, mixed waste, and mixed recyclables. The essential part of its operation is the sorting of these materials into separate commodities that are sold to other businesses at the end of the recycling process. BFI solely employs approximately 60 employees, including loader operators, equipment operators, forklift operators, and spotters. Most of these BFI employees work outside the facility, where they move materials and prepare them to be sorted inside the facility. These BFI employees are part of an existing separate bargaining unit that is represented by the Union.

The interior of the facility houses four conveyor belts, called material streams. Each stream carries a different category of materials into the facility: residential mixed recyclables, commercial mixed recyclables, dry waste process, and wet waste process. Workers provided to BFI by Leadpoint stand on platforms beside the streams and sort through the material as it passes; depending on where they are stationed, workers remove from the stream either recyclable materials or prohibited materials. Other material is automatically sorted when it passes through screens that are positioned near the conveyor belts.

As indicated, BFI, the user firm, contracts with Leadpoint, the supplier firm, to provide the workers who manually sort the material on the streams (sorters), clean the screens on the sorting equipment and clear jams (screen cleaners), and clean the facility (housekeepers).

The Union seeks to represent approximately 240 full-time, part-time, and on-call sorters, screen cleaners, and housekeepers who work at the facility. The relationship between BFI and Leadpoint is governed by a temporary labor services agreement (Agreement), which took effect in October 2009, and remains effective indefinitely. It can be terminated by either party at will with 30 days' notice. The Agreement states that Leadpoint is the sole employer of the personnel it supplies, and that nothing in the Agreement shall be construed as creating an employment relationship between BFI and the personnel that Leadpoint supplies.

B. Management Structure

BFI and Leadpoint employ separate supervisors and lead workers at the facility. BFI Operations [supervisors] . . . spend a percentage of each workday in the material stream areas, monitoring the operation and productivity of the streams. . . .

BFI and Leadpoint maintain separate human resource departments. BFI does not have an HR manager onsite. Leadpoint has an onsite HR manager who operates in a trailer (marked with the Leadpoint logo) outside the facility. Leadpoint employees use the BFI break rooms, bathrooms, and parking lot.

C. Hiring

The Agreement between BFI and Leadpoint provides that Leadpoint will recruit, interview, test, select, and hire personnel to perform work for BFI. . . . However, as to hiring, the Agreement requires Leadpoint to ensure that its personnel "have the appropriate qualifications (including certification and training) consistent with all applicable laws and instructions from [BFI], to perform the general duties of the assigned position." BFI also has the right to request that personnel supplied by Leadpoint "meet or exceed [BFI's] own standard selection procedures and tests." . . .

The Agreement also requires Leadpoint to make "reasonable efforts" not to refer workers who were previously employed by BFI and were deemed ineligible for rehire. . . . Before it refers a worker to BFI, Leadpoint is also required to ensure, in accordance with the Agreement, that she has passed, at minimum, a five-panel urinalysis drug screen, "or similar testing as agreed to in writing with [BFI's] safety, legal and commercial group." . . . After Leadpoint has referred workers, it is responsible for ensuring that they remain free from the effects of alcohol and drug use and in condition to perform their job duties for BFI. . . .

D. Discipline and Termination

Although the Agreement provides that Leadpoint has sole responsibility to counsel, discipline, review, evaluate, and terminate personnel who are assigned to BFI, it also grants BFI the authority to "reject any Personnel, and . . . discontinue the use of any personnel for any or no reason." . . .

E. Wages and Benefits

The Agreement includes a rate schedule that requires BFI to compensate Leadpoint for each worker's wage plus a specified percentage mark-up; the mark-up varies based on whether the work is performed during regular hours or as overtime. Although the Agreement provides that Leadpoint "solely determines the pay rates paid to its Personnel," it may not, without BFI's approval, "pay a pay rate in excess of the pay rate for full-time employees of [BFI] who perform similar tasks." . . .

Leadpoint employees are required to sign a benefits waiver stating they are eligible only for benefits offered by Leadpoint and are not eligible to participate in any benefit plan offered by BFI. Leadpoint provides employees with paid time-off and three paid holidays after they have worked for 2,000 hours, and the option to purchase medical, life, and disability insurance.

F. Scheduling and Hours

BFI establishes the facility's schedule of working hours. It operates three set shifts on weekdays: 4 a.m.-1 p.m., 2 p.m.-11:30 p.m., and 10:30 p.m.-7 a.m. Leadpoint is responsible for providing employees to cover all three shifts. Although Leadpoint alone schedules which employees will work each shift, Leadpoint has no input on shift schedules. . . . BFI will keep a stream running into overtime if it determines that the material on a specific stream cannot be processed by the end of a shift. A BFI manager will normally convey this decision to a Leadpoint shift supervisor; Leadpoint, in turn, determines which employees will stay on the stream to complete the overtime work.

BFI also dictates when the streams stop running so that Leadpoint employees can take breaks. . . .

The Agreement requires that Leadpoint employees must, at the end of each week, submit to Leadpoint a summary of their "hours of services rendered." Employees must obtain the signature of an authorized BFI representative attesting to the accuracy of the hours on the form. BFI may refuse payment to Leadpoint for any time claimed for which a worker failed to obtain a signature.

G. Work Processes

BFI determines which material streams will run each day and provides Leadpoint with a target headcount of workers needed. BFI also dictates the number of Leadpoint laborers to be assigned to each material stream, but Leadpoint assigns specific Leadpoint employees to specific posts. . . . During a shift, BFI might direct Leadpoint supervisors to move employees to another stream in response to processing demands.

Before each shift, BFI's [supervisors] hold meetings with Leadpoint supervisors — the onsite manager and leads — to present and coordinate the day's operating plan. During those meetings, BFI's managers dictate which streams will be operating and establish the work priorities for the shift. . . .

BFI managers set productivity standards for the material streams. . . . BFI has sole authority to set the speed of the material streams based on its ongoing assessment of the optimal speed at which materials can be sorted most efficiently. If sorters are unable to keep up with the speed of the stream, BFI — but not Leadpoint — can make various adjustments, such as slowing the speed of the stream or changing the angle of the screens. The record indicates that the speed of the streams has been a source of contention between BFI and Leadpoint employees. . . . [A BFI supervisor called] the entire line of sorters to the control room, where he directed them to work more efficiently and dismissed their requests to slow down or stop the line.

Leadpoint employees are able to stop the streams by hitting an emergency stop switch. [A BFI supervisor] testified that he has instructed Leadpoint supervisors on when it is appropriate for Leadpoint employees to use the switch. . . . [Other BFI supervisors] held a meeting with an entire line of Leadpoint employees to call attention to the frequency of their emergency stops and to direct Leadpoint employees to minimize the number of stops to reduce downtime.

BFI's managers testified that when, in the course of monitoring stream operation and productivity, they identify problems, including problems with the job performance of a Leadpoint employee, they communicate their concerns to a Leadpoint supervisor. The Leadpoint supervisor is expected to address those issues with the employees. According to the testimony of Leadpoint employees,

BFI managers have, on occasion, addressed them directly regarding job tasks and quality issues....

H. Training and Safety

When Leadpoint employees begin working at the facility, they receive an orientation and job training from Leadpoint supervisors. Periodically, they also receive substantive training and counseling from BFI managers....

As to safety, the Agreement mandates that Leadpoint require its employees to comply with BFI's safety policies, procedures, and training requirements....

V. REVISITING THE JOINT-EMPLOYER STANDARD

As the Board's view of what constitutes joint employment under the Act has narrowed, the diversity of workplace arrangements in today's economy has significantly expanded. The procurement of employees through staffing and subcontracting arrangements, or contingent employment, has increased steadily since TLI was decided. The most recent Bureau of Labor Statistics survey from 2005 indicated that contingent workers accounted for as much as 4.1 percent of all employment, or 5.7 million workers. Employment in the temporary help services industry, a subset of contingent work, grew from 1.1 million to 2.3 million workers from 1990 to 2008. As of August 2014, the number of workers employed through temporary agencies had climbed to a new high of 2.87 million, a 2 percent share of the nation's work force. Over the same period, temporary employment also expanded into a much wider range of occupations. A recent report projects that the number of jobs in the employment services industry, which includes employment placement agencies and temporary help services, will increase to almost 4 million by 2022, making it "one of the largest and fastest growing [industries] in terms of employment."

This development is reason enough to revisit the Board's current joint-employer standard. "[T]he primary function and responsibility of the Board ... is that 'of applying the general provisions of the Act to the complexities of industrial life.'" [Ford Motor Co. v. NLRB, 441 U.S. 488, 496 (1979).] If the current joint-employer standard is narrower than statutorily necessary, and if joint-employment arrangements are increasing, the risk is increased that the Board is failing in what the Supreme Court has described as the Board's "responsibility to adapt the Act to the changing patterns of industrial life." [NLRB v. J. Weingarten, Inc., 420 U.S. 251, 266 (1975).] [T]he Board has never clearly and comprehensively explained its joint-employer doctrine or, in particular, the shift in approach reflected in the current standard. Our decision today is intended to address this shortcoming....

We begin with the obvious proposition that in order to find that a statutory employer (i.e., an employer subject to the National Labor Relations Act) has a duty to bargain with a union representing a particular group of statutory employees, the Act requires the existence of an employment relationship between the employer and the employees. Section 2(3) of the Act provides that the "term 'employee' . . . shall not be limited to the employees of a particular employer, unless the Act explicitly states otherwise." . . .

In determining whether an employment relationship exists for purposes of the Act, the Board must follow the common-law agency test. The Supreme Court has made this clear in connection with Section 2(3) of the Act and its exclusion of "any individual having the status of an independent contractor" from the Act's otherwise broad definition of statutory employees. [NLRB v. United Insurance Co. of America, 390 U.S. 254, 256-258 (1968).] In determining whether a common-law employment relationship exists in cases arising under Federal statutes like the Act, the Court has regularly looked to the Restatement (Second) of Agency (1958) for guidance. Section 220(1) of the Restatement (Second) provides that a "servant is a person employed to perform services in the affairs of another and who with respect to the physical conduct in the performance of the services is subject to the other's control or right to control." . . . Thus, the Board properly considers the existence, extent, and object of the putative joint employer's control, in the context of examining the factors relevant to determining the existence of an employment relationship. Accordingly, mere "service under an agreement to accomplish results or to use care and skill in accomplishing results" is not evidence of an employment, or joint-employment, relationship.

. . . In cases where the common law would not permit the Board to find joint-employer status, we do not believe the Board is free to do so. Even where the common law does permit the Board to find joint-employer status in a particular case, the Board must determine whether it would serve the purposes of the Act to do so, taking into account the Act's paramount policy to "encourage[] the practice and procedure of collective bargaining" (in the words of Section 1). In other words, the existence of a common-law employment relationship is necessary, but not sufficient, to find joint-employer status. . . . [O]ur joint-employer standard — to the extent permitted by the common law — should encompass the full range of employment relationships wherein meaningful collective bargaining is, in fact, possible.

The core of the Board's current joint-employer standard — with its focus on whether the putative joint employer "share(s) or codetermine(s) those matters governing the essential terms and conditions of employment" — is firmly grounded in the concept of control that is central to the common-law definition of an employment relationship. The Act surely permits the Board to adopt that formulation. No federal court has suggested otherwise, and the Third Circuit in *Browning-Ferris*, of course, has endorsed this aspect of the standard.

The Board's post-*Browning-Ferris* narrowing of the joint-employer standard, however, has a much weaker footing. The Board has never looked to the common law to justify the requirements that a putative joint employer's control be exercised and that the exercise be direct and immediate, not "limited and routine." This aspect of the current standard is not, in fact, compelled by the common law — and, indeed, seems inconsistent with common-law principles. Because the Board thus is not obligated to adhere to the current standard, we must ask whether there are compelling policy reasons for doing so. The Board's prior decisions failed to offer any policy rationale at all, and we are not persuaded that there is a sound one, given the clear goals of the Act.

Under common-law principles, the right to control is probative of an employment relationship — whether or not that right is exercised. Sections 2(2) and 220(1) of the Restatement (Second) of Agency make this plain, in referring to a master as someone who "controls or has the right to control" another and to a servant as "subject to the [employer's] control or right to control". . . . The Board's joint-employer decisions requiring the exercise of control impermissibly ignore this principle. . . .

Just as the common law does not require that control must be exercised in order to establish an employment relationship, neither does it require that control (when it is exercised) must be exercised directly and immediately, and not in a limited and routine manner (as the Board's current joint-employer standard demands). Comment d ("Control or right to control") to Section 220(1) of the Restatement (Second) observes that "the control or right to control needed to establish the relation of master and servant may be very attenuated." The common law, indeed, recognizes that control may be indirect. For example, the Restatement of Agency (Second) §220, comment l ("Control of the premises") observes that "[i]f the work is done upon the premises of the employer with his machinery by workmen who agree to obey general rules for the regulation of the conduct of employees, the inference is strong that such workmen are the servants of the owner . . ." and illustrates this principle by citing the example of a coal mine owner employing miners who, in turn, supply their own helpers. Both the miners and their helpers are servants of the mine owner. As the illustration demonstrates, the common law's "subservant" doctrine addresses situations in which one employer's control is or may be exercised indirectly, where a second employer directly controls the employee. . . .

. . . Board case law suggests that in many contingent arrangements, control over employees is bifurcated between employing firms with each exercising authority over a different facet of decision making. Where the user firm owns and controls the premises, dictates the essential nature of the job, and imposes the broad, operational contours of the work, and the supplier firm, pursuant to the user's guidance, makes specific personnel decisions and administers job performance on a day-to-day basis, employees' working conditions are a byproduct of two layers of control. . . .

VI. THE RESTATED JOINT-EMPLOYER STANDARD

Having fully considered the issue and all of the arguments presented, we have decided to restate the Board's legal standard for joint-employer determinations and make clear how that standard is to be applied going forward.

We return to the traditional test used by the Board (and endorsed by the Third Circuit in *Browning-Ferris*): The Board may find that two or more entities are joint employers of a single work force if they are both employers within the meaning of the common law, and if they share or codetermine those matters governing the essential terms and conditions of employment. In evaluating the allocation and exercise of control in the workplace, we will consider the various ways in which joint employers may "share" control over terms and conditions of employment or "codetermine" them, as the Board and the courts have done in the past.

We adhere to the Board's inclusive approach in defining "essential terms and conditions of employment." The Board's current joint-employer standard refers to "matters relating to the employment relationship such as hiring, firing, discipline, supervision, and direction" [—] a nonexhaustive list of bargaining subjects. Essential terms indisputably include wages and hours, as reflected in the Act itself. Other examples of control over mandatory terms and conditions of employment found probative by the Board include dictating the number of workers to be supplied, controlling scheduling, seniority, and overtime; and assigning work and determining the manner and method of work performance. This approach has generally been endorsed by the Federal courts of appeals. . . .

The existence, extent, and object of a putative joint employer's control, of course, all may present material issues. For example, it is certainly possible that in a particular case, a putative joint employer's control might extend only to terms and conditions of employment too limited in scope or significance to permit meaningful collective bargaining. Moreover, as a rule, a joint employer will be required to bargain only with respect to such terms and conditions which it possesses the authority to control. . . .

VIII. APPLICATION OF THE RESTATED TEST

With the above principles in mind, we evaluate here whether BFI constitutes a joint employer under the Act. As always, the burden of proving joint-employer status rests with the party asserting that relationship. Having assessed all of the relevant record evidence, we conclude that the Union has met its burden of establishing that BFI is a statutory joint employer of the sorters, screen cleaners, and housekeepers at issue. BFI is an employer under common-law principles, and the facts demonstrate that it shares or codetermines those matters governing the essential terms and conditions of employment for the Leadpoint employees. In many relevant respects, its right to control is indisputable. Moreover, it has exercised that control, both directly and indirectly. Finding joint-employer status here is consistent with common-law principles, and it serves the purposes of the National Labor Relations Act. . . .

■   **Think about this:**

(W) If the staffing arrangement described in the foregoing NLRB decision results in joint employership, is there still any reason for its use?

Test Yourself

Assume Applicability of the Restatement (Third) of Agency

Questions 1-3 rely on the following facts:

DotBomb, Inc. runs an online retail business through its website, DotBomb. com. In addition to its own sales of a wide range of retail products, DotBomb sells advertising space on its site. It does so through a team of in-house sales-people, whom advertisers contact by calling a number on the "Contact Us" page of the website. (Often enough, though, DotBomb's salespeople make cold calls to potential advertisers, which they can follow up with marketing materials including their business cards and correspondence on company letterhead.) Jenny, one of the firm's best salespeople, recently scored a huge victory, con-tracting a one-year advertising deal with AutoMax, a nationwide chain of auto dealerships. Or at least she thought it was a victory, until her supervisor pointed out that according to the firm's internal sales team handbook, contracts in excess of six months require approval by DotBomb's CEO.

Meanwhile, a different sales person, Dave, has started behaving erratically lately, and hasn't made any sales in a while, so DotBomb provides him written notice that his job will be terminated and that he is no longer entitled to act on DotBomb's behalf. However, DotBomb management fears that after receipt of this notice Dave will go "rogue" and try to retaliate by committing DotBomb to a string of unfavorable advertising contracts.

1. AutoMax will be able to enforce its contract against DotBomb because:

   a. Jenny had actual authority.
   b. Jenny had apparent authority.
   c. Jenny had inherent authority.
   d. It is not possible on these facts that the contract binds DotBomb.

2. When DotBomb salespeople make cold calls that result in contracts for the sale of advertising space, the contracts are enforceable because:

   a. The salespeople have actual authority, assuming the contracts are for less than six months.
   b. The salespeople have apparent authority by virtue of the business cards and other materials they can distribute.
   c. The salespeople have apparent authority if it is customary in the indus-try for contracts of this nature to be sold by salespeople without prior approval.
   d. Answers a and b are both correct.
   e. Answers a, b, and c are all correct.

3. It should be comparatively easy for DotBomb to avoid liability for unauthorized contracts entered into by Dave, because:

   a. It should be obvious to advertisers that Dave is not authorized to bind DotBomb.
   b. Under these facts, it should be comparatively easy for DotBomb to make effective notice of withdrawal of Dave's authority.
   c. In fact, contracts made by Dave after his termination will not bind DotBomb.
   d. Under these facts, notice of withdrawal of authority would be impractical.

Questions 4-7 rely on the following facts:

Dena represents Wacky World, a family entertainment empire that operates several very popular amusement parks, with rides and attractions designed around characters from its signature animated films. Wacky World aims to build a new park in Florida, which would compete head to head with the well-known theme parks already established in Orlando. It instructs Dena to identify parcels near Orlando that might be stitched together into one block large enough for a new park. She is under orders not to disclose that she represents a principal, and not to make any purchases in excess of $100,000 without prior approval. Dena nevertheless jumps at the opportunity to buy two parcels, one from Mary and the other from Robert. She bought Mary's first, even though Mary demanded $125,000, because she was sure Wacky World would subsequently approve it. She then met with Robert, who had heard about Dena snooping around and the fairly miraculous price Mary got for her swampland. Robert asked Dena a number of probing questions, confident that she must represent a new park or some other major interest that would probably pay top dollar were its identity revealed. Dena flatly denied it, lying in fact, and insisting that the land was to be her own personal property. In the end, Dena purchased Robert's parcel too, this time paying $130,000.

4. The contract with Mary is enforceable against Wacky World because:

   a. Dena had actual authority.
   b. Dena had apparent authority.
   c. Dena made the contract on Wacky World's behalf.
   d. The contract is not enforceable.

5. The contract with Robert is unenforceable against Wacky World because:

   a. Dena lacked actual authority.
   b. Dena lacked apparent authority.
   c. Dena lied in response to Robert's questions.
   d. The contract is enforceable.

6. In any case, both contracts are enforceable against Dena.

    a. True, because she made them on behalf of an undisclosed principal.
    b. True, because she had apparent authority.
    c. False, because Dena made the contract on behalf of Wacky World.
    d. False, because she lacked actual authority.

7. Now suppose that Dena was unable to keep the secret, and eventually disclosed to both Mary and Robert, before executing contracts with them, that she represented Wacky World, forgetting to mention her directions not to disclose and not to spend more than $100,000. If the contracts are enforceable, it is because:

    a. Dena had actual authority.
    b. Either custom in the market or some other evidence suggested that Dena could proceed this way.
    c. Wacky World must have ratified them.
    d. The contracts cannot be enforceable.

Questions 8-10 rely on the following facts:

John is the owner and manager of an apartment building. Concerned about the safety of his tenants, John hires SafetyGuys, Inc., to provide security services in his building. SafetyGuys is a corporation formed for the purpose of providing security guards to private businesses. In making the arrangement, John deals directly with SafetyGuys' chief executive officer, a man named Richard, who explains to John that the security guards will be employees of SafetyGuys who will receive their instructions from their supervisor, another SafetyGuys employee. However, any agreement with SafetyGuys would be subject to John's specific requests concerning the conduct and duties of the guards, and John could make any further requests he chose during the life of the agreement.

During the first week that a SafetyGuys guard was on duty in John's building, the guard mistook Peter, a tenant, for an intruder. A scuffle ensued and the guard beat Peter severely, causing significant physical injuries. Peter sues John for money damages for his injuries.

8. What is the relationship between Richard and the security guards?

    a. Richard is their principal and they are his non-employee agents.
    b. Richard is their principal and they are his employees.
    c. Richard and the security guards are co-agents.
    d. Richard is their principal and they are his sub-agents.

9. What is the relationship between John and the security guards?

    a. John is their principal and they are his agents.
    b. John is their principal and they are his co-agents.

   c. John and the security guards are arm's-length contract parties.

   d. John and the security guards have no legal relationship.

10. Which of the following facts, if true, would be most helpful to Peter in this action?

   a. Richard, the SafetyGuys CEO, has encouraged all his guards "not to spare the rod"—that is, he has taught them that physical force is appropriate for self-defense and whenever the guards' orders are disobeyed.

   b. Peter cannot win this action.

   c. SafetyGuys is improperly incorporated and has committed federal securities fraud.

   d. John failed to inquire of Richard concerning the caliber of SafetyGuys employees.

The following questions stand alone:

11. Jim, an employee of Bill's Burger Hut (BBH), a corporation whose sole business is to own and operate a fast-food restaurant, is entrusted with operation of the french-fry cooker. One day Jim becomes incensed at a customer and savagely beats him with a spatula within the restaurant. If BBH escapes liability for the customer's injuries, it is most likely because of:

   a. Lack of an agency relationship between BBH and Jim.

   b. Lack of an employer-employee relationship between BBH and Jim.

   c. The nature of Jim's work.

   d. For reasons of public policy embodied in the concept of *respondeat superior*, BBH likely cannot escape this liability.

12. Darya is a driver for Muber, a company that provides an app for on-demand moving services. Her agreement with Muber provides that she is an independent contractor and that she will provide her own moving truck and dolly, as well as her own insurance. Muber exercises no control over the way Darya operates her vehicle or the way she loads and unloads it and cannot dictate her routes. Muber does, however, require that Darya be available to accept jobs during the hours stipulated in their agreement and that she accept all requests for jobs that she receives. Which of the following is most true?

   a. Darya is not an employee because she agreed to be an independent contractor.

   b. Darya is not an employee because she provides her own truck, dolly, and insurance.

   c. Darya is not an independent contractor because Muber controls her hours.

   d. There is not enough information to answer this question with certainty.

(Answers in Online Supplement)

13. Which of the following is *not* a reason an organization might consider using a staffing company to provide part of its workforce?

    a. Avoiding all liability from the conduct of the staffing company's employees.

    b. Avoiding recruiting and human resource expenditures.

    c. Avoiding various employee rights that are provided by statute or other legal regulation.

    d. Avoiding the need to engage in collective bargaining.

5

Further Topics in Agency

There are a number of nuances in understanding agency relationships that do not fit neatly into a discussion of its main themes. These include the ins and outs of ratification, the circumstances in which an agent's knowledge (or notice to an agent) will be imputed to the principal, the non-fiduciary duties the principal owes the agent, and the way that the agency relationship (as opposed to an agent's authority) is terminated.

Chapter Outline

A. Ratification

1. Ratification of Unauthorized Contracts
   - Ratification effective only when:
   - Ratifier had capacity at the time of the underlying act
   - Purported agent took action on ratifier's behalf
   - Ratifier had actual, subjective knowledge of all material facts
   - Ratification was made before the third party's offer is withdrawn
   - Ratification was not the result of a trick, done only to avoid loss, or done to destroy the rights of innocent third parties
   - No intervening changes in circumstances rendered ratification unfair
   - The effect of ratification is retroactive—all legal consequences are modified as if the underlying act had been fully authorized

2. Ratification of Torts
   - Ratification relates to "acts" and is not limited to contract context

B. Notice and Notification

1. "Notice" vs. "Notification"
   - "Notice" is something one has
   - "Notification" is something one gets

2. Imputation of Notice and Notification
   - Absent adversity of interest, notice and notification generally are imputed from the agent to the principal

3. The Duty to Notify
   - The agent has a fiduciary duty to report certain information to the principal

4. The Effect of Ratification on Notice and Notification
   - Imputation is retroactive in the case of ratification

C. Non-Fiduciary Rights and Remedies Between Principal and Agent

1. Principal vs. Agent
   - Most rights are fiduciary but may be added to by contract

2. Agent vs. Principal
   - Presumptive entitlement to compensation
   - General entitlement to indemnification
   - Principal owes a duty of good faith
   - Principal must not interfere with agent's work, and in some cases must provide work
   - Principal must warn agent of known risks
   - Principal must refrain from injury to agent's reputation and "self-respect"

D. Termination of the Agency Relationship

- Terminating authority is not the same as terminating the relationship
- Some duties survive termination

Test Yourself

A. Ratification

There may be times when an agent undertakes conduct purportedly on the principal's behalf but for which the principal could not legally be held responsible. This could include a contract made without actual authority and under circumstances in which belief in the agent's authority would not be reasonable, or a tort committed while not in the course of employment and not otherwise giving rise to the principal's liability. But, as previously noted in passing, a person can still become responsible for those things by "ratifying" them. Simple enough, or so it seems, but the rules present a few surprises and several technical curlicues.

The relevant rules appear in Chapter 4 of the Restatement (Third) of Agency ("Re(3)").

1. Ratification of Unauthorized Contracts

Obviously enough, one reason to ratify a contract is that the principal thinks the contract is advantageous and wants to be party to it. However, as is so often the case in agency law, a principal may take action with no such desire or intent and inadvertently ratify a contract obligation, sometimes with significant consequences.

Requisite Elements. In order to ratify a previously unauthorized contract, the would-be principal, who must have sufficient legal capacity to have been a party to the underlying contract in the first place (*see* Re(3) §4.04), must in some way manifest assent to be bound by the contract (*see* §4.01). Manifestation of assent in this context is not especially complex so long as we remember that it can be made in just as many ways as other manifestations of assent—it can be by spoken or written words, but it can also be by various kinds of conduct. To reiterate, however, because the existence of a manifestation is to be judged objectively, it does not matter whether the would-be principal means to ratify or not. Importantly, ratification can occur where the purported principal merely does nothing. For example, if the principal receives notice of facts that would cause a reasonable person to take steps to disaffirm a contract made on that person's behalf but the principal fails to do so, then the contract is ratified. The principal's manifestation need not be made to the agent or to the third party. Since the only question is whether a trier of fact could find the purported principal to have assented to the contract, any manifestation of assent made to *anyone* in any context can effect a ratification. On the other hand, even if the purported principal's conduct otherwise manifests intent to ratify, that conduct will not constitute ratification if the principal lacked knowledge of facts material to the underlying act to be ratified. *See* §4.06.

Connections: "Notice" and "Knowledge"

Re(3) §4.06 would release a purported ratifier from liability wherever he or she lacks actual "knowledge" of material facts, but comment d states that if the person ratifies despite knowledge of facts that would have led a reasonable person to investigate further, the finder of fact may find that the ratifier chose to bear the risk of lack of knowledge of material facts. As a practical matter, this sounds suspiciously like a rule that a person is held to liability when he manifests assent to a liability so long as he has mere notice of all material facts.

"Notice" is itself a term of art (*see* §5.01) and will be discussed later in this chapter.

Dear Prof.: You said the determination of ratification would be objective and then you said we should care about whether the principal lacked actual knowledge of the material facts. Isn't that subjective?

It is true that the knowledge required for an effective ratification is actual knowledge. *See* §4.06, comment b. At this point we're nonetheless really starting to get a flavor for how often agency law imposes consequences on people, sometimes very serious ones, on objective rather than subjective grounds—not for what they intended, but for what it seemed like they intended. Ask yourself again: What explains this obsession? What policy value does it serve?

■ **Think about this:**

(A) Clarice is selling her business and has authorized Alex, an attorney, to negotiate on her behalf. She has not, however, actually authorized him to agree to a sales price. When faced with the prospective buyer's threat to walk from the table if agreement to the price of $2 million isn't immediately forthcoming, Alex purports to sign the agreement as Clarice's agent. When Clarice learns of the price, she is pleasantly surprised and tells Alex that she is happy to agree. The agreement contains a number of important legal points, including a litany of representations that Clarice makes as seller. Clarice does not read the agreement nor does Alex explain the legal niceties. Has Clarice ratified the agreement?

Several other technical requirements must also be met. The contract must have been made on the purported principal's behalf, and he or she must ratify before the third party's offer is retracted. *See* §§4.03, 4.05(1). The purported principal also must ratify before there are other changes in circumstances that would cause inequity to the third party. Section 4.05 contains an apparently non-exclusive list of such changes. In addition to the third party's withdrawal from the contract (§4.05(1)), the list includes changes in circumstances that would defeat the third party's expectations (like a sudden change in the value of a thing to be sold or some large investment already made in an alternative arrangement, *see* §4.05(2)) and the expiration of some time period that determines the third party's rights or liabilities (*see* §4.05(3)). The would-be principal must agree to be subject to the whole action and not just parts of it. *See* §4.07. This rule can raise two kinds of issues. First, sometimes the agent will have committed torts or incurred other liabilities along with whatever contract has been entered into. The would-be principal cannot ratify only the beneficial contract and avoid the other liabilities. Second, where some purported agent has negotiated a series of more or less related transactions, and a purported principal manifests assent to ratify one or more of them, litigation might ensue over just how many of them have been ratified. *See id.* at comments b & c.

Finally, the person ratifying must have existed at the time of the act (this is important in the context of corporations purportedly ratifying pre-incorporation contracts). In other words, non-existent principals cannot ratify contracts retroactively to a time prior to their own existence, though otherwise incompetent principals can ratify retroactively to a time of their own incompetence so long as they gain capacity by the time of ratification. *See* §4.04. Recall, however, that even the previously non-existent principal can still *adopt* an otherwise enforceable contract made on its behalf, the difference being that the adoption takes effect only as of the date of the adoption. This is discussed further in §4.04, comment c.

Effects. Most of the legal consequences of ratification follow from the Restatement's particular formulation of its effects. Under Re(3) §4.02(1), "ratification retroactively creates the effects of actual authority." That is, ratification doesn't just render the principal subject to a contract otherwise avoidable. It automatically changes *all* legal rights and obligations, retroactively, to those that would exist had the contract been authorized from the beginning. In other words, the principal ratifies the unauthorized act, and then, *poof!*—it's as if it has been authorized all along.

The chief effect of ratification of a contract is that the principal becomes bound to it. The principal must comply with the terms of the contract, but also may enforce it against any other party to it. Ratification also modifies the relationship of the would-be principal and the would-be agent. Normally, if an agent executes an unauthorized contract on behalf of his or her principal, the act constitutes a breach of fiduciary duty and the agent will be answerable to the principal for the injuries caused. Not so upon the principal's manifestation of assent. Note, however, that ratification in itself does not relieve the agent of contract liability if in fact that agent was initially a party to the contract. Ratification also gives rise to a claim for compensation by the agent. *See* §4.02, comment b.

One other, perhaps more surprising result occurs between a purported principal and agent. The purported agent's previously unauthorized conduct followed by ratification can constitute mutual manifestation of assent to

Connections: Ratification vs. Adoption in the Corporate Context

In many circumstances, the technical inability of a principal (such as a corporation) that didn't exist at the time of a purported agent's act to ratify that act won't matter if the principal nonetheless adopts it. Sometimes, however, it does. For instance, in McArthur v. Times Printing, 51 N.W. 216 (1892), discussed in Chapter 13, the fact that the principal's liability couldn't predate its existence prevented the successful invocation of a defense based on the one-year provision of the Statute of Frauds.

Connections: When Is the Agent Liable for a Contract Entered on Behalf of a Principal?

As discussed in Chapter 4, there are circumstances in which an agent is party to a contract made on a principal's behalf even though the principal also is liable, by ratification or otherwise. This is the case when the principal is undisclosed or, unless the third party agrees to the contrary, partially disclosed or non-existent.

an agency relationship under Re(3) §1.01. In other words, even if there were no agency relationship prior to the ratification, ratification can create one, with the ongoing consequence of the agent's authority to bind the principal to further legal obligations and the agent's fiduciary responsibilities to the principal. *See* §4.01, comment b.

Finally, ratification can affect rights and liabilities as between the agent and third parties. The third party will sometimes have a breach of contract claim against an agent who executes an unauthorized contract, for the simple reason that third parties not uncommonly insist that an agent with whom they deal promise, as a part of the contract, that the agent is authorized to make the contract. Even where that promise by the agent is not explicitly bargained for, it is implied as the agent's warranty under Re(3) §6.10. If the contract is ratified, however, then there is no breach and the third party's claim is extinguished. *See* §4.02, comment e, and §6.10(1).

■ **Think about this:**

(B) Alice, acting without authority, purports to act on Principico, Inc.'s behalf when she enters into a written contract to hire Paul for one year. Principico's board subsequently ratifies the contract, congratulating Alice for using her independent judgment and moving so decisively. Within a month, Alice decides that Patricia would be a better employee than Paul. She discharges Paul and hires Patricia for one year. If Paul sues, who will be liable? If Patricia is discharged before the end of the year, who would you expect to be liable?

Timing. Ratification, again, is retroactive. *See* §4.05.

Limits. Finally, there are a few limits on the effectiveness of ratifications. Under §4.02(2), there are three circumstances in which the normal legal consequences of ratification do not follow. First, no ratification is effective in favor of a person who tricks the ratifier into the manifestation of assent. The trick might be some lie about facts material to the value or consequences of the transaction. Second, there can be cases in which a purported principal ratifies not out of belief that the underlying contract was a good deal, but because failure to do so will result in some loss. As the illustrations to §4.02, comment d suggest, this will typically be the case where the purported agent had control over the purported principal's money or other property and used it in a way that has made it hard to get back. In that case, the principal might take some action, like filing suit for breach of contract or taking part in an insolvency or bankruptcy proceeding against the third party, that could constitute ratification. Such actions will be effective as ratification against the third party, but not as to the agent. The principal will retain a claim against the agent for breach of fiduciary duty. Finally, ratification cannot be used to destroy rights of other persons acquired prior to ratification. Again, as the comments and illustrations suggest, this will commonly be the case where the would-be agent has sold the ratifier's property to an innocent third party who goes on to sell it to someone else.

BOTTICELLO V. STEFANOVICZ

Connecticut Supreme Court
411 A.2d 16 (1979)

Peters, J.

This case concerns the enforceability of an agreement for the sale of real property when that agreement has been executed by a person owning only an undivided half interest in the property. The plaintiff brought an action for specific performance against the defendants to compel conveyance of their land in accordance with the terms of a lease and option-to-purchase agreement signed by one of the defendants. . . . The defendants are now appealing from the consequent entry of a judgment ordering them to convey the real property in question to the plaintiff by warranty deed in consideration for the payment of $74,700.

The finding of the trial court discloses the following undisputed facts: The defendants, Mary and Walter Stefanovicz (hereinafter "Mary" and "Walter") in 1943 acquired as tenants in common a farm situated in the towns of Colchester and Lebanon. In the fall of 1965, the plaintiff, Anthony Botticello, became interested in the property. When he first visited the farm, Walter advised him that the asking price was $100,000. The following January, the plaintiff again visited the farm and made a counteroffer of $75,000. At that time, Mary stated that there was "no way" she could sell it for that amount. Ultimately the plaintiff and Walter agreed upon a price of $85,000 for a lease with an option to purchase; during these negotiations, Mary stated that she would not sell the property for less than that amount.

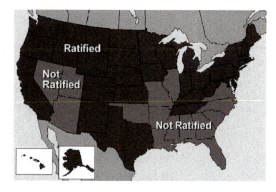

The informal agreement was finalized with the assistance of counsel for both Walter and the plaintiff. The agreement was drawn up by Walter's attorney after consultation with Walter and the plaintiff; it was then sent to, and modified by, the plaintiff's attorney. The agreement was signed by Walter and by the plaintiff. Neither the plaintiff nor his attorney, nor Walter's attorney, was then aware of the fact that Walter did not own the property outright. The plaintiff, although a successful busi-

A different kind of ratification: The (failed) Equal Rights Amendment, ratified by 30 states (as of 1979)

nessman with considerable experience in real estate never requested his attorney to do a title search of any kind, and consequently no title search was done. Walter never represented to the plaintiff or the plaintiff's attorney, or to his own attorney, that he was acting for his wife, as her agent. Mary's part ownership came to light in 1968, when a third party sought an easement over the land in question.

Shortly after the execution of the lease and option-to-purchase agreement, the plaintiff took possession of the property. He made substantial improvements on the property and, in 1971, properly exercised his option to purchase. When the defendants refused to honor the option agreement, the plaintiff commenced the present action against both Mary and Walter, seeking specific performance, possession of the premises, and damages. . . .

The plaintiff alleged, and the trial court agreed, that although Mary was not a party to the lease and option-to-purchase agreement, its terms were nonetheless binding upon her because Walter acted as her authorized agent in the negotiations, discussions, and execution of the written agreement. The defendants have attacked several findings of fact and conclusions of law, claiming that the underlying facts and applicable law do not support the court's conclusion of agency. We agree.

Agency is defined as "the fiduciary relationship which results from manifestation of consent by one person to another that the other shall act on his behalf and subject to his control, and consent by the other so to act. . . ." Restatement (Second), 1 Agency §1. Thus, the three elements required to show the existence of an agency relationship include: (1) a manifestation by the principal that the agent will act for him; (2) acceptance by the agent of the undertaking; and (3) an understanding between the parties that the principal will be in control of the undertaking. Restatement (Second), Agency §1, comment b (1958).[1]

The existence of an agency relationship is a question of fact. The burden of proving agency is on the plaintiff; and it must be proven by a fair preponderance of the evidence. Marital status cannot in and of itself prove the agency relationship. Nor does the fact that the defendants owned the land jointly make one the agent for the other.

The facts set forth in the court's finding are wholly insufficient to support the court's conclusion that Walter acted as Mary's authorized agent in the discussions concerning the sale of their farm and in the execution of the written agreement. The court's conclusion must be tested by the finding and not by the evidence. The finding indicates that when the farm was purchased, and when the couple transferred property to their sons, Walter handled many of the business aspects, including making payments for taxes, insurance, and mortgage. The finding also discloses that Mary and Walter discussed the sale of the farm, and that Mary remarked that she would not sell it for $75,000, and would not sell it for less than $85,000. A statement that one will not sell for *less than* a certain amount is by no means the equivalent of an agreement to sell for that amount. *See* Restatement (Second), Contracts §25, esp. illustration 4 (1973). Moreover, the fact that one spouse tends more to business matters than the other does not, absent other evidence of agreement or authorization, constitute the delegation of power as to an agent. What is most damaging to the plaintiff's case is the court's uncontradicted finding that, although Mary may have

---

1. Agency may be either actual or apparent. "Apparent authority is that semblance of authority which a principal, through his own acts or inadvertences, causes or allows third persons to believe his agent possesses." Lewis v. Michigan Millers Mutual Ins. Co., 228 A.2d 803 (Conn. 1967); see Restatement (Second), 1 Agency §8 (1958). Apparent authority thus must be determined by the acts of the principal rather than by the acts of the agent. Since the plaintiff has admitted that he did not know of Mary's interest in the land at the time the agreement was signed, her actions cannot form the basis for a finding of apparent authority, and the plaintiff has not pursued that theory.

acquiesced in Walter's handling of many business matters, Walter *never* signed any documents as agent for Mary prior to 1966. Mary had consistently signed any deed, mortgage, or mortgage note in connection with their jointly held property.

In light of the foregoing, it is clear that the facts found by the court fail to support its conclusion that Walter acted as Mary's authorized agent, and the conclusion therefore cannot stand.

The plaintiff argues, alternatively, that even if no agency relationship existed at the time the agreement was signed, Mary was bound by the contract executed by her husband because she ratified its terms by her subsequent conduct. The trial court accepted this alternative argument as well, concluding that Mary had ratified the agreement by receiving and accepting payments from the plaintiff, and by acquiescing in his substantial improvements to the farm. The underlying facts, however, do not support the conclusion of ratification.

Ratification is defined as "the affirmance by a person of a prior act which did not bind him but which was done or professedly done on his account." Restatement (Second), 1 Agency §82 (1958). Ratification requires "acceptance of the results of the act with an *intent* to ratify, and with *full knowledge of all the material circumstances*." (Emphasis added [by the court].) Ansonia v. Cooper, 30 A. 760 (1894).

The finding neither indicates an intent by Mary to ratify the agreement, nor establishes her knowledge of all the material circumstances surrounding the deal. At most, Mary observed the plaintiff occupying and improving the land, received rental payments from the plaintiff from time to time, knew that she had an interest in the property, and knew that the use, occupancy, and rentals were pursuant to a written agreement she had not signed. None of these facts is sufficient to support the conclusion that Mary ratified the agreement and thus bound herself to its terms. It is undisputed that Walter had the power to lease his own undivided one-half interest in the property and the facts found by the trial court could be referable to that fact alone. Moreover, the fact that the rental payments were used for "family" purposes indicates nothing more than one spouse providing for the other.

The plaintiff makes the further argument that Mary ratified the agreement simply by receiving its benefits and by failing to repudiate it. *See* Restatement (Second), 1 Agency §98 (1958). The plaintiff fails to recognize that before the receipt of benefits may constitute ratification, the other requisites for ratification must first be present. "Thus if the original transaction was not purported to be done on account of the principal, the fact that the principal receives its proceeds does not make him a party to it." Restatement (Second), 1 Agency §98, comment f (1958). Since Walter at no time purported to be acting on his wife's behalf, as is essential to effective subsequent ratification, Mary is not bound by the terms of the agreement, and specific performance cannot be ordered as to her. . . .

We turn now to the question of relief. In view of our holding that Mary never authorized her husband to act as her agent for any purpose connected with the lease and option-to-purchase agreement, recovery against her is precluded. As to Walter, the fact that his ownership was restricted to an undivided one-half interest in no way limited his capacity to contract. He contracted to convey full title and for breach of that contract he may be held liable. The facts of the case are sufficient to furnish a basis for relief to the plaintiff by specific performance or by damages. . . .

> ■ **Think about this:**
>
> *(C)* Exactly what would Mr. Botticello have needed to show to prove that Mary Stefanovicz ratified the contract Walter made?
>
> *(D)* Does the outcome in *Botticello* seem tough on the plaintiff? What would you tell a client interested in acquiring an option to purchase land to do to prevent that outcome?
>
> *(E)* What does the case tell you about the significance of marriage in determining agency? Is it in line with what reasonable people think— or should think?

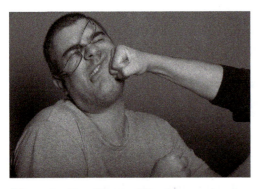

More to the Story: Ninety-Nine Problems, and Intentional Interference Is Possibly One

Although no one has sued, it has been alleged that Jay-Z's recruitment of sports figures for Roc Nations Sports sometimes constituted intentional interference with the prospective contractual advantages of the athletes' prior agents. This is an example of a situation in which the principal might very well have ratified the agent's tortious conduct.

2. Ratification of Torts

While it may seem odd, it is possible for a principal to ratify an agent's torts. It may seem odd because, by definition, an action that is ratified is one that would have no legally binding effect on the principal unless the principal ratifies, and ratification itself contains a knowledge requirement. So you might think that any principal who knows that an agent has taken tortious action not yet legally binding on the principal would simply avoid liability by carefully avoiding ratification.

Notice, though, that throughout Restatement Chapter 4 none of the rules of ratification is limited to ratification of contracts. Under §4.01, ratification is the affirmance of any prior "act," and a person ratifies that act by "manifesting assent that the act shall affect the [purported principal's] legal relations. . . ." Moreover, remember that a person can manifest such assent through a nebulous range of words and conduct, much of which may have nothing to do with the person's actual subjective desires. And so, for decades the courts have held that a person can ratify a tort as well as a contract.

Examples of ratification of torts also appear in the illustrations in Chapter 4. For example, in §4.01, comment d, illustration 1, the owner of a car lot ratifies his employee's defamatory public statements about a competitor by congratulating him on his statements.

■ **Think about this:**

(F) Joanne, Andrew's boss and good friend, has a busy and stressful job, managing a regional headquarters office of the Midwestern retail chain Sam's Drugs, Inc. Among other things, she handles purchasing of office supplies for the office, paying miscellaneous bills, and managing the office staff. (Andrew is a clerk-typist whose duties are purely clerical.) Andrew was just trying to be a good friend one day when, knowing that Joanne had had a tough stretch and knowing that she *loves* coffee, he arranged for coffee to be delivered for the office from a really great cafe around the corner. Apparently, there was a misunderstanding, as the coffee kind of kept showing up, day after day, but apparently it was all good. Joanne seemed only too pleased to take her coffee every morning for the first several days—delivered in paper cups with the cafe's logo on them—and one day even chatted with the delivery guy. Things took a turn, though, when a bill showed up for the first week's deliveries. Joanne went ballistic and canceled further deliveries. Whom can the coffee shop sue for the unpaid bill? Why?

(G) Ulysses is the proprietor of Ulysses' Used Cars. Saul is a salesman who works as an employee for Ulysses. He is only responsible for selling cars and has nothing to do with security. One day he sees a teenager "keying" an expletive into the side of an expensive used vehicle. Saul seizes a tire iron and clubs the teenager several times. When Ulysses learns of it, he says "You shouldn't have done that, but I'm really glad you did." Has Ulysses ratified the act? Suppose Saul is, instead, an independent contractor who indeed was responsible for security. Does either of the changed facts change the analysis?

B. Notice and Notification

Agents can receive "notice" of facts and events that, by way of legal fiction, constitute constructive "notice" to their principals. They also can give and receive formal legal "notifications" that satisfy legally imposed notification requirements, and these acts too can have binding legal consequences for their principals. These rules can play a very important role in business negotiations and especially in subsequent litigation. For example, if some term in some contract requires one party to provide another with notification of something in order to trigger countervailing contract obligations, then providing the notification to the party's employee or lawyer may trigger those obligations. Likewise, service of a document in litigation on a party's attorney can constitute automatic, legally binding notice to the party, and will trigger procedural time periods that begin as of the date of notice.

The relevant rules appear mainly in Chapter 5 of the Restatement.

1. "Notice" Is Something You Have; "Notification" Is Something You Get

The terms "notice" and "notification" are actually distinct terms under the Restatement, and both are explicitly defined in §5.01.

"Notice" is deemed knowledge of a fact under circumstances in which our law has decided that it is fair to treat a person as having such knowledge, whether the person does or not. Under §5.01, there are three circumstances in which this notice can be held to exist. Actual knowledge, obviously, is first. Second, a person can have "reason to know a fact." Section 5.01, comment b explains that a person has reason to know a fact if he or she could figure it out "on the basis of inferences reasonably to be drawn from [other] facts known to [the person.]" Finally, there are cases in which people "should" know a fact even if they don't, and as §5.01, comment b explains, such cases are actually different than "reason to know" cases. A person *should* know a fact when there is a duty to know it, and such a duty exists when failure to know the fact constitutes an actionable breach of a duty owed to someone else. So, for example, a financial advisor who manages the investments of private investors may have a fiduciary duty to them (assuming an agency relationship) to be aware of facts that are material to the value of the companies in which they have invested. If the advisor is ignorant of those facts, but a reasonable financial advisor would have discovered them, then the advisor is in breach. Under §5.01, the advisor therefore has notice of the fact. Note that it is conceivable that the advisor's notice of these facts might even be held against a *different* principal, represented on other matters, to whom the advisor does not owe a duty to know these facts.

"Notification," by contrast, is purely a ministerial or bureaucratic phenomenon. The giving of notification is merely a manifestation made in a form that is either specified by law or agreement, or that is "reasonable," which is intended to affect the rights between the notifier and the person notified. A good example is given in the comments following §5.01: It is an act of "notification" to file a lien against real property with the appropriate government office and in the manner specified by law, since it is intended to affect the status of the lien-filer's claims against the property vis-à-vis all the other persons who might have claims on it.

■   **Think about this:**

(H) Do you think that a notification should always be deemed to give notice of its content? Suppose it is couched in language that a layperson (that is, a non-lawyer) would not understand?

2. Imputation of Notice and Notification

In General. The primary significance in agency law of these concepts of notice and notification is that sometimes their effects can be imputed against a principal.

The imputation to a principal of facts known by an agent operates under a very general and straightforward rule. Under §5.03, *all* facts an agent knows, or has either reason or a duty to know, are imputed so long as they are material to the agent's duties for that principal, and so long as the agent is neither acting adversely to the principal nor subject to some duty to another person not to disclose those facts.[2]

 Dear Prof.: In this context, what does "material" mean?

The Restatement does not define the term, but we generally choose to be guided by the definition provided by the Supreme Court in the context of the federal securities laws: A fact is material if it is "substantially likely to be considered important by a reasonable [decision maker]." Basic, Inc. v. Levinson, 485 U.S. 224 (1988).

Notifications are imputed under similarly straightforward rules. Unless the third party is aware of the agent's adversity to the principal, notification made to an agent is effective against the principal so long as the agent had actual or apparent authority to receive it. *See* §5.02(1). Likewise, under §5.02(2), an agent with actual or apparent authority to *give* a notification can give it, and it will be legally effective as against the principal, even if the principal is unaware of it and even if it was given contrary to an explicit instruction by the principal not to give it (that is, so long as it was still made with apparent authority).

Agent's Adversity to Principal. An agent's notice of a fact is not imputed to the principal if the agent is adverse to the principal (except under the exceptions mentioned in §5.04(a)-(b)), and notifications given or received by the agent are ineffective as against the principal if the relevant third party knows or has reason to know of the adversity. The meaning of adversity is made clear in §5.04: Acting adversely means "intending to act solely for the agent's own purposes or those of another person."

■ **Think about this:**

(I) Ophelia is an office clerk for Principal, Inc. She knows she is not authorized to order supplies, but she thinks it is much more efficient for her to do that than to follow Principal's onerous requisition procedures. She therefore orders a supply of paper and writing instruments and proceeds to use them in her work for Principal. Since she knows what she is doing, is that knowledge imputed to Principal? Does that mean when no one tells her to stop that Principal has ratified her orders?

---

2. Note that if the agent's notice of a fact is not imputed to the principal because of a superior duty owed to some other person, that in itself may demonstrate a conflict of interest giving rise to fiduciary liability for the agent. Specifically, operating under a conflict of interest can violate the fiduciary duty of loyalty. This problem is discussed in Chapter 12.

3. The Duty to Notify

In some sense the legal flipside to the agency law rule of imputed notice is the fiduciary duty stated in Re(3) §8.11. The agent must use "reasonable efforts" to provide the principal with any facts of which an agent has notice (meaning, again, that the agent knows, or has reason or duty to know them) if *either* the agent knows or has reason to know the principal would want them, or they are material to the agent's duties for the principal. The only exceptions are where the principal has instructed the agent not to report those facts, *see* §8.11(1), and where disclosure of them would violate a superior duty to another.[3] Indeed, the fact of this duty to disclose is a basic justification for the imputation of notice—it makes sense to hold a principal responsible for the agent's notice, because the agent's failure to disclose material facts the agent knows or should know gives the principal a cause of action for breach of the duty in §8.11.

4. The Effect of Ratification on Notice and Notification

Finally, recall that when a principal *ratifies* previously unauthorized conduct, the result is that in every respect that conduct will be treated as if it was made with actual authority, and the act of ratification may effectively create an agency relationship where none existed before. Recall, moreover, that an effective ratification ratifies the "whole" act. This turns out to have an effect on notice, notification, and their imputation to the principal. A principal is charged with notice of a fact if his or her agent had notice of it and it was material to the agent's duties, and notifications are effective if the agent had actual or apparent authority to give or receive them. If the principal ratifies some conduct that happened to include the giving or receipt of a notification, the principal almost assuredly takes on imputation of the notification, because the ratification will retroactively authorize it. Likewise, ratification of an act will by definition render that act within the agent's "duties for the principal." Therefore, any facts of which the agent had notice at the time and which are material to the act that was ratified will be retroactively imputed to the principal.

> ■   **Think about this:**
>
> *(J)*   Years ago, just before the financial crisis of 2007-2008 and during the housing boom that preceded it, Paul was one of those many hapless, small-time investors who bought into residential real estate development as an investment opportunity. Though he actually lives and works in Southern California, he invested in two homes being built in a new development near prime ski territory in Idaho. The crash came, he lost much of his investment, and he hoped to get out as well as he could. So he listed the homes for sale with a realtor

---

3. But, note again that the presence of such superior duty might in itself constitute a conflict in violation of fiduciary duty.

named Anna. Anna—a local, and a professional in the market—was well aware of a special, wood-boring insect native to that part of the Northwest, and knew it had been a problem in the development in question, though wasn't aware if it had been discovered in either of Paul's properties. Idaho common law requires realty sellers to disclose such conditions if they are known to them. Anna executes a sale of one of Paul's houses to Tracy, another out-of-state investor (from Florida), but tells her nothing about the bugs. Sure enough, bugs turn up in the house after the deal is done, substantially reducing its value. In a claim by Tracy, is Paul liable? Why or why not?

C. Non-Fiduciary Rights and Remedies Between Principal and Agent

A principal and an agent, though in a relationship described as "fiduciary" and one commonly characterized by a special trust and confidence, will often find themselves at odds. It turns out that litigation between the parties is common, and indeed the set of legal obligations that largely make up their relationship would have little meaning if it were not for civil litigation among some principals and agents. Those obligations are enforced exclusively through private, civil liability.

Significant legal obligations within the relationship run mostly from the agent to the principal, and they can mostly be characterized as "fiduciary"—that is, they are mostly common law rights arising from substantive agency law itself, and they arise because of the agent's special role as the principal's champion and confidant. Now, this is not to imply that there is some bright and well-recognized line between fiduciary and non-fiduciary duties. There is not. For what it is worth, *Black's* defines "fiduciary duty" as

> [a] duty to act for someone else's benefit, while subordinating one's personal interests to that of the other person. It is the highest standard of duty implied by law. . . .

BLACK'S LAW DICTIONARY 625 (6th ed. 1990). So we can think of some duties within our legal system as imposing a special onus on the fiduciary in addition to those rules we must all follow in our dealings with other people. Thus, on the one hand, an agent is not allowed to take an attitude toward the principal like that implied in the phrase *caveat emptor*. It is not for the fiduciary to say that his beneficiary is a competent adult able to fend for him- or herself, and therefore that arrangements between them should be above legal challenge even if they happen to benefit the fiduciary at his beneficiary's expense. (By contrast, non-fiduciary parties to ordinary contracts are usually free to take that attitude, and the law mostly takes it for granted that they will.) Likewise, the fiduciary is not allowed to let the beneficiary float adrift in the sea of risk that is commercial affairs, because fiduciaries must take care for the interests of their beneficiaries in a way that we need not as to mere third parties. As we see elsewhere in this book, the two ideas expressed here—that a fiduciary cannot take self-serving advantage of the beneficiary and that a fiduciary must protect the beneficiary from many risks—are respectively captured in the two fundamental fiduciary duties, the duties of "loyalty" and "care."

1. Principal vs. Agent

Again, the rights of principals against their agents can almost all be characterized as "fiduciary" rights. We will learn about these duties in much more detail once we begin our general discussion of fiduciary duties in Chapter 12.

The only real exception is that the parties may have between them some contract governing their relationship, and it may bind the agent to performance in addition to the common law fiduciary obligations set out in the Restatement. Though it might seem to go without saying, the Restatement duly provides that "[a]n agent has a duty to act in accordance with the express and implied terms of any contract between the agent and the principal." Re(3) §8.07. Nothing in the official comments or Reporter's notes to §8.07 suggests that the duty stated in that section is somehow different than or in addition to the obligation of the contract itself.

2. Agent vs. Principal

It is often said that an agent is the principal's fiduciary, but not vice versa—the principal is not the agent's fiduciary. While this is surely true in a strict sense, it may be a little misleading, because principals do owe some duties to their agents that are in addition to any contract between them, and that will exist even if they have no contract at all. The principal's duties all appear in the last three provisions in Restatement Chapter 8, §§8.13-8.15.

Compensation. Most dear to the hearts of many agents will be that even in the absence of an explicit promise of compensation, the principal normally must pay some reasonable price for services rendered. Remember, first of all, that agency relationships can be created in which the agent is entitled to no compensation—the so-called gratuitous agency mentioned in Re(3) §1.04(3). However, under §8.13, comment d, a principal is presumptively obliged to pay the agent for services, and must do so unless (1) some agreement between the parties explicitly denies the duty, or (2) the parties' relationship or the trivial nature of the duties is such that a court infers an agreement denying compensation. Where the principal owes the duty but no explicit agreement between the parties sets the amount of compensation, the agent will be entitled to a fair market compensation for the value of the services rendered. *See id.* Finally, the rule is subject to a minor curlicue: Where an agent is empowered to appoint a sub-agent, the sub-agent has an implied contractual right to compensation from the appointing agent, but not from the principal. *See* §8.14, comment b.

Indemnification. A related rule is that a principal normally must indemnify the agent for losses incurred in the course of the agent's duties for the principal. For the most part, the rule seems extremely commonsensical. Roughly speaking, the principal must hold the agent harmless as against any expenses that are reasonable in light of the agent's duties. The only exceptions are where (1) the agent makes some deliberate payment that is without actual authority and is either of no benefit to the principal or was made "officiously," or (2) the agent suffers some inadvertent loss in the course of his duties but the loss is not "fairly" attributable to the principal. The agent might have additional indemnification rights by contract, *see* §8.14(1) and the comments following, and the parties can also agree by contract to limit the agent's indemnification rights, *see* §8.14(2).

Note that a theme running through §8.14 and its comments is that, barring agreement, an agent normally will not have a right to recover the agent's own ordinary costs of doing business, including the salaries of the agent's own employees. Presumably, this rule reflects the fact that principal and agent will normally agree on some compensation for the agent, from which the agent will be expected to fund his own costs.

Good Faith. The principal owes one final substantive duty toward the agent that perhaps is more like a fiduciary duty: the duty to "deal fairly and in good faith." Strictly speaking, this is the same duty of good faith implied in all contracts. However, Re(3) §8.13, comment b and §8.15 make clear that the principal's duty of good faith can be an *implied* contractual commitment even in the absence of other contract between the parties, and it can lead to some results that might seem a little surprising.

A problem to be admitted by anyone being honest is that the phrase "good faith" is so broad and amorphous as to mean not really much at all. The definition in *Black's* is almost amusing:

> **Good faith.** Good faith is an intangible and abstract quality with no technical meaning or statutory definition, and it encompasses, among other things, an honest belief, the absence of malice and the absence of design to defraud or to seek an unconscionable advantage. . . . An honest intention to abstain from taking any unconscientious advantage of another, even through technicalities of law.

Connections: Good Faith as a Matter of Corporate Law

"Good faith" has had an interesting history in the law of corporations. At least in Delaware, it now is regarded as a necessary element of the duty of loyalty owed by a corporation's officers and directors. This is discussed in Chapter 20.

BLACK'S LAW DICTIONARY 693 (6th ed. 1990). In application, it is only fair to say that the use of this term by courts and commentators is often *very* loose and nebulous.

Fortunately though, at least within the context of agency law, the emperor is not entirely without clothes, as §§8.13 and 8.15 provide explicit guidance. First, under §8.13, comment b, a principal must not unreasonably interfere with the agent's completion of work. At a minimum, the principal must *provide* work if the terms of the relationship fairly imply such an understanding. But presumably it also prohibits the principal from interfering in other ways. The principal might be tempted to do this, for example, if for some reason the principal comes to regret having hired the particular agent. Next, §8.15 says that the duty to deal "fairly and in good faith *includes*"—but is not *limited to*—a duty to warn an agent of risks either of physical harm or pecuniary loss, wherever the principal knows or reasonably should know that the risks are present in the agent's work and are unknown to the agent. Finally, under §8.15, comment d, the principal must refrain from conduct likely to injure the agent's business reputation and the agent's "self-respect." Seriously scandalous conduct or acts of notorious moral turpitude by the principal might violate this duty, as would deliberate actions by the principal to disparage or compete with the agent.

Note that the Restatement does away with a rule that had been adopted in some states, under which the duty of good faith could prevent unilateral termination of the agent under some circumstances. Section 8.15, comment b flatly states that the power to terminate in §3.10(1) is unaffected by the duty. If the termination could cause some foreseeable loss to the agent despite the agent's blamelessness, the agent will have a claim but is terminated nonetheless. This possibility is explored in illustration 1 to §8.15.

More to the Story: Power vs. Right

We all know that "might doesn't make right." The law of agency—and the law of partnership—do confer certain powers that, if exercised, are effective but nonetheless can give rise to legal liability.

■ Think about this:

(K) Penelope's Pops, Inc., is a corporation formed by Penelope to market her signature, homemade cake pops. After initial successes, she sold some shares to local investors and arranged to have an expanded board of directors with new members elected by the shareholders at large. She nevertheless tended to stick to her old ways, running the business informally as she had before. Among other things, she recently purchased a new machine for the cake pop factory, and having no corporate checks on hand, she paid for it with her own personal funds. When she seeks reimbursement, the board of directors formally disapproves it. Is the board's action legally permissible? Why or why not?

D. Termination of the Agency Relationship

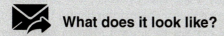 **What does it look like?**

Check the online Supplement for the following item relevant to this chapter:

■ A form of durable power of attorney

One might expect that since the *creation* of the agency relationship is such a momentous event in the law of agency, and since the Restatement devotes so much doctrinal technology to it, there would be similar fanfare surrounding the termination of the relation. On the face of the Restatement, as it happens, there is not. In fact, no provision of the Restatement explicitly mentions termination of the relationship. Instead, the Restatement sets out several rules to govern the termination of *authority. See* §§3.06-3.11, discussed elsewhere in this book. But some or all of an agent's authority could be terminated even if the agency relationship continues, so the two things—termination of agency and termination of authority—are not identical.

Instead, the nature and consequences of termination have to be teased out of several miscellaneous Restatement provisions and comments. First, it is clear both from the case law and from commentary in the Restatement that because agency must be a mutually consensual relationship, either party may terminate it at any time, even if doing so breaches some contractual obligation. Likewise, some events that automatically terminate authority also terminate agency. The death of either party automatically terminates the relationship. Likewise, at common law the incapacity of either party terminated it, though legislation in many states has modified this rule to permit so-called durable powers of attorney. Under such an instrument, a person can appoint an agent to make health care or other decisions for the principal in case the principal becomes incapacitated.

As for the legal consequences of termination, probably of chief importance is its effect on fiduciary duties. Following termination, the former agent is no longer the former principal's fiduciary, and for the most part may deal with the former principal at arm's length. *See* §8.01, comment c ("following termination . . . [the] erstwhile agent is not subject to an agent's fiduciary duties in dealings with the principal"). However, a handful of fiduciary consequences will linger. If the agent is entrusted with the principal's property for use in the execution of his assigned duties, and for whatever reason retains it for some

Connections

The fiduciary duties of an agent, which as explained here will be most often ended by termination, are examined at length in Chapter 12.

period after termination, the agent must return it and also must strictly refrain from use of the property for his own benefit. *See* §8.01, comment c; §8.04, comment b; §8.05, comment b. Likewise, if the agent comes into possession of confidential information of the principal and the agent knows the principal desires to keep it secret, even after termination the agent may not disclose it or use it for his own benefit. *See* §8.05 & comment c. Finally, a former agent may be required to continue to provide the principal with material information if the agent can reasonably foresee that the principal will expect that service to continue, unless the agent informs the principal that it will not. *See* §8.11, comment c. Other rights as between the parties normally end upon termination, including the agent's right to compensation and indemnification. The final major consequence is one we've already discussed, which is that termination ends an agent's actual authority as soon as the agent has notice of it. *See* Re(3) §§3.07-3.10, which are discussed elsewhere in this book.

The following case deals with an issue that not infrequently arises.

TOWN & COUNTRY HOUSE & HOME SERVICE, INC. V. NEWBERY

New York Court of Appeals
147 N.E.2d 724 (1958)

VAN VOORHIS, J.

This action was brought for an injunction and damages against appellants on the theory of unfair competition. The complaint asks to restrain them from engaging in the same business as plaintiff, from soliciting its customers, and for an accounting and damages. The individual appellants were in plaintiff's employ for about three years before they severed their relationships and organized the corporate appellant through which they have been operating. The theory of the complaint is that plaintiff's enterprise "was unique, personal and confidential," and that appellants cannot engage in business at all without breach of the confidential relationship in which they learned its trade secrets, including the names and individual needs and tastes of its customers.

The nature of the enterprise is house and home cleaning by contract with individual householders. Its "unique" quality consists in superseding the drudgery of ordinary house cleaning by mass production methods. The house cleaning is performed by a crew of men who descend upon a home at stated intervals of time, and do the work in a hurry after the manner of an assembly line in a factory. They have been instructed by the housewife but work without her supervision. The householder is supplied with liability insurance, the secrets of the home are kept inviolate, the tastes of the customer are served and each team of workmen is selected as suited to the home to which it is sent. The complaint says that the customer relationship is "impregnated" with a "personal and confidential aspect."

The complaint was dismissed at Special Term on the ground that the individual appellants were not subjected to negative covenants under any contract with plaintiff, and that the methods and techniques used by plaintiff in conducting its business are not confidential or secret as in the case of a scientific formula; that house cleaning and housekeeping "are old and necessary chores which accompany orderly living" and that no violation of duty was involved in soliciting plaintiff's customers by appellants after resigning from plaintiff's employ. The contacts and acquaintances with customers were held not to have been the result of a confidential relationship between plaintiff and defendants or the result of the disclosure of secret or confidential material.

By a divided vote the Appellate Division reversed, but on a somewhat different ground, namely, that while in plaintiff's employ, appellants conspired to terminate their employment, form a business of their own in competition with plaintiff and solicit plaintiff's customers for their business. The overt acts under this conspiracy were found by the Appellate Division to have been that, in pursuance of this plan, they formed the corporate appellant and bought equipment and supplies for their operations—not on plaintiff's time—but during off hours, before they had severed their relations as employees of plaintiff. The Appellate Division concluded that "it is our opinion that their agreement and encouragement to each other to carry out the course of conduct thus planned by them, and their consummation of the plan, particularly their termination of employment virtually en masse, were inimical to, and violative of, the obligations owed by them to appellant as its employees; and that therefore appellant was entitled to relief. . . ."

Although the Appellate Division implied more relief than we consider to have been warranted, we think that the trial court erred in dismissing the complaint altogether. The only trade secret which could be involved in this business is plaintiff's list of customers. Concerning that, even where a solicitor of business does not operate fraudulently under the banner of his former employer, he still may not solicit the latter's customers who are not openly engaged in business in advertised locations or whose availability as patrons cannot readily be ascertained but "whose trade and patronage have been secured by years of business effort and advertising, and the expenditure of time and money, constituting a part of the good-will of a business which enterprise and foresight have built up." (Witkop Holmes Co. v. Boyce, 61 Misc. 126, 131, *aff'd*. 131 App. Div. 922[.]. . .)

The testimony in the instant record shows that the customers of plaintiff were not and could not be obtained merely by looking up their names in the telephone or city directory or by going to any advertised locations, but had to be screened from among many other housewives who did not wish services such as respondent and appellants were equipped to render, but preferred to do their own housework. In most instances housewives do their own house cleaning. The only appeal which plaintiff could have was to those whose cleaning had been done by servants regularly or occasionally employed, except in the still rarer instances where the housewife was on the verge of abandoning doing her own work by hiring some outside agency. In the beginning, prospective customers of plaintiff were discovered by Dorothy Rossmoore, wife of plaintiff's president, by telephoning at random in "sections of Nassau that we thought would be interested in this type of cleaning, and from that we got directories, town directories, and we marked the streets that we had passed down, and I personally called, right down the list." In other words, after selecting a neighborhood which they felt was fertile for their kind of business, they would telephone to all of the residents of a street in the hope of discovering likely prospects. On the first day Mrs. Rossmoore called 52 homes. If she enlisted their interest, an appointment would be made for a personal call in order to sell them the service. At the end of the first year, only 40 to 50 customers had thus been secured. Two hundred to three hundred telephone calls netted 8 to 12 customers. Moreover, during the first year it was not possible to know how much to charge these customers with accuracy, inasmuch as the cleaning requirements of each differed from the others, so that special prices had to be set. In the beginning the customer usually suggested the price which was paid until some kind of cost accounting could demonstrate whether it should be raised or lowered. These costs were entered on cards for every customer, and this represented an accumulated body of experience of considerable value. After three years of operation, and by August, 1952, when the individual appellants resigned their employment by plaintiff, the number of customers amounted to about 240. By that time plaintiff had 7 or 8 crews doing this cleaning work, consisting of 3 men each.

Although appellants did not solicit plaintiff's customers until they were out of plaintiff's employ, nevertheless plaintiff's customers were the only ones they did solicit. Appellants solicited 20 or 25 of plaintiff's customers who refused to do business with appellants and about 13 more of plaintiff's customers who transferred their patronage to appellants. These were all the people that appellants' firm solicited. It would be different if these customers had been equally available to appellants and respondent, but, as has been related, these customers had been screened by respondent at considerable effort and expense, without which their receptivity and willingness to do business with this kind of a service organization could not be known. So there appears to be no question that plaintiff is entitled to enjoin defendants from further solicitation of its customers, or that some profits or damage should be paid to plaintiff by reason of these customers whom they enticed away.

. . . Inasmuch as the complaint asks that appellants be enjoined, severally and jointly, from engaging directly or indirectly in the business of house and home cleaning in any manner, shape or form adopted by the plaintiff, it is necessary for us to point out that plaintiff is not entitled to that much relief. The business of plaintiff has not been found to be unique either by Special Term or the Appellate Division and the evidence demonstrates that it is not so. No trade secrets are involved, as has been stated, except the customers list. . . .

It would have been courteous of appellants to have given Rossmoore advance notice that they were going to leave plaintiff's employ and engage in a competing business, but their employment was at will, which legally required no notice to be given, and rendered the employments terminable at any time at the option of either party. Plaintiff is entitled to enjoin appellants from soliciting its former customers, and to recover such damages or loss of profits as may be established to have resulted from those that have been solicited to date. Further than that the complaint is dismissed. . . .

■ **Think about this:**

(L) Zelda plans to leave her employment with Start-m-up in order to set up her own, competing company. Start-m-up has three highly trained employees (among several others) whom Zelda believes would be invaluable in her new enterprise. Before Zelda leaves Start-m-up, would it be permissible for Zelda to solicit the other employees to come work for her as soon as she exits? How about after she leaves?

 Time Out for PR

There are obvious parallels between the *Town & Country* case and the situation of a lawyer wishing to leave his or her law firm—and to take along with a few choice clients. There is, however, a twist. American Bar Association Model Rule of Professional Conduct 5.6 (Restrictions on Right to Practice) says:

> A lawyer shall not participate in offering or making:
>   (a) a partnership, shareholders, operating, employment, or other similar type of agreement that restricts the right of a lawyer to practice after termination of the relationship, except an agreement concerning benefits upon retirement; or
>   (b) an agreement in which a restriction on the lawyer's right to practice is part of the settlement of a client controversy.

Test Yourself

Assume Applicability of the Restatement (Third) of Agency

Questions 1-3 relate to the following facts:

After running a small business from her home for a few years, quite successfully, Priya took on a college student to help out, as a part-time employee. She taught the student, Alice, how to wrap the firm's products and ship them to the firm's mail-order customers, plus several other more or less clerical tasks, which Alice did entirely from the make-shift office Priya had set up in her basement. Turns out Alice found sitting down there by herself pretty boring, and so she took it on herself to make some improvements in the business—and after her initial shock, Priya found both of them actually quite desirable. Alice's biggest step was signing a lease on Priya's behalf for warehouse space in which to move the business, with rent payable monthly. A fact that Priya had shared with no one was that she'd actually been planning to take just this step, and after her initial surprise and anger at Alice wore off, she realized that Alice had actually found an ideal location at a good price. Thing is, though, the first Priya heard of it was a month after Alice did the deal, when the bill for the first month's rent showed up. Anyway, after chewing out Alice, she calmed down and said, "Ugh. Okay, it's time to bite the bullet and take this risk."

Alice's other big step was to secure a used photocopy machine for the office, which she knew to be a steal at the offering price of $2,000. Turns out, before Alice could tell Priya what she'd done, the seller called Alice and said there'd been a mistake. He would not sell the machine for less than $3,000.

1. Priya must pay the first month's rent. True or False?

   a. True, because Alice had actual authority.
   b. True, because of what she said to Alice.
   c. False, because Priya's business is a sole proprietorship.
   d. False, because of the time period in which the debt was incurred.

2. A week after moving in to the new warehouse space, Priya discovers to her horror that the building is actually full of asbestos. She can get out of the contract. True or False?

   a. True, because of the importance of this fact.
   b. True, but only if the lessor knew about the asbestos.
   c. False, because she has occupied the space.
   d. False, because she already has received the first bill without complaint.

3. Priya can buy the photocopier for $2,000. True or False?

   a. True, because of the timing of the seller's subsequent call to Alice.
   b. True, unless Alice told the seller she was acting on her own behalf.
   c. False, because of the timing of the seller's subsequent call to Alice.
   d. False, because this contract would never have been binding under any terms.

Questions 4-6 relate to the following facts:

PixCo, Inc., is a big chemicals firm based in Birmingham, Alabama. A pipe is currently leaking a dangerous substance just outside a PixCo plant building, near a stream. Under federal law, a plant owner who knows of such a condition and fails to report it is guilty of an environmental law violation. In each of the following cases, decide whether PixCo's failure to report is illegal.

4. Arno, a regulatory compliance worker at PixCo who is supposed to identify environmental risks and report them to his boss Sam, notices the leak on a routine plant inspection tour.

a. Yes, because the information is material to Arno's duties.

b. Yes, because the information is material to Arno's duties and within his scope of employment.

c. No, because Sam is not Arno's principal.

d. No, for some other reason.

5. It is Arno again that makes the discovery, but not on an official inspection tour. Instead, he notices the leak while he is on a hike for pleasure with several friends, as PixCo has adopted a new policy permitting employees and their guests to use the company's expansive, wooded grounds for recreation.

a. Yes, because the information is material to Arno's duties.

b. Yes, because all information known to employees is imputed to their employer.

c. No, because, while the information is material to Arno's duties, it is not within his scope of employment.

d. No, for some other reason.

6. This time, assume the discovery is made by Abigail, a clerk in PixCo's accounts payable department.

a. Yes, because all agents are fiduciaries.

b. Yes, because all employees are fiduciaries.

c. No, because the information is not relevant to Abigail's duties.

d. No, for some other reason.

Questions 7-8 rely on the following facts:

Paul was aghast when he learned that his friend Arnie had made a deal for him to buy an old car from Tia. (Paul and Arnie were good, long-time friends, but had never had anything like a business relationship with one another. Paul had never met Tia.) "What?!?" exclaimed Paul, when Arnie told him. "Good lord, what were you thinking?," to which Arnie replied "Dude, I got it for a hundred and forty bucks." "Oh," said Paul, falling silent. Paul later told his brother Bob (who by coincidence knew Tia socially) that he actually thought Arnie had found a rare, great opportunity. Nevertheless, Paul decided against the deal and called Tia to tell her so. That upset Tia mightily, and all the more so the next day when Bob called to ask her if the deal had gone through, repeating what Paul had told him. Tia sued Paul on the contract.

Meanwhile, Paul and Arnie's friendship had been pretty much wrecked, and they wound up each filing third-party claims against each other in the same lawsuit, Paul alleging breach of fiduciary duty and Arnie claiming a right to a "finder's fee" commission of $50 for his work in finding the car.

7. There could be no ratification in this case because:

a. Tia heard from Bob only after Paul called her.

b. Paul said what he said only to Bob, and not to Tia.

c. Paul said what he said only to Bob, and not to Arnie.

d. There could be an effective ratification in this case.

8. Which of the following claims will succeed?

    a. Paul's claim against Arnie.

    b. Arnie's claim against Paul, if $50 would be reasonable under the circumstances.

    c. Tia's claim against Paul, if her understanding of events was reasonable.

    d. Answers a and b are both correct.

    e. Answers b and c are both correct.

Part 3

The General Partnership, Other Unincorporated Entities, and the Special Problems of "Small" Business

6

Introduction to the General Partnership

The general partnership is of tremendous historic and continuing importance. Many of the newer unincorporated business forms draw on partnership law and the general partnership continues to be the default form for business entities involving more than a single owner. It is entirely possible to form a general partnership without intending it.

Chapter Outline

A. Introduction: The History and Nature of the General Partnership and the Reasons for Studying It

- General partnerships still are consciously selected by some entrepreneurs
- The general partnership is the default form when no other form is elected or, in many instances, when another form fails

B. Formation

1. In General
   - A general partnership is "an association of two or more persons to carry on as co-owners a business for profit"
   - Unless satisfying the requirements for some other form, a relationship meeting the definition of a general partnership creates a general partnership whether the parties subjectively intend it or not—that is, formation of a general partnership can be inadvertent
   - Formation of a general partnership requires no writing or other formality

2. The Default Nature of Substantive Partnership Law
   - Partnership rights largely are waivable or subject to modification by agreement

3. Some Examples in Application
    ■ Some things that are claimed to be general partnerships are not
    ■ Some things that are said not to be general partnerships are

C. Purported Partners (Formerly Known as "Partners by Estoppel")

■ Doctrine requires a "holding out"
■ Doctrine also requires reliance in entering a transaction

Test Yourself

A. Introduction: The History and Nature of the General Partnership and the Reasons for Studying It

As with agency, the partnership form of business has existed in some form or other since very ancient times. The modern general partnership is often said to have its origin in the *societas*, a form recognized in classical Roman law, which was also revived several centuries later in the so-called law merchant of the European Middle Ages. Ancient traces of similar forms can be found elsewhere, as in Islamic law.[1] The fact that this simple form of business has been so widely present, for so long and in different cultures, suggests that there is something basic in doing business that makes it valuable for co-venturers to be responsible to one another and jointly responsible to third parties with whom they deal.

Now, in the case of agency law, the reason for studying the subject was straightforward. Doctrinal agency issues remain important to daily business life. The reasons for studying the general partnership as it now exists are a bit more complex. On the one hand, this ancient form was once of signal importance in Western economies. Prior to the nineteenth century, in fact, it was virtually the only means by which entrepreneurs could venture together or jointly put their capital to work, other than through simple debtor-creditor relationships. And lenders, unlike the owners of a business, could likely earn as their return only some fixed amount of interest (as opposed to a share in the profits), and even that might be subject to limits under the law of usury. But on the other hand, a major alternative to the partnership form of business has arisen in the past few decades, and there is reason to believe that over time it may, for well-planned enterprises, tend to eclipse the general partnership. That form is the limited liability company (LLC). The LLC was introduced by state legislatures starting in the late 1970s and has quickly become very popular. The LLC initially enjoyed one special advantage over both the general partnership and the other forms of business entities that had been available up until that time: It is subject to the generally more desirable "pass-through" tax treatment that had been available only to partnerships,

---

1. *See, e.g.,* Timur Kuran, *The Absence of the Corporation in Islamic Law: Origins and Persistence,* 53 Am. J. Comp. L. 785, 785-789 (2005).

but also enjoys limited liability without any constraints on managerial participation, which up until then had been available only to corporate shareholders.

Moreover, the few other reasons that some businesses might have preferred (or been forced) to organize as general partnerships have also mostly dwindled. It was once the case that professionals—particularly doctors and lawyers—were required by their governing ethical rules to practice without limited liability. The rationale was that the risk of tort liability for professional malpractice was an important regulatory tool, and that if partners could shield themselves from their fellow partners' wrongdoing, they would fail diligently to oversee one another. That line of thinking began to meet its end during the 1980s, when large professional partnerships faced the risk of catastrophic malpractice liabilities arising from the fabled savings and loan crisis. At that time, very large law and accounting firms were really still fairly new phenomena, and the savings and loan crisis for the first time made clear the possibility that firms with hundreds of partners spread throughout the country or the world might not only be entirely wiped out over the malpractice of just one or a few partners, but that each of those hundreds of partners might be *personally* liable to satisfy all the unpaid claims. So it was during that period—before the rise of the LLC—that the state governments began to experiment with a new form that they called the "limited liability partnership" (LLP). The LLP in its early incarnations would give partners limited liability for partnership tort liabilities not stemming from their own conduct. Accordingly, since the whole purpose of the LLP was to help those professional firms now facing outsized malpractice risks, the states loosened their ethics stance and began allowing professionals to practice in limited liability forms. Nowadays, in many states, professional firms are permitted to take any form they like. In some places, they can even be traditional corporations.

Still, there is reason to believe that reports of the general partnership's death have been rather exaggerated. As shown by records of tax filings with the Internal Revenue Service, there are still quite a lot of general partnerships in the United States, and they still represent a significant proportion of all unincorporated associations that file tax returns.[2] But even as the general partnership form of

> ### Connections: Federal Tax
>
> It now is the case that any unincorporated entity can elect whether to have its income taxed to itself or to its owners. The first method is called "two-tier" or "double" taxation, because the income is taxed again if and when it is distributed to the owners. The second method is called "pass-through" or "conduit" taxation and results in only a single level of taxation. The notion that unincorporated entities can choose either form is conveyed by generally calling the taxation of those entities "check the box." This is discussed at greater length in Chapter 2 and in the online Supplement.

> ### More to the Story: What's in a Name?
>
> The fact of the matter is that, while they are governed by different statutes and usually have some differences, in most states, an LLP and an LLC now can be functionally identical.

---

2. *See* INTERNAL REVENUE SERVICE, STATISTICS OF INCOME—INTEGRATED BUSINESS DATA tbl. 1 (2013), *available at* https://www.irs.gov/statistics/soi-tax-stats-integrated-business-data (showing numbers of business entity returns by entity type for tax years 1980-2013, showing gradual decline in general partnership filings and gradual increase in LLC filings, but still showing about a half-million general partnership filings in 2013, representing about 16 percent of unincorporated entities).

business may be gradually dwindling, and indeed even if it were in danger of dying out as a form of deliberate choice for business planners (which does not currently appear to be the case), study of it would remain critical for two reasons. First, as we shall see, the general partnership is a default form. That is, a partnership is what results when would-be business associates take no steps with respect to their form of entity, and just start doing business. While the creation of a partnership of course can be planned, and many partnerships are meticulously and elaborately designed to meet particular goals, partnership is also what happens by accident. It therefore will always be important to understand partnership law, because it will govern all those businesses that lack formal governing agreements and in which no bureaucratic steps have been taken with respect to the form of entity. Second, the substantive law of partnerships remains important to understand because the more recent statutory forms of business entity tend to be based in large part on partnership concepts. Indeed, the LLP is literally just a general partnership that has made the limited liability election, and some other entity statutes (e.g., some versions of the Uniform Limited Partnership Act, discussed elsewhere in this book) incorporate some general partnership law by reference.

B. Formation

 What does it look like?

Check the online Supplement for the following item relevant to this section:

- A simple partnership agreement

1. In General

Hi There

As will be detailed in other chapters, the creation of a general partnership is quite similar to the creation of an agency relationship—so similar, in fact, that it is sometimes unclear whether the parties have created one relationship or the other. Whether or not a partnership has been formed in a given case is a question of fact that depends on the outward manifestations of intent of the parties. Ultimately, in cases of dispute, whether a partnership has been formed is a question that is judged objectively by a trier of fact. The question posed to the trier of fact is implied by Revised Uniform Partnership Act[3] (RUPA) §202(a), which contains the statutory test for partnership formation:

---

3. The Revised Uniform Partnership Act is still referred to as the "Revised Uniform Partnership Act (1997)" although it was most recently amended in 2013. It sometimes also is referred to as the "Uniform Partnership Act (1997)." There are other, earlier versions also referred to by year of proposal.

[T]he association of two or more persons to carry on as co-owners a business for profit forms a partnership, whether or not the persons intend to form a partnership.

More to the Story: The Aggregate vs. Entity Debate

Debate once raged over the seemingly obscure metaphysical question of whether, in its true nature, a partnership should be thought of as an "entity" or an "aggregate." If it was an entity in its own right, then it would exist separately from its owners. If it was merely an aggregate of them—nothing more than the sum of its parts—then it was just a fictional shorthand. Though the aggregate conception is ancient in origin, the entity view quickly gained popularity after its nineteenth-century introduction, as it could solve certain thorny doctrinal problems. It was very explicitly adopted in the first version of RUPA proposed in 1997, as well as in recent statutes governing other unincorporated entities, like Uniform Limited Liability Company Act §201. Having been resolved so clearly, and long ago, the issue is no longer much talked about.

But it turns out that it still casts some lingering shadows. Because opinion was still mixed when the original Uniform Partnership Act (UPA) was drafted in 1914, its drafters retained the aggregate concept in several respects. Notably, the death or retirement of any partner had the rather shocking consequence of "dissolving" the firm. This was so because the partnership itself was thought not to exist independently of its members, so any change in its membership required that legal recognition of the firm would cease to exist. A number of issues resulted, including complications in the enforcement of leases and other contracts the partnership might have entered. Likewise, it caused serious complexities in the definition of partners' property rights and the rights and liabilities of partners who chose to continue a firm's business after a dissolution event.

Again, the adoption of the entity concept in RUPA has been thought by most to resolve much of this anachronistic complexity, since the entity view works better as a description of current business realities. In the time of the aggregate theory's dominance, it was common that a partnership would consist of only a few partners who would devote most of their life's work to it. Its membership would thus usually be constant for a long while, and it might make sense to think of it as really no more than the sum of its parts. But nowadays, many partnerships (most of them LLPs) have hundreds or thousands of partners, and they come and go frequently. A lawyer, for example, might serve in several partnerships over an ordinary career.

Under this test, the trier of fact asks whether a reasonable person would believe the parties intended to act as "co-owners of a business for profit," based on the parties' own objective manifestations.

Since the determination is an objective one it follows that, just as in the case of agency, it is possible for persons to form a partnership without intending to, even where they explicitly deny it. Thus, even if they sign a written agreement stating that their relationship is not a partnership, so long as their other manifestations are sufficient to show an intent to create a relationship with the attributes of a partnership then one will exist. Incidentally, this fact actually distinguishes the general partnership from all other forms of multi-member business. Only the general partnership can be created without any formalities, and only the general partnership can be created by accident. All of the other forms require compliance with some bureaucratic steps. These include the filing of forms with the Secretary of State (or equivalent) and sometimes the drafting of formal agreements among the parties. Failure to comply with those formalities therefore produces an interesting consequence. Parties trying to create some other form of business, like a corporation, a limited liability company, a limited partnership, or the like, but failing some required bureaucratic compliance, will as a practical matter be likely to act as co-owners of a business for profit. In other words, they will form a general partnership, and will be subject to unlimited personal liability for all of the business's obligations.

Next, also as with agency, the question of whether a partnership has been formed is frequently litigated and has significant legal consequences. If a partnership *has* been formed, then the partners have the power to render one another liable in tort or contract to third parties, they each have management rights and a share of the profits, and they each owe fiduciary duties to one another. So, in any given case there typically will be at least one party with an incentive to deny that a partnership was created.

Such incentives were on display in one of the most venerable cases in all of partnership law, *Martin v. Peyton*, which is excerpted below. There, an investment firm, which was itself a partnership, had fallen on hard financial times owing to some unfortunate speculations. Mr. Peyton and other well-heeled friends of one of the partners (Mr. Hall) loaned the firm certain securities to be used as collateral for a bank loan. This transfer of securities was made pursuant to a contract explicitly disclaiming intent to create a partnership, but under which the lenders of the stock would receive 40 percent of the firm's profits until the loan was repaid, within a specified range (not less than $100,000 and not more than $500,000). The friends also demanded certain provisions (discussed in the opinion that follows) to protect themselves. The investment firm then failed (owing to more unfortunate speculations that in fact were prohibited by the loan agreement), and the collateral was lost. Finding no recourse against the defunct firm or its penniless partners, the firm's creditors went after the group of friends. The court's analysis nicely captures the fact-rich nature of the inquiry.

MARTIN V. PEYTON

Court of Appeals of New York
158 N.W. 77 (1927)

ANDREWS, J. . . . .

Much ancient learning as to partnership is obsolete. Today only those who are partners between themselves may be charged for partnership debts by others. (Partnership Law [Cons. Laws, ch. 39], sec. 11. [The court is referring to the

New York version of the Uniform Partnership Act (1914), which is essentially identical to RUPA for purposes of the court's analysis.]) There is one exception. Now and then a recovery is allowed where in truth such relationship is absent. This is because the debtor may not deny the claim. (Sec. 27.)

Partnership results from contract, express or implied. If denied it may be proved by the production of some written instrument; by testimony as to some conversation; by circumstantial evidence. If nothing else appears the receipt by the defendant of a share of the profits of the business is enough. (Sec. 11.)

Assuming some written contract between the parties the question may arise whether it creates a partnership. If it be complete; if it expresses in good faith the full understanding and obligation of the parties, then it is for the court to say whether a partnership exists. It may, however, be a mere sham intended to hide the real relationship. Then other results follow. In passing upon it effect is to be given to each provision. Mere words will not blind us to realities. State-ments that no partnership is intended are not conclusive. If as a whole a contract contemplates an association of two or more persons to carry on as co-owners a business for profit a partnership there is. (Sec. 10.) On the other hand, if it be less than this no partnership exists. Passing on the contract as a whole, an arrangement for sharing profits is to be considered. It is to be given its due weight. But it is to be weighed in connection with all the rest. It is not decisive. It may be merely the method adopted to pay a debt or wages, as interest on a loan or for other reasons . . . .

In the case before us the claim that the defendants became partners in the firm of Knauth, Nachod Kuhne, doing business as bankers and brokers, depends upon the interpretation of certain instruments. There is nothing in their sub-sequent acts determinative of or indeed material upon this question. And we are relieved of questions that sometimes arise. "The plaintiff's position is not," we are told, "that the agreements of June 4, 1921, were a false expression or incomplete expression of the intention of the parties. We say that they express defendants' intention and that that intention was to create a relationship which as a matter of law constitutes a partnership." Nor may the claim of the plaintiff be rested on any question of estoppel. "The plaintiff's claim," he stipulates, "is a claim of actual partnership, not of partnership by estoppel, and liability is not sought to be predicated upon article 27 of the New York Partnership Law."

Remitted then, as we are, to the documents themselves, we refer to circum-stances surrounding their execution only so far as is necessary to make them intelligible. And we are to remember that although the intention of the parties to avoid liability as partners is clear, although in language precise and definite they deny any design to then join the firm of K.N.K.; although they say their interests in profits should be construed merely as a measure of compensation for loans, not an interest in profits as such; although they provide that they shall not be liable for any losses or treated as partners, the question still remains whether in fact they agree to so associate themselves with the firm as to "carry on as co-owners a business for profit." . . .

Many other detailed agreements are contained in the papers. Are they such as may be properly inserted to protect the lenders? Or do they go further? What-

JD/MBA: Collateral and Cost

There generally is a direct relationship between perceived risk and the amount of compensation someone will demand for making funds available to an enterprise. One way of reducing risk is by pledging collateral. Another way, referred to in the case, is the purchase of "key person" insurance that will tide a company over after the death of a critical participant.

ever their purpose, did they in truth associate the respondents with the firm so that they and it together thereafter carried on as co-owners a business for profit? The answer depends upon an analysis of these various provisions.

As representing the lenders, Mr. Peyton and Mr. Freeman are called "trustees." The loaned securities when used as collateral are not to be mingled with other securities of K.N.K., and the trustees at all times are to be kept informed of all transactions affecting them. To them shall be paid all dividends and income accruing therefrom. They may also substitute for any of the securities loaned securities of equal value. With their consent the firm may sell any of its securities held by the respondents, the proceeds to go, however, to the trustees. In other similar ways the trustees may deal with these same securities, but the securities loaned shall always be sufficient in value to permit of their hypothecation for $2,000,000. If they rise in price the excess may be withdrawn by the defendants. If they fall they shall make good the deficiency.

So far there is no hint that the transaction is not a loan of securities with a provision for compensation. Later a somewhat closer connection with the firm appears. Until the securities are returned the directing management of the firm is to be in the hands of John R. Hall, and his life is to be insured for $1,000,000, and the policies are to be assigned as further collateral security to the trustees. These requirements are not unnatural. Hall was the one known and trusted by the defendants. Their acquaintance with the other members of the firm was of the slightest. These others had brought an old and established business to the verge of bankruptcy. As the respondents knew, they also had engaged in unsafe speculation. The respondents were about to loan $2,500,000 of good securities. As collateral they were to receive others of problematical value. What they required seems but ordinary caution. Nor does it imply an association in the business.

The trustees are to be kept advised as to the conduct of the business and consulted as to important matters. They may inspect the firm books and are entitled to any information they think important. Finally they may veto any business they think highly speculative or injurious. Again we hold this but a proper precaution to safeguard the loan. The trustees may not initiate any transaction as a partner may do. They may not bind the firm by any action of their own. Under the circumstances the safety of the loan depended upon the business success of K.N.K. This success was likely to be compromised by the inclination of its members to engage in speculation. No longer, if the respondents were to be protected, should it be allowed. The trustees, therefore, might prohibit it, and that their prohibition might be effective, information was to be furnished them. Not dissimilar agreements have been held proper to guard the interests of the lender.

As further security each member of K.N.K. is to assign to the trustees their interest in the firm. No loan by the firm to any member is permitted and the amount each may draw is fixed. No other distribution of profits is to be made. So that realized profits may be calculated the existing capital is stated to be $700,000, and profits are to be realized as promptly as good business practice will permit. In case the trustees think this is not done, the question is left to them and to Mr. Hall, and if they differ then to an arbitrator. There is no obligation that the firm shall continue the business. It may dissolve at any time. Again we conclude there is nothing here not properly adapted to secure the interest of the respondents as lenders. If their compensation is dependent on a percentage of the profits still provision must be made to define what these profits shall be . . . .

Finally we have the "option." It permits the respondents or any of them or their assignees or nominees to enter the firm at a later date if they desire to do so by buying 50 percent or less of the interests therein of all or any of the members at a stated price. Or a corporation may, if the respondents and the members agree, be formed in place of the firm. Meanwhile, apparently with the design of protecting the firm business against improper or ill-judged action which might render the option valueless, each member of the firm is to place his resignation in the hands of Mr. Hall. If at any time he and the trustees agree that such resignation should be accepted, that member shall then retire, receiving the value of his interest calculated as of the date of such retirement.

This last provision is somewhat unusual, yet it is not enough in itself to show that on June 4, 1921, a present partnership was created nor taking these various papers as a whole do we reach such a result. It is quite true that even if one or two or three like provisions contained in such a contract do not require this conclusion, yet it is also true that when taken together a point may come where stipulations immaterial separately cover so wide a field that we should hold a partnership exists. As in other branches of the law a question of degree is often the determining factor. Here that point has not been reached . . . .

Doing the Numbers: Calculating the Interest Rate

The "lenders" in *Martin v. Peyton* loaned securities worth $2,500,000 (in today's dollars, $30,250,000) to K.N.K. They were to be compensated with a profit share equaling not less than $100,000 nor more than $500,000. Obviously, this means that the interest they were receiving was variable, but what was the possible range of rates?

$100,000 = x% $2,500,000
$100,000/$2,500,000 = 4%

$500,000 = x% $2,500,000
$500,000/$2,500,000 = 20%

Thus, the rate could vary between 4 and 20 percent. At the high end, it would have been usurious.

JD/MBA: A Basic Tension in Organizational Design

Martin v. Peyton and our other materials on formation nicely illustrate a basic practical problem underlying partnership formation, and it also is one that has been with us since the first case in this book, *Gay Jenson Farms v. Cargill* (see Chapter 3). When one's money is at stake, the natural instinct is to protect it, and that may mean influencing decisions made about it and the uses to which it is put. The problem is that, even if you don't want it to happen this way, our social policy and the law of business entities may not permit you to involve yourself managerially while otherwise remaining merely a meddlesome but passive lender. Under our law, if one desires to wear the shoes of the owner/operator, as a force behind its choices, then one must normally bear the responsibilities as well.

■ **Think about this:**

(A) *Martin v. Peyton* strongly hints that there are some powers that a "lender" must avoid to prevent being characterized as a partner. What are they?

(B) Are there any provisions that the lenders in *Martin v. Peyton* included that made the partnership claim against them a closer case than it needed to be?

(C) Suppose that K.N.K. had been organized as a corporation rather than a partnership. Would that make it impossible for anyone to claim that Mr. Hall's friends were partners in any sort of enterprise?

(D) Do you have enough information to decide whether the lenders in *Martin v. Peyton* were partners as among themselves?

Now, consider the following RUPA provision, which is essentially the same as UPA §6 (1914):

SECTION 202. FORMATION OF PARTNERSHIP

(c) In determining whether a partnership is formed, the following rules apply:

(1) Joint tenancy, tenancy in common, tenancy by the entireties, joint property, common property, or part ownership does not by itself establish a partnership, even if the co-owners share profits made by the use of the property.

(2) The sharing of gross returns does not by itself establish a partnership, even if the persons sharing them have a joint or common right or interest in property from which the returns are derived.

(3) A person who receives a share of the profits of a business is presumed to be a partner in the business, unless the profits were received in payment:

(i) of a debt by installments or otherwise;

(ii) for services as an independent contractor or of wages or other compensation to an employee;

(iii) of rent;

(iv) of an annuity or other retirement or health benefit to a beneficiary, representative, or designee of a deceased or retired partner;

(v) of interest or other charge on a loan, even if the amount of payment varies with the profits of the business, including a direct or indirect present or future ownership of the collateral, or rights to income, proceeds, or increase in value derived from the collateral; or

(vi) for the sale of the goodwill of a business or other property by installments or otherwise.

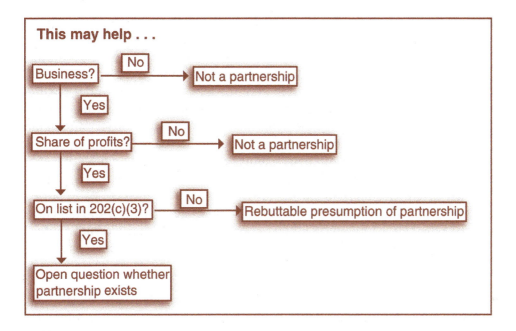

This may help . . .

Business? — No → Not a partnership

Yes ↓

Share of profits? — No → Not a partnership

Yes ↓

On list in 202(c)(3)? — No → Rebuttable presumption of partnership

Yes ↓

Open question whether partnership exists

■ **Think about this:**

(E) Is the court's opinion in *Martin v. Peyton* consistent with §202(c)?

On a slightly lighter note, the story of Sugarland highlights how significant substantive partnership law can be for anyone intending to make money with someone else, and also gives us another nice formation example:

STUCK LIKE GLUE: THE LONG EFFORT TO DISENTANGLE SUGARLAND

The hugely popular country music band Sugarland, a duo of Atlanta singer-songwriters Jennifer Nettles and Kristian Bush, enjoyed one of the quickest and most exciting journeys to stardom in contemporary music. Just one year after the group's founding in 2002, they released a break-out single called *Baby Girl*, a bittersweet, determined meditation on making it in the music business, that would be among the highest-peaking debut recordings in country-music history and, after 46 weeks, the longest-charted country single in the history of Nielsen rating system. Their 2004 debut album *Twice the Speed of Life*, which included a re-release of *Baby Girl*, ultimately went double-platinum, and they followed up just a few years later with the triple-platinum album *Enjoy the Ride.* Over time they have won a long list of major awards, including several best-new-artist awards during their initial rise. Their success was driven by a string of infectious, exuberant, mostly toe-tapping hit singles, including *Want To, Settlin',* and *Stuck Like Glue.*

More to the Story: How Not to Say "Goodbye"

Most reports put the amount in issue in the Sugarland case at $14,000,000.

As it turns out, however, Sugarland was not always just Nettles and Bush. In fact, while some of the details are disputed, the band was initially founded by another veteran Atlanta musician and one-time Indigo Girls roadie, Kristen Hall. By all accounts her initial creative contributions were as significant as her bandmates' were. She devised and trademarked the Sugarland name, or at least helped to do so, her name appearing on federal trademark filings along with Bush and Nettles. She also toured with the band through its early years, appeared in its early music videos, and wrote or co-wrote all of the songs on *Twice the Speed of Life.* However, in 2005, during the third year or so of all that success, Hall chose to leave the band, apparently following personal stresses or internal conflict. The details have never been very well explained, but in a statement at the time, Nettles and Bush said that Hall had decided to "stay home and write songs."

In 2008, about three years after her departure, Hall sued Nettles and Bush in federal court in Atlanta, seeking a share of the band's profits. The three never committed any agreement among them to writing, either at their founding or later, and they appear to have engaged in no negotiations or agreement about ongoing compensation when Hall left. Instead, their relations apparently were extremely informal from the beginning. In early 2002, Hall had simply asked Bush to join her in the band, and shortly thereafter they auditioned and invited Nettles to join as well. Each of the members contributed financially in the band's early years, and Hall paid significant expenses with her personal credit cards. She alleged in her complaint that she also acted as manager, booking agent, and tour organizer. In reply, Nettles and Bush alleged that Hall left the band in significant debt, with about $15,000 in assets but nearly $100,000 in liabilities. They alleged that they paid off those debts themselves, without contribution from Hall. In any case, while Hall's complaint nominally asked only for $1.5 million, most press accounts suggested that her total share of the band's profits—if her claims proved legally valid—could be much more.

For more details, see Janet L. Conley, *Former Band Member's Lawsuit Leaves Sour Taste for Sugarland,* Fulton Co. Daily Rep. (August 8, 2008); Kelsey Butterworth, *Whatever Happened to Sugarland's Third Member, Kristen Hall?,* Wide Open Country, February 26, 2017.

■ **Think about this:**

(F) Absent any formalities and if not a partnership, what would a band be?

Connections: We're Going to Think About This One Again, Later

The Sugarland case and the juicy legal issues it raised never saw the light of judicial day. The case settled in late 2010, almost literally on the eve of trial, for an undisclosed amount. *See* Greg Bluestein, *Sugarland Members Settle Founder's $14M Lawsuit*, Seattle Times, Nov. 14, 2010.

So the question whether there was a partnership at all was never resolved by a court. And it turns out that a number of other very interesting issues would have come up were the case to have proceeded to trial. Issues surrounding "dissolution" and valuation would have been particularly important. We shall revisit this case when we get to those problems, in Chapter 9.

---

2. The Default Nature of Substantive Partnership Law

Something we shall see again and again in our study of partnership law is that the substantive rules of the basic statute we will study—the Revised Uniform Partnership Act (RUPA), a model statute now adopted in a large majority of states—can almost always be amended by agreement, provided they concern the relations of the partners themselves. (This is also true of other modern business entity statutes, but for a long time it has been peculiarly true of partnership statutes.) Therefore, the RUPA is a "default" statute in more than one sense. First, a general partnership results when co-venturers act without taking any legal formalities, even if they don't intend it. Second, the rules that govern a partnership with no specific agreements among the partners will be the rules of the RUPA.

 Dear Prof.: You are talking about acting without any legal formalities. How about satisfying the Statute of Frauds?

It certainly is possible that some aspect of a partnership would require satisfaction of the Statute of Frauds. For instance, if the partners were to agree to form a relationship that would last for more than a year, a writing would be required. The simple formation of a partnership, however, does not trigger the Statute of Frauds.

The default nature of the RUPA and other business entity statutes invites this question: Why allow so much flexibility, on the one hand, and why do the drafters pick the particular default rules that they do for those firms that choose not to modify them? As it happens, the default rules often seem counterintuitive and poorly suited to many different sorts of business we could imagine. For example, under RUPA §401(a), in the absence of contrary agreement, all partners share equally in profits and losses regardless how much they contributed to the business, even if they put in very different contributions, bring in different amounts of business, or have different periods of seniority or eminence in their field. Likewise, under RUPA §401(h), in the absence of contrary agreement, every partner is entitled to equal participation in management. And RUPA §801(1) gives every partner in an at-will partnership a default right unilaterally to cause the dissolution and liquidation of the partnership, as a tool to force a buyout of his or her stake in the firm. Obviously, rules like these could be extremely awkward for many kinds of business that were historically organized as partnerships. Today's large law firms, for example, frequently have hundreds or even thousands of partners, and it would be extremely inconvenient if all of them had to be afforded an equal say in every day-to-day managerial decision, or if every single one of them had a unilateral right to force the liquidation of the firm when it suited them.

A way to explain all this is that the statutory default is designed for those businesses that are either likely to create partnerships by accident, or to create partnerships on purpose but without any formal agreement. By and large, those businesses will be small, deliberately informal, and operated on a more or less equal sharing basis. Moreover, they will often be businesses in which the individual identities of the partners are important to the identity of the business itself. So, it might make sense for a very small law firm to dissolve when any one of the members leaves. Another way to explain it, of course, is simply by reference to notions of judicial economy. If there are two partners, it presumably is much easier to invoke a "halfsies" rule than to try to evaluate the disparate worth of the partners' various contributions.

Of course the answer to the awkwardness of the default rules is simply drafting, drafting, drafting. No firm intended to have significant capital or commercial operations, many partners, or indefinite longevity should be without a written partnership agreement modifying those defaults that would frustrate the goals of the partners and the model of their business.

More to the Story: RUPA's Simplification Goal Part I: The Innovation of §105

RUPA's drafters sought to resolve certain persistent uncertainties under its predecessor, UPA (1914). One of their major tools is RUPA §105, which specifies which provisions of the RUPA may be modified by partnership agreements and which are mandatory.

The UPA was a default statute as well, but its default nature gave rise to quite a number of uncertainties. The UPA was a broken record in its repeated announcement that individual statute sections apply "in the absence of contrary agreement." But the courts were actually somewhat uncertain how to handle those few cases in the statute in which that phrase was not used in a given section. Sometimes the courts read its absence as a statutory directive that a given provision is not waivable, and sometimes they did not. There also was a lot of uncertainty about whether particular waivers were effective, or whether they went too far. More recent statutes have dealt with these problems by including simple lists of sections that are non-waivable, and RUPA §105 is a prime example. It begins by stating a very broad policy in favor of waivability, followed by a list of matters that partners cannot modify, or can modify only subject to specified constraints.

3. Some Examples in Application

The following cases illustrate judicial handling of formation matters, and they also nicely give some flavor for how wide and interesting the circumstances of formation disputes can be.

SIMPSON V. ERNST & YOUNG

United States District Court for the Southern District of Ohio
850 F. Supp. 648 (1994)

ORDER

STEINBURG, United States Magistrate Judge.

[Plaintiff Simpson sued the accounting firm of Ernst & Young, where he had worked as an accountant and had been formally denominated a "partner," alleging that defendant fired him in violation of age discrimination laws, including the federal Age Discrimination in Employment Act (ADEA), and the federal Employee Retirement Income Security Act (ERISA). Defendant sought summary judgment, arguing that Simpson's claims all arose under statutes protecting only "employees" and not "partners." Simpson argued that the details of his relationship with the firm did not actually constitute a partnership relationship within the meaning of the statutes under which he sued. Simpson's argument was based on the terms of a master contract governing the firm's relations with its accountants, including Simpson, which the court refers to as the "U.S. Agreement."

[Defendant itself was the product of the 1989 merger of two preexisting firms—the former Ernst & Whinny and Arthur Young firms. Simpson, previously a partner in Arthur Young, was terminated the following year as part of process of review by the merged firm's management, which resulted in termination of 127 "partners" and which one senior Ernst & Young partner described as a "lay off." Evidence showed that at the time of the merger, the merged firms' retirement benefit obligations exceeded the funds available to pay them by more than a quarter-billion dollars.] . . .

More to the Story: Once There Were Giants . . .

. . . And then they got bigger. The merger of Ernst & Whinny and Arthur Young was the first step in whittling the "Big Eight" accounting firms down to the "Big Four." Originally, the "Big Eight" included Arthur Andersen, Arthur Young & Co., Coopers & Lybrand, Ernst & Whinny, Deloitte, Haskins & Sells, Peat Marwick Mitchell, Price Waterhouse, and Touche Ross. Arthur Andersen dissolved in a puddle of shame in the wake of an early 2000s financial disaster. Klynveld Main Goerdeler (KMG) was not technically part of the "Big Eight," but later became part of the "Big Four" once it merged with Peat Marwick Mitchell to form KPMG. The other firms merged among themselves to form the titans we see today.

OPINION

I. The Court Should Apply Traditional Partnership Law Concepts in Determining Whether Simpson Was a Partner or an Employee

. . . Ernst & Young asserts that neither Simpson nor any other Party discharged during 1990 and 1991 is entitled to the protection afforded by the employment discrimination laws because these individuals are not employees, but partners. The inescapable logic of this position is that Ernst & Young claims to be free to discriminate against hundreds of its accountants due to age, race, sex, religion, national origin, and handicap because it asserts they are not employees.

Simpson, who considered himself to be a partner during his employment with Ernst & Young, now contends that he was actually an employee, as that term is defined in the law, and did not meet the legal definition of partner. He seeks the protection of the age discrimination laws. Relying on [U.S. Supreme Court precedent from other contexts, including the federal Fair Labor Standards Act] Simpson contends that the Court should use an "economic reality" test rather than traditional legal concepts in determining whether he was a partner or employee. The Sixth Circuit has described this test as "a loose formulation, leaving the determination of employment status to case-by-case resolution based on the totality of the circumstances." . . .

Ernst & Young contends that . . . Simpson's status must be determined by the application of traditional partnership law concepts. Ernst & Young claims Simpson possessed both "essential and non-essential" attributes of a partner. It argues that whatever partnership characteristics Simpson lacked, he voluntarily delegated them to the Management Committee and their absence did not destroy his partner status. Therefore, it claims, the Court has no jurisdiction over his age discrimination claims . . . .

In Nationwide Mutual Insurance Co. v. Darden, 503 U.S. 318 (1992), decided after the aforementioned cases, the Supreme Court unanimously ruled that traditional agency law criteria should be used to determine whether the plaintiff was an independent contractor or an employee under ERISA . . . .

The Court [also] distinguished the economic reality test applied in . . . cases [under the Fair Labor Standards Act] . . . [and therefore the magistrate decided to apply partnership law].

II. Traditional Partnership Law Concepts . . .

A partnership is an "association of two or more persons to carry on as co-owners a business for profit." [Here the court quoted New York's adoption of UPA §6 (1914), since the nature of the parties' relationship in this case was governed by New York law. Section 6 corresponds very closely to RUPA §202(a).] Thus, a bona fide partner is one who owns the business, i.e., an employer.

While sharing the firm's gross receipts does not establish a partnership, *id.,* [RUPA §202(c)(1)], sharing the firm's net profits may be prima facie evidence that one is a partner. *Id.,* §[202(c)(3)]. No such inference may be drawn, however, if the share of profits was received in payment of a debt, as employee wages, or as loan interest even though the amount of payment varied with the profits of the business. *Id.*

A partner is repaid his capital contribution and shares equally in the partnership's profit after all liabilities are satisfied. *Id.*

A partner receives interest on his/her capital contribution only from the date when repayment should be made. *Id.,* §[401(g)].

The partnership must indemnify a partner. *Id.,* §[401(c)].

All partners have equal rights in the management and conduct of partnership business. *Id.,* §[401(h)].

No person may become a member of a partnership without the consent of all partners. *Id.* §[402(b)].

While any difference arising as to ordinary matters connected with the partnership may be decided by a majority of the partners, no act in contravention of the agreement between the partners may be done without the consent of all partners. *Id.,* §[401(k)].

Subject to any agreement between the partners, the partnership books are kept at the principal place of the partnership's business. *Id.* [RUPA §408(a)]. Every partner must have access to and may inspect and copy any of the partnership records. *Id.* A partner has a duty to render, on demand, all information affecting the partnership. *Id.,* §[408(c)].

Partners owe a fiduciary duty to one another . . . . The nature of the fiduciary duty is such that each partner owes to the others the highest degree of fidelity, loyalty, and fairness in their mutual dealings . . . . Because of this fiduciary duty, in their dealings with one another partners cannot fall back on morals of the marketplace . . . .

The property rights of a partner are: 1) his rights in specific partnership property; 2) his interest in the partnership; and 3) his right to participate in the management of the partnership. *Id.* [Here the court cited UPA §24 (1914),

JD/MBA: Revenue vs. Profit

Use of modifiers such as "gross" and "net" add clarity—as, for example, the court does here in discussing Ernst & Young's "gross receipts." ("Gross" means total revenue, "net" means profit—revenue minus the costs of earning it.) When they are absent, however, a reference to "receipts" or "revenue" should be understood as referring to all of the amounts taken in as the result of operating a business, before deduction of the expenses to generate those amounts. "Profit" should be understood as what remains after deduction of expenses. Partners are jointly liable for all partnership debts and obligations. [The court cited a New York variation of UPA §15 (1914)], [RUPA §306]. A partner contributes toward the partnership losses according to his proportionate share in the profits. [UPA §18 (1914)], [RUPA §401(a)].

More to the Story: Partnership as a Benefit of Employment

Lest one get the wrong impression from the cite to Powell's concurrence in the *Hishon* case, it is important to note that the decision to offer partnership to an employee is one that is governed by the federal laws against discrimination. As a result, Elizabeth Anderson Hishon went on to settle for an undisclosed sum with the law firm that allegedly denied her partnership because she was a woman.

which is retained only in part in RUPA §§501 and 502.] As to specific partnership property, a partner is co-owner with his partners as a tenant in partnership. *Id.* [Again, the court cited UPA §25(1) (1914), which was discarded by the RUPA.] A partner's interest in the partnership is his share of the profits and surplus. *Id.**

While [UPA §18 (1914)] implies that certain partnership rights may be delegated by agreement, the following rights set forth in other sections are not delegable: [t]he right to access, inspection, and copying of partnership books, *id.*, §[19]; [t]he duty of partners to render to another partner on demand true and full information of all things relating to the partnership, *id.*, §[20]; [t]he fiduciary duty one partner owes another, *id.*, §[21]; [t]he right to participate in the management of the partnership, *id.*, §[24(3)], even though a partner may delegate his equal share of management and operations, *id.*, §[18(e)]; [t]he right of a partner to be a co-owner of partnership property, §[25]; and [t]he right to share the profits and surplus, *id.*, §[26].****

The Uniform Partnership Act (UPA) has been adopted by most states, including New York in 1919, as the governing body of partnership law. It sets forth, among others, the following characteristics of a partner: unlimited liability (§15); the right to share in profits and participate in management (§18(a), (e)); the right and duty to act as an agent of the other partners (§9); shared ownership (§6); and fiduciary relationship among partners (§21). The drafters of the UPA used the term "co-owners" to indicate that each partner has "the power of ultimate control." ...

The concurring opinion in Hishon v. King & Spaulding, 467 U.S. 69 (1984), also provides some guidance as to the nature of partnership. There, Justice Powell reasoned that the relationship among partners [in a law firm] should not be characterized as an employment relationship to which Title VII may apply: The relationship among law partners differs markedly from that between employer and employee . . . . The essence of the law partnership is the common conduct of a shared enterprise. The relationship among law partners contemplates that decisions important to the partnership normally will be made by common agreement . . . . Critical to this concept of a professional partnership is the partners' authority to make decisions important to the partnership. The mere labeling of an individual as a partner does not make him so . . . .

On the other hand, Wheeler v. Hurdman, 825 F.2d 257 [(10th Cir. 1987)] . . . listed factors which distinguished [plaintiff's] partnership from her prior position as an employee with the firm: 1) participation in profits and losses; 2) exposure to liability; 3) investment in the firm; 4) partial ownership of firm assets; 5)

---

* *Editors' Note*: The approach of UPA (1914) to property rights was complicated by the idea that a partnership was an aggregate of the partners rather than a separate entity.

** *Editors' Note*: This analysis of rights that are waivable and not waivable would be rather different under RUPA, since RUPA §105 simply collects an explicit list of all RUPA provisions that are not waivable. Some of the provisions non-waivable under §105 overlap with those listed in this case.

voting rights; 6) position under the partnership agreement; and 7) position under partnership laws. *Id.* Wheeler possessed the following partnership attributes: she had signed a partnership agreement; her compensation was not a salary but a share of the firm's profits paid by draw and an allocation of profits based on points; she made a genuine capital contribution; she had unlimited personal liability for partnership debts; she had the right to vote on dissolution, large mergers, admission of new partners, partner termination, shares of net profits, special distributions, and any other allocation of income; she could sign audits and tax returns; and she was reimbursed for certain club dues. *Id.* at 260.

Implicit in the Tenth Circuit's decision is the concept that, had Wheeler possessed something less than the "total bundle of partnership characteristics," she would not have been considered a bona fide partner, even though the firm so denominated her. Wheeler possessed more characteristics of a partner than did Simpson . . . . Aside from the cases Ernst & Young cited, the following cases are also pertinent.

In Fountain [v. Metcalf, Zima & Co., P.A.], 925 F.2d 1398 [(1991)], the issue was whether the plaintiff was a partner or an employee of his accounting firm under ADEA. The Eleventh Circuit held:

> [W]e look to the particular circumstances of the case at hand, . . . and, in so doing, we focus not on any label, but on the actual role played by the claimant in the operations of the involved entity and the extent to which that role dealt with traditional concepts of management, control and ownership.

Looking beyond corporate nomenclature, the Court found Fountain, one of four shareholders in a professional corporation, to be a partner based on the following facts: 1) he was compensated on the basis of a share of the firm's profits; 2) he was liable for certain debts of the firm; and 3) he had the right to vote proportionate to his ownership share on amendments to the agreement, admission of new partners, termination of partners, and distribution of profits and income. *Id.* at 1401. Fountain possessed more characteristics of a partner than Simpson . . . .

We now turn to examine the partner vs. employee characteristics Simpson possessed.

III. Simpson Was an Employee Subject to ADEA Protection

A. Simpson Did Not Make a True Capital Contribution to the Firm

Simpson never established a capital account with Ernst & Young. Therefore, we give no weight to the Partnership Agreement's reference to a Capital Account.

Simpson established an Ernst & Young U.S. Capital Account. Simpson's "capital" payment into this account was arranged by Ernst & Young and financed by Citibank. This "capital contribution" generated interest payments from Ernst & Young U.S. rather than a pro rata share of the profits. The Capital Account was not the basis for a Party's pro rata share of either profits or firm assets. Thus, Simpson's payment to Ernst & Young U.S. was more akin to a loan than a capital contribution.

Gary Stewart, a CPA and expert in the field of CPA business organizations, testified at trial that Simpson did not contribute capital but rather loaned money to Ernst & Young U.S. Stewart's opinion was based on several factors: 1) the definition of "firm capital" in Section 7 of the U.S. Agreement indicates that "amounts owing to Parties" are treated as a firm liability rather than as owner's equity; 2) when a Party withdraws from the firm, he receives only what he paid in plus interest, rather than a percentage of the value of the firm; and 3) the firm paid interest to the Parties on their Capital Accounts.

 Dear Prof.: You talked about capital and capitalization somewhere else. What does "capital" mean here?

You've seen some indication already that when people form partnerships, or new partners join existing partnerships, the new partners typically contribute some money or other property to the firm. That is called a "capital" contribution. Thus, "capital" is used here to mean money or property a firm owns and uses in doing its business. We'll learn much more about partners' capital contributions in Chapter 7. We'll also learn that partnerships commonly maintain records that include "capital accounts" for each of the partners. Such a thing is said to have been created here for plaintiff Simpson. It is simply a running record of how much a partner has put into a firm, plus a share of the firm's profits minus a share of its expenses and less any amount that has been distributed to the partner.

We view Simpson's Capital Account as a paper transaction designed to give him the appearance, but not the reality, of a partner. On its face, his substantial payment ($84,000) appears to be a capital contribution to the firm. However, Simpson did not invest one cent of his own money in the firm. The firm arranged the bank loan that Simpson signed and paid the interest on his behalf. He made no payments on the principal. Although the U.S. Agreement bound him to begin reducing the principal in his third year with Ernst & Young U.S., he was discharged before then. Although he was liable to the bank for the principal, his Capital Account at the firm was available to, and ultimately did, satisfy the debt. His yearly earnings and discharge payment were not based on the proportion [the] $84,000 contribution had to total capital investment in the firm. It appears that the primary significance of his Capital Account was not to establish Simpson's ownership interest, but to generate funds for the firm. As of the date of Simpson's termination, he had not made a true capital contribution to the firm.

B. Simpson Did Not Share in the Firm's Profits and Losses . . .

Simpson received an annual salary from Ernst & Young U.S., as determined by the Management Committee. The U.S. Agreement does not identify Simpson as a partner and specifically refers to his compensation as "salary." For state tax purposes, Ernst & Young U.S. treated Simpson's compensation as salary. For federal tax purposes, however, it treated it as a partnership distribution of earnings. This is of little significance, because under Internal Revenue Code regulations, a partnership is considered to be anything which is not a corporation, trust, or estate. 26 C.F.R. §301.7701-3(a). Simpson's salary did not vary based on the rise and fall of firm profits. There was no evidence that Simpson or any other Party were required to return any amount of salary due to declining profits. Nor was there evidence that his salary was calculated as a proportionate share of the firm's profits.

In addition to his salary from Ernst & Young U.S., Simpson was eligible to receive an "allocation" each year, also determined by the Management Committee. Neither party discussed in their memoranda the relative amounts of Simpson's salary compared to his allocation or its significance. Pursuant to the U.S. Agreement, a Party could receive advances against his/her allocation, but would have to return any advances in the event that they exceeded the allocation. The separate denominations and treatment of salary and allocation indicate that the two items are different. There is no evidence, however, that allocations were calculated from net profits or even from gross receipts. Nor is there evidence that Simpson's allocation was calculated as a proportionate share. The U.S. Agreement fails to set forth any formula for calculating allocations, leaving the determination instead to the Management Committee. Since Simpson had no right to an accounting as to how his allocation was calculated, he did not have the ability to offer evidence on this issue. It is fair to infer that, had Simpson's allocation been calculated from his proportionate share of net profits, Ernst & Young would have introduced that favorable evidence. Therefore, we conclude the allocation was comparable to a periodic bonus paid to an employee at the firm's discretion from the firm's gross revenues . . . .

C. Simpson Had No Other Indicia of an Ownership Interest in the Firm

Ernst & Young contends that Simpson's ownership rights in the firm are demonstrated by his UBT account[,] [an unbilled time account that had recorded Simpson's share of accounts receivable during his time at the Arthur Young firm]. The UBT account, however, is not indicative of his relationship with Ernst & Young since this account was a carry-over from his prior relationship with Arthur Young. Neither Ernst & Young nor Ernst & Young U.S. utilized UBT accounts. Their failure to continue a UBT arrangement demonstrates that the firms, rather than their members, owned the accounts receivable.

Ernst & Young also contends that Simpson had a contingent undivided interest in all firm assets, citing the U.S. Agreement, Section 18. That section, however, applies only upon dissolution or liquidation of the firm. When Simpson left the firm, Ernst & Young U.S. calculated his compensation in December, nine months prior to the firm's fiscal year end, using an estimate based on the prior year's figures. Thus, Simpson's discharge compensation was not measured by any ownership interest in the firm's assets but was a salary. Furthermore, Section 18 states that, upon dissolution or liquidation, the amount owing to each Party shall be computed pursuant to Section 11. The latter does not provide for a distribution of an undivided interest in firm assets. Rather, it awards a Party the amount of his Account, as determined by the Manage-

Connections: Dissolution

Under the UPA (1914) (as under RUPA), dissolution and liquidation actually were two different things. There is more on this subject in Chapter 11.

ment Committee; any allocations or interest the firm owes the Party; and the Party's proportionate allocation for the current fiscal year, less any liability the Party owes the firm, plus an "earnings charge" pursuant to Section 9 computed by the Management Committee. Simpson did not possess an undivided interest in firm assets.

Ernst & Young claims that Simpson's ownership interest in the firm is shown by his rights regarding the firm's operations. It points to the fact that Simpson could vote for amendments to the Partnership Agreement and the U.S. Agreement, dissolution of the firm, certain mergers, and members of the Advisory Council. Simpson's voting rights, however, were illusory because the Advisory Council had the right to approve and thus, implicitly, to veto any vote put to the Parties. Simpson's right to vote for members of the Advisory Council was perfunctory since the candidates were unopposed and selected by the Nominating Committee which, in turn, was selected by the Management Committee. Furthermore, the Advisory Council had no direct authority to act, serving only in an advisory capacity to the Management Committee. The Chairman selected the members of the Management Committee without any vote of the Parties, and the Management Committee selected the Chairman. The Chairman and the Management Committee managed the firm. Thus, as a practical matter, the Parties had no power to alter decisions of the Chairman and the Management Committee.

Even more illuminating are the issues for which Simpson had no vote. He had no vote for Management Committee membership. He had no vote for the admission of new partners. He had no vote on the discharge of existing partners, including himself. Finally, he had no vote on how firm members were to be compensated . . . .

D. Simpson Had No Right to Examine the Firm's Books and Records

Simpson did not have the unconditional right to examine the firm's books and records, and he was denied access to them regarding the UBT accounts. He had no right to learn the other Parties' compensation. A basic tenant of a bona fide partnership is that every partner shall at all times have access to and may inspect and copy partnership books. [RUPA §408(c).] Although some other emoluments of partnership are, under the New York [adoption of the UPA], implicitly delegable, this section is not subject to variation by agreement of the parties.

E. Simpson Had Little, If Any, Management Authority

Contrary to Ernst & Young's conclusory contentions, Simpson had few rights regarding Ernst & Young U.S.'s operations. He did not have the authority to hire, fire, or transfer even clerical workers within or without his department. The operations strategy of his department was determined by a superior. Simpson was subject to annual performance reviews. To the extent involvement in a firm's operations is indicative of being a bona fide partner, the evidence shows that Simpson's partnership interest in Ernst & Young U.S. was slim, at best . . . .

F. There Was No Fiduciary Relationship
Between the Management Committee and Simpson

Partners bear a fiduciary relationship to each other . . . . The main elements of fiduciary duty are the utmost good faith, the highest fidelity, fairness, and loyalty . . . . Ernst & Young's refusal to permit Simpson to examine books and records regarding UBTs and to obtain its attorney's opinion regarding Simpson's discharge demonstrate an absence of a fiduciary relationship between the Management Committee and Simpson.

The Management Committee's act, at the time of the merger, of privately planning to "lay-off" Parties, while at the same time assuring them good increases in 1990 and 1991, equal or better benefits, and no reduction in partners, is a vivid example of the absence of a fiduciary relationship. Simpson's discharge and that of 126 other Parties was done for two stated economic reasons: 1) to protect the continued profit of firm members who were not discharged; and 2) to encourage recruitment and retention of younger accountants, who were generally paid less, were farther away from retirement, and needed assurance they would rise to partnership status. The failure of Ernst & Young to choose other options, such as not admitting as many new accountants, or reducing Parties' compensation, belies its contention that Simpson was a bona fide partner to whom the Management Committee owed a fiduciary duty. Since bona fide partners share in profits and losses proportionately, . . . a reduction in all Parties' compensation would have been consistent with the existence of a fiduciary relationship. "Lay-off" of Parties to preserve other Parties' income is not. The fact that the Management Committee was simultaneously considering hiring accountants and terminating Parties is also indicative of the absence of a fiduciary relationship.

There is a degree of permanence associated with the status of partner that is absent from the status of employee . . . . The element of co-ownership of the firm and consequent fiduciary relationship and employment security inherent therein is absent when some Parties can be discharged, without any voice in the matter, in order to insure the financial gain of other Parties.

G. The Firm Did Not Actually Consider Simpson a Co-Owner

We are not persuaded by Ernst & Young's contention that Simpson delegated certain management responsibilities. We acknowledge that the N.Y. Partnership Law, §40(5), permits delegation of such duties, and we agree that the larger the partnership, the more delegation is to be expected . . . . Simpson, however, could not delegate rights he never possessed. Furthermore, at some point, delegation destroys partner status. While it may have been "normal business caution" to prevent Simpson from binding the firm to promissory notes by his signature and from pledging firm assets, or to require reviews of certain audits or the engagement of new clients, it was not "normal business caution" to prevent him from voting on substantive matters, to deny him a proportionate share of firm profits, to eliminate his share in the firm's accounts receivable, to deny him personnel authority, to prevent him from examining the firm's books, and to prevent him from learning what legal advice the firm's attorneys provided.

H. Simpson Agreed to Unlimited Liability for Partnership Losses

The U.S. Agreement and the Partnership Agreement provide that Simpson was jointly and individually liable for the losses of Ernst & Young U.S. and Ernst & Young respectively. On its face, this is a characteristic of partnership.

It certainly cannot, however, be considered a benefit of partnership. Furthermore, there is no evidence that Simpson or any other Party was ever called upon to accept responsibility for losses of Ernst & Young U.S. or Ernst & Young. We question the enforceability of this provision in light of the apparent lack of consideration therefor. It seems inequitable to hold an individual liable for the losses of his "partners" when that individual has no choice in determining who his partners are, no power to control the risks his "partners" take, and no right to examine the firm's books to determine what his liabilities might be. With these qualifications, Simpson's unlimited liability is a partnership attribute . . . .

J. It Is Not Necessary to Resolve Simpson's Contention That Ernst & Young Is Not Actually a Partnership

Simpson also contends that both the U.S. Agreement and the Partnership Agreement fail to establish bona fide partnerships; therefore, he is not a partner. Simpson has presented substantial evidence in this regard, much of which has been discussed above. Simpson contends that the Partnership Agreement has no specific provision regarding the distribution of earnings; it does not result in the establishment of a capital account; it provides no voting procedure for the election of the Chairman or Management Committee; and it specifically restricts the rights of the Partners to sign promissory notes or to examine the firm's books. With regard to the U.S. Agreement, Simpson contends that it has been carefully crafted to avoid creating a partnership because it includes non-CPAs as parties and state laws prohibit CPAs and non-CPAs from representing themselves as partners. The fact that we have found Simpson to be an employee does not, in and of itself, justify the conclusion that Ernst & Young and Ernst & Young U.S. are not partnerships. Because we have resolved the jurisdictional issue by finding Simpson to be an employee, it is not necessary to go further to decide whether either the entities Ernst & Young or Ernst & Young U.S. are in actuality partnerships . . . .

■ **Think about this:**

(G) Simpson argued that Ernst & Young and Ernst & Young U.S. weren't partnerships. What do you think?

(H) Was the court putting the cart before the horse in reasoning that if the management committee had treated Mr. Simpson badly, it did not have a fiduciary duty to treat him fairly? In other words, is it reasonable to say that failure to observe a fiduciary duty means that it doesn't exist?

(I) A similar question: Was the court putting the cart before the horse in reasoning that if the parties agreed that Mr. Simpson did not have the non-waivable right to inspect the firm's books and records, that he did not have that right?

(J) Is it really so clear that in covering "employees" Congress meant to exclude everyone who was a partner under state law from the protections of ADEA and ERISA? What do the federal statutes invoked in *Simpson* seem intended to protect? Why would they need to exclude partners?

(K) After reading *Simpson*, what do you think the minimal requirements of partnership status seem to be?

(L) Think about the law firms you may know or have experience with. Do you think the partners really are partners under *Simpson*?

 Time Out for PR: Partnership with Non-Lawyers

As the *Simpson* case notes, applicable ethics rules prohibited CPAs from representing themselves to be partners with non-CPAs. The American Bar Association's Model Rule of Professional Conduct 5.4 is quite detailed, and prohibits partnership (or other forms of co-ownership) with non-lawyers for the purpose of practicing law, as well as most forms of fee-sharing with non-lawyers, and employment situations in which a non-lawyer directs or regulates a lawyer's professional judgment. The District of Columbia and the state of Washington, however, have different rules that do per-mit non-lawyer participation in ownership. It appears that a firm availing itself of one of these rules will not be able to establish satellite offices in other states. In any event, if a non-Washington firm permits non-lawyers to become partners, does that mean it is not a partnership?

In the *Simpson* case, someone who thought he was a partner changed his tune. The following case presents the opposite dynamic.

IN RE MARRIAGE OF HASSIEPEN

Illinois Court of Appeals
646 N.E.2d 1348 (1995)

STEIGMANN, J.:

[Cynthia Hassiepen, petitioner, seeks an increase in child support payments from her former spouse and the father of their three children, the respondent Kevin Von Behren. Illinois statute fixes child support as a percentage of the

non-custodial parent's net income, so the question for the court is to determine Kevin's net income.]

In 1985, [after Cynthia and Kevin divorced,] Kevin began living with Brenda[,] [who would eventually become his second wife] .... [H]e and Brenda decided to start an electrical contracting business, called Von Behren Electric. Kevin started this business with only an old pickup truck and a drill which his father had given him. Brenda's credit cards were used to purchase other business supplies and materials. Brenda handled the general office work, including taking phone calls, picking up mail, preparing bills, banking, and preparing bids. Kevin performed the electrical contracting work. When they began the business, Brenda was also a court reporter, and she continued to receive income from this job for about two years thereafter.

After Kevin and Brenda began living together, they opened a joint checking account, which they used for all personal and business transactions. They did not pay themselves wages or a salary, but instead withdrew money from the account for both personal or business reasons. They put any money received into this joint account. At the time of the 1993 hearings, they continued this practice for handling money.

Von Behren Electric proved to be quite prosperous....

2. WERE KEVIN AND BRENDA BUSINESS PARTNERS?

Cynthia first argues that the trial court erred in finding that Kevin and Brenda were partners in Von Behren Electric .... Essentially, Cynthia claims that Kevin is sole owner ... and that Brenda is one of his employees. As a result, Cynthia contends that all of the [firm's] net income ... should be accorded to Kevin, not just half of this income as determined by the trial court based upon its finding that a partnership existed .... The existence of a partnership is a question of the parties' intent and is based upon all the facts and circumstances surrounding the formation of the relationship at issue. As a result, the formalities of a written partnership agreement are unnecessary to prove the existence of a partnership. A partnership arises when (1) parties join together to carry on a venture for their common benefit, (2) each party contributes property or services to the venture, and (3) each party has a community of interest in the profits of the venture.

Section 6(1) of the Uniform Partnership Act[,] [like the substantially identical RUPA §202(a),] defines a partnership as "an association of two or more persons to carry on as ... a business for profit." Further, the receipt of a share of the business profits is prima facie evidence that a person is a partner in the business. [*See* RUPA §202(c)(3).] The party asserting the existence of the partnership carries the burden of proving its existence. Because the existence of a partnership is a question of fact, a reviewing court will not overturn the trial court's determination of this question unless it is against the manifest weight of the evidence.

Cynthia points to the following facts which she claims support a conclusion that Kevin and Brenda were not partners in the Von Behren businesses: (1) prior to their marriage, Kevin and Brenda filed separate tax returns, in which Kevin reported all of the business income and Brenda reported only her court report-ing income; (2) when they filed joint tax returns after their marriage, Brenda did not report any income from either business on her separate tax schedules; (3) Kevin put "sole proprietorship" on the top (in bold letters) of his tax return schedules for 1988 through 1991; (4) no written partnership agreement exists; (5) they never filed a partnership tax return; (6) they never informed Nelson, their accountant, that they were a partnership; . . . (8) all business vehicles are titled in Kevin's name; (9) no business signs indicated that either business was a partnership; (10) business cards for Von Behren Electric, Inc., state "Kevin Von Behren/Owner"; and (11) when Kevin answered interrogatories for this case, he stated that he was sole owner and that Brenda worked for him.

Kevin asserts that the following facts support his claim that he and Brenda were partners in the Von Behren businesses: (1) in 1987, he and Brenda ver-bally agreed to "start an electrical contracting business to see if they could make some money out of it"; (2) Brenda's credit cards were used to obtain credit when they began the electrical business because he had no credit available after going through bankruptcy; (3) all money earned by the electrical business was put into their joint checking account; (4) neither he nor Brenda received wages from the electrical business; (5) Brenda gave up her court reporting career to work full-time for the business; (6) Brenda was not paid separately for her work for the business; and (7) Brenda performed integral duties for the business, including paying all bills, managing the business, coordinating employees and equipment, handling the payroll, taking phone calls, and dealing with other important mat-ters. Kevin further claims that the lack of proper written formalities for their electrical business does not negate their original agreement to "start a business and make some money together." . . .

After reviewing the evidence, the trial court found that Brenda was involved with Kevin in the electrical contracting business when it began in 1987. Also, the court noted that "Brenda was substantially and integrally involved in the Von Behren electrical business . . . and shared in the economic results of the business," and concluded that their business relationship was a partnership. Based upon our review of the record, we cannot say that this conclusion was against the manifest weight of the evidence.

Obviously, Kevin and Brenda are not sophisticated business people. While the trial court should consider the absence of written formalities, that is only one factor to consider when determining if a partnership exists. The trial court must review all facts and circumstances surrounding the formation of the busi-ness. In this case, both Kevin and Brenda provided services for the business[], Brenda provided credit for the initial operations of the business, and Kevin con-tributed assets to the business. Also, all the money earned by the business was put into their joint account and used for reinvestment in the businesses or for their personal needs. Accordingly, we conclude that the trial court did not err by finding that Kevin sustained his burden of proving that his businesses were partnerships with Brenda. Consequently, the trial court did not err in according Kevin only half of the income from the two businesses . . . .

> ■ **Think about this:**
>
> *(M)* Should marriage automatically denote partnership if both spouses are involved in a two-person business?
>
> *(N)* What evidence might have convinced the court that a partnership did not exist between Kevin and Brenda?

C. Purported Partners (Formerly Known as "Partners by Estoppel")

A separate issue analogous to the formation of a partnership is the "purported partner" theory of RUPA §308. Section 308 states a rule not unlike the "agency by estoppel" theory of the Restatement (Third) of Agency ("Re(3)") §2.05: Both sections make it possible for a person to bear vicarious liabilities, as a matter of fairness, based on their own negligent or deliberately wrongful actions, even though no partnership or agency relationship actually exists. (For this reason, the concept was actually known as "partnership by estoppel" under UPA §16. RUPA's drafters changed the name of the concept because, strictly speaking, proof of purported partnership differs in some respects from the use of the term "estoppel" in other common law contexts.) Both RUPA §308 and Re(3) §2.05 require some showing that the third party asserting such a theory made some detrimental change in reliance on some representation or wrongdoing of the defendant. However, RUPA §308 is quite a bit more complex than Re(3) §2.05, or at least it is written in a way that is more complex, and the factual scenarios to which it would apply seem likely to be quite different. Agency by estoppel will likely arise only in fairly attenuated, unusual circumstances. For example, an illustration to §2.05 suggests that an estoppel theory could be used against the owner of a furniture store for outright frauds committed by a total stranger on the premises, if he negligently allowed the culprit to pose as an agent or somehow facilitated the ruse. Purported partnership could arise in a wider range of cases, as perusal of §308(a)-(b) should suggest:

SECTION 308. LIABILITY OF PURPORTED PARTNER

(a) If a person, by words or conduct, purports to be a partner, or consents to being represented by another as a partner, in a partnership or with one or more persons not partners, the purported partner is liable to a person to whom the representation is made, if that person, relying on the representation, enters into a transaction with the actual or purported partnership. If the representation, either by the purported partner or by a person with the purported partner's consent, is made in a public manner, the purported partner is liable to a person who relies upon the purported partnership even if the purported partner is not aware of being held out as a partner to the claimant. If partnership liability results, the purported partner is liable with respect to that liability as if the purported partner were a partner. If no partnership liability results, the purported partner is liable with respect to that liability jointly and severally with any other person consenting to the representation.

(b) If a person is thus represented to be a partner in an existing partnership, or with one or more persons not partners, the purported partner is an agent of persons consenting to the representation to bind them to the same extent and in the same manner as if the purported partner were a partner with respect to persons who enter into transactions in reliance upon the representation. If all of the partners of the existing partnership consent to the representation, a partnership act or obligation results. If fewer than all of the partners of the existing partnership consent to the representation, the person acting and the partners consenting to the representation are jointly and severally liable.

The case that follows was decided under the Uniform Partnership Act (1914). UPA §16(1), which is quoted in the case, was worded slightly differently than RUPA §308(a). Would the new language have made any difference to the analysis?

YOUNG V. JONES

United States District Court of South Carolina
816 F. Supp. 1070 (1992), *aff'd sub nom.* Young v. Federal Deposit Insurance Corporation, 103 F.3d 1180 (4th Cir.), *cert. denied*, 522 U.S. 928 (1997)

HAWKINS, Chief Judge . . . .

[This is a suit against both Price Waterhouse, an entity chartered in the Bahamas ("PW-Bahamas"), and Price Waterhouse, a United States partnership doing business in several American states, including South Carolina ("PW-US").]

PW-Bahamas issued an unqualified audit letter regarding the financial statement of Swiss American Fidelity and Insurance Guaranty (SAFIG). Plaintiffs aver that on the basis of that financial statement, they deposited $550,000.00 in a South Carolina bank. Other defendants, not involved in the motions herein, allegedly sent the money from the South Carolina Bank to SAFIG. The financial statement of SAFIG was falsified. The plaintiffs' money and its investment potential has been lost to the plaintiffs and it is for these losses that the plaintiffs seek to recover damages . . . .

[PW-Bahamas, having never had any contact with South Carolina, disputed personal jurisdiction.]

However, plaintiffs assert a unique argument that the contacts of the PW-US partnership should be considered contacts by the PW-Bahamas' firm, because allegedly, the two are either a partnership in fact, or a partnership by estoppel. Accordingly, the court will address the partnership allegations and the evidence submitted on that issue . . . .

Defendants PW-US and PW-Bahamas flatly deny that a partnership exists between the two entities and have supplied, under seal, copies of relevant documents executed which establish that the two entities are separately organized. Counsel for plaintiffs admits that he has found nothing which establishes that the two entities are partners in fact. The evidence presented wholly belies plaintiffs' claims that PW-Bahamas and PW-US are operating as a partnership in fact. Thus, the court finds that there is no partnership, in fact, between PW-Bahamas and PW-US.

Then, plaintiffs make a double-edged argument that PW-US is a partner by estoppel of PW-Bahamas. On the one hand, the argument is that if the two partnerships are partners by estoppel, then the court has personal jurisdiction over PW-Bahamas, as PW-US's partner by estoppel, because PW-US has at least "minimum contacts" with South Carolina. On the other hand, the argument for estoppel seems to be that if the two partnerships are partners by estoppel then PW-US can be held liable for the negligent acts of its partner PW-Bahamas, so the claim against PW-Bahamas operates as a claim against PW-US . . . .

As a general rule, persons who are not partners as to each other are not partners as to third persons. S.C. Code Ann. §33-41-220 (Law. Co-op 1976) [UPA §7(1)]. However, a person who represents himself, or permits another to represent him, to anyone as a partner in an existing partnership or with others not actual partners, is liable to any such person to whom such a representation is made who has, on the faith of the representation, given credit to the actual or apparent partnership. S.C. Code Ann. §33-41-380(1) [UPA §16(1)] . . . .

Plaintiffs maintain that Price Waterhouse holds itself out to be a partnership with offices around the world. According to the plaintiffs, the U.S. affiliate makes no distinction in its advertising between itself and entities situated in foreign jurisdictions. The foreign affiliates are permitted to use the Price Waterhouse name and trademark. Plaintiffs urge the conclusion of partnership by estoppel from the combination of facts that Price Waterhouse promotes its image as an organization affiliated with other Price Waterhouse offices around the world and that it is common knowledge that the accounting firm of Price Waterhouse operates as a partnership.

Plaintiffs offer for illustration that PW-Bahamas and PW-US hold themselves out to be partners with one another, a Price Waterhouse brochure, picked up by plaintiffs' counsel at a litigation services seminar, that describes Price Waterhouse as one of the "world's largest and most respected professional organizations." The brochure states: "[O]ver 28,000 Price Waterhouse professionals in 400 offices throughout the world can be called upon to provide support for your reorganization and litigation efforts." Plaintiffs assert that assurances like that contained in the brochure cast Price Waterhouse as an established international accounting firm and that the image, promoted by PW-US, is designed to gain public confidence in the firm's stability and expertise.

However, the plaintiffs do not contend that the brochure submitted was seen or relied on by them in making the decision to invest. In addition, plaintiffs point to nothing in the brochure that asserts that the affiliated entities of Price

Waterhouse are liable for the acts of another, or that any of the affiliates operate within a single partnership . . . .

PW-US points out that the South Carolina statute, which was cited by plaintiffs in support of their argument for partnership by estoppel, speaks only to the creation of liability to third-persons who, in reliance upon representations as to the existence of a partnership, "[give] credit" to that partnership. There is no evidence, neither has there been an allegation, that credit was extended on the basis of any representation of a partnership existing between PW-Bahamas and the South Carolina members of the PW-US partnership. There is no evidence of any extension of credit to either PW-Bahamas or PW-US, by plaintiffs. Thus, the facts do not support a finding of liability for partners by estoppel under the statutory law of South Carolina.

Further, there is no evidence that plaintiffs relied on any act or statement by any PW-US partner which indicated the existence of a partnership with the Bahamian partnership. Finally, there is no evidence, nor is there a single allegation that any member of the U.S. Partnership had anything to do with the audit letter complained of by plaintiffs, or any other act related to the investment transaction.

The court cannot find any evidence to support a finding of partners by estoppel. Therefore, the allegations of negligence against PW-Bahamas cannot serve to hold individual members of the PW-US partnership in the suit. Without PW-US' contacts with the forum, there are insufficient contacts with South Carolina for PW-Bahamas to reasonably expected to have been haled into court here . . . .

■ **Think about this:**

(O) Would RUPA §308 seem to impose liability in more or fewer cases than UPA §16(1)?

(P) If a person were to make manifestations sufficient to support apparent authority as an agent on behalf of someone who was not his partner, could those manifestations give rise to the creation of a purported partnership?

In closing, let us note a few technical curlicues under RUPA §308. First, notice that under §308(a), slightly different consequences can follow if the representation giving rise to the purported partnership is made publicly or not. Second, §308(b) is a bit confusing.

■ **Think about this:**

(Q) What distinctions are being drawn in RUPA §308, and why?

This may help . . .

Fill in the following chart—liability yes or no?—to make sense of RUPA §308(b).

	Existing Partnership	No Existing Partnership
Person to be charged consented to the representation		
Person to be charged did not consent to the representation		

■ **Think about this:**

(R) Would one partner in an actual existing partnership have either actual or apparent authority to make representations about who is or isn't a partner?

(S) Could there ever be tort liability under RUPA §308?

Test Yourself

Assume Applicability of the Restatement (Third) of Agency and the Revised Uniform Partnership Act

Questions 1-5 rely on the following facts:

Alex and Barb, platonic friends since childhood, have begun a newsletter or "zine" for fans of their local music scene. Though they've kept their day jobs, they spend most of their free time together producing the zine, which they create each week in the garage of the house they rent together. They distribute it for free but earn revenue through sales of advertising, and more often than not break even or even turn a small profit. Their dreams are much bigger, though, and they plan for it eventually to be their sole employment. The zine was initially Alex's idea, and he put the first several issues together by himself in his dorm room while still in college. When he told Barb about it, she asked if she could help, and said, "Just tell me what to do . . . I don't know anything about this kind of stuff, so I'll just do whatever you tell me to do." They then bought some printing equipment to do a more professional job, deciding between themselves to "go halfsies" on the cost. They both worked on the actual production of each issue, made sales of advertising space, and made deliveries of the zine to newsstands, bars, and coffee shops. Alex and Barb don't keep formal books (except for the checkbook of their joint checking account, in which Alex deposits checks from advertising clients, and from which he pays expenses), and they have never written down any sort of agreement between themselves.

Barb's uncle Charlie, a well-heeled retiree, wanted to help Barb and Alex realize their dream, and he made two offers to help the zine. First, Charlie offered to give Barb and Alex the use of $5,000 in cash to cover expenses. When Barb insisted that the offer was too generous, Charlie said, "Hey, don't worry, kid. Pay it back when you can. I'm proud of you." Second, he introduced them to a friend named Paul, who runs a local nightclub. Charlie gave Barb Paul's business card and, to make a long story short, Alex and Barb were able to use Charlie's name as their introduction and land a lucrative advertising contract for the club. As a down payment, Paul sent them a check for $1,500.

For reasons known only to themselves, however, and shortly after striking their deal with Paul, Barb and Alex closed down their business and absconded with Paul's $1,500. Paul sues Charlie, the only viable defendant left to sue.

1. Which of the following suggests that Alex and Barb formed a partnership?

   a. Evidence of sharing profits.
   b. Capital contributions.
   c. Evidence of sharing losses.
   d. All of the above.
   e. Answers b and c are both correct.

2. Suppose that Paul manages to track down Alex and Barb, serves them with process, and joins them as defendants in his case against Charlie. Which of the following would be the most helpful fact for Barb in defending against liability?

   a. The means by which the firm acquired its physical assets.
   b. The means by which the firm acquired its headquarters.
   c. Decision making.
   d. The means by which the firm receives revenues.

3. Which of the following best characterizes Alex and Barb's relationship?

   a. Agency.
   b. Partnership.
   c. Some limited liability entity.
   d. It could be any of the above.
   e. It could be answer a or b.

4. Given the informal manner in which they formed their relationship, what would likely have been the biggest surprise to Alex and Barb about the legal entity that in fact they formed?

a. Alex's exposure to personal liability.
b. Barb's exposure to personal liability.
c. Barb's governance rights.
d. Answers a and c are both correct.
e. Answers b and c are both correct.

5. Paul's claim against Charlie will most likely:

a. Succeed, because of Charlie's manifestations of intent.
b. Succeed, under either the doctrine of *respondeat superior* or some other rule of vicarious liability.
c. Fail, because while vicarious liability could be an appropriate theory, the relevant evidence is likely insufficient here.
d. Fail, because of his relationship with Alex and Barb.

Questions 6-8 stand alone:

6. Because it's well worth your while to learn it before moving on, define a partnership.

7. What are the elements of a purported partnership?

8. Fill in the blanks: Receipt of _____ is presumptive evidence of the existence of a partnership. If, however, it was received as _____, _____, or _____ (there are more than three), no presumption arises.

Finance and the Sharing of Profits and Losses

The statutory default rules on the sharing of partnership profits and losses are not that hard to learn, but they can be very difficult to apply. In part, this is because they sometimes lead to unanticipated consequences that courts view as inequitable. Because of this unpredictability, it probably is best for persons forming partnerships *never* to allow the default rules to govern completely. In the case of inadvertent partnerships, of course, this advice is impossible to follow.

Chapter Outline

A. The Basic Structure of Partnership Finances: Capital Contributions, Profit Sharing, and Partnership Accounting

- The default with respect to profits is an equal shares rule
- The default with respect to losses is that they follow profits

B. The Keeping of Partnership Accounts

1. How It Works
   - The balance in a partner's account equals his or her initial contribution, plus his or her share of any profits historically earned, less his or her share of any losses historically suffered, and less any amount he or she has withdrawn
   - Partners must contribute to losses, including those of the partners' own contributions

2. Drawing Accounts and Capital Calls
   - Withdrawals are by agreement, and often recorded in a sub-account known as a "drawing account"
   - The partners may agree to mechanisms for compelling a partner to make additional contributions during the life of the partnership

3. An Example in Application
   - Courts are inclined to find the partners' financial agreements enforceable

C. The Special Problem of Loss Accounting for Services Only Partners

1. The Majority Rule
   - RUPA §401(j) provides that no partner is entitled to remuneration for services performed for the partnership, and that is the end of the matter

2. The Minority Rule
   - A minority of courts infer an implicit agreement that services only partners will not be responsible for capital losses of capital partners

D. A New "Harmonized" Rule for Capital Losses?

   - RUPA §806 evidently proposes a change in the obligation of partners to contribute toward the loss of one another's capital.

Test Yourself

A. The Basic Structure of Partnership Finances: Capital Contributions, Profit Sharing, and Partnership Accounting

For the most part, the rules of partnership finances are relatively straightforward. In a few respects, however, they can be counterintuitive.

When a partnership is formed, the partners will typically each contribute some cash, equipment, or other property to the business to get things started. It might seem reasonable to expect them to share in the profits of the business according to the proportion of their contributions. You might expect that if Partner A contributes 75 percent of a firm's start-up capital and Partner B puts in 25 percent, then A would get 75 percent of the firm's profits and B would get 25 percent.

But alas, grasshopper, it is not so simple. As a first counterintuitive point, in the statutory law of partnerships the default position is *not* that partners share profits in the same proportion as their capital contributions. Rather, under Revised Uniform Partnership Act (RUPA) §401(a), and subject to any contrary agreement among the partners, "[e]ach partner is entitled to an *equal share of the partnership distributions* and . . . is chargeable with a share of the partnership losses in proportion to the partner's share of the distributions" (emphasis added). In practical terms, this means that unless the partners provide otherwise by agreement, they will share equally in both the profits and losses of the firm regardless of how much capital they contributed when they joined.

A second counterintuitive point also arises from the language of §401. Note that this section, which is the only RUPA provision that directly addresses profit sharing, provides that the partners are each "entitled to . . . share [in] the . . . distributions and [are each] *chargeable* with a share of the . . . losses" (emphasis added). A comment to an earlier version of §401 clarified the significance of the word "chargeable": Partners are "not obligated to contribute to partnership losses before [their] withdrawal or the liquidation of the partnership, unless the partners agree otherwise." Finally, §401(j) provides that "[a] partner is not entitled to remuneration for services performed for the partnership. . . ."

It may not be immediately obvious from this language, but the practical effect of it all together is that, unless they agree otherwise, partners have no right to any proceeds from the firm other than their share of the profits, and they can get their share only after all of the firm's obligations to third parties have been satisfied. As made clear by the RUPA rules governing dissolution of partnerships (discussed in Chapter 9), liabilities to partners need not be fully "satisfied" until the firm is dissolved. This is all to say that *no partner has a default right to receive any money at all from the firm until the partner leaves the firm for good, or the firm is dissolved and its business wound up.* This is confirmed in RUPA §405(b).

Though this all may seem rather odd, the RUPA default rules might—possibly—make sense for some firms. Equal profit sharing and lack of interim payments might make sense where the partners' capital contributions are roughly equal and the partnership is some sort of investment vehicle or side business for the partners, as opposed to their sole occupation. But for many businesses, it will not be appropriate at all. Modifications of these two default rules are probably among the most common of all partnership agreement terms. For example, law firms, accounting firms, medical partnerships, and other professional businesses very commonly provide for differing profit shares to reflect seniority or the amount of business a particular partner brings in, and all kinds of firms provide for periodic profit sharing or other compensation.

Another peculiarity arises from the statutory handling of property that is owned by the partnership, including the cash and other property contributed by the partners as capital contributions. Contributions made to the firm and revenues earned by it are "partnership property" under RUPA §204. Likewise, property bought or otherwise acquired through the use of partnership property is itself presumed to be partnership property under §204(c). Importantly, appreciation in partnership property is itself partnership property. For example, say Partner A contributes a plot of land and the building on it to be used by the firm as office space. If the property appreciates by $5,000 by the time the firm is dissolved, A is not entitled to the $5,000 but rather must divide it with the other partners. Denomination of property as "partnership property" has important consequences and whether or not that denomination applies can sometimes be a little uncertain. See Chapter 8D.

B. The Keeping of Partnership Accounts

1. How It Works

The keeping of formal books in a partnership is not legally required (at least not by partnership law; *see* RUPA §405, comment), and less formal partnerships or those formed by accident may not have any recordkeeping at all. However, most firms of any substance will keep books in some way or other. A common procedure is the keeping of "capital accounts," which are a way to keep track of each partner's financial interest in the firm at any given time. Remember, in the absence of contrary agreement, a partnership will have no obligation to distribute profits or compensation until dissolution. Thus, the changing amounts in the partners' capital accounts over time do not reflect any actual payments of money to anyone. They are just a way of keeping track of the partners' changing financial rights and responsibilities at any given time. Conveniently, thinking about capital accounts will help us see the financial rules discussed above in operation.

The following is a simplified example of how the ongoing keeping of capital accounts might look in one very simple partnership, over a period of a few years.

(a) Accounts Upon Formation

Suppose that Sally and Bob establish a business together. They get things started only with a spit-and-a-handshake, believing they don't need a contract on paper or any other legal mumbo jumbo, since they are good friends. They agree orally that it will be "all for one and one for all," and that they will make their decisions together, equally.

Sally and Bob found their firm on January 1, 2019. On that day, they capitalize their business with Sally investing $60 and Bob investing $40. Thus, at this point, the firm has $100 in total assets. Let's also assume that the partnership has no other assets of any kind.

Thus, on January 1, 2019, the simplest form of the Sally-Bob partnership's capital accounts would look like this:

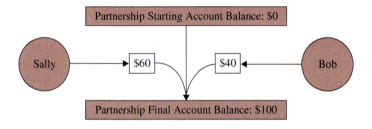

Sally-Bob Partnership Capital Account
January 1, 2019

Sally	Bob
$60	$40

(b) After a Profitable Year

In 2019, the partnership made some money. Specifically, the partnership earned $100 in total revenues. (Remember, "revenue" is a technical term meaning the total amount of money brought into a firm, regardless of any expenses or liabilities. "Profit," on the other hand, means revenue minus expenses.) The firm's total expenses for the year were $50. In other words, $100 in *revenue* minus $50 in *expenses* equals a total *profit* of $50 for the Sally-Bob firm.

Thus, on January 1, 2020, the partnership's capital account would be modified like this:

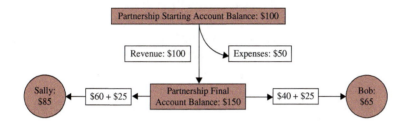

Sally-Bob Partnership Capital Account
January 1, 2020

Sally	Bob
$60 + $25	$40 + $25
(half the total profits) = $85	(half the total profits) = $65

(c) Treatment of Partnership Property and Losses

Next, let's say that the Sally-Bob firm lost money in 2020. Its total revenues again were $100, but its expenses were $150 (a loss of $50). However, let's also say that Sally contributed property with a fair market value of $100 to the firm. (Let's not worry about what the property is, or about the several technical issues that might arise concerning how its value should be properly recorded.)

Thus, on January 1, 2021, the partnership's capital account would be modified like this:

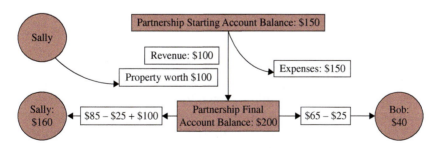

Sally-Bob Partnership Capital Account
January 1, 2021

Sally	Bob
$85 − $25 = $60 + $100 = $160	$65 − $25 = $40

(d) Upon Dissolution and Winding Up

Finally, by the end of 2021, Sally and Bob have decided that their run of luck has been so bad that they should just close their business down. (As we shall learn later, Sally and Bob will have to do what is known as a "dissolution" and a "winding up." "Dissolution" is the formal end of the partnership, following which a few different things can happen. The partners might agree to really end the business and sell its assets, but the dissolution itself is not necessarily the end of the business. It is simply the end of the partnership as it has existed, and the surviving members of the business can agree to continue it if they want. On the other hand, "winding up" means actually selling off the assets, paying off the creditors, and distributing anything that remains to the partners.)

Let's say that Sally and Bob decide during the year 2021 to dissolve their partnership and wind up the business, and that the winding up will be effective on January 1, 2022. Assume that during the year 2021 the firm exactly broke even—its total revenues were $100 and total expenses were $100. Let's also say that the firm was able to sell the item of property that Sally donated for $120 (a profit of $20).

Thus, on January 1, 2022, the partnership's capital account would be modified like this:

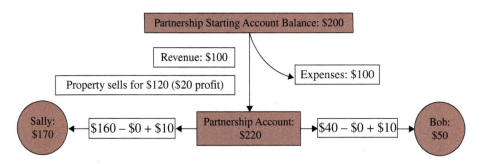

Sally-Bob Partnership Capital Account
January 1, 2022

Sally	Bob
$160 – $0 = $160 + $10 = $170	$40 – $0 = $40 + $10 = $50

(e) Accounting for "Capital" Losses

Sometimes a partnership loses so much money over its lifetime that its value on dissolution is less than the sum of the initial contributions. In that case, the partners must forfeit some of their initial capital to fully compensate their creditors. Partners in this position are said to have suffered a "capital loss." The handling of capital losses can be slightly more confusing, but exactly the same rules apply in this situation as in any other. Under the statutory default rule, partners always share profits and losses equally. Whatever the losses are at the end of the day, even if they are large enough to consume some capital, the partners must still share in them equally. This default rule applies regardless of how much each partner initially contributed, and even if it results in some of the partners owing money to the other partners.

To put some flesh on those bones, let's again consider the case of the Sally-Bob partnership, but change the facts a little bit. Recall that in the beginning, Sally put in $60 as capital and Bob put in $40. Upon formation, on January 1, 2019, their capital accounts looked like this:

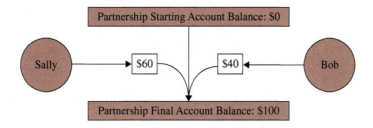

Sally-Bob Partnership Capital Account
January 1, 2019

Sally	Bob
$60	$40

But let's assume that during the year 2019, their fortunes were terrible. They earned $100 in revenue, but they incurred $150 in expenses. Things went so poorly, in fact, that Sally and Bob decided to just call it quits. On New Year's Day 2020, they dissolve, pay off the creditors, and return what's left of their initial capital to themselves. Thus, upon dissolution on January 1, 2020, their books look like this:

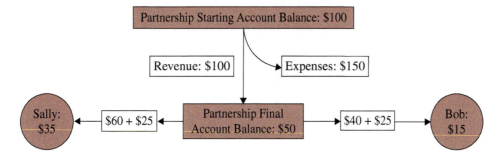

Sally-Bob Partnership Capital Account
January 1, 2020

Sally	Bob
$60 – $25 = $35	$40 – $25 = $15

Of course, it's possible that partners could lose even more money, and it's possible that they could wind up actually *owing* money. In this case, they might not only have to forfeit initial capital, but one or more of them might have to contribute additional money from their own pockets to compensate for the firm's losses. For example, let's say again that during the year 2019, the Sally-Bob partnership had revenues of $100, but in this hypothetical incurred expenses of $200. Again, they decide to dissolve at the end of the year. In that case, on January 1, 2020, the books would look like this:

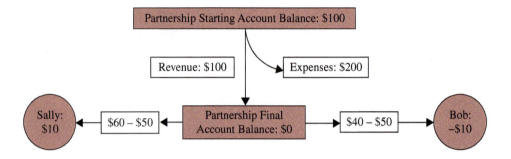

Sally-Bob Partnership Capital Account
January 1, 2020

Sally	Bob
$60 – $50 = $10	$40 – $50 = (-$10)

So Bob is in the hole. And to whom does his $10 go? In effect, it goes to Sally. It is possible—indeed, common—that a capital loss is so large that one or more of the partners' capital contributions is not only completely wiped out, but, under generally prevailing law, they must actually come up with their own money to pay other partners for their losses. A proposed change in this scheme is discussed below.

Doing the Numbers: What the Books Might Really Look Like

While we hope this exercise was useful, it is artificial. In the accounting used by most firms, the "capital account" appears only as one entry on a firm's "balance sheet." To give a flavor for how a balance sheet might look, suppose that at the firm's founding Sally and Bob made the capital contributions as indicated above. They then used $20 in cash to purchase inventory, and also purchased $30 of equipment on credit. If those are their only transactions in their first month of operation, their balance sheet would look like this at the end of the month:

Sally-Bob Partnership Balance Sheet
January 31, 2019

Assets		Liabilities	
Cash:	$ 80	Debt for Equipment:	$ 30
Inventory:	20	**Owner Equity**	
		Partner Capital	
Equipment:	30	Sally:	60
		Bob:	40
		Total Equity	$100
Total Assets	$130	Total Equity and Liabilities	$130

This financial statement is called a "balance" sheet because it literally balances the firm's assets and liabilities. The number on the bottom left (the total value of the firm's assets) will always equal the number on the bottom of the right (the owners' equity and the total outstanding liability owed to third parties). In preparing a balance sheet, one considers the firm to be an entity separate from its owners (even if it is a sole proprietorship). Accordingly, the partnership's owners are treated as persons who have enforceable claims against the firm's assets. This way, the left side of the balance sheet totals up all the firm's historical expenditures for items having continuing value. The right side shows exactly who has a legal claim to every cent of it (assuming such items as inventory and equipment will be sold at the amount paid for them, which they probably won't). There is more on the subject of balance sheets and other financial statements in the online Supplement.

■ **Think about this:**

(A) Petrus, Bill, and Jamil form a general partnership to purchase a commercial building for $100,000. Petrus and Bill each contribute $25,000; Jamil provides the rest. They do not bother to specify any agreement with respect to the sharing of profit and loss. At the end of year one, the PB&J partnership has earned $30,000 over and above its expenses for that year. What will the capital accounts look like?

(B) Suppose that the PB&J partnership loses $15,000 in year two. What will the capital accounts look like then?

(C) Return to the time the PB&J partnership is formed. On day one it purchases the building for $100,000 but fails to insure it. On day two, a fire destroys the building, leaving PB&J holding land worth $10,000. Who owes what, and to whom?

2. Drawing Accounts and Capital Calls

A few other partnership finance concepts are worthy of explanation. One is the "drawing account" and the other is the "capital call."

A "drawing account" is used when the partners have agreed to permit themselves to make withdrawals from their own capital accounts. (RUPA §405(b) makes it clear that partners do not have a right unilaterally to make withdrawals.) At the end of the year, the total in the drawing account simply is subtracted from the partner's capital account. It is, properly speaking, a type of capital account, but it always has a balance that is understood to be negative. In other words, it is better understood as something the partner has withdrawn rather than something he or she is entitled to receive in the future.

Connections: Corporate Distributions

Shareholders of corporations, like partners, cannot simply dip into the till as the spirit moves them. Although partners can make agreements about distributions, distributions to shareholders can be made only if they are authorized by the board of directors, subject to the rule that distributions cannot be made that would render the corporation insolvent. There is more about this subject in Chapter 15.

A "capital call" is a call by the partnership for the partners to make additional capital contributions. Most firms go through rough patches financially. In particular, there will be times when a firm in difficulty is unable to secure outside financing or finds the cost of available financing too high. For this reason, partnership agreements commonly include provisions requiring additional financial contributions from the partners. They typically provide that the call can be made by a majority vote of the partnership or by an executive committee of the partners. Not surprisingly, partners sometimes resist, especially if in their judgment additional capital contributions would just throw good money after bad. Therefore, a common feature in capital call provisions is some means by which partners can avoid actually paying the call if they wish. Typically, the agreement will provide that if a partner elects to refuse the capital call, it will be taken as his offer to sell his interest to the remaining partners, according to some pre-specified valuation formula, and it may also be taken as his resignation from the firm. Another common variation is that a partner may elect to have his initial capital contribution reduced by the amount of the capital call. Provisions like these make sense prospectively at the time of drafting of the partnership agreement, since none of the partners can be certain how well the business will do or when its tough times might come.

No portion of the RUPA explicitly authorizes demands for capital contribution following initial formation. Indeed, it seems likely that in the absence of an explicit agreement such a demand by less than all the partners would constitute an "act outside the ordinary course of business" and would be ineffective without unanimous vote. *See* RUPA §401(k). Clearly, however, no RUPA provision prohibits explicit capital call provisions, and they are common.

> ### ■ Think about this:
>
> *(D)* Ali and Mo start the year with $50,000 each in their capital accounts. Of that amount, $45,000 is contributed capital and $5,000 represents past profits. How much may either withdraw without the other's agreement?

3. An Example in Application

When it comes to partnership financial rights, it is often the case that the rubber hits the road only in the event of litigation. On a day-to-day basis, the partners might not actually know how their own ownership in the firm should be valued. They may not be able to know with any certainty until one of them leaves the firm or it is dissolved permanently, and even then there is often uncertainty that only a court can resolve. In general, when courts are called upon to decide these matters, they try to do the partners equity. That is, where they can, the courts will try to give each partner some reasonable estimate of the "true" value of his or her interest. However, when it comes to matters of partnership law, most courts have also proven themselves great believers in the freedom of contract. They will not rewrite partnership agreements that happen, through inadvertent or deliberately assumed risk, to disappoint a partner on dissolution or retirement. And since valuation formulas and buyout terms must be among the most frequent subjects of explicitly negotiated language, the risks are significant and lawsuits over them are frequent. Lawyers do well to heed the following advice: "It would be inequitable to require a partner to sell his interest in a partnership for a price which does not reflect its true value *unless it is clear that the partner explicitly agreed to do so*." Anderson v. Wadena Silo Co., 246 N.W.2d 45, 48 (Minn. 1976) (emphasis added).

The next case is a nice practical example of how these matters are handled, and the problems that can arise.

G&S INVESTMENTS V. BELMAN

Arizona Court of Appeals
700 P.2d 1358 (1985)

Howard, Judge.

[Decedent Thomas Nordale was one of two general partners in a limited partnership called Century Park, Ltd., which was formed to own an apartment complex. The other general partner was itself a partnership called G&S Investments. Nordale owned 25.5 percent of the firm, G&S owned 51 percent, and the remaining 33.5 percent was held by two limited partners. Trouble arose in 1979, as Nordale went through a divorce, developed a drug addiction, and began acting in ways that disrupted Century Park's business. G&S sought and a court granted judicial dissolution of Century Park so that G&S could purchase Nordale's interest and exclude him from the business. The court entered that order under the Arizona equivalent of RUPA §601(5), which authorizes judicial dissolution when a partner has persistently breached the partnership agreement or otherwise engages in conduct seriously disrupting the firm's business. While that suit was pending, Nordale died.]

. . . [Thereafter, G&S] filed a supplemental complaint invoking their right to continue the partnership and acquire Nordale's interest under article 19 of the partnership's Articles of Limited Partnership[,] . . . [which] contains the following buy-out provision:

> "The amount shall be calculated as follows:
>
> By the addition of the sums of the amount of the resigning or retiring general partner's *capital account*

Connections: Limited Partnerships

The partnership in *G&S Investments* was a limited partnership. A limited partnership has one or more general partners and one or more limited partners. General partners essentially have the rights and obligations of partners in general partnerships—so cases involving disputes among them are good authority for general partnerships, and vice versa. Limited partners generally have both limited liability (no responsibility for partnership obligations) and a limited ability to participate in management. There is more on this subject in Chapter 10.

plus an amount equal to the average of the prior three years' profits and gains actually paid to the general partner, or as agreed upon by the general partners, provided said agreed sum does not exceed the calculated sum in dollars." (Emphasis added).

[In the ensuing litigation, the trial court determined that G&S had the right to continue the business, and that it owed Nordale's estate $4,867.57 as the buyout price.]

Appellant [that is, Nordale's estate] claims that the term "capital account" in article 19(e)(2)(i) is ambiguous. The estate relies on the testimony of an accountant, Jon Young, that the term "capital account" is ambiguous merely because there is no definition of the term in the articles. He claimed that it was not clear whether the cost basis or the fair market value of the partnership's assets should be used in determining the capital account. Even on direct examination, however, Young admitted that read literally the buy-out formula takes the capital account of the deceased partner and adds to that amount the average of the prior three years' earnings. On cross-examination he admitted that generally accepted accounting principles require the partnership capital accounts be maintained on a cost basis and that he has never seen a partnership in which the capital accounts in the books and records were based on the fair market value. He also admitted that his interpretation was contrary to the literal import of the words used in the agreement and that the words used were not ambiguous and that he had no knowledge of the actual intent of the parties. The sole reason given by Young for his opinion that "capital account" should not be interpreted in accordance with its literal meaning and with generally accepted accounting principles was that he himself had never seen a buy-out provision for real property based on a cost basis of the assets.

In contrast, Gibson and Smith [the two partners who made up G&S] testified that the parties actually intended and understood "capital account" to mean exactly what it literally says, the account which shows a partner's capital contribution to the partnership plus profits minus losses. Smith, an accountant, further testified that while there is a relationship between the capital accounts and valuation of the partnership assets, the valuation of the assets does not affect the actual entries made on the capital account.

There was no dispute that Nordale's capital account showed a negative balance of $44,510.09, which the court found to be a fact and concluded that the purchase price of Nordale's interest should be calculated in accordance with article 19(e)(2), the capital account, and that his interest in the partnership was zero, instead of the fair market value of his interest in the partnership which would have amounted to the sum of $76,714.24.

Appellant contends that the conclusions of the trial court were erroneous, that fair market value should have been used instead of the balance in the capital account and that, even then, the fair market value which the court found was far in excess of the $76,714.24. We disagree with appellant and agree with the trial court's conclusions.

> ✉️ *Dear Prof.: I've heard of "historical cost" accounting.*
> *Is that what's going on here?*
>
> Correct. A major issue in *G&S Investments* was the use of "cost basis" or "historical cost" in accounting, which simply means that in keeping the books one records the value of an asset as the purchase price that was paid for it, subject to a rate of depreciation specified in prevailing accounting rules. Over time this number might diverge from the asset's fair market value (as it would, to the regret of Nordale's estate, in *G&S Investments*).

In most countries, prevailing accounting rules are promulgated by some government or expert body. In the United States they have long been set by a private body, the Financial Accounting Standards Board (FASB). The Securities and Exchange Commission requires that the financial statements filed with it be prepared in accordance with FASB standards—known as "generally accepted accounting principles" or "GAAP."

The words "capital account" are not ambiguous and clearly mean the partner's capital account as it appears on the books of the partnership. Our conclusion is further buttressed by the entire language of article 19(e)(2)(i) which requires, for a buy-out, the payment of the amount of the partner's capital account plus other sums. This is "capital account" language and not "fair market value" language. Appellant relies on the case of Mahan v. Mahan, 107 Ariz. 517, 489 P.2d 1197 (1971) for its position that even if the partnership agreement did require the buy-out on the basis of the capital account, because of the disproportion between the capital account and the fair market value of the property, equity mandates the use of the fair market value. We find that *Mahan v. Mahan, supra,* is not on point and, unfortunately, in dictum, misstates the law. *Mahan* involved the dissolution and liquidation of a partnership, not the enforcement of a buy-sell agreement. . . . [T]he *Mahan* partnership was not continued after the death of one of the partners. In a suit by the widow of the deceased partner the trial court ruled that his estate was entitled to receive only a proportional share of the book value of the partnership's assets. The supreme court reversed, holding that "book value" is used only in ascertaining the respective shares when there is an explicit contractual provision to that effect and "[h]ere there was no contractual provision mandating the use of book value."

Although it was unnecessary for the court to go any further in deciding the case, it went on to state that a contractual provision mandating the use of book value "is not used where the facts of the case make it inequitable to do so" and that such a provision would have been inequitable because the book values of the assets were disproportionate to actual values.

. . . [T]he dictum in *Mahan* misstates the law. . . . "Where the agreement stipulates that for purposes of assessing the purchase price of a partner's share by his survivors or associates the book value of such share shall be used, the courts have denied contentions for purchase prices based on real values." 60 Am. Jur. 2d Partnership §254, p. 159 (1972). . . .

Because partnerships result from contract, the rights and liabilities of the partners among themselves are subject to such agreements as they may make.

Partnership buy-out agreements are valid and binding although the purchase price agreed upon is less or more than the actual value of the interest at the time of death. Gabay v. Rosenberg, 287 N.Y.S.2d 451 (1968) (upholding a nominal purchase price of $100 where the partnership owned two parcels of improved land); In re Randall's Estate, 188 P.2d 71 (Wash. 1947) (upholding a purchase price less than one-fourth of the value of the decedent's interest).

Buy-out agreements are enforceable even when they provide that the decedent's interest shall pass to the survivors without any payment. Hale v. Wilmarth, 174 N.E. 232 (Mass. 1931) (in which the decedent held a one-fourth interest in a partnership that owned a jewelry factory); Balafas v. Balafas, 117 N.W.2d 20 (Minn. 1962) (in which the decedent had a one-half interest in a partnership that owned $700,000 worth of securities). The rationale of the cases enforcing such agreements is stated in Pailthorpe v. Tallman, 72 N.Y.S.2d 784 (1947):

> "[T]he question is not whether the executors of the Mass estate received the full net value of the interest of Mass in the partnership business as of the date of his death, but rather, did they receive for such interest the *amount contemplated* by the partners in their agreement. . . . An agreement by partners as to any matter relating to their partnership is completely controlling between them." (Emphasis in original.)

The law in Arizona is that a valid contract must be given full force and effect even if its enforcement is harsh. It is not within the power of this court to revise, modify, alter, extend or remake a contract to include terms not agreed upon by the parties.

We do not have the power to rewrite article 19 based upon subjective notions of fairness arising long after the agreement was made or because the agreement did not turn out to be an advantageous one. Modern business practice mandates that the parties be bound by the contract they enter into, absent fraud or duress. It is not the province of this court to act as a post-transaction guardian for either party. . . .

■ **Think about this:**

(E) Does the outcome in *G&S Investments* surprise you, or does it really seem like a straightforward application of contract law? (Incidentally, in case you are worrying about the introduction of parol evidence on the meaning of "capital account," Arizona has an extremely liberal approach to admission of such evidence.)

(F) Elsewhere in this book you will find substantial coverage of the partners' fiduciary duties with respect to all matters relating to the

operation and dissolution of a partnership. Was the conduct of Nordale's partners in any way unfair?

(G) This book also has in-depth coverage of the dissolution and winding up of partnerships, as well as "dissociation" (the departure of one or more partners at a time the partnership is not dissolving). The partners may, of course, agree what the appropriate buyout price is (as they did in *G&S Investments*). What would you predict would be the default in the event of failure of the partners to agree—"book" or "fair" value?

JD/MBA: Accounting and the Problem of Value

No one in *G&S Investments v. Belman*, including the trial and appellate courts, actually thought the assets of the Century Park business had no value. On the contrary, the assets, consisting mainly of an apartment building, apparently had a significant positive value, and the business appears to have been operating well into the black. The courts found the fair market value of the business to be in excess of $300,000 (since Nordale's 25.5 percent of it was $76,714.24 we solve for x in $76,714.24 = 25.5%x). The firm must also have had operating profits, because the trial court awarded Nordale's estate $4,867.57 even though his share of the "book value" of the building was ($44,510.09) and his capital account was valued at "zero." Thus, his estate left the courthouse with only a small fraction of the firm's real value.

How could that be?

The result reflects a basic problem that accountants face all the time. The value of any non–publicly traded firm is a matter of speculation until it goes up for sale and someone actually buys it. At least in principle, accounting rules are designed to play this speculation game conservatively. It is better at the end of the day to underestimate a firm's value, since then if you are surprised it is usually good news. And so, according to ordinary accounting practice, partnership assets are accounted for at their purchase price minus an assumed amount of annual depreciation and other costs, even though their real value may have actually appreciated. And, as the *G&S Investments* court observed, in the absence of contrary indication in a partnership agreement, courts generally will construe partnership accounting terms according to their commonly accepted meaning among accountants. Therefore, the "capital account" reflected in the Century Park agreement would be calculated according to ordinary accounting conventions. And accountants would recognize the building at its purchase price less assumed depreciation over time, even though as a matter of fact the fair market value of the building was going up.

C. The Special Problem of Loss Accounting for Services Only Partners

Partnership law does not require that all partners contribute cash or other property to the partnership. In fact, RUPA §402(c) provides that one can become a partner without contributing anything whatsoever. It is not uncommon that one or more partners will join a firm without making any contribution of cash or other property, but with the understanding that those partners will contribute greater amounts of labor to the firm than those investing cash or property. Default partnership rules for profit and loss sharing sometimes can pose a harsh consequence for services only partners: If the firm has suffered such losses at the time of dissolution that even some of the original capital is consumed, most jurisdictions require the services only partner to contribute cash to share in the other partners' loss of capital.

1. The Majority Rule

Under the fairly clear language of RUPA §401(a), in the absence of contrary agreement, services only partners should bear losses equally with other partners. In cases in which there is a capital loss, the result can be that services only partners will have to come up with money from their own pockets to bail out their partners. Accordingly, cases can arise in which services only partners not only lose the entire value of the time and services they devoted, but also have to pay substantial funds to other partners to share in their capital losses. This is so even though those other partners may already have recovered some substantial part of their capital contributions from the firm's remaining assets. The language of §401 would seem to compel this result, unless it is presumed that the parties to every partnership agreement intend some different result.

For example, it might be presumed that the parties intend the services only partner's services to be treated as capital, or that they each intend to bear the entire risk of their own capital loss (in which case the services only partner's risk of capital loss would be $0). But as many courts have noted, such a presumption seems at odds with the rule of §401(j) that no partner is entitled to remuneration "for services performed for the partnership." Such a presumption could also result in the arguably odd consequence that in cases in which the firm does not do well, the capital partner must not only absorb his own capital loss, but must also pay the services partner. That is, the presumption would seem to require that in capital-loss cases, the contribution of a services partner would have to be valued in some way, and it might exceed the money contributed by a capital partner. In that case, the capital partner might lose all of his money and then some, to share in the services partner's loss.

It is important to note, of course, that all of these difficulties can be fairly easily avoided by the parties by agreement, since §401 is only a default rule. That fact in itself has given many courts even more confidence in the strict reading of statutory language. Thus, most jurisdictions hold that where losses of initial capital are suffered on dissolution, a services only partner is required to contribute cash to share in the capital loss.

The majority rule is nicely explained in the frequently cited case of *Richert v. Handly*, set out below. Before you read the case, note the following facts fleshed out in earlier stages of the litigation. Plaintiff Richert and defendant Handly had formed a partnership in which Richert would pay for the timber contained on a plot of forested land, Handly would log the forest, and the two would share the profits. Richert advanced $26,842.00 for the timber and incidentals. At the end of the day, the partnership had only $17,016.88 and Richert still wanted return of his $26,842.00.

It appears that Handly was also in charge of handling the business affairs of the venture, and for whatever reason he gave Richert $10,000 out of the venture's remaining funds and handed himself $7,016.88. Richert, of course, sued. Under UPA §18(a) (which is similar for this purpose to RUPA §401(a)), partners share "losses" according to their share in the profits, and in default partnership profit is shared equally. So what was the "loss" in this case and how was it to be shared?

RICHERT V. HANDLY

Supreme Court of Washington
330 P.2d 1079 (1958)

HUNTER, J.

This is an action for an accounting and dissolution of a logging partnership. . . .

[The trial court found that the parties had agreed to share profits equally and also found:]

XII. The parties did not agree upon or specify the basis upon which losses were to be shared, nor whether the claims of one partner were to take priority over the claims of the other.

XIII. Richert [appellant] contributed a total of $26,842 for cost of timber and incidental advancements. Handly [respondent husband] used his own equipment to haul logs, as agreed by the parties, and was paid $8,673.84 for this service. Handly used his own tractor, as agreed by the parties, and was paid $9,240 for this service. There was no agreement that Handly was to be compensated for his services, in addition to his share in the profits, if any (and except for the equipment and tractor services as last hereinbefore stated), and the accounting between the parties does not disclose any such compensation.

XIV. The gross receipts from the sale of logs were $41,629.83. The disbursements were hauling (as per Finding XIII), $8,673.84; falling and bucking, $3,474.21; tractor (as per Finding XIII), $9,240.00; payroll and taxes, $4,786.56; cruising, $35.00; right of way, $200.00; commission, $500.00; paid to Richert, $10,000.00; withdrawn by Handly, $7,016.88; Total, $43,926.49.

XV. There was no agreement of the parties as to how a loss of the capital contributed by Richert in the amount of $26,842.00 was to be borne, and accordingly it cannot be determined the amount due each on the basis of their agreement. . . .

On the basis of such findings, the court concluded neither party was entitled to judgment against the other, [and] that the complaint should be dismissed. . . .

Mr. Richert has again appealed to this court from the judgment entered.

Since the trial court found that the parties had not agreed upon or specified the basis upon which losses were to be shared, or whether the claims of one partner were to take priority over the claims of the other, the provisions of the uniform partnership act are controlling. RCW 25.04.180 [UPA §18] provides:

The rights and duties of the partners in relation to the partnership shall be determined, subject to any agreement between them, by the following rules:

(1) Each partner shall be repaid his contributions, whether by way of capital or advances to the partnership property and share equally in the profits and surplus remaining after all liabilities, including those to partners, are satisfied; and must contribute toward the losses, whether of capital or otherwise, sustained by the partnership according to his share in the profits. . . .

(6) No partner is entitled to remuneration for acting in the partnership business, except that a surviving partner is entitled to reasonable compensation for his services in winding up the partnership affairs. . . .

Therefore, applying the statute to the additional facts found by the trial court, to which no error was assigned, we find the following account established:

Capital Contribution:	
Appellant Richert	$26,842.00
Respondent Handly	None
Gross Receipts From Sale of Timber	41,629.83
Expenses:	
Tractor	9,240.00
Hauling	8,673.84
Falling & Bucking	3,474.21
Payroll & Taxes	4,786.56

Cruising	35.00
Right of Way	200.00
Commission	500.00
	$26,909.61
Gross Receipts	$41,629.83
Less Expenses	26,909.61
Net Receipts	$14,720.22
Appellant's Capital Contribution	26,842.00
Less Net Receipts	14,720.22
Net Loss	$12,121.78
Appellant has received $10,000 from the venture leaving a balance due on his Capital Contribution of	$16,842.00
Less 1/2 of net loss ($12,121.78)	6,060.89
Amount respondent must reimburse appellant for loss resulting from logging venture	$10,781.11

It follows that the judgment of the trial court is incorrect, as a matter of law, under the facts found. Therefore, the judgment is reversed, and the cause remanded with directions to enter judgment in favor of the appellant in accordance with the views expressed herein.

■ **Think about this:**

(H) If this outcome was a risk that Handly actually contemplated, what might his motivation be for entering the agreement?

2. The Minority Rule

Still, some courts have sought to shield services only partners from this risk. *Kessler v. Antinora*, which follows, is a leading case on point, as is the California Supreme Court decision in *Kovacic v. Reed*, discussed at some length in the *Kessler* opinion. In any case, the comments to RUPA §401 explicitly reject the rule of *Kovacic*.

KESSLER V. ANTINORA

New Jersey Court of Appeals
653 A.2d 579 (1995)

KING, P.J.A.D.

. . . On April 15, 1987 Kessler and Antinora executed a seven-page written agreement titled "JOINT VENTURE PARTNERSHIP AGREEMENT." The

JD/MBA: Prime

"Prime" generally refers to the interest rate quoted by a bank as being the rate charged to its most creditworthy customers (although in some instances, even better deals may be available). It is adjusted according to market conditions and frequently is used as a benchmark for interest charged in other, non-bank transactions. For purposes of clarity, it would be a better idea to identify which bank's prime is the intended benchmark.

agreement contemplated a single venture: buying a lot in Wayne and building and selling a residence on it. Under the agreement Kessler agreed to "provide all necessary funds to purchase land and construct a one-family dwelling and disburse all funds to pay bills." Antinora agreed to "actually construct the dwelling and be the general contractor of the job."

The agreement provided for distribution of the proceeds of the venture:

> 9. Distribution. . . . Upon sale of [the house], and after deducting all monies expended by Robert Kessler plus insterest [sic] at prime plus one point and/or including interest or any funds borrowed for the project, not to exceed prime plus one point, engineering fees, architectural fees, legal fees, broker fees, if any, and any other costs connected with the project, the parties, Robert Kessler and Richard Antinora, shall divide the net profits as follows: . . .

Robert Kessler—sixty (60%) percent
Richard Antinora—forty (40%) percent

The agreement was silent about losses. There was no provision to compensate Antinora for any services other than the 40% profit clause.

Both parties complied with the agreement. Kessler provided the funds; Antinora supervised and delivered the finished house. This took over three years. Meanwhile, the real estate market soured. The house sold on September 1, 1991 for $420,000. The cost incurred in building and selling the house was $498,917.

Kessler was repaid all but $78,917 of the money he advanced pursuant to the contract. He also claimed unreimbursed interest of $85,440 for his self-characterized "loan" to the partnership. This claim for interest is disputed as to amount. Kessler thus claimed a total loss of $164,357. He sought and obtained his summary judgment in the Law Division for 40% of this amount, or $65,742.80. No amount was presented on the value of Antinora's services over the three-year period as general contractor.

Antinora contended that . . . both parties risked and lost their unrecovered contributions—Kessler's money and Antinora's labor. The Law Division judge disagreed and found[,] . . . [under New Jersey's adoption of UPA §18(a), which in substance is largely similar to RUPA §401(a)] that Antinora was liable for 40% of Kessler's monetary losses and inferentially rejected any recognition of Antinora's "in kind" loss. [We reverse.]

. . . We find the agreement controlling over the statute. The agreement said that upon sale of the house "and after deducting all monies expended by Robert Kessler plus interest," fees, and other costs the "parties [Kessler and Antinora] shall divide net profits" 60% and 40%. We conclude that the agreement evinced a clear intent that Kessler would be repaid his investment from the sale of the house only, not by Antinora. There is no suggestion in the agreement that any of Kessler's risked and lost money would be repaid in part by Antinora. Nor is there any suggestion that Antinora's risked labor would be repaid in part by Kessler.

We find particularly persuasive the reasoning of the California Supreme Court in Kovacik v. Reed, 315 P.2d 314 (1957). There the parties orally agreed to participate in a kitchen remodeling venture for Sears Roebuck & Company. Kovacik agreed to invest $10,000 in the venture and Reed agreed to become the job estimator and supervisor. They agreed to share the profits on a 50-50 basis. Possible losses were not discussed. Despite their efforts, the venture was unsuccessful and Kovacik sued Reed to recover one-half the money losses he endured. Kovacik prevailed in the trial court and recovered $4,340, or one-half the net monetary loss of $8,680.

The California Supreme Court acknowledged the general rule of partnership law that in the absence of an agreement, "the law presumes that partners and joint adventurers intended to participate equally in the profits and losses of the common enterprise, irrespective of any inequality in the amounts each contributed to the capital employed in the venture, with the losses being shared by them in the same proportions as they share the profits."

The California court then observed that this "general rule" did not obtain where one party contributed the money and the other the labor, stating:

> However, it appears that in the cases in which the above stated general rule has been applied, each of the parties had contributed capital consisting of either money or land or other tangible property, or else was to receive compensation for services rendered to the common undertaking which was to be paid before computation of the profits or losses. Where, however, as in the present case, one partner or joint adventurer contributes the money capital as against the other's skill and labor, all the cases cited, and which our research has discovered, hold that neither party is liable to the other for contribution for any loss sustained. Thus, upon loss of the money the party who contributed it is not entitled to recover any part of it from the party who contributed only services.

The rationale which the California decision and the earlier cited cases adopted was where one party contributes money and the other services, in the event of a loss, each loses his own capital—one in the form of money, the other in labor. A corollary view was that the parties have implicitly agreed, by their conduct and contract, to share profits and that their contributions of money and sweat equity have been valued in an equal ratio. Thus, upon the loss of both some money and labor, the loss falls upon each proportionately without any legal recourse. Thus, Kovacik lost $8,680 of his $10,000 while Reed lost all of his labor.

Likewise, in the case before us, Kessler lost some of his money—$65,472, plus disputed interest, but Antinora lost all of the value of his labor on the three-year project. . . .

While the text refers to the result in this case as the "minority" rule, remember that around one out of eight U.S. residents lives in California.

■ **Think about this:**

(I) What would you expect you would need to show a trial court to convince it there was an agreement to value services as a capital contribution?

(J) Would you say that *Kessler* presented stronger or weaker facts than *Kovacic* for a finding that the parties had agreed to value services as a capital contribution?

JD/MBA: Service Partner Contracting and the Mind-Reading Problem of Default Rules

The service partner problem is really a problem of drafting default rules. Default rules should be designed for those firms most likely to use them,* likely meaning the simplest, least formal ones. Ideally, we'd choose the rules that their members would negotiate for themselves. With service partners, it can be hard to generalize how they would provide for business failure. The problem is the range of factual scenarios—and the possible exposures to risk—they might face.**

To think about this, we might work through the different ways that a person with money and a person willing to work could cooperate to make an investment bear fruit. Imagine that Alonda, a small-town investor, would like to put up $50,000 to open a clothing store on Main Street. Brynn is an accomplished retail manager, and she's willing to run the place.

To simplify things, assume that limited liability is not an option. Alonda and Brynn would still have some options. Alonda could loan Brynn $50,000, and Brynn could open the store and make a go of it. In that case, Brynn would effectively take all the risk. She would have to repay Alonda's principal and interest, whether the business earns money or not. She might agree to that because, if the business does well, she would also get to keep the profits over and above the debt obligation and other costs. On the other hand, Alonda might invest her $50,000 into the business herself, hiring Brynn to run the place as her agent. That would effectively be the mirror image of the first arrangement, because Alonda would take the risk and keep the upside.

Then again, the parties could choose an option effectively between those two extremes. Alonda could invest her cash, Brynn could contribute her labor, and they could share the profits. That obviously is the typical service-partner

---

* Or so it is often said. *See* Robert W. Hillman, *Private Ordering Within Partnerships*, 41 U. Miami L. Rev. 425, 448 (1987).

** Bear in mind that service partners only ever really risk the value of their own personal labor. Where a "service" partner contributes other things of value, like inventory or materials or the labor of their own employees, they will either contract explicitly for the partnership to pay them for those things (as was the case in both *Richert* and *Kessler*), or those contributions will be treated as capital, whether or not the partners specifically so agreed.

scenario. If that's all we know about their relationship, one safe assumption is that neither would willingly take all the risk. But what risk would Brynn be willing to bear in exchange for only half the upside?

In this particular case, Brynn seems to be committing something of pretty significant value—her whole working life for some indefinite period. Does that imply that *Kessler* would be a better rule for this business than *Richert*? If you think so, what about cases in which the term of the partnership is definite and fairly short, or the particular labor contribution is fairly limited? With this factual context in mind, what can we safely generalize about the likely intentions of service partners, if anything?

 Time Out for PR

Do you think it is advisable to represent both partners in setting up a partnership such as the one in *Richert v. Handly* or the one in *Kessler v. Antinora*? Consider American Bar Association Model Rule of Professional Conduct 1.7 (Conflict of Interest: Current Clients), which permits concurrent representations where the lawyer reasonably believes he or she can provide diligent and competent representation to all affected clients, and the clients give informed, written consent. If such representations are not possible, is there an adverse impact on the availability of legal services?

Does it seem to you likely that the parties in *Richert* and *Kessler* were represented at all?

D. A New "Harmonized" Rule for Capital Losses?

As one final problem for this chapter, we consider a change that may be coming to the handling of capital losses. As part of its 2013 "harmonization" project, by which it meant to coordinate all of its unincorporated entity codes, the Uniform Law Commission has proposed one fairly striking change to the financial rights of partners as they long existed.

In general, the 2013 revisions preserve the traditional distribution of assets on dissolution and winding up, as it had been handled under RUPA §807 and UPA §40(b). Namely, creditors are paid first, then capital contributions are returned in full, and if anything is left over it is shared among the partners according to their profit shares. Thus, the new §806(b) says that any "surplus" after payment of creditors is first used to return the partners' contributions and then it is divided among them by their shares of distributions. So far, so good. However, new §806(e) provides that if the partnership's assets are insufficient to return all of the partners' initial capital contributions, then the "surplus" is distributed "in proportion to the value of the respective unreturned contributions. . . ." That is, the surplus is *not* shared according to their shares in the profits and losses, but in proportion to their initial capital contributions.

The major practical effect is that where initial capital contributions are unequal, the partners making smaller contributions will get more under the 2013 rule than they would have before. Moreover, they never have to contribute from their personal assets to make the other partners whole. This is because §806(c), which requires partners to contribute such amounts as will permit the partnership to satisfy its obligations, relates *only* to obligations to creditors, not partners.

Imagine a default partnership in which A initially invests $75 and B invests $25. On dissolution the business has had lifetime revenues of $100, but expenses of $150. That will leave the partnership with $50 and thus a capital loss of $50. Under the traditional law, as it had existed for more than a century, the partners would have to share it equally, meaning that each of their initial capital contributions would be reduced by $25. On dissolution, after creditors are fully satisfied, the firm's final act would be to return $50 to A and $0 to B. Thus, each would suffer the same $25 loss. Under the new §806(e), however, the "proportion [of] the value of the[ir] . . . unreturned contributions" would be that A contributed 75 percent of it and B contributed 25 percent of it. So, they would share 75/25 in the $50 of remaining surplus. The firm would return $37.50 to A and $12.50 to B.

Where the capital losses are larger, so long as they do not wipe out all the "surplus," A and B still just share in the same proportion in whatever smaller pot of assets remains. If the lifetime expenses were $190, for example, there would be a capital loss of $90, and only $10 in assets left over. Under traditional law, A would be entitled to $30—A's initial $75 minus A's $45 share of the capital loss—$20 of which B would have to supply from B's own personal assets. But under the new §806(e), the partners would just split the $10 in the same 75/25 proportion, so that A would take $7.50 and B would take $2.50, and B would owe nothing from B's personal assets. The same result follows when the losses exactly wipe out the entire surplus. If lifetime expenses were $200, the capital loss of $100 would leave no surplus at all. Under traditional law, the partners would each take a capital loss of $50, so that A would get $25 and B would owe $25, meaning that B would just pay A $25 from B's personal assets. But under the new §806(e), they would each just take their proportionate shares of nothing, which would be nothing. All the same applies to firms with service-only partners, in which those partners simply take 0 percent of the surplus. If A contributes $100, B contributes only services, and the firm then suffers some capital loss, A just takes 100 percent of any surplus. *See* RUPA §401, comment subsection (a).

This new rule, however, applies only where the losses do not exceed the total initial capital. A different loss-sharing rule is applied where they eat up more than the firm's entire value on dissolution, such that the partners must contribute from their personal assets to make creditors whole. When that is the case, there is no "surplus," so §806(e) just doesn't apply. Section 806(c) requires the partners to contribute according to their share in distributions, and §806(d) says that if any of them fail to make the required contribution, the partners who covered it for them can recover the extra they paid from the non-paying partner. The fact that they must contribute is unremarkable—again, that just restates the law as it existed. What is surprising is that at that point they contribute according to their share in distributions. In other words, the new rule for sharing according to initial contributions only applies where losses eat up some but not all of the initial capital. Where losses exceed the initial capital, partners divide the excess loss according to their share in the distributions.

The drafter's notes accompanying the 2013 revisions are maddeningly indirect on the reasons for the change, but they apparently just felt that capital losses in partnerships should be the same as in limited liability entities. That aim apparently reflects the assumption that most deliberately formed partnerships nowadays are limited liability partnerships (LLPs). (In RUPA jurisdictions, an LLP is simply a RUPA partnership in which the partners have made a no-brainer statutory election to enjoy limited liability (as explained in Chapter 11).) Therefore, the default rule chosen in §806(e) will apply to every LLP that fails to modify it. Language identical to RUPA §806(e) had already appeared in the uniform acts relating to limited liability companies (LLCs) and limited partnerships (LPs).

In any event, even the drafters admit that the new rule "in no way resembles what 'typical' partners might agree [to] . . . , especially if the partnership was never an LLP." RUPA §806, comment subsection (e). No states have yet adopted the new language, and it remains to be seen whether any will be interested in making a change of this magnitude. Pennsylvania, interestingly enough, has enacted amendments from the harmonization project, including amended §806, but changed the language of §806(e) to preserve the traditional capital loss treatment for firms that remain general partnerships. *See* 15 Pa. Code §8486(e).

■ **Think about this:**

(K) Axel and Brianna form an oral partnership with no specific mention of profits, losses, or distributions on dissolution. Axel contributes $60 and Brianna contributes $40 in initial capital. Things go poorly, alas, and on dissolution the firm's entire value is $150 and its outstanding obligations are $100. What would each of Axel and Brianna receive under the RUPA as it existed in 1997? And what would each of them get after the 2013 harmonization?

(L) Same questions, except now assume that on dissolution the firm's outstanding obligations are $300.

Test Yourself

Assume Applicability of the Revised Uniform Partnership Act (without 2013 Amendments)

Questions 1 and 2 stand alone:

1. A, B, and C form the ABC Partnership. As part of their initial agreement, they each contribute $10,000 in capital. At the time of formation, C owned a building with some unused office space. A, B, and C agree that the partnership will have the use of this office space on a month-to-month basis, in exchange for $500 per month paid from the partnership's funds. C is permitted to sell this office building at her election and to keep any profits earned thereupon. True or False?

   a. True, even though the building is partnership property.
   b. True. The building is not partnership property.
   c. False. The building is partnership property.
   d. False. She is permitted to sell the building, because she has sufficient authority to do so, but she may not retain the profits from the sale for herself.

2. When Larry joined the ABC partnership, his only capital contribution was a pick-up truck with a fair market value of $5,000. Some years later ABC agreed to sell the truck for $3,000. ABC has four members, including Larry, and they have no written partnership agreement or any other explicit agreement between them, other than to act as co-owners of a business for profit. Assume that every year since the beginning of Larry's membership, ABC's revenues have precisely equaled its expenses. At the time of the sale of the truck, what amount should be reflected in Larry's capital account?

   a. $5,000.
   b. $4,500.
   c. $3,000.
   d. None of the above.

Questions 3 and 4 relate to the following facts:

JJ&J, an at-will, default partnership among Jen, Janey, and Joe, fell on some pretty tough times last year, and also experienced personal conflicts among the partners. Jen and Janey appeared to have gotten pretty sick of the whole thing, and appeared likely to seek the firm's dissolution. In fact, they were pretty much absent during a period of about a month, and during that time Joe really had to step in and do it all himself. He estimates he spent an additional 20 hours per week working in the business. He also personally put an additional $10,000 into the firm's coffers to keep it afloat (signing a written document to the effect, with the word "Loan" written at the top, and indicating that he would be repaid "with interest," but specifying no interest rate).

3. The written document memorializing Joe's "loan" is:

    a. A breach of his fiduciary duty.
    b. Fine, and enforceable as written.
    c. Not enforceable, because one partner acting alone cannot execute such an agreement on behalf of the firm.
    d. Irrelevant, because his $10,000 will actually constitute a capital contribution.

4. To how much is Joe entitled from JJ&J, now assuming the "loan" document by its terms has become due and payable?

    a. Nothing, because his extra efforts are not compensable and, despite the word "Loan" written on the document, his $10,000 constitutes an additional capital contribution.
    b. $10,000 plus interest.
    c. $10,000 plus the value of his additional efforts.
    d. $10,000 only.

Questions 5-7 stand alone:

5. Fill in the blanks: The balance in a partner's capital account equals his or her initial contribution, plus _____, less _____, and less _____.

6. Does a partner's capital account represent an actual amount of money that the partnership has set aside? Why or why not?

7. What is the purpose of a drawing account? Does it represent an actual amount of money that the partnership has set aside? Why or why not?

8

Management and Control, and Their Legal Consequences for the Firm and Its Partners

When we think of "management" we usually think of decision-making authority. But management in business firms usually also includes some power to create liability on the part of the entity. As it turns out, that implies power to create liability for the other partners as well, if the entity cannot satisfy its obligations.

Chapter Outline

C. Tort Liability and Procedural Issues Relating to Joint and Several Liability

1. In General
   - Joint and several liability
   - Acts within the ordinary course
   - Acts that are otherwise authorized

2. The Exhaustion Rule and Procedural Aspects of Partners' Shared Liability
   - A partnership creditor must exhaust the partnership's assets before proceeding against a partner's individual assets
   - Enforcement of creditors' rights is often problematic

D. Partners' Property Rights and Relations with Partners' Creditors

   - The difference between partnership property and a partner's interest in the partnership
   - Transfer of a partner's interest is a transfer of financial entitlement only
   - Foreclosure on and sale of a partner's interest sometimes is a meaningful option

Test Yourself

A. Governance

Rights to management and control appear in both Revised Uniform Partnership Act (RUPA) §401(h) and (k), which govern voting and dispute resolution, and in the powers set out in §301 of individual partners to make arrangements that are legally binding on the partnership.

RUPA's default governance rules are radically egalitarian. For that reason they are ill suited for many businesses and frequently modified. Specifically, every partner is given "equal rights in . . . management," RUPA §401(h), and while disputes that are in the "ordinary course of business" are to be resolved by majority vote, *id.* §401(k), acts that are outside the ordinary course of business require unanimous vote. *Id.* These rules preserve substantially verbatim the counterpart rules of the Uniform Partnership Act (1914) (UPA) (*see* UPA §18(e), (h)). Partners also have unrestricted access to their firms' "books and records," RUPA §408(b), and must be provided with any other information reasonably requested, *id.* §408(c)(2). (For the UPA equivalents, see UPA §§19, 20.) For small firms these rules may be quite sensible, but they often won't be for large firms with many partners, or for those in which some partners are more senior or otherwise are thought to deserve more say. In such cases, it is common to establish voting systems that give those with larger partnership shares more votes, or to establish governing boards or officers with managerial powers.

■ **Think about this:**

Give RUPA §401 a careful reading, and then try your hand at the following problem: Three doctors, Andrew, Bob, and Cathy, intend to establish ABC Medical Partners as a general partnership in a RUPA jurisdiction. They've known each other for some time, but Andrew, by far the most senior of the three, has been in his own practice for some time. He also will likely make a substantially larger initial contribution to the firm, since he can contribute the equipment and goodwill of his existing practice, and indeed the firm's initial list of patients will consist mostly of his existing practice.

(A) Clearly, this firm does not sound like a good candidate for the default governance rules of RUPA §401. So how should the partners modify those rules? Would any of the suggestions you can think of pose problems under RUPA §105?

(B) Say that once the firm is formed and business is underway, Andrew—a pediatrician—decides he wants to try his hand at orthopedics. He wants to launch a marketing campaign to secure business in that area, and use ABC's funds to pay for it. Can he do that without talking to Bob and Cathy? If he does run it by them and one of them objects, can he do it then?

B. The Partner's Power to Bind: Creating Liabilities for One's Colleagues

 What does it look like?

Check the online Supplement for the following sample documents that are relevant to this chapter:

■ Statement of partnership authority

1. In General

The partners' most important managerial powers will often include the ability to make contracts that bind the firm. Partners all have the same power to make contracts that create joint and several liability for all the other partners. That power appears in RUPA §301. Note how closely §301 follows the Restatement rules governing the agent's authority in Restatement (Third) of Agency ("Re(3)") §§2.01-2.03. But note too certain special rules concerning property transfers in RUPA §302, and the fact that the §301 powers can be modified by "statements" under §§303 and 304. Recall too that as with much of the rest of the law of partnership, these rights are subject to some alteration by agreement among the partners.

More to the Story: RUPA's Simplification Goals II: The Public Statements System of RUPA §303

As mentioned in Chapter 1, a major goal of the drafters of the RUPA (1997) was to simplify some issues that had caused uncertainty under the UPA (1914). As was discussed in Chapter 6B, a first major step was to simplify the "default" nature of partnership law by providing the list of non-waivable terms in RUPA §105.

A second big step is the system of public statements contained in RUPA §303. The system is modeled on the familiar system of recording of real estate transfers, and RUPA anticipates that filings will be made in the same way. Section 303 aims to dispel uncertainties that, under UPA (1914), surrounded property transfers, rules requiring evidence of notice or knowledge, and the reasonableness of inferences. Many of those have to do with authority—whether a given person could be reasonably believed to have the authority to transfer property or make other deals binding the firm—or whether a person is still a member of a firm after some event of dissociation or dissolution (*see* RUPA §§704, 804). When some such statement is properly recorded in the appropriate office, its effect is typically to resolve as a matter of law questions like whether a third party knew of a limitation on a partner's authority to make a certain contract. *See, e.g.,* RUPA §303(g).

In addition to the partner's ability to bind the firm contractually, RUPA §103(e) contains rules on imputed notice and knowledge roughly comparable to those contained in Re(3) Chapter 5. As an agent of the firm, the partner's knowledge or notice of facts will in many cases be attributable to the firm as well. Similarly, statements that a partner makes to others might also bind the partnership. UPA §11 had provided explicitly that the admissions of a partner were ordinarily the admissions of the firm. RUPA does not repeat that rule or explain its absence, but an admission is probably an "act" under RUPA §301. Note that "knowledge," "notice," and "notification" are defined with precision in RUPA §103.

This may help . . .

Read RUPA §303 and then fill out this chart to describe the effect of a statement that is properly filed.

	Statement Relates to Real Property	Statement Does Not Relate to Real Property
Statement Grants Authority		
Statement Limits Authority		

Importantly, the power of an individual partner or partners acting to bind the firm under RUPA §301 is subject to the power of the other partners to disapprove or stop the partner's actions. Consider, for example, Northmon Investment Co. v. Milford Plaza Assocs., 727 N.Y.S.2d 419 (N.Y. Ct. App. 2001), where a minority of the partners tried to lease realty that was the firm's only asset for 99 years, over the majority's objection. The court found that the lease would be unenforceable even were it deemed in the firm's ordinary course of business:

> A partner's authority to bind the partnership to transactions apparently in the ordinary course of the partnership's business [as set out in UPA §9, corresponding to RUPA §301] does not affect the right of partners as between themselves to prevent contemplated transactions with third parties, or otherwise to assert their "equal rights in the management and conduct of the partnership business" [UPA §18(e), RUPA §401(h)]. Appellants cannot impose their decision to enter into this lease upon [the other partners] . . . , and, indeed, [the other partners'] right to interfere with this or any other contract or prospective contract involving the partnership is "absolute" and "privileged, excusable and justified". . . . [Moreover,] it remains that the [underlying partnership] agreement[], on [its] face, terminate[s] the partnership in 2075, many years before the contemplated 99-year lease would expire. Since such a lease cannot be deemed ordinary, respondents would not be bound by it. . . .

Id.

■ **Think about this:**

(C) Suppose, in the *Northmon* case, that the partners had filed a statement under RUPA §303 specifically disclaiming the ability of fewer than all the partners to lease or convey its real property. How would that have changed the court's analysis?

(D) Carlos and Dexter agree that Carlos is to have sole authority to order fruit and Dexter is to have sole authority to order vegetables to stock the C&D Fruit and Veggie Stand, which is operated by their general partnership. They file proper statements of authority describing exactly what authority each of them does and does not have. Carlos is temporarily ill and Dexter orders fruit from their regular supplier, Fruit-R-Us, which does not know about either the allocations of authority or the existence of the statements of authority. Carlos recovers, learns what Dexter has done, and tells Fruit-R-Us not to deliver Dexter's order. May Fruit-R-Us recover on the contract?

---

2. The Liability of Incoming Partners

Though the statute doesn't make it easy (by default, §402(b)(3) requires unanimous approval for the admission of new partners), most going firms will desire to take on new partners from time to time. A problem, though, is the degree to which a new partner should be responsible for firm obligations. RUPA §306(b) provides that "[a] person admitted as a partner into an existing partnership is not personally liable for any partnership obligation incurred before the person's admission as a partner." In other words, a new partner is liable for all firm debts, but his personal assets will not be available to satisfy debts that arose before his admission.

For what it is worth, in some cases §306(b) permits arguably superfluous or double liability. Oftentimes, a new partner will be added only to replace one who is departing—frequently as part of a single transaction in which the incoming partner buys the outgoing partner's share. In such cases, under RUPA §703(a) the departing partner will remain fully liable for all firm obligations unless released by agreement with creditors. Typically, the departing partner will have received a payout of any capital contributions made, together with a share in the firm's profits (as we shall learn at some length in Chapter 9). As a result, the firm's ready assets will be somewhat depleted. But the new partner will likely have made a capital contribution upon admission, which under §306(b) will be available to pre-admission creditors despite the new partner's lack of personal responsibility for their claims. Under §703(a) these same creditors will have access not only to the capital and profits paid out to the departing partner, but also to all of the departing partner's other personal assets.

3. Examples in Application

The following pair of cases deals with the circumstances in which one of two partners effectively can put the kibosh on the other one's plans. Clearly, it is an area for planning, although even that may not be 100 percent effective.

NATIONAL BISCUIT COMPANY, INC. V. STROUD

Supreme Court of North Carolina
249 N.C. 467 (1959)

Parker, J.

[Before the court is an order against C.N. Stroud and Earl Freeman, a partnership doing business as Stroud's Food Center, for the nonpayment of $171.04. Stroud and Freeman formed the partnership in 1953, and frequently purchased plaintiff's bread for sale to their grocery store customers. Some months prior to February 1956 Stroud advised an agent for plaintiff that he would no longer be personally responsible for bread sold to Stroud's Food Center. At Freeman's request, however, plaintiff through the same agent sold bread to the partnership during February 1956, in the amount of $171.04. Stroud and Freeman dissolved the partnership on February 25, 1956, and gave public notice of that fact in a local paper in March 1956.]

. . . There is nothing in the agreed statement of facts to indicate or suggest that Freeman's power and authority as a general partner were in any way restricted or limited

The next day was broiling, almost the last, certainly the warmest day of the summer. As my train emerged from the tunnel into sunlight, only the hot whistles of the National Biscuit Company broke the simmering hush at noon.

F. Scott Fitzgerald, The Great Gatsby

by the articles of partnership in respect to the ordinary and legitimate business of the partnership. Certainly, the purchase and sale of bread were ordinary and legitimate business of Stroud's Food Center during its continuance as a going concern. . . .

More to the Story: Contracting Rules Under UPA and RUPA, and the Old "Laundry List" Limitations

The RUPA and the former UPA (1914) treat the contracting powers of partners in almost the same way, with one significant difference. The UPA contained a list of five specific transactions that would have no effect without unanimous approval of the partners, including actions that would make it impossible for the firm to continue its business. See UPA §9(3).

Consider Patel v. Patel, 260 Cal. Rptr. 255 (Cal. App. 1989). Defendant husband and wife, owners of a hotel, formed a partnership with their son for the three of them to own it together. They did not record or otherwise publicize the fact of their partnership. Thereafter, husband and wife negotiated the hotel's sale to buyers unaware of the partnership or the son's interest in it. Their son objected, and because the hotel was the firm's only asset (and thus the firm would have no business without it), the courts applied §9(3) to bar the sale.

The purpose of RUPA's drafters in doing away with UPA's §9(3) "laundry list" was plainly to remove uncertainty for third parties dealing with partnerships, and to put the risk of those dealings more firmly on the partners. Often it will have that effect, but ask yourself: Would Patel necessarily come out differently under RUPA §301?

In Johnson v. Bernheim, 76 N.C. 139, this Court said: "A and B are general partners to do some given business; the partnership is, by operation of law, a power to each to bind the partnership in any manner legitimate to the business. If one partner go to a third person to buy an article on time for the partnership, the other partner cannot prevent it by writing to the third person not to sell to him on time; or, if one party attempt to buy for cash, the other has no right to require that it shall be on time. And what is true in regard to buying is true in regard to selling. What either partner does with a third person is binding on the partnership." . . .

Freeman as a general partner with Stroud, with no restrictions on his authority to act within the scope of the partnership business so far as the agreed statement of facts shows, had under the Uniform Partnership Act "equal rights in the management and conduct of the partnership business." Under G.S. §59-48(h) [North Carolina's adoption of UPA §18(h), which is substantially identical to RUPA §401(k),] Stroud, his co-partner, could not restrict the power and authority of Freeman to buy bread for the partnership as a going concern, for such a purchase was an "ordinary matter connected with the partnership business," for the purpose of its business and within its scope, because in the very nature of things Stroud was not, and could not be, a majority of the partners.

Therefore, Freeman's purchases of bread from plaintiff for Stroud's Food Center as a going concern bound the partnership and his co-partner Stroud. . . .

In *Crane on Partnership*, 2d Ed., p. 277, it is said: "In cases of an even division of the partners as to whether or not an act within the scope of the business should be done, of which disagreement a third person has knowledge, it seems that logically no restriction can be placed upon the power to act. The partnership being a going concern, activities within the scope of the business should not be limited, save by the expressed will of the majority deciding a disputed question; half of the members are not a majority." . . .

■ **Think about this:**

(E) Why didn't Stroud's statement to the plaintiff's agent limit Freeman's actual and apparent authority? There are separate reasons why it didn't limit actual and didn't limit apparent authority. What if there had been three partners and two of them advised a third party that the third partner had no authority to engage in a particular transaction? In other words, the number of partners is one key reason that *National Biscuit Co.* came out differently than *Northmon Investment*, which was described at the beginning of the chapter. Do you see why?

(F) Do you suppose the problem is that Stroud simply neglected to tell Freeman that he no longer agreed that Freeman had authority to order bread?

(G) Why isn't Stroud's ability not to order bread from the National Biscuit Company as legally significant as Freeman's ability to order what he wants?

The next case offers an interesting comparison. Although it may at first appear to contradict *National Biscuit Company*, it perhaps can be reconciled—so keep your eye out.

SUMMERS V. DOOLEY

Supreme Court of Idaho
481 P.2d 318 (1971)

DONALDSON, Justice.

This lawsuit, tried in the district court, involves a claim by one partner against the other for $6,000. The complaining partner asserts that he has been required to pay out more than $11,000 in expenses without any reimbursement from either the partnership funds or his partner. The expenditure in question was incurred by the complaining partner (John Summers, plaintiff-appellant) for the purpose of hiring an additional employee. The trial court denied him any relief except for ordering that he be entitled to one half $966.72 which it found to be a legitimate partnership expense.

The pertinent facts leading to this lawsuit are as follows. Summers entered a partnership agreement with Dooley (defendant-respondent) in 1958 for the purpose of operating a trash collection business. The business was operated by the two men and when either was unable to work, the non-working partner provided a replacement at his own expense. In 1962, Dooley became unable to work and, at his own expense, hired an employee to take his place. In July, 1966, Summers approached his partner Dooley regarding the hiring of an additional employee but Dooley refused. Nevertheless, on his own initiative, Summers hired the man and paid him out of his own pocket. Dooley, upon discovering that Summers had hired an additional man, objected, stating that he did not feel additional labor was necessary and refused to pay for the new employee out of the partnership funds. Summers continued to operate the business using the third man and in October of 1967 instituted suit in the district court for $6,000 against his partner, the gravamen of the complaint being that Summers has been required to pay out more than $11,000 in expenses, incurred in the hiring of the additional man, without any reimbursement from either the partnership funds or his partner. . . .

The principal thrust of appellant's contention is that in spite of the fact that one of the two partners refused to consent to the hiring of additional help, nonetheless, the non-consenting partner retained profits earned by the labors of the third man and therefore the non-consenting partner should be estopped from denying the need and value of the employee, and has by his behavior ratified the act of the other partner who hired the additional man.

The issue presented for decision by this appeal is whether an equal partner in a two man partnership has the authority to hire a new employee in disregard of the objection of the other partner and then attempt to charge the dissenting partner with the costs incurred as a result of his unilateral decision.

The State of Idaho has enacted specific statutes with respect to the legal concept known as "partnership." Therefore any solution of partnership problems should logically begin with an application of the relevant code provision.

In the instant case the record indicates that although Summers requested his partner Dooley to agree to the hiring of a third man, such requests were not honored. In fact Dooley made it clear that he was "voting no" with regard to the hiring of an additional employee.

An application of the relevant statutory provisions and pertinent case law to the factual situation presented by the instant case indicates that the trial court was correct in its disposal of the issue since a majority of the partners did not consent to the hiring of the third man. I.C. §53-318(8) [Idaho's adoption of UPA §18(h), which is substantially identical to RUPA §401(k)] provides:

> Any difference arising as to ordinary matters connected with the partnership business may be decided by a *majority of the partners* * * *. (emphasis supplied)

It is the opinion of this Court that the preceding statute is of a mandatory rather than permissive nature. This conclusion is based upon the following reasoning.

Whether a statute is mandatory or directory does not depend upon its form, but upon the intention of the legislature, to be ascertained from a consideration of the entire act, its nature, its object, and the consequences that would result from construing it one way or the other.

The intent of the legislature may be implied from the language used, or inferred on grounds of policy or reasonableness. A careful reading of the statutory provision indicates that subsection 5 bestows *equal rights in the management and conduct of the partnership business* upon all of the partners. The concept of equality between partners with respect to management of business affairs is a central theme and recurs throughout the Uniform Partnership law, I.C. §53-301 et seq., which has been enacted in this jurisdiction. Thus the only reasonable interpretation of I.C. §53-318(8) is that business differences must be decided by a majority of the partners provided no other agreement between the partners speaks to the issues.

A noted scholar has dealt precisely with the issue to be decided.

> . . . if the partners are equally divided, those who forbid a change must have their way. Walter B. Lindley, A Treatise on the Law of Partnership, Ch. II, §III, ¶24-8, p. 403 (1924). See also, W. Shumaker, A Treatise on the Law of Partnership, §97, p. 266.

In the case at bar one of the partners continually voiced objection to the hiring of the third man. He did not sit idly by and acquiesce in the actions of his partner. Under these circumstances it is manifestly unjust to permit recovery of an expense which was incurred individually and not for the benefit of the partnership but rather for the benefit of one partner.

■ Think about this:

(H) Is it clear that there was no benefit to the partnership from hiring the third man?

(I) Would the case have come out any differently if it had involved a claim against Dooley by the third man seeking unpaid salary promised to him by Summers?

(J) Suppose that the partnership had always employed a third man and Dooley had wanted to fire him. Would he have had the authority to do so?

(K) Suppose you have a client, Dante, who is entering into a partnership with Eduardo to own and operate a dive shop. Dante is not 100 percent sure that he and Eduardo will see eye to eye on such matters as the brands of inventory to carry. What would you advise him to include in the partnership agreement? Suppose Eduardo does not agree?

(L) Is there a useful role for the statement of partnership authority in resolving these issues?

Consider the following comment to RUPA §401(h) added in 2013: "[T]o the extent a partner has reason to know of a possible difference of opinion among the partner[s], Subsection (k) requires a decision by at least 'a majority of the partners' and by unanimous consent if the matter is 'outside the ordinary course of the business'" Should this change the analysis or outcome of either *National Biscuit Company or Summers* if they were being decided today?

C. Tort Liability and Procedural Issues Relating to Joint and Several Liability

1. In General

Just as with the contracting power, the partnership rules governing vicarious tort liability closely resemble those of agency law. Generally speaking, the partnership rules are simpler, mainly because they draw no distinction between "employees" and "non-employee agents." Rather, RUPA §305(a) simply makes the partnership responsible for any "loss or injury caused . . . [by] actionable conduct of a partner," so long as the partner acted either in the "ordinary course of [the firm's] business" or "with authority of the partnership." The former concept—ordinary course of business—is critical, but consider also the latter. Given what you learned above about the management powers under RUPA §401(h), what would have to be true in order for an action to be authorized even though it is outside the ordinary course of business?

In any event, cases under this rule tend to be very straightforward, but very fact-dependent. The following cases give a flavor.

GEARHART V. ANGELOFF

Ohio Court of Appeals
244 N.E.2d 802 (1969)

HUNSICKER, Presiding Judge.

In this appeal on questions of law, the chief question revolves around . . . damages . . . awarded against Robert Angeloff[] and . . . his brother, Karl, partners in the operation of a bar in the city of Akron, Summit County, Ohio. [Karl appeals.]

Tommy Gearhart, then twenty years of age, the plaintiff . . . , entered the Elbow Grille on Arlington Street, Akron, Ohio, and purchased some beer. While he was seated at the bar, another person entered the Grille and caused a disturbance. One of the defendants, Karl Angeloff . . . , a partner in the business, tried to evict the troublemaker. In the tussle that followed, Karl and the troublemaker fell to the floor. It was at that time that Robert Angeloff, a partner, obtained a revolver and shot across the bar in the direction of the two men on the floor. The bullet grazed the arm of Tommy Gearhart. The police came while Tommy Gearhart was seated at the bar. He said nothing to anyone about being shot. Tommy Gearhart left the bar, but returned with his sister in about a half hour, telling the Angeloffs that he had been shot. He then was taken by his sister to a hospital and there the abrasion on his arm was examined. He then returned home. He testified that he lost between two and three weeks' work because of the injury to his arm.

An action was commenced by Tommy Gearhart against both Robert Angeloff and Karl Angeloff for compensatory damages and punitive damages. Robert, his wife, Helen, and Karl Angeloff were partners in the operation of the Elbow Grille. There is nothing in this record which discloses that Karl Angeloff in any manner was involved in the wilful discharge of the gun. The fact that the brothers are partners does make them jointly responsible for the tortious acts of the other in a situation such as this. The maintenance of order in the bar was a normal business activity. Partners acting within the scope of the business are jointly liable for the tortious acts of another partner. . . .

■ **Think about this:**

(M) Would it make any difference if Karl had always vehemently objected to keeping a gun in the bar and in fact had no idea that Robert had one?

(N) Would it make any difference if a license for the gun was required and Robert did not have one?

The following case involves a "professional association," but under the relevant North Carolina law, vicarious tort liability of its members was determined as though they were partners in a general partnership.

HEATH V. CRAIGHILL, RENDLEMAN, INGLE & BLYTHE, P.A.

North Carolina Court of Appeals
388 S.E.2d 178 (1990)

Cozort, Judge.

. . . This lawsuit has its origins in the relationship between plaintiff M. Lee Heath, Jr., and Francis O. Clarkson, Jr., formerly a lawyer and member of Craighill, Rendleman, Clarkson, Ingle & Blythe, P.A. Beginning in 1977 Clarkson performed for Heath various legal services, including the preparation of a will, codicils, and a continuing power of attorney. Another member of the firm, Robert B. Blythe, handled real estate matters for Heath. . . .

In August 1983 Clarkson, promising a "two-to-one return," persuaded Heath to invest in an "Arab oil deal" with a "group of American investors" represented by Richard Seaman of Florida. Heath testified that when he asked about the risk, Clarkson replied: "I will minimize the risk by giving you my own promissory note." On 16 August 1983, in return for $25,000 Clarkson gave Heath a note for $50,000 payable on 30 September 1983. When the note came due, Clarkson promised an additional $12,500 in return for a two-week delay. Heath agreed to the new date and collected $62,500, representing a return on his money of one hundred and fifty percent in sixty days. In the meantime in early October, by letter dated 30 September 1983, effective the same day, Clarkson resigned from his firm. The firm allowed him to remain in its offices for about two months until he negotiated a lease on an office condominium.

Doing the Numbers: Rate of Return

With respect to Heath's first "investment," $25,000 returned $62,500, which means it earned the difference of $37,500.

$37,500 = x% of $25,000

$37,500/$25,000 = 1.5 (or 150%)

With respect to Heath's second "investment", $50,000 returned $100,000, for a difference of $50,000.

$50,000 = x% of $50,000

$50,000/$50,000 = 1 (or 100%)

With respect to Heath's third "investment," $25,000 returned $75,000, for a difference of $50,000.

$50,000 = x% of $25,000

$50,000/$25,000 = 2 (or 200%)

If the investments represented by Clarkson's "notes" were regarded as loans, the interest rate would, at the time, surely have been usurious.

Heath's final investments with Clarkson were made in November 1983. Again Clarkson proposed investment in foreign oil exploration which would yield investors a one hundred percent return. On 4 November 1983, Heath gave Clarkson $50,000 and took a note for $100,000 payable 19 December 1983. . . .

Soon afterward Clarkson solicited a final $25,000 from Heath, who declined the invitation until promised a "three-to-one return on this last phase. . . ." On 19 November 1983 Heath exchanged $25,000 for Clarkson's note in the amount of $75,000 payable 19 December 1983. . . .

Shortly after the notes came due, Clarkson wrote personal checks to pay them. His checks were dishonored. . . .

. . . A partnership is liable for loss or injury caused "by any wrongful act or omission of any partner acting in the ordinary course of business of the partnership or with the authority of his copartners. . .to the same extent as the partner so acting or omitting to act." N.C. Gen. Stat. §59-43 (1989) [UPA §13, essentially the same as

Connections: The Definition of a "Security"

The federal securities laws cover the purchase or sale of any "security." The definition of a "security" includes any "note." As the case law has developed, this sometimes— but only sometimes—extends to simple promissory notes like the ones Clarkson gave here. And so, while purely private deals like these usually avoid the registration and reporting requirements of the federal securities rules, they can remain subject to one of the most important of all securities rules, the ban on securities fraud in §10(b) of the Securities Exchange Act of 1934. There is more on this subject in Chapter 30, but the long and short of it is that Clarkson may well have violated the federal securities laws along with his other sins.

More to the Story: The Oil Embargo

Without going into too many details, it may be relevant to know that in the early 1980s the price of oil and gas was sky-high because of an embargo imposed in the Middle East.

RUPA §305(a)]. Thus, the question presented upon the trial court's grant of JNOV turns on whether, as a matter of law, there was insufficient evidence to justify a verdict that Clarkson's dealings with Heath were within the scope of authority or apparent authority conferred on Clarkson by his firm. . . .

Plaintiff submits that apparent authority to solicit money may be attributed to Clarkson from a variety of transactions and circumstances. Plaintiff alleges principally that Clarkson's letter of 4 November 1983 was written on firm stationery, and he asserts that "[o]n one occasion, James Craighill, a partner [sic] in the firm, was present with two staff members and overheard a discussion between Clarkson and Heath concerning the transactions."

Plaintiff fails to note that he was never billed by the firm for any aspect of his investments with Clarkson, including the letters of 4 November and 19 November 1988, which plaintiff characterizes as "legal opinions." The letter of 19 November was written on Clarkson's personal stationery. James Craighill testified that on or about 30 September 1983 the firm instructed its "secretaries [to] run a line through [Clarkson's] name to indicate that he was no longer with the firm. . . ." Clarkson's letter of 4 November 1983 on firm stationery was not typed by a secretary; it was written entirely in his hand.

Regarding the discussion between Clarkson and plaintiff, at which James Craighill, Janice Burton and Elizabeth Carr were present, plaintiff testified as follows:

> I made what you would call, I guess, a jestful comment, in the presence of all these people, and I said, "I'd better be careful. Frank will have me signing over all my assets to him so he can invest it with his Arab clients," to which Mr. Clarkson responded, "Yes. They're having cash flow problems in Jidda,["] to which I responded, "Yes. Those poor Arabs are only making millions instead of billions." . . . Everybody heard it. Everybody laughed. Mr. Clarkson chuckled, and Mr. Craighill grinned, and the girls sort of grinned, too, knowing that basically my comment was a jestful comment.

Ms. Burton testified that secretaries "were allowed to do personal work for the attorneys whose legal work they did." She testified further that, to the extent she knew of Clarkson's meetings with Heath, she never discussed them with other lawyers in the firm. Neither plaintiff's testimony, nor that of Ms. Burton supports his claim that other lawyers at the firm knew or "should have known about Clarkson's soliciting and accepting the money."

Finally, plaintiff cites *Zimmerman v. Hogg & Allen* in support of his argument for reinstating the verdict below. In *Zimmerman* our Supreme Court refused to allow summary judgment against a plaintiff who sought to hold a professional association liable for the stock transactions of one of its agents (Glenn L. Greene, Jr.) with the plaintiff. In its holding, the Court relied on the following facts:

> [T]he powers granted to the Professional Association by its charter were very broad powers, the exercise of which was principally in the hands of Greene; that defendant Greene, while he was on business trips to attend to the legal business of Holly Farms, accepted funds for investment purposes from employees of the corporate client; that these corporate employees were assured that such moneys would be handled through the Professional Association; that such activities by Greene, the president and principal stockholder of the Professional Association, had occurred over a period of several years; and that [shareholder-]employees of the Professional Association had knowledge of such dealings.

Zimmerman v. Hogg & Allen, 209 S.E.2d [795, 804 (1974)].

In the case below, the charter of Craighill, Rendleman, Clarkson, Ingle & Blythe, P.A., limited it to rendering legal services. Clarkson was not the principal stockholder of the professional association, nor principally in charge of its operation. He gave no assurances that money invested with him would be handled through his law firm, and plaintiff presented no credible evidence that other shareholder-employees knew or had reason to know of Clarkson's transactions with Heath. Given these facts, plaintiff's reliance on *Zimmerman* is misplaced. . . .

■ **Think about this:**

(O) Is there any argument whatsoever that Clarkson's acts were in the ordinary course of practicing law?

(P) Why might it have made a difference if Clarkson owned the largest share, or were in charge of the professional association, or made assurances that money invested with him would be handled through his law firm? Would the outcome still depend on what the other shareholders knew or should have known about what he was doing?

Although the outcome in *Heath* may be reassuring to lawyers, the outcome of the following case is less so.

ROACH V. MEAD

Supreme Court of Oregon
722 P.2d 1229 (1986)

JONES, Justice.

. . . Mead, defendant's former law partner, first represented plaintiff in December 1974 on a traffic charge and later represented plaintiff on several occasions. On November 1, 1979, Mead and defendant formed a law partner-

More to the Story: Interest Rates

Another phenomenon of the early 1980s was sky-high interest rates. Market interest rates in many instances were usurious as a matter of state law. The result was a rush by legislatures to eliminate usury laws.

ship. Mead continued to advise plaintiff on other traffic charges and on business dealings. Defendant prepared plaintiff's income tax returns.

In June 1980, plaintiff sold his meter repair business for $50,000. On November 25, 1980, plaintiff asked for Mead's advice on investing $20,000 in proceeds from the sale. Plaintiff testified that Mead told plaintiff that "he would take [the money] at 15 percent. So, I let him have it. . . . I trusted him and felt he would look out for me." Plaintiff considered Mead's advice to be legal advice; he testified that otherwise he would not have consulted an attorney.

After plaintiff agreed to the loan, Mead executed a promissory note for $20,000 payable on or before November 25, 1982, at 15 percent interest. Mead said that he would be receiving a large sum of money with which he would repay plaintiff. Mead offered to secure the loan with a second mortgage on his house, and plaintiff replied that he should do "whatever you think is best." Mead did not secure the loan. . . . Mead did not repay any money to plaintiff and later was declared bankrupt.[1]

Plaintiff sued defendant's partnership for negligence, alleging that the partnership failed to disclose the conflicting interests of plaintiff and Mead, to advise plaintiff to seek independent legal advice, to inform plaintiff of the risks involved in an unsecured loan, and to advise plaintiff that the loan would not be legally enforceable because the rate of interest was usurious[.] . . . The trial jury found defendant vicariously liable for Mead's negligence in advising plaintiff on the $20,000 loan. . . . [The Court of Appeals affirmed.] We affirm the Court of Appeals. . . .

Plaintiff contends that Mead negligently advised him about the loan and that defendant should be vicariously liable for Mead's negligent legal advice. Defendant, while conceding that Mead was negligent, argues that the transaction between plaintiff and Mead was a personal loan outside the scope of the partnership, and that the evidence did not prove that soliciting personal loans was within Mead's express, implied or apparent authority as defendant's law partner.

Oregon's Uniform Partnership Law, ORS 68.010 to 68.650, governs the liability of partnerships for the acts of partners. ORS 68.210 [Oregon's adoption of UPA §9, essentially the same as RUPA §301 for purposes of this analysis] provides in pertinent part:

> (1) Every partner is an agent of the partnership for the purpose of its business, and the act of every partner, including the execution in the partnership name of any instrument, for apparently carrying on in the usual way the business of the partnership of which the partner is a member binds the

---

1. On January 18, 1983, this court accepted Mead's resignation from the bar. He stated that he had chosen not to contest disciplinary charges alleging that he had "borrowed $45,000 from a [different] client, that he misrepresented the priority of the security given for the loan and that he subsequently forged a satisfaction of the mortgage given as security." 43 Or. St. B. Bull., June 1983, at 42. Mead was convicted of theft by deception because of the loan referred to in the disciplinary charges. *Id.*

partnership, unless the partner so acting has in fact no authority to act for the partnership in the particular matter, and the person with whom the partner is dealing has knowledge of the fact that the partner has no such authority.

(2) An act of a partner which is not apparently for the carrying on of the business of the partnership in the usual way does not bind the partnership unless authorized by the other partners. . . .

ORS 68.250 [UPA §13, essentially the same as RUPA §305(a)] provides:

Where, by any wrongful act or omission of any partner acting in the ordinary course of the business of the partnership, or with the authority of copartners, loss or injury is caused to any person, not being a partner in the partnership, or any penalty is incurred, the partnership is liable therefor to the same extent as the partner so acting or omitting to act.

ORS 68.270(1) [UPA §15, essentially the same as RUPA §306(a) in this context] provides:

All partners are liable:
(1) Jointly and severally for everything chargeable to the partnership under ORS 68.250 and 68.260.

Liability of partners for the acts of copartners is based on a principal-agent relationship between the partners and the partnership. . . . The issue in this case is whether Mead's failure to advise plaintiff on the legal consequences of the loan was "in the ordinary course of the business of the partnership."

In Croisant v. Watrud, 432 P.2d 799 (1967), this court confronted a similar issue of the vicarious liability of a partnership for the wrongful acts of a partner. In *Croisant*, the client of an accountant sued the accounting partnership, claiming damages for the accountant's breach of trust. The accountant collected income from the client's property and then made unauthorized payments to the client's husband from the money. The defendant partnership contended that the collection services were personal dealings of the accountant with the client and not part of the partnership's business. This court held:

If a third person reasonably believes that the services he has requested of a member of an accounting partnership is undertaken as a part of the partnership business, the partnership should be bound for a breach of trust incident to that employment even though those engaged in the practice of accountancy would regard as unusual the performance of such services [collecting and disbursing funds] by an accounting firm. 432 P.2d 799.

The court stated that the reasonableness of the third person's belief that "the service he seeks is within the domain of the profession is a question which must be answered upon the basis of the facts in the particular case." *Id.* at 799.

Defendant contends that *Croisant* may be distinguished from the case at bar because in *Croisant* "the misconduct occurred in the course of . . . activities which the court held could reasonably be viewed as within the scope of the accounting firm's business," while in this case "[t]here was no evidence that the act of an attorney in taking a personal loan from a client could reasonably be viewed as part of the business of a law firm." However, defendant admits that "the evidence most favorable to Plaintiff was simply that Plaintiff thought Mead was giving him investment advice and that the giving of advice regarding legal aspects of loans and investments in general is a normal part of law practice." Defendant thus concedes the validity of plaintiff's argument that plaintiff reasonably believed that investment advice was within the scope of the partnership's business; plaintiff does not contend that soliciting loans from clients was partnership business.

In the case at bar, the jury determined that plaintiff reasonably believed that the partnership's legal services included investment advice. We agree with the Court of Appeals that:

> . . . There is expert and other testimony from which the jury could have found that plaintiff relied on Mead for legal advice concerning the loan, that a lawyer seeking a loan from a client would be negligent if the lawyer did not tell the client to get independent legal advice and that a lawyer advising a client about this particular loan would seek to secure it and would warn the client of the risks involved in providing a usurious interest rate. 709 P.2d 246.

The Court of Appeals' rationale is buttressed by our decisions in bar disciplinary proceedings concerning loans from clients to lawyers. *See, e.g.* In re Montgomery, 643 P.2d 338 (1982); In re Drake, 642 P.2d 296 (1982). In *Montgomery* this court reprimanded a lawyer for failing to disclose his conflict of interest, holding that:

> When a lawyer borrows money from a non-lawyer client who is not in the business of lending money, the lawyer should assume that the client is relying on the lawyer for the legal aspects of the transaction to the same extent that the client would rely on the lawyer for advice were the client making the loan to a third person, unless the opposite is expressly stated.
>
> It would not occur to a trusting client that the lawyer would advise the client to enter into an unlawful contract. Thus, had [the client] consulted [the attorney] about a loan to a third person, although advice as to the creditworthiness of the third person would likely not be expected, advice as to the legal effect of the usurious rate of interest would likely have been given. In addition, a competent lawyer might have recommended that security be given by the borrower. 642 P.2d 296.

When a lawyer borrows money from a client, this court requires that the lawyer advise the client about the legal aspects of the loan. Mead's failure to advise plaintiff to seek independent legal advice, that loans usually should be secured and the debtor's financial status checked, and that the rate of interest was usurious were all failures of Mead as a lawyer advising his client. Because these failures occurred within the scope of the legal partnership, responsibility for Mead's negligence was properly charged to defendant as Mead's law partner. The trial court did not err in submitting the negligence issue to the jury. . . .

■ **Think about this:**

(Q) Is the *Roach* court applying a different rule than the *Heath* court?

(R) What, if anything, can one do to protect against the conduct of a law partner such as Mead?

 Time Out for PR: Business Dealings with Clients and Responsibility for the Wrongdoing of Others

The *Heath* and *Roach* cases are food for thought. The latter (in footnote 1) references a disciplinary action involving somewhat similar facts. American Bar Association Model Rule of Professional Conduct 1.8(a) (Conflict of Interest: Current Clients: Specific Rules) regulates business transactions with clients, essentially mandating the same conduct required by the *Roach* court.

Consider also the following portions of Model Rule 5.1 (Responsibilities of Partners, Managers, and Supervisory Lawyers):

(a) A partner in a law firm, and a lawyer who individually or together with other lawyers possesses comparable managerial authority in a law firm, shall make reasonable efforts to ensure that the firm has in effect measures giving reasonable assurance that all lawyers in the firm conform to the Rules of Professional Conduct.

(c) A lawyer shall be responsible for another lawyer's violation of the Rules of Professional Conduct if:

(1) the lawyer orders or, with knowledge of the specific conduct, ratifies the conduct involved; or

(2) the lawyer is a partner or has comparable managerial authority in the law firm in which the other lawyer practices, or has direct supervisory authority over the other lawyer, and knows of the conduct at a time when its consequences can be avoided or mitigated but fails to take reasonable remedial action.

2. The Exhaustion Rule and Procedural Aspects of Partners' Shared Liability

The rules of partner liability are easy to state in the abstract, but some aspects of applying them in practice can be fairly complex. It might help first to point out a few things about the collection of debts in general. First, when a plaintiff sues on some obligation and wins, even if the obligation is some very simple money debt, the mere victory on the merits is not itself an order to pay money. It does not, for example, empower the local sheriff to levy against the defendant's bank account. Of course, the debtor can pay the judgment if he or she likes, but if not, the plaintiff's only legal remedy is normally to take the additional step of seeking *execution* of the judgment. In such an action a court ordinarily will use its jurisdiction to order some garnishment of the debtor's funds or income, or order some judicial sale of the debtor's property. Every jurisdiction has some process for execution. In the federal courts, a very general power to issue writs of execution is set out in Fed. R. Civ. P. 69, and every state has either statute law or court procedural rules governing the process. While not really a new cause of action, the request for writ of execution is in some respects like the institution of a new proceeding, in which the defendant may defend on various grounds. Moreover, the court can only issue the writ against property within its jurisdictional power, so if property located in another state happens to be the defendant's only real wealth, the plaintiff may need to seek execution in the courts of that state.

As a rule, this is all simply exhausting.

It is here that rules of partner liability can both be fairly confusing and cause serious practical difficulties. So, on the one hand, it might be worth repeating the truism that all partners in general partnerships bear full personal liability for all firm obligations. However simple that truism, though, the *execution* of partnership judgments "is the least uniform—and most confusing—of all aspects of American partnership law." 2 ALAN R. BROMBERG & LARRY E. RIBSTEIN, BROMBERG AND RIBSTEIN ON PARTNERSHIP §5:53 (1994). It turns out that this is largely true because of two traditional rules.

First is the so-called exhaustion rule, which requires partnership creditors to seek execution against partnership assets only, until those assets are fully exhausted, before executing against a partner's personal assets. The difficulty of the rule often will be that creditors may become mired in lengthy court process trying to track down what may turn out to be meager or non-existent firm assets, even though the partners themselves might have large assets. The period of execution against firm assets can also provide unscrupulous partners time to conceal their own assets, or merely to suffer misfortune rendering them less able to satisfy judgments. RUPA explicitly preserves the exhaustion rule in §307(d).

Second, a rule of the UPA (1914) that is now largely defunct, and is expressly rejected by RUPA §306(a), was that a partner was "jointly and severally" liable for tort liabilities, but only "jointly" liable for all other liabilities (which as a practical matter means contract liabilities). Even though it was a mere technical procedural rule, this distinction could cause practical complications. To wit, where a liability is merely "joint," a creditor must join all the partners as defendants unless one or more of them is beyond the court's jurisdiction. Where the liability is "joint and several," suit may be filed against any one or more of the partners and any one or more of them can be held liable for the entire judgment amount. (Under RUPA §306(a), partners are jointly and severally liable for all firm liabilities.) There can, of course, be no more than a single total recovery.

The policies underlying these traditional rules are straightforward. As for exhaustion, the rule protects the personal creditors of individual partners. It might be much easier in a particular case for firm creditors to execute against the personal assets of a partner. For example, the firm might be seriously in debt, with many creditors and few assets of any value, while one of the partners is well-to-do. But the wealthy partner might have many personal creditors, and if the firm creditor is allowed to execute against some large portion of his assets, then his personal creditors will have a less creditworthy debtor on their hands. As for the joint-vs.-joint-and-several distinction, tort victims are involuntary creditors. No one chooses to be the victim of an actionable tort, and we have little freedom to choose our tortfeasors on the basis of their judgment-worthiness. Other creditors, whose claims will normally sound in contract, enter into relations with the firm voluntarily, and will have some opportunity to investigate the firm, its financial state, and the creditworthiness of its partners. It therefore struck the original drafters of the UPA as fair to saddle contract creditors with the burden of locating, serving, and suing all of the partners. In light of the practical difficulties, this perception has eroded over time.

The operation of these rules can sometimes cause serious difficulties. A case in point is the saga that culminated in Thompson v. Wayne Smith Constr., Inc., 640 N.E.2d 408 (Ind. Ct. App. 1994). Plaintiff Wayne Smith, Inc. had built two homes on Hilton Head Island in South Carolina, on behalf of an Ohio-based partnership called Woman Duberstein & Thompson (named after its three partners). Wayne Smith sued in South Carolina in 1986 over a payment dispute, securing a judgment of about $100,000 (later held to be executable with an award of post-judgment interest for a total of about $150,000). On appeal in South Carolina the judgment was held to be immediately enforceable only against the firm and not the individual partners (an application of the traditional exhaustion rule). After initial efforts at execution in South Carolina and Ohio turned up only about $2,500, which appeared to be the grand total of the firm's remaining assets, Wayne Smith commenced enforcement against the individual partners, two of them Ohio residents and the third, defendant Thompson, resident in Indiana. At length, Wayne Smith secured orders executing its claims against the personal assets of the individual partners in both states, but only after the courts of Ohio and Indiana had grappled with whether they were bound, under the Full Faith and Credit Clause of the federal Constitution, by the South Carolina appellate order rejecting immediate enforcement against the individual partners. (Both ultimately held that the South Carolina order was without prejudice, merely requiring exhaustion of firm assets before entry against individual assets, and therefore not a final judgment entitled to full faith and credit.) Still, even though Wayne Smith secured favorable judgments in both states, the judgments differed sharply in the share of liability they assessed against the individual partners. They also differed as to whether full faith and credit was owed to any aspects of the original *trial court* order from South Carolina. So, in the end, this substantively very simple contract dispute consumed nearly ten years of litigation in the trial and appellate courts of three geographically disparate states. It presumably consumed tens of thousands of dollars in fees and expenses for both sides, and led to harsh criticism by one appellate court of another as to matters of procedure, substantive partnership law, and a dispute involving the Constitution of the United States(!). All of this was over a claim that never amounted to more than about $150,000.

> ■ **Think about this:**
>
> *(S)* If you were advising a client extending credit to a partnership, and the ability to recover against the partners were an important consideration, what would you advise to avoid a *Thompson* scenario?

D. Partners' Property Rights and Relations with Partners' Creditors

The partners "own" the partnership, and they are its only owners, but during its life there is little they can really do with its assets other than use them in the course of its business. Any property that is initially contributed to the firm by the partners, plus anything the partnership buys and any revenues it earns, is "partnership property." RUPA §§203-04. While partners may use this property in the course of the firm's business, they can *only* use it for such purposes. RUPA §401(i). And while they each do literally own the assets indirectly, through their share of ownership of the firm, an individual partner has almost no right to sell or assign that partner's ownership of those assets during the life of the firm. Specifically, the only thing of value that a partner can sell or assign—and as we shall see, the only thing the partner's personal creditors can get at to satisfy their claims—is the partner's "interest "in the firm. That "interest" is merely the partner's share of distributions. RUPA §503(b). As a marketable asset, this interest is subject to some severe practical limitations. While a partner may sell this right to distributions, rights in specific partnership property cannot be assigned. RUPA §501. And the sale of a mere interest in distributions, in itself, emphatically does not make the purchaser a partner in the firm. A person can be admitted as a new partner only with the unanimous consent of all the partners, RUPA §402(b)(3). The transfer of an interest neither entitles the transferee to any managerial rights or rights to access information, RUPA §503(a)(3), nor divests the transferring partner of management rights or ownership of the firm's specific property, *see* RUPA §503(a)(2).

 Dear Prof.: I'm a little worried about this unanimity thing. Do you mean an associate can't make partner in a law firm if even one of the partners disagrees?

Unanimity is the default rule. The partners may, however, unanimously agree (in the original partnership agreement or thereafter) that subsequent admissions will be subject to some other standard, such as a majority or two-thirds vote.

Worse yet, the transferred interest will often have no value to the transferee until the firm's dissolution, and it might have no value even then. Recall that no partner has a statutory default right to interim profit sharing or compensation, so unless the agreement provides otherwise, the assignee may have to wait until dissolution and winding up to get anything. Moreover, even where there is some right to interim distributions, for the right to have any value will normally require that the firm actually turn a profit. And, of course, even under the best circumstances, the assignee is mainly dependent on the remaining partners' cooperation. If they refuse to make distributions to which the transferee is entitled, or conceal information or otherwise misbehave, there is little the transferee can do short of litigation.

That is not to say that the transferee is wholly without recourse or that transferred interests are always of little value. They may be quite valuable in firms that are profitable and are regularly distributing profits to partners. In cases where they are not, and the remaining partners misbehave, the transferee has some statutory protections. Transferees may seek judicial dissolution and winding up of the firm, RUPA §§503(b)(2), 801(5), and while the statutory language gives little guidance, it appears that this provision is designed for just those situations in which transferees are denied rightful proceeds under the interest. As we shall see when we discuss dissolution generally (see Chapter 9), the value of this right is not usually that anyone really wants to end the firm. Rather, a person can use it to force a buyout by the remaining partners.

Another strong practical incentive that will sometimes weigh in the transferee's favor is that the debtor partner appears to retain full management rights in the firm, full rights to cause dissolution and winding up, and full power to bind the firm to contract or tort liabilities. Having assigned all financial interests, however, the debtor partner may not have terribly much concern for its healthy and responsible operation, and may have unhappy relations with the remaining partners. For all these reasons, the most desirable option for the firm may be to just to get rid of the debtor partner and transferee entirely by buying them out (especially if there has been a threat of foreclosure or judicial dissolution and winding up).

Finally, as discussed below, when the transferee happens to be a partner's individual creditor, who got the interest in satisfaction of the partner's debt, that person will sometimes have certain special powers to assist in recovering on the interest. *See* RUPA §504.

ATLANTIC MOBILE HOMES, INC. V. LEFEVER

Florida Court of Appeals
481 So. 2d 1002 (1986)

Per Curiam.

At issue . . . is whether the judgment creditors of an insolvent corporate partner can attach and liquidate its interest in partnership property. The trial court ruled that the corporation's interest in partnership assets could be liquidated pursuant to section 607.274 [the liquidation provision of the Florida corporation statute]. We conclude that the trial court's order constitutes a departure from the essential requirements of the law. Therefore, we [reverse].

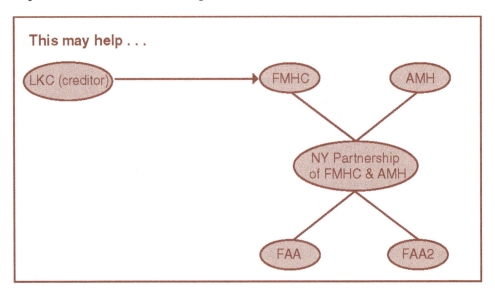

The respondents, LeFever, Krause, and Clark, obtained money judgments against Florida Mobile Home Communities, Inc. (FMHC). One of the petitioners, Atlantic Mobile Homes, Inc. is a co-partner of FMHC in a New York partnership. That partnership owns Florida Atlantic Associates and Florida Atlantic Associates Number 2, also petitioners before this court. Petitioners were not parties to the action against FMHC, nor was the partnership itself made a party. Nonetheless, the trial court fashioned an order giving petitioners thirty days in which to pay off FMHC's debt to respondents. After thirty days, if the debt remained unsatisfied, the order authorized respondents to petition the court for liquidation of FMHC's assets, including FMHC's interest in the partnership itself.

. . . Petitioners contend that . . . since respondents never sued the partnership directly, the trial court erred in ruling that some of the partnership assets could be liquidated. We agree.

Although section 607.274 authorizes a court to liquidate an insolvent corporate debtor, that authority does not extend to the liquidation of the assets of a partnership. A partner's interest in partnership assets is personal property which was subject to attachment and levy under the common law; however, Florida has adopted the Uniform Partnership Act (UPA), . . . which prohibits the attachment and liquidation of a partner's interest in a partnership unless the partnership is also a party to the action.

In order to proceed against a debtor/partner, a creditor must obtain a charging order pursuant to section 620.695, Florida Statutes (1985) [which was UPA §28, and is largely identical to RUPA §504]. Even then, the creditor cannot reach partnership assets but can only reach the debtor's share of profits from the partnership. Thus, the statutory charging order is the only means by which a judgment creditor can reach the debtor's partnership interest. . . .

In the present case, respondents did not seek a charging order against FMHC, nor did they make the partnership a party to the action. Rather, they proceeded against FMHC individually. Under section 620.68(2)(c) and section 620.695, a creditor proceeding against a partner individually cannot reach partnership assets. Consequently, we quash the trial court's order permitting the respondents to attach and liquidate FMHC's interest in the partnership. The partnership agreements, however, indicate that FMHC's liabilities have been assumed by petitioners. Therefore, this court's ruling is without prejudice to the respondents' right to sue the partnership itself.

■ **Think about this:**

(T) What, exactly, should LeFever et al. have done? Why?

As mentioned above, the transferee of a partner's interest is sometimes the partner's personal creditor, and the transfer is made in satisfaction of the partner's personal debt. A partner might make such a transfer voluntarily, to try to satisfy the debt, but the partner's creditor can also try to take it forcibly by way of the "charging order" remedy set out in RUPA §504. Such an order requires the firm to pay out the partner's interest to the creditor who secures the order, up to the unsatisfied amount of the underlying judgment debt. The problem is that a charging order gives the creditor only the same rights as would an assignment governed by §503, and the creditor too thus lacks any rights to management or information and is dependent both on the terms of the agreement as to the debtor-partner's rights and the firm's own financial fortunes.

Note that while assignees or creditors with charging orders may be entitled to distributions of profits (or capital on dissolution), they are not personally liable for the partnership's losses unless, with the consent of the existing partners, they actually become partners themselves.

 Dear Prof.: Are "individual" and "personal" creditors the same thing?

Yes. Incapable of stopping while ahead, we will go on to note that the terms generally refer to partners' creditors who have had no dealings with the partnership. To confuse things, however, once a partnership's assets are exhausted, it is not incorrect to say that the creditors of the partnership also become the creditors of the partners as individuals, given joint and several liability.

Although the UPA was less than clear on the matter, RUPA §504(c) expressly permits a court to order foreclosure on a charged partnership interest "[u]pon a showing that distributions under a charging order will not pay the judgment debt within a reasonable time. . . ." This means that the charged interest (that is, the right to receive distributions) can be sold to some willing third party. The partner whose interest is charged, the partnership, and the other partners all have the right to pay off the judgment debt in order to avert the foreclosure. It is important to remember, however, that foreclosure is an equitable remedy and courts ordinarily will, before ordering it, evaluate its likely effects on the partnership. Thus, if it is feared that an essential partner whose interest is to be sold will abandon the business, a court could decline to order a foreclosure.

■ **Think about this:**

(U) Suppose that you have a client who is an individual creditor of Perdita, the managing partner of the Perdita, Paul, and Associates law firm. Please explain to your client in plain English what the collection process may involve.

Test Yourself

Assume Applicability of the Revised Uniform Partnership Act

Questions 1-5 rely on the following facts:

Hank and his friend Biff have developed a new condiment, "Near-Death Experience Hot Sauce," for sale in local supermarkets. The idea and culinary talent mostly belong to Hank, but they agree they'll make the product using Biff's equipment, in Biff's garage. As to the costs and managerial decisions, the only thing to which they explicitly agree is that it will be "all for one and one for all."

Unfortunately, Hank knows first-hand the secret heartbreak of addiction to Unyun® brand snack treats, an artificial onion-ring-shaped snack Hank eats so compulsively that his unpaid tab at Big Billy's Qwikie-Mart is now $5,000. Much to his surprise, Biff was recently confronted by Big Billy himself at the garage/workplace where Hank and Biff make their sauce. Big Billy insisted that since he had been unable to find Hank, Biff is obliged to pay off the entire $5,000 Unyun® debt. Now, Big Billy's demand was not backed up with a threat of physical violence; Big Billy is only 4'9". Rather, Big Billy says that unless Biff pays up, he will sue.

1. The relationship between Hank and Biff is best characterized as:

    a. A mere contract, which in this case is consistent with the Statute of Frauds.
    b. An agency relationship in which Hank is principal and Biff is agent.
    c. A partnership.
    d. Something other than a partnership because in these particular circumstances a partnership agreement would have to be in writing.

2. Assuming Big Billy has not secured any sort of court order to enforce Hank's Unyun® debt, he should be able to collect:

    a. $5,000 from any of Hank, Biff, or their business.
    b. $5,000 from Hank or the business.
    c. $5,000 from the business.
    d. $5,000 from Hank.

3. Assume that Big Billy secures a court order to collect on Hank's $5,000 Unyun® debt as against Hank's interest in the hot sauce business. Such an order would:

    a. Entitle Big Billy to insist on immediate payment by the partnership of $5,000.
    b. Entitle Big Billy to one half of the excess of all assets over liabilities, upon dissolution and winding up, to a maximum of $5,000.
    c. Entitle Big Billy to one half of the excess of all assets over liabilities, upon dissolution and winding up.
    d. In fact, no such order would be available. Hank's debt is purely personal and could not be executed against the business.

4. Assume that Big Billy secures the court order described in Question 3, but Biff refuses to release any funds to Big Billy. Big Billy can, upon an appropriate showing in court:

    a. Secure a dissolution of the business.
    b. Secure a foreclosure of Hank's interest.
    c. Secure a winding up of the business.
    d. Answers a and b are both correct.
    e. Answers a, b, and c are correct.

5. Hank could have tried to settle his debt with Big Billy by:

    a. Assigning to Big Billy his interest in the business's inventory.
    b. Assigning to Big Billy his interest in the joint checking account into which Hank and Biff have deposited all of their business's revenues.
    c. Allowing Big Billy to take his place in the business completely.
    d. None of the above.

Questions 6-8 stand alone:

6. X, Y, and Z are the members of the XYZ Partnership ("XYZ"). They are each skilled craftspeople who make handmade furniture for the partnership to sell, using tools and raw materials purchased by the partnership. Z has made a chair, in the same manner in which he's made all his other products for the partnership, but he is particularly fond of this chair and does not want to part with it. Z can unilaterally refuse to sell this item, despite X and Y's desire to sell it. True or False?

   a. True. He made it and it is therefore his.
   b. True. The chair is an item of "partnership property," and the partnership cannot assign any of the partners' interests in "specific partnership property" unless it assigns all of their interests.
   c. True. *See* Revised Uniform Partnership Act §401(j).
   d. False.

7. Traditionally, the "exhaustion rule" required:

   a. For all claims, execution against partnership assets only.
   b. For contract claims, execution against partnership assets only.
   c. For contract claims, execution against partnership assets prior to execution against partners individually.
   d. For all claims, execution against partnership assets prior to execution against partners individually.

8. Shady Bros. Properties is a general partnership that invests in real estate properties for the purpose of re-selling them for profit. Late last year the only property in Shady Bros.' ownership was a downtown retail building. Scott, one of the three general partners at Shady Bros., meets a willing buyer for the downtown building, and unilaterally executes an agreement for immediate sale of the property. The sale agreement most likely is:

   a. Unenforceable. Scott lacked authority for this kind of transaction.
   b. Unenforceable because of the nature of Shady Bros.' business.
   c. Enforceable because of the nature of Shady Bros.' business.
   d. None of the above.

9

Dissolution and Winding Up

The end of the partnership and the attending to of its final affairs can be among the most complicated matters in partnership law. This is so because it is at this time that the partners' interests are most in conflict, and most at odds with those of the firm's creditors.

Chapter Outline

A. Introduction

- The most important policy goals of partnership dissolution rules are:
    - Preservation of the partners' own liquidity
    - Protection of partnership creditors

B. RUPA's Distinctions Among Dissociation, Dissolution, and Winding Up

- Dissociation is an event triggered by departure of a partner
- Dissolution marks the end of the partnership
- Winding up is a process that occurs only after dissolution, and is different than dissolution

C. Certain Technicalities and Practical Realities Surrounding Dissociation, Dissolution, and Winding Up

1. What Dissolution Is Usually About: Investor Liquidity and Bargaining in the Shadow of the Law
    - The partners generally are free to agree about consequences, either up front or after the fact
    - RUPA provides for very specific default outcomes

2. The Mechanics of Valuation
    - Valuing liabilities
    - Valuing goodwill

3. The Requirement of Reduction to Cash
   - Reducing assets to cash permits payment of obligations

4. The Wrongful Dissociation Issue
   - Wrongful dissolution results in damages and loss of certain rights

D. Some Examples, Including Fiduciary Issues and Wrongful Termination

- Statutory rules are applied to clean up partners' failure to observe formalities
- "Bad faith" dissolution has consequences

E. Post-Break-up Arrangements and the "Continuing" Firm

1. Post-Dissolution Continuation in General
   - Winding up in the absence of agreement to the contrary

2. Powers and Liabilities of the Dissolved or Continuing Firm and the Departing Partners
   - Powers and liabilities following dissolution and winding up are a function of which acts are appropriate for winding up and/or within apparent authority
   - Powers and liabilities following dissociation where no dissolution occurs
     - The dissociating partner's actual authority is terminated; apparent authority is more complicated
     - The dissociating partner continues to have liability for pre-dissociation obligations of the partnership, but does not have liability for post-dissociation obligations absent certain circumstances involving a third party's reasonable belief

3. Partnership Mergers, Exchanges of Interest, and Conversions
   - Partnerships can merge with other entities
   - Interests in partnerships can be exchanged, *en masse*, for interests in other entities
   - Partnerships can be converted to other business entities
     - The partners and the new entity generally have continuing liability for the obligations of the partnership
     - Mergers, exchanges of interest, and conversions generally are not to be treated as dissolutions

Test Yourself

What does it look like?

Check the online Supplement for the following sample documents that are relevant to this chapter:

- A sample dissolution agreement.

A. Introduction

Above all, two policy concerns are paramount in the law of dissolution:

1. *Liquidity:* The rules by which a partnership can be ended and its assets dissolved govern the liquidity of partners' investment in the firm. Unless a partner has some leverage to force actual liquidation of firm assets, the partner's investment in the firm will be largely illiquid in most cases.
2. *Creditors:* Events surrounding the end of a firm's life or the end of a partner's association with it give rise to the most acute and most complicated issues concerning individual partners' liabilities to third parties.

Keeping these concerns in mind will be of great help when the details start to seem overwhelming.

B. RUPA's Distinctions Among Dissociation, Dissolution, and Winding Up

As a first step in understanding the subject matters of this chapter, it is wise to learn the meaning of three terms of art employed by the Revised Uniform Partnership Act (RUPA)[1]:

Breaking up is hard to do.

Breaking up is hard to do, and also sometimes doctrinally complex.

1. *Dissociation:* The event of a partner leaving the firm and discarding the status of partner.
2. *Dissolution:* The formal, legal end of the firm's existence, which ordinarily requires that its ordinary business cease and that the partners proceed to a winding up.

---

1. As in all other chapters in this book, references to RUPA are to the Uniform Partnership Act (1997) with amendments through 2013.

3. *Winding Up:* The actual liquidation of the business. The assets are applied to satisfy creditors, and the remainder is to be distributed to the partners in cash.

RUPA set up this three-part system to resolve certain confusing problems under the Uniform Partnership Act (1914) (UPA). Under the UPA, any change in a partnership's personnel caused a *dissolution*—at least as a matter of legal principle, the firm was considered to have ceased its existence, and, in the absence of an agreement to the contrary, the partners were under an obligation actually to liquidate. This could happen whenever a partner died, went bankrupt, became mentally unfit, or just decided to quit. In practice, the harsh consequences of this rule could often be avoided by those partners who wanted to continue the firm, so long as they could scrape together enough cash to buy out the departing partner's interest.

Still, the automatic dissolution rule caused a lot of hassle and uncertainty, all the more so as time wore on, and larger and more complex partnerships became common. It could also give one partner what seemed like unfair leverage over others. And it was based entirely on a legal fiction that in many cases was pretty far from the reality—the so-called aggregate theory manifest in some portions of the UPA, under which partnerships had no independent existence as entities in their own right, and were conceived of as no more than the collection of the partners themselves. Adding the "dissociation" concept to resolve some of the inconvenience of UPA dissolution was one of the major aspects in which RUPA replaced the "aggregate" theory with an "entity" theory of the partnership.

 Dear Prof.: What do you mean by "firm"?

This is not a term with any legal definition. We use it as economists and businesspeople commonly use it, to mean simply any business entity.

RUPA §801(1), a key provision governing dissolution, says that when a dissociation is caused by any of the events described in RUPA §601(2)-(10), it does not cause a dissolution of the partnership. It does have other consequences. As soon as the dissociation occurs, the dissociating partner loses all management rights, and no longer owes the partnership most fiduciary duties. RUPA §603(b). Likewise, the dissociating partner largely loses the ability to bind the firm to contracts or subject it to tort liability. Such ability as is retained depends essentially on the extent of lingering apparent authority. This means that if a dissociated partner creates post-dissociation liabilities, the other partners will likely have redress against the dissociated partner.

Perhaps the most important consequence of dissociation in the absence of dissolution is that the partnership must, under §701, buy out the dissociating partner's interest. To repeat, however, since no dissolution occurs, the remaining partners are free to continue business as they otherwise would have. Thus, as a consequence of RUPA's entity theory of partnership, personnel changes that result from things like a partner's death, bankruptcy, expulsion by the other partners, or termination (in the case of a partner that is a corporation or other juridical entity) have no effect on the firm's status as a going entity.

 Dear Prof.: What happens if one partner in a two-partner partnership dissociates?

When you're alone you're alone. When you're alone you ain't nothing but alone.
>   Bruce Springsteen, *When You're Alone*, from the *Tunnel of Love* album

A partnership is defined as "an association of two or more persons to carry on as co-owners a business for profit." RUPA §101(11). Thus, as a logical matter, when only one owner remains, a partnership cannot exist and has dissolved. *See* Corrales v. Corrales, 98 Cal. App. 4th 221 (2011). RUPA §801(6), however, now provides that a one-person partnership can continue for 90 days before dissolution is triggered.

However, RUPA preserves one very important means of dissociation that *does* cause dissolution, reflecting a value that runs deeply in the traditions of partnership law. Section 601(1) preserves the power of any partner unilaterally to dissociate, and under §801(1), in the case of a so-called at-will partnership such voluntary withdrawal always causes dissolution. (As an aside, note that, as §602(a) makes clear, any partner can withdraw at any time, even if doing so is a breach of contract among the partners. "Wrongful" breaches are further discussed below.)

 Dear Prof.: How about a partnership that is not at will?

By negative implication from RUPA §801(1), if a partner dissociates from a partnership for a term or undertaking—that is, a partnership that the partners agree will not be dissolved before a particular time or completion of a particular goal, and that therefore is not at will—he or she does not have the right to force a dissolution. RUPA §801(2) provides that after such a dissociation the remaining partners can trigger a winding up within 90 days if at least one-half of them vote to do so. (Thereafter, unanimous assent is required.)

Connections: LLCs and Corporations

Although there are many similarities between RUPA and the Uniform Limited Liability Company Act (ULLCA), they are different on this point. ULLCA §701 does *not* give members the default right to force dissolution. See Chapter 11.

With respect to the dissolution of closely held corporations, see Chapter 27.

Where dissociation is not wrongful, a partner can often use the power of unilateral dissolution as a fairly mighty weapon. Upon an event of dissolution, the partnership must proceed to winding up unless dissolution is rescinded by the unanimous consent of all partners. *See* RUPA §§802, 803. The winding-up process culminates in payment of the partnership's debts and payment "in money" of any amounts to which partners are entitled. *See* RUPA §806. Thus, following dissolution and in the absence of contrary agreement, every partner who has not wrongfully dissociated can *force* the partnership to sell all of its assets, to reduce them to cash. In many cases, that will give a dissociating partner quite a lot of leverage against the others, especially if the others would like to continue the firm. They will be able to continue the business only under two circumstances. First, they might come to some agreement with the dissociating partner as to the terms of a buyout. Alternately, if sale of the partnership's business as a going concern will bring more money than a piecemeal sale of its assets, the remaining partners might make the highest offer to purchase the partnership's business on terms producing enough cash to pay off its debts and the claim of the dissociating partner.

There is a reason that this special power of unilateral dissolution was preserved, despite adoption of the entity theory in the RUPA in 1997. Among the most salient features of the traditional partnership is this special tool of liquidity. It allows partners quickly to force a liquidation of their investment in the firm (assuming that the investment has a positive value). That distinguishes partnership from several other business entity forms, and makes it sharply distinct from the closely held corporation (in which equity investments are more or less totally illiquid except in the unusual circumstance where a shareholder can force a judicial dissolution).

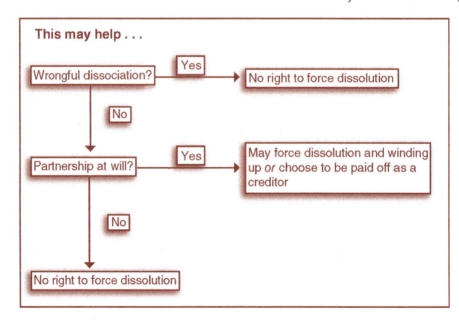

> ■ **Think about this (assuming all situations are governed by the default rules of RUPA):**
>
> *(A)* Kim, your client, is a partner in an at-will general partnership with Kourtney and Khloé. She is unhappy with some of the choices they have made and would like to withdraw. Please explain to her what her options are.
>
> *(B)* Assume, instead, that Kim's partnership with Kourtney and Khloé is for a term of two years. At the end of the first year, she wants to withdraw even though her agreement does not permit it. What are her options?

C. Certain Technicalities and Practical Realities Surrounding Dissociation, Dissolution, and Winding Up

1. What Dissolution Is Usually About: Investor Liquidity and Bargaining in the Shadow of the Law

> *Dear Prof.: Bargaining in the shadow of the law?*
>
> In a famous law review article, two professors observed that in some circumstances explicit legal rules themselves are often less important in defining outcomes than they are in shaping and setting the boundaries for negotiation among parties. Dissociation and dissolution work very much in that way. Actual negotiated outcomes in practice are routinely different than one might imagine if the only thing one had ever done is read the RUPA provisions. *See* Robert H. Mnookin & Lewis Kornhauser, *Bargaining in the Shadow of the Law: The Case of Divorce*, 88 YALE L.J. 950 (1979).
>
> In fact, call me Captain Obvious, but the partners can, by agreement, completely avoid most of the rules described thus far, including the one calling for dissolution by voluntary withdrawal from an at-will partnership.

It is important to appreciate that a partnership break-up is not necessarily the end of the firm. As noted above, if a non-wrongful dissociation triggers dissolution, a unanimous agreement by the partners can rescind it. RUPA §803(b). In the event of a wrongful dissociation (one before the end of the partnership's agreed upon term or undertaking) or dissociation pursuant to one of the events specified in §601(6)-(10), a majority of the non-dissociating partners can choose to avoid dissolution entirely. RUPA §801(2).

The major issue involved in a dissociation will often be a hotly disputed valuation of the departing partner's investment, and the matter of whether the continuing partners can come up with enough cash to pay it off. Ordinarily, the departing partner will not have any particular desire to cause the business to be *really* liquidated, so long as there is enough cash to satisfy the partner's needs and so long as there is adequate protection from lingering liabilities to third parties (on that, much more below). But the power to *threaten* an actual liquidation is the departing partner's best tool in leveraging a better payout.

Doing the Numbers: Paying a Dissociating Partner

Assume that Angelina contributed $9,000 to an at-will general partnership owned by herself, Brad, and Chuck. Brad and Chuck each contributed property valued at $9,000. Because they have no agreement to the contrary, they share profits and losses equally. Very little happens, although the partnership spends $3,000 in advertising. Happily, however, the property Brad contributed has doubled in value. Angelina decides to withdraw. She agrees to waive dissolution, a decision with which Brad and Chuck agree. What will Angelina receive?

First, calculate the partner's capital accounts as of the date of dissociation: $9,000 − $1,000 = $8,000 each, for a total of $24,000.

Then, calculate the maximum amount that would be generated by liquidating the partnership's assets, including by way of sale as a going concern. Assume that piecemeal liquidation would bring the highest amount. The partnership has $6,000 in cash, plus Chuck's contributed property at $9,000 and Brad's contributed property at $18,000, for a total of $33,000.

Of that amount, $24,000 would be required to pay the partners' claims for contributed capital, leaving profit of $9,000 to be allocated three ways.

Thus, Angelina will receive $8,000 + $3,000 = $11,000. (This happens to be 1/3 of the $33,000 liquidation price but that is not how the facts will always sort out.)

Because this problem of valuation will often be so divisive and uncertain, RUPA's drafters included a special dispute resolution procedure that at least sometimes should make it go more simply. Under §701, the partners must negotiate the value of the departing partner's interest, which is to approximate the value that that partner would receive if the firm were either liquidated or sold as a going concern, whichever is greater. Anticipating that the parties will often disagree on that value, §701(e) sets in motion a resolution process if the parties are deadlocked. If they have not reached agreement within 120 days after a written demand for payment, then the partnership *must* either pay the dissociated partner the amount it believes the payout to be worth, or tender an offer to pay that amount in cases of wrongful dissociation. ("Wrongful" dissociation will be discussed further below, in Section C4 of this chapter.) Subsection (f) says that if the dissociation was wrongful, and the partnership is entitled under subsection (h) to defer the payout until the expiration of an agreed upon term or undertaking, then the partnership only has to send the dissociating partner a written estimate of what the payout will be. The payment or offer of payment must be accompanied by supporting documents and a statement that it constitutes payment in full unless the dissociating party commences action for a judicial valuation within 120 days of the payment or tender. If the partnership fails to make the requisite payment or offer of payment, then under §701(i) the dissociating party may likewise commence such an action within one year of the written demand for payment.

What incentive does the partnership have to make a realistic estimate in its §701(e)-(f) payment or offer of payment? At least one incentive is that the dissociating partner's payout value accrues interest from the time of dissociation to the time of actual payment. §701(b). Note as well the last few lines in §701(i) relating to the assessment of fees and expenses.

> ■ **Think about this:**
>
> *(C)* What other incentives might the partnership have to make a realistic estimate?

There is an important piece of the puzzle still to be described. If a partner has voluntarily withdrawn from an at-will partnership, then a dissolution and winding up are called for by §801(1). In order to avoid that effect by agreement under §802(b), the dissociating partner must also agree to waive the winding up. In other words, the §701 process and its simplified dispute resolution procedure do not even get started unless the dissociating partner first agrees to start it by waiving the winding up. If that partner has reason to believe that valuation will be unreasonably low, or lower than he might like, then that partner might have quite an incentive not to waive it. Again, the power unilaterally to force winding up is an important source of leverage. Likewise, the only really sure-fire protection from personal responsibility for the firm's ongoing liabilities is a winding up. Only through that procedure, for the most part, are the creditors actually paid off in cash and the liabilities actually disposed of. So, if a person dissociates from a firm with a lot of value but also significant or significantly risky liabilities, insisting on the winding up might be the best bet.

> ■ **Think about this:**
>
> *(D)* A withdrawing partner might not want to force a winding up if there are large liabilities but not a lot of value in the firm. Can you explain why?

All this begs the question, of course, whether the continuing partners have any leverage of their own, and indeed they do: The power of unilateral dissolution is tempered by certain other realities. The dissolving partner will have some measure of his own assets tied up in the firm and will have an interest in whatever profits and goodwill it currently retains. Causing dissolution when the firm's business is suffering, when it has large outstanding liabilities, or when market conditions cause its assets to be undervalued can result in the departing partner taking less than his share is really worth, and perhaps in taking nothing or even *owing* money, to cover his share of the firm's existing liabilities. So if the firm happens to be on hard times or for some other reason has little actual value, even in total liquidation, the departing partner's threat of unilateral dissolution does not carry much weight.

Even when times are good, a dissociating partner trying to hold out for more money can only play so much hardball. While he or she can threaten to force an actual liquidation, and while the continuing partners would ordinarily like to avoid that for any number of reasons, the continuing partners can always ultimately just say: fine, go ahead. Section 802(e) permits any partner to request judicial supervision of the winding up—which would prevent the dissociating partner from just going off and selling the assets and absconding with proceeds or engaging in other funny business—and §410(b) empowers any partner to seek an "accounting" of the partnership affairs, which amounts to a judicial valuation of the firm and each partner's stake in it. Using those tools, the continuing partners can make their case to a judge that the dissociating partner's demands are too high, and it very well may be that the dissociating partner who bargains too hard and winds up with such a judicial determination will be disappointed.

As may be becoming clear, an important facet of this law of dissolution and winding up is that in many firms it turns out to be one of the only sources of real power to be held by individual partners. The reason is simple, and it reflects certain basic realities about the nature of the general partnership. On the one hand, interests in a general partnership would otherwise be highly illiquid. In the absence of contrary agreement, RUPA §§402(b)(3) and 503 make it difficult to sell any partnership interest for its fair value, because unless the remaining partners unanimously agree to admit a purchaser as a full partner in the firm, that purchaser is entitled only to purchase the departing partner's right to receive distributions, and will be unable to participate or interfere in management. For these and other reasons, even if a partner can find a buyer for her interest, she will likely be able to get only a fraction of its value.

■ **Think about this:**

(E) Given its value to individual partners as perhaps their only real source of power, would there ever be a case in which you would counsel a client to agree to give up the right of unilateral dissolution at the time the partnership is being entered?

Finally, dissolving partners occasionally might be following yet one other strategy: to coerce their own complete takeover of the business. As observed by Professor Ribstein, "[t]his can occur in a number of circumstances where the non-dissociating partners cannot practically replace the resources removed from the firm by the dissociating partner. . . ." So, for example, "the remaining partners may be unable to pay for the dissociating partner's interest without selling the firm's assets, to replace unique assets that were owned by the partner, to restore the creditworthiness attributable to the personal wealth of the dissociating partner, or to replace the dissociating partner's managerial skills." Larry E. Ribstein, *A Statutory Approach to Partner Dissociation*, 65 Wash. U. L.Q. 357, 384 (1987). A case we'll read presently, the famous California Supreme Court decision in Page v. Page, 359 P.2d 41 (Cal. 1961), is a classic example of this situation. Another example (which, like *Page*, also involves laundry and is cited by Professor Ribstein) was Cude v. Couch, 588 S.W.2d 554 (Tenn. 1977), where a dissolving partner was able to buy out the partnership's laundromat business because he owned the premises and refused to lease them to his partner or any other buyer of the business.

It is worth noting that the mechanism under RUPA §803(b) that permits buy-out-in-lieu-of-liquidation merely makes explicit what had been implicit under the UPA. Even under that statute, it had been very common for dissolving partnerships to be preserved by some number of the partners who were treated as having created a new partnership that purchased the business of the old partnership. This artifice was another reflection of the UPA's aggregate theory. That theory required that a partnership retain the same membership to remain the same partnership. So the loss of even one partner caused the original partnership no longer to exist, even if the business continued in otherwise identical form. This, in turn, sometimes caused problems with, for example, contracts the partnership had entered that provided that the rights under them could not be assigned.

 ### Time Out for PR: Ends, Means, and Complications

Imagine yourself as an attorney explaining to an impatient businessperson exactly how much he or she needs to know to make decisions about some of the matters described in this chapter. Are there some decisions you might be tempted to make for them in order to simplify the discussion? Consider American Bar Association Model Rules of Professional Conduct 1.2(a) and 1.4.

Rule 1.2 Scope of Representation and Allocation of Authority Between Client and Lawyer

(a) Subject to paragraphs (c) and (d), a lawyer shall abide by a client's decisions concerning the objectives of representation and, as required by Rule 1.4, shall consult with the client as to the means by which they are to be pursued. A lawyer may take such action on behalf of the client as is impliedly authorized to carry out the representation.

Rule 1.4 Communication

(a) A lawyer shall: . . .

(2) reasonably consult with the client about the means by which the client's objectives are to be accomplished; . . .

(3) keep the client reasonably informed about the status of the matter; . . .

(b) A lawyer shall explain a matter to the extent reasonably necessary to permit the client to make informed decisions regarding the representation.

2. The Mechanics of Valuation

When the firm is wound up, or when a partner dissociates and is entitled to a buyout under RUPA §701, the value of the individual partners' interests must be determined. Although not required, it may be the case that the partnership maintains the type of capital accounts described in Chapter 7. These accounts consist of each partner's initial capital contribution, plus the appropriate allocation of profits (or losses), minus any distributions that were made to the partner during the course of the partnership. The partners may have agreed that buyout prices are governed by capital accounts or some other mechanism. If not, the default rule of §701(b) provides that the purchase price must be determined as if the firm were wound up—by liquidation of assets or sale as a going concern, whichever would produce the highest value—on the day of dissociation and accounts were settled under §807(b). Under that section, the amount produced by winding up under the appropriate method is first to be applied to satisfy creditors. Any surplus then is applied to return unrepaid contributions by the partners. Any overage will be allocated among the partners according to their rights to participate in distributions (which is in equal shares unless otherwise agreed).

We should consider as well two technical issues in valuation. First, a special problem of valuation in the case of dissociation that does not cause dissolution is that the parties must make some estimate of the firm's existing liabilities as of the date of dissociation. This can sometimes be a little complicated, because some of those liabilities will require performances that have not come due as of the date of dissolution. How much, if any, of the future liability

JD/MBA: The Time Value of Money

The comments to RUPA §701 indicates that amounts payable in the future should be discounted to "present value." This acknowledges that payment of a lesser amount now is equivalent in value to payment of a greater amount in the future (since the money paid now presumably can be invested). Present value calculators are readily available online and elsewhere; using them requires selection of an assumed rate at which money currently received can be invested.

should the departing partner bear? For example, suppose that a partnership, the ABC firm, had entered into a two-year lease for one of its machine shop locations, and that the rent is $500 per month, payable monthly. One partner, Alan, dissociates. On the day of his dissociation, only one half of the lease had expired and been paid for. Alan likely will strenuously disavow any part of the remaining liability, since it would require reduction of his payout by $2,000 (one-third of the $6,000 remaining).

The general rule in these cases has been that pre-dissolution contracts bind a departing partner, and courts seem rarely to deviate from that rule. There is some authority in some jurisdictions, however, that where some obligation is a periodic and continuing one extending well into the firm's future, the unpaid portion of it is not properly chargeable against the departing partner's interest. *See generally* 2 ALAN R. BROMBERG & LARRY E. RIBSTEIN, BROMBERG AND RIBSTEIN ON PARTNERSHIP §7.14(b) (2014).

A second technicality is that the rule that buyout valuation is based on the higher of liquidation value or sale of the going business means that the firm's "goodwill" must be calculated. Goodwill is the amount that a buyer of a profitable ongoing business is willing to pay over and above the liquidation value of its assets. It is paid because the purchaser values not only the assets themselves, but the likelihood that when kept in the business those assets will continue to generate profits. (It is only in the case of a continuing firm that the parties must estimate "goodwill," since it only exists as a separate asset where the firm is not yet fully liquidated. Where the firm is actually sold intact to a third party, the value of its goodwill will be included as a component of the purchase price, and does not need to be separately estimated.)

In a few jurisdictions, this causes a special problem in the case of *professional* firms. At one time, most courts held that a departing professional partner could receive a payout like any other partner, but could *never* be compensated for any part of the firm's goodwill, and indeed many courts held as a matter of law that professional firms simply have no "going concern" value at all. The rule had two rationales. First, to some large extent the prospective goodwill of a professional firm is in the actual talents and skills of its partners, because the goodwill of any firm is really just a present estimate of its ability to make profits in the future. Professional partners who depart in effect take their future profit-making ability with them, and so their share of "goodwill" is already reflected in their own abilities. Second, in at least some professions (law, for example) ethical rules prohibit the sharing of fees with anyone except another professional with whom one is a partner. In any event, the common law rule has been rejected by most jurisdictions. *See, e.g.*, Spayd v. Turner, Granzlow & Hollenkamp, 482 N.E.2d 1232 (Ohio 1985) (recounting the history of the common law rule and formally rejecting it under Ohio law; adopting the rule that prospective goodwill can be valued and liquidated even in professional partnerships).

JD/MBA: Accounting for Goodwill

Even though it may be perfectly clear that a third party would be willing to pay for a company's "goodwill," it is not carried as an asset on the company's own books. If, however, one company buys the business of another and pays more than the identifiable tangible and intangible assets are worth, the excess is carried as an asset, subject to periodic testing for continuing value.

As noted in the text, an estimate of goodwill generally is taken into account in valuing a departing partner's share.

Time Out for PR: Dividing Fees

As the text indicates, there indeed are limits on attorneys' ability to divide fees. Read American Bar Association Model Rule of Professional Conduct 1.5(e) and accompanying comment 8. As a practical matter, what does Rule 1.5(e) mean for the arrangements lawyers can make to pay a departing partner?

Rule 1.5 Fees

(e) A division of a fee between lawyers who are not in the same firm may be made only if:

(1) the division is in proportion to the services performed by each lawyer or each lawyer assumes joint responsibility for the representation;

(2) the client agrees to the arrangement, including the share each lawyer will receive, and the agreement is confirmed in writing; and

(3) the total fee is reasonable.

Comment 8. Paragraph (e) does not prohibit or regulate division of fees to be received in the future for work done when lawyers were previously associated in a law firm.

As the *Spayd* majority noted, the traditional rule arose at a time when professional persons would commonly join one partnership early in their careers and remain there until their retirement. By contrast, it is nowadays more common for practicing professionals to change jobs several times during their careers, even after attaining partnership. Therefore, the usual practice under modern law is to hold that the existence or not of goodwill in any sort of partnership is simply a question of fact. The question for the trier of fact in any case is whether a buyer for the firm would pay more for it than the book value of its assets. The trier should normally find that a professional firm lacks measurable goodwill only where its future expectation of earnings resides *solely* in the professional skills of the individual partners (as opposed to the brand value of the firm name or its established network of clients or the like). In such a case, the departing partner will in essence automatically take an appropriate share of goodwill with her upon departure. *See generally* 2 Bromberg & Ribstein, *supra*, at §7.13(c)(2).

3. The Requirement of Reduction to Cash

RUPA §807(f) specifies that winding up payments to partners are to be made "in money." The fundamental idea of winding up is that each partner is entitled not only to a share of the firm's economic value, but to be completely and unambiguously freed of legal ties to former partners and the firm's creditors. The case of Hill v. Brown, 520 N.E.2d 1038 (Ill. Ct. App. 1988), nicely illustrates this rule and its rationale. Plaintiff and defendant partnered in harvesting cattle embryos for transplantation to recipient cows. The firm's sole asset, in which they had equal shares, was the prize cow from which they got the embryos. They agreed mutually that their relationship should come to an end, but disagreed how the firm should be wound up. Defendant, who had possession of the cow, insisted that the asset should be auctioned off in two separate 50 percent ownership interests, pointing to language in the written partnership agreement stating that if they could not negotiate a friendly settlement for liquidation, the firm's assets would be auctioned "in halves" (though, as the court speculated, defendant's real motive may have been that he desired continued access to the prize cow, but wouldn't have enough ready cash to buy her outright). The court disagreed, and accepted plaintiff's view, ordering liquidation by a sale of 100 percent ownership of the cow. As the court explained, "[c]omplete liquidation of the partnership property as a unit . . . is the most efficient and equitable method," and speculated that the "in halves" method might not "insure[] a wind up of the business of the partnership." 520 N.E.2d at 1041.

■ **Think about this:**

(F) Why was the court so concerned about the risk that plaintiff and defendant would each wind up purchasing one of two 50 percent interests? Couldn't that still be a liquidation? If that happened, what might be their relationship following the sale?

---

4. The Wrongful Dissociation Issue

Finally, one last distinction, mentioned briefly above, deserves further thought. Some partnerships are formed for a "term or undertaking." The partners might agree that the firm will exist for a stated period of time or that it will exist at least until some specific date. Likewise, they might agree that it will exist until they have accomplished some particular task, like construction of a building. If any partner dissociates before such a date or before achieving such an objective, it is a breach of the partnership agreement and certain negative consequences will follow. There are two small doctrinal issues in this connection. First, the courts carefully construe language that purportedly establishes a fixed term. In particular, language to the effect that the firm will exist *no later than* some date does *not* create a fixed term, and the firm may be unilaterally dissolved earlier without breach of the agreement. Second, although expiration of an agreed-upon term or undertaking is a cause of dissolution under RUPA §801(2)(C), §803(b) provides for continuation after dissolution by unanimous agreement of the partners. Such an agreement presumably could be implied in cases in which the partners agree to a fixed term but then continue business after its passing.

Dissociation in breach of the agreement is called "wrongful dissociation." RUPA §602(b). The consequences for the wrongfully dissociating partner are several. The main consequence is that damages caused by the breach will be recoverable under RUPA §602(c). The wrongfully dissociating partner is also denied the right to seek winding up except by court order under RUPA §803(e). This can be a significant penalty because it entitles the continuing partners to refuse to pay out the dissociating partner's share until expiration of the term or undertaking. RUPA §701(h). Subsection 701(h), however, provides the dissociating partner some protection—during the period in which the payout is deferred, the continuing parties must provide "adequate[] secur[ity]" for the payout and cause it to accrue interest.

Where there is no specified term or undertaking, the partnership is said to be "at will." Unilateral dissolution of an at-will partnership has no negative statutory consequences for the dissolving partner.

D. Some Examples, Including Fiduciary Issues and Wrongful Termination

As you might expect, even rules as specific as those described above still leave plenty to fight about. The following case addresses what happens when the parties deal with dissolution too casually.

SHAR'S CARS, L.L.C. V. ELDER

Utah Court of Appeals
97 P.3d 724 (2004)

GREENWOOD, J.

[In January 1998, Jeffrey Birschbach and his wife began a used car dealership that they called Shar's Cars, L.L.C. (The court refers to Birschbach and Shar's Cars collectively as "Plaintiffs.") They had dealings with Deloy Elder and Bruce Rutherford, who were in business together as used car wholesalers. (The court refers to their business as the Elder/Rutherford partnership.) By oral agreement in early 1998, Birschbach and the Elder/Rutherford partnership agreed to sell cars from the same lot, doing business as Shar's Cars, though maintaining the separate existence of the two businesses. In mid-August, Elder left the business and ended his partnership with Rutherford. Shortly thereafter, Rutherford and Birschbach agreed to carry on the business together. The Elder/Rutherford partnership's bank account was closed, and the remaining balance was either transferred to Birschbach and Rutherford's new business account, or used to pay off partnership debts. The business faltered, however, and by mid-October Birschbach closed down Shar's Cars. With one exception, Elder was not involved in closing the business or repayment

Things fall apart; the center cannot hold;

Mere anarchy is loosed upon the world.

WILLIAM BUTLER YEATS, THE SECOND COMING

of any of the Elder/Rutherford debts. This action originated as a suit against Plaintiffs by one of the firm's many creditors, as a part of which Plaintiffs then filed a third-party action against Rutherford and Elder. The trial court held that at the point of Elder's departure in August 1998 the firm's total net loss was $45,000, and that only $22,500 of that amount would be entered as a judgment against Elder.]

A. PARTIAL RELEASE OF ELDER'S LIABILITY

Plaintiffs challenge the trial court's determination that Elder was released from liability for partnership debts incurred after August 31, 1998. In announcing its findings, the trial court noted that while Rutherford, Elder, and Birschbach never formally agreed to release Elder from all partnership liabilities, the court expressly found that Elder was "not responsible for anything after August 31st of 1998, that there was in fact a new agreement." Based on the evidence in the record and case law, the trial court correctly concluded that Elder was not liable for any debts incurred after his departure.

Normally, a partnership continues to exist until it has completed the statutory dissolution and winding up process. In this case, the parties did not follow the normal dissolution and winding up process. However, Elder's departure effectuated a dissolution of the Elder/Rutherford partnership. Upon Elder's departure, the partnership's bank account was closed and partnership assets were either used to pay debts, or transferred to a new bank account. However, rather than formally winding up the partnership, Rutherford essentially carried on the partnership by bringing in Birschbach as a new partner.

In MacKay v. Hardy, 973 P.2d 941 (Utah 1998), the Utah Supreme Court stated:

> Under general partnership principles, a withdrawing or "outgoing" partner is not liable for partnership debts which arise after dissolution: "On the dissolution of a partnership by the withdrawal or retirement of a partner, the outgoing partner sustains no further relation to the remaining or continuing partners whereby they can exercise any authority binding on him, in the absence of circumstances giving rise to an estoppel. Thus, a partner is not personally liable for partnership debts where the partnership is dissolved before the inception of the debt, at least where notice of the dissolution is given to third parties who have dealings with the partnership."

In this case, the trial court found that during the formation of the new agreement between Birschbach and Rutherford, it was known, accepted, and agreed that Elder was no longer involved in the partnership. This finding was based in part on the oral agreement between the two after Rutherford informed Birschbach of Elder's departure. Further, the subsequent actions of Rutherford and Birschbach demonstrate an intent to carry on a partnership without Elder's involvement. Because Elder was not involved with the partnership after August 1998, the trial court correctly limited his liability to debts incurred prior to the dissolution of the Elder/Rutherford partnership.

B. PARTNERSHIP LIABILITY

Plaintiffs next assert that the trial court erred when it concluded that Elder was only liable for one-half of the partnership's debt. Plaintiffs contend that there is no basis for this conclusion under Utah's partnership law because partners are jointly liable for all debts. We agree.

Connections: Revisiting the Sugarland Case

Now that we've got *Shar's Cars* and some statutory mechanics under our belts, let us think a bit more about a case we considered earlier in this book—the dispute among the founders of the country music group Sugarland (see Chapter 6B). Recall that plaintiff Kristen Hall founded the band with defendants Jennifer Nettles and Kristian Bush in 2002. She left it in December 2005, when the band had yet to make it big, apparently to write music on her own. Then in 2008, after the band achieved breakout success without her, Hall sued Nettles and Bush for what she claimed to be her share of the spoils.

By most accounts, Hall's complaint demanded $14 million for her share of profits derived since the band parted ways, plus unspecified damages for what the complaint described as defendants' "de facto dissolution" of the partnership. As to that, she argued that the firm was dissolved when defendants "excluded Hall from all aspects of the partnership business."

Again, the case never made it to trial. But if it had, what would Hall have to prove to recover these claimed amounts? And if you represented Nettles and Bush, what would be your version of the legal events?

Utah law clearly provides that "[t]he dissolution of a partnership does not of itself discharge the existing liability of any partner." Under the Utah Uniform Partnership Act, partners are jointly, rather than jointly and severally, liable for all debts and obligations of the partnership. . . . Thus, "upon each partner rests an absolute liability for the whole amount of every debt due from the partnership and although originally a joint contract, it may be separate as to its effects."

The trial court determined that $45,000 was owed by the partnership for a specified time period. Then, without explanation, the trial court "split that in half," and ordered Elder to pay $22,500. Because the partnership did not have any available assets, under the "joint liability" principles outlined above, the trial court should have found Elder individually liable for 100 per cent of the damages for that time period.

Elder provided no authority to support the proposition that when a partnership's assets are insufficient or depleted, the individual partners are only liable for a share of the debt proportionate to their share of the partnership. Therefore, the trial court erred by limiting Elder's liability to one-half of the partnership's obligations.

C. DAMAGES OF NET LOSS RATHER THAN UNPAID EXPENSES

Plaintiffs next argue that the trial court abused its discretion by calculating the damages based on the partnership's net loss rather than outstanding debts at the time Elder left the partnership. More specifically, they argue that the trial court did not award damages based on the parties' agreement which called for the partnership to pay all expenses incurred in the operation of the business.

Under Utah partnership law, upon dissolution of a partnership, "each partner . . . may have the partnership property applied to discharge its liabilities." In this case, while the Elder/Rutherford partnership did not go through the formal winding up process as outlined in Utah's Uniform Partnership Act, the partnership was clearly dissolved when Elder left. The record indicates that when Elder left in August 1998, he closed the partnership bank account and turned over his interest in any partnership assets, including money, inventory, and records. To accept the Plaintiffs' argument, and award damages based on unpaid expenses, would result in a windfall for Birshbach and would ignore Elder's partnership interests at the time of dissolution which Elder is entitled to have applied against the partnership liabilities. See MacKay v. Hardy, 896 P.2d 626, 631 (Utah 1995) (holding that trial court erred in apportioning partnership's post-dissolution profits because its award resulted in improper windfall to one partner after failing to consider profits attributable to other partner's efforts). Therefore, the trial court did not abuse its discretion when it used the expert's net loss calculations rather than unpaid expenses in awarding damages. . . .

Doing the Numbers: Unpaid Expenses vs. Net Loss

Assume that Partner A and Partner B each contribute $50,000 to the AB Partnership, for a total of $100,000.

The partnership then expends the entire amount trying to make a go of its business, plus $50,000 it borrows from a bank, and makes no money whatsoever.

The partnership thus has lost $150,000. Its unpaid expenses are $50,000.

Now, assume that the partnership expended the same $150,000, $100,000 of which was contributed by the partners and $50,000 of which was borrowed. It earned $160,000, all of which was withdrawn by the partners in equal amounts.

The partnership has no net loss; instead it has net income of $10,000. Its unpaid expenses still are $50,000.

■ **Think about this:**

(G) Exactly why are unpaid expenses and net loss different amounts?

(H) Which one was higher in this case?

(I) Could the converse ever be true?

Very different outcomes can follow depending on whether a partnership is for a term or undertaking, as opposed to at will. The following case is a classic, in part because it so clearly reveals the types of motivation that may underlie a dissolution.

PAGE V. PAGE

Supreme Court of California
359 P.2d 41 (1961)

TRAYNOR, Justice.

Plaintiff and defendant are partners in a linen supply business in Santa Maria, California. Plaintiff appeals from a judgment declaring the partnership to be for a term rather than at will.

The partners entered into an oral partnership agreement in 1949. Within the first two years each partner contributed approximately $43,000 for the purchase of land, machinery, and linen needed to begin the business. From 1949 to 1957 the enterprise was unprofitable, losing approximately $62,000. The partnership's major creditor is a corporation, wholly owned by plaintiff, that supplies the linen and machinery necessary for the day-to-day operation of the business. This corporation holds a $47,000 demand note of the partnership. The partnership operations began to improve in 1958. The partnership earned $3,824.41 in that year and $2,282.30 in the first three months of 1959. Despite this improvement plaintiff wishes to terminate the partnership.

The Uniform Partnership Act provides that a partnership may be dissolved "By the express will of any partner when no definite term or particular undertaking is specified." Corp. Code, §15031, subd. (1)(b). [UPA §31(1)(b), which is preserved in slightly modified form by RUPA §601(1).] The trial court found that the partnership is for a term, namely, "such reasonable time as is necessary to enable said partnership to repay from partnership profits, indebtedness incurred for the purchase of land, buildings, laundry and delivery equipment and linen for the operation of such business...." Plaintiff correctly contends that this finding is without support in the evidence.

Defendant testified that the terms of the partnership were to be similar to former partnerships of plaintiff and defendant, and that the understanding of these partnerships was that "we went into partnership to start the business and let the business operation pay for itself, put in so much money, and let the business pay itself out." There was also testimony that one of the former partnership agreements provided in writing that the profits were to be retained until all obligations were paid.

Upon cross-examination defendant admitted that the former partnership in which the earnings were to be retained until the obligations were repaid was substantially different from the present partnership. The former partnership was a limited partnership and provided for a definite term of five years and a partnership at will thereafter. Defendant insists, however, that the method of operation of the former partnership showed an understanding that all obligations were to be repaid from profits. He nevertheless concedes that there was no understanding as to the term of the present partnership in the event of losses. He was asked: "[W]as there any discussion with reference to the continuation of the business in the event of losses?" He replied, "Not that I can remember." He was then asked, "Did you have any understanding with Mr. Page, your brother, the plaintiff in this action, as to how the obligations were to be paid if there were losses?" He replied, "Not that I can remember. I can't remember discussing that at all. We never figured on losing, I guess."

Viewing this evidence most favorably for defendant, it proves only that the partners expected to meet current expenses from current income and to recoup their investment if the business were successful.

Defendant contends that such an expectation is sufficient to create a partnership for a term under the rule of Owen v. Cohen, 119 P.2d 713. In that case we held that when a partner advances a sum of money to a partnership with the understanding that the amount contributed was to be a loan to the partnership and was to be repaid as soon as feasible from the prospective profits of the business, the partnership is for the term reasonably required to repay the loan. It is true that *Owen v. Cohen, supra,* and other cases hold that partners may impliedly agree to continue in business until a certain sum of money is earned, or one or more partners recoup their investments, or until certain debts are paid, or until certain property could be disposed of on favorable terms. In each of these cases, however, the implied agreement found support in the evidence.

In *Owen v. Cohen, supra,* the partners borrowed substantial amounts of money to launch the enterprise and there was an understanding that the loans would be repaid from partnership profits. In Vangel v. Vangel, [116 Cal. App. 2d 615], one partner loaned his co-partner money to invest in the partnership with the understanding that the money would be repaid from partnership profits. In Mervyn Investment Co. v. Biber, [184 Cal. 637], one partner contributed all the capital, the other contributed his services, and it was understood that upon the repayment of the contributed capital from partnership profits the partner who contributed his services would receive a one-third interest in the partnership assets. In each of these cases the court properly held that the partners impliedly promised to continue the partnership for a term reasonably required to allow the partnership to earn sufficient money to accomplish the understood objective. In Shannon v. Hudson, [161 Cal. App. 2d 44], the parties entered into a joint venture to build and operate a motel until it could be sold upon favorable and mutually satisfactory terms, and the court held that the joint venture was for a reasonable term sufficient to accomplish the purpose of the joint venture.

In the instant case, however, defendant failed to prove any facts from which an agreement to continue the partnership for a term may be implied. The understanding to which defendant testified was no more than a common hope that the partnership earnings would pay for all the necessary expenses. Such a hope does not establish even by implication a "definite term or particular undertaking". . . . All partnerships are ordinarily entered into with the hope that they will be profitable, but that alone does not make them all partnerships for a term and obligate the partners to continue in the partnerships until all of the losses over a period of many years have been recovered.

Defendant contends that plaintiff is acting in bad faith and is attempting to use his superior financial position to appropriate the now profitable business of the partnership. Defendant has invested $43,000 in the firm, and owing to the long period of losses his interest in the partnership assets is very small. The fact that plaintiff's wholly-owned corporation holds a $47,000 demand note of the partnership may make it difficult to sell the business as a going concern. Defendant fears that upon dissolution he will receive very little and that plaintiff, who is the managing partner and knows how to conduct the operations of the partnership, will receive a business that has become very profitable because of the establishment of Vandenberg Air Force Base in its vicinity. Defendant charges that plaintiff has been content to share the losses but now that the business has become profitable he wishes to keep all the gains.

There is no showing in the record of bad faith or that the improved profit situation is more than temporary. In any event these contentions are irrelevant to the issue whether the partnership is for a term or at will. Since, however, this action is for a declaratory judgment and will be the basis for future action by the parties, it is appropriate to point out that defendant is amply protected by the fiduciary duties of co-partners.

Even though the Uniform Partnership Act provides that a partnership at will may be dissolved by the express will of any partner (Corp. Code, §15031, subd. (1) (b)), this power, like any other power held by a fiduciary, must be exercised in good faith.

We have often stated that "partners are trustees for each other, and in all proceedings connected with the conduct of the partnership every partner is bound to act in the highest good faith to his copartner, and may not obtain any advantage over him in the partnership affairs by the slightest misrepresentation, concealment, threat, or adverse pressure of any kind."...

A partner at will is not bound to remain in a partnership, regardless of whether the business is profitable or unprofitable. A partner may not, however, by use of adverse pressure "freeze out" a co-partner and appropriate the business to his own use. A partner may not dissolve a partnership to gain the benefits of the business for himself, unless he fully compensates his co-partner for his share of the prospective business opportunity. . . .

. . . [I]n the instant case, plaintiff has the power to dissolve the partnership by express notice to defendant. If, however, it is proved that plaintiff acted in bad faith and violated his fiduciary duties by attempting to appropriate to his own use the new prosperity of the partnership without adequate compensation to his co-partner, the dissolution would be wrongful and the plaintiff would be liable as provided by subdivision (2)(a) of Corporations Code, §15038 [UPA §38(2)(a), providing recourse to non-wrongfully-dissolving partners, preserved in RUPA §602(c)] for violation of the implied agreement not to exclude defendant wrongfully from the partnership business opportunity.

The judgment is reversed.

■ **Think about this:**

(J) What will the Page brother resisting dissolution need to show to establish his brother acted wrongfully?

The *Page* case dealt with a strategic dissolution, as does the next. *Cadwalader*, however, involves the expulsion of one partner by others who meant to continue the firm. It was decided under the UPA, which had little to say directly on the subject. As you read, think carefully about the way the court, and the parties, seem to have used the terms "expulsion" and "dissolution." Be sure to keep in mind that even though the withdrawal of a partner under the UPA dissolved the partnership, the partners could agree what the consequences of dissolution would be.

CADWALADER, WICKERSHAM & TAFT V. BEASLEY

Florida Court of Appeals
728 So. 2d 253 (1998)

POLEN, Judge.

. . . [In 1989, James Beasley, already an established Florida estate planning lawyer, joined the Palm Beach office of Cadwalader, Wickersham & Taft (CW&T), as a partner. Unfortunately, CW&T, a storied, very large New York-based outfit that remains one of the world's leading law firms, found the Palm Beach office unprofitable and by 1994 resolved to close it. Beasley objected, arguing that CW&T lacked the legal authority to expel him.]

. . . CW&T [then] sent a memorandum to Beasley informing him that he was still a partner in the firm. It then offered Beasley either relocation within the firm but in the New York or Wash-

Wall Street in 1792, the place and time of the founding of the firm later to be known as Cadwalader, Wickersham & Taft

ington, D.C. offices, or, a compensation/severance package which included his return of capital, departure bonus, and full shares through December 31, 1994. He was presented with a written withdrawal agreement confirming the same. Beasley, a member of both the Florida and New York bars, rejected the same as impractical.

Settlement negotiations between CW&T and Beasley then continued. On November 9, he sued the firm for fraud and breach of fiduciary duty, among other counts. On November 10, 1994, CW&T sent a letter to Beasley informing him to vacate the premises by 5:00 P.M. the next day. The letter specifically prohibited him from continuing to represent himself as associated with the firm.

[Beasley won a bench verdict finding that CW&T anticipatorily breached its partnership agreement by announcing closure of the Palm Beach office and actually breached it with the letter of November 10. The court awarded him more than $2.5 million,] . . . broken down as follows:

— Beasley's paid-in capital of $194,193, plus interest at the rate as defined in the partnership agreement to the date of judgment [$42,199]	$ 236,392.00
— his percentage interest in the firm's accounts receivable, work-in-progress, office building and other assets	$ 867,110.00
— his profits attributable to the use of his right in the property of the dissolved partnership	$ 935,261.52
— punitive damages	$ 500,000.00
— attorney's fees and costs	$1,108,247.92

I. WHETHER BEASLEY WAS EXPELLED OR VOLUNTARILY WITHDREW

Under New York Partnership Law's adoption of the Uniform Partnership Act (UPA), partners have no common law or statutory right to expel or dismiss another partner from the partnership; they may, however, provide in their partnership agreement for expulsion under prescribed conditions which must be strictly applied. Absent such a provision, as here, the removal of a partner may be accomplished only through dissolution of the firm.

The evidence supports Judge Cook's finding that CW&T intended to remove Beasley as a partner in the firm when it announced it was closing its Palm Beach office by year-end 1994. This finding, in turn, supports the conclusion that CW&T anticipatorily expelled Beasley from the firm. . . . In reaching this conclusion, we necessarily reject CW&T's argument that Beasley voluntarily withdrew from the firm rather than having been expelled. Beasley had been practicing exclusively in South Florida for 22 years, where he built a substantial client base. As the trial court observed, to suddenly uproot to New York or Washington and leave his clients and contacts behind, as the court suggested, would have severely diminished his rainmaking abilities. Under these circumstances, we conclude that his rejecting the offer as impractical was not tantamount to a voluntary withdrawal.

Even assuming that CW&T did not anticipatorily breach the agreement on August 29, 1994, we conclude that the November 10, 1994 letter actually expelled him. Even though CW&T notes that Beasley planned on eventually leaving the firm even before it announced the decision to close the Palm Beach office, and that he most likely would not have stayed past 1994, the record does not reflect that he actually had definite plans to leave.

We further reject CW&T's argument that Beasley's suing the firm on November 9, 1994 was tantamount to a voluntary withdrawal. Since CW&T does not dispute the lack of frivolousness of Beasley's lawsuit, but merely takes issue with its allegations, we find its argument unpersuasive.

II. THE AWARD OF INTEREST

CW&T then argues the trial court erred in finding that a dissolution occurred and contends that, as a "withdrawn partner" pursuant to the agreement,

Beasley was entitled to only his paid-in capital. Even if dissolution had occurred, it argues he still only would be entitled to an amount significantly less than that awarded to him. Beasley disputes that he was a "withdrawn" partner pursuant to the agreement, and contends that dissolution was mandated.

Under the partnership agreement, a "withdrawn Partner" is anyone "who was a Partner under this or a prior Firm Agreement." More specifically, the agreement provides that a partner, upon 60 days written notice, may withdraw from the firm at the end of any fiscal year. CW&T argues that, under these provisions, Beasley was technically a withdrawn partner and, thus, was only entitled to his capital contribution plus interest under Paragraph F(2)(a)(i) of the agreement. We, instead, agree with Judge Cook that the term "withdrawn" neither contemplated nor encompassed a partner expelled in the same manner as Beasley, especially since Beasley never provided any written notice of a voluntary withdrawal, and since CW&T conceded at trial that it did not treat Beasley as a "withdrawn partner" after his departure.

Antidissolution Provision

CW&T then argues that concluding a dissolution occurred would conflict with that portion of the agreement which states, "Neither withdrawal of a Partner nor the death of a Partner, *nor any other event* shall cause dissolution of the Firm [unless 75 percent of the remaining partners agreed in writing]." (Emphasis added.) It reasons that expulsion of a partner, however wrongful, is an "event" for purposes of this antidissolution clause. We disagree, for to construe this anti-dissolution provision strictly would recognize an implicit expulsion provision where no provision exists. Such an interpretation would be inconsistent with existing law.

 Dear Prof.: The court's heading for this section is "The Award of Interest" and it affirms the award of "interest in the amount of $867,110." Calculating interest doesn't really seem to be what's going on. What gives?

The court owes us a bit of an apology. What it really is talking about in this section is the value of Beasley's *interest in the partnership*, over and above his capital contribution.

Even if the provision were broad enough to cover expulsions, we believe Beasley would still be allowed to seek dissolution of the partnership. Under New York law, any partner has the right to a formal accounting as to partnership affairs if he is wrongfully excluded from the partnership business or possession of its property by his co-partners, or "[w]henever other circumstances render it just and reasonable." N.Y. Partnership Law §44 (McKinney 1993) [UPA §22, preserved in RUPA §405(b)]. Thus, a wrongful exclusion of one partner by a co-partner from participation in the conduct of the business may be grounds for judicial dissolution.

Since Beasley was expelled, his damages are to be assessed under §71 of New York Partnership Law [the final dissolution provisions, preserved in RUPA §807], and not under the partnership agreement. Since there is competent, substantial evidence in the record to support both the method and result used to calculate his interest in the firm's assets, we affirm the award of interest in the amount of $867,110.00.

III. THE AWARD OF PROFITS

Under New York law, when a partnership continues following the expulsion of a partner, that partner has the right to receive the value of his partnership interest as of the date of dissolution, either with interest from the date of dissolution, or, at his election, the profits attributable to the use of his right in the property of the dissolved partnership. N.Y. Partnership Law §73 (McKinney 1993). . . .

Strictly construing this statute, Beasley was entitled to either interest on the value of his interest in the dissolved partnership ($867,110) or profits attributable to the use of his right in the property of the firm on top of the $867,110. Beasley elected to receive the profits attributable to his use through the date of judgment instead of interest at 3% over prime (as defined in the agreement).* Based on his expert, Mr. Burgher, having calculated the profits attributable to the use of his right in the property based on the firm's total earnings to reflect what Beasley's total income would have been had he stayed at the firm from November, 1994 through May, 1996, the court awarded Beasley profits in the amount of $935,261.52.

CW&T argues that, as a matter of law, awarding Beasley $935,261.52 in "profits" based on this calculation was incorrect. Relying on Kirsch v. Leventhal, 586 N.Y.S.2d 330 (1992), it reasons that Beasley should not be entitled to profits resulting from the postdissolution services of the remaining partners. We agree. To the extent that some of the firm's postdissolution profits may be attributable to the postdissolution efforts, skill, and diligence of the remaining partners, the firm's fee as a result of those services should not be proportionately attributable to the use of the departing partner's right in the property of the dissolved partnership. . . .**

---

* *Editors' Note*: Section 73 was New York's adoption of UPA §42, and the election discussed here is no longer available under RUPA. Its purpose may have been to encourage the continuing partners to conclude buyout negotiations quickly, as it would put the risk of delay more firmly on them. They couldn't benefit from delay, if the firm's profits turned out to be higher during the period of their delay than the rate of interest would have been. Anyway, RUPA's drafters did away with this election, perhaps because RUPA's procedures for negotiating the buyout of a dissociating partner, set out in §701(e), (g), and (i), include other means to encourage speedy resolution.

** *Editors' Note*: Beasley argued that this case law shouldn't apply because of CW&T's wrongdoing. The court disagreed, finding both parties to have behaved poorly, even though it emphatically found CW&T's conduct to be worse than Beasely's. [Court:] The final judgment clearly shows Judge Cook's determination of the relative equities of the parties' positions when he found, "If Beasley has dirt under his fingernails, CW & T was up to its' (sic) elbows in the dung heap."

IV. THE IMPOSITION OF PUNITIVE DAMAGES

. . . Under New York law, the nature of the conduct which justifies an award of punitive damages is conduct having a high degree of moral culpability, or, in other words, conduct which shows a "conscious disregard of the rights of others or conduct so reckless as to amount to such disregard." CW&T is correct in arguing that punitive damages are generally recovered only after compensatory damages have been awarded; however, since the purpose of punitive damages is to both punish the wrongdoer and deter others from such wrongful behavior, as a matter of policy, courts have the discretion to award punitive damages even where compensatory damages are found lacking.

We believe CW&T should not be insulated from the consequences of its wrongdoing simply because Beasley suffered no compensatory damages. As the court found, CW&T "was participating in a clandestine plan to wrongfully expel some partners for the financial gain of other partners. Such activity cannot be said to be honorable, much less to comport with the 'punctilio of an honor.'" Because these findings establish that CW&T consciously disregarded the rights of Beasley, we affirm the award of punitive damages. . . .

> **Connections: "Punctilio of an Honor"**
>
> Partners are, of course, in a fiduciary relationship. The court in *Cadwalader* is quoting, without attribution, Justice Cardozo's encapsulation of the duty owed as "the punctilio of an honor the most sensitive" (alternatively characterized as "the duty of the finest loyalty"). Meinhard v. Salmon, 164 N.E. 545 (1928). Fiduciary duty in unincorporated entities is covered in more detail in Chapter 12.

■ **Think about this:**

(K) The court says, "Absent such a[n expulsion] provision, as here, the removal of a partner may be accomplished only through dissolution of the firm." What does the court really mean?

(L) The partnership agreement provided: "Neither withdrawal of a Partner nor the death of a Partner, nor any other event shall cause dissolution of the Firm [unless 75 percent of the remaining partners agreed in writing]." What did the partners really mean?

(M) Would the case have come out any differently if RUPA, rather than the UPA, applied?

E. Post-Break-up Arrangements and the "Continuing" Firm

Again, neither a partner's dissociation nor any event of dissolution in itself necessarily means the end of the business, and in fact partnership businesses often continue after dissolution events. How these matters are worked out raises some special issues, and one of them—the liabilities issue considered in subsection 2 to follow—is unusually thorny.

1. Post-Dissolution Continuation in General

Consider a simple example. Imagine that Alan is one partner in a three-member at-will RUPA firm, the ABC partnership. Let's assume that ABC owns and operates a small manufacturing outfit, producing specialty metal components for industrial machines. Its assets are a machine shop with a few hundred thousand dollars' worth of machinery and stock, and it employs 20 machinists and other employees. Alan desires to depart the business, but the other two partners, Barb and Camille, want to continue. Alan's departure will cause dissolution, and in the absence of contrary agreement he would be within his statutory rights to insist on winding up and a payout of his own interest in cash. Carrying all the way through with liquidation to cash, however, sometimes will mean the end of the business as a going concern, so it would behoove Barb and Camille to come up with some other arrangement.

 Dear Prof.: Why would Alan insist on a winding up rather than a negotiated buyout?

He might do that for at least a few reasons. First, he may fear that a mere buyout of his interest will be insufficient to protect him from his continuing liabilities to creditors, even with releases or promises of indemnification, a point we will consider below. Second, negotiations with Barb and Camille over a friendly buyout might simply stall. If Barb and Camille are unwilling to meet the minimum that Alan demands, he might take the gamble that winding up will produce a better value for his share.

However, as we learned earlier in the chapter, RUPA §803(b) permits the partners to rescind dissolution if they can work out the terms of dissociation to their (more or less) mutual satisfaction. First, Barb and Camille simply can come up with enough cash to pay Alan some amount that they agree his share in the business to be worth. In such a buyout, Alan will almost surely insist that Barb and Camille assume all of his liability for the firm's obligations. This is the result contemplated by the buyout procedure that we discussed earlier, from §701. Second, even if Alan insists on dissolution and winding up, Barb and Camille could put the firm up for sale and just make sure that they themselves make the best offer for the entire firm. In such a case, they may set off their own share of the firm's assets against the purchase price, and therefore pay only the net due to Alan. The result should be that they wind up paying about the same that they would have paid through friendly negotiation, though all three take the risk that actual liquidation would have resulted in some drastically different price. There is also the risk that Barb and Camille won't be able to come up with enough cash to buy it away from some higher bidder.

In any event, it should be borne in mind that RUPA provides more than enough flexibility for partners to craft solutions prospectively, as part of their original partnership agreement, to avoid some of the uncertainty and acrimony that otherwise are normal features of dissolution. Buyout provisions for departing partners are very common, and they typically include some formula to value the departing partner's interest.

In any case, each of these resolutions raises a difficult little set of legal issues under the RUPA concerning the ongoing rights and liabilities of the dissolving firm and the new rights and liabilities of the continuing firm.

2. Powers and Liabilities of the Dissolved or Continuing Firm and the Departing Partners

Legally, one fairly complex consequence of dissolution and continuation is its effect on the continuing liabilities of the original business and on the partners' ability to create new liabilities. The problem had been *profoundly* complex under UPA (1914), but has been improved substantially under RUPA. Note that all of the following rules make fairly heavy use of the terms "notice" and "knowledge," and that those terms are elaborately defined in RUPA §102.

 Dear Prof.: What transactions are "appropriate for winding up the business"?

They could include lots of miscellaneous steps useful in reducing the firm's assets to cash, and resolving all of its outstanding liabilities. So, the firm may sell partnership property, receive payments from debtors, file suit against debtors, pay creditor's claims or compromise them and negotiate their release, and so on.

Powers and Liabilities Following Dissolution and Winding Up. Where an event of dissolution occurs and no agreement is reached to rescind it, the consequence for ongoing liabilities is reasonably straightforward. Under RUPA §802(a), an event of dissolution requires that the partnership's ordinary business cease and that the partners begin winding up. Accordingly, any partner "act" that occurs after an event of dissolution binds the partnership only if it is (1) appropriate for winding up the business or (2) within that partner's apparent authority. Apparent authority is defined in this case as authority that the partner would have had under RUPA §301 *if* the other party does not have "notice" of the dissolution. *See* §804(2). Recall that an act is binding under RUPA §301 if it is "apparently . . . in the ordinary course of the partnership business or business of the kind carried on by the partnership. . . ." "Notice," if not otherwise acquired, is deemed by §103(d) to occur 90 days after the filing of a "statement of dissolution" under §802.

So, an event of dissolution might occur, and then a partner for one reason or another might execute a new agreement purporting to bind the firm, or otherwise incur liability. Even if the new liability has nothing to do with winding up the firm—say it constitutes a contract for new work to be performed by the firm—it is enforceable against the partnership and potentially against the partners' personal assets if it was made with apparent authority. However, under §805(a), a partner with "knowledge" of the dissolution who incurs a liability through apparent authority is liable to the other partners for the full amount of any "damage caused to the partnership arising from the liability."

> ■ **Think about this:**
>
> *(N)* How come? For what reason of policy does RUPA penalize the partner who makes a post-dissolution obligation not appropriate for winding up only where the partner had actual, subjective knowledge of dissolution?

Powers and Liabilities Following Dissociation Where No Dissolution Occurs. Slightly more complex rules apply where a partner dissociates but the dissociation does not cause dissolution. These rules apply where dissociation is caused by an event listed in §601 that does not cause dissolution. But they also apply to voluntary dissociation under §601(1) if the partners rescind dissolution under §803(b). In any such case, the parties will be subject to rules that govern their power to bind one another and their exposure to liability for the firm's obligations.

With respect to the dissociating partner's ongoing liabilities, RUPA states two stark rules. First, dissociation itself does not affect the dissociating partner's responsibilities for *pre*-dissociation liabilities. RUPA §603(c). They continue, and may be executed against his or her personal assets if the partnership assets are insufficient to satisfy them, and they will so continue unless an agreement with creditors releasing the partner has been reached under §703(c) or (d). Second, the dissociated partner cannot be held liable for *post*-dissociation partnership liabilities except in the limited circumstances stated in §703(a). Namely, for a period of two years following dissolution, such a liability can bind the dissociated partner if the other party to the transaction reasonably believed he or she was still a partner, and that other person lacked both notice of the dissolution and such constructive notice of it as might occur if a "statement of dissociation" is on file under §704. Under §103(d), such notice is deemed to occur 90 days after the filing of the statement.

There also is of course a consequence for the dissociating partner's power to bind the ongoing firm. Section 603(b) has the effect of immediately ending the dissociating partner's status as partner. It terminates the partner's management rights and most fiduciary duties. It likewise plainly has the effect of ending the dissociating partner's *actual* authority to bind the firm, though RUPA nowhere says so in those explicit terms. Rather, it provides that the dissociating partner has apparent authority under a statutory definition exactly matching the test just mentioned from §703(b). Here, under §702(a), the partner can create liabilities any time within two years after dissociation that will bind the partnership, if the act would have been binding under §301 and the other party reasonably believed in the dissociating partner's authority and lacked notice or constructive knowledge of the dissociation. However, the dissociated partner will be liable under §702(b) to the other partners for any damages caused to the partnership.

In Application. To continue the hypothetical from above, Alan, Barb, and Camille will retain full personal liability for all pre-dissociation obligations of the ABC firm. What happens to those liabilities following the dissociation depends on just exactly how Barb and Camille cash out Alan's interest. Again assuming they didn't provide for dissociation situations in their agreement, there are basically two ways in which they can do so. On the one hand, the three of them might negotiate a friendly settlement in which Barb and Camille purchase Alan's interest, following an agreement under §803(b) to rescind dissolution. In that case, in all likelihood, none of the firm's outstanding debts will be immediately satisfied. Technically, under §603(a), each of the three of them would remain fully personally liable for all of those debts. However, the partnership is required under §701(d) to indemnify Alan if any such liabilities go unsatisfied. In the alternative, the three of them might be able to secure releases of Alan's continuing liabilities, as contemplated by §703(c) or (d). In effect, the consideration that Alan pays in exchange for this release or indemnification is the amount by which his buyout payment is reduced to reflect his share of existing liabilities.

On the other hand, Alan might not agree to rescind dissolution under §803(b). Assuming his dissociation was not wrongful, it is his right to refuse. In that case, again the three partners retain their full personal liability for partnership obligations, as is explicit in §806(c). Section 802(a) requires that, because dissolution has not been rescinded, the ordinary business of the firm cease and winding up proceed. The winding-up procedures in §806 require that the assets be applied to satisfy creditors prior to any distributions to partners. So, assuming the firm is not in the red at the time of winding up, Alan will be free and clear of pre-dissolution partnership liabilities upon winding up; they will all have been satisfied. Now, since Barb and Camille want to keep the firm going, they in all likelihood would attempt to buy the firm themselves, which would mean coming up with enough cash to buy out Alan's share and satisfy all debts outstanding at the time of winding up. (All that said, they presumably would be free to agree with Alan, if he could be convinced, to enter an indemnity agreement or releases with creditors under §703(c) or (d), rather than actually paying off creditors.)

■   **Think about this:**

(O) Release by creditors is substantially preferable to indemnification by the partnership. Do you see why?

In either of these two scenarios, it would remain possible for any of the three partners to take actions that will bind the others, though the details will differ in small ways depending on which scenario is followed. If there is a non-dissolving buyout under §701, then for two years after his dissociation Alan could bind the firm to acts apparently in the firm's ordinary business, so long as the third party has no knowledge or constructive notice of dissociation. But if he did so, Alan would be liable to the firm for any damages caused under §702(b). Likewise, Alan could find himself responsible for partnership obligations within two years of dissociation if the third party reasonably believed he was still a partner and lacked knowledge or constructive notice. *See* §703(b). But in that case, Alan would also would be entitled to indemnity under §701(d), or some comparable arrangement negotiated by the parties.

The event of a dissolution raises roughly the same issues, but triggers different statutory rules. Each of the three partners could freely make binding obligations for the purpose of winding up under §804(a), and under §804(b) they could make any other contract apparently for the firm's ordinary business so long as the other parties lacked notice of the dissolution. Again, the partner who made a contract not for the purpose of winding up would be responsible for damages caused thereby under §805(a) if at the time of the transaction the partner had knowledge of the dissolution.

To illustrate the effect of the "knowledge" requirement, imagine that Alan states his intention to dissolve to Barb, and makes clear that he will not waive winding up. The partnership will at that moment have "notice" of an event causing dissolution for purposes of §801(1), and Barb herself would plainly have "knowledge" of it. But suppose that Camille had been off on a business trip, and before she got news of Alan's announcement, she inks a deal for a large supply contract with a new client. That contract would not be for the purpose of winding up, and so would be enforceable only if it were made with Camille's apparent authority under §804(a). But Camille would not have "knowledge" of the dissolution at that point, because §102 defines "knowledge" to mean actual knowledge. Camille thus would have no liability under §805(a).

What happens, however, if Barb and Camille buy the firm as part of the winding-up process and *then* make a substantial new contract? Could Alan be responsible for that? Strictly speaking, Barb and Camille will have begun a new firm, since the old one was dissolved and under §802(a) the old firm was not even legally permitted to continue its ordinary business. But to any third party it would likely appear that just the same business was underway as had ever been, and so one wonders whether something comparable to the two-year window of liability for dissociated partners under §703(b) would apply, either by operation of §703(b) itself or by judicial application of common law agency principles. It also is possible that §804(a) means that Alan could be bound without regard to a two-year window. Neither the statute nor its comments clearly say.

In any case, the wise course for all parties in a RUPA jurisdiction would be to file the relevant "statement" reflecting changes in authority. *See* §§704, 805.

3. Partnership Mergers, Exchanges of Interest, and Conversions

Partnerships can merge with one another and with other entities and also can be converted into other business entity forms. Both kinds of transaction are quite common. UPA (1914) gave these matters no explicit consideration, and so firms and their lawyers were left essentially to make up the law by which they should occur on the fly. The result was a lot of complexity and a lot of uncertainty. RUPA has attempted to deal with these transactions in in its Article 11. Article 11 also deals with "exchanges of interest" in which one entity acquires another, often by offering its own securities to the owners of the acquired entity.

Article 11 reflects an attempt to harmonize RUPA's requirements with respect to the covered transactions with the requirements of the Uniform Limited Liability Company Act (ULLCA), the Uniform Limited Partnership Act (ULPA), and the Model Business Corporations Act (MBCA). The idea is that it should be possible to combine and/or convert the different business entities in essentially the same way. The rules are relatively complex, and are subject to the acknowledgment in RUPA §§1102 through 1104 that other laws may apply and the same results can be achieved through different means. A few comments follow on the subjects of mergers and conversions, but the details of these matters, as well as the subject of exchanges of interest, are beyond the scope of this book. We bring them up here primarily to make the point that the drafters of RUPA do not mean for the transactions involved to be classified as dissolutions.

Merger. "Merger" means the combination of two or more firms into one. In a merger of two partnerships—or the merger of a partnership with an entity of some other form, like a limited liability company or a corporation—the owners must agree among themselves as to which assets of the combining firms will be owned by the merged firm, how the resulting firm will be governed, how the owners will be compensated for selling their interests into the resulting firm, and how they will handle the ongoing liabilities of the predecessor firms.

Such a deal can be structured in a number of ways, depending on designs of the parties. It might merge all of the assets of the two firms into one, and the resulting combination might be governed by some collection of the previous firm's governing bodies. Or, it may in effect merge one of the firms out of existence, cashing out that firm's owners and absorbing all of its assets into the other, in which case the other firm might be thought of as the "acquiring" firm. Or it could be some more complex deal in which only some of the owners and assets of the predecessor firms are combined, while other owners go off on their own and other assets are sold, perhaps to third parties. One of the most important issues, which RUPA deals with in §1106, is assuring the protection of pre-merger creditors.

Conversion. A partnership can be "converted" into some other business entity form. Again, the UPA (1914) provided no explicit rules on point, so the consequences of conversion had to be pieced together from the statute and from whatever agreement the parties made.

RUPA has simplified these matters. By far the simplest conversion transaction is conversion to limited liability partnership form. This conversion in fact

Connections: Consult an Expert

Note that a partnership-to-corporation conversion will trigger at least some rules of federal securities law, since stock in a corporation is virtually always a "security." Usually, however, it should be easy to avoid the registration and reporting requirements of the federal securities laws, because a conversion of this kind will not typically involve sale of securities to the public.

Note too that different kinds of conversion can have different federal tax consequences. These are just some of the relevant technical details surrounding merger and conversion that are beyond the scope of this book.

is covered by its own RUPA article, Article 9, and can be accomplished by filing a simple registration form with the Secretary of State.

Incorporation of a general partnership is also a common conversion, and has generated a fair bit of litigation. Typically, it is accomplished by the creation of a new corporation under the general incorporation statute of the state in which the business intends to proceed. The partners then simply exchange their own partnership shares for stock in the new entity, and then (1) the corporation will be the owner of all the assets and goodwill of the former firm, and (2) the former partners will be owners of the corporation in the same proportion that they owned the partnership.

The popularity of the limited liability company also has led to many conversions to LLC form, and they likely will become only more common. The ULLCA has long provided that organizations converted to LLCs are the same entity that existed before the conversion, and RUPA §1146 provides that any converted entity is the same as the converting entity.

A separate issue is what effect a conversion will have on the partners' individual liabilities and the liabilities of their converted firm. Since general partnership conversion to some other form almost by definition means conversion to a form with limited liability, the question arises whether the pre-conversion liabilities can somehow be avoided by the conversion itself. As for the partners themselves, RUPA §1146(d) provides that they cannot limit their own pre-conversion liabilities. Moreover, §1146(a)(3) provides that the converted entity is liable for the former firm's debts.

■ **Think about this:**

(P) Bob and Hank's business, "Bob & Hank's Beans 'n Franks," is a RUPA general partnership with no written agreement. It has substantial tangible assets, consisting mainly of a fleet of hot-dog carts and inventory, plus leased storage and operating space in a downtown warehouse building. The business is going great, but unfortunately Hank's health has taken a turn for the worse, and he wants to retire. As a practical matter, that means he needs to withdraw from the business and extract the value of his interest in it, to fund his retirement. He has asked you what his options might be. For what it's worth, Bob and Hank's relations are quite good, but they've never kept particularly careful books and have never had any formal accounting or audit, and so Hank has no especially precise estimate of the value of his share.

What's your advice?

Test Yourself

Assume Applicability of the Revised Uniform Partnership Act

1. When they formed the A & B Company, a general partnership, A contributed $250 cash in capital and B contributed $50 cash in capital. Their partnership was formed solely with a handshake and a mutual oral promise that it would be "all for one and one for all, share and share alike." When they dissolved and wound up their business, following payment of creditors there remained only $100. To how much are A and B entitled of this amount?

   a. A: $250; B: $50—they are each entitled to a return of their initial capital.
   b. A: $150; B: ($50)—A will take the $100 in remaining proceeds and B will have to contribute $50 to cover the shortfall.
   c. A: $75; B: $25—they should share 3 to 1, since that was the ratio of their capital contributions.
   d. A: $50; B: $50—since they did not agree otherwise, they share profits and losses equally.

2. X and Y form a partnership in a UPA (1914) jurisdiction for the purpose of speculating on certain real estate investments. To establish their partnership X and Y execute a written partnership agreement. A provision of this agreement entitled "Duration and Termination" provides that "the XY partnership shall exist no longer than two years." Y, however, is fed up at the end of the first year of business and informs X of his decision to leave the firm. X wishes to continue the firm for the full two years. The agreement contains no terms relating to retirement, buyout or post-dissolution continuation.

   Y will be entitled to a buyout of his partnership interest, but it will be reduced by the value of:

   a. Damages caused.
   b. The goodwill of the XY Partnership.
   c. Damages and goodwill.
   d. Neither damages nor goodwill.

3. A, B, and C form a partnership, which they call the ABC Partnership. The partnership is formed with the purpose of building an office building. The major source of operating capital for ABC is a $5 million bank loan, which is taken out immediately after ABC's formation. The anticipation of the partners is that the building will be sold on completion, though ABC may rent it out as office space for some period until a suitable buyer is found. The partners anticipate that ABC will not engage in any other sort of business.

   After five years, shortly before completion of the building (and, incidentally, shortly before the last of the $5 million bank loan will be spent on construction expenses), A retires. According to the partnership agreement, A is entitled to a buyout equaling the value of his capital account at the time of retirement. Much to his surprise, however, he learns only at that point that the value stated in his capital account is "$0," even though the market value of the building upon completion will be quite significant. A's outside accountant reviews the partnership's books and assures him that the statement in his capital account is correct.

This result:

a. Probably gives rise to a cause of action on A's part against his partners.
b. Suggests self-interested misconduct on the part of B and C.
c. Should have been expected.
d. Might have been expected, though if A is surprised, then it probably suggests mismanagement by B and C.

Questions 4-6 rely on the following facts:

Flarnstein, Jehozephat & Cadiddlehopper Dental Associates (FJ&C) is a general partnership engaged in the provision of dental services. FJ&C's founding partners formed their partnership using a printed form partnership agreement that they purchased at a bookstore, and that they did not read carefully. Among many other things, their agreement contained the following two clauses:

> "This partnership shall exist no longer than five years from the effective date stated herein."
> "Every partner, at his or her election, shall be entitled to an annual distribution, from partnership funds, of $5,000."

The founding partners created FJ&C when they signed their partnership agreement on January 1, 2012. Camille Cadiddlehopper, one of the founding partners, sent a letter to her partners dated December 2018, requesting her distribution of $5,000, even though none of the partners had previously requested such a thing. In response, another founding partner named Filbert Flarnstein immediately insists upon dissolution and winding up of FJ&C.

4. Is FJ&C a partnership at will? Did it even still exist at the time of the events now in dispute?

5. Is Camille entitled to receive her $5,000?

6. What is the effect of Filbert's effort to dissolve? Will he owe damages? Can he seek a winding up?

10

The Limited Partnership

The limited partnership (LP) plays a much different and narrower role in contemporary law than the other entities featured in this book. The history of the LP and the reasons for its decline nonetheless are important to the story of our arrival at the present busy profusion of entities. Its continuing use also happens to remain strong in a few special contexts—specifically, venture capital, oil and gas exploration, and family estate planning.

Chapter Outline

A. The History of the Limited Partnership and Its Two Narrow Roles Under Modern Law

1. History

2. Current Significance
   - Once a common choice and still significant as an economic matter, the LP is now used mainly for family businesses as a matter of estate planning and to pool investments in certain real estate and energy businesses

B. Tax Rationales for Current LP Applications

1. The Family LP

2. The Investment LP
   - Publicly traded, or "master," limited partnerships
   - Privately held investment limited partnerships

C. Other Attributes

1. Formation, Governance, and the "Control Rule"
   - Formation of a limited partnership is fairly simple, although drafting the limited partnership agreement is not

- Absent agreement to the contrary, governance of a limited partnership is in the hands of the general partner(s)
- There are two different approaches to the limited partner's ability to participate in control

2. Fiduciary Duty and "Derivative" Litigation
   - General partners owe fiduciary duties; limited partners do not
   - Limited partners may, after unsatisfied demand on the general partner(s), sue on behalf of the limited partnership

3. Securities Law
   - The interest of a limited partner usually is a security

4. Distributions and Creditor Protections
   - There are limits on a limited partnership's distributions to its partners, designed for the protection of creditors

5. Exit and Liquidity
   - Unless provided for by agreement, the partners in a limited partnership have limited exit rights and therefore limited liquidity

Test Yourself

 What does it look like?

Check the online Supplement for the following sample documents that are relevant to this chapter:

- A simple limited partnership agreement
- A registration statement filed under the federal securities laws relating to a publicly traded limited partnership agreement

A. The History of the Limited Partnership and Its Two Narrow Roles Under Modern Law

The limited partnership (LP) is like a general partnership except that some of its members, known as "limited partners," enjoy the same limited liability as corporate shareholders. The limited partners make capital contributions and are entitled to share in the firm's profits, but are nominally barred from participating in management. An LP is required to have at least one "general partner," to whom all management is entrusted and who will bear full personal liability for the firm's obligations.

The LP once played an important role in American law, as it was for many years the primary vehicle through which investors could enjoy the "upside" that is the main benefit of equity ownership, but also remain passive *and* enjoy pass-through taxation. That role was eclipsed during the 1980s and 1990s, with the rise of the limited liability company (LLC) and the limited liability partnership (LLP).

But there is still ample reason to study the LP. For one thing, LPs remain common and economically significant. While they are now in the minority among firms, there still really are quite a lot of them—about a half-million, with more than 10 million partners (by comparison to about 2 million LLCs, 3 million general partnerships, and 5 million corporations). *See* 1 LARRY E. RIBSTEIN & ROBERT R. KEATINGE, RIBSTEIN AND KEATINGE ON LIMITED LIABILITY COMPANIES §2.1 (2012). And not only that, that small set of firms generates a *huge* amount of money. Limited partnerships earn nearly a third of the profits earned by all unincorporated entities (other than sole proprietorships), even though they are only about one-eighth of those firms by number. They also contain within them nearly half of the partners in all partnerships. *See* Ron DeCarlo & Nina Shumofsky, *Partnership Returns 2012, in* INTERNAL REVENUE SERVICE, STATISTICS OF INCOME BULLETIN, Winter 2015.

More to the Story: The LP in Antiquity and Its Role in a World of Nobility and Religious Constraint

The LP is another very old entity form, mentioned in European law as early as 1160. One very interesting aspect of its ancient origin is essentially political. It was perceived during the European Middle Ages that for neither the nobility nor the clergy was it particularly dignified to be involved directly in trade, since the then-newly emerging mercantile class was generally comprised of people of lower birth. The clergy and others were also sometimes barred by religious rules from trade or lending money at interest. But the problems this caused were two. First, much of the money available to fund the new commercial world was in the hands of nobles and the clergy, and second, they themselves wanted to take advantage of the new opportunities for gain. That dilemma, as it happens, was really just one manifestation of an eternal verity running throughout business law. As Bromberg and Ribstein put it:

> Since business employs both capital and services that may come from very different sources, a need exists for a form of association that permits capital investment without responsibility for services or management and without liability for losses beyond the amount invested.

3 ALAN R. BROMBERG & LARRY E. RIBSTEIN, BROMBERG AND RIBSTEIN ON PARTNERSHIP §11.02(a) (2006). And so, it occurred to the embarrassed nobility from a very early time that something like the limited partnership—a means for passive investment with neither operational duties nor liability exposure—could permit them to put their money quietly to work without openly transgressing social norms.

And for another thing, it turns out that LPs still suit the particular needs of clients in two narrow circumstances: investment limited partnerships with sophisticated investor-owners, and family limited partnerships created to hold investment assets in connection with individuals' estate planning.

1. History

While earlier instances had long been set up informally by contract, the LP form appears to have first been formally recognized, by statute, only in a French act of 1673. That French provision is often said to have inspired the first American appearance, which was in New York in 1828. A problem for American business at that time was that there was no such thing in U.S. law as the generally available *corporate* form. Prior to the late nineteenth century, in most states a corporation could be created only by special act of the state legislature. The "general incorporation" statutes with which we are now familiar—under which a corporation free to engage in any business can be formed by the simple filing of a document with a state agency—did not arise until much later. So, when the LP was introduced it was the only generally available form in which a person could safely act as a passive investor and yet enjoy a share of a firm's profits. Before, the only options were to engage in general partnership, with its promise of profit sharing but unlimited personal risk, or simply to loan money under contract, an arrangement that provided some guarantee of interest payments and no risk of personal liability, but also no hope of sharing in the "upside" if the venture went well.

More to the Story: A One-Time Different Role for the LP in Tax Planning

During the 1970s and 1980s, the LP was used extensively as a tax avoidance vehicle. It could provide tax benefits for certain kinds of investments that other forms could not—or at least the promoters of those investment vehicles so promised. The LP enjoyed a few decades of great popularity for real estate investment, mineral exploration, and other ventures that tended to generate large tax losses, but the maneuver was drastically limited by the Tax Reform Act of 1986 (adopted at the behest of Ronald Reagan, of all people), which limited several special deductions and benefits. The tax schemes of the 1970s and 1980s also turned out to be seriously disappointing to many investors either because their particular partnership arrangements involved unsound business plans or were held by courts to be impermissible tax avoidance schemes. *See generally* 2 BROMBERG & RIBSTEIN, *supra*, at §8.01(f).

As explained below, the 1986 Act left some narrow benefits intact, and they largely explain the LP's continued relevance outside the realm of estate planning for family businesses.

---

2. Current Significance

But as mentioned, things have changed. The place of the LP in American law has gone through several distinct phases. While originally it may have been a valuable option for passive investment, that role was largely supplanted once general incorporation came about, since in a corporation there is no need to retain even one member with unlimited liability. Later it came to be of use in several more creative ways. In the mid-twentieth century it was discovered that an LP with a corporate general partner owned and operated by the limited partners could combine limited liability for all human partners, control of the business by the limited partners, and pass-through taxation (see the diagram to follow). It accomplished these things all long before introduction of the limited liability company (as to which, see Chapter 11). But in later years, especially after the LLC and permissive Treasury rules made both limited liability and favorable tax treatment very widely available, LPs came to play even more esoteric roles, primarily in investment arrangements under which limited partnership shares were publicly traded but for a time enjoyed special tax benefits.

This may help . . .

The LP with an Incorporated General Partner: The Mid-Century Brass Ring of Tax-Optimized Full Limited Liability

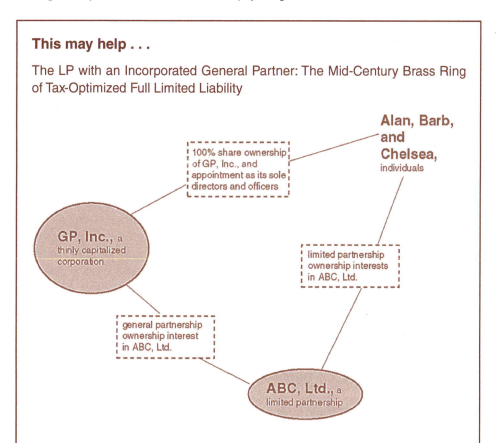

Assume that Alan, Barb, and Chelsea establish a corporation, GP, Inc., in which they purchase all the shares of stock and appoint themselves its sole directors and officers. They then cause GP, Inc. to create a limited partnership, ABC, Ltd., issue a small general partnership ownership interest to GP, Inc., and issue to themselves the LP's limited partnership ownership interests. The only operating business of the enterprise will be conducted by ABC, Ltd., and only it will earn any revenues (though it will then distribute its profits to the partners). Assuming that GP, Inc. is capitalized with enough assets to avoid a finding that it is a fraudulent sham, they now have total control of an entity with full limited liability, and can lose no more than the limited value of GP, Inc.'s capital, but in which they also enjoy pass-through taxation. It will be useful to ask yourself why these results follow, and also to note that if GP, Inc. indeed is a sham a court might choose to disregard it and impose liability on its owners (known as "piercing the veil," discussed in Chapter 16).

In any case, the described combination of attributes is not such a big deal in this age of LLCs and LLPs, but it was in the days when this arrangement first appeared.

As we shall see in the next section, most LPs in use today fall in one or the other of two categories. They are either family business entities designed to minimize estate taxes or investment firms that typically hold real estate or other substantial, durable assets. Indeed, there has been some suggestion of a need for change in LP law to reflect its narrower contemporary role. The Uniform Law Commission has issued what purported to be a drastically revised version of the Uniform Limited Partnership Act. The drafters said this:

> The new Act has been drafted for a world in which limited liability partnerships and limited liability companies can meet many of the needs formerly met by limited partnerships. This Act therefore targets two types of enterprises that seem largely beyond the scope of LLPs and LLCs: (i) sophisticated, manager-entrenched commercial deals whose participants commit for the long term, and (ii) estate planning arrangements (family limited partnerships). This Act accordingly assumes that, more often than not, people utilizing it will want: (i) strong centralized management, strongly entrenched, and (ii) passive investors with little control over or right to exit the entity. The Act's rules, and particularly its default rules, have been designed to reflect these assumptions.

That said, that statute, ULPA (2001),[1] doesn't seem to change that much in the way of substantive law. In some ways, the changes it makes even seem at odds with the stated goal of "manager-entrenched" business plans, since it actually makes it easier for limited partners to involve themselves fully in management. It had long been the law that if limited partners interfered significantly in management, they would be treated as general partners and take on full personal liability. ULPA (2001) (since adopted in just under half the states) did away with

---

1. ULPA (2001) was, like the Uniform Partnership Act (1997), and the Uniform Limited Liability Company Act (2006), amended in 2013 to harmonize all three Acts with each other and with the Model Business Corporations Act.

that rule, although, as a default matter, limited partners do not have management rights.

It is worth noting here that the biggest substantive innovation of ULPA (2001) is that it allows an electing limited partnership to confer limited liability on its general partners, thus becoming a limited liability limited partner (LLLP). There is more on this change below.

 Dear Prof.: What about the S Corp?

You might be wondering why the LP was so important for tax planning prior to the LLC, given that another American entity form—the S Corporation—long predated the LLC, and might seem to have offered similar advantages. So-named because its tax treatment is governed by Subchapter S of the Internal Revenue Code, the S Corp also combined pass-through taxation with limited liability for all of its owners. But in fact, the S Corp traditionally was a problematic alternative, especially when it was first introduced. It did not even appear until 1958, and was subject to extensive restrictions. As initially enacted, an S Corp could have only one class of stock, no more than ten shareholders, no non-resident alien shareholder, and no non-human persons as shareholders. Those restrictions were loosened over time, but even by the time that LLCs began to flourish, an S Corp could have no more than 35 members.

That is not to say the S Corp has become irrelevant in the age of LLCs. It remains quite popular; in fact, S Corps now substantially outnumber C Corps. The reason appears to be one of tax avoidance, associated with the so-called Edwards-Gingrich tax shelter. This was elaborated a bit in Chapter 2.

B. Tax Rationales for Current LP Applications

For years and years, the role of the LP in the U.S. economy has been driven by the Internal Revenue Code. At least since the rise of the LLP and the LLC, there has been no real reason to use the LP unless some special combination of its peculiar characteristics as an entity and its tax treatment make it the right choice. Briefly put, its peculiar entity characteristics are that it usually entails uncommonly tough, deeply entrenched management—the general partners hold their position indefinitely, with no need for election or re-election by the limited partners—leaving the limited partners essentially no management role except to bring derivative lawsuits for breach of duty (as to which see below). As for its tax treatment, that has changed a bit over time. At present, the LP remains a pass-through entity, although it has been stripped of certain special benefits it once may have offered. It still has a few tricks up its federal taxation sleeve, however, and they largely drive the two uses to which LPs are still commonly put.

1. The Family LP

The Rice family, which endowed Rice University, has for years maintained a highly successful family limited partnership.

The structure of the LP, with a powerful, entrenched general partner making the decisions, and limited partners who make no decisions and have no liability, is very appealing to owners of family businesses who want to give the bulk of their business during life to their children as limited partners, but retain control as the general partner. Among other benefits, the fact that assets (even including publicly traded stock) are held by an entity the interests in which are not freely tradable can translate into valuation discounts in determining the gift or estate tax due.

2. The Investment LP

A more complex problem is why investment LPs—entities formed to invest the limited partners' money in some business or asset—still thrive in certain contexts. As mentioned above, LPs lost a lot of their federal tax razzle-dazzle when a particular advantage they previously enjoyed was repealed. Specifically, the Tax Reform Act of 1986 took away the ability of an LP to become publicly traded but still provide the limited partners with pass-through tax treatment (in effect allowing them to invest like corporate shareholders, but without the double-tax disadvantage). The Act also did away with some special deductions and benefits for LPs. Accordingly, since the Act, most LPs simply offer the same federal income tax treatment as general partnerships, LLPs, and LLCs.

But as mentioned, the LP still has something to offer even outside the family business context. Understanding it will take some explaining.

The Larger Tax Issue and the Rise of "Master Limited Partnerships" in Energy and Real Estate. The 1986 Act broadly required "publicly traded partnerships" to be taxed like C corporations—and therefore to pay two-tier tax. I.R.C. §7704(a). As a practical matter, that was the end of most publicly traded LPs. Once pass-through treatment is lost there is no benefit to operating a publicly traded firm in LP form that would outweigh the administrative burdens it would entail. But §7704 carved out one narrow class of businesses that can still be pursued in LP form and enjoy pass-through tax. Under §7704(c), so long as a firm earns most of its money in exploration, development, or distribution of minerals or natural resources, including real estate, and has done so in all of its years of operation, it may be publicly traded without triggering double tax. *See* I.R.C. §7704(d)(1) (defining permissible lines of business). And so there has arisen a small but highly profitable world of publicly traded firms known as "master limited partnerships" or "MLPs." Together they market limited partner interests to several million passive investors. Their interests are traded on the New York Stock Exchange, Nasdaq, and other exchanges.

As a practical matter, most MLPs engage in energy businesses, and indeed they now mainly focus on a narrow subset within it—they mostly own pipelines or other intermediary transportation businesses. The reason is that MLP investors are mostly hunting for very high-income investments, meaning that an MLP must be able to maintain and distribute a consistently, reliably large cash flow. But to keep pass-through treatment it must earn that cash from one of the mineral or natural resources businesses permitted under §7704(d)(1). It turns out that most such businesses—except for distribution—have pretty volatile returns. Nevertheless, despite the heavy focus on the subset of energy distribution, MLPs have engaged in plenty of other businesses, including agriculture and real estate holdings, embracing things as far-flung as amusement parks and cemeteries. *See generally* John Goodgame, *Master Limited Partnership Governance*, 60 Bus. Law. 471 (2009).

Sand Hill Road, in Menlo Park, California, is home to a large number of venture capitalists, many organized as limited partnerships. Microsoft, Facebook, Amazon, Twitter, Instagram, and Skype all found seed money on Sand Hill Road.

Private Investment LPs. For having said all that, there might still be some reason to choose the LP form for use on a privately held basis, and indeed there appears still to be some non-trivial incidence of privately held investment LPs. There could be several explanations. For one thing, the LP offers an off-the-shelf management structure with an unusually entrenched management and unusually inert investors. It might appeal to parties seeking to invest in assets to hold long-term. Another benefit for some firms is that while an individual general partner that receives distributions must generally pay the federal self-employment tax on them, a general partner can simply arrange to hold a small general partnership interest and comparatively large proportion of limited partnership interests—distributions to which are *not* subject to self-employment tax.

 Dear Prof.: Self-employment tax?

People who are self-employed must pay this tax on their income, to make up for the fact that no employer is withholding the so-called payroll taxes from their wages. The payroll taxes fund Social Security and Medicare.

And so, it turns out that many venture capital firms and leveraged buyout companies—firms that pool very large amounts of money from wealthy investors, and invest it in promising start-ups or use it to take over other companies entirely—choose to operate as limited partnerships. Venture capital firms pool money for purposes of investing in new enterprises known as "portfolio companies." As part of their model, venture capitalists demand that the general partner of the venture capital firm be given heavy managerial involvement in their portfolio companies. Leveraged buyout companies pool investor funds with borrowed money to acquire controlling interests in companies that already are established. The term "leverage" is examined at length elsewhere in the book, but for present can be understood simply as meaning "using borrowed money."

■ **Think about this:**

(A) Why might venture capital and leveraged buyout firms choose to operate as limited partnerships?

(B) In the case of investment LPs, a substantial benefit seems to be gotten where the firm's main business is to buy and hold some large, durable asset, which will depreciate over time. Tax law and accounting rules will allow the firm to treat the asset as if it is losing value, and this has a benefit for the partners. The effect is enhanced if the firm makes this investment through a lot of leverage—that is, by borrowing some of the money used to buy the assets. Can you explain why? Why would those two features—depreciation and borrowed capital—tend to generate tax benefits for the partners? Remember Tax Assumption 1 from Chapter 2.

(C) In discussing investment LPs, an implicit theme is to ask why firms even today would choose the LP form and accept its downside of unlimited liability for at least one general partner. The apparent tension is that the same tax benefits should be available if the firm were organized as one of the limited liability entities now widely available, the LLP or the LLC. (And as we shall see in Chapter 11, such an entity could be chosen even in the case of a publicly traded partnership that enjoys single taxation, which does not have to be an LP—it can be organized as an LLC that has elected to be manager-managed and taxed as a partnership.)

But must this trade-off really be made? Can you think of a way that an MLP or a privately held investment LP could avoid or minimize the drawback of the general partner's full liability?

C. Other Attributes

1. Formation, Governance, and the "Control Rule"

Under current law the formation of an LP is very simple, though it involves some risk for the limited partners. The creation of the firm requires the filing with the Secretary of State of a document usually called the "certificate of limited partnership." In general, the certificate must contain only bare-bones information, including the firm's name and the location and identities of its general partners. *See* ULPA (2001) §201. The certificate can contain anything else that the general partners desire to include, but because it is publicly filed and because limited partnerships are permitted (not required) also to have internal, confidential partnership agreements in addition to the certificate, they generally choose to include as little as is legally permitted. Limited partnership *agreements*, by contrast, are often complex, detailed, and long.

Note that under §207 the LP comes into existence as soon as the certificate is "fil[ed] . . . in the office of the Secretary of State," and under §210 the Secretary is required to file the certificate upon receipt and payment of filing fees, unless the Secretary finds that the certificate does not satisfy the Act. But §210 clearly contemplates that there may be a period of time (the Act recommends 15 days) before the Secretary must acknowledge filing or give a reason for rejection. Mistakes can be made in the drafting of certificates, and, even though the statutory requirements are simple, LP certificates are commonly filed with errors that cause them to be rejectable by the Secretary or subject to challenge in later litigation as ineffective to create the LP, even if the Secretary initially accepted them.

The consequences for failure to file, or for failure of substantial compliance even when the certificate is accepted for filing by the Secretary, can be severe for the limited partners. Namely, the firm will be held to be a general partnership, and therefore the would-be limited partners will have full liability and the default rules of the general partnership statute will govern unless modified by some provision in the partnership agreement. *See generally* 3 Bromberg & Ribstein, *supra*, at §§12.02-12.04. The same is true, of course, if the person responsible for the filing simply forgets to file. But there is an escape hatch for the limited partners in these situations. Under ULPA (2001) §306, a would-be limited partner can avoid general partner treatment for subsequent obligations of the partnership if he or she either causes a certificate of limited partnership to be filed, or files a statement of withdrawal from the partnership. With respect to obligations incurred before any such filing, the would-be limited partner will be liable only to persons who entered transaction with the firm believing in good faith that the would-be limited partner was actually a general partner.

As for liabilities and management powers, §403 of the Revised Uniform Limited Partnership Act of 1976 with 1985 amendments (RULPA) simply provided that absent contrary agreement general partners have both the powers and the liabilities to third parties that they would have as partners in a general partnership. By contrast, ULPA

Connections: LLLPs

Once the members of LLCs and the partners in general partnerships were able to claim limited liability, there seemed little reason to leave the general partners in limited partnerships shivering in the cold. The result was the final acquiescence of the Uniform Law Commission and some legislatures, who cried uncle and permitted the limited liability limited partnership (LLLP). The LLLP is further discussed below and in Chapter 11D.

More to the Story: The "Linkage" Issue

For most of its modern history (that is, since the nearly universal adoption of the original Uniform Limited Partnership Act (1914)), LP law has been parasitic on general partnership law. Still today, in the more than 25 jurisdictions that maintain RULPA, when situations arise as to which no RULPA provision governs, the state's general partnership law fills in the gap. *See* RULPA §1105. ULPA (2001) removed the linkage provision and filled in for itself all the gaps that previously had been governed by the general partnership statute.

(2001) in §404 provides for joint and several liability for all general partners unless the limited partnership has made the LLLP election, and in §406 specifically grants the general partners equal rights to manage, with all matters relating to the activities and affairs of the partnership to be decided exclusively by the general partner or, if there is more than one, a majority of the general partners.

Under either version, limited partners ordinarily have no authority to bind the partnership to contracts or torts, but may be granted voting rights by the agreement on any matter. *See* ULPA (2001) §302; RULPA §302. In the absence of agreement they have no voting rights at all except in a handful of cases. For example, under RULPA, a unanimous vote of all the partners can dissolve the firm, even in contravention of the agreement. *See* RULPA §801(3). Under ULPA (2001) §801(2), dissolution can be achieved by a unanimous vote of the general partners and a majority vote of the limited partners.

 Dear Prof.: Wait a minute. Why are you suddenly talking about two different versions of the same Act? And why is the earlier version called "Revised"?

As always, a great question! Because there was an earlier version of the Uniform Limited Partnership Act (the original "ULPA"), the edition adopted in 1976 was named the "Revised Uniform Limited Partnership Act." When we use the term "RULPA," we always refer to the 1976 version with 1985 amendments. When yet another version was adopted in 2001, some folks wanted to call it "Re-RULPA," but its drafters felt otherwise. Just over half the states still follow RULPA, but the number of ULPA (2001) adherents is slowly growing. As noted above, the two versions are quite similar, but where there are significant differences we'll be sure to spell them out. This is one of those places.

One way in which RULPA and ULPA (2001) seem to differ has to do with the so-called control rule, under which a limited partner may pay a price for "participat[ing] in the control of the business." That price is being treated as a general partner. RULPA §303(a). Read the following excerpts from §303 and then think about the various ways a limited partner may get into—or keep out of—hot water.

SECTION 303. LIABILITY TO THIRD PARTIES (RULPA)

(a) Except as provided in subsection (d), a limited partner is not liable for the obligations of a limited partnership unless he [or she] is also a general partner or, in addition to the exercise of his [or her] rights and powers as a limited partner, he [or she] participates in the control of the business.

However, if the limited partner participates in the control of the business, he [or she] is liable only to persons who transact business with the limited partnership reasonably believing, based upon the limited partner's conduct, that the limited partner is a general partner.

(b) A limited partner does not participate in the control of the business within the meaning of subsection (a) solely by doing one or more of the following:

(1) being a contractor for or an agent or employee of the limited partnership or of a general partner or being an officer, director, or shareholder of a general partner that is a corporation;

(2) consulting with and advising a general partner with respect to the business of the limited partnership; . . .

(6) proposing, approving, or disapproving, by voting or otherwise, one or more of the following matters: . . .

(ii) the sale, exchange, lease, mortgage, pledge, or other transfer of all or substantially all of the assets of the limited partnership other than in the ordinary course of its business;

(iii) the incurrence of indebtedness by the limited partnership other than in the ordinary course of its business;

(iv) a change in the nature of the business;

(v) the admission or removal of a general partner; . . .

(ix) matters related to the business of the limited partnership not otherwise enumerated in this subsection (b), which the partnership agreement states in writing may be subject to the approval or disapproval of limited partners; . . .

(c) The enumeration in subsection (b) does not mean that the possession or exercise of any other powers by a limited partner constitutes participation by him [or her] in the business of the limited partnership.

(d) A limited partner who knowingly permits his [or her] name to be used in the name of the limited partnership, except under circumstances permitted by Section 102(2), is liable to creditors who extend credit to the limited partnership without actual knowledge that the limited partner is not a general partner.

■ **Think about this:**

(D) Boris and Claudio form a limited partnership. Boris is the initial general partner and Claudio is the initial limited partner. Boris subsequently purchases an additional interest as a limited partner. What effect will this have on his liability as a general partner? Why would he do it?

(E) Boris and Claudio form a limited partnership. Boris is the initial general partner and Claudio is the initial limited partner. They have an agreement that Boris will act on behalf of Claudio and subject to his control (in other words, as his agent) in all things related to the

partnership. If Boris, at Claudio's direction, enters into a contract that turns out badly, who will be liable? Does it matter what the third party with whom the contract was entered knew or thought?

(F) Boris and Claudio form a limited partnership. Boris is the initial general partner and Claudio is the initial limited partner. The limited partnership agreement provides that Claudio has a veto power over any business decision to be made by Boris. If Boris enters into a contract that Claudio does not veto, and that turns out badly, who will be liable? Does it matter what the third party with whom the contract was entered knew or thought?

(G) Does it appear that a limited partner of a duly formed limited partnership ever could be liable for the partnership's tort obligations?

In contrast to RULPA §303, ULPA (2001) §303 reads in relevant part as follows:

SECTION 303. LIABILITY TO THIRD PARTIES (ULPA (2001))

(a) A debt, obligation, or other liability of a limited partnership is not the debt, obligation, or other liability of a limited partner. A limited partner is not personally liable, directly or indirectly, by way of contribution or otherwise, for a debt obligation, or other liability of the partnership solely by reason of being or acting as a limited partner, even if the limited partner participates in the management and control of the limited partnership. . . .

Would this change any of your answers to Think About This Problems D through G?

The following case is a classic, decided under the language of the original Uniform Limited Partnership Act of 1916. As you read it, think about what its outcome would be under RULPA §303 and under ULPA (2001) §303.

HOLZMAN V. DE ESCAMILLA

California Court of Appeal
81 Cal. App. 2d 858 (1948)

MARKS, J.

This is an appeal by James L. Russell and H. W. Andrews from a judgment decreeing they were general partners in Hacienda Farms Limited, a limited partnership, from February 27 to December 1, 1943, and as such were liable as general partners to the creditors of the partnership.

Early in 1943, Hacienda Farms Limited was organized as a limited partnership, with Ricardo de Escamilla as the general partner and James L. Russell and H. W. Andrews as limited partners.

The partnership went into bankruptcy in December, 1943, and Lawrence Holzman was appointed and qualified as trustee of the estate of the bankrupt. On November 13, 1944, he brought this action for the purpose of determining that Russell and Andrews, by taking part in the control of the partnership business, had become liable as general partners to the creditors of the partnership. The trial court found in favor of the plaintiff on this issue and rendered judgment to the effect that the three defendants were liable as general partners. . . .

De Escamilla was raising beans on farm lands near Escondido at the time the partnership was formed. The partnership continued raising vegetable and truck crops which were marketed principally through a produce concern controlled by Andrews.

The record shows the following testimony of de Escamilla:

> "A. We put in some tomatoes. Q. Did you have a conversation or conversations with Mr. Andrews or Mr. Russell before planting the tomatoes? A. We always conferred and agreed as to what crops we would put in. . . . Q. Who determined that it was advisable to plant watermelons? A. Mr. Andrews. . . . Q. Who determined that string beans should be planted? A. All of us. There was never any planting done—except the first crop that was put into the partnership as an asset by myself, there was never any crop that was planted or contemplated in planting that wasn't thoroughly discussed and agreed upon by the three of us; particularly Andrews and myself."

De Escamilla further testified that Russell and Andrews came to the farms about twice a week and consulted about the crops to be planted. He did not want to plant peppers or eggplant because, as he said, "I don't like that country for peppers or eggplant; no, sir," but he was overruled and those crops were planted. The same is true of the watermelons.

Shortly before October 15, 1943, Andrews and Russell requested de Escamilla to resign as manager, which he did, and Harry Miller was appointed in his place.

Hacienda Farms Limited maintained two bank accounts, one in a San Diego bank and another in an Escondido bank. It was provided that checks could be drawn on the signatures of any two of the three partners. It is stated in plaintiff's brief, without any contradiction (the checks are not before us) that money was withdrawn on 20 checks signed by Russell and Andrews and that all other checks except three bore the signatures of de Escamilla, the general partner, and one of the other defendants. The general partner had no power to withdraw money without the signature of one of the limited partners.

Section 2483 of the Civil Code provides as follows:

> "A limited partner shall not become liable as a general partner unless, in addition to the exercise of his rights and powers as a limited partner, he takes part in the control of the business."

The foregoing illustrations sufficiently show that Russell and Andrews both took "part in the control of the business." The manner of withdrawing money from the bank accounts is particularly illuminating. The two men had absolute power to withdraw all the partnership funds in the banks without the knowledge or consent of the general partner. Either Russell or Andrews could take control of the business from de Escamilla by refusing to sign checks for bills contracted by him and thus limit his activities in the management of the business. They required him to resign as manager and selected his successor. They were active in dictating the crops to be planted, some of them against the wish of de Escamilla. This clearly shows they took part in the control of the business of the partnership and thus became liable as general partners.

Judgment affirmed.

■ **Think about this:**

(H) *Holzman* was a case decided under the original ULPA. How would you expect it to come out under RULPA? Under ULPA (2001)?

2. Fiduciary Duty and "Derivative" Litigation

Duties. On the surface, fiduciary duties in the LP are straightforward. Superficially, the only real difference from fiduciary duties in the general partnership is that the limited partners owe no fiduciary duties at all unless they become involved in the firm's management, and even then only to the extent of their involvement. Limited partners remain free to compete with the business or take opportunities that the business might desire, and sales of limited partnership interests between them are arm's-length transactions. *See* 4 BROMBERG & RIBSTEIN, *supra*, at §16.07(a).

Connections: Fiduciary Duties of Care and Loyalty

A fiduciary—one who is charged with the legal obligation to act in another's best interest rather than her own—owes duties including a duty of care (a duty to act with reasonable care) and a duty of loyalty (which includes a duty to avoid unfair self-dealing and avoid usurping opportunities). There is more on these subjects in Chapter 12.

Connections: The Business Judgment Rule

Different fiduciaries are subject to somewhat different rules when it comes to the duty of care. Trustees are probably subject to the most stringent standards. By contrast, fiduciaries in most business entities are given substantial deference when it comes to their business judgments. This is called the "business judgment rule" and is discussed at greater length in the corporate context in Chapter 18.

Connections: The Duty to Avoid Disloyal Behavior

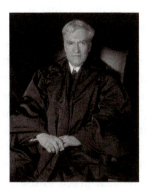

It may seem somewhat odd to say that the duty of loyalty is enhanced in the context of limited partnerships, since in the general partnership context it has been lyrically described by Justice Cardozo as "a duty of the finest loyalty" and "the punctilio of honor the most sensitive." Nonetheless, that standard was enunciated in a context in which one partner was completely passive, and Cardozo noted that for a managing partner the "rule of undivided loyalty" was "relentless and supreme." Meinhard v. Salmon, 164 N.E. 545 (N.Y. 1928).

Justice Cardozo

In considering the duty of the general partners, however, it is important to note that LPs are in many respects quite different than general partnerships, and different in ways relevant to fiduciary duty. In general partnerships, the partners are by default one another's equals, and all have direct personal stakes in the firm's affairs and fortunes. In many LPs, especially where the general partners were also the founding promoters of the firm, not only are the limited partners not their equals, they are likely to see the firm and its goals differently. A personally invested general partner often will see the firm as part of some larger enterprise or some larger family of firms, and may have intentions as to the future of its business after the LP itself is dissolved or all the limited partners are bought out. Those intentions might not complement the personal interests of the limited partners. One commentator put it in these rather stark terms:

> Self-dealing and conflicts of interest are endemic to the limited partnership. Limited partnerships "are born in conflicts of interest, live in conflicts of interest, and sometimes poof out of existence in conflicts of interest." . . . The general partners are typically the organizing entrepreneurs or promoters. They may be affiliated with the sellers of the enterprise's assets, and are frequently involved in multiple, potentially competing related enterprises. This may be good, bad, or indifferent. Categorical prohibitions of conflicting interests might be a coherent response to all this, but a potentially fatal one as well for whatever assumed benefits of flexibility in capital formation the form provides. Categorical permission for conflicting interests might also be a coherent response, but one running all the risks that "fiduciary ideology" is supposed to prevent. What is desired is a scheme for containing conflicts, a fairness-promoting regime that ensures, to the extent possible, that investors in the limited partnership are not being exploited, overreached, or taken advantage of by the managers of their money.

Daniel S. Reynolds, *Loyalty and Limited Partnership*, 34 U. KAN. L. REV. 1, 25 (1985).

Accordingly, in two ways the general partner's duties are unusual and not like those in general partnerships. First, many courts have said that because the general partner holds most or all of the managerial power, she takes on *more* fiduciary duty. It appears that for the most part the courts have imposed only the same duty of *care* on general partners as they do in general partnerships—that is, the informed business judgment of a general partner is not subject to judicial second-guessing, and an informed business judgment that simply turns out to be wrong will not expose the general partner who made it to liability. *See* 4 BROMBERG & RIBSTEIN, *supra*, at §16.07(f). However, courts sometimes say that they impose on them more exacting duties of loyalty and disclosure. Some courts have reached the related conclusion that limited partnership agreements should be construed against the general partners. That is, in cases of ambiguity, a court should prefer the interpretation that would benefit a limited partner in litigation with a general partner. *See, e.g.*, SI Mgmt. L.P. v. Wininger, 707 A.2d 37 (Del. 1998).

Second, however, there is one context in which a general partner's duties are probably *lower* in the LP context. Because it is so clearly anticipated in the very nature of the limited partnership that the general and limited partners are not one another's equals and are not engaged in the same bond of mutual commitment as in general partnership, some courts say that in transactions between partners *as individuals*, fiduciary duties are relaxed. The prime example will be the purchase by a general partner of the interests of one or more limited partners. For example, in Exxon Corp. v. Burglin, 4 F.3d 1294, 1301 (5th Cir. 1993), a general partner purchased the shares of limited partners in an oil exploration venture without disclosing information in its possession suggesting the future value of the shares was substantially greater than it paid. After upholding very broad fiduciary waivers and finding no violation of the duty of good faith, the court added, as a concluding bit of support for its findings, this fairly strong language:

> . . . [T]he standard of conduct for a general partner is somewhat lower when acting in an adversarial relationship with the limited partners. In regard to the buyout offer, Exxon was not acting on behalf of the partnership, representing both its and the limited partners' interests. If it were, the duty of good faith and fair dealing necessarily would be high, to avoid the problem of a general partner's self-dealing.
>
> In this case, however, Exxon was buying out the limited partners' interests. It is logical to expect that the relationship would be somewhat adversarial. The limited partners must have realized that Exxon would try to secure the best deal it could and that this goal was adverse to their interests.

Id. at 1301.

Nevertheless, most courts in this context will still require the general partner to disclose material facts, and impose some obligation to pay a "fair" price. "Fair" price means a price approximating market value under the circumstances, and also implies that the general partner should not coerce the limited partners into sale at discount. *See generally* 4 BROMBERG & RIBSTEIN, *supra*, at §16.07(g). Dicta in *Burglin* suggest that even that court would take this view, as the court rather pointedly observed that in that case defendant general partner did not coerce the limited partners and gave them opportunities to verify the value for themselves.

Enforcement: The "Derivative" Lawsuit.

Fiduciary duties are enforced exclusively through civil lawsuits. The bringing of a lawsuit is a management function that will normally be beyond the authority of a limited partner, and so as with other lawsuits a fiduciary claim in the name of the LP would normally have to be initiated by a general partner. The problem is that only general partners owe fiduciary duties, and so where duties are breached there usually will be no person with an interest in seeking judicial relief who is also authorized to bring suit in the firm's name.

Connections: The Corporate Shareholder's Derivative Suit

The LP derivative suit is very similar to the shareholder derivative suit recognized in corporate law, as to which the law is much more developed and which we cover at much greater length in Chapter 22.

Limited partnership law deals with this problem through the so-called derivative suit. In such a case, a limited partner brings suit on behalf of the firm, and her right to act as plaintiff is said to "derive" from the rights of the firm. The details are somewhat more involved than it will be worth our while to pursue, so we will do with this summary. A limited partner who owned her partnership share at the time of the challenged conduct may sue under ULPA (2001) §902, after making an unsuccessful "demand" on the general partners to initiate the action. If there is a recovery, it actually belongs to the partnership, though where derivative suit is successful §906 permits the court to award the plaintiff expenses and a reasonable attorney's fee. ULPA (2001), unlike RULPA, specifically contemplates a role for a "litigation committee" appointed by the partnership to intervene in derivative litigation on the partnership's behalf. ULPA (2001) §905. Such a committee could cause the litigation to be dismissed if the members of the committee were "disinterested and independent and that the committee acted in good faith, independently, and with reasonable care. . . ." *Id.*

Though not explicitly required by statute, limited partnership case law has made relatively clear that where a claim brought by a limited partner really asserts a right that belongs to the firm, it *must* be brought as a derivative action. This is important because if the limited partner either failed to make any required demand on the general partner or if it can be shown that she did not own her share at the time of the challenged conduct, the suit is dismissible.

An Example in Application. As noted earlier in this chapter, it is not unusual to utilize a corporate general partner for purposes of insulating all the individuals involved in a limited partnership from liability for the partnership's obligations. Corporations, of course, are fictional human beings and must be operated by real people. The next case addresses the range of duties those real people may owe.

IN RE USACAFES, LP LITIGATION

Court of Chancery of Delaware
600 A.2d 43 (1991)

ALLEN, Chancellor.

These consolidated actions arise out of the October 1989 purchase by Metsa Acquisition Corp. of substantially all of the assets of USACafes, L.P., a Delaware limited partnership (the "Partnership") at a cash price of $72.6 million or $10.25

per unit. Plaintiffs are holders of limited partnership units. They bring these cases as class actions on behalf of all limited partnership unitholders except defendants. The relief sought includes, inter alia, the imposition of constructive trusts on certain funds received by defendants in connection with the Metsa sale and an award of damages to the class resulting from the sale.

The Partnership was formed in the 1986 reorganization of the business of USA-Cafes, Inc., a Nevada corporation. Also formed as part of that reorganization was USACafes General Partner, Inc. (the "General Partner"), a Delaware corporation that acts as the general partner of the Partnership. Both the Partnership and the General Partner are named as defendants in this action. A second category of defendants is composed of Sam and Charles Wyly, brothers who together own all of the stock of the General Partner, sit on its board, and who also personally, directly or indirectly, own 47% of the limited partnership units of the Partnership. Sam Wyly chairs the Board of the General Partner.

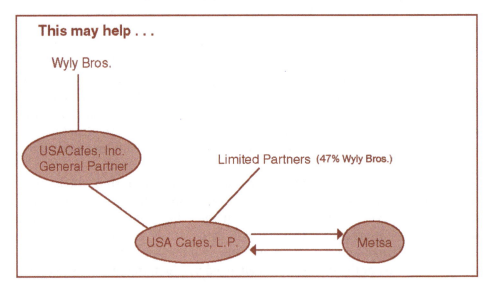

The third category of defendants are four other individuals who sit on the board of directors of the General Partner. All of these persons are alleged to have received substantial cash payments, loan forgiveness, or other substantial personal benefits in connection with the 1989 Metsa purchase.

The last of the defendants is Metsa, the buyer of the Partnership's assets. Metsa is not alleged to be related in any way to the Wylys or any other defendant except as a buyer in the transaction under review.

THE THEORIES OF THE AMENDED COMPLAINT

. . . The first and most central theory involves an alleged breach of the duty of loyalty. In essence, it claims that the sale of the Partnership's assets was at a low price, favorable to Metsa, because the directors of the General Partner all received substantial side payments that induced them to authorize the sale of the Partnership assets for less than the price that a fair process would have yielded. . . . In sum, it is alleged that between $15 and $17 million was or will be paid to the directors and officers of the General Partner by or with the approval of Metsa; those payments are alleged to constitute financial inducements to the directors of the General Partner to refrain from searching for a higher offer to the Partnerships. Plaintiffs add that, even assuming that Metsa was the buyer willing to pay the best price, some part at least of these "side payments" should have gone to the Partnership. . . .

Presently pending are several motions. First, the Wyly defendants and the other director defendants move under Rule 12(b)(6) to dismiss the breach of fiduciary duty claims in the amended complaint asserting that, while the General Partner admittedly did owe fiduciary duties to the limited partners, they as directors of the General Partner owe no such duties to those persons. The whole remedy of the limited partners for breach of the duties of loyalty and care, it is said, is against the General Partner only and not its directors. . . .

I turn first to the director defendants' motion to dismiss for failure to state a claim with respect to the sale of the Partnership's assets. The gist of this motion is the assertion that the directors of the General Partner owed the limited partners no duty of loyalty or care. In their view their only duty of loyalty was to the General Partner itself and to its shareholders (i.e., the Wyly brothers). Thus, in alleging that the director defendants breached duties of loyalty and care running to them, the directors say the limited partners have asserted a legal nullity.

In my opinion the assertion by the directors that the independent existence of the corporate General Partner is inconsistent with their owing fiduciary duties directly to limited partners is incorrect. Moreover, even were it correct, their position on this motion would have to be rejected in any event because the amended complaint expressly alleges that they personally participated in the alleged breach by the General Partner itself, which admittedly did owe loyalty to the limited partners.

The first basis of this holding is the more significant. While I find no corporation law precedents directly addressing the question whether directors of a corporate general partner owe fiduciary duties to the partnership and its limited partners, the answer to it seems to be clearly indicated by general principles and by analogy to trust law. I understand the principle of fiduciary duty, stated most generally, to be that one who controls property of another may not, without implied or express agreement, intentionally use that property in a way that benefits the holder of the control to the detriment of the property or its beneficial owner. There are, of course, other aspects—a fiduciary may not waste property even if no self interest is involved and must exercise care even when his heart is pure but the central aspect of the relationship is, undoubtedly, fidelity in the control of property for the benefit of another.

The law of trusts represents the earliest and fullest expression of this principle in our law, but courts of equity have extended it appropriately to achieve substantial justice in a wide array of situations. Thus, corporate directors, even though not strictly trustees, were early on regarded as fiduciaries for corporate stockholders. When control over corporate property was recognized to be in the hands of shareholders who controlled the enterprise, the fiduciary obligation was found to extend to such persons as well.

While the parties cite no case treating the specific question whether directors of a corporate general partner are fiduciaries for the limited partnership, a large number of trust cases do stand for a principle that would extend a fiduciary duty to such persons in certain circumstances. The problem comes up in trust law because modernly corporations may serve as trustees of express trusts. Thus, the question has arisen whether directors of a corporate trustee may personally owe duties of loyalty to cestui que trusts of the corporation. A leading authority states the accepted answer:

> . . . The directors and officers are in a fiduciary relation not merely to the [corporation] . . . but to the beneficiaries of the trust administered by the [corporation].

4 A. Scott & W. Fratcher, The Law of Trusts §326.3, at 304-306 (4th ed. 1989) (citing cases) ["Scott on Trusts"].

The theory underlying fiduciary duties is consistent with recognition that a director of a corporate general partner bears such a duty towards the limited partnership. That duty, of course, extends only to dealings with the partnership's property or affecting its business, but, so limited, its existence seems apparent in any number of circumstances. Consider, for example, a classic self-dealing transaction: assume that a majority of the board of the corporate general partner formed a new entity and then caused the general partner to sell partnership assets to the new entity at an unfairly small price, injuring the partnership and its limited partners. Can it be imagined that such persons have not breached a duty to the partnership itself? And does it not make perfect sense to say that the gist of the offense is a breach of the equitable duty of loyalty that is placed upon a fiduciary? It appears true that the same result might be rationalized as aider and abettor liability, but I am unsure what such indirection would add that is useful where a self-dealing transaction or other diversion of partnership property is alleged. Indeed in some instances, for example the use by a director of confidential information concerning the partnership's business not yet known by the board of the general partner, there may be no breach of loyalty or care by the general partner itself to abet, yet there may be director liability to the partnership by the director. *Cf.* cases cited at 4 Scott on Trusts §326.3, at n.7.

Two courts have, in fact, held a sole shareholder/director of a corporate general partner personally liable for breach of fiduciary duty to limited partners, although without much discussion of the issue here considered. . . . While these authorities extend the fiduciary duty of the general partner to a controlling shareholder, they support as well, the recognition of such duty in directors of the General Partner who, more directly than a controlling shareholder, are in control of the partnership's property. It is not necessary here to attempt to delineate the full scope of that duty. It may well not be so broad as the duty of the director of a corporate trustee. But it surely entails the duty not to use control over the partnership's property to advantage the corporate director at the expense of the partnership. That is what is alleged here. . . .

I therefore conclude that the amended complaint does allege facts which if true establish that the director defendants have breached fiduciary obligations imposed upon them as directors of a Delaware corporation or have participated in a breach of such duties by the General Partner. The amended complaint does, in my opinion, state a claim upon which relief can be granted.

> ■ **Think about this:**
>
> *(I)* What arguments might you have presented to support the argument that the directors and/or controlling shareholders of a corporate general partner should *not* be found to owe fiduciary duties to the limited partnership?
>
> *(J)* Can you think of any stronger arguments in support of Chancellor Allen's conclusion than "does it not make perfect sense"?

3. Securities Law

One of the most important consequences of organizing a business as an LP is that, unlike most other unincorporated entity forms, LPs are routinely subject to federal securities law. To summarize a fairly complex issue dealt with elsewhere in this book, that body of law regulates transactions involving "securities," as it defines them. All kinds of things can be "securities," and investment interests in which the investor is mainly passive—not actually involved in management or other operations within the business—are typically "securities." The partnership interests of limited partners, in fact, are almost always "securities." The consequences of this fact can be quite serious, because compliance with securities law is expensive and entails substantial public disclosures to be prepared and filed with the Securities and Exchange Commission. This is called the "registration" requirement.

But it turns out that LPs can frequently avoid this result. Securities law provides several exemptions to the registration requirement, mainly designed to protect small businesses that do not market their membership interests to the public at large. In particular, promoters of LPs often seek to sell limited partnership interests only to some small group of wealthy and sophisticated investors, who are then barred from re-selling them for a period of time. In cases like this, significant disclosures about the firm still must be made to the investors themselves, and misrepresentation must be assiduously avoided. Selling securities through this non-public avenue is known as "private placement," and knowing how to perfect a private placement without triggering applicability of federal securities law is an essential tool for the business counselor.

4. Distributions and Creditor Protections

The default profit-sharing rule for limited partnerships is the opposite of—or, at any rate, different than—the equal shares rule followed for general partnerships. Absent contrary agreement, profits are shared by both general and limited partners in the same proportion as their contributions. *See* ULPA (2001) §810(b). If interim distributions are made and the agreement does not provide otherwise, they must be made in proportion to capital contributions. *See id.* §503.

No partner has a statutory default right to interim distributions. Moreover, while at least the limited partners will normally receive some periodic interim distributions, and may even have a right to them under the partnership agreement, ULPA (2001) §504 provides that distributions cannot be made where they would render the firm unable to pay its debts when due or where the payment would cause its liabilities to third parties to exceed its assets. Moreover, a person receiving a distribution that would be improper under §504 is personally liable to repay the limited partnership the amount that exceeds the amount the statute permits.

5. Exit and Liquidity

Absent contrary agreement, a general partner may withdraw at will, although written notice to all the other partners is required. Withdrawal in violation of the partnership agreement entitles the firm to seek damages the general partner caused by breach. Under RULPA, limited partners could withdraw only on six months' written notice to each general partner. *See* RULPA §§602-603. ULPA (2001) is tougher: Limited partners cannot withdraw before completion of winding up. ULPA (2001) §601(a).

Absent contrary agreement, the interest of either a general or limited partner is freely assignable. As is the case with general partnerships, the assignment gives the assignee no managerial powers or rights, though in the case of a limited partner interest this is a small concern since limited partners have essentially no managerial role (though the assignee likely would be unable to exercise the derivative litigation rights of a partner, which might in a particular case be a significant shortcoming). Charging orders are available under ULPA (2001) §703 that are essentially similar to charging orders under general partnership law.

More important, if the partnership agreement permits it, an assignee of either a general or limited partner's interest may become a limited partner. In this latter case, a limited partner's share can actually become a fairly liquid asset, and as discussed, limited partnerships have often been publicly traded. In these cases, the only real limit on liquidity will have to do with the value and future prospects of the partnership itself, the extent of the general partner's discretionary powers, and the likelihood that the firm will distribute interim proceeds to the limited partners.

On the flip side, there may be terms in the partnership agreement forbidding any type of transfer or requiring prior general partner approval. In addition, rules of federal securities law limit trading in unregulated securities. Generally, where limited partner shares that constitute "securities" are sold under an exemption from the federal securities laws, as discussed above, they cannot be easily resold.

Limited partners generally have little power to dissolve and general partners have less power to dissolve than they would in a general partnership. Limited partners can cause dissolution only by seeking judicial order under ULPA (2002) §801(6) or RULPA §802. Under RULPA, dissolution occurs on the withdrawal of a general partner unless the remaining partners unanimously agree to continue within 90 days. RULPA §801(4). Under ULPA (2001) §801(2), provided there is at least one continuing general partner, withdrawal of a general partner does not cause dissolution unless there is a vote within 90 days by the holders of a majority of partnership interests to wind up the limited partnership's affairs. Thus, limited partnerships lack the powerful liquidity measure of unilateral dissolution observed in general partnerships.

Room to Argue: Do ULPA (2001) and Its LLLP Election Invite the End of Multiple Unincorporated Entity Alternatives?

Two significant changes in ULPA (2001) remove what had been the hallmarks of the LP that made it genuinely different than other unincorporated limited liability entities: The code did away with the traditional "control" rule, granting new managerial freedom to the limited partners, and it adopted a new rule that even general partners may now elect to enjoy full limited liability. (That is, under ULPA (2001), an LP can elect to be a "limited liability limited partnership" or LLLP.) These two changes beg a few rather large questions. First, one must wonder why, in an ULPA (2001) jurisdiction, LPs and LLLPs would still be needed, given the availability of LLCs and LLPs. An LP with a limited liability general partner and fully managerially involved limited partners would be hard to distinguish in any meaningful way from either an LLP or a member-managed limited LLC (though occasionally there will be small state regulatory differences, like the fact that in some states an LLC must pay state franchise tax but LLPs and LLLPs do not). It seems obvious, given the growing convergence of model unincorporated business statutes toward a regime in which any business can quite easily achieve full limited liability with full managerial involvement and yet still claim pass-through taxation, that the drafters of uniform business statutes foresee a day on which some single "unified" statute would govern all unincorporated businesses. That is in fact a course that many commentators have urged.

Test Yourself

(Answers in Online Supplement)

Assume Applicability of the Revised Uniform Limited Partnership Act

1. ABC, Ltd., a limited partnership formed under a relatively bare-bones partnership agreement that left most terms of the state limited partnership statute unmodified, manufactures gaskets for the automobile industry. Jane is ABC's sole general partner and Paula is its sole limited partner.

   a. On March 1, a car maker that is one of ABC's chief customers informs ABC of a defect affecting a large batch of gaskets. The customer demands repayment of their value, whereas ABC happens to be sufficiently low on cash at the moment that satisfying the obligation could make the firm insolvent. Alarmed at these events, on March 3 Paula engages a law firm to represent ABC in what seems to be shaping up to be litigation, and she also makes overtures to the car maker's executives to try to work out a compromise. If the car maker reduces its claim to judgment, and the value of it exceeds the net value of ABC, Ltd., for how much of the excess are Jane and Paula each liable?

b. Assume that the gasket conflict is resolved amicably, but that it caused lasting strife between Jane and Paula. At wit's end, Paula decides her only option is to quit ABC altogether. Never one to stand on formalities, she visits Jane in person to give her the sad news. Paula demands reduction of the value of her partnership share to cash, with payment within the month. What effect?

2. XYZ, Ltd., is a limited partnership with a corporate general partner and 275 limited partners, all of whom are individuals and none of whom have any other relation to the general partner, and all the limited partnership shares are currently traded on the New York Stock Exchange. Mark is one of those limited partners.

a. Two years ago, XYZ had a very tough year, and it failed to distribute any profits at all to its limited partners. Incensed, Mark brings suit, asserting that he was entitled to a distribution of $5,000. What must be true in order for Mark's lawsuit to recover the unpaid distribution to succeed?

b. At the end of its last taxable year, XYZ distributed $10,000 of its profits to Mark. Will those profits be subject to two-tier taxation? Do you have enough information to know?

3. PQR, L.P., is a limited partnership. The agreement of limited partnership provides that the limited partners are entitled to receive annual distributions equal to no less than 20 percent of the amount of their capital contributions. At the end of year one, the distributions are made, leaving PQR, L.P. unable to pay its creditors. If the creditors sue the limited partners, must they return their distributions?

4. Larry is a limited partner in Limited, L.P., a limited partnership. He also is the 100 percent shareholder of Limited, Inc., the corporate general partner, as well as its only director and president. At a Rotary Club luncheon, he meets Sue, a supplier of a product that Limited, L.P., uses. He hands her a business card that says "Larry, Limited Partner, Limited, L.P." Larry subsequently phones Sue, identifies himself as "Larry from Limited." He reminds her where they met and places a large order. The order is delivered and the product is used, but not paid for. If Limited, L.P., is unable to pay, will Sue be able to recover from Larry? If so, under what theory or theories? Does it matter whether RULPA or ULPA (2001) applies?

11

The Limited Liability Company, Its Special Attributes, and Other Modern Alternatives

Every state now has a limited liability company (LLC) statute, and in all states the LLC combines the desirable features of pass-through taxation and limited liability for all members. Because LLC statutes give LLC members great flexibility in structuring their firms as they see fit, they can make them closely resemble either a general partnership or a corporation, or many things in between. This chapter investigates the differences between LLCs and general partnerships, and between them and corporations, and explains why they exist and how they can be made to (almost) disappear. There are, however, quite a few other entity forms available under current law and a number of strategic issues in using them to achieve client goals. The trend seems to be toward diminishing distinctions among the various entity forms. Suggestions have been made to do away with these distinctions altogether.

Chapter Outline

A. Introduction

B. Primary Characteristics and Differences from Other Entities

1. Flexible Governance and the Election Between "Member-Management" and "Manager-Management"

2. Fiduciary Duties

303

3. Corporate Litigation Attributes: Derivative Actions and "Piercing the Veil"

4. Distributions, Transferability, Liquidity, and Exit

C. The LLC in the Courts: "Hybrid-ness" and Other Metaphysics

D. Series LLCs

E. Other Modern Alternatives

1. The LLP

2. The PC, the "Medical Corporation," and Similar Entities

3. The LLLP

4. The LPA

F. Future Trends: The End of Distinguishable Business Entity Forms?

Test Yourself

 What does it look like?

Check the online Supplement for the following sample documents that are relevant to this chapter:

- Certificate of organization for a limited liability company
- A limited liability company operating agreement

A. Introduction

In a way, the limited liability company (LLC) has been with us throughout this book. Though it is relatively new, it has quickly found itself in a sort of default position, and discussion of any other entity usually raises the question why a business would prefer it to the LLC. In most states, for most businesses, there is normally little reason to choose another entity unless some practical or legal issue requires it. Thus, though it first appeared only in a 1977 Wyoming statute and did not come really into its own until ten years later, when the Treasury Department formally agreed to tax it as a partnership, it is roughly tied with the general partnership as the most common unincorporated entity in the United States. So, on some level, a question is always with us: Why would one choose anything else?

More to the Story: The History of the LLC

Every state now has an LLC statute. However, the early LLC statutes varied quite a lot, and even now significant state-to-state variations remain. It turns out that the continuing variation in the states is to some extent just a lingering anachronism, an artifact of a long struggle for permissive tax treatment. When the Treasury Department first granted the LLC pass-through tax treatment, it did so through the so-called Kintner rules, under which favorable treatment was allowed only if, under an entity's organizing documents and the state statute under which it was formed, it had more attributes common to partnerships than to corporations. The entity would be double-taxed if it had three of the four following traits: limited liability, centralized management, continuity of life (that is, the entity would not terminate on the death or dissociation of a member), and free transferability of shares. At the time, state legislatures were eager to ensure that their in-state LLCs could meet the Kintner rules. Many of the state statutes were therefore full of what now seem like peculiar or unnecessary restrictions concerning such matters as dissolution and transferability. To make a long story short, the Treasury Department finally relented. In 1997 it replaced the Kintner rules with a simpler and much more permissive approach, permitting unincorporated entities simply to elect pass-through treatment under the so-called check-the-box rule (see Chapter 2). But some states have been slow to do away with the many otherwise undesirable technicalities that were originally meant to placate the Treasury Department.

One problem for us, explained in the "More to the Story" box on this page, is the still non-trivial variation among state LLC statutes. It may lessen with the spread of the Uniform Law Commission's Uniform Limited Liability Company Act (ULLCA), which was first promulgated in 1995 and then substantially revised in 2006. Although adopted in a minority of the states, since federal tax law no longer requires the many peculiarities that once drove state statutory complexity, it should spread more broadly soon. In this chapter, we consider the ULLCA (2006) as amended in 2013.

B. Primary Characteristics and Differences from Other Entities

The LLC's chief attributes are that it enjoys limited liability, like a corporation, and pass-through tax treatment, like a partnership. But countless other legal issues come up in its formation and operation that must be answered somehow, and a *large* number of them will find no clear answer in the LLC statute in a given state or in the organizational documents of most LLCs. The courts accordingly have been faced with a bit of a dilemma in

litigation involving them (and in fact the same dilemma comes up with the other unincorporated forms, like the limited liability partnership, the limited partnership association, the professional corporation, and so on). For the most part, the courts have said that when such an issue arises they will resolve it as best they can through analogy to either the law of partnerships or the law of corporations. They say this because the LLC is very literally a hybrid of both, combining characteristics borrowed from the two areas. Incidentally, many LLC statutes are either silent or agnostic on this point—they leave it up to the courts whether to analogize to corporate, partnership, or some other law. A case in point is ULLCA §111, which provides that "[u]nless displaced by particular provisions of this [Act], the principles of law and equity supplement this [Act]." We discuss this issue a bit further below, and present an example of a court working through just such an analysis, in Section C.

Legislatures have also been sensitive to this hybrid nature, and have sought to combine the most desirable aspects of both entities in the LLC. Accordingly, in the years since the check-the-box rules freed them to serve constituents' desires, rather than those of the Treasury Department, legislatures have gradually molded the LLC in a way that borrows from both traditions (and typically allows LLC members to choose aspects from either).

Connections: Federal Securities Law in General and with Respect to Publicly Traded LLCs

Like limited partners' interests in LPs, ownership interests in manager-managed LLCs are passive investments, and therefore are often "securities," with all the attendant consequences under federal and state securities laws. Care is generally taken in the sale of such interests to bring them within the exceptions to the securities laws' registration requirements. Membership interests in genuinely member-managed LLCs, because they are not passive in nature, are not "securities." These matters are covered in more detail in Chapter 28.

In fact, just as with limited partnerships, see Chapter 10C, manager-managed LLCs can even be publicly traded. Bear in mind that to do so the creators of the LLC must modify the default LLC rules for transferability, and they must comply with the full range of federal securities laws. But so long as these requirements are met, an LLC's shares can be traded just like publicly traded corporate stock, and can be listed on securities exchanges. And while, as a result of the same rule that applies to LPs, a publicly traded LLC normally loses pass-through tax status by issuing public shares, see I.R.C. §7704(a), it can retain that status if it makes most of its money in the energy or natural resources businesses in which publicly traded partnerships can engage under I.R.C. §7704(d).

1. Flexible Governance and the Election Between "Member-Management" and "Manager-Management"

A truly key, distinguishing feature of the LLC is its flexible management structure. It can accomplish a range of management structures to which other statutory forms do not as readily lend themselves. As we have seen, a running problem in business entity statutes is that they must attempt to capture some default conception of the firms that they will govern, and the default ought to be fairly realistically true to the needs and characteristics of those firms most likely to rely on the default provisions. But every firm will have its own peculiar characteristics, and some firms are highly idiosyncratic.

First of all, ULLCA is extremely flexible in providing that virtually all of its rules are merely defaults. Following the Revised Uniform Partnership Act (RUPA) very closely, ULLCA §110(a) provides that with the exception of the 11 specific items listed in §110(c), *any* provision of the ULLCA may be modified or waived completely by agreement.

Next, ULLCA effectively contemplates that an LLC can have any management structure its members desire, though there have come to be certain standard models. Under ULLCA, an LLC need not have any formal agreement governing the members' relations. They must only file a "certificate of organization" with the Secretary of State or equivalent, the required contents of which are even more minimal than those of a certificate of limited partnership under RULPA §201(a). *See* ULLCA §201(b) (setting out required information in LLC certificate). But not only will most LLCs have internal operating agreements, they will also normally be long and detailed, and because virtually everything in ULLCA can be modified in the agreement, the members are free to set up virtually any management structure they desire.

ULLCA provides two basic (and very general) default options for the management structure of the company, and choosing between them has a number of legal consequences. The ULLCA definitions provision, §102, distinguishes between a "member-managed limited liability company," §102(12), and a "manager-managed limited liability company," §102(10). Obviously enough, the former is managed in the same way that general partnerships are managed—by equal member participation unless otherwise agreed. *See* §407(b). The latter is managed by persons hired to manage in exchange for salary, one or more of whom may be non-members of the firm. *See* §407(c). The election of one or the other form is simply made in the operating agreement; in the absence of any agreement, the statutory default is member-management. *See* ULLCA §407(a). By default, member-managed firms have largely the same governance structure as default general partnerships. Members have equal participation in management, ordinary disputes are resolved by majority, and acts outside the ordinary course of business require

Connections: Bare-Bones Filings, But *Looooong* Operating Agreements

Most LLCs have written internal membership agreements, and most of them are quite long and detailed. In this way, LLCs are like LPs and many general partnerships, which also tend to have long operating agreements. (Technically, ULLCA §102(13) provides that agreements among the members modifying ULLCA provisions may be oral, so long as they are unanimous, but a purely oral membership agreement would be unusual.)

unanimity. *See* §407(b). In manager-managed firms, the managers are equal managers with power to bind, though taking actions outside the ordinary course of business requires unanimous consent of the *members*. *See* §407(c)(3).

Within this extremely flexible governance regime—which really would permit basically limitless variation—certain relatively standard models have begun to emerge. Ribstein and Keatinge explain that

> [w]hile the management structure of an LLC is limited only by the owners' imagination, there are three "fundamental" or typical structures: a corporate or "representative management" structure; a limited partnership or "entrenched management" structure; and a general partnership or "direct management" structure.

1 Larry E. Ribstein & Robert R. Keatinge, Ribstein and Keatinge on Limited Liability Companies §2.3 (2015).

■ **Think about this:**

(A) While it may not be immediately clear, each of the three models described by Ribstein and Keatinge could actually be set up in either a member-managed or manager-managed LLC. Do you see why? Ask yourself, for example, what a member-managed "corporate" management structure would look like, and how it would differ from a manager-managed "corporate" management structure. Keep in mind as you think about this that there is no requirement for all LLC members to have the same management status.

Note, by the way, ULLCA §201(a)'s explicit recognition that an LLC can be formed and owned by one person, meaning that a sole proprietorship can take LLC status and so enjoy limited liability. (This is of course true with corporations as well—one person may incorporate a sole proprietorship, continuing to own it as 100 percent shareholder.)

■ **Think about this:**

(B) Imogene forms a one-person LLC for the purpose of carrying on business as a masseuse. While administering a massage, she negligently causes injury to a client. If the LLC does not have adequate assets to pay any judgment against it, are Imogene's personal assets at risk?

(C) Ike forms a one-person LLC for the purpose of carrying on business as a masseur. He wants to buy a new table and other equipment, for which the LLC must borrow funds. The lender demands a personal guarantee. If the LLC does not have enough assets to pay off the debt, are Ike's personal assets at risk?

(D) Exactly what good does it do for a sole proprietorship to be reformed as an LLC?

The case that follows was an early decision under the Delaware LLC statute. It took a strong position that the goal of the LLC is to maximize flexibility of governance and members' freedom in contracting to design their firms as they see fit.

ELF ATOCHEM NORTH AMERICA, INC. V. JAFFARI

Supreme Court of Delaware
727 A.2d 286 (1999)

VEASEY, Chief Justice:

. . .

FACTS

Plaintiff below—appellant Elf Atochem North America, Inc., a Pennsylvania Corporation ("Elf")[—]manufactures and distributes solvent-based maskants to the aerospace and aviation industries throughout the world. Defendant below—appellee Cyrus A. Jaffari[—]is the president of Malek, Inc., a California Corporation. Jaffari had developed an innovative, environmentally-friendly alternative to the solvent-based maskants that presently dominate the market.

For decades, the aerospace and aviation industries have used solvent-based maskants in the chemical milling process. Recently, however, the Environmental Protection Agency ("EPA") classified solvent-based maskants as hazardous chemicals and air contaminants. To avoid conflict with EPA regulations, Elf considered developing or distributing a maskant less harmful to the environment.

In the mid-nineties, Elf approached Jaffari and proposed investing in his product and assisting in its marketing. Jaffari found the proposal attractive since his company, Malek, Inc., possessed limited resources and little international sales expertise. Elf and Jaffari agreed to undertake a joint venture that was to be carried out using a limited liability company as the vehicle.

On October 29, 1996, Malek, Inc. caused to be filed a Certificate of Formation with the Delaware Secretary of State, thus forming Malek LLC, a Delaware limited liability company under the Act. The certificate of formation is a relatively brief and formal document that is the first statutory step in creating the LLC as a separate legal entity. The certificate does not contain a comprehensive agreement among the parties, and the statute contemplates that the certificate of formation is to be complemented by the terms of the Agreement.

Next, Elf, Jaffari and Malek, Inc. entered into a series of agreements providing for the governance and operation of the joint venture. Of particular importance to this litigation, Elf, Malek, Inc., and Jaffari entered into the Agreement, a comprehensive and integrated document of 38 single-spaced pages setting forth detailed provisions for the governance of Malek LLC, which is not itself a signatory to the Agreement. Elf and Malek LLC entered into an Exclusive Distributorship Agreement in which Elf would be the exclusive, worldwide distributor for Malek LLC. The Agreement provides that Jaffari will be the manager of Malek LLC. Jaffari and Malek LLC entered into an employment agreement providing for Jaffari's employment as chief executive officer of Malek LLC.

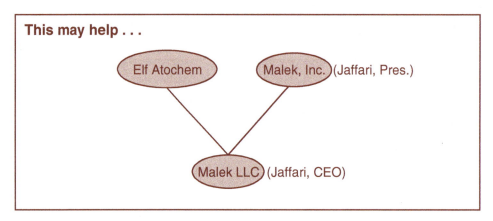

The Agreement is the operative document for purposes of this Opinion, however. Under the Agreement, Elf contributed $1 million in exchange for a 30 percent interest in Malek LLC. Malek, Inc. contributed its rights to the water-based maskant in exchange for a 70 percent interest in Malek LLC.

The Agreement contains an arbitration clause covering all disputes. The clause, Section 13.8, provides that "any controversy or dispute arising out of this Agreement, the interpretation of any of the provisions hereof, or the action or inaction of any Member or Manager hereunder shall be submitted to arbitration in San Francisco, California." Section 13.8 further provides: "No action based upon any claim arising out of or related to this Agreement shall be instituted in any court by any Member except (a) an action to compel arbitration or (b) an action to enforce an award obtained in an arbitration proceeding." The Agreement also contains a forum selection clause, Section 13.7, providing that all members consent to: "exclusive jurisdiction of the state and federal courts sitting in California in any action on a claim arising out of, under or in connection with this Agreement or the transactions contemplated by this Agreement, provided such claim is not required to be arbitrated pursuant to Section 13.8"; and personal jurisdiction in California. The Distribution Agreement contains no forum selection or arbitration clause.

ELF'S SUIT IN THE COURT OF CHANCERY

On April 27, 1998, Elf sued Jaffari and Malek LLC, individually and derivatively on behalf of Malek LLC, in the Delaware Court of Chancery, seeking equitable remedies. Among other claims, Elf alleged that Jaffari breached his fiduciary duty to Malek LLC, pushed Malek LLC to the brink of insolvency by withdrawing funds for personal use, interfered with business opportunities, failed to make disclosures to Elf, and threatened to make poor quality maskant and to violate environmental regulations. Elf also alleged breach of contract, tortious interference with prospective business relations, and (solely as to Jaffari) fraud.

The Court of Chancery granted defendants' motion to dismiss based on lack of subject matter jurisdiction. The court held that Elf's claims arose under the Agreement, or the transactions contemplated by the agreement, and were directly related to Jaffari's actions as manager of Malek LLC. Therefore, the court found that the Agreement governed the question of jurisdiction and that only a court of law or arbitrator in California is empowered to decide these claims. Elf now appeals the order of the Court of Chancery dismissing the complaint . . . .

GENERAL SUMMARY OF BACKGROUND OF THE ACT

. . . The [Delaware LLC] Act can be characterized as a "flexible statute" because it generally permits members to engage in private ordering with substantial freedom of contract to govern their relationship, provided they do not contravene any mandatory provisions of the Act. Indeed, the LLC has been characterized as the "best of both worlds."[1] . . .

POLICY OF THE DELAWARE ACT

The basic approach of the Delaware Act is to provide members with broad discretion in drafting the Agreement and to furnish default provisions when the members' agreement is silent. The Act is replete with fundamental provisions made subject to modification in the Agreement (e.g. "unless otherwise provided in a limited liability company agreement.") . . . .

FREEDOM OF CONTRACT

Section 18-1101(b) of the Act . . . provides that "[i]t is the policy of [the Act] to give the maximum effect to the principle of freedom of contract and to the enforceability of limited liability company agreements." Accordingly, the following observation relating to limited partnerships applies as well to limited liability companies:

> The Act's basic approach is to permit partners to have the broadest possible discretion in drafting their partnership agreements and to furnish answers only in situations where the partners have not expressly made provisions in their partnership agreement. Truly, the partnership agreement is the cornerstone of a Delaware limited partnership, and effectively constitutes the entire agreement among the partners with respect to the admission of partners to, and the creation, operation and termination of, the limited partnership. Once partners exercise their contractual freedom in their partnership agreement, the partners have a great deal of certainty that their partnership agreement will be enforced in accordance with its terms.

In general, the commentators observe that only where the agreement is inconsistent with mandatory statutory provisions will the members' agreement be invalidated. Such statutory provisions are likely to be those intended to protect third parties, not necessarily the contracting members. As a framework for

---

1. [Martin I. Lubaroff & Paul M. Altman, *Delaware Limited Liability Companies*, in DELAWARE LAW OF CORPORATIONS & BUSINESS ORGANIZATIONS, §20.1 (R. Franklin Balotti & Jesse A. Finkelstein eds., 1998)].

decision, we apply that principle to the issues before us, without expressing any views more broadly . . . .

Malek LLC's Failure to Sign the Agreement Does Not Affect the Members' Agreement Governing Dispute Resolution

Elf argues that because Malek LLC, on whose behalf Elf allegedly brings these claims, is not a party to the Agreement, the derivative claims it brought on behalf of Malek LLC are not governed by the arbitration and forum selection clauses of the Agreement.

Elf argues that Malek LLC came into existence on October 29, 1996, when the parties filed its Certificate of Formation with the Delaware Secretary of State. The parties did not sign the Agreement until November 4, 1996. Elf contends that Malek LLC existed as an LLC as of October 29, 1996, but never agreed to the Agreement because it did not sign it. Because Malek LLC never expressly assented to the arbitration and forum selection clauses within the Agreement, Elf argues it can sue derivatively on behalf of Malek LLC pursuant to 6 Del. C. §18-1001.

We are not persuaded by this argument. Section 18-101(7) defines the limited liability company agreement as "any agreement, written or oral, of the member or members as to the affairs of a limited liability company and the conduct of its business." Here, Malek, Inc. and Elf, the members of Malek LLC, executed the Agreement to carry out the affairs and business of Malek LLC and to provide for arbitration and forum selection.

Notwithstanding Malek LLC's failure to sign the Agreement, Elf's claims are subject to the arbitration and forum selection clauses of the Agreement. The Act is a statute designed to permit members maximum flexibility in entering into an agreement to govern their relationship. It is the members who are the real parties in interest. The LLC is simply their joint business vehicle. This is the contemplation of the statute in prescribing the outlines of a limited liability company agreement . . . .

Classification by Elf of Its Claims as Derivative Is Irrelevant

. . . Although Elf correctly points out that Delaware law allows for derivative suits against management of an LLC, Elf contracted away its right to bring such an action in Delaware and agreed instead to dispute resolution in California . . . . Sections 13.7 and 13.8 of the Agreement do not distinguish between direct and derivative claims. They simply state that the members may not initiate any claims outside of California. Elf initiated this action in the Court of Chancery in contravention of its own contractual agreement. As a result, the Court of Chancery correctly held that all claims, whether derivative or direct, arose under, out of or in connection with the Agreement, and thus are covered by the arbitration and forum selection clauses . . . .

The Argument That Chancery Has "Special" Jurisdiction for Derivative Claims Must Fail

Elf claims that 6 Del. C. §§18-110(a), 18-111 and 18-1001 vest the Court of Chancery with subject matter jurisdiction over this dispute . . . . Elf is correct that 6

Del. C. §§18-110(a) and 18-111 vest jurisdiction with the Court of Chancery in actions involving removal of managers and interpreting, applying or enforcing LLC agreements respectively. As noted above, Section 18-1001 provides that a party may bring derivative actions in the Court of Chancery. Such a grant of jurisdiction may have been constitutionally necessary if the claims do not fall within the traditional equity jurisdiction. Nevertheless, for the purpose of designating a more convenient forum, we find no reason why the members cannot alter the default jurisdictional provisions of the statute and contract away their right to file suit in Delaware . . . . We hold that, because the policy of the Act is to give the maximum effect to the principle of freedom of contract and to the enforceability of LLC agreements, the parties may contract to avoid the applicability of Sections 18-110(a), 18-111, and 18-1001.

Validity of Section 13.7 of the Agreement Under 6 Del. C. §18-109(d)

Elf argues that Section 13.7 of the Agreement, which provides that each member of Malek LLC "consents to the exclusive jurisdiction of the state and federal courts sitting in California in any action on a claim arising out of, under or in connection with this Agreement or the transactions contemplated by this Agreement" is invalid under Delaware law. Elf argues that Section 13.7 is invalid because it violates 6 Del. C. §18-109(d).

Subsection 18-109(d) is part of Section 18-109 relating to "Service of process on managers and liquidating trustee." It provides:

> In a written limited liability company agreement or other writing, a manager or member may consent to be subject to the nonexclusive jurisdiction of the courts of, or arbitration in, a specified jurisdiction, or the exclusive jurisdiction of the courts of the State of Delaware, or the exclusivity of arbitration in a specified jurisdiction or the State of Delaware.

Section 18-109(d) does not expressly state that the parties are prohibited from agreeing to the exclusive subject matter jurisdiction of the courts or arbitration fora of a foreign jurisdiction. Thus, Elf contends that Section 18-109(d) prohibits vesting exclusive jurisdiction in a court outside of Delaware, which the parties have done in Section 13.7.

We decline to adopt such a strict reading of the statute. Assuming, without deciding, that Section 109(d) relates to subject matter jurisdiction and not merely in personam jurisdiction, it is permissive in that it provides that the parties "may" agree to the non-exclusive jurisdiction of the courts of a foreign jurisdiction or to submit to the exclusive jurisdiction of Delaware. In general, the legislature's use of "may" connotes the voluntary, not mandatory or exclusive, set of options. The permissive nature of Section 18-109(d) complements the overall policy of the Act to give maximum effect to the parties' freedom of contract. Although Section 18-109(d) fails to mention that the parties may agree to the exclusive jurisdiction of a foreign jurisdiction, the Act clearly does not state that the parties must agree to either one of the delineated options for subject matter jurisdiction. Had the General Assembly intended to prohibit the parties from vesting exclusive jurisdiction in arbitration or court proceedings in another state, it could have proscribed such an option. The Court of Chancery did not err in declining to strike down the validity of Section 13.7 or Section 13.8 of the Agreement . . . .

■ **Think about this:**

(E) Does *Elf Atochem* mean that there are no limits on what an LLC's members may agree to? If there are limits, what are they?

(F) Does *Elf Atochem* mean that an LLC's members may disregard the formality of having the entity sign agreements to which it is to be bound?

(G) Suppose that Mr. Jaffari, acting on behalf of Malek, Inc., and Ms. X, acting on behalf of Elf Atochem North America, Inc., had orally agreed that all matters related to the affairs of Malek LLC were to be arbitrated in California. Under the reasoning of *Elf Atochem*, would that agreement be enforceable?

2. Fiduciary Duties

As with the limited partnership, fiduciary duties in LLCs largely follow the law of general partnerships, but with one major distinction. ULLCA §409(a) provides that members of *member-managed* companies owe only the fiduciary duties described in §409(b) and (c), which lay out essentially the duties owed by partners in general partnerships. However, in a *manager-managed* company, the members owe no duties at all to the company or one another, except to perform their obligations under the operating agreement in good faith. *See* §409(d), (i)(6). Instead, the managers hired to manage the firm for them owe the same fiduciary duties that member-managers would have owed in their place (which is to say, the duties of care and loyalty, under §409(b) and (c)). Where a member in a manager-managed firm is given some management rights under an operating agreement, that person bears the ordinary obligations under §409(b) and (c) to the extent of his role in management.

These rules again reflect the hybrid partnership-corporate character of the LLC. A member-managed firm is like a partnership, and so the members bear the duties of

> **Connections: Incorporating the "Business Judgment Rule" for LLCs**
>
> The fiduciary duties of LLC members in member-managed firms, or managers in manager-managed firms, incorporate the "business judgment rule for partnerships." Under that rule, a fiduciary with no conflict of interest is personally liable for losses only when caused by actions that were not reasonably informed, were not "rationally" related to the best interests of the company, or were knowingly illegal. The rule is further discussed in Chapter 12.

partners, but in a manager-managed firm the members have in essence the status of corporate shareholders, who generally owe no fiduciary duties but rely on the fiduciary obligations of the corporate officers employed by the firm to protect their interests.

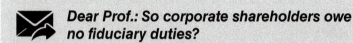

Dear Prof.: So corporate shareholders owe no fiduciary duties?

This is not the case. Sometimes shareholders do owe fiduciary duties (see, especially, Chapters 23 and 26)—but they usually don't.

3. Corporate Litigation Attributes: Derivative Actions and "Piercing the Veil"

LLCs pose special problems in litigation, and two important ones are dealt with by rules borrowed from corporate law. First, individual LLC members, especially in manager-managed firms, can face difficulty ensuring that the interests of the LLC are protected. In this, they face a problem just like one faced by shareholders in a corporation. To deal with it, code drafters have borrowed the corporate law concept of "derivative" litigation. The managers of manager-managed LLCs hold the management powers, and members who do not themselves serve as managers have essentially none. The decision to file a lawsuit is a managerial act, and so it can be exercised only by managers. So, while non-manager members are protected in principle by the fiduciary duties of their managers, when those duties are breached the only people with authority to enforce them are often the breaching managers themselves.

They are unlikely to sue themselves, so the law permits non-member managers to bring "derivative" lawsuits against them. (There can also be cases in which the firm's managers fail to assert rights against third parties, which members might then choose to assert derivatively, as for example where a manager fails to enforce a contract against a party because that party is the manager's associate or family member.) It turns out that limited partners in limited partnerships have the same problem, and so they too usually have rights to enforce fiduciary and other duties derivatively. ULLCA §§802-806 set out a derivative litigation right for members that is essentially the same as the right held by corporate shareholders, and is more or less identical to the derivative rules of RULPA §§1002-1005. See Chapter 10C.

> **Connections: Corporate Derivative Litigation and Veil-Piercing**
>
> Both doctrines discussed here are better developed in the corporate law context, and we discuss that elaborate and extensive case law elsewhere. The corporate derivative suit is discussed in Chapter 22, and the corporate piercing-the-veil rule is discussed in Chapter 16.

Room to Argue: The Benefits of Limited Liability

There is some amount of academic controversy about whether limited liability is the unmitigated good that state legislatures seem to think it is, or whether the risk of "moral hazard"—the temptations to benefit without reckoning with third-party costs—is too great. There is more on this subject in the online Supplement. What one believes about limited liability in general presumably affects how liberally one would choose to see veil-piercing invoked.

Specifically, where a member can show some injury to the LLC—as opposed to an injury to the member's own interests, not affecting other members, which must be brought as a direct action, *see* ULLCA §901—the member can sue in place of the LLC. Before bringing suit, the member must make a "demand" of the managers that they address the problem internally, and must then plead either that the demand was refused or that it would have been "futile." *See* §802.

Second, a quite different problem is posed by an under-capitalized LLC sued by creditors for its debts. Not uncommonly an LLC will incur liability to a plaintiff that the LLC's assets cannot cover, while the members themselves might have significant personal assets that can cover the shortfall. Ordinarily, this is just the situation that limited liability is supposed to address, and so creditors cannot execute their unsatisfied claims against the members' personal property. But at times the rule can seem sufficiently unfair that the courts deploy an equitable doctrine to avoid it, known as "piercing the veil." The doctrine was long available under corporate law, and under the case law of most jurisdictions it is possible to "pierce the veil" of the LLC's limited liability protection.

Generally speaking, a court will pierce the veil where the owners of the firm have not respected it as a separate entity. Relevant evidence includes whether they have commingled their personal funds with the entity's funds, whether they have commingled the entity's funds with those of other entities under their control, whether they have used the entity for personal purposes or to advance the interests of other entities they control, whether the entity is grossly under-capitalized, and whether they have observed formalities in the running of its business, such as the holding of proper meetings and keeping of proper books. Cases in which the courts are willing to pierce the veil typically involve either truly pathological laxity in administrative affairs, or outright fraud, such as the transfer of assets among different entities to hide them from creditors.

The following case gives the flavor of the way courts deal with the basic question of whether veil-piercing is permissible in the LLC context. It also introduces the proud role of Wyoming in the LLC story. Perhaps most important, it exemplifies the problems that arise when new forms of business join older ones without any particular, continuing effort to reconcile relevant statutory requirements.

KAYCEE LAND AND LIVESTOCK V. FLAHIVE

Supreme Court of Wyoming
46 P.3d 323 (2002)

KITE, Justice.

[Plaintiff Kaycee Land and Livestock contracted to allow Flahive Oil & Gas, LLC, to use the surface of its land. Kaycee sued in federal district court for environmental damage the LLC allegedly caused, and seeks to hold Roger Flahive, its managing member, personally liable, since the LLC now has no assets. No fraud is alleged. Uncertain how Wyoming would handle the issue, the district court certified to the state supreme court whether Flahive could be personally liable.] . . .

The question presented is limited to whether, in the absence of fraud, the remedy of piercing the veil is available against a company formed under the Wyoming Limited Liability Company Act (Wyo. Stat. Ann. §§17-15-101 to -144).* To answer this question, we must first examine the development of the doctrine within Wyoming's corporate context. As a general rule, a corporation is a separate entity distinct from the individuals comprising it. Wyoming statutes governing corporations do not address the circumstances under which the veil can be pierced. However, since 1932, this court has espoused the concept that a corporation's legal entity will be disregarded whenever the recognition thereof in a particular case will lead to injustice . . . .

Wyoming courts, as well as courts across the country, have typically utilized a fact driven inquiry to determine whether circumstances justify a decision to pierce a corporate veil. This case comes to us as a certified question in the abstract with little factual context, and we are asked to broadly pronounce that there are no circumstances under which this court will look through a failed attempt to create a separate LLC entity and prevent injustice. We simply cannot reach that conclusion and believe it is improvident for this court to prohibit this remedy from applying to any unforeseen circumstance that may exist in the future.

We have long recognized that piercing the corporate veil is an equitable doctrine. The concept of piercing the corporate veil is a judicially created remedy for situations where corporations have not been operated as separate entities as contemplated by statute and, therefore, are not entitled to be treated as such. The determination of whether the doctrine applies centers on whether there is an element of injustice, fundamental unfairness, or inequity. The concept developed through common law and is absent from the statutes governing corporate organization. *See* Wyo. Stat. Ann. §§17-16-101 to -1803. Appellee Roger Flahive suggests that, by the adoption of §17-16-622(b)—a provision from the revised Model Business Corporation Act—the Wyoming legislature intended to explicitly authorize piercing in the corporate context and, by inference, prevent its application in the LLC context. A careful review of the statutory language and legislative history leads to a different conclusion. Section 17-16-622(b) reads: "Unless otherwise provided in the articles of incorporation, a shareholder of a corporation is not personally liable for the acts or debts of the corporation except that he may become personally liable by reason of his own acts or conduct." Mr. Flahive contrasts that language with the LLC statute which simply states the underlying principle of limited liability for individual members and managers. Wyo. Stat. Ann. §17-15-113. Section 17-15-113 provides:

> Neither the members of a limited liability company nor the managers of a limited liability company managed by a manager or managers are liable under a judgment,

---

* *Editors' Note:* Wyoming has subsequently adopted the ULLCA.

decree or order of a court, or in any other manner, for a debt, obligation or liability of the limited liability company.

However, we agree with Commentator Gelb that: "It is difficult to read statutory §17-15-113 as intended to preclude courts from deciding to disregard the veil of an improperly used LLC." Harvey Gelb, *Liabilities of Members and Managers of Wyoming Limited Liability Companies*, 31 Land & Water L. Rev. 133 at 142 (1996).

Section 17-16-622—the statute relied upon by Mr. Flahive as indicating legislative intent to allow piercing of the corporate veil—when considered in the context of its legislative history, provides no support for the conclusion that the legislature intended in any way to limit application of the common-law doctrine to LLCs. As previously explained, §17-16-622 was adopted from the revised Model Business Corporation Act, and the comments therein clarify that subsection (b) "sets forth the basic rule of nonliability of shareholders for corporate acts or debts that underlies modern corporation law" and "recognizes that such liability may be assumed voluntarily or by other conduct." 1 Model Bus. Corp. Act Ann. §6.22 at 6-94 to 6-95 (Supp. 1997) . . . . The official comments in the revised Model Business Corporation Act specifically recognize the separate existence of the common law by stating: "Shareholders may also become liable for corporate obligations by their voluntary actions or by other conduct under the common law doctrine of 'piercing the corporate veil.'" *Id.* at 6-96 . . . .

With the dearth of legislative consideration on this issue in Wyoming, we are left to determine whether applying the well established common law to LLCs somehow runs counter to what the legislature would have intended had it considered the issue. In that regard, it is instructive that: "Every state that has enacted LLC piercing legislation has chosen to follow corporate law standards and not develop a separate LLC standard." Philip P. Whynott, The Limited Liability Company §11:140 at 11-5 (3rd ed. 1999). Statutes which create corporations and LLCs have the same basic purpose—to limit the liability of individual investors with a corresponding benefit to economic development. Statutes created the legal fiction of the corporation being a completely separate entity which could act independently from individual persons. If the corporation were created and operated in conformance with the statutory requirements, the law would treat it as a separate entity and shelter the individual shareholders from any liability caused by corporate action, thereby encouraging investment. However, courts throughout the country have consistently recognized certain unjust circumstances can arise if immunity from liability shelters those who have failed to operate a corporation as a separate entity . . . .

We can discern no reason, in either law or policy, to treat LLCs differently than we treat corporations. If the members and officers of an LLC fail to treat it as a separate entity as contemplated by statute, they should not enjoy immunity from individual liability for the LLC's acts that cause damage to third parties. Most, if not all, of the expert LLC commentators have concluded the doctrine of piercing the veil should apply to LLCs . . . . It also appears that most courts faced with a similar situation—LLC statutes which are silent and facts which suggest the LLC veil should be pierced—have had little trouble concluding the common law should be applied and the factors weighed accordingly . . . .

Certainly, the various factors which would justify piercing an LLC veil would not be identical to the corporate situation for the obvious reason that many of the organizational formalities applicable to corporations do not apply to LLCs. The LLC's operation is intended to be much more flexible than a corporation's. Factors relevant to determining when to pierce the corporate veil have developed over time in a multitude of cases. It would be inadvisable in this case, which lacks a complete factual context, to attempt to articulate all the possible factors to be applied to LLCs in Wyoming in the future . . . . Determinations of fact are within the trier of fact's province. The district court must complete a fact intensive inquiry and exercise its equitable powers to determine whether piercing the veil is appropriate under the circumstances presented in this case . . . .

No reason exists in law or equity for treating an LLC differently than a corporation is treated when considering whether to disregard the legal entity. We conclude the equitable remedy of piercing the veil is an available remedy under the Wyoming Limited Liability Company Act.

■ **Think about this:**

(H) The court finds no reason to treat an LLC differently than a corporation. Can you think of one? Or was the attempt made by appellant Flahive frivolous?

(I) If it were up to you to decide the grounds that would suffice to disregard the veil of limited liability, what would they be?

It is worth noting that ULLCA §304(b) now provides that the failure of an LLC to observe formalities is not a ground for imposing liability on any of its members or managers.

4. Distributions, Transferability, Liquidity, and Exit

A feature of defining significance for any business is how easily its participants can exit. That question really just translates to how liquid a member's investment is, and liquidity in turn depends on (a) how easily the member's interest can be sold in full to a buyer, or in the alternative, (b) how easily the member can force buyout of the interest by the firm.

For better or worse, this problem of exit has been the subject of much state variation, as explained in the "More to the Story" box on the following page. For the reasons explained there, the default rules of most early state LLC statutes and of ULLCA (1994) largely follow the structure of general partnership law. That is to say, by default, LLC member interests under those statutes are quite liquid. Even though they are not freely transferrable to third parties, members may dissociate at will and are entitled to payment of their interest by the firm.

ULLCA §701. But some more modern statutes prohibit member dissociation altogether, while ULLCA (2006), and some other more recent statutes, permit dissociation but provide that it does *not* cause dissolution. The dissociating member rather is treated as a mere transferee, with no managerial rights and no enforceable buyout right. This "Hotel California" rule—under which you can check out, but you can never leave—preserves the dissociating member's right to receive any interim distributions the firm provides, but does not require a buyout of that member's interest or a return of any capital until dissolution. (One might wonder then why a member would bother to dissociate in such a state. The reason is to avoid fiduciary obligations and other contractual obligations of members, and so, for example, a member might dissociate in order to become free to compete with the LLC in its business.)[2]

In any case, LLC interests are freely transferable in the absence of contrary agreement, *see* ULLCA §502(a), but as in other unincorporated firms the transferee will receive only a right to the transferor's distributions from the firm. Again, where the agreement provides for transfer of full membership rights, the only real restraints on liquidity will be the nature of the firm itself and restrictions imposed by federal securities law. As to the latter, the major restriction is that interests in manager-managed LLCs will usually be freely tradable only if they are registered.

For all these reasons, membership in a default LLC can be either relatively liquid or quite illiquid, depending on whether the jurisdiction recognizes a right of mandatory buyout. In those states without it, along with the fact that, as with general and limited partnerships, LLC members have no default right to interim distributions, ULLCA §404(b), LLC members are at somewhat increased risk of minority oppression, akin to that in closely held corporations.

More to the Story: The Evolution of Exit Rules and the Hotel California Provision

As with so many issues in LLC law, rules on dissolution have evolved along with the gradual loosening of federal tax rules. Initially, the rules pressured states to impose partnership-style features in their LLC statutes, since LLCs were more likely to get pass-through treatment the more they "looked like" general partnerships. Accordingly, the early LLC statutes typically granted strong rights of unilateral dissolution. (For discussion of unilateral dissolution in the general partnership, see Chapter 9.) But with the coming of check-the-box taxation, and given that many businesses will find the unilateral dissolution power a serious nuisance, LLC statutes have begun to do away with it. Hence the rules mentioned in the text, some states providing no default dissociation right at all, and some permitting only "Hotel California" withdrawal.

---

2. See generally Ribstein & Keatinge, supra, at §11.2; Douglas K. Moll, *Minority Oppression and the Limited Liability Company: Learning (or Not) from Close Corporation History*, 40 Wake Forest L. Rev. 883, 927-940 (2005).

■ **Think about this:**

(J) As mentioned in the "More to the Story" box above, many states now follow quite different dissolution rules for LLCs and general partnerships. Whether or not any state legislator actually thought it through this far, there is an intriguing theoretical justification for the difference. It may reflect perhaps the most fundamental difference between the general partnership and the LLC—that general partners are vicariously liable for their firms' debts. That being the case, do you see why LLC members don't really *need* an individual dissolution power, in the same way that general partners do, however much they might personally value liquidity?

(K) The relative illiquidity of LLC interests will be a drawback for some firms, especially in Hotel California states, but as with most other matters of LLC structure it is easy to modify. In fact, an LLC can be arranged with very freely transferrable interests that could trade just like shares of corporate stock, and indeed, LLCs can be and sometimes are publicly traded. What default rules would have to be modified to reach that result?

(L) Explain to yourself how the following can be true: Given the flexibility of management structure and rules for distribution in most LLC statutes, an LLC can have a hierarchical corporate-type management structure and a partnership-type financial structure with capital accounts, variable distributions, and changing profit-sharing percentages or a partnership-type management structure with fungible equity interests that resemble shares of stock.

LLCs frequently are praised for their flexibility and lack of requisite formalities. It is important that these attributes not be taken too far, as the following case indicates.

NEW HORIZONS SUPPLY COOP. V. HAACK

Wisconsin Court of Appeals
1999 WL 33499 (Unpublished)

DEININGER, J.

[Defendant Haack and her brother Robert Koch formed Kickapoo Valley Freight, LLC (Kickapoo). Haack signed a fuel supply contract with plaintiff New Horizons Supply Cooperative (New Horizons), identifying Kickapoo as responsible for payment, but signing her own name without indication whether she meant to take on personal liability. Kickapoo later dissolved, leaving no assets and leaving $1,009.99 owing to New Horizons, for which New Horizons secured a small claims court judgment against Haack personally. She now appeals. New

Horizons put on testimony that when it sought payment, Haack described Kickapoo as a "partnership," said it had been dissolved, and that she "planned to assume responsibility" for the debt. Haack further admitted in testimony that she told New Horizons she "would try to take care" of it. To prove the existence of the LLC, Haack could produce only a state tax registration certificate and some state agency correspondence, and admitted she had neither filed the "articles of dissolution" permitted by state statute nor notified creditors of the dissolution. The small claims court held her personally liable because it was "piercing the corporate veil," and stated as its reason that there was no attempt properly to dissolve and because Kickapoo elected partnership taxation.] . . .

. . . [W]e are called upon to decide a legal question: Were Haack's testimony and exhibits sufficient to establish a defense under §183.0304, Stats., which provides that "a member or manager of a limited liability company is not personally liable for any debt, obligation or liability of the limited liability company"? [The court first acknowledges that despite the paucity of evidence, a factfinder could find that Kickapoo was properly formed as an LLC, and that it existed at the time the debt was incurred. The court also rejected the decision below to "pierce the veil," as it appeared to have been based improperly on little more than Kickapoo's election of partnership taxation.] Rather, we conclude that entry of judgment against Haack on the New Horizons' claim was proper because she failed to establish that she took appropriate steps to shield herself from liability for the company's debts following its dissolution and the distribution of its assets . . . .

The record is devoid . . . of any evidence showing that appropriate steps were taken upon the dissolution of the company to shield its members from liability for the entity's obligations. Although it appears that filing articles of dissolution is optional, see §183.0906, Stats., the order for distributing the company's assets following dissolution is fixed by statute, and the company's creditors enjoy first priority, see §183.0905, Stats. A dissolved limited liability company may "dispose of known claims against it" by filing articles of dissolution, and then providing written notice to its known creditors containing information regarding the filing of claims. See §183.0907, Stats. The testimony at trial indicates that Haack knew of New Horizons' claim at the time Kickapoo Valley was dissolved. It is also clear from the record that articles of dissolution for Kickapoo Valley Freight LLC were not filed, nor was the cooperative formally notified of a claim filing procedure or deadline.

Section 183.0909, Stats., provides in relevant part as follows:

> A claim not barred under §183.0907 or 183.0908 may be enforced under this section against any of the following: . . .
>
> (2) If the dissolved limited liability company's assets have been distributed in liquidation, a member of the limited liability company to the extent of the member's proportionate share of the claim or to the extent of the assets of the limited liability company distributed to the member in liquidation, whichever is less, but a member's total liability for all claims under this section may not exceed the total value of assets distributed to the member in liquidation.

It appears from the record that certain of Kickapoo Valley's assets were sold, and that the proceeds from that sale were remitted to the bank which held a lien on the company's truck. There is nothing in the record, however, showing the disposition of other company assets, such as cash and accounts receivable. New Horizons' witness testified that, in October 1997, Haack had claimed to be attempting to collect the accounts of the dissolved company and hoped to pay the instant debt from those proceeds. We do not know the value of the accounts receivable in question, however, or the amounts of any other company debts to which the proceeds of the accounts may have been applied, because Haack presented no testimony on the issue.

In this regard, we agree with the trial court's comments regarding the lack of evidence in the record to show that Kickapoo Valley's affairs were properly wound up following its dissolution occasioned by Robert Koch's dissociation from the enterprise. Although Kickapoo Valley Freight LLC may have been properly formed and operated as an entity separate and distinct from its owners, Haack did not establish that she distributed the entity's assets in accordance with §183.0905, Stats., following Kickapoo's dissolution. Her failure to employ the procedures outlined in §§183.0906 and .0907, Stats., left her vulnerable to New Horizons' claim under §183.0909(2), Stats., absent proof that the value of any assets of the dissolved company she received were exceeded by the cooperative's claim . . . .

> ◼ **Think about this:**
>
> *(M)* Can it possibly be correct that Haack needed to show that the cooperative's claim exceeded the value of any assets she received?
>
> *(N)* Does the court's assessment of the burden of proof strike you as the correct one?
>
> *(O)* Of what relevance is Kickapoo's tax treatment?

The most recent version of the ULLCA reflects concern with the possibility that members will distribute an LLC's assets to themselves before the entity is dissolved, leaving creditors unpaid. Section 405 imposes two tests, both of which must be satisfied assuming the distribution is made:

- The LLC still must be able to pay its debts as they become due in the ordinary course of its business; and
- Its total assets must be no less than the sum of its total liabilities plus the amount that would be needed to satisfy the dissolution preferences of any member (or transferee) whose rights are superior to those of the persons receiving the distribution.

Section 406 imposes liability in the amount of any distribution in violation of §405 on any member or manager who consented to it.

C. The LLC in the Courts: "Hybrid-ness" and Other Metaphysics

Notice that in both of the preceding cases, *Kaycee Land and Livestock* and *New Horizons Supply*, a major issue was whether the courts should import a well-established doctrine from corporate law—piercing the veil. It turns out that this same sort of problem has been very common throughout LLC litigation. And so, for our purposes the significance of a case like *Cortez*, which follows, is not really the specific rule it adopts. More important is its approach to the problem that LLCs resemble both corporations and partnerships. Sometimes, even when the local LLC statute specifically addresses an issue, it will not be clear whether a court should apply the rule that applies to corporations or the rule that applies to partnerships. Courts in these cases often decide by asking whether, under the particular circumstances of the case, the LLC was acting more like one or more like the other.

CORTEZ V. NACCO MATERIALS HANDLING GROUP, INC.

Supreme Court of Oregon
337 P.3d 111 (Or. 2014)

KISTLER, J.

[Plaintiff sues Swanson Group, Inc., which wholly owns his employer, Sun Studs, LLC, for a workplace accident in which he was struck by a forklift operated by another Sun Studs employee. The forklift was sold to Sun Studs by Nacco Materials Handling Group. Sun Studs is one of several lumber mills owned by Swanson, all of which are organized as freestanding, member-managed LLCs. Though Swanson is the sole member of each LLC, and is formally a manager of each of them, each mill also has its own supervisory employees, who are responsible for day-to-day operations. Plaintiff, though he received a workers' compensation award with respect to Sun Studs, alleged that Swanson was liable for negligently failing (or for negligently failing to require Sun Studs) to provide a safe workplace and for failing to provide competent safety personnel. The court here affirms dismissal of the negligence claim against Swanson.]

Because Sun Studs is currently organized as a limited liability company (LLC), we discuss that form of organization briefly before setting out the facts. An LLC is a relatively new form of business organization . . . . The persons who own an LLC are its "members." . . . The members can manage the LLC themselves, or they can appoint a manager or group of managers to manage the company . . . . The statutes accordingly distinguish between member-managed and manager-managed LLCs.

LLCs share many attributes of limited partnerships, but they differ from that form of business organization in at least one respect: in Oregon, a "member or manager [of an LLC] is not personally liable for a . . . liability of the [LLC] solely by reason of being or acting as a member or manager." . . .

Regarding safety, Swanson provided the LLCs that it owned with a safety manual, which stated general policies and served as a "template" that each LLC could customize to its particular operations. Swanson delegated day-to-day responsibility for safety at Sun Studs to Sun Studs' mill manager and HR director. Specifically, Swanson delegated responsibility "to [Sun Studs' mill manager and HR director] to carry out the safety program and to follow as close as they can the template provided by [Swanson]." It was "up to [Sun Studs' mill manager and HR director] to identify and rectify any safety violations or unsafe workplace issues or safety hazard type issues" at the worksite.

[Swanson concedes on appeal that plaintiff created a triable issue of fact as to Sun Studs' negligence, and also that Swanson had the authority, as the member-manager of Sun Studs, to require Sun Studs to provide safer conditions.] . . . Swanson notes, however, that ORS 63.165(1) [a provision of the Oregon LLC statute] shields LLC members and managers from personal liability for "acting" as a member-manager.[3] Swanson reasons that, under ORS 63.165(1), "merely having the authority to require the LLC to prevent a workplace accident . . . is not sufficient for personal liability to attach to a managing-member for every act of negligence that arises out of the operations of the LLC's business."

Swanson argues that it will be liable as Sun Studs' member-manager only when an officer or director of a corporation would be liable for a corporate employee's negligence—that is, only if Swanson "actively participated" in Sun Studs' negligence. Swanson contends that the evidence on summary judgment does not permit an inference that it either actually knew of the conditions at Sun Studs that allegedly led to plaintiff's injuries or that it actively participated in the creation of those conditions.

Plaintiff takes a different view of both ORS 63.165(1) and the evidence. He argues that the sole function of ORS 63.165(1) is to make clear that LLC members and managers are immune from vicarious liability for the LLC's debts, obligations, and liabilities. Plaintiff reasons that, to the extent a member or a manager is independently liable to an employee or a third party, ORS 63.165(1) provides no protection from that liability. As a corollary to that argument, plaintiff contends that . . . a reasonable juror could infer that Swanson "retain[ed] control over job site safety" and, having retained control, failed to provide (or to require Sun Studs to provide) a safe workplace . . . .

A. STATUTORY IMMUNITY UNDER ORS 63.165(1)

In interpreting ORS 63.165(1), we begin, as we customarily do, with the text and context of ORS 63.165(1) and then turn to that statute's legislative history . . . .

---

3. An LLC member can be a passive owner of the LLC, much like a corporate shareholder. Alternatively, an LLC member can manage the LLC either in a member-managed LLC or in a manager-managed LLC, if the member is designated as the manager of the manager-managed LLC . . . . We assume that the issues that arise from extending immunity to LLC members and managers for "acting" in those capacities primarily will involve persons (whether members or managers) who manage the LLC.

1. Text

ORS 63.165(1) provides:

> "The debts, obligations and liabilities of a limited liability company, whether arising in contract, tort or otherwise, are solely the debts, obligations and liabilities of the limited liability company. A member or manager is not personally liable for a debt, obligation or liability of the limited liability company solely by reason of being or acting as a member or manager."

In many respects, the two sentences in subsection (1) mirror each other. The first sentence provides that the "debts, obligations and liabilities" of an LLC are "solely" the debts, obligations, and liabilities of the LLC. The second sentence provides that a member or a manager of an LLC is not personally liable for the LLC's debts, obligations, and liabilities "solely by reason of being or acting as a member or manager" of the LLC. Each sentence makes clear, in a different way, that a member or a manager of an LLC is not vicariously liable for the LLC's debts, obligations, and liabilities, as a general partner will be vicariously liable for the partnership's obligations.

The use of the word "being" in the second sentence in ORS 63.165(1) is consistent with that interpretation. Merely "being" a member or manager does not make that person liable for the LLC's obligations. However, the use of the word "acting" in the second sentence interjects ambiguity into the text. On the one hand, "acting" could mean that a member or manager is not personally liable for any debts, obligations or liabilities of the LLC that arise solely by reason of the "actions" that a member or manager takes in that person's official capacity. Read broadly, the phrase "acting as a member or manager" would provide members and managers immunity not only from vicarious liability but also from personal liability for their actions in managing an LLC.

On the other hand, the word "acting" may play a more modest role. It may simply confirm that a member or manager of an LLC is not vicariously liable for the LLC's debts, obligations, and liabilities. Specifically, the word "acting" could serve to make clear that, unlike a limited partner who will become vicariously liable if he or she participates in the control of the business, a member or manager of an LLC will not be vicariously liable for actively managing the LLC's business.... The text, specifically the word "acting," is capable of more than one interpretation, and we turn to the context.

2. Context

The context does little to clarify the text's meaning. Essentially, it reveals that, as initially enacted in 1993, ORS 63.165(1) shielded an LLC member or manager from liability for the LLC's obligations only for "being" a member or manager.... As noted, granting immunity for "being" a member or manager implies only that the grant of immunity extends to vicarious liability.

In 1999, the legislature amended the part of ORS 63.165 (1993) at issue by adding the word "acting."... As discussed above, the addition of the word "acting" could have been intended to expand the scope of ORS 63.165(1) to include not only immunity from vicarious liability but also immunity from liability for all "actions" that a member or manager of an LLC takes in his or her official capacity. Alternatively, the legislature could have added "acting" to make clear that a member or manager of an LLC will not be vicariously liable either for "being" a member or manager of an LLC or for "acting" as such, i.e., for exercising control over the LLC. That is, the legislature may have wanted only to clarify that a member or manager of an LLC enjoys greater immunity than a limited partner does . . . . Because the context does not resolve the ambiguity inherent in the text of ORS 63.165(1), we turn to the statute's legislative history.

3. Legislative History

The legislative history of ORS 63.165 shows that the 1993 legislature enacted the initial version of that statute to protect members and managers from vicarious liability for the LLC's obligations even when the member or manager actively managed the LLC. A member of a taskforce charged with advising the legislature on LLCs told the 1993 House Judiciary Subcommittee on Civil Law:

> "The limited liability company gives flexibility for members to participate as little or as much as they wish . . . as opposed to a limited partner[ship] where the limited partner[s] cannot [participate] without running the risk of becoming general partners."

. . . The legislative history of the 1999 amendments to the LLC statutes does not reveal an intent to depart from that original understanding. Rather, a member of the LLC taskforce told the 1999 legislature that the proposed amendments to ORS 63.165 merely "clarifie[d] the provisions [of the 1993 LLC statute] that members and managers do not have personal liability for obligations of the LLC." . . .

In clarifying ORS 63.165(1), the 1999 legislature relied on the recently published Uniform Limited Liability Company Act (ULLCA) (1996) and adopted verbatim subsections 303(a) and (b) from that uniform statute. The comment to those 1996 ULLCA provisions sheds some light on the 1999 legislature's intent . . . .

The relevant part of the comment to Section 303 explains:

> "A member or manager is responsible for acts or omissions to the extent those acts or omissions would be actionable in contract or tort against the member or manager if that person were acting in an individual capacity. Where a member or manager delegates or assigns the authority or duty to exercise appropriate company functions, the member or manager is ordinarily not personally liable for the acts or omissions of the officer, employee, or agent [of the LLC] if the member or manager has complied with the duty of care set forth in Section 409(c)."

ULLCA §303 comment (1996). The first sentence in the comment makes clear that the use of the word "acting" in section 303 of the ULLCA, and by extension in ORS 63.165(1), was not intended to immunize members and managers from personal liability for their actions in managing an LLC. Rather, members and managers remain personally liable for the actions that they take on behalf of an LLC to the same extent that they would be liable "if [they] were acting in an individual capacity."

Having identified that, as a general rule, members or managers will remain personally liable for their own acts, the comment goes on to identify one instance in which members or managers ordinarily will not be personally liable. The second sentence quoted above recognizes that, when a member or manager of an LLC delegates authority to carry out company functions, as an officer or director of a corporation might, the member or manager ordinarily will not be personally liable for a subordinate's negligence. We do not read the second sentence as establishing statutory immunity in that situation. Rather, the second sentence recognizes that, as a matter of common law, a member or manager ordinarily will not be personally liable for a subordinate's negligence . . . .

Considering the text, context, and legislative history of ORS 63.165(1), we conclude that the 1999 amendments to ORS 63.165 did not change its substance but instead confirmed the 1993 legislature's original intent. Unlike limited partners, members or managers who participate in or control the business of an LLC will not, as a result of those actions, be vicariously liable for the LLC's debts, obligations, or liabilities. However, a member or manager remains responsible for his or her acts or omissions to the extent those acts or omissions would be actionable against the member or manager if that person were acting in an individual capacity . . . . Because ORS 63.165(1) does not shield Swanson from responsibility for its own negligent acts in managing Sun Studs, we turn to the question whether, as a matter of Oregon negligence law, there was evidence from which a reasonable juror could find that Swanson was liable for the injuries that plaintiff suffered.

B. OREGON NEGLIGENCE LAW

. . . Swanson argues, and plaintiff does not dispute, that this court has recognized that "[a] director of a corporation is not liable for any tort of other subordinate agents in which he did not participate." Pelton v. Gold Hill Canal Co., 72 Or. 353, 357-58, 142 P. 769 (1914) . . . .

Swanson argues that, in acting as the member-manager of Sun Studs, its role was comparable to that of a corporate officer and should be judged by the same standard. We agree with both the premise and conclusion of that argument. As Swanson's argument implicitly recognizes, an LLC gives its members flexibility in choosing a management structure . . . . In this case, the evidence on summary judgment showed that Swanson had adopted a corporate model; that is, in managing safety at Sun Studs, Swanson acted in the same way that an officer in a corporation would. Swanson delegated primary responsibility for safety to Sun Studs' HR director and

---

Connections: Supervisor Liability and the Common Law of Agency

The court in this part of the opinion refers to the basic rule that officers of a corporation are not personally liable for its debts, including tort liabilities incurred in their workplaces, unless they personally participate or supervise conduct causing liability.

This does not actually reflect the rule of corporation law we refer to as "limited liability," which limits the liabilities only of shareholders. It is rather just a rule of the common law of agency. Do you see why?

mill manager but retained oversight authority of their implementation of Swanson's safety policies. Having agreed with Swanson's premise, we also agree with its conclusion that the negligence standards that apply to corporate officers and managers apply to Swanson.

Turning to the applicable common-law negligence standard, we note that this court has held that a director or an officer of a corporation will be liable for a subordinate's tortious acts if the officer knew of those acts or participated in them . . . . In this case, a reasonable juror could infer that Swanson "participated" in worksite safety at Sun Studs in three respects: Swanson formulated a general safety policy that it directed Sun Studs to implement; it delegated primary authority for safety at Sun Studs to Sun Studs' HR director and mill manager; and Swanson undertook to oversee those persons' implementation of Swanson's general safety policies. However, there was no evidence from which a reasonable juror could infer that Swanson negligently had formulated the general safety plan that it directed Sun Studs to implement. Similarly, a reasonable juror could not infer that Swanson negligently delegated primary responsibility for safety to Sun Studs' HR director and mill manager . . . . Finally, there was no evidence from which a reasonable juror could infer that Swanson negligently exercised the oversight authority that it retained over Sun Studs' implementation of Swanson's safety policies . . . .[4]

One final point deserves mention. The "participation" doctrine . . . rests on a distinction between misfeasance and nonfeasance . . . . As the California Court of Appeal explained in Towt v. Pope, 168 Cal. App. 2d 520, 336 P.2d 276 (1959), "[i]n the absence of active participation in an act of misfeasance, generally an officer of a corporation is not personally liable to a third person for nonfeasance." *Id.* at 283. As noted, one potential problem with the participation doctrine is that it is sometimes difficult to categorize a specification of negligence as either nonfeasance or misfeasance . . . . Another potential problem is that the doctrine can foreclose any inquiry into an officer's negligent failure to carry out an assigned task . . . .

Initially, most American courts adopted the participation doctrine to determine when an officer or manager will be liable for a subordinate or fellow employee's negligence . . . . A substantial number of jurisdictions still adhere to it . . . . Other jurisdictions have rejected or modified the doctrine . . . . Those courts that have rejected or modified the doctrine have not always been consistent in articulating a new standard; however, they have recognized, as a general rule, that an officer or manager whose assigned task is the supervision of others

---

4. As discussed below, the "participation" standard that this court stated in Pelton turns on a distinction between misfeasance, which is actionable, and nonfeasance, which is not. It is sometimes difficult, however, to classify a specification of negligence as either misfeasance or nonfeasance. Evidence that Swanson undertook to oversee Sun Studs' implementation of Swanson's general safety policies illustrates that difficulty. We assume, for the purposes of resolving plaintiff's negligence claim, that Swanson's undertaking constituted "participation" even though it is arguable that, if Swanson were negligent, any error on its part lay in its failure to supervise, namely its nonfeasance.

will be liable for a negligent failure to carry out that task even though that failure could be characterized as nonfeasance . . . .[5]

In this case, both plaintiff and Swanson have framed their arguments on the assumption that plaintiff must prove participation or knowledge on Swanson's part to prevail on his negligence claim . . . . Applying the standard on which the parties' arguments rest, we hold that plaintiff's negligence claim fails . . . . Our negligence cases have held that, in the absence of knowledge or participation, corporate officers and directors are not liable for their employees' negligence. That is so even though corporate officers, having delegated responsibility to others to carry out tasks, retain the right to control how those tasks are carried out . . . .

We summarize our conclusions briefly. ORS 63.165 immunizes members and managers of an LLC from vicarious liability for the debts, obligations, and liabilities of that LLC. LLC members and managers, however, remain personally liable for their acts and omissions to the extent those acts or omissions would be actionable against the member or manager if that person were acting in an individual capacity. Even though ORS 63.165 does not shield Swanson from liability for its own negligence in managing Sun Studs, Swanson acted towards Sun Studs in the same way that an officer of a corporation would. Applying the negligence standard applicable to corporate officers, we conclude that the evidence on summary judgment does not permit an inference that Swanson either had actual knowledge of the conditions that resulted in plaintiff's injury or actively participated in creating them . . . .

■ **Think about this:**

(P) The court seemed to find *Cortez* a fairly hard case—hard enough to resort to context and legislative history, even though a statute explicitly addressed the question before it—because the role of an LLC member-manager is not exactly analogous to the role of the typical corporate shareholder. Can you see why the two roles are not the same?

(Q) There are no necessarily correct answers to the following questions, but they are useful to think about. Under the circumstances of the *Cortez* case, why did Swanson Group, Inc., make itself a member-manager of

---

5. The Restatement [Third of Agency] sets out the following principles:

"[T]he fact that A is the President of P Corporation does not in itself subject A to liability for E [an employee's] violation of the Fair Housing Act. In contrast, if A directs or participates in an action that violates the Act, A is subject to liability. However, an agent whose assigned function within an organization includes the supervision of others may be subject to liability when a failure by the agent properly to supervise breaches a duty that the agent owes to a third party."

Restatement at §7.01 comment d.

Sun Studs and its other LLCs, rather than a non-manager member? Did it necessarily make that choice deliberately? If so, did it make a good choice?

(R) The plaintiff's claim in *Cortez* is not a claim for "piercing the veil." Remember, piercing the veil is a doctrine from corporate law that is generally available as against LLC members, when the circumstances are appropriate. The plaintiff's claim against Swanson Group is based on a different theory. Do you see why? What separate showings would plaintiff have to have made for a piercing theory to succeed?

D. Series LLCs

Delaware pioneered the invention of the Series LLC (SLLC) in 1997 and has had a limited number of imitators (most recently numbering 11). The basic idea is that a "master" LLC makes a single state filing permitting it to add additional "series" simply by amending its operating agreement. The master and series are a single legal entity, even though each series has its own members, assets, and debts. This limits the cost of formation and operation, as only one filing fee is required, as well as only one franchise tax. At the same time, the risks of each series are limited to its own assets. This structure, often likened to a honeycomb, frequently is used by real estate developers working on multiple projects, as well as by companies with a number of separately branded products.

The SLLC structure also facilitates the registration of membership interests under the federal securities laws, since the Securities and Exchange Commission permits the entire organization to be registered pursuant to a single registration statement. This is popular with investment companies wishing to offer a number of separate investment funds. The public generally is not permitted to purchase interests in the master LLC but is invited to invest in one or more offered funds, each of which is a separate series.

For federal tax purposes, however, each series is regarded as a separate entity; accordingly, careful records of each series' assets, liabilities, and income must be kept. Even more important, these records are critical in order to assure that the cell walls are not broached for purposes of imposing cross-series liability.

E. Other Modern Alternatives

To give a flavor for the many other organizational alternatives available under current law, here are just a few of the more common ones:

1. The LLP

We have referred to the limited liability partnership (LLP) throughout the book. The LLP is simply a general partnership, governed by the state partnership statute of the state where it is created, and is identical to the general partnership in every respect except one. If the firm is formed in a state whose statute allows it, the partners may make a simple election to be treated as an LLP, and they will thereafter each enjoy some degree of limited liability for the firm's obligations. The election is made by the filing of a simple document with the Secretary of State. As far as RUPA is concerned, the most important functional difference between a general partnership and an LLP is set out in §306(c):

SECTION 306. PARTNER'S LIABILITY

(c) A debt, obligation, or other liability of a partnership incurred while the partnership is a limited liability partnership is solely the debt, obligation, or other liability of the limited liability partnership. A partner is not personally liable, directly or indirectly, by way of contribution or otherwise, for a debt, obligation, or other liability of the limited liability partnership solely by reason of being or acting as a partner. This subsection applies: (1) despite anything inconsistent in the partnership agreement that existed immediately before the vote or consent required to become a limited liability partnership under Section 901(b); and (2) regardless of the dissolution of the limited liability partnership.

The other notable distinctions between a general partnership and an LLP formed under RULPA are that the latter is subject to ongoing reporting requirements and limits on distributions to the partners similar to those applicable to LLCs.

The original LLP statutory provisions arose at about the time of the initial LLC statutes, and accompanied the easing of certain traditional professional ethics rules. Until about the early 1980s, ethical rules governing many professions prohibited professionals from practicing in limited liability entities. The rationale was that liability for professional malpractice (which, interestingly, is usually just liability for breach of the fiduciary duty of care) serves an important regulatory role. It incentivizes professionals to take more care on behalf of their clients, limiting the agency costs that might otherwise interfere. Moreover, where two or more professionals practice together, the risk of joint and several professional liability compels them all to monitor one another, which should again serve to protect their clients' interests.

This all began to change during the early 1980s, when the truly gargantuan professional firms we know today began to appear—law firms and accounting firms with hundreds or even thousands of partners. At the same time, there happened to arise a series of very significant public scandals involving claims that lawyers or accountants had abetted serious financial wrongdoing, chief among them the so-called savings and loan crisis. In the litigation that ensued, many of those professionals were named as defendants, and the potential liabilities not infrequently ran into the hundreds of millions of dollars. So the specter was raised of huge general partnerships, involving hundreds or thousands of professionals spread across the country or even internationally, facing liabilities that would completely bankrupt their firms and the partners themselves through the misdeeds of only one or a few partners whom most of the rest of the partners had not even met. States responded to this crisis by loosening requirements that professionals practice only in full-liability forms, and then by creating the LLP.

The initial LLP statutes were mostly what came to be known as "partial shield" statutes, in that they protected partners only from their fellow partners' torts, and not from contract responsibilities. These original statutes were mostly pretty quickly replaced by "full shield" statutes, which provide limited liability for all firm liabilities.

More to the Story and Doing the Numbers: The Obligation to Return Capital

Section 306(c) and its limitation on liability for the partners in an LLP appears in Article 3 of RUPA—Relations of Partners to Persons Dealing with Partnerships. At least some courts considering the pre-2013 version of RUPA were not inclined to extend the limitation to the relations among the partners (which is the subject of Article 4). This means that, unless they agree otherwise, the partners in an LLP might be required to reach into their own pockets to reimburse one another for lost capital.

Assume that X contributes $100,000 and Y contributes only services to the XY LLP. Their agreement calls for the equal sharing of profits. Unfortunately, the entire $100,000 is lost. RUPA's default rules (in §§401 and 807) prevent Y from recovering for services and charge each partner with 50 percent of the loss. This means that X has a capital account of $100,000 − $50,000 = $50,000. Y has a capital account of 0 − $50,000 = ($50,000). Y must contribute $50,000 to be paid to X.

It can be argued that §306(c) says that partners in a limited liability partnership are not liable "by contribution or otherwise" for losses by the LLP, so Y should not have to cough up any of X's lost capital. Although the weight of the very limited authority is to the contrary, a comment to RUPA (2013) §306(c) states that "there is no distinction [between] a claim arising from an LLP's debt to a commercial creditor [and] a partner's claim that the LLP has failed to return a contribution. . . ."

The moral of the story is that this is a matter to be addressed by agreement.

More to the Story: Piercing the Veil

Of course, as soon as one acquires something, a new worry blooms: Suppose I lose it? Just as is the case with corporations and limited liability companies, there may be circumstances in which a court finds it unfair for one or more individuals to claim the shield of limited liability. RUPA §306(d) was added in 2013 to provide that the failure of an LLP to observe formalities is not a ground for imposing liability on any of its partners. However, there could be other bases for piercing the veil of an LLP, as there are for corporations and other limited liability entities.

Vic Fuentes, a member of Pierce the Veil. Pierce the Veil, a post-hardcore, progressive rock, emo, screamo band (their description, not ours), was formed in 2006 and released its latest album in 2016.

An interesting question is why we really need both the LLP and the LLC, and what differences between them there might be. In fact, a side-by-side comparison of RUPA and the ULLCA as harmonized through 2013 suggests they can be very similar indeed. The answers are a bit complicated and vary by state. In some states, the LLP is available only to professionals, and some states also still recognize only "partial shield" LLPs. And finally, there are sometimes minor state law bureaucratic differences between the LLP and the LLC, such as the rule in some states that LLCs must pay the corporate franchise tax but LLPs do not.[6]

2. The PC, the "Medical Corporation," and Similar Entities

The professional corporation is similar to the traditional corporation, but its shareholder members must be practicing professionals. Its use remains significant

---

6. *See generally* Jennifer L. Johnson, *Limited Liability for Lawyers: General Partners Need Not Apply*, 51 Bus. Law. 85 (1995).

mainly in health care, where state licensure laws still frequently require that health care professionals not engage in the practice of medicine except in certain permitted organizational forms. Significantly, most PC statutes provide that while the shareholders of the firm enjoy limited liability for some firm debts, they remain jointly and severally liable for "services rendered." In short, they each remain fully liable for professional malpractice committed by any one of them. Several states have also created special entity forms for particular professions, including not uncommonly the "medical corporation," designed specifically for private medical practices.

Courts have often held that despite their title, the PC and related entities are not simply special subspecies of corporation. They are rather hybrids of corporation and partnership law specially designed to suit the needs of professionals. In particular, when the form was first conceived in the 1960s, it actually gave its members certain tax benefits available to corporations and their employees but not available to general partnerships (those tax advantages have largely disappeared with changes in tax law).

Given this hybrid nature, in cases where neither a state's professional corporation statute nor any agreement among the shareholders clearly controls, a court might make reference to partnership law by analogy. This has occurred quite commonly as to problems associated with dissolution and the parceling out of the value of unfinished business among departing shareholders. Another common problem has been whether PC shareholders should have rights like employees (for example, under state and federal employment discrimination statutes).[7]

 Time Out for PR: Limitations on Liability

The present American Bar Association rule on limitation of liability is as follows:

Rule 1.8 Conflict of Interest: Current Clients: Specific Rules

. . .

> (h) A lawyer shall not:
> (1) make an agreement prospectively limiting the lawyer's liability to a client for malpractice unless the client is independently represented in making the agreement; or

---

7. For a nice discussion of these issues, see Christopher C. Wang, Comment, *Breaking Up Is Hard to Do: Allocating Fees from the Unfinished Business of a Professional Corporation*, 67 U. CHI. L. REV. 1367 (1997); John Narducci, The Application of Antidiscrimination Statutes to Shareholders of Professional Corporations: Forcing Fellow Shareholders Out of the Club, 55 FORDHAM L. REV. 839 (1987), and for a nice summary of the history of the PC and similar entities, see Wang, supra, at 1373-1375.

(2) settle a claim or potential claim for such liability with an unrepresented client or former client unless that person is advised in writing of the desirability of seeking and is given a reasonable opportunity to seek the advice of independent legal counsel in connection therewith.

One might argue that if a lawyer enters into a representation agreement on behalf of the limited liability entity with which he is associated, he runs afoul of this rule, but that is not how it is read.

It is important to note that, as far as the Model Rules are concerned, a lawyer is not completely free of liability for the misconduct of other lawyers in a limited liability entity.

Rule 5.1: Responsibilities of a Partner or Supervisory Lawyer

. . .

(c) A lawyer shall be responsible for another lawyer's violation of the Rules of Professional Conduct if:

(1) the lawyer orders or, with knowledge of the specific conduct, ratifies the conduct involved; or

(2) the lawyer is a partner or has comparable managerial authority in the law firm in which the other lawyer practices, or has direct supervisory authority over the other lawyer, and knows of the conduct at a time when its consequences can be avoided or mitigated but fails to take reasonable remedial action.

(Rule 5.3 provides a parallel in the case of non-lawyer employees.) The Model Rules are not intended to be used to determine civil liability, but often are considered as speaking to the conduct of a reasonable lawyer.

3. The LLLP

As if desiring to prove the limitless possible length and variety of the acronyms they can devise, a handful of legislatures and the Uniform Law Commission have given blessing to the "limited liability limited partnership." In short, an LLLP is simply a limited partnership (discussed at length in Chapter 10) in which the general partner also enjoys limited liability. A growing number of states have followed the most recent version of the Uniform Limited Partnership Act in permitting a limited partnership to make the LLLP election in the certificate of limited partnership. In others, it is possible for a preexisting limited partnership simply to make an LLP filing to procure limited liability for its general partners. Just as is true of LLCs and LLPs, failure to follow formalities does not jeopardize the limited liability of either an LLLP's general partners or its limited partners. Abuse of the form by other conduct would.

4. The LPA

The "limited partnership association" is actually a bit of an old peculiarity, in that it appeared a long time ago and remains available in a few states, but has never much been used. The LPA was an experiment first proposed in Pennsylvania in 1874 and then quickly followed in Ohio, Michigan, and New Jersey. It introduced a form that resembled in some respects the general partnership but also provided limited liability. It imported certain other features of the corporate law of the day that were thought to make it a desirable alternative to the general partnership, like easy transferability of ownership shares and management by a small corps of elected managers who did not even have to be shareholders.

The LPA is, if nothing else, an interesting object lesson in the history of business entity law. The intriguing question is why the LPA never really caught on, even though it permits what is essentially a partnership form of organization that also provides limited liability for all of its members (recall that the LP form was widely available at the time, but required a fully liable general partner). In part, the lack of success seems to reflect the fact that limited liability, however much it may seem to have been the business planner's holy grail, may not always be all that it is cracked up to be,[8] and also because when the form first appeared tax law was very different and limited liability could be gotten through general incorporation without the same significant tax costs. But even more interesting is why its creators *thought* the LPA would take off. They appear to have created it to combine with the general partnership those features of incorporation then most desired. Chief among its purported advantages were that it permitted the creation of a limited liability entity without the great technical difficulty that at that time plagued the creation of corporations under the newly emerging general incorporation statutes. Likewise, the LPA could own property and sue and be sued in its own name—features unavailable under the partnership law of the time because of the then-dominant aggregate theory.[9]

F. Future Trends: The End of Distinguishable Business Entity Forms?

Notice a trend lurking throughout this extensive mass of ever-evolving business entity statutes, a trend that has been noted elsewhere in this book. Under current law, most any business, so long as it has no need for very large capitalization, can now secure limited liability, pass-through taxation, management by limited liability members, and flexible governance. In fact, a given business can often get this same result if organized in any one of several different ways. A consequence is that the statute books and the case reporters simply overflow

---

8. An interesting meditation on that point, for the inquiring student, is Thomas E. Rutledge, *Limited Liability (Or Not): Reflections on the Holy Grail*, 51 S.D. L. Rev. 417 (2006).

9. *See generally* Edward R. Schwartz, *The Limited Partnership Association—An Alternative to the Corporation for the Small Business with "Control" Problems?*, 20 Rutgers L. Rev. 29 (1965).

with profuse, overlapping, often redundant laws, which occasionally contain apparent inconsistencies or conflicts.

> ■ **Think about this:**
>
> *(Q)* It will be useful to explain to yourself why each of the following entities provides limited liability, managerial involvement of limited liability members, and pass-through taxation:
>
> (1) the member-managed LLC;
> (2) in those states that recognize it, the full-shield LLP;
> (3) in those states that recognize it, the LPA;
> (4) the LP with a marginally capitalized corporate general partner owned and managed by the limited partners;
> (5) the LLLP in those states that permit it;
> (6) a traditional corporation in which all shareholders are employed as employees whose salaries consume the firm's whole profits (and which can therefore deduct enough to leave it with no taxable income, roughly approximating pass-through tax treatment);
> (7) the S corporation (a special form recognized by Subchapter S of the Internal Revenue Code, which resembles a traditional corporation but also enjoys pass-through taxation), in which the shareholders hold management positions; and, to a somewhat more complicated extent,
> (8) an LP in those jurisdictions that now permit unrestrained managerial involvement by the limited partners (i.e., those that have adopted ULPA (2001) or the equivalent).
>
> Remember, too, that all of these entity forms permit very flexible management structure, great flexibility as to profit sharing, transferability, and rules for dissolution, and broad waivability of fiduciary duties.

To be frank, it is fairly difficult to find any really meaningful justification for this bizarre range of entity laws, with its many redundancies and overlaps. Often, the reasons that entrepreneurs choose one form of unincorporated entity over another can seem fairly miscellaneous and picayune. Sometimes the choice is driven by those remaining professional ethical rules that still limit the forms in which some professionals can practice, and sometimes it is driven by state tax and regulatory issues that may treat different entities differently (e.g., some states impose their franchise tax on the corporation and the LLC, but not the LLP). One common reason for choosing the LLP rather than the LLC has been that in some states the conversion from GP to LLP is much simpler—it requires merely the filing of a form, rather than drafting a complex contractual arrangement and, depending on the jurisdiction, the creation of an entirely new entity—and so those businesses already practicing as GPs have an incentive to choose it. Occasionally, it is driven by some federal regulation or a rule of a commercial exchange, or some other comparatively obscure concern. One practitioner recounts a fairly exotic example this way:

> . . . [S]ome years ago, I created an entity structure for the ownership and operation of an agricultural enterprise by three individuals. In order to satisfy the three parameters of (i) compliance with (and maximization of benefit under) applicable federal agricultural subsidy regulations, (ii) limitation of owner liability, and (iii) minimization of federal income tax and state franchise tax liability, the structure used seven different related entities. The enterprise was set up as a joint venture ([which in this case was simply a] general partnership [with a limited purpose]) among three limited partnerships. The 99% limited partnership interest in each limited partnership was owned by one of the three individuals involved in the operation of the enterprise and the 1% general partner of each limited partnership was an S corporation, wholly owned and managed by the respective individual, who was also the limited partner of the limited partnership. The joint venture satisfied the federal agricultural subsidy regulatory limitations on business entity form and maximized the availability of the subsidies; the limited partnerships and use of corporate general partners satisfied concerns about limitation of owner liability; and the use of a joint venture, limited partnerships, and S corporations with the overwhelming percentage of ownership weighted toward the individual limited partners had the effect of minimizing both federal income taxes to the entities and the assessment of state franchise taxes. The franchise tax bill was three percent of what it would have been had the corporations alone been used to limit liability [since the state franchise tax was assessed only against corporations, and was based on the number of shares issued to each shareholder, which in this case was one for each S corporation] . . . . [Still,] the filing fees for forming the various entities totaled more than $3,000 in excess of the cost of creating the joint venture alone and more than $2,000 in excess of the cost of using a joint venture consisting of corporations (the agriculture regulations [required that the subsidized entity, which in this case was the joint venture among the limited partnerships, had to be a partnership or other unincorporated entity, and could not be] a single corporation).

Thomas F. Blackwell, *The Revolution Is Here: The Promise of a Unified Business Entity Code*, 24 J. Corp. L. 333, 337 n.13 (1998).

Various suggestions and efforts have been made to bring some order to this chaos. Though its ambitions for the moment remain narrow, the Uniform Laws Commission has put in place a Committee on the Harmonization of Business Entity Acts, with an aim to bringing some order. This is why the uniform acts governing partnerships, limited partnerships, and limited liability companies all were amended in 2013. That group, however, as yet has no apparent goal to eliminate any of the several unincorporated entity forms currently available under uniform statutes, and has only worked to harmonize definitions and other elements common across the different acts. More ambitious proposals have been made by others, up to and

---

Room to Argue: Impounding the Value of Law

It sometimes is asserted that the market value of securities reflects assumptions about the efficiency of the governing entity law. For instance, scholars have studied the "value" of incorporating in Delaware rather than some other state. The market might also value corporations *as corporations* rather than as some other entity. Using less traditional forms might then come with a price tag. You can read more about this subject in the online Supplement.

including doing away with the varying forms of business entity, by way of some single, centralizing statute that would authorize only one unincorporated entity form. Some advocates believe in this reform a *lot*, one of them having written a self-described "unificationist manifesto." Blackwell, *supra*, at 335. The proposals come in various forms, though their point generally is to put forward one comparatively simple entity form that would enjoy limited liability, pass-through tax treatment, and flexible governance, and more or less to do away with all the others. The major defense of these proposals has mainly been just that they would make the law simpler.[10] Interestingly, almost all such proposals envision that while there could be some simple, unified statutory regime setting out only one form of unincorporated entity, there would still remain a separate regime for the traditional corporation. This is so for at least two major reasons. First, federal law all but requires it. The federal government would still demand freedom to directly tax at least one broad class of business profits under Subchapter C, and the complex, comprehensive law of federal securities regulation and the investment culture that surround it are closely tied to the law of the traditional corporation. Second, there is a need for an entity permitting passive investment with a default governance structure designed for investor protection.

Anyway, any really serious unifying reform seems unlikely to come anytime soon. Among other things, critics of "unification" or "rationalization" argue that the current availability of several different default forms, with their separate bodies of case law, is useful because there are in fact so many different kinds of businesses and so many different reasons that various combinations of entrepreneurs and investors come together. Another argument is that, for the time being, maintaining a variety of choices provides a form of useful experimentation.

Moreover, there apparently is not actually that much demand for the change. Though various arguments are made in its favor, the basic argument for reform seems to be that it would just tidy up our legal doctrine. Moreover, though many proposals have been made and much debated, they come mainly from academics. The business community and the practicing transactional bar seem comfortable enough with the state of play. On the other side of the ledger are potentially very serious risks. Foremost would be dramatic uncertainty and risk of unintended consequences during some possibly quite long period of transition. Also, a unified statutory regime would have to account somehow for the fact that even after its adoption there would remain literally millions of unincorporated business entities still organized under the already existing welter of business entity statutes. In some way or other, all those firms would need to be able to convert themselves to the new unified entity, and conversions can raise many complex, unpredictable, and costly issues. And indeed,

Connections: Civ Pro

For purposes of federal diversity jurisdiction, a corporation is a citizen of its state of incorporation and its primary place of business. Unincorporated entities, including LLCs, are citizens of every state in which a member is domiciled.

---

10. *See, e.g.*, Blackwell, *supra*; Robert R. Keatinge, *Universal Business Organization Legislation: Will It Happen? Why and When*, 23 Del. J. Corp. L. 29 (1998); Mark J. Loewenstein, *A New Direction for State Corporate Codes*, 68 U. Colo. L. Rev. 453 (1997); John H. Matheson & Brent A. Olson, *A Call for a Unified Business Organization Law*, 65 Geo. Wash. L. Rev. 1 (1996).

since nowadays most businesses of any size will have some business dealings in more than one state, and in any given state there will be many thousands of out-of-state businesses at work, the regime would only really be "unified" if some *uniform* statute were developed and then rapidly adopted by all states.

Test Yourself

1. Jim and Joe created a two-member default LLC in a ULLCA state, called Happy Time Amusements, LLC (Happy Time). Happy Time manufactures large, arcade-style video game consoles that it distributes to arcades and other public venues. Happy Time has elected to be taxed as a partnership. After a successful first year of operations, Jim believes he and Joe both ought to receive payments from the substantial profits the firm earned. Joe is opposed, and Jim is prepared to sue.

   a. Given the facts stated, is Happy Time a manager-managed or member-managed firm?
   b. Could Happy Time become publicly traded while remaining an LLC? Would it have to make any changes to its governance or organizational structure? And assuming it could, could it retain pass-through tax status?
   c. Given the facts stated, how much will Jim win in his suit for a distribution of profits?

2. Why do you suppose only a manager-managed LLC can be publicly traded?

3. Bob is an attorney hired by several individual investors. They desire to establish a firm, to be known as XYZ, LLC as a manager-managed limited liability company. Bob drafts the articles of association and instructs his paralegal to file them with his state's Secretary of State, on May 1. The paralegal does so, and the next morning Bob phones the investors to tell them. On May 4, two of the investors execute a lease for office space to serve as XYZ's headquarters. They signed only in their representative capacities, as officers of XYZ, making clear that they did not personally intend to take liability. The following week, on May 9, Bob receives a notice from the Secretary of State indicating that the articles of association were drafted incorrectly and will be rejected, requiring resubmission. The next day, May 10, XYZ's financing falls through, and the investors decide to abandon the project.

Who, if anyone, is liable on the lease for office space?

4. Alice, Bo, and Conchita file the necessary paperwork to create the ABC LLC under state law. They subsequently enter into an operating agreement containing a clause agreeing that all disputes relating to the LLC will

be subject to arbitration in a state other than the one in which the LLC was formed. Alice, Bo, and Conchita sign the agreement, but there is no signature line for the LLC. Which of the following is most true?

a. ABC LLC will be subject to the arbitration clause described.

b. Alice, Bo, and Conchita will be subject to the arbitration clause described.

c. Neither answer a nor answer b is true.

d. Both answers a and b are true.

5. Which of the following represents advice that you would give a client? (Assume that all of the business forms alluded to would be available, and mark all choices that would apply.)

a. There are circumstances in which a general partnership would be a better choice than an LLP.

b. There are circumstances in which a limited partnership would be a better choice than an LLLP.

c. There are circumstances in which either an LLP or an LLC could accomplish the same goals.

d. There is never a reason to prefer a Subchapter S corporation to an LLC.

6. True, false, or indeterminable? An LLP is to a general partnership what an LLLP is to a limited partnership.

7. True, false, or indeterminable? An LLC is more like a limited partnership than it is like a corporation.

8. True, false, or indeterminable? Adoption of LLP status means that no partner may be called upon to contribute amounts that will permit the partnership to satisfy its obligations.

12

Fiduciary Duties in Agency and Unincorporated Entities

In all agency relationships and within all business entities, the law imposes special requirements of loyalty and care on certain persons. These requirements are known as "fiduciary duties." The duties that apply are by and large the same, regardless what sort of business entity or relationship is involved, with only a few significant differences. This chapter covers them as they apply in all entities except the corporation. Fiduciary duties in corporations raise some special issues, and we cover them later in the book.

Chapter Outline

A. Introduction to Fiduciary Duties and Their Great Generality in Business Organizations Law

1. In General
   - The duties are very general, but they don't *always* apply in the same way
   - There are some specific sub-rules within the general duties of care and loyalty
2. A Few Clarifications Before Getting Started

B. The Duty of Care

1. The Agent's Duty of Care
2. The Business Judgment Rule and the Standard of Care of Entity Managers

C. The Duty of Loyalty: The General Cause of Action and Several Special Rules

1. The Intrinsic Fairness Test: The Basic Duty of Loyalty Claim for General Interested Transactions

2. The Five Special Loyalty Rules
   - Excess benefits
   - Duty not to compete
   - Business opportunities
   - Loyalty obligations as to the principal's property
   - Loyalty obligations as to the principal's confidences

D. Fiduciary Situations Requiring Disclosure

E. Waiver

1. Agency

2. Partnerships and Other Unincorporated Entities: The Law as It Was, Under UPA (1914)

3. The Somewhat New World of RUPA §105

F. Remedies and Procedural Issues

1. In General

2. Two Special Partnership Remedial Rules: The Accounting and the Accounting Rule

Test Yourself

A. Introduction to Fiduciary Duties and Their Great Generality in Business Organizations Law

1. In General

Connections: Corporate Fiduciary Rules

Because corporate fiduciary duties raise some special issues, and we think they are best understood if studied as a part of corporate law generally, we defer them until Part 4.

A basic policy problem underlying all business arrangements, and the reason we have fiduciary duties, is the "agency cost" problem. Any time that one person employs the assistance of another, there is a likelihood that the services rendered will be somehow less or different than what was desired. An employee, a manager, a business firm's executive, or anyone else engaged to perform a service often won't have quite the incentive for diligence and care as the person employing them might hope. (As we observed in the Introduction, describing the issue this way is not without its political baggage.

Whether the real problem in business entities is shirking under-
lings or bosses that exploit them is a hot controversy, and not one
we address. But the law, for better or worse, takes agency cost seriously through fiduciary rules.) Worse yet, people entrusted with
the affairs of others will sometimes face temptation for deliberate
wrongdoing. They may have access to those persons' money, for
example, or confidential information that can be exploited for
their own personal gain.

So, the law imposes fiduciary duties in relationships in which
one person, who is called a "fiduciary," is required by law to take
special care in his or her dealings with some other person (in this
book we refer to that other person as the beneficiary of the fiduciary's duties). Specifically, it imposes two general duties on all
fiduciaries:

Peter Jakob Horemans,
Sleeping Kitchen Maid

- the duty of **care**, which requires that in all of the fiduciary's
  conduct related to the fiduciary relationship, the fiduciary act with some
  specified level of caution to protect the beneficiary's interests, and provides that if the beneficiary is injured by the fiduciary in some way, the
  beneficiary may have legal recourse; and
- the duty of **loyalty**, which requires that in conduct related to the fiduciary relationship, the fiduciary act only in the beneficiary's interests
  (e.g., the fiduciary cannot try to earn secret profits or take bribes in connection with services for the beneficiary).

 ***Dear Prof.: What about the "duty of disclosure"?
Haven't I heard of that?***

It is sometimes said that fiduciaries owe one other duty, in addition to
the two we discuss. This is a duty of disclosure, pursuant to which fiduciaries must ensure that the beneficiary knows important facts. But we
think disclosure is better thought of as just a component of the other
two duties. Where the fiduciary is acting under a conflict of interest,
he or she may have an obligation to disclose the conflict and facts surrounding it, but that is just a reflection of the duty of loyalty. And in the
absence of a conflict, the fiduciary might have to advise the beneficiary
of this or that, but only where a reasonably prudent fiduciary would do
so under the circumstances. This obligation would just reflect the duty
of care.

Fiduciary duties are enforced exclusively through civil lawsuits—they
are not enforced by any government authorities. When suit is brought
against a fiduciary, it is very literally just a tort cause of action. *See* Restatement (Second) of the Law of Torts §874 & comment b (1979) ("A fiduciary

who commits a breach of his duty as a fiduciary is guilty of tortious conduct to the person for whom he should act."). Indeed, one of the major duties we'll discuss, the duty of care, is literally a cause of action for "negligence," and the courts often so describe it. The only way in which it differs from the more familiar rule against negligence you studied in Torts class is in the "duty" element.

Recall that to bring the general cause of action for negligence, the plaintiff must prove the following:

- That defendant bore a **duty** (in the case of simple negligence, the duty we all bear of reasonable care to avoid injury to others in their person or property);
- That defendant breached that duty, meaning defendant took some action not in conformity with it;
- That plaintiff suffered an injury; and
- That defendant's breach was the proximate **cause** of plaintiff's injury.

It turns out that causes of action for breach of fiduciary duty also more or less always take this rough form. Thus, for example, the cause of action for legal malpractice, which is a cause of action for breach of the lawyer's fiduciary duty of care, looks like this:

- Duty (in this case, the duty of care that a reasonably prudent attorney would exercise in the representation under the circumstances);
- Breach;
- Injury; and
- Proximate cause.

A cause of action for breach of any other fiduciary duty is usually structured in just the same way, the only difference being the content of the "duty" element. Our basic job for this chapter is to learn about that content in the context of the laws of agency and unincorporated entities.

2. A Few Clarifications Before Getting Started

The Duties Are Very General, But They Don't *Always* Apply in the Same Way. As you will see, the cases we excerpt involve a variety of relationships—some of them involve agencies, some involve general partnerships, some limited partnerships, and so on—but they each apply the same fiduciary rules pretty much interchangeably. But that is not to say that there are no distinctions among the rules as they apply in different relationships, and indeed there are a few variations that are fairly significant.

Most importantly, not everyone in every business relationship is everyone else's fiduciary.

Connections: Fiduciary Relations in Corporations

As we shall pursue at length in Part 4, a special rule governs who owes fiduciary duties in corporations. There are three classes of such persons: (a) members of the board of directors, (b) officers of the corporation (like the CEO, vice presidents, etc.), and (c) "controlling" shareholders. Interestingly, these persons owe their duties *to the corporation*, and not to the shareholders individually, an often academic point that occasionally matters a lot.

Ordinary shareholders usually do not owe fiduciary duties to anyone, though as explained in Chapter 26, under a special rule in some jurisdictions, shareholders in *closely held* corporations owe one another fiduciary duties as if they were partners in a partnership. Special duties may also arise in the context of sales of control. See Chapter 23.

- In **agency** relationships, fiduciary duties run in only one direction: An agent is a fiduciary of his or her principal, but the principal is not the agent's fiduciary.
- All partners in general partnerships owe fiduciary duties to all of the other partners.
- As discussed in Chapter 10, limited partnerships are managed by one or more "general partners," but also take investments from passive investors called "limited partners." General partners owe the same fiduciary duties that they would in a general partnership, but the limited partners are not fiduciaries unless they participate in management, and then only to the extent of their involvement.
- As discussed in Chapter 11, limited liability companies can usually be structured either as "member-managed" or "manager-managed" companies. Where the former option is chosen, the firm is more like a general partnership, and its members are one another's fiduciaries. Where the latter is chosen, the firm is more like a corporation, and the members are not fiduciaries. In that case, only the managers that the firm hires owe fiduciary duties.

A separate thing to bear in mind, and a fact well demonstrated in the cases below, is that fiduciary duty is always fact-sensitive and context-specific. Even though it can fairly, roughly be said that all fiduciaries owe the same *general* duties, the nature of the particular relationship determines the scope of a fiduciary's duty in any particular context. *See* Restatement (Third) of Agency ("Re(3)") §1.01, comment e ("Any agent has power over the principal's interests to a greater or lesser degree. This determines the scope in which fiduciary duty operates."); §8.01, comment c ("Fiduciary obligation, although a general concept, . . . var[ies] depending on the parties' agreement and the scope of the parties' relationship."). Thus, for example, a person employed by a corporation as a janitor in one of its facilities, a realtor representing a home buyer, and the vice president of a multi-state banking enterprise are all agents, and on an abstract level they all owe the same fiduciary duties. But the extent of their duties—the degree of diligence and honesty they must exercise and the range of subject matters in which their duties apply—will vary a *lot*.

And finally, fiduciaries working in particular professions are often subject to rules other than the law of agency or partnership that will affect their fiduciary duties. Notably, lawyers in every state are subject to extensive codes of professional responsibility minutely regulating their relationships of agency to their clients.

There Are Some Specific Sub-Rules Within the General Duties of Care and Loyalty. While again it is true in a general sense that all fiduciaries owe two fiduciary duties, the law in particular areas often sets out very specific sub-rules to flesh them out, and some statements of the specific sub-rules are not very clear about which general duty is being elaborated. So, for example, Chapter 8 of the Restatement (Third) of Agency contains 11 specific sections (§§8.02-8.12) detailing the agent's duties. Each of them can be characterized as stating a fiduciary obligation, and each can be characterized as elaborations on either the duty of care or the duty of loyalty. But this latter fact can be hard to see from the specific text of any one provision.

B. The Duty of Care

The duty of care is fairly straightforward. As we have said, it is really just a tort rule against negligence. One special distinction we'll draw, however, is that managers of all unincorporated entities (and managers of corporations) owe a standard of care entitling them to more deference than agents in general. This is because of what is known as the "business judgment rule." In fact, the standard is so deferential that proving liability against such managers for care violations is extremely difficult.

More to the Story: Gratuitous Agents and Fiduciary Duty

Recall from our discussion of agency law in general that agency relations can be formed even though the agent works for free. In those circumstances, the agent is known as a "gratuitous agent." Perhaps surprisingly, the same fiduciary duties apply, and apply in the same general way, to all agents, whether they are paid or not. *See* §8.01, comment c; *see also* §8.08, comment e.

1. The Agent's Duty of Care

The agent's basic obligation is to use "reasonable care" in the performance of his duties. Under Restatement (Third) §8.08, an agent must act with that "care, competence, and diligence" that would be "normally exercised" by other agents "in similar circumstances." This obligation of reasonable care implies certain particular obligations. First, the duty of care includes within it a "competence" component, under which a person must possess at least the specific skills reasonably to be expected of persons undertaking similar tasks. *See* §8.08, comment c. Likewise, where an agent represents to the principal some special skill or knowledge, the agent is legally obliged to use it, even if to do so would require some greater effort than the "reasonable" care required of other agents.

As mentioned, the care obligation (and loyalty, as we shall see) is fleshed out in certain more specific rules that apply in particular situations. Section 8.10 requires the agent to avoid conduct that would embarrass the principal or otherwise damage the "principal's enterprise." Under §8.11 the agent must use reasonable efforts to provide the principal with facts of which the agent has notice if they are material to the agent's duties or if the agent knows or has reason to know the principal would want to know them. Likewise, §8.09 requires the agent to act only with actual authority and comply with lawful instructions. Interestingly, comments following §8.09 make clear that an agent must comply with the principal's lawful orders (i.e., those that would not require the agent himself to commit a crime or otherwise incur liability), even where the order would in some way breach a contract between principal and agent. For the most part, these special-case subsidiary rules also apply as part of the care obligations of entity managers. For example, it is a breach of a general partner's duty of care to take action beyond her authority under the partnership agreement. This is analogous to the agent's duty to obey lawful orders.

2. The Business Judgment Rule and the Standard of Care of Entity Managers

Again, probably the most significant difference between the fiduciary duties of agents and those of business entity managers is that managers owe a lower duty of care. For example, §404(c) of the Revised Uniform Partnership Act (RUPA) captures the entire law of partnership care in the following terse sentence:

> A partner's duty of care to the partnership and the other partners . . . is limited to refraining from engaging in grossly negligent or reckless conduct, intentional misconduct, or a knowing violation of law.

This provision codifies longstanding case law. (The original UPA (1914) did not mention the duty of care, and it was left to the common law.) It is also captured in other modern entity statutes, and states the rule that probably applies to the managers of all unincorporated entities. *See, e.g.,* Uniform Limited Liability Company Act §409(c); Uniform Limited Partnership Act (2001) §409(c). The duty is commonly analogized to the duty of care owed by corporate officers and directors to their corporations, which is likewise lower than the reasonable care standard that normally governs agents. In the corporate context, the law is much better developed. Corporate officers and directors owe a duty of care to their corporations, but their compliance is judged under the so-called business judgment rule. Under

> **Connections: The Duty of Care and the Business Judgment Rule in Corporations**
>
> The duty of care and the business judgment rule in the corporate context are dealt with at length in Chapter 18.

that rule, wherever the officer or director makes a conscious business decision that is:

(1) not self-interested,
(2) reasonably informed,
(3) rationally related to the best interests of the corporation, and
(4) not knowingly wrongful or illegal,

then it does not breach the duty of care. American Law Institute, *Principles of Corporate Governance* §4.01(c). In other words, a corporate fiduciary normally cannot breach the duty merely through mistaken judgment in making a business decision, even if it turns out to be catastrophically wrong. (This is the effect of the word "rationally" in element three—a decision must be *irrational* to breach the duty.) Normally, they can breach it only by failing to be reasonably informed about the decision or by making a decision that deliberately serves some purpose other than the best interests of the firm. Because most courts have analogized the partners' duty of care to that of corporate fiduciaries, the partnership standard of care is often known as the "business judgment rule for partnerships." *See generally* 1 ALAN R. BROMBERG & LARRY E. RIBSTEIN, BROMBERG AND RIBSTEIN ON PARTNERSHIP §6.07(f) (2001).

So, in a nutshell, a partner is not liable to the partnership for mistakes of merely negligent mismanagement. A partner will breach the duty of care only by acting extremely carelessly in the actual deliberation of the decision (e.g., by acting without good information), by making a decision for some purpose other than the firm's best interests, by acting beyond authority, or by breaching some term of the partnership agreement.

■ **Think about this:**

Why on earth should this be?

(A) As we discussed in Chapter 8, partners by default enjoy a statutory right to equal participation in management, RUPA §401(h), and they each bear full personal liability for the firm's losses. Do you see why that justifies denying the partners a cause of action to recover the firm's losses from the partner who caused them? If this seems like a hard question to answer, ask yourself first what underlying policy of a liability rule *would* make partners personally liable for the entirety of losses they negligently caused (as opposed merely to sharing the liability proportionately with the other partners).

(B) But what explains the business judgment rule for firms in which managers don't bear any personal liability, which is true in corporations and all other full limited-liability entities? Indeed, corporate officers

and the managers of manager-managed LLCs don't even share in the firm's profits or losses, unless they also happen to own ownership interests. Why in those cases might it be desirable to excuse managers from after-the-fact responsibility for losses they cause, even though arguably they lack the same acute incentive for good judgment that general partners have by virtue of their pecuniary stake in their firms? To help you think through your answer, consider the following:

(i) What might be the downside for a firm if its managers were unduly cautious?

(ii) Investors don't have to put all their money in one business. Could there be an advantage to investors' ability to diversify in freeing up their managers to take risks?

(iii) Remember that fiduciary liability is assessed only after the fact, by judges and jurors. Does that matter?

C. The Duty of Loyalty: The General Cause of Action and Several Special Rules

A Shifting Burden

Like the duty of care, the duty of loyalty imposes both (1) a very general duty governing actions taken on the beneficiary's behalf while subject to a "conflict of interest," and (2) several special rules tailored to specific situations.

The "general" duty can be stated in roughly this way: Where no other special rule applies to a given situation, the cause of action for breach of the duty of loyalty has two elements. First, plaintiff (who will be the purported beneficiary) must show that the defendant owed plaintiff a duty of loyalty, and that while subject to that duty defendant acted under a conflict of interest. Second, if plaintiff makes that showing, the burden of proof shifts to the defendant to show that his conduct was nevertheless "fair" to the plaintiff. As to element one, whether there is a conflict of interest is fact sensitive, but normally it can be shown only in the following three specific circumstances:

(a) The defendant had a direct interest in a transaction in which the defendant also acted on the beneficiary's behalf,

(b) A close associate or relative of the defendant had such a direct interest, or

(c) The defendant owed fiduciary duties to two or more persons whose interests in some transaction were adverse.

Time Out for PR: Concurrent Conflicts

The American Bar Association Model Rules of Professional Conduct address the representation of clients with adverse interests in the following terms:

Rule 1.7 Conflict of Interest: Current Clients

(a) Except as provided in paragraph (b), a lawyer shall not represent a client if the representation involves a concurrent conflict of interest. A concurrent conflict of interest exists if:

(1) the representation of one client will be directly adverse to another client; or

(2) there is a significant risk that the representation of one or more clients will be materially limited by the lawyer's responsibilities to another client, a former client or a third person or by a personal interest of the lawyer.

(b) Notwithstanding the existence of a concurrent conflict of interest under paragraph (a), a lawyer may represent a client if:

(1) the lawyer reasonably believes that the lawyer will be able to provide competent and diligent representation to each affected client;

(2) the representation is not prohibited by law;

(3) the representation does not involve the assertion of a claim by one client against another client represented by the lawyer in the same litigation or other proceeding before a tribunal; and

(4) each affected client gives informed consent, confirmed in writing.

It should be obvious that if a representation involving a concurrent conflict proceeds, the lawyer still will owe fiduciary duties to each affected client.

As to element two, the defendant can show that a transaction is "fair" by showing that the beneficiary got the same treatment that might have been available in the open market, and that he was not coerced, misled, or otherwise taken advantage of.

More to the Story: Limits on Common Law Fiduciary Obligations in Modern Entity Statutes

Modern entity statutes strive to render entity law as much a creature of contract as possible, as opposed to legal mandate. And so, among other things, they have limited the degree to which judges can import fiduciary rules by way of common law lawmaking. The original UPA (1914) had mentioned a few fiduciary issues in its §§20-21, but what it had to say was quite limited, and much of the partner's fiduciary obligation was left to common law. Quite to the contrary, RUPA §409 states with clarity that *all* fiduciary duties among partners are contained within it. That is to say, in jurisdictions where it is adopted, the legislature directs that the common law does not add to the duties that §409 provides. (There is no reason, however, that partners cannot add additional duties by contract, and they might sometimes so desire. As to whether they can *subtract* from the duties in §409, see the materials on "waiver," below.) Other modern entity statutes contain similar provisions.

This general duty of loyalty cause of action is applicable only where no other special loyalty rule applies. In the case of agency law, there are at least five such special rules. They appear in Restatement (Third) of Agency §§8.02, 8.04, and 8.05.

1. a duty not to derive **excess benefits** (with respect to agents, this duty is set out in Re(3) §8.02);
2. a duty not to take **business opportunities** (also contained in Re(3) §8.02);
3. a duty not to **compete** with the principal (Re(3) §8.04);
4. duties with respect to the principal's **property** (Re(3) §8.05);
5. a duty not to exploit the principal's **confidences** (also contained in Re(3) §8.05).

 Time Out for PR: Safeguarding Property and Confidences

Among other duties clearly identifiable as fiduciary in nature, the American Bar Association Model Rules of Professional Conduct have provisions dealing with the safeguarding of client property (Model Rule 1.15) and, of course, confidences (Model Rule 1.6). Model Rule 1.8(b) specifically prohibits using a client's confidences to the client's disadvantage without informed consent. A number of states have opted to maintain the stricter standard stated in the predecessor to the Model Rules and also prohibit use of a client's confidences to the lawyer's own advantage.

These same specific sub-rules also apply, in probably more or less the same way, to managers in all unincorporated entities. For example, RUPA §409(b) says that the following are a general partner's duties of loyalty:

(1) to account to the partnership and hold as trustee for it any property, profit, or benefit derived by the partner in the conduct and winding

up of the partnership business or derived from a use by the partner of partnership property, including the appropriation of a partnership opportunity;

(2) to refrain from dealing with the partnership in the conduct or winding up of the partnership business as or on behalf of a party having an interest adverse to the partnership; and

(3) to refrain from competing with the partnership in the conduct of the partnership business before the dissolution of the partnership.

This section surely captures all five of the specific loyalty obligations imposed on agents by the Restatement (Third), as well as the generic standard for conflicted transactions. Subsection (1) plainly accommodates the "excess benefit" and "business opportunity" rules of Re(3) §8.02. Thus, the partner may not receive kickbacks or bribes in connection with partnership business (the excess benefit rule), and may not appropriate investment opportunities that properly belong to the partnership. Subsection (1) also incorporates the rule against use of partnership property for personal use or personal benefit, reflected as to agents in Re(3) §8.05. It also incorporates the similar duty not to exploit confidences for the partner's own benefit. For example, a partner may not profit from the use of a trade secret or confidential list of customers that belongs to the partnership. As for agents, this same duty appears in Re(3) §8.05. Subsection (2) then restates the basic rule conflicts of interest in general. And subsection (3) restates the duty not to compete, imposed on agents by Re(3) §8.04.

A helpful way to think about the little battery of rules making up the duty of loyalty might be to work through the following flow chart, as it applies to any duty of loyalty problem:

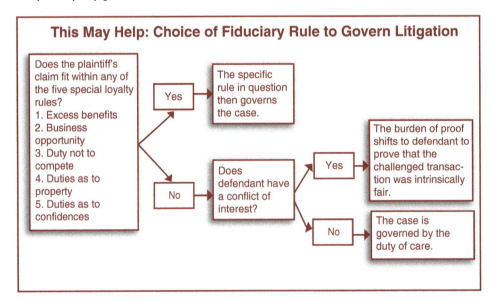

This May Help: Choice of Fiduciary Rule to Govern Litigation

Does the plaintiff's claim fit within any of the five special loyalty rules?
1. Excess benefits
2. Business opportunity
3. Duty not to compete
4. Duties as to property
5. Duties as to confidences

Yes → The specific rule in question then governs the case.

No → Does defendant have a conflict of interest?

Yes → The burden of proof shifts to defendant to prove that the challenged transaction was intrinsically fair.

No → The case is governed by the duty of care.

1. The Intrinsic Fairness Test: The Basic Duty of Loyalty Claim for General Interested Transactions

The *Labovitz* case, which follows, illustrates the application of the basic rule involving "interested" or "self-dealing" transactions. Bear in mind, as you read, that it was decided before the promulgation of RUPA in 1997.

LABOVITZ V. DOLAN

Illinois Court of Appeals
545 N.E.2d 304 (1989)

Justice SCARIANO delivered the opinion of the court:

We have for decision in this case the issue, as posited by the plaintiffs, of whether management discretion granted solely and exclusively to a general partner in a limited partnership agreement authorizes the general partner to use economic coercion to cause his limited partner investors to sell their interests to him at a bargain price.

Plaintiffs as limited partners invested over $12 million dollars in a cablevision programming limited partnership sponsored and syndicated by defendant general partner Dolan. In 1985 the partnership reported earnings of over $34 million dollars, and in 1986 it had earnings of just under $18 million dollars, as a result of which each of the limited partners was required to report his pro rata share on his personal income tax returns for those years.

Plaintiffs claim that although the partnership had cash available to fund the limited partners' tax obligations, Dolan elected to make only a nominal distribution of cash to cover such liability; accordingly, in 1985 and in 1986 the limited partners were required to pay taxes almost entirely from their own funds on income retained by the partnership. In late November of 1986 an affiliate owned and controlled by Dolan offered to buy out the interests of the limited partners for approximately two-thirds of their book value. Over 90% of the limited partners accepted the offer, but simultaneously filed suit claiming Dolan's tactics to be a breach of his fiduciary duty to them. The circuit court dismissed plaintiffs' complaint with prejudice pursuant to Section 2-619(a)(9) of our Code of Civil Procedure, holding that Dolan's acts were within the broad discretion granted him under the terms of the partnership agreement. Plaintiffs appeal from that ruling.

The limited partnership in this case, Cablevision Programming Investments (CPI) was organized for the purpose of investing in entities that produce and acquire programming for marketing and distribution to cable

> ### JD/MBA: Book Value
>
> Perhaps obviously, "book value" refers to the value of an ownership interest shown on the "books" of the company that is owned. "Books" are the accounting records (which hopefully are kept in accordance with generally accepted accounting practices). In the case of a partnership, the book value of each interest will reflect the amount paid by the partner, plus his or her share of profits, and less his or her share of losses and any distributions that he or she has received from the partnership. This can differ wildly from what a third party would be willing to pay to step into the partner's shoes.

Connections: Federal Securities Laws

The limited partnership interests were sold pursuant to an exemption from the registration requirements of the federal securities laws. Certain disclosure requirements still applied. These matters are dealt with in Chapter 28.

Doing the Numbers: Partnership Accounting

We are told that the limited partners paid $200,000 for each of their units in 1980. We also know that there was per unit taxable income of $415,331 in 1985 and $216,750 in 1986. This totals $832,081. Deducting $24,000 for the amounts distributed leaves $808,081.

The book value per unit, however, is only $405,000. The difference must have to do with the pre-1985 losses. This reconciles with the court's statement that the limited partners were afforded "tax benefits" from 1980 through 1984.

If the limited partners sold their units for more than the amount in their accounts, they would have a taxable gain. Because they sold for $271,870, they had a loss for tax purposes of $133,130. This would be available to offset other taxable income.

and other pay television services . . . . The 263 page Private Placement Memorandum (PPM) . . . advised investors that their rights and obligations "are governed by the Articles of Limited Partnership" (the Articles), which were bound as an exhibit to the PPM, and added, in a section entitled "Projected Results of Operations of Cablevision Programming Investments," that:

"The Partnership, Cablevision and its affiliates' intended policy is to make cash distributions to partners each year in an amount approximating the amount of taxable income reflected each year, after providing for adequate working capital requirements deemed necessary by the General Partners. Although the projections assume that this policy can be followed in the future, there are significant contingencies relating to many factors which, from time to time, may prohibit any distributions, including, but not limited to cash, cash availability, general working capital requirements, lending restrictions and revised costs and capital requirements."

The Articles provided that Dolan will have "full responsibility and exclusive and complete discretion in the management and control of the business and affairs of the partnership"; that "Dolan in his sole discretion shall determine the availability of Cash Flow for distribution to partners"; that they "contain the entire understanding among the partners and supersede any prior understanding and/or written or oral agreements among them"; and that Dolan would be liable to the limited partners for his willful misconduct but not for "errors in judgment or for any acts or omissions that do not constitute willful misconduct."

CPI limited partnership interests were offered and sold only to "wealthy and sophisticated investors." . . . Prospective investors were apprised in the PPM that the "offering and the operations of the entities summarized [therein] are complex," and that a "thorough understanding of such matters is essential in order for prospective investors to evaluate the merits and risks of the offering." . . .

An examination of a limited partner's "K-1" tax form reveals that from 1980 through 1984 CPI provided no cash to the limited partners but did afford them some tax benefits. In 1985, each partner was required to report a taxable income of $415,331 per unit, while Dolan distributed only $12,000 per unit; and in 1986 the partners were required to report a taxable income of $216,750 per unit, while again receiving a distribution of only $12,000 per unit.

On November 25, 1986 Cablevision Systems Corporation (CSC), owned and controlled by Dolan, made an offer to purchase all of the CPI limited partnership interests for $271,870 per unit . . . . The offer disclosed that "Dolan and his affiliates would derive substantial benefits in connection with the offer" and that "although the partnership was potentially very valuable . . . it was extremely difficult to determine its true value since it was likely that current assumptions would not materialize and that unanticipated events and circumstances would occur." . . . The articles provided that a limited partner could not sell or otherwise transfer his interest in the partnership without the prior written consent of the general partners. More than 90% of the limited partners elected to accept CSC's offer and sold their interests in CPI to CSC . . . .

Plaintiffs appeal the order of dismissal, contending that since "'discretion' can never be exercised in breach of a fiduciary duty," the trial court erred in holding that the PPM and the Articles granted Dolan the discretion to treat his limited partners as he did, without permitting a trial that would inquire into his intent regarding the fairness of the transactions at issue . . . .

Plaintiffs point out that the PPM provides that:

> Distributions of Cash Flow of the Partnership and Cablevision will be made at such times and in such amounts as Charles F. Dolan, as the individual General Partner of both partnerships, in his sole discretion shall determine, subject to any restrictions on distributions to partners contained in loan agreements which may be entered into by Cablevision as a condition to its borrowings and which restrictions are not ascertainable at this time . . . .
>
> The Partnership, Cablevision and its affiliates' intended policy is to make cash distributions to partners each year in an amount approximating the amount of taxable income reflected each year, after providing for adequate working capital requirements deemed necessary by the General Partners.

Thus, plaintiffs argue, Dolan made it clear in the PPM that he intended to distribute cash flow annually when not required to meet current obligations; accordingly his "discretion" to distribute cash flow was limited by his fiduciary duties to his partners . . . .

However, defendants assert, this argument is seriously impaired by the fact that the Articles, and not the PPM defined the partners' rights and obligations, pointing to Section 15.10 of the Articles which provides in pertinent part: "These Articles contain the entire understanding among the partners and supersedes [sic] any prior understandings and/or written or oral agreements among them respecting the within subject matter." . . .

Defendants claim that although the "rights and obligations of the Investors are governed by the Articles," the PPM was merely "intended to furnish information to the proposed investors with respect to the investment described." Thus, defendants contend, the PPM is entirely consistent with the Articles' grant of sole discretion to Dolan to determine how partnership proceeds should be allocated . . . .

Defendants' further response to plaintiffs is that the general partner's specific authority to determine how partnership proceeds should be allocated was not inconsistent with any fiduciary duty owed by Dolan to the plaintiffs, insisting that partners have the right to establish among themselves, by a partnership agreement, their rights, duties and obligations . . . . Dolan was given, they continue, "the sole discretion to determine whether partnership proceeds were needed to fund related entities or could be distributed as cash to the limited partners so that he would have the flexibility needed to meet and anticipate the ever-changing business conditions in the industry," and in deciding how to allocate partnership proceeds, "Dolan was called upon to exercise his business judgment in anticipating future needs, expanding profitable areas and exploring promising new fields." Plaintiffs now attempt, defendants claim, "to second-guess Dolan's business judgment with respect to whether proceeds withheld from distribution were needed for the sound operation of CPI's business affairs and to have the court do likewise."

OPINION

[The court first held that] the language in the Articles standing alone does not deprive plaintiffs of the trial they seek against Dolan for breach of fiduciary duty. [The law governing fiduciary waivers is considered later in this chapter.] We therefore agree with plaintiffs that the trial court did not give due consideration to Dolan's duty as general partner to exercise the highest degree of honesty and good faith in his handling of partnership assets, and instead treated the parties as arm's length strangers . . . , holding that no inquiry could be made into the fairness of the transactions at issue because of the language in the Articles regarding Dolan's discretion. Yet "in any fiduciary relationship, the burden of proof shifts to the fiduciary to show by clear and convincing evidence that a transaction is equitable and just." . . . Indeed, cases cited and relied upon by defendants hold that "where there is a question of breach of a fiduciary duty of a managing partner, all doubts will be resolved against him, and the managing partner has the burden of proving his innocence." . . .

. . . Plaintiffs' complaint in essence charges that Dolan, as general partner, owed plaintiffs, his limited partners, a fiduciary duty "to distribute available cash flow to his partners in 1983 through 1986," which duty he breached because "he never intended to pay cash flow to the limited partners," thus "forcing or squeezing his limited partners into accepting his below book value offer" to buy out their interests, to their financial damage. The complaint goes on to allege that by Dolan's selling of the 85 limited partnership units at $200,000 per unit, $17,000,000 was realized as capital for the partnership. After deducting $2,000,000 to pay fees to Dolan and to reimburse him for attorney and accounting fees and other costs incurred in the preparation of the PPM, the sum of $15,000,000 remained as the partnership's capital. In addition to the cash flow generated by operations, the partnership and its related entities realized cash as follows: $20,000,000 in 1983 by selling interests in two related entities to a subsidiary of The Washington Post. In 1985 there was a $31,600,000 gain upon the sale of an interest in a related entity to a subsidiary of CBS, Inc., plus $50,000,000 when a lawsuit against Ted Turner and MGM was settled. In 1986 approximately $20,000,000 was paid to the partnership by MGM/UA Home Entertainment Group in exchange for a license option agreement, and $3,500,000 in exchange for the termination of a distribution agreement.

In 1985 the partnership showed income of $2,778,000 exclusive of the gain on the sale of assets, and after allowing for depreciation of $1,289,000. During 1986 the balance in the partnership cash account increased $11,000,000; receivables from parties "related" to Dolan and the partnership increased $3,600,000; and long term notes receivable increased $9,000,000. For the year ending December 31, 1986, partnership net income was $17,658,000 and working capital increased by $10,220,000. A footnote to the financial statement for the year ended December 31, 1985, discloses that Dolan retained significant amounts of money [$19,139,000] within the partnership which were loaned to "related parties[.]" . . . We can think of no reason as to why these allegations should not be found to be sufficient to encompass the claim raised on this appeal, and sufficient also to apprise defendants thereof . . . .

JD/MBA: Distinguishing Income and Cash Flow

An entity's income and its cash flow are two quite different things. Note, for instance, that the limited partnership took in $20 million in cash in 1983 by selling interests in two related entities. We know, however, that the partnership had no income for that year and in fact generated a tax loss.

It is customary for an entity's financial statements to include both an income statement and a statement of cash flows. You can read more about this in the online Supplement.

Dear Prof.: Cash? The court seems, in that third to the last paragraph, to be saying that the limited partnership had at least $140.1 million in cash. Where would they keep it all?

You might possibly remember the old Scrooge McDuck comics and be envisioning Scrooge diving in heaps of coins in his money bin—indubitably not what was going on here. "Cash" refers to "cash equivalents," which include amounts on deposit in banks. (In addition, it is not clear that the court is carefully distinguishing the flow of cash and the recognition of gains on sale.)

◼ Think about this:

(C) Which facts do you think were most important to the appellate court in *Labovitz*?

(D) Would you expect the analysis in *Labovitz* to differ under RUPA?

(E) Does the opinion in *Labovitz* mean that the defendants are liable? If not, what do they have to prove?

2. The Five Special Loyalty Rules

The Excess Benefits Rule. As to this first of the "special" loyalty rules we will study, *see* Re(3) §8.02 or entity statutes like RUPA §409(b)(1). The following often-cited case nicely illustrates the basic rule in operation, and the remedies available to the beneficiary.

BRITISH AMERICAN & EASTERN CO. V. WIRTH, LTD.

United States Court of Appeals for the Second Circuit
592 F.2d 75 (1979)

LUMBARD, Circuit Judge:

[Plaintiff Frederick Sunley acted through the British American & Eastern Co., Inc. as his "alter ego," according to the court. Sunley had for many years been U.S. representative of an Australian steel mill known as VMW. As he was getting on in years, he arranged with defendant Manfred Wirth to take over his responsibilities. To help Wirth transition into that role, Sunley agreed to work as Wirth's agent for a time, assisting him in VMW's U.S. affairs. Relations deteriorated, and in this case Sunley sues for commissions to which he believes he was entitled as Wirth's agent.] . . .

Wirth ceased making the payments to Sunley required by the contract in January, 1976. Sunley then sued for breach of contract. The district court awarded Sunley $27,085.84 in damages and Wirth now appeals . . . .

Wirth's second contention on appeal is that Sunley's claim for compensation should be barred because Sunley sought and received commercial bribes from Non-Ferrous, a customer of Wirth, in exchange for increasing Non-Ferrous' allocation of scarce aluminum. Wirth further contends that Sunley should be required to turn over to Wirth the payments Sunley received as bribes. Sunley responds that Wirth failed to establish that payments received from Non-Ferrous were improper or a breach of contract. The district court made no finding as to whether these payments were bribes or were merely payments for services rendered, on the ground that even if they were bribes, acceptance of these payments did not breach the contract because Wirth could show no injury caused by their receipt. Thus the district court treated the allegations of bribe-taking as irrelevant to Sunley's contract claim.

Wirth's allegations of bribe-taking, however, are not irrelevant if Sunley's relationship with Wirth was that of an agent or fiduciary. An agent's contract action for compensation from his principal can be defeated if the principal shows that the agent breached his trust by accepting from the principal's customers, without the principal's knowledge, monies intended to influence the agent's actions concerning a matter affecting the principal's interest . . . . In addition, where there is an agency relationship, the principal is entitled to recover any monies paid as commercial bribes to his agent . . . .

Although the district court indicated in its review of Wirth's libel claim that Sunley was an independent contractor and not an agent, we hold that in his dealings with Non-Ferrous Sunley acted as Wirth's agent. An agent serves under the control and supervision of his principal; so long as he acts within the ambit of his authority to represent his principal, he binds him. Such was the case with Sunley's dealings with Non-Ferrous once his agreement with Wirth took effect. The trial record indicates that Sunley was empowered to take orders from Non-Ferrous and from other customers for Wirth's account . . . . This is the essence of the agency relation . . . . Indeed, Sunley handled customer relations on Wirth's behalf in a number of ways, as he was hired to do, from assessing their supply needs to informing them of changes in the way Wirth planned to handle import duties. As Wirth's agent, Sunley also had supervisory authority over Wirth's secretarial staff. Accordingly, if Sunley accepted payments from Non-Ferrous designed to influence the way in which he fulfilled his duties as Wirth's agent, Wirth is entitled to recover those payments and Sunley is barred from recovering on the contract.

The district court, however, did not decide whether the payments Sunley received from Non-Ferrous were actually bribes because it concluded that Wirth had not shown direct injury from the alleged bribe-taking. We hold that finding clearly erroneous. Even if, as the district court hypothesized, Non-Ferrous did not attribute Sunley's actions to Wirth, any customer such as Non-Ferrous would certainly prefer to do business with a company which employs salesmen who do not demand extra payments for themselves. In addition, where there is an agency relationship, the principal need not show injury through bribe-taking in order to defend against an action by the agent for compensation or to prevail in an action to recover the amount of the bribes. The strong public policy against all kinds of bribery requires that injury be presumed under these circumstances. The acceptance by an agent of secret payments to himself for doing what he is already under an obligation to do is obviously destructive to the relationship with his principal and contrary to dealing fairly with customers of the principal. Accordingly, the purpose and the propriety of the payments to Sunley should be determined by the district court on remand . . . .

 Time Out for PR: Accepting Compensation from One Other Than the Client

American Bar Association Model Rule 1.8(f) reads as follows:

> (f) A lawyer shall not accept compensation for representing a client from one other than the client unless:
>   (1) the client gives informed consent;
>   (2) there is no interference with the lawyer's independence of professional judgment or with the client-lawyer relationship; and
>   (3) information relating to representation of a client is protected as required by Rule 1.6.

Does this seem to have any relation to the *British American* case?

■ **Think about this:**

(F) Stella, a traveling sales representative for Compuserver, invites Paolo, a purchasing agent for Consumco, out for a fancy lunch to discuss Compuserver's new product line. Stella insists on paying the bill. If she does, will Paolo be in breach of his duty to Consumco?

Duty Not to Compete. Generally, the duty of loyalty prohibits a fiduciary from competing with the beneficiary in its business. This implies fairly obviously that the fiduciary should not sell a product or service in direct competition with the beneficiary. But one of the more surprising aspects of this duty is that while a *former* partner, employee, or other agent is permitted to compete with the beneficiary after the fiduciary relationship has ended, the current fiduciary risks breach if she engages in preparations for future competition before the relationship is over. This duty is commonly implicated in situations in which a current employee or partner is disgruntled or desirous of setting off on her own, but before doing so takes steps to set up the new business. Merely making arrangements is generally okay—renting office space or printing business cards, for example—but problems arise where preparatory conduct looks more like actual competition. Contacting a current employer's clients to encourage them to follow the defector, for example, is a common basis for a fiduciary claim, as are efforts to steal away the employer's other valued employees.

GRAPHIC DIRECTIONS, INC. V. BUSH

Colorado Court of Appeals
862 P.2d 1020 (1993)

Opinion by Chief Judge STERNBERG.

[Defendants Bush and Dickerson had both worked as officers of plaintiff Graphic Directions, Inc. (GDI), a small graphic design business. After several years of employment, Bush made plans to leave GDI to start his own business. He discussed his plans with defendant Dickerson, and together they left the firm, taking another employee named Roche with them to found a competing graphics business, which they called Concepts 3.] . . .

I.

In order to recover on a claim for breach of fiduciary duty, a plaintiff must prove: 1) that the defendant was acting as a fiduciary of the plaintiff; 2) that he breached a fiduciary duty to the plaintiff; 3) that the plaintiff incurred damages; and 4) that the defendant's breach of fiduciary duty was a cause of the plaintiff's damages. CJI-Civ. 2d 26:1 (1989) . . . .

B.

Although the evidence was not overwhelming, we conclude that it was sufficient to support the jury's conclusion that Bush and Dickerson breached their fiduciary duty to GDI.

While still employed, an employee may make preparations to compete after termination of his employment and may advise current customers that he will be leaving. However, pre-termination solicitation of customers for a new competing business violates the employee's duty of loyalty. Jet Courier Service, Inc. v. Mulei[, 771 P.2d 486 (Colo. 1989)].

Indeed the very heart of the *Mulei* decision is to give vitality to an employee's duty of loyalty to his employer . . . . [In that case,] the supreme court placed great reliance on the Restatement (Second) of Agency §393 comment e (1958) and held that this court and the trial court had "applied an unduly narrow legal standard in holding [the employee's] duty of loyalty . . . ." The supreme court ordered the case remanded to the trial court to determine whether the pre-termination customer meetings were "impermissible solicitation" or "allowable preparation for competition."

In denying Bush and Dickerson's motions for a directed verdict and for judgment notwithstanding the verdict, the court determined that circumstantial evidence would permit an inference that they solicited customers prior to terminating their employment with GDI, causing some customers to transfer their business to Concepts 3. Therefore, under the supreme court holding in *Mulei*, the trial court in this case would have erred had it resolved the issue as one of law and granted either a directed verdict or a judgment notwithstanding the verdict.

The record supports the court's conclusion that there was competent evidence to support the verdict that Bush and Dickerson had breached their fiduciary duty to GDI. Thus, although we might have reached a different conclusion, the jury verdict may not be disturbed.

C.

Nevertheless, although the evidence was sufficient to establish the existence and the breach of a fiduciary duty, we agree with Bush and Dickerson that, as a matter of law, the evidence of damages was insufficient to permit the claim to go to the jury.

. . . [T]he claimant must submit "substantial evidence [of injury resulting from fiduciary breach through competition with the beneficiary], which together with reasonable inferences to be drawn therefrom, provides a reasonable basis for computation of the damage." . . .

Damages for lost profits are measured by the loss of net profits, meaning net earnings or the excess of returns over expenditures, but not lost gross profits or gross sales revenues. Further, a business has the ability to produce specific historical records showing customary net profits from which a reasonably reliable estimate of its losses can be made . . . .

GDI's evidence concerning its damages consisted of testimony from its accountant and president. The accountant testified that the company lost $173,337 in net taxable profits in the eighteen months following the defendants' departure. The president's testimony which referred to the amount and percentage of the sales volume lost from GDI's reduced customer base is not a measure of its lost profits . . . . [S]ee also Western Cities Broadcasting, Inc. v. Schueller, 849 P.2d 44 (Colo. 1993) (Plaintiff failed to connect evidence of value of business to issue of claimed lost profits from lease involving business.).

Nor did GDI provide financial statements that would have allowed the jury to compare the company's historical income and expenses with the income and expenses in the months following the departure of Bush and Dickerson . . . .

Additionally, it is axiomatic that before damages for lost profits may be awarded, one who seeks them must establish that the damages are traceable to and are the direct result of the wrong to be redressed . . . . GDI's accountant testified that he did not have an opinion as to whether the losses were caused by Bush and Dickerson's conduct and stated he had not related his calculation of the loss of net taxable profits to the lost customers. Nor is there evidence establishing a causal link between all the lost sales and Bush and Dickerson's solicitation of customers. At least four of the "lost" customers continued to do some business with GDI, and GDI presented no evidence that eight other "lost" customers did any business with Concepts 3. [The court accordingly overturns GDI's recovery.]

■ **Think about this:**

(G) Is it all right for a departing agent to take the principal's customer lists and thereafter use them, provided he or she does not contact the customers before departure?

(H) What would someone have to show to establish damages under *Graphic Directions*? Does it seem to you that recovery ever would be possible?

(I) Why must one prove damages under the anti-competition rule but not under the excess benefits rule?

Business Opportunities. Restatement §8.02, which generally prohibits the taking by an agent of "material benefits" from third parties in connection with the agency, also sets out the duty-of-loyalty obligation not to take business opportunities that fairly should be given to the beneficiary. Comment d provides that an opportunity should be first offered to the beneficiary "when either the nature of the opportunity or the circumstances under which the agent learned of it require that the agent offer the opportunity to the principal." It goes on to approve of the habit of many courts of making this determination by using the test set out in the American Law Institute's *Principles of Corporate Governance* §5.05(b). Paraphrasing that provision, with a few words changed to make it applicable to non-corporate contexts, it provides as follows:

(b) *Definition* . . . . For purposes of this Section, a [business] opportunity [that fairly belongs to the beneficiary] means:

(1) Any opportunity to engage in a business activity of which a [fiduciary] becomes aware, either:

(A) In connection with the performance of functions as a [fiduciary], or under circumstances that should reasonably lead the [fiduciary] to believe that the person offering the opportunity expects it to be offered to the [beneficiary]; or

(B) Through the use of [the beneficiary's] information or property, if the resulting opportunity is one that the [fiduciary] should reasonably be expected to believe would be of interest to the [beneficiary]; or

(2) Any opportunity to engage in a business activity of which a [fiduciary] becomes aware and knows is closely related to a business in which the [beneficiary] is engaged or expects to engage.

Generally, a fiduciary may take the opportunity for himself if he first adequately discloses it and the nature of the conflict, and the beneficiary rejects the opportunity. As Re(3) §8.02, comment e points out, the remedy for an improperly taken opportunity is simply for the principal to take it from the agent, and provide the agent "reimbursement." The word "reimbursement" plainly indicates that the agent is not entitled to any appreciation in the value of the investment between the time he acquired it and the time the principal took it from him.

The case that appears below is perhaps the most famous in all of business law. Its sweeping language is invoked broadly throughout the fiduciary duties case law (for instance, there are many references to it in the unedited version of the *Labovitz* case, set out above). And within the opinion—decided four-to-three—the court touches several important duty-of-loyalty matters, including the duty to disclose material facts while in a conflict of interest (a point we'll revisit below). But it also nicely illustrates the business opportunity rule, and so we consider it in detail here. An interesting question will be whether this old case, seeming to consist as it does only of broad platitudes that lack the crisp detail of a modern code like the ALI *Principles*, is consistent with the rule of §5.05(b). At the end we'll ask you a few questions about whether the case would come out the same or differently under the ALI *Principles*.

MEINHARD V. SALMON

New York Court of Appeals
164 N.E. 545 (1928)

CARDOZO, Ch. J.

On April 10, 1902, Louisa M. Gerry leased to the defendant Walter J. Salmon the premises known as the Hotel Bristol at the northwest corner of Forty-second street and Fifth avenue in the city of New York. The lease was for a term of twenty years, commencing May 1, 1902, and ending April 30, 1922. The lessee

Hotel Bristol, 42nd and Fifth Ave.

undertook to change the hotel building for use as shops and offices at a cost of $200,000. Alterations and additions were to be accretions to the land.

Salmon, while in course of treaty with the lessor as to the execution of the lease, was in course of treaty with Meinhard, the plaintiff, for the necessary funds. The result was a joint venture with terms embodied in a writing. Meinhard was to pay to Salmon half of the moneys requisite to reconstruct, alter, manage and operate the property. Salmon was to pay to Meinhard 40 per cent of the net profits for the first five years of the lease and 50 per cent for the years thereafter. If there were losses, each party was to bear them equally. Salmon, however, was to have sole power to "manage, lease, underlet and operate" the building. There were to be certain pre-emptive rights for each in the contingency of death.

The two were coadventurers, subject to fiduciary duties akin to those of partners. As to this we are all agreed. The heavier weight of duty rested, however, upon Salmon. He was a coadventurer with Meinhard, but he was manager as well. During the early years of the enterprise, the building, reconstructed, was operated at a loss. If the relation had then ended, Meinhard as well as Salmon would have carried a heavy burden. Later the profits became large with the result that for each of the investors there came a rich return. For each, the venture had its phases of fair weather and of foul. The two were in it jointly, for better or for worse.

When the lease was near its end, Elbridge T. Gerry had become the owner of the reversion. He owned much other property in the neighborhood, one lot adjoining the Bristol Building on Fifth avenue and four lots on Forty-second street. He had a plan to lease the entire tract for a long term to some one who would destroy the buildings then existing, and put up another in their place. In the latter part of 1921, he submitted such a project to several capitalists and dealers. He was unable to carry it through with any of them. Then, in January, 1922, with less than four months of the lease to run, he approached the defendant Salmon. The result was a new lease to the Midpoint Realty Company, which is owned and controlled by Salmon, a lease covering the whole tract, and involving a huge outlay. The term is to be twenty years, but successive covenants for renewal will extend it to a maximum of eighty years at the will of either party. The existing buildings may remain unchanged for seven years. They are then to be torn down, and a new building to cost $3,000,000 is to be placed upon the site. The rental, which under the Bristol lease was only $55,000, is to be from $350,000 to $475,000 for the properties so combined. Salmon personally guaranteed the performance by the lessee of the covenants of the new lease until such time as the new building had been completed and fully paid for.

The lease between Gerry and the Midpoint Realty Company was signed and delivered on January 25, 1922. Salmon had not told Meinhard anything about it. Whatever his motive may have been, he had kept the negotiations to himself. Meinhard was not informed even of the bare existence of a project. The first that he knew of it was in February when the lease was an accomplished fact. He then made demand on the defendants that the lease be held in trust as an asset of the venture, making offer upon the trial to share the personal obligations incidental to the guaranty. The demand was followed by refusal, and later by this suit. A referee gave judgment for the plaintiff, limiting the plaintiff's interest in the lease, however, to 25 per cent. The limitation was on the theory that the plaintiff's equity was to be restricted to one-half of so much of the value of the lease as was contributed or represented by the occupation of the Bristol site. Upon cross-appeals to the Appellate Division, the judgment was modified so as to enlarge the equitable interest to one-half of the whole lease. With this enlargement of plaintiff's interest, there went, of course, a corresponding enlargement of his attendant obligations. The case is now here on an appeal by the defendants.

> **Room to Argue: He's So Fine**
>
> It sometimes is argued that the fiduciary duty Cardozo describes is not only unrealistic but, from an economic standpoint, undesirable. Some also have challenged it as unduly paternalistic and tending to exclude the legitimate interests of third parties. You can read more about this in the online Supplement.

Joint adventurers, like copartners, owe to one another, while the enterprise continues, the duty of the finest loyalty. Many forms of conduct permissible in a workaday world for those acting at arm's length, are forbidden to those bound by fiduciary ties. A trustee is held to something stricter than the morals of the market place. Not honesty alone, but the punctilio of an honor the most sensitive, is then the standard of behavior. As to this there has developed a tradition that is unbending and inveterate. Uncompromising rigidity has been the attitude of courts of equity when petitioned to undermine the rule of undivided loyalty by the "disintegrating erosion" of particular exceptions. Only thus has the level of conduct for fiduciaries been kept at a level higher than that trodden by the crowd. It will not consciously be lowered by any judgment of this court.

The owner of the reversion, Mr. Gerry, had vainly striven to find a tenant who would favor his ambitious scheme of demolition and construction. Baffled in the search, he turned to the defendant Salmon in possession of the Bristol, the keystone of the project. He figured to himself beyond a doubt that the man in possession would prove a likely customer. To the eye of an observer, Salmon held the lease as owner in his own right, for himself and no one else. In fact he held it as a fiduciary, for himself and another, sharers in a common venture. If this fact had been proclaimed, if the lease by its terms had run in favor of a partnership, Mr. Gerry, we may fairly assume, would have laid before the partners, and not merely before one of them, his plan of reconstruction. The pre-emptive privilege, or, better, the pre-emptive opportunity, that was thus an incident of the enterprise, Salmon appropriated to himself in secrecy and silence. He might have warned Meinhard that the plan had been submitted, and that either would be free to compete for the award. If he had done this, we do not need to say whether he would have been under a duty, if successful in the competition, to hold the lease so acquired for the benefit of a venture then about to end, and thus prolong by indirection its responsibilities and duties. The trouble about his conduct is that he excluded his coadventurer from any chance to compete, from any chance to enjoy the opportunity for benefit that had come to him alone by virtue of his agency. This chance, if nothing more, he was under a duty to concede. The price of its denial is an extension of the trust at the option and for the benefit of the one whom he excluded.

No answer is it to say that the chance would have been of little value even if seasonably offered. Such a calculus of probabilities is beyond the science of the chancery. Salmon, the real estate operator, might have been preferred to Meinhard, the woolen merchant. On the other hand, Meinhard might have offered better terms, or reinforced his offer by alliance with the wealth of others. Perhaps he might even have persuaded the lessor to renew the Bristol lease alone, postponing for a time, in return for higher rentals, the improvement of adjoining lots. We know that even under the lease as made the time for the enlargement of the building was delayed for seven years. All these opportunities were cut away from him through another's intervention. He knew that Salmon was the manager. As the time drew near for the expiration of the lease, he would naturally assume from silence, if from nothing else, that the lessor was willing to extend it for a term of years, or at least to let it stand as a lease from year to year. Not impossibly the lessor would have done so, whatever his protestations of unwillingness, if Salmon had not given assent to a project more attractive. At all events, notice of termination, even if not necessary, might seem, not unreasonably, to be something to be looked for, if the business was over and another tenant was to enter. In the absence of such notice, the matter of an extension was one that would naturally be attended to by the manager of the enterprise, and not neglected altogether. At least, there was nothing in the situation to give warning to any one that while the lease was still in being, there had come to the manager an offer of extension which he had locked within his breast to be utilized by himself alone. The very fact that Salmon was in control with exclusive powers of direction charged him the more obviously with the duty of disclosure, since only through disclosure could opportunity be equalized. If he might cut off renewal by a purchase for his own benefit when four months were to pass before the lease would have an end, he might do so with equal right while there remained as many years. He might steal a march on his comrade under cover of the darkness, and then hold the captured ground. Loyalty and comradeship are not so easily abjured . . . .

We have no thought to hold that Salmon was guilty of a conscious purpose to defraud. Very likely he assumed in all good faith that with the approaching end of the venture he might ignore his coadventurer and take the extension for himself. He had given to the enterprise time and labor as well as money. He had made it a success. Meinhard, who had given money, but neither time nor labor, had already been richly paid. There might seem to be something grasping in his insistence upon more. Such recriminations are not unusual when coadventurers fall out. They are not without their force if conduct is to be judged by the common standards of competitors. That is not to say that they have pertinency here. Salmon had put himself in a position in which thought of self was to be renounced, however hard the abnegation. He was much more than a coadventurer. He was a managing coadventurer. For him and for those like him, the rule of undivided loyalty is relentless and supreme. A different question would be here if there were lacking any nexus of relation between the business conducted by the manager and the opportunity brought to him as an incident of management. For this problem, as for most, there are distinctions of degree. If Salmon had received from Gerry a proposition to lease a building at a location far removed, he might have held for himself the privilege thus acquired, or so we shall assume. Here the subject-matter of the new lease was an extension and enlargement of the subject-matter of the old one. A managing coadventurer appropriating the benefit of such a lease without warning to his partner might fairly expect to be reproached with conduct that was underhand, or lacking, to say the least, in reasonable candor, if the partner were to surprise him in the act of signing the new instrument. Conduct subject to that reproach does not receive from equity a healing benediction.

A question remains as to the form and extent of the equitable interest to be allotted to the plaintiff. The trust as declared has been held to attach to the lease which was in the name of the defendant corporation. We think it ought to attach at the option of the defendant Salmon to the shares of stock which were owned by him or were under his control. The difference may be important if the lessee shall wish to execute an assignment of the lease, as it ought to be free to do with the consent of the lessor. On the other hand, an equal division of the shares might lead to other hardships. It might take away from Salmon the power of control and management which under the plan of the joint venture he was to have from first to last. The number of shares to be allotted to the plaintiff should, therefore, be reduced to such an extent as may be necessary to preserve to the defendant Salmon the expected measure of dominion. To that end an extra share should be added to his half.

Subject to this adjustment, we agree with the Appellate Division that the plaintiff's equitable interest is to be measured by the value of half of the entire lease, and not merely by half of some undivided part. A single building covers the whole area. Physical division is impracticable along the lines of the Bristol site, the keystone of the whole. Division of interests and burdens is equally impracticable. Salmon, as tenant under the new lease, or as guarantor of the performance of the tenant's obligations, might well protest if Meinhard, claiming an equitable interest, had offered to assume a liability not equal to Salmon's, but only half as great. He might justly insist that the lease must be accepted by his coadventurer in such form as it had been given, and not constructively divided into imaginary fragments. What must be yielded to the one may be demanded by the other. The lease as it has been executed is single and entire. If confusion has resulted from the union of adjoining parcels, the trustee who consented to the union must bear the inconvenience . . . .

The judgment should be modified by providing that at the option of the defendant Salmon there may be substituted for a trust attaching to the lease a trust attaching to the shares of stock, with the result that one-half of such shares together with one additional share will in that event be allotted to the defendant Salmon and the other shares to the plaintiff, and as so modified the judgment should be affirmed with costs.

ANDREWS, J. (dissenting).

. . . Were this a general partnership between Mr. Salmon and Mr. Meinhard I should have little doubt as to the correctness of this result assuming the new

Photo Credit: Gryffindor
500 Fifth Avenue,
constructed in
1929-1931 on the site of
the Bristol

lease to be an offshoot of the old. Such a situation involves questions of trust and confidence to a high degree; it involves questions of good will; many other considerations. As has been said, rarely if ever may one partner without the knowledge of the other acquire for himself the renewal of a lease held by the firm, even if the new lease is to begin after the firm is dissolved. Warning of such an intent, if he is managing partner, may not be sufficient to prevent the application of this rule.

We have here a different situation governed by less drastic principles. I assume that where parties engage in a joint enterprise each owes to the other the duty of the utmost good faith in all that relates to their common venture. Within its scope they stand in a fiduciary relationship. I assume prima facie that even as between joint adventurers one may not secretly obtain a renewal of the lease of property actually used in the joint adventure where the possibility of renewal is expressly or impliedly involved in the enterprise. I assume also that Mr. Meinhard had an equitable interest in the Bristol Hotel lease. Further, that an expectancy of renewal inhered in that lease. Two questions then arise. Under his contract did he share in that expectancy? And if so, did that expectancy mature into a graft of the original lease? To both questions my answer is "no." . . .

It seems to me that the venture so inaugurated had in view a limited object and was to end at a limited time. There was no intent to expand it into a far greater undertaking lasting for many years. The design was to exploit a particular lease. Doubtless in it Mr. Meinhard had an equitable interest, but in it alone. This interest terminated when the joint adventure terminated. There was no intent that for the benefit of both any advantage should be taken of the chance of renewal—that the adventure should be continued beyond that date. Mr. Salmon has done all he promised to do in return for Mr. Meinhard's undertaking when he distributed profits up to May 1, 1922. Suppose this lease, nonassignable without the consent of the lessor, had contained a renewal option. Could Mr. Meinhard have exercised it? Could he have insisted that Mr. Salmon do so? Had Mr. Salmon done so could he insist that the agreement to share losses still existed or could Mr. Meinhard have claimed that the joint adventure was still to continue for twenty or eighty years? I do not think so. The adventure by its express terms ended on May 1, 1922. The contract by its language and by its whole import excluded the idea that the tenant's expectancy was to subsist for the benefit of the plaintiff. On that date whatever there was left of value in the lease reverted to Mr. Salmon, as it would had the lease been for thirty years instead of twenty. Any equity which Mr. Meinhard possessed was in the particular lease itself, not in any possibility of renewal. There was nothing unfair in Mr. Salmon's conduct.

I might go further were it necessary. Under the circumstances here presented, had the lease run to both the parties, I doubt whether the taking by one of a renewal without the knowledge of the other would cause interference by a court of equity. An illustration may clarify my thought. A and B enter into a joint venture to resurface a highway between Albany and Schenectady. They rent a parcel of land for the storage of materials. A, unknown to B, agrees with the lessor to rent that parcel and one adjoining it after the venture is finished, for an iron foundry. Is the act unfair? Would any general statements, scattered here and there through opinions dealing with other circumstance, be thought applicable? In other words, the mere fact that the joint venturers rent property together does not call for the strict rule that applies to general partners. Many things may excuse what is there forbidden. Nor here does any possibility of renewal exist as part of the venture. The nature of the undertaking excludes such an idea . . . .

■ **Think about this:**

(J) Do Cardozo and Andrews disagree about the standard of conduct to be applied?

(K) Was Meinhard bound by the terms of the new lease as soon as Salmon entered it?

(L) Does Cardozo's analysis reconcile with the ALI approach set out before the case?

(M) Does either Cardozo's or Andrew's approach reconcile with RUPA's statement, in §409, of the duties of partners?

(N) Suppose Eldridge Gerry, wildly impressed with the success at the Bristol location, had asked Salmon to lease and develop a vacation property in the Bahamas. Does Meinhard get to share the opportunity? Must Salmon tell him about it?

 Dear Prof.: Punctilio? Abnegation? Benediction? Really?

Roll your eyes as you will, Justice Cardozo's paean to fiduciary duty provides some of the most-quoted language you will see in this or any other book on the subject of business associations.

Loyalty Obligations as to the Principal's Property and Confidences. Finally, the duty of loyalty requires the fiduciary not to use the beneficiary's property or confidences for personal benefit, and to keep the beneficiary's confidences secret even where disclosing them would be of no benefit to the fiduciary. *See* Re(3) §8.05; *cf.* RUPA §409(b)(1). Note the rule stated in comments to §8.05 that this duty survives termination so long as the agent retains property or confidences, and it seems likely that where the circumstances are right it could precede the relationship if such things were entrusted to a prospective fiduciary. (The circumstances would seem right for such a result if they suggested that the relationship was likely to come into being and both parties understood the beneficiary's expectation that the duty would be honored.) *See* Re(3) §8.01, comment c.

Note, too, that the duty to keep confidences can itself be the basis for an actionable conflict of interest. There may be times when a fiduciary represents two separate principals and learns a confidence from one that might be of material interest to the other, in which case the fiduciary is prohibited by Re(3) §8.05 from disclosing the first beneficiary's confidence, but might otherwise be under a duty under §8.11 to disclose it to the second beneficiary. While under §8.11(2) an agent is relieved of the disclosure duty where disclosure would violate a duty to someone else, §8.03, comment b points out that the agent's position in such a case "is not tenable . . . ." "[C]onsequently," it continues, "[the agent] must withdraw" from the representations, though it may be that the agent could withdraw from only one and thereby avoid the conflict. For example, in this hypothetical the agent could presumably withdraw from the second relationship, retain the first, and simply keep the first principal's secret. Common situations of this kind of conflict include the representation by an investment advisor of two businesses that are competing with one another, or representation by an attorney of two spouses in their estate planning.

D. Fiduciary Situations Requiring Disclosure

It probably bears repeating that the "duty of disclosure," such as it is, might really better be thought of as a particular manifestation of either the duty of care or the duty of loyalty, depending on the circumstances. Which duty is at issue in a given case depends on whether the failure to disclose was made in connection with a conflict of interest. If so, the duty of loyalty will control, and the fiduciary will bear the burden of showing fairness to the principal. If not, then the obligation to disclose is subject only to the fiduciary's duty of care. Note, incidentally, that in the agency context a particular Restatement provision governs the duty of care disclosure obligation. *See* Re(3) §8.11. Admittedly, on close reading, the rule appears not to state much other than that the agent's duty to disclose is a duty to take reasonable care under the circumstances, but §8.11 and the comments following set out a few technical points that are worth observing.

The following cases will explore a few aspects of the duty of loyalty disclosure obligation (as, incidentally, did *Meinhard v. Salmon*).

WALTER V. HOLIDAY INNS, INC.

United States Court of Appeals for the Third Circuit
985 F.2d 1232 (1993)

SLOVITER, Chief Judge.

Plaintiffs are several individuals and a corporation who formed a 50-50 partnership with Holiday Inns, Inc. (Holiday) in 1979 to develop and operate

Harrah's Marina Hotel and Casino in Atlantic City, New Jersey. In 1981, plaintiffs sold their 49% interest in the partnership to Holiday. In 1983, plaintiffs sold their remaining 1% interest to Holiday. In 1985, four years after the first sale, by which time the hotel/casino complex had become highly profitable, they filed this suit claiming that in the buy-out transaction Holiday committed common law fraud, violated federal securities laws, and breached the fiduciary duty it owed to plaintiffs. After plaintiffs presented their case, the district court granted Holiday's motion for judgment as a matter of law on the breach of fiduciary duty claim. *See* Walter v. Holiday Inns, Inc., 784 F. Supp. 1159 (D.N.J. 1992). At the conclusion of the trial, the jury decided for Holiday on the remaining claims. Plaintiffs appeal . . . .

I. FACTS AND PROCEDURAL HISTORY

In August 1978, shortly after New Jersey legalized gambling, the plaintiffs purchased a tract of land with the intent of developing a hotel and casino complex at a marina in Atlantic City. Plaintiffs then created two New Jersey corporations (L & M Walter Enterprises, Inc. and Bayfield Enterprises, Inc.) and had both entities form a general partnership known as Marina Associates. After looking for a suitable partner to develop the casino, plaintiffs sold Bayfield Enterprises to Holiday on January 30, 1979 and entered into a 50-50 Partnership Agreement with the hotel chain. Both parties agreed to make an initial capital contribution of $2 million each to the partnership business.

The partners successfully obtained a $75 million loan for the project from Midlantic National Bank, which later advanced an additional $20 million to the partnership. Construction commenced in early 1980 and proceeded at a rapid pace.

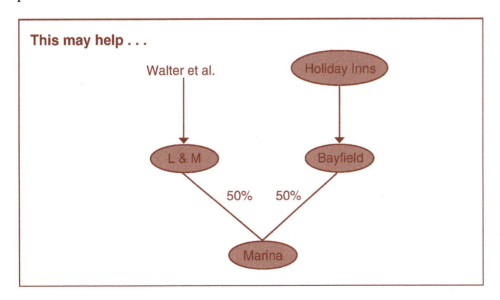

While the construction of the casino was progressing, the partners executed several documents that defined the nature of their relationship. Pursuant

JD/MBA: Dilution

"Dilution" can refer to a diminution in either the control or value of a person's interest in a firm. A person's interest can be diluted when new investors are brought in, or, as in *Walter*, for other reasons. In the case of a general partnership interest, dilution would not occur without the consent of the affected partner.

to a Memorandum of Understanding dated June 6, 1980, the partners agreed to advance in equal shares additional capital to the casino on an as-needed basis to cover project development (pre-opening) or operating (post-opening) cash shortfalls. If one partner was unable to meet its share, the other could advance the funds and then serve a written "cash call" letter on the non-contributing partner. The Memorandum provided that a failure to comply with a strict timetable for repayment of the cash call would result in a dilution of the non-contributing partner's interest in the casino, with the degree of dilution linked to the total amount of the cash call. The conditions for relief from dilution because of failure to meet a project development cash call were more formidable than those for an operating cash call.

A second Memorandum of Understanding dated June 20, 1980 set forth how the casino was to be managed. The day-to-day operations were turned over to Harrah's, Inc., a subsidiary of Holiday. The more important management and financing decisions remained with the partnership's Executive Committee, which was composed of two Holiday executives and two of the plaintiffs, Louis Walter and Lance Walter. The Executive Committee's decision-making power included, inter alia, overseeing the completion of the casino's construction and development, approving capital expenditures for replacement and expansion that exceeded 4% of total revenues for any year, the creation of long-term debt, and the creation of short-term debt for working capital in excess of $2 million.

The hotel and casino complex opened its doors to the public on November 22, 1980, before all of the construction was completed. However, construction costs rose substantially over budget, and financial concerns mounted. At a meeting of the Executive Committee in January 1981, the plaintiffs were presented with financial projections for the casino. Walter Haybert, the Chief Financial Officer of Marina Associates, presented "a 'worst case' projection of profit and loss for 1981 with related projections of monthly cash flow." He explained the need to substantially supplement working capital in the project development budget.

Shortly thereafter, two separate cash call letters were issued formally demanding that plaintiffs make equity contributions to the project. The first letter advised that an equity contribution of $18.8 million was required to cover expenditures in connection with the project development budget (plaintiffs' half being $9.4 million). The second letter, which cited Marina Associates' negative cash flow, was a call for cash increments due from November 1980 to May 1981 totaling $15.7 million (plaintiffs' share being $7.85) to cover operating shortfalls for the project.

Plaintiffs determined not to supply their share of the funds requested, allegedly relying on Holiday's pessimistic predictions about the financial prospects of the Marina. As a result, Holiday advanced its own funds to cover the shortfalls, and plaintiffs' partnership interest was diluted pursuant to the formula specified in the partners' prior agreements.

At the same January 1981 Executive Committee meeting, the partners also approved an Information Flow Agreement that specified the items of partnership financial data, such as financial statements and internal audit reports, that would be provided to the plaintiffs.

The financial situation presented at the January 1981 Executive Committee Meeting apparently precipitated plaintiffs' efforts to sell their interest in the casino to outside investors. However, there is some evidence in the record that in 1980 plaintiffs had approached Holiday and others to purchase plaintiffs' partnership interest. After the January 1981 meeting, negotiations with Holiday resumed at plaintiffs' request. They continued until the parties agreed on the terms of a buy-out on May 9, 1981, whereby Holiday agreed to acquire plaintiffs' 49% interest in the partnership for payments to plaintiffs of $1.75 million per year for twenty years, which plaintiffs calculate had a present value of $10.9 million. In July 1983, plaintiffs sold their remaining 1% interest to Holiday for an additional $1.8 million.

Sometime after the 1981 buy-out, the casino became a profitable enterprise. Under New Jersey law, the casino's profits and losses were a matter of public record and plaintiffs implicitly concede that they were aware of the highly profitable operations of Marina from 1982 to 1984. Nevertheless, plaintiffs did not challenge the buy-out transaction until this suit was brought in 1985. In that period, they sold their remaining 1% interest to Holiday and continued to do business with Holiday elsewhere. Louis Walter claims he was prompted to file this action by a newspaper article in which Donald Trump, the owner of another casino, suggested that Holiday had taken advantage of the plaintiffs in connection with the 1981 buy-out . . . .

. . . [T]he essence of plaintiffs' claims is that Holiday failed to provide them with certain information that they needed to negotiate the buy-out transaction from an equal position with Holiday. They also assert that Holiday had designed a "cash call strategy" to force the buy-out on terms unfavorable to plaintiffs . . . .

> **JD/MBA: Present Value**
>
> The court refers to plaintiffs' claim that their buyout agreement with Holiday had a "present value." The right to receive some payment in the future is said to have a "present" value, and the present value of a future payment is always assumed to be smaller than its face value, because we assume that a person could invest some smaller amount of money today, at some rate of interest or some rate of return, and have more money in hand by the time that future payment comes due than the initial amount invested. Accordingly, we say a dollar in hand today is more valuable than one received in the future. Just how much more valuable is the function of the assumed rate of return on investment. There are a variety of online and other present value calculators available, and we discuss it further in the online Supplement.

II. DISCUSSION

A. Asserted Fiduciary Duty

. . . We . . . focus . . . on the heart of this case—the nature of the obligations, if any, owed by Holiday to plaintiffs in connection with the negotiations leading to Holiday's buy-out of plaintiffs' interest . . . .

Since the mid-19th century, New Jersey courts have recognized that in order to set aside the sale of a partnership interest on the ground of breach of

Connections: The Federal Securities Laws

TSC Indus. is a case involving the federal securities laws and states the definition of "materiality" that applies throughout those laws (discussed at more length in Part 7). In fact, the *Walter* plaintiffs also made federal securities claims.

fiduciary duty, "it is essential that the misrepresentation or concealment should be . . . in regard to a fact material to the contract." . . . Even if Holiday had some fiduciary obligation to plaintiffs and Holiday had the burden of proving that this duty was not breached, if the evidence plaintiffs produced at trial showed that under the circumstances none of the alleged misstatements or omissions would have been material to their decision to sell their partnership interest to Holiday or that Holiday had no obligation to do more than it did, we must affirm.

B. Applicable Legal Principles

Materiality cannot be determined in a vacuum. In business transactions, what is material must be evaluated in the context in which the statements or omissions occurred. *See* TSC Indus., Inc. v. Northway, Inc., 426 U.S. 438, 449 (1976) (omitted fact is material if there is a "substantial likelihood that, under all the circumstances, the omitted fact would have assumed actual significance in the deliberations of the reasonable shareholder"). This is true as well in partnership buy-outs. 2 Alan R. Bromberg & Larry E. Ribstein, BROMBERG & RIBSTEIN ON PARTNERSHIP §6.06, at 6:64 (1988) (in partnership buy-out transactions, "[e]ven if a partner was subject to a duty of full disclosure and failed to disclose every fact in connection with a particular transaction, there is no liability unless the nondisclosed facts were such as might be expected to have induced action or forbearance by the other partners—that is, were material").

As a general proposition courts and commentators have recognized that in determining whether a fiduciary duty has been breached by a material misstatement or by a failure to disclose a material fact, the sophistication of the complaining partner and the degree of access to partnership records are key factors to be considered . . . .

As leading commentators in the law of partnerships have stated, "The extent of the duty to disclose depends on the circumstances of the individual case . . . [and] may depend on the degree to which the nondisclosing partner managed the business and thus was familiar with the relevant information, and on the knowledgeability or degree of expertise of the party to whom the duty of disclosure is owed."

The plaintiffs stipulated that at the relevant times "each of the plaintiffs was a highly sophisticated and experienced investor," and the record amply bears that out. In light of this concession we need only examine the extent of plaintiffs' access to the partnership records.

Plaintiffs contend that they were passive partners while Holiday was the managing partner with exclusive control over all financial information concerning the casino. If that were in fact the case, we believe that New Jersey would hold Holiday to a more stringent fiduciary standard in connection with the buy-out than if the partners bargained from equal positions. However, we find insufficient evidence in the record to support plaintiffs' factual assertion, even viewing the facts in the light most favorable to the plaintiffs.

Those portions of the record that plaintiffs have cited to support their claim of passivity reveal that although the day-to-day operations of the casino were under Holiday's control through its subsidiary, Harrah's, Inc., the most important decisions regarding the planning and financial management remained with the partnership's Executive Committee on which plaintiffs served equally with defendants . . . . The record also shows that plaintiffs requested and received volumes of financial data pursuant to the Information Flow Agreement that provided them with ample data by which to assess the partnership's financial situation . . . .

In fact, plaintiffs' access to the partnership's records was specifically assured by Section 5.1 of the 1979 Partnership Agreement which states: The Partnership will at all times maintain, at the Hotel, complete and accurate books of account . . . . Such books and records shall be made available for inspection and copying by the Partners, or their duly authorized representatives, during business hours.

Plaintiffs produced no evidence that they were ever denied access to any information on the casino's past or present financial situation. On the contrary, there is evidence that they were specifically notified that their independent auditors could examine the partnership records . . . . We therefore proceed on the basis that plaintiffs had unrestricted access to all past and current information regarding the partnership and its financial operations . . . .

With these general principles in mind, we proceed with an item by item analysis of the specific facts that plaintiffs claim would have been material to their decision to sell their half share of the casino to Holiday. We do so mindful of our prior assertion that "[o]nly when the disclosures or omissions are so clearly unimportant that reasonable minds could not differ should the ultimate issue of materiality be decided as a matter of law." Craftmatic Sec. Litig. v. Kraftsow, 890 F.2d 628, 641 (3d Cir. 1989) . . . .

C. The Alleged Misrepresentations and Nondisclosures

1. The Boxer Report

Plaintiffs have devoted considerable argument to Holiday's failure to provide them with copies of the financial projections contained in the Boxer Report. The Report, prepared prior to the 1981 buy-out, was a 35 year financial forecast prepared by the defendants, based on the current financial statements and projected growth, which projected large cash flows and high profits for the hotel/casino project. It also contained two ten-year projections of substantial, albeit differing, profits.

To support their assertion that this was an omission material to their buy-out decision, plaintiffs point to Sturman's testimony that "the Holiday projections would have been very, very meaningful to me[.] I would recognize that it is a projection but it would have been the best guess of a very sophisticated gaming entity and . . . so I would have given them some credibility." . . .

As for the relevance of the Boxer Report to the plaintiffs' decision, nothing indicates that plaintiffs would have placed any greater reliance on the Boxer projections than on the numerous other forecasts that Holiday had previously disclosed or that plaintiffs themselves had prepared through their independent auditors. Herbert Sturman and Charles Solomonson, a senior Vice President and Chief Financial Officer at Holiday, testified to Louis Walter's disdain for financial projections, such as the two 10-year financial projections that Holiday had previously commissioned in the spring of 1979 and which it provided to plaintiffs. Moreover, the Boxer Report was simply a projection based on the volumes of financial information already in plaintiffs' possession. Plaintiffs have not shown why the forecast prepared for them by their independent auditor in June 1980 was not an equally reliable predictor.

Of course, we recognize that every negotiator would like to have all the information upon which his or her counterpart is proceeding, but that is a far cry from materiality in the legal sense. That depends, instead, on whether plaintiffs had access to the raw data upon which they could make their own projections. The record shows they did . . . .

In light of the applicable law and all of the evidence presented, we hold that no reasonable jury could have concluded that Holiday's failure to make the Boxer Report available to plaintiffs was a breach of any fiduciary duty owed by Holiday.

2. Failure to Disclose 1981 Cash Flow Projection

We reach a similar result with respect to plaintiffs' assertion that Holiday failed to disclose a 1981 cash flow projection for the casino that was prepared by Marina Associates and presented to the Gaming Committee of Holiday's Board of Directors in January 1981 . . . .

3. Transaction Audit Review Group Report

Plaintiffs contend that Holiday failed to disclose its Transaction Audit Review Group Report, which was completed on May 28, 1981. This review was undertaken to establish the reasons for the multi-million dollar project development cost overrun. The Report revealed that mismanagement by casino employees under Holiday's control was a significant cause of the cost overruns that precipitated Marina Associates' cash calls on plaintiffs. Plaintiffs claim that they would have had a stronger negotiating position against Holiday had they known of the Report, and could have resisted Holiday's dilution threats . . . .

Even if we infer, as plaintiffs ask us to do, that the study and analysis were done before the buy-out, plaintiffs had the opportunity to discover the relevant facts regarding the cost overruns but failed to avail themselves of this opportunity. Thus, they have no basis to complain that the Report was not provided to them when it was completed after the buy-out . . . .

We conclude therefore that the record fails to support plaintiffs' argument that Holiday made any material misrepresentations or omitted providing material facts that it had a duty to disclose to plaintiffs. Thus we conclude that the district court did not err in granting judgment as a matter of law on plaintiffs' claim of breach of fiduciary duty . . . .

> ■ **Think about this:**
>
> *(O)* What facts most clearly distinguish this case from *Meinhard v. Salmon*? Or is the court simply applying a different standard?
>
> *(P)* What would you advise a client in Holiday's position to disclose to a partner from whom a partnership interest is being purchased?

As always, when you are presented with more than one case on the same topic, think carefully about what the later one adds to the topic.

APPLETREE SQUARE I LIMITED PARTNERSHIP V. INVESTMARK, INC.

Minnesota Court of Appeals
494 N.W.2d 889 (1993)

CRIPPEN, Judge.

Appletree Square One Limited Partnership purchased a commercial office building which is contaminated with asbestos fireproofing materials. Purchasers sued the sellers on various theories of fraud for failing to disclose the presence and hazards of asbestos. Purchasers appeal from summary judgment dismissing each of their claims. We reverse.

FACTS

Appletree Square I Limited Partnership was formed September 21, 1981, to purchase and operate One Appletree Square, a 15-story office building. The partnership was organized under the 1976 Uniform Limited Partnership Act, MINN. STAT. §§322A.01-.87 (1980). Appellants represent the partnership and its affiliates who purchased the property (purchasers). Respondents represent the builders and sellers of the property (sellers), who held interests in the [purchaser limited] partnership when sale transactions occurred.

This suit is based on two transactions. The building sale occurred in 1981. In 1985, a further acquisition was made by sale of a 25 percent interest in the Appletree partnership. An affiliate of the purchasers, CRI, represented them in both transactions; CRI is a real estate syndication firm. During negotiations for the sale of the property in 1981, CRI wrote a letter to sellers requesting "any information that you have not already sent to us which would be material to our investors' participation in this development." In response, CRI was told to inspect the building and the records, because the sellers "ha[d] no way of knowing what information would be material to your investors' participation."

In 1986, the purchasers learned that the structural steel in the building had been coated with asbestos-based fireproofing, which was deteriorating and releasing fibers. The cost of abatement was estimated at ten million dollars.

In their subsequent suit, the purchasers alleged that the sellers were liable for failing to disclose the presence and danger of asbestos. The purchasers sought recovery of damages under theories of breach of contract; violation of the Limited Partnership Act, MINN. STAT. §322A.17 (1990); violation of the Deceptive Trade Practices Act, MINN. STAT. §325D.44 (1990); fraud and misrepresentation; and negligent misrepresentation . . . .

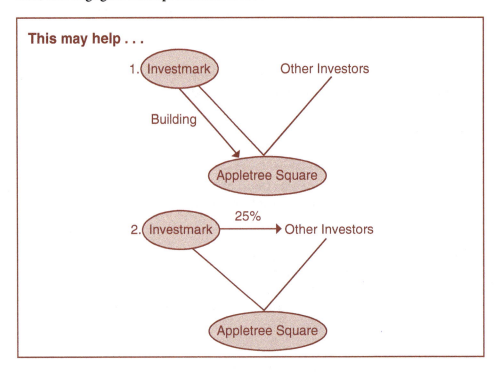

ANALYSIS

This appeal turns on whether respondents had a fiduciary duty to disclose to appellants the presence and danger of asbestos . . . .

1. Common Law Duty of Disclosure

Absent a fiduciary relationship, one party to a transaction has "no duty to disclose material facts to the other." . . . In this case, appellants and respondents were partners in a limited partnership. The relationship of partners is fiduciary and partners are held to high standards of integrity in their dealings with each other . . . . Parties in a fiduciary relationship must disclose material facts to each other . . . . Where a fiduciary relationship exists, silence may constitute fraud . . . . Under the common law, respondents had a duty to disclose information regarding asbestos if they knew about it.

Uniform Limited Partnership Act and Duties of Disclosure

The trial court held that the Uniform Limited Partnership Act changed the common law duties of disclosure. MINN. STAT. §322A.28(2) (1990) states that limited partners have the right, "upon reasonable demand," to obtain information from the general partners. This statute mirrors the disclosure requirement in the Uniform Partnership Act and should be interpreted similarly. *See* MINN. STAT. §323.19 (1990). The trial court held that because appellants did not demand information about asbestos, respondents had no obligation to disclose the information.

The trial court's holding is contradicted by a proper interpretation of the disclosure statute. MINN. STAT. §322A.28(2) addresses the narrow duty of partners to respond to requests for information. It does not negate a partner's broad common law duty to disclose all material facts . . . .

2. Knowledge of Sellers

The evidence here is sufficient to create a genuine fact issue of whether respondents knew of the presence of asbestos in the building and knew before the 1985 transaction of the danger now associated with this use of the substance . . . .

Justifiable Reliance

The trial court determined that any alleged breach of a partner's duty to disclose was defeated by evidence that the purchasers inadequately investigated the transaction. The trial court held as a matter of law that appellants were not justified in relying on respondents to disclose the presence and danger of asbestos. The court based its decision on the fact that respondents told appellants to conduct their own investigation and on its finding that appellants were sophisticated buyers. A fiduciary's duty is defined "with reference to the experience and intelligence of the person to whom the duty is owed." . . .

The record here does not permit the holding as a matter of law that appellants were not justified in relying on respondents. The sellers designed and built the building and thus may have had superior knowledge about the asbestos. The buyers' expertise appears to have been in the area of finance and marketing. In an affidavit, respondent's former vice president who had supervised the construction of the building stated:

> CRI and its affiliates were involved in only the financial aspects of development and they would have looked to Ellerbe companies for information regarding asbestos or any other information about construction materials or hazards in One Appletree Square.

The unique qualifications of the buyers and sellers in this case create questions of fact regarding the relative sophistication of the parties. The factfinder must weigh this evidence to determine whether the buyers' reliance on disclosures was reasonable.

There is no compelling evidence that either the building specifications or a visual inspection of the building should have revealed the asbestos. Moreover, although the purchasers had partnership authority over management of the building prior to the 1985 partnership interest buyout, respondents were managers in fact from 1972 (when the building was constructed) to 1985. To discover asbestos on their own, appellants would have had to know enough to ask about it or know enough to have various building materials tested.

Finally, the fact that respondents told appellants to investigate did not make appellants' reliance unreasonable as a matter of law. Respondents' statement did not specifically tell appellants not to rely on them. Moreover, even if respondents had told appellants not to rely on them, that statement would not necessarily make reliance unreasonable. Evidence in the record permits a finding that respondents had superior knowledge and knew appellants did not know about the asbestos. These are fact questions which must be answered to determine whether respondents neglected their fiduciary duty to inform appellants . . . .

■ **Think about this:**

(Q) What would make reliance on the sellers in *Appletree Square* unreasonable?

(R) Is the *Appletree Square* court applying the same standard as the court in *Walter v. Holiday Inns*?

E. Waiver

 What does it look like?

Check the online Supplement for the following sample documents that are relevant to this section:

■ Provisions from a partnership agreement limiting the duty of loyalty
■ An excerpt from an attorney's engagement letter purportedly waiving conflicts

It is possible in any fiduciary relationship for the parties to limit the fiduciary's duties by agreement. Moreover, they can limit *any* fiduciary duties—if they like, they can limit the fiduciary's responsibility for inadvertent losses (i.e., limit the duty of care), give the fiduciary some freedom to act on his own pecuniary behalf (i.e., limit the duty of loyalty), or free the fiduciary from the burden of keeping the beneficiary apprised of material facts (i.e., limit the care-based disclosure obligation). Fiduciary waivers can be critically important in some relationships or for some fiduciaries, because fiduciary liability is so fact-sensitive and so dependent on the sensibilities of a given trier of fact that it can be very hard to predict. Lawyers, for example, especially those practicing in large firms, often find it useful to seek waiver of conflicts of interest, simply because the possibilities of conflict become hard to predict when many lawyers with many clients are involved. Quite frequently, lawyers ask their clients to waive potential conflicts or other fiduciary risks even where they believe the merits of any potential problem would be weak, as pure prophylactic.

However, waiver or consent is also subject to limits. Many courts say that while they will tolerate (that is, enforce) some fiduciary waivers, they will not allow the parties to utterly remove the fiduciary character of an otherwise fiduciary relationship. They also will often inquire into the degree to which the beneficiary was informed of issues relevant to the waiver, whether it was given freely, and whether it is consistent with public policy.

More to the Story: Careful Definitions of Scope

Bear in mind that carefully defining the scope of a relationship may be as good as—or better than—a waiver. Fiduciary duties are, after all, owed only within that scope. Recall that then-Judge Cardozo was willing to assume that Salmon owed Meinhard no duty with respect to a leasing opportunity "at a location far removed."

 Time Out for PR: Waiver and Prospective Waiver

American Bar Association Model Rule 1.8(h) has this to say relative to the subject of malpractice waivers:

> A lawyer shall not:
> (1) make an agreement prospectively limiting the lawyer's liability to a client for malpractice unless the client is independently represented in making the agreement; or
> (2) settle a claim or potential claim for such liability with an unrepresented client or former client unless that person is advised in writing of the desirability of seeking and is given a reasonable opportunity to seek the advice of independent legal counsel in connection therewith.

There is a different rule—1.7(b)—dealing with waivers of conflict of interest:

> Notwithstanding the existence of a concurrent conflict of interest under paragraph (a), a lawyer may represent a client if:
> (1) the lawyer reasonably believes that the lawyer will be able to provide competent and diligent representation to each affected client;
> (2) the representation is not prohibited by law;
> (3) the representation does not involve the assertion of a claim by one client against another client represented by the lawyer in the same litigation or other proceeding before a tribunal; and
> (4) each affected client gives informed consent, confirmed in writing.

It is important to note that if a client challenges a prospective conflict waiver, the waiver quite frequently is struck down as being insufficiently informed.

1. Agency

In the case of agency law, the Restatement draws a strong and explicit distinction between waivers of care and waivers of loyalty, and puts much tighter limits on the latter. Under Re(3) §8.06, a principal can consent to conduct that would otherwise violate the loyalty duties under §§8.01-8.05, but only if the fiduciary, when it sought consent, dealt in good faith, made the disclosure required in §8.06(1)(a)(ii), and otherwise behaved fairly. Moreover, under §8.06(1)(b), principals are usually prohibited from giving very general or blanket waivers to loyalty breaches. They may only consent either to one specific act by the agent, or to a specific class of such actions that could be reasonably expected in the ordinary course of the agent's duties. Note a few particular curlicues on this rule. First, after-the-fact waivers are not only permitted, but they appear to be preferred for reasons stated in §8.06, comment b. Second, in fiduciary litigation the agent will bear the burden of proving the requisite elements of valid waiver under §8.06. Finally, an agent who seeks waiver of a conflict that would be prohibited under §8.03 must disclose it in sufficient time to allow the principal to judge whether to proceed with the transaction in question and whether to engage a different agent.

If thou faint in the day of adversity thy strength is small.

THE BIBLE, PROVERBS, 24:10

Note also that there is one special case of loyalty waiver contained in §8.06. Strictly speaking, the Restatement's explicit conflict-of-interest rule, which appears in §8.03, only bars the agent from standing in a position that is *adverse* to the principal and is adverse *in a transaction connected with the agency relationship.* "Adversity" is defined in comment c to that section to mean either that the agent has a "substantial economic interest" in a party opposed to the principal in a given transaction (or, by definition, *is* the party opposed to the principal), or that the opposing party is the agent's close friend or relative. The clear meaning of "opposed to" in this definition is that the other party is either an opposing party in litigation or is on the other side of some commercial or similar transaction. In other words, §8.03 relates only to specific situations of strong adversity. By contrast, §8.06(2) requires that any time an agent serves more than one principal, regardless of who the principals are and what their interests may be, the agent must disclose to each of them that the agent represents other principals and such other facts as may "reasonably affect the principal's judgment."

Waivers of care are more permissive under the Restatement. Section 8.08, which contains the Restatement's basic statement of the standard of care, begins with the simple clarification that it is "[s]ubject to any agreement with the principal . . . ." The comments following point out that §8.08 permits general, blanket modifications of the "[reasonable] care, competence and diligence" standard, and permits them to be made without the disclosures that would be required under §8.06(1)(b).

2. Partnerships and Other Unincorporated Entities: The Law as It Was, Under UPA (1914)

In the law of partnerships, RUPA has worked a fairly major innovation in the case of fiduciary waiver. It had been clear under the UPA that at least some waivers were acceptable, but the statute itself was more or less silent on the issue. Most individual provisions of the UPA stated or implied that they could be modified by agreement, but the UPA actually said very little about fiduciary duties. A few duties were explicitly mentioned and were, by their terms, non-waivable. The rest, however, was up to the courts.

Most UPA jurisdictions imposed some additional case law limits on fiduciary waiver. Most courts would not allow partners to "destroy the fiduciary character" of a partnership through general waivers of all duty, and they also guarded their prerogative to disregard those waivers they considered contrary to public policy. A court desiring to take such a course has basically two options. First, the court can argue that any fiduciary waiver, since it is, after all, a term in a contract, must be interpreted in light of the implied covenant of good faith that is read into all contracts. In the law of contracts, the covenant of good faith requires that a party purporting to interpret a particular contract provision (such as a fiduciary waiver) must interpret it in a way that remains fair to the other party. Second, a court can read a fiduciary waiver narrowly, on the theory that where there is any ambiguity in the meaning of such a waiver, public policy requires the narrow reading.

 Dear Prof.: Please remind me why we are still talking about the UPA.

Around 40 states have adopted the RUPA, but around 10 have not (Louisiana has adopted neither, but its partnership law has elements of both). In addition, some states adopting RUPA have opted to keep some aspects of the UPA.

In the case of fiduciary waiver, an additional reason to pay some attention to the case law as it existed under UPA is that a number of the leading cases happened to be decided under that statute, and continue to exert influence.

Probably one of the better known decisions refusing to enforce a broad fiduciary waiver is the *Appletree Square* case, excerpted above. The partnership agreement provided that the general partners would "provide the partners with all information that reasonably may be requested." Again, in that case both the buyers and the sellers of a piece of commercial realty happened to hold partnership interests in a partnership formed to manage the property. The sellers, despite their fiduciary status, failed to disclose that the building was contaminated with asbestos. Under the partnership agreement, the general partners were required only to "provide the partners with all information that may reasonably be requested," and because the limited partners never explicitly requested information about asbestos or other environmental burdens, defendants argued that they were under no duty to disclose it. In frequently quoted language, the court disagreed:

> Partners may change their common law and statutory duties by incorporating such changes in their partnership agreement. *See* MINN. STAT. §322A.33 . . . . However, where the major purpose of a contract clause is to shield wrongdoers from liability, the clause will be set aside as against public policy . . . . Additionally, while "partners are free to vary many aspects of their relationship . . . they are not free to destroy its fiduciary character." . . .
>
> To hold that partners may replace their broad duty of disclosure with a narrow duty to render information upon demand would destroy the fiduciary character of their relationship, and it would also invite fraud. Unless partners knew what questions to ask, they would have no right to know material information about the business. In this case, if respondents knew the building was contaminated with asbestos and if they reasonably should have known their partners did not know about the asbestos, they may have breached their fiduciary duty of disclosure . . . .

Appletree Square I Limited Partnership v. Investmark, Inc., 494 N.W.2d 889, 893 (Minn. Ct. App. 1993). *Labovitz v. Dolan*, which also appeared earlier in this chapter, contained another well-known disavowal of a fiduciary provision. There a limited partnership agreement provided that the general partner held "exclusive and complete discretion in the management and control of the business," and further that "in his sole discretion [he could] determine the availability of Cash Flow for distribution to partners . . . ." However, on the plaintiffs' allegations that defendant Dolan had used this discretion to coerce them economically in selling their interests to him at depressed prices, the court showed little sympathy for Dolan's waiver arguments. The court wrote:

> It is no answer . . . that partners have the right to establish among themselves their rights, duties and obligations, as though the exercise of that right releases, waives or delimits somehow, the high fiduciary duty owed to them by a general partner . . . . Dolan's sole discretion . . . was encumbered by a supreme fiduciary duty of fairness, honesty, good faith and loyalty to his partners. Language in an agreement such as "sole discretion" does not metamorphose the document into an unrestricted license to engage in self-dealing at the expense of those to whom the managing partner owes such a duty. Defendants cite no authority, and we find none, for the proposition that there can be an a priori waiver of fiduciary duties in a partnership . . . .

Labovitz v. Dolan, 545 N.E.2d 304, 310 (Ill. Ct. App. 1989).

Other courts, however, were much more tolerant of waiver, some apparently willing to allow partners to do away with fiduciary duties altogether. A leading case to that effect is Exxon Corp. v. Burglin, 4 F.3d 1294 (5th Cir. 1993). There, defendant Exxon had been general partner in a limited partnership that owned oil and gas leases on land in Alaska. During the existence of the limited partnership, Exxon learned of the discovery of significant oil resources under the land, but disclosed to the limited partners (all individual persons) only that it was "encouraged" by ongoing exploration. Some time later, but before oil production on the property, Exxon and the limited partners agreed to a purchase by Exxon of their limited partnership shares. Exxon offered to allow the limited partners to seek outside valuation of their interests or, in the alternative, to wait and see how much oil would actually be produced, but they declined. Once drilling began, it became clear that the value of the limited partnership interests was dramatically greater than what Exxon had paid, and there was no apparent dispute that Exxon knew or could have predicted as much when it purchased them.

The partnership agreement limited Exxon's duties. As to the disclosure claim raised by plaintiffs, it provided that while Exxon owed each limited partner an annual report of "nonconfidential information" relevant to the value of their shares, it said that "no Limited Partner shall have the right to any confidential information concerning the Leases." The agreement, according to the court, gave Exxon sole discretion to determine what information was "confidential," in the following language: "[T]he General Partner shall not be obligated to furnish any information concerning subsurface structure, reserves or other information concerning the Leases which the General Partner believes would be in the best interest of the Partnership or of the General Partner to be kept confidential."

Applying Alaska law, the court first noted that "[t]he Partnership Agreement was negotiated by highly sophisticated parties who bargained for the terms of the agreement at arm's length with the assistance of counsel," and that because, on the court's view, "the terms of the Partnership Agreement do not violate public policy and are not illegal or unconscionable," the only question was "whether Exxon's actions were in accordance with the provisions of that agreement." The court found that they were, and also explicitly held that Exxon's actions did not even violate the duty of good faith and fair dealing.

3. The Somewhat New World of RUPA §105

RUPA adopted an innovation meant to clear up all this uncertainty. RUPA §105 lists *all* provisions that are non-waivable, throughout the *entire* RUPA. That is, it lists not only those fiduciary duties that are non-waivable, but all RUPA provisions that are non-waivable. Every single other statutory provision throughout RUPA may therefore be modified or waived by the parties. Section 105(c)(6) forbids the elimination of the contractual obligation of good faith and fair dealing (but does permit the partnership agreement to prescribe standards, if not manifestly unreasonable, by which the performance of the obligation is to be measured). Section 105(c)(5) prohibits the alteration or elimination of the duty of loyalty or the duty of care, except as otherwise provided in §105(d). Section 105(d)(3), however, provides that, unless manifestly unreasonable, the partnership agreement may:

(A) alter or eliminate the aspects of the duty of loyalty stated in Section 409(b);

(B) identify specific types or categories of activities that do not violate the duty of loyalty; (C) alter the duty of care, but may not authorize conduct involving bad faith, willful or intentional misconduct, or knowing violation of law; and (D) alter or eliminate any other fiduciary duty.

The cross-referenced section, §409(b), states that the duty of loyalty *includes* the duty not to usurp partnership opportunities, the duty to avoid conflicts of interest in dealing with the partnership, and the duty to refrain from competing with the partnership. A comment to §409(b) observes:

> UPA (1997) §404 [a predecessor to §409] had deviated substantially from UPA (1914) by purporting to codify all fiduciary duties owed by partners. This approach had a number of problems. Most notably, the exhaustive list of fiduciary duties left no room for the fiduciary duty owed by partners to each other—i.e., "the punctilio of an honor the most sensitive"). Meinhard v. Salmon, 164 N.E. 545, 546 (N.Y. 1928).

It is clear, then, that §409(b)'s list of duties is not exhaustive. Because §105(d)(3) permits limits on those aspects of the duty of loyalty "stated in Section 409(b)," one might think that, under the most recent version of the RUPA, the duty of loyalty owed *among partners* cannot be altered or eliminated. This is not the case, however. A comment to §105(d)(3) clarifies that any aspect of the duty of loyalty not stated in §409(b) is an "other fiduciary duty" referred to in §105(d)(3)(D).

The comments to §105(d)(3) also make it clear that "a properly drafted partnership agreement may substantially alter and even eliminate fiduciary duties." There are, however, two important limitations.

> First, arrangements subject to this subsection may not be "manifestly unreasonable." . . . Second, the partnership agreement may not transform the relationship *inter se* partners and the partnership into an entirely arm's length arrangement. For example, displacement of fiduciary duties is effective only to the extent that the displacement is stated clearly and with particularity. This rule is fundamental in the jurisprudence of fiduciary duty.

Section 105(e) provides the standard for determining (as a matter of law) when a term of a partnership agreement is "manifestly unreasonable." "The court . . . may invalidate the term only if, in light of the purposes and business of the partnership, it is readily apparent that: (A) the objective of the term is unreasonable; or (B) the term is an unreasonable means to achieve the term's objective."

It is worth noting that a few jurisdictions have gone farther than RUPA §105, and have made fiduciary duties completely optional. Notably, Delaware's general partnership statute now permits "the limitation or elimination of any and all liabilities for breach . . . of duties (including fiduciary duties) . . . ." Del. Gen. P'ship L. §15-103(f).

> ■ **Think about this:**
>
> *(S)* Under what circumstances would you advise a client to enter into a general partnership agreement eliminating all liabilities of the partners to one another?
>
> *(T)* Suppose Josef and Jen both live in a state other than Delaware. They enter into a general partnership agreement calling for the elimination of liability to one another and stipulate they would like the agreement to be governed by Delaware law. If there subsequently is litigation in their home state over whether the elimination of liability was effective, what result would you expect?

F. Remedies and Procedural Issues

1. In General

Fiduciary duties are normally enforced by after-the-fact civil litigation for money damages. In a few specific cases, special remedies rules apply, mainly in cases in which the beneficiary is entitled to recover the entire value of some ill-gotten gain without proof of injury. One of these is imposition of a constructive trust until the gain in question (frequently a business opportunity) is relinquished to the beneficiary.

Punitive damages are available where the conduct is "outrageous, because of the defendant's evil motive or his reckless indifference to the rights of others." Restatement (Second) of the Law of Torts §908 (1979).

There are, however, some special remedies rules. In the agency context, a principal may seek injunction to prevent ongoing fiduciary breach and may recover secret profits skimmed away by a disloyal agent, including by using the principal's property without paying for its value. (In the latter case, the agent can in effect be forced to pay rent for such use; *see* Re(3) §8.01, comment d(1).) A principal also may use a fiduciary breach as a basis to avoid paying compensation for any work performed during the period of breach. These issues are each elaborated in Re(3) §8.01, comment d. Fiduciary breach, as it happens, is always a "material" breach of any contract between principal and agent, *see* Re(3)§8.01, comment d(1), so the principal always may use it as a reason to terminate the contract.

2. Two Special Partnership Remedial Rules: The Accounting and the Accounting Rule

Partners are entitled by statute to a special procedure designed to protect their interests: the "accounting." An "accounting" is an equitable proceeding in which a court examines the financial affairs of the firm and renders judgment as to all debts owing among partners. Because an accounting resolves *all* issues within the firm, and because it will often require valuation of speculative assets, rights, and liabilities, the proceeding tends to be drawn out, unpredictable, and expensive.

Nevertheless, RUPA §410(b) explicitly preserves the right of any partner to seek an accounting, apparently at any time.

A second special partnership feature is an antiquated rule no longer followed even in most of the remaining UPA jurisdictions, and done away with completely in RUPA: the "accounting rule." The courts at common law had long handled internal partnership disputes very cautiously. Under the accounting rule, as it came to be known, courts refused to entertain individual claims between partners, whether for fiduciary breach or anything else, on a case-by-case basis. Instead, a partner asserting any claim against another partner that related to the partnership business had to seek a full accounting. The rationales commonly stated were (1) that since the affairs of the partnership and the partners' mutual obligations could be quite complex, one could not really know who owed what to whom without a full accounting, and (2) that a suit between partners was confusingly like a person suing himself. In any case, the rule could be very cumbersome in practice, especially where only simple claims were at issue or where the partnership itself was complex.

The rule sometimes produced not just cost and inconvenience, but harsh unfairness. In particular, sometimes the personal creditor of a partner would take an assignment of the partner's rights against the firm in satisfaction of its claims. But if the partnership then failed to pay, a court following the traditional rule might refuse any remedy at all. On the one hand, the court might require that the right could only be enforced through an accounting, since it is a right among partners, but on the other hand that under the plain language of the UPA, third-party creditors lacked standing to seek accounting because they are not partners.

For all these reasons, the accounting rule has now been rejected by a majority of jurisdictions. The rule is explicitly rejected by RUPA §410(b) and comments thereto.

■ **Think about this:**

(U) Review the court's remedy in *Meinhard v. Salmon*. What other possibilities might you have suggested? What would you expect Meinhard and Salmon to do going forward?

Test Yourself

Assume Applicability of the Restatement (Third) of Agency and the Revised Uniform Partnership Act

1. X, Y, and Z form the XYZ partnership. They establish their firm through a written partnership agreement, but it contains very little except their agreement to form the business for profit with themselves as members.

The business is engaged in oil and gas exploration, and its main activity is identifying new oil and gas deposits and selling them to oil companies. The partners, however, have made money in other ways, such as investment in securities and loans to other promising start-ups. Though they didn't provide for it explicitly in their agreement, they each understand that they will share all management responsibilities equally. Z recently invested a significant amount of the firm's liquid cash in publicly traded securities, which ultimately lost a lot of money, and the loss of which turned out to be of no tax benefit to the firm.

X and Y sue Z for the entire amount of the loss. This lawsuit most likely will:

a. Succeed, because Z will be unable to prove the fairness of the transaction.
b. Succeed, because of the substantive standard of care that applies to partners' managerial decisions.
c. Succeed, because this particular sort of transaction would require specific authorization of the other partners.
d. Fail.

2. On the facts of the previous question, assume instead that Z invested the money in a chain of ice cream stores, indulging a childhood dream of entering that business. His action:

a. Breached his fiduciary duty of care.
b. Breached his fiduciary duty of loyalty.
c. Did not breach a duty, though he will be personally responsible for any losses.
d. Did not breach a duty, and he will bear no personal liability for it.

3. Miguel was hired as chief executive of Greenwood, LLC, a prominent Chicago real-estate development firm. Greenwood is a manager-managed Illinois limited liability company. Miguel was lured to the position with a lucrative contract, renewable annually, still with six months before its expiration in the current year. While his tenure at Greenwood has generally been a success, Miguel recently made some regrettable headlines. While addressing an industry social gathering covered by the Chicago press, and having apparently gotten quite intoxicated, Miguel made both a series of inflammatory sexual and racial comments and a number of statements boasting of his managerial role at Greenwood.

What remedies might Greenwood have against Miguel?

a. Termination, despite his contract.
b. Damages.
c. Both.
d. Neither.

4. On the facts of the previous question, assume that it was not Miguel who spoke off-color at the industry gathering, but Melinda, a

Greenwood member and a retiree who resides most of the year in North Carolina.

What remedies might Greenwood have against Melinda?

a. Termination of her membership.
b. Damages.
c. Both.
d. Neither.

5. ABC, LLP is a dental practice organized as a limited liability partnership, owned by three practicing dentists named Anil, Barb, and Chuck. Unfortunately, during its brief lifetime, ABC has been an unhappy little family. In particular, conflict between Anil and Barb has led Barb to decide to leave the firm and begin her own solo practice. When she first came to this resolve, some months ago, she sent a letter to each of the patients whom she'd served while working at ABC, advising them that she'd soon be in her own practice and accepting new patients. (She never told Anil or Chuck that she'd sent this letter.) In the intervening months, she's taken several other steps to start her new venture, including securing office space, leasing office equipment, and entering into a substantial, long-term contract with a business printer to print business cards and advertising materials.

Which of the following statements is true?

a. Barb's letter violated her duty of care.
b. Barb's letter violated her duty of loyalty.
c. Barb's letter and printing contract, both conducted in secret, violated her duty of disclosure.
d. Barb's letter and printing contract violated her duty of loyalty.
e. None of Barb's actions violated a fiduciary duty.

6. On the facts of the previous question, assume that one of the events that so soured Anil and Barb's relationship was Anil's unilateral decision to make himself a loan from ABC's bank account, pursuant to a written contract that he wrote and executed himself. The contract obliged him to repay the principal within six months, at 4.25 percent interest. Had he gotten the loan from a bank, he likely would have paid something in the range of 4 percent to 4.5 percent interest. Only after executing the writing, withdrawing the funds, and spending them did Anil disclose the facts to Barb and Chuck.

Which of the following is most likely to be true?

a. The loan is illegal because Anil did not disclose it to Barb and Chuck before he executed it.
b. The loan is automatically illegal, regardless of any other facts.
c. The loan is illegal because it is not "intrinsically fair."
d. The loan is not illegal.

Questions 7-10 rely on the following facts:

For some time, Julie has successfully run a chain of laundromats in Wisconsin and Minnesota, and she wants to expand her business into jukeboxes placed in bars and restaurants. But since that market is already rather saturated in her area, she thinks her best bet is to buy in to an existing operation. To help her find one, she engages a business broker named Guadalupe. Guadalupe's standard contract provides that she works according to her client's directions in return for a stated compensation, that she works only in a fully disclosed capacity—making clear to sellers that she represents a client—and that she is not responsible for damages arising from conflict of interest. Guadalupe identifies not one but two promising opportunities for Julie, the American Amusements Company and Coin-Op Entertainment, Inc. The owners of American Amusements offer Guadalupe a bonus commission of $1,000 if she can convince Julie to buy their business; the owners of Coin-Op offer her no commission. Guadalupe tells Julie of the American Amusements opportunity, and since the $100,000 purchase price is pretty clearly below market value, Julie jumps at it and buys it outright. Thereafter, Guadalupe purchases the Coin-Op business herself. She never told Julie about Coin-Op, because she believed American Amusements was the better deal, as its purchase price was higher but, in Guadalupe's opinion, it was of no greater value than American Amusements.

7. Julie discovers that Guadalupe accepted the $1,000 payment and sues for breach of fiduciary duty. She may recover:

  a. $1,000.
  b. $1,000 plus damages.
  c. Nothing, because Julie purchased the American Amusements at less than market value.
  d. Nothing, because Guadalupe's contract waived the relevant fiduciary duty.

8. The waiver in Guadalupe's contract is effective:

  a. True.
  b. False because the relevant duty is usually non-waivable.
  c. False, because of its scope.
  d. It's actually irrelevant, because Guadalupe is not Julie's agent.

9. By purchasing Coin-Op, Guadalupe improperly took a business opportunity that belonged to Julie.

  a. Probably true, because she learned of it in the course of her duties for Julie.
  b. Probably true, because she learned of it using Julie's property or confidences.
  c. Probably false, because it was not as good a deal as American Amusements.
  d. Probably false, for some other reason.

10. Guadalupe's purchase and operation of Coin-Op is separate a violation of her duty not to compete with Julie.

   a. Probably true, because of how she learned of the opportunity.

   b. Probably true, because of the subject matter of her duties.

   c. Probably false, because of the times at which relevant events occurred.

   d. Probably false, for some other reason.

Part 4

The Corporation

13

Incorporation, Organization, and Promoter Issues

Like all important forms of business other than the sole proprietorship and the general partnership, the corporation can be formed only by the filing of a particular document with a state government. Also, as with other limited liability entities, this seemingly ministerial bureaucratic step actually has quite significant legal consequences. If the members of the business fail to file the requisite document, or if they fail to comply with the relevant requirements for its filing, they may believe that they are acting as a corporation but will not be—with consequences.

Chapter Outline

A. Where to Incorporate and Incorporation Procedure

1. Where to Incorporate?
   - The internal affairs doctrine
   - The preeminence of Delaware
   - Was the success of Delaware a race to the top or a race to the bottom?

2. Incorporation Procedure
   - Incorporation by postcard
   - You get what you pay for

B. Promoters and Pre-Incorporation Liabilities

- Liability of co-promoters
- Refreshers in agency and contract law: when and how does the corporation become liable?

C. Liability as the Result of Defective Incorporation

- Corporations de jure
- Corporations de facto

- Corporations by estoppel
- The passive vs. active distinction

D. Promoter Liability to Investors and the Corporation Itself

- Securities fraud
- Promoters' fraud

Test Yourself

A. Where to Incorporate and Incorporation Procedure

The filing to be made to form a corporation—usually known as the "articles of incorporation"[1]—can itself be a detailed and important document in the life of the business. The articles are basically constitution-like. They normally set out the basic design of the business's governance and its capital structure (that is, the number and kinds of shares of stock the company can sell to raise money), and they may set out fairly detailed rules governing virtually any matter within the corporation.

 What does it look like?

Check the online Supplement for the following sample documents that are relevant to this chapter:

- Articles of Incorporation
- Bylaws
- Minutes of an organizational meeting
- Copy of a certificate for corporate shares

Generally speaking, however, incorporators of corporations will prefer to keep the articles as simple as is legally permitted. There are two reasons. First, the articles normally can be amended only after majority votes of the board of directors and shareholders, and in any corporation with a significant number of shareholders this can be burdensome (for management) and unpredictable. Second, most business planners will want the business to have as much legal flexibility as possible, because it can be hard to predict what sorts of transactions might be desirable in the future. For these reasons, such limitations or

---

1. The articles of incorporation are also sometimes known as the "certificate of incorporation" or "corporate charter," depending on the term used in the particular state's corporation statute.

rules as are thought desirable are normally placed in the company's bylaws or board resolutions rather than its articles. Still, a number of strategic and practical considerations go into the seemingly simple process of drafting and filing the articles.

1. Where to Incorporate?

A question of some significance for many corporations is where they should incorporate—which state they should choose as their place of incorporation. The state need not be the same as the state where the corporation keeps its offices or otherwise does business, and therefore every business has at least the theoretical option of shopping around for the most favorable state regulatory regime in which to establish itself, even if it has no other contact with that state. However, incorporating out of state imposes a number of costs, and is therefore not to be taken lightly. Ultimately, the choice usually boils down to local incorporation—incorporating in the state where the business primarily will be operated—or Delaware.

For small businesses that do business mainly within one state, local incorporation is the logical choice. Incorporating out of state (e.g., an Ohio business incorporating under the laws of Delaware) imposes a number of costs that will significantly outweigh any advantage of Delaware substantive corporate law for most small businesses. State income taxes and the "franchise" taxes that most corporations have to pay to their state of incorporation will be the same for in-state and foreign corporations, but the local business incorporated in Delaware will have to pay taxes both to the state of operation and to Delaware. Moreover, Delaware franchise taxes are non-trivially higher than those in many states. A number of other regulatory costs are involved, such as having to make a filing qualifying the corporation as a "foreign" corporation to transact business in its headquarter state, and filing annual regulatory compliance documents with two states instead of one. Also, by incorporating in Delaware a business necessarily submits itself to the personal jurisdiction of the courts of that state and may be forced to defend suit there, a problem that could impose prohibitive costs on the typical small business.

Nevertheless, many small businesses outside Delaware are still incorporated under Delaware law. This may reflect a mistaken calculus of the costs and benefits of incorporating there. Alternatively, it may simply reflect the founders' ambitions for future growth.

More to the Story: Why I Care

Because of the internal affairs doctrine, which has nothing to do with dirty cops.

Simply put, it is a choice of law principle providing that, no matter where a corporation is sued, the law of the state of incorporation governs the "internal affairs" of the corporation *unless* the outcome is repugnant to the state hosting the litigation.

What, however, is an "internal affair"?

Some people find it useful to think of the corporation as an artificial person animated by real human beings and the legal relationships between them. Those legal relationships are the corporation's "internal affairs." They include the rights and duties of directors, officers, and shareholders, but not the corporation's obligations to third parties—including its employees and other creditors.

Connections: Piercing the Corporate Veil

"Piercing the corporate veil" refers to imposing liability for a corporation's debts on its shareholders. Should this be a question of internal affairs?

Room to Argue

There is a rich literature on how Delaware achieved its preeminence, and whether it was a matter of winning a race to the bottom (of laxity) or a race to the top (through enablement of private ordering). You can read more about that in the online Supplement.

In addition, it's worth noting that other states still sometimes try to attract incorporation business volume through various strategies.

For larger businesses with multi-state or multi-national operations, the costs of incorporating in one state and qualifying to do business in others will be comparatively trivial, and the advantages of incorporating in Delaware frequently outweigh them. These advantages are commonly said to include the sophistication of Delaware's Court of Chancery and its Secretary of State in dealing with corporate matters, the breadth and depth of the established Delaware law of corporations, and the general flexibility and business-friendliness of Delaware law.

■ Think about this:

(A) Belinda, who has been blind since birth, is the president of Hypo Corp., which is incorporated in Delaware. She has a contract to serve in the position for two more years. Most of the directors and officers of the corporation live in New Jersey, which is where the board meets for convenience. Most of the actual business of Hypo Corp. is conducted in New York, which is where most of the shareholders live. The board of directors decides to replace Belinda as president; she believes it is, in part, due to her disability. What law or laws will govern the outcome if Belinda decides to sue?

---

2. Incorporation Procedure

Under contemporary law, incorporation is itself a simple process. At least one person—known by statute as an "incorporator"—must file a document known as the "articles of incorporation" (or, in some states the "certificate of incorporation" or "charter") with the Secretary of State (or equivalent official) in the state where the business will be incorporated. There is nothing magical about being an "incorporator." That person need do no more than sign and cause the physical (or, in most states, electronic) delivery of the articles to the filing authority. Indeed the incorporator of record often will be simply a paralegal or junior attorney in the office of the attorney who prepared the articles. After the articles are filed, there is nothing for the incorporator(s) to do other than name the initial board of directors (and, if so inclined, adopt bylaws). If the initial board was named in the articles, the incorporator usually just goes the way of the dodo.

Incorporation by Postcard

It sometimes is said that the Model Business Corporation Act (MBCA) and similar statutes permit "incorporation by postcard." This certainly conveys that not much is required in a valid set of articles.

But the image is a bit dated, and might better capture things if it were "incorporation by email." Most, if not all, jurisdictions accept electronic filings, and there are many online providers who will provide both preparation and filing service for nominal fees. (They also will serve as the corporation's registered agent.)

The postcard concept also fails to reflect the old wisdom that you get what you pay for. Corporate planners have freedom to include any number of discretionary provisions, and wherever more than one founder is involved it is wise to consider them.

Incorporation was not always so easy. Historically, most states required quite a bit of bureaucratic compliance, including the requirement in many states that the incorporators file notice in a county government office of every county in which the company would do business. In addition, publication (and sometimes multiple publications) of the articles of incorporation in newspapers sometimes was required. The idea was to give notice to creditors that if they dealt with the business they would not have recourse against the shareholders' personal assets in case of the company's insolvency. But these requirements were onerous and easily flubbed, and therein was the serious rub. If the incorporators failed to comply with even one of the many, tedious incorporation requirements, the corporation could fail to come into existence and the incorporators could face unexpected personal liability.

Bureaucratic requirements of this kind are almost completely a thing of the past. The incorporation procedure in Model Act jurisdictions is a good example of the simple and highly permissive incorporation procedure in modern corporation statutes. Peruse MBCA §§1.25, 2.01-2.06, 3.01-3.02, 4.01, and 6.01, and then . . .

More to the Story: What Comes Next?

Although filing the articles of incorporation completes creation of the corporation, there are a number of steps to take before operation as a corporation actually can begin. These include naming directors (unless the directors are named in the articles themselves). The directors then elect officers, adopt bylaws, authorize the sale of shares, and (as is practically required) designate a corporate bank account. (*See* MBCA §2.05.) These steps usually take place at an organizational meeting, which can take place through unanimous written consent. (*See* MBCA §2.05(b).)

■ Think about this:

(B) Amanda Ahn and Bill Boca want to form a new corporation in State X, which follows the MBCA. They intend to carry on business as a food truck, parked on Bank Street, selling tacos. They decide that the

corporation should issue 100 shares of common stock to each of the two founders and should be authorized to sell up to 100,000 shares of preferred stock to future investors. Will the following articles of incorporation accomplish their purpose? Do they contain anything you wouldn't advise?

ARTICLES OF INCORPORATION

1. The name of the corporation is First Bank Corp.
2. The duration of First Bank Corp. is perpetual.
3. First Bank Corp. is authorized to issue 100,200 shares.
4. The name of the registered agent of First Bank Corp. is Amanda Ahn, and the address of the registered office of First Bank Corp. is P.O. Box 555, Hypo City, State X.
5. The name and address of the incorporator of First Bank Corp. are Bill Boca, P.O. Box 444, Hypo City, State X.
6. The purpose of First Bank Corp. is the sale of Mexican food.
7. The powers of First Bank Corp. include, upon the consent of the directors, the ability to donate the assets of the corporation to the homeless population of Hypo City.

Bill Boca April 1, 20__.

Bill submits the articles on the day they are signed. He is told that it will be a few days before the Secretary of State's office can check to see if they are in legal compliance. Suppose, whether the articles are valid are not, that the Secretary of State's office deems them valid and stamps them as "approved" on the fourth day after submission.[2] When—if at all—did the corporation come into existence?

This may help . . .

INCORPORATION CHECKLIST

✓ State chosen
✓ Incorporator(s) meeting residency requirement, if any
✓ Qualifying name
✓ Articles of Incorporation including
  o Name of corporation
  o Name and address of incorporator

2. In some states, the relevant statute provides that the corporation does not exist until the Secretary has issued some additional document acknowledging incorporation. Confusingly, in some states the document that is issued will be called the "certificate of incorporation," even though in some other states that term is used to describe the corporation's articles themselves.

- o Name and address of registered agent
- o Number and class of authorized shares, including par value, if any
- o Discretionary items, often including the initial directors and provisions limiting the liability of officers and directors
- ✓ Filing fee

Dear Prof.: Your hypothetical mentioned common and preferred stock. What's the difference?

We cover this topic at length in Chapter 15. For present purposes, assume that the holders of preferred stock have the right to payment of dividends and/or liquidation distributions that must be satisfied before the holders of common stock receive anything. Assume too that the holders of common stock have superior rights vis-à-vis corporate control.

Time Out for PR

Amanda and Bill evidently represented themselves. Could the same attorney have represented both Amanda and Bill? Is that the right way to frame the question? If you need more information, what might it be? *See* American Bar Association Model Rules 1.7 (Conflict of Interest: Current Client) and 1.13 (Organization as Client).

B. Promoters and Pre-Incorporation Liabilities

As the term is used in corporation law, a "promoter" is a person who acts on behalf of a business before it is incorporated. A promoter might borrow money, enter into contracts, hire potential employees, rent office or factory space, and so on, all with the idea that these transactions will be of use to the business once it is incorporated. Sometimes more than one promoter will work on behalf of the business before its incorporation, in which case they are known as co-promoters. This can all raise a basic legal problem: As a practical matter, there will often be a flurry of activity for a promoter to attend to while the business is getting itself set up, and only one of the many things going on in the promoter's busy life will be attending to the legal formality of incorporation. Thus, a range of potential liabilities might surface before the corporation itself comes into existence. The legal questions are who takes on those liabilities and, if there are two or more co-promoters, what are their relations to one another?

Connections: What Is a Partnership?

The definition of a partnership is "an association of two or more persons to carry on as co-owners a business for profit."

In general, when a promoter executes a contract or commits a tort in connection with the business prior to its incorporation, that promoter is usually personally liable for it, and all of his or her co-promoters are liable for it, too. In addition, if co-promoters act on behalf of a business before it is incorporated, they take on fiduciary duties to one another. Pre-incorporation liabilities can therefore include tort and contract liabilities to third parties, shared among the co-promoters jointly and severally, and fiduciary liabilities as between the co-promoters. Ask yourself: This all being the case, in what form of business entity must these co-promoters be operating prior to incorporation? Separately, as a practical matter, given that a person who acts as a promoter prior to incorporation takes on fairly significant personal risks (especially if he or she is working with one or more co-promoters), why would he or she do such a thing?

The promoter's liability for pre-incorporation obligations is a matter of agency law and sometimes of substantive contract law, as explained by the following excerpt:

AMERICAN LAW INSTITUTE RESTATEMENT (THIRD) OF THE LAW AGENCY

§6.04 Principal Does Not Exist or Lacks Capacity

Unless the third party agrees otherwise, a person who makes a contract with a third party purportedly as an agent on behalf of a principal becomes a party to the contract if the purported agent knows or has reason to know that the purported principal does not exist or lacks capacity to be a party to a contract.

This does not, of course, indicate how a third party must manifest agreement that a promoter is not liable, which will be determined as a matter of fact.

■ **Think about this:**

(C) Pablo Perez intends to form Perez Hilton, Inc., to operate a hotel. Before the articles of incorporation are filed, he enters into a contract with Art Andrews, an architect, pursuant to which Andrews agrees to design the hotel for a substantial fee. Perez signs "Pablo Perez, agent for Perez Hilton, Inc., a corporation to be formed." Andrews subsequently drafts the design, and Perez makes partial payment out of a personal checking account. Has Andrews agreed not to hold Perez liable? What should Perez have done to make the matter clearer? How might Andrews have responded?

The case that follows is a classic, but reaches the same conclusion one would expect today. Note carefully the possibility that "official" corporate actors can bind the corporation by acting relatively informally.

MCARTHUR V. TIMES PRINTING CO.

Supreme Court of Minnesota
51 N.W. 216 (1892)

MITCHELL, J.

The complaint alleges that about October 1, 1889, the defendant contracted with plaintiff for his services as advertising solicitor for one year; that in April, 1890, it discharged him, in violation of the contract. The action is to recover damages for the breach of the contract. The answer sets up two defenses: (1) That plaintiff's employment was not for any stated time, but only from week to week; (2) that he was discharged for good cause. Upon the trial there was evidence reasonably tending to prove that in September, 1889, one C.A. Nimocks and others were engaged as promoters in procuring the organization of the defendant company to publish a newspaper; that, about September 12th, Nimocks, as such promoter, made a contract with plaintiff, in behalf of the contemplated company, for his services as advertising solicitor for the period of one year from and after October 1st,—the date at which it was expected that the company would be organized; that the corporation was not, in fact, organized until October 16th, but that the publication of the paper was commenced by the promoters October 1st, at which date plaintiff, in pursuance of his arrangement with Nimocks, entered upon the discharge of his duties as advertising solicitor for the paper; that after the organization of the company he continued in its employment in the same capacity until discharged, the following April; that defendant's board of directors never took any formal action with reference to the contract made in its behalf by Nimocks, but all of the stockholders, directors, and officers of the corporation knew of this contract at the time of its organization, or were informed of it soon afterwards, and none of them objected to or repudiated it, but, on the contrary, retained plaintiff in the employment of the company without any other or new contract as to his services.

There is a line of cases which hold that where a contract is made in behalf of, and for the benefit of, a projected corporation, the corporation, after its organization, cannot become a party to the contract, either by adoption or ratification of it . . . . This, however, seems to be more a question of name than of substance; that is, whether the liability of the corporation, in such cases, is to be placed on the grounds of its adoption of the contract of its promoters, or upon some other ground, such as equitable estoppel. This court, in accordance with what we deem sound reason, as well as the weight of

Connections: Corporate Formalities

Formal methods can be used to take corporate action. These methods have predictable results and are what a lawyer generally would advise. As this case indicates, informal acts also can have consequences.

authority, has held that, while a corporation is not bound by engagements made on its behalf by its promoters before its organization, it may, after its organization, make such engagements its own contracts. And this it may do precisely as it might make similar original contracts; formal action of its board of directors being necessary only where it would be necessary in the case of a similar original contract. That it is not requisite that such adoption or acceptance be express, but it may be inferred from acts or acquiescence on part of the corporation, or its authorized agents, as any similar original contract might be shown . . . . The right of the corporate agents to adopt an agreement originally made by promoters depends upon the purposes of the corporation and the nature of the agreement. Of course, the agreement must be one which the corporation itself could make, and one which the usual agents of the company have express or implied authority to make. That the contract in this case was of that kind is very clear; and the acts and acquiescence of the corporate officers, after the organization of the company, fully justified the jury in finding that it had adopted it as its own.

The defendant, however, claims that the contract was void under the statute of frauds, because, "by its terms, not to be performed within one year from the making thereof," which counsel assumes to be September 12th,—the date of the agreement between plaintiff and the promoter. This proceeds upon the erroneous theory that the act of the corporation, in such cases, is a ratification, which relates back to the date of the contract with the promoter, under the familiar maxim that "a subsequent ratification has a retroactive effect, and is equivalent to a prior command." . . . Although the acts of a corporation with reference to the contracts made by promoters in its behalf before its organization are frequently loosely termed "ratification," yet a "ratification," properly so called, implies an existing person, on whose behalf the contract might have been made at the time. There cannot, in law, be a ratification of a contract which could not have been made binding on the ratifier at the time it was made, because the ratifier was not then in existence . . . . What is called "adoption," in such cases, is, in legal effect, the making of a contract of the date of the adoption, and not as of some former date. The contract in this case was, therefore, not within the statute of frauds . . . .

───────────────

■ **Think about this:**

(D) Building on Problem C, above, suppose that Perez Hilton, Inc. is duly formed and begins hotel construction, using a design provided by Art Andrews, who has been only partially paid. Do you think Perez Hilton, Inc. must pay for the design? How about Pablo Perez, the promoter who entered the contract?

C. Liability as the Result of Defective Incorporation

Pre-incorporation liability for promoters will often seem quite harsh, especially in two instances. First, sometimes promoters fail to incorporate for innocent reasons, such as making technical errors in the articles that they filed with the Secretary of State. Alternatively, they may simply forget to file. Second, one or more of the "co-promoters" might be a person who really only intended to be a passive investor in the business and took no part in managing it. It can seem unfair to hold such a person liable for managerial acts taken by other promoters.

The courts, using their powers of equity, have come up with a few solutions to these problems. One of these is the "corporation by estoppel" theory, which is explained in the materials that follow. Though neither the *Robertson* nor *Timberline* case actually applies this theory—and *Robertson* holds that it does not exist in the relevant jurisdiction—the doctrine is in fact alive and well, and is applied by many courts.

There is another doctrine that at one time provided an equitable defense to pre-incorporation liability for defective incorporation—the so-called de facto corporation doctrine. The idea was that even if the promoters had failed to incorporate properly, the courts would give them a break and recognize limited liability on their behalf if they could make the requisite showings, which are set out in *Robertson*. The rationale of the doctrine reflected the fact that at one time incorporation was complicated and easily frustrated by mere mistakes of red tape that did not obviously injure anyone with whom the promoters might be dealing. The doctrine is now largely unnecessary, as indicated in *Robertson*.

You will see that the following cases find two particular provisions of the then-current MBCA to be very important. They were precursors to the two modern provisions set out immediately below:

MODEL BUSINESS CORPORATIONS ACT

§2.03 Incorporation

(a) Unless a delayed effective date is specified, the corporate existence begins when the articles of incorporation are filed.

(b) The secretary of state's filing of the articles of incorporation is conclusive proof that the incorporators satisfied all conditions precedent to incorporation except in a proceeding by the state to cancel or revoke the incorporation or involuntarily dissolve the corporation.

§2.04 Liability for Preincorporation Transactions

All persons purporting to act as or on behalf of a corporation, knowing there was no incorporation under this Act, are jointly and severally liable for all liabilities created while so acting.

The case below provides an excellent history of the relevant doctrines, and illustrates what might be thought of as the "mid-century modern" minimalist approach to giving new order to the area. As you read, keep in mind the questions of what result seems most fair, as well as what approach will most likely influence the conduct of real-life human beings.

ROBERTSON V. LEVY

District of Columbia Court of Appeals
197 A.2d 443 (1964)

HOOD, Chief Judge.

On December 22, 1961, Martin G. Robertson and Eugene M. Levy entered into an agreement whereby Levy was to form a corporation, Penn Ave. Record Shack, Inc., which was to purchase Robertson's business. Levy submitted articles of incorporation to the Superintendent of Corporations on December 27, 1961, but no certificate of incorporation was issued at this time. Pursuant to the contract an assignment of lease was entered into on December 31, 1961, between Robertson and Levy, the latter acting as president of Penn Ave. Record Shack, Inc. On January 2, 1962, the articles of incorporation were rejected by the Superintendent of Corporations but on the same day Levy began to operate the business under the name Penn Ave. Record Shack, Inc. Robertson executed a bill of sale to Penn Ave. Record Shack, Inc. on January 8, 1962, disposing of the assets of his business to that "corporation" and receiving in return a note providing for installment payments signed "Penn Ave. Record Shack, Inc. by Eugene M. Levy, President." The certificate of incorporation was issued on January 17, 1962. One payment was made on the note. The exact date when the payment was made cannot be clearly determined from the record, but presumably it was made after the certificate of incorporation was issued. Penn Ave. Record Shack, Inc. ceased doing business in June 1962 and is presently without assets. Robertson sued Levy for the balance due on the note . . . . In holding for the defendant the trial court found that [§139 of the 1950 Model Act*], relied upon by Robertson, did not apply and further that Robertson was estopped to deny the existence of the corporation.

The case presents the following issues on appeal: Whether the president of an "association" which filed its articles of incorporation, which were first rejected but later accepted, can be held personally liable on an obligation entered into by the "association" before the certificate of incorporation has been issued, or whether the creditor is "estopped" from denying the existence of the

---

* *Editors' Note*: This section read as follows:

§139. Unauthorized Assumption of Corporate Powers. All persons who assume to act as a corporation without authority so to do shall be jointly and severally liable for all debts and liabilities incurred or arising thereof.

How is this different from the current version, §2.04?

"corporation" because, after the certificate of incorporation was issued, he accepted the first installment payment on the note.

The Business Corporation Act of the District of Columbia, Code 1961, Title 29, is patterned after the Model Business Corporation Act . . . . On this appeal, we are concerned with an interpretation of [§§50* and 139 of the 1950 Model Act] . . . .

For a full understanding of the problems raised, some historical grounding is not only illuminative but necessary. In early common law times private corporations were looked upon with distrust and disfavor. This distrust of the corporate form for private enterprise was eventually overcome by the enactment of statutes which set forth certain prerequisites before the status was achieved, and by court decisions which eliminated other stumbling blocks. Problems soon arose, however, where there was substantial compliance with the prerequisites of the statute, but not complete formal compliance. Thus the concepts of . . . de facto corporations, and of "corporations by estoppel" came into being . . . .

A de facto corporation is one which has been defectively incorporated and thus is not de jure . . . . [T]he requisites for a corporation de facto are: (1) A valid law under which such a corporation can be lawfully organized;* (2) An attempt to organize thereunder; (3) Actual user of the corporate franchise. Good faith in claiming to be and in doing business as a corporation is often added as a further condition. A de facto corporation is recognized for all purposes except where there is a direct attack by the state in a quo warranto proceeding. The concept of de facto corporation has been roundly criticized . . . .

Cases continued to arise, however, where the corporation was not de jure, where it was not de facto because of failure to comply with one of the four requirements above, but where the courts, lacking some clear standard or guideline, were willing to decide on the equities of the case. Thus another concept arose, the so-called "corporation by estoppel." This term was a complete misnomer. There was no corporation, the acts of the associates having failed even to colorably fulfill the statutory requirements; there was no estoppel in the pure sense of the word because generally there was no holding out followed by reliance on the part of the other party. Apparently estoppel can arise whether or not a de facto corporation has come into existence. Estoppel problems arose where the certificate of incorporation had been issued as well as where it had not been issued, and under the following general conditions: where the "associ-

---

This may help . . .

Robertson v. Levy Timeline

12/22	Agreement to form corporation for purposes of purchasing business
12/27	**Articles submitted**
12/31	Acceptance of lease assignment in corporate name
1/2	**Articles rejected**
1/8	Transfer of assets in return for note executed in corporate name
1/17	**Articles accepted**

How did this timing injure Plaintiff Robertson?

---

* *Editors' Note*: Section 50 essentially was the same as §2.03 of the current MBCA.

* *Editors' Note*: This is a requirement that shows just how antiquated the de facto corporation doctrine now is—it obviously arose prior to the time when all U.S. jurisdictions had adopted general incorporation statutes, which was sometime around the turn of the twentieth century.

ation" sues a third party and the third party is estopped from denying that the plaintiff is a corporation; where a third party sues the "association" as a corporation and the "association" is precluded from denying that it was a corporation; where a third party sues the "association" and the members of that association cannot deny its existence as a corporation where they participated in holding it out as a corporation; where a third party sues the individuals behind the "association" but is estopped from denying the existence of the "corporation"; where either a third party, or the "association" is estopped from denying the corporate existence because of prior pleadings.

One of the reasons for enacting modern corporation statutes was to eliminate problems inherent in the . . . de facto and estoppel concepts . . . .

The first portion of [MBCA §50] sets forth a sine qua non regarding compliance. No longer must the courts inquire into the equities of a case to determine whether there has been "colorable compliance" with the statute. The corporation comes into existence only when the certificate has been issued. Before the certificate issues, there is no corporation de jure, de facto or by estoppel. After the certificate is issued under [§50], the de jure corporate existence commences . . . .

The authorities which have considered the problem are unanimous in their belief that [§§50 and 139] have put to rest de facto corporations and corporations by estoppel. Thus the Comment to section 50 of the Model Act, after noting that de jure incorporation is complete when the certificate is issued, states that:

> "Since it is unlikely that any steps short of securing a certificate of incorporation would be held to constitute apparent compliance, the possibility that a de facto corporation could exist under such a provision *is remote.*" [Emphasis provided.]

Similarly, Professor Hornstein in his work on Corporate Law and Practice (1959) observes at §29 that: "Statutes in almost half the jurisdictions have virtually eliminated the distinction between de jure and de facto corporations [citing §139 of the Model Act]." . . .

The portion of [§50] which states that the certificate of incorporation will be "conclusive evidence" that all conditions precedent have been performed eliminates the problems of estoppel and de facto corporations once the certificate has been issued. The existence of the corporation is conclusive evidence against all who deal with it. Under [§139], if an individual or group of individuals assumes to act as a corporation before the certificate of incorporation has been issued, joint and several liability attaches. We hold, therefore, that the impact of these sections, when considered together, is to eliminate the concepts of estoppel and de facto corporateness under the Business Corporation Act of the District of Columbia. It is immaterial whether the third person believed he was dealing with a corporation or whether he intended to deal with a corporation.[3] The

---

3. In the present case, Robertson admitted intending to deal with a corporation.

certificate of incorporation provides the cut off point; before it is issued, the individuals, and not the corporation, are liable.

Turning to the facts of this case, Penn Ave. Record Shack, Inc. was not a corporation when the original agreement was entered into, when the lease was assigned, when Levy took over Robertson's business, when operations began under the Penn Ave. Record Shack, Inc. name, or when the bill of sale was executed. Only on January 17 did Penn Ave. Record Shack, Inc. become a corporation. Levy is subject to personal liability because, before this date, he assumed to act as a corporation without any authority so to do. Nor is Robertson estopped from denying the existence of the corporation because after the certificate was issued he accepted one payment on the note. An individual who incurs statutory liability on an obligation under [§139] because he has acted without authority, is not relieved of that liability where, at a later time, the corporation does come into existence by complying with section [§50]. Subsequent partial payment by the corporation does not remove this liability.

The judgment appealed from is reversed with instructions to enter judgment against the appellee on the note and for damages proved to have been incurred by appellant for breach of the lease.

Reversed with instructions.

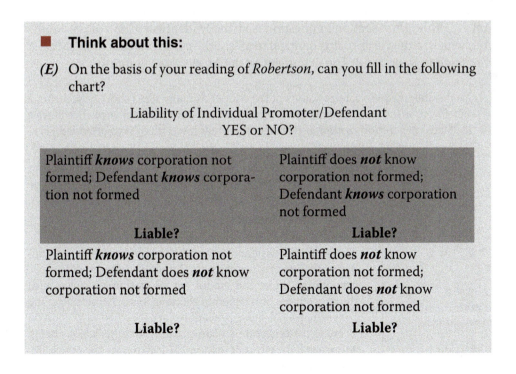

Think about this:

(E) On the basis of your reading of *Robertson*, can you fill in the following chart?

Liability of Individual Promoter/Defendant
YES or NO?

Plaintiff **knows** corporation not formed; Defendant **knows** corporation not formed	Plaintiff does **not** know corporation not formed; Defendant **knows** corporation not formed
Liable?	**Liable?**
Plaintiff **knows** corporation not formed; Defendant does **not** know corporation not formed	Plaintiff does **not** know corporation not formed; Defendant does **not** know corporation not formed
Liable?	**Liable?**

The next case, *Timberline*, involves essentially the same statutory language as *Robertson*, though decided in a different jurisdiction several years later. Ask yourself whether it represents the same reading or a different one.

TIMBERLINE EQUIPMENT CO. V. DAVENPORT

Supreme Court of Oregon
514 P.2d 1109 (1973)

DENECKE, Justice.

Plaintiff brought this action for equipment rentals against the defendant Dr. Bennett and two others. In addition to making a general denial, Dr. Bennett alleged as a defense that the rentals were to a de facto corporation, Aero-Fabb Corp., of which Dr. Bennett was an incorporator, director and shareholder. He also alleged plaintiff was estopped from denying the corporate character of the organization to whom plaintiff rented the equipment. The trial court held for plaintiff. Dr. Bennett, only, appeals.

On January 22, 1970, Dr. Bennett signed articles of incorporation for Aero-Fabb Co. The original articles were not in accord with the statutes and, therefore, no certificate of incorporation was issued for the corporation until June 12, 1970, after new articles were filed. The leases were entered into and rentals earned during the period between January 22nd and June 12th.

Prior to 1953 Oregon had adopted the common-law doctrine that prohibited a collateral attack on the legality of a defectively organized corporation which had achieved the status of a de facto corporation . . . .

In 1953 the legislature adopted the Oregon Business Corporation Act . . . . Th[e] [first section in question is virtually identical to §56 of the Model Act, which in turn is virtually identical to §50 of the earlier version of the MBCA discussed in *Robertson*]. The Comment to the Model Act . . . states: . . .

> Under the unequivocal provisions of the Model Act, any steps short of securing a certificate of incorporation would not constitute apparent compliance. Therefore a de facto corporation ***cannot exist*** under the Model Act. [Emphasis provided.] . . .

The [second relevant section is virtually identical to §146 of the Model Act, in turn identical to §139 of the earlier version of the MBCA discussed in *Robertson*]. The Comment states:

This section is designed to prohibit the application of any theory of de facto incorporation. The only authority to act as a corporation under the Model Act arises from completion of the procedures prescribed in sections 53 to 55 inclusive. The consequences of those procedures are specified in section 56 as being the creation of a corporation. No other means being authorized, the effect of section 146 is to negate the possibility of a de facto corporation.

Abolition of the concept of de facto incorporation, which at best was fuzzy, is a sound result. No reason exists for its continuance under general corporate laws, where the process of acquiring de jure incorporation is both simple and clear. The vestigial appendage should be removed.

This may help . . .

Timberline Equipment Co. v. Davenport Timeline

1/22   Articles signed and thereafter unsuccessfully filed

1/23-   Leases entered in
6/11   corporate name

6/12   Corporate existence begins

How did this timing injure Plaintiff Timberline?

[The court then cites *Robertson* with approval in holding that the cited provisions ended the common law doctrine of de facto corporation.]

The defendant also contends that the plaintiff is estopped to deny that it contracted with a corporation . . . .

The doctrine of "corporation by estoppel" has been recognized by this court but never fully dissected . . . . Corporation by estoppel is a difficult concept to grasp and courts and writers have "gone all over the lot" in attempting to define and apply the doctrine . . . .

As several writers have pointed out, in order to apply the doctrine correctly, the cases must be classified according to who is being charged with estoppel . . . .

When a defendant seeks to escape liability to a corporation plaintiff by contending that the plaintiff is not a lawful corporate entity, courts readily apply the doctrine of corporation by estoppel. Thompson Optical Institute v. Thompson, 237 P. 965 (Ore. 1925), well illustrates the equity of the doctrine in this class of cases. R. A. Thompson carried on an optical business for years. He then organized a corporation to buy his optical business and subscribed to most of the stock in this corporation. He chaired the first meeting at which the Board resolved to purchase the business from him. The corporation and Thompson entered into a contract for the sale of the business which included a covenant by Thompson not to compete. Thereafter, Thompson sold all of his stock to another individual. Some years later Thompson re-entered the optical business in violation of the covenant not to compete. The corporation brought suit to restrain Thompson from competing. Thompson defended upon the ground that the corporation had not been legally organized. We held, "The defendant cannot be heard to challenge the validity of the contract or the proper organization of the corporation." . . .

The fairness of estopping a defendant such as Thompson from denying the corporate existence of his creation is apparent.

On the other hand, when individuals such as the defendants in this case seek to escape liability by contending that the debtor is a corporation, Aero-Fabb Co., rather than the individual who purported to act as a corporation, the courts are more reluctant to estop the plaintiff from attacking the legality of the alleged debtor corporation . . . .

The most appealing explanation of why the plaintiff may be estopped is based upon the intention of the parties. The creditor plaintiff contracted believing it could look for payment only to the corporate entity. The associates, whatever their relationship to the supposed corporate entity, believed their only potential liability was the loss of their investment in the supposed corporate entity and that they were not personally liable . . . .

From the plaintiff-creditor's viewpoint, such reasoning is somewhat tenuous. The creditor did nothing to create the appearance that the debtor was a legal corporate entity. The creditor formed its intention to contract with

Room to Argue: Intent of the Parties

Does someone who enters into a contract with a corporation signal an intention not to hold any individual personally liable?

Do you think someone who deals with a corporation is likely to demand some sort of price concession for giving up access to the assets of the shareholders?

Assumptions about these matters often are critical to the analytic method of law and economics. You can read more about this in the online Supplement, but keep reading for the trial court's take on the facts in this case.

a debtor corporate entity because someone associated with the debtor represented, expressly or impliedly, that the debtor was a legal corporate entity.

We need not decide whether the doctrine of corporation by estoppel would apply in such a case as this. The trial court found that if this doctrine was still available under the Business Corporation Act defendants did not prove all the elements necessary for its application, and, moreover, it would be inequitable to apply the doctrine . . . .

Under the explanation stated above for the application of the doctrine of estoppel in this kind of case, it is necessary that the plaintiff believe that it was contracting with a corporate entity. The evidence on this point is contradictory and the trial court apparently found against defendants.

The trial court found, and its findings are supported by the evidence, that all the defendants were partners prior to January 1970 and did business under the name "Aero-Fabb Co." Not until June 1970 were the interests in this partnership assigned to the corporation "Aero-Fabb Co." and about the same time the assumed business name "Aero-Fabb Co." was cancelled.

The trial court found, and the evidence supported the finding, that two of the leases entered into by plaintiff were with "Kenneth L. Davenport, dba Aero-Fabb Co." The other was with "Kenneth L. Davenport, dba Aero-Fabb Corp." "Aero-Fabb Corp." was never the corporate name; the name of the corporation for which a certificate was finally issued was "Aero-Fabb Co." The correspondence and records of plaintiff sometimes referred to the debtor as "Aero-Fabb Co." and others as "Aero-Fabb Corp."

Plaintiff's bookkeeper testified that she thought it was a corporation because, "This was the way the information was given to me." It is uncertain whether the information was given to her by someone employed by plaintiff or by a company with whom she made a credit check. In any event, plaintiff's salesman said Mr. Davenport, speaking for the organization, stated several times that he was in a partnership with Drs. Gorman and Bennett. The salesman was dubious and checked the title to the land on which the debtors' operation was being conducted and found it was in the name of the three defendants as individuals.

A final question remains: Can the plaintiff recover against Dr. Bennett individually?

In the first third of this century the liability of persons associated with defectively organized corporations was a controversial and well-documented legal issue. The orthodox view was that if an organization had not achieved de facto status and the plaintiff was not estopped to attack the validity of the corporate status of the corporation, all shareholders were liable as partners. This court, however, rejected the orthodox rule. In Rutherford v. Hill, 29 P. 546 (Ore. 1892), we held that a person could not be held liable as a partner merely because he signed the articles of incorporation though the corporation was so defectively formed as to fall short of de facto status. The court stated that under this rule a mere passive stockholder would not

Connections: Corporate Knowledge

Plaintiff Timberline is a corporation, and some issues in this case depend on the legal fiction that it did or did not "know" certain facts. How do you know what a corporation thinks or believes? The laws of agency are helpful with respect to what information acquired by an agent is imputed to the principal. Nonetheless, issues presented by corporate state of mind can be extremely problematic, particularly in criminal prosecutions.

be held liable as a partner. We went on to observe, however, that if the party actively participated in the business he might be held liable as a partner.

This controversy subsided 30 or 40 years ago probably because the procedure to achieve de jure corporate status was made simpler; so the problem did not arise.

The Model Act [followed by Oregon] solve[s] the problem as follows:

> All persons who assume to act as a corporation without the authority of a certificate of incorporation issued by the Corporation Commissioner, shall be jointly and severally liable for all debts and liabilities incurred or arising as a result thereof.

We have found no decisions, comments to the Model Act, or literature attempting to explain the intent of this section.

We find the language ambiguous. Liability is imposed on "(a)ll persons who assume to act as a corporation." Such persons shall be liable "for all debts and liabilities incurred or arising as a result thereof."

A Passive Investor

We conclude that the category of "persons who assume to act as a corporation" does not include those whose only connection with the organization is as an investor. On the other hand, the restriction of liability to those who personally incurred the obligation sued upon cannot be based upon logic or the realities of business practice. When several people carry on the activities of a defectively organized corporation, chance frequently will dictate which of the several active principals directly incurs a certain obligation or whether an employee, rather than an active principal, personally incurs the obligation.

We are of the opinion that the phrase, "persons who assume to act as a corporation" should be interpreted to include those persons who have an investment in the organization and who actively participate in the policy and operational decisions of the organization. Liability should not necessarily be restricted to the person who personally incurred the obligation.

The trial court found that Dr. Bennett "acted in the business venture which was subsequently incorporat[ed] on June 12, 1970." . . .

There is evidence from which the trial court could have found that while Drs. Bennett and Gorman, another defendant, entrusted the details of management to Davenport, they endeavored to and did retain some control over his management. All checks required one of their signatures. Dr. Bennett frequently visited the site and observed the activity and the presence of the equipment rented by plaintiff. He met with the organization's employees to discuss the operation of the business. Shortly after the equipment was rented and before most of the rent had accrued, Dr. Bennett was informed of the rentals and given an opinion that they were unnecessary and ill-advised. Drs. Bennett and Gorman thought they had Davenport and his management "under control."

This evidence all supports the finding that Dr. Bennett was a person who assumed to act for the organization and the conclusion of the trial court that Dr. Bennett is personally liable.

Affirmed.

Let's return now to the current version of the MBCA. Re-read §2.04, set out before *Robertson*, and consider the following excerpted Official Comment to that provision:

OFFICIAL COMMENT

Incorporation under modern statutes is so simple and inexpensive that a strong argument may be made that nothing short of filing articles of incorporation should create the privilege of limited liability. A number of situations have arisen, however, in which the protection of limited liability arguably should be recognized even though the simple incorporation process established by modern statutes has not been completed. [These include situations in which the participants honestly and reasonably but erroneously believe the articles had been filed, etc.]

[A]fter a review of these situations, it seemed appropriate to impose liability only on persons who act as or on behalf of corporations "knowing" that no corporation exists . . . .

While no special provision is made in section 2.04, the section does not foreclose the possibility that persons who urge defendants to execute contracts in the corporate name knowing that no steps to incorporate have been taken may be estopped to impose personal liability on individual defendants . . . .

How might the new language change the outcome in *Robertson* or *Timberline*, if at all? Does it open the door to use of the corporation de facto doctrine? How might it apply in the following (presumably familiar) scenario?

> ■ **Think about this:**
>
> *(F)* Pablo Perez intends to form Perez Hilton, Inc., to operate a hotel. Before the articles of incorporation are filed, he enters into a contract with Art Andrews, an architect, pursuant to which Andrews agrees to design the hotel for a substantial fee. Perez signs "Pablo Perez, agent for Perez Hilton, Inc." Andrews does not know the corporation has not yet been formed. If Perez Hilton, Inc. subsequently is duly formed and begins hotel construction, using the design provided by Art Andrews, who has not yet been paid, will Perez Hilton, Inc. be liable? How about Pablo Perez? Suppose Pablo has a "silent partner"—how about him or her?
>
> *(G)* On the basis of your reading of *Robertson*, *Timberline*, and the current version of MBCA §2.04, can you fill in the following chart? Are your results the same as when you filled it in before?

Liability of Individual Promoter/Defendant YES or NO?	
Plaintiff **knows** corporation not formed; Defendant **knows** corporation not formed **Liable?**	Plaintiff does **not** know corporation not formed; Defendant **knows** corporation not formed **Liable?**
Plaintiff **knows** corporation not formed; Defendant does **not** know corporation not formed **Liable?**	Plaintiff does **not** know corporation not formed; Defendant does **not** know corporation not formed **Liable?**

D. Promoter Liability to Investors and the Corporation Itself

Thus far, you have read about a promoter's risk of liability for transactions entered when he knows the corporation does not yet exist, including fiduciary liabilities to co-promoters. You also have read about liability risk when the incorporation process is botched.

There are two other common grounds for promoter liability. One simply is based on misrepresentation and/or certain types of non-disclosure to investors, which are illegal under all kinds of common and statutory laws, including the federal securities laws.

The other has a certain glamour factor associated with it, probably because of a case in which two courts came to different conclusions on exactly the same set of facts. (Neither case discussed here was a federal securities law case; the federal securities laws as we now know them were adopted in the 1930s and 1940s, and the primary rule against misrepresentation and non-disclosure was adopted in 1934. These two cases were common law fraud cases, but they raise issues similar to those that now might be faced under the law of federal securities fraud.) In Old Dominion Copper Mining & Smelting Co. v. Lewinsohn, 210 U.S. 206 (1908), the United States Supreme Court found that corporate promoters were not liable *to the corporation*, unlike the Massachusetts Supreme Court in Old Dominion Copper Mining & Smelting Co. v. Bigelow, 89 N.E. 193 (1909), *aff'd*, 225 U.S. 111 (1912). The type of liability at issue is usually referred to as *promoter's fraud*. The (grossly simplified) fact pattern involved a group of corporate promoters purchasing property and promptly selling it at a significantly higher price to a corporation they had formed and exclusively owned. It was contemplated at the time of the sale that shares would also be offered to the public without disclosure of the promoters' profit.

Connections: Stock Is a Security

Corporate stock is virtually always a security for purposes of the federal securities laws, and misrepresentation (including some non-disclosures) in connection with its purchase or sale can turn a situation into a federal case.

Connections: The Duty of Loyalty

There are materials in Chapters 12, 19, and 20 on the fiduciary duty of loyalty, both in general and in the context of corporate officers and directors.

As the U.S. Supreme Court saw it, the promoters could not have defrauded the corporation because those acting on the corporation's behalf (the promoters themselves) had all the relevant information. Later investors might have a claim against the corporation or the promoters for deceit, but the corporation itself was not deceived. In the view of the Massachusetts Supreme Court, however, the promoters owed the corporation a fiduciary duty (presumably because they were acting on its behalf in approving the sale) that was breached by agreeing to a sale at an unfair price at a time when sales to uninformed investors were contemplated. Looking at it this way, the Massachusetts result might be a bit narrower than, but would still dovetail with, the general fiduciary duty of loyalty, which requires that a fiduciary's transactions with a beneficiary be on fair terms, as well as involve full disclosure.

■ Think about this:

(H) Penelope Pettigrew is planning to start business as a land developer, and acquires a large parcel for $1 million. She also takes other steps toward starting the business, including lining up contracts for office space and services, the obligations for which would cost her an additional $200,000. She then has a change of heart. She has heard that Start-up Co., Inc., a firm with which she has not otherwise been involved, is interested in commencing land development, so she offers the land and contract rights to Start-up Co. for $2 million. Do you think Pettigrew has done anything wrong? Does it matter what she told the representatives of Start-up Co. about her purchase of the land?

 ### *Time Out for PR*

Suppose an attorney working on an incorporation is offered an opportunity to purchase shares in the corporation he or she is forming. As a matter of legal ethics, what should he or she keep in mind?

Hint: The attorney-client relationship is **fiduciary** in nature. The nature of fiduciary duties are explored elsewhere in this text. Also consider ABA Model Rule 1.8(a):

(a) A lawyer shall not enter into a business transaction with a client or knowingly acquire an ownership, possessory, security or other pecuniary interest adverse to a client unless:

(1) the transaction and terms on which the lawyer acquires the interest are fair and reasonable to the client and are fully disclosed

(Answers in Online Supplement)

and transmitted in writing in a manner that can be reasonably understood by the client;

(2) the client is advised in writing of the desirability of seeking and is given a reasonable opportunity to seek the advice of independent legal counsel on the transaction; and

(3) the client gives informed consent, in a writing signed by the client, to the essential terms of the transaction and the lawyer's role in the transaction, including whether the lawyer is representing the client in the transaction.

Hint: The attorney may well be a member of a **partnership** or an **LLC**, or may be **employed** by another attorney or entity. This means duties may be owed to other lawyers or the employing entity.

Test Yourself

Assume Applicability of the Most Current Version of the Model Business Corporations Act

Questions 1-3 rely on the following facts:

Frieda believes she has a great idea for a new business: Frieda's Frozen Fish Pops! Frieda doesn't have any money, however; just an idea and a lot of ambition. Fortunately for Frieda, her mother is a person of some means and has already told Frieda she'd be glad to invest in the business. Her mother does not care what form of business Frieda chooses, so Frieda tells her mom she's going to incorporate, and some days later, in exchange for a check for a substantial sum, Frieda gives her mom a stack of stock certificates indicating that she's a shareholder.

Newly infused with her mother's cash, Frieda goes about her efforts to get Frieda's Frozen Fish Pops up and running, and, among many other steps she takes, she signs a lease for retail space. At length, however, her business goes awry and Frieda never makes enough money to pay any rent on the lease.

Incidentally, Frieda lied to her mother and never filed any articles of incorporation.

1. Is Frieda liable on the lease she signed?

a. Yes.
b. Yes, unless Frieda told the lessor the corporation had not yet been formed.
c. Yes, unless Frieda told the lessor she was acting on behalf of a corporation.
d. No, unless Frieda told the lessor the corporation had not yet been formed.

2. Is Frieda's mother personally liable on the lease signed by Frieda?

    a. Yes, because promoters are always liable under pre-incorporation contracts.

    b. Yes, because promoters are partners by operation of law, and are jointly and severally liable for liabilities to third parties, even where they have been dishonest with one another.

    c. No, because only Frieda signed the lease.

    d. No, because Frieda's mother lacked knowledge about the true legal status of Frieda's Frozen Fish Pops.

3. Suppose (changing the facts stated above) that Frieda did file articles of incorporation subsequent to the date she entered the lease agreement, and that the articles were accepted by the Secretary of State before Frieda's business went awry. Is Frieda liable on the lease she signed?

    a. Yes, because at the time the lease was signed she knew the corporation had not been formed.

    b. No, because the lessor was not harmed by the delay in filing.

    c. Yes, unless the lessor knew the corporation had not yet been formed and agreed not to hold Frieda liable.

    d. Yes, and so is Frieda's mother.

Question 4 stands alone:

4. In Model Business Corporation Act jurisdictions, a corporation comes into existence:

    a. When the incorporators indicate their desire to incorporate by spoken words, written words, or conduct.

    b. When articles of incorporation are delivered or mailed to the Secretary of State.

    c. When two or more persons agree to act as co-owners of a corporation for profit.

    d. When articles of incorporation are filed by the Secretary of State.

Questions 5-9 rely on the following facts:

Some time ago, Joe Johnson and his friend Bill Baxter started a business selling leather apparel, called "Johnson's Leather." Joe put up the money for the business and has pretty much called the shots. Bill didn't put in any money, but agreed he would contribute his physical labor. In return, each week since they started Joe has given Bill $100 in cash from the company's receipts. They never wrote down any agreement between them. The business is located in a Model Business Corporation Act (MBCA) jurisdiction.

Last week was a crazy one for Johnson's Leather. The following things happened:

Monday:	Joe drafted and filed articles of incorporation on behalf of the business, naming it "Johnson's Leather, Inc.," and filed them with the Secretary of State. The articles specified that Joe would be the corporation's initial director.
Tuesday:	Joe signed two written agreements, signing both "By Joe Johnson, CEO, Johnson's Leather, Inc." First, he signed a contract with Bill promising a paycheck of $100 per week in exchange for his continued labor, for the next year. Second, he signed a written agreement with his longtime supplier of leather handbags, Gucci, providing for a large purchase of new bags.
Wednesday:	A clerk from the Secretary of State's office called to tell Joe the articles of incorporation had been rejected for technical reasons.
Thursday:	Joe filed corrected articles of incorporation and they were immediately accepted for filing by the office of the Secretary of State.
Friday:	Joe cut a check in the amount of $100, payable to Bill, drawn on the company's bank account.

5. Prior to the events of last week, Bill was:

   a. A partner in a partnership.
   b. An employee of a sole proprietorship.
   c. An employee of a partnership.
   d. A shareholder.

6. If Bill now has an enforceable right to payment as against Joe, for the next year, it is because of:

   a. MBCA §2.01.
   b. MBCA §2.04.
   c. The common law of agency.
   d. Answers b and c are both correct.

7. If Bill now has an enforceable right to payment as against Johnson's Leathers, Inc., it is because of:

   a. Informal ratification.
   b. Informal adoption.
   c. Explicit novation.
   d. None of the above.

8. If the handbag supply agreement is unenforceable as against Joe, it is because of:

a. Ratification.
b. Adoption.
c. Facts believed to be true by Gucci.
d. None of the above.

9. If the handbag supply agreement is unenforceable as against Johnson's Leathers, Inc., it is because of:

a. MBCA §2.01.
b. MBCA §2.04.
c. The common law of agency.
d. None of the above.

14

Corporate Power and Purpose

Corporations (like other limited liability entities) exist . . . why? Is it to achieve social goals? To make money for their owners? To achieve the former via means of the latter? The early view was that corporations could exist only for limited and specifically identified social purposes. This chapter explores the transition in thinking about this topic, covering both twentieth- and twenty-first-century developments.

Chapter Outline

A. Purpose, Power, and the Doctrine of *Ultra Vires*

- There is a difference between power and purpose
- The doctrine of *ultra vires* is of declining importance but still worth knowing

B. The Common Law of Corporate Purpose

- Is the purpose of the corporation to make money for shareholders?
- Who gets to decide how the corporate purpose is best achieved?

C. Corporate Constituency Statutes and Benefit Corporations

- Sometimes permission isn't enough
- Doing well by doing good

A. Purpose, Power, and the Doctrine of *Ultra Vires*

Corporations were first chartered for limited purposes—such as the construction and operation of railways—that were viewed as publicly beneficial but not matters in which governments themselves wanted to invest. To ensure that these purposes were achieved, and because agglomerations of capital were viewed with some suspicion, charters closely circumscribed both corporate purposes and the powers that corporations could exercise in achieving them. Acts that were outside the power of the corporation (including for the reason that they were not in furtherance of its purpose) were known as *ultra vires*—legally unenforceable because undertaken with no legal power.

A.P. SMITH MFG. CO. V. BARLOW

Supreme Court of New Jersey
98 A.2d 581 (1953)

JACOBS, Justice.

The Chancery Division, in a well-reasoned opinion by Judge Stein, determined that a donation by the plaintiff The A.P. Smith Manufacturing Company to Princeton University was *intra vires*. . . .

Photographic credit: Smallbones, cropped by Inabluemn
At the end of fiscal year 2014, Princeton's endowment stood at $21 billion.

The company was incorporated in 1896 and is engaged in the manufacture and sale of valves, fire hydrants and special equipment, mainly for water and gas industries. Its plant is located in East Orange and Bloomfield and it has approximately 300 employees. Over the years the company has contributed regularly to the local community chest and on occasions to Upsala College in East Orange and Newark University, now part of Rutgers, the State University. On July 24, 1951 the board of directors adopted a resolution which set forth that it was in the corporation's best interests to join with others in the 1951 Annual Giving to Princeton University, and appropriated the sum of $1,500 to be transferred by the corporation's treasurer to the university as a contribution towards its maintenance. When this action was questioned by stockholders the corporation instituted a declaratory judgment action in the Chancery Division and trial was had in due course.

Mr. Hubert F. O'Brien, the president of the company, testified that he considered the contribution to be a sound investment, that the public expects corporations to aid philanthropic and benevolent institutions, that they obtain good will in the community by so doing, and that their charitable donations create favorable environment for their business operations. In addition, he expressed the thought that in contributing to liberal arts institutions, corporations were furthering their self-interest in assuring the free flow of properly trained personnel for administrative and other corporate employment. Mr. Frank W. Abrams, chairman of the board of the Standard Oil Company of New Jersey, testified that corporations are expected to acknowledge their public responsibilities in support of the essential elements of our free enterprise system. He indicated that it was not "good business" to disappoint "this reasonable and justified public expectation," nor was it good business for corporations "to take substantial benefits from their membership in the economic community while avoiding the normally accepted obligations of citizenship in the social community." Mr. Irving S. Olds, former chairman of the board of the United States Steel Corporation, pointed out that corporations have a self-interest in the maintenance of liberal education as the bulwark of good government. He stated that "Capitalism and free enterprise owe their survival in no small degree to the existence of our private, independent universities" and that if American business does not aid in their maintenance it is not "properly protecting the long-range interest of its stockholders, its employees and its customers." Similarly, Dr. Harold W. Dodds, President of Princeton University, suggested that if private institutions of higher learning were replaced by governmental institutions our society would be vastly dif-

More to the Story: The "Red Scare"

Senator Joseph McCarthy
In Office 1947-1957

Though it remains fairly muted in the opinion, a theme very plainly in the background of the *A.P. Smith* case was 1950s-era fears over the spread of Communism and its threat to democratic institutions. In 1953, when the case was decided, the "second red scare" was in full swing.

ferent and private enterprise in other fields would fade out rather promptly. Further on he stated that "democratic society will not long endure if it does not nourish within itself strong centers of non-governmental fountains of knowledge, opinions of all sorts not governmentally or politically originated. If the time comes when all these centers are absorbed into government, then freedom as we know it, I submit, is at an end."

The objecting stockholders have not disputed any of the foregoing testimony nor the showing of great need by Princeton and other private institutions of higher learning and the important public service being rendered by them for democratic government and industry alike. Similarly, they have acknowledged that for over two decades there has been state legislation on our books which expresses a strong public policy in favor of corporate contributions such as that being questioned by them. Nevertheless, they have taken the position that (1) the plaintiff's certificate of incorporation does not expressly authorize the contribution and under common-law principles the company does not possess any implied or incidental power to make it, and (2) the New Jersey statutes which expressly authorize the contribution may not constitutionally be applied to the plaintiff, a corporation created long before their enactment. . . .

Room to Argue:
The Profit Motive

Is society inevitably furthered by the existence of corporations with "the end of private profit"? There is a substantial literature on this subject and you can read more about it in the online Supplement.

It is worth noting that some state legislatures have specifically provided that a corporation's decision makers can take into account the interests of "constituencies" other than shareholders (such as employees and the community). In addition, several states now recognize the "benefit corporation," which can be organized for the dual purpose of profit and accomplishing social goals such as production of clean energy.

In his discussion of the early history of business corporations Professor Williston refers to a 1702 publication where the author stated flatly that "The general intent and end of all civil incorporations is for better government." And he points out that the early corporate charters, particularly their recitals, furnish additional support for the notion that the corporate object was the public one of managing and ordering the trade as well as the private one of profit for the members. . . . However, with later economic and social developments and the free availability of the corporate device for all trades, the end of private profit became generally accepted as the controlling one in all businesses other than those classed broadly as public utilities. . . . As a concomitant the common-law rule developed that those who managed the corporation could not disburse any corporate funds for philanthropic or other worthy public cause unless the expenditure would benefit the corporation. . . . During the 19th Century when corporations were relatively few and small and did not dominate the country's wealth, the common-law rule did not significantly interfere with the public interest. But the 20th Century has presented a different climate. . . . Control of economic wealth has passed largely from individual entrepreneurs to dominating corporations, and calls upon the corporations for reasonable philanthropic donations have come to be made with increased public support. In many instances such contributions have been sustained by the courts within the common-law doctrine upon liberal findings that the donations tended reasonably to promote the corporate objectives. . . .

[The court then summarizes cases recognizing (indirect) corporate benefits generated by donations that would produce an educated workforce, lead to goodwill of influential citizens and patrons, avoid the loss of prestige that would follow if a corporation's competitor made unmatched contributions, and lead to the goodwill of workers. It also recognizes a trend toward regarding a corporation as having the same powers as an individual.]

When the wealth of the nation was primarily in the hands of individuals they discharged their responsibilities as citizens by donating freely for charitable purposes. With the transfer of most of the wealth to corporate hands and the imposition of heavy burdens of individual taxation, they have been unable to keep pace with increased philanthropic needs. They have therefore, with justification, turned to corporations to assume the modern obligations of good citizenship in the same manner as humans do. Congress and state legislatures have enacted laws which encourage corporate contributions, and much has recently been written to indicate the crying need and adequate legal basis therefor. . . . In actual practice corporate giving has correspondingly increased. Thus, it is estimated that annual corporate contributions throughout the nation aggregate over 300 million dollars with over 60 million dollars thereof going to universities and other educational institutions. Similarly, it is estimated that local community chests receive well over 40% of their contributions from corporations; these contributions and those made by corporations to the American Red Cross, to Boy Scouts and Girl Scouts, to 4-H Clubs and similar organizations have almost invariably been unquestioned.

During the first world war corporations loaned their personnel and contributed substantial corporate funds in order to insure survival; during the depression of the '30s they made contributions to alleviate the desperate hardships of the millions of unemployed; and during the second world war they again contributed to insure survival. They now recognize that we are faced with other, though nonetheless vicious, threats from abroad which must be withstood without impairing the vigor of our democratic institutions at home and that otherwise victory will be pyrrhic indeed. More and more they have come to recognize that their salva-

More to the Story: Threats from Abroad

Anti-Communist propaganda could get . . . well, interesting . . .

At the Sign of THE UNHOLY THREE

Are you willing to PUT IN PAWN to the UNHOLY THREE all of the material, mental and spiritual resources of this GREAT REPUBLIC?

tion rests upon sound economic and social environment which in turn rests in no insignificant part upon free and vigorous non-governmental institutions of learning. It seems to us that just as the conditions prevailing when corporations were originally created required that they serve public as well as private interests, modern conditions require that corporations acknowledge and discharge social as well as private responsibilities as members of the communities within which they operate. Within this broad concept there is no difficulty in sustaining, as incidental to their proper objects and in aid of the public welfare, the power of corporations to contribute corporate funds within reasonable limits in support of academic institutions. But even if we confine ourselves to the terms of the common-law rule in its application to current conditions, such expenditures may likewise readily be justified as being for the benefit of the corporation; indeed, if need be the matter may be viewed strictly in terms of actual survival of the corporation in a free enterprise system. The genius of our common law has been its capacity for growth and its adaptability to the needs of the times. Generally courts have accomplished the desired result indirectly through the molding of old forms. Occasionally they have done it directly through frank rejection of the old and recognition of the new. But whichever path the common law has taken it has not been found wanting as the proper tool for the advancement of the general good. . . .

[The court then describes New Jersey's adoption of legislation from 1930 through 1950 progressively liberalizing the ability of corporations to make charitable contributions, culminating in a statute permitting reasonable contributions provided that the contribution shall not be permissible if the donee institution owns more than 10 percent of the voting stock of the donor and that a contribution shall not exceed 1 percent of capital and surplus unless the excess is authorized by the stockholders.] To insure that the grant of express power in the 1950 statute would not displace pre-existing power at common law or otherwise, the Legislature provided that the "act shall not be construed as directly or indirectly minimizing or interpreting the rights and powers of corporations, as heretofore existing, with reference to appropriations, expenditures or contributions of the nature above specified." . . .

The appellants contend that the foregoing New Jersey statutes may not be applied to corporations created before their passage. Fifty years before the incorporation of The A.P. Smith Manufacturing Company our Legislature provided that every corporate charter thereafter granted "shall be subject to alteration, suspension and repeal, in the discretion of the legislature." . . . A similar reserved power was placed into our State Constitution in 1875. . . . [Later cases] have repeatedly recognized that where justified by the advancement of the public interest the reserved power may be invoked to sustain later charter alterations even though they affect contractual rights between the corporation and its stockholders and between stockholders *inter se.* . . .

State legislation adopted in the public interest and applied to pre-existing corporations under the reserved power has repeatedly been sustained by the United States Supreme Court above the contention that it impairs the rights of stockholders and violates constitutional guarantees under the Federal Constitution. . . .

It seems clear to us that the public policy supporting the statutory enactments under consideration is far greater and the alteration of pre-existing rights of stockholders much lesser than in the cited cases sustaining various exercises of the reserve power. In encouraging and expressly authorizing reasonable charitable contributions by corporations, our State has not only joined with other states in advancing the national interest but has also specially furthered the interests of its own people who must bear the burdens of taxation resulting from increased state and federal aid upon default in voluntary giving. It is significant that in its enactments the State had not in anywise sought to impose any compulsory obligations or alter the corporate objectives. And since in our view the corporate power to make reasonable charitable contributions exists under modern conditions, even apart from express statutory provision, its enactments simply constitute helpful and confirmatory declarations of such power, accompanied by limiting safeguards.

In the light of all of the foregoing we have no hesitancy in sustaining the validity of the donation by the plaintiff. There is no suggestion that it was made indiscriminately or to a pet charity of the corporate directors in furtherance of personal rather than corporate ends. On the contrary, it was made to a preeminent institution of higher learning, was modest in amount and well within the limitations imposed by the statutory enactments, and was voluntarily made in the reasonable belief that it would aid the public welfare and advance the interests of the plaintiff as a private corporation and as part of the community

---

Connections: Fiduciary Duty

The officers and directors of a corporation owe the entity—and sometimes, it is said, its shareholders—certain fiduciary duties. These include the duty of loyalty (which has to do with avoiding or limiting conflicts of interest) and the duty of care (which requires acting in a manner reasonably calculated to be in the corporations' best interests). The *A.P. Smith* court notes that the donation was neither indiscriminate nor to a pet charity. Does that have more to do with fiduciary duty than with corporate power and purpose? Does it make a difference?

in which it operates. We find that it was a lawful exercise of the corporation's implied and incidental powers under common-law principles and that it came within the express authority of the pertinent state legislation. As has been indicated, there is now widespread belief throughout the nation that free and vigorous non-governmental institutions of learning are vital to our democracy and the system of free enterprise and that withdrawal of corporate authority to make such contributions within reasonable limits would seriously threaten their continuance. Corporations have come to recognize this and with their enlightenment have sought in varying measures, as has the plaintiff by its contribution, to insure and strengthen the society which gives them existence and the means of aiding themselves and their fellow citizens. Clearly then, the appellants, as individual stockholders whose private interests rest entirely upon the well-being of the plaintiff corporation, ought not be permitted to close their eyes to present-day realities and thwart the long-visioned corporate action in recognizing and voluntarily discharging its high obligations as a constituent of our modern social structure.

———————

The Model Business Corporations Act contains the following provisions, which would seem to sustain the outcome in the *A.P. Smith* case:

MODEL BUSINESS CORPORATIONS ACT

§3.01 Purposes

(a) Every corporation incorporated under this Act has the purpose of engaging in any lawful business unless a more limited purpose is set forth in the articles of incorporation.

§3.02 General Powers

Unless its articles of incorporation provide otherwise, every corporation has perpetual duration and succession in its corporate name and has the same powers as an individual to do all things necessary or convenient to carry out its business and affairs. . . . [Section 3.02 goes on to enumerate a number of examples, including the power to make donations for the public welfare or for charitable, scientific, or educational purposes.]

§3.04 Ultra Vires

(a) Except as provided in subsection (b), the validity of corporate action may not be challenged on the ground that the corporation lacks or lacked power to act.

(b) A corporation's power to act may be challenged:

    (1) in a proceeding by a shareholder against the corporation to enjoin the act;

(2) in a proceeding by the corporation, directly, derivatively, or through a receiver, trustee, or other legal representative, against an incumbent or former director, officer, employee, or agent of the corporation; or

(3) in a proceeding by the attorney general under section 14.30.

(c) In a shareholder's proceeding under subsection (b)(1) to enjoin an unauthorized corporate act, the court may enjoin or set aside the act, if equitable and if all affected persons are parties to the proceeding, and may award damages for loss (other than anticipated profits) suffered by the corporation or another party because of enjoining the unauthorized act.

More to the Story: Con Law

If a corporation has the same powers as an individual, does it have the same rights? For instance, does it have a Fifth Amendment right against self-incrimination? A First Amendment right to free speech? The answers seem to be "no" and "yes." Grossly simplified, the general line of demarcation has to do with the individual rights of shareholders and their freedom to associate. In other words, if a right would be available to a group of individuals, it often will be available to a corporation.

Still, since (as discussed in Chapter 13) the internal affairs of a corporation generally are governed by state law, would it be possible for a state legislature to provide that corporations formed in that state do **not** have rights under the federal Constitution?

■ **After examining the foregoing provisions, think about this:**

(A) Could a corporation formed in an MBCA jurisdiction give away all of its assets?

(B) Could a corporation formed in an MBCA jurisdiction enter into a contract to pay an employee less than the legal minimum wage?

(C) Suppose Glenda has invested in Monstro, Inc., a corporation formed in a state following the MBCA. Glenda discovers that Monstro is, in a foreign country, exploiting child labor in a manner generally understood to be a violation of human rights. Is there anything Glenda can do about it?

(D) Suppose, instead, that Glenda discovers Monstro has given a very large gift to Princeton University. Assume, further, that a majority of the directors, as well as many of their children, are graduates of Princeton. Does Glenda have any legal complaint?

(E) MachineCo manufactures specialty machines that other companies buy to use in manufacturing their products. MachineCo recently contracted with BuyerCo to produce a large, very expensive, one-of-a-kind mill

press that BuyerCo wants to use to make lava lamps. MachineCo has hit a snag, though, with a labor disturbance in its plant. As a result, making the mill press (on which MachineCo hasn't even begun work) will be much more expensive than anticipated, and MachineCo will lose money on the contract. To its surprise, MachineCo's lawyer discovered that BuyerCo's articles of incorporation include a purposes clause providing that BuyerCo is formed for the sole purpose of manufacturing ceiling fans.

Can MachineCo refuse to perform, or defend a breach of contract action by BuyerCo for failure to perform, on the theory that the contract was illegal *ab initio*?

 Time Out for PR

Although individuals generally are free to represent themselves in litigation "pro se," representation of someone else is usually only permitted if the representative is an attorney admitted to practice law before the court in question. The question sometimes arises whether a corporation—which has all the power of an individual—can represent itself in court. The answer generally is "no."

Assume that Laverne is a lawyer admitted to practice in State X. She also is the 100 percent shareholder and president of Bestco, Inc., which is incorporated in and being sued in State Y.

Consult American Bar Association Model Rules 5.5 (Unauthorized Practice of Law; Multijurisdictional Practice of Law) and 8.5 (Disciplinary Authority; Choice of Law). Would Laverne be in violation of Rule 5.5 if she represented Bestco in the State Y litigation? If so, what does Rule 8.5 tell you about which jurisdiction might discipline her?

 Time Out for PR, Continued

In addition, is there an argument that Laverne might have a proprietary interest in the outcome of litigation in violation of Model Rule 1.8(i) (Conflict of Interest: Current Clients: Specific Rules)?

As a final consideration, is there any possibility that Laverne might have a prohibited conflict of interest under Model Rule 1.7 (Conflict of

Interest: Current Clients)? That is, is there some chance her personal interest might get in the way of her representing Bestco? Would that also be true if she were representing the company in a non-litigation context—say, negotiating a supply contract on Bestco's behalf? Or negotiating with a minority shareholder for the repurchase of shares?

 Dear Prof.: You provided the relevant MBCA provisions, but are the laws of most jurisdictions generally the same on these matters?

Remember, if the laws of an important state differ significantly from the MBCA, we will signal it. Consider the following excerpts from the Delaware General Corporation Law:

§121 General powers.

(a) In addition to the powers enumerated in §122 of this title, every corporation, its officers, directors and stockholders shall possess and may exercise all the powers and privileges granted by this chapter or by any other law or by its certificate of incorporation, together with any powers incidental thereto, so far as such powers and privileges are necessary or convenient to the conduct, promotion or attainment of the business or purposes set forth in its certificate of incorporation. . . .

§122 Specific powers.

Every corporation created under this chapter shall have power to: . . . (9) Make donations for the public welfare or for charitable, scientific or educational purposes, and in time of war or other national emergency in aid thereof. . . .

Would you regard these provisions as saying something different than MBCA §3.02?

B. The Common Law of Corporate Purpose

The following case appears to be the most notorious authority for one of the most important (and, to some, controversial) rules of corporate law: what it means for a corporation's fiduciaries to make decisions "in the best interests of the corporation." In fact, the *A.P. Smith* court cited it for the modern view of corporate purpose.

The plaintiffs, the Dodge brothers, were minority shareholders in the Ford Motor Company. At the time, Henry Ford, president of the company, owned 58 percent of the outstanding capital stock.

DODGE V. FORD MOTOR CO.

Supreme Court of Michigan
170 N.W. 668 (1919)

OSTRANDER, C.J. . . .

[As the "Doing the Numbers" box and the discussion below indicate, the Ford Motor Company had huge cash reserves at the time the complaint in the matter was filed. The board of directors had begun to implement a plan involving replicating its existing plant and expanding its operations to include "vertical integration" — that is, smelting its own iron ore for the purpose of producing car parts. Plaintiff shareholders objected, believing that some of the company's large cash surplus should be distributed as dividends. The trial court ordered a dividend equivalent to one-half of accumulated cash surplus at the end of the preceding fiscal year, less the aggregate amount of "special" dividends paid in the interim. It also enjoined further progress on the smelting venture (evidently) as *ultra vires* for a corporation formed for the purpose of manufacturing cars, and prohibited any future increase in fixed capital assets as exceeding the amount permitted by a statute requiring a corporation's capital stock to be between $1,000 and $50,000,000. The holding of liquid assets, "(including accumulations of and from the earnings and profits of regular business operations from time to time) by the defendant, Ford Motor Company, in excess of such as may be reasonably required in the proper conduct and carrying on of the business and operations of said corporation in connection with, and by the use of, the fixed capital assets, limited as aforesaid, [was] likewise [found] without authority of law and [was] permanently and absolutely restrained and enjoined, and said defendant corporation and its board of directors, the individual defendants herein and their respective successors in office, [were] directed and commanded to declare and distribute, as dividends to the stockholders, any such excess" thereafter accruing.

The Supreme Court of Michigan found the statutory limit on capital stock applicable only upon such stock's initial issuance. With respect to the *ultra vires* argument it observed that it was not technically raised by the pleadings; more importantly, if a car manufacturing company could buy car parts it should be able to smelt the ore to make them, even though the smelted product could not be sold to third parties. The reasoning of the court with respect to the accumulation of fixed and liquid assets is set out below.]

As we regard the testimony as failing to prove any violation of anti-trust laws or that the alleged policy of the company, if successfully carried out, will involve a monopoly other than such as accrues to a concern which makes what the public demands and sells it at a price which the public regards as cheap or reasonable, the case for plaintiffs must rest upon the claim, and the proof in support of it, that the proposed expansion of the business of the corporation, involving the further use of profits as capital, ought to be enjoined because inimical to the best interests of the company and its shareholders, and upon the further claim that in any event the withholding of the special dividend asked for by plaintiffs is arbitrary action of the directors requiring judicial interference. . . .

Doing the Numbers: The Amount Available for Distribution

The unedited case contains substantially more financial information than this edited version. Still, it is possible to approximately recreate the corporation's balance sheet from the facts given.

Ford Motor Co. Balance Sheet for Year Ended July 31, 1916

ASSETS

Cash and other current assets	$54,000,000
Plant, equipment and other assets	$78,000,000
TOTAL ASSETS	$132,000,000

LIABILITIES AND OWNERS' EQUITY

TOTAL LIABILITIES	$18,000,000
OWNERS' EQUITY	
Stated Capital	$2,000,000
Earned Surplus	$112,000,000
TOTAL OWNERS' EQUITY	$114,000,000
TOTAL LIABILITIES AND OWNERS' EQUITY	$132,000,000

So what?

It's always good to see that balance sheets really do balance. The balance sheet also gives you a picture of how much money was lawfully available for dividends—at the time of the case, the amount of owners' equity in excess of stated capital (the sum of the par value of the outstanding shares), or $112 million. Adjusted for inflation, that would be about $2.4 billion today. The Dodge brothers, you see, were frustrated that the company in which they invested had the equivalent of about two-and-a-half billion dollars sitting around (more than a billion of it in cash), and wasn't sharing any with shareholders.

In Morawetz on Corporations (2d Ed.) §447, it is stated:

It may often be reasonable to withhold part of the earnings of a corporation in order to increase its surplus fund, when it would not be reasonable to withhold all the earnings for that purpose. The shareholders forming an ordinary business corporation expect to obtain the profits of their investment in the form of regular dividends. To withhold the entire profits merely to enlarge the capacity of the company's business would defeat their just expectations. After the business of a corporation has been brought to a prosperous condition, and necessary provision has been made for future prosperity, a reasonable share of the profits should be applied in the payment of regular dividends, though a part may be reserved to increase the surplus and enlarge the business itself. . . .

When plaintiffs made their complaint and demand for further dividends, the Ford Motor Company had concluded its most prosperous year of business. The demand for its cars at the price of the preceding year continued. It could make and could market in the year beginning August 1, 1916, more than 500,000 cars. Sales of parts and repairs would necessarily increase. The cost of materials was likely to advance, and perhaps the price of labor; but it reasonably might have expected a profit for the year of upwards of $60,000,000. It had assets of more than $132,000,000, a surplus of almost $112,000,000, and its cash on hand and municipal bonds were nearly $54,000,000. Its total liabilities, including capital stock, was a little over $20,000,000. It had declared no special dividend during the business year except the October, 1915, dividend. It had been the practice, under similar circumstances, to declare larger dividends. Considering only these facts, a refusal to declare and pay further dividends appears to be not an exercise of discretion on the part of the directors, but an arbitrary refusal to do what the circumstances required to be done. These facts and others call upon the directors to justify their action, or failure or refusal to act. In justification, the defendants have offered testimony tending to prove, and which does prove, the following facts: It had been the policy of the corporation for a considerable time to annually reduce the selling price of cars, while keeping up, or improving, their quality. As early as in June, 1915, a general plan for the expansion of the productive capacity of the concern by a practical duplication of its plant had been talked over by the executive officers and directors and agreed upon; not all of the details having been settled, and no formal action of directors having been taken. The erection of a smelter was considered, and engineering and other data in connection therewith secured. In consequence, it was determined not to reduce the selling price of cars for the year beginning August 1, 1915, but to maintain the price and to accumulate a large surplus to pay for the proposed expansion of plant and equipment, and perhaps to build a plant for smelting ore. It is hoped, by Mr. Ford, that eventually 1,000,000 cars will be annually produced. The contemplated changes will permit the increased output.

The plan, as affecting the profits of the business for the year beginning August 1, 1916, and thereafter, calls for a reduction in the selling price of the cars. It is true that this price might be at any time increased, but the plan called for the reduction in price of $80 a car. The capacity of the plant, without the additions thereto voted to be made (without a part of them at least), would produce more than 600,000 cars annually. This number, and more, could have been sold for $440 instead of $360, a difference in the return for capital, labor, and materials employed of at least $48,000,000. In short, the plan does not call for and

The car in question was the "Model T."

Henry Ford

is not intended to produce immediately a more profitable business, but a less profitable one; not only less profitable than formerly, but less profitable than it is admitted it might be made. The apparent immediate effect will be to diminish the value of shares and the returns to shareholders.

It is the contention of plaintiffs that the apparent effect of the plan is intended to be the continued and continuing effect of it, and that it is deliberately proposed, not of record and not by official corporate declaration, but nevertheless proposed, to continue the corporation henceforth as a semi-eleemosynary institution and not as a business institution. In support of this contention, they point to the attitude and to the expressions of Mr. Henry Ford.

Mr. Henry Ford is the dominant force in the business of the Ford Motor Company. No plan of operations could be adopted unless he consented, and no board of directors can be elected whom he does not favor. . . . A business, one of the largest in the world, and one of the most profitable, has been built up. It employs many men, at good pay.

[The court here quotes from a company press release.] "My ambition," said Mr. Ford, "is to employ still more men, to spread the benefits of this industrial system to the greatest possible number, to help them build up their lives and their homes. To do this we are putting the greatest share of our profits back in the business."

"With regard to dividends, the company paid sixty per cent. on its capitalization of two million dollars, or $1,200,000, leaving $58,000,000 to reinvest for the growth of the company. This is Mr. Ford's policy at present, and it is understood that the other stockholders cheerfully accede to this plan."

He had made up his mind in the summer of 1916 that no dividends other than the regular dividends should be paid, "for the present." [And the court takes the following quotations from a deposition of Mr. Ford.]

> "**Q.** For how long? Had you fixed in your mind any time in the future, when you were going to pay—
> "**A.** No.
> "**Q.** That was indefinite in the future?
> "**A.** That was indefinite; yes, sir."

The record, and especially the testimony of Mr. Ford, convinces that he has to some extent the attitude towards shareholders of one who has dispensed and distributed to them large gains and that they should be content to take what he chooses to give. His testimony creates the impression, also, that he thinks the Ford Motor Company has made too much money, has had too large profits, and that, although large profits might be still earned, a sharing of them with the public, by reducing the price of the output of the company, ought to be undertaken. We have no doubt that certain sentiments, philanthropic and altruistic, creditable to Mr. Ford, had large influence in determining the policy to be pursued by the Ford Motor Company—the policy which has been herein referred to.

. . . There should be no confusion (of which there is evidence) of the duties which Mr. Ford conceives that he and the stockholders owe to the general public and the duties which in law he and his codirectors owe to protesting, minority stockholders. A business corporation is organized and carried on primarily for the profit of the stockholders. The powers of the directors are to be employed for that end. The discretion of directors is to be exercised in the choice of means to attain that end, and does not extend to a change in the end itself, to the reduction of profits, or to the nondistribution of profits among stockholders in order to devote them to other purposes.

There is committed to the discretion of directors, a discretion to be exercised in good faith, the infinite details of business, including the wages which shall be paid to employees, the number of hours they shall work, the conditions under which labor shall be carried on, and the price for which products shall be offered to the public.

In 1915, the Dodge Brothers Motor Company was ranked second to the Ford Motor Company in U.S. car sales. Pancho Villa drove a 1915 Touring Car.

It is said by appellants that the motives of the board members are not material and will not be inquired into by the court so long as their acts are within their lawful powers. As we have pointed out, and the proposition does not require argument to sustain it, it is not within the lawful powers of a board of directors to shape and conduct the affairs of a corporation for the merely incidental benefit of shareholders and for the primary purpose of benefiting others, and no one will contend that, if the avowed purpose of the defendant directors was to sacrifice the interests of shareholders, it would not be the duty of the courts to interfere.

We are not, however, persuaded that we should interfere with the proposed expansion of the business of the Ford Motor Company. In view of the fact that the selling price of products may be increased at any time, the ultimate results of the larger business cannot be certainly estimated. The judges are not business experts. It is recognized that plans must often be made for a long future, for expected competition, for a continuing as well as an immediately profit-

Connections: Purpose Under the Statutes

What does this all have to do with the statutes providing that corporations can be formed for any lawful purpose?

John and Horace Dodge

1915 Dodge Brothers Motor Company Touring Car

Connections: The Duty of Care

When we discuss the duty of care owed by a corporation's fiduciaries, in Chapter 18, we will note that those fiduciaries are required to take action rationally related to the best interests of the company. For so long as it appears that the company will be a continuing enterprise, this arguably requires maximization of long-term share value—as *Dodge v. Ford* suggests.

able venture. The experience of the Ford Motor Company is evidence of capable management of its affairs. It may be noticed, incidentally, that it took from the public the money required for the execution of its plan, and that the very considerable salaries paid to Mr. Ford and to certain executive officers and employees were not diminished. We are not satisfied that the alleged motives of the directors, in so far as they are reflected in the conduct of the business, menace the interests of shareholders. It is enough to say, perhaps, that the court of equity is at all times open to complaining shareholders having a just grievance. . . .

The decree of the court below fixing and determining the specific amount to be distributed to stockholders is affirmed. . . .

■ **Think about this:**

(F) Suppose that Henry Ford, rather than reducing the price of cars, wanted to cause the Ford Motor Company to donate a substantial amount of its profits to charity. Does it matter how large the gift is? Does it matter who the recipient is? Alternatively, be reminded that the events complained of in *Dodge v. Ford Motor Co.* transpired as the winds of war were sweeping toward the United States. Suppose Henry Ford, in a fit of patriotism, had decided to lower the price of a foreseeably large number of cars sold to the U.S. military. Would that pass muster?

(G) Interestingly, *Dodge v. Ford* was decided at a time of fervent popular concern over "big business." Perceived abuses by the railroads and the business "trusts" of the 1870s and 1880s had led to adoption of the Sherman Antitrust Act in 1890, but when that law failed to stop the "Great Merger Movement" of 1895-1905—during which upwards of 1,800 business firms disappeared into new combinations and whole sectors were reshaped, often enough leaving only one or a few firms dominant over them—renewed popular clamor against big business was among the most important political pressures of the day. The issue was a key focus of the presidential election of 1912, and one of Woodrow Wilson's first major initiatives as President was the 1914 adoption of the Clayton Act, to toughen merger and other antitrust rules, and creation of the Federal Trade Commission in the same year, the more vigorously to enforce them.

But not everyone agreed with antagonism to large business and accumulation of wealth. So ask yourself: Is the result in *Dodge v. Ford* consistent with that popular sentiment, or in tension with it?

Time Out for PR

Read American Bar Association Model Rule 3.3(a)(3) (Candor Toward the Tribunal). If you had been Henry Ford's lawyer in *Dodge v. Ford Motor Co.*, what would you have counseled him to say on the stand in order to avoid any charge that you had offered false evidence? How many questions should you ask him about his true motives?

C. Corporate Constituency Statutes and Benefit Corporations

In the 1980s, a wave of attempted hostile takeovers caused corporate managers to lobby state legislatures for the authority to base decisions on what was best for a corporation on matters in addition to corporate profitability. The idea was to permit the decision to resist a takeover to rest on grounds including loss of jobs and the effects on communities of plant closures. This type of legislation became quite popular: Over 40 states now have some version of what has come to be known as a "corporate constituency" statute. Interestingly, most of these statutes are not textually limited to the takeover context, instead applying to all corporate decision making. Also interesting is the fact that Delaware does not have such a statute. What Delaware has instead is a wealth of common law on the subject of corporate decision making in general, as well as on specific duties in the face of proposed takeovers.

Set out below are excerpts from the law of Pennsylvania, the earliest adopter of corporate constituency legislation.

PENNSYLVANIA BUSINESS CORPORATIONS LAW

§1715. Exercise of powers generally.

(a) General rule.—In discharging the duties of their respective positions, the board of directors, committees of the board and individual directors of a business corporation may, in considering the best interests of the corporation, consider to the extent they deem appropriate:

(1) The effects of any action upon any or all groups affected by such action, including shareholders, employees, suppliers, customers and creditors of the corporation, and upon communities in which offices or other establishments of the corporation are located.

(2) The short-term and long-term interests of the corporation, including benefits that may accrue to the corporation from its long-term plans and the

> **Connections: Mergers and Acquisitions**
>
> As discussed in Part 5, when a corporation is faced with the prospect of being acquired, its managers must decide how to respond in a manner that is consistent with both their fiduciary duty of care and their fiduciary duty of loyalty.

Room to Argue: Too Far or Not Far Enough?

Do corporate constituency statutes go too far, giving rise to the possibility that corporations will be managed inefficiently?

Or, on the other hand, do they not go far enough, as they generally permit, but do not require, consideration of non-shareholder interests and do not give other constituents any enforceable rights?

You can read more about this debate in the online Supplement.

possibility that these interests may be best served by the continued independence of the corporation.

(3) The resources, intent and conduct (past, stated and potential) of any person seeking to acquire control of the corporation.

(4) All other pertinent factors.

(b) Consideration of interests and factors.—The board of directors, committees of the board and individual directors shall not be required, in considering the best interests of the corporation or the effects of any action, to regard any corporate interest or the interests of any particular group affected by such action as a dominant or controlling interest or factor. . . .

§1717. Limitation on standing.

The duty of the board of directors, committees of the board and individual directors . . . is solely to the business corporation and may be enforced directly by the corporation or may be enforced by a shareholder, as such, by an action in the right of the corporation, and may not be enforced directly by a shareholder or by any other person or group. . . .

■ **Think about this:**

(H) Assume that the events complained of in *Dodge v. Ford Motor Co.* transpired in Pennsylvania after the adoption of the statutory provisions set out above. Would either the form of argument or the outcome of the case be likely to change?

Connections: A Shareholder's Right to Sue

When it appears that a corporation's best interests are not being well served by its decision makers, the decision makers themselves are not likely to object. As discussed in Chapters 15 and 22, the conditions under which shareholders may complain—suing "derivatively" on behalf of the corporation—vary depending on the jurisdiction.

Unrelated to takeover concerns, since 2010 at least 19 jurisdictions have adopted legislation enabling the creation of what are generally referred to as "benefit corporations," or "B-corporations." The following is an excerpt from Delaware's General Corporate Law providing a good sense of the thrust of these statutes.

§362 Public benefit corporation defined; contents of certificate of incorporation.

(a) A "public benefit corporation" is a for-profit corporation organized under and subject to the requirements of this chapter that is intended to produce a public benefit or public benefits and to operate in a responsible and sustainable manner. To that end, a public benefit corporation shall be managed in a manner that balances the stockholders' pecuniary interests, the best interests of those materially affected by the corporation's conduct, and the public benefit or public benefits identified in its certificate of incorporation. In the certificate of incorporation, a public benefit corporation shall:

(1) Identify within its statement of business or purpose pursuant to §102(a)(3) of this title 1 or more specific public benefits to be promoted by the corporation; and

(2) State within its heading that it is a public benefit corporation.

(b) "Public benefit" means a positive effect (or reduction of negative effects) on 1 or more categories of persons, entities, communities or interests (other than stockholders in their capacities as stockholders) including, but not limited to, effects of an artistic, charitable, cultural, economic, educational, environmental, literary, medical, religious, scientific or technological nature. "Public benefit provisions" means the provisions of a certificate of incorporation contemplated by this subchapter.

(c) The name of the public benefit corporation shall, without exception, contain the words "public benefit corporation," or the abbreviation "P.B.C.," or the designation "PBC," which shall be deemed to satisfy the requirements of §102(a)(l)(i) of this title.

■ **Think about this:**

(1) Assume that you are a legislator in a state that has not yet adopted either a corporate constituency statute or a statute enabling the creation of B-corporations. Do you think that your jurisdiction *should* adopt one or the other? How about both?

 Dear Prof.: You didn't spend much time on either corporate constituency statutes or benefit corporations. Does that mean they aren't very important?

As far as corporate constituency statutes are concerned, the answer is that they have given rise to a lot of commentary, but popularly are perceived as not changing much about day-to-day managerial focus on the all-important bottom line (that's the one at the bottom of the corporation's income statement). They may or may not embolden managers to resist more takeovers than otherwise would be the case.

On the other hand, the surging interest in benefit corporations might be the start of something big. It simply is too soon to tell.

Test Yourself

1. If someone were to say "the purpose of the corporation is to make money for its shareholders," he or she would, as a legal matter:

   a. generally be correct.
   b. be correct unless the relevant jurisdiction had adopted a corporate constituency statute.
   c. be correct only if the relevant jurisdiction had adopted a corporate constituency statute.
   d. generally be incorrect.

2. Which of the following most accurately describes the doctrine of *ultra vires*?

   a. The doctrine of *ultra vires* is totally defunct.
   b. The doctrine of *ultra vires* is useful in preventing the making of over-large corporate gifts.
   c. The doctrine of *ultra vires* generally presses the founders of corporations to form them for the broadest purpose possible.
   d. The doctrine of *ultra vires* can only be invoked by shareholders and not by the corporation itself.

3. PC, Inc., is limited in its articles of incorporation to the business of manufacturing and selling pollution control equipment. Which of the following is most true?

   a. PC, Inc.'s purpose is not valid because it arguably is in the public interest, rather than the best interests of shareholders.
   b. PC, Inc., lawfully may engage in any business its managers choose because of the permissive nature of modern statutes.
   c. PC, Inc., lawfully may engage only in the business of manufacturing and selling pollution control equipment.
   d. PC, Inc.'s issuance of debt would be *ultra vires* because it is something other than the manufacture or sale of pollution control equipment.

Questions 4 and 5 relate to the following facts:

Harry owns 75 percent of the stock of Harry Corp.; his ex-wife Esther owns the rest. Harry is the president and controls the board of directors. Harry decides he wants to donate to a worthy cause the maximum amount of the corporation's substantial income that will be deductible for federal income tax purposes. When he can't find a cause quite worthy enough, he decides to create his own foundation, to be known as the Harry Charitable Foundation (HCF). The purpose of the HCF is to operate a ranch so that children from homeless shelters in urban locations can spend time in another type of environment.

4. Harry explains to Esther that the board will be unable to declare dividends in the near future because it has determined that it needs to reinvest all of the company's earnings in excess of the intended donation in expanding Harry Corp.'s facilities. Esther consults you about whether a suit demanding that the board be ordered to pay dividends would be successful. Your advice to her is that:

   a. The board's determination with respect to reinvestment is unlikely to be second-guessed by a court.
   b. The board's determination with respect to the charitable donation is unlikely to be second-guessed by a court.
   c. Answers a and b are both correct.
   d. Neither answer a nor answer b is correct.

5. If the donation is made and Esther brings litigation, which of the following is most likely to be true?

   a. The gift will be found to be a breach of fiduciary duty.
   b. The gift will be found to be *ultra vires*.
   c. Answers a and b are both correct.
   d. Neither answer a nor b is correct.

15

Introduction to Shares, Shareholders, and Corporate Debt

A business can raise the money it needs to operate in a variety of ways, and the choices it makes have a lot of consequences. When a business takes in money from a certain source or in a certain way, it can raise issues under several different doctrines of corporation law. We will spend much of the coming chapters digging deeply into each of these various matters. Because it can be hard to get your head around it all, this chapter provides an overview of the various considerations, at a fairly high, introductory level of abstraction.

There essentially are two ways that any business can raise money (other than just by retaining its earnings): by issuing equity or by issuing debt. This chapter describes the methods of issuing both, and introduces a series of the rights and attributes of each. Understanding it all is important in designing the particular portfolio of tools a business uses to fund itself—a process we might describe as planning its capital structure. In reading through all this, it is important to keep in mind that although we discuss certain accepted characteristics of debt and equity, their details can be widely varied. The kinds of instruments firms employ to raise money are limited by not much more than financiers' imaginations. You should also remember that virtually all businesses fund themselves not just in one way or the other, but through varying combinations of debt, equity, and retained earnings. In any case, the choice to raise money in each way poses its own special set of legal issues, and its own set of pros and cons.

Chapter Outline

A. Shares and Shareholders

1. Issuance of Shares
   - Sales of stock by closely held corporations
   - Public offerings

2. Types of Shares
   - Common stock
   - Preferred stock

3. Shareholder Rights
   - Distributions
   - Preemptive rights
   - Dilution

4. Par Value

5. Limited Liability and the Obligation to Pay for Shares
   - "Watered stock" liability

6. Introduction to the Control Rights of Shareholders
   - The traditional role of shareholders

7. Introduction to the Shareholder's Right to Sue
   - Direct claims
   - Derivative claims

B. Corporate Debt

1. Debt and Debt Securities
   - Private debt
   - Public issuance of debt
   - Interest rates and the price of debt

2. Equity vs. Debt and the Basic Strategy of Capital Structure
   - Distinctions between debt and equity
   - The concept of leverage

Test Yourself

A. Shares and Shareholders

We begin with the first of the two major means of raising external funding, the sale of equity. "Equity" means "ownership," and in principle an owner of a firm's equity is an owner of the firm. When a corporation sells equity interests, they are commonly called "shares" or "stock."

We begin by briefly exploring the mechanics of stock sales, and then the different kinds of stock that can be issued. We then explore a series of special rights and protections shareholders enjoy, like rules surrounding distributions and dilution by new issuances. Probably the most significant equity attribute we'll discuss, at least in terms of its legal complexity, is a rule very dear to the average shareholder: limited liability. In particular, we look over two ways in which shareholders can *lose* limited liability—the doctrines of "watered stock" and "piercing the veil." Finally, we consider the role of shareholders in governing the corporation, which for present purposes consists of two broad powers. First, shareholders enjoy some limited rights to participate in internal decision making. As we stress, however, their participation is really very limited. It consists more or less exclusively of their right to vote at properly convened shareholder meetings, and then only on matters properly presented for their decision. Second, shareholders have a right to sue on behalf of the corporation when they believe it is being governed badly. Such suits are called "derivative," and derivative litigation is the primary means by which the fiduciary duties of corporate officers and directors are enforced.

Again, all these matters will be explored in greater depth in later chapters. The point for now is to lay them out for an initial survey.

1. Issuance of Shares

In surveying the mechanics of share sales, we begin with a basic distinction—sales by closely held companies and those by publicly traded companies. Strictly speaking, as a matter of corporation law, they are the same. The corporation first must ensure that the shares are authorized in its articles of incorporation, and then cause their issuance pursuant to a resolution of the board of directors. In practice, however, they differ quite a bit.

 Dear Prof.: You mentioned "closely held" and "publicly traded" companies. What's the difference?

Basically, a "closely held" company has few shareholders and active involvement of shareholders in management. Neither is true of a "publicly traded" company. There is more detail on this subject elsewhere in this book.

Sales of Stock by Closely Held Corporations. This will often be quite a simple affair. The closely held company will normally sell shares upon its formation to some small group of people, often including only the promoter or promoters and a close group of associates or family. The sales themselves will normally constitute simple contractual sales—shares of stock are issued in exchange for immediately delivered consideration, which, in most jurisdictions, now can include cash, a promissory note, tangible or intangible property, or an agreement to provide services. The only bureaucratic requirement is that

Connections: Federal Securities Laws

Corporate stock is virtually **always** a security for purposes of the federal securities laws. Although there frequently will be exemptions from registration available for the sale of stock by a closely held company, there is **never** an exemption from the federal laws against securities fraud. See Chapters 28 and 30.

corporations normally record stock sales in the "stock transfer record," a book normally kept by the corporate secretary or some other officer.

Public Offerings. By contrast, when a corporation decides to sell shares to the public at large, the transaction will be complex and time consuming. It also usually triggers complex and ongoing obligations under the federal securities laws, compliance with which is expensive in terms of legal and accountant fees as well as executive time.

A public offering (known as an "initial public offering" or "IPO" if it is a corporation's first such offering) usually also involves an additional party. The "underwriter," which is normally an investment bank, both advises the issuing corporation as to how to structure the transaction and price the securities, and aids in the distribution of the securities to be sold. The corporation itself does not usually sell securities directly to the investing public. Rather, the underwriter provides the corporation with cash and then markets the company's securities to the public. Corporations use this procedure because a public offering requires a large infrastructure and financial industry contacts that would be inefficient for businesses to maintain in-house, but which the investment bank maintains and uses every time it acts as an underwriter.

 Dear Prof.: You mentioned "investment banks." What are those?

Although the distinctions have eroded, in gross terms, "commercial banks" accept depositors' funds and deploy them for investment subject to banking regulations. They are not supposed to act as underwriters. "Investment banks" do not accept depositors' funds and do fulfill the underwriting function described in the text.

Connections: Derivative Litigation

There are a lot of bells and whistles associated with shareholders' rights to sue for breach of a duty owed to the corporation, rather than for breach of their own rights. Such suits are known as "derivative" suits and are discussed at length in Chapter 22.

2. Types of Shares

Every for-profit corporation is empowered to sell shares of itself (often referred to as "stock"). Every share at least theoretically represents an ownership interest in the corporation, meaning a right to benefit from the corporation's ownership of all of its assets and the use of those assets to produce profits. Ownership of stock can also give the shareholder a right to participate in the corporation's management, most importantly by voting to elect members of the board of directors. Likewise, holders of stock in some circumstances are entitled to bring lawsuits to enforce duties that the corporation's fiduciaries owe to the corporation. (These lawsuits are referred to as "derivative" lawsuits.) The shareholders therefore frequently are characterized as the corporation's owners, and at least in some sense its board and management work on their behalf.

For our purposes, and very generally speaking, there are two broad categories of stock. Before discussing them individually, it is good to remember that modern corporation law permits very wide flexibility for corporate planners to design securities as they see fit. Therefore, while we can generalize about different kinds of stock, these are generalizations only. There really are no precise terms of art to describe different kinds of security.

Where the corporation has more than one class of stock, the articles must authorize each class and define their terms. Model Business Corporations Act (MBCA) §6.01(a).

More to the Story: What Is "Ownership"?

A partnership is an association of two or more persons to carry on as co-owners a business for profit. "Ownership" in that context tends to confer on the owners more rights to participate in management than does ownership by shareholders. There is more on this subject elsewhere in this text.

The members of a limited liability company (LLC) have the rights set out in the entity's formational documents. Depending on how the members have designed their firm, their rights may closely resemble those of partners or those of shareholders, but they might also look not that much like either. Limited liability companies also are covered at length elsewhere in this text.

Moreover, there is a huge—verging on overwhelming—body of literature discussing the relationship of corporations to their shareholders and other stakeholders. Some of this literature disputes the characterization of shareholders as owners. You can read more about this in the online Supplement.

 ### What does it look like?

Check the online Supplement for the following items that are relevant to the issuance of shares:

- Articles of Incorporation provisions establishing multiple classes of stock
- Copy of a stock certificate for preferred stock
- Instructions for how to calculate a Delaware corporation's franchise fees

The two broad categories of shares are common stock and preferred stock.

Common Stock. Generally speaking, shares of common stock have a governance role in the corporation: They are entitled to vote at shareholder meetings.

Common stock also normally has a right to receive residual proceeds upon dissolution and liquidation of a corporation. On the other hand, common shares generally have no legal interest in receiving dividends (the corporation may pay them dividends any time it wishes if it is legally able to do so, but it is not required to do so provided it is not withholding them in bad faith).

More to the Story: Participating and Convertible Preferred

There are some common variations among types of preferred stock. Holders of "participating" preferred have rights to share in what is distributed to common shareholders in addition to the amounts to which their preferences entitle them.

Likewise, "convertible" preferred shares can, on specified terms, be converted into common shares. When might conversion be desirable to the investor? You can read more in the online Supplement, but the basic idea is that if a corporation reaches a stage of predictable profitability, the common shareholder's rights to the residue of what the company earns will be more valuable than the preferred shareholder's legally prior, but limited, rights.

Preferred Stock. Preferred stock normally does not vote, and indeed, holders of preferred stock do not usually invest because they are interested in participating in management. Rather, the value of preferred stock is thought to be in its financial attributes. First, preferred stock often is "preferred" on the basis of a dividend "preference." Thus, a share of preferred stock may entitle its owner to a fixed dividend each year—say, $10 per share—*if* the board of directors decides the corporation can and will pay dividends that year. Dividend preferences generally must be satisfied before the common shareholders can receive distributions. These preferences are either **cumulative** (meaning that for each year the corporation fails to pay the preference, it will be added to the next year's preference) or **non-cumulative** (meaning that if a dividend is not declared in a given year, the right to receive it is lost). Often, preferred shareholders may gain voting rights—and sometimes exclusive voting rights—if preferred dividends have gone unpaid for some specified period.

Preferred stock often also enjoys a "liquidation preference." If so, when the corporation is dissolved and its assets sold, the preferred shareholders will be entitled to payment of some fixed sum per share out of any proceeds remaining after the payment of creditors. That preference must be paid before the common shareholders receive any share of the liquidation proceeds. However, once the preferred have received their preference they are not entitled to receive any further liquidation proceeds, and the entire remainder goes to the common stock.

The mechanics of the design and issuance of shares are set out in MBCA §§6.01-6.03 and 6.21. *See also* Delaware Gen. Corp. L. §§151-152 and 161. Peruse these sections and then:

■ **Think about this:**

(A) Abdullah Al Salir and Berta Blomquist have decided to form a corporation in order to carry on the business of operating an upscale tea shop to be known as A&B Tea. Berta will provide the necessary financial backing in the amount of $2 million, payable immediately, and Abdullah will run the tea shop. They further agree that Abdullah will receive a salary of $100,000 per year in equal monthly installments

so long as he runs the tea shop, and that, after payment of Abdullah's salary and other corporate expenses, Berta will be entitled to all corporate earnings until her initial investment is repaid. Thereafter, profits will be shared 50/50. Control of the corporation is to be equally shared at all times. Is there some way to accomplish what Abdullah and Berta desire solely utilizing common and preferred stock, coupled with an employment contract for Abdullah? What does their proposed deal suggest about the "real" value of Abdullah's services?

This may help . . .

Debt and Equity

Preferred stock is often said to resemble "debt" more than it resembles "equity." The usual differences (dealt with in more detail elsewhere in this text) between debt and equity may quickly be summarized:

> **Debt** usually must be repaid, and its holders usually are entitled to ongoing compensation, known as "interest," until the principal is fully paid. Interest is deductible for tax purposes by the entity that pays it.
> **Equity** usually is not subject to repayment, and sharing of profits is at the discretion of the board of directors. Payments made to equity holders are not tax deductible.

One reason that preferred stock resembles debt is that it is often issued for a term of years, whereupon it can or must be **redeemed**, if the corporation has adequate funds.

---

3. Shareholder Rights

It was mentioned above, but well worth reiterating, that neither common nor preferred shareholders have any judicially enforceable right to receive distributions from the corporation unless the board of directors determines that it is lawful and desirable for such a distribution to be made. If these determinations are made and a distribution is declared, the relevant class or classes of shareholders essentially become creditors of the corporation to the extent of the amount declared. The only real qualification to this analysis is that the board of directors may not withhold distributions in bad faith (i.e., to starve the shareholders into selling their shares back to the corporation or to the directors themselves).

JD/MBA: Dividend vs. Distribution

Some people use the terms "distribution" and "dividend" as synonyms. That is not especially accurate. A dividend is a sub-type of distribution representing allocation of corporate profits. Under appropriate circumstances, a corporation may also distribute (that is, return) shareholders' investments by buying back their shares or simply by declaring distributions in excess of accumulated earnings. In addition, upon dissolution, a corporation's residual assets (after repayment of creditors) will be distributed to shareholders.

The tests governing the legality of corporate distributions are discussed in the online Supplement. The basic idea, though, is to prevent the directors from distributing to the shareholders amounts that are owed to creditors (and to prevent distributing to common shareholders amounts that are owed to preferred shareholders).

More to the Story: Par Value and Legal Consideration for Shares

Issuance of shares generally used to be more complicated than it is now, and this is still the case in some jurisdictions. One of the complications was that shares could only be issued for "par," a subject briefly discussed in the next section (Section A4). Another was that certain types of payment, including promissory notes and future services, were not legal consideration for shares. You can read more about both subjects in the online Supplement.

But shareholders do have some legal rights as shareholders. First, courts initially considering the issue concluded that, as property owners, common shareholders enjoyed a right (though not an obligation) to acquire a proportional number of shares out of any subsequent offering of the same class. This right is known as the "**preemptive**" right. Preemptive rights are now governed by statute, with MBCA §6.30 representing a typical approach. Basically, whether or not a corporation's shareholders have preemptive rights is a matter of choice (exercised when drafting the Articles of Incorporation).

Even where the incorporators have elected not to grant themselves preemptive rights in the articles, shareholders still have rights against **unfair dilution**. "Dilution" occurs when the value of a holder's shares is reduced by the sale of new shares for some lesser value. That is, as explained in the "Doing the Numbers" box, if a corporation issues new shares at a price lower than the current value of the outstanding shares, it will have the effect of pulling down the value of the existing shares. That said, there may be situations where a shareholder claims a dilution that hasn't occurred, as well as situations in which the board of directors' decision to issue new shares (often to themselves) at a given price indeed is unfair (and thus a breach of fiduciary duty).

Doing the Numbers: Dilution 101

Susana owns 100 shares (or 100 percent) of Xco, Inc.'s outstanding shares. Each of her shares is worth $100 (for a total of $100,000).

If Xco, Inc. issues an additional 100 shares for $50 each ($50,000 in total), the new worth of the corporation presumably is $150,000 ($100,000 + $50,000—the additional value in the company coming from the $50 per share that investors paid for the new shares).

When that amount is divided by the 200 shares outstanding after the issuance, it appears that Susana's shares each are worth only $75. (The online Supplement moves on to Dilution 102 and beyond.)

Do note, however, that a decision whether dilution really has occurred cannot be based solely on the basis of the shares' "book value" (the amount shown in the corporation's financial records). This is because the company's records generally reflect historic cost rather than current value.

Dear Prof.: You mentioned "outstanding" shares. Are they as great as they sound?

"Outstanding" shares are shares that a corporation has issued and has not repurchased or otherwise reacquired. Under some regimes, shares that have been issued and reacquired but not formally retired by the corporation are known as "treasury stock" or "treasury shares." Under the current MBCA, treasury shares do not exist. The only distinction is between "authorized" shares (those authorized by the articles of incorporation) and the number of those shares that are issued and outstanding.

■ **Think about this:**

(B) Annika Alvarez and Bo Brandenburg each own 50 percent of HypoCorp. Bo is the only director. Annika and Bo each paid $1,000 for each of the 20 shares outstanding. Bo would like to raise more capital (both he and Annika are tapped out), and the only person who seems to be interested is Charlene Cheng. Charlene, however, is only willing to pay $500 per share. Is there anything wrong with making the sale? If you were advising Bo, what questions would you ask him?

(C) Ainsley Alreeba and Bebe Bjorn each own 50 percent of Example, Inc. Each paid $50,000 for her shares. The company invested all $100,000 in Blackacre, which now is worth a mere $75,000. If Carlos Cramer wants to become a one-third owner by purchasing newly issued shares from Example, Inc., what is the logical price?

4. Par Value

There continues in American law a somewhat—well, completely—anachronistic concept known as "par value." There is no particularly good reason to study it, since it no longer has any real legal significance in MBCA jurisdictions or most others, except that corporations do in fact continue to issue par value stock, and discussing it a bit may spare you confusion. It turns out that in most states the only legal consequence of stating a par value is that it affects calculation of the franchise tax.

Basically, a corporation's founders, if they so desire, can assign an arbitrary value to the company's shares of stock. This is known as "par" value. The articles of incorporation thus can say, by fiat, that the shares have a par value of $1 per share, or one cent or $100 or whatever is chosen. Until about the 1970s, the statement of a par value had serious legal consequences. Shares could not be sold at less than par, and distributions to shareholders could never reduce the assets of the corporation to less than par. These rules were meant to protect creditors. Any creditor could inquire as to the number of shares outstanding and assume that a certain amount of money had been paid into the corporation, against which a claim could be executed. But par value and the legal rules surrounding it came under heavy criticism for much of the twentieth century.

For one thing, their value as creditor protection was dubious. While shareholders couldn't just return all their investment to themselves, no rule could prevent the amounts they paid in from being lost through operations. And in fact, though stock couldn't be sold at *less* than par, it could be sold for more. And of course, successful companies tend to build up some store of retained earnings over time. So, the actual wealth held by a company would often be much, much larger than the amount initially paid in as par, perhaps many years earlier, and the amount representing par would often be so small as to be meaningless to the creditors, particularly of large companies.

Doing the Numbers: Par Value and Stated Capital

Although par value has lost most of its legal significance, it is still reflected in corporate accounts:

Bookit, Inc.'s articles authorize 1 million shares with a par value of $1.00 per share. Bookit has issued 1,000 shares at a price of $10 per share, for a total of $10,000. Of that amount, $1,000 is recorded in Bookit's accounting records in the stated capital (or capital stock) account, and $9,000 goes in the capital surplus (or additional paid-in capital account). Both are sub-categories of "paid-in capital," and sensibly are distinguished, for record-keeping purposes, from the amounts of capital that a corporation has borrowed or earned.

The online Supplement contains readings amplifying this and other matters of corporate accounting.

In any event, the modern approach to par is to make it completely discretionary and, as far as the MBCA is concerned, irrelevant to both issue price and distributions to shareholders. Still, corporate founders may choose, in the articles of incorporation, whether the shares of the corporation do or do not have par value and, if they do, what that par value is. The amount of capitalization received as "par" in a given corporation, and particularly in publicly held companies, is likely to be fairly small in relation to the company's overall capitalization and in relation to its overall liabilities.

It would be reasonable to ask why corporations ever adopt par value, as it seems arbitrary and of little significance. The chief reason is simple: In some states, notably including Delaware, calculation of the state's franchise tax may be affected by the par value of a company's authorized or outstanding shares of stock.

 Dear Prof.: You made reference to "capital" and "capitalization." What did you mean?

This is a little tricky. A corporation's "capitalization" or "capital" generally includes the amounts that shareholders have paid for the shares (known as "paid-in capital"), the amounts that long-term creditors have loaned to the corporation, and the amounts that the corporation has earned but not distributed to shareholders (usually referred to as "earned surplus" or "retained earnings"). Sometimes, however, people use "capitalization" and "capital" to include only the amounts that "belong" to shareholders, and not the amounts that have been advanced by long-term creditors. Compounding the confusion is the concept of "working capital," which is the amount by which a company's liquid assets exceed its short-term liabilities. The online Supplement goes into more detail on these matters.

5. Limited Liability and the Obligation to Pay for Shares

> **More to the Story: A Shareholder's Other Roles**
>
> Remember that shareholders may play other roles in a corporation and will need to be aware of the prospect of liability in their other capacities.

All shareholders in a corporation enjoy limited liability. Generally, this concept is quite simple. Unlike the owner of a sole proprietorship or partners in a general partnership, shareholders cannot be required to contribute their own personal assets for obligations of the corporation that the business itself cannot cover. There are two situations, however, in which the courts have held that shareholders can be held to account for the company's debts, even if the company was properly organized as a corporation. One of these is when a court decides, for equitable reasons, to disregard the corporate entity. This is known as "piercing the corporate veil" and is the subject of its own chapter. The other is described below.

At a time when corporations generally were precluded from selling stock at less than its "par" value (that is, the arbitrary value stated in the articles of incorporation), courts recognized that shareholders who acquired shares for less than par should be liable for the difference. This liability generically was known as "watered stock liability" (although there were more specific terms based on the type or amount of consideration the corporation actually did receive). The following case talks about par value, but also invokes a (now typical) relevant statute that can apply whether or not shares have par value. The case also makes the point that even if there are no grounds for "piercing the corporate veil" to disregard the limited liability of shareholders, requiring said shareholders to pay for their shares is a different matter.

HANEWALD V. BRYAN'S, INC.

Supreme Court of North Dakota
429 N.W.2d 414 (1988)

MESCHKE, Justice.

Harold E. Hanewald appealed from that part of his judgment for $38,600 plus interest against Bryan's, Inc. which refused to impose personal liability upon Keith, Joan, and George Bryan for that insolvent corporation's debt. We reverse the ruling that Keith and Joan Bryan were not personally liable.

On July 19, 1984, Keith and Joan Bryan incorporated Bryan's, Inc. to "engage in and operate a general retail clothing, and related items, store. . . ." The Certificate of Incorporation was issued by the Secretary of State on July 25, 1984.

The first meeting of the board of directors elected Keith Bryan as president and Joan Bryan as secretary-treasurer of Bryan's, Inc. George Bryan was elected vice-president, appointed registered agent, and designated manager of the prospective business. The Articles of Incorporation authorized the corporation to issue "100 shares of common stock with a par value of $1,000 per share" with "total authorized capitalization [of] $100,000.00." Bryan's, Inc. issued 50 shares of stock to Keith Bryan and 50 shares of stock to Joan Bryan. The trial court found that "Bryan's, Inc. did not receive any payment, either in labor, services, money, or property, for the stock which was issued."

On August 30, 1984, Hanewald sold his dry goods store in Hazen to Bryan's, Inc. Bryan's, Inc. bought the inventory, furniture, and fixtures of the business for $60,000, and leased the building for $600 per month for a period of five years. Bryan's, Inc. paid Hanewald $55,000 in cash and gave him a promissory note for $5,000, due August 30, 1985, for the remainder of the purchase price. The $55,000 payment to Hanewald was made from a loan by the Union State Bank of Hazen to the corporation, personally guaranteed by Keith and Joan Bryan.

Doing the Numbers: Par Value and the Balance Sheet

Assume the dry goods business really was worth $60,000. The corporation's assets also included $10,000 in cash loaned by the Bryans, for a total of $70,000.

The creditors' claims against this amount were as follows: $55,000 owed to a bank, $5,000 owed to Hanewald, and $10,000 owed to the Bryans—again totaling $70,000.

The online Supplement goes into additional detail on corporate accounting, but an early corporate "balance sheet" (but for the complication of par value) would have looked something like this:

ASSETS		LIABILITIES	
Cash	$10,000	Debt to Bank	$55,000
Store	60,000	Debt to Hanewald	5,000
Total	$70,000	Debt to Bryans	10,000
		Total	$70,000
		EQUITY	
		Total	$70,000

The convention of accounting for par value, however, would force an entry of $100,000 in a "Stated Capital" sub-account under "Equity." This would throw the balance sheet out of balance unless an asset entry were made for something like "Shareholder's Debt for Failure to Pay for Shares."

Bryan's, Inc. began operating the retail clothing store on September 1, 1984. The business, however, lasted only four months with an operating loss of $4,840. In late December 1984, Keith and Joan Bryan decided to close the Hazen store. Thereafter, George Bryan, with the assistance of a brother and local employees, packed and removed the remaining inventory and delivered it for resale to other stores in Montana operated by the Bryan family. Bryan's, Inc. sent a "Notice of

Rescission" to Hanewald on January 3, 1985, in an attempt to avoid the lease. The corporation was involuntarily dissolved by operation of law on August 1, 1986, for failure to file its annual report with the Secretary of State.

Bryan's, Inc. did not pay the $5,000 promissory note to Hanewald but paid off the rest of its creditors. Debts paid included the $55,000 loan from Union State Bank and a $10,000 loan from Keith and Joan Bryan. The Bryan loan had been, according to the trial court, "intended to be used for operating costs and expenses."

Hanewald sued the corporation and the Bryans for breach of the lease agreement and the promissory note, seeking to hold the Bryans personally liable. The defendants counterclaimed, alleging that Hanewald had fraudulently misrepresented the business's profitability in negotiating its sale. After a trial without a jury, the trial court entered judgment against Bryan's, Inc. for $38,600 plus interest on Hanewald's claims and ruled against the defendants on their counterclaim. The defendants have not cross appealed these rulings.

The trial court, however, refused to hold the individual defendants personally liable for the judgment against Bryan's, Inc., stating: "Bryan's, Inc. was formed in a classic manner, the $10,000.00 loan by Keith Bryan being more than sufficient operating capital. Bryan's Inc. paid all obligations except the obligation to Hanewald in a timely fashion, and since there was no evidence of bad faith by the Bryans, the corporate shield of Bryan's Inc. should not be pierced." Hanewald appealed from the refusal to hold the individual defendants personally liable.

Insofar as the judgment fails to impose personal liability upon Keith and Joan Bryan, the corporation's sole shareholders, we agree with Hanewald that the trial court erred. We base our decision on the Bryans' statutory duty to pay for shares that were issued to them by Bryan's, Inc.

Organizing a corporation to avoid personal liability is legitimate. Indeed, it is one of the primary advantages of doing business in the corporate form. . . . However, the limited personal liability of shareholders does not come free. As this court [has] said . . . , "[t]he mere formation of a corporation, fixing the amount of its capital stock, and receiving a certificate of incorporation, do not create anything of value upon which the company can do business." It is the shareholders' initial capital investments which protects their personal assets from further liability in the corporate enterprise. . . . Thus, generally, shareholders are not liable for corporate debts beyond the capital they have contributed to the corporation. . . .

This protection for corporate shareholders was codified in the statute in effect when Bryan's, Inc. was incorporated and when this action was commenced, former §10-19-22, N.D.C.C.:

> Liability of subscribers and shareholders.—A holder of or subscriber to shares of a corporation shall be under no obligation to the corporation or its creditors with respect to such shares other than the obligation to pay to the corporation the full consideration for which such shares were issued or to be issued. . . .

In this case, Bryan's, Inc. was authorized to issue 100 shares of stock each having a par value of $1,000. Keith Bryan and Joan Bryan, two of the original incorporators and members of the board of directors, were each issued 50

Doing the Numbers, Continued

Bryan's, Inc., lost $4,840 through four months of operations, paid $55,000 to the Bank, and $10,000 to the Bryans. This is $69,840 (leaving $160 that evidently was paid to someone other than Hanewald).

This means the company still owed Hanewald $5,000 from the original purchase price plus $33,600 for four years and eight months of future rent.

If the Bryans had paid par value for their shares, the corporation would have had an additional $100,000, which easily would have been enough to pay Hanewald.

shares. The trial court determined that "Bryan's Inc. did not receive any payment, either in labor, services, money, or property, for the stock which was issued." Bryans have not challenged this finding of fact on this appeal. We hold that Bryans' failure to pay for their shares in the corporation makes them personally liable under §10-19-22, N.D.C.C., for the corporation's debt to Hanewald. . . .

. . . This court [also has] held that creditors could directly enforce shareholders' liabilities to pay for shares held by them under statutes analogous to §10-19-22. We believe that the shareholder liability created by §10-19-22 may likewise be enforced in a direct action by a creditor of the corporation.

. . . One commentator has observed: "For a corporation to issue its stock as a gratuity violates the rights of existing stockholders who do not consent, and is a fraud upon subsequent subscribers, and upon subsequent creditors who deal with it on the faith of its capital stock. The former may sue to enjoin the issue of the stock, or to cancel it if it has been issued, and has not reached the hands of a bona fide purchaser; and the latter, according to the weight of authority, may compel payment by the person to whom it was issued, to such extent as may be necessary for the payment of their claims." . . . The shareholder "is liable to the extent of the difference between the par value and the amount actually paid," and "to such an extent only as may be necessary for the satisfaction of" the creditor's claim. . . .

The defendants asserted, and the trial court ruled, that the $10,000 loan from Keith and Joan Bryan to the corporation was nevertheless "more than sufficient operating capital" to run the business. However, a shareholder's loan is a debt, not an asset, of the corporation. Where, as here, a loan was repaid by the corporation to the shareholders before its operations were abandoned, the loan cannot be considered a capital contribution. . . .

We conclude that the trial court, having found that Keith and Joan Bryan had not paid for their stock, erred as a matter of law in refusing to hold them personally liable for the corporation's debt to Hanewald. The debt to Hanewald does not exceed the difference between the par value of their stock and the amount they actually paid. Therefore, we reverse in part to remand for entry of judgment holding Keith and Joan Bryan jointly and severally liable for the entire corporate debt to Hanewald. The judgment is otherwise affirmed.

This may help . . .

CHECKLIST FOR ISSUANCE OF SHARES

✓ Number and type of shares authorized in Articles of Incorporation
✓ Preemption rights, if any, observed
✓ Determination by Board that consideration to be paid is adequate, and verification that it is actually received
✓ Existing shareholders treated fairly
✓ Full disclosure to new investors, including any dilution of investment

---

MBCA §6.22 is similar to the North Dakota statute quoted in the case. Assume that the MBCA applies, and then

■ **Think about this:**

(D) Would the case have come out any differently if the shares of Bryan's, Inc., had not had par value?

(E) Would the case have come out any differently if the Bryans had forgiven the $10,000 loan they made to the corporation?

(F) Yco, Inc.'s articles of incorporation authorize the issuance of 10,000 shares of $1 par stock. Shelley, who is a director and the president of Yco, agrees to pay $2 per share for all 10,000 shares. She has been issued all 10,000 shares but has not paid a penny. Adrian loans Yco $10,000 and demands that Shelley personally guarantee repayment, which Shelley agrees to do. Ben sells inventory to Yco in exchange for a promissory note for $5,000. Yco dissolves without paying either Adrian or Ben. How much do you suppose Shelley owes, and who can collect it? On what theory or theories?

(G) Suppose that while Yco was in operation, Shelley also was employed by Yco to drive its truck while making deliveries on its behalf. She drives the truck negligently and causes $50,000 of property damage to Carlos. Will Shelley be liable for the damage? Does it depend on whether she paid the agreed upon amount for her shares?

(H) Further suppose that while Yco was in operation, Shelley entered into a contract for $5,000 of supplies for Yco's use, neglecting to mention that she was acting on behalf of Yco. Yco uses the supplies. Will Shelly be liable to pay for them? Does it depend on whether she paid the agreed upon amount for her shares?

6. Introduction to the Control Rights of Shareholders

The mechanics of corporate governance, including just how shareholders are expected to take the actions they are permitted to take, are dealt with elsewhere in this text. Some of the procedures traditionally required can seem tedious and dry, and indeed in the case of very small companies it can seem absurd to follow all the requirements set out for meetings and voting. Nonetheless, a recurring theme in the law of corporations is that it can be very important to comply with corporate formalities, even when they seem unnecessary.

The following is a case in point, but more importantly illustrates the historic approach toward the role of the shareholder in corporate governance.

GASHWILER V. WILLIS

Supreme Court of California
33 Cal. 11 (1867)

By the Court, SAWYER, J.:

The Rawhide Ranch Gold and Silver Mining Company is a corporation duly organized under the statutes of California, for the purpose of carrying on the business of mining. On the 29th of April, 1865, a special meeting of the stockholders of the corporation was held, pursuant to notice, at the office of the company, at which all the stockholders were present. At this meeting of the stockholders, all the stockholders being present and all the capital stock represented, a resolution was unanimously adopted authorizing S. S. Turner, T. N. Willis and James J. Hodges, Trustees of said corporation, for and on behalf of said corporation, to sell and convey to D. W. Barney the mine, mill, buildings, mining implements, and appurtenances belonging to said company. In pursuance of said resolution, and without any other authority shown, on the 5th of June following a conveyance was executed by said Turner, Willis, and Hodges, Trustees, the commencement and form of execution of which are as follows:

JD/MBA: What's in a Name?

The California statute enabling formation of the corporation involved in this case used, at the time, the terms "trustees" and "board of trustees" for what, in the case of a for-profit entity, we more usually refer to as "directors" and "board of directors." The terms "trustees" and "board of trustees" generally are reserved for the nonprofit equivalents.

"This indenture, made the 5th day of June, A. D. 1865, between the Rawhide Ranch Gold and Silver Mining Company, a corporation under the laws of the State of California, by S. S. Turner, T. N. Willis and James J. Hodges, Trustees of said corporation, who are duly authorized and empowered by resolution and order of said corporation to sell and convey," etc.

"In witness whereof we, as the Trustees of and for and on behalf of said corporation, have hereunto set our hands and seal (the said corporation having no seal) the day and year first above written.

T. N. WILLIS. [L. S.]
JAMES J. HODGES. [L. S.]
S. S. TURNER. [L. S.]

Trustees of the Rawhide Ranch Gold and Silver Mining Company."

On the trial, after proving the adoption of the resolution before referred to at a meeting of the stockholders, as stated, the plaintiffs offered said deed in evidence, and defendants objected to its introduction on the three grounds—that it did not appear to be the act or deed of the corporation; that it had not the signature of the corporation, and that it was not sealed with the corporate seal but with the individual seals of the Trustees. The Court sustained the objection and excluded the deed, to which ruling plaintiffs excepted; and this ruling presents the question to be determined.

Under the view we take, it will only be necessary to consider the first ground of the objection, and the question is, does the instrument in question appear to be the act or deed of the corporation? If not, it was properly excluded, and the judgment must be affirmed. It is claimed by respondents that no authority is shown in the parties executing to execute the deed on behalf of the corporation. If the deed of a natural person, purporting to have been executed by an attorney in fact, were offered in evidence, it would, clearly, be inadmissible, without first showing the authority of the attorney. The recital of the authority in the deed itself would furnish no evidence whatever of its existence. The same is true of an artificial person—a corporation—at least, where the corporate seal is not affixed. . . . The authority of the Trustees to execute the instrument in question must, therefore, affirmatively appear, or it does not appear to be the act or deed of the corporation.

We are not aware of anything in the law, independent of any authority expressly conferred by the corporation, which authorizes Turner, Willis and Hodges, in their official character as Trustees, to execute the instrument in question on behalf of the corporation. No law of the kind has been called to our attention, and we do not understand that any is claimed by appellants' counsel to exist. And there is nothing in the nature of those offices, as connected with the object and business of the company, from which a general power in the Trustees, when not acting as a Board, to sell and convey the mine, mill and other property of the company, could be implied. The parties executing the instrument, then, if they had any authority in the premises, must have derived it from some corporate act; and the only act proved or relied on is the resolution adopted at the stockholders' meeting before mentioned. This was a meeting of the stockholders only. It was called as such, and the proceedings all appear to have been conducted as a stockholders' meeting. The resolution authorizing the sale and conveyance of the mine, etc., in question, was adopted by the stockholders, as such, at said meeting, and not by the Board of Trustees, or at any meeting of said Board. The Board of Trustees do not appear to have ever acted at all upon the matter in the character of a Board, but the testimony shows that they acted in pursuance of the said resolution adopted at the meeting of stockholders.

More to the Story: Seals

At one time both corporate and individual seals had evidentiary value with respect to whether signatures were valid and authorized. This has, with rare statutory exceptions, ceased to be the case in this country.

Connections: An Agent's Representations of Authority

In general, representations of authority by an agent are not effective. See Chapter 4.

Too Many Hats?

The problem manifest in this case is sometimes known as having "too many hats"—and confusing them.

More to the Story: Enforceable Shareholders' Agreements

As discussed in Chapter 25, there are more modern cases in which courts sometimes have permitted enforcement of unanimous shareholder agreements with respect to matters within the purview of the board of directors. Litigation is not, however, a substitute for planning.

In addition, most jurisdictions now explicitly authorize direct shareholder management by statute, though the statutory requirements must be followed carefully.

Section five of the Act authorizing the formation of corporations for mining purposes provides: "That the corporate powers of the corporation shall be exercised by a Board of not less than three Trustees, who shall be stockholders," etc. And section seven provides that: "A majority of the whole number of Trustees shall form a Board for the transaction of business, and every decision of a majority of the persons duly assembled as a Board shall be valid as a corporate act." Conferring authority to sell and convey the corporate property is the exercise of a corporate power, and under these provisions the "corporate powers of the corporation" are to be exercised by the Board of Trustees when the majority are "duly assembled as a Board." When thus assembled and acting the decision of the majority "shall be valid as a corporate act." We find nothing in the Act authorizing the stockholders, either individually or collectively in a stockholders' meeting, to perform corporate acts of the character in question. The property in question was the property of the artificial being created by the statute. The whole title was in the corporation. The stockholders were not in their individual capacities owners of the property as tenants in common, joint tenants, copartners or otherwise. This proposition is so plain that no citation of authorities is needed. Had the stockholders all executed a deed to the property, they could have conveyed no title, for the reason that it was not in them and what they could not do themselves they could not by resolution or otherwise authorize another to do for them. The corporation could only act— could only speak—through the medium prescribed by law, and that is its Board of Trustees.... It is said, however, that the Trustees were also all present and participated in the proceedings at the stockholders' meeting and assented to the resolution; that the resolution therefore was approved by all of the constituents of the corporation, and the powers of the corporation were exhaustively exercised. But they were acting in their individual characters as stockholders, and not as a Board of Trustees. In this character they were not authorized to perform a corporate act of the kind in question.... The power to sell and convey could only be conferred by the Trustees when assembled and acting as a Board. This is the mode prescribed. As a Board they could perform valid corporate acts, and confer authority within the province of their powers, upon the Trustees individually or upon any other parties to perform acts as the agents of the corporation....

Judgment affirmed.

As *Gashwiler* implies, a fundamental rule of American corporate law is that management of the corporation is vested above all in the board of directors. In fact, though it is old and in some ways idiosyncratic, the California statute at issue in *Gashwiler* remains fairly prototypical (*see*, for instance, MBCA §8.01(b)). Certain specific matters, however, usually are reserved by statute for shareholder vote, usually involving fundamental matters such as election of directors, amendment of the articles of incorporation and bylaws, and approval of at least some corporate combinations.

> ■ **Think about this:**
>
> *(I)* Peruse the table of contents of the MBCA, thinking about the types of matters upon which shareholders might logically be given the right to vote. Then, browse the statutes themselves to see if your intuitions were correct.

7. Introduction to the Shareholder's Right to Sue

Obviously, shareholders are entitled to enforce their own personal rights as shareholders. Thus, for instance, if money were distributed to common shareholders without regard for the monetary preference rights of preferred shareholders, the holders of preferred shares would have a cause of action.

But whether the *corporation* should bring a lawsuit is ordinarily left to the discretion of the officers and directors, even where some wrong has been done to the company that affects share values. That makes sense, and is consistent with the fundamental primacy of the board, as captured in cases like *Gashwiler*. But the rule conceals a significant problem. There are times when harm might be done that should be redressed, but likely will not be, because it was caused by the officers and directors themselves. Above all, breaches of fiduciary duties owed by the directors and officers would typically go uncorrected if their only remedy were lawsuits brought by the corporation as plaintiff, within management's own discretion. Directors and officers that actually breach a duty are not very likely to authorize suit against themselves, and might also resist suit against other directors or officers, with whom they often will be close. The problem doesn't only come up in fiduciary cases, though. For example, a corporation that is the victim of a tort or breach of contract might fail to sue if the defendant happens to be personally close with the company's management. For these reasons, the courts, using their powers in equity, have fashioned the so-called derivative lawsuit, by which shareholders can sometimes sue on their corporation's behalf, derivatively.

The following excerpt from Cohen v. Beneficial Industrial Loan Corp., 337 U.S. 541 (1949), describes the reasoning.

> As business enterprise increasingly sought the advantages of incorporation, management became vested with almost uncontrolled discretion in handling other people's money. The vast aggregate of funds committed to corporate control came

to be drawn to a considerable extent from numerous and scattered holders of small interests. The director was not subject to an effective accountability. That created strong temptation for managers to profit personally at expense of their trust. The business code became all too tolerant of such practices. Corporate laws were lax and were not self-enforcing, and stockholders, in face of gravest abuses, were singularly impotent in obtaining redress of abuses of trust.

Equity came to the relief of the stockholder, who had no standing to bring civil action at law against faithless directors and managers. Equity, however, allowed him to step into the corporation's shoes and to seek in its right the restitution he could not demand in his own. It required him first to demand that the corporation vindicate its own rights, but when, as was usual, those who perpetrated the wrongs also were able to obstruct any remedy, equity would hear and adjudge the corporation's cause through its stockholder with the corporation as a defendant, albeit a rather nominal one. This remedy, born of stockholder helplessness, was long the chief regulator of corporate management and has afforded no small incentive to avoid at least grosser forms of betrayal of stockholders' interests. It is argued, and not without reason, that without it there would be little practical check on such abuses.

Unfortunately, the remedy itself provided opportunity for abuse, which was not neglected. Suits sometimes were brought not to redress real wrongs, but to realize upon their nuisance value. They were bought off by secret settlements in which any wrongs to the general body of share owners were compounded by the suing stockholder, who was mollified by payments from corporate assets. These litigations were aptly characterized in professional slang as "strike suits." And it was said that these suits were more commonly brought by small and irresponsible than by large stockholders, because the former put less to risk and a small interest was more often within the capacity and readiness of management to compromise than a large one.

We need not determine the measure of these abuses or the evils they produced on the one hand or prevented and redressed on the other. The Legislature of New Jersey, like that of other states, considered them sufficient to warrant some remedial measures.

While the idea of derivative litigation is fairly straightforward in the abstract, the procedural details are quite complicated and are dealt with at length in their own chapter (Chapter 22). The parties will care a great deal about proving whether a suit is derivative or not, and it is because of those procedural details. They always burden the shareholder plaintiff, and they give defendants a series of powerful tools to dismiss. Accordingly, the parties expend enormous energy fighting over the question. For now, it is sufficient to recognize that if the gravamen of the complaint is injury to the corporation the suit is derivative, but "if the injury is one to the plaintiff as a stockholder and to him individually and not to the corporation," the suit is individual in nature. 13 Fletcher, Private Corporation §5911 (1970 Rev. Vol.). There are, however, many cases illustrating that the distinction between derivative and direct causes of action can be harder than it seems, and that the results courts reach can be surprising.

Dear Prof.: I don't feel good about this. Can't you just come right out and tell me how to tell the difference between direct and derivative claims?

Not really. The fact of the matter is that courts may be influenced by policy considerations—including some alluded to in the excerpt above—which in turn can be affected by some of the procedural bells and whistles (dealt with elsewhere in the text; see Chapter 22) associated with derivative litigation. For now, take heart from the assurance that the nature of a claim is not very often the subject of much real doubt. Your gut instinct as to whether a cause of action is derivative or direct is usually pretty reliable.

■ **Think about this:**

(J) Latoya Litigious owns shares in Derivco, Inc. She is upset because Derivco has not declared any dividends for the last three years. She believes that dividends are being withheld in bad faith because the directors wish to force her to sell her shares. Assuming she has a claim, is it derivative, direct, or both?

B. Corporate Debt

The other of the two major means by which any company can raise external funds is by borrowing it—that is, by issuing debt. In some ways, borrowing is like a flip-side of raising money through selling equity. In any case, debt is interesting and important and, indeed, a large percentage of American corporations raise more money through debt than through equity. Issuing it presents its own legal issues, but, strictly as a matter of corporate law, it does not trigger the same range of special doctrinal problems as does the sale of stock. So what we discuss in this section will really be more a set of pros and cons. Selling equity and selling debt pose different problems and advantages for both a corporation and its investors. It is important for transactional lawyers to understand them.

 What does it look like?

Check the online Supplement for the following sample documents that are relevant to the subject of corporate debt:

■ A copy of a bond
■ A copy of a typical trust Indenture
■ A prospectus relating to the public sale of debt securities

1. Debt and Debt Securities

Any form of business can, under the right circumstances, raise money through debt. Most obviously, any business can request a loan from a bank or other private third-party lender, businesses that qualify can apply for a loan or guaranty from the federal Small Business Administration or from one of its many state government counterparts, and often small businesses will receive loans from the owners themselves or from their friends, family, or close acquaintances. A two-party loan of this nature is usually just a contract, and the primary question from the perspective of corporate law is whether the party representing the corporation has authority to enter into the contract and, if not, what the consequences might be.

Less familiar may be the raising of funds through debt securities. There are actually quite a range of different investment vehicles that could be called debt securities, but the most common is the bond. Although, as a technical matter, any form of business might issue bonds, they primarily are issued by corporations. In simple terms, a bond represents a secured, long-term obligation of the corporation to repay principal and interest. It will state a face value amount of

---

Doing the Numbers: Rates of Return and Market Price

The amount someone is willing to pay for a bond logically relates to the interest rate it bears. If current interest rates are 10 percent for loans of a certain risk level, a $100 bond with a 10 percent interest rate ("Bond A") will sell for $100. If interest rates drop to 5 percent, Bond A's resale price will rise to $200. How do we know?

Bond A is paying $10 annually.

$$\$10 = .10(\$100)$$

Bond A will continue to pay $10 annually, even though an investor putting $100 into new bonds would expect to get only $5.

$$\$5 = .05(\$100)$$

A would-be purchaser of Bond A expecting only the prevailing 5 percent return will make the following calculation:

$$\$10 = .05(X)$$

We solve for X by dividing both sides of the equation by .05:

$$\$10/.05 = X, \text{ or } \$200 = X$$

principal—say, $100—a maturation date—the date by which the principal must be fully paid—and a rate of interest.[1]

Although a corporation usually offers its bonds for sale at their face value, it is quite usual for "fixed rate" bonds (those with interest rates that do not fluctuate based on market conditions) thereafter to trade at either a premium above, or a discount below, face value. This is so for two reasons. First, the market's view of the risk that the corporation will become insolvent or otherwise be unable to repay the loan may change. The purchaser will want to be appropriately compensated for bearing that risk, and since the rate of interest does not change, the price of the bond must. Second, market rates of interest and going rates of return on other investments also change over time. Again, if the bond is fixed rate, the appropriate adjustment can only take place in the price the bond purchaser pays.

Connections: Federal Securities Laws

Debt securities are frequently publicly traded, just like shares of stock, and also are subject to federal securities regulation. The exact rules that apply (except for those prohibiting fraud) sometimes differ depending on whether a security is equity or debt.

Sometimes private loans also involve the issuance of securities. Then, the anti-fraud provisions of the federal securities laws apply, even though the registration requirements do not. See Chapter 30.

Procedurally, a public issuance of debt securities looks just like a public offering of stock, and involves the assistance of an investment bank (which is again known, as in the case of stock offerings, as an "underwriter") in placing the debt with purchasers. There is, in the case of debt, an additional player known as the "indenture trustee." The trustee, which is usually a bank or trust company, is appointed in the master loan contract under which the bonds are issued, known as the "indenture." The indenture sets out rights and obligations between the corporation and the debt-holders, most of which serve to protect the holders' interests. Normally, the indenture will put limitations on the corporation's ability to take on new debt or engage in major transactions that could impair its ability to repay existing debt-holders. The indenture trustee will often have certain obligations under the indenture, including to see that timely payments are made to the bondholders, and may have duties to take action against the corporation to protect the interests of the holders.

---

2. Equity vs. Debt, and the Basic Strategy of Capital Structure

One might wonder why corporations need access to more than one avenue for raising capital. Indeed, the more deeply one gets into the study of

---

1. A bond is nearly identical to another instrument called the debenture. The only difference is that one (the bond) is secured with collateral and the other (the debenture) is not, and even then true debentures are often referred to as "bonds."

JD/MBA: Tax Consequences

The distinction between debt and equity can have significant tax consequences. Tax payments made by corporations to their lenders are considered a cost of doing business in order to produce income for the corporation's owners, and therefore are deductible by the corporation. Payments made to equity investors, by contrast, are not deductible. The tax authorities have therefore often challenged deductions for payments made to security holders when those securities arguably look more like equity than like debt, and the courts have had to sort out how to draw the distinction.

The online Supplement contains more information on this and other matters related to the subject of corporate finance.

Give me a lever long enough and a fulcrum on which to place it, and I shall move the world.
—*Archimedes*

Archimedes, Thoughtful, by *Fetti* (1620)

corporate finance the more surprising it becomes just how numerous and varied the different kinds of instruments are. The variety of instruments available to the investing public is now simply so huge that it can be difficult even to tell whether a particular one is "equity" or "debt."

The most important reason for this range of options is probably that different kinds of investors have different needs and interests, and corporations want flexibility to raise funds from all of them. Moreover, corporations differ in the degree to which investors will see them as desirable investments, and therefore different corporations will have different levels of bargaining strength with respect to the terms they can extract from their investors. Different vehicles to raise money therefore allow corporations and their investors to tune their relationships very finely to suit the circumstances.

The basic distinction, however, is this. Equity tends to put the risk of an investment more on the investors, but leaves them with the benefit of the "upside." The holders of shares of common stock, for example, generally have no right to receive dividends (although dividends cannot be withheld in bad faith), and will receive them only at the corporation's pleasure. Moreover, if the business fails they generally will lose some or all of their investment. The positive side of it is that if the business does very well, the returns (the "upside") belong mainly to the common shareholders. Debt, by contrast, puts the risk on the company, but ordinarily gives investors none of the upside. The company bears the risk because payments of interest and principal are contractually enforceable obligations whether or not it has profits from which to pay them. But because lenders are entitled only to the fixed returns for which they negotiated, all the cream of excess profits belongs to the common shareholders.

It is important to note that debt can have very valuable benefits for the company. First, as explained in the "Doing the Numbers" box on the next page, debt can be a very profitable means to raise money, so long as the corporation can earn returns that exceed the interest to be paid. This phenomenon is known as "leverage." Finally, an important reason that corporations need debt financing is that many companies, especially large ones, simply can't raise all the money they need through equity financing. There is a market-based limit to how much a company can raise by selling ownership in itself.

Doing the Numbers: The Magical But Risky Profitability of Leverage

Imagine that ABC Corp. invests in a new project that will cost $1 million. The firm invests $100,000 of its own ready cash, and borrows the rest at an interest rate of 5 percent annually, payable in one year. The project pays off very handsomely, returning not only the original $1 million cost, but an additional $145,000, an overall profit of about 15 percent.

But from ABC's point of view, the rate of profit it personally enjoys is *100 percent.* The interest owed its lenders will be $45,000 (5 percent of their principal of $900,000), leaving $100,000 profit on ABC's initial investment of only $100,000 of its own money.

So, you might wonder, why doesn't everybody fund all business endeavors with as much debt as they can get? The answer, aside from the fact that lenders will not consider every business creditworthy enough to lend it lots of money, is that debt is very risky. Principal and interest must be timely paid, whether there are profits or not, on pain of litigation and potential insolvency. In this hypothetical, for example, ABC must earn at least $45,000 in one year on a $1 million project—a sizeable return—before it earns the first penny for itself.

From the corporation's perspective, this all raises certain issues of strategy. Every corporation, as a practical matter, must sell shares of stock, and they all do so, as an initial matter, because the core group of promoters of the corporation desires to be its owners and the beneficiaries of its expected upside. However, many corporations will need more money than they can raise through sales of stock, and many will want to put some limits on the number of persons entitled to share in the spoils. Many will want to take advantage of leverage. Moreover, there are large pools of money in the world—contributed by groups of investors and institutions—that a particular corporation will be able to reach only by taking on debt—that is, only by limiting the risk of the debt's purchasers, but guaranteeing a rate of return.

■ **Think about this:**

(K) Assume that the founders of Mathco, Inc., who intend to own 100 percent of its shares, want to raise $1 million. They believe Mathco then will be able to earn $100,000 per year (which, incidentally, is 10 percent of $1 million). They know that Mathco could borrow $500,000 from a local bank at an interest rate of 5 percent ($25,000 annually). Should they cause Mathco to borrow the money or should they try to come up with it all themselves? Why might the bank be willing to charge only 5 percent if there are investments that could produce 10 percent?

(L) Suppose that you are advising Big Bank, which is thinking about loaning $500,000 to Dinky Corp. Dinky Corp. is owned by Rielle Riche, who has paid $100,000 for all of the company's outstanding stock. What might you suggest that Big Bank consider?

Connections: Other Rights That Protect Creditors

The law protects creditors in a few special ways beyond the rights contained in their loan contracts. First, once a corporation is insolvent (generally meaning unable to pay its debts as they come due), creditors may be (and in Delaware clearly are) able to bring actions derivatively on behalf of the corporation. According to the Delaware Supreme Court, speaking in *North American Catholic Educational Programming Foundation, Inc. v. Gheewalla*, 930 A.2d 92, 101-102 (2007):

> The corporation's insolvency "makes the creditors the principal constituency injured by any fiduciary breaches that diminish the firm's value." Therefore, equitable considerations give creditors standing to pursue derivative claims against the directors of an insolvent corporation. Individual creditors of an insolvent corporation have the same incentive to pursue valid derivative claims on its behalf that shareholders have when the corporation is solvent.

This right to sue on behalf of the insolvent corporation specifically includes a right to recover any agreed-upon but unpaid consideration for shares.

Moreover, as discussed elsewhere in this text (see Chapter 14C), creditors are—like employees and customers—some of the constituents whose interests may be considered by corporate managers in determining the corporation's overall best interests.

Finally, creditors also enjoy a number of protections under state and federal bankruptcy laws, as well as laws that prohibit "fraudulent conveyances."

Test Yourself

Assume Applicability of the Most Current Version of the Model Business Corporations Act

1. Preferred stock is more like debt than like equity because:

   a. It earns fixed periodic returns, casts no vote, and is not subject to federal securities law.

b. It earns fixed periodic returns and must be retired according to its terms.

c. It earns fixed periodic returns and enjoys a liquidation preference.

d. Preferred stock does not resemble debt.

2. NewCo's articles of incorporation authorize the issuance of up to 100,000 shares of $1 par value stock. NewCo issues 10,000 shares to Ali for $5,000 and 10,000 shares to Bonita in exchange for her promise to work for one year. After the year has passed and Bonita has performed the work, NewCo incurs a debt to Big Bank of $15,000, which it ultimately is unable to pay. If Big Bank sues both Ali and Bonita, which of the following is most likely to be true?

a. Big Bank will recover $5,000 from Ali and $10,000 from Bonita.

b. Big Bank will recover nothing from Ali but will recover $10,000 from Bonita.

c. Big Bank will recover $5,000 from Ali but will recover nothing from Bonita.

d. Big Bank will not recover from either Ali or Bonita.

3. Start-up, Inc.'s articles of incorporation authorize the issuance of up to 100,000 shares of $5 par value stock. There is nothing else in the articles that would affect the answer to this question. Start-up issued ten shares, at a price of $1,000 per share, to each of Angus and Bo and subsequently became quite profitable. It has attracted the attention of Carl, who is willing to pay $200,000 for ten shares. Angus, the only director, decides to cause Start-up to issue the shares to Carl on those terms. Which of the following is most likely to be true?

a. Bo has the right to insist that an equal number of shares be offered to him on the same terms.

b. Bo has the right to prevent the sale to Carl.

c. Bo has no rights with respect to the sale to Carl.

d. Bo has the right to require that the sale to Carl be made at a fair price.

4. Which of the following statements is most true with regard to the similarities and differences between debt and equity?

a. Payments to shareholders are deductible, while payments to creditors are not.

b. Debt usually must be paid off according to a specific schedule, while equity need not.

c. The amounts that may be paid to creditors are subject to legal limits, while the amounts that may be distributed to shareholders are not.

d. It is always preferable to hold debt rather than equity.

5. Carlos is a creditor of Sketchy Co., while Sara is a shareholder. There is substantial doubt as to whether Sketchy Co. will be able to pay off its debt to Carlos as it comes due. Which of the following statements is most likely to be true?

    a. The directors of Sketchy Co. owe a duty to Carlos to see that the company's debt to him is paid.
    b. If Sketchy Co. cannot pay Carlos, Sara will be obligated to do so.
    c. In the event Sketchy Co. actually becomes insolvent, Carlos's claims as a creditor will be satisfied before Sara's claims as a shareholder.
    d. In the event Sketchy Co. actually becomes insolvent, Carlos's claims as a creditor will be satisfied before Sara's claims as a shareholder only if he is a bondholder.

6. Hugham holds 51 percent of the shares of Votex, Inc. He also is one of the two members of the board of directors, but is not an officer. If he learns of a piece of property that he believes Votex should purchase,

    a. He can enter into a binding purchase contract in the name of Votex, Inc., signing as its majority shareholder.
    b. Whether he can enter into a binding purchase contract in the name of Votex, Inc., depends on whether the shares he holds are common or preferred.
    c. He can enter into a binding purchase contract in the name of Votex, Inc., signing as a member of the board of directors.
    d. He cannot, without the approval of the other director, enter into a binding purchase contract in the name of Votex, Inc.

7. Delilah is one of Derivicorp's shareholders. She is disgruntled (the opposite of gruntled!) to learn that the board of directors has announced that it has authorized a contract to purchase property in downtown Detroit. Delilah thinks this is a terrible investment and plans to sue. Which of the following is most true?

    a. Delilah's claim is direct.
    b. Delilah's claim is derivative.
    c. Delilah will win if she is a preferred shareholder.
    d. Delilah will win if she is a common shareholder.

16

Piercing the Veil of Limited Liability

Limited liability looms large among factors motivating the choice to incorporate. Courts, however, have resisted the idea that all that is required to claim the privilege of limited liability is to file a "magic" piece of paper. The proprietors of limited liability vehicles must generally also dot their i's and cross their t's in the ongoing management of their firms, at the risk of being held to have disregarded their independent existence. They also need to be aware of the courts' general concern with guarding against inequity.

Chapter Outline

A. Introduction

- Various theories of shareholder liability
- "True piercing" and the factors approach
- The role of inequity
- Piercing other entities
- Enterprise liability
- Insurance and undercapitalization

B. Advanced Topics in Piercing the Corporate Veil

1. Who Can Be a Defendant?
   - The significance of control

2. Shareholder Direct Liability
   - What does the statute say?

Connections: Agency Law

An agent is one who acts on behalf of, and subject to the control of, another (who is known as a principal). In general, principals are liable for many of an agent's torts, including those the principal directs or authorizes and those of an employee acting within the scope of employment. In addition, a principal is liable for any contract an agent is actually or apparently authorized to enter on the principal's behalf. For more detail, see Part 2 of this text.

Test Yourself

A. Introduction

The doctrine generally referred to as "piercing the corporate veil" is somewhat unpredictable and subject to a variety of articulations. Complicating the picture is the fact that sometimes courts say they are piercing the corporate veil to impose liability on shareholders when liability could be imposed simply on the basis of an agency relationship. In other words, the shareholder could be acting as an agent on the corporation's behalf. Alternately, the corporation could be acting as the shareholder's agent. In addition, sometimes a shareholder will be liable not on account of veil piercing, but instead because he or she has been called upon to personally guarantee a corporate debt. Yet another possibility is that a shareholder will be liable to a corporate creditor because he or she simply failed to pay the originally agreed-upon purchase price of his or her shares.

The *Baatz* case provides a good overview of some of the main theories of shareholder liability.

BAATZ V. ARROW BAR

Supreme Court of South Dakota
452 N.W.2d 138 (1990)

SABERS, Justice.

Kenny and Peggy Baatz (Baatz), appeal from summary judgment dismissing Edmond, LaVella, and Jacquette Neuroth, as individual defendants in this action.

FACTS

Kenny and Peggy were seriously injured in 1982 when Roland McBride crossed the center line of a Sioux Falls street with his automobile and struck them while they were riding on a motorcycle. McBride was uninsured at the time of the accident and apparently is judgment proof.

Baatz alleges that Arrow Bar served alcoholic beverages to McBride prior to the accident while he was already intoxicated. Baatz commenced this action in 1984, claiming that Arrow Bar's negligence in serving alcoholic beverages to McBride contributed to the injuries they sustained in the accident. Baatz supports his claim against Arrow Bar with the affidavit of Jimmy Larson. Larson says he knew McBride and observed him being served alcoholic beverages in the Arrow Bar during the afternoon prior to the accident, while McBride was intoxicated. . . .

Edmond and LaVella Neuroth formed the Arrow Bar, Inc. in May 1980. During the next two years they contributed $50,000 to the corporation pursuant to a stock subscription agreement. The corporation purchased the Arrow Bar business in June 1980 for $155,000 with a $5,000 down payment. Edmond and LaVella executed a promissory note personally guaranteeing payment of the $150,000 balance. In 1983 the corporation obtained bank financing in the amount of $145,000 to pay off the purchase agreement. Edmond and LaVella again personally guaranteed payment of the corporate debt. Edmond is the president of the corporation, and Jacquette Neuroth serves as the manager of the business. Based on the enactment of [South Dakota Codified Laws] 35-4-78 and 35-11-1 and [ultimately incorrect] advice of counsel, the corporation did not maintain dram shop liability insurance at the time of the injuries to Kenny and Peggy.

Doing the Numbers: Arrow Bar's Balance Sheet

Assume the bar business was worth the $155,000 paid for it. The corporation's assets also included $50,000 (evidently in cash) contributed by the Neuroths, $5,000 of which went toward the purchase of the bar. This means the bar's known assets at the time of the accident were around $200,000.

The only acknowledged creditor's claim against this amount was the $150,000 debt owed to the seller of Arrow Bar, leaving $50,000 to satisfy other creditors.

The online Supplement goes into additional detail on corporate accounting, but a (simplified) corporate "balance sheet" prepared immediately after the bar's purchase would have looked something like this:

ASSETS		LIABILITIES	
Cash	$ 45,000	Debt to Seller	$150,000
Bar	155,000	Total	$150,000
Total	$200,000		
		EQUITY	$50,000
		Total	$200,000

In 1987 the trial court entered summary judgment in favor of Arrow Bar and the individual defendants. Baatz appealed that judgment and we reversed and remanded to the trial court for trial. . . . Shortly before the trial date, Edmond, LaVella, and Jacquette moved for and obtained summary judgment dismissing them as individual defendants. Baatz appeals. We affirm. . . .

1. Individual Liability as Employees

SDCL 35-4-78 protects persons from the risk of injury or death resulting from intoxication enhanced by the particular sale of alcoholic beverages. . . .

Accordingly, the statute "establishes a standard of care or conduct, a breach of which is negligence as a matter of law." . . . That standard of care may be breached either by the liquor licensee or an employee of the licensee. . . .

Neuroths claim there is no evidence that they individually violated the standard of care created by SDCL 35-4-78. They claim the licensee is the corporation, Arrow Bar, Inc., leaving them liable only if one of them, as an employee, served alcoholic beverages to McBride while he was intoxicated. They claim the record is void of any evidence indicating that any one of them served McBride on the day of the accident.

Baatz argues that this court's decision in [an earlier case] allowed a cause of action against both the liquor licensee and the licensee's employees. Baatz claims that each of the Neuroths admitted in deposition to being an employee of the corporation. Consequently, under his reasoning, a cause of action may be brought against the Neuroths in their individual capacities. . . . While a cause of action may be brought against a licensee's employee, it must be established that that employee violated the standard of care established by the statute. Employee status alone is insufficient to sustain a cause of action. Baatz failed to offer evidence that any of the Neuroths personally served McBride on the day of the accident.

Baatz also argues that Jacquette Neuroth, as manager of the bar, is liable under the doctrine of respondeat superior. Under this doctrine, an employer may be liable for the conduct of an employee. . . . However, in this case, Jacquette Neuroth is not the employer. The employer of the individuals who may have served McBride is the corporation, Arrow Bar, Inc. Therefore, Baatz' argument misapplies the doctrine of respondeat superior.

2. Individual Liability by Piercing the Corporate Veil

1905 Mademoiselle Lo in body-stocking and veil

Baatz claims that even if Arrow Bar, Inc. is the licensee, the corporate veil should be pierced, leaving the Neuroths, as the shareholders of the corporation, individually liable. A corporation shall be considered a separate legal entity until there is sufficient reason to the contrary. . . . When continued recognition of a corporation as a separate legal entity would "produce injustices and inequitable consequences," then a court has sufficient reason to pierce the corporate veil. . . . Factors that indicate injustices and inequitable consequences and allow a court to pierce the corporate veil are:

(1) fraudulent representation by corporation directors;
(2) undercapitalization;
(3) failure to observe corporate formalities;
(4) absence of corporate records;
(5) payment by the corporation of individual obligations; or
(6) use of the corporation to promote fraud, injustice, or illegalities. . . .

Baatz advances several arguments to support his claim that the corporate veil of Arrow Bar, Inc. should be pierced, but fails to support them with facts, or misconstrues the facts.

First, Baatz claims that since Edmond and LaVella personally guaranteed corporate obligations, they should also be personally liable to Baatz. However, the personal guarantee of a loan is a contractual agreement and cannot be enlarged to impose tort liability. Moreover, the personal guarantee creates individual liability for a corporate obligation, the opposite of factor 5), above. As such, it supports, rather than detracts from, recognition of the corporate entity.

Baatz also argues that the corporation is simply the alter ego of the Neuroths, and [that] . . . the corporate veil should be pierced. Baatz' discussion of the law is adequate, but he fails to present evidence that would support a decision in his favor in accordance with that law. When an individual treats a corporation "as an instrumentality through which he [is] conducting his personal business," a court may disregard the corporate entity. . . . Baatz fails to demonstrate how the Neuroths were transacting personal business through the corporation. In fact, the evidence indicates the Neuroths treated the corporation separately from their individual affairs.

Baatz next argues that the corporation is undercapitalized. Shareholders must equip a corporation with a reasonable amount of capital for the nature of the business involved. . . . Baatz claims the corporation was started with only $5,000 in borrowed capital, but does not explain how that amount failed to equip the corporation with a reasonable amount of capital. In addition, Baatz fails to consider the personal guarantees to pay off the purchase contract in the amount of $150,000, and the $50,000 stock subscription agreement. There simply is no evidence that the corporation's capital in whatever amount was inadequate for the operation of the business. . . . [S]imply asserting that the corporation is undercapitalized does not make it so. Without some evidence of the inadequacy of the capital, Baatz fails to present specific facts demonstrating a genuine issue of material fact. . . .

Finally, Baatz argues that Arrow Bar, Inc. failed to observe corporate formalities because none of the business' signs or advertising indicated that the business was a corporation. Baatz cites SDCL 47-2-36 as requiring the name of any corporation to contain the word corporation, company, incorporated, or limited, or an abbreviation for such a word. In spite of Baatz' contentions, the corporation is in compliance with the statute because its corporate name—Arrow Bar, Inc.—includes the abbreviation of the word incorporated. Furthermore, the "mere failure upon occasion to follow all the forms prescribed by law for the conduct of corporate activities will not justify" disregarding the corporate entity. . . . Even if the corporation is improperly using its name, that alone is not a sufficient reason to pierce the corporate veil. This is especially so where,

Connections: Other Entities

Corporate shareholders are not, of course, the only modern investors who expect to enjoy limited liability—so do the members of limited liability companies and the partners in limited liability partnerships. It makes perfect sense to predict that courts would invoke the same considerations in determining when limited liability should be disregarded in these other contexts—and they do.

as here, there is no relationship between the claimed defect and the resulting harm. . . .

In summary, Baatz fails to present specific facts that would allow the trial court to find the existence of a genuine issue of material fact. There is no indication that any of the Neuroths personally served an alcoholic beverage to McBride on the day of the accident. Nor is there any evidence indicating that the Neuroths treated the corporation in any way that would produce the injustices and inequitable consequences necessary to justify piercing the corporate veil. In fact, the only evidence offered is otherwise. Therefore, we affirm summary judgment dismissing the Neuroths as individual defendants. . . .

HENDERSON, Justice (dissenting).

This corporation has no separate existence. It is the instrumentality of three shareholders, officers, and employees. Here, the corporate fiction should be disregarded. . . .

A corporate shield was here created to escape the holding of this Court relating to an individual's liability in a dram shop action. . . . As a result of this holding, the message is now clear: Incorporate, mortgage the assets of a liquor corporation to your friendly banker, and proceed with carefree entrepreneuring. . . .

Peggy Baatz, a young mother, lost her left leg; she wears an artificial limb; Kenny Baatz, a young father, has had most of his left foot amputated; he has been unable to work since this tragic accident. Peggy uses a cane. Kenny uses crutches. Years have gone by since they were injured and their lives have been torn asunder.

Room to Argue: Is Limited Liability Good or Bad?

Is limited liability an unmitigated good, because it encourages investments that might not otherwise occur? Or does it create the risk of "moral hazard"? That is, because investors can avoid some of the risk of the investment but enjoy all of the possible upside, are they just encouraged to gamble on investments that would be better avoided? You can read more about this argument in the online Supplement.

Assume that it were proven in the *Baatz* case that all three Neuroths *knew* that employees of Arrow Bar, Inc., regularly served intoxicated patrons, and did nothing to prevent it. Is there anything wrong with that? Is it any better or worse than the act of the bartender who individually served the drinks? Do the answers have anything to do with whether dram shop liability is good or bad?

Uninsured motorist was drunk, and had a reputation of being a habitual drunkard; Arrow Bar had a reputation of serving intoxicated persons. (Supported by depositions on file). An eyewitness saw uninsured motorist in an extremely intoxicated condition, shortly before the accident, being served by Arrow Bar. . . .

Are the Neuroths subject to personal liability? It is undisputed, by the record, that the dismissed defendants (Neuroths) are immediate family members and stockholders of Arrow Bar. By pleadings, . . . it is expressed that the dismissed defendants are employees of Arrow Bar. Seller of the Arrow Bar would not accept Arrow Bar, Inc., as buyer. Seller insisted that the individual incorporators, in their individual capacity be equally responsible for the selling price. Thus, the individuals are the real party in interest and the corporate entity, Arrow Bar, Inc., is being used to justify any wrongs perpetrated by the incorporators in their individual capacity. Conclusion: Fraud is perpetrated upon the public. At a deposition of Edmond Neuroth (filed in this record), this "President" of "the corporation" was asked why the Neuroth family incorporated. His answer: "Upon advice of counsel, as a shield against individual liability." . . .

Clearly, it appears a question arises as to whether there is a fiction established to escape our previous holdings and the intent of our State Legislature. Truly, there are fact questions for a jury to determine: (1) negligence or no negligence of the defendants and (2) did the Neuroth family falsely establish a corporation to shield themselves from individual liability, i.e., do facts in this scenario exist to pierce the corporate veil? . . .

Therefore, I respectfully dissent.

■ Think about this:

(A) Suppose that Arrow Bar, Inc.'s past transactions are as stated in the case and that, for whatever reason, Peggy and Kenny Baatz do not succeed in recovering anything from the corporation. Edmond Neuroth then enters into a contract on behalf of Arrow Bar to purchase a piece of property in exchange for $5,000 loaned to the corporation by Edmond and LaVella, and a promissory note in the amount of $150,000. The contract and promissory note are signed "Edmond Neuroth for Arrow Bar." Sidney Smith, the elderly man selling the property, does not inquire as to what type of entity Arrow Bar might be and is not sophisticated enough to ask for a personal guarantee. If Arrow Bar is not sufficiently profitable to make the scheduled payments on the promissory note, what might you expect to happen?

 Time Out for PR

Peggy and Kenny Baatz in fact were represented by an attorney throughout the proceedings involving Arrow Bar, Inc. and the Neuroth family. Consider ABA Model Rules 1.1 and 3.1 and the question of whether the attorney's conduct was problematic.

> ### Rule 1.1 Competence
>
> A lawyer shall provide competent representation to a client. Competent representation requires the legal knowledge, skill, thoroughness and preparation reasonably necessary for the representation.
>
> ### Rule 3.1 Meritorious Claims and Contentions
>
> A lawyer shall not bring or defend a proceeding, or assert or controvert an issue therein, unless there is a basis in law and fact for doing so that is not frivolous, which includes a good faith argument for an extension, modification or reversal of existing law. . . .

Although there are cases in some jurisdictions stating that no single factor is enough to justify piercing the corporate veil, it is clear that undercapitalization is extremely significant. In some states, undercapitalization coupled with a finding that injustice will result if the shareholders are not found liable does appear to be sufficient to justify a pierce. The *Walkovszky* case is a classic, both for its discussion of the undercapitalization issue and for its treatment of a potentially viable theory of "horizontal" piercing, between sibling corporations.

WALKOVSZKY V. CARLTON

New York Court of Appeals
223 N.E.2d 6 (1966)

FULD, Judge.

This case involves what appears to be a rather common practice in the taxicab industry of vesting the ownership of a taxi fleet in many corporations, each owning only one or two cabs.

The complaint alleges that the plaintiff was severely injured four years ago in New York City when he was run down by a taxicab owned by the defendant Seon Cab Corporation and negligently operated at the time by the defendant Marchese. The individual defendant, Carlton, is claimed to be a stockholder of 10 corporations, including Seon, each of which has but two cabs registered in its name, and it is implied that only the minimum automobile liability insurance required by law (in the amount of $10,000) is carried on any one cab. Although seemingly independent of one another, these corporations are alleged to be "operated . . . as a single entity, unit and enterprise" with regard to financing, supplies, repairs, employees and garaging, and all are named as defendants. . . . The plaintiff asserts that he is also entitled to hold their stockholders personally liable for the damages sought because the multiple corporate structure constitutes an unlawful attempt "to defraud members of the general public" who might be injured by the cabs.

The defendant Carlton has moved . . . to dismiss the complaint on the ground that as to him it "fails to state a cause of action." The court at Special Term granted the motion but the Appellate Division, by a divided vote, reversed, holding that a valid cause of action was sufficiently stated. The defendant Carlton appeals to us, from the nonfinal order, by leave of the Appellate Division on a certified question.

The law permits the incorporation of a business for the very purpose of enabling its proprietors to escape personal liability . . . but, manifestly, the privilege is not without its limits. Broadly speaking, the courts will disregard the corporate form, or, to use accepted terminology, "pierce the corporate veil," whenever necessary "to prevent fraud or to achieve equity". . . . In determining whether liability should be extended to reach assets beyond those belonging to the corporation, we are guided, as Judge Cardozo noted, by "general rules of agency". . . . In other words, whenever anyone uses control of the corporation to further his own rather than the corporation's business, he will be liable for the corporation's acts "upon the principle of respondeat superior applicable even where the agent is a natural person". . . . Such liability, moreover, extends not only to the corporation's commercial dealings but to its negligent acts as well.

In [Mangan v. Terminal Trans. Sys., Inc., 268 N.Y.S. 666 (Ct. App. N.Y. 1936),] the plaintiff was injured as a result of the negligent operation of a cab owned and operated by one of four corporations affiliated with the defendant Terminal. Although the defendant was not a stockholder of any of the operating companies, both the defendant and the operating companies were owned, for the most part, by the same parties. The defendant's name (Terminal) was conspicuously displayed on the sides of all of the taxis used in the enterprise and, in point of fact, the defendant actually serviced, inspected, repaired and dispatched them. These facts were deemed to provide sufficient cause for piercing the corporate veil of the operating company—the nominal owner of the cab which injured the plaintiff—and holding the defendant liable. The operating companies were simply instrumentalities for carrying on the business of the defendant without imposing upon it financial and other liabilities incident to the actual ownership and operation of the cabs. . . .

In the case before us, the plaintiff has explicitly alleged that none of the corporations "had a separate existence of their own" and, as indicated above, all are named as defendants. However, it is one thing to assert that a corporation is a fragment of a larger corporate combine which actually conducts the business. (See Berle, The Theory of Enterprise Entity, 47 Col. L. Rev. 343, 348-350.) It is quite another to claim that the corporation is a "dummy" for its individual stockholders who are in reality carrying on the business in their personal capacities for purely personal rather than corporate ends. . . . Either circumstance would justify treating the corporation as an agent and piercing the corporate veil to reach the principal but a different result would follow in each case. In the first, only a larger corporate entity would be held financially responsible while, in the other, the stockholder would be personally liable. Either the stockholder is conducting the business in his individual capacity or he is not. If he is, he will be liable; if he is not, then it does not matter—insofar as his personal liability is

Room to Argue: Is the Enterprise Entity Concept Good or Bad?

Is the enterprise entity concept discussed by the court well-recognized law and/or a good idea? There is more on this subject in the online Supplement.

concerned—that the enterprise is actually being carried on by a larger "enterprise entity." (See Berle, The Theory of Enterprise Entity, 47 Col. L. Rev. 343.)

At this stage in the present litigation, we are concerned only with the pleadings[.] . . . Reading the complaint in this case most favorably and liberally, we do not believe that there can be gathered from its averments the allegations required to spell out a valid cause of action against the defendant Carlton.

The individual defendant is charged with having "organized, managed, dominated and controlled" a fragmented corporate entity but there are no allegations that he was conducting business in his individual capacity. Had the taxicab fleet been owned by a single corporation, it would be readily apparent that the plaintiff would face formidable barriers in attempting to establish personal liability on the part of the corporation's stockholders. The fact that the fleet ownership has been deliberately split up among many corporations does not ease the plaintiff's burden in that respect. The corporate form may not be disregarded merely because the assets of the corporation, together with the mandatory insurance coverage of the vehicle which struck the plaintiff, are insufficient to assure him the recovery sought. If Carlton were to be held individually liable on those facts alone, the decision would apply equally to the thousands of cabs which are owned by their individual drivers who conduct their businesses through corporations organized pursuant to section 401 of the Business Corporation Law, Consol. Laws, c. 4 and carry the minimum insurance required by subdivision 1 (par. (a)) of section 370 of the Vehicle and Traffic Law, Consol. Laws, c. 71. These taxi owner-operators are entitled to form such corporations . . . , and we agree with the court at Special Term that, if the insurance coverage required by statute "is inadequate for the protection of the public, the remedy lies not with the courts but with the Legislature." It may very well be sound policy to require that certain corporations must take out liability insurance which will afford adequate compensation to their potential tort victims. However, the responsibility for imposing conditions on the privilege of incorporation has been committed by the Constitution to the Legislature (N.Y. Const., art. X, §1) and it may not be fairly implied, from any statute, that the Legislature intended, without the slightest discussion or debate, to require of taxi corporations that they carry automobile liability insurance over and above that mandated by the Vehicle and Traffic Law. . . .

More to the Story: A Shareholder's Other Roles

If an individual incorporates a single-cab business and drives the cab, will his or her liability be limited to the assets of the corporation?

This is not to say that it is impossible for the plaintiff to state a valid cause of action against the defendant Carlton. However, the simple fact is that the plaintiff has just not done so here. While the complaint alleges that the separate corporations were undercapitalized and that their assets have been intermingled, it is barren of any "sufficient[] [allegation]" that the defendant Carlton and his associates are actually doing business in their individual capacities, shuttling their personal funds in and out of the corporations "without regard to formality and to suit their immediate convenience." . . . Such a "perversion of the privilege to do business in a corporate form" . . . would justify imposing personal liability on the individual stockholders. . . . Nothing of the sort has in fact been charged, and it cannot reasonably or logically be inferred from the happenstance that the business of Seon Cab Corporation may actually be carried on by a larger corporate entity composed of many corporations which, under general principles of agency, would be liable to each other's creditors in contract and in tort. . . .

In March 2017, under pressure from Uber, the price of a single taxi medallion in New York City fell to $241,000 from a former high of approximately $1.3 million.

. . . If it is not fraudulent for the owner-operator of a single cab corporation to take out only the minimum required liability insurance, the enterprise does not become either illicit or fraudulent merely because it consists of many such corporations. The plaintiff's injuries are the same regardless of whether the cab which strikes him is owned by a single corporation or part of a fleet with ownership fragmented among many corporations. Whatever rights he may be able to assert against parties other than the registered owner of the vehicle come into being not because he has been defrauded but because, under the principle of respondeat superior, he is entitled to hold the whole enterprise responsible for the acts of its agents.

In sum, then, the complaint falls short of adequately stating a cause of action against the defendant Carlton in his individual capacity.

The order of the Appellate Division should be reversed, with costs in this court and in the Appellate Division, the certified question answered in the negative and the order of the Supreme Court, Richmond County, reinstated, with leave to serve an amended complaint.

KEATING, Judge (dissenting).

The defendant Carlton, the shareholder here sought to be held for the negligence of the driver of a taxicab, was a principal shareholder and organizer of the defendant corporation which owned the taxicab. The corporation was one of 10 organized by the defendant, each containing two cabs and each cab having the "minimum liability" insurance coverage mandated by section 370 of the Vehicle and Traffic Law. The sole assets of these operating corporations are the vehicles themselves and they are apparently subject to mortgages.[1]

From their inception these corporations were intentionally undercapitalized for the purpose of avoiding responsibility for acts which were bound to arise as a result of the operation of a large taxi fleet having cars out on the street 24 hours a day and engaged in public transportation. And during the course of the corporations' existence all income was continually drained out of the corporations for the same purpose.

The issue presented by this action is whether the policy of this State, which affords those desiring to engage in a business enterprise the privilege of limited

---

1. It appears that the medallions, which are of considerable value, are judgment proof. (Administrative Code of City of New York, §436-2.0.)

Connections: Distributions to Shareholders

In general, distributions to shareholders may not be made if they will render the corporation unable to pay its debts as they come due. Might that be the real issue?

liability through the use of the corporate device, is so strong that it will permit that privilege to continue no matter how much it is abused, no matter how irresponsibly the corporation is operated, no matter what the cost to the public. I do not believe that it is.

Under the circumstances of this case the shareholders should all be held individually liable to this plaintiff for the injuries he suffered. . . . At least, the matter should not be disposed of on the pleadings by a dismissal of the complaint. "If a corporation is organized and carries on business without substantial capital in such a way that the corporation is likely to have no sufficient assets available to meet its debts, it is inequitable that shareholders should set up such a flimsy organization to escape personal liability. The attempt to do corporate business without providing any sufficient basis of financial responsibility to creditors is an abuse of the separate entity and will be ineffectual to exempt the shareholders from corporate debts. It is coming to be recognized as the policy of law that shareholders should in good faith put at the risk of the business unencumbered capital reasonably adequate for its prospective liabilities. If capital is illusory or trifling compared with the business to be done and the risks of loss, this is a ground for denying the separate entity privilege." (Ballantine, Corporations (rev. ed., 1946), §129, pp. 302-303.) . . .

The defendant Carlton claims that, because the minimum amount of insurance required by the statute was obtained, the corporate veil cannot and should not be pierced despite the fact that the assets of the corporation which owned the cab were "trifling compared with the business to be done and the risks of loss" which were certain to be encountered. I do not agree.

The Legislature in requiring minimum liability insurance of $10,000, no doubt, intended to provide at least some small fund for recovery against those individuals and corporations who just did not have and were not able to raise or accumulate assets sufficient to satisfy the claims of those who were injured as a result of their negligence. It certainly could not have intended to shield those individuals who organized corporations, with the specific intent of avoiding responsibility to the public, where the operation of the corporate enterprise yielded profits sufficient to purchase additional insurance. Moreover, it is reasonable to assume that the Legislature believed that those individuals and corporations having substantial assets would take out insurance far in excess of the minimum in order to protect those assets from depletion. Given the costs of hospital care and treatment and the nature of injuries sustained in auto collisions, it would be unreasonable to assume that the Legislature believed that the minimum provided in the statute would in and of itself be sufficient to recompense "innocent victims of motor vehicle accidents . . . for the injury and financial loss inflicted upon them."

The defendant, however, argues that the failure of the Legislature to increase the minimum insurance requirements indicates legislative acquiescence in this scheme to avoid liability and responsibility to the public. In the absence of a clear legislative statement, approval of a scheme having such serious consequences is not to be so lightly inferred. . . .

The defendant contends that a decision holding him personally liable would discourage people from engaging in corporate enterprise. . . . The only types of corporate enterprises that will be discouraged as a result of a decision allowing the individual shareholder to be sued will be those such as the one in question, designed solely to abuse the corporate privilege at the expense of the public interest.

For these reasons I would vote to affirm the order of the Appellate Division.

■ Think about this:

(B) Is the majority in *Carlton* applying the same test applied in *Baatz*? How about the dissent?

(C) Suppose that Pablo Perez wants to own and operate a hotel chain known as the Perez Hiltons. The hotels will be identical in look and feel but for their locations in different cities. They will use the same suppliers and the same reservation system and will be advertised as a chain rather than as individual hotels. Pablo's plan is to separately incorporate each hotel and to form an additional corporation that will arrange supply, advertising, and other contracts for the entire chain. Since no statute requires hotels to carry insurance, he does not plan to have any of the corporations purchase any. What do you think of his plan? As his attorney, what suggestions might you make?

(D) Suppose, in the *Walkovszky* case, that each corporation had contracted for the minimum mandated insurance, but the company issuing the policies had gone bankrupt before Carlton made his claim. Would that have changed the outcome? Should it? Suppose the insurance company had gone bankrupt two years before Carlton's injury and the corporation's managers had notice of that fact? Is this any different than a corporation starting out with a substantial amount of cash that is contributed by shareholders and subsequently lost through unsuccessful operations?

(E) Suppose, in the *Walkovszky* case, that there were no statute mandating minimum insurance. Would that have changed the outcome? Should it?

(F) When the New York General Assembly adopted the minimum insurance rule discussed in *Walkovszky*, what policy issues do you think it had in mind, and was it thinking about a case like this one? What's your best argument that the General Assembly's purposes in adopting that statute suggest that it is not relevant to resolution of this case?

Time Out for PR

Was any of the advice you thought of giving Pablo business advice, as opposed to legal advice? Is it your obligation to consider business angles a client might have missed? *See* ABA Model Rules 1.1 (Competence) and 2.1.

Rule 2.1 Advisor

In representing a client, a lawyer shall exercise independent professional judgment and render candid advice. In rendering advice, a lawyer may refer not only to law but to other considerations such as moral, economic, social and political factors, that may be relevant to the client's situation.

This may help . . .

PLANNER'S CHECKLIST I

Have you given good advice about the need to . . .

A. Consider statutory alternatives to forming a corporation OR
B. Abide by the following? (The redundancy is worth it.)
  ✓ Observe corporate formalities
  ✓ Keep records
  ✓ Declare any distributions
  ✓ Maintain separate individual and corporate bank accounts
  ✓ Adequately capitalize/insure against liability
  ✓ Avoid using corporate funds for personal purposes
  ✓ Wear the right hat

B. Advanced Topics in Piercing the Corporate Veil

1. Who Can Be a Defendant?

One issue that does not come up very often, but which turns out to be fairly important, is just whom a plaintiff can hold accountable for a company's debts. It is almost always the case that named defendants in veil-piercing cases are shareholders in the corporation, and it is uncontroversial that shareholders may be held personally responsible when the veil is pierced. But what about officers and directors? Indeed, what about persons who have no formal relationship with a corporation but nonetheless effectively control it?

Some courts have read the range of possible defendants broadly. The *Freeman* case, which follows, held that veil-piercing liability can extend beyond the shareholders, and indeed beyond all formal limits.

FREEMAN V. COMPLEX COMPUTING CO.

United States Court of Appeals for the Second Circuit
119 F.3d 1044 (1997)

MINER, Circuit Judge.

Defendant-appellant Jason Glazier appeals from a judgment entered in the United States District Court for the Southern District of New York (Kaplan, J.) to the extent that the judgment compels him to arbitrate the claims made against him by plaintiff-appellee-cross-appellant Daniel Freeman. The claims were asserted under the provisions of a contract between Freeman and defendant Complex Computing Company, Inc. ("C3"). The court found that, although Glazier was neither an employee, officer, director, nor shareholder of C3, his control and dominion over C3 warranted the piercing of the corporate veil in order to impose personal liability upon him. . . .

BACKGROUND

While pursuing graduate studies under a fellowship at Columbia University in the early 1990s, Glazier co-developed computer software with potential commercial value and negotiated with Columbia to obtain a license for the software. Columbia apparently was unwilling to license software to a corporation of which Glazier was an officer, director, or shareholder. Nonetheless, Columbia was willing to license the software to a corporation that retained Glazier as an independent contractor. The licensed corporation then could sublicense the product to others for profit.

Accordingly, in September of 1992, C3 was incorporated, with an acquaintance of Glazier's as the sole shareholder and initial director, and Seth Akabas (a partner of Glazier's counsel in this action) as the president, treasurer and assistant secretary. In November of 1992, another corporation, Glazier, Inc., of which Glazier was the sole shareholder, entered into an agreement with C3 (the "consulting agreement").[2] Under the consulting agreement, Glazier, Inc. was retained as an independent contractor (titled as C3's "Scientific Advisor") to develop and market Glazier's software, which was licensed from Columbia, and to provide support services to C3's clients. Glazier was designated the sole

---

2. Although the consulting agreement was between C3 and Glazier, Inc., numerous provisions in the agreement made express reference to Glazier personally. For example, the consulting agreement provided that it was terminable if Glazier himself was unable to perform or supervise performance of Glazier, Inc.'s obligations. Also, the agreement defined the royalties to which Glazier, Inc. was entitled as revenues received by C3 in connection with products developed, or services rendered, by Glazier, Inc. or by Glazier personally.

signatory on C3's bank account, and was given a written option to purchase all of C3's stock for $2,000.

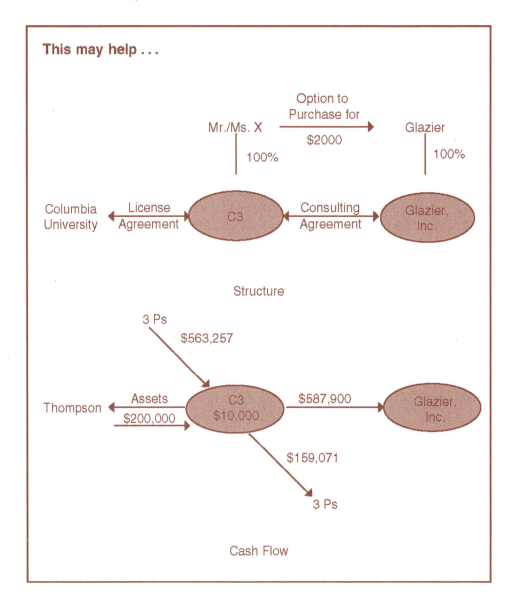

In September of 1993, C3 entered into an agreement with Freeman (the "C3-Freeman Agreement"), under which Freeman agreed to sell and license C3's computer software products for a five-year term. In exchange, C3 agreed to pay Freeman commissions on the revenue received by C3 over a ten-year period from the client-base developed by Freeman, including the revenue received from sales and licensing, maintenance and support services. The C3-Freeman Agreement included provisions relating to Freeman's compensation if C3 terminated the agreement prior to its expiration, or if C3 made a sale that did not result in revenues because of a future merger, consolidation, or stock acquisition. The agreement included an arbitration clause. . . .

. . . Although C3's president signed the C3-Freeman Agreement, Glazier personally signed the periodic amendments to [it]. . . .

In October of 1994, C3 gave Freeman the requisite 60-days notice of the termination of its agreement with him. The letter of termination, signed by Glazier, explained that C3's exercise of its option to terminate Freeman's employment was "an action to combat the overly generous termination clause we committed to, and to force a renegotiation of your sales contract."

[The assets of C3 subsequently were sold, and the available proceeds paid to Glazier through Glazier, Inc., as consulting fees. As a consequence of this and earlier payments made by C3 to Glazier, Inc., for consulting services, C3 was left with approximately $10,000 in assets. The exact amounts are detailed by the court below.]

In May of 1995, Freeman commenced the action giving rise to this appeal. . . . He estimated that he currently was due more than $100,000, and that the moneys due him in the future under the agreement would be in excess of $5 million.

. . . [D]efendants [who included C3, Glazier, and Thompson, the purchaser of C3's assets,] responded by seeking a stay of the action pending arbitration. Defendants contended that Freeman was obliged to arbitrate his claims against C3 in accordance with the terms of the C3-Freeman Agreement. . . . Freeman then moved to compel all three defendants to arbitrate. . . . Defendants countered that the arbitration clause in the agreement did not bind either Glazier or Thompson because neither one was a signatory to the C3-Freeman Agreement.

. . . The district court found that Glazier was subject to the arbitration clause of the C3-Freeman Agreement because he "did not merely dominate and control C3—to all intents and purposes, he was C3" and because he held the "sole economic interest of any significance" in the corporation. . . . The district court intended the judgment to "dispose[ ] of all claims asserted herein between and among [Freeman, C3 and Glazier]." . . .

[The district court further found that Thompson was an entity separate from C3, and that under no legal or equitable theory could Thompson be held to have assumed C3's obligations to Freeman. Accordingly, the district court entered an order] directing Freeman, C3 and Glazier to proceed to arbitration. This appeal and cross-appeal followed. . . .

II. Piercing the Corporate Veil

[The parties agreed that corporate law issues would be governed by New York law.]

Glazier argues on appeal that the district court erred in piercing the corporate veil to compel him to arbitrate Freeman's claims pursuant to the arbitration provision of the C3-Freeman Agreement. First, he contends that he cannot be held liable on a veil-piercing theory because he is neither a shareholder, officer, director or employee of C3. Second, Glazier argues that the district court's determination that he controlled C3 does not justify piercing the corporate veil in the absence of a factual finding that he used his control over C3 to wrong Freeman. We reject the former contention, but agree that the district court erred

Connections: The Internal Affairs Doctrine

If the parties hadn't agreed on the applicable law, the court would have had to make the choice, in which it probably would have been guided by the internal affairs doctrine. This is a choice of law principle providing that the law of the state of incorporation will govern a corporation's "internal affairs." It has often been applied in the context of veil-piercing litigation.

- Is liability of shareholders or others for corporate debts *really* an internal affair?
- Should the law to be applied depend on whether the claim is in tort or contract?
- On the other hand, does it *really* seem to make a difference which state's law is invoked?

JD/MBA: Income vs. Revenue

Some people—like the author of the *Freeman* opinion—use the terms "income" and "revenue" as synonyms. This is not recommended. "Revenue" refers to the entire amount received from regular operations, before deduction of expenses. "Income," by contrast, has a variety of meanings (e.g., "net income" and "operating income"). They are more specifically described in the online Supplement. What they have in common, however, is that certain expenses already have been deducted.

in piercing the corporate veil before finding that Glazier used his domination of C3 to wrong Freeman. . . .

A. Glazier's Equitable Ownership of C3

Glazier contends that he should not be held personally liable under a veil-piercing theory because he is not a shareholder, officer, director, or employee of C3. We reject this argument.

New York courts have recognized for veil-piercing purposes the doctrine of equitable ownership, under which an individual who exercises sufficient control over the corporation may be deemed an "equitable owner," notwithstanding the fact that the individual is not a shareholder of the corporation. . . . [A] nonshareholder defendant may be, "in reality," the equitable owner of a corporation where the nonshareholder defendant "exercise[s] considerable authority over [the corporation] . . . to the point of completely disregarding the corporate form and acting as though [its] assets [are] his alone to manage and distribute." . . .

Because Glazier "exercised considerable authority over [the corporation] . . . to the point of completely disregarding the corporate form and acting as though [its] assets were his alone to manage and distribute," . . . he is appropriately viewed as C3's equitable owner for veil-piercing purposes. If there were board meetings, no minutes were kept from August 1994 through May 1995. Glazier agreed to personally indemnify C3's sole shareholder and director against any liability arising from the performance of his duties as C3's director. The president of C3 never attended a meeting of the Board of Directors. No shareholder received dividends or other distributions, despite the corporate income of $563,257 in 1994[3] and $200,000 from the assets sale to Thomson.

Glazier used C3 to sell his intellectual product and powers, including the software that he had co-developed at Columbia and which Columbia licensed to C3. Through payments from C3 to Glazier, Inc., he received the vast majority of the resulting revenues.[4] Both Glazier, Inc. and C3 were located at Glazier's apartment, and Glazier was the sole signatory on C3's bank account.

---

3. From this revenue, C3 paid $66,541 in development costs, $18,332 in royalties, presumably to Columbia, $53,875 in sales commissions, $20,323 in legal fees, and $397,900 to Glazier, Inc. in consulting fees.

4. The consulting agreement provided that C3 would not pay anyone compensation unless Glazier, Inc. had first received its share in full.

Glazier, Inc.'s consulting agreement with C3 expressly provided that it was terminable if Glazier himself was unable to perform or supervise the performance of Glazier, Inc.'s obligations to C3, which were described as "marketing [C3's] software products, developing new software products, enhancing [C3's] existing software products, and providing support services to [C3's] clients." These obligations essentially described C3's entire business. . . .

The district court found that "[t]o regard [Glazier] as anything but the sole stockholder and controlling person of C3 would be to exalt form over substance." . . . Under the unique facts of the instant case, viewed in their totality, we agree that it is appropriate to treat Glazier as an "equitable owner" for veil-piercing purposes. . . .

B. Piercing the C3 Veil

The presumption of corporate independence and limited shareholder liability serves to encourage business development. . . . Nevertheless, that presumption will be set aside, and courts will pierce the corporate veil under certain limited circumstances. . . . Specifically, such "[l]iability . . . may be predicated either upon a showing of fraud or upon complete control by the dominating [entity] that leads to a wrong against third parties." . . . As we [have elsewhere] explained . . . to pierce the corporate veil under New York law, a plaintiff must prove that "(1) [the owner] ha[s] exercised such control that the [corporation] has become a mere instrumentality of the [owner], which is the real actor; (2) such control has been used to commit a fraud or other wrong; and (3) the fraud or wrong results in an unjust loss or injury to plaintiff." *Id.* (internal quotation omitted).

To the extent that we have restated this test [to provide for veil-piercing] . . . "in two broad situations: to prevent fraud or other wrong, or where a parent dominates and controls a subsidiary," . . . the element of domination and control never was considered to be sufficient of itself to justify the piercing of a corporate veil. Unless the control is utilized to perpetrate a fraud or other wrong, limited liability will prevail. . . .

In determining whether "complete control" exists, we have considered such factors as: (1) disregard of corporate formalities; (2) inadequate capitalization; (3) intermingling of funds; (4) overlap in ownership, officers, directors, and personnel; (5) common office space, address and telephone numbers of corporate entities; (6) the degree of discretion shown by the allegedly dominated corporation; (7) whether the dealings between the entities are at arm's length; (8) whether the corporations are treated as independent profit centers; (9) payment or guarantee of the corporation's debts by the dominating entity, and (10) intermingling of property between the entities. . . . No one factor is decisive. . . . In this case, there is little question that Glazier exercised "complete control" over C3.

As discussed in the context of equitable ownership, the record is replete with examples of Glazier's control over C3. Therefore, the district court's finding of control was not erroneous. However, the district court erred in the decision to pierce C3's corporate veil solely on the basis of a finding of domination and control. "While complete domination of the corporation is the key to piercing the corporate veil, . . . such domination, standing alone, is not enough; some showing of a wrongful or unjust act toward plaintiff is required." . . . Thus, while we accept the district court's factual finding that Glazier controlled C3, we remand to the district court the issue of whether Glazier used his control over C3 to commit a fraud or other wrong that resulted in unjust loss or injury to Freeman. Though there is substantial evidence of such wrongdoing, a finding on this issue must be made in the first instance by the district court before veil-piercing occurs. We therefore remand to the district court with instructions to determine whether Glazier used his control over C3 to commit a fraud or other wrong that resulted in an unjust loss or injury to Freeman. . . .

 Dear Prof.: The court mentioned the terms "parent" and "subsidiary." I think I know what they mean, but I thought I'd better check.

When one corporation owns or controls another, by owning a majority of its stock, we say that it is a "parent" corporation, and the other is its "subsidiary." The parent-subsidiary terminology is not used where one corporation owns less than a controlling share of another (as in cases where it has simply purchased a minority of shares for investment purposes). Note that *Freeman* itself involves no parents or subsidiaries.

■ **Think about this:**

(G) Does *Freeman* apply the same test as *Baatz*?

(H) The only shareholder of C3 was Glazier's nameless acquaintance ("Mr. or Ms. X"), who also was the only director of C3. If Freeman had tried to recover from Mr. or Ms. X, would he likely have succeeded?

2. Shareholder Direct Liability

The following case involves a civil action by the United States to enforce the Comprehensive Environmental Response, Compensation, and Liability Act of 1980 (CERCLA) against the corporate parent of a polluting subsidiary. The Court discusses the prospect of piercing the corporate veil, but it also identifies a theory for shareholder liability not reflected in the cases presented above. As you read, you will want to be very attentive to when the Court is talking about veil-piercing and when it is talking about something else. When you encounter the "new" theory, ask yourself whether there is anything about this decision that limits it to the federal environmental context. In other words, is there anything in the CERCLA statute itself that requires this result, or would this theory be available in other contexts?

UNITED STATES V. BESTFOODS

United States Supreme Court
524 U.S. 51 (1998)

SOUTER, J.

The United States brought this action for the costs of cleaning up industrial waste generated by a chemical plant. The issue before us, under the Comprehensive Environmental Response, Compensation, and Liability Act of 1980 (CERCLA), 94 Stat. 2767, as amended, 42 U.S.C. §9601 et seq., is whether a parent corporation that actively participated in, and exercised control over, the operations of a subsidiary may, without more, be held liable as an operator of a polluting facility owned or operated by the subsidiary. We answer no, unless the corporate veil may be pierced. But a corporate parent that actively participated in, and exercised control over, the operations of the facility itself may be held directly liable in its own right as an operator of the facility.

I.

In 1980, CERCLA was enacted in response to the serious environmental and health risks posed by industrial pollution. . . . If it satisfies certain statutory conditions, the United States may, for instance, use the "Hazardous Substance Superfund" to finance cleanup efforts . . . which it may then replenish by suits brought under §107 of the Act against, among others, "any person who at the time of disposal of any hazardous substance owned or operated any facility." . . . So, those actually "responsible for any damage, environmental harm, or injury from chemical poison [may be charged with] the cost of their actions". . . . The phrase "owner or operator" is defined only by tautology, however, as "any person owning or operating" a facility . . . and it is this bit of circularity that prompts our review. . . .

II.

In 1957, Ott Chemical Co. (Ott I) began manufacturing chemicals at a plant near Muskegon, Michigan, and its intentional and unintentional dumping of hazardous substances significantly polluted the soil and ground water at the site. In 1965, respondent CPC International Inc. [which subsequently changed its name to "Bestfoods"] . . . incorporated a wholly owned subsidiary to buy Ott I's assets in exchange for CPC stock. The new company, also dubbed Ott Chemical Co. (Ott II), continued chemical manufacturing at the site, and continued to pollute its surroundings. CPC kept the managers of Ott I, including its founder, president, and principal shareholder, Arnold Ott, on board as officers of Ott II. Arnold Ott and several other Ott II officers and directors were also given positions at CPC, and they performed duties for both corporations.

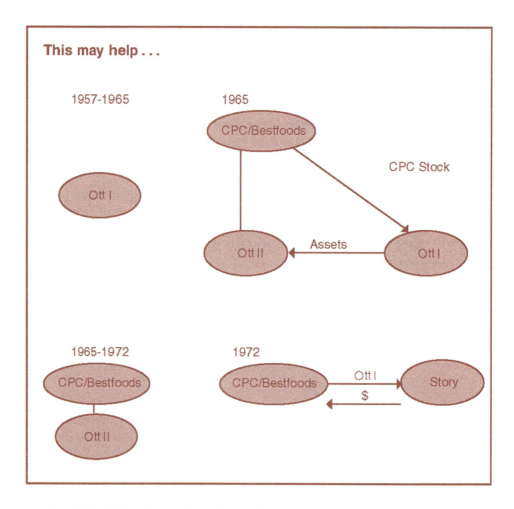

In 1972, CPC sold Ott II to Story Chemical Company, which operated the Muskegon plant until its bankruptcy in 1977. Shortly thereafter, when respondent Michigan Department of Natural Resources (MDNR) . . . examined the site for environmental damage, it found the land littered with thousands of leaking and even exploding drums of waste, and the soil and water saturated with noxious chemicals. . . .

By 1981, the federal Environmental Protection Agency had undertaken to see the site cleaned up, and its long-term remedial plan called for expenditures well into the tens of millions of dollars. To recover some of that money, the United States filed this action under §107 in 1989. . . . (By that time, Ott I and Ott II were defunct.) . . . [T]he trial focused on the issues of whether CPC . . . as the parent corporation[] of Ott II . . . had "owned or operated" the facility within the meaning of §107(a)(2).

The District Court said that operator liability may attach to a parent corporation both directly, when the parent itself operates the facility, and indirectly, when the corporate veil can be pierced under state law. . . . The court explained that, while CERCLA imposes direct liability in situations in which the corporate veil cannot be pierced under traditional concepts of corporate law, "the statute and its legislative history do not suggest that CERCLA rejects entirely the crucial limits to liability that are inherent to corporate law." . . .

. . . [In holding CPC liable as an operator under §107(a)(2)] the court found it particularly telling that CPC selected Ott II's board of directors and populated its executive ranks with CPC officials, and that a CPC official, G.R.D. Williams, played a significant role in shaping Ott II's environmental compliance policy.

After a divided panel of the Court of Appeals for the Sixth Circuit reversed in part . . ., that court granted rehearing en banc and vacated the panel decision. . . . This time, 7 judges to 6, the court again reversed the District Court in part. . . . The majority remarked on the possibility that a parent company might be held directly liable as an operator of a facility owned by its subsidiary: "At least conceivably, a parent might independently operate the facility in the stead of its subsidiary; or, as a sort of joint venturer, actually operate the facility alongside its subsidiary." . . . But the court refused to go any further and rejected the District Court's analysis. . . . Applying Michigan veil-piercing law, the Court of Appeals decided that neither CPC nor Aerojet . . . was liable for controlling the actions of its subsidiaries, since the parent and subsidiary corporations maintained separate personalities and the parents did not utilize the subsidiary corporate form to perpetrate fraud or subvert justice.

> ### Connections: The Internal Affairs Doctrine and Other Choices of Law
>
> - The internal affairs doctrine provides that the law of the state of incorporation will govern a corporation's "internal affairs."
> - You will have learned in civil procedure that federal courts are not required to follow state law in answering federal questions.
> - In (omitted) footnote 9 to the *Bestfoods* opinion, the Court noted that "[t]here is significant disagreement among courts and commentators over whether, in enforcing CERCLA's indirect liability, courts should borrow state law, or instead apply a federal common law of veil piercing. . . . Since none of the parties challenges the Sixth Circuit's holding that CPC . . . incurred no derivative liability, the question is not presented in this case and we do not address it further."

We granted certiorari . . . to resolve a conflict among the Circuits over the extent to which parent corporations may be held liable under CERCLA for operating facilities ostensibly under the control of their subsidiaries. . . . We now vacate and remand.

III.

It is a general principle of corporate law deeply "ingrained in our economic and legal systems" that a parent corporation (so-called because of control through ownership of another corporation's stock) is not liable for the acts of its subsidiaries. . . . [I]t is hornbook law that "the exercise of the 'control' which stock ownership gives to the stockholders . . . will not create liability beyond the assets of the subsidiary. That 'control' includes the election of directors, the making of by-laws . . . and the doing of all other acts incident to the legal status of stockholders. Nor will a duplication of some or all of the directors or executive officers be fatal." . . . Although this respect for corporate distinctions when the subsidiary is a polluter has been severely criticized in the literature, . . . nothing in CERCLA purports to reject this bedrock principle, and against this venerable common-law backdrop, the congressional silence is audible. . . . The Government has indeed made no claim that a corporate parent is liable as an owner or an operator under §107 simply because its subsidiary is subject to liability for owning or operating a polluting facility.

But there is an equally fundamental principle of corporate law, applicable to the parent-subsidiary relationship as well as generally, that the corporate veil may be pierced and the shareholder held liable for the corporation's conduct when, inter alia, the corporate form would otherwise be misused to accomplish certain wrongful purposes, most notably fraud, on the shareholder's behalf. . . . Nothing in CERCLA purports to rewrite this well-settled rule, either. CERCLA is thus like many another congressional enactment in giving no indication that "the entire corpus of state corporation law is to be replaced simply because a plaintiff's cause of action is based upon a federal statute," . . . and the failure of the statute to speak to a matter as fundamental as the liability implications of corporate ownership demands application of the rule that "[i]n order to abrogate a common-law principle, the statute must speak directly to the question addressed by the common law". . . . The Court of Appeals was accordingly correct in holding that when (but only when) the corporate veil may be pierced, . . . may a parent corporation be charged with derivative CERCLA liability for its subsidiary's actions. . . .

Arizona Donnie Barker
a/k/a "Ma" Barker

"Ma" Barker was the mother of four members of the "Karpis-Barker" gang. After she died in a shoot-out with the FBI in 1935, J. Edgar Hoover called her "the most vicious, dangerous and resourceful criminal brain of the last decade."

The most ridiculous story in the annals of crime is that Ma Barker was the mastermind behind the Karpis-Barker gang. . . . She wasn't a leader of criminals or even a criminal herself. There is not one police photograph of her or set of fingerprints taken while she was alive. . . . [S]he knew we were criminals but her participation in our careers was limited to one function: when we traveled together, we moved as a mother and her sons. What could look more innocent?

ALVIN KARPIS, with BILL TRENT, THE ALVIN KARPIS STORY 80-91 (1971).

IV.

A.

If the Act rested liability entirely on ownership of a polluting facility, this opinion might end here; but CERCLA liability may turn on operation as well as ownership, and nothing in the statute's terms bars a parent corporation from direct liability for its own actions in operating a facility owned by its subsidiary. As Justice (then-Professor) Douglas noted almost 70 years ago, derivative liability cases are to be distinguished from those in which "the alleged wrong can seemingly be traced to the parent through the conduit of its own personnel and management" and "the parent is directly a participant in the wrong complained of." . . . In such instances, the parent is directly liable for its own actions. . . . The fact that a corporate subsidiary happens to own a polluting facility operated by its parent does nothing, then, to displace the rule that the parent "corporation is [itself] responsible for the wrongs committed by its agents in the course of its business," Mine Workers v. Coronado Coal Co., 259 U.S. 344, 395 (1922), and whereas the rules of veil piercing limit derivative liability for the actions of another corporation, CERCLA's "operator" provision is concerned primarily with direct liability for one's own actions. . . . It is this direct liability that is properly seen as being at issue here.

Under the plain language of the statute, any person who operates a polluting facility is directly liable for the costs of cleaning up the pollution. . . . This is so regardless of whether that person is the facility's owner, the owner's parent corporation or business partner, or even a saboteur who sneaks into the facility at night to discharge its poisons out of malice. If any such act of operating a corporate subsidiary's facility is done on behalf of a parent corporation, the existence of the parent-subsidiary relationship under state corporate law is simply irrelevant to the issue of direct liability. . . .

This much is easy to say: the difficulty comes in defining actions sufficient to constitute direct parental "operation." Here of course we may again rue the uselessness of CERCLA's definition of a facility's "operator" as "any person . . . operating" the facility, 42 U.S.C. §9601(20)(A)(ii), which leaves us to do the best we can to give the term its "ordinary or natural meaning." Bailey v. United States, 516 U.S. 137, 145 (1995). In a mechanical sense, to "operate" ordinarily means "[t]o control the functioning of; run: operate a sewing machine." American Heritage Dictionary 1268 (3d ed. 1992). . . . And in the organizational sense more obviously intended by CERCLA, the word ordinarily means "[t]o conduct the affairs of; manage: operate a business." American Heritage Dictionary, supra, at 1268; see also Webster's New International Dictionary, supra, at 1707 ("to manage"). So, under CERCLA, an operator is simply someone who directs the workings of, manages, or conducts the affairs of a facility. To sharpen the definition for purposes of CERCLA's concern with environmental contamination, an operator must manage, direct, or conduct operations specifically related to pollution, that is, operations having to do with the leakage or disposal of hazardous waste, or decisions about compliance with environmental regulations.

B

With this understanding, we are satisfied that the Court of Appeals correctly rejected the District Court's analysis of direct liability. But we also think that the appeals court erred in limiting direct liability under the statute to a parent's sole or joint venture operation, so as to eliminate any possible finding that CPC is liable as an operator on the facts of this case.

1

By emphasizing that "CPC is directly liable under section 107(a)(2) as an operator because CPC actively participated in and exerted significant control over Ott II's business and decision-making," . . . the District Court applied the "actual control" test of whether the parent "actually operated the business of its subsidiary," . . . as several Circuits have employed it. . . .

The well-taken objection to the actual control test, however, is its fusion of direct and indirect liability; the test is administered by asking a question about the relationship between the two corporations (an issue going to indirect liability) instead of a question about the parent's interaction with the subsidiary's facility (the source of any direct liability). If, however, direct liability for the parent's operation of the facility is to be kept distinct from derivative liability for the subsidiary's own operation, the focus of the enquiry must necessarily be different under the two tests. "The question is not whether the parent operates the subsidiary, but rather whether it operates the facility, and that operation is evidenced by participation in the activities of the facility, not the subsidiary. Control of the subsidiary, if extensive enough, gives rise to indirect liability under piercing doctrine, not direct liability under the statutory language." . . . The District Court was therefore mistaken to rest its analysis on CPC's relationship with Ott II, premising liability on little more than "CPC's 100-percent ownership of Ott II" and "CPC's active participation in, and at times majority control over, Ott II's board of directors." . . . The analysis should instead have rested on the relationship between CPC and the Muskegon facility itself.

In addition to (and perhaps as a reflection of) the erroneous focus on the relationship between CPC and Ott II, even those findings of the District Court that might be taken to speak to the extent of CPC's activity at the facility itself are flawed, for the District Court wrongly assumed that the actions of the joint officers and directors are necessarily attributable to CPC. The District Court emphasized the facts that CPC placed its own high-level officials on Ott II's board of directors and in key management positions at Ott II, and that those individuals made major policy decisions and conducted day-to-day operations at the facility: "Although Ott II corporate officers set the day-to-day operating policies for the company without any need to obtain formal approval from CPC,

CPC actively participated in this decision-making because high-ranking CPC officers served in Ott II management positions." . . .

In imposing direct liability on these grounds, the District Court failed to recognize that "it is entirely appropriate for directors of a parent corporation to serve as directors of its subsidiary, and that fact alone may not serve to expose the parent corporation to liability for its subsidiary's acts." . . .

This recognition that the corporate personalities remain distinct has its corollary in the "well established principle [of corporate law] that directors and officers holding positions with a parent and its subsidiary can and do 'change hats' to represent the two corporations separately, despite their common ownership." . . . Since courts generally presume "that the directors are wearing their 'subsidiary hats' and not their 'parent hats' when acting for the subsidiary," . . . it cannot be enough to establish liability here that dual officers and directors made policy decisions and supervised activities at the facility. The Government would have to show that, despite the general presumption to the contrary, the officers and directors were acting in their capacities as CPC officers and directors, and not as Ott II officers and directors, when they committed those acts. . . . The District Court made no such enquiry here, however, disregarding entirely this time-honored common-law rule.

In sum, the District Court's focus on the relationship between parent and subsidiary (rather than parent and facility), combined with its automatic attribution of the actions of dual officers and directors to the corporate parent, erroneously, even if unintentionally, treated CERCLA as though it displaced or fundamentally altered common-law standards of limited liability. Indeed, if the evidence of common corporate personnel acting at management and directorial levels were enough to support a finding of a parent corporation's direct operator liability under CERCLA, then the possibility of resort to veil piercing to establish indirect, derivative liability for the subsidiary's violations would be academic. There would in essence be a relaxed, CERCLA-specific rule of derivative liability that would banish traditional standards and expectations from the law of CERCLA liability. But, as we have said, such a rule does not arise from congressional silence, and CERCLA's silence is dispositive.

2

We accordingly agree with the Court of Appeals that a participation-and-control test looking to the parent's supervision over the subsidiary, especially one that assumes that dual officers always act on behalf of the parent, cannot be used to identify operation of a facility resulting in direct parental liability. Nonetheless, a return to the ordinary meaning of the word "operate" in the organizational sense will indicate why we think that the Sixth Circuit stopped short when it confined its examples of direct parental operation to exclusive or joint ventures, and declined to find at least the possibility of direct operation by CPC in this case.

In our enquiry into the meaning Congress presumably had in mind when it used the verb "to operate," we recognized that the statute obviously meant something more than mere mechanical activation of pumps and valves, and must be read to contemplate "operation" as including the exercise of direction over the facility's activities. . . . The Court of Appeals recognized this by indicating that a parent can be held directly liable when the parent operates the facility in the stead of its subsidiary or alongside the subsidiary in some sort of a joint venture. . . . We anticipated a further possibility above, however, when we observed that a dual officer or director might depart so far from the norms of parental influence exercised through dual officeholding as to serve the parent, even when ostensibly acting on behalf of the subsidiary in operating the facility. . . . Yet another possibility, suggested by the facts of this case, is that an agent of the parent with no hat to wear but the parent's hat might manage or direct activities at the facility.

Identifying such an occurrence calls for line-drawing yet again, since the acts of direct operation that give rise to parental liability must necessarily be distinguished from the interference that stems from the normal relationship between parent and subsidiary. Again norms of corporate behavior (undisturbed by any CERCLA provision) are crucial reference points. Just as we may look to such norms in identifying the limits of the presumption that a dual officeholder acts in his ostensible capacity, so here we may refer to them in distinguishing a parental officer's oversight of a subsidiary from such an officer's control over the operation of the subsidiary's facility. "[A]ctivities that involve the facility but which are consistent with the parent's investor status, such as monitoring of the subsidiary's performance, supervision of the subsidiary's finance and capital budget decisions, and articulation of general policies and procedures, should not give rise to direct liability." . . . The critical question is whether, in degree and detail, actions directed to the facility by an agent of the parent alone are eccentric under accepted norms of parental oversight of a subsidiary's facility.

There is, in fact, some evidence that CPC engaged in just this type and degree of activity at the Muskegon plant. The District Court's opinion speaks of an agent of CPC alone who played a conspicuous part in dealing with the toxic risks emanating from the operation of the plant. G.R.D. Williams worked only for CPC; he was not an employee, officer, or director of Ott II, . . . and thus, his actions were of necessity taken only on behalf of CPC. The District Court found that "CPC became directly involved in environmental and regulatory matters through the work of . . . Williams, CPC's governmental and environmental affairs director. Williams . . . became heavily involved in environmental issues at Ott II." . . . He "actively participated in and exerted control over a variety of Ott II environmental matters," . . . and he "issued directives regarding Ott II's responses to regulatory inquiries". . . .

We think that these findings are enough to raise an issue of CPC's operation of the facility through Williams's actions, though we would draw no ultimate conclusion from these findings at this point. Not only would we be deciding in the first instance an issue on which the trial and appellate courts did not focus, but the very fact that the District Court did not see the case as we do suggests that there may be still more to be known about Williams's activities. Indeed, even as the factual findings stand, the trial court offered little in the way of concrete detail for its conclusions about Williams's role in Ott II's environmental affairs, and the parties vigorously dispute the extent of Williams's involvement. Prudence thus counsels us to remand, on the theory of direct operation set out here, for reevaluation of Williams's role, and of the role of any other CPC agent who might be said to have had a part in operating the Muskegon facility.[5]

V

The judgment of the Court of Appeals for the Sixth Circuit is vacated, and the case is remanded with instructions to return it to the District Court for further proceedings consistent with this opinion.

■ **Think about this:**

(I) What if the laws of all 50 states were amended to provide that a corporation's subsidiaries could be directly managed by the parent's officers and directors entirely for the benefit of the corporation? Would that be a good idea? Would it change the outcome in *Bestfoods*?

(J) Suppose that someone had thought to elect G.R.D. Williams an unpaid officer of Ott II? Or caused Ott II to enter into a paid consulting arrangement with him? Would that have changed the outcome?

(K) Suppose that a state statute provides that anyone owning or operating a bar will be liable for injuries caused by persons served alcohol by the bar while obviously intoxicated. Assume further that Peggy and Kenny are riding on a motorcycle that is struck by someone who patronized Arrow Bar, Inc., while obviously intoxicated. What would Peggy and Kenny have to show to recover damages from the shareholders of Arrow Bar, Inc.? How about from the corporation's directors, officers, and/or managerial employees?

---

5. There are some passages in the District Court's opinion that might suggest that, without reference to Williams, some of Ott II's actions in operating the facility were in fact dictated by, and thus taken on behalf of, CPC[:] . . . "CPC officials engaged in . . . missions to Ott II in which Ott II officials received instructions on how to improve and change"; . . . "CPC executives who were not Ott II board members also occasionally attended Ott II board meetings." But nothing in the District Court's findings of fact, as written, even comes close to overcoming the presumption that Ott II officials made their decisions and performed their acts as agents of Ott II. Indeed, the finding that "Ott II corporate officers set the day-to-day operating policies for the company without any need to obtain formal approval from CPC," . . . indicates just the opposite. Still, the Government is, of course, free on remand to point to any additional evidence, not cited by the District Court, that would tend to establish that Ott II's decision-makers acted on specific orders from CPC.

> **This may help . . .**
>
> ### PLANNER'S CHECKLIST II
>
> In addition to being a shareholder, will your client be . . .
>
> ✓ A guarantor?
> ✓ An agent of the corporation?
> ✓ The corporation's principal for some personal matter?
> ✓ Liable for corporate debts by reason of some statute?

Test Yourself

Assume Applicability of the Most Current Version of the Model Business Corporations Act

1. BigCo, Inc., a publicly traded holding company, owns 100 percent of the shares of LilCo, a corporation engaged in oil exploration. LilCo's board is appointed and elected entirely by BigCo. BigCo has often instructed LilCo's board to distribute funds to BigCo, without interest, when BigCo is in need of cash. Recently, LilCo announced that because of poor earnings it will be unable adequately to fund employee pension obligations, which are a contractual obligation of LilCo. LilCo's employees bring a "piercing the corporate veil" cause of action against BigCo and its shareholders for this breach of contract. This action most likely will:

   a. Succeed with respect to both BigCo and its shareholders.
   b. Succeed with respect to BigCo but not its shareholders.
   c. Succeed with respect to BigCo's shareholders but not with respect to BigCo.
   d. Fail.

Questions 2-4 rely on the following facts:

AgBeast, Inc., a publicly traded corporation, is a holding company operating in a variety of agricultural lines of business. An AgBeast subsidiary called LilMoo Corp. owns and operates several mid-sized dairy farms. AgBeast's CEO, Bob, happened to be visiting LilMoo's headquarters last year and was surprised to learn that LilMoo's delivery drivers had been instructed never to exceed a posted speed limit. Knowing that one of LilMoo's most significant problems was customer anger over poor delivery times, Bob drafted a memo to all

LilMoo drivers instructing them to drive at up to ten miles over any posted limit, whenever feasible. Bob insisted that the memo be distributed immediately on LilMoo letterhead.

Shortly thereafter, a LilMoo employee named Biff, a delivery driver for the company, drove a LilMoo delivery truck at ten miles over a posted speed limit. During this delivery, which was in the normal course of his duties, Biff struck and seriously injured a pedestrian.

2. Which of the following facts, if true, would most help the injured pedestrian to get recovery directly from AgBeast?

   a. AgBeast has occasionally caused LilMoo to make distributions to AgBeast when AgBeast itself has had cash-flow needs.
   b. Bob is an employee of LilMoo.
   c. Bob is not an employee of LilMoo.
   d. The CEO and chairman of LilMoo is also an AgBeast director.

3. Assume that under the new LilMoo delivery driving policy, injuries involving LilMoo drivers increased 400 percent. On those facts, Bob's wrongdoing would strongly support piercing AgBeast's corporate veil. True or False?

   a. True. The doctrine of piercing the veil is applied very flexibly to "prevent fraud or injustice."
   b. True. The facts suggest that Bob considered LilMoo to be AgBeast's "alter ego."
   c. False. On these facts, there could be no showing that LilMoo was AgBeast's "alter ego."
   d. False, for some other reason.

4. Assume that AgBeast has caused LilMoo to sell its products exclusively to other AgBeast subsidiaries, and to do so at cost. As a result, LilMoo has never operated at a profit. Which of the following is most true?

   a. Even if LilMoo's veil is not pierced so as to impose liability on AgBeast, it is possible that liability might be imposed on the AgBeast subsidiaries receiving LilMoo's product at cost.
   b. The additional facts assumed for purposes of this question do not affect the likelihood that liability for Biff's accident might be imposed on AgBeast.
   c. Provided that LilMoo's directors held regular meetings, kept minutes, assured that all business was transacted in the corporate name, and made no illegal distributions to AgBeast or its other subsidiaries, LilMoo's veil cannot be pierced.
   d. LilMoo's veil cannot be pierced to impose liability for a tort obligation such as the one incurred as the result of Biff's accident.

Questions 5 and 6 stand alone:

5. Chas and Jana decide to incorporate for the purpose of operating a limousine service. Each pays $1,000 to the corporation and receives 1,000 shares of stock. In addition, Chas lends $15,000 to the corporation. The $15,000 is used for the down payment on a limousine the corporation purchases.

   One week after the service begins, the limousine is involved in an accident, resulting in two wrongful death judgments against the corporation. Jana was driving the limo at the time of the accident. These judgments exceed the corporation's liability insurance (which is $1 million) by $500,000. The corporation then files a voluntary bankruptcy petition.

   Based on the foregoing, which of the following statements is most likely to be correct?

   a. Chas and Jana are personally liable for the corporation's debts.
   b. Assuming strict adherence to the necessary formalities for incorporation and the conduct of corporate business, Chas and Jana have no personal liability.
   c. The existence of a statute mandating a certain level of insurance for a limousine service could have some relevance to a court's willingness to pierce the corporation's veil.
   d. There are no grounds for imposing personal liability on Chas and Jana.

6. Fill in the Blanks: Three of the factors taken into account by courts in deciding whether to pierce a corporate veil are _____, _____, and _____.

17

The Basics of Corporate Governance

The traditional form of corporate governance is easy to describe. The shareholders elect members of the board of directors, who make broad policy decisions but do not participate in day-to-day management. The board, in turn, hires and supervises managers to run the business and execute the board's policies. The laws that structure the governance roles of these constituencies within the corporation are the subject of this chapter. We also shall see, however, that the simple model of corporate governance conceals a much more complex reality.

Chapter Outline

A. Traditional Roles

- Shareholders elect directors
- Management by or under the direction of the board
- Officers are the agents of the corporation

B. Action by Shareholders

1. Meetings
   - Types of meetings
   - Notice and record dates
   - Record and beneficial owners
   - Quorum requirements
   - Proxy voting
   - Waivers
   - Voting requirements: other than election of directors
   - Voting requirements: election of directors
   - Cumulative vs. straight voting

2. Action Without a Meeting
   - Written consent
   - Electronic consent

C. Action by the Board of Directors

1. Planned Action by the Board
   - Action at a meeting
     - Physical meetings
     - Meetings by conference call
   - Action without a meeting
     - Unanimous written consent

2. Unplanned Action by the Board
   - Creating apparent authority through inaction

D. Action by Officers

- Action by the board creates authority for actions of officers
- The president: the ordinary/extraordinary distinction
- The secretary: attests to authority of other officers

Test Yourself

A. Traditional Roles

The starting point is to reemphasize the traditional allocation of duties among the constituents. Shareholders elect the board of directors and vote on certain matters allocated to them by statute or, in some cases, the Articles of Incorporation. In the traditional model, they are not supposed to make management decisions. The board is expected to manage the corporation's business, which it does by making decisions that create authority on the part of the corporation's agents — most notably its officers.

 Dear Prof.: It sounds as though there may also be non-traditional forms of corporate governance. Is that correct?

Yes. What is described in this chapter is the default model. Alternative forms usually are available if a corporation's shares are not publicly traded. These alternatives are discussed in Part 6 of this book.

Connections: Board Primacy and Its Significance Throughout Corporate Law

We already encountered the foundational rule of board primacy in Chapter 15. In *Gashwiler v. Willis*, we learned that shareholders cannot make decisions relating to corporate management—even all of them, unanimously—unless specifically authorized to do so by statute.

This rule runs throughout the law and explains several other doctrines. It is a fundamental justification for the "business judgment rule," which states the highly deferential standard of corporate fiduciaries' duty of care (see Chapter 18); it explains the requirement that shareholder derivative plaintiffs first make a "demand" for relief from their management before going to court (see Chapter 22); and it underlies the requirement that even the most major events in a corporation's life—such as merger with another company, sale of all its assets, and dissolution—are not submitted to shareholder vote until first recommended by the board (see Chapter 23).

Before we get to the specific powers and obligations of these corporate constituencies, we introduce one very basic policy rule, concerning the primacy of the board of directors. Model Business Corporations Act §8.01(b) provides: "All corporate powers shall be exercised by or under the authority of the board of directors of the corporation, and the business and affairs of the corporation shall be managed by or under the direction, and subject to the oversight, of the board of directors. . . ." The rule will underlie much of the rest of corporate law. It is elaborated in the following case.

MCQUADE V. STONEHAM

New York Court of Appeals
263 N.Y. 323 (1934)

POUND, Ch. J.

The action is brought to compel specific performance of an agreement between the parties, entered into to secure the control of National Exhibition Company, also called the Baseball Club (New York Nationals or "Giants"). This was one of Stoneham's enterprises which used the New York polo grounds for its home games. McGraw was manager of the Giants. McQuade was at the time the contract was entered into a City Magistrate. He resigned December 8, 1930.

Defendant Stoneham became the owner of 1,306 shares, or a majority of the stock of National Exhibition Company. Plaintiff and defendant McGraw each purchased seventy shares of his stock. Plaintiff paid Stoneham $50,338.10 for the stock he purchased. As a part of the transaction the agreement in

Official Giants' Logo 1918-1920.
The team moved to San Francisco in 1954.

question was entered into. It was dated May 21, 1919. Some of its pertinent provisions are

> "VIII. The parties hereto will use their best endeavors for the purpose of continuing as directors of said Company and as officers thereof the following:
>
> Directors:
> Charles A. Stoneham,
> John J. McGraw,
> Francis X. McQuade,
> with the right to the party of the first part [Stoneham] to name all additional directors as he sees fit.
>
> Officers:
> Charles A. Stoneham, President,
> John J. McGraw, Vice-President,
> Francis X. McQuade, Treasurer.
>
> IX. No salaries are to be paid to any of the above officers or directors, except as follows:
>
> President:
> $45,000
> Vice-President:
> 7,500
> Treasurer:
> 7,500
>
> X. There shall be no change in said salaries, no change in the amount of capital, or the number of shares, no change or amendment of the by-laws of the corporation or any matters regarding the policy of the business of the corporation or any matters which may in anywise affect, endanger or interfere with the rights of minority stockholders, excepting upon the mutual and unanimous consent of all of the parties hereto."

In pursuance of this contract Stoneham became president and McGraw vice-president of the corporation. McQuade became treasurer. In June, 1925, his salary was increased to $10,000 a year. He continued to act until May 2, 1928, when Leo J. Bondy was elected to succeed him. The board of directors consisted of seven men. The four outside of the parties hereto were selected by Stoneham and he had complete control over them. At the meeting of May 2, 1928, Stoneham and McGraw refrained from voting, McQuade voted for himself and the other four voted for Bondy. Defendants did not to keep their agreement with McQuade to use their best efforts to continue him as treasurer. On the contrary, he was dropped with their entire acquiescence. At the next stockholders' meeting he was dropped as a director although they might have elected him.

The courts below have refused to order the reinstatement of McQuade, but have given him damages for wrongful discharge, with a right to sue for future damages.

The cause for dropping McQuade was due to the falling out of friends. McQuade and Stoneham had disagreed. The trial court has found in substance that their numerous quarrels and disputes did not affect the orderly and efficient administration of the business of the corporation; that plaintiff was removed because he had antagonized the dominant Stoneham by persisting in challenging his power over the corporate treasury and for no misconduct on his part. The court also finds that plaintiff was removed by Stoneham for protecting the corporation and its minority stockholders. We will assume that Stoneham put him out when he might have retained him, merely in order to get rid of him.

Defendants say that the contract in suit was void because the directors held their office charged with the duty to act for the corporation according to their best judgment and that any contract which compels a director to vote to keep any particular person in office and at a stated salary is illegal. Directors are the exclusive executive representatives of the corporation, charged with administration of its internal affairs and the management and use of its assets. They manage the business of the corporation. (Gen. Corp. Law; Cons. Laws, ch. 23, §27.) "An agreement to continue a man as president is dependent upon his continued loyalty to the interests of the corporation." (Fells v. Katz, 256 N.Y. 67, 72.) So much is undisputed.

Plaintiff contends that the converse of this proposition is true and that an agreement among directors to continue a man as an officer of a corporation is not to be broken so long as such officer is loyal to the interests of the corporation and that, as plaintiff has been found loyal to the corporation, the agreement of defendants is enforceable.

Although it has been held that an agreement among stockholders whereby it is attempted to divest the directors of their power to discharge an unfaithful employee of the corporation is illegal as against public policy, it must be equally true that the stockholders may not, by agreement among themselves, control the directors in the exercise of the judgment vested in them by virtue of their office to elect officers and fix salaries. Their motives may not be questioned so long as their acts are legal. The bad faith or the improper motives of the parties does not change the rule. (Manson v. Curtis, 223 N.Y. 313, 324.) Directors may not by agreements entered into as stockholders abrogate their independent judgment.

Stockholders may, of course, combine to elect directors. That rule is well settled. As Holmes, Ch. J., pointedly said: "If stockholders want to make their power felt, they must unite. There is no reason why a majority should not agree to keep together." The power to unite is, however, limited to the election of directors and is not extended to contracts whereby limitations are placed on the power of directors to manage the business of the corporation by the selection of agents at defined salaries.

The minority shareholders whose interests McQuade says he has been punished for protecting, are not, aside from himself, complaining about his discharge. He is not acting for the corporation or for them in this action. It is impossible to see how the corporation has been injured by the substitution of Bondy as treasurer in place of McQuade. As McQuade represents himself in this action and seeks redress for his own wrongs, "we prefer to listen to [the corporation and the minority stockholders] before any decision as to their wrongs." (Faulds v. Yates, 57 Ill. 416, 421.)

It is urged that we should pay heed to the morals and manners of the market place to sustain this agreement and that we should hold that its violation gives rise to a cause of action for damages rather than base our decision on any outworn notions of public policy. Public policy is a dangerous guide in determining the validity of a contract and courts should not interfere lightly with the freedom of competent parties to make their own contracts. We do not close our eyes to the fact that such agreements, tacitly or openly arrived at, are not uncommon, especially in close corporations where the stockholders are doing business for convenience under a corporate organization. We know that majority stockholders, united in voting trusts, effectively manage the business of a corporation by choosing trustworthy directors to reflect their policies in the corporate management. Nor are we unmindful that McQuade has, so the court has found, been shabbily treated as a purchaser of stock from Stoneham. We have said: "A trustee is held to something stricter than the morals of the market place" (Meinhard v. Salmon, 249 N.Y. 458, 464), but Stoneham and McGraw were not trustees for McQuade as an individual. Their duty was to the corporation and its stockholders, to be exercised according to their unrestricted lawful judgment. They were under no legal obligation to deal righteously with McQuade if it was against public policy to do so.

The courts do not enforce mere moral obligations, nor legal ones either, unless someone seeks to establish rights which may be waived by custom and for convenience. We are constrained by authority to hold that a contract is illegal and void so far as it precludes the board of directors, at the risk of incurring legal liability, from changing officers, salaries or policies or retaining individuals in office, except by consent of the contracting parties. On the whole, such a holding is probably preferable to one which would open the courts to pass on the motives of directors in the lawful exercise of their trust.

A further reason for reversal exists. [McQuade was a City Magistrate and required by statute to devote his whole time and capacity to the duties of his office.]

The judgment of the Appellate Division and that of the Trial Term should be reversed and the complaint dismissed, with costs in all courts.

LEHMAN, J. (concurring).

I concur in the decision of the court on the second ground stated in the opinion. I desire to state the reasons why I do not accept the first ground. . . .

There can, I think, be no doubt that shareholders owning a majority of the corporate stock may combine to obtain and exercise any control which a single owner of such stock could exercise. What may lawfully be done by an individual may ordinarily be lawfully done by a combination, but no combination is legal if formed to accomplish an illegal object. No such combination or agreement may "contravene any express charter or statutory provision or contemplate any fraud, oppression or wrong against other stockholders or other illegal object." (*Manson v. Curtis*, supra.)

. . . The majority stockholders can compel no action by the directors, but at the expiration of the term of office of the directors the stockholders have the power to replace them with others whose actions coincide with the judgment or desires of the holders of a majority of the stock. The theory that directors exercise in all matters an independent judgment in practice often yields to the fact that the choice of directors lies with the majority stockholders and thus gives the stockholders a very effective control of the action by the board of directors. In truth the board of directors may check the arbitrary will of those who would otherwise completely control the corporation, but cannot indefinitely thwart their will.

A contract which destroys this check contravenes "express charter or statutory provisions" and is, therefore, illegal. A contract which merely provides that stockholders shall in combination use their power to achieve a legitimate purpose is not illegal. They may join in the election of directors who, in their opinion, will be in sympathy with the policies of the majority stockholders and who, in the choice of executive officers, will be influenced by the wishes of the majority stockholders. The directors so chosen may not act in disregard of the best interests of the corporation and its minority stockholders, but with that limitation they may and, in practice, usually are swayed by the wishes of the majority. Otherwise there would be no continuity of corporate policy and no continuity in management of corporate affairs.

The contract now under consideration provides, in a narrow field, for corporate action within these limitations. . . . It does constrain the parties while acting as directors to vote for officers in a predetermined manner, but there is no suggestion that such vote would not accord with their best judgment and be in the interests of the corporation. It is subject to the implied condition that the officers so elected will be loyal to the corporation. (Fells v. Katz, 256 N.Y. 67.) It binds the directors only in a matter where freedom is a fiction rather than a fact. If this contract is unenforceable and contrary to public policy, then every purchase of a substantial block of stock upon the promise of the majority stockholders that the purchaser will be elected a director and officer of the corporation is likewise against public policy.

. . . A contract which merely provides for the election of fit officers and adhesion to particular policy determined in advance constitutes an agreement by which men in combination exercise a power which could be lawfully exercised if lodged in a single man. It is legal if designed to protect legitimate interests without wrong to others. Public policy should be governed by facts, not abstractions. The contract is, in my opinion, valid. It is unenforceable only because it resulted in an employment which was itself illegal. . . .

Connections

In Chapter 25 you will read about the modern alternatives available to the shareholders of closely held corporations. Notably, statutes like MBCA §7.32 permit unanimous shareholder agreements to dispense with the board of directors. In exchange, the shareholders assume all of the directors' duties.

■   **Think about this:**

(A) Note that in the foregoing case no one seems to have been complaining about Paragraph X of the shareholders' agreement. If someone had, what would its fate have been pursuant to the majority's analysis? How about pursuant to the analysis of the concurring opinion?

(B) Suppose that the parties had not agreed to use their best efforts to continue the designated officers, but had agreed only to vote for directors who announced in advance that they intended to vote for the designated officers. Would that have been all right?

(C) Suppose that Stoneham, McGraw, and McQuade had not said anything about officers in their shareholders' agreement. Instead, they entered into a separate "directors' agreement" in which they agreed to vote for one another as officers with the desired salaries. Would that have overcome the majority's objection?

(D) Assuming that McQuade was not a City Magistrate, is there any way that he could have achieved his objective of long-term employment as a salaried treasurer of the National Exhibition Company?

B. Action by Shareholders

Despite their ordinarily passive role, shareholders do occasionally exercise important rights in the management of their firms. Their most important role is probably the election of directors, but they also must be consulted at times of fundamental change, including charter amendment, merger, or dissolution. But to have validity, shareholders' exercise of these powers must comply with statutorily mandated procedures for voting their shares. Their votes must be cast at shareholder meetings, which must be properly noticed and administered.

1. Meetings

 What does it look like?

Check the online Supplement for the following sample documents that are relevant to this section:

■ Notice of an annual meeting
■ Proxy statement
■ Form of proxy

Types of Meetings. Annual meetings of shareholders are to be held at the time stated in, or fixed in accordance with, the bylaws (MBCA §7.01). The primary purpose of the annual meeting is to elect directors, although any other legitimate shareholder business also can be brought before the shareholders. Failure to hold an annual meeting does not affect the validity of corporate action. In other words, the members of the board of directors simply hold over in office.

Special shareholders' meetings also can be called by the board of directors, by anyone authorized in the bylaws or articles to call a meeting, or at the request of some percentage (usually 10 percent) of the votes entitled to be cast on the issue to come before the meeting (MBCA §7.02). On application of a shareholder, a court may order a meeting that otherwise should have been held but was not (MBCA §7.03).

This may help . . .

After reading the accompanying text you should feel comfortable with the following terms:

> Record Date
> Record Holder
> Beneficial Holder
> Street Name
> Quorum
> Proxy
> Voting Requirements
> Voting Group
> Class Voting
> Cumulative Voting
> Straight Voting

Notice and Record Dates. The first step in holding either an annual or special meeting is to determine who is entitled to vote and thus who will receive notice of the meeting. From the corporation's standpoint, the process is simple. First, the Articles of Incorporation should be consulted to determine the voting rights of the various classes of shares (if there is more than one class). Then, the board of directors should set a date (known as the "record date") as of which the corporation's records will be consulted to determine the identity of the shareholders. Most statutes provide that the record date must be set, and notice must be given, within a certain number of days of the meeting. For instance, the MBCA provides that the record date cannot be more than 70 days before the meeting, and that notice must be given between 10 and 60 days of the meeting. *See* §§7.07 and 7.05. Notice of an annual meeting generally need not state the meeting's purpose (§7.05(b)), but the notice of a special meeting must do so (§7.05(c)), and only business that is fairly within what is described can be conducted at the meeting (§7.02(d)).

Record and Beneficial Owners, and the Bureaucratic Challenge of Voting Rights in Publicly Traded Companies. The names appearing in the corporation's records on the record date determine who has the right to vote (and receive notice), at least as far as the corporation is concerned. Keeping track of these owners is usually simple in closely held companies. In publicly traded companies, the sheer volume of daily trading complicates matters, and understanding how transfer of ownership and voting rights are handled calls for some background and some terminology.

More to the Story: The Still-Lingering Tradition of Paper Stock Certificates

The root of the problem discussed here is that corporations, in principle, can still issue paper stock certificates to represent ownership, and where a certificate is issued a trade entails its delivery from seller to buyer. Paper certificates were once generally required, but most statutes now merely permit and do not require them. *See, e.g.*, MBCA §6.25(a).

Connections: Law Governing Ownership and Transfer

The rules by which the "clearing functions" described here are performed—the rules that determine who actually owns a share of stock at a given point in time, and how it is transferred—are not actually rules of the state law of corporations. They are matters of commercial law, governed in almost all states by Article 8 of the Uniform Commercial Code.

Connections: Law and Technology

By the time of the next edition of this casebook, it is quite likely that blockchain technology will have significantly altered the landscape. According to DTCC, "DTCC believes [blockchain] technology represents a generational opportunity to re-imagine the post-trade infrastructure." http://www.dtcc.com/ blockchain. Projects are underway to implement use of the technology in the United States and elsewhere. Delaware legislation has authorized use of blockchain technology for tracking share ownership and processing secured loans.

Prior to the early 1970s, stock brokerages executing trades for their clients had to handle the physical delivery of stock certificates, and the burdens were sometimes significant. The brokerages solved this problem by creating a central clearing-house system, through which the vast majority of trades are now made with electronic record keeping. Specifically, they set up a holding company known as the Depository Trust & Clearing Corporation (DTCC), owned by the banks and brokerages that used its services, and over time DTCC came to operate through several subsidiaries that handle clearing of various kinds of securities trades. One of the subsidiaries is the Deposit Trust Company (DTC), which in turn operates through a subsidiary known as Cede & Company. Cede & Co. happens to be the largest nominal owner of stock of most publicly traded corporations in the United States, acting as it does on behalf of so many clients of so many stockbrokers.

It is useful to know a few special terms used to identify the players within this clearing system. Corporations usually must keep track of the owners of their stock, and the person identified in corporate records as the owner of a given share is known as its "record owner" or "record holder." But the record holder is not necessarily the *real* owner, and where stock is cleared through a clearing process like the one just described, the record owner is not the real owner. The person who really "owns" the stock in the vernacular sense—that is, the person who paid for it, and who enjoys the benefits of ownership, including the ultimate right to dividends and voting—is called the "beneficial owner" or "beneficial holder." But for the sake of convenience, the beneficial owner might appoint its stock broker to act as record owner, or the stock may be cleared through another intermediary such as Cede & Co., which would then be the record owner. When a stock is held by the broker or any other intermediary, the stock is said to be held in "street name" (an allusion to Wall Street).

The record owner must forward voting materials and dividends or distributions to the beneficial owner.

This process of clearing through intermediaries is depicted in the "This may help" box on the following page.

Quorum Requirements. In order for shareholders to take valid action at a meeting, a quorum requirement must be satisfied. A "quorum" is some minimum number of shares entitled to vote on an issue that must be represented at the meeting in order for the results of a vote to be valid. Under the MBCA, the default is simple majority—a majority of shares entitled to vote must be present or represented by a proxy at the meeting. Considering

This may help . . . Clearing of Publicly Traded Stock: Trading in Street Name Through Cede & Co.

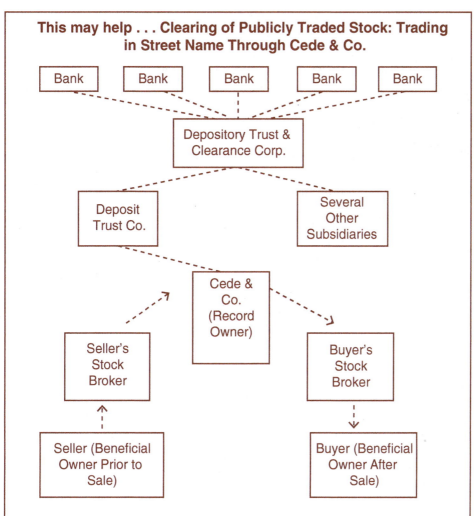

By no means are all "street name" or other trades of public stock cleared in this particular way, but a large proportion of them are, and most other trades executed through intermediaries work in more or less the same way. Where Cede & Co. is used, a share of stock is owned by Seller, who is a client of a stock broker. The broker has already engaged Cede & Co. to act as record owner, strictly for the sake of convenience. When Seller desires to sell, it instructs its broker to execute the trade, and upon identifying Buyer, who is also represented by a stock brokerage firm, Seller's broker directs Cede & Co. to make a change in its books switching the stock's beneficial owner-ship to Buyer.

Sometimes brokers simply own street name securities in their own name, so that they themselves appear as record owner, and sometimes they use inermediaries other than Cede & Co. But in those other cases, trades work in much the same way.

In 2003, Yuri Malenchenko was orbiting earth on the International Space Station when he married Ekaterina Dmitrieva by proxy in Texas, thus becoming the first person to marry in outer space.

MBCA §7.25 and §7.27 in tandem, however, you will see a trap for the unwary: While §7.25 appears to suggest the quorum requirement could be adjusted up or down by the Articles of Incorporation, it is clear from §7.27 that only an increase is possible. Once formed, a quorum generally is assumed to be present for the rest of the meeting.

Proxies. Proxies are used in a variety of situations. As a practical matter, publicly held corporations must use them for shareholder meetings. In order to meet the quorum requirement, management must solicit enough proxies. In publicly traded firms, solicitation of proxies triggers federal securities laws rules under the Securities Exchange Act of 1934, dealt with in Chapter 29. Even the shareholders of companies with very few shareholders may rely on proxy voting as a convenience. In addition, in some circumstances proxy voting is useful for establishing control arrangements. For instance, a corporation's lender might insist that the majority shareholder(s) grant the lender a proxy for the duration of the loan.

Obviously, in the situation just described, the lender would want to be sure that the grant of voting authority was irrevocable for the term of the loan and that the lender had discretion over how votes would be cast. This example helps focus on the distinctions between revocable and irrevocable proxies, and between those that are grants of discretion and those that are grants to vote only in a specified manner. The following provision deals, among other things, with irrevocability.

This may help . . .

Sometimes, you just may need to ask what the speaker means.

"Proxy" sometimes is used to refer to the person to whom a shareholder gives voting authority. Sometimes it is used to refer to the piece of paper executed to evidence voting authority on the part of the holder. Sometimes it is used to refer to the grant of authority itself. The MBCA uses it only in the first sense, preferring "appointment form" and "appointment" for the latter two uses.

MBCA §7.22 Proxies

(a) A shareholder may vote the shareholder's shares in person or by proxy.
(b) A shareholder or the shareholder's agent or attorney-in-fact may appoint a proxy to vote or otherwise act for the shareholder by signing an appointment form. . . .

(c) An appointment of a proxy is effective when a signed appointment form . . . is received by the inspector of election or the officer or agent of the corporation authorized to tabulate votes. An appointment is valid for 11 months unless a longer period is expressly provided in the appointment form. (d) An appointment of a proxy is revocable unless the appointment form . . . states that it is irrevocable and the appointment is coupled with an interest. Appointments coupled with an interest include the appointment of:

(i) a pledgee;

(ii) a person who purchased or agreed to purchase the shares;

(iii) a creditor of the corporation who extended it credit under terms requiring the appointment;

(iv) an employee of the corporation whose employment contract requires the appointment; or

(v) a party to a voting agreement created under section 7.31 [which permits shareholders to agree how to vote their shares]. . . .

Historically, the law has exhibited antipathy to "vote selling" in both political and corporate contexts. The idea that irrevocable proxies must be "coupled with an interest" took hold in the corporate realm. When you look at the list of things qualifying as an "interest" and think about what they have in common, you easily will discern that the idea is to link the interest of the proxy holder to the corporation's own interest. Thus, would-be corporate competitors are supposed to be unable to buy off shareholders in order to vote their shares for an incompetent board, in favor of a transaction that would be unfavorable to the shareholders as a whole, etc.

This may help . . .

The primary actions shareholders take:

- Vote for or to remove directors
- "Sanitize" management's self-dealing transactions
- Adopt advisory resolutions
- Approve directors' recommendations of:
  - Amendments to Articles of Incorporation
  - Corporate combinations
  - Sale of substantially all the assets
  - Liquidations

Waivers. In any event, what happens if the quorum requirement is satisfied by shareholders attending in person or represented by proxy, but one or more shareholders complain that they did not receive notice of the meeting? The law generally requires only that notice be sent to the record holder at the record address, not that it be received. If notice was not sent to one or more shareholders, however, or was defective, the meeting cannot take place unless the lack/defect is waived. Attendance at a meeting without stating an objection usually constitutes a waiver.

Voting Requirements and Types of Voting: Matters Other Than the Election of Directors. Voting requirements, like quorum requirements, can be increased in the Articles of Incorporation, but under the MBCA the default rule is that a majority of the votes cast on a matter (even if less than a majority of a quorum) will prevail on matters other than elections of directors. MBCA §7.25(c). The hypothetical in the box below will both illustrate this rule and suggest how the MBCA resolves such questions as whether one can break a quorum by leaving a meeting once it has begun.

Doing the Numbers: Quorum and Voting Requirements

Suppose that Hypo Corp. has 100 shares of a single class of shares outstanding. Notice of a meeting to vote on a proposed amendment to the Articles of Incorporation is duly given.

> 51 shares are represented at the meeting.
> The owners of 20 shares leave the meeting.
> The owners of 20 shares abstain.
> Six shares are voted in favor of the amendment; five are voted against.
> The motion carries.

Calculations can be a little more difficult — but still nothing like rocket science — when a corporation has more than one class of shares. If this is the case, nothing substitutes for in-depth perusal of both the relevant statutory provision(s) and the Articles of Incorporation. One generalization, however, is that if a vote would affect the rights of a class of shareholders, they will get a class vote on the matter, which effectively constitutes a veto power. Another way to describe this is to say that the affected class constitutes a voting group. This is the terminology adopted by the MBCA, which helps eliminate confusion when either the statute or the articles provide that, in some situations, two or more classes will vote together as a single voting group. For instance, under the MBCA, if two or more classes are affected similarly by an amendment of the Articles of Incorporation, they will vote as a single voting group unless the Articles of Incorporation or the board of directors requires otherwise. §10.04(c).

Doing the Numbers: Voting Groups

Exemplary, Inc. has three classes of outstanding shares. There are 100 outstanding shares of common, 100 outstanding shares of Class A preferred, which is nonvoting and senior to the common shares, and 200 outstanding shares of Class B preferred, which is voting and senior to both the common and the Class A shares. The directors of Exemplary approve and recommend to the shareholders an amendment to the Articles of Incorporation that would increase the rights of the Class A shares, still leaving them subordinate to the Class B shares. Notice of a meeting to vote on the proposed amendment is given to all three classes. On the day of the meeting, 60 shares of common, 60 shares of Class A, and 120 shares of Class B are represented at the meeting (for a total of 240). Assuming no one leaves the meeting and all shares will be voted, what minimum number of votes will it take to authorize the amendment?

Analysis

The common stock gets a class vote — as its own voting group — because the rights of a superior class are being increased. §10.04(a)(6) and (b). Thus, 31 common shares must be voted in favor.

The Class A shares get a class vote — comprise a voting group — because the rights of the class are being changed. §10.04(a)(3) and (b). This is true even though Class A otherwise is nonvoting. §10.04(d). Thus, 31 Class A shares must be voted in favor.

The Class B shares do get to vote, but not as a class. If exactly 31 common shares and 31 Class A shares are voted in favor, 59 Class B shares also must be voted in favor. This will total 121, which is a majority of 240.

Voting Requirements and Types of Voting: Election of Directors.

The usual rule is that directors are elected by a plurality of votes cast, rather than by a majority. This simply means that, if there are x positions to be filled, the x nominees who receive the most votes will be elected, even if none of them receives a majority of the votes cast. MBCA §7.28. This allows elections to occur notwithstanding a number of candidates far exceeding the positions to be filled. For instance, if there are nine nominees for three positions, there is a good chance that none of them will get a majority of votes cast. Election by plurality also permits cumulative voting, which is required by statute in some states: For instance, California requires cumulative voting if a corporation has fewer than 600 shareholders. Somewhat oddly, in a few states, cumulative voting is

Results of the 1992 United States Presidential Election

Bill Clinton—43%   George H.W. Bush—37.5%   Ross Perot—18.9%

even required by the state constitution. In most states, however, and under the MBCA, cumulative voting rights only exist if the Articles of Incorporation so require. Cumulative voting is best understood after a description of the alternative — straight voting. The descriptions below assume that there is nothing in the articles that addresses voting rights other than the presence or absence of a provision electing cumulative voting.

Straight Voting. When voting is straight, each share gets one vote for each opening on the board. This means that a majority shareholder, or group of shareholders who act together and constitute a majority, can elect every member of the board.

Cumulative Voting. When voting is cumulative, each share gets one vote for each opening on the board, but the votes can be — you guessed it — cumulated and cast for fewer than all openings. This means that if the numbers are right, a minority interest or interests can succeed in achieving at least some board representation. The key to understanding why — and how — cumulative voting works is to recognize that elections of directors, like the election of the United States President, are not a question of voting for or against. Although in the heat of the political moment it may feel otherwise, one really only votes "for" a candidate.

Doing the Numbers: Straight and Cumulative Voting

Assume that Straightco, Inc., has 100 shares of common stock outstanding. A owns 60 and B owns 40. Straightco is incorporated in an MBCA state, and the articles say nothing about cumulative voting. There are three positions on the board of directors.

> A casts 60 votes for each of Al, Ali, and Alix. B casts 40 votes for each of Bo, Bob, and Bobi. Of the six nominees, Al, Ali, and Alix are elected by plurality.

Assume that Cumulcorp has 100 shares of common stock outstanding. C owns 60 and D owns 40. Cumulcorp is incorporated in an MBCA state, and the articles elect cumulative voting. There are three positions on the board of directors.

> C is entitled to 60 votes for each of three positions, or 180 votes. C casts 60 votes each for Cal, Calvin, and Callista.
> D is entitled to 40 votes for each of three positions, or 120 votes. D cumulates them and casts them for a single position, giving all 120 votes to Dan.
> Dan will be elected to the board, and there will be a three-way tie between Cal, Calvin, and Callista for the other two positions. The tie may be

resolved by the withdrawal of one of the candidates or by a run-off election.

There is no way — repeat no way — for C to cast more than 121 votes for any of C's candidates and still have enough to elect two more.

There is a formula that allows one to predict outcomes in various cumulative voting scenarios. It is explored in some detail in the online Supplement.

Having the right to cumulate votes is not, however, the same as having the right to elect a candidate. The effectiveness of cumulative voting obviously depends on the number of shares outstanding, the various coalitions owners may form, and the number of positions to be filled. Thus, the issuance of additional shares or a reduction in the number of directors will reduce the efficacy of cumulative voting. Another strategy employed by majority shareholders is to amend the Articles of Incorporation to provide that members of the board serve staggered terms of two or three years (similar to the election of United State Senators). Obviously, this reduces the number of directorial positions to be filled in any given election. *See* MBCA §8.06.

■ **Think about this:**

(E) The concept of cumulative voting did not originate in corporate law. It actually was developed by political theorists attempting to devise ways for minorities to achieve representation. Pondering the pros and cons in the political context may assist in seeing some of the pros and cons in the corporate setting as well.

---

2. Action Without a Meeting

Some of the procedures described above can be tedious, and indeed in very small companies it can seem absurd actually to follow all the requirements set out above. As a general matter, tedious or not, planners should be careful to comply with all requisite formalities — filing the Articles of Incorporation, holding meetings, giving notice of meetings, etc. In the case of shareholder action, however, there is a handy shortcut that sometimes can be employed. The MBCA provision set out below is clear enough to speak for itself.

§7.04 Action Without Meeting

(a) Action required or permitted by this Act to be taken at a shareholders' meeting may be taken without a meeting if the action is taken by all the shareholders entitled to vote on the action. The action must be evidenced

by one or more written consents bearing the date of signature and describing the action taken, signed by all the shareholders entitled to vote on the action, and delivered to the corporation for inclusion in the minutes or filing with the corporate records.

(b) The articles of incorporation may provide that any action required or permitted by this Act to be taken at a shareholders' meeting may be taken without a meeting, and without prior notice, if consents in writing setting forth the action so taken are signed by the holders of outstanding shares having not less than the minimum number of votes that would be required to authorize or take the action at a meeting at which all shares entitled to vote on the action were present and voted. . . .

Electronic transmissions can qualify as signed written consents. MBCA §7.04(b).

■ **Think about this:**

(F) Is the number of votes necessary to take action by written consent the same as or different from the number necessary to take action at a meeting held with due notice?

C. Action by the Board of Directors

 What does it look like?

Check the online Supplement for the following sample documents that are relevant to this section:

■ Notice of a directors' meeting
■ Bylaw provisions relating to directors' meetings

This section discusses the various methods pursuant to which the board can act. Before getting to the specific methods, there are a few background points to address, all of which are covered in MBCA Chapter 8A. First, the modern rule is that the number of board members (which can be as few as one) can be set by either the Articles of Incorporation or the bylaws. The articles can establish qualifications for board members, such as whether they must be shareholders.

Board members are permitted to resign at any time and can be removed by the shareholders (at a meeting called for that purpose) either with or without cause, unless the articles provide for removals only for cause. Judicial removal also is a possibility. Unless the articles provide otherwise, vacancies can be filled by the shareholders, the board, or, "if the directors remaining in office constitute fewer than a quorum of the board, they may fill the vacancy by the affirmative vote of a majority of all the directors remaining in office." §8.10(a). Directors' terms generally expire at the next annual meeting of shareholders (unless they are serving for staggered terms), but directors may continue to serve until a successor is elected and qualifies or there is a decrease in the number of directors.

> ***Dear Prof.: What's so special about the language you specifically quoted in the last paragraph?***

It was adopted in reaction to an (in)famous case in which two of the remaining three members of a four-member board successfully filled the vacant seat even though the third member, in order to prevent a quorum, refused to attend the meeting at which the seat was filled.

> ***But, Prof.: The language seems to say that you would need to satisfy a quorum requirement unless the number left in office is less than a quorum. That doesn't cover the case you described.***

Exactly!

1. Planned Action by the Board

For planning purposes, there are three ways for a board of directors to take action. One is to hold a physical meeting. Another is to hold a meeting by conference call. The third is to act by unanimous written consent. All are equally valid for purposes of either approving an act in advance or ratifying it after the fact.

(a) Action at a Meeting

Physical Meetings. Shareholder meetings and board meetings differ in several technical details. *See* MBCA §8.24. For one, although the default rule with respect to a quorum is a majority of the number of board members that is fixed or prescribed, variances can be set out in the bylaws, as well as in the Articles of Incorporation. In addition, the quorum requirement can be reduced to as little as one-third. Unless the voting requirement is increased in the articles or bylaws, action can be taken by a majority present (as opposed to a majority of the votes cast), provided the quorum requirement is satisfied when the vote is taken. No notice need be given of regularly scheduled meetings and only two days' notice need precede special meetings. Perhaps most important, there is no mechanism for voting by proxy.

■ **Think about this:**

(G) Why do the differences between shareholders' meetings and directors' meetings exist? A few of them are set out in the following chart.

Shareholders' Meetings	Directors' Meetings
Quorum assumed to continue once formed	Quorum must be present when action taken
Quorum must be a majority or higher	Quorum may be as low as one-third
Quorum changes only in articles	Quorum changes in articles or bylaws

Meetings by Conference Call.

In a concession to convenience and twentieth-century technology, MBCA §8.20(b) provides that directors' meetings may be held by any means that allows the directors simultaneously to hear one another.

■ **Think about this:**

(H) Does this mean corporations can't have deaf directors?

(I) Would a meeting by Skype be valid?

(J) Would a meeting by online chat be valid?

Committee Action. It is quite usual for boards of any significant size to delegate certain functions to committees. As a matter of fact, it is even required that the boards of corporations that have registered securities under the Securities Exchange Act of 1934 create audit committees. This is a committee of what are commonly known as "outside" or "independent" directors — that is, directors who do not have any other material or pecuniary relationship with the corporation or a related party. Its function is to select the corporation's outside audit firm and to receive its report.

MBCA §8.25 is a typical statute authorizing the creation of board committees. It also is typical in providing that there are certain functions that cannot be delegated to a committee. These include authorizing distributions (other than pursuant to a method or formula approved by the full board), proposing shareholder action where shareholder action is required, filling vacancies on the board, and adopting, amending, or repealing bylaws.

> **This may help . . .**
>
> Independent and outside directors generally are the same thing. They are directors who are not employed by, and have no other relationships with, the corporation or its related parties (as opposed to "inside directors," who serve as both directors and employees of the corporation).
>
> Disinterested directors are something different. To say that a director is disinterested just means that the director has no personal interest in the subject of some particular transaction. The director may or may not also be independent or outside.

(b) Action Without a Meeting

Directors, like shareholders, may act by written consent. Unlike shareholders, however, the consent must be unanimous and, under the MBCA, there is no provision permitting electronic transmission of consent.

2. Unplanned Action by the Board

Recall that the directors elect the officers and authorize them to take certain acts on behalf of the corporation. Authority can be inherent in a position, sometimes as a matter of statute. More frequently, authority can be actual, based on the officers' reasonable understanding of the corporate principal's manifestations to them — which typically will be a matter of how the board conducts itself. Authority also can be apparent, based on a reasonable third party's understanding of the corporate principal's manifestations to them. What is reasonably understood is not always congruent with what is intended. Therefore, the board must be wary of standing by in light of conduct by officers of which they reasonably could be expected to be aware.

> **Connections: Agency Law**
>
> Fictional entities, including corporations, can only act through agents. The principles of agency are examined at length elsewhere in this text.

■ **Peruse MBCA Chapter 8B and think about this:[1]**

(K) Starco stockbrokers, attempting to market one million common shares to be issued by Durmac, offered 500,000 shares to Ennis Corp. at $50 per share. Already the owner of a substantial interest in Durmac, Ennis's financial condition was such as to make a large, immediate acquisition of additional shares of Durmac desirable.

Ennis's bylaws provided that a quorum consists of five out of its seven directors. After 24 hours' notice to the four "inside" directors, but without notice to the three "outside" directors, a special emergency board of directors meeting was held. Inside directors Almon, Barnes, and Chester, armed with a proxy executed by director Drake, the fourth inside director, attended the meeting. Also present was Owens, an outside director. The directors present voted unanimously (including the Drake proxy) to purchase 400,000 additional Durmac shares. At the end of the meeting, Owens signed a waiver of notice.

Immediately following the meeting, Ennis purchased and paid for 400,000 shares of Durmac stock at $50 per share. Preston and Quentin, the two outside directors who did not attend the meeting subsequently consented in writing to the purchase.

What defects in the process followed can you identify? Was the purchase ultimately approved in a manner that you would recommend?

D. Action by Officers

 What does it look like?

Check the online Supplement for the following sample document relevant to this section:
■ Bylaw provisions describing duties and authority of officers

In contrast to the shareholders and directors, the function and legal attributes of corporate officers are quite simple: They are agents of the corporation.

---

1. This hypothetical is based on one originally appearing in *Siegel's Corporations and Other Business Entities* (Theresa Gabaldon ed., 5th ed. 2012).

The material in this section makes that point and investigates the authority of two particular officers — the president (the subject of the first case noted below) and the secretary (the subject of the second). Although it is quite usual for a corporation to have at least these two officers, modern statutes typically do not require a corporation to have specific officers. Under the MBCA, all that is necessary is that a corporation have at least one officer who has the authority to prepare the minutes of shareholders' and directors' meetings and to authenticate corporate records. §8.40(c).

LEE v. JENKINS BROS.

United States Court of Appeals for the Second Circuit
268 F.2d 357 (1959)

MEDINA, Circuit Judge.

[In 1919, the Crane Company agreed to sell its Bridgeport, Connecticut, plant to a New Jersey corporation, Jenkins Brothers. Jenkins Brothers felt it needed to employ competent personnel, and sought to employ Lee, the business manager of Crane Company. Yardley, the President of Jenkins Brothers and a substantial stockholder, met with Lee at a hotel on June 1, 1920, and sought to entice him to join Jenkins Brothers. Also present was a vice president and his wife, though at the time of the trial in October 1957 only Lee was alive to describe the conversation.] . . .

Lee testified:

> "As far as the pension that I had earned with Crane Company he said the company (Jenkins Brothers) would pay that pension (and) if they didn't or, if anything came up, he would assume the liability himself he would guarantee payment of the pension; and in consideration of that promise I agreed to go to work for Jenkins Bros. on June 1, 1920.
>
> "The amount of the pension referred to by Mr. Yardley was a maximum of $1500 a year and that would be paid me when I reached the age of 60 years; regardless of what happened in the meantime, if I were with the company or not, I would be given a credit for those 13 years of service with the maximum pension of $1500." . . .

This agreement was never reduced to writing.

Lee's prospects with Jenkins turned out to be just about as bright as he had hoped. He subsequently became vice president and general manager in charge of manufacturing and a director of the company. At that time he was receiving a salary of $25,000 from Jenkins, $8,000 more from an affiliate, plus an annual 10 per cent bonus. In 1945, however, after 25 years with Jenkins, Lee was discharged at the age of 55. . . .

Connections

An agent's actual authority is based on manifestations by the principal to the agent.

By contrast, an agent's apparent authority is based on manifestations by the principal to a third party.

A title might manifest the same thing to the agent and to third parties.

See Chapter 4.

In the discussion which follows we assume, *arguendo*, that there was evidence sufficient to support a finding that Yardley orally agreed on behalf of the corporation that Lee would be paid at the age of 60 a pension not to exceed $1500, and that Yardley's words "regardless of what happens" were, as Lee contends, to be interpreted as meaning that Lee would receive this pension even if he were not working for Jenkins at the time the pension became payable. Jenkins asserts that Yardley had no authority to bind it to such an "extraordinary" contract, express, implied, or apparent and the trial court so found. There is nothing in the proofs submitted by Lee to warrant any finding of actual authority in Yardley. The Certificate of Incorporation and By-Laws of Jenkins are not in evidence nor was any course of conduct shown as between the corporation and Yardley. Accordingly, on the phase of the case now under discussion, we are dealing only with apparent authority. See 2 Fletcher, Cyclopedia Corporations, Section 449 (Perm. Ed. 1954)....

The ascertainment of the Connecticut law on this critical question of Yardley's apparent authority is a far from simple task. The Connecticut cases have not yet quite come to grips with the question.... Hence, it is necessary to consult the "general" law on the subject, on the assumption that, if a general rule can be found, Connecticut would follow it....

Our question on this phase of the case then boils itself down to the following: can it be said as a matter of law that Yardley as president, chairman of the board, substantial stockholder and trustee and son-in-law of the estate of the major stockholder, had no power in the presence of the company's most interested vice president to secure for a "reasonable" length of time badly needed key personnel by promising an experienced local executive a life pension to commence in 30 years at the age of 60, even if Lee were not then working for the corporation, when the maximum liability to Jenkins under such a pension was $1500 per year.

A survey of the law on the authority of corporate officers does not reveal a completely consistent pattern. For the most part the courts perhaps have taken a rather restrictive view on the extent of powers of corporate officials, ... but the dissatisfaction with such an approach has been manifested in a variety of exceptions such as ratification, ... estoppel, ... and promissory estoppel....

The rule most widely cited is that the president only has authority to bind his company by acts arising in the usual and regular course of business but not for contracts of an "extraordinary" nature.... The substance of such a rule lies in the content of the term "extraordinary" which is subject to a broad range of interpretation.

The growth and development of this rule occurred during the late nineteenth and early twentieth centuries when the potentialities of the corporate form of enterprise were just being realized. ... As the corporation became a more common vehicle for the conduct of business it became increasingly evident that many corporations, particularly small closely held ones, did not normally function in the formal ritualistic manner hitherto envisaged. While the boards of directors still nominally controlled corporate affairs, in reality officers and managers frequently ran the business with little, if any, board supervision. The natural consequence of such a development was that third parties commonly relied on the authority of such officials in almost all the multifarious transactions in which corporations engaged. The pace of modern business life was too swift to insist on the approval by the board of directors of every transaction that was in any way "unusual."

The judicial recognition given to these developments has varied considerably. Whether termed "apparent authority" or an "estoppel" to deny authority, many courts have noted the injustice caused by the practice of permitting corporations to act commonly through their executives and then allowing them to disclaim an agreement as beyond the authority of the contracting officer, when the contract no longer suited its convenience. . . . Other courts, however, continued to cling to the past with little attempt to discuss the unconscionable results obtained or the doctrine of apparent authority. . . . Such restrictive views have been generally condemned by the commentators. . . .

The summary of holdings pro and con in general on the subject of what are and what are not "extraordinary" agreements is inconclusive at best. . . . But the pattern becomes more distinct when we turn to the more limited area of employment contracts.

It is generally settled that the president as part of the regular course of business has authority to hire and discharge employees and fix their compensation. . . . In so doing he may agree to hire them for a specific number of years if the term selected is deemed reasonable. . . . But employment contracts for life or on a "permanent" basis are generally regarded as "extraordinary" and beyond the authority of any corporate executive if the only consideration for the promise is the employee's promise to work for that period. . . . Jenkins would have us analogize the pension agreement involved herein to these generally condemned lifetime employment contracts because it extends over a long period of time, is of indefinite duration, and involves an indefinite liability on the part of the corporation.

It is not surprising that lifetime employment contracts have met with substantial hostility in the courts, for these contracts are often oral, uncorroborated, vague in important details and highly improbable. Accordingly, the courts have erected a veritable array of obstacles to their enforcement. They have been construed as terminable at will, . . . too indefinite to enforce, . . . ultra vires, . . . lacking in mutuality or consideration, . . . abandoned or breached by subsequent acts, . . . and the supporting evidence deemed insufficient to go to the jury, . . . as well as made without proper authority. . . .

Where reasons have been given to support the conclusion that lifetime employments are "extraordinary," and hence made without authority, a scrutiny of these reasons may be helpful for their bearing on the analogous field of pension agreements. It is said that: they unduly restrict the power of the shareholders and future boards of directors on questions of managerial policy; they subject the corporation to an inordinately substantial amount of liability; they run for long and indefinite periods of time. Of these reasons the only one applicable to pension agreements is that they run for long and indefinite periods of time. There the likeness stops. Future director or shareholder control is in no way impeded; the amount of liability is not disproportionate; the agreement was not only not unreasonable but beneficial and necessary to the corporation; and pension contracts are commonly used fringe benefits in employment contracts. Moreover, unlike the case with life employment contracts, courts have often gone out of their way to find pension promises binding and definite even when labeled gratuitous by the employer. The consideration given to the employee involved is not at all dependent on profits or sales, nor does it involve some other variable suggesting director discretion.

In this case Lee was hired at a starting salary of $4,000 per year plus a contemplated pension of $1500 per year in thirty years. Had Lee been hired at a starting salary of $10,000 per year the cost to the corporation over the long run would have been substantially greater, yet no one could plausibly contend that such an employment contract was beyond Yardley's authority. . . .

Almost Doing the Numbers: The Time Value of Money

"The time value of money" is an important financial principle based on the assumption that money has earning potential—at a minimum it can be placed in an interest-bearing savings account. Thus, it is common to agree to pay a larger sum in the future in order to forgo paying a smaller sum today. Interest rates in 1920, when the alleged agreement was entered, were over 15 percent. The online Supplement describes how to calculate the present value of an agreement to pay a sum in the future, given an assumed interest rate (the easiest way is to use an online calculator). The present value of an agreement to pay $1,500 in 30 years was around $22. If, as the court hypothesizes, Lee might have agreed to forgo $6,000 of salary for even a single year it would have financed a $1,500 pension for over 270 years.

Apparent authority is essentially a question of fact. It depends not only on the nature of the contract involved, but the officer negotiating it, the corporation's usual manner of conducting business, the size of the corporation and the number of its stockholders, the circumstances that give rise to the contract, the reasonableness of the contract, the amounts involved, and who the contracting third party is, to list a few but not all of the relevant factors. In certain instances a given contract may be so important to the welfare of the corporation that outsiders would naturally suppose that only the board of directors (or even the shareholders) could properly handle it. It is in this light that the "ordinary course of business" rule should be given its content. Beyond such "extraordinary" acts, whether or not apparent authority exists is simply a matter of fact.

Accordingly, we hold that, assuming there was sufficient proof of the making of the pension agreement, Connecticut, in the particular circumstances of this case, would probably take the view that reasonable men could differ on the subject of whether or not Yardley had apparent authority to make the contract, and that the trial court erred in deciding the question as a matter of law. We do not think Connecticut would adopt any hard and fast rule against apparent authority to make pension agreements generally, on the theory that they were in the same category as lifetime employment contracts. . . .

■ **Think about this:**

(L) Rachel is a commercial real estate agent handling the listing of a large office building. She is authorized by the owner to accept the first offer of $4,500,000 or more. She is contacted by Priscilla, who introduces herself as the president of Acquisico, Inc., and makes an offer of $5 million for the office building. Rachel has heard of Acquisico and knows that it is in the business of buying, renovating, and reselling commercial properties. Does Rachel need to ask Priscilla any questions before she accepts the offer and takes the property off the market?

The following case almost certainly will teach you to have profound respect for the role of the corporate secretary.

IN RE DRIVE IN DEVELOPMENT CORP.

United States Court of Appeals for the Seventh Circuit
371 F.2d 215 (1966)

SWYGERT, Circuit Judge.

The principal question in this appeal relates to the circumstances which may bind a corporation to a guaranty of the obligations of a related corporation when it is contended that the corporate officer who executed the guaranty had no authority to do so. The facts giving rise to the question underlie a claim filed by the National Boulevard Bank of Chicago in an arrangement proceeding under chapter XI of the Bankruptcy Act, 11 U.S.C. §§701-799, in which the Drive In Development Corporation was the debtor. National Boulevard's claim was disallowed by the referee, whose decision was confirmed by the district court.

Drive In was one of four subsidiary companies controlled by Tastee Freez Industries, Inc., a holding company that conducted no business of its own. . . .

[The officers of Drive In executed a guarantee of payment to induce National Boulevard Bank to make a loan to Drive In's parent corporation. The guarantee was executed by one Maranz on behalf of Drive In, as "Chairman," and one Dick attested to its execution as Secretary. National Boulevard requested a copy of the authorizing resolution of the board of directors of Drive In. A copy, certified by Dick with the corporate seal affixed, was duly delivered. No such resolution, however, was contained in Drive In's corporate minute book, and the directors'

Although once required to authenticate documents the execution of which had been authorized by the board of directors, corporate seals generally no longer have any legal significance.

testimony left it uncertain as to whether any such resolution had ever been considered or approved at a directors meeting. National Boulevard advanced substantial sums under the guaranty.]

Turning to the merits of the objections to National Boulevard's claim, the referee found that Drive In's minute book did not show that a resolution authorizing Maranz to sign the guaranty was adopted by the directors and that Dick could not recall a specific directors' meeting at which such a resolution was approved. From these findings, the referee concluded that Maranz, who signed the guaranty on behalf of Drive In, had no authority, "either actual or implied or apparent," to bind Drive In. This conclusion was erroneous. Drive In was estopped to deny Maranz' express authority to sign the guaranty because of the certified copy of a resolution of Drive In's board of directors purporting to grant such authority furnished to the bank by Dick, whether or not such a resolution was in fact formally adopted. Dick was the secretary of the corporation. Generally, it is the duty of the secretary to keep the corporate records and to make proper entries of the actions and resolutions of the directors. Therefore it was within the authority of Dick to certify that a resolution such as challenged here was adopted. Statements made by an officer or agent in the course of a transaction in which the corporation is engaged and which are within the scope of his authority are binding upon the corporation. Consequently Drive In was estopped to deny the representation made by Dick in the certificate forwarded to National Boulevard, in the absence of actual or constructive knowledge on the part of the bank that the representation was untrue. . . .

The objectors argue that since William Schneider, a vice president of National Boulevard, requested Dick to furnish the certified copy of a resolution granting authority to execute the guaranty, and since Hugh Driscoll, another vice president of National Boulevard, was also a director of Tastee Freez and was familiar with the organization of the subsidiaries, the bank was somehow in a position to know that no resolution had in fact been adopted by Drive In's board of directors. These facts, however, fall far short of proving such knowledge on the part of National Boulevard.

. . . Although intercorporate contracts of guaranty do not usually occur in the regular course of commercial business, here the interrelationship of Tastee Freez and its subsidiaries presented a situation in which the guaranty was not so unusual as would ordinarily obtain. Furthermore, the realities of modern corporate business practices do not contemplate that those who deal with officers or agents acting for a corporation should be required to go behind the representations of those who have authority to speak for the corporation and who verify the authority of those who presume to act for the corporation. . . .

The order of the district court confirming the referee's order is reversed in part and affirmed in part.

> ■ **Think about this:**
>
> *(M)* How could Drive In have protected itself from the acts of the wily Dick?
>
> *(N)* Did National Boulevard Bank conduct itself in a manner you would recommend?

Test Yourself

Assume Applicability of the Most Current Version of the Model Business Corporations Act

Also assume that there is nothing relevant in the corporation's articles or bylaws unless you are told to the contrary.

1. At the request of a shareholder, a corporation's secretary has called a special meeting pursuant to MBCA §7.02, for the properly noticed purpose of voting on the removal of a particular director for cause. At the meeting, the removal is defeated. One of the shareholders present then moves that the shareholders vote to endorse the current board. The motion is:

   a. Out of order because it was not covered by the notice of the meeting.
   b. Out of order because it does not relate to legitimate shareholder action.
   c. Permissible only if the moving shareholder owns at least 5 percent of the stock of the corporation.
   d. Permissible because it is so innocuous.

2. Joe, John, and Jim are three shareholders of XYZ, Inc., and together they own 45 percent of its shares. They know that voting together they can control a large portion of the company's board of directors. They also know that Joe is brightest among them and most involved in the company's affairs, so they provide in a written agreement among them that they will each vote all of the shares at each annual shareholders' meeting exactly as Joe directs them to do. This arrangement is legally unenforceable because:

   a. It is void as against public policy.
   b. There are shareholders who are not parties to it.
   c. It is unsupported by consideration.
   d. On these facts there is no obvious reason that this arrangement would be legally unenforceable.

3. Nellie owns 50 percent of the shares of the N&N Corporation. Nancy owns the other 50 percent. Both have served on the two-person board of directors for some years. Nancy refuses to attend shareholders' meetings.

   a. Nellie can elect both directors at the next annual meeting.
   b. Nellie can elect both directors at the next annual meeting unless the corporation's articles provide for cumulative voting.
   c. Nellie can elect one director at the next annual meeting if the corporation's articles provide for cumulative voting.
   d. No annual meeting can be held.

4. Which of the following best characterizes the enforceability of a shareholders' agreement providing that they will elect themselves as directors, and that as directors they will vote for the maximum dividends legally allowable?

   a. Enforceable, because shareholders are permitted to bind themselves as to any matter on which they are entitled to vote.
   b. Enforceable, because directors are permitted to bind themselves as to any matter on which they are entitled to vote.
   c. Enforceable because both election of directors and declaration of dividends are legitimate shareholder actions.
   d. Unenforceable if the corporation is publicly traded.

5. BigCo's board of directors has 13 authorized seats, 9 of which are currently filled. A quorum of BigCo's board is:

   a. 13.
   b. 7.
   c. 6.
   d. 5.

6. ABC, Inc., has 100 shares of stock outstanding. Assuming that the votes of all shares represented at a meeting are cast either for or against a proposal, the absolute minimum number of shares that must be voted in favor of a proposal for it to carry is:

   a. 1.
   b. 26.
   c. 51.
   d. 100.

7. XYZ, Inc.'s board of directors has nine seats, two of which are unfilled. The absolute minimum number of votes at any meeting of this board needed to take effective action is:

   a. One.
   b. Three.

c. Four.

d. Five.

8. Due to recent retirements, five of the nine authorized seats on ABC Corp.'s board are currently unfilled, and the annual shareholders' meeting will not be held for another seven months. ABC's board:

a. Cannot take legally effective action on behalf of the corporation until the annual shareholders' meeting.

b. Can take legally effective action on behalf of the corporation only by calling a special shareholders' meeting.

c. Can take legally effective action on behalf of the corporation by appointing one new director to the board.

d. None of the above.

18

Fiduciary Duties in the Corporate Context: The Duty of Care

The introductory material in this chapter describes who owes fiduciary duties in the corporate context, to whom they are owed, and, in very general terms, how they are enforced. The main focus of the chapter, however, is the first of the two traditional duties: the duty of care. The duty of loyalty (the second of the major traditional fiduciary duties) is the subject of its own two chapters.

Briefly, the duty of care requires that in all actions in connection with the fiduciary's official duties, the fiduciary will exercise a certain degree of legally required caution to be sure that the action is in the company's best interests and will not cause it harm.

Chapter Outline

A. Fiduciary Duty and Introduction to the Duty of Care

- A fiduciary must act on behalf of another, who is known as the beneficiary
- There is a traditional division between the duties of care and loyalty
- In general, duties are owed to the corporation rather than its individual shareholders
- An action based on breach of the duty of care is akin to an action for negligence

B. The Duty of Care and the Failure to Act

- Failure to act is actionable when there is a duty to act

- Directors must exercise the degree of diligence, care, and skill that an ordinarily prudent person would exercise under similar circumstances in like positions
- Directors are under a continuing duty to stay informed and cannot close their eyes to misconduct by other corporate actors

C. The Duty of Care, Decisions That Turn Out Badly, and the Business Judgment Rule

1. A Traditional Approach
   - The courts will not interfere with the directors' honest business judgment unless there is a showing of fraud, illegality, or conflict of interest

2. The Business Judgment Rule and Its Possible Limits
   - It is not always clear whether the business judgment rule is a rule of abstention for judges or a standard of conduct for corporate fiduciaries
   - There is a limit on the business judgment rule for illegal acts
   - There is a theoretical limit on the business judgment rule for "wasteful" acts
   - A lack of informed process has consequences

D. Legislative Responses to Officer and Director Liability

- Limits on monetary liability for breaches of the duty of care (but not bad faith)
- Redefining the duty of care

E. Oversight, Monitoring, and the Duty of Care

- Decisions about oversight and monitoring are business decisions
- Utter failure to invest in oversight would evidence lack of good faith

Test Yourself

A. Fiduciary Duty and Introduction to the Duty of Care

The directors and officers are "corporate fiduciaries." This means that they are entrusted with a duty to act in the corporation's best interests. It is traditional to characterize this duty as having two main components: the duty of care and the duty of loyalty. The duty of care requires that in all actions related to the fiduciary's official duties, the fiduciary will exercise a certain degree of legally required caution. The duty of loyalty imposes special, strict burdens on the fiduciary when acting in connection with his or her official duties while under a "conflict of interest."

A few questions seem obvious up front: First, who owes the traditional duties? They apply to all officers and directors of the corporation, and they apply in essentially the same way to each. In fact, all agents of a corporation, in addition to its officers, are fiduciaries and owe duties of care and loyalty (although they are not afforded the protection of the "business judgment rule" described below). Moreover, as discussed elsewhere in this book, the law generally holds "controlling shareholders" to be corporate fiduciaries and to owe the same duties as officers and directors.

Connections: Good Faith and Disclosure

Fiduciaries sometimes also are said to owe a miscellany of other duties, including *good faith* and *disclosure*. As a theoretical matter, they sometimes are described as subsumed in the duty of loyalty, but sometimes the duty of disclosure is characterized as part of the duty of care. In any event, the duty of disclosure is not very often enforced as a matter of the state law of fiduciary duty. Rather, because the disclosure failures that can give rise to liability often also violate federal securities law, the law of disclosure is largely a matter of the federal law of "securities fraud" and "proxy regulation," discussed elsewhere in this book.

During the past several decades, the courts have developed new twists on fiduciary obligations that govern in special situations. In some states, they include a duty between shareholders in closely held corporations, a duty owed by a controlling shareholder, and the special duties that officers and directors owe when their company is facing a hostile takeover attempt. These rules also are discussed elsewhere in this book.

A second question is to whom are these duties owed? Even though courts sometimes say that fiduciaries owe their duties "to the corporation and its shareholders," it generally is more correct to regard a corporate fiduciary as owing fiduciary duties only to the corporation. This means that when shareholders complain about breaches of the duty of care or loyalty they must bring "derivative" suits on the corporation's behalf. Importantly, even when the shareholder wins in a derivative suit alleging breach of fiduciary duty, any money damages recovered are paid by the defendant fiduciary directly to the corporation, and the plaintiff is entitled to none of it. This is so even though a frequent basis for fiduciary claims is that some management action caused an injury to the corporation that in turn caused share prices to fall.

It is often said that a claim for breach of the duty of care is really just a cause of action for "negligence." We will use that observation as a helpful starting point, but it is important to recognize that not all courts describe it in the same way, and there can be complications with respect to establishing cause.

It will be useful to recall the general cause of action for negligence you learned in Torts class, since the duty of care claim works in the same way. A negligence plaintiff must prove the following:

- That defendant bore a **duty** (in the case of simple negligence, the duty we all bear to take reasonable care to avoid foreseeable injury to other persons in their person or property);
- That defendant **breached** that duty, meaning defendant took some action not in conformity with it;
- That plaintiff suffered an **injury**; and
- That defendant's breach was the **actual and proximate cause** of plaintiff's injury.

Causes of action for breach of fiduciary duty also take roughly this form. Thus, a cause of action for breach of a corporate duty of care is structured the same way, with the main challenge presented by the content of the "duty" element.

 Time Out for PR

Lawyers are, of course, fiduciaries for their clients. A cause of action for legal malpractice sometimes is brought as a breach of contract claim. More usually, it is a claim based on breach of the lawyer's duty of care, and it is structured as follows:

- Duty (in this case, the duty to exercise the care that a reasonably prudent attorney would exercise in the representation under the circumstances);
- Breach;
- Injury; and
- Actual and proximate cause

Before turning to the content of the duty of care, however, it is important to recognize that since the 1980s it generally has been possible for corporations to place provisions in their Articles of Incorporation eliminating monetary liability for breach of an officer's or director's duty of care. (See, for instance, MBCA §2.02(b)(4) and Del. Corp. Code §102(b)(7).) These statutes are discussed elsewhere in the text. Many companies have taken advantage of the statutes' invitation. However, it is not possible to eliminate monetary liability for breach of the duty of loyalty. In consequence, plaintiffs' lawyers often attempt to characterize an act that traditionally would have been assessed in terms of negligence as a matter of disloyalty.

B. The Duty of Care and the Failure to Act

When one thinks about negligence it is usual to think about an act that is poorly performed — say, driving a car, installing electrical wiring, or the like. In the corporate fiduciary context, the analogue generally would be making a decision, and the argument is about a decision that is poorly made. Sometimes, however, it may be negligent to *fail* to act when there is a duty to do so. The following case makes the point that such a duty is imposed on corporate directors, but explores its parameters without fully defining them. Pay attention to the acts that the court suggests may be necessary for directors to protect themselves from liability.

FRANCIS v. UNITED JERSEY BANK

Supreme Court of New Jersey
432 A.2d 814 (1981)

POLLOCK, J.

The primary issue on this appeal is whether a corporate director is personally liable in negligence for the failure to prevent the misappropriation of trust funds by other directors who were also officers and shareholders of the corporation.

Plaintiffs are trustees in bankruptcy of Pritchard & Baird Intermediaries Corp. (Pritchard & Baird), a reinsurance broker or intermediary. Defendant Lillian P. Overcash is the daughter of Lillian G. Pritchard and the executrix of her estate. At the time of her death, Mrs. Pritchard was a director and the largest single shareholder of Pritchard & Baird. Because Mrs. Pritchard died after the institution of suit but before trial, her executrix was substituted as a defendant. United Jersey Bank is joined as the administrator of the estate of Charles Pritchard, Sr., who had been president, director and majority shareholder of Pritchard & Baird.

This litigation focuses on payments made by Pritchard & Baird to Charles Pritchard, Jr. and William Pritchard, who were sons of Mr. and Mrs. Charles Pritchard, Sr., as well as officers, directors and shareholders of the corporation. Claims against Charles, Jr. and William are being pursued in bankruptcy proceedings against them. . . .

. . . [T]he initial question is whether Mrs. Pritchard was negligent in not noticing and trying to prevent the misappropriation of funds held by the corporation in an implied trust. A further question is whether her negligence was the proximate cause of the plaintiffs' losses. Both lower courts found that she was liable in negligence for the losses caused by the wrongdoing of Charles, Jr. and William. We affirm.

> **STATE OF NEW JERSEY, PLAINTIFF V. CHARLES H. PRITCHARD, JR. AND WILLIAM G. PRITCHARD, DEFENDANTS**
>
> The brothers were charged with 111 counts of conversion, fraud, and embezzlement. After a four-week jury trial, they were acquitted on all counts.

I

The matrix for our decision is the customs and practices of the reinsurance industry and the role of Pritchard & Baird as a reinsurance broker. Reinsurance involves a contract under which one insurer agrees to indemnify another for loss sustained under the latter's policy of insurance. Insurance companies that insure against losses arising out of fire or other casualty seek at times to minimize their exposure by sharing risks with other insurance companies. Thus, when the face amount of a policy is comparatively large, the company may enlist one or more insurers to participate in that risk. Similarly, an insurance company's loss potential and overall exposure may be reduced by reinsuring a part of an entire class of policies (e.g., 25% of all of its fire insurance policies). The selling insurance company is known as a ceding company. The entity that assumes the obligation is designated as the reinsurer.

The reinsurance broker arranges the contract between the ceding company and the reinsurer. . . . In most instances, the ceding company and the reinsurer do not communicate with each other, but rely upon the reinsurance broker. . . . The reinsurance business was described by an expert at trial as having "a magic aura around it of dignity and quality and integrity." A telephone call which might be confirmed by a handwritten memorandum is sufficient to create a reinsurance obligation. . . .

. . . [T]he corporation operated as a close family corporation with Mr. and Mrs. Pritchard and their two sons as the only directors. After the death of Charles, Sr. in 1973, only the remaining three directors continued to operate as the board. Lillian Pritchard inherited 72 of her husband's 120 shares in Pritchard & Baird, thereby becoming the largest shareholder in the corporation with 48% of the stock. . . .

Contrary to the industry custom of segregating funds, Pritchard & Baird commingled the funds of reinsurers and ceding companies with its own funds. All monies (including commissions, premiums and loss monies) were deposited in a single account. . . . Starting in 1970, however, Charles, Jr. and William begin to siphon ever-increasing sums from the corporation under the guise of loans. As of January 31, 1970, the "loans" to Charles, Jr. were $230,932 and to William were $207,329. At least by January 31, 1973, the annual increase in the loans exceeded annual corporate revenues. By October 1975, the year of bankruptcy, the "shareholders' loans" had metastasized to a total of $12,333,514.47 [taken from funds held in trust for clients].

The trial court rejected the characterization of the payments as "loans." 162 N.J. Super. at 365, 392 A.2d 1233. No corporate resolution authorized the "loans," and no note or other instrument evidenced the debt. Charles, Jr. and William paid no interest on the amounts received. The "loans" were not repaid or reduced from one year to the next; rather, they increased annually. . . .

Mrs. Pritchard was not active in the business of Pritchard & Baird and knew virtually nothing of its corporate affairs. She briefly visited the corporate offices in Morristown on only one occasion, and she never read or obtained the annual financial statements. She was unfamiliar with the rudiments of reinsurance and made no effort to assure that the policies and practices of the corporation, particularly pertaining to the withdrawal of funds, complied with industry custom or relevant law. Although her husband had warned her that Charles, Jr. would "take the shirt off my back," Mrs. Pritchard did not pay any attention to her duties as a director or to the affairs of the corporation.

After her husband died in December 1973, Mrs. Pritchard became incapacitated and was bedridden for a six-month period. She became listless at this time and started to drink rather heavily. Her physical condition deteriorated, and in 1978 she died. The trial court rejected testimony seeking to exonerate her because she "was old, was grief-stricken at the loss of her husband, sometimes consumed too much alcohol and was psychologically overborne by her sons." That court found that she was competent to act and that the reason Mrs. Pritchard never knew what her sons "were doing was because she never made the slightest effort to discharge any of her responsibilities as a director of Pritchard & Baird."

III

Individual liability of a corporate director for acts of the corporation is a prickly problem. Generally directors are accorded broad immunity and are not insurers of corporate activities. The problem is particularly nettlesome when a third party asserts that a director, because of nonfeasance, is liable for losses caused by acts of insiders, who in this case were officers, directors and shareholders. Determination of the liability of Mrs. Pritchard requires findings that she had a duty to the clients of Pritchard & Baird, that she breached that duty and that her breach was a proximate cause of their losses.

The New Jersey Business Corporation Act, which took effect on January 1, 1969, was a comprehensive revision of the statutes relating to business corporations. One section, N.J.S.A. 14A:6-14, concerning a director's general obligation, makes it incumbent upon directors to discharge their duties in good faith and with that degree of diligence, care and skill which ordinarily prudent men would exercise under similar circumstances in like positions....

... In addition to requiring that directors act honestly and in good faith, the New York courts [interpreting the statute on which the New Jersey statute was based] recognized that the nature and extent of reasonable care depended upon the type of corporation, its size and financial resources. Thus, a bank director [is] held to stricter accountability than the director of an ordinary business....

As a general rule, a director should acquire at least a rudimentary understanding of the business of the corporation. Accordingly, a director should become familiar with the fundamentals of the business in which the corporation is engaged.... Because directors are bound to exercise ordinary care, they cannot set up as a defense lack of the knowledge needed to exercise the requisite degree of care. If one "feels that he has not had sufficient business experience to qualify him to perform the duties of a director, he should either acquire the knowledge by inquiry, or refuse to act."

More to the Story: Special Duties

Banks, of course, accept depositors' funds in trust. In addition, bank directors often are subject to specified statutory duties (including a duty to prevent violations of banking law).

Directors are under a continuing obligation to keep informed about the activities of the corporation. Otherwise, they may not be able to participate in the overall management of corporate affairs.... Directors may not shut their eyes to corporate misconduct and then claim that because they did not see the misconduct, they did not have a duty to look. The sentinel asleep at his post contributes nothing to the enterprise he is charged to protect....

Directorial management does not require a detailed inspection of day-to-day activities, but rather a general monitoring of corporate affairs and policies.... Accordingly, a director is well advised to attend board meetings regularly. Indeed, a director who is absent from a board meeting is presumed to concur in action taken on a corporate matter, unless he files a "dissent with the secretary of the corporation within a reasonable time after learning of such action." N.J.S.A. 14A:6-13 (Supp. 1981-1982). Regular attendance does not mean that directors must attend every meeting, but that directors should attend meetings as a matter of practice. A director of a publicly held corporation might be expected to attend regular monthly meetings, but a director of a small, family corporation might be asked to attend only an annual meeting. The point is that one of the responsibilities of a director is to attend meetings of the board of which he or she is a member....

While directors are not required to audit corporate books, they should maintain familiarity with the financial status of the corporation by a regular review of financial statements.... The review of financial statements, however, may give rise to a duty to inquire further into matters revealed by those statements.... Upon discovery of an illegal course of action, a director has a duty to object and, if the corporation does not correct the conduct, to resign....

In certain circumstances, the fulfillment of the duty of a director may call for more than mere objection and resignation. Sometimes a director may be required to seek the advice of counsel.... Sometimes the duty of a director may require more than consulting with outside counsel. A director may have a duty to take reasonable means to prevent illegal conduct by co-directors; in any appropriate case, this may include threat of suit....

A director's duty of care does not exist in the abstract, but must be considered in relation to specific obligees. In general, the relationship of a corporate director to the corporation and its stockholders is that of a fiduciary.... Shareholders have a right to expect that directors will exercise reasonable supervision and control over the policies and practices of a corporation. The institutional integrity of a corporation depends upon the proper discharge by directors of those duties.

While directors may owe a fiduciary duty to creditors also, that obligation generally has not been recognized in the absence of insolvency.... With certain corporations, however, directors are deemed to owe a duty to creditors and other third parties even when the corporation is solvent. Although depositors of a bank are considered in some respects to be creditors, courts have recognized that directors may owe them a fiduciary duty.... Directors of nonbanking corporations may owe a similar duty when the corporation holds funds of others in trust....

As a reinsurance broker, Pritchard & Baird received annually as a fiduciary millions of dollars of clients' money which it was under a duty to segregate. To this extent, it resembled a bank rather than a small family business. Accordingly, Mrs. Pritchard's relationship to the clientele of Pritchard & Baird was akin to that of a director of a bank to its depositors....

As a director of a substantial reinsurance brokerage corporation, she should have known that it received annually millions of dollars of loss and premium funds which it held in trust for ceding and reinsurance companies. Mrs. Pritchard should have obtained and read the annual statements of financial condition of Pritchard & Baird. Although she had a right to rely upon financial statements prepared in accordance with N.J.S.A. 14A:6-14, such reliance would not excuse her conduct. The reason is that those statements disclosed on their face the misappropriation of trust funds.

Doing the Numbers (Sort of): Pritchard & Baird Balance Sheet

The court seems quite sure that anyone who looked at the financial statements would have seen something amiss. What might they have looked like? According to the trial court, "All statements reflected the fact that the corporation had virtually no assets and that liabilities vastly exceeded assets." That sounds like the balance sheet (which does, after all, have to balance) would be a less exaggerated version of something like this:

Assets	$ 0	Liabilities	
		Amounts owed to customers	$12,000,000
		Equity	($12,000,000)
Total Assets	$ 0	Total Liabilities and Equity	$ 0

It does seem that a reader might say, "Oh, I wonder what happened to the money we were supposed to be holding in trust?" In fact, however, the balance sheet more likely looked something like this:

Assets		Liabilities	
Amount receivable from shareholders	$12,000,000	Amounts owed to customers	$12,000,000
		Equity	$ 0
Total Assets	$12,000,000	Total Liabilities and Equity	$12,000,000

This presentation means that the reader does not have to wonder where the trust funds went.

From those statements, she should have realized that, as of January 31, 1970, her sons were withdrawing substantial trust funds under the guise of "Shareholders' Loans." The financial statements for each fiscal year commencing with that of January 31, 1970, disclosed that the working capital deficits and the "loans" were escalating in tandem. Detecting a misappropriation of funds would not have required special expertise or extraordinary diligence; a cursory reading of the financial statements would have revealed the pillage. Thus, if Mrs. Pritchard had read the financial statements, she would have known that her sons were converting trust funds. When financial statements demonstrate that insiders are bleeding a corporation to death, a director should notice and try to stanch the flow of blood.

In summary, Mrs. Pritchard was charged with the obligation of basic knowledge and supervision of the business of Pritchard & Baird. Under the circumstances, this obligation included reading and understanding financial statements, and making reasonable attempts at detection and prevention of the illegal conduct of other officers and directors. She had a duty to protect the clients of Pritchard & Baird against policies and practices that would result in the misappropriation of money they had entrusted to the corporation. She breached that duty.

IV

Nonetheless, the negligence of Mrs. Pritchard does not result in liability unless it is a proximate cause of the loss. . . . Analysis of proximate cause requires an initial determination of cause-in-fact. Causation-in-fact calls for a finding that the defendant's act or omission was a necessary antecedent of the loss, i.e., that if the defendant had observed his or her duty of care, the loss would not have occurred. . . . W. Prosser, Law of Torts §41 at 238 (4 ed. 1971). Further, the plaintiff has the burden of establishing the amount of the loss or damages caused by the negligence of the defendant. . . . Thus, the plaintiff must establish not only a breach of duty, "but in addition that the performance by the director of his duty would have avoided loss, and the amount of the resulting loss." . . .

Cases involving nonfeasance present a much more difficult causation question than those in which the director has committed an affirmative act of negligence leading to the loss. Analysis in cases of negligent omissions calls for determination of the reasonable steps a director should have taken and whether that course of action would have averted the loss. . . .

In this case, the scope of Mrs. Pritchard's duties was determined by the precarious financial condition of Pritchard & Baird, its fiduciary relationship to its clients and the implied trust in which it held their funds. Thus viewed, the scope of her duties encompassed all reasonable action to stop the continuing conversion. Her duties extended beyond mere objection and resignation to reasonable attempts to prevent the misappropriation of the trust funds.

A leading case discussing causation where the director's liability is predicated upon a negligent failure to act is Barnes v. Andrews, 298 F. 614 (S.D.N.Y.

1924). In that case the court exonerated a figurehead director who served for eight months on a board that held one meeting after his election, a meeting he was forced to miss because of the death of his mother. Writing for the court, Judge Learned Hand distinguished a director who fails to prevent general mismanagement from one such as Mrs. Pritchard who failed to stop an illegal "loan":

> When the corporate funds have been illegally lent, it is a fair inference that a protest would have stopped the loan, and that the director's neglect caused the loss. But when a business fails from general mismanagement, business incapacity, or bad judgment, how is it possible to say that a single director could have made the company successful, or how much in dollars he could have saved? (*Id.* at 616-617). . . .

In assessing whether Mrs. Pritchard's conduct was a legal or proximate cause of the conversion, "(l)egal responsibility must be limited to those causes which are so closely connected with the result and of such significance that the law is justified in imposing liability." . . . Such a judicial determination involves not only considerations of causation-in-fact and matters of policy, but also common sense and logic. . . .

Within Pritchard & Baird, several factors contributed to the loss of the funds: comingling of corporate and client monies, conversion of funds by Charles, Jr. and William and dereliction of her duties by Mrs. Pritchard. The wrongdoing of her sons, although the immediate cause of the loss, should not excuse Mrs. Pritchard from her negligence which also was a substantial factor contributing to the loss. Restatement (Second) of Torts, supra, §442B, comment b. Her sons knew that she, the only other director, was not reviewing their conduct; they spawned their fraud in the backwater of her neglect. Her neglect of duty contributed to the climate of corruption; her failure to act contributed to the continuation of that corruption. Consequently, her conduct was a substantial factor contributing to the loss.

. . . Where a case involves nonfeasance, no one can say "with absolute certainty what would have occurred if the defendant had acted otherwise." . . . Nonetheless, where it is reasonable to conclude that the failure to act would produce a particular result and that result has followed, causation may be inferred. . . . We conclude that even if Mrs. Pritchard's mere objection had not stopped the depredations of her sons, her consultation with an attorney and the threat of suit would have deterred them. That conclusion flows as a matter of common sense and logic from the record. Whether in other situations a director has a duty to do more than protest and resign is best left to case-by-case determinations. In this case, we are satisfied that there was a duty to do more than object and resign. Consequently, we find that Mrs. Pritchard's negligence was a proximate cause of the misappropriations. . . .

■ **Think about this:**

(A) Mrs. Pritchard was the mother of Charles, Jr. and William. Does that make her conduct more suspicious than if she were not related to them?

(B) Suppose that in setting up a corporation to be owned 50/50 by Abigail and Ben, the advising attorney noted the possibility of a deadlock if Abigail and Ben served as the only two directors. Abigail and Ben therefore decide to ask Claudio, a mutual friend, to serve as a director in order to break ties if necessary. He agrees, and then proceeds to conduct himself precisely like Mrs. Pritchard, while Abigail and Ben proceed to conduct themselves exactly like Mrs. Pritchard's two sons. The business of the corporation is acting as a reinsurance broker. Has Claudio violated the duty of care?

(C) Would your answer to Problem B change if the business of the corporation were manufacturing widgets, and the money embezzled by Abigail and Ben were cash that was prepaid by customers?

(D) Would your answer to Problem B change if, rather than embezzling money, Abigail and Ben bankrupted the company by horribly mismanaging it?

(E) The *Francis* court makes what politely might be described as a big, hairy deal out of cause. Is that really necessary? On the other hand, does it seem that cause is very difficult to prove in a case like *Francis*? What would a plaintiff need to prove in a case like Problem D?

(F) Why was it necessary for the court to establish that Mrs. Pritchard owed a duty to the company's clients?

(G) What advice would you give to someone contemplating joining the board of a small, closely held business as to how to make sure he or she is satisfying the duty of care? How would your advice change if you were talking about an international financial institution known for participating in complicated financial hedging?

C. The Duty of Care, Decisions That Turn Out Badly, and the Business Judgment Rule

Most of the work of directors and officers involves making decisions. Decisions call for a decision-making process, which then can be called into question and, in appropriate circumstances, deemed negligent. If an inadequate process nonetheless resulted in an outcome that was not injurious to the corporation (that is, did not actually cause it any damage), no one is likely to find it worthwhile to complain. On the other hand, faultless process can yield decisions that, with the benefit of hindsight, turn out to be "bad," or even disastrous. A third possibility is that a bad process results in an equally bad judgment. In some cases, of course, the lines between process and substance are blurred or disappear entirely.

1. A Traditional Approach

As you read the following case, think about whether the complaint is process-based or substance-based — or both.

SHLENSKY v. WRIGLEY

Appellate Court of Illinois
237 N.E.2d 776 (1968)

SULLIVAN, Justice.

This is an appeal from a dismissal of plaintiff's amended complaint on motion of the defendants. The action was a stockholders' derivative suit against the directors for negligence and mismanagement. The corporation was also made a defendant. Plaintiff sought damages and an order that defendants cause the installation of lights in Wrigley Field and the scheduling of night baseball games.

Plaintiff is a minority stockholder of defendant corporation, Chicago National League Ball Club (Inc.), a Delaware corporation with its principal place of business in Chicago, Illinois. Defendant corporation owns and operates the major league

A Recent Photograph of Wrigley Field

professional baseball team known as the Chicago Cubs. The corporation also engages in the operation of Wrigley Field, the Cubs' home park, the concessionaire sales during Cubs' home games, television and radio broadcasts of Cubs' home games, the leasing of the field for football games and other events and receives its share, as visiting team, of admission moneys from games played in other National League stadia. The individual defendants are directors of the Cubs and have served for varying periods of years. Defendant Philip K. Wrigley is also president of the corporation and owner of approximately 80% of the stock therein.

Plaintiff alleges that since night baseball was first played in 1935 nineteen of the twenty major league teams have scheduled night games. In 1966, out of a total of 1620 games in the major leagues, 932 were played at night. Plaintiff alleges that every member of the major leagues, other than the Cubs, scheduled substantially all of its home games in 1966 at night, exclusive of opening days, Saturdays, Sundays, holidays and days prohibited by league rules. Allegedly

More to the Story?: The Curse of the Billy Goat

The Chicago Cubs had not won the World Series in 108 years before their 2016 victory, and are the only major North American professional sports team to have experienced a championship drought of this duration.

The Cubs' fortunes on the field took a particular downturn after Billy Sianis and his pet goat were ejected from a game in 1945. Mr. Sianis reportedly laid "the curse of the Billy Goat" on the team and in the following two decades the Cubs' record was especially dismal.

Connections: The Purpose of the Corporation

In Dodge v. Ford, 170 N.W. 668 (Mich. Sup. Ct. 1919), Henry Ford's controlled board of directors voted to withhold dividends in order (according to Ford) to reduce the cost of cars to the American consumer. The court ordered that a dividend be paid because the purpose of the corporation "is to make money for its stockholders." It also ruled, however, that withholding dividends in order to finance a plant expansion was a legitimate exercise of business judgment by the directors. What seems to be different here?

this has been done for the specific purpose of maximizing attendance and thereby maximizing revenue and income.

The Cubs, in the years 1961-65, sustained operating losses from its direct baseball operations. Plaintiff attributes those losses to inadequate attendance at Cubs' home games. He concludes that if the directors continue to refuse to install lights at Wrigley Field and schedule night baseball games, the Cubs will continue to sustain comparable losses and its financial condition will continue to deteriorate.

Plaintiff alleges that, except for the year 1963, attendance at Cubs' home games has been substantially below that at their road games, many of which were played at night.

Plaintiff compares attendance at Cubs' games with that of the Chicago White Sox, an American League club, whose weekday games were generally played at night. The weekend attendance figures for the two teams was similar; however, the White Sox week-night games drew many more patrons than did the Cubs' weekday games.

Plaintiff alleges that the funds for the installation of lights can be readily obtained through financing and the cost of installation would be far more than offset and recaptured by increased revenues and incomes resulting from the increased attendance.

Plaintiff further alleges that defendant Wrigley has refused to install lights, not because of interest in the welfare of the corporation but because of his personal opinions "that baseball is a 'daytime sport' and that the installation of lights and night baseball games will have a deteriorating effect upon the surrounding neighborhood." It is alleged that he has admitted that he is not interested in whether the Cubs would benefit financially from such action because of his concern for the neighborhood, and that he would be willing for the team to play night games if a new stadium were built in Chicago.

Plaintiff alleges that the other defendant directors, with full knowledge of the foregoing matters, have acquiesced in the policy laid down by Wrigley and have permitted him to dominate the board of directors in matters involving the installation of lights and scheduling of night games, even though they knew he was not motivated by a good faith concern as to the best interests of defendant corporation, but solely by his personal views set forth above. It is charged that the directors are acting for a reason or reasons contrary and wholly unrelated to the business interests of the corporation; that such arbitrary and capricious acts constitute mismanagement and waste of corporate assets, and that the directors have been negligent in failing to exercise reasonable care and prudence in the management of the corporate affairs.

The question on appeal is whether plaintiff's amended complaint states a cause of action. It is plaintiff's position that fraud, illegality and conflict of interest are not the only bases for a stockholder's derivative action against the directors. Contrariwise, defendants argue that the courts will not step in and interfere with honest business judgment of the directors unless there is a showing of fraud, illegality or conflict of interest.

The cases in this area are numerous and each differs from the others on a factual basis. However, the courts have pronounced certain ground rules which appear in all cases and which are then applied to the given factual situation. The court in Wheeler v. The Pullman Iron & Steel Co., 143 Ill. 197, 207, 32 NE 420 said:

> Every one purchasing or subscribing for stock in a corporation impliedly agrees that he will be bound by the acts and proceedings done or sanctioned by a majority of the shareholders, or by the agents of the corporation duly chosen by such majority, within the scope of the powers conferred by the charter, and courts of equity will not undertake to control the policy or business methods of a corporation, although it may be seen that a wiser policy might be adopted and the business more successful if other methods were pursued. . . .

The standards set in Delaware are also clearly stated in the cases. In Davis v. Louisville Gas & Electric Co., 6 NJ Misc. 706, 142 A 654, . . . [t]he court said on page 659:

> We have then a conflict in view between the responsible managers of a corporation and an overwhelming majority of its stockholders on the one hand and a dissenting minority on the other — a conflict touching matters of business policy. . . . The response which courts make to such applications is that it is not their function to resolve for corporations questions of policy and business management. The directors are chosen to pass upon such questions and their judgment *unless shown to be tainted with fraud* is accepted as final. The judgment of the directors of corporations enjoys the benefit of a presumption that it was formed in good faith and was designed to promote the best interests of the corporation they serve. (Emphasis supplied.) . . .

Plaintiff in the instant case argues that the directors are acting for reasons unrelated to the financial interest and welfare of the Cubs. However, we are not satisfied that the motives assigned to Philip K. Wrigley, and through him to the other directors, are contrary to the best interests of the corporation and the stockholders. For example, it appears to us that the effect on the surrounding neighborhood might well be considered by a director who was considering the patrons who would or would not attend the games if the park were in a poor neighborhood. Furthermore, the long run interest of the corporation in its property value at Wrigley Field might demand all efforts to keep the neighborhood from deteriorating. By these thoughts we do not mean to say that we have decided that the decision of the directors was a correct one. That is beyond

our jurisdiction and ability. We are merely saying that the decision is one properly before directors and the motives alleged in the amended complaint showed no fraud, illegality or conflict of interest in their making of that decision. . . . [W]e feel that unless the conduct of the defendants at least borders on one of the elements, the courts should not interfere. . . .

Finally, we do not agree with plaintiff's contention that failure to follow the example of the other major league clubs in scheduling night games constituted negligence. Plaintiff made no allegation that these teams' night schedules were profitable or that the purpose for which night baseball had been undertaken was fulfilled. Furthermore, it cannot be said that directors, even those of corporations that are losing money, must follow the lead of the other corporations in the field. Directors are elected for their business capabilities and judgment and the courts cannot require them to forego their judgment because of the decisions of directors of other companies. Courts may not decide these questions in the absence of a clear showing of dereliction of duty on the part of the specific directors and mere failure to "follow the crowd" is not such a dereliction. . . .

■ Think about this:

(H) The plaintiffs contended that the directors of the Chicago National League Ball Club (Inc.) were fully informed of all other facts alleged (and, indeed, they seem rather obvious). Suppose, however, that one of the directors was supine (think about Mrs. Pritchard in *Francis*). Would he or she be in violation of the duty of care? Would it be worthwhile for anyone to complain about it?

(I) It is not unusual for major league baseball teams to recruit talent from other countries. Suppose that the directors of the Chicago National League Ball Club (Inc.) were convinced by Mr. Wrigley, a space enthusiast, that the Cubs should construct a satellite seeking interest from intergalactic ball players. Assuming that the directors were fully informed of the likelihood of success (or lack thereof), might Shlensky successfully sue them for breach of the duty of care?

(J) Suppose that the directors of the Chicago National League Ball Club (Inc.) were convinced by Mr. Wrigley to lower the price of tickets in order to make it easier for more people to afford them. Might Shlensky successfully sue them for breach of the duty of care?

2. The Business Judgment Rule and Its Possible Limits

(a) Differing Formulations

Though not specifically naming it, *Shlensky* clearly applies a fundamental corporate law doctrine known as the business judgment rule (BJR). The BJR is a special rule that relates to the conduct of corporate fiduciaries when they make conscious business decisions. In effect, the BJR requires that courts defer to the substantive business judgments of corporate fiduciaries. Thus, courts will virtually never find a breach of the duty of care for a substantive business decision that is only "wrong" in the sense that it turned out to be poor judgment. The practical result is that when corporate fiduciaries do their jobs in some procedural sense, it really doesn't matter just how foolish their decisions turn out to be.

A problem in studying the BJR is that different courts describe it in very different terms, and even their own internal formulations can be very confusing. For example, the Delaware courts have referred to the BJR as a rebuttable presumption that fiduciaries have acted as required by the duty of care. How is that any different than saying that the plaintiff has to prove his or her case? Other courts and commentators have described the BJR as some sort of presumption, a standard for judicial review, or a standard of conduct to be observed by the fiduciaries themselves. When it is viewed as a standard of conduct, there also superficially appears to be uncertainty about what happens when the standard has not been satisfied — must the defendant's conduct then be judged under the "reasonable person" standard of *Francis*, or is there a breach of the duty of care *per se*? Conveniently, these distinctions turn out to make little, if any, practical difference.

Also conveniently, the ALI Principles of Corporate Governance set out a neat and thorough summary of the duty of care that appears to incorporate the BJR as it is commonly applied:

AMERICAN LAW INSTITUTE PRINCIPLES OF CORPORATE GOVERNANCE

§4.01 . . .

(c) A director or officer who makes a business judgment in good faith fulfills the duty under this Section if the director or officer:

(1) is not interested in the subject of the business judgment;

(2) is informed with respect to the subject of the business judgment to the extent the director or officer reasonably believes to be appropriate under the circumstances; and

(3) rationally believes that the business judgment is in the best interests of the corporation.

(b) Illegality or Other Wrongdoing

An addition could be made to the otherwise very satisfactory codification of the BJR in ALI *Principles* §4.01: Courts have often said that acts of corporate fiduciaries that are knowingly wrongful or criminal are not protected by the BJR. It is somewhat less clear exactly under what standard such acts should be judged—if not the BJR, then the reasonable person standard? Or do such acts breach the duty of care *per se*? It is, however, a safe bet that if a fiduciary's crime results in significant penalties or other harms to the corporation, the fiduciary will be called to account for those harms personally. For example, in Miller v. American Telephone & Telegraph Co., 507 F.2d 759 (3d Cir. 1974), the court explained that:

> The suit centered upon the failure of AT&T to collect an outstanding debt of some $1.5 million owed to the company by the Democratic National Committee ("DNC") for communications services provided by AT&T during the 1968 Democratic national convention. . . .
>
>   . . . The failure to collect was alleged to have involved a breach of the defendant directors' duty to exercise diligence in handling the affairs of the corporation, to have resulted in affording a preference to the DNC in collection procedures in violation of §202(a) of the Communications Act of 1934, 47 U.S.C. §202(a) (1970), and to have amounted to AT&T's making a "contribution" to the DNC in violation of a federal prohibition on corporate campaign spending. . . .
>
>   Had plaintiffs' complaint alleged only failure to pursue a corporate claim, application of the sound business judgment rule would support the district court's ruling that a shareholder could not attack the directors' decision. Where, however, the decision not to collect a debt owed the corporation is itself alleged to have been an illegal act, different rules apply. When New York law regarding such acts by directors is considered in conjunction with the underlying purposes of the particular statute involved here, we are convinced that the business judgment rule cannot insulate the defendant directors from liability. . . .
>
>   Roth v. Robertson, 118 N.Y.S. 351 (Sup. Ct. 1909), illustrates the proposition that even though committed to benefit the corporation, illegal acts may amount to a breach of fiduciary duty in New York. In *Roth*, the managing director of an amusement park company had allegedly used corporate funds to purchase the silence of persons who threatened to complain about unlawful Sunday operation of the park. Recovery from the defendant director was sustained on the ground that the money was an illegal payment. . . .

Republican Richard Nixon was the winner of the 1968 presidential election.

Somewhat more surprising is a rule applied by many courts that, while a fiduciary may breach the duty of care by any knowingly wrongful or criminal act that causes the corporation injury, the fiduciary will not be liable to the corporation in money damages if the "injury" was on net profitable. For example, suppose a particular corporation's factory is causing pollution in violation of federal environmental law. The company could comply with the law by installing new equipment at a cost of $1 million. Violation of the law will at most result in a penalty of $500,000. If the board of directors consciously chooses to violate the law, the company might face criminal liability, but still will have saved $500,000, and the conduct therefore would be profitable on net. Many courts would hold that while the directors have violated their duty of care, they are not answerable for it in money damages.

■   **Think about this:**

(K) What might be the rationale for this rule? As a policy matter, does it seem to be correct?

(L) Suppose the directors of a corporation are considering whether to comply with a law prohibiting U.S. corporations and their subsidiaries from paying bribes to foreign officials, even if the bribes are legal in the official's home country. The directors believe that the economic benefit of paying bribes would be huge and the penalties for doing so would be far less. The directors seek your advice as to the prospect of their personal liability. What would you tell them?

(M) Suppose the directors of a corporation are considering whether to comply with a new pollution control law. The cost of compliance clearly will exceed any possible penalty for non-compliance. Is there a reasonable argument that it would breach the duty of care if the board chooses compliance?

   Time Out for PR

American Bar Association Model Rule of Professional Conduct 1.13, available in the online Supplement, addresses the responsibility of a lawyer in dealing with corporate constituents. What, if anything, does it suggest about dealing with a board of directors that wishes to cause a corporation to engage in illegal conduct that is on net profitable?

   Model Rule 1.16, also available in the online Supplement, describes the circumstances in which an attorney must decline or withdraw from a representation. What, if anything, should it suggest to an attorney who is consulted about an economic breach of law?

(c) Rationality and the Doctrine of Waste

Aside from a situation involving knowingly wrongful or criminal conduct, will the BJR ever permit judicial review of a business judgment? One old case, *Litwin v. Allen*, is famous as one of the few examples of duty of care liability ostensibly based on nothing but a bad business decision. Understood that way, it is highly unusual.

In fact, it is so unusual that a number of commentators have tried to explain it as the court's response to a concern with an unarticulated conflict of interest. An alternative explanation is that the directors of banking corporations owe a higher standard of care than otherwise would be the case. A third possibility is that the case actually would be better classified as one involving a knowingly wrongful act.

Consider the following factual background. J.P. Morgan & Co. ("Morgan") was a banking institution that had heavily invested in the "Van Sweringen empire," a large part of which consisted of stock of the Alleghany Corporation ("Alleghany"). Alleghany needed funds but was precluded by its Articles of Incorporation from incurring any more debt. Morgan devised a plan to "put Alleghany in funds" by having it sell assets consisting of convertible, interest-bearing bonds issued by the Missouri Pacific Company. The catch was that Alleghany wanted a six-month option to repurchase the bonds. From Alleghany's standpoint, this had the same functional effect as a loan secured by the bonds, since the income it would forgo on the bonds simply would be received by the functional lender to compensate it for the use of its funds for the six months until the bonds were repurchased (effectively repaying the loan). One critical difference, however, was that Alleghany was not obliged to make the repurchase — if it were, it would be in violation of its debt restriction.

Morgan did not wish to bear the entire risk of the transaction, and involved other banks, including Guaranty Trust Company ("Trust"). Partners in Morgan owned approximately 13,500 shares of Trust out of 900,000 outstanding. Two partners in Morgan also sat on the board of Trust and on the executive committee of that board (but were distinctly a minority of both). In addition, a number of the other directors of Trust were described as "long established clients or friends" of Morgan and its partners. It is clear that Morgan frequently involved Trust and its individual directors and officers in transactions, including other transactions with Alleghany and/or the Van Sweringens. The trial court in *Litwin v. Allen* nonetheless specifically found that there had been no improper influence brought to bear on Trust by Morgan. (Incidentally, the two firms were merged in 1959, many years after the case.)

LITWIN v. ALLEN

Supreme Court of New York
25 N.Y.S.2d 667 (1940)

More to the Story?: Shareholder Liability

At the time of the occurrences in *Litwin*, shareholders of New York banking corporations did not enjoy—that is, did not have—limited liability for their shareholders.

Shientag, Justice.

[This was a derivative action brought by persons owning 36 of the 900,000 outstanding shares of the stock of a New York bank, the Guaranty Trust Company ("Trust Company"). Defendants included the company's directors and members of the banking firm of J.P. Morgan & Co. The complaint sought to impose liability on the defendants for losses incurred as a result of four transactions. The portions of the opinion set forth below relate to the justice's general discussion and the single transaction for which liability was imposed.]

[T]he main transactions attacked in this case . . . took place in October 1930. There had been a crash in the stock market in October, 1929. In April 1930, there was an upswing in the market. Shortly thereafter there began a slow but steady decline until October, 1930, when there was another severe break. The real significance of what was taking place was, generally speaking, missed at the time, but is plain in retrospect. Forces were at work which for the most part were unforeseeable. Men who were judging conditions in October, 1930, by what had been the course and the experience of past panics thought that the bottom had been reached and that the worst of the depression was over; that any change would be for the better and that recovery might reasonably be envisaged for the near future. Experience turned out to be fallacious and judgment proved to be erroneous; but that did not become apparent until some time in 1931. In order to judge the transactions complained of, therefore, we must not only hold an inquest on the past but, what is much more difficult, we must attempt to take ourselves back to the time when the events here questioned occurred and try to put ourselves in the position of those who engaged in them. . . .

[D]irectors are liable for negligence in the performance of their duties. Not being insurers, directors are not liable for errors of judgment or for mistakes while acting with reasonable skill and prudence. It has been said that a director is required to conduct the business of the corporation with the same degree of fidelity and care as an ordinarily prudent man would exercise in the management of his own affairs of like magnitude and importance. . . .

Undoubtedly, a director of a bank is held to stricter accountability than the director of an ordinary business corporation. A director of a bank is entrusted with the funds of depositors, and the stockholders look to him for protection from the imposition of personal liability. But clairvoyance is not required even of a bank director. The law recognizes that the most conservative director is not infallible, and that he will make mistakes, but if he uses that degree of care ordinarily exercised by prudent bankers he will be absolved from liability although his opinion may turn out to have been mistaken and his judgment faulty.

Finally, in order to determine whether transactions approved by a director subject him to liability for negligence, we must "look at the facts as they exist at the time of their occurrence, not aided or enlightened by those which subsequently take place". . . . "A wisdom developed after an event, and having it and its consequences as a source, is a standard no man should be judged by." . . .

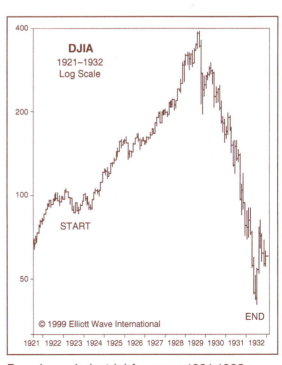

Dow Jones Industrial Averages 1921-1932

II. THE MISSOURI PACIFIC BOND TRANSACTION . . .

Not being able to [take] a loan [because of debt restrictions in its charter], the way that Alleghany could raise the necessary funds was by sale of some of the securities that it held. Among them was a large block of about $23,500,000 of Missouri Pacific convertible 5½ debentures. These were unsecured and subordinate to other Missouri Pacific bond issues. They were convertible into common stock at the rate of ten shares for each $1,000 bond. . . . At one time in 1929, the bonds had sold as high as 124 and had never gone below par except in November 1929 when they sold at 97. Between October 1 and October 10, 1930 Missouri Pacific common stock had dropped from 53 to 44. There was a decline in the bonds from 113 in April 1930 to 107 on October 1, 1930, and thereafter a decline of about two more points to 105½ by the date of the consummation of the transaction we are considering on October 16, 1930. . . .

Doing the Numbers: Price and Rate of Return

The amount someone is willing to pay for a bond logically relates to the interest rate it bears. If current interest rates are 10 percent for loans of a certain risk level, a $100 bond with a 10 percent interest rate ("Bond A") will sell for $100. If interest rates drop to 5 percent, Bond A's resale price will rise to $200. How do we know?

Bond A is paying $10 annually.

$$\$10 = .10(\$100)$$

Bond A will continue to pay $10 annually, even though an investor putting $100 into new bonds would expect to get only $5.

$$\$5 = .05(\$100).$$

A would-be purchaser of Bond A expecting only the prevailing 5 percent return will make the following calculation:

$$\$10 = .05(\times)$$

We solve for $\times$ by dividing both sides of the equation by .05:

$$\$10/.05 = \times$$

$$\$200 = \times$$

So what?

The bonds in *Litwin*, when sold to the bank, had a market value *above* their face, or "par" amount. This means that they bore an above-market interest rate. It also means that when the bank paid only the face amount of the bonds, it received a bargain.

The decline in the market continued. On October 23, 1930, when the Executive Committee of the Trust Company approved the transaction the Missouri Pacific bonds were at 103 7/8. On November 5, 1930, when the Board of Directors of the Trust Company gave its approval, the bonds sold for 102 7/8. . . . At the end of the six months' period, on April 16, 1931, the bonds sold at 86 high and 81 low. . . .

[The court then discusses precedents establishing that, as a matter of common law, it is unlawful for a bank to sell assets with an obligation to repurchase them.]

Although . . . there is no case precisely in point, it would seem that if it is against public policy for a bank, anxious to dispose of some of its securities, to agree to buy them back at the same price, it is even more so where a bank purchases securities and gives the seller the option to buy them back at the same price, thereby incurring the entire risk of loss with no possibility of gain other than the interest derived from the securities during the period that the bank holds them. Here, if the market price of the securities should rise, the holder of the repurchase option would exercise it in order to recover his securities from the bank at the lower price at which he sold them to the bank. If the market price should fall, the seller holding the option will not exercise it and the bank will sustain the loss. Thus, any benefit of a sharp rise in the price of the securities is assured the seller and any risk of heavy loss is inevitably assumed by the bank. If such an option agreement as is here involved were sustained, it would force the bank to set aside for six months whatever securities it had purchased. A bank certainly could not free itself from this obligation by engaging in a "short sale." In other words, while a resale option would force a bank to freeze an amount of cash equal to the selling price of the securities sold by it, a repurchase option would force a bank to freeze the securities themselves for the period of the option. In both situations the true financial condition of the bank could not be determined wholly from its books. It would depend upon the fluctuations of the market. In both cases there is a contingent liability which the balance sheet does not show. . . .

It seems clear on principle as well as analogous authority that, although they differ in certain respects, either kind of option would be held *ultra vires* and unenforceable against a bank.

Plaintiffs urge that if the purchase subject to the option is found to be *ultra vires*, that finding, in and of itself, imposes absolute liability upon the defendants. It is doubtful whether any such strict rule would apply where directors as here, act honestly and particularly where no violation of a statute is involved. . . .

Directors are not in the position of trustees of an express trust who, regardless of good faith, are personally liable for losses arising from an infraction of their trust deed. . . . If liability is to be imposed on these directors it should rest on a more solid foundation. I find liability in this transaction because the entire arrangement was so improvident, so risky, so unusual and unnecessary as to be contrary to fundamental conceptions of prudent banking practice. A bank director when appointed or elected takes oath that he will, so far as the duty devolves on him "diligently and honestly administer the affairs of the bank or trust company." Banking Law, §117. The oath merely adds solemnity to the obligation which the law itself imposes. Honesty alone does not suffice; the honesty of the directors in this case is unquestioned. But there must be more than honesty—there must be diligence, and that means care and prudence, as well. This transaction, it has been said, was unusual; it was unique, yet there is nothing in the record to indicate that the advice of counsel was sought. It is not surprising that a precedent cannot be found dealing with such a situation.

What sound reason is there for a bank, desiring to make an investment, short term or otherwise, to buy securities under an arrangement whereby any appreciation will inure to the benefit of the seller and any loss will be borne by the bank? The five and one-half point differential is no answer. It does not meet the fundamental objection that whatever loss there is would have to be borne by the Bank and whatever gain would go to the customer. There is more here than a question of business judgment as to which men might well differ. The directors plainly failed in this instance to bestow the care which the situation demanded. Unless we are to do away entirely with the doctrine that directors of a bank are liable for negligence in administering its affairs liability should be imposed in connection with this transaction. . . .

■ **Think about this:**

(N) Was the court putting the cart before the horse by finding that a really bad business decision was *ultra vires* for a bank? Or was the real evil, as the court suggests, non-disclosure?

(O) Hypo Inc. is a corporation formed for the purpose of investing in securities and real estate. The directors decide to cause Hypo to purchase a large number of the shares of Newco, an unrelated entity. The purchase is privately transacted and, in order to bring the transaction within an exemption from the registration requirements of the federal securities laws, Hypo agrees that it will not resell the shares for a period of one year, unless an opinion of counsel is obtained that a resale will not destroy the exemption. The shares of Newco decline substantially in value before Hypo is able to resell them. Have the directors violated their duty of care?

(P) Better Bank Co. believes that interest rates are going to go up. The board of directors authorizes an agreement pursuant to which the floating rate of interest Better Bank is paying on an existing debt is exchanged ("swapped") for the fixed interest rate that Counterparty, Inc., is paying on one of its existing debts. If interest rates do go up, Better Bank will benefit. If they go down, all benefit inures to Counterparty. Have the directors violated the duty of care?

Plaintiffs often invoke the doctrine of "corporate waste" in an attempt to impose liability for exchanges of corporate property for consideration (particularly services) so disproportionately small as to lie beyond the range at which any reasonable person would make an exchange. This may be inconsistent with some articulations of the BJR, but links up nicely with the third requirement of the ALI formulation set out toward the beginning of this section: The director must rationally believe that the business judgment made is in the best interests of the corporation. These attempts usually fail, though, because courts seldom are convinced that there is no rational justification for a directorial decision.

(d) Lack of Informed Process

The following case, *Smith v. Van Gorkom*, suggests a different reason why the business judgment rule may not always protect directors. Essentially, it is because the decision was not the result of an informed process.

It will be helpful before we get into the case to introduce a basic background idea. At issue in this case is what is often called a "control premium." The idea is simple enough: Having control of a corporation — that is, owning a large enough percentage of its voting stock that one effectively controls its board of directors and therefore its management — gives a person a certain special value beyond the sum total value of the individual shares themselves. This is so because control can in and of itself be quite profitable, for a few reasons. First, there are times when the individual assets of a corporation are actually worth more than the business as a going concern. This may be because the business has been poorly managed or because its product or service for some reason has lost its former value. In such cases, it can be quite profitable to purchase a controlling share in the corporation as a going concern and then sell off all or some of its assets. Second, and maybe somewhat less depressing, acquiring ownership might be valuable precisely because prior management had run the business poorly. If so, the going stock value might be depressed and control might be purchased at a comparative bargain. If the purchaser can then run the business better, it will reap the value of an increased price for its stock. Either way, a person seeking to buy a controlling share in a corporation will normally have to pay substantially more per share than if the person were merely buying individual shares. If shareholders know the buyer is seeking to establish control, they have every incentive to hold out for a price higher than the going share price. This excess in price for purchases of control is called the "control premium."

Ironically, in *Smith v. Van Gorkom*, the company appears to have been well managed enough, but it had generated investment tax credits that it and its consolidated enterprises were unable to use because of other tax rules reducing its taxable income (although not its cash flow). These credits would have value if the company were acquired by an entity with significant taxable income. Some combination of the value of these credits and the concept of the control premium justified a proposed purchase price of more than 150 percent of the prevailing market price — about which the shareholder plaintiffs complained!

JD/MBA: Investment Tax Credits and Accelerated Depreciation

Investment tax credits are intended to stimulate investment in certain types of assets. There are a wide and constantly changing variety of credits, some of which are industry specific. The basic idea is that they offset not only taxable income that might be generated with the assets, but other income as well. As *Van Gorkom* suggests, they even can be used to offset income earned by certain affiliated entities (and can be carried over from year to year).

The cost of acquiring income-producing property generally can be used to reduce the income an entity reports for tax purposes. The expense of acquiring property with an expected useful life of more than one year generally must be allocated across the years the property will remain in service. Accelerated depreciation permits the allocation of some or all of the expense to the earlier years of useful life and is another strategy for encouraging investment in certain types of assets.

Trans Union, the corporation at issue in *Van Gorkom*, had so much accelerated depreciation that it could not use its investment tax credits.

SMITH v. VAN GORKOM

Supreme Court of Delaware
488 A.2d 858 (1985)

HORSEY, Justice (for the majority):

This appeal from the Court of Chancery involves a class action brought by shareholders of the defendant Trans Union Corporation ("Trans Union" or "the Company"), originally seeking rescission of a cash-out merger of Trans Union into the defendant New T Company ("New T"), a wholly-owned subsidiary of the defendant, Marmon Group, Inc. ("Marmon"). Alternate relief in the form of damages is sought against the defendant members of the Board of Directors of Trans Union, New T, and Jay A. Pritzker and Robert A. Pritzker, owners of Marmon. . . .

I.

[As noted above, owing to its accelerated depreciation of equipment, Trans Union had unused tax credits that could be used by an acquirer. Van Gorkom, the CEO of Trans Union, was interested in finding such an acquirer, and was advised by the chief financial officer that a "leveraged buyout" might be possible at a price between $50 and $60 per share.]

. . . Van Gorkom stated that he would be willing to take $55 per share for his own 75,000 shares. He vetoed the suggestion of a leveraged buy-out by Management, however, as involving a potential conflict of interest for Management. Van Gorkom, a certified public accountant and lawyer, had been an officer of Trans Union for 24 years, its Chief Executive Officer for more than 17 years, and Chairman of its Board for 2 years. It is noteworthy in this connection that he was then approaching 65 years of age and mandatory retirement. . . .

Doing the Numbers: Leveraged Buyouts

The term "leveraged buyout" literally refers to using debt to purchase control of a company. It frequently (as in this case) is used to refer to an acquisition of control with debt that can be repaid entirely out of the cash generated by the acquired entity. To price a leveraged buyout that is to be entirely financed by debt, you would need to answer the following questions:

1. How much cash can the acquired company reliably generate per year? Let's artificially assume that it's $10 million. This is the amount that the purchaser can pay in annual "debt service" (combined principal and interest).
2. How much can the purchaser borrow given the ability to pay annual debt service of $10 million? This is a function of prevailing interest rates and assumed repayment schedules, as well as the creditworthiness of the borrower. Let's just as artificially assume it's between $50 million and $60 million.
3. How many shares are necessary to acquire the desired level of control? Let's (artificially!) assume it's 1 million and that this number represents 100 percent ownership.

Dividing the amount of debt calculated in 2 by the number of shares calculated in 3 gives a price range of $50-$60 per share.

So what?

Does the amount you can afford to pay for an asset necessarily match the amount that it's worth?

Van Gorkom decided to meet with Jay A. Pritzker, a well-known corporate takeover specialist and a social acquaintance [to determine whether Pritzker would be interested in purchasing Trans Union for $55 per share.] . . . Van Gorkom did so without consulting either his Board or any members of Senior Management except one: Carl Peterson, Trans Union's Controller. Telling

Peterson that he wanted no other person on his staff to know what he was doing, but without telling him why, Van Gorkom directed Peterson to calculate the feasibility of a leveraged buy-out at an assumed price per share of $55. Apart from the Company's historic stock market price,[1] and Van Gorkom's long association with Trans Union, the record is devoid of any competent evidence that $55 represented the per share intrinsic value of the Company.

. . . However, Van Gorkom stated that to be sure that $55 was the best price obtainable, Trans Union should be free to accept any better offer. Pritzker demurred, stating that his organization would serve as a "stalking horse" for an "auction contest" only if Trans Union would permit Pritzker to buy [a large number of] shares of Trans Union stock at [or around] market price which Pritzker could then sell to any higher bidder. After further discussion on this point, Pritzker told Van Gorkom that he would give him a more definite reaction soon. . . .

On Thursday, September 18, Van Gorkom met again with Pritzker. . . . At this point, Pritzker insisted that the Trans Union Board act on his merger proposal within the next three days, stating to Van Gorkom: "We have to have a decision by no later than Sunday [evening, September 21] before the opening of the English stock exchange on Monday morning." Pritzker's lawyer was then instructed to draft the merger documents, to be reviewed by Van Gorkom's lawyer, "sometimes with discussion and sometimes not, in the haste to get it finished."

On Friday, September 19, . . . Van Gorkom retained James Brennan, Esquire, to advise Trans Union on the legal aspects of the merger. Van Gorkom did not consult with William Browder, a Vice-President and director of Trans Union and former head of its legal department, or with William Moore, then the head of Trans Union's legal staff.

On Friday, September 19, Van Gorkom called a special meeting of the Trans Union Board for noon the following day. He also called a meeting of the Company's Senior Management to convene at 11:00 A.M., prior to the meeting of the Board. [The Board was not informed of the purpose of the meeting and] Van Gorkom did not invite Trans Union's investment banker, Salomon Brothers or its Chicago-based partner, to attend.

[At the Senior Management meeting,] reaction to the Pritzker proposal was completely negative. . . .

Ten directors served on the Trans Union Board, five inside (defendants Bonser, O'Boyle, Browder, Chelberg, and Van Gorkom) and five outside (defendants Wallis, Johnson, Lanterman, Morgan and Reneker). All directors were present at the meeting, except O'Boyle who was ill. Of the outside directors, four were corporate chief executive officers and one was the former Dean of the University of Chicago Business School. None was an investment banker or trained financial analyst. All members of the Board were well informed about

---

1. The common stock of Trans Union was traded on the New York Stock Exchange. Over the five year period from 1975 through 1979, Trans Union's stock had traded within a range of a high of $39 1/2 and a low of $24 1/4. Its high and low range for 1980 through September 19 (the last trading day before announcement of the merger) was $38 1/4-$29 1/2.

the Company and its operations as a going concern. They were familiar with the current financial condition of the Company, as well as operating and earnings projections reported in the recent Five Year Forecast. The Board generally received regular and detailed reports and was kept abreast of the accumulated investment tax credit and accelerated depreciation problem.

Van Gorkom began the Special Meeting of the Board with a twenty-minute oral presentation. Copies of the proposed Merger Agreement were delivered too late for study before or during the meeting. He reviewed the Company's ITC and depreciation problems and the efforts theretofore made to solve them. He discussed his initial meeting with Pritzker and his motivation in arranging that meeting. Van Gorkom did not disclose to the Board, however, the methodology by which he alone had arrived at the $55 figure, or the fact that he first proposed the $55 price in his negotiations with Pritzker. . . . Van Gorkom took the position that putting Trans Union "up for auction" through a 90-day market test would validate a decision by the Board that $55 was a fair price. He told the Board that the "free market will have an opportunity to judge whether $55 is a fair price." Van Gorkom framed the decision before the Board not as whether $55 per share was the highest price that could be obtained, but as whether the $55 price was a fair price that the stockholders should be given the opportunity to accept or reject. . . .

Attorney Brennan advised the members of the Board that they might be sued if they failed to accept the offer and that a fairness opinion was not required as a matter of law.

Romans attended the meeting as chief financial officer of the Company. He told the Board that he had not been involved in the negotiations with Pritzker and knew nothing about the merger proposal until the morning of the meeting; that his studies did not indicate either a fair price for the stock or a valuation of the Company; that he did not see his role as directly addressing the fairness issue; and that he and his people "were trying to search for ways to justify a price in connection with such a [leveraged buyout] transaction, rather than to say what the shares are worth." . . . Romans told the Board that, in his opinion, $55 was "in the range of a fair price," but "at the beginning of the range." . . .

The Board meeting of September 20 lasted about two hours. Based solely upon Van Gorkom's oral presentation, [Vice President] Chelberg's supporting representations, Romans' oral statement, Brennan's legal advice, and their knowledge of the market history of the Company's stock, the directors approved the proposed Merger Agreement. However, the Board later claimed to have attached two conditions to its acceptance: (1) that Trans Union reserved the right to accept any better offer that was made during the market test period; and (2) that Trans Union could share its proprietary information with any other potential bidders. While the Board now claims to have reserved the right to accept any better offer received after the announcement of the Pritzker agreement (even though the minutes of the meeting do not reflect this), it is undisputed that the Board did not reserve the right to actively solicit alternate offers. [Moreover, it appears that the agreement later was amended to provide that Trans Union could not share its proprietary information with other bidders.]

Interior of the Chicago Lyric Opera

The Merger Agreement was executed by Van Gorkom during the evening of September 20 at a formal social event that he hosted for the opening of the Chicago Lyric Opera. Neither he nor any other director read the agreement prior to its signing and delivery to Pritzker. . . . [Subsequent amendments to the agreement were approved by the board without reading them, and subsequent attempts by an investment banker to find other viable suitors for Trans Union were unsuccessful.]

. . . On January 26, Trans Union's Board met and, after a lengthy meeting, voted to proceed with the Pritzker merger. . . . On February 10, the stockholders of Trans Union approved the Pritzker merger proposal. Of the outstanding shares, 69.9% were voted in favor of the merger; 7.25% were voted against the merger; and 22.85% were not voted.

II.

We turn to the issue of the application of the business judgment rule to the September 20 meeting of the Board. . . .

Under Delaware law, the business judgment rule is the offspring of the fundamental principle, codified in 8 Del. C. §141(a), that the business and affairs of a Delaware corporation are managed by or under its board of directors. . . . In carrying out their managerial roles, directors are charged with an unyielding fiduciary duty to the corporation and its shareholders. . . . The business judgment rule exists to protect and promote the full and free exercise of the managerial power granted to Delaware directors. . . . The rule itself "is a presumption that in making a business decision, the directors of a corporation acted on an informed basis, in good faith and in the honest belief that the action taken was in the best interests of the company." . . . Thus, the party attacking a board decision as uninformed must rebut the presumption that its business judgment was an informed one.

The determination of whether a business judgment is an informed one turns on whether the directors have informed themselves "prior to making a business decision, of all material information reasonably available to them."

Under the business judgment rule there is no protection for directors who have made "an unintelligent or unadvised judgment." . . . A director's duty to inform himself in preparation for a decision derives from the fiduciary capacity in which he serves the corporation and its stockholders. . . . Since a director is vested with the responsibility for the management of the affairs of the corporation, he must execute that duty with the recognition that he acts on behalf of others. Such obligation does not tolerate faithlessness or self-dealing. But fulfillment of the fiduciary function requires more than the mere absence of bad faith or fraud. Representation of the financial interests of others imposes on a director an affirmative duty to protect those interests and to proceed with a critical eye in assessing information of the type and under the circumstances present here. . . .

Thus, a director's duty to exercise an informed business judgment is in the nature of a duty of care, as distinguished from a duty of loyalty. Here, there were no allegations of fraud, bad faith, or self-dealing, or proof thereof. Hence, it is presumed that the directors reached their business judgment in good faith, . . . and considerations of motive are irrelevant to the issue before us.

The standard of care applicable to a director's duty of care has also been recently restated by this Court. In *Aronson*, supra, we stated:

> While the Delaware cases use a variety of terms to describe the applicable standard of care, our analysis satisfies us that under the business judgment rule director liability is predicated upon concepts of gross negligence. (footnote omitted) 473 A.2d at 812.

We again confirm that view. We think the concept of gross negligence is also the proper standard for determining whether a business judgment reached by a board of directors was an informed one. . . .

III. . . .

On the record before us, we must conclude that the Board of Directors did not reach an informed business judgment on September 20, 1980 in voting to "sell" the Company for $55 per share pursuant to the Pritzker cash-out merger proposal. Our reasons, in summary, are as follows:

The directors (1) did not adequately inform themselves as to Van Gorkom's role in forcing the "sale" of the Company and in establishing the per share purchase price; (2) were uninformed as to the intrinsic value of the Company; and (3) given these circumstances, at a minimum, were grossly negligent in approving the "sale" of the Company upon two hours' consideration, without prior notice, and without the exigency of a crisis or emergency.

As has been noted, the Board based its September 20 decision to approve the cash-out merger primarily on Van Gorkom's representations. None of the directors, other than Van Gorkom and Chelberg, had any prior knowledge that the purpose of the meeting was to propose a cash-out merger of Trans Union. No members of Senior Management were present, other than Chelberg, Romans and Peterson; and the latter two had only learned of the proposed sale an hour earlier. Both general counsel Moore and former general counsel Browder attended the meeting, but were equally uninformed as to the purpose of the meeting and the documents to be acted upon.

Without any documents before them concerning the proposed transaction, the members of the Board were required to rely entirely upon Van Gorkom's 20-minute oral presentation of the proposal. No written summary of the terms of the merger was presented; the directors were given no documentation to support the adequacy of $55 price per share for sale of the Company; and the Board had before it nothing more than Van Gorkom's statement of his understanding of the substance of an agreement which he admittedly had never read, nor which any member of the Board had ever seen.

Under 8 Del. C. §141(e), "directors are fully protected in relying in good faith on reports made by officers."* . . . The term "report" has been liberally construed to include reports of informal personal investigations by corporate officers. . . . However, there is no evidence that any "report," as defined under §141(e), concerning the Pritzker proposal, was presented to the Board on September 20. Van Gorkom's oral presentation of his understanding of the terms of the proposed Merger Agreement, which he had not seen, and Romans' brief oral statement of his preliminary study regarding the feasibility of a leveraged buy-out of Trans Union do not qualify as §141(e) "reports" for these reasons: The former lacked substance because Van Gorkom was basically uninformed as to the essential provisions of the very document about which he was talking. Romans' statement was irrelevant to the issues before the Board since it did not purport to be a valuation study. At a minimum for a report to enjoy the status conferred by §141(e), it must be pertinent to the subject matter upon which a board is called to act, and otherwise be entitled to good faith, not blind, reliance. Considering all of the surrounding circumstances — hastily calling the meeting without prior notice of its subject matter, the proposed sale of the Company without any prior consideration of the issue or necessity therefor, the urgent time constraints imposed by Pritzker, and the total absence of any documentation whatsoever — the directors were duty bound to make reasonable inquiry of Van Gorkom and Romans, and if they had done so, the inadequacy of that upon which they now claim to have relied would have been apparent.

The defendants rely on the following factors to sustain the Trial Court's finding that the Board's decision was an informed one: (1) the magnitude of the premium or spread between the $55 Pritzker offering price and Trans Union's current market price of $38 per share. . . .

A substantial premium may provide one reason to recommend a merger, but in the absence of other sound valuation information, the fact of a premium alone does not provide an adequate basis upon which to assess the fairness of an offering price. Here, the judgment reached as to the adequacy of the premium was based on a comparison between the historically depressed Trans Union market price and the amount of the Pritzker offer. Using market price as a basis for concluding that the premium adequately reflected the true value of the Company was a clearly faulty, indeed fallacious, premise, as the defendants' own evidence demonstrates.

The record is clear that before September 20, Van Gorkom and other members of Trans Union's Board

JD/MBA: Valuation

There are any number of ways to value investments. There is more in the online Supplement on this subject.

---

* *Editors' Note:* 8 Del. C. §141(e) now more broadly permits reliance on information, opinions, and statements of officers, employees, and certain others. The new language would not seem to dictate a different result.

knew that the market had consistently undervalued the worth of Trans Union's stock, despite steady increases in the Company's operating income in the seven years preceding the merger.... The parties do not dispute that a publicly-traded stock price is solely a measure of the value of a minority position and, thus, market price represents only the value of a single share. Nevertheless, on September 20, the Board assessed the adequacy of the premium over market, offered by Pritzker, solely by comparing it with Trans Union's current and historical stock price.... [T]here was no call by the Board, either on September 20 or thereafter, for any valuation study or documentation of the $55 price per share as a measure of the fair value of the Company in a cash-out context....

We do not imply that an outside valuation study is essential to support an informed business judgment; nor do we state that fairness opinions by independent investment bankers are required as a matter of law. Often insiders familiar with the business of a going concern are in a better position than are outsiders to gather relevant information; and under appropriate circumstances, such directors may be fully protected in relying in good faith upon the valuation reports of their management.... Here, the record establishes that the Board did not request its Chief Financial Officer, Romans, to make any valuation study or review of the proposal to determine the adequacy of $55 per share for sale of the Company....

None of the directors, Management or outside, were investment bankers or financial analysts. Yet the Board did not consider recessing the meeting until a later hour that day (or requesting an extension of Pritzker's Sunday evening deadline) to give it time to elicit more information as to the sufficiency of the offer, either from inside Management (in particular Romans) or from Trans Union's own investment banker, Salomon Brothers, whose Chicago specialist in merger and acquisitions was known to the Board and familiar with Trans Union's affairs.

Thus, the record compels the conclusion that on September 20 the Board lacked valuation information adequate to reach an informed business judgment as to the fairness of $55 per share for sale of the Company....

We hold, therefore, that the Trial Court committed reversible error in applying the business judgment rule in favor of the director defendants in this case.

On remand, the Court of Chancery shall conduct an evidentiary hearing to determine the fair value of the shares represented by the plaintiffs' class, based on the intrinsic value of Trans Union on September 20, 1980.... Thereafter, an award of damages may be entered to the extent that the fair value of Trans Union exceeds $55 per share....

McNEILLY, Justice, dissenting:

The majority opinion reads like an advocate's closing address to a hostile jury. And I say that not lightly. Throughout the opinion great emphasis is directed only to the negative, with nothing more than lip service granted the positive aspects of this case.... The majority has spoken and has effectively said that Trans Union's Directors have been the victims of a "fast shuffle" by Van Gorkom and

Pritzker. That is the beginning of the majority's comedy of errors. The first and most important error made is the majority's assessment of the directors' knowledge of the affairs of Trans Union and their combined ability to act in this situation under the protection of the business judgment rule. . . . At the time the merger was proposed the inside five directors had collectively been employed by the Company for 116 years and had 68 years of combined experience as directors. . . . The five "outside" directors had 78 years of combined experience as chief executive officers, and 53 years cumulative service as Trans Union directors. . . . Directors of this caliber are not ordinarily taken in by a "fast shuffle." . . .

I have no quarrel with the majority's analysis of the business judgment rule. It is the application of that rule to these facts which is wrong. An overview of the entire record, rather than the limited view of bits and pieces which the majority has exploded like popcorn, convinces me that the directors made an informed business judgment which was buttressed by their test of the market.

■ **Think about this:**

(Q) The board of directors of Targuette, Inc., has, for several days, debated the merits of permitting the company to be acquired by Acquisico at a price of $25 per share. It has fully informed itself by, among other things, consulting with lawyers and investment bankers. According to the investment bankers, $25 is within a range of fairness. The board is evenly divided and ultimately decides the matter by flipping a coin. Will their decision be protected by the business judgment rule?

In portions of the case not included above, the court indicated (1) that since the inside and outside directors took a unified position the court would not attempt to draw distinctions between them for purposes of determining whether they were entitled to the protection of the BJR; and (2) the fact that the shareholders had approved the board's decision did not constitute ratification because they had not been fully informed. The court regarded the failure to fully inform the shareholders as an additional breach of fiduciary duty on the part of the directors of Trans Union.

The court in *Van Gorkom* directed the lower court to determine whether the fair value of Trans Union stock exceeded the $55 per share price at which the company had been sold, and to enter an appropriate order. Presumably, if the fair value of the stock did not exceed $55, no harm would have been caused. In a subsequent, similar case (which actually involved a transaction taking place prior to the one complained of in *Van Gorkom*), the Delaware Supreme Court indicated that if the business judgment rule did not protect the directors' judgment with respect to the terms of the transaction they approved, the plaintiff did not need to prove causation of damage. Cede & Co., Cinerama, Inc. v. Technicolor, Inc., 634 A.2d 345 (Del. 1993). Instead, the directors carried the burden with respect to showing the inherent fairness of the transaction, as they would whenever the plaintiff showed a violation of duty. (As a logical matter, of course, the plaintiff still would be required to put on evidence that the price approved was too low, or there would be no damage to calculate.)

Connections—and Predictions!

Corporate litigation. Suppose that a disgruntled shareholder asks the board of directors of Hypo Corp. to initiate a lawsuit against Supply, Inc., which has breached its contract with Hypo Corp. The board refuses. Should its judgment be protected by the BJR? Probably so, assuming a reasonable decision-making process.

Suppose that a disgruntled shareholder asks the board of directors of Hypo Corp. to initiate a lawsuit against the members of the board for having made terrible business decisions. The board refuses. Should its judgment be protected by the BJR? As we'll see, courts and legislatures have devised special rules for this type of case, which clearly involves a conflict of interest.

Changes in control. Suppose Acquisico proposes a merger pursuant to which it will acquire control of Targuette, Inc., and replace all the members of Targuette's board of directors. The board of Targuette refuses to consider the matter. Should its judgment be protected by the BJR? Once again, the fear that the board has a conflict of interest has prompted special approaches.

D. Legislative Responses to Officer and Director Liability

In response to what directors perceived as excessive liability risks created by the *Van Gorkom* case, many state legislatures moved to ameliorate the crisis. They enacted laws that, in one way or another, decreased directors' liability risks. These sometimes are referred to as "exculpation" provisions. More popularly, they are called "raincoat" provisions. At least two types of statutes emerged. First, as illustrated by Delaware's General Corporation Law §102(b)(7), some statutes allow individual corporations, typically through shareholder action, to include in their articles a provision limiting their directors' monetary liability for various types of wrongdoing not involving lack of loyalty, lack of good faith, or illegality. A second type of statute actually alters the standards of fiduciary duties imposed on all corporate directors, typically lowering the standard of conduct for the duty of care. Virginia Code Ann. §13.1-690(A) is such a statute. Both types are further examined in Chapter 21. The advent of these statutes provided incentives for plaintiffs' attorneys to recharacterize what previously would have been duty of care claims as something else—quite often claims under the duty of loyalty.

E. Oversight, Monitoring, and the Duty of Care

Sometimes it may be possible to say that a fiduciary, like the supine Mrs. Pritchard, did absolutely nothing. More commonly, officers and directors will have done *something* to comply with their fiduciary obligations, and the question becomes whether they did enough. Is deciding how much effort to invest itself a decision entitled to the protection of the business judgment rule? *Smith v. Van Gorkom* seems to suggest that it is not, although the dissent surely could be read as suggesting that it is. In any event, when courts have been asked to decide how much effort boards are required to invest in oversight and monitoring, there indeed has been a tendency to defer, subject to the stated requirement that the conditions of the business judgment rule (including good faith) be satisfied.

In re Caremark International Inc. Derivative Litigation, 698 A.2d 959 (Del. Ch. 1996), showcased a company that had incurred large liabilities for paying for referred business in violation of federal regulations. Plaintiff shareholders sued the company's directors for failure to detect the illegal kickbacks going on under their noses, seeking to hold them accountable for the large penalties the company had to pay to the federal government. In approving a proposed settlement, Chancellor (now Professor) Allen was required to assess the strength of the claim that the directors had violated the duty of care. In doing so, he discussed an important decision by the Delaware Supreme Court and delivered his own influential interpretation:

> In 1963, the Delaware Supreme Court in *Graham v. Allis-Chalmers Mfg. Co.* addressed the question of potential liability of board members for losses experienced by the corporation as a result of the corporation having violated the antitrust laws of the United States. There was no claim in that case that the directors knew about the behavior of subordinate employees of the corporation that had resulted in the liability. Rather, as in this case, the claim asserted was that the directors ought to have known of it and if they had known they would have been under a duty to bring the corporation into compliance with the law and thus save the corporation from the loss. The Delaware Supreme Court concluded that, under the facts as they appeared, there was no basis to find that the directors had breached a duty to be informed of the ongoing operations of the firm. In notably colorful terms, the court stated that "absent cause for suspicion there is no duty upon the directors to install and operate a corporate system of espionage to ferret out wrongdoing which they have no reason to suspect exists." . . .

> How does one generalize this holding today? Can it be said today that, absent some ground giving rise to suspicion of violation of law, that corporate directors have no duty to assure that a corporate information gathering and reporting systems exists which represents a good faith attempt to provide senior management and the Board with information respecting material acts, events or conditions within the corporation, including compliance with applicable statutes and regulations? I certainly do not believe so. I doubt that such a broad generalization of the *Graham* holding would have been accepted by the Supreme

Court in 1963. The case can be more narrowly interpreted as standing for the proposition that, absent grounds to suspect deception, neither corporate boards nor senior officers can be charged with wrongdoing simply for assuming the integrity of employees and the honesty of their dealings on the company's behalf. . . .

A broader interpretation of *Graham v. Allis-Chalmers* — that it means that a corporate board has no responsibility to assure that appropriate information and reporting systems are established by management — would not, in any event, be accepted by the Delaware Supreme Court in 1996, in my opinion. In stating the basis for this view, I start with the recognition that in recent years the Delaware Supreme Court has made it clear — especially in its jurisprudence concerning takeovers, from *Smith v. Van Gorkom* through *Paramount Communications v. QVC* — the seriousness with which the corporation law views the role of the corporate board. Secondly, I note the elementary fact that relevant and timely information is an essential predicate for satisfaction of the board's supervisory and monitoring role under Section 141 of the Delaware General Corporation Law. . . .

In light of these developments, it would, in my opinion, be a mistake to conclude that our Supreme Court's statement in *Graham* concerning "espionage" means that corporate boards may satisfy their obligation to be reasonably informed concerning the corporation, without assuring themselves that information and reporting systems exist in the organization that are reasonably designed to provide to senior management and to the board itself timely, accurate information sufficient to allow management and the board, each within its scope, to reach informed judgments concerning both the corporation's compliance with law and its business performance.

Obviously the level of detail that is appropriate for such an information system is a question of business judgment. And obviously too, no rationally designed information and reporting system will remove the possibility that the corporation will violate laws or regulations, or that senior officers or directors may nevertheless sometimes be misled or otherwise fail reasonably to detect acts material to the corporation's compliance with the law. But it is important that the board exercise a good faith judgment that the corporation's information and reporting system is in concept and design adequate to assure the board that appropriate information will come to its attention in a timely manner as a matter of ordinary operations, so that it may satisfy its responsibility.

Thus, I am of the view that a director's obligation includes a duty to attempt in good faith to assure that a corporate information and reporting system, which the board concludes is adequate, exists, and that failure to do so under some circumstances may, in theory at least, render a director liable for losses caused by non-compliance with applicable legal standards. I now turn to an analysis of the claims asserted with this concept of the directors' duty of care, as a duty satisfied in part by assurance of adequate information flows to the board, in mind. . . .

In order to show that the Caremark directors breached their duty of care by failing adequately to control Caremark's employees, plaintiffs would have to show either (1) that the directors knew or (2) should have known that violations of law were occurring and, in either event, (3) that the directors took no steps in a good faith effort to prevent or remedy that situation, and (4) that such failure proximately resulted in the losses complained of. . . .

[After verifying that the Caremark directors did not know about the violations, Chancellor Allen turned to the question of whether they should have known, addressing it in terms of a possible failure to monitor.]

Connections: Internal Controls

Since the early 2000s, corporations that have registered securities under the Securities Exchange Act of 1934 (essentially, what are known as "publicly held" companies) have been required to obtain an independent audit of their financial and other managerial control systems. Under these circumstances, how likely is it that the board of a publicly held company will ever be liable under Chancellor Allen's "utter failure" test?

2. Failure to monitor: Since it does appear that the Board was to some extent unaware of the activities that led to liability, I turn to a consideration of the other potential avenue to director liability that the pleadings take: director inattention or "negligence." Generally where a claim of directorial liability for corporate loss is predicated upon ignorance of liability creating activities within the corporation, as in *Graham* or in this case, in my opinion only a sustained or systematic failure of the board to exercise oversight — such as an utter failure to attempt to assure a reasonable information and reporting system exists — will establish the lack of good faith that is a necessary condition to liability. Such a test of liability — lack of good faith as evidenced by sustained or systematic failure of a director to exercise reasonable oversight — is quite high. But, a demanding test of liability in the oversight context is probably beneficial to corporate shareholders as a class, as it is in the board decision context, since it makes board service by qualified persons more likely, while continuing to act as a stimulus to good faith performance of duty by such directors.

Apparently, in the unlikely event that the board of a large corporation had "utterly failed" to establish a reasonable information and reporting system, Chancellor Allen would be willing to say that the directors had lacked good faith. This presumably would (1) mean they would lose the protection of the business judgment rule vis-à-vis how the corporate oversight system was designed, and (2) open them to a charge that they should have known of the violations. Perhaps, though, if a reasonable system would not have detected the violations, the directors still could escape liability — Chancellor Allen did not need to reach that scenario. (But note again that in Cede & Co., Cinerama, Inc. v. Technicolor, Inc., 634 A.2d 345 (Del. 1993), the Delaware Supreme Court indicated that where the business judgment rule does not apply, the plaintiff need not prove causation.) Neither was he called upon to observe that, if lack of good faith were shown, it would be possible to obtain monetary damages even in the face of an articles provision adopted pursuant to the Delaware "raincoat" provision, §102(b)(7).

■ **Think about this:**

(R)   Compare *In re Caremark* to *Francis v. United Jersey Bank.* Consider in particular Chancellor Allen's emphasis on a "lack of good faith . . . [as] a necessary condition to liability." Did he intend in this language just to adopt the general standard of care for fiduciary inaction, or is it different? Does it go easier or harder on defendants? And if he did impose a different standard, why?

(S)   Suppose the financial statements of a small corporation clearly reveal "Loans to Officers" in a very large amount. The directors do not inquire into the circumstances under which the loans were made or are being repaid. If the corporation subsequently becomes insolvent, need the directors fear liability in Delaware?

Test Yourself

Assume Applicability of the Most Current Version of the Model Business Corporations Act

Questions 1-3 rely on the following facts:

The Los Angeles Machine Company (LAMC) is a major producer of industrial machinery. In order to save costs, its board of directors decides to relocate the factory to a fairly remote area in the Mojave Desert. Because LAMC relies on its skilled labor force, it is reluctant to lay off all of its employees or lose them in the move. At the same time, the prospect of moving from LAMC's urban location to a remote desert area will be unattractive to many of the company's employees.

After a lengthy and detailed process of study, the board decides to build a "company town" surrounding its new factory. Houses are built for employees and sold to them at cost, stores are built to provide a variety of consumer goods at reasonable prices, and a new entertainment complex is constructed, with sports and theater facilities that the board expects to be used by employees as well as for sports and entertainment events sponsored by the corporation.

1. A stockholder of LAMC brings a derivative suit challenging the development of the new company town. If the suit proceeds to the merits, the stockholder most likely will:

   a. Win, because the board is favoring the employees over the stockholders.
   b. Win, because there is a strong argument that the board has breached its duty of care.
   c. Lose, because such expenditures are within the legitimate range of the board's business judgment.
   d. Lose, because the expenditures obviously are fair.

2. Despite the allure of this company town, not all of the company's employees wish to move. In order to help these employees find new jobs, or obtain training for new careers if similar jobs are unavailable, the board retains a professional career counseling and vocational training firm, for a period of a year, at a cost of approximately 10 percent of LAMC's net income. A stockholder again sues derivatively. If the suit proceeds to the merits, the shareholder most likely will:

   a. Win, because a business corporation is not a charitable endeavor; therefore the expenditures are *ultra vires*.
   b. Win, because the corporation owes no legally enforceable duty to its employees.
   c. Lose, because the board rationally could have decided that such expenditures were in the corporation's long-term interest.
   d. Lose, because the corporation has the right to do anything that an individual could do.

3. Suppose that the board's planning process before deciding to move the plant, build the company town, and retain the career counseling and vocational training firm was not "a lengthy and detailed process of study." Instead, these decisions were made in a two-hour meeting following a presentation by the chief executive officer, who has a vacation home in the Mojave Desert. If a stockholder were to bring a derivative suit seeking to impose monetary liability on the members of the board, the stockholder probably would:

   a. Lose if LAMC's Articles of Incorporation contain a "raincoat" provision.
   b. Lose, whether or not LAMC's Articles of Incorporation contain a "raincoat" provision.
   c. Win, because the directors breached their duty of care.
   d. Lose, because the business judgment rule would protect the board's decision.

Questions 4-6 stand alone:

4. Fill in the Blanks: The duty of care obligates corporate directors to act with the _____, _____, and _____ of an ordinary person in similar circumstances.

5. Fill in the Blanks: A "raincoat" provision can protect a director from monetary liability for breaches of the duty of _____ but not for breaches of the duty of _____.

6. Fill in the Blanks: The theoretical limits on the application of the business judgment rule include _____ and _____.

19

The Duty of Loyalty and Conflicts of Interest: Self-Dealing Transactions and Corporate Opportunities

As the word "loyalty" is commonly used, the concept is quite broad. Consider, for a moment, what it is to be disloyal:

> **Disloyal:** lacking in loyalty; *also*: showing an absence of allegiance, devotion, obligation, faith, or support <his *disloyal* refusal to help his friend>[1]

All kinds of bad things a fiduciary might do could fit within a definition this broad. One can imagine, for example, that remarks freely denigrating one's employer might be characterized as disloyal, even though they might not involve what is usually thought of as a conflict of interest.

As a matter of tradition, however, the *legal* duty of loyalty has been triggered only when a fiduciary acts under a "conflict of interest." And "conflict of interest," though not particularly well defined, is now usually fit within specific, familiar confines. Two broad and fairly well-cabined categories of conflicted conduct have been identified, and each is dealt with in corporate law contexts

---

1. http://www.merriam-webster.com/dictionary/disloyal.

under its own legal standard. These two categories—interested transactions and corporate opportunity transactions—are the subject of this chapter.

Chapter Outline

A. Introduction to the Duty of Loyalty

- Differences between conflicts of interest and other duty of loyalty scenarios
- Differences between "interested" or "self-dealing" transactions and "corporate opportunity" transactions
    - Indicative facts
    - Tests
- Remedies

B. "Interested" or "Self-Dealing" Transactions

1. In General
    - What is self-dealing?

2. Ratification
    - Multiple meanings
    - Burden-shifting devices

C. Corporate Opportunities

- The "line-of-business" test
- The "fairness" test
- The "line-of-business plus fairness" test
- The ALI approach

Test Yourself

A. Introduction to the Duty of Loyalty

We turn now to the second of the two major, traditional fiduciary duties: the duty of loyalty. As noted at the start of the chapter, invocation of the duty usually appears in one of two contexts, both involving alleged conflicts of interest on the part of a corporate fiduciary. These are "interested" transactions and "corporate opportunity" transactions. A less well-defined, but oft-mentioned category (which probably also could be used as an umbrella term for breaches of the other two types) appears to be acts in "bad faith" or acts "not in good faith." It is covered in the next chapter, along with the state law approach to insider trading, which involves a failure to disclose.

As we shall see in the *Sinclair* case below, identifying conflicts can be tricky. Nonetheless, knowing whether one is present can be of outcome-determinative significance because, in the absence of a conflict, the plaintiff usually has a cause of action only under the duty of care. There, the business judgment rule stands ready to drape its comforting veil over the substance of any informed decision. By contrast, the substantive standards that govern litigation under the duty of loyalty are more plaintiff-friendly.

Although the task sometimes is more difficult than the following will imply, on many occasions identifying the presence of a conflict is straightforward. Your gut instinct as to whether a conflict is present in a given case will usually be quite reliable. Conflicts usually fall into the following categories:

- Cases in which the fiduciary has some direct pecuniary interest in a transaction that involves the corporation—for example, the fiduciary receives a loan of money from the company or sells his or her own property to the company;
- Cases in which the fiduciary is related to or closely associated with a person who has a direct personal stake in a transaction that involves the corporation—for example, a director votes in favor of a lucrative employment contract for his or her father;
- Cases in which the fiduciary owes duties both to the corporation and to another person involved in a transaction with the corporation—for example, a director also happens to serve as director of another company that is doing business with the corporation; and
- Cases in which the fiduciary has taken something that belongs to the corporation and used it for the fiduciary's own benefit—for example, an officer takes a new process developed by the corporation and incorporates it in the manufacture of a product by the fiduciary's own, individually held business.

The first three examples are varieties of "interested" transactions. They are judged pursuant to the "entire fairness" or "intrinsic fairness" standard. The usual remedy for a breach of the duty of loyalty in this context is voiding the tainted transaction.

The fourth example involves the usurpation of a corporate opportunity— essentially, the investment by the fiduciary in an opportunity that properly should have been left open for the corporation. Illegal usurpations are governed by standards that vary somewhat from state to state, but the usual remedy is to impose a constructive trust. This means that the fiduciary holds the opportunity in trust for the corporation and must account for all profits.

 Dear Prof.: Does "account" for profits mean "keep track" of them?

An "accounting" is actually a judicial proceeding, in which a fiduciary must disgorge profits that rightfully belong to a beneficiary. It frequently is called for in partnership and agency contexts, and where corporate fiduciaries are found to have breached their loyalty duties, courts often impose as a remedy that they "account" for ill-gotten gains by disgorging them.

B. "Interested" or "Self-Dealing" Transactions

1. In General

The modern state of the law of interested transactions is nicely captured in the *Lewis* case, appearing immediately below. The remedy is unusual, but the transaction involved is easily identified as falling in the "interested" category, and the opinion showcases the very clear and usual resolution of the issue presented.

LEWIS V. S.L. & E., INC.

United States Court of Appeals for the Second Circuit
629 F.2d 764 (1980)

KEARSE, Circuit Judge:

This case arises out of an intra-family dispute over the management of two closely-held affiliated corporations. Plaintiff Donald E. Lewis ("Donald"), a shareholder of S.L. & E., Inc. ("SLE"), appeals from judgments entered against him in the United States District Court for the Western District of New York, Harold P. Burke, Judge, after a bench trial of his derivative claim against directors of SLE, and of a claim asserted against him by the other corporation, Lewis General Tires, Inc. ("LGT"), which intervened in the suit. The defendants Alan E. Lewis ("Alan"), Leon E. Lewis, Jr. ("Leon, Jr."), and Richard E. Lewis ("Richard"), are the brothers of Donald; they were, at pertinent times herein, directors of SLE and officers, directors and shareholders of LGT. Donald charged that his brothers had wasted the assets of SLE by causing SLE to lease business premises to LGT from 1966 to 1972 at an unreasonably low rental. LGT was permitted to intervene in the action, and filed a complaint seeking specific performance of an agreement by Donald to sell his SLE stock to LGT in 1972. The district court held that Donald had failed to prove waste by the defendant directors, and entered judgment in their favor. . . .

On appeal, Donald argues that the district court improperly allocated to him the burden of proving his claims of waste, and that since defendants failed to prove that the transactions in question were fair and reasonable, he was entitled to judgment. . . . We agree with each of these contentions, and therefore reverse and remand.

I

For many years Leon Lewis, Sr., the father of Donald and the defendant directors, was the principal shareholder of SLE and LGT. LGT, formed in 1933, operated a tire dealership in Rochester, New York. SLE, formed in 1943, owned the land and complex of buildings at 260 East Avenue in Rochester. This property was SLE's only significant asset. Prior to 1956 LGT occupied SLE's premises without benefit of a lease; the rent paid was initially $200 per month, and had increased over the years to $800 per month by 1956, when additional parcels were added. On February 28, 1956, SLE granted LGT a 10-year lease on the newly expanded property ("the Property"), for a rent of $1200 per month, or $14,400 per year. Under the terms of the lease, SLE was responsible for payment of real estate taxes on the Property, while all other current expenses were to be borne by the tenant, LGT.[2]

This may help . . .

Ownership of SLE and LGT

1962

| Owners | { Richard, Alan, Leon, Jr, Donald, Margaret, Carol | Richard, Alan, Leon, Jr, Leon, Sr. } | Owners |

| Directors | { Richard, Alan, Leon, Jr, Leon, Sr., Henry E. | Richard, Alan, Leon, Jr, Leon, Sr., Henry E. } | Directors |

(SLE)   (LGT)

1967

| Owners | { Richard, Alan, Leon, Jr, Donald, Margaret, Carol | Richard, Leon, Jr. } | Owners |

| Directors | { Richard, Alan, Leon, Jr, Leon, Sr., Henry E. | Richard, Alan, Leon, Jr, Leon, Sr., Henry E. } | Directors |

(SLE)   (LGT)

1973

| Owners | { Donald, Richard, Leon, Jr. | Richard, Leon, Jr. } | Owners |

| Directors | { Richard, Leon, Jr, | Richard, Leon, Jr. } | Directors |

(SLE)   (LGT)

---

2. It appears that SLE was also responsible for payments due on a mortgage on the Property. In addition, LGT charged SLE for the costs of certain capital improvements, such as the major structural repairs to the principal building's facade, carried out in 1969.

In 1962, [SLE cashed out a minority shareholder and] Leon Lewis, Sr., transferred his SLE stock, 90 shares in all, to his six children (defendants Richard, Alan and Leon, Jr., plaintiff Donald, and two daughters, Margaret and Carol), giving 15 shares to each. At that time Richard, Alan and Leon, Jr., were already shareholders, officers and directors of LGT. Contemporaneously with their receipt of SLE stock, all six of the children entered into a "shareholders' agreement" with LGT, under which each child who was not a shareholder of LGT on June 1, 1972 would be required to sell his or her SLE shares to LGT, within 30 days of that date, at a price equal to the book value of the SLE stock as of June 1, 1972.

LGT's lease on the SLE property expired on February 28, 1966. At that time the directors of SLE were Richard, Alan, Leon, Jr., Leon, Sr., and Henry Etsberger; these five were also the directors of LGT. In 1966 Alan owned 44% of LGT, Richard owned 30%, Leon, Jr., owned 19%, and Leon, Sr., owned 7%. From 1967 to 1972 Richard owned 61% of LGT and Leon, Jr., owned the remaining 39%. When the lease expired in 1966, no new lease was entered into. LGT nonetheless continued to occupy the property and to pay SLE at the old rate, $14,400 per year. According to the defendants' testimony at trial, there was never any thought or discussion among the SLE directors of entering into a new lease or of increasing the rent. Richard testified: "We never gave consideration to a new lease." From all that appears, the defendant directors viewed SLE as existing purely for the benefit of LGT. Richard testified, for example, that although real estate taxes rose sharply during the period 1966-1971, from approximately $7,800 to more than $11,000, to be paid by SLE out of its constant $14,400 rental income, raising the rent was never mentioned. He testified that SLE was "only a shell to protect the operating company (LGT)." When this suit was commenced there had not been a formal meeting of either the shareholders or the directors of SLE since 1962. Richard, Alan and Leon, Jr., had largely ignored SLE's separate corporate existence and disregarded the fact that SLE had shareholders who were not shareholders of LGT and who therefore could not profit from actions that used SLE solely for the benefit of LGT.

Neither Donald nor his sisters ever owned LGT stock. As the June 1972 date approached for the required sale of their SLE stock to LGT, Donald apparently came to believe that SLE's book value was lower than it should have been. He sought SLE financial information from Richard, who had been president of SLE since 1967. Richard refused to provide information. Donald therefore refused to sell his SLE shares in 1972,[3] and commenced this shareholders' derivative action in the district court in August 1973, basing jurisdiction on diversity of citizenship. The sole claim raised in the complaint was that the defendant directors had wasted the assets of SLE by "grossly undercharging" LGT for the latter's occupancy and use of the Property. . . .

There ensued an eight-day bench trial, at which plaintiff sought to prove, by the testimony of several expert witnesses, that the fair rental value of the

---

3. Donald's sisters Carol and Margaret sold their SLE shares to LGT in 1972 and 1973 respectively. Alan, who had sold his LGT stock in 1967, sold his SLE stock to LGT in 1972.

Property was greater than the $14,400 per year that SLE had been paid by LGT. Defendants sought to show that the rental paid was reasonable, by offering evidence concerning the financial straits of LGT, the cost to LGT of operating the Property, the general economic decline of the East Avenue neighborhood, and rentals paid on two other properties in that neighborhood. LGT presented expert testimony that the value of plaintiff's stock as of June 1972, assuming a successful defense of the derivative claims, was $15,650.

. . . On this basis, the court held that Donald had failed to establish the rental value of the Property during the period at issue, and that defendants were therefore entitled to judgment on the derivative claims. Implicit in the district court's ruling, granting judgment for defendants upon plaintiff's failure to prove waste, was a determination that plaintiff bore the burden of proof on that issue. . . .

II

Turning first to the question of burden of proof, we conclude that the district court erred in placing upon plaintiff the burden of proving waste. Because the directors of SLE were also officers, directors and/or shareholders of LGT, the burden was on the defendant directors to demonstrate that the transactions between SLE and LGT were fair and reasonable. . . .

Under normal circumstances the directors of a corporation may determine, in the exercise of their business judgment, what contracts the corporation will enter into and what consideration is adequate, without review of the merits of their decisions by the courts. The business judgment rule places a heavy burden on shareholders who would attack corporate transactions. But the business judgment rule presupposes that the directors have no conflict of interest. When a shareholder attacks a transaction in which the directors have an interest other than as directors of the corporation, the directors may not escape review of the merits of the transaction. At common law such a transaction was voidable unless shown by its proponent to be fair, and reasonable to the corporation. [New York Business Corporations Law] §713, in both its current and its prior versions, carries forward this common law principle, and provides special rules for scrutiny of a transaction between the corporation and an entity in which its directors are directors or officers or have a substantial financial interest.

The current version of §713 . . . , which became effective on September 1, 1971, and governs at least so much of the dealing between SLE and LGT as occurred after that date, expressly provides that a contract between a corporation and an entity in which its directors are interested may be set aside unless the proponent of the contract "shall establish affirmatively that the contract or transaction was fair and reasonable as to the corporation at the time it was approved by the board. . . ." §713(b). Thus when the transaction is challenged in a derivative action against the interested directors, they have the burden of proving that the transaction was fair and reasonable to the corporation.

The same was true under the predecessor to §713(b), former §713(a)(3), which was in effect prior to September 1, 1971. Section 713(a)(3) was not explicit as to the burden of proof, but simply stated that a transaction with interested directors would not be voidable "If the contract or transaction is fair and reasonable as to the corporation at the time it is approved by the board. . . ." The consensus among the commentators was that §713(a)(3) carried forward the common law rule, which placed the burden of proof as to fairness on the interested directors. . . . We agree with this construction. . . .

During the entire period 1966-1972, Richard, Alan and Leon, Jr., were directors of both SLE and LGT; there were no SLE directors who were not also directors of LGT. Richard, Alan and Leon, Jr., were all shareholders of LGT in 1966, and from 1967 to 1972 Richard and Leon, Jr., were the sole shareholders of LGT. Under BCL §713, therefore, Richard, Alan and Leon, Jr., had the burden of proving that $14,400 was a fair and reasonable annual rent for the SLE property for the period February 28, 1966 through June 1, 1972.

Our review of the record convinces us that defendants failed to carry their burden. . . . Thus, Donald is not required to sell his SLE shares to LGT without such upward adjustment in the June 1, 1972, book value of SLE as may be necessary to reflect the amount by which the fair rental value of the Property exceeded $14,400 in any of the years 1966-1972. . . .

■ **Think about this:**

(A) Alan Lewis sold his shares in LGT in 1967 and his shares in SLE in 1972. Under what theory did he have a conflict of interest? Was it because he was Richard and Leon's brother? Wasn't he Donald's brother too?

(B) In a family-owned corporation, is it ever possible to find a disinterested decision maker?

(C) The relevant statute requires the proponent of a contract to show it was fair and reasonable at the time it was approved by the board. When was the contract in *Lewis* approved?

Although it is easy to see the directorial interest at stake in *Lewis*, other cases are more complex. The *Sinclair* decision, appearing below, is a casebook standard. It states a test for the existence of conflict of interest that is highly influential, although oft-criticized in academic circles.

SINCLAIR OIL CORP. V. LEVIEN

Supreme Court of Delaware
280 A.2d 717 (1971)

WOLCOTT, Chief Justice.

This is an appeal by the defendant, Sinclair Oil Corporation (hereafter Sinclair), from an order of the Court of Chancery, 261 A.2d 911, in a derivative action requiring Sinclair to account for damages sustained by its subsidiary,

Sinclair Venezuelan Oil Company (hereafter Sinven), organized by Sinclair for the purpose of operating in Venezuela, as a result of dividends paid by Sinven, the denial to Sinven of industrial development, and a breach of contract between Sinclair's wholly-owned subsidiary, Sinclair International Oil Company, and Sinven.

Sinclair, operating primarily as a holding company, is in the business of exploring for oil and of producing and marketing crude oil and oil products. At all times relevant to this litigation, it owned about 97% of Sinven's stock. The plaintiff owns about 3000 of 120,000 publicly held shares of Sinven. Sinven, incorporated in 1922, has been engaged in petroleum operations primarily in Venezuela and since 1959 has operated exclusively in Venezuela.

Sinclair nominates all members of Sinven's board of directors. The Chancellor found as a fact that the directors were not independent of Sinclair. Almost without exception, they were officers, directors, or employees of corporations in the Sinclair complex. By reason of Sinclair's domination, it is clear that Sinclair owed Sinven a fiduciary duty. Sinclair concedes this.

The Chancellor held that because of Sinclair's fiduciary duty and its control over Sinven, its relationship with Sinven must meet the test of intrinsic fairness. The standard of intrinsic fairness involves both a high degree of fairness and a shift in the burden of proof. Under this standard the burden is on Sinclair to prove, subject to careful judicial scrutiny, that its transactions with Sinven were objectively fair.

Sinclair argues that the transactions between it and Sinven should be tested, not by the test of intrinsic fairness with the accompanying shift of the burden of proof, but by the business judgment rule under which a court will not interfere with the judgment of a board of directors unless there is a showing of gross and palpable overreaching. A board of directors enjoys a presumption of sound business judgment, and its decisions will not be disturbed if they can be attributed to any rational business purpose. A court under such circumstances will not substitute its own notions of what is or is not sound business judgment.

We think, however, that Sinclair's argument in this respect is misconceived. When the situation involves a parent and a subsidiary, with the parent controlling the transaction and fixing the terms, the test of intrinsic fairness, with its resulting shifting of the burden of proof, is applied. The basic situation for the application of the rule is the one in which the parent has received a benefit to the exclusion and at the expense of the subsidiary.

Recently, this court dealt with the question of fairness in parent-subsidiary dealings in Getty Oil Co. v. Skelly Oil Co., [267 A.2d 883 (Del. Supr. 1970)]. In that case, both parent and subsidiary

Connections: Controlling Shareholders

Courts commonly treat controlling shareholders as if they owe the same fiduciary duties as the directors they control, and that typically is more or less accurate. When the controlling shareholder is selling control, however, rather than managing the corporation, the discussion is different. Sales of control are discussed elsewhere in this book.

A Shifting Burden

were in the business of refining and marketing crude oil and crude oil products. The Oil Import Board ruled that the subsidiary, because it was controlled by the parent, was no longer entitled to a separate allocation of imported crude oil. The subsidiary then contended that it had a right to share the quota of crude oil allotted to the parent. We ruled that the business judgment standard should be applied to determine this contention. Although the subsidiary suffered a loss through the administration of the oil import quotas, the parent gained nothing. The parent's quota was derived solely from its own past use. The past use of the subsidiary did not cause an increase in the parent's quota. Nor did the parent usurp a quota of the subsidiary. Since the parent received nothing from the subsidiary to the exclusion of the minority stockholders of the subsidiary, there was no self-dealing. Therefore, the business judgment standard was properly applied.

A parent does indeed owe a fiduciary duty to its subsidiary when there are parent-subsidiary dealings. However, this alone will not evoke the intrinsic fairness standard. This standard will be applied only when the fiduciary duty is accompanied by self-dealing—the situation when a parent is on both sides of a transaction with its subsidiary. Self-dealing occurs when the parent, by virtue of its domination of the subsidiary, causes the subsidiary to act in such a way that the parent receives something from the subsidiary to the exclusion of, and detriment to, the minority stockholders of the subsidiary.

We turn now to the facts. The plaintiff argues that, from 1960 through 1966, Sinclair caused Sinven to pay out such excessive dividends that the industrial development of Sinven was effectively prevented, and it became in reality a corporation in dissolution.

More to the Story: Permissible Dividends

The Delaware statute permitted making distributions to shareholders out of net profits or surplus. Without getting too far into the weeds, surplus includes both the amount the corporation has earned (including the appreciation in value of its property) and not distributed, and the amount the shareholders have paid for their shares in excess of par value. The rules are different under the Model Act, although the permissible distribution amounts will not vary all that much. There is more on this subject in the online Supplement.

From 1960 through 1966, Sinven paid out $108,000,000 in dividends ($38,000,000 in excess of Sinven's earnings during the same period). The Chancellor held that Sinclair caused these dividends to be paid during a period when it had a need for large amounts of cash. Although the dividends paid exceeded earnings, the plaintiff concedes that the payments were made in compliance with 8 Del. C. §170, authorizing payment of dividends out of surplus or net profits. However, the plaintiff attacks these dividends on the ground that they resulted from an improper motive—Sinclair's need for cash. The Chancellor, applying the intrinsic fairness standard, held that Sinclair did not sustain its burden of proving that these dividends were intrinsically fair to the minority stockholders of Sinven.

Since it is admitted that the dividends were paid in strict compliance with 8 Del. C. §170, the alleged excessiveness of the payments alone would not state a cause of action. Nevertheless, compliance with the applicable statute may not, under all circumstances, justify all dividend payments. If a plaintiff can meet his burden of proving that a dividend cannot be grounded on any reasonable business objective, then the courts can and will interfere with the board's decision to pay the dividend.

Sinclair contends that it is improper to apply the intrinsic fairness standard to dividend payments even when the board which voted for the dividends is completely dominated. . . .

We do not accept the argument that the intrinsic fairness test can never be applied to a dividend declaration by a dominated board, although a dividend declaration by a dominated board will not inevitably demand the application of the intrinsic fairness standard. If such a dividend is in essence self-dealing by the parent, then the intrinsic fairness standard is the proper standard. For example, suppose a parent dominates a subsidiary and its board of directors. The subsidiary has outstanding two classes of stock, X and Y. Class X is owned by the parent and Class Y is owned by minority stockholders of the subsidiary. If the subsidiary, at the direction of the parent, declares a dividend on its Class X stock only, this might well be self-dealing by the parent. It would be receiving something from the subsidiary to the exclusion of and detrimental to its minority stockholders. This self-dealing, coupled with the parent's fiduciary duty, would make intrinsic fairness the proper standard by which to evaluate the dividend payments.

Consequently it must be determined whether the dividend payments by Sinven were, in essence, self-dealing by Sinclair. The dividends resulted in great sums of money being transferred from Sinven to Sinclair. However, a proportionate share of this money was received by the minority shareholders of Sinven. Sinclair received nothing from Sinven to the exclusion of its minority stockholders. As such, these dividends were not self-dealing. We hold therefore that the Chancellor erred in applying the intrinsic fairness test as to these dividend payments. The business judgment standard should have been applied.

We conclude that the facts demonstrate that the dividend payments complied with the business judgment standard and with 8 Del. C. §170. The motives for causing the declaration of dividends are immaterial unless the plaintiff can show that the dividend payments resulted from improper motives and amounted to waste. The plaintiff contends only that the dividend payments drained Sinven of cash to such an extent that it was prevented from expanding.

The plaintiff proved no business opportunities which came to Sinven independently and which Sinclair either took to itself or denied to Sinven. As a matter of fact, with two minor exceptions which resulted in losses, all of Sinven's operations have been conducted in Venezuela, and Sinclair had a policy of exploiting its oil properties located in different countries by subsidiaries located in the particular countries.

From 1960 to 1966 Sinclair purchased or developed oil fields in Alaska, Canada, Paraguay, and other places around the world. The plaintiff contends that these were all opportunities which could have been taken by Sinven. The Chancellor concluded that Sinclair had not proved that its denial of expansion opportunities to Sinven was intrinsically fair. He based this conclusion on the following findings of fact. Sinclair made no real effort to expand Sinven. The excessive dividends paid by Sinven resulted in so great a cash drain as to effectively deny to Sinven any ability to expand. During this same period Sinclair actively pursued a company-wide policy of developing through its subsidiaries new sources of revenue, but Sinven was not permitted to participate and was confined in its activities to Venezuela.

However, the plaintiff could point to no opportunities which came to Sinven. Therefore, Sinclair usurped no business opportunity belonging to Sinven. Since Sinclair received nothing from Sinven to the exclusion of and detriment to Sinven's minority stockholders, there was no self-dealing. Therefore, business judgment is the proper standard by which to evaluate Sinclair's expansion policies.

Since there is no proof of self-dealing on the part of Sinclair, it follows that the expansion policy of Sinclair and the methods used to achieve the desired result must, as far as Sinclair's treatment of Sinven is concerned, be tested by the standards of the business judgment rule. Accordingly, Sinclair's decision, absent fraud or gross overreaching, to achieve expansion through the medium of its subsidiaries, other than Sinven, must be upheld.

Even if Sinclair was wrong in developing these opportunities as it did, the question arises, with which subsidiaries should these opportunities have been shared? No evidence indicates a unique need or ability of Sinven to develop these opportunities. The decision of which subsidiaries would be used to implement Sinclair's expansion policy was one of business judgment with which a court will not interfere absent a showing of gross and palpable overreaching. No such showing has been made here.

Next, Sinclair argues that the Chancellor committed error when he held it liable to Sinven for breach of contract.

In 1961 Sinclair created Sinclair International Oil Company (hereafter International), a wholly-owned subsidiary used for the purpose of coordinating all of Sinclair's foreign operations. All crude purchases by Sinclair were made thereafter through International.

On September 28, 1961, Sinclair caused Sinven to contract with International whereby Sinven agreed to sell all of its crude oil and refined products to International at specified prices. The contract provided for minimum and maximum quantities and prices. The plaintiff contends that Sinclair caused this contract to be breached in two respects. Although the contract called for payment on receipt, International's payments lagged as much as 30 days after receipt. Also, the contract required International to purchase at least a fixed minimum amount of crude and refined products from Sinven. International did not comply with this requirement.

Clearly, Sinclair's act of contracting with its dominated subsidiary was self-dealing. Under the contract Sinclair received the products produced by Sinven, and of course the minority shareholders of Sinven were not able to share in the receipt of these products. If the contract was breached, then Sinclair received these products to the detriment of Sinven's minority shareholders. We agree with the Chancellor's finding that the contract was breached by Sinclair, both as to the time of payments and the amounts purchased. . . .

Under the intrinsic fairness standard, Sinclair must prove that its causing Sinven not to enforce the contract was intrinsically fair to the minority shareholders of Sinven. Sinclair has failed to meet this burden. Late payments were clearly breaches for which Sinven should have sought and received adequate damages. As to the quantities purchased, Sinclair argues that it purchased all the products produced by Sinven. This, however, does not satisfy the standard of intrinsic fairness. Sinclair has failed to prove that Sinven could not possibly have produced or someway have obtained the contract minimums. As such, Sinclair must account on this claim. . . .

We will therefore reverse that part of the Chancellor's order that requires Sinclair to account to Sinven for damages sustained as a result of dividends paid between 1960 and 1966, and by reason of the denial to Sinven of expansion during that period. We will affirm the remaining portion of that order and remand the cause for further proceedings.

■ **Think about this:**

(D) The court in *Sinclair* acknowledges that "[a] parent does indeed owe a fiduciary duty to its subsidiary when there are parent-subsidiary dealings." If there are no minority shareholders of the subsidiary, is the existence of this duty in any way meaningful?

(E) The court's example about paying dividends on one class of stock but not another seems like a bit of a slow pitch. Can you imagine any instance in which paying dividends on a single class would involve self-dealing, as far as the Delaware Supreme Court is concerned?

(F) Assume that Fay controls the board of Fiscal, Inc., because she owns a majority of its common stock. Fiscal also has a class of redeemable, non-voting, preferred shares that are entitled to annual dividends, when declared, of $15 per share before the common can receive any dividends. Fay is aware that market conditions have changed and that it now would be possible to sell preferred shares for the same face value but with an annual preference of only $10 per share. May Fay cause the board to redeem the outstanding preferred and then to sell the new class?

(G) Assume that Gadget, Inc., has two classes of shares: common and preferred. The widely held common class has voting rights, and the preferred does not. The preferred shares are redeemable and are entitled to annual dividends, when declared, of $15 per share before the common can receive any dividends. The market has changed, and it now would be possible to sell preferred shares for the same face value but with an annual preference of only $10 per share. The board of directors fears that if it does not redeem the outstanding preferred

and sell the new class, the common shareholders will become dissatisfied and, perhaps, vote the directors out of office. Would it be a breach of any duty to follow through with this redemption and sale?

(H) The court in *Sinclair* says the standard for reviewing a parent's allocation of opportunities among its subsidiaries is "tested by the standards of the business judgment rule" and will be respected "absent a showing of gross and palpable overreaching." Can you imagine what "gross and palpable overreaching" might be in this context? What do you suppose the word "palpable" is supposed to add?

A word or two about intrinsic fairness. One might start with the question, what is the difference between "fair" and "intrinsically fair"? The courts obviously are trying to make a point when they use the latter term, more or less pioneered in Delaware. As explained in *Sinclair*, "intrinsic fairness" requires both "a high degree of fairness" and a shift in the burden of proof. The shift in burden is important and relatively easy to understand. What, however, is a "high degree" of fairness? Although not well illustrated by *Sinclair*, it generally is accepted that under this test the defendant must prove both substantive fairness and procedural fairness. The "intrinsic fairness" test therefore is sometimes also known as the "entire fairness" test. The Court in Weinberger v. UOP, Inc., 457 A.2d 701, 710 (Del. Supr. 1983), put it this way:

> When directors of a Delaware corporation are on both sides of a transaction, they are required to demonstrate their utmost good faith and the most scrupulous inherent fairness of the bargain. . . .
>
> The requirement of fairness is unflinching in its demand that where one stands on both sides of a transaction, he has the burden of establishing its entire fairness, sufficient to pass the test of careful scrutiny by the courts.

Lewis v. S.L. & E., Inc., which we read above, gives a nice flavor for the kinds of evidence by which defendants can show "substantive" fairness. The question was whether LGT, Inc., which operated the tire business, was paying proper rent to SLE, Inc., which owned the property on which it sat. The parties accordingly put on testimony of real estate specialists from Rochester, New York (where the business was located) to establish fair market rent for similar land there. The court found the evidence inadequate to meet defendants' burden, but made clear that if the rent had matched going rents for similar land in the local market, then it would have been substantively fair. From the standpoint of procedural fairness, defendants should try to show that either their beneficiaries or a disinterested decision maker was made fully aware of the transaction at issue and the nature of the conflict, and that no appropriate record-keeping or decision-making procedures were sidestepped.

Time Out for PR

Lawyers are, of course, fiduciaries for their clients, and their transactions with them are said to be "constructively fraudulent." This means, as a matter of common law, that they can be set aside unless the attorney makes the appropriate showing. The Model Rules of Professional Conduct take a parallel approach, providing in Rule 1.8(a) that it is a breach of ethics to enter into a transaction with a client unless:

(1) the transaction and terms on which the lawyer acquires the interest are fair and reasonable to the client and are fully disclosed and transmitted in writing in a manner that can be reasonably understood by the client;

(2) the client is advised in writing of the desirability of seeking and is given a reasonable opportunity to seek the advice of independent legal counsel on the transaction; and

(3) the client gives informed consent, in a writing signed by the client, to the essential terms of the transaction and the lawyer's role in the transaction, including whether the lawyer is representing the client in the transaction.

2. Ratification

It should be apparent that not every corporate transaction involving a conflict of interest violates the duty of loyalty—those that satisfy the "inherent fairness" test do not. Moreover, the chances of a violation can be reduced through a procedure known as "ratification." What, however, is ratification?

- One common meaning is "approval after the fact"; for instance, if an agent made a contract that wouldn't bind the principal, because the agent lacked authority, the principal may subsequently "ratify" the contract, by either specifically approving it or, in some circumstances, knowingly accepting the benefits without complaint. This type of ratification essentially has the same effect as approval before the act is taken. Ratifications of this kind are common in principal-agent relationships, and were dealt with in Chapter 5.
- Another usage is to describe a second approval that is legally required to complete a process. For instance, a vote by the board of directors recommending an amendment of the Articles of Incorporation may require "ratification"—a second vote—by the shareholders.
- Sometimes the term is used to describe an approval that is not required for the act to be effective, but may play a role in insulating the act against later challenge. For example, where a corporate fiduciary loans money to the company or engages in any number of other simple, interested

transactions, there likely is no need for anyone else to do anything. But as we shall see, this type of ratification may be sought voluntarily or may be made a term of a contract.

The amount of information provided to a ratifying party is an issue in determining a ratification's legal effect.

Sometimes the types of ratification overlap. Thus, a shareholder vote required by statute to complete a transaction might also play a role in preserving the transaction against later attack on the grounds that it involved an interested party.

Delaware dealt with some ratification problems in a statute, D.G.C.L. §144, that is not atypical of statutes in other states.[4] As you read it, think about what it is actually trying to accomplish. One problem it addressed was uncertainty at common law as to whether interested transactions should be void or voidable automatically, whether they were fair or not, and whether an interested director's participation at a meeting would render approval of those transactions ineffective. Remember, sometimes shareholder or board approval is necessary for a transaction to have legal effect, regardless whether there is any conflict at stake. This is a good reminder that general rules for approving transactions—such as quorum and other requirements—apply to self-interested transactions and must be satisfied in addition to whatever requirements are associated with the self-interest problem.

DELAWARE GENERAL CORPORATION LAW D.C.A., TITLE 8, CH. 1

§144 Interested directors; quorum.

(a) No contract or transaction between a corporation and 1 or more of its directors or officers, or between a corporation and any other corporation, partnership, association, or other organization in which 1 or more of its directors or officers, are directors or officers, or have a financial interest, shall be void or voidable solely for this reason, or solely because the director or officer is present at or participates in the meeting of the board or committee which authorizes the contract or transaction, or solely because any such director's or officer's votes are counted for such purpose, if:

(1) The material facts as to the director's or officer's relationship or interest and as to the contract or transaction are disclosed or are known to the board of directors or the committee, and the board or committee in good faith authorizes the contract or transaction by the affirmative votes of a majority of the disinterested directors, even though the disinterested directors be less than a quorum; or

---

This may help . . .

Remember to ask:

✓ Was there corporate authorization?
✓ Was there ratification of any self-dealing?

---

4. The Model Business Corporation took a more elaborate approach, but it has had little influence.

(2) The material facts as to the director's or officer's relationship or interest and as to the contract or transaction are disclosed or are known to the stockholders entitled to vote thereon, and the contract or transaction is specifically approved in good faith by vote of the stockholders; or

(3) The contract or transaction is fair as to the corporation as of the time it is authorized, approved or ratified, by the board of directors, a committee or the stockholders.

(b) Common or interested directors may be counted in determining the presence of a quorum at a meeting of the board of directors or of a committee which authorizes the contract or transaction.

Obviously, the statute presupposes approval by the board, a committee, or the shareholders of the transaction in question. Sometimes such approval is required for a transaction to have any effect. But note that many interested transactions undertaken by a fiduciary will be binding on the corporation simply because the fiduciary acted with sufficient agency authority to bind it, and will be legally effective whether or not there is any separate approval by the board or the shareholders. Section 144 seems not to address such cases, but the next case, *Marciano v. Nakash*, does.

MARCIANO V. NAKASH

Supreme Court of Delaware
535 A.2d 400 (1987)

WALSH, Justice.

This is an appeal from a decision of the Court of Chancery which validated a claim in liquidation of Gasoline, Ltd. ("Gasoline"), a Delaware corporation, placed in custodial status pursuant to 8 Del. C. §226 by reason of a deadlock among its board of directors. Fifty percent of Gasoline is owned by Ari, Joe, and Ralph Nakash (the "Nakashes") and fifty percent by Georges, Maurice, Armand and Paul Marciano (the "Marcianos"). The Vice Chancellor ruled that $2.5 million in loans made by the Nakashes faction to Gasoline were valid and enforceable debts of the corporation, notwithstanding their origin in self-dealing transactions....

Connections: Deadlock

Fifty-fifty ownership and an even number of directors constitute a recipe for deadlock. The statutory remedies include placement in custodial status and in some cases dissolution. Deadlock and dissolution are the subject of another chapter in this book.

I

... The liquidation proceeding marked the end of a joint venture launched in 1984 by the Marcianos and the Nakashes to market designer jeans and sportswear. Through a solely owned corporation called Guess? Inc. ("Guess"), the California based Marcianos had been engaged in the design and distribution of stylized jeans for several years. In 1983 they decided to form a separate division to market copies

Gasoline jeans were particularly known for their stylish two-tone designs.

of Guess creations in a broader retail market. In order to secure financing and broaden market exposure the Marcianos entered into negotiations with the New York based Nakash brothers, the owners of Jordache Enterprises, Inc. a leading manufacturer of jeans. Ultimately, it was agreed that the Nakashes would receive fifty percent of the stock of Guess for a consideration of $4.7 million. As a result, the three Nakash brothers joined three of the Marcianos on the Guess board of directors.

Similarly, when Gasoline was formed, stock ownership and board composition was shared equally by the two families. Although corporate control and direction were equally divided, from an operational standpoint Gasoline functioned in New York under the Nakashes' operational guidance while the parent, Guess, continued under the primary attention of the Marcianos. Differences between the two factions quickly surfaced with resulting deadlocks at the director level of both Guess and Gasoline. . . .

Without consulting the Marcianos [who previously had refused to guarantee Gasoline's debts], the Nakashes advanced approximately $2.3 million of their personal funds to Gasoline to enable the corporation to pay outstanding bills and acquire inventory. [The debt to the Nakashes and their controlled entities subsequently increased.] . . . At the time of the court-ordered sale of assets, the Nakashes and their entities were general creditors of Gasoline. If allowed in full the Nakashes' claim will exhaust Gasoline's assets, leaving nothing for its shareholders.

The parties agree that the loans made by the Nakashes to Gasoline were interested transactions. . . . It is also not disputed that, given the control deadlock, the questioned transactions did not receive majority approval of Gasoline's directors or shareholders. The Marcianos argue that the loan transaction is voidable at the option of the corporation notwithstanding its fairness or the good faith of its participants. A review of this contention, rejected by the Court of Chancery, requires analysis of the concept of director self-dealing under Delaware law.

II

It is a long-established principle of Delaware corporate law that the fiduciary relationship between directors and the corporation imposes fundamental limitations on the extent to which a director may benefit from dealings with the corporation he serves. Guth v. Loft, Inc., Del. Supr., 5 A.2d 503 (1939). Thus, the "voting [for] and taking" of compensation may be deemed "constructively fraudulent" in the absence of shareholder ratification, or statutory or bylaw authorization. Cahall v. Lofland, Del. Ch., 114 A. 224, 232 (1921). Perhaps the strongest condemnation of interested director conduct appears in Potter v. Sanitary Co. of America, Del. Ch., 194 A. 87 (1937), a decision which the Marcianos advance as definitive of the rule of per se voidability. In *Potter* the Court of Chancery characterized transactions between corporations having common directors and officers "constructively fraudulent," absent shareholder ratification.

Support can also be found for the per se rule of voidability in this Court's decision in Kerbs v. California Eastern Airways Inc., Del. Supr., 90 A.2d 652 (1952). The *Kerbs* court, in considering the validity of a profit sharing plan, ruled that the self-interest of the directors who voted on the plan caused the transaction to be voidable. The court concluded that the profit sharing plan was voidable based on the common law rule that the vote of an interested director will not be counted in determining whether the challenged action received the affirmative vote of a majority of the board of directors. *Id.* at 658.

The principle of per se voidability for interested transactions, which is sometimes characterized as the common law rule, was significantly ameliorated by the 1967 enactment of Section 144 of the Delaware General Corporation Law [set out above]. The Marcianos argue that section 144(a) provides the only basis for immunizing self-interested transactions and since none of the statute's component tests are satisfied the stricture of the common law per se rule applies. The Vice Chancellor agreed that the disputed loans did not withstand a section 144(a) analysis but ruled that the common law rule did not invalidate transactions determined to be intrinsically fair. We agree that section 144(a) does not provide the only validation standard for interested transactions.

It overstates the common law rule to conclude that relationship, alone, is the controlling factor in interested transactions. Although the application of the per se voidability rule in early Delaware cases resulted in the invalidation of interested transactions, the result was not dictated simply by a tainted relationship. Thus in *Potter*, the Court, while adopting the rule of voidability, emphasized that interested transactions should be subject to close scrutiny. Where the undisputed evidence tended to show that the transaction would advance the personal interests of the directors at the expense of stockholders, the stockholders, upon discovery, are entitled to disavow the transaction. *Potter*, 194 A. at 91. Further, the court examined the motives of the defendant directors and the effect the transaction had on the corporation and its shareholders. *Id.*

In other Delaware cases, decided before the enactment of section 144, interested director transactions were deemed voidable only after an examination of the fairness of a particular transaction vis-à-vis the nonparticipating shareholders and a determination of whether the disputed conduct received the approval of a noninterested majority of directors or shareholders. Keenan v. Eshleman, Del. Supr., 2 A.2d 904, 908 (1938); Blish v. Thompson Automatic Arms Corp., Del. Supr., 64 A.2d 581, 602 (1948); *Kerbs*, 90 A.2d at 658. The latter test is now crystallized in the ratification criteria of section 144(a), although the non-quorum restriction of *Kerbs* has been superceded by the language of subparagraph (b) of section 144.

The Marcianos view compliance with section 144 as the sole basis for avoiding the per se rule of voidability. The Court of Chancery rejected this contention and we agree that it is not consonant with Delaware corporate law. This Court in Fliegler v. Lawrence, Del. Supr., 361 A.2d 218 (1976), a post-section 144 decision, refused to view section 144 as either completely preemptive of the common law duty of director fidelity or as constituting a grant of broad immunity. As we stated in *Fliegler*: "It merely removes an 'interested director' cloud when its terms are met and provides against invalidation of an agreement 'solely' because such a director or officer is involved." *Id.* at 222. In *Fliegler* this Court applied a two-tiered analysis: application of section 144 coupled with an intrinsic fairness test.

If section 144 validation of interested director transactions is not deemed exclusive, as *Fliegler* clearly holds, the continued viability of the intrinsic fairness test is mandated not only by fact situations, such as here present, where shareholder deadlock prevents ratification but also where shareholder control by interested directors precludes independent review. Indeed, if an independent committee of the board, contemplated by section 144(a)(1) is unavailable, the sole forum for demonstrating intrinsic fairness may be a judicial one. See Merritt v. Colonial Foods, Inc., Del. Ch., 505 A.2d 757, 764 (1986). In such situations the intrinsic fairness test furnishes the substantive standard against which the evidential burden of the interested directors is applied. . . .

This case illustrates the limitation inherent in viewing section 144 as the touchstone for testing interested director transactions. Because of the shareholder deadlock, even if the Nakashes had attempted to invoke section 144, it was realistically unavailable. The ratification process contemplated by section 144 presupposes the functioning of corporate constituencies capable of providing assents. Just as the statute cannot "sanction unfairness" neither can it invalidate fairness if, upon judicial review, the transaction withstands close scrutiny of its intrinsic elements.[5] . . .

———————

It is worth reiterating that the multiple uses of the term "ratification" may partially explain the complexity of governing law. Although *Wheelabrator*, below, can be a little hard to understand, Chancellor Jacobs's opinion is an erudite and authoritative summary of the law.

IN RE WHEELABRATOR TECHNOLOGIES, INC. SHAREHOLDERS LITIGATION

Court of Chancery of Delaware
663 A.2d 1194 (1995)

JACOBS, Vice Chancellor. . . .

[Waste Management, Inc. ("Waste") was a 22 percent holder of Wheelabrator Technologies, Inc. (WTI). Waste elected four of WTI's eleven directors. A merger of the two companies was proposed. The seven non-Waste directors of

———————

5. Although in this case none of the curative steps afforded under section 144(a) were available because of the director-shareholder deadlock, a non-disclosing director seeking to remove the cloud of interestedness would appear to have the same burden under section 144(a)(3), as under prior case law, of proving the intrinsic fairness of a questioned transaction which had been approved or ratified by the directors or shareholders. Folk, The Delaware General Corp. Law: A Commentary and Analysis, 86 (1972). On the other hand, approval by fully-informed disinterested directors under section 144(a)(1), or disinterested stockholders under section 144(a)(2), permits invocation of the business judgment rule and limits judicial review to issues of gift or waste, with the burden of proof upon the party attacking the transaction.

WTI met and approved the merger (in a fashion the court found to satisfy duty of care standards). The four WTI directors joined the meeting, and the entire board re-approved the transaction. The shareholders subsequently also approved the transaction after receiving a proxy statement the court found to satisfy disclosure requirements. The discussion that follows relates only to the effect of the shareholder vote on the claim that the transaction should be avoided as a violation of the duty of loyalty.]

> **Connections: M&A**
>
> Corporate acquisitions present special considerations that are considered further in Part 5 of this book.

The question of whether or not shareholder ratification should operate to extinguish a duty of loyalty claim cannot be decided in a vacuum, divorced from the broader issue of what generally are the legal consequences of a fully-informed shareholder approval of a challenged transaction. The Delaware case law addressing that broader topic is not reducible to a single clear rule or unifying principle. Indeed, the law in that area might be thought to lack coherence because the decisions addressing the effect of shareholder "ratification" have fragmented that subject into three distinct compartments, only one of which involves "claim extinguishment."

The basic structure of stockholder ratification law is, at first glance, deceptively simple. Delaware law distinguishes between acts of directors (or management) that are "void" and acts that are "voidable." As the Supreme Court stated in Michelson v. Duncan, 407 A.2d 211, 218-19 (1979):

> The essential distinction between voidable and void acts is that the former are those which may be found to have been performed in the interest of the corporation but beyond the authority of management, as distinguished from acts which are ultra vires, fraudulent, or waste of corporate assets. The practical distinction, for our purposes, is that voidable acts are susceptible to cure by shareholder approval while void acts are not. (citations omitted).

One possible reading of *Michelson* is that all "voidable" acts are "susceptible to cure by shareholder approval." Under that reading, shareholder ratification might be thought to constitute a "full defense" (407 A.2d at 219) that would automatically extinguish all claims challenging such acts as a breach of fiduciary duty. Any such reading, however, would be overbroad, because the case law governing the consequences of ratification does not support that view and, in fact, is far more complex.

The Delaware Supreme Court has found shareholder ratification of "voidable" director conduct to result in claim-extinguishment in only two circumstances. The first is where the directors act in good faith, but exceed the board's de jure authority. . . . The second circumstance is where the directors fail "to reach an informed business judgment" in approving a transaction.

Except for these two situations, no party has identified any type of board action that the Delaware Supreme Court has deemed "voidable" for claim extinguishment purposes. More specifically, no Supreme Court case has held that shareholder ratification operates automatically to extinguish a duty of loyalty claim. To the contrary, the ratification cases involving duty of loyalty claims have uniformly held that the effect of shareholder ratification is to alter the standard of review, or to shift the burden of proof, or both. Those cases further frustrate any effort to describe the "ratification" landscape in terms of a simple rule.

The ratification decisions that involve duty of loyalty claims are of two kinds: (a) "interested" transaction cases between a corporation and its directors (or between the corporation and an entity in which the corporation's directors are also directors or have a financial interest), and (b) cases involving a transaction between the corporation and its controlling shareholder.

Regarding the first category, 8 Del. C. §144(a)(2) pertinently provides that an "interested" transaction of this kind will not be voidable if it is approved in good faith by a majority of disinterested stockholders. Approval by fully informed, disinterested shareholders pursuant to §144(a)(2) invokes "the business judgment rule and limits judicial review to issues of gift or waste with the burden of proof upon the party attacking the transaction." Marciano v. Nakash, Del. Supr., 535 A.2d 400, 405 n. 3 (1987). The result is the same in "interested" transaction cases not decided under §144:

> Where there has been independent shareholder ratification of interested director actions, the objecting stockholder has the burden of showing that no person of ordinary sound business judgment would say that the consideration received for the options was a fair exchange for the options granted.

Michelson, 407 A.2d at 224. . . .

The second category concerns duty of loyalty cases arising out of transactions between the corporation and its controlling stockholder. Those cases involve primarily parent-subsidiary mergers that were conditioned upon receiving "majority of the minority" stockholder approval. In a parent-subsidiary merger, the standard of review is ordinarily entire fairness, with the directors having the burden of proving that the merger was entirely fair. But where the merger is conditioned upon approval by a "majority of the minority" stockholder vote, and such approval is granted, the standard of review remains entire fairness, but the burden of demonstrating that the merger was unfair shifts to the plaintiff. . . . That burden-shifting effect of ratification has also been held applicable in cases involving mergers with a de facto controlling stockholder, and in a case involving a transaction other than a merger. . . .

Having determined what effect shareholder ratification does not have, the Court must now determine what effect it does have. The plaintiffs argue that their duty of loyalty claim is governed by the entire fairness standard, with ratification operating only to shift the burden on the fairness issue to the plaintiffs. That is incorrect, because

A Shifting Burden

this merger did not involve an interested and controlling stockholder. . . . The participation of the controlling interested stockholder is critical to the application of the entire fairness standard because . . . the potential for process manipulation by the controlling stockholder, and the concern that the controlling stockholder's continued presence might influence even a fully informed shareholder vote, justify the need for the exacting judicial scrutiny and procedural protection afforded by the entire fairness form of review. . . .

This may help . . .

This is one way — but only one — of thinking about what the court seemed to be saying in *Wheelabrator*. The starting point, of course, is that one is considering an interested transaction.

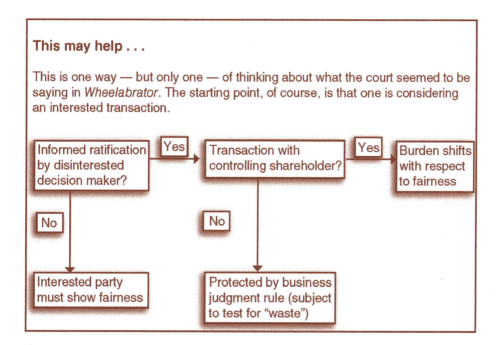

Think about this:

(I) Who had the burden of proof in *Wheelabrator*? What did the "burdened" party need to show to win?

(J) Suppose that the plaintiff was able to show that the merger price in *Wheelabrator* clearly was unfair and was approved only because most of the shareholders did not read their proxy materials and, instead, simply cast their votes as management suggested? Would that make a difference to the outcome?

A few other nuances have been added by subsequent Delaware case law. Some are explained in litigation involving a loan made to a corporation, known as The Nostalgia Network (TNN), by two of its directors. The loans were made at a time when TNN was in dire financial straits and all of its directors believed emergency action was called for. The company had received outside advice that there was no realistic chance of outside financing, and so as a last resort two of the directors—Salkind and Oolie—loaned their own money. They proposed the initial loan terms, though those terms were modified through negotiation with the firm. The loans were then unanimously approved by TNN's four-member board of directors, including Salkind and Oolie.

In Cooke v. Oolie, 1997 WL 367034 (Del. Ch. 1997), plaintiffs were TNN shareholders who alleged that Salkind and Oolie had violated their duty of loyalty, and argued that notwithstanding the purported "ratification" by the independent directors, Salkind and Oolie bore the burden of proving their loans' "intrinsic fairness." The court disagreed, explaining as follows:

> . . . [E]ven if a board's action falls within the safe harbor of [Delaware General Corporate Code] section 144, the board is not entitled to receive the protection of the business judgment rule. Compliance with section 144 merely shifts the burden to the plaintiffs to demonstrate that the transaction was unfair. . . .
>
> The fact that plaintiffs do not challenge the independence of the approving directors does not automatically entitle the defendants to rely on the safe harbor of section 144 or automatically shift to the plaintiffs the burden of showing that the transaction was unfair. . . . [Section] 144(a)(1) provides that a transaction between a corporation and one (or more) of its directors shall not be void solely because that director participated in authorizing the transaction if:
>
>> The material facts as to his relationship or interest and as to the contract or transaction are disclosed or known to the board of directors or to the committee, and the board or committee in good faith authorizes the contract or transaction by the affirmative votes of a majority of the disinterested directors, even though the disinterested directors be less than a quorum.
>
> Whether a transaction has been approved under the circumstances described above depends upon the particular facts of the case. There is no question here that the interests of Oolie and Salkind were known to the other Board members. Moreover, the evidence does not suggest . . . that the approving Board members were personally interested in the transaction or beholden to Oolie or Salkind. But for me to conclude that the disinterested directors' approval of the transaction shifted the burden of demonstrating the unfairness of the transaction to the plaintiffs, the defendants must demonstrate that they are entitled to rely on section 144(a)(1). That is, they carry the burden of demonstrating that the directors approving the loan were "truly independent, fully informed, and had the freedom to negotiate at arm's length." Evidence that the "action taken as though each of the contending parties had in fact exerted its bargaining power against the other at arm's length is strong evidence that the transaction meets the test of fairness."

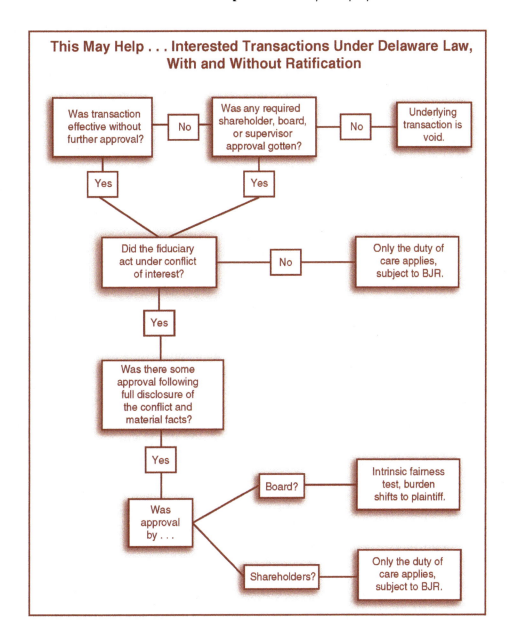

This May Help . . . Interested Transactions Under Delaware Law, With and Without Ratification

Think about this:

(K) Suppose that three members of a five-member board of directors are willing to loan the corporation much-needed funds. The two "disinterested" directors think it is a good idea. How should the approval be structured?

C. Corporate Opportunities

In the words of the Supreme Court of Delaware in the *Broz* case, presented below, "[c]ases involving a claim of usurpation of a corporate opportunity range over a multitude of factual settings. Hard and fast rules are not easily crafted to deal with such an array of complex situations." That has not stopped courts— and others, such as the American Law Institute—from trying to develop clearer guidance.

BROZ V. CELLULAR INFORMATION SYSTEMS, INC.

Supreme Court of Delaware
673 A.2d 148 (1996)

VEASEY, Chief Justice:

In this appeal, we consider the application of the doctrine of corporate opportunity. The Court of Chancery decided that the defendant, a corporate director, breached his fiduciary duty by not formally presenting to the corporation an opportunity which had come to the director individually and independent of the director's relationship with the corporation. Here the opportunity was not one in which the corporation in its current mode had an interest or which it had the financial ability to acquire, but, under the unique circumstances here, that mode was subject to change by virtue of the impending acquisition of the corporation by another entity.

We conclude that, although a corporate director may be shielded from liability by offering to the corporation an opportunity which has come to the director independently and individually, the failure of the director to present the opportunity does not necessarily result in the improper usurpation of a corporate opportunity. We further conclude that, if the corporation is a target or potential target of an acquisition by another company which has an interest and ability to entertain the opportunity, the director of the target company does not have a fiduciary duty to present the opportunity to the target company. Accordingly, the judgment of the Court of Chancery [holding that Broz diverted a corporate opportunity properly belonging to CIS and imposing a constructive trust] is REVERSED.

I. THE CONTENTIONS OF THE PARTIES AND THE DECISION BELOW

Robert F. Broz ("Broz") is the President and sole stockholder of RFB Cellular, Inc. ("RFBC"), a Delaware corporation engaged in the business of providing cellular telephone service in the Midwestern United States. At the time of the conduct at issue in this appeal, Broz was also a member of the board of directors of plaintiff below-appellee, Cellular Information Systems, Inc. ("CIS"). CIS is a publicly held Delaware corporation and a competitor of RFBC. [CIS was fully aware of Broz' relationship with RFBC.]

The conduct before the Court involves the purchase by Broz of a cellular telephone service license for the benefit of RFBC.[6] The license in question, known as the Michigan-2 Rural Service Area Cellular License ("Michigan-2"), is issued by the Federal Communications Commission ("FCC") and entitles its holder to provide cellular telephone service to a portion of northern Michigan. [The Michigan-2 license was offered to RFBC but not to CIS; CIS was disregarded because of its known financial difficulties. Broz discussed the opportunity with the chief executive officer of CIS and two of its board members, all of whom confirmed that CIS would not be interested. In addition, all of the CIS directors testified that they each would have responded the same way, if asked.] CIS brought an action against Broz and RFBC for equitable relief, contending that the purchase of this license by Broz constituted a usurpation of a corporate opportunity properly belonging to CIS, irrespective of whether or not CIS was interested in the Michigan-2 opportunity at the time it was offered to Broz.

The principal basis for the contention of CIS is that PriCellular, Inc. ("PriCellular"), another cellular communications company which was contemporaneously engaged in [a friendly] acquisition of CIS, was interested in the Michigan-2 opportunity. [Essentially, PriCellular and RFBC engaged in a bidding war, which RFBC won, while PriCellular's purchase of CIS was pending completion of its financing. Nine days after RFBC's purchase, PriCellular closed its acquisition of CIS. Prior to that point, PriCellular owned no equity interest in CIS. Subsequent to the consummation of the PriCellular tender offer for CIS, members of the CIS board of directors, including Broz, were discharged and replaced with a slate of PriCellular nominees.] CIS contends that, in determining whether the Michigan-2 opportunity rightfully belonged to CIS, Broz was required to consider the interests of PriCellular insofar as those interests would come into alignment with those of CIS as a result of PriCellular's acquisition plans. . . .

IV. APPLICATION OF THE CORPORATE OPPORTUNITY DOCTRINE

The doctrine of corporate opportunity represents but one species of the broad fiduciary duties assumed by a corporate director or officer. A corporate fiduciary agrees to place the interests of the corporation before his or her own in appropriate circumstances. In light of the diverse and often competing obligations faced by directors and officers, however, the corporate opportunity doctrine arose as a means of defining the parameters of fiduciary duty in instances of potential conflict. The classic statement of the doctrine is derived from the venerable case of Guth v. Loft, Inc.[, 5 A.2d 503 (Del. 1939)]. In *Guth*, this Court held that:

---

6. The Court recognizes that the actual purchase of the Michigan-2 license was consummated by RFBC as a corporate entity, rather than by Broz acting as an individual for his own benefit. Broz is, however, the sole party in interest in RFBC and all actions taken by RFBC, including the acquisition of Michigan-2, are accomplished at the behest of Broz. Therefore, insofar as the purchase of Michigan-2 is concerned, the Court will not distinguish between the actions of Broz and those of RFBC in analyzing Broz' alleged breach of fiduciary duty.

if there is presented to a corporate officer or director a business opportunity which the corporation is financially able to undertake, is, from its nature, in the line of the corporation's business and is of practical advantage to it, is one in which the corporation has an interest or a reasonable expectancy, and, by embracing the opportunity, the self-interest of the officer or director will be brought into conflict with that of the corporation, the law will not permit him to seize the opportunity for himself. *Guth*, 5 A.2d at 510-11.

The corporate opportunity doctrine, as delineated by *Guth* and its progeny, holds that a corporate officer or director may not take a business opportunity for his own if: (1) the corporation is financially able to exploit the opportunity; (2) the opportunity is within the corporation's line of business; (3) the corporation has an interest or expectancy in the opportunity; and (4) by taking the opportunity for his own, the corporate fiduciary will thereby be placed in a position inimicable to his duties to the corporation. The Court in *Guth* also derived a corollary which states that a director or officer may take a corporate opportunity if: (1) the opportunity is presented to the director or officer in his individual and not his corporate capacity; (2) the opportunity is not essential to the corporation; (3) the corporation holds no interest or expectancy in the opportunity; and (4) the director or officer has not wrongfully employed the resources of the corporation in pursuing or exploiting the opportunity. *Guth*, 5 A.2d at 509.

Thus, the contours of this doctrine are well established. It is important to note, however, that the tests enunciated in *Guth* and subsequent cases provide guidelines to be considered by a reviewing court in balancing the equities of an individual case. No one factor is dispositive, and all factors must be taken into account insofar as they are applicable. Cases involving a claim of usurpation of a corporate opportunity range over a multitude of factual settings. Hard and fast rules are not easily crafted to deal with such an array of complex situations. . . . In the instant case, we find that the facts do not support the conclusion that Broz misappropriated a corporate opportunity.

We note at the outset that Broz became aware of the Michigan-2 opportunity in his individual and not his corporate capacity. As the Court of Chancery found, "Broz did not misuse proprietary information that came to him in a corporate capacity nor did he otherwise use any power he might have over the governance of the corporation to advance his own interests." This fact is not the subject of serious dispute. In fact, it is clear from the record that Mackinac did not consider CIS a viable candidate for the acquisition of Michigan-2. Accordingly, Mackinac did not offer the property to CIS. In this factual posture, many of the fundamental concerns undergirding the law of corporate opportunity are not present (e.g., misappropriation of the corporation's proprietary information). The burden imposed upon Broz to show adherence to his fiduciary duties to CIS is thus lessened to some extent. . . . Nevertheless, this fact is not dispositive. . . .

We turn now to an analysis of the factors relied on by the trial court. First, we find that CIS was not financially capable of exploiting the Michigan-2 opportunity. . . . The record shows that CIS was in a precarious financial position at the time Mackinac presented the Michigan-2 opportunity to Broz. Having recently emerged from lengthy and contentious bankruptcy proceedings, CIS was not in a position to commit capital to the acquisition of new assets. Further, the loan agreement entered into by CIS and its creditors severely limited the discretion of CIS as to the acquisition of new assets and substantially restricted the ability of CIS to incur new debt....

Second, while it may be said with some certainty that the Michigan-2 opportunity was within CIS' line of business, it is not equally clear that CIS had a cognizable interest or expectancy in the license.[7] Under the third factor laid down by this Court in *Guth*, for an opportunity to be deemed to belong to the fiduciary's corporation, the corporation must have an interest or expectancy in that opportunity.... At the time the opportunity was presented, CIS was actively engaged in the process of divesting its cellular license holdings. CIS' articulated business plan did not involve any new acquisitions. Further, as indicated by the testimony of the entire CIS board, the Michigan-2 license would not have been of interest to CIS even absent CIS' financial difficulties and CIS' then current desire to liquidate its cellular license holdings. Thus, CIS had no interest or expectancy in the Michigan-2 opportunity....

Finally, the corporate opportunity doctrine is implicated only in cases where the fiduciary's seizure of an opportunity results in a conflict between the fiduciary's duties to the corporation and the self-interest of the director as actualized by the exploitation of the opportunity. In the instant case, Broz' interest in acquiring and profiting from Michigan-2 created no duties that were inimicable to his obligations to CIS. Broz, at all times relevant to the instant appeal, was the sole party in interest in RFBC, a competitor of CIS. CIS was fully aware of Broz' potentially conflicting duties. Broz, however, comported himself in a manner that was wholly in accord with his obligations to CIS. Broz took care not to usurp any opportunity which CIS was willing and able to pursue. Broz sought only to compete with an outside entity, PriCellular, for acquisition of an opportunity which both sought to possess. Broz was not obligated to refrain from competition with PriCellular. Therefore, the totality of the circumstances indicates that Broz did not usurp an opportunity that properly belonged to CIS.

A. Presentation to the Board: . . .

The teaching of *Guth* and its progeny is that the director or officer must analyze the situation ex ante to determine whether the opportunity is one rightfully

---

7. The language in the *Guth* opinion relating to "line of business" is less than clear:

> Where a corporation is engaged in a certain business, and an opportunity is presented to it embracing an activity as to which it has fundamental knowledge, practical experience and *ability to pursue*, which, logically and naturally, is adaptable to its business *having regard for its financial position*, and *is consonant with its reasonable needs and aspirations for expansion*, it may properly be said that the opportunity is within the corporation's line of business.

Guth, 5 A.2d at 514 (emphasis supplied). This formulation of the definition of the term "line of business" suggests that the business strategy and financial well-being of the corporation are also relevant to a determination of whether the opportunity is within the corporation's line of business. Since we find that these considerations are decisive under the other factors enunciated by the Court in *Guth*, we do not reach the question of whether they are here relevant to a determination of the corporation's line of business.

belonging to the corporation. If the director or officer believes, based on one of the factors articulated above, that the corporation is not entitled to the opportunity, then he may take it for himself. Of course, presenting the opportunity to the board creates a kind of "safe harbor" for the director, which removes the specter of a post hoc judicial determination that the director or officer has improperly usurped a corporate opportunity. Thus, presentation avoids the possibility that an error in the fiduciary's assessment of the situation will create future liability for breach of fiduciary duty. It is not the law of Delaware that presentation to the board is a necessary prerequisite to a finding that a corporate opportunity has not been usurped. . . .

B. Alignment of Interests Between CIS and PriCellular:

. . . Broz was under no duty to consider the interests of PriCellular when he chose to purchase Michigan-2. As stated in *Guth*, a director's right to "appropriate [an] . . . opportunity depends on the circumstances existing at the time it presented itself to him without regard to subsequent events." *Guth*, 5 A.2d at 513. At the time Broz purchased Michigan-2, PriCellular had not yet acquired CIS. Any plans to do so would still have been wholly speculative. Accordingly, Broz was not required to consider the contingent and uncertain plans of PriCellular in reaching his determination of how to proceed. . . .

In reaching our conclusion on this point, we note that certainty and predictability are values to be promoted in our corporation law. Broz, as an active participant in the cellular telephone industry, was entitled to proceed in his own economic interest in the absence of any countervailing duty. The right of a director or officer to engage in business affairs outside of his or her fiduciary capacity would be illusory if these individuals were required to consider every potential, future occurrence in determining whether a particular business strategy would implicate fiduciary duty concerns. In order for a director to engage meaningfully in business unrelated to his or her corporate role, the director must be allowed to make decisions based on the situation as it exists at the time a given opportunity is presented. Absent such a rule, the corporate fiduciary would be constrained to refrain from exploiting any opportunity for fear of liability based on the occurrence of subsequent events. This state of affairs would unduly restrict officers and directors and would be antithetical to certainty in corporation law. . . .

■ Think about this:

(L) The test described in *Broz* is known as the "line of business" test. Is that an accurate name?

(M) Suppose that at the time Broz acquired the Michigan-2 license PriCellular already had acquired a majority interest in CIS. Would that have made a difference to the analysis?

> *(N)* Nita is a director of Night Corp., which owns and operates a chain of hotels. While so serving, she reads in a real estate ad that there is a hotel property for sale that would be of great interest to Night Corp. She knows, however, that Night does not currently have enough cash to buy it. She resigns from Night Corp.'s board and then purchases the property for herself. Is that any sort of problem?

Delaware is, of course, Delaware, and its case law is important in its own right, due to the large number of corporations governed by its law. It also has a great deal of influence on decisions in other jurisdictions. In the area of corporate opportunity, however, its influence is less pronounced, because the line of business test has been so heavily criticized. The court in the following case discusses competing approaches, and adopts one that it hopes will provide more clarity.

NORTHEAST HARBOR GOLF CLUB, INC. V. HARRIS

Supreme Judicial Court of Maine
661 A.2d 1146 (1995)

ROBERTS, Justice.

Northeast Harbor Golf Club, Inc., appeals from a judgment entered in the Superior Court (Hancock County, Atwood, J.) following a nonjury trial. The Club maintains that the trial court erred in finding that Nancy Harris did not breach her fiduciary duty as president of the Club by purchasing and developing property abutting the golf course. Because we today adopt principles different from those applied by the trial court in determining that Harris's activities did not constitute a breach of the corporate opportunity doctrine, we vacate the judgment.

I. THE FACTS

Nancy Harris was the president of the Northeast Harbor Golf Club, a Maine corporation, from 1971 until she was asked to resign in 1990. The Club also had a board of directors that was responsible for making or approving significant policy decisions. The Club's only major asset was a golf course in Mount Desert. During Harris's tenure as president, the board occasionally discussed the possibility of developing some of the Club's real estate in order to raise money. Although Harris was generally in favor of tasteful development, the board always "shied away" from that type of activity.

In 1979, Robert Suminsby informed Harris that he was the listing broker for the Gilpin property, which comprised three noncontiguous parcels located among the fairways of the golf course. The property included an unused right-of-way on which the Club's parking lot and clubhouse were located. It was also encumbered by an easement in favor of the Club allowing foot traffic from the green of one hole to the next tee. Suminsby testified that he contacted Harris because she was the president of the Club and he believed that the Club would be interested in buying the property in order to prevent development.

Harris immediately agreed to purchase the Gilpin property in her own name for the asking price of $45,000. She did not disclose her plans to purchase the property to the Club's board prior to the purchase. She informed the board at its annual August meeting that she had purchased the property, that she intended to hold it in her own name, and that the Club would be "protected." The board took no action in response to the Harris purchase. . . .

In 1984, while playing golf with the postmaster of Northeast Harbor, Harris learned that a parcel of land owned by the heirs of the Smallidge family might be available for purchase. The Smallidge parcel was surrounded on three sides by the golf course and on the fourth side by a house lot. It had no access to the road. . . . Harris testified that she told a number of individual board members about her attempt to acquire the Smallidge parcel. At a board meeting in August 1985, Harris formally disclosed to the board that she had purchased the Smallidge property. . . . Again, the board took no formal action as a result of Harris's purchase. Harris acquired the Smallidge property from ten heirs, paying a total of $60,000. In 1990, Harris paid $275,000 for the lot and building separating the Smallidge parcel from the road in order to gain access to the otherwise landlocked parcel.

The trial court expressly found that the Club would have been unable to purchase either the Gilpin or Smallidge properties for itself, relying on testimony that the Club continually experienced financial difficulties, operated annually at a deficit, and depended on contributions from the directors to pay its bills. On the other hand, there was evidence that the Club had occasionally engaged in successful fund-raising, including a two-year period shortly after the Gilpin purchase during which the Club raised $115,000. The Club had $90,000 in a capital investment fund at the time of the Smallidge purchase.

. . . At the time the Club filed this suit, the property was divided into 11 lots, some owned by Harris and others by her children who are also defendants in this case. Harris estimated the value of all the real estate at the time of the trial to be $1,550,000. . . . Plans of Harris and her family for development of the other parcels are unclear, but the local zoning ordinance would permit construction of up to 11 houses on the land as currently divided.

After Harris's plans to develop [the property] became apparent, the board grew increasingly divided concerning the propriety of development near the golf course. . . . In particular, John Schafer, a Washington, D.C., lawyer and long-time member of the board, took issue with Harris's conduct. He testified that he had relied on Harris's representations at the time she acquired the properties that she would not develop them. According to Schafer, matters came to a head in August 1990 when a number of directors concluded that Harris's development plans irreconcilably conflicted with the Club's interests. As a result, Schafer and two other directors asked Harris to resign as president. In April 1991, after a substantial change in the board's membership, the board authorized the instant lawsuit against Harris for the breach of her fiduciary duty to act in the best interests of the corporation. The board simultaneously resolved that the proposed housing development was contrary to the best interests of the corporation. . . .

The trial court found that Harris had not usurped a corporate opportunity because the acquisition of real estate was not in the Club's line of business. Moreover, it found that the corporation lacked the financial ability to purchase the real estate at issue. Finally, the court placed great emphasis on Harris's good faith. It noted her long and dedicated history of service to the Club, her personal oversight of the Club's growth, and her frequent financial contributions to the Club. The court found that her development activities were "generally . . . compatible with the corporation's business." This appeal followed.

II. THE CORPORATE OPPORTUNITY DOCTRINE

Corporate officers and directors bear a duty of loyalty to the corporations they serve. As Justice Cardozo explained the fiduciary duty in Meinhard v. Salmon, 249 N.Y. 458, 164 N.E. 545, 546 (1928):

Justice Cardozo

> A trustee is held to something stricter than the morals of the marketplace. Not honesty alone, but the punctilio of an honor the most sensitive, is then the standard of behavior. As to this there has developed a tradition that is unbending and inveterate.

Maine has embraced this "unbending and inveterate" tradition. Corporate fiduciaries in Maine must discharge their duties in good faith with a view toward furthering the interests of the corporation. They must disclose and not withhold relevant information concerning any potential conflict of interest with the corporation, and they must refrain from using their position, influence, or knowledge of the affairs of the corporation to gain personal advantage. . . .

Various courts have embraced different versions of the corporate opportunity doctrine. The test applied by the trial court and embraced by Harris is generally known as the "line of business" test. The seminal case applying the line of business test is Guth v. Loft, Inc., 5 A.2d 503 (Del. 1939). In *Guth*, the Delaware Supreme Court adopted an intensely factual test stated in general terms as follows:

> [I]f there is presented to a corporate officer or director a business opportunity which the corporation is financially able to undertake, is, from its nature, in the line of the corporation's business and is of practical advantage to it, is one in which the corporation has an interest or a reasonable expectancy, and, by embracing the opportunity, the self-interest of the officer or director will be brought into conflict with that of his corporation, the law will not permit him to seize the opportunity for himself.

Id. at 511. The "real issue" under this test is whether the opportunity "was so closely associated with the existing business activities . . . as to bring the transaction within that class of cases where the acquisition of the property would throw the corporate officer purchasing it into competition with his company." *Id.* at 513. The Delaware court described that inquiry as "a factual question to be decided by reasonable inferences from objective facts." *Id.*

The line of business test suffers from some significant weaknesses. First, the question whether a particular activity is within a corporation's line of business is conceptually difficult to answer. The facts of the instant case demonstrate that difficulty. The Club is in the business of running a golf course. It is not in the business of developing real estate. In the traditional sense, therefore, the trial court correctly observed that the opportunity in this case was not a corporate opportunity within the meaning of the *Guth* test. Nevertheless, the record would support a finding that the Club had made the policy judgment that development of surrounding real estate was detrimental to the best interests of the Club. The acquisition of land adjacent to the golf course for the purpose of preventing future development would have enhanced the ability of the Club to implement that policy. The record also shows that the Club had occasionally considered reversing that policy and expanding its operations to include the development of surrounding real estate. Harris's activities effectively foreclosed the Club from pursuing that option with respect to prime locations adjacent to the golf course.

Second, the *Guth* test includes as an element the financial ability of the corporation to take advantage of the opportunity. The court in this case relied on the Club's supposed financial incapacity as a basis for excusing Harris's conduct. Often, the injection of financial ability into the equation will unduly favor the inside director or executive who has command of the facts relating to the finances of the corporation. Reliance on financial ability will also act as a disincentive to corporate executives to solve corporate financing and other problems. In addition, the Club could have prevented development without spending $275,000 to acquire the property Harris needed to obtain access to the road.

The Massachusetts Supreme Judicial Court adopted a different test in Durfee v. Durfee & Canning, Inc., 323 Mass. 187, 80 N.E.2d 522 (1948). The *Durfee* test has since come to be known as the "fairness test." According to *Durfee*, the

> true basis of governing doctrine rests on the unfairness in the particular circumstances of a director, whose relation to the corporation is fiduciary, taking advantage of an opportunity [for her personal profit] when the interest of the corporation justly call[s] for protection. This calls for application of ethical standards of what is fair and equitable . . . in particular sets of facts.

Id. at 529. As with the *Guth* test, the *Durfee* test calls for a broad-ranging, intensely factual inquiry. The *Durfee* test suffers even more than the *Guth* test from a lack of principled content. It provides little or no practical guidance to the corporate officer or director seeking to measure her obligations.

The Minnesota Supreme Court elected "to combine the 'line of business' test with the 'fairness' test." Miller v. Miller, 301 Minn. 207, 222 N.W.2d 71, 81 (1974). It engaged in a two-step analysis, first determining whether a particular opportunity was within the corporation's line of business, then scrutinizing "the equitable considerations existing prior to, at the time of, and following the officer's acquisition." *Id.* The *Miller* court hoped by adopting this approach "to ameliorate the often-expressed criticism that the [corporate opportunity] doctrine is vague and subjects today's corporate management to the danger of unpredictable liability." *Id.* In fact, the test adopted in *Miller* merely piles the uncertainty and vagueness of the fairness test on top of the weaknesses in the line of business test.

Despite the weaknesses of each of these approaches to the corporate opportunity doctrine, they nonetheless rest on a single fundamental policy. At bottom, the corporate opportunity doctrine recognizes that a corporate fiduciary should not serve both corporate and personal interests at the same time. . . . The various formulations of the test are merely attempts to moderate the potentially harsh consequences of strict adherence to that policy. It is important to preserve some ability for corporate fiduciaries to pursue personal business interests that present no real threat to their duty of loyalty.

III. THE AMERICAN LAW INSTITUTE APPROACH

In an attempt to protect the duty of loyalty while at the same time providing long-needed clarity and guidance for corporate decisionmakers, the American Law Institute has offered the most recently developed version of the corporate opportunity doctrine. Principles of Corporate Governance §5.05 (May 13, 1992), provides as follows:

§5.05 Taking of Corporate Opportunities by Directors or Senior Executives

(a) *General Rule.* A director [§1.13] or senior executive [§1.33] may not take advantage of a corporate opportunity unless:

(1) The director or senior executive first offers the corporate opportunity to the corporation and makes disclosure concerning the conflict of interest [§1.14(a)] and the corporate opportunity [§1.14(b)];

(2) The corporate opportunity is rejected by the corporation; and

(3) Either:

(A) The rejection of the opportunity is fair to the corporation;

(B) The opportunity is rejected in advance, following such disclosure, by disinterested directors [§1.15], or, in the case of a senior executive who is not a director, by a disinterested superior, in a manner that satisfies the standards of the business judgment rule [§4.01(c)]; or

(C) The rejection is authorized in advance or ratified, following such disclosure, by disinterested shareholders [§1.16], and the rejection is not equivalent to a waste of corporate assets [§1.42].

(b) *Definition of a Corporate Opportunity.* For purposes of this Section, a corporate opportunity means:

(1) Any opportunity to engage in a business activity of which a director or senior executive becomes aware, either:

(A) In connection with the performance of functions as a director or senior executive, or under circumstances that should reasonably lead the director or senior executive to believe that the person offering the opportunity expects it to be offered to the corporation; or

(B) Through the use of corporate information or property, if the resulting opportunity is one that the director or senior executive should reasonably be expected to believe would be of interest to the corporation; or

(2) Any opportunity to engage in a business activity of which a senior executive becomes aware and knows is closely related to a business in which the corporation is engaged or expects to engage. . . .

The central feature of the ALI test is the strict requirement of full disclosure prior to taking advantage of any corporate opportunity. *Id.*, §5.05(a)(1). "If the opportunity is not offered to the corporation, the director or senior executive will not have satisfied §5.05(a)." *Id.*, cmt. to §5.05(a). The corporation must then formally reject the opportunity. *Id.*, §5.05(a)(2). The ALI test is discussed at length and ultimately applied by the Oregon Supreme Court in Klinicki v. Lundgren, 298 Or. 662, 695 P.2d 906 (1985). As *Klinicki* describes the test, "full disclosure to the appropriate corporate body is . . . an absolute condition precedent to the validity of any forthcoming rejection as well as to the availability to the director or principal senior executive of the defense of fairness." *Id.* at 920. . . .

The ALI test defines "corporate opportunity" broadly. It includes opportunities "closely related to a business in which the corporation is engaged." *Id.*, §5.05(b). It also encompasses any opportunities that accrue to the fiduciary as a result of her position within the corporation. *Id.* This concept is most clearly illustrated by the testimony of Suminsby, the listing broker for the Gilpin property, which, if believed by the factfinder, would support a finding that the Gilpin property was offered to Harris specifically in her capacity as president of the Club. If the factfinder reached that conclusion, then at least the opportunity to acquire the Gilpin property would be a corporate opportunity. The state of the record concerning the Smallidge purchase precludes us from intimating any opinion whether that too would be a corporate opportunity.

Under the ALI standard, once the Club shows that the opportunity is a corporate opportunity, it must show either that Harris did not offer the opportunity to the Club or that the Club did not reject it properly. If the Club shows that the board did not reject the opportunity by a vote of the disinterested directors after full disclosure, then Harris may defend her actions on the basis that the taking of the opportunity was fair to the corporation. *Id.*, §5.05(c). If Harris failed to offer the opportunity at all, however, then she may not defend on the basis that the failure to offer the opportunity was fair. *Id.*, cmt. to §5.05(c).

The *Klinicki* court viewed the ALI test as an opportunity to bring some clarity to a murky area of the law. *Klinicki*, 695 P.2d at 915. We agree, and today we follow the ALI test. The disclosure-oriented approach provides a clear procedure whereby a corporate officer may insulate herself through prompt and complete disclosure from the possibility of a legal challenge. The requirement of disclosure recognizes the paramount importance of the corporate fiduciary's duty of loyalty. At the same time it protects the fiduciary's ability pursuant to the proper procedure to pursue her own business ventures free from the possibility of a lawsuit. . . .

Remanded for further proceedings consistent with the opinion herein.

———————————

The trial court held for the Club on remand. The Maine Supreme Court on appeal concluded that the Gilpin and Smallidge lots were "corporate opportunities" under Maine's new test and that defendant accordingly breached her fiduciary duty by not offering them to the Club. However, the court also held that the Club's action was barred by the statute of limitations.

> ■ **Think about this:**
>
> *(O)* Suppose that Mrs. Harris had purchased a piece of property adjoining the Club's golf course and had opened a meat packing plant on it. Would that present a corporate opportunity issue?
>
> *(P)* How would the *Northeast Harbor* case likely have come out under *Guth*? How about the meat-packing hypothetical?

Test Yourself

Questions 1-3 rely on the following facts:

ABC, Inc., a Delaware corporation, owns 65 percent of the voting stock of another Delaware company, XYZ, Inc. Another 25 percent of XYZ's shares are owned by the California Public Employees Retirement System ("CalPERS"), a major pension fund, which is not otherwise affiliated with either company. An XYZ bylaw provides that board candidates will be nominated by any shareholder with more than 50 percent of XYZ's voting stock. XYZ's Articles of Incorporation contain what commonly is known as a "raincoat" provision.

CalPERS has brought suit against ABC and against XYZ's entire board. CalPERS seeks money damages against ABC and an injunction against the XYZ directors, to remedy what CalPERS believes was an improperly motivated distribution of dividends to XYZ's shareholders. CalPERS puts on uncontroverted evidence that (1) at the time of the dividends, ABC was in great need of ready cash, and (2) the dividends in question exceeded XYZ's entire revenues for the year.

(Answers in Online Supplement)

1. ABC:

   a. Owes no fiduciary obligations to XYZ.
   b. Owes fiduciary duties in light of its ability to elect the board of directors.
   c. Is probably not a controlling shareholder of XYZ, in light of the consolidated, institutional ownership of the minority shares.
   d. None of the above.

2. Assuming that ABC does owe fiduciary duties to XYZ, in the CalPERS suit, ABC:

   a. Must show that the dividends were "intrinsically fair."
   b. Will win unless CalPERS can show that the dividends were "intrinsically unfair."
   c. Will be liable because dividends in excess of revenues are waste.
   d. Must defend its actions under the business judgment rule.

3. In the CalPERS suit, the XYZ directors:

   a. Must show that the dividends were "intrinsically fair."
   b. Will win unless CalPERS can show that the dividends were "intrinsically unfair."
   c. May be liable for monetary damages because the "raincoat" provision will not protect them.
   d. Must defend their actions under the business judgment rule.

Questions 4-6 rely on the following facts:

Tough Guys, Inc., a closely held company incorporated in Delaware, produces a magazine called Tough Guys Weekly. Tough Guys's CEO, Rufus McPiercedlip, recently got a call from a friend asking whether Tough Guys might be interested in investing in a new start-up magazine, to be called You Wouldn't Want to Meet Me in a Dark Alley, Illustrated. The friend tells Rufus that the company, Dark Alley, Inc., has a 10 percent block of its own stock set aside for purchase by the right investor, and would like it to go to someone with knowledge of the business, who could provide advice and insight from time to time. In fact, it occurs to Rufus that the new magazine would likely be a direct competitor of Tough Guys Weekly, and that it would hardly be wise for Tough Guys, Inc., to encourage its own competition. Rufus, however, is a man who knows how to hedge his bets, and he thinks this new magazine is likely to be a profitable enterprise, so without telling anyone at Tough Guys, Inc., he arranges to buy the 10 percent stake in Dark Alley with his own personal funds.

Billy Bob Tattooson is among the founders and is still a shareholder in Tough Guys, Inc., though he has been largely uninvolved in the company's affairs for some time. Billy Bob learns of Rufus's investment and he brings suit, alleging that in fact Tough Guys, Inc., should have been given the opportunity to invest in the 10 percent block of stock.

4. If the matter goes to trial, which of the following would be most damaging to Rufus?

    a. Dark Alley, Inc., was looking for an investor experienced in the magazine business.

    b. Rufus's friend contacted him in his official capacity as CEO of Tough Guys, Inc.

    c. Dark Alley's business probably will compete with Tough Guys's business.

    d. Rufus's failure to offer the Dark Alley investment opportunity to Tough Guys, Inc.

5. Rufus's purchase of the 10 percent block of stock creates a conflict of interest. True or False?

    a. True, because his fiduciary obligations to Tough Guys, Inc. may now be in conflict with his fiduciary obligations to Dark Alley, Inc.

    b. True, because his fiduciary obligations to Tough Guys, Inc. may be at odds with his own pecuniary interest.

    c. Answers a and b are both correct.

    d. False.

6. If Tough Guys, Inc., were incorporated in a state following the ALI approach to corporate opportunity, which of the following would be most damaging to Rufus at trial?

    a. Dark Alley, Inc., was looking for an investor experienced in the magazine business.

    b. Rufus's friend contacted him in his official capacity as CEO of Tough Guys, Inc.

    c. Dark Alley's business probably will compete with Tough Guys's business.

    d. Rufus's failure to offer the Dark Alley investment opportunity to Tough Guys, Inc.

Questions 7-10 rely on the following facts:

John is the chief executive officer and chairman of the board of BigCo, a publicly traded Delaware corporation. John believes the company should adopt a new compensation package in order to attract top quality young executives. In particular, he would like the company to adopt a plan he has devised that would entitle all executives of the company to receive shares of BigCo's stock as annual bonus compensation, based on performance. Concerned about structuring the plan properly, John seeks the opinion of an outside law firm and an outside corporate financial advisor. After some weeks of study, both reply favorably on the proposal and suggest it would be both legal and in the company's best interests. In particular, the financial advisor suggested that similar plans are in place at many similarly sized firms in BigCo's industry.

BigCo's board of directors has thirteen authorized seats, nine of which are currently filled. Of those nine, five are outside directors. At the meeting at which the stock compensation plan was first considered by the board, seven directors attended, including the four inside directors. After receiving a lengthy report from the same attorney and financial advisor who had given John their opinions, the seven board members present voted unanimously in favor of the stock compensation plan. The board members were concerned about potential conflicts of interest, however, so the three outside directors present then convened separately to consider the proposal again, and they unanimously approved it.

7. At the initial board meeting at which the stock compensation plan was first adopted, four of the seven board members who voted had conflicts of interest, and therefore the board's vote was ineffective and the plan in fact was not adopted. True or False?

    a. True, because the board lacked a quorum as to the stock compensation plan.
    b. True, because the conflicted votes cannot be counted, and therefore the plan did not receive a majority of the votes.
    c. True, unless the plan was later presented to the full board and approved again.
    d. False.

8. The subsequent vote by outside directors was ineffective as a ratification. True or False?

    a   True, because the board did not formally delegate authority to the committee.
    b. True, because the committee lacked a quorum.
    c. True, because the board that appointed the committee lacked a quorum.
    d. False.

9. The opinions presented by the outside attorney and financial advisor are relevant to which of the following:

    a. The substantive fairness of the plan.
    b. The procedural fairness of the plan.
    c. Compliance with the duty of care of the outside directors.
    d. All of the above.
    e. Answers a and b are correct.

10. If John is personally sued for his role in establishing the stock compensation plan, what standard will govern his liability?

    a. Intrinsic fairness, as to which John bears the burden of proof.
    b. Intrinsic fairness, as to which the plaintiff bears the burden of proof.
    c. Business judgment rule.
    d. John cannot be liable—ratification by the outside directors renders him immune from suit.

Questions 11-13 stand alone:

11. Marge N. O'Verra, a statistician and accountant by trade, has formed an accounting firm she calls Count de Monet, Inc. Marge has made herself CEO, sole director, and sole shareholder of Count de Monet. As she makes an outlandish number of errors, however, she thought it wise to secure some reliable source of White Out® correction fluid. For this purpose she formed a company with her friend Bob to provide this and other office supplies, which they call Supply, Inc. Bob was just a passive investor. He took 49 percent of Supply, Inc.'s stock and allowed Marge to act as CEO and sole director. If Bob were to sue Marge to challenge a contract for White Out® between Count de Monet, Inc. and Supply, Inc., which of the following facts, if true, would be most helpful to Marge in defending herself?

    a. In her capacity as CEO and director of Count de Monet, she observed all "corporate formalities."
    b. In her capacity as CEO and director of Supply, Inc., she observed all "corporate formalities."
    c. The contract's terms were comparable to those offered to other companies on similar supply arrangements.
    d. She really should not worry too much about such a suit, because it will be governed by the business judgment rule.

12. A corporate vice president who is also the treasurer of the corporation makes a loan of company funds to his best friend, subject to a stated rate of interest to be paid by the friend, to help the friend start a new business. The vice president:

    a. Has violated a fiduciary duty.
    b. Has probably violated a fiduciary duty if he did not disclose the loan to the company.
    c. Has violated a fiduciary duty unless the loan was rationally related to the best interests of the company.
    d. May not have violated a fiduciary duty if the interest is comparable to market rates.

13. In Delaware, informed, disinterested ratification of *ultra vires* board action renders the action:

    a. Void.
    b. Voidable at the election of the corporation.
    c. Subject to duty of care scrutiny under the business judgment rule.
    d. Impervious to legal challenge.

Further Problems in the Duty of Loyalty: Good Faith and Disclosure

20

In this chapter, we consider a few further issues that remain rather less settled than those in the last chapter. They can be thought of as problems in the duty of loyalty.

Duty of loyalty questions are basically simple when they involve the two traditional contexts we learned about in Chapter 19: "interested" transactions, in which a fiduciary makes some decision on behalf of the corporation while under a conflict of interest, and those in which a fiduciary takes some business opportunity that might benefit the corporation.

But a few other obligations, often said to be fiduciary, have been less clear. They became the focus of much controversy following legislative changes of the late 1980s, when a nation-wide stampede of state legislatures empowered corporations to limit directors' monetary liability exposure. While the resulting statutes—the so-called raincoat or exculpation statutes, such as Delaware's §102(b)(7), discussed further in Chapter 21—permitted limits on duty of care exposure, they typically still required full exposure to liability for breaches of loyalty and good faith. So it suddenly seemed important—especially to plaintiffs' attorneys—to explore applications of the duty of loyalty outside the traditional contexts of interested transactions and corporate opportunity. This led to speculation that "good faith" might be a loyalty obligation or some sort of freestanding duty of its own, and that there could be a duty to make disclosures that is not part of the duty of care. Both of those questions received much attention since the 1980s, and both have gotten at least some clarification from the courts. We explore them both in this chapter.

Chapter Outline

A. Good Faith

- A staple of the common law
- A pre-condition to satisfaction of the duty of loyalty

B. Disclosure

- A fiduciary is required to make full disclosure to the beneficiary about all matters related to the beneficiary's business
- Corporate fiduciaries sometimes owe a state corporate law duty of disclosure to the corporation's shareholders and prospective shareholders
- In Delaware, only deliberate (and possibly reckless) non-disclosure is a breach of the duty of loyalty

Test Yourself

A. Good Faith

The duty of "good faith" has been much raised and ill defined, but now seems, at least in Delaware, to be taking on discernible parameters. The following two cases—*In re The Walt Disney Co. Derivative Litigation* and *Stone v. Ritter*—are landmarks and worthy of careful attention.

The *In re The Walt Disney Co. Derivative Litigation* spanned almost ten years. The facts giving rise to it go on for 24 double-spaced pages in the final decision of the Delaware Supreme Court but can be grossly summarized as follows. In 1995, The Walt Disney Company entered into a five-year agreement employing Michael Ovitz, the hot-shot majority owner of a premier talent agency, as Disney's president. The agreement was approved by the Compensation Committee and the full board in a process that fairly could be called "expedited" (apparently consuming no more than an hour of discussion). Ovitz's services were deemed unsatisfactory, and he was terminated without cause 16 months later, triggering a pre-negotiated severance payment valued at around $130 million (which could have been avoided only if he were shown to be grossly negligent or malfeasant). Some of Disney's shareholders brought derivative claims against Ovitz, complaining, among other things, that his pre-negotiation of a bloated severance package

Michael Ovitz received over $300,000 in severance for each day he was employed by Disney.

was a breach of fiduciary duty. With respect to that particular claim, Ovitz was absolved of liability on the grounds that although he was privy to private Disney information during the negotiation, he did not assume the duties of a fiduciary until he actually assumed the position of president.

The shareholders also claimed that the members of the board had breached fiduciary duties and committed waste in connection with the handling of Ovitz's hiring and firing. The portion of the Delaware Supreme Court's opinion set forth below struggles with the claims relating to his hiring. (Those related to his firing and establishing waste were disposed of quite readily.)

IN RE THE WALT DISNEY CO. DERIVATIVE LITIGATION

Supreme Court of Delaware
906 A.2d 27 (2006)

. . . As earlier noted, the appellants' core argument in the trial court was that the Disney defendants' approval of [Ovitz's employment agreement] . . . and election of Ovitz as President were not entitled to business judgment rule protection, because those actions were either grossly negligent or not performed in good faith. The Court of Chancery rejected these arguments, and held that the appellants had failed to prove that the Disney defendants had breached any fiduciary duty. For clarity of presentation we address the claimed errors relating to the fiduciary duty of care rulings separately from those that relate to the directors' fiduciary duty to act in good faith.

1. THE DUE CARE DETERMINATIONS

. . . The appellants claim that the Chancellor erred by: (1) treating as distinct questions whether the plaintiffs had established by a preponderance of the evidence either gross negligence or a lack of good faith. . . .

This argument is best understood against the backdrop of the presumptions that cloak director action being reviewed under the business judgment standard. Our law presumes that "in making a business decision the directors of a corporation acted on an informed basis, in good faith, and in the honest belief that the action taken was in the best interests of the company." Those presumptions can be rebutted if the plaintiff shows that the directors breached their fiduciary duty of care or of loyalty or acted in bad faith. If that is shown, the burden then shifts to the director defendants to demonstrate that the challenged act or transaction was entirely fair to the corporation and its shareholders.

Because no duty of loyalty claim was asserted against the Disney defendants, the only way to rebut the business judgment rule presumptions would be to show that the Disney defendants had either breached their duty of care or had not acted in good faith. At trial, the plaintiff-appellants attempted to establish both grounds, but the Chancellor determined that the plaintiffs had failed to prove either. . . .

[The court here determined that it was not error for the Chancellor to have determined that the defendants had been adequately informed and thus were not in breach of the duty of care.]

2. THE GOOD FAITH DETERMINATIONS

The Court of Chancery held that the business judgment rule presumptions protected the decisions of the compensation committee and the remaining Disney directors, not only because they had acted with due care but also because they had not acted in bad faith. That latter ruling, the appellants claim, was reversible error because the Chancellor formulated and then applied an incorrect definition of bad faith.

In its Opinion the Court of Chancery defined bad faith as follows:

> Upon long and careful consideration, I am of the opinion that the concept of intentional dereliction of duty, a conscious disregard for one's responsibilities, is an appropriate (although not the only) standard for determining whether fiduciaries have acted in good faith. Deliberate indifference and inaction in the face of a duty to act is, in my mind, conduct that is clearly disloyal to the corporation. It is the epitome of faithless conduct.

. . . The appellants also assert that the Chancellor erred by imposing upon them the burden of proving that the Disney directors acted in bad faith. That argument fails because our decisions clearly hold that for purposes of rebutting the business judgment presumptions, the plaintiffs have the burden of proving bad faith. . . .

The appellants essentially concede that their proof of bad faith is insufficient to satisfy the standard articulated by the Court of Chancery. That is why they ask this Court to treat a failure to exercise due care as a failure to act in good faith. Unfortunately for appellants, that "rule," even if it were accepted, would not help their case. If we were to conflate these two duties and declare that a breach of the duty to be properly informed violates the duty to act in good faith, the outcome would be no different, because, as the Chancellor and we now have held, the appellants failed to establish any breach of the duty of care. . . . To say it differently, even if the Chancellor's definition of bad faith were erroneous, the error would not be reversible because the appellants cannot satisfy the very test they urge us to adopt.

For that reason, our analysis of the appellants' bad faith claim could end at this point. In other circumstances it would. This case, however, is one in which the duty to act in good faith has played a prominent role, yet to date is not a well-developed area of our corporate fiduciary law. . . . Because of the increased recognition of the importance of good faith, some conceptual guidance to the corporate community may be helpful. For that reason we proceed to address the merits of the appellants' second argument.

The precise question is whether the Chancellor's articulated standard for bad faith corporate fiduciary conduct—intentional dereliction of duty, a conscious disregard for one's responsibilities—is legally correct. In approaching that question, we note that the Chancellor characterized that definition as "an appropriate (although not the only) standard for determining whether fiduciaries have acted in good faith." That observation is accurate and helpful, because as a matter of simple logic, at least three different categories of fiduciary behavior are candidates for the "bad faith" pejorative label.

The first category involves so-called "subjective bad faith," that is, fiduciary conduct motivated by an actual intent to do harm. That such conduct constitutes classic, quintessential bad faith is a proposition so well accepted in the liturgy of fiduciary law that it borders on axiomatic. We need not dwell further on this category, because no such conduct is claimed to have occurred, or did occur, in this case.

The second category of conduct, which is at the opposite end of the spectrum, involves lack of due care—that is, fiduciary action taken solely by reason of gross negligence and without any malevolent intent. In this case, appellants assert claims of gross negligence to establish breaches not only of director due care but also of the directors' duty to act in good faith. Although the Chancellor found, and we agree, that the appellants failed to establish gross negligence, to afford guidance we address the issue of whether gross negligence (including a failure to inform one's self of available material facts), without more, can also constitute bad faith. The answer is clearly no. From a broad philosophical standpoint, that question is more complex than would appear, if only because (as the Chancellor and others have observed) "issues of good faith are (to a certain degree) inseparably and necessarily intertwined with the duties of care and loyalty. . . ." But, in the pragmatic, conduct-regulating legal realm which calls for more precise conceptual line drawing, the answer is that grossly negligent conduct, without more, does not and cannot constitute a breach of the fiduciary duty to act in good faith. The conduct that is the subject of due care may overlap with the conduct that comes within the rubric of good faith in a psychological sense, but from a legal standpoint those duties are and must remain quite distinct. Both our legislative history and our common law jurisprudence distinguish sharply between the duties to exercise due care and to act in good faith, and highly significant consequences flow from that distinction. . . .

That leaves the third category of fiduciary conduct, which falls in between the first two categories of (1) conduct motivated by subjective bad intent and (2) conduct resulting from gross negligence. This third category is what the Chancellor's definition of bad faith—intentional dereliction of duty, a conscious disregard for one's responsibilities—is intended to capture. The question is whether such misconduct is properly treated as a non-exculpable, nonindemnifiable violation of the fiduciary duty to act in good faith. In our view it must be, for at least two reasons.

First, the universe of fiduciary misconduct is not limited to either disloyalty in the classic sense (i.e., preferring the adverse self-interest of the fiduciary or of a related person to the interest of the corporation) or gross negligence. Cases have arisen where corporate directors have no conflicting self-interest in a decision, yet engage in misconduct that is more culpable than simple inattention or failure to be informed of all facts material to the decision. To protect the interests of the corporation and its shareholders, fiduciary conduct of this kind, which does not involve disloyalty (as traditionally defined) but is qualitatively more culpable than gross negligence, should be proscribed. A vehicle is needed to address such violations doctrinally, and that doctrinal vehicle is the duty to act in good faith. The Chancellor implicitly so recognized in his Opinion, where he identified different examples of bad faith as follows:

> The good faith required of a corporate fiduciary includes not simply the duties of care and loyalty, in the narrow sense that I have discussed them above, but all actions required by a true faithfulness and devotion to the interests of the corporation and its shareholders. A failure to act in good faith may be shown, for instance, where the fiduciary intentionally acts with a purpose other than that of advancing the best interests of the corporation, where the fiduciary acts with the intent to violate applicable positive law, or where the fiduciary intentionally fails to act in the face of a known duty to act, demonstrating a conscious disregard for his duties. There may be other examples of bad faith yet to be proven or alleged, but these three are the most salient.

Those articulated examples of bad faith are not new to our jurisprudence. Indeed, they echo pronouncements our courts have made throughout the decades. Second, the legislature has also recognized this intermediate category of fiduciary misconduct, which ranks between conduct involving subjective bad faith and gross negligence. Section 102(b)(7)(ii) of the DGCL expressly denies money damage exculpation for "acts or omissions not in good faith or which involve intentional misconduct or a knowing violation of law." By its very terms that provision distinguishes between "intentional misconduct" and a "knowing violation of law" (both examples of subjective bad faith) on the one hand, and "acts . . . not in good faith," on the other. Because the statute exculpates directors only for conduct amounting to gross negligence, the statutory denial of exculpation for "acts . . . not in good faith" must encompass the intermediate category of misconduct captured by the Chancellor's definition of bad faith.

For these reasons, we uphold the Court of Chancery's definition as a legally appropriate, although not the exclusive, definition of fiduciary bad faith. We need go no further. To engage in an effort to craft (in the Court's words) "a definitive and categorical definition of the universe of acts that would constitute bad faith" would be unwise and is unnecessary to dispose of the issues presented on this appeal. . . .

■ **Think about this:**

(A) After reading this opinion, does it seem that the duty of good faith is part of the duty of care, part of the duty of loyalty, or a separate duty? Does it make any difference?

(B) Would it have been possible, given what you know of the facts in *Disney*, to articulate a straight-face claim based on self-dealing or corporate opportunity?

(C) Suppose an elderly woman, depressed and subject to drinking heavily, serves on the board of a company that handles large sums in trust. She does not go to meetings and does not read financial statements, and thus fails to discover that her sons, who manage the business, have taken huge loans from the company that they are unable to repay. Has she acted with gross negligence or in bad faith? And, as a practical matter, would it make a difference?

 Time Out for PR

Although modern "raincoat" provisions seem to beg litigators to think creatively, there are limits—sort of. Model Rule of Professional Conduct 3.1 (Meritorious Claims and Contentions) provides that "[a] lawyer shall not bring or defend a proceeding, or assert or controvert an issue therein, unless there is a basis in law and fact for doing so that is not frivolous, which includes a good faith argument for an extension, modification or reversal of existing law. . . ."

In fact, following *Disney*, many academics concluded that good faith was a separate duty and rushed to speculate about its possible applications. *Stone v. Ritter* caused a course correction.

STONE V. RITTER

Supreme Court of Delaware
911 A.2d 362 (2006)

HOLLAND, Justice:

[AmSouth and a banking subsidiary paid $50 million in fines and civil penalties for failure to file "suspicious activity reports" in connection with a particular investment scheme conducted by a third party and involving some of the subsidiary's custodial trust accounts. It appears to have been conceded that the company's internal controls were inadequate to detect the scheme, but the trial court found no facts showing that the board ever was aware that AmSouth's internal controls were inadequate, or that these inadequacies would result in illegal activity. The Stones, who were shareholders of AmSouth, brought an action derivatively on behalf of the corporation against its directors. They did not make a demand on the board first, arguing that it would have been futile to do so since they would be required to decide whether to sue themselves. According to applicable Delaware law, "futility" is assessed as a matter of how likely it is that the board in fact would face liability on the underlying claim.

Because AmSouth's articles of incorporation contained a "raincoat" provision, the directors were exculpated for breaches of the duty of care, but not for conduct not in good faith or for breach of the duty of loyalty. The court thus is required to address whether the board's alleged conduct falls into one of these latter two categories.] . . .

GRAHAM AND CAREMARK

Graham [v. Allis-Chalmers Mfg., Inc., 188 A.2d 125 (Del. 1963),] was a derivative action brought against the directors of Allis-Chalmers for failure to prevent violations of federal anti-trust laws by Allis-Chalmers employees. There was no claim that the Allis-Chalmers directors knew of the employees' conduct that resulted in the corporation's liability. Rather, the plaintiffs claimed that the Allis-Chalmers directors *should have known* of the illegal conduct by the corporation's employees. In *Graham*, this Court held that *"absent cause for suspicion* there is no duty upon the directors to install and operate a corporate system of espionage to ferret out wrongdoing which they have no reason to suspect exists."

In [In re] Caremark International Inc. Derivative Litigation, [698 A.2d 959 (Del. Ch. 1996),] . . . [t]he plaintiffs claimed that the Caremark directors should have known that certain officers and employees of Caremark were involved in violations of the federal Anti-Referral Payments Law. That law prohibits health care providers from paying any form of remuneration to induce the referral of Medicare or Medicaid patients. The plaintiffs claimed that the *Caremark* directors breached their fiduciary duty for having "allowed a situation to develop and continue which exposed the corporation to enormous legal liability and that in so doing they violated a duty to be active monitors of corporate performance." . . .

The *Caremark* Court opined it would be a "mistake" to interpret this Court's decision in *Graham* to mean that:

> corporate boards may satisfy their obligation to be reasonably informed concerning the corporation, without assuring themselves that information and reporting systems exist in the organization that are reasonably designed to provide to senior management and to the board itself timely, accurate information sufficient to allow management and the board, each within its scope, to reach informed judgments concerning both the corporation's compliance with law and its business performance.

To the contrary, the Caremark Court stated, "it is important that the board exercise a good faith judgment that the corporation's information and reporting system is in concept and design adequate to assure the board that appropriate information will come to its attention in a timely manner as a matter of ordinary operations, so that it may satisfy its responsibility." The Caremark Court recognized, however, that "the duty to act in good faith to be informed cannot be thought to require directors to possess detailed information about all aspects of the operation of the enterprise." The Court of Chancery then formulated the following standard for assessing the liability of directors where the directors are unaware of employee misconduct that results in the corporation being held liable:

> Generally where a claim of directorial liability for corporate loss is predicated upon ignorance of liability creating activities within the corporation, as in *Graham* or in this case, . . . only a sustained or systematic failure of the board to exercise oversight—such as an utter failure to attempt to assure a reasonable information and reporting system exists—will establish the lack of good faith that is a necessary condition to liability.

CAREMARK STANDARD APPROVED

As evidenced by the language quoted above, the *Caremark* standard for so-called "oversight" liability draws heavily upon the concept of director failure to act in good faith. That is consistent with the definition(s) of bad faith recently approved by this Court in . . . [In re The Walt Disney Company Derivative Litigation, 906 A.2d 27 (2006)], where we held that a failure to act in good faith requires conduct that is qualitatively different from, and more culpable than, the conduct giving rise to a violation of the fiduciary duty of care (i.e., gross negligence). . . .

It is important, in this context, to clarify a doctrinal issue that is critical to understanding fiduciary liability under *Caremark* as we construe that case. The phraseology used in *Caremark* and that we employ here—describing the lack of good faith as a "necessary condition to liability"—is deliberate. The purpose of that formulation is to communicate that a failure to act in good faith is not conduct that results, *ipso facto*, in the direct imposition of fiduciary liability. The failure to act in good faith may result in liability because the requirement to act in good faith "is a subsidiary element[,]" i.e., a condition, "of the fundamental duty of loyalty." It follows that because a showing of bad faith conduct, in the sense described in *Disney* and *Caremark*, is essential to establish director oversight liability, the fiduciary duty violated by that conduct is the duty of loyalty.

This view of a failure to act in good faith results in two additional doctrinal consequences. First, although good faith may be described colloquially as part of a "triad" of fiduciary duties that includes the duties of care and loyalty,[1] the obligation to act in good faith does not establish an independent fiduciary duty that stands on the same footing as the duties of care and loyalty. Only the latter two duties, where violated, may directly result in liability, whereas a failure to act in good faith may do so, but indirectly. The second doctrinal consequence is that the fiduciary duty of loyalty is not limited to cases involving a financial or other cognizable fiduciary conflict of interest. It also encompasses cases where the fiduciary fails to act in good faith. As the Court of Chancery aptly put it in *Guttman*, "[a] director cannot act loyally towards the corporation unless she acts in the good faith belief that her actions are in the corporation's best interest."[2]

---

1. *See* Cede & Co. v. Technicolor, Inc., 634 A.2d 345, 361 (Del. 1993).
2. Guttman v. Huang, 823 A.2d 494, 506 n. 34 (Del. Ch. 2003).

We hold that *Caremark* articulates the necessary conditions predicate for director oversight liability: (a) the directors utterly failed to implement any reporting or information system or controls; *or* (b) having implemented such a system or controls, consciously failed to monitor or oversee its operations thus disabling themselves from being informed of risks or problems requiring their attention. In either case, imposition of liability requires a showing that the directors knew that they were not discharging their fiduciary obligations. Where directors fail to act in the face of a known duty to act, thereby demonstrating a conscious disregard for their responsibilities, they breach their duty of loyalty by failing to discharge that fiduciary obligation in good faith. . . .

REASONABLE REPORTING SYSTEM EXISTED

The . . . Report [prepared for AmSouth by outside auditor KPMG] evaluated the various components of AmSouth's longstanding [Banking Secrecy Act/ Anti-Money Laundering] compliance program. The KPMG Report reflects that AmSouth's Board dedicated considerable resources to the BSA/AML compliance program and put into place numerous procedures and systems to attempt to ensure compliance. [Various components of the program are discussed here at length.] . . . Further, the Board's Audit and Community Responsibility Committee (the "Audit Committee") oversaw AmSouth's BSA/AML compliance program on a quarterly basis. The KPMG Report states that "the BSA Officer presents BSA/AML training to the Board of Directors annually," and the "Corporate Security training is also presented to the Board of Directors." . . . [One of the policies adopted by the board] directs all AmSouth employees to immediately report suspicious transactions or activity to the BSA/AML Compliance Department or Corporate Security. . . .

The KPMG Report—which the plaintiffs explicitly incorporated by reference into their derivative complaint—refutes the assertion that the directors "never took the necessary steps . . . to ensure that a reasonable BSA compliance and reporting system existed." . . . Although there ultimately may have been failures by employees to report deficiencies to the Board, there is no basis for an oversight claim seeking to hold the directors personally liable for such failures by the employees.

With the benefit of hindsight, the plaintiffs' complaint seeks to equate a bad outcome with bad faith. The lacuna in the plaintiffs' argument is a failure to recognize that the directors' good faith exercise of oversight responsibility may not invariably prevent employees from violating criminal laws, or from causing the corporation to incur significant financial liability, or both, as occurred in *Graham, Caremark* and this very case. In the absence of red flags, good faith in the context of oversight must be measured by the directors' actions "to assure a reasonable information and reporting system exists" and not by second-guessing after the occurrence of employee conduct that results in an unintended adverse outcome. Accordingly, we hold that the Court of Chancery properly applied *Caremark* and dismissed the plaintiffs' derivative complaint. . . .

Dear Prof.: Do plaintiffs ever win in Delaware?

Sure—if they're suing in the U.S. District Court for patent infringement. There, the success rate has been as high as 62.5 percent. On the other hand, in a 2001 study of executive compensation claims, plaintiffs in Delaware state court won at some stage of the relevant legal proceedings about one-third of the time if the corporation in question was publicly held and about one-half the time if the corporation was closely held. This was about the same result as for executive compensation litigation brought elsewhere. *See* Randall S. Thomas & Kenneth J. Martin, *Litigating Challenges to Executive Pay: An Exercise in Futility?*, 79 WASH. U. L.Q. 569 (2001).

■ **Think about this:**

(D) Why is it important for the Delaware Supreme Court to tell us that the duty of good faith does not stand alone?

(E) The court in *Stone v. Ritter* discusses what good faith requires in the absence of red flags. What would it require in the presence of such flags?

(F) Suppose that Fatimah is a member of the board of Fessco, and intentionally reveals to the federal government that Fessco has engaged in certain criminal activity. The result is bad publicity and a huge fine—and a big whistleblower's award for Fatimah. Has Fatimah acted in bad faith and/or otherwise violated her duty of loyalty?

(G) Gino is a member of the board of directors of Gigantico, which uses a product known as Flarp in its manufacturing process. He is a scientist who, for recreational purposes, has made careful study of the properties of Gloop. Gigantico now is considering switching from Flarp to Gloop. Gino knows this would result in an unacceptably high level of product failures, but he says nothing because he does not want the responsibility. Has Gino acted in bad faith or otherwise violated his duty of loyalty?

B. Disclosure

As we have said elsewhere, fiduciaries must sometimes disclose information to their principals, and it is sometimes said that they therefore owe a "duty of disclosure." Like the obligation of good faith, it became desirable to plaintiffs to explore whether this disclosure duty might exist distinctly from the duty of care, as part of the duties of loyalty or good faith, or as some freestanding duty. If so, they might still secure monetary relief for breaches of it, even under the raincoat and exculpation statutes of the 1980s. As with good faith, there had not previously been much clarity on these questions, and they thus became the focus of much judicial attention.

Some circumstances in which an agent must disclose are straightforward and are simply consequences of the traditional duty of care or loyalty. An agent owes "a general duty of full disclosure respecting matters affecting the principal's interests"—a duty of care obligation—and must not "us[e] the relationship to benefit his personal interest, except with the full knowledge and consent of the principal"—an aspect of the duty of loyalty. United Teachers Associates Insurance Co. v. MacKeen & Bailey, Inc., 99 F.3d 645, 650 (5th Cir. 1996); *see also* Restatement (Third) of Agency §§8.03, comment b; 8.11 (codifying these same rules, the first as a care obligation and the second as a loyalty obligation). In the context of self-dealing transactions, it is fairly obvious how these requirements play out. If the fiduciary fails to disclose her own interest in a transaction on the principal's behalf, and if the principal has not consented, the transaction may be avoided for loyalty breach. It also is clear how the same principles apply in the context of corporate opportunity. If an opportunity belongs to the corporation (as to which there can be some question), it can (probably) only be taken with the entity's consent, a consent that requires disclosure of the conflict and all material facts. Both situations regularly are dealt with under the rubric of the duty of loyalty.

But there are some other situations in which courts have required disclosure—either to the corporation or to third parties—that do not fit quite so neatly into the traditional mold. In particular, the two cases that follow deal with transactions with third parties—shareholders and prospective shareholders—and give insight into how courts struggle with situations that are neither self-dealing nor corporate opportunity *per se*. Note, in particular, that these two cases, though they are often thought of as companion cases, actually deal with different factual scenarios, and at issue are two different causes of action.

GOODWIN V. AGASSIZ

Massachusetts Supreme Judicial Court
186 N.E. 659 (1933)

RUGG, C.J.

A stockholder in a corporation seeks in this suit relief for losses suffered by him in selling shares of stock in Cliff Mining Company by way of accounting, rescission of sales, or redelivery of shares. The named defendants are MacNaughton, a resident of Michigan not served or appearing, and Agassiz, a resident of this Commonwealth, the active party defendant.

. . . The defendants, in May, 1926, purchased through brokers on the Boston stock exchange seven hundred shares of stock of the Cliff Mining Company which up to that time the plaintiff had owned. Agassiz was president

Connections: Federal Securities Law

The reader may identify this fact pattern as involving alleged "insider trading." For what may be obvious reasons, most insider trading litigation is a matter of federal law. It is the subject of another chapter in this book.

and director and MacNaughton a director and general manager of the company. They had certain knowledge, material as to the value of the stock, which the plaintiff did not have. The plaintiff contends that such purchase in all the circumstances without disclosure to him of that knowledge was a wrong against him. That knowledge was that an experienced geologist had formulated in writing in March, 1926, a theory as to the possible existence of copper deposits under conditions prevailing in the region where the property of the company was located. [The theory was kept private in order to allow another company of which the defendants were officers to pursue options on land. Notwithstanding the theory, an exploration on Cliff Mining's own property was completed unsuccessfully in May, 1926, with public announcement of that fact.] Both [defendants] felt that the theory had value and . . . that, if there was any merit in the geologist's theory, the price of Cliff Mining Company stock in the market would go up. Its stock was quoted and bought and sold on the Boston stock exchange. Pursuant to agreement, they bought many shares of that stock through agents on joint account.

The plaintiff first learned of the closing of exploratory operations on property of the Cliff Mining Company from an article in a paper on May 15, 1926, and immediately sold his shares of stock through brokers. It does not appear that the defendants were in any way responsible for the publication of that article. The plaintiff did not know that the purchase was made for the defendants and they did not know that his stock was being bought for them. There was no communication between them touching the subject. The plaintiff would not have sold his stock if he had known of the geologist's theory. The finding is express that the defendants were not guilty of fraud, that they committed no breach of duty owed by them to the Cliff Mining Company, and that that company was not harmed by the nondisclosure of the geologist's theory, or by their purchases of its stock, or by shutting down the exploratory operations.

The contention of the plaintiff is that the purchase of his stock in the company by the defendants without disclosing to him as a stockholder their knowledge of the geologist's theory, their belief that the theory had value, the keeping secret the existence of the theory, discontinuance by the defendants of exploratory operations begun in 1925 on property of the Cliff Mining Company and their plan ultimately to test the value of the theory, constitute actionable wrong for which he as stockholder can recover. . . .

The directors of a commercial corporation stand in a relation of trust to the corporation and are bound to exercise the strictest good faith in respect to its property and business. The contention that directors also occupy the position of trustee toward individual stockholders in the corporation is plainly contrary to repeated decisions of this court and cannot be supported. In Smith v. Hurd, 12 Met. 371, 384, it was said by Chief Justice Shaw: "There is no legal privity, relation, or immediate connexion, between the holders of shares in a bank, in their individual capacity, on the one side, and the directors of the bank on the other. The directors are not the bailees, the factors, agents or trustees of such individual stockholders." . . . The principle thus established is supported by an imposing weight of authority in other jurisdictions. . . . A rule holding that directors are trustees for individual stockholders with respect to their stock prevails in comparatively few States; but in view of our own adjudications it is not necessary to review decisions to that effect.

While the general principle is as stated, circumstances may exist requiring that transactions between a director and a stockholder as to stock in the corporation be set aside. The knowledge naturally in the possession of a director as to the condition of a corporation places upon him a peculiar obligation to observe every requirement of fair dealing when directly buying or selling its stock. Mere silence does not usually amount to a breach of duty, but parties may stand in such relation to each other that an equitable responsibility arises to communicate facts. Purchases and sales of stock dealt in on the stock exchange are commonly impersonal affairs. An honest director would be in a difficult situation if he could neither buy nor sell on the stock exchange shares of stock in his corporation without first seeking out the other actual ultimate party to the transaction and disclosing to him everything which a court or jury might later find that he then knew affecting the real or speculative value of such shares. Business of that nature is a matter to be governed by practical rules. Fiduciary obligations of directors ought not to be made so onerous that men of experience and ability will be deterred from accepting such office. Law in its sanctions is not coextensive with morality. It cannot undertake to put all parties to every contract on an equality as to knowledge, experience, skill and shrewdness. It cannot undertake to relieve against hard bargains made between competent parties without fraud.

On the other hand, directors cannot rightly be allowed to indulge with impunity in practices which do violence to prevailing standards of upright business men. Therefore, where a director personally seeks a stockholder for the purpose of buying his shares without making disclosure of material facts within his peculiar knowledge and not within reach of the stockholder, the transaction will be closely scrutinized and relief may be granted in appropriate instances. Strong v. Repide, 213 U.S. 419. *See also*, Old Dominion Copper Mining Smelting Co. v. Bigelow, 203 Mass. 159, 194-95. The applicable legal principles "have almost always been the fundamental ethical rules of right and wrong." Robinson v. Mollett, L.R. 7 H.L. 802, 817.

The precise question to be decided in the case at bar is whether on the facts found the defendants as directors had a right to buy stock of the plaintiff, a stockholder. Every element of actual fraud or misdoing by the defendants is negatived by the findings. Fraud cannot be presumed; it must be proved. The facts found afford no ground for inferring fraud or conspiracy. The only knowledge possessed by the defendants not open to the plaintiff was the existence of a theory formulated in a thesis by a geologist as to the possible existence of copper deposits where certain geological conditions existed common to the property of the Cliff Mining Company and that of other mining companies in its neighborhood. This thesis did not express an opinion that copper deposits would be found at any particular spot or on property of any specified owner. Whether that theory was sound or fallacious, no one knew, and so far as appears has never been demonstrated. The defendants made no representations to anybody about the theory. No facts found placed upon them any obligation to disclose the theory. . . . The Cliff Mining Company was not harmed by the nondisclosure. There would have been no advantage to it, so far as appears, from a disclosure. The disclosure would have been detrimental to the interests of another mining corporation in which the defendants were directors. . . . Disclosure of the theory, if it ultimately was proved to be erroneous or without foundation in fact, might involve the defendants in litigation with those who might act on the hypothesis that it was correct. The stock of the Cliff Mining Company was bought and sold on the stock exchange. The identity of buyers and seller of the stock in question in fact was not known to the parties and perhaps could not readily have been ascertained. The defendants caused the shares to be bought through brokers on the stock exchange. They said nothing to anybody as to the reasons actuating them. The plaintiff was no novice. He was a member of the Boston stock exchange and had kept a record of sales of Cliff Mining Company stock. He acted upon his own judgment in selling his stock. He made no inquiries of the defendants or of other officers of the company. The result is that the plaintiff cannot prevail.

■ **Think about this:**

(H) Suppose that Agassiz and McNaughton were the only two members of Cliff Mining Company who knew about the geologist's theory. They negotiate with the company to purchase its shares directly without disclosing the theory. Would they be in breach of their duty of loyalty?

(I) What if Agassiz and McNaughton, instead of purchasing shares of Cliff Mining Company, had decided to purchase real property on the basis of the geologist's theory?

(J) Would the outcome of the case have been different if Goodwin and Agassiz had met face to face?

In reading the next case, which frequently appears as a companion to *Goodwin v. Agassiz*, be careful to distinguish the claim being made from the one made in *Goodwin*.

DIAMOND V. OREAMUNO

New York Court of Appeals
24 N.Y.2d 494 (1969)

Chief Judge FULD.

Upon this appeal from an order denying a motion to dismiss the complaint as insufficient on its face, the question presented—one of first impression in this court—is whether officers and directors may be held accountable to their corporation for gains realized by them from transactions in the company's stock as a result of their use of material inside information.

The complaint was filed by a shareholder of Management Assistance, Inc. (MAI) asserting a derivative action against a number of its officers and directors to compel an accounting for profits allegedly acquired as a result of a breach of fiduciary duty. It charges that two of the defendants—Oreamuno, chairman of the board of directors, and Gonzalez, its president—had used inside information, acquired by them solely by virtue of their positions, in order to reap large personal profits from the sale of MAI shares and that these profits rightfully belong to the corporation. Other officers and directors were joined as defendants on the ground that they acquiesced in or ratified the assertedly wrongful transactions.

MAI is in the business of financing computer installations through sale and lease back arrangements with various commercial and industrial users. Under its lease provisions, MAI was required to maintain and repair the computers but, at the time of this suit, it lacked the capacity to perform this function itself and was forced to engage the manufacturer of the computers, International Business Machines (IBM), to service the machines. As a result of a sharp increase by IBM of its charges for such service, MAI's expenses for August of 1966 rose considerably and its net earnings declined from $262,253 in July to $66,233 in August, a decrease of about 75%. This information, although earlier known to the defendants, was not made public until October of 1966. Prior to the release of the information, however, Oreamuno and Gonzalez sold off a total of 56,500 shares of their MAI stock at the then current market price of $28 a share.

After the information concerning the drop in earnings was made available to the public, the value of a share of MAI stock immediately fell from the $28 realized by the defendants to $11. Thus, the plaintiff alleges, by taking advantage of their privileged position and their access to confidential information, Oreamuno and Gonzalez were able to realize $800,000 more for their securities than they would have had this inside information not been available to them. Stating that the defendants were "forbidden to use [such] information . . . for their own personal profit or gain," the plaintiff brought this derivative action seeking to have the defendants account to the corporation for this difference. . . .

In reaching a decision in this case, we are, of course, passing only upon the sufficiency of the complaint and we necessarily accept the charges contained in that pleading as true.

It is well established, as a general proposition, that a person who acquires special knowledge or information by virtue of a confidential or fiduciary relationship with another is not free to exploit that knowledge or information for his own personal benefit but must account to his principal for any profits derived therefrom. . . . This, in turn, is merely a corollary of the broader principle, inherent in the nature of the fiduciary relationship, that prohibits a trustee or agent from extracting secret profits from his position of trust.

In support of their claim that the complaint fails to state a cause of action, the defendants take the position that, although it is admittedly wrong for an officer or director to use his position to obtain trading profits for himself in the stock of his corporation, the action ascribed to them did not injure or damage MAI in any way. Accordingly, the defendants continue, the corporation should not be permitted to recover the proceeds. They acknowledge that, by virtue of the exclusive access which officers and directors have to inside information, they possess an unfair advantage over other shareholders and, particularly, the persons who had purchased the stock from them but, they contend, the corporation itself was unaffected and, for that reason, a derivative action is an inappropriate remedy.

It is true that the complaint before us does not contain any allegation of damages to the corporation but this has never been considered to be an essential requirement for a cause of action founded on a breach of fiduciary duty.... This is because the function of such an action, unlike an ordinary tort or contract case, is not merely to compensate the plaintiff for wrongs committed by the defendant but, as this court declared many years ago (Dutton v. Willner, 52 N.Y. 312, 319), "to *prevent* them, by removing from agents and trustees all inducement to attempt dealing for their own benefit in matters which they have undertaken for others, or to which their agency or trust relates." (Emphasis supplied.)

Just as a trustee has no right to retain for himself the profits yielded by property placed in his possession but must account to his beneficiaries, a corporate fiduciary, who is entrusted with potentially valuable information, may not appropriate that asset for his own use even though, in so doing, he causes no injury to the corporation. The primary concern, in a case such as this, is not to determine whether the corporation has been damaged but to decide, as between the corporation and the defendants, who has a higher claim to the proceeds derived from the exploitation of the information. In our opinion, there can be no justification for permitting officers and directors, such as the defendants, to retain for themselves profits which, it is alleged, they derived solely from exploiting information gained by virtue of their inside position as corporate officials....

The defendants maintain that extending the prohibition against personal exploitation of a fiduciary relationship to officers and directors of a corporation will discourage such officials from maintaining a stake in the success of the corporate venture through share ownership, which, they urge, is an important incentive to proper performance of their duties. There is, however, a considerable difference between corporate officers who assume the same risks and obtain the same benefits as other shareholders and those who use their privileged position to gain special advantages not available to others. The sale of shares by the defendants for the reasons charged was not merely a wise investment decision which any prudent investor might have made. Rather, they were assertedly able in this case to profit solely because they had information which was not available to any one else— including the other shareholders whose interests they, as corporate fiduciaries, were bound to protect.

Although no appellate court in this State has had occasion to pass upon the precise question before us, the concept underlying the present cause of action is hardly a new one.... Under Federal law (Securities Exchange Act of 1934, §16[b]), for example, it is conclusively presumed that, when a director, officer or 10% shareholder buys and sells securities of his corporation within a six-month

> **Connections: Short-swing Trading**
>
> The purchase and sale (or sale and purchase) of securities within less than six months is known as "short-swing trading" and is addressed in more detail in Chapter 32.

period, he is trading on inside information. The remedy which the Federal statute provides in that situation is precisely the same as that sought in the present case under State law, namely, an action brought by the corporation or on its behalf to recover all profits derived from the transactions. . . . In Brophy v. Cities Serv. Co. (31 Del. Ch. 241), . . . the Chancery Court of Delaware allowed a similar remedy in a situation not covered by the Federal legislation. One of the defendants in that case was an employee who had acquired inside information that the corporate plaintiff was about to enter the market and purchase its own shares. On the basis of this confidential information, the employee, who was not an officer and, hence, not liable under Federal law, bought a large block of shares and, after the corporation's purchases had caused the price to rise, resold them at a profit. The court sustained the complaint in a derivative action brought for an accounting, stating that "[p]ublic policy will not permit an employee occupying a position of trust and confidence toward his employer to abuse that relation to his own profit, regardless of whether his employer suffers a loss" (31 Del. Ch., at p. 246). And a similar view has been expressed in the Restatement, 2d, Agency (§388, comment c):

> "c. Use of confidential information. An agent who acquires confidential information in the course of his employment or in violation of his duties has a duty . . . to account for any profits made by the use of such information, although this does not harm the principal. . . . So, if [a corporate officer] has 'inside' information that the corporation is about to purchase or sell securities, or to declare or to pass a dividend, profits made by him in stock transactions undertaken because of his knowledge are held in constructive trust for the principal."

Connections: An Agent's Use of Confidential Information

Oreamuno is cited in the Reporter's notes to Restatement (Third) of Agency §8.05, a provision in the Restatement's fiduciary duties article, which is entitled "Use of Principal's Property; Use of Confidential Information." Subsection 2 of §8.05 captures the same rule as the one stated in the comment that the court cites here, from the Restatement (Second).

Re(3) §8.05(2) provides that:

> An agent has a duty . . . (2) not to use or communicate confidential information of the principal for the agent's own purposes or those of a third party.

Other comments to Re(3) §8.05—like the quoted comments from the Restatement (Second)—make clear that an appropriate remedy is accounting for profits. That is, that the fiduciary must fork over ill-gotten gains to the beneficiary, regardless of any showing of harm. Section 8.05 is also discussed in Chapter 12C.

In the present case, the defendants may be able to avoid liability to the corporation under section 16(b) of the Federal law since they had held the MAI shares for more than six months prior to the sales. Nevertheless, the alleged use of the inside information to dispose of their stock at a price considerably higher than its known value constituted the same sort of "abuse of a fiduciary relationship" as is condemned by the Federal law. Sitting as we are in this case as a court of equity, we should not hesitate to permit an action to prevent any unjust enrichment realized by the defendants from their allegedly wrongful act. . . .

■ Think about this:

(K) Given the reasoning and holding in this case, would you expect most corporate opportunity litigation brought in New York to be fairly easily resolved in the plaintiff's favor?

It is critical to note that both *Goodwin* and *Diamond* involved intentional non-disclosures. At least in Delaware, it seems to be the case that intentional (and possibly reckless) non-disclosure is a matter of the duty of loyalty, while other types of non-disclosure are not. *See* Arnold v. Society for Savings Bancorp, Inc., 650 A.2d 1270 (1994). This makes a difference as to whether "raincoat" provisions exculpating officers and directors from some types of liability apply.

Test Yourself

1. Meds for Feds, Inc., a Delaware corporation, is one of the prescription medicine insurers from among which federal employees may choose. Its directors receive a report from a whistleblower that the company is paying kickbacks to certain federal benefit administrators to push for employees to elect Meds for Feds coverage. They reason that, although the practice clearly is illegal, it is resulting in great success for Meds for Feds, and that any fine the company might have to pay would be less than the amount the kickbacks earn. They therefore decline to implement any program to detect or prevent kickbacks. Which of the following is most true?

   a. The failure to implement a program to detect or prevent kickbacks may be a breach of the directors' duty of good faith.
   b. Whether or not a company should have a program to detect or prevent kickbacks is entirely within the business judgment of the directors.
   c. The directors have satisfied the duty of good faith because they are aware that kickbacks are being paid.
   d. The directors are in violation of their duty of good faith and are required to disclose that violation to the shareholders.

(Answers in Online Supplement)

2. Theo, a director of Hypoxico, a New York corporation that is publicly traded, learns that Fidel, the chief financial officer, has been "cooking the books" to make Hypoxico appear much more profitable than it really is. Which of the following is most true?

a. Theo must disclose the information he has acquired to the public.
b. Theo must disclose the information he has acquired to the rest of the board of directors.
c. Theo has no obligation to disclose the information he has acquired unless he is engaged in a transaction involving Hypoxico or its shares.
d. Theo has no obligation to disclose the information he has acquired.

3. At least in Delaware, breach of the duty of good faith:

a. Is a breach of the duty of care.
b. Is a breach of the duty of loyalty.
c. Can give rise to an award of monetary damages.
d. Answers b and c are both correct.

4. The intentional failure of a fiduciary to disclose material information:

a. Makes ratification of a transaction ineffective.
b. Will give rise to an award of monetary damages.
c. Cannot stand alone as a breach of fiduciary duty, but may make ratification of a transaction ineffective.
d. Is prima facie evidence of a breach of the duty of care.

5. The duties of good faith and disclosure:

a. Give rise to actions for monetary damages.
b. Do not give rise to actions for monetary damages.
c. Are subsumed in the duty of loyalty.
d. Are traditionally recognized fiduciary duties.

21

Exculpation, Indemnification, and Insurance

Many states have tried to ease corporate fiduciaries' litigation risks. One approach is to allow corporations to provide their fiduciaries with insurance coverage for their official acts. Another approach is to permit (and sometimes require) corporations to indemnify them when they are sued for fiduciary breach or for other reasons related to their functions. A third solution has been to permit corporations to limit the circumstances in which their fiduciaries may be held liable—a process often referred to as "exculpation."

Chapter Outline

A. Introduction

- Corporate officers and directors are exposed to significant risks, especially under the federal securities laws

B. Insurance

- Arguably creates moral hazard
- Is not available against all risks
- Is provided at a price affected by the insurer's assessment of a corporation's governance structure and corporate culture

C. Indemnification

1. Dealing with a Typical Statute
   - The typical statute is quite complex and requires careful reading

2. Interpretive Issues
   - What is the meaning of "success"?
   - What is the meaning of "by reason of"?

D. Exculpation—Raincoat Provisions Revisited

- One type of exculpation involves limiting monetary damages
- Another type redefines duty

Test Yourself

A. Introduction

Corporate officers and directors should assume their positions with the knowledge that they are exposed to a certain amount of litigation risk. Some of that risk relates to the discharge of their fiduciary duties, but there are other sources as well. For instance, federal environmental law can impose liability on those making relevant decisions about the operation of polluting facilities, and there are specific requirements for the fiduciaries of banks. Probably the most significant sources, however, are the federal securities laws.

As the sidebar indicates, liability can be monstrous. (It is important to note, however, that in many cases reports of settlements aggregate claims against issuers as well as their officers and directors, and may also include figures for other actors such as accounting and underwriting firms.)

State statutes play a role in making a corporate fiduciary's risks manageable. Thus, they permit the limitation of monetary liability for some forms of fiduciary breach. They cannot, of course, eliminate liability arising under federal law, but they do permit, and sometimes require, corporations to hold their officers and directors harmless against some types of expense. Perhaps most important, they clearly permit corporations to insure their officers and directors. Virtually all publicly held companies carry directors and officers insurance, and virtually all claims against those covered are settled within policy limits.[1]

Largest Securities Settlements in the United States

(All settlements are the cumulative result of multiple suits—some suits are still outstanding.)

Company	Amount paid out
Enron	$8,138,000,000
WorldCom	$7,640,000,000
Cendant	$3,591,000,000
AOL Time Warner	$3,724,000,000

Sources: Cornerstone Report, "D&O Litigation Trends in 2006"/ Aon, June 2009; Cornerstone Report, "Securities Class Action Settlements in 2013."

---

1. Tom Baker & Sean J. Griffith, *Predicting Corporate Governance Risk: Evidence from the Directors' and Officers' Liability Insurance Market*, 74 U. Chi. L. Rev. 487, 533 (2007).

What does it look like?

Check the online Supplement for the following sample documents that are relevant to this chapter:

■ A directors and officers insurance policy
■ Bylaws provisions relating to the indemnification of officers and directors

B. Insurance

At one time there was doubt whether corporations should be permitted to provide officers and directors with liability insurance. The concern was that it would create "moral hazard"—basically, that the insureds would be less careful in the discharge of their duties if they did not have to reckon with the consequences. Nonetheless, modern statutes clearly do allow the practice, and what is called "D&O" insurance has been widely purchased since the 1960s. The Delaware statute below is quite typical.

DELAWARE GENERAL CORPORATION LAW D.C.A., TITLE 8, CH. 1

§145 Indemnification of Officers, Directors, Employees and Agents; Insurance

(g) A corporation shall have power to purchase and maintain insurance on behalf of any person who is or was a director, officer, employee or agent of the corporation, or is or was serving at the request of the corporation as a director, officer, employee or agent of another corporation, partnership, joint venture, trust or other enterprise against any liability asserted against such person and incurred by such person in any such capacity, or arising out of such person's status as such, whether or not the corporation would have the power to indemnify such person against such liability under this section.

Although there are some interpretive issues, such as what kinds of liability would be characterized as "arising out of such person's status," the provision makes it clear that the

Common D&O Exclusions

■ Fraud
■ Intentional non-compliant acts
■ Illegal remuneration or personal profit
■ Property damage and bodily harm (except corporate manslaughter)
■ Legal action already taken when the policy begins
■ Claims made under a previous policy
■ Claims covered by other insurance

ability to insure is quite broad, and clearly is broader than a corporation's power to directly indemnify its directors, officers, employees, and agents (as we shall see below). It evidently would be possible to insure directors for deliberate violations of their fiduciary duties and of the federal securities laws—if insurance companies were willing to issue the policies at a tolerable price.

Consider the following excerpt from a 2007 article in the University of Chicago Law Review summarizing the results of an extensive empirical study:[2]

> First, we find that D&O insurers seek to price policies according to the risk posed by each corporate insured and that, in doing so, they make a detailed inquiry into the corporate governance practices of the prospective insured. The underwriting process thus transforms the insured's expected losses from shareholder litigation into an annual cost. Because this cost is, in part, a function of the quality of the insured's corporate governance practices, it fulfills a necessary condition for advancing the deterrence objectives of corporate and securities law. Second, our findings also provide evidence that the merits do matter in corporate and securities litigation. D&O insurers have the greatest at stake in that question, and their conduct in risk assessment and pricing demonstrates a belief that the merits matter. Third, and finally, our findings offer a unique perspective on what (if anything) matters in corporate governance, underscoring the role of "deep governance" variables such as "culture" and "character" in contrast to the formal governance structures commonly emphasized in previous scholarship.

In other words, it should be understood that insurers do pay attention to such matters as corporate governance, although not in the precise way lawyers think about it. Moreover, since insurance companies do not issue policies covering, for example, intentional violations of law and acts resulting in personal profit, there are still financial incentives for insured officers and directors to "behave themselves." These incentives are in addition to reputational concern and a logical desire to stay out of litigation entirely.

C. Indemnification

1. Dealing with a Typical Statute

To "indemnify" someone essentially is to compensate him or her for a loss. Technically, providing insurance as permitted in §145(g) is a kind of indemnification. But what we more commonly think of as indemnification is to make a direct payment, and indemnifications of officers and directors of this kind have been somewhat more tightly controlled by state legislatures. The following provisions from the (quite typical) Delaware statute specify when direct payments are permitted or required, but leave to the corporation the method of accomplishing them. It is usual both to insure a company's officers and directors

---

2. *Id.* at 489-490.

and to carry insurance to reimburse the company for any amounts it must pay directly.

Pay close attention to the various details contained in D.G.C.L. §145, and ask: Why did the Delaware General Assembly see fit to draw these many distinctions and exceptions?

DELAWARE GENERAL CORPORATION LAW D.C.A., TITLE 8, CH. 1

§145 Indemnification of Officers, Directors, Employees and Agents; Insurance

(a) A corporation shall have power to indemnify any person who was or is a party . . . to any . . . action, suit or proceeding . . . (other than an action by or in the right of the corporation) by reason of the fact that the person is or was a director, officer, employee or agent of the corporation . . . against expenses (including attorneys' fees), judgments, fines and amounts paid in settlement actually and reasonably incurred by the person . . . if the person acted in good faith and in a manner the person reasonably believed to be in or not opposed to the best interest of the corporation, and, with respect to any criminal action or proceeding, had no reasonable cause to believe that the person's conduct was unlawful. . . .

(b) A corporation shall have power to indemnify any person who was or is a party . . . to any . . . action or suit by or in the right of the corporation . . . by reason of the fact that the person is or was a director, officer, employee or agent of the corporation . . . against expenses (including attorney's fees) actually and reasonably incurred by the person in connection with the defense or settlement of such action or suit if the person acted in good faith and in a manner the person reasonably believed to be in or not opposed to the best interest of the corporation and except that no indemnification shall be made in respect of any claim . . . as to which such person shall have been adjudged to be liable to the corporation. . . .

> **Connections**
>
> Delaware law permits corporations to limit the liability of directors and officers for monetary liability for breach of fiduciary duty. However, no limitation is permitted for breaches of the duty of loyalty. See Chapters 19 and 20.

(c) To the extent that a present or former director or officer of a corporation has been successful on the merits or otherwise in defense of any action . . . referred to in subsections (a) and (b) of this section . . . such person shall be indemnified. . . .

(e) Expenses (including attorneys' fees) incurred by an officer or director in defending any civil, criminal, administrative or investigative action, suit or proceeding may be paid by the corporation in advance of the final disposition of such action, suit or proceeding upon receipt of an undertaking by or on behalf of such director or officer to repay such amount if it shall ultimately be determined that such person is not entitled to be indemnified by the corporation as authorized in this section. Such expenses (including attorneys' fees) incurred by former directors and officers or other employees and agents may be so paid upon such terms and conditions, if any, as the corporation deems appropriate.

(f) The indemnification and advancement of expenses provided by, or granted pursuant to, the other subsections of this section shall not be deemed exclusive of any other rights to which those seeking indemnification or advancement of expenses may be entitled under any bylaw, agreement, vote of stockholders or disinterested directors or otherwise, both as to action in such person's official capacity and as to action in another capacity while holding such office. . . .

Section 145 presents a good opportunity to design a flow chart. A logical starting point would be determining whether the liability for which indemnification is sought is "by reason of the fact" that the would-be recipient is on the list of covered individuals. If so, and the would-be recipient has been "successful on the merits or otherwise," that is the end of the matter: He or she is entitled to indemnification. After that, things get a little trickier, but it should be obvious that a distinction must be made between those causes of action that are brought "by or on behalf" of a corporation and those that are not.

■ **Whether you choose to develop your own flow chart or not, think about this:**

(A) DCA, Inc., a Delaware corporation, has a provision in its Articles of Incorporation providing for indemnification to the fullest extent permitted by law. Its directors are sued derivatively for violating the duty of loyalty by reason of their total failure to supervise DCA's employees, notwithstanding red flags that would have put them on notice that embezzlement was taking place. The directors lose and seek indemnification for the amount of damages owed plus the cost of their unsuccessful defense. Must DCA pay?

(B) DCB, Inc., a Delaware corporation, has a provision in its Articles of Incorporation providing for indemnification to the fullest extent permitted by law. Its directors are sued derivatively for violating the duty of loyalty by reason of their total failure to supervise DCB's employees, notwithstanding red flags that would have put them on notice that embezzlement was taking place. The directors win and seek indemnification for the cost of their successful defense. Must DCB pay?

(C) DCC, Inc., a Delaware corporation, has a provision in its Articles of Incorporation providing for indemnification to the fullest extent permitted by law. Its directors are sued derivatively for violating the duty of loyalty by reason of their total failure to supervise DCC's employees, notwithstanding red flags that would have put them on notice that embezzlement was taking place. The matter is settled at 50 percent of the amount claimed and the directors seek indemnification for the amount of the settlement plus the cost of their defense. Must DCC pay?

(D) DCD, Inc., a Delaware corporation, has a provision in its Articles of Incorporation providing for indemnification to the fullest extent permitted by law. Its directors are sued by shareholders who purchased their shares in an offering involving defective disclosure documents. Federal securities laws provide that a company's directors are liable in such a situation unless they prove that they acted reasonably. DCD's directors fail to establish their defense and seek indemnification for the amount of damages owed plus the cost of their unsuccessful defense. Must DCD pay?

(E) DCE, Inc., a Delaware corporation, has a provision in its Articles of Incorporation providing for indemnification to the fullest extent permitted by law. Its directors are sued by shareholders who purchased their shares in an offering involving defective disclosure documents. Federal securities laws provide that a company's directors are liable in such a situation unless they prove that they acted reasonably. DCE's directors establish their defense and seek indemnification for the cost of their defense. Must DCE pay?

(F) DCF, Inc., a Delaware corporation, has a provision in its Articles of Incorporation providing for indemnification to the fullest extent permitted by law. Its directors are sued by shareholders who purchased their shares in an offering involving defective disclosure documents. Federal securities laws provide that a company's directors are liable in such a situation unless they prove that they acted reasonably. The matter is settled at 50 percent of the amount claimed and the directors seek indemnification for the amount of the settlement plus the cost of their defense. Must DCF pay?

(G) DCG, Inc., is a Delaware corporation that has no provision in its Articles of Incorporation addressing indemnification. If DCG were in each of the positions described in Problems A through F, how would your answers change?

Before moving on, it is worth noting that the Securities and Exchange Commission takes the position that it is against public policy to indemnify anyone against liability under the federal securities laws, but at least one court has disagreed. It does not take the same position with respect to insurance.

> **Connections: Federal Securities Regulation**
>
> Liability under the federal securities laws is discussed in Part 7 of this book.

2. Interpretive Issues

Section 145 and its ilk are complex statutes. The complexity is enhanced by the use of terms requiring interpretation. The next case addresses what it means to be "successful."

WALTUCH V. CONTICOMMODITY SERVICES, INC.

United States Court of Appeals for the Second Circuit
88 F.3d 87 (1996)

JACOBS, Circuit Judge:

Famed silver trader Norton Waltuch spent $2.2 million in unreimbursed legal fees to defend himself against numerous civil lawsuits and an enforcement proceeding brought by the Commodity Futures Trading Commission (CFTC). In this action under Delaware law, Waltuch seeks indemnification of his legal expenses from his former employer. The district court denied any indemnity, and Waltuch appeals.

As vice-president and chief metals trader for Conticommodity Services, Inc., Waltuch traded silver for the firm's clients, as well as for his own account. In late 1979 and early 1980, the silver price spiked upward as the then-billionaire Hunt brothers and several of Waltuch's foreign clients bought huge quantities of silver futures contracts. Just as rapidly, the price fell until (on a day remembered in trading circles as "Silver Thursday") the silver market crashed. Between 1981 and 1985, angry silver speculators filed numerous lawsuits against Waltuch and Conticommodity, alleging fraud, market manipulation, and antitrust violations. All of the suits eventually settled and were dismissed with prejudice, pursuant to settlements in which Conticommodity paid over $35 million to the various suitors. Waltuch himself was dismissed from the suits with no settlement contribution. His unreimbursed legal expenses in these actions total approximately $1.2 million.

Waltuch was also the subject of an enforcement proceeding brought by the CFTC, charging him with fraud and market manipulation. The proceeding was settled, with Waltuch agreeing to a penalty that included a $100,000 fine and a six-month ban on buying or selling futures contracts from any exchange floor. Waltuch spent $1 million in unreimbursed legal fees in the CFTC proceeding.

Waltuch brought suit in the United States District Court for the Southern District of New York (Lasker, J.) against Conticommodity and its parent company, Continental Grain Co. (together "Conti"), for indemnification of his unreimbursed expenses. . . .

Unlike §145(a), which grants a discretionary indemnification power, §145(c) affirmatively requires corporations to indemnify its officers and directors for the "successful" defense of certain claims:

> To the extent that a director, officer, employee or agent of a corporation has been successful on the merits or otherwise in defense of any action, suit or proceeding referred to in subsections (a) and (b) of this section, or in defense of any claim, issue or matter therein, he shall be indemnified against expenses (including attorneys' fees) actually and reasonably incurred by him in connection therewith. . . .

Waltuch argues that he was "successful on the merits or otherwise" in the private lawsuits, because they were dismissed with prejudice without any payment or assumption of liability by him. Conti argues that the claims against

Waltuch were dismissed only because of Conti's $35 million settlement payments, and that this payment was contributed, in part, "on behalf of Waltuch."

The district court agreed with Conti that "the successful settlements cannot be credited to Waltuch but are attributable solely to Conti's settlement payments. It was not Waltuch who was successful, but Conti who was successful for him." 833 F. Supp. at 311. The district court held that §145(c) mandates indemnification when the director or officer "is vindicated," but that there was no vindication here:

> Vindication is also ordinarily associated with a dismissal with prejudice without any payment. However, a director or officer is not vindicated when the reason he did not have to make a settlement payment is because someone else assumed that liability. Being bailed out is not the same thing as being vindicated.

Id. We believe that this understanding and application of the "vindication" concept is overly broad and is inconsistent with a proper interpretation of §145(c).

No Delaware court has applied §145(c) in the context of indemnification stemming from the settlement of civil litigation. One lower court, however, has applied that subsection to an analogous case in the criminal context, and has illuminated the link between "vindication" and the statutory phrase, "successful on the merits or otherwise." In Merritt-Chapman & Scott Corp. v. Wolfson, 321 A.2d 138 (Del. Super. Ct. 1974), the corporation's agents were charged with several counts of criminal conduct. A jury found them guilty on some counts, but deadlocked on the others. The agents entered into a "settlement" with the prosecutor's office by pleading *nolo contendere* to one of the counts in exchange for the dropping of the rest. *Id.* at 140. The agents claimed entitlement to mandatory indemnification under §145(c) as to the counts that were dismissed. In opposition, the corporation raised an argument similar to the argument raised by Conti:

> [The corporation] argues that the statute and sound public policy require indemnification only where there has been vindication by a finding or concession of innocence. It contends that the charges against [the agents] were dropped for practical reasons, not because of their innocence. . . .
>
> The statute requires indemnification to the extent that the claimant "has been successful on the merits or *otherwise*." Success is vindication. In a criminal action, any result other than conviction must be considered success. Going behind the result, as [the corporation] attempts, is neither authorized by subsection (c) nor consistent with the presumption of innocence.

Id. at 141 (emphasis added).

Although the underlying proceeding in *Merritt* was criminal, the court's analysis is instructive here. The agents in *Merritt* rendered consideration—their guilty plea on one count—to achieve the dismissal of the other counts. The court considered these dismissals both "success" and (therefore) "vindication," and refused to "go[ ] behind the result" or to appraise the reason for the success. In equating "success" with "vindication," the court thus rejected the more expansive view of vindication urged by the corporation. Under *Merritt's* holding, then, vindication, when used as a synonym for "success" under §145(c), does not mean moral exoneration. Escape from an adverse judgment or other detriment, for whatever reason, is determinative. According to *Merritt*, the only question a court may ask is what the result was, not why it was.[3] . . .

Conti's contention that, because of its $35 million settlement payments, Waltuch's settlement without payment should not really count as settlement without payment, is inconsistent with the rule in *Merritt*. Here, Waltuch was sued, and the suit was dismissed without his having paid a settlement. Under the approach taken in *Merritt*, it is not our business to ask why this result was reached. Once Waltuch achieved his settlement gratis, he achieved success "on the merits or otherwise." And, as we know from *Merritt*, success is sufficient to constitute vindication (at least for the purposes of §145(c)). Waltuch's settlement thus vindicated him.

The concept of "vindication" pressed by Conti is also inconsistent with the fact that a director or officer who is able to defeat an adversary's claim by asserting a technical defense is entitled to indemnification under §145(c). In such cases, the indemnitee has been "successful" in the palpable sense that he has won, and the suit has been dismissed, whether or not the victory is deserved in merits terms. If a technical defense is deemed "vindication" under Delaware law, it cannot matter why Waltuch emerged unscathed, or whether Conti "bailed [him] out," or whether his success was deserved. Under §145(c), mere success is vindication enough.

This conclusion comports with the reality that civil judgments and settlements are ordinarily expressed in terms of cash rather than moral victory. No doubt, it would make sense for Conti to buy the dismissal of the claims against Waltuch along with its own discharge from the case, perhaps to avoid further expense or participation as a non-party, potential cross-claims, or negative publicity. But Waltuch apparently did not accede to that arrangement, and Delaware law cannot allow an indemnifying corporation to escape the mandatory indemnification of subsection (c) by paying a sum in settlement on behalf of an unwilling indemnitee. . . .

For all of these reasons, we agree with Waltuch that he is entitled to indemnification under §145(c) for his expenses pertaining to the private lawsuits. . . .

■ **Think about this:**

(H) DCH, Inc., a Delaware corporation, has a provision in its Articles of Incorporation providing for indemnification to the fullest extent permitted by law. DCH and its president are sued by the federal

---

3. Our adoption of Merritt's interpretation of the statutory term "successful" does not necessarily signal our endorsement of the result in that case. The Merritt court sliced the case into individual counts, with indemnification pegged to each count independently of the others. We are not faced with a case in which the corporate officer claims to have been "successful" on some parts of the case but was clearly "unsuccessful" on others, and therefore take no position on this feature of the Merritt holding.

government as "operators" of a polluting facility. The claims ultimately are dropped because of the statute of limitations. The president seeks indemnification for the cost of his defense. Must DCH pay?

Another issue that has come up has to do with liability or expense incurred "by reason" of a covered status. *Heffernan* illustrates how difficult this determination can be.

HEFFERNAN V. PACIFIC DUNLAP GNB CORP.

United States Court of Appeals for the Seventh Circuit
965 F.2d 369 (1992)

ESCHBACH, Senior Circuit Judge.

Litigation is an occupational hazard for corporate directors, albeit one that may often be shifted to the corporation through indemnification. In this diversity case, we consider whether Delaware law precludes a former director from obtaining indemnification from the corporations he served. For the reasons that follow, we hold that the district court prematurely dismissed this case under Rule 12(b)(6) by concluding that it was one in which the director could prove no set of facts entitling him to indemnification. Accordingly, we reverse and remand for further proceedings.

I.

Daniel E. Heffernan is a former director and 6.7% shareholder of GNB Holdings, Inc. (Holdings) and its wholly-owned subsidiary, GNB Inc. (GNB). [A] third firm, Pacific Dunlop Holdings, Inc. (Pacific)[, which owned 92 percent of Holdings' stock, entered into an agreement (the Stock Purchase Agreement) with Heffernan and others to acquire the rest of Holdings' shares.]

In September 1990, Pacific sued Heffernan and [others] under section 12[(a)](2) of the Securities Act of 1933 and under Illinois securities law. Pacific sought to rescind its purchase [under the Stock Purchase Agreement] on the ground that [it] was materially misleading in regard to its disclosure of certain liabilities facing Holdings and GNB. Heffernan requested indemnification and an advance on his litigation expenses from Holdings and GNB pursuant to section 145 of the Delaware General Corporation Law and the companies' corporate bylaws. When Holdings refused (and GNB failed to respond to) Heffernan's request, he initiated this action against the two companies seeking to establish his rights to indemnification and advances.

Under Delaware law, "a corporation may indemnify any person who was or is a party to any [suit] by reason of the fact that he is or was a director . . ." §145(a). Holdings' and GNB's bylaws make mandatory the provision for permissive indemnification in section 145(a). Holdings' bylaws state that "the Corporation shall, to the fullest extent permitted by the Delaware General Corporation law . . . indemnify and hold harmless any person who is or was a party [to] any [suit] by reason of his status as, or the fact that he is or was or has agreed to become, a director [of] the Corporation or of an affiliate, and as to acts performed in the course of the [director's] duty to the Corporation. . . ." GNB's bylaws simply state that "[t]he corporation shall indemnify its officers, directors, employees and agents to the extent permitted by the law of Delaware."

Heffernan does not argue that there is a material difference between the statutory requirement that a director be sued "by reason of the fact that" he was a director and Holdings' bylaw requirement that a director be sued "by reason of his status as, or the fact that" he was a director. And Holdings' brief footnote argument that its bylaw standard is narrower in scope than the statutory one fails in light of its bylaws' stated objective to indemnify directors "to the fullest extent permitted" by Delaware law. Thus, we focus our inquiry on whether Pacific may have sued Heffernan "by reason of the fact that" he was a director of Holdings and GNB.

II.

The district court dismissed Heffernan's complaint, holding that he was not entitled to indemnification under the terms of the statute and bylaws because he had been sued for "wrongs he committed as an individual, not as a director." Furthermore, the district court reasoned that because "Heffernan's status as a director is not a necessary element of the section 12[(a)](2) claim" he was not sued by reason of the fact that he was a director. On appeal, Heffernan argues that although he was sued over a transaction in which he sold his own stock in Holdings, it does not necessarily follow as a matter of law that he was not sued "by reason of the fact that" he was a director of Holdings and GNB. He asserts that Delaware's "by reason of the fact that" phrase reaches Pacific's suit against him because the suit involves his status as a director. Conversely, appellees Holdings and GNB contend that Pacific's complaint against Heffernan has nothing whatsoever to do with Heffernan's former status as a director for Holdings and GNB. They argue that Delaware's "by reason of the fact that" requirement means that a director must be sued for a breach of duty to the corporation or for a wrong committed on behalf of the corporation to be entitled to indemnification. Accordingly, Holdings and GNB assert that Heffernan is not entitled to indemnification because the "sale of his stock was a personal transaction which did not involve his duties or status as a director." . . .

III.

To determine whether Heffernan was sued "by reason of the fact" that he was a director of Holdings and GNB, we begin by reviewing the allegations in the underlying action's complaint. Here, the underlying complaint is based on Heffernan's sale of his shares in Holdings to Pacific pursuant to the Stock Purchase Agreement. More specifically, Pacific contends that Heffernan violated section 12[(a)](2) of the Securities Act by selling those securities pursuant to a misleading prospectus—that is, the Stock Purchase Agreement. Under section 12[(a)](2), a person who offers or sells a security through a prospectus or oral communication containing a material misrepresentation or omission may be liable to the purchaser. To avoid liability, the seller must prove that he did not know, and in the exercise of reasonable care could not have known, of the misrepresentation or omission.

In complaining of Heffernan's alleged failure to disclose environmental and other liabilities of Holdings and GNB in the Stock Purchase Agreement, Pacific's complaint repeatedly states that Heffernan's status as a director put him in a position where, in the performance of his duties as a director, he either learned or should have learned of those liabilities. Because Pacific realleges these provisions under both counts of its complaint, its argument that Heffernan's status as a director was not specifically alleged in the complaint is without merit. Moreover, assuming for the moment that Pacific's section 12[(a)](2) claim against Heffernan is viable, his status as a director is directly relevant to his defense. As noted earlier, to avoid liability under section 12[(a)](2), a defendant must prove that he did not know, and in the exercise of reasonable care could not have known, of the misrepresentation or omission. The defendant's position gives content to the term "reasonable care." For instance, reasonable care for a director requires more than does reasonable care for an individual owning a few shares of stock with no other connection to the corporation. It is accordingly no answer to our inquiry as to whether Heffernan was sued "by reason of the fact that" he was a director to label his participation in Pacific's acquisition of Holdings a "personal" transaction. Despite the fact that Heffernan sold his own shares to Pacific, a nexus exists between Heffernan's status as a director and Pacific's suit.

Moreover, the transaction at the heart of Pacific's complaint is not a purely personal transaction of Heffernan's. Despite Holdings' and GNB's arguments to the contrary, Heffernan was not "trading securities for his own account" in the usual meaning of that phrase. That is, this is not a situation in which Heffernan maintained a personal trading portfolio and encountered litigation over his individual sale of a security in an unrelated company. . . . Rather, this was a structured sale of control transaction pursuant to one agreement—all of the stock that Pacific acquired in this transaction was pursuant to the Stock Purchase Agreement. We decline to distort the context in which Pacific's complaint arose by accepting Holdings' and GNB's unsupported invitation to carve Pacific's acquisition of Holdings' into various component parts.

Furthermore, neither the specific statutory provision under which a director is sued nor the mere form of the underlying complaint is dispositive of his right to indemnification. The logical extension of the district court's reliance on the "necessary elements" of section 12[(a)](2) in denying Heffernan indemnification as a matter of law is that Delaware did not intend for any suit under section 12[(a)](2) to fall within its indemnification provisions. Delaware's case-by-case approach to indemnification counsels against such a formalistic gloss. Otherwise, a director could be forced to bear the costs of unfounded, harassing litigation just because the particular cause of action does not specify a breach of a duty to the corporation, regardless of the connection between the suit and the individual's service as a director. As a practical matter, it is unsurprising that Pacific's complaint is not more explicit in its reliance on Heffernan's role as a director of Holdings and GNB. Because Pacific now controls Holdings and

GNB, those three corporations' interests are aligned; thus Pacific has the incentive and opportunity to structure its complaint so as to avoid triggering its subsidiaries' duty of indemnification. Nevertheless, artful drafting cannot disguise the fact that the gravamen of Pacific's complaint is that Heffernan, at least in part because he was a director of Holdings and GNB, either knew or should have known that Holdings and GNB may be subject to environmental and other liabilities inadequately reflected in the Stock Purchase Agreement. We recognize that because Heffernan wore [multiple] hats . . . his director status may not be the only reason that he was sued by Pacific. But at this stage of this litigation, we cannot, as a matter of law, rule out the fact that it may have been one reason.

IV.

Having established that Pacific's complaint is connected to Heffernan's status as a director, we now turn to whether Delaware's "by reason of" requirement necessarily requires more than the nexus present here. Without delineating the precise contours of the "by reason of" phrase, we conclude that it may be broad enough to encompass the litigation that Heffernan has incurred, at least in part, because of his status as a director of Holdings and GNB. Both the language and the purpose of Delaware's indemnification statute support interpreting its scope expansively.

First, Delaware is no neophyte in corporate law matters. Had it desired to limit permissible indemnification solely to those suits in which a director is sued for breaching a duty of his directorship or for certain enumerated causes of action, it would have jettisoned the supple "by reason of the fact that" phrase in favor of more specific language. Had Delaware desired to so limit its indemnification statute, we are confident that it could have found the words. Holdings and GNB have given us no reason to doubt that Delaware's choice of language was anything but purposeful and strategic. We believe that Delaware's "by reason of the fact that" phrase is broad enough to encompass suits against a director in his official capacity as well as suits against a director that arise more tangentially from his role, position or status as a director. Flexibility of language is vexing as well as liberating. In employing its "by reason of" phrase, Delaware is able to cover a myriad of potential factual scenarios that cannot be anticipated ex ante by the legislature or by corporate officials in drafting their articles and bylaws. The task of giving content to that flexible phrase, however, falls on the courts when the parties encounter interpretive differences.

Finally, we think that the policy of Delaware's indemnification statute supports permitting Heffernan to proceed to establish his right to advances and indemnification from Holdings and GNB. One of the primary purposes of Delaware's indemnification statute is to encourage capable individuals "to serve as corporate directors, secure in the knowledge that expenses incurred by them in upholding their honesty and integrity as directors will be borne by the corporation they serve." MCI Telecommunications Corp. v. Wanzer, 1990 Del. Super. Lexis 222 (citations omitted). Additionally, the statute ought to promote the "desirable end that corporate officials will resist what they consider unjustified suits and claims, secure in the knowledge that their reasonable expenses will be borne by the corporation they have served if they are vindicated." *Id.* Delaware has effectuated these policies by gradually expanding its indemnification provisions to cover the everchanging contexts in which a director may encounter litigation. See Hibbert v. Hollywood Park, Inc., 457 A.2d 339 (Del. 1983) (indemnification provided to directors acting as plaintiffs). See generally Veasey, Finkelstein & Bigler, Delaware Supports Directors with a Three-Legged Stool of Limited Liability, Indemnification and Insurance, 42 Bus. Law. 401 (1987). The district court's restrictive interpretation of Heffernan's claim diminishes the broad and expansive flavor of Delaware's indemnification provisions. . . .

Reversed and Remanded.

D. Exculpation—Raincoat Provisions Revisited

In the wake of *Smith v. Van Gorkom*, a 1985 Delaware Supreme Court decision finding directors of a publicly held company to have been grossly negligent in approving the sale of the company (see Chapter 18), many state legislatures moved to ease a perceived crisis in access to directors and officers insurance. Wholly in addition to the insurance and indemnification rules that already existed, they enacted laws that, in one way or another, decreased directors' liability risks. At least two types of statutes emerged. We discuss a few of these provisions elsewhere in the
book, and have often referred to them by their nickname: They are commonly known as "raincoat" provisions. Here we get a bit more into the nitty-gritty of their details.

First, as illustrated by Delaware's General Corporation Law §102(b)(7) (reprinted in the box below), some statutes allow individual corporations, typically through shareholder action, to include in their articles a provision limiting their directors' liability for various types of wrongdoing not involving lack of loyalty or illegality. The following case considers the broad effect of such a provision.

ARNOLD V. SOCIETY FOR SAVINGS BANCORP, INC.

Supreme Court of Delaware
650 A.2d 1270 (1994)

Chief Justice:

In this appeal from a judgment of the Court of Chancery in favor of defendants we consider the contention of plaintiff below-appellant Robert H. Arnold ("plaintiff") that the trial court erred in granting defendants' summary judgment motion and denying his own. This suit arose out of a merger (the "Merger") of BBC Connecticut Holding Corporation ("BBC"), a wholly-owned Connecticut subsidiary of Bank of Boston Corporation ("BoB"), a Massachusetts corporation, into Society for Savings ("Society"), a wholly-owned Connecticut subsidiary of Society for Savings Bancorp, Incorporated ("Bancorp"), a Delaware corporation. In accordance with the Merger, Bancorp ultimately merged with BoB. Plaintiff was at all relevant times a Bancorp stockholder. Plaintiff named as defendants Bancorp, BoB, BBC, and twelve of fourteen members of Bancorp's board of directors (collectively "defendants"). . . .

Plaintiff's central claim is that the trial court erred in holding that certain alleged omissions and misrepresentations in the Merger proxy statement [constituted fiduciary breaches by the defendants]. Also at issue on this appeal is whether or not the individual defendants can be held liable if a disclosure violation is found in view of the exemption from liability provision in Bancorp's certificate of incorporation, adopted pursuant to 8 Del. C. §102(b)(7) ("Section 102(b)(7)"). For the reasons set forth below, . . . [we] hold that, in all events, the limitation provision in Bancorp's certificate of incorporation shields the individual defendants from personal liability for the disclosure violation found to exist in this case. . . .

DELAWARE GENERAL CORPORATION LAW D.C.A., TITLE 8, CH. 1

§102(b) In addition to the matters required to be set forth in the certificate of incorporation by subsection (a) of this section, the certificate of incorporation may also contain any or all of the following matters: . . .

(7) A provision eliminating or limiting the personal liability of a director to the corporation or its stockholders for monetary damages for breach of fiduciary duty as a director, provided that such provision shall not eliminate or limit the liability of a director:

(i) For any breach of the director's **duty of loyalty** to the corporation or its stockholders;

(ii) for acts or omissions **not in good faith** or which involve **intentional misconduct or a knowing violation of law**;

(iii) under §174 of this title [relating to declaration of dividends when certain tests are not satisfied]; or

(iv) for any transaction from which the director derived an **improper personal benefit**. . . .

VI. SECTION 102(b)(7) PROTECTION

Plaintiff argues that the exemption from liability in Bancorp's certificate of incorporation, adopted pursuant to Section 102(b)(7), does not extend to disclosure claims, and that, even if the provision so extended, the individual defendants' conduct here falls within two exceptions. . . .

A. Application of Section 102(b)(7) to Disclosure Claims

Article XIII of Bancorp's certificate of incorporation . . . parallels the language in Section 102(b)(7). . . . Plaintiff claims that the legislative history of Section 102(b)(7) supports his argument that the shield is not applicable here. Plaintiff's argument, however, bypasses a logical step in statutory analysis. . . . A court should not resort to legislative history in interpreting a statute where statutory language provides unambiguously an answer to the question at hand. . . .

In the instant case, plaintiff's claim that Section 102(b)(7) does not extend to disclosure violations must be rejected as contrary to the express, unambiguous language of that provision. Section 102(b)(7) provides protection "for breach of fiduciary duty." Given that the fiduciary disclosure requirements were well-established when Section 102(b)(7) was enacted and were nonetheless not excepted expressly from coverage, there is no reason to go beyond the text of the statute. Thus, claims alleging disclosure violations that do not otherwise fall within any exception are protected by Section 102(b)(7) and any certificate of incorporation provision (such as Article XIII) adopted pursuant thereto. In any event, nothing in the legislative history of the adoption of Section 102(b)(7) is inconsistent with the result we reach herein.

B. Applicability of the Exceptions to Section 102(b)(7)

Plaintiff argues that the individual defendants' conduct implicates the duty of loyalty and the proscription against knowing, intentional violations of law. . . . He argues that the individual defendants' conduct falls within the exceptions in Section 102(b)(7)(i) & (ii) because they: (i) "improperly interfer[ed] with the voting process by knowingly or deliberately failing to make proper disclosure"; [and] (ii) acted in bad faith and recklessly. . . .

The individual defendants counter that plaintiff's claims are essentially conclusory for there is no affirmative proof that they knowingly or deliberately failed to disclose facts they knew were material. That is, they argue that they balanced in good faith which facts to disclose against those to withhold as immaterial. . . .

Plaintiff's claims are not supported by the record or Delaware law. The individual defendants did not violate the duty of loyalty under the facts of this case. . . . Plaintiff's intentional violation argument is unsupported by the record. . . .

Arnold seems to suggest that if non-disclosure is intentional (or possibly reckless?) it would implicate the duty of loyalty. Otherwise, it involves some other fiduciary duty.

A second type of statute actually alters the standards of fiduciary duties imposed on all corporate directors, typically lowering the standard of conduct. Virginia Code Ann. §13.1-690(A) is such a statute and is the subject of the following case. Ask yourself, as you read it, whether §13.1-690(A) actually differs from the standard embodied in the traditional business judgment rule.

VIRGINIA CODE ANNOTATED

§13.1-690 General Standards of Conduct for Director

(A) A director shall discharge his duties as a director, including his duties as a member of a committee, in accordance with his good faith business judgment in the best interests of the corporation. . . .

WLR FOODS, INC. V. TYSON FOODS, INC.

United States Court of Appeals for the Fourth Circuit
65 F.3d 1172 (1995)

MURNAGHAN, Circuit Judge.

The instant case arose from an attempt by Tyson Foods, Inc. ("Tyson"), a nationwide poultry producer, to acquire WLR Foods, Inc. ("WLR"), a chicken and turkey producer. In early 1994, Tyson engaged in extensive discussions with certain members of WLR's Board of Directors ("the WLR Board") in an attempt to arrange a merger between Tyson and WLR. The WLR Board, resistant to the idea of being acquired by Tyson, adopted various defensive measures to protect WLR against the takeover. Tyson eventually presented a tender offer directly to

the stockholders of WLR, but withdrew the offer several months later, claiming that, due to actions taken by the WLR Board, Tyson's offering price was no longer reflective of the value of WLR's stock. Tyson now challenges several rulings of the district court, which found that the defensive tactics adopted by the WLR Board were a valid legal means by which to respond to the threatened takeover of WLR by Tyson. . . .

III. THE BUSINESS JUDGMENT STATUTE

In its next assignment for error, Tyson challenges the district court's finding that the Virginia Business Judgment Statute, Va. Code Ann. §13.1-690 ("§690"), allows an inquiry only into the processes employed by corporate directors in making their decisions regarding a takeover, and not into the substance of those decisions. Pursuant to that interpretation, the district court denied Tyson access during discovery to the substantive content of the materials used by the WLR Board in responding to Tyson's takeover attempt. . . .

. . . The district court held that under the standard articulated in §690, only the good faith business judgment of the directors was at issue in Tyson's claims, and the rationality *vel non* of the decision ultimately reached by the WLR Board was not relevant. The district court thus permitted Tyson to inquire into the procedures followed by the WLR directors during their investigation of Tyson's offer that indicated whether or not they were considering the offer in good faith, but did not allow Tyson access to the actual substantive information that was used by the directors in making their decision regarding the offer.

We find that the district court did not abuse its discretion in limiting discovery in the instant case. First, it is clear from the language of §690 that the actions of a director are to be judged by his or her good faith in performing corporate duties, and not by the substantive merit of the director's decisions themselves. Tyson concedes that good faith is the relevant standard under §690. However, according to Tyson, although §690 itself does not focus on whether a director's decision is substantively correct, knowledge of the substantive content of the information that was available to the director is necessary in order to determine whether the decision was made in good faith. Tyson claims that a litigant cannot prove a director's lack of good faith without having access to all of the information on which the director relied.

In essence, Tyson hopes to prove lack of good faith in the instant case by showing that, based upon the substantive information received by the WLR Board, the Board should have reached a different result. However, that argument imports an aspect into the Virginia standard of director conduct that is not part of Virginia law. It reduces, and nearly eliminates, the ability to rely, in good faith, on experts. Whether a different person would have come to a different conclusion given the information that a director had before him is simply irrelevant to the determination of whether a director in Virginia has acted in good faith in fulfilling his corporate duties.

In fact, it is precisely such a comparison between a director and the hypothetical reasonable person that the Virginia legislature explicitly chose to reject when it enacted §690. . . . The business judgment rule contained in the Model Act, like §690, is based upon a director's good faith. By referring to an "ordinarily prudent person" and the director's "reasonabl[e] belie[f] concerning the corporation's best interests," however, the Model Act makes clear that one of the ways in which a litigant may prove that a director did not exercise good faith is by showing that a director's decision is irrational, i.e., that the decision does not comport with what a reasonable person would do under similar circumstances.

Section 690, however, contains no reference to the "reasonable person." In fact, the Virginia legislature expressly chose to reject the Model Act standard. . . .

The term "reasonable" is intentionally not used in the standard. It thereby eliminates comparison of the conduct in question with idealized standard and removes the question of how great a deviation from this idealized standard is acceptable.

[*See* Daniel T. Murphy, *The New Virginia Stock Corporation Act: A Primer*, 20 U. RICH. L. REV. 67, 108 (1985).] (Under §690, "[t]he trier of fact need only find good faith and determine whether the conduct in question was a product of the director's own business judgment of what is in the best interest of the corporation. The director's conduct or decision is not to be analyzed in the context of whether a reasonable man would have acted similarly"); *id.* ("The statute . . . may . . . protect the utterly inept, but well-meaning, good faith director."). Directors' actions in Virginia are not to be judged for their reasonableness, and we, like the district court, reject Tyson's attempt to inject such a standard into Virginia law. . . .

■ **Think about this:**

(1) The directors of Chicken, Inc., a Virginia corporation, have, for several days, debated the merits of permitting the company to be acquired by Poultrico at a price of $25 per share. The board has fully informed itself by, among other things, consulting with lawyers and investment bankers. According to the investment bankers, $25 is within a range of fairness. The board is evenly divided and ultimately decides the matter by flipping a coin. Has the board breached any duty for which it might be liable in monetary damages?

> *(J)* Imagine the same facts as in Problem I except that the company instead is Delaware Chicken, Inc., a Delaware corporation that has made the election under Delaware's §102(b)(7). Has the board breached any duty for which it might be liable in monetary damages?

Test Yourself

For each of the following questions, assume that the corporation's Articles of Incorporation provide for indemnification to the fullest extent permitted by law.

1. A director of a Delaware corporation found guilty of materially misleading statements or omissions in communications with shareholders, in violation of a federal securities law, likely:

    a. Must be indemnified by the corporation for any fines, costs, and attorney's fees.

    b. Can be indemnified by the corporation for any fines, fees, or costs, at the corporation's election.

    c. Must be indemnified by the corporation for attorney's fees and costs, but cannot be indemnified for any fines.

    d. None of the above.

2. The reason a Delaware corporation is not permitted to indemnify a "director, officer, employee or agent" who loses a fiduciary cause of action is that:

    a. Defendants must be "successful on the merits or otherwise" to be indemnified.

    b. Indemnification is never permitted with respect to fiduciary causes of action.

    c. Where defendant loses, indemnification would cost the company more than the funds it recovers in money damages.

    d. In fact, Delaware corporations are permitted to indemnify such persons under such circumstances.

3. Several of the employees of Hypoxico, Inc., are found to have engaged in a pattern of paying illegal bribes to local officials. Any reasonable director would have been aware of what was going on, but director Francis was oblivious because, although he went to meetings, he simply didn't understand the first thing about Hypoxico or its business. Which of the following is most likely to be true?

    a. Francis has breached no duty if Hypoxico is a Virginia corporation, but may have breached a duty if Hypoxico is incorporated in Delaware.

    b. Francis has breached a duty even if Hypoxico is a Virginia corporation.

   c. Francis has breached no duty if Hypoxico is either a Virginia or a Delaware corporation.

   d. None of the above.

4. Which of the following statements is most true?

   a. A Delaware corporation must not indemnify its fiduciaries against third-party claims if the fiduciaries acted in conscious violation of law.

   b. A Delaware corporation must not indemnify its fiduciaries against third-party claims if the fiduciaries acted in conscious violation of criminal law.

   c. A Delaware corporation must indemnify its fiduciaries against third-party claims unless the fiduciaries acted in conscious violation of law.

   d. A Delaware corporation must indemnify its fiduciaries against third-party claims unless the fiduciaries acted in conscious violation of criminal law.

5. [Short Answer] Explain the difference between the Delaware and Virginia approaches to the exculpation of officers and directors.

22

Derivative Litigation

The concept of "derivative" litigation implicitly has recurred throughout this book, particularly in connection with fiduciary litigation. It also was expressly introduced in Chapter 15's overview of shareholder rights. While the idea is fairly straightforward in the abstract, the procedural details of derivative litigation are somewhat complicated. This chapter will work out the major complications, while giving thought to why those complications have arisen.

Chapter Outline

A. Introduction

- In general, derivative litigation is brought by a shareholder to assert a corporation's rights
- Procedural requirements associated with derivative litigation burden shareholders, making it preferable to characterize an action as direct, rather than derivative

B. Distinguishing Derivative Suits

- Most cases are clear, infrequently cases arise that are not at all
- Some facts give rise to both derivative and direct claims
- Possible clues:
  - Does the claim relate to exceeding power or to breach of duty?
  - To whom was a breached duty owed?
  - What remedy is sought?

C. The Demand Requirement: Demand and Futility Under Delaware Law and the MBCA's Universal Demand Requirement

1. Demand and Futility in Delaware

2. Other Methods: "Universal Demand" Under the MBCA and the New York Approach

D. The Directors' Authority to Dismiss Derivative Litigation

- A committee of independent directors generally has the power to dismiss derivative litigation, subject to the satisfaction of a jurisdiction's relevant test
- Some tests are deferential and some are not

Test Yourself

A. Introduction

Every state has a rule substantially similar to Delaware Chancery Court Rule 23.1 (and a nearly identical rule appears as Federal Rule of Civil Procedure 23.1). Sometimes these rules appear in a particular state's corporation statute rather than in its rules of court. As you'll see from reading the rule, derivative suits require compliance with a number of procedural steps, and if they are not taken their failure is a basis for dismissal without prejudice. These procedural requirements always burden the shareholder plaintiff. Therefore, defendant fiduciaries will very much want, and plaintiffs will very much want to avoid, characterization of a lawsuit as derivative.

DELAWARE CHANCERY COURT RULES

Rule 23.1 Derivative Actions by Shareholders

In a derivative action brought by 1 or more shareholders or members to enforce a right of a corporation or of an unincorporated association, the corporation or association having failed to enforce a right which may properly be asserted by it, the complaint shall allege that the plaintiff was a shareholder or member at the time of the transaction of which the plaintiff complains or that the plaintiff's share or membership thereafter devolved on the plaintiff by operation of law. The complaint shall also allege with particularity the efforts, if any, made by the plaintiff to obtain the action the plaintiff desires from the directors or comparable authority and the reasons for the plaintiff's failure to obtain the action or for not making the effort.

The action shall not be dismissed or compromised without the approval of the Court, and notice by mail, publication or otherwise of the proposed dismissal or compromise shall be given to shareholders or members in such manner as the Court directs; except that if the dismissal is to be without prejudice or with prejudice to the plaintiff only, then such dismissal shall be ordered without notice thereof if there is a showing that no compensation in any form has passed directly or indirectly from any of the defendants to the plaintiff or plaintiff's attorney and that no promise to give any such compensation has been made.

Perusal of Rule 23.1 reveals the following important points:

- Derivative litigation is undertaken to enforce a right of a corporation that the corporation is not pursuing.
- Derivative litigation may only be brought by a plaintiff who was a shareholder at the time of the complained-about event (or, essentially, by the heir of such a shareholder).
- A prospective plaintiff must ask the directors or a comparable authority to pursue the matter or explain why the request was not made—that is, shareholder must either make "demand" or explain why demand would have been "futile."
- The pleading of demand and futility must be done with particularity.
- Once derivative litigation has commenced it cannot be withdrawn or settled without court approval.

Some interpretive questions can be easily discerned and have relatively clear answers. For instance, who counts as a shareholder? Only the record owner or beneficial owners as well? What happens if a corporation is in so much financial trouble that any recovery necessarily will be for the benefit of creditors? In general, the answers to these questions are that beneficial owners have standing and so do receivers in bankruptcy.

Other questions may be obvious but turn out to be harder to address. These include how to tell whether a right belongs to the corporation rather than a shareholder, as well as what reasons will constitute an adequate explanation for why the shareholder did not demand that the directors launch the suit.

Connections: Unincorporated Entities

As Rule 23.1 makes clear, derivative litigation also can be brought on behalf of unincorporated entities. Whether a member of such an entity can sue derivatively depends on its governing statute and sometimes case law in its state of formation, but where a member enjoys that right, its lawsuit is largely the same as a corporate shareholder's derivative suit.

More to the Story: State Nuances

Statutes authorizing derivative litigation frequently have additional i's to be dotted and t's to be crossed. Even when they do not, judicial decisions may complicate matters. As a result, the nuances of derivative litigation can vary from state to state with respect to such matters as whether a plaintiff shareholder must own a minimum number of shares, must have held those shares both at the time of the transaction complained of and at the time of suit, and must post security for the expenses of the corporation—which is a nominal defendant—and the other defendants.

Dear Prof.: Why are we concentrating on Delaware rather than the MBCA?

As you know, many of the largest corporations are incorporated in Delaware. It consequently is home to a great deal of derivative litigation, and its courts have decided a large range of questions that derivative litigation poses, often with influence beyond its borders. The choices it has made sometimes differ from the MBCA approach—these are matters addressed later in the chapter.

What does it look like?

- A form of demand for action by the board of directors
- A complaint filed in derivative litigation

B. Distinguishing Derivative Suits

The following case is a classic that will help guide us in the basic operation of deciding when a case is derivative and when it is not (shareholder suits that are not derivative are said to be "direct"). Generally speaking, a suit must be brought as a derivative suit when the shareholder plaintiff seeks to enforce rights that belong to the corporation rather than to the shareholder in his or her personal capacity. A suit may be brought as a direct suit when the plaintiff seeks to enforce rights that are owed to plaintiff in his or her personal capacity.

Flying Tiger Line, the defendant corporation in this case, was named after a successful World War II volunteer fighter squadron. Its members founded the cargo airline in 1945. The airline was purchased by FedEx in the 1980s and is now defunct.

EISENBERG V. FLYING TIGER LINE, INC.

United States Court of Appeals for the Second Circuit
451 F.2d 267 (1971)

KAUFMAN, Circuit Judge:

Max Eisenberg, a resident of New York, "as stockholder of The Flying Tiger Line, Inc. [Flying Tiger], on behalf of himself and all other stockholders of said corporation similarly situated" commenced this action in the Supreme Court of the State of New York to enjoin the effectuation of a plan of reorganization and merger. Flying Tiger, a Delaware corporation with its principal place of business in California, removed the action to the District Court for the Eastern District of New York.

Flying Tiger pleaded several affirmative defenses and moved for an order to require Eisenberg to comply with New York Business Corporation Law §627, which requires a plaintiff suing derivatively on behalf of a corporation to post security for the corporation's costs. Judge Travia granted the motion without opinion and afforded Eisenberg thirty days to post security in the sum of $35,000. Eisenberg did not comply, his action was dismissed and he appeals. We find Eisenberg's cause of action to be personal and not derivative within the meaning of §627. We therefore reverse the dismissal.

In this action, Eisenberg is seeking to overturn a reorganization and merger which Flying Tiger effected in 1969. He charges that a series of corporate maneuvers were intended to dilute his voting rights. In order to achieve this end, he alleges, Flying Tiger in July 1969 organized a wholly owned Delaware subsidiary, the Flying Tiger Corporation ("FTC"). In August, FTC in turn organized a wholly-owned subsidiary, FTL Air Freight Corporation ("FTL"). The three Delaware corporations then entered into a plan of reorganization, subject to stockholder approval, by which Flying Tiger merged into FTL and only FTL survived. A proxy statement dated August 11 was sent to stockholders, who approved the plan by the necessary two-thirds vote at the stockholders' meeting held on September 15.

Upon consummation of this merger Flying Tiger ceased as the operating company, FTL took over operations and Flying Tiger shares were converted into an identical number of FTC shares. Thereafter, FTL changed its name to "Flying Tiger Line, Inc.," for the obvious purpose of continuing without disruption the business previously conducted by Flying Tiger. The approximately 4,500,000 shares of the company traded on the New York and Pacific Coast stock exchanges are now those of the holding company, FTC, rather than those of the operating company, Flying Tiger. The effect of the merger is that business operations are now confined to a wholly owned subsidiary of a holding company whose stockholders are the former stockholders of Flying Tiger.

It is of passing interest that Eisenberg contends that the end result of this complex plan was to deprive minority stockholders of any vote or any influence over the affairs of the newly spawned company. Flying Tiger insists the plan was devised to bring about diversification without interference from the Civil Aeronautics Board, which closely regulates air carriers, and to better use available tax benefits. Even if any of these motives prove to be relevant, the alleged illegality is not relevant to the questions before this court. We are called on to decide, assuming Eisenberg's complaint is sufficient on its face, only whether he should have been required to post security for costs as a condition to prosecuting his action.

> ## Connections: Proxies
>
> Shareholders may cast their votes in person or by **proxy**. When the shareholders of a publicly traded corporation are asked to vote by proxy, federal law requires the use of a regulated informational document known as a "proxy statement." There is more on this subject elsewhere in this text. See Chapter 29.

> ## Connections: Mergers
>
> Mergers can involve issuances of shares of corporations related to those of the merger partners. See Chapter 23.

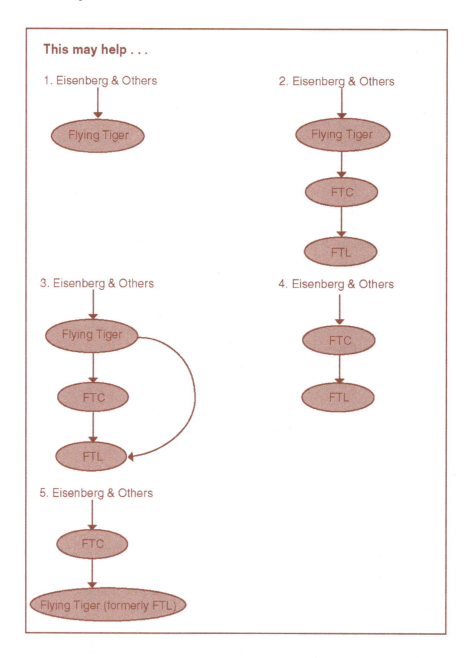

[The court then determined that the law of the state of New York controlled the matter.]

Eisenberg argues, however, that New York courts would refuse to invoke §627 in the instant case because the section applies exclusively to derivative actions specified in Business Corporation Law §626. He urges that his class action is representative and not derivative.

We are told that if the gravamen of the complaint is injury to the corporation the suit is derivative, but "if the injury is one to the plaintiff as a stockholder and to him individually and not to the corporation," the suit is individual in nature and may take the form of a representative class action. 13 Fletcher, Private Corporation §5911 (1970 Rev. Vol.). This generalization is of little use in our case which is one of those "borderline cases which are more or less troublesome to classify." *Id.* The essence of Eisenberg's claimed injury is that the reorganization has deprived him and fellow stockholders of their right to vote on the operating company affairs and that this right in no sense ever belonged to Flying Tiger itself. This right, he says, belonged to the stockholders per se. Flying Tiger notes, however, that the stockholders were harmed, if at all, only because their company was dissolved, and their vote can be restored only if that company is revived. It insists, therefore, that stockholders are affected only secondarily or derivatively because we must first breathe life back into their dissolved corporation before the stockholders can be helped. . . .

. . . In Lazar [v. Knolls Cooperative Section No. 2, Inc., 130 N.Y.S.2d 407, 410 (Sup. Ct. 1954)], a stockholder sought to force directors to call a stockholders' meeting. The court stated security for costs could not be required where a plaintiff

> "does not challenge acts of the management on behalf of the corporation. He challenges the right of the present management to exclude him and other stockholders from proper participation in the affairs of the corporation. He claims that the defendants are interfering with the plaintiff's rights and privileges as stockholders."

In substance, this is a similar to what Eisenberg challenges here. . . .

Other New York cases which have distinguished between derivative and representative actions are of some interest. In Horwitz v. Balaban, 112 F. Supp. 99 (S.D.N.Y. 1949), a stockholder sought to restrain the exercise of conversion rights that the corporation had granted to its president. The court found the action representative and refused to require security, setting forth the test as "[w]here the corporation has no right of action by reason of the transaction complained of, the suit is representative, not derivative." *Id.* at 101. Similarly, actions to compel the dissolution of a corporation have been held representative, since the corporation could not possibly benefit therefrom. . . . Lennan v. Blakely, 80 N.Y.S.2d 288 (Sup. Ct. 1948), teaches that an action by preferred stockholders against directors is not derivative. And Lehrman v. Godchaux Sugars, Inc., [138 N.Y.S. 163 (Sup. Ct. 1955)] discloses that an action by a stockholder complaining that a proposed recapitalization would unfairly benefit holders of another class of stock was representative. . . .

Eisenberg's position is even stronger than it would be in the ordinary merger case. In routine merger circumstances the stockholders retain a voice in the operation of the company, albeit a corporation other than their original choice. Here, however, the reorganization deprived him and other minority stockholders of any voice in the affairs of their previously existing operating company. . . .

Furthermore, we view as an objective of a requirement for security for costs the prevention of strike suits and collusive settlements. Where directors are sued for mismanagement, the risk of personal monetary liability is a strong motive for bringing the suit and inducing settlement. Here, no monetary damages are sought, and no individuals will be liable. . . .

. . . We believe Eisenberg's action should not have been dismissed for failure to post security pursuant to §627.

Reversed.

 Dear Prof.: Derivative vs. representative? Is there a difference?

The court here uses the term "representative" to refer to class actions and similar lawsuits in which named plaintiffs effectively assert the interests of themselves and others, and distinguishes them from derivative actions. A derivative action generally is not a class action, even though any recovery by the shareholder plaintiff is likely to affect the interests of all shareholders equally.

The Second Circuit referred to the fact pattern in *Eisenberg* as "troublesome." There are many others that further illustrate the fact that the distinction between derivative and direct causes of action can be harder than it seems. Sometimes, as in the *Grimes* case, which follows, the results courts reach can be surprising. It would be wrong, however, to suggest that this question is the subject of much real doubt very often. Your gut instinct as to whether a cause of action is derivative or direct is usually pretty reliable. It is worth reading a case like *Grimes*, though, to try to understand why a court will sometimes go to such lengths to treat a case as direct when it was so seemingly obviously derivative.

GRIMES V. DONALD

Delaware Supreme Court
673 A.2d 1207 (1996)

VEASEY, Chief Justice:

[DSC Communications Corp. entered into an Employment Agreement with James Donald, its CEO. Under the contract's terms, Donald was entitled to very substantial severance payments if in his good faith judgment there was "substantial interference . . . by the Board . . . in [his] carrying out" the general management and affairs of DSC. Grimes, a shareholder in DSC, brought an action seeking a declaration that the Agreement was invalid and seeking an award of damages. He alleged that the Board had breached its fiduciary duties by abdicating its authority to Donald and that it had breached its fiduciary duties by failing to exercise due care, by committing waste, and by paying excessive compensation.]

As required by Court of Chancery Rule 23.1, Grimes alleges in his complaint that he wrote to the Board on September 23, 1993 and demanded that the Board abrogate the Agreements . . . [which the Board, in a letter dated November 8, 1993, refused to do.]

. . . We agree that the Court of Chancery appropriately analyzed the abdication claim as a direct—as distinct from a derivative—claim.

Courts have long recognized that the same set of facts can give rise both to a direct claim and a derivative claim. . . . The due care, waste and excessive compensation claims asserted here are derivative and will be considered as such. . . . The abdication claim, however, is a direct claim. In order to reach this conclusion, we believe a further exploration of the distinction between direct and derivative claims is appropriate. . . .

> **Connections: Fiduciary Duty**
>
> As we explore at length in Chapters 18 through 20, a corporation's officers and directors owe it fiduciary duties, including duties of care and loyalty. Terms such as "waste" and "excessive compensation" are sometimes used to invoke these duties in particular fact patterns (the latter of which is obvious).

As the Court of Chancery has noted: "Although the tests have been articulated many times, it is often difficult to distinguish between a derivative and an individual action." . . . The distinction depends upon "'the nature of the wrong alleged' and the relief, if any, which could result if plaintiff were to prevail." . . . To pursue a direct action, the stockholder-plaintiff "must allege more than an injury resulting from a wrong to the corporation." . . .

The American Law Institute ("ALI") Principles of Corporate Governance: Analysis and Recommendations (1992) ("Principles") is helpful in this instance. Section 7.01 of the Principles undertakes to state the common law with respect to the distinction between direct and derivative actions. *Id.* §7.01, cmt. a. The Comment also discusses a situation relevant to the case *sub judice*:

> In some instances, actions that essentially involve the structural relationship of the shareholder to the corporation . . . may also give rise to a derivative action when the corporation suffers or is threatened with a loss. One example would be a case in which a corporate official knowingly acts in a manner that the certificate of incorporation [or the Delaware General Corporation Law] denied the official authority to do, thereby violating both specific restraints imposed by the shareholders [or the GCL] and the official's duty of care.

Id., cmt. c. The Comment further notes that, "courts have been more prepared to permit the plaintiff to characterize the action as direct when the plaintiff is seeking only injunctive or prospective relief." *Id.*, cmt. d.

With respect to the abdication claim, Grimes seeks only a declaration of the invalidity of the Agreements. Monetary recovery will not accrue to the corporation as a result. Chancellor Seitz illustrated this distinction in Bennett [v. Breuil Petroleum Corp., Del. Ch., 99 A.2d 236, 241 (1953).] The Court of Chancery there allowed the plaintiff-stockholder to proceed individually on his claim that stock was issued for an improper purpose and entrenchment; he proceeded derivatively on his claim that the stock was issued for an insufficient price. . . .

[The court then rejected the plaintiff's abdication claim, on the merits. Its analysis of his derivative claims appears below.]

————————

In 2004, in Tooley v. Donaldson, Lufkin & Jenrette, Inc., 845 A.2d 1031 (2004), the Delaware Supreme Court confirmed the outcome in *Grimes* and approved the following test (while rejecting a competing formulation):

> That is, a court should look to the nature of the wrong and to whom the relief should go. The stockholder's claimed direct injury must be independent of any alleged injury to the corporation. The stockholder must demonstrate that the duty breached was owed to the stockholder and that he or she can prevail without showing an injury to the corporation.

This means that shareholders seeking to bring direct claims are going to have to establish that the defendants owed duties directly to them, as well as (or instead of) to the corporation.

> ■ **Think about this:**
>
> *(A)* Allison, a shareholder of Aco, Inc., is concerned that the board of directors of Aco is about to issue shares of Aco at a price that is less than the price she paid. If she sues to enjoin the sale, will her suit be direct or derivative?
>
> *(B)* Boris, is a shareholder of Bco, Inc., which was formed for the limited purpose of acting as a holding company. He learns that the board of directors of Bco has resolved to take the corporation in a new direction—operating a fleet of taco trucks. If he sues to enjoin the change of business, will his suit be direct or derivative?
>
> *(C)* Celina was a shareholder of Cco, Inc. Following approval by the board of directors and the shareholders of Cco, the corporation was merged into Dco, Inc. Celina, who voted against the merger, believes that the shareholders were not adequately informed either of how sloppy the board's approval procedure had been or the fact that the Dco shares they would receive would have less value than the Cco shares they gave up. If Celina sues the former board of Cco, is her action direct or derivative? Does it matter what remedy she seeks?

  Time Out for PR

When an action is derivative it is quite likely to be the case that any benefit that could inure to an individual shareholder will be minimal. Why, then, are such suits ever brought? It is said by some that derivative litigation is driven by the interest of plaintiffs' lawyers in generating legal fees. To the extent this claim is true, it presents two problems.

One is the process by which a lawyer might go about finding a share-holder to act as nominal plaintiff. In this regard, consider American Bar Association Model Rule 7.3(a):

> (a) A lawyer shall not by in person, live telephone or real-time electronic contact solicit professional employment when a significant motive for the lawyer's doing so is the lawyer's pecuniary gain, unless the person con-tacted:
>
>   (1) is a lawyer; or
>
>   (2) has a family, close personal, or prior professional relationship with the lawyer.

Moreover, in some class action and derivative cases, courts have declined to confirm a potential named plaintiff's standing on the grounds that he or she is too closely affiliated with the attorney bringing suit and thus is not the "moving force" behind the action.

A second problem is that the nominal plaintiff will have little interest in either being liable for attorney's fees or for advancing the costs of litigation. Contingent fees are permissible. Although banned for decades, advancing costs on a contingent basis now is permissible under Model Rule 1.8(e). It may, however, be debatable exactly what expenses can be advanced. For instance, there is a difference among jurisdictions as to whether an attorney can advance fees for other, cooperating attorneys.

C. The Demand Requirement: Demand and Futility Under Delaware Law and the MBCA's Universal Demand Requirement

Courts and legislatures consider the corporation's decision to sue to be a busi-ness matter ordinarily reserved to the entity's usual decision makers. And so, in most cases, a disgruntled shareholder cannot simply go to court on the compa-ny's behalf. She must first notify the directors of her complaint and leave it in their hands. As the courts have sometimes explained, this "demand" require-ment reflects perhaps corporation law's most fundamental policy, the require-ment that ultimate decision-making authority be left in the board of directors. However, such a system may seem to make less sense where the members of the board are called upon to decide whether to sue themselves (or their close relatives, friends, etc.). "Demand" in that case might seem pointless, and indeed Delaware and some other states will excuse demand where circumstances strongly indicate that we cannot trust a company's sitting management to make decisions in its best interests.

As we shall see later on, the Model Business Corporation Act, to avoid the uncertainty and expense of demand futility litigation, has taken rather a different approach: "universal demand," under which plaintiff shareholders must always make demand, no matter how hopeless it might be.

1. Demand and Futility in Delaware

Appearing below is the portion of *Grimes v. Donald*, part of which we read above, containing the court's views on those of Mr. Grimes's claims that had to be brought derivatively: due care, waste, and excessive compensation. As you will recall, his claims were based on an agreement granting CEO James Donald the authority to generally manage DSC Communications Corporation and allowing him to claim a sizable severance package if he deemed the board to have unreasonably interfered with his management.

As you shall see, *Grimes* relies heavily on an earlier Delaware Supreme Court case, Aronson v. Lewis, 473 A.2d 805 (Del. 1984). *Aronson* first set out the court's test for when demand is "futile," and while *Grimes* elaborated on the test and answered some lingering questions under it, *Aronson* remains the seminal case.

Plaintiff in *Aronson* sued the entire board of Meyers Parking System, Inc., challenging employment and loan transactions between Meyers and one of its directors, Leo Fink, who owned 47 percent of its outstanding stock. The plaintiff contended that these transactions were approved "only because Fink personally selected each director and officer of Meyers" and that (1) because of that domination, (2) because the board had approved the agreements, and (3) because all members of the board were being sued, demand should be excused as futile. Applying the rule that demand can only be excused where facts are alleged with particularity that create a reasonable doubt that the directors' decision "today" would be entitled to the protections of the business judgment rule, *Aronson* made it clear that the fact that the directors were named as defendants was not sufficient to create that doubt. Neither was the fact that they approved the complained-of transaction nor the fact that they had been selected by the other party to the transaction.

It is easy to see why excusing demand if the directors are named would simply create too big a loophole. Naming as defendants the directors who approved a challenged transaction seems, however, to implicate their self-interest, rendering the business judgment rule inapplicable. The *Aronson* court, however, reasoned that if the underlying transaction would be protected by the business judgment rule, there would be nothing for the directors to fear and thus no reason to doubt their business judgment on the

Futility (or The Sinking of the Titan), by Morgan Robertson, is an 1898 novella about the fictional ocean liner Titan, which sinks in the North Atlantic after striking an iceberg. The book was written 14 years before the sinking of the Titanic. Both the fictional Titan and the Titanic were described as the largest craft afloat; neither carried enough lifeboats.

question of whether to pursue litigation. The fact that the transaction was with the shareholder who elected them was not, by itself, enough to remove the protection of the business judgment rule, since the directors were entitled to a presumption of independence. According to the court,

> there must be coupled with the allegation of control such facts as would demonstrate that through personal or other relationships the directors are beholden to the controlling person. . . . Thus, it is not enough to charge that a director was nominated by or elected at the behest of those controlling the outcome of a corporate election. That is the usual way a person becomes a corporate director. It is the care, attention and sense of individual responsibility to the performance of one's duties, not the method of election, that generally touches on independence.

Instead, the court announced the now-controlling formulation under which Delaware plaintiffs must plead futility. Plaintiff must plead facts with particularity creating "a reasonable doubt . . . that: (1) the directors are disinterested and independent and (2) the challenged transaction was otherwise the product of a valid exercise of business judgment."

Plaintiff was, however, granted leave to amend his complaint.

GRIMES V. DONALD

Delaware Supreme Court
673 A.2d 1207 (1996)

Veasey, Chief Justice:

. . . III. GRIMES' DEMAND ON THE BOARD WITH RESPECT TO THE DERIVATIVE CLAIM CONCEDED THAT DEMAND WAS REQUIRED

The complaint alleges that Grimes made a pre-suit demand on the Board in the September 29, 1993, letter quoted above. In summary, the letter described the relevant provisions of the Donald Agreements and demanded that the Board "take immediate steps to abrogate" the cited sections of the Agreements. The Court of Chancery held that, by "making demand upon the board, plaintiff has in effect conceded that the board was in a position to consider and act upon his demand." *Grimes*, 20 Del. J. Corp. L. at 772 (citing Spiegel v. Buntrock, Del. Supr., 571 A.2d 767, 775 (1990)). Contending that demand was excused, Grimes later filed suit alleging waste, excessive compensation and due care claims arising out of the Agreements. But the Chancellor held that Grimes waived his right to argue that demand was excused with respect to these claims because he had already made demand that the agreements be abrogated as unlawful. *Id.* We agree.

A. The Demand Requirement in Perspective

Because the prolix (43 page) complaint tends to confuse the issues in this case, it is appropriate to restate, as a matter of background, the Delaware jurisprudence relating to stockholder derivative litigation.

If a claim belongs to the corporation, it is the corporation, acting through its board of directors, which must make the decision whether or not to assert the claim. "[T]he derivative action impinges on the managerial freedom of directors." Pogostin v. Rice, Del. Supr., 480 A.2d 619, 624 (1984). "[T]he demand requirement is a recognition of the fundamental precept that directors manage the business and affairs of the corporation." Aronson v. Lewis, Del. Supr., 473 A.2d 805, 812 (1984).

A stockholder filing a derivative suit must allege either that the board rejected his pre-suit demand that the board assert the corporation's claim or allege with particularity why the stockholder was justified in not having made the effort to obtain board action. This is a "basic principle of corporate governance" and is a matter of substantive law embodied in the procedural requirements of Chancery Rule 23.1. One ground for alleging with particularity that demand would be futile is that a "reasonable doubt" exists that the board is capable of making an independent decision to assert the claim if demand were made. The basis for claiming excusal would normally be that: (1) a majority of the board has a material financial or familial interest; (2) a majority of the board is incapable of acting independently for some other reason such as domination or control;[1] or (3) the underlying transaction is not the product of a valid exercise of business judgment. If the stockholder cannot plead such assertions consistent with Chancery Rule 11, after using the "tools at hand"[2] to obtain the necessary information before filing a derivative action, then the stockholder must make a pre-suit demand on the board.

The demand requirement serves a salutary purpose. First, by requiring exhaustion of intracorporate remedies, the demand requirement invokes a species of alternative dispute resolution procedure which might avoid litigation altogether. Second, if litigation is beneficial, the corporation can control the proceedings. Third, if demand is excused or wrongfully refused, the stockholder will normally control the proceedings.

The jurisprudence of *Aronson* and its progeny is designed to create a balanced environment which will: (1) on the one hand, deter costly, baseless suits by creating a screening mechanism to eliminate claims where there is only a suspicion expressed solely in conclusory terms; and (2) on the other hand, permit suit

---

1. Rales v. Blasband, Del. Supr., 635 A.2d 927, 936 (1993). Demand is not excused simply because plaintiff has chosen to sue all directors. *Id.* Likewise, a plaintiff cannot necessarily disqualify all directors simply by attacking a transaction in which all participated. Pogostin v. Rice, 480 A.2d at 627. To hold otherwise would permit plaintiffs to subvert the particularity requirements of Rule 23.1 simply by designating all the directors as targets.

2. In *Rales* we undertook to describe some of those "tools at hand":

> Although derivative plaintiffs may believe it is difficult to meet the particularization requirement of *Aronson* because they are not entitled to discovery to assist their compliance with Rule 23.1, *see Levine*, 591 A.2d at 208-10, they have many avenues available to obtain information bearing on the subject of their claims. For example, there is a variety of public sources from which the details of a corporate act may be discovered, including the media and governmental agencies such as the Securities and Exchange Commission. In addition, a stockholder who has met the procedural requirements and has shown a specific proper purpose may use the summary procedure embodied in 8 Del. C. §220 to investigate the possibility of corporate wrongdoing....

by a stockholder who is able to articulate particularized facts showing that there is a reasonable doubt either that (a) a majority of the board is independent for purposes of responding to the demand, or (b) the underlying transaction is protected by the business judgment rule. *Aronson* introduced the term "reasonable doubt" into corporate derivative jurisprudence. Some courts and commentators have questioned why a concept normally present in criminal prosecution would find its way into derivative litigation. Yet the term is apt and achieves the proper balance. Reasonable doubt can be said to mean that there is a reason to doubt.[3] This concept is sufficiently flexible and workable to provide the stockholder with "the keys to the courthouse" in an appropriate case where the claim is not based on mere suspicions or stated solely in conclusory terms.

> **Connections: The Business Judgment Rule**
>
> The business judgment rule is a doctrine covered at length in connection with the duty of care. When its conditions are satisfied, courts will refrain from "second-guessing" the content of directorial decisions. Does it seem to be operating any differently here?

B. Wrongful Refusal Distinguished from Excusal

Demand has been excused in many cases in Delaware under the *Aronson* test. The law regarding wrongful refusal is not as well developed, however. Although Delaware law does not require demand in every case[4] because Delaware does have the mechanism of demand excusal, it is important that the demand process be meaningful. Therefore, a stockholder who makes a demand is entitled to know promptly what action the board has taken in response to the demand. A stockholder who makes a serious demand and receives only a peremptory refusal has the right to use the "tools at hand" to obtain the relevant corporate records, such as reports or minutes, reflecting the corporate action and related information in order to determine whether or not there is a basis to assert that demand was wrongfully refused. In no event may a corporation assume a position of neutrality and take no position in response to the demand.

If a demand is made, the stockholder has spent one—but only one—"arrow" in the "quiver." The spent "arrow" is the right to claim that demand is excused. The stockholder does not, by making demand, waive the right to claim that demand has been wrongfully refused.

Simply because the composition of the board provides no basis *ex ante* for the stockholder to claim with particularity and consistently with Rule 11 that

---

3. Stated obversely, the concept of reasonable doubt is akin to the concept that the stockholder has a "reasonable belief" that the board lacks independence or that the transaction was not protected by the business judgment rule. The concept of reasonable belief is an objective test and is found in various corporate contexts. *See* 8 Del. C. §145(a) (b). . . .

4. The ALI *Principles* and the American Bar Association's *Model Business Corporation Act* §7.42(1), both are premised upon the concept of universal demand—that is, a requirement that demand must be made in every case. The *Principles* and the *Model Act* then go in directions which are different from Delaware law and different from each other in determining the manner in which derivative litigation is to be conducted or terminated after demand has been made. In reversing the decision of the United States Court of Appeals for the Seventh Circuit, which had adopted the universal demand rule in a derivative suit under the Investment Company Act of 1940, the Supreme Court of the United States held that state law applied and analyzed the implications of the universal demand rule compared with the traditional rule exemplified by Delaware law. Kamen v. Kemper Fin. Svcs., Inc., 500 U.S. 90, 101-08 (1991).

it is reasonable to doubt that a majority of the board is either interested or not independent, it does not necessarily follow *ex post* that the board in fact *acted* independently, disinterestedly or with due care in response to the demand. A board or a committee of the board may *appear* to be independent, but may not always *act* independently.[5] If a demand is made and rejected, the board rejecting the demand is entitled to the presumption of the business judgment rule unless the stockholder can allege facts with particularity creating a reasonable doubt that the board is entitled to the benefit of the presumption. If there is reason to doubt that the board acted independently or with due care in responding to the demand, the stockholder may have the basis *ex post* to claim wrongful refusal. The stockholder then has the right to bring the underlying action with the same standing which the stockholder would have had, *ex ante*, if demand had been excused as futile.

C. Application to This Case

In the case before the Court, plaintiff made a pre-suit demand. Later, however, plaintiff contended that demand was excused. Under the doctrine articulated by this Court in Spiegel v. Buntrock, [571 A.2d 767,] plaintiff, by making a demand, waived his right to contest the independence of the board. As the Court of Chancery properly held, plaintiff may not bifurcate his theories relating to the same claim. Thus, demand having been made as to the propriety of the Agreements, it cannot be excused as to the claim that the Agreements constituted waste, excessive compensation or was the product of a lack of due care.

The Court of Chancery implicitly applied a test analogous to *res judicata* to determine whether Grimes' demand letter conceded that demand was required for all legal theories arising out of the set of facts described in the demand letter. We believe this to be a correct approach. The alternative claims raised in the complaint fit squarely within the same transactional rubric as the demand since all of the claims, however denominated, arise out of the Agreements. . . .

In *Spiegel*, this Court held that "[a] shareholder who makes a demand can no longer argue that demand is excused." 571 A.2d at 775. Permitting a stockholder to demand action involving only one theory or remedy and to argue later that demand is excused as to other legal theories or remedies arising out of the same set of circumstances as set forth in the demand letter would create an undue risk of harassment.

In this case, the Board of DSC considered and rejected the demand. After investing the time and resources to consider and decide whether or not to take action in response to the demand, the Board is entitled to have its decision analyzed under the business judgment rule unless the presumption of that rule can be rebutted. Grimes cannot avoid this result by holding back or bifurcating legal theories based on precisely the same set of facts alleged in the demand.

---

5. *See* Kahn v. Lynch Communication Sys., Del. Supr., 638 A.2d 1110, 1120-21 (1994) ("independent committee" of the board did not act independently when it succumbed to threat of controlling stockholder, thus invoking entire fairness analysis rather than business judgment rule).

Since Grimes made a pre-suit demand with respect to all claims arising out of the Agreements, he was required by Chancery Rule 23.1 to plead with particularity why the Board's refusal to act on the derivative claims was wrongful. The complaint recites the Board's rejection of Grimes' demand and proceeds to assert why Grimes disagrees with the Board's conclusion. The complaint generally asserts that the refusal could not have been the result of an adequate, good faith investigation since the Board decided not to act on the demand. Such conclusory, *ipse dixit*, assertions are inconsistent with the requirements of Chancery Rule 23.1. The complaint fails to include particularized allegations which would raise a reasonable doubt that the Board's decision to reject the demand was the product of a valid business judgment. . . .

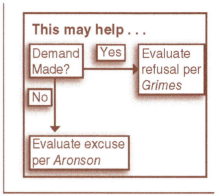

■   **Think about this:**

(D) The court in *Grimes* refers to the loss of one arrow from the plaintiff's quiver, since making demand concedes the independence of the board. Is there ever more than one arrow in the quiver at one time? Consider the diagram in the sidebar.

(E) How is the test that will be applied to tell if demand is excused any different from the one that is applied to tell if refusal was wrongful?

2. Other Methods: "Universal Demand" Under the MBCA and the New York Approach

The Model Business Corporations Act, to avoid the uncertainty and expense of demand futility litigation under a rule like the *Aronson* rule, has adopted a "universal demand" rule. *See* MBCA §7.42. Essentially, a shareholder must make written demand and wait 90 days before filing suit unless demand is earlier rejected, or the corporation would be irreparably injured by the wait. What happens if the directors reject the demand? Presumably, the shareholder is free to file suit, but will do so with the knowledge that the corporation promptly will move to dismiss it. MBCA §7.44 specifies the circumstances under which such a motion is to be granted and is discussed in Section D, below.

And finally, New York takes an approach that is at least facially different than that of the MBCA or Delaware. In Marx v. Akers, 666 N.E.2d 1034 (1996), the court put it this way:

(1) Demand is excused because of futility when a complaint alleges with particularity that a majority of the board of directors is interested in the challenged transaction.

Director interest may either be self-interest in the transaction at issue . . . or a loss of independence because a director with no direct interest in a transaction is "controlled" by a self-interested director. (2) Demand is excused because of futility when a complaint alleges with particularity that the board of directors did not fully inform themselves about the challenged transaction to the extent reasonably appropriate under the circumstances. . . . (3) Demand is excused because of futility when a complaint alleges with particularity that the challenged transaction was so egregious on its face that it could not have been the product of sound business judgment of the directors.

Whether this formulation would lead to different outcomes than the Delaware approach may be arguable. The *Marx* court applied its own test in concluding that demand was excused in the context of directors voting on their own compensation. (It nonetheless went on to hold that no cause of action had been stated.)

■ **Think about this:**

(F) Suppose that the act of directors voting on their own compensation is challenged in Delaware. Would demand be excused?

D. The Directors' Authority to Dismiss Derivative Litigation

Suppose a private plaintiff has successfully navigated the demand requirement and has filed a derivative cause of action. Under what circumstances does the board have power to dismiss it? The trio of cases below give insight into this subject.

AUERBACH V. BENNETT

New York Court of Appeals
393 N.E.2d 994 (1979)

Jones, Judge. . . .

In the summer of 1975 the management of General Telephone & Electronics Corporation, in response to reports that numerous other multinational companies had made questionable payments to public officials or political parties in foreign countries, directed that an internal preliminary investigation be made to ascertain whether that corporation had engaged in similar transactions. On the basis of the report of this survey, received in October, 1975, management brought the issue to the attention of the corporation's board of directors. At a meeting held on November 6 of that year the board referred the matter to the board's audit committee. The audit committee retained as its special counsel the Washington, D.C., law firm of Wilmer, Cutler & Pickering which had not previously acted as counsel to the corporation. With the assistance of such special counsel and Arthur Andersen & Co., the corporation's outside auditors, the audit committee engaged in an investigation into the corporation's worldwide operations, focusing on whether, in the period January 1, 1971 to December 31, 1975, corporate funds had been (1) paid directly or indirectly to any political party or person or to any officer, employee, shareholder or director of any governmental or private customer, or (2) used to reimburse any officer of the corporation or other person for such payments.

On March 4, 1976 the audit committee released its report which was filed with the Securities and Exchange Commission and disclosed to the corporation's shareholders in a proxy statement prior to the annual meeting of shareholders held in April, 1976. The audit committee reported that it had found evidence that in the period from 1971 to 1975 the corporation or its subsidiaries had made payments abroad and in the United States constituting bribes and kickbacks in amounts perhaps totaling more than 11 million dollars and that some of the individual defendant directors had been personally involved in certain of the transactions.

Almost immediately Auerbach [for whom Stanley Wallenstein was later substituted], a shareholder in the corporation, instituted the present shareholders' derivative action on behalf of the corporation against the corporation's directors, Arthur Andersen & Co., and the corporation. The complaint alleged that in connection with the transactions reported by the audit committee defendants, present and former members of the corporation's board of directors and Arthur Andersen & Co., are liable to the corporation for breach of their duties to the corporation and should be made to account for payments made in those transactions.

> **More to the Story: Nominal Plaintiffs and Defendant**
>
> The shareholder bringing a derivative action is the "nominal" plaintiff—the corporation is the real party in interest. The corporation usually is aligned as a "nominal" defendant to assure that it receives adequate notice.

On April 21, 1976 the board of directors of the corporation adopted a resolution creating a special litigation committee "for the purpose of establishing a point of contract between the Board of Directors and the Corporation's General Counsel concerning the position to be taken by the Corporation in certain litigation involving shareholder derivative claims on behalf of the Corporation against certain of its directors and officers" and authorizing that committee "to take such steps from time to time as it deems necessary to pursue its objectives including the retention of special outside counsel." The special committee comprised three disinterested directors who had joined the board after the challenged transactions had occurred. The board subsequently additionally vested in the committee "all of the authority of the Board of Directors to determine, on behalf of the Board, the position that the Corporation shall take with respect to the derivative claims alleged on its behalf" in the present and similar shareholder derivative actions.

The special litigation committee reported under date of November 22, 1976. It found that defendant Arthur Andersen & Co. had conducted its examination of the corporation's affairs in accordance with generally accepted auditing standards and in good faith and concluded that no proper interest of the corporation or its shareholders would be served by the continued assertion of a claim against it. The committee also concluded that none of the individual defendants had violated the New York State statutory standard of care, that none had profited personally or gained in any way, that the claims asserted in the present action are without merit, that if the action were allowed to proceed the time and talents of the corporation's senior management would be wasted on lengthy pretrial and trial proceedings, that litigation costs would be inordinately high in view of the unlikelihood of success, and that the continuing publicity could be damaging to the corporation's business. The committee determined that it would not be in the best interests of the corporation for the present derivative action to proceed, and, exercising the authority delegated to it, directed the corporation's general counsel to take that position in the present litigation as well as in pending comparable shareholders' derivative actions. . . . On May 13, 1977 Supreme Court, Special Term, granted the motions of all defendants and dismissed the complaint on the merits. . . .

As all parties and both courts below recognize, the disposition of this case on the merits turns on the proper application of the business judgment doctrine, in particular to the decision of a specially appointed committee of disinterested directors acting on behalf of the board to terminate a shareholders' derivative action. . . .

In this instance our inquiry, to the limited extent to which it may be pursued, has a two-tiered aspect. The complaint initially asserted liability on the part of defendants based on the payments made to foreign governmental customers and privately owned customers, some unspecified portions of which were allegedly passed on to officials of the customers, i.e., the focus was on first-tier bribes and kickbacks. Then subsequent to the service of the complaint there came the report of a special litigation committee, particularly appointed by the corporation's board of directors to consider the merits of the present and similar shareholders' derivative actions, and its determination that it would not be in the best interests of the corporation to press claims against defendants based on their possible first-tier liability. The motions for summary judgment were predicated principally on the report and determination of the special litigation committee and on the contention that this second-tier corporate action insulated the first-tier transactions from judicial inquiry and was itself subject to the shelter of the business judgment doctrine. . . .

This may help . . .

Eating a cake from the top down.

TIER TWO
Decision to dismiss

TIER ONE

Underlying asserted "bad act"

It appears to us that the business judgment doctrine, at least in part, is grounded in the prudent recognition that courts are ill equipped and infrequently called on to evaluate what are and must be essentially business judgments. . . . Derivative claims against corporate directors belong to the corporation itself. As with other questions of corporate policy and management, the decision whether and to what extent to explore and prosecute such claims lies within the judgment and control of the corporation's board of directors. . . .

In the present case we confront a special instance of the application of the business judgment rule and inquire whether it applies in its full vigor to shield from judicial scrutiny the decision of a three-person minority committee of the board acting on behalf of the full board not to prosecute a shareholder's derivative action. The record in this case reveals that the board is a 15-member board, and that the derivative suit was brought against four of the directors. Nothing suggests that any of the other directors participated in any of the challenged first-tier transactions. Indeed the report of the audit committee on which the complaint is based specifically found that no other directors had any prior knowledge of or were in any way involved in any of these transactions. Other directors had, however, been members of the board in the period during which the transactions occurred. Each of the three director members of the special litigation committee joined the board thereafter.

The business judgment rule does not foreclose inquiry by the courts into the disinterested independence of those members of the board chosen by it to make the corporate decision on its behalf[—]here the members of the special litigation committee. Indeed the rule shields the deliberations and conclusions of the chosen representatives of the board only if they possess a disinterested independence and do not stand in a dual relation which prevents an unprejudicial exercise of judgment.

We examine then the proof submitted by defendants. It is not disputed that the members of the special litigation committee were not members of the corporation's board of directors at the time of the first-tier transactions in question. . . . None of the three had had any prior affiliation with the corporation. Notwithstanding the vigorous and imaginative hypothesizing and innuendo of counsel there is nothing in this record to raise a triable issue of fact as to the independence and disinterested status of these three directors.

The contention of Wallenstein that any committee authorized by the board of which defendant directors were members must be held to be legally infirm and may not be delegated power to terminate a derivative action must be rejected. In the very nature of the corporate organization it was only the existing board of directors which had authority on behalf of the corporation to direct the investigation and to assure the cooperation of corporate employees, and it is only that same board by its own action or as here pursuant to authority duly delegated by it which had authority to decide whether to prosecute the claims against defendant directors. The board in this instance, with slight adaptation, followed prudent practice in observing the general policy that when individual members of a board of directors prove to have personal interests which may conflict with the interests of the corporation, such interested directors must be excluded while the remaining members of the board proceed to consideration and action. . . . Courts have consistently held that the business judgment rule applies where some directors are charged with wrongdoing, so long as the remaining directors making the decision are disinterested and independent. . . .

To accept the assertions of the intervenor and to disqualify the entire board would be to render the corporation powerless to make an effective business judgment with respect to prosecution of the derivative action. The possible risk of hesitancy on the part of the members of any committee, even if composed of outside, independent, disinterested directors, to investigate the activities of fellow members of the board where personal liability is at stake is an inherent, inescapable, given aspect of the corporation's predicament. To assign responsibility of the dimension here involved to individuals wholly separate and apart from the board of directors would, except in the most extraordinary circumstances, itself be an act of default and breach of the nondelegable fiduciary duty owed by the members of the board to the corporation and to its shareholders, employees and creditors. For the courts to preside over such determinations would similarly work an ouster of the board's fundamental responsibility and authority for corporate management.

We turn then to the action of the special litigation committee itself which comprised two components. First, there was the selection of procedures appropriate to the pursuit of its charge, and second, there was the ultimate substantive decision, predicated on the procedures chosen and the data produced thereby, not to pursue the claims advanced in the shareholders' derivative actions. The latter, substantive decision falls squarely within the embrace of the business judgment doctrine, involving as it did the weighing and balancing of legal, ethical, commercial, promotional, public relations, fiscal and other factors familiar to the resolution of many if not most corporate problems. To this extent the conclusion reached by the special litigation committee is outside the scope of our review. Thus, the courts cannot inquire as to which factors were considered by that committee or the relative weight accorded them in reaching that substantive decision. . . .

As to the other component of the committee's activities, however, the situation is different. . . . As to the methodologies and procedures best suited to the conduct of an investigation of facts and the determination of legal liability, the courts are well equipped by long and continuing experience and practice to make determinations. In fact they are better qualified in this regard than are corporate directors in general. Nor do the determinations to be made in the adoption of procedures partake of the nuances or special perceptions or comprehensions of business judgment or corporate activities or interests. The question is solely how appropriately to set about to gather the pertinent data.

While the court may properly inquire as to the adequacy and appropriateness of the committee's investigative procedures and methodologies, it may not under the guise of consideration of such factors trespass in the domain of business judgment. At the same time those responsible for the procedures by which the business judgment is reached may reasonably be required to show that they have pursued their chosen investigative methods in good faith. What evidentiary proof may be required to this end will, of course, depend on the nature of the particular investigation, and the proper reach of disclosure at the instance of the shareholders will in turn relate inversely to the showing made by the corporate representatives themselves. The latter may be expected to show that the areas and subjects to be examined are reasonably complete and that there has been a good-faith pursuit of inquiry into such areas and subjects. What has been uncovered and the relative weight accorded in evaluating and balancing the several factors and considerations are beyond the scope of judicial concern. Proof, however, that the investigation has been so restricted in scope, so shallow in execution, or otherwise so Pro forma or halfhearted as to constitute a pretext or sham, consistent with the principles underlying the application of the business judgment doctrine, would raise questions of good faith or conceivably fraud which would never be shielded by that doctrine.

   . . . On the submissions made by defendants in support of their motions, we do not find either insufficiency or infirmity as to the procedures and methodologies chosen and pursued by the special litigation committee. That committee promptly engaged eminent special counsel to guide its deliberations and to advise it. The committee reviewed the prior work of the audit committee, testing its completeness, accuracy and thoroughness by interviewing representatives of Wilmer, Cutler & Pickering, reviewing transcripts of the testimony of 10 corporate officers and employees before the Securities and Exchange Commission, and studying documents collected by and work papers of the Washington law firm. Individual interviews were conducted with the directors found to have participated in any way in the questioned payments, and with representatives of Arthur Andersen & Co. Questionnaires were sent to and answered by each of the corporation's nonmanagement directors. At the conclusion of its investigation the special litigation committee sought and obtained pertinent legal advice from its special counsel. The selection of appropriate investigative methods must always turn on the nature and characteristics of the particular subject being investigated, but we find nothing in this record that requires a trial of any material issue of fact concerning the sufficiency or appropriateness of the procedures chosen by this special litigation committee. Nor is there anything in this record to raise a triable issue of fact as to the good-faith pursuit of its examination by that committee. . . .

■ **Think about this:**

(G) Is the court in *Auerbach* applying the business judgment rule in exactly the same way we encountered it in discussing the duty of care?

(H) Suppose that Henrietta has brought a derivative claim against the directors of HCo, Inc., a New York corporation, claiming that they voted themselves a gigantic and unjustified salary increase. HCo forms a special litigation committee composed of directors added after the vote in question. They move to dismiss Henrietta's claim. Who needs to show what?

   Auerbach was decided in 1979 and, for the most part, seems a logical extrapolation of traditional doctrines. When Delaware got its chance to resolve the same issues it went a different way.

ZAPATA CORP. V. MALDONADO

Supreme Court of Delaware
430 A.2d 779 (1981)

QUILLEN, Justice:

This is an interlocutory appeal from an order entered on April 9, 1980, by the Court of Chancery denying appellant-defendant Zapata Corporation's (Zapata) alternative motions to dismiss the complaint or for summary judgment. The issue to be addressed has reached this Court by way of a rather convoluted path.

In June, 1975, William Maldonado, a stockholder of Zapata, instituted a derivative action in the Court of Chancery on behalf of Zapata against ten officers and/or directors of Zapata, alleging, essentially, breaches of fiduciary duty. Maldonado did not first demand that the board bring this action, stating instead such demand's futility because all directors were named as defendants and allegedly participated in the acts specified. In June, 1977, Maldonado commenced an action in the United States District Court for the Southern District of New York against the same defendants, save one, alleging federal security law violations as well as the same common law claims made previously in the Court of Chancery.

By June, 1979, four of the defendant-directors were no longer on the board, and the remaining directors appointed two new outside directors to the board. The board then created an "Independent Investigation Committee" (Committee), composed solely of the two new directors, to investigate Maldonado's actions, as well as a similar derivative action then pending in Texas, and to determine whether the corporation should continue any or all of the litigation. The Committee's determination was stated to be "final, . . . not . . . subject to review by the Board of Directors and . . . in all respects . . . binding upon the Corporation."

Following an investigation, the Committee concluded, in September, 1979, that each action should "be dismissed forthwith as their continued maintenance is inimical to the Company's best interests. . . ." Consequently, Zapata moved for dismissal or summary judgment in the three derivative actions. . . . On March 18, 1980, the Court of Chancery . . . denied Zapata's motions, holding that Delaware law does not sanction this means of dismissal. More specifically, it held that the "business judgment" rule is not a grant of authority to dismiss derivative actions and that a stockholder has an individual right to maintain derivative actions in certain instances. Maldonado v. Flynn, Del. Ch., 413 A.2d 1251 (1980) (herein *Maldonado*). Pursuant to the provisions of Supreme Court Rule 42, Zapata filed an interlocutory appeal with this Court shortly thereafter. . . . [W]e agree that this Court can and should attempt to resolve the particular question of Delaware law. As the Vice Chancellor noted, 413 A.2d at 1257, "it is the law of the State of incorporation which determines whether the directors have this power of dismissal, Burks v. Lasker, 441 U.S. 471 (1979)." We limit our review in this interlocutory appeal to whether the Committee has the power to cause the present action to be dismissed.

We begin with an examination of the carefully considered opinion of the Vice Chancellor which states, in part, that the "business judgment" rule does not confer power "to a corporate board of directors to terminate a derivative suit," 413 A.2d at 1257. His conclusion is particularly pertinent because several federal courts, applying Delaware law, have held that the business judgment rule enables boards (or their committees) to terminate derivative suits, decisions now in conflict with the holding below.

As the term is most commonly used, and given the disposition below, we can understand the Vice Chancellor's comment that "the business judgment rule is irrelevant to the question of whether the Committee has the authority to compel the dismissal of this suit." 413 A.2d at 1257. Corporations, existing because of legislative grace, possess authority as granted by the legislature. Directors of Delaware corporations derive their managerial decision-making power, which encompasses decisions whether to initiate, or refrain from entering, litigation, from 8 Del. C. §141(a). This statute is the fount of directorial powers. The "business judgment" rule is a judicial creation that presumes propriety, under certain circumstances, in a board's decision. Viewed defensively, it does not create authority. In this sense the "business judgment" rule is not relevant in corporate decision making until after a decision is made. It is generally used as a defense to an attack on the decision's soundness. The board's managerial decision making power, however, comes from §141(a). The judicial creation and legislative grant are related because the "business judgment" rule evolved to give recognition and deference to directors' business expertise when exercising their managerial power under §141(a).

In the case before us, although the corporation's decision to move to dismiss or for summary judgment was, literally, a decision resulting from an exercise of the directors' (as delegated to the Committee) business judgment, the question of "business judgment," in a defensive sense, would not become relevant until and unless the decision to seek termination of the derivative lawsuit was attacked as improper. . . . This question was not reached by the Vice Chancellor because he determined that the stockholder had an individual right to maintain this derivative action. . . .

Thus, the focus in this case is on the power to speak for the corporation as to whether the lawsuit should be continued or terminated. As we see it, this issue in the current appellate posture of this case has three aspects: the conclusions of the Court below concerning the continuing right of a stockholder to maintain a derivative action; the corporate power under Delaware law of an authorized board committee to cause dismissal of litigation instituted for the benefit of the corporation; and the role of the Court of Chancery in resolving conflicts between the stockholder and the committee.

Accordingly, we turn first to the Court of Chancery's conclusions concerning the right of a plaintiff stockholder in a derivative action. We find that its determination that a stockholder, once demand is made and refused, possesses an independent, individual right to continue a derivative suit for breaches of fiduciary duty over objection by the corporation, *Maldonado*, 413 A.2d at 1262-63, as an absolute rule, is erroneous. . . .

Consistent with the purpose of requiring a demand, a board decision to cause a derivative suit to be dismissed as detrimental to the company, after demand has been made and refused, will be respected unless it was wrongful.[6] . . .

The question to be decided becomes: When, if at all, should an authorized board committee be permitted to cause litigation, properly initiated by a derivative stockholder in his own right, to be dismissed? As noted above, a board has the power to choose not to pursue litigation when demand is made upon it, so long as the decision is not wrongful. If the board determines that a suit would be detrimental to the company, the board's determination prevails. Even when demand is excusable, circumstances may arise when continuation of the litigation would not be in the corporation's best interests. Our inquiry is whether, under such circumstances, there is a permissible procedure under §141(a) by which a corporation can rid itself of detrimental litigation. If there is not, a single stockholder in an extreme case might control the destiny of the entire corporation. . . . But, when examining the means, including the committee mechanism examined in this case, potentials for abuse must be recognized. This takes us to the second and third aspects of the issue on appeal. . . .

At the risk of stating the obvious, the problem is relatively simple. If, on the one hand, corporations can consistently wrest bona fide derivative actions away from well-meaning derivative plaintiffs through the use of the committee mechanism, the derivative suit will lose much, if not all, of its generally-recognized effectiveness as an intra-corporate means of policing boards of directors. . . . If, on the other hand, corporations are unable to rid themselves of meritless or harmful litigation and strike suits, the derivative action, created to benefit the corporation, will produce the opposite, unintended result. . . . It thus appears desirable to us to find a balancing point where bona fide stockholder power to bring corporate causes of action cannot be unfairly trampled on by the board of directors, but the corporation can rid itself of detrimental litigation.

As we noted, the question has been treated by other courts as one of the "business judgment" of the board committee. If a "committee, composed of independent and disinterested directors, conducted a proper review of the matters before it, considered a variety of factors and reached, in good faith, a business judgment that (the) action was not in the best interest of (the corporation)," the action must be dismissed. See, e.g., Maldonado v. Flynn, supra, 485 F. Supp. at 282, 286. The issues become solely independence, good faith, and reasonable investigation. The ultimate conclusion of the committee, under that view, is not subject to judicial review.

We are not satisfied, however, that acceptance of the "business judgment" rationale at this stage of derivative litigation is a proper balancing point. While we admit an analogy with a normal case

Viva Zapata! A movie of this name and starring Marlon Brando was made in 1952. It was based on the life of Emiliano Zapata, an iconic figure of the Mexican Revolution.

---

6. In other words, when stockholders, after making demand and having their suit rejected, attack the board's decision as improper, the board's decision falls under the "business judgment" rule and will be respected if the requirements of the rule are met. That situation should be distinguished from the instant case, where demand was not made, and the power of the board to seek a dismissal, due to disqualification, presents a threshold issue. . . . We recognize that the two contexts can overlap in practice.

respecting board judgment, it seems to us that there is sufficient risk in the realities of a situation like the one presented in this case to justify caution beyond adherence to the theory of business judgment.

The context here is a suit against directors where demand on the board is excused. We think some tribute must be paid to the fact that the lawsuit was properly initiated. It is not a board refusal case. Moreover, this complaint was filed in June of 1975 and, while the parties undoubtedly would take differing views on the degree of litigation activity, we have to be concerned about the creation of an "Independent Investigation Committee" four years later, after the election of two new outside directors. Situations could develop where such motions could be filed after years of vigorous litigation for reasons unconnected with the merits of the lawsuit.

Moreover, notwithstanding our conviction that Delaware law entrusts the corporate power to a properly authorized committee, we must be mindful that directors are passing judgment on fellow directors in the same corporation and fellow directors, in this instance, who designated them to serve both as directors and committee members. The question naturally arises whether a "there but for the grace of God go I" empathy might not play a role. And the further question arises whether inquiry as to independence, good faith and reasonable investigation is sufficient safeguard against abuse, perhaps subconscious abuse. . . .

Whether the Court of Chancery will be persuaded by the exercise of a committee power resulting in a summary motion for dismissal of a derivative action, where a demand has not been initially made, should rest, in our judgment, in the independent discretion of the Court of Chancery. We thus steer a middle course between those cases which yield to the independent business judgment of a board committee and this case as determined below which would yield to unbridled plaintiff stockholder control. In pursuit of the course, we recognize that "(t)he final substantive judgment whether a particular lawsuit should be maintained requires a balance of many factors ethical, commercial, promotional, public relations, employee relations, fiscal as well as legal." Maldonado v. Flynn, supra, 485 F. Supp. at 285. But we are content that such factors are not "beyond the judicial reach" of the Court of Chancery which regularly and competently deals with fiduciary relationships, disposition of trust property, approval of settlements and scores of similar problems. We recognize the danger of judicial overreaching but the alternatives seem to us to be outweighed by the fresh view of a judicial outsider. Moreover, if we failed to balance all the interests involved, we would in the name of practicality and judicial economy foreclose a judicial decision on the merits. At this point, we are not convinced that is necessary or desirable.

After an objective and thorough investigation of a derivative suit, an independent committee may cause its corporation to file a pretrial motion to dismiss in the Court of Chancery. The basis of the motion is the best interests of the corporation, as determined by the committee. The motion should include a thorough written record of the investigation and its findings and recommendations. Under appropriate Court supervision, akin to proceedings on summary judgment, each side should have an opportunity to make a record on the motion. As to the limited issues presented by the motion noted below, the moving party should be prepared to meet the normal burden under Rule 56 that there is no genuine issue as to any material fact and that the moving party is entitled to dismiss as a matter of law. The Court should apply a two-step test to the motion.

First, the Court should inquire into the independence and good faith of the committee and the bases supporting its conclusions. Limited discovery may be ordered to facilitate such inquiries. The corporation should have the burden of proving independence, good faith and a reasonable investigation, rather than presuming independence, good faith and reasonableness. If the Court determines either that the committee is not independent or has not shown reasonable bases for its conclusions, or, if the Court is not satisfied for other reasons relating to the process, including but not limited to the good faith of the committee, the Court shall deny the corporation's motion. If, however, the Court is satisfied under Rule 56 standards that the committee was independent and showed reasonable bases for good faith findings and recommendations, the Court may proceed, in its discretion, to the next step.

The second step provides, we believe, the essential key in striking the balance between legitimate corporate claims as expressed in a derivative stockholder suit and a corporation's best interests as expressed by an independent investigating committee. The Court should determine, applying its own independent business judgment, whether the motion should be granted. This means, of course, that instances could arise where a committee can establish its independence and sound bases for its good faith decisions and still have the corporation's motion denied. The second step is intended to thwart instances where corporate actions meet the criteria of step one, but the result does not appear to satisfy its spirit, or where corporate actions would simply prematurely terminate a stockholder grievance deserving of further consideration in the corporation's interest. The Court of Chancery of course must carefully consider and weigh how compelling the corporate interest in dismissal is when faced with a non-frivolous lawsuit. The Court of Chancery should, when appropriate, give special consideration to matters of law and public policy in addition to the corporation's best interests.

If the Court's independent business judgment is satisfied, the Court may proceed to grant the motion, subject, of course, to any equitable terms or conditions the Court finds necessary or desirable. . . .

Connections: A Shifting Burden

Burden shifting is something we encountered in the duty of loyalty context. Essentially, once a plaintiff establishes that a transaction involved self-dealing, the burden shifted to the corporate fiduciary to establish the entire fairness of a transaction—although involving a disinterested decision maker on the corporation's behalf can have the effect of shifting the burden back.

■ **Think about this:**

(I) *Aronson* was decided after *Zapata*. Is *Zapata* a case that would satisfy *Aronson*'s standards for excusing demand?

(J) Suppose that Maldonado, the plaintiff in *Zapata*, had made demand on the corporation, which then formed a special litigation committee composed of independent directors. The special litigation committee concluded that it was in the corporation's best interests to dismiss the litigation. What test will apply?

This may help . . . in thinking about the relationship of Aronson, Grimes, and Zapata:

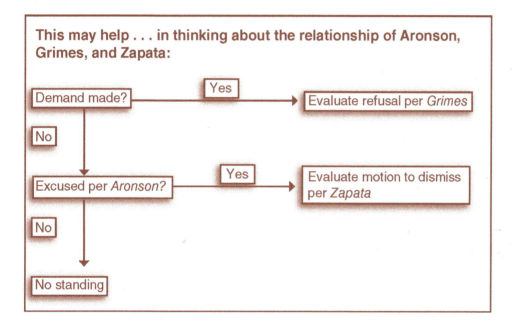

One might expect that *Zapata* would be influential, and indeed it was. Still, there are jurisdictions that found it imperfect.

ALFORD V. SHAW

Supreme Court of North Carolina
358 S.E.2d 323 (1987)

MARTIN, Justice.

The sole issue raised by this appeal is whether a special litigation committee's decision to terminate plaintiff minority shareholders' derivative action against defendant corporate directors is binding upon the courts. . . .

The recent trend among courts which have been faced with the choice of applying an *Auerbach*-type rule of judicial deference or a *Zapata*-type rule of judicial scrutiny has been to require judicial inquiry on the merits of the special litigation committee's report. . . .

... We interpret the trend away from *Auerbach* among other jurisdictions as an indication of growing concern about the deficiencies inherent in a rule giving great deference to the decisions of a corporate committee whose institution symbiosis with the corporation necessarily affects its ability to render a decision that fairly considers the interest of the plaintiffs forced to bring suit on behalf of the corporation. Such concerns are legitimate ones and, upon further reflection, we find that they must be resolved not by slavish adherence to the business judgment rule, but by careful interpretation of the provisions of our own Business Corporation Act. We conclude from our analysis of the pertinent statutes that a modified *Zapata* rule, requiring judicial scrutiny of the merits of the litigation committee's recommendation, is most consistent with the intent of our legislature and is therefore the appropriate rule to be applied in our courts....

Although the recommendation of the special litigation committee is not binding on the court, in making this determination the court may choose to rely on such recommendation. To rely blindly on the report of a corporation-appointed committee which assembled such materials on behalf of the corporation is to abdicate the judicial duty to consider the interests of shareholders imposed by the statute. This abdication is particularly inappropriate in a case such as this one, where shareholders allege serious breaches of fiduciary duties owed to them by the directors controlling the corporation....

The *Zapata* Court limited its two-step judicial inquiry to cases in which demand upon the corporation was futile and therefore excused. However, we find no justification for such limitation in our statutes.... Thus, court approval is required for disposition of all derivative suits, even where the directors are not charged with fraud or self-dealing, or where the plaintiff and the board agree to discontinue, dismiss, compromise, or settle the lawsuit.

While *Auerbach* was the first high court decision to consider the power of the board to dismiss derivative actions, and while *Zapata* was as closely watched as most corporate law decisions of the Delaware Supreme Court, *Alford* now appears to state the majority rule. Consider the following provision from the Model Business Corporations Act relating to dismissal of derivative litigation:

MODEL BUSINESS CORPORATIONS ACT

§7.44 Dismissal

(a) A derivative proceeding shall be dismissed by the court on motion by the corporation if one of the groups specified in subsection §7.44(b) or subsection §7.44(e) has determined in good faith, after conducting a reasonable inquiry upon which its conclusions are based, that the maintenance of the derivative proceeding is not in the best interests of the corporation.

(b) Unless a panel is appointed pursuant to subsection §7.44(e), the determination in subsection §7.44(a) shall be made by: (1) a majority vote of independent directors present at a meeting of the board of directors if the independent directors constitute a quorum; or (2) a majority vote of a committee consisting of two or more independent directors appointed by majority vote of independent directors present at a meeting of the board of directors, whether or not such independent directors constituted a quorum.

(c) If a derivative proceeding is commenced after a determination has been made rejecting a demand by a shareholder, the complaint shall allege with particularity facts establishing either (1) that a majority of the board of directors did not consist of independent directors at the time the determination was made or (2) that the requirements of subsection §7.44(a) have not been met.

(d) If a majority of the board of directors does not consist of independent directors at the time the determination is made, the corporation shall have the burden of proving that the requirements of subsection §7.44(a) have been met.

(e) The court may appoint a panel of one or more independent persons upon motion by the corporation to make a determination whether the maintenance of the derivative proceeding is in the best interests of the corporation. In such case, the plaintiff shall have the burden of proving that the requirements of subsection §7.44(a) have not been met.

Although not set out here, there is a helpful commentary to this section making it clear, among other things, that the language in (a) indeed requires that the conclusions referred to must be based on the called-for inquiry. Nonetheless, the section does not authorize a court to review the determination for reasonableness.

■ **Think about this:**

(K) How does the MBCA approach seem to differ from the approaches represented in *Auerbach*, *Zapata*, and *Auer*?

(L) Considering only the context of cases brought where demand is excused, would you expect more or fewer dismissals to be granted under the MBCA approach, compared to *Zapata*?

 Dear Prof.: Do special litigation committees always choose not to pursue litigation?

The cynics among us always suspected that might be the case, but it turns out not to be so. Consider the following, taken from an article based on a study of special litigation committee (SLC) decisions from 1993 to 2006:

The data indicate that SLCs do not uniformly decide to dismiss derivative litigation. They sought some form of formal relief much more frequently than heretofore recognized: approximately forty percent of the time, SLCs pursued or settled claims against one or more defendants.

A broader claim about SLC behavior—that, even if they do not dismiss claims, they may nevertheless take it easy on defendants by failing to pursue claims diligently or by settling claims for nothing—also finds no support in the data. When SLCs decided to pursue claims or settle them, the company received meaningful financial recoveries. SLCs thus do not appear to be in the business of letting defendants off the hook, either by dismissing claims or by pressing them with no zeal.

The SLC decision is not the final procedural development in cases, and a majority of all cases subject to their review eventually end up settled, not dismissed. Dismissal is not even the most common outcome when the SLC decides to seek dismissal of the claims. What has been viewed as the great engine for dismissing shareholder derivative cases actually ends up resulting in mostly settlements.

The pattern of recoveries in settlement suggests that SLCs may be more sensitive to the merits of shareholder claims than has been recognized before. Company recoveries were large in the median instance when SLCs decided to pursue claims, modest when they decided to settle claims, and zero when they decided to dismiss claims. To the extent that settlement values correlate with merit, SLCs pursue strong claims, dismiss weak ones, and settle close ones.

The data also indicate one important reason why a company might use an SLC: cases in which an SLC is appointed are resolved much more quickly than derivative cases generally. This suggests SLCs may function as a form of alternative dispute resolution.

Minor Myers, *The Decisions of the Corporate Special Litigation Committees: An Empirical Investigation*, 84 IND. L.J. 1309, 1311 (2009).

Test Yourself

1. Joe, a shareholder in a large consumer products manufacturer called ABC, Inc., is planning a derivative lawsuit. The company is incorporated in a state following the Model Business Corporations Act. First, Joe calls ABC's Consumer Complaints Department and speaks with a consumer help representative named I. Kent Bebothered. Joe explains to Mr. Bebothered, in some detail, why he believes that fiduciary duties have been breached. Which of the following most accurately describes Joe's situation?

a. Joe's phone call probably constitutes effective shareholder "demand" because there is no required form in which demand must be made.

b. Joe's phone call probably does not constitute effective shareholder "demand" because of Mr. Bebothered's position within the company.

c. Joe's phone call does not constitute effective shareholder "demand" because it is not in writing.

d. Answers b and c are both true.

Questions 2-5 rely on the following set of facts:

Paul Plaintiff owns one share of stock in DotBomb, Inc., a publicly held Delaware company that launched a briefly successful internet service that since has failed and gone through bankruptcy. Paul, who is not the sharpest knife in the drawer, bought his share shortly after DotBomb emerged from those bankruptcy proceedings, not knowing that the company had gone through difficult times. In fact, at the time of his purchase, Paul was under the impression that DotBomb's website was still active and profitable, and accordingly he bought his share at the high price of $15. At that point, however, DotBomb was actually engaged in no business whatsoever, and Paul has discovered that if he were to try to sell his share of stock, it would be worth something more like 5¢. Paul has also learned that the company has given up any plans to resume its business, and in fact its board has already voted to recommend to the shareholders that they dissolve the company.

Frustrated, Paul decides legal action is required. First, he makes a number of telephone calls to the company's board and management, and manages to speak with a few of the company's directors and senior officers. To each of these persons Paul states his complaint, and insists that if the board votes in favor of dissolving the company either he or someone within the company should sue the board members for breach of fiduciary duty. Some days later Paul received a letter from DotBomb's General Counsel that stated in polite but firm language that the company had considered his views and had decided to take no legal action.

Paul immediately files suit, naming each member of the board of directors and all of the senior officers of DotBomb, alleging that their failure to exercise adequate care caused the drop in value of his stock price. DotBomb's board directs the company's General Counsel to file a motion to dismiss.

2. Which of the following best characterizes Paul's lawsuit?

a. On only the facts as given, it is a derivative suit as to which demand is required.

b. On only the facts as given, it is a derivative suit as to which demand is futile.

c. Paul need not make demand because the harm he alleges is loss of his share value, which is a personal injury.

d. None of the above.

3. What risk did Paul take by communicating directly with DotBomb's management?

 a. That he will have admitted as a matter of law that his demand was inadequate.
 b. That he will have admitted as a matter of law that demand was futile.
 c. That he will have admitted as a matter of law that the suit should be dismissed unless the board's motion was irrational, uninformed, or conflicted.
 d. None at all—in fact it was wise for him to do so, since demand plainly is required in this case.

4. In considering the board's motion, what standard will the court most likely employ to decide whether or not to dismiss Paul's complaint?

 a. As in other majority jurisdictions, this court will apply *Alford v. Shaw*.
 b. The *Zapata* rule for demand-required cases.
 c. The *Zapata* rule for demand-excused cases.
 d. None of the above.

5. Could Paul have brought a derivative action to challenge the decisions that led the company into bankruptcy in the first place?

 a. Yes, though he would be unlikely to win because the relevant conduct would likely be judged under the business judgment rule.
 b. Yes, and he would be likely to win, since business choices leading to bankruptcy were likely so bad as not to be "rationally related to the best interests of the corporation."
 c. No, because on these special facts he could not possibly make out a substantive cause of action.
 d. No, for procedural reasons.

6. ABC, Inc., a Delaware corporation, owns 65 percent of the voting stock of another company, XYZ, Inc. Another 25 percent of the shares are owned by the California Public Employees Retirement System ("CalPERS"), a major pension fund, which is not otherwise affiliated with either company. An XYZ bylaw provides that board candidates will be nominated by any shareholder with more than 50 percent of XYZ's voting stock.

CalPERS has brought suit against ABC and against XYZ's entire board. CalPERS seeks money damages against ABC and injunction against the XYZ directors, all to remedy what CalPERS believes was an improperly motivated distribution of dividends to XYZ's shareholders. CalPERS puts on uncontroverted evidence that (1) at the time of the dividends, ABC was in great need of ready cash, and (2) the dividends in question exceeded XYZ's entire revenues for the year.

The CalPERS suit is:
a. Entirely derivative in nature.
b. Necessarily direct as to the XYZ defendants.
c. Entirely direct in nature.
d. Direct as to ABC.

7. Jenny, a shareholder in the Delaware holding company known as BigCo, Inc., believes that a recent, spectacularly failed investment by BigCo was the fault of the company's bumbling board of directors, and she sues each of them for breach of fiduciary duty. Among many other things, her complaint alleges the following: "Internal remedies would be ineffective because the entire board are incompetent, and because they each only do the bidding of BigCo's chief executive officer, who is also named as defendant herein." Jenny has one share of BigCo's one million shares of stock, and the lawsuit is the first that anyone within the company has ever heard of her. On only these facts, Jenny's failure to seek intracorporate remedies:

a. Is irrelevant in this particular case.
b. Does not really matter, because the CEO and each of the directors are all named defendants.
c. Is fatal to her lawsuit because of the manner in which she pleaded the facts.
d. Automatically triggers the first prong of *Zapata*.

Part 5

Corporate Control Transactions

23

Corporate Control Transactions, Part I: Introduction, Negotiated Transactions, and Sales of Control

This is one of two chapters dealing with a set of special transactions often thought of as "corporate acquisitions." This nomenclature is somewhat misleading because it does not connote just any old transaction in which corporations acquire things. For the most part, the buying of things by corporations is legally uninteresting. For example, nothing about a purchase of, say, paper clips or raw materials or electricity for the factory plant or whatever raises much of an issue of corporation law, except for the minor question of whether the corporate employee who executes the purchase contract had authority to do so. Instead what we mean by "corporate acquisition," and what is indeed very interesting as a matter of corporate law, is the acquisition of another corporation. This chapter provides an introduction to acquisition transactions in general, and gives detailed consideration to negotiated transactions and the duties of controlling shareholders. The next chapter deals with takeovers that are hostile.

Chapter Outline

A. Introduction

- Major types of transaction:
    - Purchase of assets
    - Share exchange
    - Merger
    - Consolidation
    - Tender offer
    - Private purchases of control shares

B. Statutory Framework

- Mergers
- Share exchanges
- Sales of substantially all the assets

C. The De Facto Merger Doctrine

- Substance over form
- The Delaware approach

D. The Freeze-Out Merger

- Duties of the majority
- Appraisal rights

E. Sales of Control

Test Yourself

 What does it look like?

Check the online Supplement for the following sample documents that are relevant to this chapter:

- Articles of merger
- A proxy statement describing a proposed merger

A. Introduction

In this overview of corporate control acquisitions, we will study five major kinds of transactions:

Purchase of Assets. First, one company can effectively acquire another simply by buying up all of the target's assets and goodwill. When this occurs, the seller corporation will remain in existence, but it will no longer have any hard assets. (Though, as a result of the transaction, it will now have one significant asset—cash or the acquiring corporation's shares.)

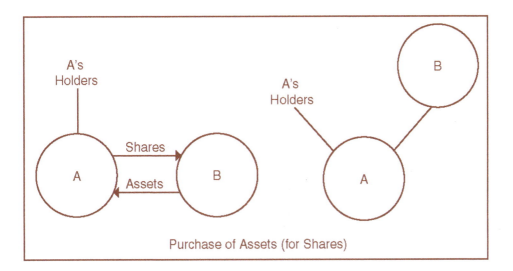

Purchase of Assets (for Shares)

Share Exchange. A corporation or person may buy all of the shares of another corporation through a "share exchange." The consideration given for the shares acquired can be cash, stock, or other securities. The share exchange is effected when the would-be buyer proposes a "plan of share exchange" to the board of the target corporation, the board recommends the plan to the shareholders, and the shareholders approve it by majority vote. Upon approval, the target corporation continues to exist as a separate entity, but all its shares will be held by the acquiror. (If the acquiror is itself a corporation, this would result in the target being a wholly-owned subsidiary.) As we shall see, the critical and quite surprising feature of the share exchange is that because it can be approved by only a majority vote, a large minority of shareholders may be forced to sell their shares even though they don't want to.

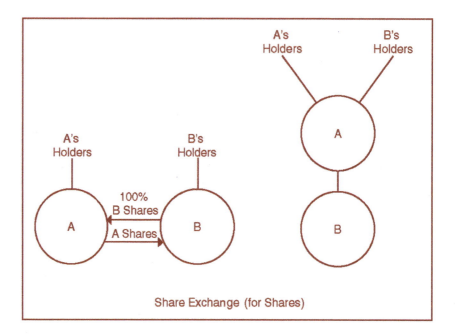

Share Exchange (for Shares)

Merger. A merger is rather like a share exchange. The board of a company to be merged must propose a plan of merger to its shareholders and they may approve it by majority vote. When approved, the shareholders of a company to be merged will exchange their shares for shares in the newly merged entity (or sometimes for other consideration, like cash or non-equity securities). The chief difference between a merger and a share exchange is that following the merger, one or both of the previously existing corporations will cease to exist. Mergers can be structured in two ways:

Merger:

A true merger occurs when corporation A merges into corporation B. Corporation B will still exist in substantially its original form, but corporation A will no longer exist as a separate entity.

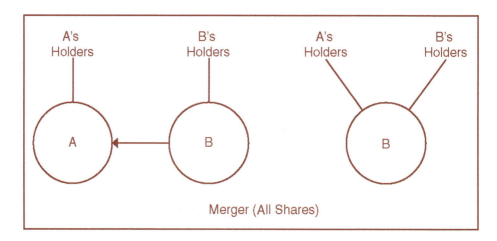

Merger (All Shares)

Consolidation:

Following a consolidation, both of the original companies cease to exist, and together they form a new corporation.

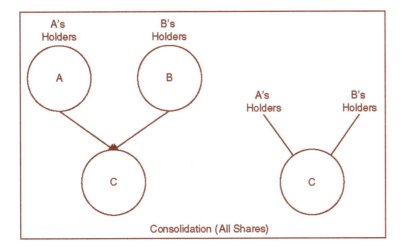

Consolidation (All Shares)

Tender Offer. A tender offer is an open market offer to purchase some or all of the outstanding shares of a corporation's stock. It does not require acquiescence of the board—indeed, where a target company has no controlling shareholder, it is the primary means to acquire control without board approval—and it does not effect a change in control until the tender offer proponent acquires a controlling share of stock through individual purchases from shareholders. As we shall see, the fact that a tender offer does not require board approval of the target company is quite significant—it is for this reason that tender offers are often considered "hostile takeovers." Tender offers are highly regulated as a matter of federal law. The primary state issues have to do with the duties of management in resisting them.

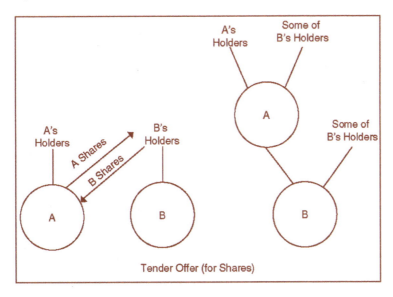

Tender Offer (for Shares)

Private Purchase of Control Shares. Finally, a purchaser may negotiate privately with the owner or owners of shares sufficient to transfer control of a corporation. Consideration for the sale could take any form. The primary issues associated with this type of transaction relate to the duties of those who are selling control.

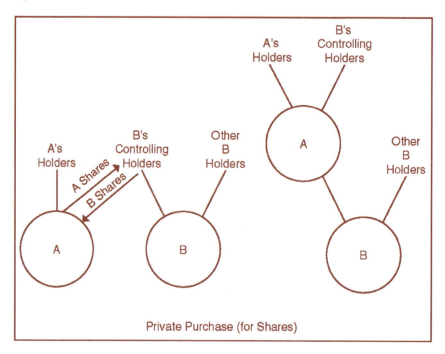

Private Purchase (for Shares)

This chapter concentrates on "friendly" acquisitions—those control transactions that either require acquiescence by the target company's management or consist of the direct purchase of shares from a controlling shareholder or group.

The several different forms that these transactions can take can have vastly different legal consequences. Corporate planners choose among them to suit the parties' interests. For example, structuring a deal as a merger can have tax benefits. (There is some tendency to describe mergers as "tax-free" but that is a dangerous generalization; moreover, some of the other types of transaction can be designed to eliminate tax consequences.) In many other aspects, however, the merger traditionally has been seen as having disadvantages. First, mergers require the approval of the shareholders in at least one of the corporations, and frequently the shareholders of both. Second, when one company merges into another, it takes all of its liabilities along with it. In other words, the survivor corporation will take on all of the liabilities of its merger partner as its own. This is true neither of the share exchange nor, in most cases, the purchase of assets. Finally, mergers trigger the so-called appraisal remedy, pursuant to which dissenting shareholders of the target company can seek to convince a court that the consideration they were offered was inadequate, and that they should receive more.

For these reasons, as discussed below, there have been many instances in which corporate planners have sought to structure a transaction that is for practical purposes a merger as if it were something else, most commonly a purchase of assets. The drafters of the Model Business Corporation Act have attempted to discourage such subterfuge by limiting the legal distinctions among these different transactions. Thus, share exchanges and sales of all assets also require approval of the target company's shareholders, and both also trigger appraisal rights. The transfer of liabilities, however, remains a vital difference—it still occurs only in mergers.

B. Statutory Framework

The methods of accomplishing mergers, share exchanges, and sales of substantially all of the assets of a corporation are governed by Chapters 11 (mergers and share exchanges), 12 (disposition of assets), and 13 (appraisal rights) of the Model Business Corporation Act. Many questions can be answered simply by reading the statute. The following brief summaries nonetheless may come in handy—*if* one keeps in mind that these are generalities and that there are a number of specific exceptions.

In the case of a merger (including a consolidation), a plan must be approved by the board of directors of both of the entities involved. The plan then is submitted for approval by the shareholders of any entity that will not survive. Shareholders of a surviving corporation generally are given a vote only if the merger requires an amendment to the Articles of Incorporation (if, for instance, additional shares must be authorized), the attributes of the shares they own will be changed, or the transaction involves the issuance of more than 20 percent of the shares of a class previously outstanding. After the requisite approvals, articles of merger must be filed with the appropriate state office (wherever Articles of Incorporation are filed). Upon acceptance for filing or some later date specified in the articles of merger, the merger will become effective by operation of law. The survivor becomes the owner of all real and personal property, and becomes subject to all of the liabilities, of each corporation that is merged into it.

There is, however, an important exception to the steps detailed above in the case of a parent merging with a 90 percent controlled subsidiary or causing the merger of two or more such subsidiaries: then, no approval is required by either the directors or the shareholders of the subsidiary(ies).

The steps for a share exchange closely follow those for a merger. Approval of a plan by both boards must be followed by the approval of the shareholders of the corporation that is being acquired. Approval by the acquiring corporation's shareholders only is required if the acquiror's articles must be amended, if the attributes of what the existing shareholders own will change (generally not the case), or the issuance of more than 20 percent of the stock already outstanding will be involved. The plan must be filed with the requisite state office, whereupon the situation differs from that with a merger, since a share exchange does not affect the separate existence of the parties or automatically transfer the acquired corporation's property or liabilities to the acquiror.

The statutes dealing with the disposition of substantially all of a corporation's assets require a somewhat careful reading. First, §12.01 specifies that, unless the Articles of Incorporation provide to the contrary, no approval of the shareholders of a corporation is required to sell or otherwise dispose of all of a corporation's assets in the usual and regular course of business. Then, §12.02 provides that a disposition of assets *does* require both directorial and shareholder approval if it will leave the corporation without a significant continuing business activity. At least some guidance is given on just what that means:

§12.02 Shareholder Approval of Certain Dispositions

(a) . . . A corporation will conclusively be deemed to have retained a significant continuing business activity if it retains a business activity that represented, for the corporation and its subsidiaries on a consolidated basis, at least (i) 25% of total assets at the end of the most recently completed fiscal year, and (ii) either 25% of either income from continuing operations before taxes or 25% of revenues from continuing operations, in each case for the most recently completed fiscal year.

Unlike the other change in control transactions, there is no need to file evidence of the deal with the state authorities, and the statute is silent on the question of "successor liability." Although the general rule that has judicially evolved is to the effect that the purchaser of assets does not involuntarily assume the seller's liabilities, there are a few anti-abuse exceptions, including the de facto merger doctrine.

The right to "opt out" of a transaction and receive the appraised right of one's shares essentially is tied to the right to vote on a merger, share exchange, or sale of assets. There are two major exceptions. One is for what generally may be described as "publicly traded" shares, but the exception is subject to its own exception for "interested transactions." The definition of "interested transaction" is quite complex, but includes transactions in which management gets financial benefits not available to the shareholders generally. The second major instance in which appraisal rights are not available is when the Articles of Incorporation provide to the contrary. The provisions dealing with how appraisal rights are to be exercised and how the value of shares is to be appraised are among the most detailed of the entire Model Act.

 Dear Prof.: About these "questions that can be answered by reading the statute" that you referred to above—what do we really have to know?

Your own professor will tell you and may make use of a number of hypotheticals available in the teacher's manual. Here is an example:

ABC, Inc., has 100 shares of stock outstanding. If a proposal to merge ABC into another corporation is presented to its shareholders, what is the absolute minimum number of shares that must be voted in favor in order for the proposal to be approved?

To answer the question, you would look at Chapter 11 (mergers and share exchanges) and encounter §11.04 (action on a plan of merger of share exchange). Sub-section (e) deals with shareholder voting, and you would see that the general rule is a majority of a quorum. You would also see that a greater number could be required by the articles or the board of directors when it adopted the plan of merger. The question is somewhat confusingly worded (isn't that always the way?), but evidently refers to the general rule, since the articles or board could call only for a greater number. You aren't told what ABC's quorum requirement is, but since the usual rule is a majority—subject, once again, only to being increased—the answer is 26 (assuming no fractional voting).

The more interesting question is why the board would ever require a higher number of shareholders than absolutely necessary to approve a plan it already has endorsed. Often it will be because a transaction involves a majority shareholder. Then, the board often imposes a "majority of the minority" requirement for reasons that will become clear.

C. The De Facto Merger Doctrine

Corporate planners sometimes try to structure a merger as if it were something else—most commonly as merely a purchase by one company of the assets of another. The goal is to avoid the rights of shareholders to vote on the transaction and to get appraisal rights if it is approved, and to avoid taking on the preexisting liabilities of the target corporation. Hence the courts have devised the "de facto merger" doctrine, which is explained in the following cases.

FARRIS V. GLEN ALDEN CORP.

Supreme Court of Pennsylvania
143 A.2d 25 (1958)

Cohen, Justice.

We are required to determine on this appeal whether, as a result of a "Reorganization Agreement" executed by the officers of Glen Alden Corporation and List Industries Corporation, and approved by the shareholders of the former company, the rights and remedies of a dissenting shareholder accrue to the plaintiff.

Glen Alden is a Pennsylvania corporation engaged principally in the mining of anthracite coal and lately in the manufacture of air conditioning units and fire-fighting equipment. In recent years the company's operating revenue has declined substantially, and in fact, its coal operations have resulted in tax loss carryovers of approximately $14,000,000. In October 1957, List, a Delaware holding company owning interests in motion picture theaters, textile companies and real estate, and to a lesser extent, in oil and gas operations, warehouses and aluminum piston manufacturing, purchased through a wholly owned subsidiary 38.5% of Glen Alden's outstanding stock.[1] This acquisition enabled List to place three of its directors on the Glen Alden board.

On March 20, 1958, the two corporations entered into a "reorganization agreement," subject to stockholder approval, which contemplated the following actions:

1. Glen Alden is to acquire all of the assets of List, excepting a small amount of cash reserved for the payment of List's expenses in connection with the transaction. These assets include over $8,000,000 in cash held chiefly in the treasuries of List's wholly owned subsidiaries.

2. In consideration of the transfer, Glen Alden is to issue 3,621,703 shares of stock to List. List in turn is to distribute the stock to its shareholders at a ratio of five shares of Glen Alden stock for each six shares of List stock. In order to accomplish the necessary distribution, Glen Alden is to increase the authorized number of its shares of capital stock from 2,500,000 shares to 7,500,000 shares without according pre-emptive rights to the present shareholders upon the issuance of any such shares.

3. Further, Glen Alden is to assume all of List's liabilities including a $5,000,000 note incurred by List in order to purchase Glen Alden stock in 1957, outstanding stock options, incentive stock options plans, and pension obligations.

4. Glen Alden is to change its corporate name from Glen Alden Corporation to List Alden Corporation.

5. The present directors of both corporations are to become directors of List Alden.

6. List is to be dissolved and List Alden is to then carry on the operations of both former corporations.

Two days after the agreement was executed notice of the annual meeting of Glen Alden to be held on April 11, 1958, was mailed to the shareholders together with a proxy statement analyzing the reorganization agreement and recommending its approval as well as approval of certain amendments to Glen Alden's articles of incorporation and bylaws necessary to implement the agreement. At this meeting the holders of a majority of the outstanding shares, (not including those owned by List), voted in favor of a resolution approving the reorganization agreement. On the day of the shareholders' meeting, plaintiff, a shareholder of Glen Alden, filed a complaint in equity against the corporation and its officers seeking to enjoin them temporarily until final hearing, and perpetually thereafter, from executing and carrying out the agreement.

The gravamen of the complaint was that the notice of the annual shareholders' meeting did not conform to the

Connections: Proxy Regulation

A publicly held corporation rarely will be able to take shareholder action without solicitation of proxies. The process, as well as the form and content of the proxy and proxy statement are matters of federal regulation.

---

1. Of the purchase price of $8,719,109, $5,000,000 was borrowed.

requirements of the Business Corporation Law, 15 P.S. §2852-1 et seq., in three respects: (1) It did not give notice to the shareholders that the true intent and purpose of the meeting was to effect a merger or consolidation of Glen Alden and List; (2) It failed to give notice to the shareholders of their right to dissent to the plan of merger or consolidation and claim fair value for their shares, and (3) It did not contain copies of the text of certain sections of the Business Corporation Law as required.[2]

By reason of these omissions, plaintiff contended that the approval of the reorganization agreement by the shareholders at the annual meeting was invalid and unless the carrying out of the plan were enjoined, he would suffer irreparable loss by being deprived of substantial property rights.[3]

The defendants answered admitting the material allegations of fact in the complaint but denying that they gave rise to a cause of action because the transaction complained of was a purchase of corporate assets as to which shareholders had no rights of dissent or appraisal. For these reasons the defendants then moved for judgment on the pleadings.[4]

The court below concluded that the reorganization agreement entered into between the two corporations was a plan for a de facto merger, and that therefore the failure of the notice of the annual meeting to conform to the pertinent requirements of the merger provisions of the Business Corporation Law rendered the notice defective and all proceedings in furtherance of the agreement void. Wherefore, the court entered a final decree denying defendants' motion for judgment on the pleadings, entering judgment upon plaintiff's complaint and granting the injunctive relief therein sought. This appeal followed.

When use of the corporate form of business organization first became widespread, it was relatively easy for courts to define a "merger" or a "sale of assets" and to label a particular transaction as one or the other. . . . But prompted by the desire to avoid the impact of adverse, and to obtain the benefits of favorable, government regulations, particularly federal tax laws, new accounting and legal techniques were developed by lawyers and accountants which interwove the elements characteristic of each, thereby creating hybrid forms of corporate amalgamation. Thus, it is no longer helpful to consider an individual transaction in the abstract and solely by reference to the various elements therein determine whether it is a "merger" or a "sale." Instead, to determine properly the nature of a corporate transaction, we must refer not only to all the provisions

---

2. The proxy statement included the following declaration: "Appraisal Rights. In the opinion of counsel, the shareholders of neither Glen Alden nor List Industries will have any rights of appraisal or similar rights of dissenters with respect to any matter to be acted upon at their respective meetings."

3. The complaint also set forth that the exchange of shares of Glen Alden's stock for those of List would constitute a violation of the pre-emptive rights of Glen Alden shareholders as established by the law of Pennsylvania at the time of Glen Alden's incorporation in 1917. The defendants answered that under both statute and prior common law no pre-emptive rights existed with respect to stock issued in exchange for property.

4. Counsel for the defendants concedes that if the corporation is required to pay the dissenting shareholders the appraised fair value of their shares, the resultant drain of cash would prevent Glen Alden from carrying out the agreement. On the other hand, plaintiff contends that if the shareholders had been told of their rights as dissenters, rather than specifically advised that they had no such rights, the resolution approving the reorganization agreement would have been defeated.

of the agreement, but also to the consequences of the transaction and to the purposes of the provisions of the corporation law said to be applicable. We shall apply this principle to the instant case.

Section 908, subd. A of the Pennsylvania Business Corporation Law provides: "If any shareholder of a domestic corporation which becomes a party to a plan of merger or consolidation shall object to such plan of merger or consolidation . . . such shareholder shall be entitled to . . . [the fair value of his shares upon surrender of the share certificate or certificates representing his shares]."

. . . [W]hen a corporation combines with another so as to lose its essential nature and alter the original fundamental relationships of the shareholders among themselves and to the corporation, a shareholder who does not wish to continue his membership therein may treat his membership in the original corporation as terminated and have the value of his shares paid to him. . . .

Does the combination outlined in the present "reorganization" agreement so fundamentally change the corporate character of Glen Alden and the interest of the plaintiff as a shareholder therein, that to refuse him the rights and remedies of a dissenting shareholder would in reality force him to give up his stock in one corporation and against his will accept shares in another? If so, the combination is a merger within the meaning of section 908, subd. A of the corporation law. . . .

If the reorganization agreement were consummated plaintiff would find that the "List Alden" resulting from the amalgamation would be quite a different corporation than the "Glen Alden" in which he is now a shareholder. Instead of continuing primarily as a coal mining company, Glen Alden would be transformed, after amendment of its articles of incorporation, into a diversified holding company whose interests would range from motion picture theaters to textile companies, Plaintiff would find himself a member of a company with assets of $169,000,000 and a long-term debt of $38,000,000 in lieu of a company one-half that size and with but one-seventh the long-term debt.

While the administration of the operations and properties of Glen Alden as well as List would be in the hands of management common to both companies, since all executives of List would be retained in List Alden, the control of Glen Alden would pass to the directors of List; for List would hold eleven of the seventeen directorships on the new board of directors.

As an aftermath of the transaction plaintiff's proportionate interest in Glen Alden would have been reduced to only two-fifths of what it presently is because of the issuance of an additional 3,621,703 shares to List which would not be subject to pre-emptive rights. In fact, ownership of Glen Alden would pass to the stockholders of List who would hold 76.5% of the outstanding shares as compared with but 23.5% retained by the present Glen Alden shareholders.

Perhaps the most important consequence to the plaintiff, if he were denied the right to have his shares redeemed at their fair value, would be the serious financial loss suffered upon consummation of the agreement. While the present book value of his stock is $38 a share after combination it would be worth only $21 a share. In contrast, the shareholders of List who presently hold stock with a total book value of $33,000,000 or $7.50 a share, would receive stock with a book value of $76,000,000 or $21 a share.

Under these circumstances it may well be said that if the proposed combination is allowed to take place without right of dissent, plaintiff would have his stock in Glen Alden taken away from him and the stock of a new company thrust upon him in its place. He would be projected against his will into a new enterprise under terms not of his own choosing. It was to protect dissident shareholders against just such a result that this Court one hundred years ago in the *Lauman* case, and the legislature thereafter in section 908, subd. A, granted the right of dissent. And it is to accord that protection to the plaintiff that we conclude that the combination proposed in the case at hand is a merger within the intendment of section 908, subd. A.

Nevertheless, defendants contend that the 1957 amendments to sections 311 and 908 of the corporation law preclude us from reaching this result and require the entry of judgment in their favor. Subsection F of section 311 dealing with the voluntary transfer of corporate assets provides: "The shareholders of a business corporation which acquires by sale, lease or exchange all or substantially all of the property of another corporation by the issuance of stock, securities or otherwise shall not be entitled to the rights and remedies of dissenting shareholders. . . ."

And the amendment to section 908 reads as follows: "The right of dissenting shareholders . . . shall not apply to the purchase by a corporation of assets whether or not the consideration therefor be money or property, real or personal, including shares or bonds or other evidences of indebtedness of such corporation. The shareholders of such corporation shall have no right to dissent from any such purchase." . . .

. . . [W]e will not blind our eyes to the realities of the transaction. Despite the designation of the parties and the form employed, Glen Alden does not in fact acquire List, rather, List acquires Glen Alden. . . .

We hold that the combination contemplated by the reorganization agreement, although consummated by contract rather than in accordance with the statutory procedure, is a merger within the protective purview of sections 908, subd. A and 515 of the corporation law. The shareholders of Glen Alden should have been notified accordingly and advised of their statutory rights of dissent and appraisal. The failure of the corporate officers to take these steps renders the stockholder approval of the agreement at the 1958 shareholders' meeting invalid. The lower court did not err in enjoining the officers and directors of Glen Alden from carrying out this agreement.

The *Farris* case dealt with the rights of shareholders. The doctrine also has been invoked for the protection of creditors. For instance, in Knapp v. North American Rockwell Corp., 506 F.2d 361 (3d Cir. 1974), plaintiff was an individual injured by a machine manufactured by an entity that sold substantially all of its assets for the stock of North American Rockwell Corp. (Rockwell). Plaintiff was allowed to recover against Rockwell. The original manufacturer had, pursuant to agreement with Rockwell, dissolved and distributed all of its Rockwell shares to its shareholders 18 months after the initial transaction. The court applied what the parties acknowledged was the controlling principle of law:

The general rule is that "a mere sale of corporate property by one company to another does not make the purchaser liable for the liabilities of the seller not assumed by it." . . . There are, however, certain exceptions to this rule. Liability for obligations of a selling corporation may be imposed on the purchasing corporation when (1) the purchaser expressly or impliedly agrees to assume such obligations; (2) the transaction amounts to a consolidation or merger of the selling corporation with or into the purchasing corporation; (3) the purchasing corporation is merely a continuation of the selling corporation; or (4) the transaction is entered into fraudulently to escape liability for such obligations. (Quoting Shane v. Hobam, Inc., 332 F. Supp. 526 (E.D. Pa. 1971) (decided under New York law)).

Although prior cases had focused on whether the selling corporation had gone out of existence immediately following the challenged transaction, the Third Circuit was not persuaded that was a critical consideration, given that dissolution of the selling corporation was part of the original plan and that, as a public policy matter, Rockwell was better equipped to spread the loss than was the plaintiff. The court reasoned that Rockwell could have bargained with its transferor for the transfer of insurance coverage, as well as its other assets.

The general rule is, of course, the general rule. There have been an increasing number of cases invoking the stated exceptions—meaning that avoidance of successor liability has become an important part of mergers and acquisitions planning.

 Time Out for PR

Would it be ethical to assist a client in structuring a transaction that could have been a merger as something else, specifically to avoid giving a group of shareholders a right to vote? Or to transfer assets free of encumbering liabilities to the transferor's mangled tort victims? While you're thinking about that, . . .

■ **Think about this:**

(A) Why should a corporation ever be able to transfer its assets without the associated liabilities?

(B) Suppose that Hypoco, Inc., a manufacturer of garden lawn mowers, has "hard" assets with a liquidation value of $1 million. It has been operating very profitably, and making regular large distributions to its shareholders. As recently as a month ago, Giant Gardener, Inc., offered to buy Hypoco's entire business for $3 million. Now, Hypoco learns of a terrible runaway mower accident clearly attributable to negligence by a Hypoco employee. It is told that it probably owes tort liabilities of $4 million to the mangled victims. Assuming Hypoco "self-insures" (a euphemism for having no insurance from third parties), what is the best possible outcome for the victims?

The case below portrays the de facto merger doctrine in (in)action in Delaware.

HARITON V. ARCO ELECTRONICS, INC.

Supreme Court of Delaware
188 A.2d 123 (1963)

SOUTHERLAND, Chief Justice.

This case involves a sale of assets under §271 of the corporation law, 8 Del. C. It presents for decision the question presented, but not decided, in Heilbrunn v. Sun Chemical Corporation, Del., 150 A.2d 755. It may be stated as follows:

A sale of assets is effected under §271 in consideration of shares of stock of the purchasing corporation. The agreement of sale embodies also a plan to dissolve the selling corporation and distribute the shares so received to the stockholders of the seller, so as to accomplish the same result as would be accomplished by a merger of the seller into the purchaser. Is the sale legal?

The facts are these:

The defendant Arco and Loral Electronics Corporation, a New York corporation, are both engaged, in somewhat different forms, in the electronic equipment business. In the summer of 1961 they negotiated for an amalgamation of the companies. As of October 27, 1961, they entered into a "Reorganization Agreement and Plan." The provisions of this Plan pertinent here are in substance as follows:

1. Arco agrees to sell all its assets to Loral in consideration (inter alia) of the issuance to it of 283,000 shares of Loral.
2. Arco agrees to call a stockholder's meeting for the purpose of approving the Plan and the voluntary dissolution.
3. Arco agrees to distribute to its stockholders all the Loral shares received by it as a part of the complete liquidation of Arco.

At the Arco meeting all the stockholders voting (about 80%) approved the Plan. It was thereafter consummated.

Plaintiff, a stockholder who did not vote at the meeting, sued to enjoin the consummation of the Plan on the grounds (1) that it was illegal, and (2) that it was unfair. The second ground was abandoned. Affidavits and documentary evidence were filed, and defendant moved for summary judgment and dismissal of the complaint. The Vice Chancellor granted the motion and plaintiff appeals.

The question before us we have stated above. Plaintiff's argument that the sale is illegal runs as follows:

The several steps taken here accomplish the same result as a merger of Arco into Loral. In a "true" sale of assets, the stockholder of the seller retains the right to elect whether the selling company shall continue as a holding company. Moreover, the stockholder of the selling company is forced to accept an investment in a new enterprise without the right of appraisal granted under the merger statute. §271 cannot therefore be legally combined with a dissolution proceeding under §275 and a consequent distribution of the purchaser's stock. Such a proceeding is a misuse of the power granted under §271, and a de facto merger results.

The foregoing is a brief summary of plaintiff's contention.

Plaintiff's contention that this sale has achieved the same result as a merger is plainly correct. The same contention was made to us in Heilbrunn v. Sun Chemical Corporation, Del., 150 A.2d 755. Accepting it as correct, we noted that this result is made possible by the overlapping scope of the merger statute and section 271, mentioned in Sterling v. Mayflower Hotel Corporation, 93 A.2d 107. We also adverted to the increased use, in connection with corporate reorganization plans, of §271 instead of the merger statute....

We now hold that the reorganization here accomplished through §271 and a mandatory plan of dissolution and distribution is legal. This is so because the sale-of-assets statute and the merger statute are independent of each other. They are, so to speak, of equal dignity, and the framers of a reorganization plan may resort to either type of corporate mechanics to achieve the desired end. This is not an anomalous result in our corporation law. As the Vice Chancellor pointed out, the elimination of accrued dividends, though forbidden under a charter amendment . . . may be accomplished by a merger....

We are in accord with the Vice Chancellor's ruling, and the judgment below is affirmed.

The *Hariton* case obviously deals with the claims of a disappointed shareholder. It is worth noting that the Delaware General Corporate Law (unlike the MBCA) makes provision for appraisal rights in the context of mergers but not for asset sales.

The court's analysis in *Hariton* seems somewhat cut and dried. Would a Delaware court be as unmoved by the plight of an Arco creditor? Suppose, for instance, that a piece of electronic equipment had malfunctioned, leading to an electrical fire that destroyed a home and caused grievous injury. Would we see the same deference to the choice of the framers of a reorganization plan? Perhaps surprisingly, Delaware does not seem to have an established approach—or much case law at all—on the issue of the liability of successor corporations. It does, however, have fairly intricate statutes dealing with dissolution and provisions for creditors' claims.

> ■ **Think about this:**
>
> Biff was driving recently in his Roadstar 2000 station wagon, when all four wheels fell off, the brakes failed, and the hood popped open, obstructing his view. He skidded into a ditch and suffered serious injuries. He would now like to bring a tort action for products liability against the car's maker, to recover for his injuries.

Two years before Biff suffered his accident, Road Motors, Inc., the maker of his car, entered into a transaction with another company called Megabeast Motors Corp. Megabeast, a publicly traded Delaware corporation, issued 500,000 of its own shares as consideration for purchase of the bulk of Road Motors's assets (its manufacturing facilities, its inventory, its patent rights, and so on). Pursuant to the transaction, Road Motors retained $1 million in cash to pay whatever liabilities remained after the transaction. Finally, also pursuant to the transaction, Road Motors's board issued an in-kind dividend to the company's shareholders consisting of all the shares of Megabeast stock received, and then recommended that they vote to dissolve Road Motors. The shareholders so voted, and Road Motors was dissolved.

(C) Strictly as a matter of the rules provided in statutory corporate law, does Biff have a basis of recovery in tort against Megabeast?

(D) Regardless of how the transaction will be treated as a matter of statutory corporate law, can Biff can still recover against Megabeast?

(E) Despite the risk of taking on Road Motors's pre-transaction liabilities, is there any reason Megabeast might have proposed to structure the transaction formally as a merger?

D. The Freeze-Out Merger

One result—and sometimes goal—of a merger is the cashing out of an unneeded or unwanted minority interest. The following is the classic case in the area:

WEINBERGER V. UOP, INC.

Supreme Court of Delaware
457 A.2d 701 (1983)

MOORE, Justice:

This post-trial appeal was reheard en banc from a decision of the Court of Chancery. It was brought by the class action plaintiff below, a former shareholder of UOP, Inc., who challenged the elimination of UOP's minority shareholders by a cash-out merger between UOP and its majority owner, The Signal Companies, Inc. Originally, the defendants in this action were Signal, UOP, certain officers and directors of those companies, and UOP's investment banker, Lehman Brothers Kuhn Loeb, Inc. The present Chancellor held that the terms of the merger were fair to the plaintiff and the other minority shareholders of UOP. Accordingly, he entered judgment in favor of the defendants.

Numerous points were raised by the parties, but we address only the following questions presented by the trial court's opinion:

1) The plaintiff's duty to plead sufficient facts demonstrating the unfairness of the challenged merger;
2) The burden of proof upon the parties where the merger has been approved by the purportedly informed vote of a majority of the minority shareholders;
3) The fairness of the merger in terms of adequacy of the defendants' disclosures to the minority shareholders;
4) The fairness of the merger in terms of adequacy of the price paid for the minority shares and the remedy appropriate to that issue; and
5) The continued force and effect of Singer v. Magnavox Co., Del. Supr., 380 A.2d 969, 980 (1977), and its progeny.

In ruling for the defendants, the Chancellor re-stated his earlier conclusion that the plaintiff in a suit challenging a cash-out merger must allege specific acts of fraud, misrepresentation, or other items of misconduct to demonstrate the unfairness of the merger terms to the minority. We approve this rule and affirm it.

The Chancellor also held that even though the ultimate burden of proof is on the majority shareholder to show by a preponderance of the evidence that the transaction is fair, it is first the burden of the plaintiff attacking the merger to demonstrate some basis for invoking the fairness obligation. We agree with that principle. However, where corporate action has been approved by an informed vote of a majority of the minority shareholders, we conclude that the burden entirely shifts to the plaintiff to show that the transaction was unfair to the minority. . . . But in all this, the burden clearly remains on those relying on the vote to show that they completely disclosed all material facts relevant to the transaction. . . .

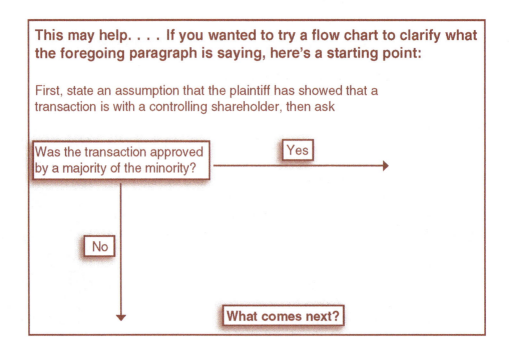

This may help. . . . If you wanted to try a flow chart to clarify what the foregoing paragraph is saying, here's a starting point:

First, state an assumption that the plaintiff has showed that a transaction is with a controlling shareholder, then ask

Was the transaction approved by a majority of the minority? — Yes →

No ↓

What comes next?

I. . . .

Signal is a diversified, technically based company operating through various subsidiaries. Its stock is publicly traded on the New York, Philadelphia and Pacific Stock Exchanges. UOP, formerly known as Universal Oil Products Company, was a diversified industrial company engaged in various lines of business, including petroleum and petro-chemical services and related products, construction, fabricated metal products, transportation equipment products, chemicals and plastics, and other products and services including land development, lumber products and waste disposal. Its stock was publicly held and listed on the New York Stock Exchange.

In 1974 Signal sold one of its wholly-owned subsidiaries for $420,000,000 in cash. While looking to invest this cash surplus, Signal became interested in UOP as a possible acquisition. Friendly negotiations ensued, and . . . [i]n the arm's length bargaining that followed, an understanding was reached whereby Signal agreed to purchase from UOP 1,500,000 shares of UOP's authorized but unissued stock at $21 per share.

This purchase was contingent upon Signal making a successful cash tender offer for 4,300,000 publicly held shares of UOP, also at a price of $21 per share. This combined method of acquisition permitted Signal to acquire 5,800,000 shares of stock, representing 50.5% of UOP's outstanding shares. . . . Immediately before the announcement of the tender offer, UOP's common stock had been trading on the New York Stock Exchange at a fraction under $14 per share . . . and the resulting tender offer was greatly oversubscribed. However, Signal limited its total purchase of the tendered shares so that, when coupled with the stock bought from UOP, it had achieved its goal of becoming a 50.5% shareholder of UOP.

Although UOP's board consisted of thirteen directors, Signal nominated and elected only six. Of these, five were either directors or employees of Signal. The sixth, a partner in the banking firm of Lazard Freres & Co., had been one of Signal's representatives in the negotiations and bargaining with UOP concerning the tender offer and purchase price of the UOP shares.

However, the president and chief executive officer of UOP retired during 1975, and Signal caused him to be replaced by James V. Crawford, a long-time employee and senior executive vice president of one of Signal's wholly-owned subsidiaries. Crawford succeeded his predecessor on UOP's board of directors and also was made a director of Signal.

By the end of 1977 Signal basically was unsuccessful in finding other suitable investment candidates for its excess cash, and by February 1978 considered that it had no other realistic acquisitions available to it on a friendly basis. Once again its attention turned to UOP.

> **Connections: Tender Offers**
>
> Tender offers often are thought of as hostile transactions because they do not require approval by the target's board of directors. They can, however, be part of a cordially negotiated plan in which the target's management may endorse the terms of the tender offer. In any event, tender offers for the shares of publicly held companies are subject to federal regulation.

The trial court found that at the instigation of certain Signal management personnel, including William W. Walkup, its board chairman, and Forrest N. Shumway, its president, a feasibility study was made concerning the possible acquisition of the balance of UOP's outstanding shares. This study was performed by two Signal officers, Charles S. Arledge, vice president (director of planning), and Andrew J. Chitiea, senior vice president (chief financial officer). Messrs. Walkup, Shumway, Arledge and Chitiea were all directors of UOP in addition to their membership on the Signal board.

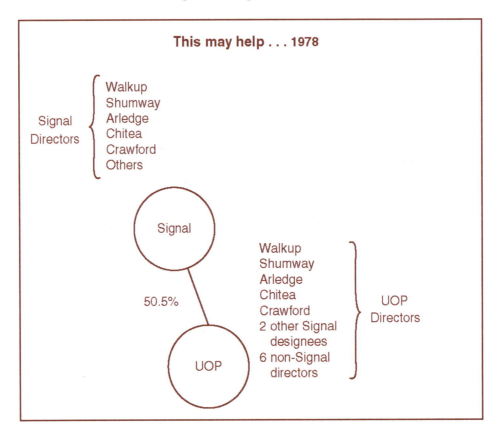

Arledge and Chitiea concluded that it would be a good investment for Signal to acquire the remaining 49.5% of UOP shares at any price up to $24 each. Their report was discussed between Walkup and Shumway who, along with Arledge, Chitiea and Brewster L. Arms, internal counsel for Signal, constituted Signal's senior management. In particular, they talked about the proper price to be paid if the acquisition was pursued, purportedly keeping in mind that as UOP's majority shareholder, Signal owed a fiduciary responsibility to both its own stockholders as well as to UOP's minority. It was ultimately agreed that a meeting of Signal's executive

Connections: The Duties of a Controlling Shareholder

The fiduciary duty of a majority shareholder is well established. Insofar as it controls management, it owes the same duties of care and loyalty.

committee would be called to propose that Signal acquire the remaining outstanding stock of UOP through a cash-out merger in the range of $20 to $21 per share. [In none of the negotiations that followed was there any mention of Arledge and Chitiea's figure of as much as $24.] . . .

. . . For many reasons, Signal's management concluded that the acquisition of UOP's minority shares provided the solution to a number of its business problems.

Thus, it was the consensus [at Signal's Executive Committee meeting of February 8, 1978, which Crawford attended,] that a price of $20 to $21 per share would be fair to both Signal and the minority shareholders of UOP. Signal's executive committee authorized its management "to negotiate" with UOP "for a cash acquisition of the minority ownership in UOP, Inc., with the intention of presenting a proposal to [Signal's] board of directors . . . on March 6, 1978." [Signal subsequently issued two press releases referring to its negotiations with UOP, the first referring to UOP's then-closing price of $14.50 and the second referring to Signal's recommended offering price of $20 to $21 per share.] . . .

Between Tuesday, February 28, 1978 and Monday, March 6, 1978, a total of four business days, Crawford spoke by telephone with all of UOP's non-Signal, i.e., outside, directors. Also during that period, Crawford retained Lehman Brothers to render a fairness opinion as to the price offered the minority for its stock. He gave two reasons for this choice. First, the time schedule between the announcement and the board meetings was short (by then only three business days) and since Lehman Brothers had been acting as UOP's investment banker for many years, Crawford felt that it would be in the best position to respond on such brief notice. Second, James W. Glanville, a long-time director of UOP and a partner in Lehman Brothers, had acted as a financial advisor to UOP for many years. Crawford believed that Glanville's familiarity with UOP, as a member of its board, would also be of assistance in enabling Lehman Brothers to render a fairness opinion within the existing time constraints.

Crawford telephoned Glanville, who gave his assurance that Lehman Brothers had no conflicts that would prevent it from accepting the task. Glanville's immediate personal reaction was that a price of $20 to $21 would certainly be fair, since it represented almost a 50% premium over UOP's market price. Glanville sought a $250,000 fee for Lehman Brothers' services, but Crawford thought this too much. After further discussions Glanville finally agreed that Lehman Brothers would render its fairness opinion for $150,000.

During this period Crawford also had several telephone contacts with Signal officials. In only one of them, however, was the price of the shares discussed. In a conversation with Walkup, Crawford advised that as a result of his communications with UOP's non-Signal directors, it was his feeling that the price would have to be the top of the proposed range, or $21 per share, if the approval of UOP's outside directors was to be obtained. But again, he did not seek any price higher than $21.

Glanville assembled a three-man Lehman Brothers team to do the work on the fairness opinion. These persons examined relevant documents and information concerning UOP, including its annual reports and its Securities and Exchange Commission filings from 1973 through 1976, as well as its audited financial statements for 1977, its interim reports to shareholders, and its recent and historical market prices and trading volumes. In addition, on Friday, March 3, 1978, two members of the Lehman Brothers team flew to UOP's headquarters in Des Plaines, Illinois, to perform a "due diligence" visit, during the course of which they interviewed Crawford as well as UOP's general counsel, its chief financial officer, and other key executives and personnel.

As a result, the Lehman Brothers team concluded that "the price of either $20 or $21 would be a fair price for the remaining shares of UOP." They telephoned this impression to Glanville, who was spending the weekend in Vermont. . . .

On March 6, 1978, both the Signal and UOP boards were convened to consider the proposed merger. Telephone communications were maintained between the two meetings. . . . Arledge and Chitiea, along with Signal's other designees on UOP's board, participated by conference telephone. All of UOP's outside directors attended the meeting either in person or by conference telephone.

First, Signal's board unanimously adopted a resolution authorizing Signal to propose to UOP a cash merger of $21 per share as outlined in a certain merger agreement and other supporting documents. This proposal required that the merger be approved by a majority of UOP's outstanding minority shares voting at the stockholders meeting at which the merger would be considered, and that the minority shares voting in favor of the merger, when coupled with Signal's 50.5% interest would have to comprise at least two-thirds of all UOP shares. Otherwise the proposed merger would be deemed disapproved.

UOP's board then considered the proposal. Copies of the agreement were delivered to the directors in attendance, and other copies had been forwarded earlier to the directors participating by telephone. They also had before them UOP financial data for 1974-1977, UOP's most recent financial statements, market price information, and budget projections for 1978. In addition they had Lehman Brothers' hurriedly prepared fairness opinion letter finding the price of $21 to be fair. Glanville, the Lehman Brothers partner, and UOP director, commented on the information that had gone into preparation of the letter.

Signal also suggests that the Arledge-Chitiea feasibility study, indicating that a price of up to $24 per share would be a "good investment" for Signal, was discussed at the UOP directors' meeting. The Chancellor made no such finding, and our independent review of the record, detailed infra, satisfies us by a preponderance of the evidence that there was no discussion of this document at UOP's board meeting. Furthermore, it is clear beyond peradventure that nothing in that report was ever disclosed to UOP's minority shareholders prior to their approval of the merger.

After consideration of Signal's proposal, Walkup and Crawford left the meeting to permit a free and uninhibited

Connections: A Shifting Burden

In self-dealing cases, the usual effect of the approval of a disinterested decision maker is to shift the burden with respect to fairness.

exchange between UOP's non-Signal directors. Upon their return a resolution to accept Signal's offer was then proposed and adopted. While Signal's men on UOP's board participated in various aspects of the meeting, they abstained from voting. However, the minutes show that each of them "if voting would have voted yes."

. . . Despite the swift board action of the two companies, the merger was not submitted to UOP's shareholders until their annual meeting on May 26, 1978. . . .

As of the record date of UOP's annual meeting, there were 11,488,302 shares of UOP common stock outstanding, 5,688,302 of which were owned by the minority. At the meeting only 56%, or 3,208,652, of the minority shares were voted. Of these, 2,953,812, or 51.9% of the total minority, voted for the merger, and 254,840 voted against it. When Signal's stock was added to the minority shares voting in favor, a total of 76.2% of UOP's outstanding shares approved the merger while only 2.2% opposed it.

> **Connections: Federal Securities Regulation**
>
> Proxy solicitation is a time-consuming process that, in the case of publicly held corporations, requires submission of documents to the Securities and Exchange Commission.
>
> If a merger involves issuance of shares of the acquiror (which the merger in *Weinberger* did not), those shares would have to be registered with the Commission—sometimes also a time-consuming process.

By its terms the merger became effective on May 26, 1978, and each share of UOP's stock held by the minority was automatically converted into a right to receive $21 cash.

II.

A.

A primary issue mandating reversal is the preparation by two UOP directors, Arledge and Chitiea, of their feasibility study for the exclusive use and benefit of Signal. This document was of obvious significance to both Signal and UOP. Using UOP data, it described the advantages to Signal of ousting the minority at a price range of $21-$24 per share. . . .

Having written those words, solely for the use of Signal, it is clear from the record that neither Arledge nor Chitiea shared this report with their fellow directors of UOP. We are satisfied that no one else did either. This conduct hardly meets the fiduciary standards applicable to such a transaction. . . .

The Arledge-Chitiea report speaks for itself in supporting the Chancellor's finding that a price of up to $24 was a "good investment" for Signal. It shows that a return on the investment at $21 would be 15.7% versus 15.5% at $24 per share. This was a difference of only two-tenths of one percent, while it meant over $17,000,000 to the minority. Under such circumstances, paying UOP's minority shareholders $24 would have had relatively little long-term effect on Signal, and the Chancellor's findings concerning the benefit to Signal, even at a price of $24, were obviously correct.

Certainly, this was a matter of material significance to UOP and its shareholders. Since the study was prepared by two UOP directors, using UOP information for the exclusive benefit of Signal, and nothing whatever was done to disclose it to the outside UOP directors or the minority shareholders, a question of breach of fiduciary duty arises. This problem occurs because there were common Signal-UOP directors participating, at least to some extent, in the UOP board's decision-making processes without full disclosure of the conflicts they faced.[5]

B.

In assessing this situation, the Court of Chancery was required to:

> examine what information defendants had and to measure it against what they gave to the minority stockholders, in a context in which "complete candor" is required. In other words, the limited function of the Court was to determine whether defendants had disclosed all information in their possession germane to the transaction in issue. And by "germane" we mean, for present purposes, information such as a reasonable shareholder would consider important in deciding whether to sell or retain stock. . . .
>
> . . . Completeness, not adequacy, is both the norm and the mandate under present circumstances.

Lynch v. Vickers Energy Corp., Del. Supr., 383 A.2d 278, 281 (1977). This is merely stating in another way the long-existing principle of Delaware law that these Signal designated directors on UOP's board still owed UOP and its shareholders an uncompromising duty of loyalty. . . .

Given the absence of any attempt to structure this transaction on an arm's length basis, Signal cannot escape the effects of the conflicts it faced, particularly when its designees on UOP's board did not totally abstain from participation in the matter. There is no "safe harbor" for such divided loyalties in Delaware. When directors of a Delaware corporation are on both sides of a transaction, they are required to demonstrate their utmost good faith and the most scrupulous inherent fairness of the bargain. The requirement of fairness is unflinching in its demand that where one stands on both sides of a transaction, he has the burden of establishing its entire fairness, sufficient to pass the test of careful scrutiny by the courts. . . .

There is no dilution of this obligation where one holds dual or multiple directorships, as in a parent-subsidiary context. Levien v. Sinclair Oil Corp., Del. Ch., 261 A.2d 911, 915 (1969). Thus, individuals who act in a dual capacity as directors of two corporations, one of whom is parent and the other subsidiary, owe the same duty of good management to both corporations, and in the absence of an independent negotiating structure, or the directors' total absten-

---

5. Although perfection is not possible, or expected, the result here could have been entirely different if UOP had appointed an independent negotiating committee of its outside directors to deal with Signal at arm's length. Since fairness in this context can be equated to conduct by a theoretical, wholly independent, board of directors acting upon the matter before them, it is unfortunate that this course apparently was neither considered nor pursued. Particularly in a parent-subsidiary context, a showing that the action taken was as though each of the contending parties had in fact exerted its bargaining power against the other at arm's length is strong evidence that the transaction meets the test of fairness. . . .

tion from any participation in the matter, this duty is to be exercised in light of what is best for both companies. The record demonstrates that Signal has not met this obligation.

C.

The concept of fairness has two basic aspects: fair dealing and fair price. The former embraces questions of when the transaction was timed, how it was initiated, structured, negotiated, disclosed to the directors, and how the approvals of the directors and the stockholders were obtained. The latter aspect of fairness relates to the economic and financial considerations of the proposed merger, including all relevant factors: assets, market value, earnings, future prospects, and any other elements that affect the intrinsic or inherent value of a company's stock. However, the test for fairness is not a bifurcated one as between fair dealing and price. All aspects of the issue must be examined as a whole since the question is one of entire fairness. However, in a non-fraudulent transaction we recognize that price may be the preponderant consideration outweighing other features of the merger. Here, we address the two basic aspects of fairness separately because we find reversible error as to both.

D.

Part of fair dealing is the obvious duty of candor. . . . Moreover, one possessing superior knowledge may not mislead any stockholder by use of corporate information to which the latter is not privy. Delaware has long imposed this duty even upon persons who are not corporate officers or directors, but who nonetheless are privy to matters of interest or significance to their company. With the well-established Delaware law on the subject, and the Court of Chancery's findings of fact here, it is inevitable that the obvious conflicts posed by Arledge and Chitiea's preparation of their "feasibility study," derived from UOP information, for the sole use and benefit of Signal, cannot pass muster.

The Arledge-Chitiea report is but one aspect of the element of fair dealing. How did this merger evolve? It is clear that it was entirely initiated by Signal. The serious time constraints under which the principals acted were all set by Signal. It had not found a suitable outlet for its excess cash and considered UOP a desirable investment, particularly since it was now in a position to acquire the whole company for itself. For whatever reasons, and they were only Signal's, the entire transaction was presented to and approved by UOP's board within four business days. Standing alone, this is not necessarily indicative of any lack of fairness by a majority shareholder. It was what occurred, or more properly, what did not occur, during this brief period that makes the time constraints imposed by Signal relevant to the issue of fairness.

What Makes a Classic?

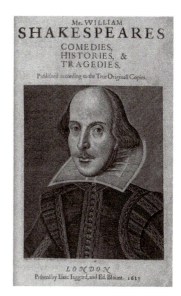

Me. WILLIAM
SHAKESPEARES
COMEDIES,
HISTORIES, &
TRAGEDIES.
Published according to the True Originall Copies.

LONDON
Printed by Isaac Iaggard, and Ed. Blount. 1623

Whatever that certain something is, this case's discussion of "fairness" certainly has it, and is oft-quoted.

The structure of the transaction, again, was Signal's doing. So far as negotiations were concerned, it is clear that they were modest at best. Crawford, Signal's man at UOP, never really talked price with Signal, except to accede to its management's statements on the subject, and to convey to Signal the UOP outside directors' view that as between the $20-$21 range under consideration, it would have to be $21. The latter is not a surprising outcome, but hardly arm's length negotiations. Only the protection of benefits for UOP's key employees and the issue of Lehman Brothers' fee approached any concept of bargaining.

As we have noted, the matter of disclosure to the UOP directors was wholly flawed by the conflicts of interest raised by the Arledge-Chitiea report. All of those conflicts were resolved by Signal in its own favor without divulging any aspect of them to UOP.

This cannot but undermine a conclusion that this merger meets any reasonable test of fairness. The outside UOP directors lacked one material piece of information generated by two of their colleagues, but shared only with Signal. True, the UOP board had the Lehman Brothers' fairness opinion, but that firm has been blamed by the plaintiff for the hurried task it performed, when more properly the responsibility for this lies with Signal. There was no disclosure of the circumstances surrounding the rather cursory preparation of the Lehman Brothers' fairness opinion. . . .

Finally, the minority stockholders were denied the critical information that Signal considered a price of $24 to be a good investment. Since this would have meant over $17,000,000 more to the minority, we cannot conclude that the shareholder vote was an informed one. Under the circumstances, an approval by a majority of the minority was meaningless. . . .

Given these particulars and the Delaware law on the subject, the record does not establish that this transaction satisfies any reasonable concept of fair dealing, and the Chancellor's findings in that regard must be reversed.

E.

Turning to the matter of price, plaintiff also challenges its fairness. His evidence was that on the date the merger was approved the stock was worth at least $26 per share. In support, he offered the testimony of a chartered investment analyst who used two basic approaches to valuation: a comparative analysis of the premium paid over market in ten other tender offer-merger combinations, and a discounted cash flow analysis.

In this breach of fiduciary duty case, the Chancellor perceived that the approach to valuation was the same as that in an appraisal proceeding. Consistent with precedent, he rejected plaintiff's method of proof and accepted defendants' evidence of value as being in accord with practice under prior case law. This means that the so-called "Delaware block" or weighted average method was employed wherein the elements of value, i.e., assets, market price, earnings, etc., were assigned a particular weight and the resulting amounts added to determine the value per share. This procedure has been in use for decades. However, to the extent it excludes other generally accepted techniques used in the financial community and the courts, it is now clearly outmoded. It is time we recognize this in appraisal and other stock valuation proceedings and bring our law current on the subject.

While the Chancellor rejected plaintiff's discounted cash flow method of valuing UOP's stock, as not corresponding with "either logic or the existing law," it is significant that this was essentially the focus, i.e., earnings potential of UOP, of Messrs. Arledge and Chitiea in their evaluation of the merger. Accordingly, the standard "Delaware block" or weighted average method of valuation, formerly employed in appraisal and other stock valuation cases, shall no longer exclusively control such proceedings. We believe that a more liberal approach must include proof of value by any techniques or methods which are generally considered acceptable in the financial community and otherwise admissible in court, subject only to our interpretation of 8 Del. C. §262(h), infra. This will obviate the very structured and mechanistic procedure that has heretofore governed such matters.

Fair price obviously requires consideration of all relevant factors involving the value of a company. . . . Until the $21 price is measured on remand by the valuation standards mandated by Delaware law, there can be no finding at the present stage of these proceedings that the price is fair. Given the lack of any candid disclosure of the material facts surrounding establishment of the $21 price, the majority of the minority vote, approving the merger, is meaningless.

The plaintiff has not sought an appraisal, but rescissory damages. . . . While a plaintiff's monetary remedy ordinarily should be confined to the more liberalized appraisal proceeding herein established, we do not intend any limitation on the historic powers of the Chancellor to grant such other relief as the facts of a particular case may dictate. The appraisal remedy we approve may not be adequate in certain cases, particularly where fraud, misrepresentation, self-dealing, deliberate waste of corporate assets, or gross and palpable overreaching are involved. Under such circumstances, the Chancellor's powers are complete to fashion any form of equitable and monetary relief as may be appropriate, including rescissory damages. Since it is apparent that this long completed transaction is too involved to undo, and in view of the Chancellor's discretion, the award, if any, should be in the form of monetary damages based upon entire fairness standards, i.e., fair dealing and fair price. . . .

III.

Finally, we address the matter of business purpose. The defendants contend that the purpose of this merger was not a proper subject of inquiry by the trial court. The plaintiff says that no valid purpose existed—the entire transaction was a mere subterfuge designed to eliminate the minority. The Chancellor ruled otherwise, but in so doing he clearly circumscribed the thrust and effect of *Singer*. . . .

In view of the fairness test, . . . the expanded appraisal remedy now available to shareholders, and the broad discretion of the Chancellor to fashion such relief as the facts of a given case may dictate, we do not believe that any additional meaningful protection is afforded minority shareholders by the business purpose requirement. . . . Accordingly, such requirement shall no longer be of any force or effect.

The judgment of the Court of Chancery, finding both the circumstances of the merger and the price paid the minority shareholders to be fair, is reversed. The matter is remanded for further proceedings consistent herewith. . . .

The footnote to *Weinberger* set out above is worth re-reading, at least in part:

> [T]he result here could have been entirely different if UOP had appointed an independent negotiating committee of its outside directors to deal with Signal at arm's length. Since fairness in this context can be equated to conduct by a theoretical, wholly independent, board of directors acting upon the matter before them, it is unfortunate that this course apparently was neither considered nor pursued.

Does this mean that entire fairness then would be established, since a price determined by such a fair process could never be wrong? Or was the court merely observing that although both aspects of entire fairness still would need to be investigated (in an unbifurcated manner, of course), it was likely that the determination of a completely independent negotiating committee would pass muster? The latter interpretation is given support by Kahn v. Lynch Communication Sys. Inc., 638 A.2d 1110 (Del. 1984). There, the Delaware Supreme Court rejected the idea that an independent negotiating committee would be entitled to the deference of the business judgment rule; rather, entire fairness is the test. However, informed approval by an independent committee (like informed approval by disinterested shareholders) shifts the burden on the issue of entire fairness from the controlling shareholder to the complaining minority—with the important proviso that the committee must have real bargaining power.

Then, however, came *Kahn v. M & F Worldwide Corp.*:

KAHN V. M & F WORLDWIDE CORP.

Supreme Court of Delaware
88 A.3d 635 (2014)

HOLLAND, Justice: . . .

We hold that business judgment is the standard of review that should govern mergers between a controlling stockholder and its corporate subsidiary, where the merger is conditioned *ab initio* upon both the approval of an independent, adequately-empowered Special Committee that fulfills its duty of care; and the uncoerced, informed vote of a majority of the minority stockholders. We so conclude for several reasons.

First, entire fairness is the highest standard of review in corporate law. It is applied in the controller merger context as a substitute for the dual statutory protections of disinterested board and stockholder approval, because both protections are potentially undermined by the influence of the controller. However, as this case establishes, that undermining influence does not exist in every controlled merger setting, regardless of the circumstances. The simultaneous deployment of the procedural protections employed here create a countervailing, offsetting influence of equal—if not greater—force. That is, where the controller irrevocably and publicly disables itself from using its control to dictate the outcome of the negotiations and the shareholder vote, the controlled merger then acquires the shareholder-protective characteristics of third-party, arm's-length mergers, which are reviewed under the business judgment standard.

Simultaneous Deployment of Procedural Protections

Second, the dual procedural protection merger structure optimally protects the minority stockholders in controller buyouts. As the Court of Chancery explained:

> [W]hen these two protections are established up-front, a potent tool to extract good value for the minority is established. From inception, the controlling stockholder knows that it cannot bypass the special committee's ability to say no. And, the controlling stockholder knows it cannot dangle a majority-of-the-minority vote before the special committee late in the process as a deal-closer rather than having to make a price move.

Third, and as the Court of Chancery reasoned, applying the business judgment standard to the dual protection merger structure:

> . . . is consistent with the central tradition of Delaware law, which defers to the informed decisions of impartial directors, especially when those decisions have been approved by the disinterested stockholders on full information and without coercion. Not only that, the adoption of this rule will be of benefit to minority stockholders because it will provide a strong incentive for controlling stockholders to accord minority investors the transactional structure that respected scholars believe will provide them the best protection, a structure where stockholders get the benefits of independent, empowered negotiating agents to **bargain for the best price and say no** if the agents believe the deal is not advisable for any proper reason, plus the critical ability to determine for themselves whether to accept any deal that their negotiating agents recommend to them. A transactional structure with both these protections is fundamentally different from one with only one protection.

Fourth, the underlying purposes of the dual protection merger structure utilized here and the entire fairness standard of review both converge and are fulfilled at the same critical point: **price.** Following *Weinberger v. UOP, Inc.*, this Court has consistently held that, although entire fairness review comprises the dual components of fair dealing and fair price, in a non-fraudulent transaction "price may be the preponderant consideration outweighing other features of the merger." 457 A.2d 701, 711 (Del. 1983). The dual protection merger structure requires two price-related pretrial determinations: first, that a fair price was achieved by an empowered, independent committee that acted with care; and, second, that a fully-informed, uncoerced majority of the minority stockholders voted in favor of the price that was recommended by the independent committee.

THE NEW STANDARD SUMMARIZED

To summarize our holding, in controller buyouts, the business judgment standard of review will be applied *if and only if:* (i) the controller conditions the procession of the transaction on the approval of both a Special Committee and a majority of the minority stockholders; (ii) the Special Committee is independent; (iii) the Special Committee is empowered to freely select its own advisors and to say no definitively; (iv) the Special Committee meets its duty of care in negotiating a fair price; (v) the vote of the minority is informed; and (vi) there is no coercion of the minority.

If a plaintiff that can plead a reasonably conceivable set of facts showing that any or all of those enumerated conditions did not exist, that complaint would state a claim for relief that would entitle the plaintiff to proceed and conduct discovery. If, after discovery, triable issues of fact remain about whether either or both of the dual procedural protections were established, or if established were effective, the case will proceed to a trial in which the court will conduct an entire fairness review.

This approach is consistent with *Weinberger*, [Kahn v. Lynch Comc'n Sys., Inc., 638 A.2d 1110 (Del. 1994)], and their progeny. A controller that employs and/or establishes only one of these dual procedural protections would continue to receive burden-shifting within the entire fairness standard of review framework. Stated differently, unless *both* procedural protections for the minority stockholders are established *prior to trial*, the ultimate judicial scrutiny of controller buyouts will continue to be the entire fairness standard of review.

Having articulated the circumstances that will enable a controlled merger to be reviewed under the business judgment standard, we next address whether those circumstances have been established as a matter of undisputed fact and law in this case.

DUAL PROTECTION INQUIRY

To reiterate, in this case, the controlling stockholder conditioned its offer upon the MFW Board agreeing, *ab initio*, to both procedural protections, *i.e.*, approval by a Special Committee and by a majority of the minority stockholders. For the combination of an effective

---

More to the Story: A Professional Plaintiff

Alan Russell Kahn has been called a "quasi-mythical figure[]" by the Delaware Court of Chancery. In re Revlon, Inc. S'holders Litig., 990 A.2d 940, 943 n.3 (Del. Ch. 2010). Between 2002 and 2012 alone, he individually served as plaintiff in 42 shareholder lawsuits, many involving transactions with controlling shareholders. His career as a plaintiff, however, began much earlier. He is the son of "the world's oldest investor," Irving Kahn, who died in 2014 at the age of 109. There is more in the online Supplement about "professional" plaintiff shareholders and the legal ethics issues they present.

committee process and majority-of-the-minority vote to qualify (jointly) for business judgment review, each of these protections must be effective singly to warrant a burden shift.

We begin by reviewing the record relating to the independence, mandate, and process of the Special Committee. In Kahn v. Tremont Corp., this Court held that "[t]o obtain the benefit of burden shifting, the controlling stockholder must do more than establish a perfunctory special committee of outside directors." [694 A.2d 422, 429 (Del. 1997).]

Rather, the special committee must "function in a manner which indicates that the controlling stockholder did not dictate the terms of the transaction and that the committee exercised real bargaining power 'at an arms-length.'" [*Id.*] As we have previously noted, deciding whether an independent committee was effective in negotiating a price is a process so fact-intensive and inextricably intertwined with the merits of an entire fairness review (fair dealing and fair price) that a pretrial determination of burden shifting is often impossible. Here, however, the Defendants have successfully established a record of independent committee effectiveness and process that warranted a grant of summary judgment entitling them to a burden shift prior to trial.

We next analyze the efficacy of the majority-of-the-minority vote, and we conclude that it was fully informed and not coerced. That is, the Defendants also established a pretrial majority-of-the-minority vote record that constitutes an independent and alternative basis for shifting the burden of persuasion to the Plaintiffs.

[The court's extensive discussion of both the independent committee determination and the majority of the minority vote are omitted.]

BOTH PROCEDURAL PROTECTIONS ESTABLISHED

Based on a highly extensive record, the Court of Chancery concluded that the procedural protections upon which the Merger was conditioned—approval by an independent and empowered Special Committee and by a[n] uncoerced informed majority of MFW's minority stockholders—had both been undisputedly established prior to trial. We agree and conclude the Defendants' motion for summary judgment was properly granted on all of those issues.

BUSINESS JUDGMENT REVIEW PROPERLY APPLIED

We have determined that the business judgment rule standard of review applies to this controlling stockholder buyout. Under that standard, the claims against the Defendants must be dismissed unless no rational person could have believed that the merger was favorable to MFW's minority stockholders. In this case, it cannot be credibly argued (let alone concluded) that no rational person would find the Merger favorable to MFW's minority stockholders.

———

As always, it is important to remember that Delaware is not the only fish in the corporate sea, although it does entertain a substantial percentage of important corporate litigation. Thus, in Coggins v. New England Patriots Football

Club, Inc., 492 N.E.2d 1112 (Mass. 1986), the Massachusetts Supreme Judicial Court chose to differ with Delaware, holding that in evaluating a freeze-out merger the court first must be satisfied that the transaction had a legitimate business purpose. Only then should it proceed to the question of fairness to the minority, given the totality of the circumstances. The court also ruled that the normally appropriate relief for an impermissible freeze-out merger is rescission. In *Coggins*, however, too much time had passed for rescission to fairly accommodate the intervening interests of third parties and the plaintiffs were granted rescissory damages.

The question of remedy may, after reading the material above, still seem a bit mysterious. One question that may occur is why it makes a difference whether a plaintiff receives rescissory damages or an amount determined through the appraisal mechanism. In light of the flexible approach toward valuation indicated in *Weinberger* itself, it may not—assuming the plaintiff wins. If, however, a plaintiff has not taken advantage of the appraisal mechanism (which has firm cut-off dates for filing) and loses in litigation challenging the transaction, he, she, or it will be stuck with the terms the shareholder vote has approved. This is a risk a shareholder might nevertheless choose to take when the defendants allegedly engaged in bad faith conduct going beyond "mere inadequacy of price." In Rabkin v. Phillip A. Hunt Chemical Corporation, 498 A.2d 1099 (Del. 1985), for instance, the defendant controlling shareholder had been committed, by contract with the issuer, to pay $25 per share for the minority interests if it purchased those interests within one year of acquiring its initial stake of 63.4 percent. The controlling shareholder had, instead, waited until the expiration of the one-year term before initiating a freeze-out merger at $20 per share. Since the plaintiffs were arguing a contractual right rather than "questions of valuation which are the traditional subjects of an appraisal," the Delaware Supreme Court felt they were within the wriggle room left by *Weinberger*. Thus, the plaintiffs were not limited to appraisal rights.

The drafters of the MBCA tried to be a bit clearer on the issue of whether appraisal is an exclusive remedy, providing as follows:

§13.40 Other Remedies Limited

(a) The legality of a proposed or completed corporate action described in section 13.02(a) [which includes mergers, share exchanges, and dispositions of assets] may not be contested, nor may the corporate action be enjoined, set aside or rescinded, in a legal or equitable proceeding by a shareholder after the shareholders have approved the corporate action.

(b) Subsection (a) does not apply to a corporate action that: (1) was not authorized and approved in accordance with the applicable provisions of: (i) chapter 9 [domestication and conversion], 10 [amendment of the articles], 11 [mergers and share exchanges], or 12 [dispositions of assets]; (ii) the articles of incorporation or bylaws; or (iii) the resolution of the board of directors authorizing the corporate action; (2) was procured as a result of fraud, a material misrepresentation, or an omission of a material fact necessary to make statements made, in light of the circumstances in which they were made, not misleading; (3) is an interested transaction, unless it has been [approved by informed, disinterested directors or shareholders as provided in chapter 8]; or (4) is approved by less than unanimous consent of the voting shareholders pursuant to section 7.04 [permitting shareholder actions without meetings] if [the challenge to the corporate is brought within a specified time frame by a shareholder who did not consent].

More to the Story: History and Controversy of the Appraisal-Rights Market Exception

Under §13.02(b), shareholders in publicly traded companies have no appraisal rights at all (so long as the acquiring person is not an interested party, and so long as the only consideration they must accept is cash or liquid securities). The MBCA first adopted a market exception to appraisal rights in its 1969 version, and a few states followed it, but it was deleted in 1978. The drafters in 1978 stated their view that market valuation had often been inadequate to prevent abuse of dissenting shareholders, apparently finding markets to be unreliable short-term judges of value during extraordinary periods like pending takeover transactions. Delaware's Supreme Court, however, thereafter created its own market exception by case law—in Weinberger v. UOP, Inc., 457 A.2d 701 (Del. 1983), which we read above—and then in 1999 the MBCA re-adopted the market exception that still appears as §13.02(b).

The reason, according to the official comment to the 1999 amendment, was the same as it had been in 1969. Public shareholders already enjoy a great deal of liquidity and benefit from a valuation mechanism that ought to be as reliable as a judge's opinion in an appraisal proceeding. So they don't need appraisal—they can sell prior to a disfavored transaction, and if they don't, markets should properly value their shares thereafter. And indeed, in states with no market exception, where public shareholders have sought appraisal the courts have often said that the market price was dispositive of the shares' true value, and so plaintiffs would have been better off just selling their shares. The drafters in 1999 were apparently no longer persuaded by the criticism the market exception had drawn in its 1969-1978 career.

The official comment makes it clear that remedies (such as injunctions) sought before a corporate action is effected are not precluded. The comment also states that the statute "does not address remedies, if any, that shareholders may have against directors or other persons as a result of the corporate action." Another problem, of course, is that minority shareholders may claim that they did not have full information, with a resultant failure to satisfy a requirement fairly implicit in the provisions describing how to procedurally accomplish a merger.

Appraisal statutes, including the MBCA and Delaware provisions, provide that shareholders invoking their rights are to receive the "fair value" of their shares. The MBCA specifies in §13.01 that the determination is to be made "immediately before the effectuation of the corporate action to which the shareholder objects" and "without discounting for lack of marketability or minority status." D.G.C.L. §262(h) excludes "any element of value arising from the accomplishment or expectation of the merger," but is silent as to the significance of minority status. In Cede & Co. v. Technicolor, Inc., 684 A.2d 289 (1996), however, the Delaware Supreme Court permitted value added by a controlling shareholder subsequent to its initial purchase of its shares to be considered—effectively permitting the dissenting minority to share in the "control premium." In Armstrong v. Marathon Oil Co., 513 N.E.2d 776 (1987), the Ohio Supreme Court held to the contrary in an opinion resulting in an appraisal calculation that was substantially less than the amount offered in the questioned merger.

■ **Think about this (it may sound somewhat familiar at first):**

Road Motors, Inc., a Delaware corporation, entered into a transaction with another company called Megabeast Motors Corp. Megabeast, a publicly traded Delaware corporation, issued 500,000 of its own shares as consideration for purchase of the bulk of Road Motors's assets (its manufacturing facilities, its inventory, its patent rights, and so on). Pursuant to the transaction, Road Motors retained $1 million in cash to pay whatever liabilities remained after the transaction. Finally, also pursuant to the transaction, Road Motors's board issued an in-kind dividend to the company's shareholders consisting of all the shares of Megabeast stock received, and then recommended that they vote to dissolve Road Motors. The shareholders so voted, and Road Motors was dissolved.

(F) If they so choose, could Road Motors's shareholders bring a legal action to challenge the company's acquisition, alleging that they should have been entitled to voting or appraisal rights?

(G) If they so choose, could Megabeast's shareholders bring a legal action to challenge the company's acquisition of Road Motors, alleging that they should have been entitled to voting or appraisal rights?

(H) Would it make a difference in either Problem F or Problem G if Road Motors and Megabeast were incorporated in a state following the Model Business Corporation Act?

E. Sales of Control

Officers and directors are not the only persons subject to the traditional duties of care and loyalty. Those duties are also imposed on a "controlling shareholder," most often because the directors they elect (and sometimes the officers they appoint) function effectively as the controlling shareholder's agents. As illustrated by *Weinberger*, above, these duties frequently pinch in parent-subsidiary mergers. This section, however, considers the pinch when the controlling shareholder is not seeking to merge—he, she, or it simply is trying to sell out at the highest amount possible.

We begin our study of this issue with an older case, *Perlman v. Feldmann*. It should be noted up front that *Perlman* is no longer within the mainstream as to the main issue addressed—whether a controlling shareholder may sell a controlling stake in the company and keep whatever "control premium" the buyer is willing to pay. The current law on that point, observed pretty much everywhere, is set forth in the *Zetlin* case, below. (Note that *Zetlin* largely restates the view of Judge Swan, dissenting in *Perlman*.)

However, *Perlman* very nicely sets up the issues surrounding controlling shareholders and also provides a nice example of how the courts determine when a shareholder has "control" sufficient to trigger fiduciary duties.

> ## Connections: Shareholder Duties
>
> *Perlman* and *Zetlin* both involve the controlling shareholders of publicly held corporations. Courts in some states—notably *not* including Delaware—recognize fiduciary duties akin to those of partners on the part of all shareholders of closely held corporations.

PERLMAN V. FELDMANN

United States Court of Appeals for the Second Circuit
219 F.2d 173 (1955)

CLARK, Chief Judge.

This is a derivative action brought by minority stockholders of Newport Steel Corporation to compel accounting for, and restitution of, allegedly illegal gains which accrued to defendants as a result of the sale in August, 1950, of their controlling interest in the corporation. The principal defendant, C. Russell Feldmann, who represented and acted for the others, members of his family,[6] was at that time not only the dominant stockholder, but also the chairman of the board of directors and the president of the corporation. Newport, an Indiana corporation, operated mills for the production of steel sheets for sale to manufacturers of steel products, first at Newport, Kentucky, and later also at other places in Kentucky and Ohio. The buyers, a syndicate organized as Wilport Company, a Delaware corporation, consisted of end-users of steel who were interested in securing a source of supply in a market becoming ever tighter in the Korean War. Plaintiffs contend that the consideration paid for the stock included compensation for the sale of a corporate asset, a power held in trust for the corporation by Feldmann as its fiduciary. This power was the ability to control the allocation of the corporate product in a time of short supply, through control of the board of directors; and it was effectively transferred in this sale by having Feldmann procure the resignation of his own board and the election of Wilport's nominees immediately upon consummation of the sale.

---

6. The stock was not held personally by Feldmann in his own name, but was held by the members of his family and by personal corporations. The aggregate of stock thus had amounted to 33% of the outstanding Newport stock and gave working control to the holder. The actual sale included 55,552 additional shares held by friends and associates of Feldmann, so that a total of 37% of the Newport stock was transferred.

The present action represents the consolidation of three pending stockholders' actions in which yet another stockholder has been permitted to intervene. Jurisdiction below was based upon the diverse citizenship of the parties. Plaintiffs argue here, as they did in the court below, that in the situation here disclosed the vendors must account to the non-participating minority stockholders for that share of their profit which is attributable to the sale of the corporate power. Judge Hincks denied the validity of the premise, holding that the rights involved in the sale were only those normally incident to the possession of a controlling block of shares, with which a dominant stockholder, in the absence of fraud or foreseeable looting, was entitled to deal according to his own best interests. Furthermore, he held that plaintiffs had failed to satisfy their burden of proving that the sales price was not a fair price for the stock *per se*. Plaintiffs appeal from these rulings of law which resulted in the dismissal of their complaint.

The essential facts found by the trial judge are not in dispute. Newport was a relative newcomer in the steel industry with predominantly old installations which were in the process of being supplemented by more modern facilities. Except in times of extreme shortage Newport was not in a position to compete profitably with other steel mills for customers not in its immediate geographical area. Wilport, the purchasing syndicate, consisted of geographically remote end-users of steel who were interested in buying more steel from Newport than they had been able to obtain during recent periods of tight supply. The price of $20 per share was found by Judge Hincks to be a fair one for a control block of stock, although the over-the-counter market price had not exceeded $12 and the book value per share was $17.03. But this finding was limited by Judge Hincks' statement that "what value the block would have had if shorn of its appurtenant power to control distribution of the corporate product, the evidence does not show." It was also conditioned by his earlier ruling that the burden was on plaintiffs to prove a lesser value for the stock.

Both as director and as dominant stockholder, Feldmann stood in a fiduciary relationship to the corporation and to the minority stockholders as beneficiaries thereof. . . . His fiduciary obligation must in the first instance be measured by the law of Indiana, the state of incorporation of Newport. . . . Although there is no Indiana case directly in point, the most closely analogous one emphasizes the close scrutiny to which Indiana subjects the conduct of fiduciaries when personal benefit may stand in the way of fulfillment of trust obligations. In Schemmel v. Hill, 169 N.E. 678, 682, 683, McMahan, J., said: "Directors of a business corporation act in a strictly fiduciary capacity. Their office is a trust. When a director deals with his corporation, his acts will be closely scrutinized. . . . Directors of a corporation are its agents, and they are governed by the rules of law applicable to other agents, and, as between themselves and their principal, the rules relating to honesty and fair dealing in the management of the affairs of their principal are applicable. They must not, in any degree, allow their official conduct to be swayed by their private interest, which must yield to official duty. . . . In a transaction between a director and his corporation, where he acts for himself and his principal at the same time in a matter connected with the relation between them, it is presumed, where he is thus potential on both sides of the contract, that self-interest will overcome his fidelity to his principal, to his own benefit and to his principal's hurt." And the judge added: "Absolute and most scrupulous good faith is the very essence of a director's obligation to his corporation. The first principal duty arising from his official relation is to act in all things of trust wholly for the benefit of his corporation."

In Indiana, then, as elsewhere, the responsibility of the fiduciary is not limited to a proper regard for the tangible balance sheet assets of the corporation, but includes the dedication of his uncorrupted business judgment for the sole benefit of the corporation, in any dealings which may adversely affect it. . . . Although the Indiana case is particularly relevant to Feldmann as a director, the same rule should apply to his fiduciary duties as majority stockholder, for in that capacity he chooses and controls the directors, and thus is held to have assumed their liability. . . . This, therefore, is the standard to which Feldmann was by law required to conform in his activities here under scrutiny.

It is true, as defendants have been at pains to point out, that this is not the ordinary case of breach of fiduciary duty. We have here no fraud, no misuse of confidential information, no outright looting of a helpless corporation. But on the other hand, we do not find compliance with that high standard which we have just stated and which we and other courts have come to expect and demand of corporate fiduciaries. In the often-quoted words of Judge Cardozo: "Many forms of conduct permissible in a workaday world for those acting at arm's length, are forbidden to those bound by fiduciary ties. A trustee is held to something stricter than the morals of the market place. Not honesty alone, but the punctilio of an honor the most sensitive, is then the standard of behavior. As to this there has developed a tradition that is unbending and inveterate. Uncompromising rigidity has been the attitude of courts of equity when petitioned to undermine the rule of undivided loyalty by the 'disintegrating erosion' of particular exceptions." Meinhard v. Salmon, 164 N.E. 545, 546. The actions of defendants in siphoning off for personal gain corporate advantages to be derived from a favorable market situation do not betoken the necessary undivided loyalty owed by the fiduciary to his principal.

Justice Cardozo

The corporate opportunities of whose misappropriation the minority stockholders complain need not have been an absolute certainty in order to support this action against Feldmann. If there was possibility of corporate gain, they are entitled to recover. In Young v. Higbee Co., 324 U.S. 204, 65 S. Ct. 594, two stockholders appealing the confirmation of a plan of bankruptcy reorganization were held liable for profits received for the sale of their stock pending determination of the validity of the appeal. They were held accountable for the excess of the price of their stock over its normal price, even though there was no indication that the appeal could have succeeded on substantive grounds. And in Irving Trust Co. v. Deutsch, 2 Cir., 73 F.2d 121, 124, an accounting was required of corporate directors who bought stock for themselves for corporate use, even though there was an affirmative showing that the corporation did not have the finances itself to acquire the stock. Judge Swan speaking for the court pointed out that "The defendants' argument, contrary to Wing v. Dillingham (5

Cir., 239 F. 54), that the equitable rule that fiduciaries should not be permitted to assume a position in which their individual interests might be in conflict with those of the corporation can have no application where the corporation is unable to undertake the venture, is not convincing. If directors are permitted to justify their conduct on such a theory, there will be a temptation to refrain from exerting their strongest efforts on behalf of the corporation since, if it does not meet the obligations, an opportunity of profit will be open to them personally."

This rationale is equally appropriate to a consideration of the benefits which Newport might have derived from the steel shortage. In the past Newport had used and profited by its market leverage by operation of what the industry had come to call the "Feldmann Plan." This consisted of securing interest-free advances from prospective purchasers of steel in return for firm commitments to them from future production. The funds thus acquired were used to finance improvements in existing plants and to acquire new installations. In the summer of 1950 Newport had been negotiating for cold-rolling facilities which it needed for a more fully integrated operation and a more marketable product, and Feldmann plan funds might well have been used toward this end.

Further, as plaintiffs alternatively suggest, Newport might have used the period of short supply to build up patronage in the geographical area in which it could compete profitably even when steel was more abundant. Either of these opportunities was Newport's, to be used to its advantage only. Only if defendants had been able to negate completely any possibility of gain by Newport could they have prevailed. It is true that a trial court finding states: "Whether or not, in August, 1950, Newport's position was such that it could have entered into 'Feldmann Plan' type transactions to procure funds and financing for the further expansion and integration of its steel facilities and whether such expansion would have been desirable for Newport, the evidence does not show." This, however, cannot avail the defendants, who—contrary to the ruling below—had the burden of proof on this issue, since fiduciaries always have the burden of proof in establishing the fairness of their dealings with trust property. . . .

Defendants seek to categorize the corporate opportunities which might have accrued to Newport as too unethical to warrant further consideration. It is true that reputable steel producers were not participating in the gray market brought about by the Korean War and were refraining from advancing their prices, although to do so would not have been illegal. But Feldmann plan transactions were not considered within this self-imposed interdiction; the trial court found that around the time of the Feldmann sale Jones & Laughlin Steel Corporation, Republic Steel Company, and Pittsburgh Steel Corporation were all participating in such arrangements. In any event, it ill becomes the defendants to disparage as unethical the market advantages from which they themselves reaped rich benefits.

We do not mean to suggest that a majority stockholder cannot dispose of his controlling block of stock to outsiders without having to account to his corporation for profits or even never do this with impunity when the buyer is an interested customer, actual or potential, for the corporation's product. But when the sale necessarily results in a sacrifice of this element of corporate good will and consequent unusual profit to the fiduciary who has caused the sacrifice, he should account for his gains. So in a time of market shortage, where a call on a corporation's product commands an unusually large premium, in one form or another, we think it sound law that a fiduciary may not appropriate to himself the value of this premium. Such personal gain at the expense of his coventurers seems particularly reprehensible when made by the trusted president and director of his company. In this case the violation of duty seems to be all the clearer because of this triple role in which Feldmann appears, though we are unwilling to say, and are not to be understood as saying, that we should accept a lesser obligation for any one of his roles alone.

Hence to the extent that the price received by Feldmann and his codefendants included such a bonus, he is accountable to the minority stockholders who sue here. . . . And plaintiffs, as they contend, are entitled to a recovery in their own right, instead of in right of the corporation (as in the usual derivative actions), since neither Wilport nor their successors in interest should share in any judgment which may be rendered. . . . Defendants cannot well object to this form of recovery, since the only alternative, recovery for the corporation as a whole, would subject them to a greater total liability.

The case will therefore be remanded to the district court for a determination of the question expressly left open below, namely, the value of defendants' stock without the appurtenant control over the corporation's output of steel. We reiterate that on this issue, as on all others relating to a breach of fiduciary duty, the burden of proof must rest on the defendants. Judgment should go to these plaintiffs and those whom they represent for any premium value so shown to the extent of their respective stock interests. . . .

SWAN, Circuit Judge (dissenting).

With the general principles enunciated in the majority opinion as to the duties of fiduciaries I am, of course, in thorough accord. But, as Mr. Justice Frankfurter stated in Securities and Exchange Comm. v. Chenery Corp., 318 U.S. 80, 85, "to say that a man is a fiduciary only begins analysis; it gives direction to further inquiry. To whom is he a fiduciary? What obligations does he owe as a fiduciary? In what respect has he failed to discharge these obligations?" My brothers' opinion does not specify precisely what fiduciary duty Feldmann is held to have violated or whether it was a duty imposed upon him as the dominant stockholder or as a director of Newport. Without such specification I think that both the legal profession and the business world will find the decision confusing and will be unable to foretell the extent of its impact upon customary practices in the sale of stock.

The power to control the management of a corporation, that is, to elect directors to manage its affairs, is an inseparable incident to the ownership of a majority of its stock, or sometimes, as in the present instance, to the ownership of enough shares, less than a majority, to control an election. Concededly a majority or dominant shareholder is ordinarily privileged to sell his stock at the best price obtainable from the purchaser. In so doing he acts on his own behalf, not as an agent of the corporation. If he knows or has reason to believe that the purchaser intends to exercise to the detriment of the corporation the power of management acquired by the purchase, such knowledge or reasonable suspicion will terminate the dominant shareholder's privilege to sell and will create a duty not to transfer the power of management to such purchaser. The duty seems to me to resemble the obligation which everyone is under not to assist another to commit a tort rather than the obligation of a fiduciary. But whatever the nature of the duty, a violation of it will subject the violator to liability for damages sustained by the corporation. Judge Hincks found that Feldmann had no reason to think that Wilport would use the power of management it would acquire by the purchase to injure Newport, and that there was no proof that it ever was so used. Feldmann did know, it is true, that the reason Wilport wanted the stock was to put in a board of directors who would be likely to permit Wilport's members to purchase more of Newport's steel than they might otherwise be able to get. But there is nothing illegal in a dominant shareholder purchasing from his own corporation at the same prices it offers to other customers. That is what the members of Wilport did, and there is no proof that Newport suffered any detriment therefrom.

My brothers say that "the consideration paid for the stock included compensation for the sale of a corporate asset," which they describe as "the ability to control the allocation of the corporate product in a time of short supply, through control of the board of directors; and it was effectively transferred in this sale by having Feldmann procure the resignation of his own board and the election of Wilport's nominees immediately upon consummation of the sale." The implications of this are not clear to me. If it means that when market of a corporation's product are such as to induce users to wish to buy a controlling block of stock in order to be able to purchase part of the corporation's output at the same mill list prices as are offered to other customers, the dominant stockholder is under a fiduciary duty not to sell his stock, I cannot agree. For reasons already stated, in my opinion Feldmann was not proved to be under any fiduciary duty as a stockholder not to sell the stock he controlled.

Feldmann was also a director of Newport. Perhaps the quoted statement means that as a director he violated his fiduciary duty in voting to elect Wilport's nominees to fill the vacancies created by the resignations of the former directors of Newport. As a director Feldmann was under a fiduciary duty to use an honest judgment in acting on the corporation's behalf. A director is privileged to resign, but so long as he remains a director he must be faithful to his fiduciary duties and must not make a personal gain from performing them. Consequently, if the price paid for Feldmann's stock included a payment for voting to elect the new directors, he must account to the corporation for such payment, even though he honestly believed that the men he voted to elect were well qualified to serve as directors. He can not take pay for performing his fiduciary duty. There is no suggestion that he did do so, unless the price paid for his stock was more than its value. . . .

The final conclusion of my brothers is that the plaintiffs are entitled to recover in their own right instead of in the right of the corporation. This appears to be completely inconsistent with the theory advanced at the outset of the opinion, namely, that the price of the stock "included compensation for the sale of a corporate asset." If a corporate asset was sold, surely the corporation should recover the compensation received for it by the defendants. Moreover, if the plaintiffs were suing in their own right, Newport was not a proper party. . . .

The following case exemplifies the modern approach.

ZETLIN V. HANSON HOLDINGS, INC.

New York Court of Appeals
397 N.E.2d 387 (1979)

MEMORANDUM.

The order of the Appellate Division should be affirmed, with costs.

Plaintiff Zetlin owned approximately 2% of the outstanding shares of Gable Industries, Inc., with defendants Hanson Holdings, Inc., and Sylvestri together with members of the Sylvestri family, owning 44.4% of Gable's shares. The defendants sold their interests to Flintkote Co. for a premium price of $15 per share, at a time when Gable was selling on the open market for $7.38 per share. It is undisputed that the 44.4% acquired by Flintkote represented effective control of Gable.

Recognizing that those who invest the capital necessary to acquire a dominant position in the ownership of a corporation have the right of controlling that corporation, it has long been settled law that, absent looting of corporate assets, conversion of a corporate opportunity, fraud or other acts of bad faith, a controlling stockholder is free to sell, and a purchaser is free to buy, that controlling interest at a premium price.

Certainly, minority shareholders are entitled to protection against such abuse by controlling shareholders. They are not entitled, however, to inhibit the legitimate interests of the other stockholders. It is for this reason that control shares usually command a premium price. The premium is the added amount an investor is willing to pay for the privilege of directly influencing the corporation's affairs.

In this action plaintiff Zetlin contends that minority stockholders are entitled to an opportunity to share equally in any premium paid for a controlling interest in the corporation. This rule would profoundly affect the manner in which controlling stock interests are now transferred. It would require, essentially, that a controlling interest be transferred only by means of an offer to all stockholders, i.e., a tender offer. This would be contrary to existing law and if so radical a change is to be effected it would best be done by the Legislature.

■ **Think about this:**

(I) Is it clear that, if applied to the facts of *Perlman*, the *Zetlin* approach would lead to a different result?

(J) Jerry owns 51 percent of the voting stock of Supposal, Inc. He is approached by Blain, who is well known for acquiring the majority interest in corporations and causing them to liquidate in order to turn quick profits on his investment. Minority shareholders in such deals, who may have owned their shares for some time, receive their pro rata portion of the liquidation proceeds, but often have undesirable, unexpected tax consequences. Supposal shares are selling on the open market for $25 per share. Blain offers Jerry $27 per share. May Jerry accept the offer?

(K) Kerry owns 51 percent of Assumpsit, Inc., an up-and-coming manufacturer of sump pumps. She is approached by Pump It Up, Inc., a competitor of Assumpsit, and is offered a price of $15 per share. The prevailing market price is $10. She does not know, but strongly suspects, that Pump It Up will either operate Assumpsit in a manner advantageous to itself or merge with it at terms that will not be very desirable to the minority shareholders. May she accept the offer?

(L) Larry owns 51 percent of Surmise Corp., a software company. He can, and does, elect all seven members of the board of directors. He is approached by Mary, who would like to serve on the board in order to earn directors' fees and to enhance her resume. She offers to pay him one-quarter of the fees she earns for each year he elects her. May Larry elect Mary and take the payment?

Test Yourself

1. In Model Act jurisdictions, which of the following states the difference in consequences between mergers and share exchanges?

   a. In mergers, the acquiring company takes on the target company's pre-acquisition liabilities.
   b. Share exchanges do not trigger appraisal rights.
   c. Answers a and b are both correct.
   d. Neither answer a nor answer b is correct.

2. Myron is a shareholder in a closely held corporation called XYZ, Inc., which has one class of common voting stock. Myron is annoyed that 51 percent of the shares of the company were recently voted in favor of a one-for-one share exchange for the stock of ZYX, Inc. ZYX is a publicly held

company the shares of which are trading at $10 per share. Myron believes that his stock is worth more than that, so he should wait and try to sell it at a higher price. True or False?

a. True. The pendency of a share exchange would likely give rise to a "control premium" and the value of Myron's stock to a third party is probably quite high.
b. True, but only because ZYX is a publicly held company.
c. False, because close corporation stock is illiquid and therefore Myron could probably not sell it for much.
d. False for some other reason.

3. XYZ, a Delaware diversified holding company, owns a number of subsidiaries, including ABC, which is incorporated in a Model Act jurisdiction. XYZ owns 92 percent of ABC's voting stock. If XYZ desires to merge ABC into itself, ABC's shareholders need not be offered the right to vote on the plan. True or False?

a. False, unless ABC's articles will not be amended and its shareholders will retain the same number of shares with the same rights and attributes.
b. False for some other reason.
c. True.
d. This question cannot be answered without knowing the requirements for short-form merger under Delaware law.

4. Appraisal is a dissenting shareholder's exclusive remedy following a tender offer. True or False?

a. True. This rule is required by statute law governing corporate acquisitions.
b. True. This rule is required by common law governing corporate acquisitions.
c. False. The shareholder will have other remedies in addition to appraisal if he or she can prove some fraud or other misconduct in connection with the tender offer.
d. False. A tender offer is not an event triggering appraisal rights.

Questions 5-8 rely on the following facts:

A leading maker of vision care equipment that is not very concerned with its consumers' personal desires, C.F. Eyecare, Inc., is incorporated in a Model Act jurisdiction. C.F. Eyecare has 4,000 outside shareholders who hold between them about 35 million shares. Those 35 million shares in total have a market value of about $350 million. Another corporation, the large diversified holding company known as XYZ, Inc., enters into an agreement with the management of C.F. Eyecare under which XYZ will purchase all the assets of C.F. Eyecare in exchange for shares of XYZ. Following the purchase, C.F. Eyecare agreed that it would distribute its XYZ stock as an in-kind dividend to its shareholders, and then it would dissolve. This plan was recommended by C.F. Eyecare's board to its shareholders, and they approved it by a vote of more than 70 percent. The plan was not submitted to XYZ's shareholders, but 75 percent of XYZ's stock is owned by one man who favored the plan.

John is a former shareholder of C.F. Eyecare who voted against the plan and is now unhappy with his shares of XYZ stock. He thinks the shares he received did not reflect the fair market value of the C.F. Eyecare stock that he formerly held, and he brings a lawsuit against C.F. Eyecare and XYZ seeking payment of the fair market value of his stock.

5. Defendants move to dismiss John's lawsuit, alleging that he is not entitled to this kind of relief. How should a court rule on this motion?

   a. Grant it, because John no longer holds any shares and therefore lacks standing.
   b. Grant it if John failed to make demand on the board of directors of either company.
   c. Grant it for some other reason.
   d. Deny it. In Model Act jurisdictions, appraisal is an appropriate remedy in cases such as this and that is essentially what he is seeking.

6. In a jurisdiction that recognizes the "de facto merger" doctrine, the transaction between XYZ and C.F. Eyecare could be described as a "de facto merger." True or False?

   a. True, because the nature of the business in which C.F. Eyecare's former shareholders now own stock has changed.
   b. True, because C.F. Eyecare's former shareholders now have a very different relationship with the management of the company in which they own stock.
   c. True, because C.F. Eyecare's shareholders were entitled to vote as to the transaction.
   d. All of the above answers are correct.
   e. Answers a and b are both correct.

7. If this transaction were held to be a "de facto merger," how would John's situation be changed?

   a. He would be entitled to appraisal.
   b. He would be entitled to voting rights.
   c. Answers a and b are both correct.
   d. His situation would be unchanged.
   e. None of the above.

8. Failure to submit the transaction to vote by XYZ's shareholders is:

   a. Relevant to whether they will enjoy appraisal rights.
   b. Relevant to whether XYZ's controlling shareholder breached any fiduciary duties.
   c. Likely irrelevant to the legal soundness of the transaction itself, since even in Model Act jurisdictions acquiring-firm shareholders are normally not entitled to vote on purchases of assets.
   d. All of the above.
   e. Answers b and c are both correct.

(Answers in Online Supplement)

24

Corporate Control Transactions, Part II: Tender Offers, Tender Offer Defenses, and Special Fiduciary Duties in Hostile Takeover Situations

An important distinction between the tender offer and many other corporate control transactions is that the tender offer does not require the acquiescence of the board of directors of the target company. In other words, a third party can literally buy the company out from management, and this is why "tender offers" are often "hostile" takeovers. This chapter describes the mechanics of a tender offer, briefly reviews the federal scheme for regulating them, and highlights the conflict of interest that can arise between the management as a group and the company's shareholders when preparing for, or directly facing, a hostile takeover.

Chapter Outline

A. Introduction

1. The Tender Offer and Other Hostile Acquisitions of Control
   - Offers for cash or shares
   - Two-tier tender offers

2. Federal Regulatory Scheme
   - Disclosure
   - Anti-fraud
   - Regulation of terms

3. Inherent Conflicts of Interest

B. The Traditional *Cheff* Rule

- Danger to corporate policy or effectiveness
- Good faith and reasonable investigation

C. Modern Developments

1. Background

2. "New" Fiduciary Duties: *Unocal*, *Revlon*, and Refinements
   - The revised *Cheff-Unocal* rule: good faith investigation plus reasonable response
   - *Revlon*: the duty to auction
   - Sale of control

D. Anti-Takeover Legislation and the State-Federal Interface
   - Corporate constituency statutes
   - Delaware §203
   - Control share statutes
   - The danger of preemption and/or the impermissible burdening of interstate commerce

Test Yourself

 What does it look like?

Check the online Supplement for the following sample documents that are relevant to this chapter:

- Tender offer disclosure statement

A. Introduction

1. The Tender Offer and Other Hostile Acquisitions of Control

The tender offer was introduced in another chapter, but it is worth revisiting. A tender offer is an open market offer to purchase some or all of the outstanding shares of a corporation's stock. It does not require acquiescence of the board, and it does not effect a change in control until the tender offer proponent acquires a controlling share of stock through individual purchases from shareholders. Sometimes the acquiror is content with simply maintaining that control position, but sometimes it will seek to merge the target into itself, perhaps for efficiency, for the purpose of eliminating the minority shareholders, or for some combination of factors. Tender offers are not the only method of taking over control without management acquiescence, of course. Control shares might be acquired in a privately negotiated transaction. In addition, it is possible for the holders of a minority position simply to wage a proxy battle to oust incumbent directors and replace them with others who are more amenable to the goals of the insurgent camp. Proxy battles involving companies that are registered under the Securities Exchange Act of 1934 ('34 Act) are regulated primarily by federal law and are dealt with in a different chapter.

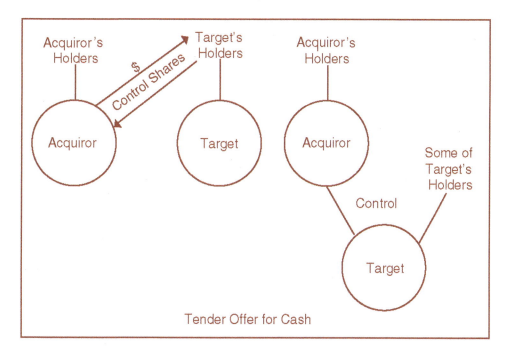

Tender Offer for Cash

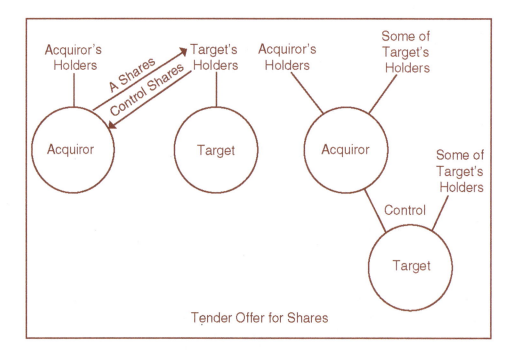

Tender Offer for Shares

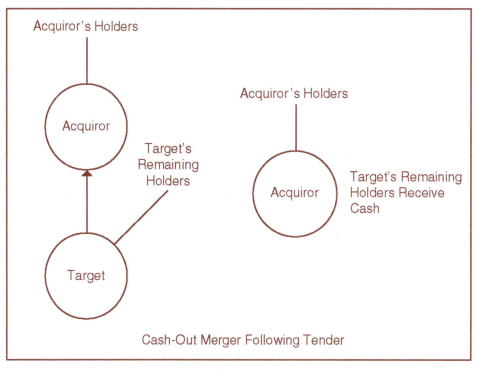

Cash-Out Merger Following Tender

2. Federal Regulatory Scheme

Tender offers for the shares of companies registered under the '34 Act, like proxy battles, are highly regulated as a matter of federal law. The primary state issues have to do with the duties of management in guarding against or resist-ing them. Before turning to them it is worth a few moments to understand the broad strokes of the federal scheme.

Tender offers in which the acquiring company offers its securities in exchange for shares in the target (often called "stock tender offers") always have been subject to the registration requirements of the Securities Act of 1933. Prior to 1968, however, tender offers in which the target's shareholders were offered cash (generally called "cash tender offers") were unregulated. That changed in 1968 when Congress passed the Williams Act, which amended the '34 Act by the addition of three types of provisions:

- Those requiring various disclosures to the target firm's sharehold-ers (including disclosure relating to intent to eliminate the remaining minority shareholders after the acquisition);
- Those mandating certain provisions that must be a part of all tender offers (such as a rule that all shareholders responding to the tender offer must receive the best price offered at any time while the tender offer is open); and
- One prohibiting various kinds of fraudulent conduct in connection with tender offers (which has been used to justify a rule that a tender offer must be left open for at least 20 days).

3. Inherent Conflicts of Interest

There are reasons that a tender offer as such, as opposed to a merger, share exchange, or assets purchase, only sometimes will be "friendly." If the target company's board is amenable to some friendly acquisition, then it can almost surely be accomplished with less expense and risk to the prospective acquiror than through a tender offer. Because a tender offer, once launched, must be left open for at least 20 days—as required by the Williams Act—there is ample time for competing tenders to be launched. Thus, if a prospective acquiror has put time and effort into identifying a good prospect that it believes harbors unex-ploited value, beginning a tender offer essentially waves a flag attracting the attention of other would-be corporate suitors. The result can be a bidding war, which the initial prospective acquiror would very much like to avoid.

Something important to understand about tender offer cases, then, is that a special sort of conflict of interest can arise: a conflict between the management as a group and the company's shareholders. When a hostile takeover attempt is pending, the target company's management is likely to feel quite threatened. Most pressingly, they may lose their jobs during the inevitable post-acquisition reor-ganization. This will typically be a much more acute concern for officers of the company and inside directors than for outside directors. Officers depend for their living on their executive position, whereas outside directors earn only a much smaller amount of their living from their compensation as directors. Even if the officers and directors do not lose their positions, they are likely to lose control and autonomy they previously had. On the other hand, the shareholders might have a strong pecuniary interest in seeing a tender offer happen—or better yet a tender offer bidding war—because of the "control premium" that typically is paid.

Peter Jakob Horemans,
Sleeping Kitchen Maid

This is an example of a basic agency cost problem. Remember that as a basic principle of corporation law the officers and directors of the corporation are duty-bound to serve the best interests of the corporation, even at the expense of their own personal interests, and their most basic obligation in this respect is to protect the value of the shareholders' investment. This is so even when it means they might lose their jobs.

But what if officers and directors of the target company really, genuinely believe that a pending hostile takeover is bad for the company's future, and their fears are well founded? Can they try to stop it? Or should it be up to the judgments made by individual shareholders in deciding how to respond to a tender offer?

We shall see the courts' answers to these questions in the sections that follow.

B. The Traditional *Cheff* Rule

Heaven forfend that a textbook be either boring or redundant, but there is value to reconsidering the basics of an officer or director's fiduciary duties. As we have seen many times, the corporate fiduciary's traditional obligations were thought to consist of two fundamental duties:

- The **duty of care** requires the fiduciary to use that skill, diligence, and prudence of a reasonable person in similar circumstances. Where the decision maker takes some conscious action, and is not financially interested in the outcome, the business judgment rule protects the substance of any rational decision.
- The **duty of loyalty** prevents unfair self-dealing and unfair usurpation of corporate opportunities. In general, the burden of proving fairness falls on an interested decision maker. If a transaction involving a corporate fiduciary was approved by a disinterested decision maker (that is, if it was "ratified"), however, the burden of proving unfairness usually falls on the party challenging the transaction.

These duties have been the subject of judicial contemplation in at least two areas, in addition to that of the hostile tender offer, that involve what might be thought of as structural bias on the part of management. These are the decision whether to bring or dismiss derivative litigation against members of management and the freeze-out merger. If your class already has covered either or both of these subjects, you might want to take a moment to think about what the rules in those areas would prompt you to predict in the context of the hostile tender offer.

The following is a case that did not actually involve a tender offer. Rather, the prospective acquiror had followed a strategy of open-market purchases leading corporate management to fear what might happen next. The tactic of purchasing shares, either on the open market or through tender offer, and then offering to sell them back to management at a premium price in order to prevent an unwanted takeover is known as "greenmail."

 Dear Prof.: A couple of things. First, what's the difference between an open-market purchase and a tender offer? Second, it looks like the next umpteen cases are from Delaware and have most of the facts edited out. What's up with that?

First, an open-market purchase is made anonymously and with no fanfare through existing venues, such as stock exchanges or stockbrokers. A tender offer typically is publicly announced and responses—the tenders of the shares—do not go through the standard channels. They go straight to the agent of the tender offeror. An interesting question, incidentally, is why non-tender-offer purchases on the open market are kept so quiet. Do you see the reason?

As to the second question, as you know, many of the largest corporations are incorporated in Delaware. It consequently is home to a great deal of the litigation involving corporate acquisitions of a size big enough to be worth very seriously fighting over.

Finally, it is an open secret that the Delaware courts are extremely sensitive to the importance of their decisions and to the fact that the stakes are so high in the world of corporate acquisition that strategies for executing and resisting such acquisitions are sophisticated and ever-changing. In addition, their decisions are often rendered in the course of battles for control and thus under severe time constraints. Their response, in many instances, is to emphasize that their decisions are narrowly fact-specific. The idea is to decide cases rather than establish sweeping precedents, and the result is opinions that are very long. It may seem perverse, then, to summarize the facts so closely. We nonetheless made the judgment to do so and have put longer, but still edited versions, in the online Supplement. We expect that your professor may want to assign one or more of these longer versions.

CHEFF V. MATHES

Supreme Court of Delaware
199 A.2d 548 (1964)

CAREY, Justice.

This is an appeal from the decision of the Vice-Chancellor in a derivative suit holding certain directors of Holland Furnace Company [Holland] liable for loss allegedly resulting from improper use of corporate funds to purchase shares of the company. . . .

[The case is a derivative action against the directors of Holland for buying shares of the company back from a prospective acquiror at a premium price. The prospective acquiror was Arnold H. Maremont (Maremont), acting through Motor Products Corporation. Maremont was known for acquiring companies and quickly liquidating them, but represented when he first approached Holland that he was interested in a merger that would modernize it and improve its profitability, which was slowly rebounding from a decline following a post–World War II building boom. The decision to resist his proposed takeover was made by six of a seven-member board composed of both inside" and "outside" directors, notwithstanding the willingness of one of the directors, Mrs. Cheff, to put personal resources into buying out Maremont.]

On February 6, 1958, plaintiffs, owners of 60 shares of Holland stock, filed a derivative suit in the court below naming all of the individual directors of Holland, Holland itself and Motor Products Corporation as defendants. The complaint alleged that all of the purchases of stock by Holland in 1957 were for the purpose of insuring the perpetuation of control by the incumbent directors. The complaint requested that the transaction between Motor Products and Holland be rescinded and, secondly, that the individual defendants account to Holland for the alleged damages. . . .

Under the provisions of 8 Del. C. §160, a corporation is granted statutory power to purchase and sell shares of its own stock. Such a right, as embodied in the statute, has long been recognized in this State. The charge here is not one of violation of statute, but the allegation is that the true motives behind such purchases were improperly centered upon perpetuation of control. In an analogous field, courts have sustained the use of proxy funds to inform stockholders of management's views upon the policy questions inherent in an election to a board of directors, but have not sanctioned the use of corporate funds to advance the selfish desires of directors to perpetuate themselves in office. Similarly, if the actions of the board were motivated by a sincere belief that the buying out of the dissident stockholder was necessary to maintain what the board believed to be proper business practices, the board will not be held liable for such decision, even though hindsight indicates the decision was not the wisest course. On the other hand, if the board has acted solely or primarily because of the desire to perpetuate themselves in office, the use of corporate funds for such purposes is improper. . . .

Our first problem is the allocation of the burden of proof to show the presence or lack of good faith on the part of the board in authorizing the purchase of shares. Initially, the decision of the board of directors in authorizing a purchase was presumed to be in good faith and could be overturned only by a conclusive showing by plaintiffs of fraud or other misconduct. . . . However, in Bennett v. Propp, [Del., 187 A.2d 405], we stated:

> We must bear in mind the inherent danger in the purchase of shares with corporate funds to remove a threat to corporate policy when a threat to control is involved. The directors are of necessity confronted with a conflict of interest, and an objec-

tive decision is difficult. . . . Hence, in our opinion, the burden should be on the directors to justify such a purchase as one primarily in the corporate interest. . . .

To say that the burden of proof is upon the defendants is not to indicate, however, that the directors have the same "self-dealing interest" as is present, for example, when a director sells property to the corporation. The only clear pecuniary interest shown on the record was held by Mr. Cheff, as an executive of the corporation, and Trenkamp, as its attorney. The mere fact that some of the other directors were substantial shareholders does not create a personal pecuniary interest in the decisions made by the board of directors, since all shareholders would presumably share the benefit flowing to the substantial shareholder. Accordingly, these directors other than Trenkamp and Cheff, while called upon to justify their actions, will not be held to the same standard of proof required of those directors having personal and pecuniary interest in the transaction. . . .

Plaintiffs urge that the sale price was unfair in view of the fact that the price was in excess of that prevailing on the open market. However, as conceded by all parties, a substantial block of stock will normally sell at a higher price than that prevailing on the open market, the increment being attributable to a "control premium." Plaintiffs argue that it is inappropriate to require the defendant corporation to pay a control premium, since control is meaningless to an acquisition by a corporation of its own shares. However, it is elementary that a holder of a substantial number of shares would expect to receive the control premium as part of his selling price, and if the corporation desired to obtain the stock, it is unreasonable to expect that the corporation could avoid paying what any other purchaser would be required to pay for the stock. In any event, the financial expert produced by defendant at trial indicated that the price paid was fair and there was no rebuttal. . . .

The question then presented is whether or not defendants satisfied the burden of proof of showing reasonable grounds to believe a danger to corporate policy and effectiveness existed by the presence of the Maremont stock ownership. It is important to remember that the directors satisfy their burden by showing good faith and reasonable investigation; the directors will not be penalized for an honest mistake of judgment, if the judgment appeared reasonable at the time the decision was made.

[The court then evaluated the defendants' contentions that (1) Maremont's attention was causing unrest on the part of Holland's employees, and (2) there was a threat by Maremont to Holland's sales policies, which the board considered vital to success and found them reasonable, particularly in light of Maremont's poor reputation and his attempt, at one, point to deceive Holland's representative about his intentions.]

Accordingly, we are of the opinion that the evidence presented in the court below leads inevitably to the conclusion that the board of directors, based upon direct investigation, receipt of professional advice, and personal observations of the contradictory action of Maremont and his explanation of corporate purpose, believed, with justification, that there was a reasonable threat to the continued existence of Holland, or at least existence in its present form, by the plan of Maremont to continue building up his stock holdings. . . .

[T]he Vice-Chancellor found that the purpose of the acquisition was the improper desire to maintain control, but, at the same time, he exonerated those individual directors whom he believed to be unaware of the possibility of using non-corporate funds to accomplish this purpose. . . . If the actions were in fact improper because of a desire to maintain control, then the presence or absence of a non-corporate alternative is irrelevant, as corporate funds may not be used to advance an improper purpose even if there is no non-corporate alternative available. Conversely, if the actions were proper because of a decision by the board made in good faith that the corporate interest was served thereby, they are not rendered improper by the fact that some individual directors were willing to advance personal funds if the corporation did not. . . .

Accordingly, the judgment of the court below is reversed and remanded with instruction to enter judgment for the defendants.

■ **Think about this:**

(A) What, precisely, is it the defendant's burden to show in a case in which the plaintiff contends "entrenchment" was the motive for resisting a takeover? Does it make a difference whether he or she is an inside director?

(B) What, precisely, must the plaintiff show in order to win a case based on the claim that the defendants sought to entrench themselves?

C. Modern Developments

1. Background

In the past 30 years or so, a lot has changed.

For example, in reading the full version of the *Cheff* case one gets the impression that during the 1950s and 1960s a corporate "raider" like Maremont was not very well thought of in communities of business executives. Indeed, a major social change has occurred in recent decades, as a result of which corporate transactions that were once nearly unheard of have become quite common. Namely, there was a time when a hostile takeover—an attempt to take away a business from a group who didn't want it to be sold—was, at best, poor etiquette.

That began to change in the mid-1970s, and by the 1980s both friendly and hostile takeovers were much more common than ever before. Along with these changes came new institutions. In particular, new investment banks sprang up (investment banks are institutions that fund corporate transactions, rather than sell mortgage loans and hold deposits for retail customers) and existing banks that had been smaller, fringe entities came to be major players. Likewise, law firms came to specialize in corporate takeovers—frequently known as "Mergers and Acquisitions" or "M&A" firms. Counseling businesses about M&A transactions, both as to how to plan desired takeovers and how to defend against unwanted hostile ones, became a huge business for law firms, especially several large ones located in New York City. During the 1980s and throughout much of the 1990s, this huge increase in legal business caused major law firms to go on a feeding frenzy to hire new associates, contributing, in part, to an increase in law school attendance that now seems to be "correcting" itself.

In any event, these developments give rise to two matters that call for attention. The first is that a new slang-language of terms sprang up in the financial press and in legal parlance to describe the various kinds of transactions and strategies employed. A quick overview of these terms will help ease the reading of the case law to follow. Second, the courts themselves were faced with what was basically a new world of corporate behavior and corporate risks, and they had to consider whether the old, familiar *Cheff* rule was up to dealing with it.

The following comprises a non-comprehensive list of common takeover terms:

- ☐ **Back-end Transaction:** The second tier of a two-tiered tender offer (see below), in which the consideration to be offered to shareholders is usually less desirable than that offered in the first tier, with the purpose of pressuring shareholders to sell during the first tier.
- ☐ **Greenmail:** Use of a threatened tender offer to extort an inflated price for a buy-back of the potential tender offeror's holding of the target's shares. The greenmailer may be able to effectively coerce a control premium on that buyout, even though his share may be only a fairly small minority share.
- ☐ **Golden Parachute:** An employment contract with a highly favorable package of benefits that is triggered by termination, a takeover, or some other specified event. Golden parachute contracts are often offered to high-ranking managers and set to trigger by tender offers or acquisitions of substantial share blocs, with the purpose of discouraging hostile tender offers. They arguably also serve to encourage the executives who will receive them to consider the merits of a hostile takeover more dispassionately.
- ☐ **Junk Bond:** A bond issued by a corporation that is very high risk (meaning that there is a high likelihood that the corporation will default on the bond, and be unable to pay the principal and interest owed under it), but that in return pays a very high rate of interest. Junk bonds have often been used to finance takeovers. For example, a small company might attempt a hostile takeover of a large one. In order to raise the funds needed to buy a controlling percentage of the target company's outstanding shares, the small company might sell a large number of its bonds to third parties. The bonds might be considered "junk" because the odds that the small company could acquire the

large target under that new debt burden *and* turn enough of a profit to pay off all of its bonds would raise a substantial risk of failure. In order to induce investors to buy its bonds under those circumstances, the small company might have to pay a very high rate of interest on the bonds (further adding to the risk, but making the bonds very valuable to investors if the company is able to pull it all off and actually pay what it owes to the bondholders).

☐ **Leveraged Buyout:** Purchase of a company financed by debt, typically to be paid off by the target company's own revenues or assets.

☐ **Lock-Up:** Contractual arrangement with a third party that will transfer some or all of the target company's value in the event that some other party attempts a hostile takeover. The term can include a variety of devices, such as a sale of the company's most prized assets (or "crown jewels") or sale of control.

☐ **Poison Pill:** Basically any provision, which can be in the articles, the bylaws, or simply in a contract arrangement, that renders a target corporation less desirable to a potential tender offeror.

☐ **Short Form Merger:** Merger of a subsidiary into its parent, which requires no shareholder vote (cf. MBCA §11.05).

☐ **Takeover Defense:** Any sort of legal arrangement within a corporation to forestall hostile takeover. This could include the "poison pill," described above, as well as any other sort of provision in the Articles of Incorporation or in contractual arrangements with shareholders or third parties that would make it more difficult for a takeover proponent to acquire the company.

☐ **Target Company:** The company that is sought to be acquired in any sort of corporate control transaction.

☐ **Two-Tier Tender Offer:** A two-part transaction in which, during the first part, a takeover proponent makes a tender offer for enough of the company's outstanding shares that the takeover proponent will have voting control of the company. In the second tier, the proponent will propose a plan of merger or share exchange that would force the remaining outstanding shareholders to accept some consideration that is less desirable than that which was offered to sellers during the first tier. The objective is to scare shareholders into selling during the first tier, presumably for less than they would be willing to accept were they not selling under pressure. This is a bit of a misnomer, incidentally, in that only the first tier is truly a tender offer. The second tier is a merger or share exchange.

☐ **White Knight:** Any third party to whom the management of a target corporation turns as a buyer preferable to some would-be tender offeror.

Connections: Staggering the Board

Although the lingo set out above might create the impression that all anti-takeover devices are highly specialized, this is not the case. For instance, staggering the election of directors commonly is justified as a way to make sure that there is continuity in decision making, but it also can deter takeovers. Thus, if the board is divided into two or more classes, each standing for election in a different year, and the Articles of Incorporation provide that directors are subject to removal only for cause, anyone acquiring control will have to wait through at least two election cycles before replacing a majority of the directors.

Time Out for PR

Martin (Marty) Lipton, of the Wachtell, Lipton firm, is credited with the invention of the poison pill. He and his firm also were involved in many of the most significant takeover transactions of the last several decades. The firm is notable for, among other things, operating without a written partnership agreement, refusing to open any office outside of New York City, and charging a (very lucrative) percentage-of-transaction fee—for instance, in 1988 it charged a client $20 million for two weeks of work.

American Bar Association Rule 1.5 (Fees) provides:

> (a) A lawyer shall not make an agreement for, charge, or collect an unreasonable fee or an unreasonable amount for expenses. The factors to be considered in determining the reasonableness of a fee include the following: (1) the time and labor required, the novelty and difficulty of the questions involved, and the skill requisite to perform the legal service properly; . . . (4) the amount involved and the results obtained; . . .
> (7) the experience, reputation, and ability of the lawyer or lawyers performing the services. . . .

In reading the subsequent cases involving various anti-takeover strategies and tactics, keep in mind that the issue generally is whether a given takeover defense violates the defendants' fiduciary duties, not whether the corporation had authority to adopt it. Moran v. Household International, Inc., 500 A.2d 1346 (Del. 1985), a case that is not set out, made the point that Delaware General Corporate Law §157 grants broad authority for the adoption of a variety of defensive measures. A similar point is made in the *Unocal* case, which is the first case below.

2. "New" Fiduciary Duties: *Unocal, Revlon,* and Refinements

The mid-1980s introduced a flurry of litigation related to anti-takeover defenses. *Unocal* took the existing *Cheff* approach and added something of its own. A non-trivial fact in the background of this case is that the dominating owner of the

T. Boone Pickens

Mesa family of companies—and therefore the person who was effectively the real party in interest in the effort to take over Unocal—was a man named T. Boone Pickens. Pickens had already become fairly notorious during the 1980s as an aggressive takeover artist and greenmailer.

UNOCAL CORP. V. MESA PETROLEUM

Supreme Court of Delaware
493 A.2d 946 (1985)

MOORE, Justice.

We confront an issue of first impression in Delaware—the validity of a corporation's self-tender for its own shares which excludes from participation a stockholder making a hostile tender offer for the company's stock.

The Court of Chancery granted a preliminary injunction to the plaintiffs, Mesa Petroleum Co., Mesa Asset Co., Mesa Partners II, and Mesa Eastern, Inc. (collectively "Mesa"), enjoining an exchange offer of the defendant, Unocal Corporation (Unocal) for its own stock. The trial court concluded that a selective exchange offer, excluding Mesa, was legally impermissible. . . .

I.

The factual background of this matter bears a significant relationship to its ultimate outcome.

On April 8, 1985, Mesa, the owner of approximately 13% of Unocal's stock, commenced a two-tier "front loaded" cash tender offer for 64 million shares, or approximately 37%, of Unocal's outstanding stock at a price of $54 per share. The "back-end" was designed to eliminate the remaining publicly held shares by an exchange of securities purportedly worth $54 per share. However, pursuant to an order entered by the United States District Court for the Central District of California on April 26, 1985, Mesa issued a supplemental proxy statement to Unocal's stockholders disclosing that the securities offered in the second-step merger would be highly subordinated, and that Unocal's capitalization would differ significantly from its present structure. Unocal has rather aptly termed such securities "junk bonds."

Unocal's board consists of eight independent outside directors and six insiders. [Over a period of several days it considered an appropriate response, and on April 15, 1985, the board unanimously adopted a resolution providing] that if Mesa acquired 64 million shares of Unocal stock through its own offer (the Mesa Purchase Condition), Unocal would buy the remaining 49% outstanding for an exchange of debt securities having an aggregate par value of $72 per share. The board resolution also stated that the offer would be subject to other conditions that had been described to the board at the meeting, or which were deemed necessary by Unocal's officers, including the exclusion of Mesa from the proposal (the Mesa exclusion). . . .

Unocal's exchange offer was commenced on April 17, 1985, and Mesa promptly challenged it by filing this suit in the Court of Chancery. . . . On April

29, 1985, the Vice Chancellor temporarily restrained Unocal from proceeding with the exchange offer unless it included Mesa. . . .

III.

We begin with the basic issue of the power of a board of directors of a Delaware corporation to adopt a defensive measure of this type. Absent such authority, all other questions are moot. Neither issues of fairness nor business judgment are pertinent without the basic underpinning of a board's legal power to act.

The board has a large reservoir of authority upon which to draw. Its duties and responsibilities proceed from the inherent powers conferred by 8 Del. C. §141(a), respecting management of the corporation's "business and affairs." Additionally, the powers here being exercised derive from 8 Del. C. §160(a), conferring broad authority upon a corporation to deal in its own stock. From this it is now well established that in the acquisition of its shares a Delaware corporation may deal selectively with its stockholders, provided the directors have not acted out of a sole or primary purpose to entrench themselves in office. . . .

Finally, the board's power to act derives from its fundamental duty and obligation to protect the corporate enterprise, which includes stockholders, from harm reasonably perceived, irrespective of its source. . . . Thus, we are satisfied that in the broad context of corporate governance, including issues of fundamental corporate change, a board of directors is not a passive instrumentality.

Given the foregoing principles, we turn to the standards by which director action is to be measured. In Pogostin v. Rice, Del. Supr., 480 A.2d 619 (1984), we held that the business judgment rule, including the standards by which director conduct is judged, is applicable in the context of a takeover. *Id.* at 627. . . .

When a board addresses a pending takeover bid it has an obligation to determine whether the offer is in the best interests of the corporation and its shareholders. In that respect a board's duty is no different from any other responsibility it shoulders, and its decisions should be no less entitled to the respect they otherwise would be accorded in the realm of business judgment. . . . There are, however, certain caveats to a proper exercise of this function. Because of the omnipresent specter that a board may be acting primarily in its own interests, rather than those of the corporation and its shareholders, there is an enhanced duty which calls for judicial examination at the threshold before the protections of the business judgment rule may be conferred.

. . . In the face of this inherent conflict directors must show that they had reasonable grounds for believing that a danger to corporate policy and effectiveness existed because of another person's stock ownership. Cheff v. Mathes, 199 A.2d [548,] 554-55 [(1964)]. However, they satisfy that burden "by showing good faith and reasonable investigation. . . ." *Id.* at 555. Furthermore, such proof is materially enhanced, as here, by the approval of a board comprised of a majority of outside independent directors who have acted in accordance with the foregoing standards. . . .

IV.

A.

. . . The restriction placed upon a selective stock repurchase is that the directors may not have acted solely or primarily out of a desire to perpetuate themselves in office. . . . Of course, to this is added the further caveat that inequitable action may not be taken under the guise of law. . . . The standard of proof established in *Cheff v. Mathes* . . . is designed to ensure that a defensive measure to thwart or impede a takeover is indeed motivated by a good faith concern for the welfare of the corporation and its stockholders, which in all circumstances must be free of any fraud or other misconduct. Cheff v. Mathes, 199 A.2d at 554-55. However, this does not end the inquiry.

B.

A further aspect is the element of balance. If a defensive measure is to come within the ambit of the business judgment rule, it must be reasonable in relation to the threat posed. This entails an analysis by the directors of the nature of the takeover bid and its effect on the corporate enterprise. Examples of such concerns may include: inadequacy of the price offered, nature and timing of the offer, questions of illegality, the impact on "constituencies" other than shareholders (i.e., creditors, customers, employees, and perhaps even the community generally), the risk of nonconsummation, and the quality of securities being offered in the exchange. While not a controlling factor, it also seems to us that a board may reasonably consider the basic stockholder interests at stake, including those of short term speculators, whose actions may have fueled the coercive aspect of the offer at the expense of the long term investor.[1] Here, the threat posed was viewed by the Unocal board as a grossly inadequate two-tier coercive tender offer coupled with the threat of greenmail.

Room to Argue: Are Hostile Takeovers Good for Shareholders?

The court's footnote is well worth reading, although the studies it refers to are dated. There is indeed a great deal of controversy over the costs and benefits of hostile acquisitions. You can read more about this in the online Supplement.

---

1. There has been much debate respecting such stockholder interests. One rather impressive study indicates that the stock of over 50 percent of target companies, who resisted hostile takeovers, later traded at higher market prices than the rejected offer price, or were acquired after the tender offer was defeated by another company at a price higher than the offer price. Moreover, an update . . . of this study, involving the stock prices of target companies that have defeated hostile tender offers during the period from 1973 to 1982 demonstrates that in a majority of cases the target's shareholders benefited from the defeat. The stock of 81% of the targets studied has, since the tender offer, sold at prices higher than the tender offer price. When adjusted for the time value of money, the figure is 64%. See Lipton & Brownstein, supra ABA Institute at 10. The thesis being that this strongly supports application of the business judgment rule in response to takeover threats. There is, however, a rather vehement contrary view.

Specifically, the Unocal directors had concluded that the value of Unocal was substantially above the $54 per share offered in cash at the front end. Furthermore, they determined that the subordinated securities to be exchanged in Mesa's announced squeeze out of the remaining shareholders in the "back-end" merger were "junk bonds" worth far less than $54. It is now well recognized that such offers are a classic coercive measure designed to stampede shareholders into tendering at the first tier, even if the price is inadequate, out of fear of what they will receive at the back end of the transaction. Wholly beyond the coercive aspect of an inadequate two-tier tender offer, the threat was posed by a corporate raider with a national reputation as a "greenmailer."

In adopting the selective exchange offer, the board stated that its objective was either to defeat the inadequate Mesa offer or, should the offer still succeed, provide the 49% of its stockholders, who would otherwise be forced to accept "junk bonds," with $72 worth of senior debt. We find that both purposes are valid.

However, such efforts would have been thwarted by Mesa's participation in the exchange offer. First, if Mesa could tender its shares, Unocal would effectively be subsidizing the former's continuing effort to buy Unocal stock at $54 per share. Second, Mesa could not, by definition, fit within the class of shareholders being protected from its own coercive and inadequate tender offer.

Thus, we are satisfied that the selective exchange offer is reasonably related to the threats posed. It is consistent with the principle that "the minority stockholder shall receive the substantial equivalent in value of what he had before." Sterling v. Mayflower Hotel Corp., Del. Supr., 93 A.2d 107, 114 (1952). This concept of fairness, while stated in the merger context, is also relevant in the area of tender offer law. Thus, the board's decision to offer what it determined to be the fair value of the corporation to the 49% of its shareholders, who would otherwise be forced to accept highly subordinated "junk bonds," is reasonable and consistent with the directors' duty to ensure that the minority stockholders receive equal value for their shares.

V.

Mesa contends that it is unlawful, and the trial court agreed, for a corporation to discriminate in this fashion against one shareholder. It argues correctly that no case has ever sanctioned a device that precludes a raider from sharing in a benefit available to all other stockholders. However, as we have noted earlier, the principle of selective stock repurchases by a Delaware corporation is neither unknown nor unauthorized. . . . The only difference is that heretofore the approved transaction was the payment of "greenmail" to a raider or dissident posing a threat to the corporate enterprise. All other stockholders were denied such favored treatment, and given Mesa's past history of greenmail, its claims here are rather ironic.

However, our corporate law is not static. It must grow and develop in response to, indeed in anticipation of, evolving concepts and needs. Merely because the General Corporation Law is silent as to a specific matter does not mean that it is prohibited. . . . In the days when *Cheff* [was] decided . . . the favored attack of a raider was stock acquisition followed by a proxy contest. Various defensive tactics, which provided no benefit whatever to the raider, evolved. Thus, the use of corporate funds by management to counter a proxy battle was approved. . . . Litigation, supported by corporate funds, aimed at the raider has long been a popular device.

More recently, as the sophistication of both raiders and targets has developed, a host of other defensive measures to counter such ever mounting threats has evolved and received judicial sanction. These include defensive charter amendments and other devices bearing some rather exotic, but apt, names: Crown Jewel, White Knight, Pac Man, and Golden Parachute. Each has highly selective features, the object of which is to deter or defeat the raider.

Thus, while the exchange offer is a form of selective treatment, given the nature of the threat posed here the response is neither unlawful nor unreasonable. If the board of directors is disinterested, has acted in good faith and with due care, its decision in the absence of an abuse of discretion will be upheld as a proper exercise of business judgment.

To this Mesa responds that the board is not disinterested, because the directors are receiving a benefit from the tender of their own shares, which because of the Mesa exclusion, does not devolve upon all stockholders equally. See Aronson v. Lewis, Del. Supr., 473 A.2d 805, 812 (1984). However, Mesa concedes that if the exclusion is valid, then the directors and all other stockholders share the same benefit. The answer of course is that the exclusion is valid, and the directors' participation in the exchange offer does not rise to the level of a disqualifying interest. . . .

VI.

In conclusion, there was directorial power to oppose the Mesa tender offer, and to undertake a selective stock exchange made in good faith and upon a reasonable investigation pursuant to a clear duty to protect the corporate enterprise. Further, the selective stock repurchase plan chosen by Unocal is reasonable in relation to the threat that the board rationally and reasonably believed was posed by Mesa's inadequate and coercive two-tier tender offer. Under those circumstances the board's action is entitled to be measured by the standards of the business judgment rule. Thus, unless it is shown by a preponderance of the evidence that the directors' decisions were primarily based on perpetuating themselves in office, or some other breach of fiduciary duty such as fraud, overreaching, lack of good faith, or being uninformed, a Court will not substitute its judgment for that of the board. . . .

■   **Think about this:**

(C) What, exactly, did *Unocal* add to *Cheff*? Why do you suppose the court thought it was necessary? Had something changed since 1964?

(D) If the *Unocal* test had been applied in the *Cheff* case, what would the result have been?

In both of the cases presented so far in this chapter, the defensive action of the board was upheld, and one might suspect that there was no defense that would not pass judicial muster. As *Revlon* illustrates, however, that conclusion is too hasty.

REVLON, INC. V. MACANDREWS & FORBES HOLDINGS, INC.

Supreme Court of Delaware
506 A.2d 173 (1986)

MOORE, Justice:

In this battle for corporate control of Revlon, Inc. (Revlon), the Court of Chancery enjoined certain transactions designed to thwart the efforts of Pantry Pride, Inc. (Pantry Pride) to acquire Revlon. The defendants are Revlon, its board of directors, and Forstmann Little & Co. and the latter's affiliated limited partnership (collectively, Forstmann). The injunction barred consummation of an option granted Forstmann to purchase certain Revlon assets (the lock-up option), a promise by Revlon to deal exclusively with Forstmann in the face of a takeover (the no-shop provision), and the payment of a $25 million cancellation fee to Forstmann if the transaction was aborted. The Court of Chancery found that the Revlon directors had breached their duty of care by entering into the foregoing transactions and effectively ending an active auction for the company. The trial court ruled that such arrangements are not illegal per se under Delaware law, but that their use under the circumstances here was impermissible. We agree. . . . Thus, we granted this expedited interlocutory appeal to consider for the first time the validity of such defensive measures in the face of an active bidding contest for corporate control. Additionally, we address for the first time the extent to which a corporation may consider the impact of a takeover threat on constituencies other than shareholders. . . .

In our view, lock-ups and related agreements are permitted under Delaware law where their adoption is untainted by director interest or other breaches of fiduciary duty. The actions taken by the Revlon directors, however, did not meet this standard. Moreover, while concern for various corporate constituencies is proper when addressing a takeover threat, that principle is limited by the requirement that there be some rationally related benefit accruing to the stockholders. We find no such benefit here.

Thus, under all the circumstances we must agree with the Court of Chancery that the enjoined Revlon defensive measures were inconsistent with the directors' duties to the stockholders. Accordingly, we affirm.

I.

[Pantry Pride made overtures relating to a friendly acquisition, but was rebuffed, perhaps because the chief executive officer of Revlon personally disliked

Ronald O. Perelman, chairman of the board and chief executive officer of Pantry Pride. Pantry Pride's board then authorized Perelman to launch a hostile tender offer at $45 per share. Lazard Freres, Revlon's investment banker, advised the Revlon directors that $45 per share was a grossly inadequate price for the company, and that Pantry Pride's financial strategy for acquiring Revlon would be through "junk bond" financing followed by a break-up of Revlon and the disposition of its assets. The board, acting on the advice of experts, undertook a variety of defensive measures. The first was a program to repurchase up to 5 million (later raised to 10 million) of its nearly 30 million outstanding shares. The consideration for the exchange was a combination of subordinated Notes with a favorable interest rate and one-tenth of a share of convertible preferred stock. The program was vastly oversubscribed, and acceptance of tenders was pro rated. The new Notes contained covenants that limited Revlon's ability to incur additional debt, sell assets, or pay dividends unless otherwise approved by the "independent" (non-management) members of the board.

The second defensive measure was adoption of a "poison pill"—a Note Purchase Rights Plan distributing to each Revlon shareholder as a dividend one Note Purchase Right (the Rights) for each share of common stock, with the Rights entitling the holder to exchange one common share for a $65 principal Revlon note at 12 percent interest with a one-year maturity. The Rights would become effective whenever anyone acquired beneficial ownership of 20 percent or more of Revlon's shares, unless the purchaser acquired all the company's stock for cash at $65 or more per share. In addition, the Rights would not be available to the acquiror, and prior to the 20 percent triggering event the Revlon board could redeem the rights for 10 cents each.

The court ultimately determined that both the exchange and the Rights plans withstood *Cheff/Unocal* analysis: After reasonable investigation, the board had reason to believe there was a threat to corporate policy and effectiveness and both defenses were reasonable in relation to the threat. It noted, with approval, that the defenses spurred Pantry Pride to increase its bids.

Pantry Pride continued its hostile campaign for control, notwithstanding the exchange and Rights plans, indeed increasing its bids. The Revlon board determined to negotiate with other parties. The directors, on October 3, 1983,] unanimously agreed to a leveraged buyout by Forstmann. The terms of this accord were as follows: each stockholder would get $56 cash per share; management would purchase stock in the new company by the exercise of their Revlon "golden parachutes"; Forstmann would assume Revlon's $475 million debt incurred by the issuance of the Notes; and Revlon would redeem the Rights and waive the Notes covenants for Forstmann or in connection with any other offer superior to Forstmann's. The board did not actually remove the covenants at the October 3 meeting, because Forstmann then lacked a firm commitment on its financing, but accepted the Forstmann capital structure, and indicated that the outside directors would waive the covenants in due course. Part of Forstmann's plan was to sell Revlon's Norcliff Thayer and Reheis divisions to American Home Products for $335 million. Before the merger, Revlon was to sell its cosmetics and fragrance division to [an agreed-upon third party] for $905 million. These transactions would facilitate the purchase by Forstmann or any other acquiror of Revlon.

When the merger, and thus the waiver of the Notes covenants, was announced, the market value of these securities began to fall. The Notes, which originally traded near par, around 100, dropped to 87.50 by October 8. One director later reported (at the October 12 meeting) a "deluge" of telephone calls from irate noteholders, and on October 10 the Wall Street Journal reported threats of litigation by these creditors.

Pantry Pride countered with a new proposal on October 7, raising its $53 offer to $56.25, subject to nullification of the Rights, a waiver of the Notes covenants, and the election of three Pantry Pride directors to the Revlon board. On October 9, representatives of Pantry Pride, Forstmann and Revlon conferred in an attempt to negotiate the fate of Revlon, but could not reach agreement. At this meeting Pantry Pride announced that it would engage in fractional bidding and top any Forstmann offer by a slightly higher one. It is also significant that Forstmann, to Pantry Pride's exclusion, had been made privy to certain Revlon financial data. Thus, the parties were not negotiating on equal terms.

Again privately armed with Revlon data, Forstmann met on October 11 with Revlon's special counsel and investment banker. On October 12, Forstmann made a new $57.25 per share offer, based on several conditions. The principal demand was a lock-up option to purchase Revlon's Vision Care and National Health Laboratories divisions for $525 million, some $100-$175 million below the value ascribed to them by Lazard Freres, if another acquiror got 40% of Revlon's shares. Revlon also was required to accept a no-shop provision. The Rights and Notes covenants had to be removed as in the October 3 agreement. There would be a $25 million cancellation fee to be placed in escrow, and released to Forstmann if the new agreement terminated or if another acquiror got more than 19.9% of Revlon's stock. Finally, there would be no participation by Revlon management in the merger. In return, Forstmann agreed to support the par value of the Notes, which had faltered in the market, by an exchange of new notes. Forstmann also demanded immediate acceptance of its offer, or it would be withdrawn. The board unanimously approved Forstmann's proposal because: (1) it was for a higher price than the Pantry Pride bid, (2) it protected the noteholders, and (3) Forstmann's financing was firmly in place. The board further agreed to redeem the rights and waive the covenants on the preferred stock in response to any offer above $57 cash per share. The covenants were waived, contingent upon receipt of an investment banking opinion that the Notes would trade near par value once the offer was consummated.

Pantry Pride, which had initially sought injunctive relief from the Rights plan on August 22, filed an amended complaint on October 14 challenging the lock-up, the cancellation fee, and the exercise of the Rights and the Notes covenants. Pantry Pride also sought a temporary restraining order to prevent Revlon from placing any assets in escrow or transferring them to Forstmann. Moreover, on October 22, Pantry Pride again raised its bid, with a cash offer of $58 per share conditioned upon nullification of the Rights, waiver of the covenants, and an injunction of the Forstmann lock-up.

On October 15, the Court of Chancery prohibited the further transfer of assets, and eight days later enjoined the lock-up, no-shop, and cancellation fee provisions of the agreement. The trial court concluded that the Revlon directors had breached their duty of loyalty by making concessions to Forstmann, out of concern for their liability to the noteholders, rather than maximizing the sale price of the company for the stockholders' benefit.

II. . . .

D.

[W]hen Pantry Pride increased its offer to $50 per share, and then to $53, it became apparent to all that the break-up of the company was inevitable. The Revlon board's authorization permitting management to negotiate a merger or buyout with a third party was a recognition that the company was for sale. The duty of the board had thus changed from the preservation of Revlon as a corporate entity to the maximization of the company's value at a sale for the stockholders' benefit. This significantly altered the board's responsibilities under the Unocal standards. It no longer faced threats to corporate policy and effectiveness, or to the stockholders' interests, from a grossly inadequate bid. The whole question of defensive measures became moot. The directors' role changed from defenders of the corporate bastion to auctioneers charged with getting the best price for the stockholders at a sale of the company.

III.

This brings us to the lock-up with Forstmann and its emphasis on shoring up the sagging market value of the Notes in the face of threatened litigation by their holders. Such a focus was inconsistent with the changed concept of the directors' responsibilities at this stage of the developments. The impending waiver of the Notes covenants had caused the value of the Notes to fall, and the board was aware of the noteholders' ire as well as their subsequent threats of suit. The directors thus made support of the Notes an integral part of the company's dealings with Forstmann, even though their primary responsibility at this stage was to the equity owners.

The original threat posed by Pantry Pride—the break-up of the company— had become a reality which even the directors embraced. Selective dealing to fend off a hostile but determined bidder was no longer a proper objective. Instead, obtaining the highest price for the benefit of the stockholders should have been the central theme guiding director action. Thus, the Revlon board could not make the requisite showing of good faith by preferring the noteholders and ignoring its duty of loyalty to the shareholders. The rights of the former already were fixed by contract. The noteholders required no further protection, and when the Revlon board entered into an auction-ending lock-up agreement with Forstmann on the basis of impermissible considerations at the expense of the shareholders, the directors breached their primary duty of loyalty.

The Revlon board argued that it acted in good faith in protecting the noteholders because *Unocal* permits

---

More to the Story: Doesn't Revlon Still Exist?

Pantry Pride subsequently changed its name to "Revlon Group, Inc." and did indeed sell off four of Revlon, Inc.'s divisions.

consideration of other corporate constituencies. Although such considerations may be permissible, there are fundamental limitations upon that prerogative. A board may have regard for various constituencies in discharging its responsibilities, provided there are rationally related benefits accruing to the stockholders. However, such concern for non-stockholder interests is inappropriate when an auction among active bidders is in progress, and the object no longer is to protect or maintain the corporate enterprise but to sell it to the highest bidder.

Revlon also contended that . . . it had contractual and good faith obligations to consider the noteholders. However, any such duties are limited to the principle that one may not interfere with contractual relationships by improper actions. Here, the rights of the noteholders were fixed by agreement, and there is nothing of substance to suggest that any of those terms were violated. The Notes covenants specifically contemplated a waiver to permit sale of the company at a fair price. The Notes were accepted by the holders on that basis, including the risk of an adverse market effect stemming from a waiver. Thus, nothing remained for Revlon to legitimately protect, and no rationally related benefit thereby accrued to the stockholders. Under such circumstances we must conclude that the merger agreement with Forstmann was unreasonable in relation to the threat posed.

A lock-up is not per se illegal under Delaware law. . . . Such options can entice other bidders to enter a contest for control of the corporation, creating an auction for the company and maximizing shareholder profit. Current economic conditions in the takeover market are such that a "white knight" like Forstmann might only enter the bidding for the target company if it receives some form of compensation to cover the risks and costs involved. . . . However, while those lock-ups which draw bidders into the battle benefit shareholders, similar measures which end an active auction and foreclose further bidding operate to the shareholders' detriment. . . .

The Forstmann option had a similar destructive effect on the auction process. Forstmann had already been drawn into the contest on a preferred basis, so the result of the lock-up was not to foster bidding, but to destroy it. . . . While Forstmann's $57.25 offer was objectively higher than Pantry Pride's $56.25 bid, the margin of superiority is less when the Forstmann price is adjusted for the time value of money. In reality, the Revlon board ended the auction in return for very little actual improvement in the final bid. The principal benefit went to the directors, who avoided personal liability to a class of creditors to whom the board owed no further duty under the circumstances. Thus, when a board ends an intense bidding contest on an insubstantial basis, and where a significant by-product of that action is to protect the directors against a perceived threat of personal liability for consequences stemming from the adoption of previous defensive measures, the action cannot withstand the enhanced scrutiny which *Unocal* requires of director conduct.

In addition to the lock-up option, the Court of Chancery enjoined the no-shop provision as part of the attempt to foreclose further bidding by Pantry Pride. The no-shop provision, like the lock-up option, while not per se illegal, is impermissible under the *Unocal* standards when a board's primary duty becomes that of an auctioneer responsible for selling the company to the highest bidder. The agreement to negotiate only with Forstmann ended rather than intensified the board's involvement in the bidding contest.

It is ironic that the parties even considered a no-shop agreement when Revlon had dealt preferentially, and almost exclusively, with Forstmann throughout the contest. After the directors authorized management to negotiate with other parties, Forstmann was given every negotiating advantage that Pantry Pride had been denied: cooperation from management, access to financial data, and the exclusive opportunity to present merger proposals directly to the board of directors. Favoritism for a white knight to the total exclusion of a hostile bidder might be justifiable when the latter's offer adversely affects shareholder interests, but when bidders make relatively similar offers, or dissolution of the company becomes inevitable, the directors cannot fulfill their enhanced Unocal duties by playing favorites with the contending factions. Market forces must be allowed to operate freely to bring the target's shareholders the best price available for their equity. Thus, as the trial court ruled, the shareholders' interests necessitated that the board remain free to negotiate in the fulfillment of that duty. . . .

V.

In conclusion, the Revlon board was confronted with a situation not uncommon in the current wave of corporate takeovers. A hostile and determined bidder sought the company at a price the board was convinced was inadequate. The initial defensive tactics worked to the benefit of the shareholders, and thus the board was able to sustain its *Unocal* burdens in justifying those measures. However, in granting an asset option lock-up to Forstmann, we must conclude that under all the circumstances the directors allowed considerations other than the maximization of shareholder profit to affect their judgment, and followed a course that ended the auction for Revlon, absent court intervention, to the ultimate detriment of its shareholders. No such defensive measure can be sustained when it represents a breach of the directors' fundamental duty of care. . . . In that context the board's action is not entitled to the deference accorded it by the business judgment rule. The measures were properly enjoined. . . .

■ **Think about this:**

(E) It is customary to refer to distinct "*Unocal*" and "*Revlon*" duties. Are they really something different from the duty of care and loyalty? Or just a way to discharge the traditional duties in specific contexts?

(F) When would you apply *Unocal* and when would you apply *Revlon*? Are they mutually exclusive?

It probably is obvious that, after *Revlon*, further litigation would be necessary to establish precisely when the duty to "auction" a corporation for the best price would be triggered. In Paramount Communications, Inc. v. Time, Inc., 571 A.2d 1140 (1989) (usually referred to as "*Time-Warner*"), the Delaware Supreme Court returned to the issue, again in the context of an emergency review of a Chancellor's decision with respect to injunctive relief.

Time, Inc. (Time), had been considering a plan of global expansion for some time. In March 1989, after protracted negotiations, the board approved a merger agreement with Warner Communications, Inc. (Warner). At the same time, it adopted several defensive measures and, at the insistence of Warner, a "no-shop" clause preventing Time from considering any other consolidation proposal. In May, proxy materials relating to the merger were sent to Time's shareholders. In June, Paramount Communications, Inc. (Paramount) bid $175 per share for all of Time's outstanding shares—$49 in excess of the then market price of $126. Time's board viewed the offer as inadequate, to have undesirable conditions, and to be a threat to "Time culture." As to the latter, which would play an important role in the court's reasoning, the "Time culture" was the tradition of editorial independence of Time's flagship product, Time magazine. The firm considered preservation of that independence key to the value of its brand. Time wished to pursue its combination with Warner, proposing to make an all-cash offer for 51 percent of Warner's shares (which would not require approval by Time's shareholders), to be followed by a purchase of the remainder with a combination of cash and securities. The acquisition would require Time to assume 7-10 billion dollars' worth of debt, eliminating a significant benefit of the original merger agreement. Paramount raised its bid to $200 per share, which Time's board continued to reject as inadequate. Paramount and two groups of shareholder plaintiffs sought to enjoin Time's tender for Warner, arguing that it violated the board's *Unocal* duties. The non-Paramount plaintiffs also argued that the board's *Revlon* duties had been triggered when it first agreed to a merger with Warner.

The court determined that the first merger agreement did not trigger *Revlon* duties, as no "bust up" or dissolution had become "inevitable" in the sense that it had in *Revlon*, despite the fact that Time's board itself had voluntarily initiated the deal. Rather, the merger represented a strategic plan of expansion. Thus, the transaction was protected by the business judgment rule. Moreover, the court did not find "in Time's [subsequent] recasting of its merger agreement with Warner from a share exchange to a share purchase a basis to conclude that Time had either abandoned its strategic plan or made a sale of Time inevitable." Even though the merged company would be large, "recent takeover cases have proven that acquisition of the combined company might nonetheless be possible." As a result, "*Unocal* alone applies to determine whether the business judgment rule attaches to the revised agreement." 571 A.2d 1140, 1151 (Del. 1989).

The following excerpt provides the court's *Unocal* analysis.

PARAMOUNT COMMUNICATIONS, INC. V. TIME, INC.

Supreme Court of Delaware
571 A.2d 1140 (1989)

HORSEY, Justice: . . .

We turn now to plaintiffs' *Unocal* claim. . . .

In *Unocal*, we held that before the business judgment rule is applied to a board's adoption of a defensive measure, the burden will lie with the board to prove (a) reasonable grounds for believing that a danger to corporate policy and effectiveness existed; and (b) that the defensive measure adopted was reasonable in relation to the threat posed. Directors satisfy the first part of the *Unocal* test by demonstrating good faith and reasonable investigation. We have repeatedly stated that the refusal to entertain an offer may comport with a valid exercise of a board's business judgment. . . .

[The court concluded that refusal to deal with Paramount did not demonstrate either lack of good faith or reasonable investigation, since Time's long-term global expansion plan previously had led it to consider and reject a number of possible merger partners, including Paramount.]

Unocal involved a two-tier, highly coercive tender offer. In such a case, the threat is obvious: shareholders may be compelled to tender to avoid being treated adversely in the second stage of the transaction. . . . In subsequent cases, the Court of Chancery has suggested that an all-cash, all-shares offer, falling within a range of values that a shareholder might reasonably prefer, cannot constitute a legally recognized "threat" to shareholder interests sufficient to withstand a *Unocal* analysis. . . . In those cases, the Court of Chancery determined that whatever threat existed related only to the shareholders and only to price and not to the corporation.

From those decisions by our Court of Chancery, Paramount and the individual plaintiffs extrapolate a rule of law that an all-cash, all-shares offer with values reasonably in the range of acceptable price cannot pose any objective threat to a corporation or its shareholders. Thus, Paramount would have us hold that only if the value of Paramount's offer were determined to be clearly inferior to the value created by management's plan to merge with Warner could the offer be viewed—objectively—as a threat.

Implicit in the plaintiffs' argument is the view that a hostile tender offer can pose only two types of threats: the threat of coercion that results from a two-tier offer promising unequal treatment for nontendering shareholders; and the threat of inadequate value from an all-shares, all-cash offer at a price below what a target board in good faith deems to be the present value of its shares. Since Paramount's offer was all-cash, the only conceivable "threat," plaintiffs argue, was inadequate value. We disapprove of such a narrow and rigid construction of *Unocal*, for the reasons which follow.

Plaintiffs' position represents a fundamental misconception of our standard of review under *Unocal* principally because it would involve the court in substituting its judgment as to what is a "better" deal for that of a corporation's board of directors. To the extent that the Court of Chancery has recently done so in certain of its opinions, we hereby reject such approach as not in keeping with a proper *Unocal* analysis. . . . The open-ended analysis mandated by *Unocal* is not intended to lead to a simple mathematical exercise: that is, of comparing the discounted value of Time-Warner's expected trading price at some future date with Paramount's offer and determining which is the higher. Indeed, in our view, precepts underlying the business judgment rule militate against a court's engaging in the process of attempting to appraise and evaluate the relative merits of a long-term versus a short-term investment goal for shareholders. To engage in such an exercise is a distortion of the *Unocal* process and, in particular, the application of the second part of *Unocal*'s test, discussed below.

In this case, the Time board reasonably determined that inadequate value was not the only legally cognizable threat that Paramount's all-cash, all-shares offer could present. Time's board concluded that Paramount's eleventh hour offer posed other threats. One concern was that Time shareholders might elect to tender into Paramount's cash offer in ignorance or a mistaken belief of the strategic benefit which a business combination with Warner might produce. Moreover, Time viewed the conditions attached to Paramount's offer as introducing a degree of uncertainty that skewed a comparative analysis. Further, the timing of Paramount's offer to follow issuance of Time's proxy notice was viewed as arguably designed to upset, if not confuse, the Time stockholders' vote. Given this record evidence, we cannot conclude that the Time board's decision of June 6 that Paramount's offer posed a threat to corporate policy and effectiveness was lacking in good faith or dominated by motives of either entrenchment or self-interest. . . .

We turn to the second part of the *Unocal* analysis. The obvious requisite to determining the reasonableness of a defensive action is a clear identification of the nature of the threat. As the Chancellor correctly noted, this "requires an evaluation of the importance of the corporate objective threatened; alternative methods of protecting that objective; impacts of the 'defensive' action, and other relevant factors." It is not until both parts of the *Unocal* inquiry have been satisfied that the business judgment rule attaches to defensive actions of a board of directors. As applied to the facts of this case, the question is whether the record evidence supports the Court of Chancery's conclusion that the restructuring of the Time-Warner transaction, including the adoption of several preclusive defensive measures, was a reasonable response in relation to a perceived threat.

Paramount argues that, assuming its tender offer posed a threat, Time's response was unreasonable in precluding Time's shareholders from accepting the tender offer or receiving a control premium in the immediately foreseeable future. Once again, the contention stems, we believe, from a fundamental misunderstanding of where the power of corporate governance lies. Delaware law confers the management of the corporate enterprise to the stockholders' duly elected board representatives. 8 Del. C. §141(a). The fiduciary duty to manage a corporate enterprise includes the selection of a time frame for achievement of corporate goals. That duty may not be delegated to the stockholders. Directors are not obliged to abandon a deliberately conceived corporate plan for a short-term shareholder profit unless there is clearly no basis to sustain the corporate strategy.

Although the Chancellor blurred somewhat the discrete analyses required under *Unocal*, he did conclude that Time's board reasonably perceived Paramount's offer to be a significant threat to the planned Time-Warner merger and that Time's response was not "overly broad." We have found that even in light of a valid threat, management actions that are coercive in nature or force upon shareholders a management-sponsored alternative to a hostile offer may be struck down as unreasonable and nonproportionate responses. . . .

Here, on the record facts, the Chancellor found that Time's responsive action to Paramount's tender offer was not aimed at "cramming down" on its shareholders a management-sponsored alternative, but rather had as its goal the carrying forward of a pre-existing transaction in an altered form. Thus, the response was reasonably related to the threat. The Chancellor noted that the revised agreement and its accompanying safety devices did not preclude Paramount from making an offer for the combined Time-Warner company or from changing the conditions of its offer so as not to make the offer dependent upon the nullification of the Time-Warner agreement. Thus, the response was proportionate. We affirm the Chancellor's rulings as clearly supported by the record. Finally, we note that although Time was required, as a result of Paramount's hostile offer, to incur a heavy debt to finance its acquisition of Warner, that fact alone does not render the board's decision unreasonable so long as the directors could reasonably perceive the debt load not to be so injurious to the corporation as to jeopardize its well being. . . .

■ **Think about this:**

(G) Suppose (however unlikely it may be) that the *only* possible objection to a transaction is that it involves inadequate value for the shareholders. Would *Unocal* be triggered? If not, what test would apply?

(H) Why is deciding that a cash offer is bad for shareholders a matter for the board, rather than the shareholders, to decide?

(I) What point was the court trying to make in its discussion of long-term and short-term objectives?

Hopefully, it is crystal clear at this point that, in a hostile takeover situation, the directors bear the burden of establishing good faith and reasonable investigation. In *Time-Warner*, the Time board's reasonable investigation preceded the threatened takeover by Paramount, but was a reasonable investigation nonetheless. In the following case, the Delaware Supreme Court returned to the subject of reasonable investigation, as well as the question of when the *Revlon* duty to auction a target company would attach.

PARAMOUNT COMMUNICATIONS, INC. V. QVC NETWORK, INC.

Supreme Court of Delaware
637 A.2d 34 (1993)

VEASEY, Chief Justice.

In this appeal we review an order of the Court of Chancery dated November 24, 1993 . . . preliminarily enjoining certain defensive measures designed to facilitate a so-called strategic alliance between Viacom Inc. ("Viacom") and Paramount Communications Inc. ("Paramount") approved by the board of directors of Paramount (the "Paramount Board" or the "Paramount directors") and to thwart an unsolicited, more valuable, tender offer by QVC Network Inc. ("QVC"). In affirming, we hold that the sale of control in this case, which is at the heart of the proposed strategic alliance, implicates enhanced judicial scrutiny of the conduct of the Paramount Board under Unocal Corp. v. Mesa Petroleum Co., Del. Supr., 493 A.2d 946 (1985), and Revlon, Inc. v. MacAndrews & Forbes Holdings, Inc., Del. Supr., 506 A.2d 173 (1986). We further hold that the conduct of the Paramount Board was not reasonable as to process or result. . . .

I. FACTS

[Paramount was a publicly traded entertainment conglomerate with a 15-person board including 11 outside directors. . . . Following its unsuccessful bid to acquire Time, Inc., it turned to other possibilities and identified Viacom, the owner of a number of cable television channels, as a desirable merger partner. It apparently had not considered QVC, which sells merchandise through a televised shopping channel. After negotiation, and with the advice of experts, the Paramount board unanimously approved the Original Merger Agreement whereby Paramount would merge with and into Viacom. As part of the deal, the board agreed to amend its "poison pill" Rights Agreement to exempt the proposed merger with Viacom. It also agreed to (1) a "no-shop" provision; (2) a $100 million Termination Fee payable to Viacom if Paramount's shareholders did not approve the deal or a competing transaction interfered; and (3) a Stock Option Agreement which granted to Viacom an option to purchase approximately 19.9 percent (23,699,000 shares) of Paramount's outstanding common stock at highly favorable terms if any of the triggering events for the Termination Fee occurred. The merger was announced, and described by Viacom's controlling shareholder and CEO as a "marriage" that would "never be torn asunder" and that could be broken only by a "nuclear attack." The controlling shareholder/ CEO, who would continue to hold a controlling position in the merged entity, specifically contacted QVC to dissuade it from making a competing bid.

QVC nonetheless proposed a competing merger, but quickly moved to the announcement of an] $80 cash tender offer for 51 percent of Paramount's outstanding shares (the "QVC tender offer"). Each remaining share of Paramount common stock would be converted into 1.42857 shares of QVC common stock in a second-step merger. The tender offer was conditioned on, among other things, the invalidation of the Stock Option Agreement, which was worth over $200 million by that point.

Confronted by QVC's hostile bid, which on its face offered over $10 per share more than the consideration provided by the Original Merger Agreement, Viacom [negotiated an Amended Merger Agreement. It called for an $80 per share cash tender offer by Viacom for 51 percent of Paramount's stock, and another improved the merger consideration. It did not eliminate or modify the "no shop" provision, the Termination Fee, or the Stock Option Agreement, although a few new rights for the Paramount board to revoke the deal were included.

A bidding war followed.] On November 6, 1993, Viacom unilaterally raised its tender offer price to $85 per share in cash and offered a comparable increase

in the value of the securities being proposed in the second-step merger. At a telephonic meeting held later that day, the Paramount Board agreed to recommend Viacom's higher bid to Paramount's stockholders.

QVC responded to Viacom's higher bid on November 12 by increasing its tender offer to $90 per share and by increasing the securities for its second-step merger by a similar amount. . . . At its meeting on November 15, 1993, the Paramount Board determined that the new QVC offer was not in the best interests of the stockholders. The purported basis for this conclusion was that QVC's bid was excessively conditional. The Paramount Board did not communicate with QVC regarding the status of the conditions because it believed that the No-Shop Provision prevented such communication in the absence of firm financing. Several Paramount directors also testified that they believed the Viacom transaction would be more advantageous to Paramount's future business prospects than a QVC transaction. Although a number of materials were distributed to the Paramount Board describing the Viacom and QVC transactions, the only quantitative analysis of the consideration to be received by the stockholders under each proposal was based on then-current market prices of the securities involved, not on the anticipated value of such securities at the time when the stockholders would receive them.[2]

The preliminary injunction hearing in this case took place on November 16, 1993. On November 19, [QVC Chairman and CEO Barry] Diller wrote to the Paramount Board to inform it that QVC had obtained financing commitments for its tender offer and that there was no antitrust obstacle to the offer. On November 24, 1993, the Court of Chancery issued its decision granting a pre-

---

2. The market prices of Viacom's and QVC's stock were poor measures of their actual values because such prices constantly fluctuated depending upon which company was perceived to be the more likely to acquire Paramount.

liminary injunction in favor of QVC and the plaintiff stockholders. This appeal followed.

II. APPLICABLE PRINCIPLES OF ESTABLISHED DELAWARE LAW

The General Corporation Law of the State of Delaware (the "General Corporation Law") and the decisions of this Court have repeatedly recognized the fundamental principle that the management of the business and affairs of a Delaware corporation is entrusted to its directors, who are the duly elected and authorized representatives of the stockholders. . . . Under normal circumstances, neither the courts nor the stockholders should interfere with the managerial decisions of the directors. The business judgment rule embodies the deference to which such decisions are entitled.

Nevertheless, there are rare situations which mandate that a court take a more direct and active role in overseeing the decisions made and actions taken by directors. In these situations, a court subjects the directors' conduct to enhanced scrutiny to ensure that it is reasonable. The decisions of this Court have clearly established the circumstances where such enhanced scrutiny will be applied. The case at bar implicates two such circumstances: (1) the approval of a transaction resulting in a sale of control, and (2) the adoption of defensive measures in response to a threat to corporate control.

A. The Significance of a Sale or Change of Control

When a majority of a corporation's voting shares are acquired by a single person or entity, or by a cohesive group acting together, there is a significant diminution in the voting power of those who thereby become minority stockholders. Under the statutory framework of the General Corporation Law, many of the most fundamental corporate changes can be implemented only if they are approved by a majority vote of the stockholders. . . .

In the absence of devices protecting the minority stockholders, stockholder votes are likely to become mere formalities where there is a majority stockholder. For example, minority stockholders can be deprived of a continuing equity interest in their corporation by means of a cash-out merger. Absent effective protective provisions, minority stockholders must rely for protection solely on the fiduciary duties owed to them by the directors and the majority stockholder, since the minority stockholders have lost the power to influence corporate direction through the ballot. The acquisition of majority status and the consequent privilege of exerting the powers of majority ownership come at a price. That price is usually a control premium which recognizes not only the value of a control block of shares, but also compensates the minority stockholders for their resulting loss of voting power.

In the case before us, the public stockholders (in the aggregate) currently own a majority of Paramount's voting stock. Control of the corporation is not vested in a single person, entity, or group, but vested in the fluid aggregation of unaffiliated stockholders. In the event the Paramount-Viacom transaction is consummated, the public stockholders will receive cash and a minority equity voting position in the surviving corporation. Following such consummation, there will be a controlling stockholder who will have the voting power to: (a) elect directors; (b) cause a break-up of the corporation; (c) merge it with another company; (d) cash-out the public stockholders; (e) amend the certificate of incorporation; (f) sell all or substantially all of the corporate assets; or (g) otherwise alter materially the nature of the corporation and the public stockholders' interests. Irrespective of the present Paramount Board's vision of a long-term strategic alliance with Viacom, the proposed sale of control would provide the new controlling stockholder with the power to alter that vision.

Because of the intended sale of control, the Paramount-Viacom transaction has economic consequences of considerable significance to the Paramount stockholders. Once control has shifted, the current Paramount stockholders will have no leverage in the future to demand another control premium. As a result, the Paramount stockholders are entitled to receive, and should receive, a control premium and/or protective devices of significant value. There being no such protective provisions in the Viacom-Paramount transaction, the Paramount directors had an obligation to take the maximum advantage of the current opportunity to realize for the stockholders the best value reasonably available.

B. The Obligations of Directors in a Sale or Change of Control Transaction

The consequences of a sale of control impose special obligations on the directors of a corporation. In particular, they have the obligation of acting reasonably to seek the transaction offering the best value reasonably available to the stockholders. The courts will apply enhanced scrutiny to ensure that the directors have acted reasonably. . . .

In the sale of control context, the directors must focus on one primary objective—to secure the transaction offering the best value reasonably available for the stockholders—and they must exercise their fiduciary duties to further that end. The decisions of this Court have consistently emphasized this goal. . . .

In pursuing this objective, the directors must be especially diligent. In particular, this Court has stressed the importance of the board being adequately informed in negotiating a sale of control. . . . Moreover, the role of outside, independent directors becomes particularly important because of the magnitude of a sale of control transaction and the possibility, in certain cases, that management may not necessarily be impartial. . . .

In determining which alternative provides the best value for the stockholders, a board of directors is not limited to considering only the amount of cash involved, and is not required to ignore totally its view of the future value of a strategic alliance. Instead, the directors should analyze the entire situation and evaluate in a disciplined manner the consideration being offered. Where stock or other non-cash consideration is involved, the board should try to quantify its value, if feasible, to achieve an objective comparison of the alternatives. In addition, the board may assess a variety of practical considerations relating to each alternative, including [such factors as feasibility, and the bidder's identity, background, and plans for the corporation].

C. Enhanced Judicial Scrutiny of a Sale or Change of Control Transaction

Board action in the circumstances presented here is subject to enhanced scrutiny. Such scrutiny is mandated by: (a) the threatened diminution of the current stockholders' voting power; (b) the fact that an asset belonging to public stockholders (a control premium) is being sold and may never be available again; and (c) the traditional concern of Delaware courts for actions which impair or impede stockholder voting rights. . . .

The key features of an enhanced scrutiny test are: (a) a judicial determination regarding the adequacy of the decisionmaking process employed by the directors, including the information on which the directors based their decision; and (b) a judicial examination of the reasonableness of the directors' action in light of the circumstances then existing. The directors have the burden of proving that they were adequately informed and acted reasonably.

. . . A court applying enhanced judicial scrutiny should be deciding whether the directors made a reasonable decision, not a perfect decision. If a board selected one of several reasonable alternatives, a court should not second-guess that choice even though it might have decided otherwise or subsequent events may have cast doubt on the board's determination. Thus, courts will not substitute their business judgment for that of the directors, but will determine if the directors' decision was, on balance, within a range of reasonableness. . . .

D. *Revlon* and *Time-Warner* Distinguished

The Paramount defendants and Viacom assert that the fiduciary obligations and the enhanced judicial scrutiny discussed above are not implicated in this case in the absence of a "break-up" of the corporation, and that the order granting the preliminary injunction should be reversed. This argument is based on their erroneous interpretation of our decisions in *Revlon* and *Time-Warner*. . . .

[The court then explained that *Revlon* had involved a break-up but that its reasoning was not limited to that scenario, and that the original stock-for-stock merger proposed in *Time-Warner* had not involved a sale of control because "Time would be owned by a fluid aggregation of unaffiliated stockholders both before and after the merger."]

Accordingly, when a corporation undertakes a transaction which will cause: (a) a change in corporate control; or (b) a break-up of the corporate entity, the directors' obligation is to seek the best value reasonably available to the stockholders. This obligation arises because the effect of the Viacom-Paramount transaction, if consummated, is to shift control of Paramount from the public stockholders to a controlling stockholder, Viacom. Neither *Time-Warner* nor any other decision of this Court holds that a "break-up" of the company is essential to give rise to this obligation where there is a sale of control.

III. BREACH OF FIDUCIARY DUTIES BY PARAMOUNT BOARD

[The court concluded that in negotiating the Original Merger Agreement the Paramount board was negotiating for change in control, but agreed to deal-protective devices that would prevent it from discharging its duty to seek the best available value for its shareholders. Those aspects of the agreement therefore were invalid and unenforceable and did not provide a reason not to actively negotiate with QVC as well as Viacom. Agreeing to and complying with those terms resulted in an unreasonable process. In the view of the court, the unreasonable process also resulted in an unreasonable result:]

By November 12, 1993, the value of the revised QVC offer on its face exceeded that of the Viacom offer by over $1 billion at then current values. This significant disparity of value cannot be justified on the basis of the directors' vision of future strategy, primarily because the change of control would supplant the authority of the current Paramount Board to continue to hold and implement their strategic vision in any meaningful way. Moreover, their uninformed process had deprived their strategic vision of much of its credibility. . . .

V. CONCLUSION . . .

It is the nature of the judicial process that we decide only the case before us—a case which, on its facts, is clearly controlled by established Delaware law. Here, the proposed change of control and the implications thereof were crystal clear. In other cases they may be less clear. The holding of this case on its facts, coupled with the holdings of the principal cases discussed herein where the issue of sale of control is implicated, should provide a workable precedent against which to measure future cases. . . .

■ **Think about this:**

(J) What is the critical difference between *Time-Warner* and this case—that is, why does *Revlon* attach to these facts, but not those in *Time-Warner*?

(K) Suppose that Viacom had not been controlled by a single shareholder. Instead, it is held by a fluid aggregation of unaffiliated stockholders. Suppose, too, that the plaintiff shareholders of Paramount will be entirely cashed out as a result of a combined tender offer and second-tier merger. Will *Revlon* apply?

The foregoing represent just a very few of the relevant Delaware cases, but they are popularly regarded as among the most influential in the field. They have been joined by the following case. Note that *Lyondell*, like *Cheff v. Mathes*, involves a derivative action for damages rather than an attempted injunction. This means that it was necessary for the court to distinguish between possible breaches of the duty of care (for which no damages would be available, given a raincoat provision in the target company's Articles of Incorporation) and breach of the duty of good faith (which could give rise to damages).

LYONDELL CHEMICAL COMPANY V. RYAN

Supreme Court of Delaware
970 A.2d 235 (2009)

BERGER, Justice:

We accepted this interlocutory appeal to consider a claim that directors failed to act in good faith in conducting the sale of their company. The Court of Chancery decided that "unexplained inaction" permits a reasonable inference that the directors may have consciously disregarded their fiduciary duties. The trial court expressed concern about the speed with which the transaction was consummated; the directors' failure to negotiate better terms; and their failure to seek potentially superior deals. But the record establishes that the directors were disinterested and independent; that they were generally aware of the company's value and its prospects; and that they considered the offer, under the time constraints imposed by the buyer, with the assistance of financial and legal advisors. At most, this record creates a triable issue of fact on the question of whether the directors exercised due care. There is no evidence, however, from which to infer that the directors knowingly ignored their responsibilities, thereby breaching their duty of loyalty. Accordingly, the directors are entitled to the entry of summary judgment.

FACTUAL AND PROCEDURAL BACKGROUND

Before the merger at issue, Lyondell Chemical Company ("Lyondell") was the third largest independent, publicly traded chemical company in North America. Dan Smith ("Smith") was Lyondell's Chairman and CEO. Lyondell's other ten directors were independent and many were, or had been, CEOs of other large, publicly traded companies. Basell AF ("Basell") is a privately held Luxembourg company owned by Leonard Blavatnik ("Blavatnik") through his ownership of Access Industries. Basell is in the business of polyolefin technology, production and marketing.

In April 2006, Blavatnik told Smith that Basell was interested in acquiring Lyondell. A few months later, Basell sent a letter to Lyondell's board offering $26.50-$28.50 per share. Lyondell determined that the price was inadequate and that it was not interested in selling. During the next year, Lyondell prospered and no potential acquirors expressed interest in the company. In May 2007, an Access affiliate filed a Schedule 13D with the Securities and Exchange Commission disclosing its right to acquire an 8.3% block of Lyondell stock owned by Occidental Petroleum Corporation. The Schedule 13D also disclosed Blavatnik's interest in possible transactions with Lyondell.

Connections: Federal Securities Regulation

Section 13(d) of the Securities Exchange Act of 1934 is one of the sections intended to regulate tender offers. It is an "early warning" provision requiring anyone acquiring beneficial ownership of in excess of 5 percent of a registered class of shares to file Schedule 13D. One of the disclosures required relates to intent to make further acquisitions.

In response to the Schedule 13D, the Lyondell board immediately convened a special meeting. The board recognized that the 13D signaled to the market that the company was "in play,"[3] but the directors decided to take a "wait and see" approach. [A period passed during which Blavatnik made a series of proposals, culminating in an offer of] $48 per share. Under Blavatnik's proposal, Basell would require no financing contingency, but Lyondell would have to agree to a $400 million break-up fee and sign a merger agreement by July 16, 2007.

Smith called a special meeting of the Lyondell board on July 10, 2007 to review and consider Basell's offer. The meeting lasted slightly less than one hour, during which time the board reviewed valuation material that had been prepared by Lyondell management for presentation at the regular board meeting, which was scheduled for the following day. The board also discussed the Basell offer, the status of [Basell's attempt to acquire another, unrelated chemical company], and the likelihood that another party might be interested in Lyondell. The board instructed Smith to obtain a written offer from Basell and more details about Basell's financing. . . . [At a subsequent meeting, also lasting less than an hour, t]he board decided that it was interested, authorized the retention of Deutsche Bank Securities, Inc. ("Deutsche Bank") as its financial advisor, and instructed Smith to negotiate with Blavatnik.

. . . From July 12-July 15 the parties negotiated the terms of a Lyondell merger agreement; Basell conducted due diligence; Deutsche Bank prepared a "fairness" opinion; and Lyondell conducted its regularly scheduled board meeting. The Lyondell board discussed the Basell proposal again on July 12, and later instructed Smith to try to negotiate better terms. Specifically, the board wanted a higher price, a go-shop provision [permitting it to actively solicit other offers], and a reduced break-up fee. As the trial court noted, Blavatnik was "incredulous." He had offered his best price, which was a substantial premium, and the deal had to be concluded on his schedule. As a sign of good faith, however, Blavatnik agreed to reduce the break-up fee from $400 million to $385 million.

On July 16, 2007, the board met to consider the Basell merger agreement. Lyondell's management, as well as its financial and legal advisers, presented reports analyzing the merits of the deal. The advisors explained that, notwithstanding the no-shop provision in the merger agreement, Lyondell would be able to consider any superior proposals that might be made because of [a] . . . "fiduciary out" provision[,] [a provision in the merger agreement that permits the target board to pull out of a deal if it determines the deal would breach its *Unocal* or *Revlon* duties not to do so]. In addition, Deutsche Bank reviewed valuation models derived from "bullish" and more conservative financial projections. Several of those valuations yielded a range that did not even reach $48 per share,

---

3. On the day that the 13D was made public, Lyondell's stock went from $33 to $37 per share.

and Deutsche Bank opined that the proposed merger price was fair. Indeed, the bank's managing director described the merger price as "an absolute home run." Deutsche Bank also identified other possible acquirors and explained why it believed no other entity would top Basell's offer. After considering the presentations, the Lyondell board voted to approve the merger and recommend it to the stockholders. At a special stockholders' meeting held on November 20, 2007, the merger was approved by more than 99% of the voted shares. . . .

DISCUSSION

The class action complaint challenging this $13 billion cash merger alleges that the Lyondell directors breached their "fiduciary duties of care, loyalty and candor . . . and . . . put their personal interests ahead of the interests of the Lyondell shareholders." Specifically, the complaint alleges that: 1) the merger price was grossly insufficient; 2) the directors were motivated to approve the merger for their own self-interest;[4] 3) the process by which the merger was negotiated was flawed; 4) the directors agreed to unreasonable deal protection provisions; and 5) the preliminary proxy statement omitted numerous material facts. The trial court rejected all claims except those directed at the process by which the directors sold the company and the deal protection provisions in the merger agreement.

The remaining claims are but two aspects of a single claim, under Revlon v. MacAndrews & Forbes Holdings, Inc., 506 A.2d 173,182 (Del 1986), that the directors failed to obtain the best available price in selling the company. As the trial court correctly noted, *Revlon* did not create any new fiduciary duties. It simply held that the "board must perform its fiduciary duties in the service of a specific objective: maximizing the sale price of the enterprise." The trial court reviewed the record, and found that Ryan might be able to prevail at trial on a claim that the Lyondell directors breached their duty of care. But Lyondell's charter includes an exculpatory provision, pursuant to 8 Del. C. §102(b)(7), protecting the directors from personal liability for breaches of the duty of care. Thus, this case turns on whether any arguable shortcomings on the part of the Lyondell directors also implicate their duty of loyalty, a breach of which is not exculpated. Because the trial court determined that the board was independent and was not motivated by self-interest or ill will, the sole issue is whether the directors are entitled to summary judgment on the claim that they breached their duty of loyalty by failing to act in good faith.

This Court examined "good faith" in two recent decisions. In In re Walt Disney Co. Deriv. Litig., 906 A.2d 27 (Del. 2006), the Court discussed the range of conduct that might be characterized as bad faith, and concluded that bad faith encompasses not only an intent to harm but also intentional dereliction of duty. . . . A few months later, in Stone v. Ritter, 911 A.2d 362 (Del. 2006), this Court addressed the concept of bad faith in the context of an "oversight" claim.

---

4. The directors' alleged financial interest is the fact that they would receive cash for their stock options.

We adopted the standard articulated ten years earlier, in In re Caremark Int'l Deriv. Litig., 698 A.2d 959, 971 (Del. Ch. 1996):

> [W]here a claim of directorial liability for corporate loss is predicated upon ignorance of liability creating activities within the corporation . . . only a sustained or systematic failure of the board to exercise oversight—such as an utter failure to attempt to assure a reasonable information and reporting system exists—will establish the lack of good faith that is a necessary condition to liability.

The *Stone* Court explained that the *Caremark* standard is fully consistent with the *Disney* definition of bad faith. *Stone* also clarified any possible ambiguity about the directors' mental state, holding that "imposition of liability requires a showing that the directors knew that they were not discharging their fiduciary obligations." 911 A.2d at 370.

The Court of Chancery recognized these legal principles, but it denied summary judgment in order to obtain a more complete record before deciding whether the directors had acted in bad faith. Under other circumstances, deferring a decision to expand the record would be appropriate. Here, however, the trial court reviewed the existing record under a mistaken view of the applicable law. Three factors contributed to that mistake. First, the trial court imposed *Revlon* duties on the Lyondell directors before they either had decided to sell, or before the sale had become inevitable. Second, the court read *Revlon* and its progeny as creating a set of requirements that must be satisfied during the sale process. Third, the trial court equated an arguably imperfect attempt to carry out *Revlon* duties with a knowing disregard of one's duties that constitutes bad faith. . . .

The trial court found the directors' failure to act during the two months after the filing of the Basell Schedule 13D critical to its analysis of their good faith. The court pointedly referred to the directors' "two months of slothful indifference despite knowing that the Company was in play," and the fact that they "languidly awaited overtures from potential suitors. . . ." In the end, the trial court found that it was this "failing" that warranted denial of their motion for summary judgment. . . .

The problem with the trial court's analysis is that *Revlon* duties do not arise simply because a company is "in play." The duty to seek the best available price applies only when a company embarks on a transaction—on its own initiative or in response to an unsolicited offer—that will result in a change of control. Basell's Schedule 13D did put the Lyondell directors, and the market in general, on notice that Basell was interested in acquiring Lyondell. The directors responded by promptly holding a special meeting to consider whether Lyondell should take any action. The directors decided that they would neither put the company up for sale nor institute defensive measures to fend off a possible hostile offer. Instead, they decided to take a "wait and see" approach. That decision was an entirely appropriate exercise of the directors' business judgment. The time for action under *Revlon* did not begin until July 10, 2007, when the directors began negotiating the sale of Lyondell.

The Court of Chancery focused on the directors' two months of inaction, when it should have focused on the one week during which they considered

Basell's offer. During that one week, the directors met several times; their CEO tried to negotiate better terms; they evaluated Lyondell's value, the price offered and the likelihood of obtaining a better price; and then the directors approved the merger. The trial court acknowledged that the directors' conduct during those seven days might not demonstrate anything more than lack of due care. But the court remained skeptical about the directors' good faith—at least on the present record. That lingering concern was based on the trial court's synthesis of the *Revlon* line of cases, which led it to the erroneous conclusion that directors must follow one of several courses of action to satisfy their *Revlon* duties.

There is only one *Revlon* duty—to "[get] the best price for the stockholders at a sale of the company." No court can tell directors exactly how to accomplish that goal, because they will be facing a unique combination of circumstances, many of which will be outside their control. . . . [O]ur courts have highlighted both the positive and negative aspects of various boards' conduct under *Revlon*. The trial court drew several principles from those cases: directors must "engage actively in the sale process," and they must confirm that they have obtained the best available price either by conducting an auction, by conducting a market check, or by demonstrating "an impeccable knowledge of the market."

The Lyondell directors did not conduct an auction or a market check, and they did not satisfy the trial court that they had the "impeccable" market knowledge that the court believed was necessary to excuse their failure to pursue one of the first two alternatives. . . . But, as noted, there are no legally prescribed steps that directors must follow to satisfy their *Revlon* duties. Thus, the directors' failure to take any specific steps during the sale process could not have demonstrated a conscious disregard of their duties. More importantly, there is a vast difference between an inadequate or flawed effort to carry out fiduciary duties and a conscious disregard for those duties.

Directors' decisions must be reasonable, not perfect. "In the transactional context, [an] extreme set of facts [is] required to sustain a disloyalty claim premised on the notion that disinterested directors were intentionally disregarding their duties." In re Lear Corp. S'holder Litig., 2008 WL 4053221 at *11 (Del. Ch.). The trial court denied summary judgment because the Lyondell directors' "unexplained inaction" prevented the court from determining that they had acted in good faith. But, if the directors failed to do all that they should have under the circumstances, they breached their duty of care. Only if they knowingly and completely failed to undertake their responsibilities would they breach their duty of loyalty. The trial court approached the record from the wrong perspective. Instead of questioning whether disinterested, independent directors did everything that they (arguably) should have done to obtain the best sale price, the inquiry should have been whether those directors utterly failed to attempt to obtain the best sale price.

Viewing the record in this manner leads to only one possible conclusion. The Lyondell directors met several times to consider Basell's premium offer. They were generally aware of the value of their company and they knew the chemical company market. The directors solicited and followed the advice of their financial and legal advisors. They attempted to negotiate a higher offer even though all the evidence indicates that Basell had offered a "blowout" price. Finally, they approved the merger agreement, because "it was simply too good not to pass along [to the stockholders] for their consideration." We assume, as we must on summary judgment, that the Lyondell directors did absolutely nothing to prepare for Basell's offer, and that they did not even consider conducting a market check before agreeing to the merger. Even so, this record clearly establishes that the Lyondell directors did not breach their duty of loyalty by failing to act in good faith. In concluding otherwise, the Court of Chancery reversibly erred.

■ **Think about this:**

(L) Suppose the court had been asked to decide whether the proposed acquisition should be enjoined. Would you expect a different outcome?

(M) What would you advise a director in the position of Lyondell's board to do differently, if anything?

D. Anti-Takeover Legislation and the State-Federal Interface

In the 1980s, the surge in attempted hostile takeovers caused corporate managers to lobby state legislatures for the authority to base decisions on what was best for a corporation on matters in addition to corporate profitability. The idea was to permit the decision to resist a takeover to rest on grounds including loss of jobs and the effects on communities of plant closures. This type of legislation became quite popular: Over 40 states now have some version of what has come to be known as a "corporate constituency" statute. Interestingly, most of these statutes are not textually limited to the takeover context, instead applying to all corporate decision making. Also interesting is the fact that Delaware does not have such a statute.

What Delaware has instead, in addition to its wealth of common law on fiduciary duties in the face of proposed takeovers, is Delaware General Corporation Law §203. In a nutshell (attributable to Professor Steven Bainbridge[5]):

Section 203 prohibits a Delaware corporation from entering into a business combination for a period of three years after an offeror becomes an interested stockholder. Business combination is defined to include freezeout mergers and other common post-acquisition transactions. Interested shareholder is defined, subject to various exceptions, as the owner of 15% or more of the target's outstanding shares.

The section does, however, permit business combinations in the event of board approval, approval by two-thirds of the voting stock held by other than the inter-

---

5. http://www.professorbainbridge.com/professorbainbridgecom/2009/11/the-constitutionality
-of-the-delaware-takeover-statute.html.

ested stockholder, or if upon consummation of the transaction in which a stock-holder became an interested stockholder the interested stockholder owned at least 85 percent of the company's theretofore outstanding voting stock.

Another type of anti-takeover statute is a "control share" statute. Such a statute is described, and evaluated for constitutionality, in the following case. The "Williams Act" references are to the provisions of the Securities Exchange Act of 1934, described earlier in this chapter, regulating tender offers. Acting under the authority conferred under one of those provisions, the Securities and Exchange Commission adopted a rule requiring tender offers for the shares of publicly traded companies to remain open for 20 days. The statute itself provides that tender offers cannot stay open longer than 60 days.

CTS CORPORATION V. DYNAMICS CORPORATION OF AMERICA

Supreme Court of the United States
481 U.S. 69 (1987)

Justice POWELL delivered the opinion of the Court.

This case presents the questions whether the Control Share Acquisitions Chapter of the Indiana Business Corporation Law is pre-empted by the Williams Act, or violates the Commerce Clause of the Federal Constitution.

I

A

On March 4, 1986, the Governor of Indiana signed a revised Indiana Business Corporation Law. That law included the Control Share Acquisitions Chapter (Indiana Act or Act). Beginning on August 1, 1987, the Act will apply to any corporation incorporated in Indiana, unless the corporation amends its articles of incorporation or bylaws to opt out of the Act. . . . [T]he Act applies only to "issuing public corporations." The term "corporation" includes only businesses incorporated in Indiana. An "issuing public corporation" is defined as: a corporation that has: (1) one hundred (100) or more shareholders; (2) its principal place of business, its principal office, or substantial assets within Indiana; and (3) either: (A) more than ten percent (10%) of its shareholders resident in Indiana; (B) more than ten percent (10%) of its shares owned by Indiana residents; or (C) ten thousand (10,000) shareholders resident in Indiana."

The Act focuses on the acquisition of "control shares" in an issuing public corporation. Under the Act, an entity acquires "control shares" whenever it acquires shares that, but for the operation of the Act, would bring its voting power in the corporation to or above any of three thresholds: 20%, 33⅓%, or 50%. An entity that acquires control shares does not necessarily acquire voting rights. Rather, it gains those rights only "to the extent granted by resolution approved by the shareholders of the issuing public corporation." Section 9 requires a majority vote of all disinterested shareholders holding each class of stock for passage of such a resolution. The practical effect of this requirement is to condition acquisition of control of a corporation on approval of a majority of the pre-existing disinterested shareholders.

The shareholders decide whether to confer rights on the control shares at the next regularly scheduled meeting of the shareholders, or at a specially scheduled meeting. The acquiror can require management of the corporation to hold such a special meeting within 50 days if it files an "acquiring person statement," requests the meeting, and agrees to pay the expenses of the meeting. If the shareholders do not vote to restore voting rights to the shares, the corporation may redeem the control shares from the acquiror at fair market value, but it is not required to do so. Similarly, if the acquiror does not file an acquiring person statement with the corporation, the corporation may, if its bylaws or articles of incorporation so provide, redeem the shares at any time after 60 days after the acquiror's last acquisition.

B

On March 10, 1986, appellee Dynamics Corporation of America (Dynamics) owned 9.6% of the common stock of appellant CTS Corporation, an Indiana corporation. On that day, six days after the Act went into effect, Dynamics announced a tender offer for another million shares in CTS; purchase of those shares would have brought Dynamics' ownership interest in CTS to 27.5%. . . .

[Dynamics then sued in the United States District Court for the Northern District of Illinois, challenging the constitutionality of the Indiana Act on the grounds of federal preemption and unreasonable burden on interstate commerce. The District Court found the statute unconstitutional on both grounds, and the Seventh Circuit affirmed.]

II

The first question in this case is whether the Williams Act pre-empts the Indiana Act. . . .

C . . .

The Indiana Act operates on the assumption, implicit in the Williams Act, that independent shareholders faced with tender offers often are at a disadvantage. By allowing such shareholders to vote as a group, the Act protects them from the coercive aspects of some tender offers. If, for example, shareholders believe that a successful tender offer will be followed by a purchase of nontendering shares at a depressed price, individual shareholders may tender their shares—even if they doubt the tender offer is in the corporation's best interest—to protect themselves from being forced to sell their shares at a depressed price. . . . [I]n such a situation under the Indiana Act, the shareholders as a group, acting in the corporation's best interest, could reject the offer, although individual shareholders might be inclined to accept it. The desire of the Indiana Legislature to protect shareholders of Indiana corporations from this type of coercive offer does not conflict with the Williams Act. Rather, it furthers the federal policy of investor protection.

. . . [T]he Indiana Act does not give either management or the offeror an advantage in communicating with the shareholders about the impending offer. The Act also does not impose an indefinite delay on tender offers. Nothing in the Act prohibits an offeror from consummating an offer on the 20th business day, the earliest day permitted under applicable federal regulations. Nor does the Act allow the state government to interpose its views of fairness between willing buyers and sellers of shares of the target company. Rather, the Act allows shareholders to evaluate the fairness of the offer collectively.

D

The Court of Appeals based its finding of pre-emption on its view that the practical effect of the Indiana Act is to delay consummation of tender offers until 50 days after the commencement of the offer. As did the Court of Appeals, Dynamics reasons that no rational offeror will purchase shares until it gains assurance that those shares will carry voting rights. Because it is possible that voting rights will not be conferred until a shareholder meeting 50 days after commencement of the offer, Dynamics concludes that the Act imposes a 50-day delay. This, it argues, conflicts with the shorter 20-business-day period established by the SEC as the minimum period for which a tender offer may be held open. We find the alleged conflict illusory.

The Act does not impose an absolute 50-day delay on tender offers, nor does it preclude an offeror from purchasing shares as soon as federal law permits. If the offeror fears an adverse shareholder vote under the Act, it can make a conditional tender offer, offering to accept shares on the condition that the shares receive voting rights within a certain period of time. . . .

. . . [T]he Indiana Act provides that full voting rights will be vested—if this eventually is to occur—within 50 days after commencement of the offer. This period is within the 60-day maximum period Congress established for tender offers in [the Williams Act]. We cannot say that a delay within that congressionally determined period is unreasonable. . . . [A]ccordingly, we hold that the Williams Act does not pre-empt the Indiana Act.

III

As an alternative basis for its decision, the Court of Appeals held that the Act violates the Commerce Clause of the Federal Constitution. . . .

A

The principal objects of dormant Commerce Clause scrutiny are statutes that discriminate against interstate commerce. The Indiana Act is not such a statute. It has the same effects on tender offers whether or not the offeror is a domiciliary or resident of Indiana. . . . [B]ecause nothing in the Indiana Act imposes a greater burden on out-of-state offerors than it does on similarly situated Indiana offerors, we reject the contention that the Act discriminates against interstate commerce.

B

This Court's recent Commerce Clause cases also have invalidated statutes that adversely may affect interstate commerce by subjecting activities to inconsistent regulations. The Indiana Act poses no such problem. So long as each State regulates voting rights only in the corporations it has created, each corporation will be subject to the law of only one State. No principle of corporation law and practice is more firmly established than a State's authority to regulate domestic corporations, including the authority to define the voting rights of shareholders. Accordingly, we conclude that the Indiana Act does not create an impermissible risk of inconsistent regulation by different States.

C

The Court of Appeals did not find the Act unconstitutional for either of these threshold reasons. Rather, its decision rested on its view of the Act's potential to hinder tender offers. We think the Court of Appeals failed to appreciate the significance for Commerce Clause analysis of the fact that state regulation of corporate governance is regulation of entities whose very existence and attributes are a product of state law. . . . [E]very State in this country has enacted laws regulating corporate governance. By prohibiting certain transactions, and regulating others, such laws necessarily affect certain aspects of interstate commerce. This necessarily is true with respect to corporations with shareholders in States other than the State of incorporation. . . .

It thus is an accepted part of the business landscape in this country for States to create corporations, to prescribe their powers, and to define the rights that are acquired by purchasing their shares. A State has an interest in promoting stable relationships among parties involved in the corporations it charters, as well as in ensuring that investors in such corporations have an effective voice in corporate affairs.

There can be no doubt that the Act reflects these concerns. The primary purpose of the Act is to protect the shareholders of Indiana corporations. It does this by affording shareholders, when a takeover offer is made, an opportunity to decide collectively whether the resulting change in voting control of the corporation, as they perceive it, would be desirable. A change of management may have important effects on the shareholders' interests; it is well within the State's role as overseer of corporate governance to offer this opportunity. The autonomy provided by allowing shareholders collectively to determine whether the takeover is advantageous to their interests may be especially beneficial where a hostile tender offer may coerce shareholders into tendering their shares. . . .

Dynamics argues in any event that the State has "'no legitimate interest in protecting the nonresident shareholders.'" . . . We agree that Indiana has no interest in protecting nonresident shareholders of nonresident corporations. But this Act applies only to corporations incorporated in Indiana. We reject the contention that Indiana has no interest in providing for the shareholders of its corporations the voting autonomy granted by the Act. Indiana has a substantial interest in preventing the corporate form from becoming a shield for unfair business dealing. Moreover, . . . the Indiana Act applies only to corporations that have a substantial number of shareholders in Indiana. Thus, every application of the Indiana Act will affect a substantial number of Indiana residents, whom Indiana indisputably has an interest in protecting. . . .

IV

On its face, the Indiana Control Share Acquisitions Chapter evenhandedly determines the voting rights of shares of Indiana corporations. The Act does not conflict with the provisions or purposes of the Williams Act. To the limited extent that the Act affects interstate commerce, this is justified by the State's interests in defining the attributes of shares in its corporations and in protecting shareholders. Congress has never questioned the need for state regulation of these matters. Nor do we think such regulation offends the Constitution. Accordingly, we reverse the judgment of the Court of Appeals. . . .

■　**Think about this:**

(N) If you were advising a state legislature seeking to adopt anti-takeover legislation, what guidelines would you suggest?

As was to be expected, after *CTS* a number of states copied the Indiana statute. Because so many publicly held corporations are incorporated in Delaware but headquartered elsewhere, however, and because Delaware has not passed a control share acquisition statute, some states were pressured by Delaware corporations to pass an Indiana-type statute and to extend its application to them. One state that passed such a statute was Tennessee, whose Control Share Acquisition Act, adopted in 1988, was made applicable to foreign corporations that have their principal office and substantial assets in Tennessee. Within a few months, however, the Tennessee statute was found to violate the Commerce Clause insofar as it related to foreign corporations, thus dampening the hopes of corporations around the country that they would be able to get the benefits of a control share acquisition statute anywhere except in their state of incorporation.

Statutes of a different design, such as Delaware's §203, have been tested only to a limited extent in the federal courts of appeal, and have not been tested at all before the Supreme Court. Thus far, however, they have been upheld. Nonetheless, uncertainty remains about how far—and in what direction—states permissibly can go with takeover legislation.

Test Yourself

Questions 1-5 rely on the following facts:

Sitting Duck, Inc., is a publicly traded Delaware corporation. Shortly after the company was formed, its board of directors received a presentation from an outside investment banker, advising them that because of the nature of the company's business, it was likely to enjoy large cash flows and might have a large amount of cash on hand at any given time. The banker's advice was that Sitting Duck was therefore at a serious risk of hostile takeover.

Fortunately, Sitting Duck's outside law firm specializes in making companies frustratingly difficult targets for would-be acquirors. The firm, Ima, Paine, LLP, advised Sitting Duck to adopt a plan under which, upon the acquisition by any person of more than 20 percent of Sitting Duck's outstanding stock, all shareholders would be entitled immediately to exchange each share of stock for a Sitting Duck corporate bond. The bonds would have a $100 principal value, one-year maturity period, and would pay 17.5 percent interest. The plan was explicitly made revocable at the board's election. The board referred this "Rights Plan" to a committee of its outside directors, who adopt it unanimously.

Recently, Sitting Duck's management was dismayed to learn that Greedy McGreederson, a notorious corporate greenmailer, had already acquired 5 percent of the company's outstanding stock and that he would shortly initiate a tender offer for the rest. McGreederson soon announced a front-loaded, two-tier tender offer, in which he would first acquire another 46 percent of the company's stock, and then merge Sitting Duck into his own holding company. Pursuant to the plan of merger, McGreederson's holding company would acquire the remaining 49 percent of Sitting Duck shares by exchanging them for junk bonds, which McGreederson claims will be equal in value to the Sitting Duck shares so acquired. On the same day that he announced his tender offer, McGreederson filed suit in Delaware Chancery Court seeking injunction of the Rights Plan.

Now at wit's end, Sitting Duck's board contacts WiteNite Industries, Inc., another publicly traded company, to negotiate a friendly merger plan. The two companies quickly strike an agreement under which Sitting Duck will be merged into WiteNite. The parties agreed that if Sitting Duck were to breach the contract, WiteNite would receive a cancellation fee of $100 million.

1. In McGreederson's challenge to the Rights Plan, to what standard should Sitting Duck's outside directors be held?

   a. Reasonable care, because no tender offer was pending when the plan was adopted.
   b. The business judgment rule, because no tender offer was pending when the plan was adopted.
   c. The *Cheff* standard.
   d. The *Unocal* standard.
   e. The *Revlon* standard.

2. Even without the defenses adopted by Sitting Duck's board, Greedy McGreederson could not go forward with the takeover transaction that he proposed. True or False?

   a. True. A transaction of this nature would require approval of Sitting Duck's shareholders.
   b. True. The second tier of McGreederson's plan involves a merger, which would call for board approval.
   c. False. Despite the board's refusal to cooperate with McGreederson's takeover, on these facts he would likely be able to get a court order requiring the board to cooperate.
   d. False for some other reason.

3. Why would Sitting Duck adopt the Rights Plan as a way to deter a hostile takeover?

   a. Because it will increase the number of voting shares McGreederson will have to buy to secure control.
   b. Because it will decrease the number of voting shares McGreederson will have to buy to secure control.
   c. Because it will tend to make Sitting Duck more expensive to purchase.
   d. None of the above.

4. Assume that the initial adoption of the Rights Plan is subject to the *Revlon* standard. Would it be consistent with the board's duties under that standard?

   a. Probably, as shown by the fact that a hostile tender offer in fact was made, and it was highly coercive in nature.
   b. Probably, because the Rights Plan was revocable at the board's election.
   c. Probably not, because the Rights Plan plainly was not "proportional" to any "threat to corporate policy and effectiveness."
   d. No, because there is no evidence that the board in good faith determined that there was a "threat to corporate policy and effectiveness."

5. If one of WiteNite's shareholders sues WiteNite's outside directors in connection with the WiteNite merger agreement, under what standard should the court judge her liability?

   a. *Revlon*, because the huge cancellation fee renders the merger "inevitable."
   b. *Unocal*, because Sitting Duck and WiteNite are both publicly traded; there will be no "change of control."
   c. Intrinsic fairness.
   d. Business judgment rule.

6. Fill in the Blanks: A purchase of a company financed by debt is known as a _____ _____.

7. [Short Answer] When does the *Revlon* duty attach?

Part 6

Special Considerations in the Close Corporation Context

25

Special Considerations in the Close Corporation Context, Part I: Planning for Control

Close corporations are in all legal respects corporations just as much as are publicly traded ones. Their owners, however, have tended to think of them and run them as if they were partnerships. The various formalities traditionally associated with operating a corporation often prove a poor fit—a problem for which most modern statutes provide workable solutions. Where a firm elects one of these modern statutory alternatives, the result is an entity functionally similar to a limited liability partnership or limited liability company. Still, care must be taken to avoid some very predictable difficulties that arise when there are a few shareholders and no ready market for shares.

Chapter Outline

A. Introduction

- The definition of a close corporation
  - A small number of holders
  - No ready market for shares
  - Overlap of shareholders and management

- Predictable difficulties
  - Failure to comply with formalities
  - Deadlock
  - Oppression of minorities

B. Direct Management by Shareholders

- The traditional approach to shareholder agreements relating to management
- Traditional restrictions on shareholder agreements have been relaxed over time in many states
- Integrated close corporation statutes provide one model
- Modern statutes provide flexibility—when followed

C. Voting Trusts and Other Control Devices

1. The Statutory Voting Trust
   - Sometimes employed for creditor protection
   - To be distinguished from illegal voting trusts

2. The Structural Tie-Breaker
   - Non-economic stock

3. Voting and Arbitration Agreements
   - Enforcement by specific performance or irrevocable proxy

D. Other Planning Possibilities

- Employment agreements
- Buy-sell agreements

Test Yourself

A. Introduction

There are numerous definitions of the "close" corporation, but they tend to converge along the lines set out in Donahue v. Rodd Electrotype of New England, Inc., 328 N.E.2d 505 (Mass. 1975): "We deem a close corporation to be typified by: (1) a small number of stockholders; (2) no ready market for the corporate stock; and (3) substantial majority stockholder participation in the management, direction and operations of the corporation."

In corporations of this sort, a variety of issues tend to present themselves. These include, at a minimum, impatience with the notion that the shareholder-managers should separate their roles, and the difficulty of obtaining an exit when there is disagreement over management matters. Because of the lack of a ready market for shares, it also is said that close corporations are rife with opportunities for unscrupulous majorities to oppress helpless minorities. Moreover, lurking on the beams of the traditional corporate governance structure are a variety of possible difficulties. For instance, an even number of directors or a 50/50 split of shares between two shareholders poses the prospect of deadlock. It also is the case that shareholders sometimes will look at the overall design and become apprehensive about losing control.

Planning for control of the close corporation is the subject of this chapter. Other chapters deal with the problems of oppression, resolving unplanned-for deadlock, and dissolution.

 ### What does it look like?

Check the online Supplement for the following sample documents that are relevant to this chapter:

- A shareholder voting agreement
- A voting trust agreement
- A buy-sell agreement
- A stock certificate bearing a legend

 ### Dear Prof.: Does "close corporation" mean the same thing as "closely held corporation"?

Sometimes! Sometimes "closely held" and "close" are used interchangeably to refer to a corporation satisfying the *Donahue* definition. Sometimes they are used interchangeably as the opposite of "publicly held." If so, you need to know what the speaker thinks makes a corporation "public." Is it more than a few holders or is it registration under the Securities Exchange Act of 1934? There may be some tendency to use "close corporation" in the *Donahue* sense and "closely held corporation" in the "non-public" sense but you shouldn't count on it as a reliable distinction.

B. Direct Management by Shareholders

It is easy to describe the traditional corporate governance structure: The shareholders elect the directors, who elect and control the officers. This structure often does not suit the needs or interests of small-firm shareholders very well. Most importantly, it does not contemplate participation by shareholders in management—that is the job of the corporation's directors. This is a nicety frequently lost on the constituents of close corporations and it is not at all unusual for the shareholders of such corporations both to disregard corporate formalities and to attempt to make binding agreements affecting management. With respect to the latter, any number of arrangements can be managed to suit the needs of individual investors and, by and large, the courts are tolerant of them. In closely held companies, especially where all of the shareholders are parties to or in some way consent to a particular structural arrangement, the courts are likely to defer to it, or at least to try to find some way to uphold it. The three cases that follow are examples both of the kinds of arrangements that might be used to serve the parties' needs and the approach of courts to them.

After these cases, we will also consider a Model Business Corporation Act rule, under §7.32, that broadly authorizes shareholder agreements to modify default governance rules, indeed permitting shareholders to dispense with their board of directors entirely.

CLARK V. DODGE

New York Court of Appeals
199 N.E. 641 (1936)

The action is for the specific performance of a contract between the plaintiff Clark and the defendant Dodge, relating to the affairs of the two defendant corporations. . . . The two corporate defendants[,] [Bell & Co., Inc. and Hollings-Smith Company, Inc.,] are New Jersey corporations manufacturing medicinal preparations by secret formulae. The main office, factory, and assets of both corporations are located in the state of New York.

In 1921, and at all times since, Clark owned 25% and Dodge 75% of the stock of each corporation. Dodge took no active part in the business, although he was a director, and through ownership of their qualifying shares, controlled the other directors of both corporations. He was the president of Bell & Co., Inc., and nominally general manager of Hollings-Smith Company, Inc. The plaintiff, Clark, was a director and held the offices of treasurer and general manager of Bell & Co., Inc., and also had charge of the major portion of the business of Hollings-Smith Company, Inc. The formulae and methods of manufacture of the medicinal preparations were known to him alone.

Under date of February 15, 1921, Dodge and Clark, the sole owners of the stock of both corporations, entered into a written agreement under seal, which after reciting the stock ownership of both parties, the desire of Dodge that Clark should continue in the efficient management and control of the business of Bell & Co., Inc., so long as he should "remain faithful, efficient and competent to so manage and control the said business"; and his further desire that Clark should not be the sole custodian of a specified formula, but should share his knowledge thereof and of the method of manufacture with a son of Dodge, provided, in substance, as follows: That Dodge during his lifetime and, after his death, a trustee to be appointed by his will, would so vote his stock and so vote as a director that the plaintiff (a) should continue to be a director of Bell & Co., Inc.; and (b) should continue as its general manager so long as he should be "faithful, efficient and competent"; (c) should during his life receive one-fourth of the net income of the corporations either by way of salary or dividends; and (d) that no unreasonable or incommensurate salaries should be paid to other officers or agents which would so reduce the net income as materially to affect Clark's profits. Clark on his part agreed to disclose the specified formula to the son and to instruct him in the details and methods of manufacture; and, further, at the end of his life to bequeath his stock—if no issue survived him—to the wife and children of Dodge.

It was further provided that the provisions in regard to the division of net profits and the regulation of salaries should also apply to the Hollings-Smith Company.

The complaint alleges due performance of the contract by Clark and breach thereof by Dodge in that he has failed to use his stock control to continue Clark as a director and as general manager, and has prevented Clark from receiving his proportion of the income, while taking his own, by causing the employment of incompetent persons at excessive salaries, and otherwise.

The relief sought is reinstatement as director and general manager and an accounting by Dodge and by the corporations for waste and for the proportion of net income due plaintiff, with an injunction against further violations.

The only question which need be discussed is whether the contract is illegal as against public policy within the decision in McQuade v. Stoneham, 189 N.E. 234, upon the authority of which the complaint was dismissed by the Appellate Division.

"The business of a corporation shall be managed by its board of directors." General Corporation Law §27. That is the statutory norm. Are we committed by the McQuade Case to the doctrine that there may be no variation, however slight or innocuous, from that norm, where salaries or policies or the retention of individuals in office are concerned? There is ample authority supporting that doctrine, and something may be said for it, since it furnishes a simple, if arbitrary, test. Apart from its practical administrative convenience, the reasons upon which it is said to rest are more or less nebulous. Public policy, the intention of the Legislature, detriment to the corporation, are phrases which in this connection mean little. Possible harm to bona fide purchasers of stock or to creditors or to stockholding minorities have more substance; but such harms are absent in many instances. If the enforcement of a particular contract damages nobody—not even, in any perceptible degree, the public—one sees no reason for holding it illegal, even though it impinges slightly upon the broad provision of section 27. Damage suffered or threatened is a logical and practical test, and has come to be the one generally adopted by the courts. . . . Where the directors are the sole stockholders, there seems to be no objection to enforcing an agreement among them to vote for certain people as officers. . . . The opinion in Manson v. Curtis, 119 N.E. 559, 562, closed its discussion by saying: "The rule that all the stockholders by their universal consent may do as they choose with the corporate concerns and assets, provided the interests of creditors are not affected, because they are the complete owners of the corporation, cannot be invoked here." That was because all the stockholders were not parties to the agreement there in question. So, where the public was not affected, "the parties in interest, might, by their original agreement of incorporation, limit their respective rights and powers," even where there was a conflicting statutory standard. Ripin v. United States Woven Label Co., 98 N.E. 855, 857. . . .

Except for the broad dicta in the McQuade opinion, we think there can be no doubt that the agreement here in question was legal and that the complaint states a cause of action. There was no attempt to sterilize the board of directors, as in the Manson and McQuade cases. The only restrictions on Dodge were (a) that as a stockholder he should vote for Clark as a director—a perfectly legal contract; (b) that as director he should continue Clark as general manager, so long as he proved faithful, efficient and competent—an agreement which could harm nobody; (c) that Clark should always receive as salary or dividends one-fourth of the "net income." For the purpose of this motion, it is only just to construe that phrase as meaning whatever was left for distribution after the directors had in good faith set aside whatever they deemed wise; (d) that no salaries to other officers should be paid, unreasonable in amount or incommensurate with services rendered—a beneficial and not a harmful agreement.

If there was any invasion of the powers of the directorate under that agreement, it is so slight as to be negligible; and certainly there is no damage suffered by or threatened to anybody. The broad statements in the McQuade opinion, applicable to the facts there, should be confined to those facts. . . .

The court in Clark obviously thought that it was critical that the agreement involved all (both) of the shareholders, but it still found it necessary to take the time to evaluate the actual restrictions imposed. In a case over a decade later, the same approach led the court to conclude that a unanimous shareholder agreement giving one shareholder full authority to manage the corporation went too far and indeed "sterilized" the directors in a manner offensive to public policy. Long Park, Inc. v. Trenton-New Brunswick Theatres Co., 77 N.E.2d 633 (N.Y. 1948).

The step-by-step approach in Galler, below, is similar. It is important to note that in Galler there was an employee shareholder—Rosenberg—who was not party to the challenged agreement. Keep a careful eye out for his appearances in the court's discussion.

 Dear Prof.: The agreement in Clark v. Dodge was between shareholders. Is a shareholders' agreement the same thing as a voting agreement?

There is a lot of loose talk about shareholders' agreements, voting agreements, voting trusts, and pooling agreements. Voting agreements and pooling agreements are the same thing—agreements by shareholders about how to vote shares. It certainly isn't improper to call them shareholders' agreements. Shareholders, however, may also agree about other things, such as buying and selling shares. When an agreement is about voting and something else, it wouldn't be surprising for someone still to refer to it as a voting or pooling agreement, although I probably wouldn't. The point of the case, obviously, is what shareholders can validly agree about with respect to managing the entity, given that statutes provide corporations are to be managed by their directors.

Finally, a "voting trust" is a special animal, governed by special statutory requirements. We shall return to it later.

GALLER V. GALLER

Supreme Court of Illinois
203 N.E.2d 577 (1964)

UNDERWOOD, Justice.

Plaintiff, Emma Galler, sued in equity for an accounting for specific performance of an agreement made in July, 1955, between plaintiff and her husband, of one part, and defendants, Isadore A. Galler and his wife, Rose, of the other. Defendants appealed from a decree of the superior court of Cook County granting the relief prayed. The First District Appellate Court reversed the decree and denied specific performance, affirming in part the order for an accounting, and modifying the order awarding master's fees. . . .

There is no substantial dispute as to the facts in this case. From 1919 to 1924, Benjamin and Isadore Galler, brothers, were equal partners in the Galler Drug Company, a wholesale drug concern. In 1924 the business was incorporated under the Illinois Business Corporation Act, each owning one half of the outstanding 220 shares of stock. In 1945 each contracted to sell 6 shares to an employee, Rosenberg, at a price of $10,500 for each block of 6 shares, payable within 10 years. They guaranteed to repurchase the shares if Rosenberg's employment were terminated, and further agreed that if they sold their shares, Rosenberg would receive the same price per share as that paid for the brothers' shares. Rosenberg was still indebted for the 12 shares in July, 1955, and continued to make payments on account even after Benjamin Galler died in 1957 and after the institution of this action by Emma Galler in 1959. Rosenberg was not involved in this litigation either as a party or as a witness, and in July of 1961, prior to the time that the master in chancery hearings were concluded, defendants Isadore and Rose Galler purchased the 12 shares from Rosenberg. A supplemental complaint was filed by the plaintiff, Emma Galler, asserting an equitable right to have 6 of the 12 shares transferred to her and offering to pay the defendants one half of the amount that the defendants paid Rosenberg. The parties have stipulated that pending disposition of the instant case, these shares will not be voted or transferred. For approximately one year prior to the entry of the decree by the chancellor in July of 1962, there were no outstanding minority shareholder interests.

In March, 1954, Benjamin and Isadore, on the advice of their accountant, decided to enter into an agreement for the financial protection of their

Unsurprisingly, a number of close corporation cases involve family members.

immediate families and to assure their families, after death of either brother, equal control of the corporation. [In July 1955, the agreement was executed.] . . .

Shortly after Benjamin's death, Emma went to the office and demanded the terms of the 1955 agreement be carried out. Isadore told her that anything she had to say could be said to Aaron, [Isadore's son, who worked in the business,] who then told her that his father would not abide by the agreement. He offered a modification of the agreement by proposing the salary continuation payment but without her becoming a director. When Emma refused to modify the agreement and sought enforcement of its terms, defendants refused and this suit followed.

During the last few years of Benjamin's life both brothers drew an annual salary of $42,000. Aaron, whose salary was $15,000 as manager of the warehouse prior to September, 1956, has since the time that Emma agreed to his acting as president drawn an annual salary of $20,000. In 1957, 1958, and 1959 a $40,000 annual dividend was paid. Plaintiff has received her proportionate share of the dividend.

The July, 1955, agreement in question here, entered into between Benjamin, Emma, Isadore and Rose, recites that Benjamin and Isadore each own 47½ of the issued and outstanding shares of the Galler Drug Company, an Illinois corporation, and that Benjamin and Isadore desired to provide income for the support and maintenance of their immediate families. . . . The essential features of the contested portions of the agreement are substantially as set forth in the opinion of the Appellate Court: (2) that the bylaws of the corporation will be amended to provide for a board of four directors; that the necessary quorum shall be three directors; and that no directors' meeting shall be held without giving ten days notice to all directors. (3) The shareholders will cast their votes for the above named persons (Isadore, Rose, Benjamin and Emma) as directors at said special meeting and at any other meeting held for the purpose of electing directors. (4, 5) In the event of the death of either brother his wife shall have the right to nominate a director in place of the decedent. (6) Certain annual dividends will be declared by the corporation. The dividend shall be $50,000 payable out of the accumulated earned surplus in excess of $500,000. If 50% of the annual net profits after taxes exceeds the minimum $50,000, then the directors shall have discretion to declare a dividend up to 50% of the annual net profits. If the net profits are less than $50,000, nevertheless the minimum $50,000 annual dividend shall be declared, providing the $500,000 surplus is maintained. Earned surplus is defined. (9) The certificates evidencing the said shares of Benjamin Galler and Isadore Galler shall be a legend that the shares are subject to the terms of this agreement. (10) A salary continuation agreement shall be entered into by the corporation which shall authorize the corporation upon the death of Benjamin Galler or Isadore Galler, or both, to pay a sum equal to twice the salary of such officer, payable monthly over a five-year period. Said sum shall be paid to the widow during her widowhood, but should be paid to such widow's children if the widow remarries within the five-year period. (11, 12)....

The Appellate Court found the 1955 agreement void because "the undue duration, stated purpose and substantial disregard of the provisions of the Corporation Act outweigh any considerations which might call for divisibility" and held that "the public policy of this state demands voiding this entire agreement."

While the conduct of defendant towards plaintiff was clearly inequitable, the basically controlling factor is the absence of an objecting minority interest, together with the absence of public detriment....

In Schumann-Heink v. Folsom, 159 N.E. 250, 254, we said:

> In considering whether any contract is against public policy, it should be remembered that it is to the interests of the public that persons should not be unnecessarily restricted in their freedom to make their own contracts. Agreements are not held to be void, as being contrary to public policy, unless they be clearly contrary to what the constitution, the statutes, or the decisions of the courts have declared to be the public policy, or unless they be manifestly injurious to the public welfare. Courts must act with care in extending those rules which say that a given contract is void because against public policy, since, if there be one thing more than any other which public policy requires, it is that men of full age and competent understanding shall have the utmost liberty of contract, and that their contracts, when entered into fairly and voluntarily, shall be held sacred and shall be enforced by the courts....

The power to invalidate the agreements on the grounds of public policy is so far reaching and so easily abused that it should be called into action to set aside or annul the solemn engagement of parties dealing on equal terms only in cases where the corrupt or dangerous tendency clearly and unequivocally appears upon the face of the agreement itself or is the necessary inference from the matters which are expressed, and the only apparent exception to this general rule is to be found in those cases where the agreement, though fair and unobjectionable on its face, is a part of a corrupt scheme and is made to disguise the real nature of the transaction....

... [T]here has been a definite, albeit inarticulate, trend toward eventual judicial treatment of the close corporation as sui generis. Several shareholder-director agreements that have technically "violated" the letter of the Business Corporation Act have nevertheless been upheld in the light of the existing practical circumstances, i.e., no apparent public injury, the absence of a complaining minority interest, and no apparent prejudice to creditors. However, we have thus far not attempted to limit these decisions as applicable only to close corporations and have seemingly implied that general considerations regarding judicial supervision of all corporate behavior apply.

The practical result of this series of cases, while liberally giving legal efficacy to particular agreements in special circumstances notwithstanding literal "violations" of statutory corporate law, has been to inject much doubt and uncertainty into the thinking of the bench and corporate bar of Illinois concerning shareholder agreements....

It is therefore necessary, we feel, to discuss the instant case with the problems peculiar to the close corporation particularly in mind.

It would admittedly facilitate judicial supervision of corporate behavior if a strict adherence to the provisions of the Business Corporation Act were required in all cases without regard to the practical exigencies peculiar to the close corporation. However, courts have long ago quite realistically, we feel, relaxed their attitudes concerning statutory compliance when dealing with close corporate behavior, permitting "slight deviations" from corporate "norms" in order to give legal efficacy to common business practice. . . .

Numerous helpful textual statements and law review articles dealing with the judicial treatment of the close corporation have been pointed out by counsel. One article concludes with the following:

> New needs compel fresh formulation of corporate "norms." There is no reason why mature men should not be able to adapt the statutory form to the structure they want, so long as they do not endanger other stockholders, holders, creditors, or the public, or violate a clearly mandatory provision of the corporation laws. In a typical close corporation the stockholders' agreement is usually the result of careful deliberation among all initial investors. In the large public-issue corporation, on the other hand, the "agreement" represented by the corporate charter is not consciously agreed to by the investors; they have no voice in its formulation, and very few ever read the certificate of incorporation. Preservation of the corporate norms may therefore be necessary for the protection of the public investors.

Hornstein, "Stockholders' Agreements in the Closely Held Corporation," 59 Yale L. Journal, 1040, 1056. . . .

Perhaps, as has been vociferously advanced, a separate comprehensive statutory scheme governing the close corporation would best serve here. . . .

At any rate, however, the courts can no longer fail to expressly distinguish between the close and public-issue corporation when confronted with problems relating to either. What we do here is to illuminate this problem—before the bench, corporate bar, and the legislature, in the context of a particular fact situation. To do less would be to shirk our responsibility, to do more would, perhaps be to invade the province of the legislative branch.

We now, in the light of the foregoing, turn to specific provisions of the 1955 agreement.

The Appellate Court correctly found many of the contractual provisions free from serious objection, and we need not prolong this opinion with a discussion of them here. That court did, however, find difficulties in the stated purpose of the agreement as it relates to its duration, the election of certain persons to specific offices for a number of years, the requirement for the mandatory declaration of stated dividends (which the Appellate Court held invalid), and the salary continuation agreement.

Since the question as to the duration of the agreement is a principal source of controversy, we shall consider it first. The parties provided no specific termination date, and while the agreement concludes with a paragraph that its terms "shall be binding upon and shall inure to the benefits of the legal representatives, heirs and assigns of the parties," this clause is, we believe, intended to be operative only as long as one of the parties is living. It further provides that it shall be so construed as to carry out its purposes, and we believe these must be determined from a consideration of the agreement as a whole. Thus viewed, a fair construction is that its purposes were accomplished at the death of the survivor of the parties. While these life spans are not precisely ascertainable, and the Appellate Court noted Emma Galler's life expectancy at her husband's death was 26.9 years, we are aware of no statutory or public policy provision against stockholder's agreements which would invalidate this agreement on that ground. . . . While defendants argue that the public policy evinced by the legislative restrictions upon the duration of voting trust agreements should be applied here, this agreement is not a voting trust, but as pointed out by the dissenting justice in the Appellate Court, is a straight contractual voting control agreement which does not divorce voting rights from stock ownership. . . .

> ### Connections: Formal Voting Trusts
>
> Voting trust statutes provide a planning vehicle for shareholders (frequently at the insistence of corporate creditors) to transfer voting rights to an appointed trustee. The traditional limit on the length of such a trust was ten years.

The clause that provides for the election of certain persons to specified offices for a period of years likewise does not require invalidation. In Kantzler v. Bensinger, 73 N.E. 874, this court upheld an agreement entered into by all the stockholders providing that certain parties would be elected to the offices of the corporation for a fixed period. In Faulds v. Yates, 57 Ill. 416, we upheld a similar agreement among the majority stockholders of a corporation, notwithstanding the existence of a minority which was not before the court complaining thereof. . . .

We turn next to a consideration of the effect of the stated purpose of the agreement upon its validity. The pertinent provision is: "The said Benjamin A. Galler and Isadore A. Galler desire to provide income for the support and maintenance of their immediate families." Obviously, there is no evil inherent in a contract entered into for the reason that the persons originating the terms desired to so arrange their property as to provide post-death support for those dependent upon them. Nor does the fact that the subject property is corporate stock alter the situation so long as there exists no detriment to minority stock interests, creditors or other public injury. It is however, contended by defendants that the methods provided by the agreement for implementation of the stated purpose are, as a whole, violative of the Business Corporation Act to such an extent as to render it void in toto.

The terms of the dividend agreement require a minimum annual dividend of $50,000, but this duty is limited by the subsequent provision that it shall be operative only so long as an earned surplus of $500,000 is maintained. It may be noted that in 1958, the year prior to commencement of this litigation, the corporation's net earnings after taxes amounted to $202,759 while its earned surplus was $1,543,270, and this was increased in 1958 to $1,680,079 while earnings were $172,964. The minimum earned surplus requirement is designed for the protection of the corporation and its creditors, and we take no exception to the contractual dividend requirements as thus restricted. . . .

The salary continuation agreement is a common feature, in one form or another, of corporate executive employment. It requires that the widow should receive a total benefit, payable monthly over a five-year period, aggregating twice the amount paid her deceased husband in one year. This requirement was likewise limited for the protection of the corporation by being contingent upon the payments being income tax-deductible by the corporation. The charge made in those cases which have considered the validity of payments to the widow of an officer and shareholder in a corporation is that a gift of its property by a noncharitable corporation is in violation of the rights of its shareholders and ultra vires. Since there are no shareholders here other than the parties to the contract, this objection is not here applicable, and its effect, as limited, upon the corporation is not so prejudicial as so require its invalidation. . . .

We hold defendants must account for all monies received by them from the corporation since September 25, 1956, in excess of that theretofore authorized. . . .

> ■ **Think about this:**
>
> *(A)* Would there be any reason for Rosenberg to have been concerned about the agreement the Gallers had made? If you were the judge and Rosenberg had not already sold his shares, would you still find the agreement enforceable?
>
> *(B)* If you applied the Clark test to the Galler facts, would you get the same result as Galler?
>
> *(C)* If you applied the Galler test to the Clark facts, would you get the same result as Clark?

Some states, like Delaware, have made special statutory schemes available for the shareholders of closely held corporations. These schemes, known as "integrated close corporation statutes," permit direct shareholder management (in exchange for assumption of the fiduciary duties of directors). For a variety of reasons use of these statutes has been limited. For one thing, entrepreneurs dreaming of the big time may prefer to form under the "regular" corporate scheme, thus preparing to seamlessly transition into life as something other than a close corporation if the business is successful. On the other hand, persons who want informal management structures and have no desire to "go public" in the foreseeable future may choose the format of a limited liability company.

The following case tells the story of a corporation that could have elected under a close corporation statute but, for whatever reason, did not.

RAMOS V. ESTRADA

California Court of Appeal
10 Cal. Rptr. 2d 833 (1992)

GILBERT, J.

Defendants Tila and Angel Estrada appeal a judgment which states they breached a written corporate shareholder voting agreement. We hold that a corporate shareholders' voting agreement may be valid even though the corporation is not technically a close corporation. We affirm.

[The Estradas were parties to a shareholder voting agreement entered into by a group (the "Broadcast Group") of shareholders owning slightly over 50 percent of Television, Inc. The Estradas defected, electing to cast their votes with those of a competing group of shareholders (the "Ventura Group"). The Broadcast Group agreement provided that failure to observe its terms constituted an election to sell the non-compliant shareholder's shares pursuant to the agreement's buy-sell terms.]

The Estradas contend that the June Broadcast Agreement is void because it constitutes an expired proxy which the Estradas validly revoked. . . .

Corporations Code section 178 defines a proxy to be "a written authorization signed . . . by a shareholder . . . giving another person or persons power to vote with respect to the shares of such shareholder." (Italics added.)

Section 7.1 of the June Broadcast Agreement details the voting arrangement among the shareholders. It states, in pertinent part: "The Stockholders agree that they shall consult with each other prior to voting their shares in the Company. They shall attempt in good faith to reach a consensus as to the outcome of any such vote. . . . In the case of all votes of Stockholders they agree that, following consultation and compliance with the other provisions of this paragraph, they will all vote their stock in the manner voted by a majority of the Stockholders." (Second italics in original.)

No proxies are created by this agreement. The agreement has the characteristics of a shareholders' voting agreement expressly authorized by section 706, subdivision (a) for close corporations. Although the articles of incorporation do not contain the talismanic statement that "This corporation is a close corporation," the arrangements of this corporation, and in particular this voting agreement, are strikingly similar to ones authorized by the code for close corporations.

Section 706, subdivision (a) states, in pertinent part: "an agreement between two or more shareholders of a close corporation, if in writing and signed by the parties thereto, may provide that in exercising any voting rights the shares held by them shall be voted as provided by the agreement, or as the parties may agree or as determined in accordance with a procedure agreed upon by them. . . ."

JD/MBA: Taxation

Close corporations usually can make an election for tax purposes that will get them essentially the same (favorable) treatment as limited liability companies. "Essentially," however, is not the same as "exactly." There are minor ways in which taxation of a limited liability company can be superior from the owners' standpoint.

Connections: Buy-Sell Agreements

Because of the difficulty of finding a market for the shares of a close corporation, it often is advisable for the shareholders to provide for one themselves, entering into an agreement that specifies the triggers and terms for mandatory buyouts by the company or the other shareholders. In some circumstances, shareholders who haven't set up mandatory buyouts might still want an option on the departing holders' shares. Both arrangements are known as "buy-sell" agreements.

Even though this corporation does not qualify as a close corporation, this agreement is valid and binding on the Estradas. Section 706, subdivision (d) states: "This section shall not invalidate any voting or other agreement among shareholders . . . which agreement . . . is not otherwise illegal."

The legislative committee comment regarding section 706, subdivision (d) states that "[t]his subdivision is intended to preserve any agreements which would be upheld under court decisions even though they do not comply with one or more of the requirements of this section, including voting agreements of corporations other than close corporations." (West's Ann. Corp. Code, §706 (1990) p. 330, italics added.) . . .

The instant agreement is valid, enforceable and supported by consideration. It states, in pertinent part, that the stockholders entered into the agreement for the purposes of "limiting the transferability of . . . stock in the Company, ensuring that the Company does not pass into the control of persons whose interests might be incompatible with the interests of the Company and of the Stockholders, establishing their mutual rights and obligations in the event of death, and establishing a mechanism for determining how the Stockholders' voting rights . . . shall be exercised. . . ."

Section 7.2 of the agreement states that "[t]he Stockholders understand and acknowledge that the purpose of the foregoing arrangement is to preserve their relative voting power in the Company. . . . Accordingly, in the event that a Stockholder fails to abide by this arrangement for whatever reason, that failure shall constitute on [sic] irrevocable election by the Stockholder to sell his stock in the Company, triggering the same rights of purchase provided in Article IV above."

The agreement calls for enforcement by specific performance of its terms because the stock is not readily marketable. Section 709, subdivision (c) expressly permits enforcement of shareholder voting agreements by such equitable remedies. It states, in pertinent part: "The court may determine the person entitled to the office of director or may order a new election to be held or appointment to be made, may determine the validity, effectiveness and construction of voting agreements . . . and the right of persons to vote and may direct such other relief as may be just and proper."

The Estradas contend that the forced sale provision is unconscionable and oppressive. They portray themselves as naive, small-town business people who were forced to sign an adhesion agreement without reviewing its contents.

Substantial evidence supports the findings that Tila Estrada has been a licensed real estate broker. She is an astute businesswoman experienced with contracts concerning real property. The consent and signatures of the Estradas to the agreement were not procured by fraud, duress or other wrongful conduct of Ramos. The Estradas read and discussed with other members of Broadcast Group, and with their own counsel, the voting, buy/sell and other provisions of the agreement and the January Broadcast Agreement, as well as various drafts of these documents, and they freely signed these agreements. . . .

The June Broadcast Agreement, including its voting and buy/sell provisions, was unanimously executed after the Estradas had a full and fair opportunity to consider it in its entirety. As the trial court found, the buy out provisions at issue here are valid, favored by courts and enforceable by specific performance. . . .

The Estradas breached the agreement by their written repudiation of it. Their breach constituted an election to sell their Television Inc. shares in accordance with the terms of the buy/sell provisions in the agreement. This election does not constitute a forfeiture—they violated the agreement voluntarily, aware of the consequences of their acts and they are provided full compensation, per their agreement. The judgment is affirmed. Costs to Ramos.

Note that the agreement in Ramos related to the voting of shares, rather than the usurpation of board authority, so it is not surprising that it was upheld. It nonetheless suggests one way to deal with the existence of a statutory scheme that the parties chose not to—or simply didn't—use.

A similar case in New York puts a coda on the Clark and Long Park line. In Zion v. Kurtz, 405 N.E.2d 199 (1980), the New York Court of Appeals was required to consider an arrangement giving a minority shareholder a veto over any change in the business of a Delaware corporation. The Delaware integrated close corporation statute would have authorized such an arrangement if it were contained in the Articles of Incorporation of an electing close corporation, but the election had not been made. The majority of the court concluded that the existence of Delaware's integrated close corporation statute (like the existence of New York's own, similar, statute) indicated that there was no public policy against shareholder involvement in management. Absent any "intervening rights" of third parties (including other shareholders who weren't parties to the arrangement), it saw no reason not to order the Articles of Incorporation to be revised as those of an electing close corporation—or more simply, to estop the shareholder who wished to disregard the arrangement from relying on the non-election.

> **Connections: The Internal Affairs Doctrine**
>
> The internal affairs doctrine provides that the law of the state of incorporation controls a corporation's governance matters. However, the rule is subject to a public policy override if it would lead to a result against the public policy of the jurisdiction in which litigation takes place.

The dissent in *Zion* essentially urged that if one wished a statutory result, one should follow the statute, and that the legislature had reasons for its design, including, on a prophylactic basis, notice to third parties. Twelve years later, the Supreme Court of Delaware faced a case involving shareholders seeking a court-ordered buyout of the shares of a corporation on the grounds that it was a close corporation. Noting that the company had not elected statutory close corporation status, the court said this:

> In 1967, when the Delaware General Corporation Law was significantly revised, a new Subchapter XIV entitled "Close Corporations; Special Provisions," became a part of that law for the first time. . . . Subchapter XIV is a narrowly constructed

statute which applies only to a corporation which is designated as a "close corporation" in its certificate of incorporation, and which fulfills other requirements, including a limitation to 30 on the number of stockholders, that all classes of stock have to have at least one restriction on transfer, and that there be no "public offering." 8 Del. C. §342. Accordingly, subchapter XIV applies only to "close corporations," as defined in section 342. "Unless a corporation elects to become a close corporation under this subchapter in the manner prescribed in this subchapter, it shall be subject in all respects to this chapter, except this subchapter." 8 Del. C. §341. The corporation before the Court in this matter, is not a "close corporation." Therefore it is not governed by the provisions of Subchapter XIV.

Nixon v. Blackwell, 626 A.2d 1366 (1992).

■ **Think about this:**

(D) Does *Nixon* mean that *Zion* was wrongly decided? If so, why would anyone talk about *Zion*?

Finally, the Model Business Corporation Act and some other statutes now permit shareholders to enter agreements modifying default governance rules. MBCA §7.32. Such agreements may go so far as to entirely dispense with the board of directors (in which case the shareholders assume the directors' fiduciary duties). The shareholders must, however, unanimously agree. Subsequent purchasers are to be informed of the existence of the agreement by reason of a notice on the face or back of the share certificate or, if the shares are not represented by certificate, in a separate information statement. A purchaser who receives the requisite notice is deemed to know about the agreement. If, however, notice is not given and the purchaser otherwise does not know about the agreement, the purchaser has a right of rescission.

Connections: Legends

A notice placed on a stock certificate is known as a "legend." Legends are used for a variety of purposes, including restricting share transfers if certain conditions—such as compliance with federal securities laws—are not satisfied.

What, then, is the point of reading cases like *Clark* and *Galler*? That is, why worry about comparatively old cases dealing with mere incursions into board authority when the Model Act now permits doing away with the board entirely? There are several reasons. First, there will be many situations in which not all the shareholders are interested in precisely the same arrangements, or any agreement at all, even in small companies. Second, the shareholders might simply make a mistake in drafting a §7.32 agreement, and fail to comply with some statutory requirement, in which case the traditional public policy rule surrounding shareholder agreements will apply.

■ **Think about this:**

(E) Would the arrangement in *Clark* be enforceable under the MBCA?

(F) How about the arrangement in *Galler*?

(G) Imagine that you are among the promoters founding a small company, which you intend to incorporate, and it is contemplated that you and your colleagues each will take a minority percentage of the shares. Bearing in mind that a key policy purpose of boards of directors is protection of minority shareholders, if you were to agree to a §7.32 agreement eliminating your company's board, what other protections should you seek for yourself? Having thought through that question, ask yourself this: Might it be wise to seek the same kinds of protections even if the traditional board is left in place? If you do seek those protections, what might be necessary to make sure your agreement putting them in place is enforceable?

C. Voting Trusts and Other Control Devices

Sometimes shareholders will seek (or be asked by creditors) to bind themselves as to how they will vote on matters that themselves are perfectly fair game for shareholder action. Sometimes they will seek to provide for tie-breaking devices more elaborate than simply providing for an odd number of directors. This section discusses the statutory voting trust (mentioned above) and the use of arbitrators to resolve control disputes. It also describes the method one set of shareholders adopted as a tie-breaking device that seems to have disastrously misfired.

1. The Statutory Voting Trust

The following is a fairly typical statute governing the formation of a voting trust. It should be read with the knowledge that courts traditionally were wary that other control devices could be voting trusts that should have complied with relevant statutes but failed to do so.

REVISED MODEL BUSINESS CORPORATION ACT

§7.30. Voting Trusts

(a) One or more shareholders may create a voting trust, conferring on a trustee the right to vote or otherwise act for them, by signing an agreement setting out the provisions of the trust (which may include anything consistent with its purpose) and transferring their shares to the trustee. When a voting trust agreement is signed, the trustee shall prepare a list of the names and addresses of all owners of beneficial interests in the trust, together with the number and class of shares each transferred to the trust, and deliver copies of the list and agreement to the corporation's principal office.

(b) A voting trust becomes effective on the date the first shares subject to the trust are registered in the trustee's name.

(c) Limits, if any, on the duration of a voting trust shall be as set forth in the voting trust. A voting trust that became effective when this Act provided a 10-year limit on its duration remains governed by the provisions of this section concerning duration then in effect, unless the voting trust is amended to provide otherwise by unanimous agreement of the parties to the voting trust.

■ **Think about this:**

(H) What good does it do anyone to notify the corporation that the voting trust exists?

(I) Why does the corporation need to know who the beneficial owners of a voting trust are?

(J) Why should there be any time limit imposed on a voting trust?

Part of the explanation of the voting trust requirements has to do with an antipathy to vote-selling that also underlies the rule that a proxy cannot be made irrevocable unless it is "coupled with an interest." This is a subject governed by statutes (such as MBCA §7.22) that generally require the proxy holder to have some relationship with the corporation that more or less parallels the incentives of an owner.

■ **Think about this:**

(K) Really, what's so bad about selling a vote?

---

2. The Structural Tie-Breaker

The voting trust rules are given further consideration in the following case, which turns out not to involve a voting trust after all. Lehrman considers the Delaware voting trust statute, which is quite similar to an earlier version of MBCA §7.30 imposing a ten-year limit on the existence of a voting trust.

LEHRMAN V. COHEN

Supreme Court of Delaware
222 A.2d 800 (1966)

HERRMANN, Justice.
The primary problem presented on this appeal involves the applicability of the Delaware Voting Trust Statute. Other questions involve the legality of stock

having voting power but no dividend or liquidation rights except repayment of par value, and an alleged unlawful delegation of directorial duties and powers.

These are the material facts:

Giant Food Inc. (hereinafter the "Company") was incorporated in Delaware in 1935 by the defendant N. M. Cohen and Samuel Lehrman, deceased father of the plaintiff Jacob Lehrman. From its inception, the Company was controlled by the Cohen and Lehrman families, each of which owned equal quantities of the voting stock, designated Class AC (held by the Cohen family) and Class AL (held by the Lehrman family) common stock. The two classes of stock have cumulative voting rights and each is entitled to elect two members of the Company's four-member board of directors.

Over the years, as may have been expected, there were differences of opinion between the Cohen and Lehrman families as to operating policies of the Company. Samuel Lehrman died in 1949; each of his children inherited part of his stock in the Company; but a dispute arose among the children regarding an inter vivos gift of certain shares made to the plaintiff by his father shortly before his death. To eliminate the Lehrman family dispute and its possible disruption of the affairs of the Company, an arrangement was made which settled the dispute and permitted the plaintiff to acquire all of the outstanding Class AL stock, thereby vesting in him voting power equal to that held by the Cohen family. The arrangement involved repurchase by the Company of the stock held by the plaintiff's brothers and sister, their relinquishment of any claim to the stock gift, and an equalizing surrender of certain stock by the Cohens to the Company for retirement. An essential part of the arrangement, upon the insistence of the Cohens, was the establishment of a fifth directorship to obviate the risk of deadlock which would have continued if the equal division of voting power between AL and AC stock were continued.

To implement the arrangement, on December 31, 1949, the Company's certificate of incorporation was amended, inter alia, to create a third class of voting stock, designated Class AD common stock, entitled to elect the fifth director. Article Fourth of the amendment to the certificate of incorporation provided for the issuance of one share of Class AD stock, having a par value of $10 and the following rights and powers:

> The holder of Class AD common stock shall be entitled to all of the rights and privileges pertaining to common stock without any limitations, prohibitions restrictions or qualifications except that the holder of said Class AD stock shall not be entitled to receive any dividends declared and paid by the corporation, shall not be entitled to share in the distribution of assets of the corporation upon liquidation or dissolution either partial or final, except to the extent of the par value of said Class AD common stock, and in the election of Directors shall have the right to vote for and elect one of the five Directors hereinafter provided for.
>
> The corporation shall have the right, at any time, to redeem and call in the Class AD stock by paying to the holder thereof the par value of said stock, provided however, that such redemption or call shall be authorized and directed by the affirmative vote of four of the five Directors hereinafter provided for.

By resolution of the board of directors, the share of Class AD stock was issued forthwith to the defendant Joseph B. Danzansky, who had served as counsel to the Company since 1944. All corporate action regarding the creation and the issuance of the Class AD stock was accomplished by the unanimous vote of the AC and AL stockholders and of the board of directors. In April 1950, pursuant to the arrangement, Danzansky voted his share of AD stock to elect himself as the Company's fifth director; and he served as such until the institution of this action in 1964. During that entire period, the AC and AL stock have been voted to elect two directors each. From 1950 through 1964, Danzansky regularly attended board meetings, raised and discussed general items of business, and voted on all issues as they came before the board. He was not obliged to break any deadlock among the directors prior to October 1, 1964 because no such deadlock arose before that date.

Beginning in December 1959, 200,000 shares of non-voting common stock of the Company were sold in a public issue for over $3,000,000. Each prospectus published in connection with the public issue contained the following statement:

> "Common Stock AD is not a participating stock, and the only purpose for the provision and issuance of such stock is to prevent a deadlock in case the Directors elected by the Common Stock AC and the Directors elected by the Common Stock AL cannot reach an agreement." . . .

From the outset and until October 1, 1964, the defendant N. M. Cohen was president of the Company. On that date, a resolution was adopted at the Company's annual stockholders' meeting to give Danzansky a fifteen year executive employment contract at an annual salary of $67,600, and options for 25,000 shares of the non-voting common stock of the Company. The AC and AD stock were voted in favor and the AL stock was voted against the resolution. At a directors meeting held the same day, Danzansky was elected president of the Company by a 3-2 vote, the two AL directors voting in opposition. On December 11, 1964, Danzansky resigned as director and voted his share of AD stock to elect as the fifth director. Millard F. West, Jr., a former AL director and investment banker whose firm was one of the underwriters of the public issue of the Company's stock. The newly constituted board ratified the election of Danzansky as president; and, on January 27, 1965, after the commencement of this action and after a review and report by a committee consisting of the new AD director and one AL director, Danzansky's employment contract was approved and adopted with certain modifications.

Connections: Self-Dealing

There were two board votes taken to authorize Danzansky's election as president. The second clearly was prompted by this lawsuit, which characterized Danzansky's original vote for himself as a type of self-dealing—which, of course, it was. The opinion does not address that issue.

The plaintiff brought this action on December 11, 1964, basing it upon two claims: The First Claim charges that the creation, issuance, and voting of the one share of Class AD stock resulted in an arrangement illegal under the law of this State for the reasons hereinafter set forth. . . . The Second Claim, addressed to the events of October 1, 1964, charges that the election of Danzansky as president of the Company and his employment contract violated the terms of the 1959 deadlock-breaking arrangement, as made between the holders of the AC and AL stock, and constituted breaches of contract and fiduciary duty. The plaintiff and the defendants filed cross-motions for summary judgment as to the First Claim. The Court of Chancery, after considering the contentions now before us and discussed Infra, granted summary judgment in favor of the defendants and denied the plaintiff's motion for summary judgment. The plaintiff appeals.

I.

The plaintiff's primary contention is that the Class AD stock arrangement is, in substance and effect, a voting trust; that, as such, it is illegal because not limited to a ten year period as required by the Voting Trust Statute. The defendants deny that the AD stock arrangement constitutes a disguised voting trust; but they concede that if it is, the arrangement is illegal for violation of the Statute. Thus, issue is clearly joined on the point.

The criteria of a voting trust under our decisions have been summarized by this Court in Abercrombie v. Davies, 130 A.2d 338 (1957). The tests there set forth, accepted by both sides of this cause as being applicable, are as follows: (1) the voting rights of the stock are separated from the other attributes of ownership; (2) the voting rights granted are intended to be irrevocable for a definite period of time; and (3) the principal purpose of the grant of voting rights is to acquire voting control of the corporation.

Adopting and applying these tests, the plaintiff says, as to the first element, that the AD arrangement provides for a divorcement of voting rights from beneficial ownership of the AC and AL stock; that the creation and issuance of the share of AD stock is tantamount to a pooling by the AC and AL stockholders of a portion of their voting stock and giving it to a trustee, in the person of the AD stockholder, to vote for the election of the fifth director; that after the creation of the AD stock, the AC and AL stockholders each hold but 40% of the voting power, and the AD stockholder holds the controlling balance of 20%; that the AD stock has no property rights except the right to a return of the $10 paid as the par value; and that, therefore, there has been a transfer of the voting rights devoid of any participating property rights. So runs the argument of the plaintiff in support of his contention that the first of the Abercrombie criteria for a voting trust is met.

The contention is unacceptable. The AD arrangement did not separate the voting rights of the AC or the AL stock from the other attributes of ownership of those classes of stock. Each AC and AL stockholder retains complete control over the voting of his stock; each can vote his stock directly; no AL or AC stockholder is divested of his right to vote his stock as he sees fit; no AL or AC stock can be voted against the shareholder's wishes; and the AL and AC stock continue to elect two directors each.

The AD stock arrangement, as we view it, became a part of the capitalization of the Company. The fact that there is but a single share, or that the par value is nominal, is of no legal significance; the one share and the $10 par value might have been multiplied many times over, with the same consequence. It is true that the creation of the separate class of AD stock may have diluted the voting Power which had previously existed in the AC and AL stock—the usual consequence when additional voting stock is created—but the creation of the new class did not divest and separate the voting rights which remain vested in each AC and AL shareholder, together with the other attributes of the ownership of that stock. The fallacy of the plaintiff's position lies in his premise that since the voting power of the AC and AL stock was reduced by the creation of the AD stock, the percentage of reduction became the res of a voting trust. In any recapitalization involving the creation of additional voting stock, the voting power of the previously existing stock is diminished; but a voting trust is not necessarily the result.

Since the holders of the Class AC and Class AL stock of the Company did not separate the voting rights from the other attributes of ownership of those classes when they created the Class AD stock, the first Abercrombie test of a voting trust is not met.

. . . Having held that the AC and AL stockholders have not divested themselves of their voting rights, although they may have diluted their voting powers, we do not reach the remaining Abercrombie tests, both of which assume the divestiture of voting rights.

In the final analysis, the essence of the question raised by the plaintiff in this connection is this: Is the substance and purpose of the AD stock arrangement sufficiently close to the substance and purpose of §218 to warrant its being subjected to the restrictions and conditions imposed by that Statute? The answer is negative not only for the reasons above stated, but also because §218 regulates trusts and pooling agreements amounting to trusts, not other and different types of arrangements and undertakings possible among stockholders. The AD Stock arrangement is neither a trust nor a pooling agreement.

We hold, therefore, that the Class AD stock arrangement is not controlled by the Voting Trust Statute.

II.

The plaintiff's second point is that even if the Class AD stock arrangement is not a voting trust in substance and effect, the AD stock is illegal, nevertheless, because the creation of a class of stock having voting rights only, and lacking any substantial participating proprietary interest in the corporation, violates the public policy of this State as declared in §218.

The fallacy of this argument is twofold: First, it is more accurate to say that what the law has disfavored, and what the public policy underlying the Voting Trust Statute means to control, is the separation of the vote from the stock—not from the stock ownership. Clearly, the AD stock arrangement is not violative of that public policy. Secondly, there is nothing in §218, either expressed or implied, which requires that all stock of a Delaware corporation must have both voting rights and proprietary interests. Indeed, public policy to the contrary seems clearly expressed by 8 Del. C. §151(a) which authorizes, in very broad terms, such voting powers and participating rights as may be stated in the certificate of incorporation. Non-voting stock is specifically authorized by §151(a); and in the light thereof, consistency does not permit the conclusion, urged by the plaintiff, that the present public policy of this State condemns the separation of voting rights from beneficial stock ownership. . . .

We conclude that the plaintiff's contention in this regard cannot withstand the force and effect of §151(a). In our view, that Statute permits the creation of stock having voting rights only, as well as stock having property rights only. . . .

We are told that if the AD stock arrangement is allowed thus to stand, our Voting Trust Statute will become a "dead letter" because it will be possible to evade and circumvent its purpose simply by issuing a class of non-participating voting stock, as was done here. We have three negative reactions to this argument:

First, it presupposes a divestiture of the voting rights of the AC and AL stock—an untenable supposition as has been stated. Secondly, it fails to take into account the main purpose of a Voting Trust Statute: to avoid secret, uncontrolled combinations of stockholders formed to acquire voting control of the corporation to the possible detriment of non-participating shareholders. It may not be said that the AD stock arrangement contravenes that purpose. Finally on this point, if we misconceive the legislative intent, and if the AD stock arrangement in this case reveals a loophole in §218 which should be plugged, it is for the General Assembly to accomplish—not for us to attempt by interstitial judicial legislation. . . .

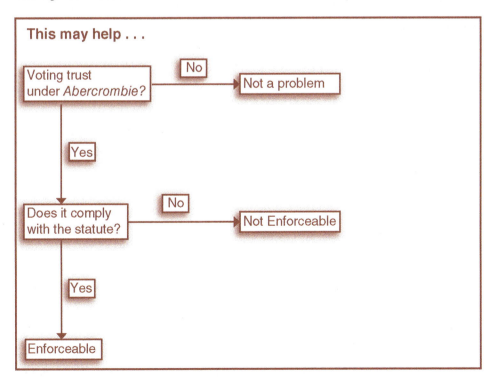

■ Think about this:

(L) Does *Lehrman* have anything to do with vote-selling?

(M) The Cohens are the ones who insisted on the creation of the fifth directorship. If it had not been created, what do you think would have happened with respect to the election of president?

(N) If you were advising the shareholders before the amendment of the articles to create class AD, is that what you would have advised?

 Time Out for PR

Hmmmm. Where to start? Perhaps at the beginning.

Who was Danzansky representing when advising that class AD be created (assuming it was indeed his advice)?

Was it good advice?

Was it a professional conflict of interest for him to buy the AD share?

Was it a professional conflict of interest for him to vote himself into the presidency?

Would it have been a professional conflict of interest to resign as a lawyer in order to vote himself into the presidency?

3. Voting and Arbitration Agreements

The *Ringling* case involves a voting (or pooling) agreement that was not unanimous and that anticipated the possibility of discord with an arbitration proviso that, like the arrangement in Lehrman, probably did not achieve precisely what the parties intended. It also implicates other control devices, including voting trusts and cumulative voting.

RINGLING BROS.-BARNUM & BAILEY COMBINED SHOWS V. RINGLING

Supreme Court of Delaware
53 A.2d 441 (1947)

Connections: Formal Voting Trusts

The agreement between Mrs. Ringling and Mrs. Haley was entered after their shares had been subjected to a statutory voting trust created for the benefit of creditors.

PEARSON, Judge.

The Court of Chancery was called upon to review an attempted election of directors at the 1946 annual stockholders meeting of the corporate defendant. The pivotal questions concern an agreement between two of the three present stockholders, and particularly the effect of this agreement with relation to the exercise of voting rights by these two stockholders. At the time of the meeting, the corporation had outstanding 1000 shares of capital stock held as follows: 315 by petitioner Edith Conway Ringling; 315 by defendant Aubrey B. Ringling Haley (individually or as executrix and legatee of a deceased husband); and 370 by defendant John Ringling North. The purpose of the meeting was to elect the entire board of seven directors. The shares could be voted cumulatively. Mrs. Ringling asserts that by virtue of the operation of an agreement between her and Mrs. Haley, the latter was bound to vote her shares for an adjournment of the meeting, or in the alternative, for a certain slate of directors. Mrs. Haley contends that she was not so bound for reason that the agreement was invalid, or at least revocable.

Alf Ringling

The two ladies entered into the agreement in 1941. It makes like provisions concerning stock of the corporate defendant and of another corporation, but in this case, we are concerned solely with the agreement as it affects the voting of stock of the corporate defendant. The agreement recites that each party was the owner "subject only to possible claims of creditors of the estates of Charles Ringling and Richard Ringling, respectively" (deceased husbands of the parties), of 300 shares of the capital stock of the defendant corporation; that in 1938 these shares had been deposited under a voting trust agreement which would terminate in 1947, or earlier, upon the elimination of certain liability of the corporation; that each party also owned 15 shares individually; that the parties had "entered into an agreement in April 1934 providing for joint action by them in matters affecting their ownership of stock and interest in" the corporate defendant; that the parties desired "to continue to act jointly in all matters relating to their stock ownership or interest in" the corporate defendant (and the other corporation). The agreement then provides as follows:

Al Ringling

Charles
Ringling

> Now, Therefore, in consideration of the mutual covenants and agreements hereinafter contained the parties hereto agree as follows: . . .
>
> 2. In exercising any voting rights to which either party may be entitled by virtue of ownership of stock or voting trust certificates held by them in either of said corporation, each party will consult and confer with the other and the parties will act jointly in exercising such voting rights in accordance with such agreement as they may reach with respect to any matter calling for the exercise of such voting rights.
>
> 3. In the event the parties fail to agree with respect to any matter covered by paragraph 2 above, the question in disagreement shall be submitted for arbitration to Karl D. Loos, of Washington, D.C. as arbitrator and his decision thereon shall be binding upon the parties hereto. Such arbitration shall be exercised to the end of assuring for the respective corporations good management and such participation therein by the members of the Ringling family as the experience, capacity and ability of each may warrant. The parties may at any time by written agreement designate any other individual to act as arbitrator in lieu of said Loos.
>
> 4. Each of the parties hereto will enter into and execute such voting trust agreement or agreements and such other instruments as, from time to time they may deem advisable and as they may be advised by counsel are appropriate to effectuate the purposes and objects of this agreement.
>
> 5. This agreement shall be in effect from the date hereof and shall continue in effect for a period of ten years unless sooner terminated by mutual agreement in writing by the parties hereto. . . .

Otto
Ringling

John
Ringling

Connections: Cumulative Voting

Cumulative voting is an additional control device. When voting for directors is straight, the holder(s) of a majority of the shares voting can elect all the directors. When it is cumulative, each holder gets a number of votes equal to the number of shares held multiplied by the number of vacancies to be filled, and may choose to pile those votes on just a few candidates. See the court's original footnote for the math!

The Mr. Loos mentioned in the agreement is an attorney and has represented both parties since 1937, and, before and after the voting trust was terminated in late 1942, advised them with respect to the exercise of their voting rights. At the annual meetings in 1943 and the two following years, the parties voted their shares in accordance with mutual understandings arrived at as a result of discussions. In each of these years, they elected five of the seven directors. Mrs. Ringling and Mrs. Haley each had sufficient votes, independently of the other, to elect two of the seven directors. By both voting for an additional candidate, they could be sure of his election regardless of how Mr. North, the remaining stockholder, might vote.[1]

Some weeks before the 1946 meeting, they discussed with Mr. Loos the matter of voting for directors. They were in accord that Mrs. Ringling should cast sufficient votes to elect herself and her son; and that Mrs. Haley should elect herself and her husband; but they did not agree upon a fifth director. The day before the meeting, the discussions were continued, Mrs. Haley being represented by her husband since she could not be present because of illness. In a conversation with Mr. Loos, Mr. Haley indicated that he would make a motion for an adjournment of the meeting for sixty days, in order to give the ladies additional time to come to an agreement about their voting. On the morning of the meeting, however, he stated that because of something Mrs. Ringling had done, he would not consent to a postponement. Mrs. Ringling then made a demand upon Mr. Loos to act under the third paragraph of the agreement "to arbitrate the disagreement" between her and Mrs. Haley in connection with the manner in which the stock of the two ladies should be voted. At the opening of the meeting, Mr. Loos read the written demand and stated that he determined and directed that the stock of both ladies be voted for an adjournment of sixty days. Mrs. Ringling then made a motion for adjournment and voted for it. Mr. Haley, as proxy for his wife, and Mr. North voted against the motion. Mrs. Ringling (herself or through her attorney, it is immaterial which,) objected to the voting of Mrs. Haley's stock in any manner other than in accordance with Mr. Loos' direction. The chairman ruled that the stock could not be voted contrary to such direction, and declared the motion for adjournment had carried. Nevertheless, the meeting proceeded to the election of directors. Mrs. Ringling stated that she would continue in the meeting "but without prejudice to her position with respect to the voting of the stock

---

1. Each lady was entitled to cast 2205 votes (since each had the cumulative voting rights of 315 shares, and there were 7 vacancies in the directorate). The sum of the votes of both is 4410, which is sufficient to allow 882 votes for each of 5 persons. Mr. North, holding 370 shares, was entitled to cast 2590 votes, which obviously cannot be divided so as to give to more than two candidates as many as 882 votes each. It will be observed that in order for Mrs. Ringling and Mrs. Haley to be sure to elect five directors (regardless of how Mr. North might vote) they must act together in the sense that their combined votes must be divided among five different candidates and at least one of the five must be voted for by both Mrs. Ringling and Mrs. Haley.

and the fact that adjournment had not been taken." Mr. Loos directed Mrs. Ringling to cast her votes

> 882 for Mrs. Ringling,
> 882 for her son, Robert, and
> 441 for a Mr. Dunn,

who had been a member of the board for several years. She complied. Mr. Loos directed that Mrs. Haley's votes be cast

> 882 for Mrs. Haley,
> 882 for Mr. Haley, and
> 441 for Mr. Dunn.

Instead of complying, Mr. Haley attempted to vote his wife's shares

> 1103 for Mrs. Haley, and
> 1102 for Mr. Haley.

Mr. North voted his shares

> 864 for a Mr. Woods,
> 863 for a Mr. Griffin, and
> 863 for Mr. North.

The chairman ruled that the five candidates proposed by Mr. Loos, together with Messrs. Woods and North, were elected. The Haley-North group disputed this ruling insofar as it declared the election of Mr. Dunn; and insisted that Mr. Griffin, instead, had been elected. A director's meeting followed in which Mrs. Ringling participated after stating that she would do so "without prejudice to her position that the stockholders' meeting had been adjourned and that the directors' meeting was not properly held." Mr. Dunn and Mr. Griffin, although each was challenged by an opposing faction, attempted to join in voting as directors for different slates of officers. Soon after the meeting, Mrs. Ringling instituted this proceeding.

The Vice Chancellor determined that the agreement to vote in accordance with the direction of Mr. Loos was valid as a "stock pooling agreement" with lawful objects and purposes, and that it was not in violation of any public policy of this state. He held that where the arbitrator acts under the agreement and one party refuses to comply with his direction, "the Agreement constitutes the willing party . . . an implied agent possessing the irrevocable proxy of the recalcitrant party for the purpose of casting the particular vote." It was ordered that a new election be

More to the Story

Behind the Scenes at the Circus

The antipathy between the Haleys and Ringlings is said to be attributable to a horrific circus fire in 1944, as the result of which Mr. Haley went to prison for negligent manslaughter. Mr. Haley sought a suspended sentence, claiming the circus needed him in order to make enough money to pay damages. Mrs. Ringling's son, who was the president of the corporation, stated at sentencing that the company would run just fine without Mr. Haley.

held before a master, with the direction that the master should recognize and give effect to the agreement if its terms were properly invoked.

Before taking up defendants' objections to the agreement, let us analyze particularly what it attempts to provide with respect to voting, including what functions and powers it attempts to repose in Mr. Loos, the "arbitrator." The agreement recites that the parties desired "to continue to act jointly in all matters relating to their stock ownership or interest in" the corporation. The parties agreed to consult and confer with each other in exercising their voting rights and to act jointly—that is, concertedly; unitedly; towards unified courses of action—in accordance with such agreement as they might reach. Thus, so long as the parties agree for whom or for what their shares shall be voted, the agreement provides no function for the arbitrator. His role is limited to situations where the parties fail to agree upon a course of action. In such cases, the agreement directs that "the question in disagreement shall be submitted for arbitration" to Mr. Loos "as arbitrator and his decision thereon shall be binding upon the parties." These provisions are designed to operate in aid of what appears to be a primary purpose of the parties, "to act jointly" in exercising their voting rights, by providing a means for fixing a course of action whenever they themselves might reach a stalemate.

Should the agreement be interpreted as attempting to empower the arbitrator to carry his directions into effect? Certainly there is no express delegation or grant of power to do so, either by authorizing him to vote the shares or to compel either party to vote them in accordance with his directions. The agreement expresses no other function of the arbitrator than that of deciding questions in disagreement which prevent the effectuation of the purpose "to act jointly." The power to enforce a decision does not seem a necessary or usual incident of such a function. Mr. Loos is not a party to the agreement. It does not contemplate the transfer of any shares or interest in shares to him, or that he should undertake any duties which the parties might compel him to perform. They

---

Connections: The Test for a Voting Trust

Recall from *Lehrman*, above, that the test for an illegal voting trust was stated in Abercrombie v. Davies, 130 A.2d 338 (Del. 1957): (1) the voting rights of the stock are separated from the other attributes of ownership; (2) the voting rights granted are intended to be irrevocable for a definite period of time; and (3) the principal purpose of the grant of voting rights is to acquire voting control of the corporation.

---

provided that they might designate any other individual to act instead of Mr. Loos. The agreement does not attempt to make the arbitrator a trustee of an express trust. What the arbitrator is to do is for the benefit of the parties, not for his own benefit. Whether the parties accept or reject his decision is no concern of his, so far as the agreement or the surrounding circumstances reveal. We think the parties sought to bind each other, but to be bound only to each other, and not to empower the arbitrator to enforce decisions he might make.

From this conclusion, it follows necessarily that no decision of the arbitrator could ever be enforced if both parties to the agreement were unwilling that it be enforced, for the obvious reason that there would be no one to enforce it. Under the agreement, something more is required after the arbitrator has given his decision in order that it should become compulsory: at least one of the parties must determine that such decision shall be carried into effect. Thus, any "control" of the voting of the shares, which is reposed in the arbitrator, is substantially limited in action under the agreement in that it is subject to the overriding power of the parties themselves.

The agreement does not describe the undertaking of each party with respect to a decision of the arbitrator other than to provide that it "shall be binding upon the parties." It seems to us that this language, considered with relation to its context and the situations to which it is applicable, means that each party promised the other to exercise her own voting rights in accordance with the arbitrator's decision. The agreement is silent about any exercise of the voting rights of one party by the other. The language with reference to situations where the parties arrive at an understanding as to voting plainly suggests "action" by each, and "exercising" voting rights by each, rather than by one for the other. There is no intimation that this method should be different where the arbitrator's decision is to be carried into effect. Assuming that a power in each party to exercise the voting rights of the other might be a relatively more effective or convenient means of enforcing a decision of the arbitrator than would be available without the power, this would not justify implying a delegation of the power in the absence of some indication that the parties bargained for that means. The method of voting actually employed by the parties tends to show that they did not construe the agreement as creating powers to vote each other's shares; for at meetings prior to 1946 each party apparently exercised her own voting rights, and at the 1946 meeting, Mrs. Ringling, who wished to enforce the agreement, did not attempt to cast a ballot in exercise of any voting rights of Mrs. Haley. We do not find enough in the agreement or in the circumstances to justify a construction that either party was empowered to exercise voting rights of the other.

Having examined what the parties sought to provide by the agreement, we come now to defendants' contention that the voting provisions are illegal and revocable. They say that the courts of this state have definitely established the doctrine "that there can be no agreement, or any device whatsoever, by which the voting power of stock of a Delaware corporation may be irrevocably separated from the ownership of the stock, except by an agreement which complies with Section 18 of the Corporation Law, and except by a proxy coupled with an interest. They . . . contend that the doctrine is derived from Section 18 itself, Rev. Code of Del. 1935. The statute reads, in part, as follows:

> Sec. 18. Fiduciary Stockholders; Voting Power of; Voting Trusts:
> . . . One or more stockholders may by agreement in writing deposit capital stock of an original issue with or transfer capital stock to any person or persons, or corporation or corporations authorized to act as trustee, for the purpose of vesting in said person or persons, corporation or corporations, who may be designated Voting Trustee or Voting Trustees, the right to vote thereon for any period of time determined by such agreement, not exceeding ten years, upon the terms and conditions stated in such agreement. Such agreement may contain any other lawful provisions not inconsistent with said purpose. . . . Said Voting Trustees may vote upon the stock so issued or transferred during the period in such agreement specified; stock standing in the names of such Voting Trustees may be voted either in person or by

proxy, and in voting said stock, such Voting Trustees shall incur no responsibility as stockholder, trustee or otherwise, except for their own individual malfeasance."[2]

In our view, neither the cases nor the statute sustain the rule for which the defendants contend. Their sweeping formulation would impugn well-recognized means by which a shareholder may effectively confer his voting rights upon others while retaining various other rights. For example, defendants' rule would apparently not permit holders of voting stock to confer upon stockholders of another class, by the device of an amendment of the certificate of incorporation, the exclusive right to vote during periods when dividends are not paid on stock of the latter class. The broad prohibitory meaning which defendants find in Section 18 seems inconsistent with their concession that proxies coupled with an interest may be irrevocable, for the statute contains nothing about such proxies. The statute authorizes, among other things, the deposit or transfer of stock in trust for a specified purpose, namely, "vesting" in the transferee "the right to vote thereon" for a limited period; and prescribes numerous requirements in this connection. Accordingly, it seems reasonable to infer that to establish the relationship and accomplish the purpose which the statute authorizes, its requirements must be complied with. But the statute does not purport to deal with agreements whereby shareholders attempt to bind each other as to how they shall vote their shares. Various forms of such pooling agreements, as they are sometimes called, have been held valid and have been distinguished from voting trusts. We think the particular agreement before us does not violate Section 18 or constitute an attempted evasion of its requirements, and is not illegal for any other reason. Generally speaking, a shareholder may exercise wide liberality of judgment in the matter of voting, and it is not objectionable that his motives may be for personal profit, or determined by whims or caprice, so long as he violates no duty owed his fellow shareholders. The ownership of voting stock imposes no legal duty to vote at all. A group of shareholders may, without impropriety, vote their respective shares so as to obtain advantages of concerted action. They may lawfully contract with each other to vote in the future in such way as they, or a majority of their group, from time to time determine. Reasonable provisions for cases of failure of the group to reach a determination because of an even division in their ranks seem unobjectionable. The provision here for submission to the arbitrator is plainly designed as a deadlock-breaking measure, and the arbitrator's decision cannot be enforced unless at least one of the parties (entitled to cast one-half of their combined votes) is willing that it be enforced. We find the provision reasonable. It does not appear that the agreement enables the parties to take any unlawful advantage of the outside shareholder, or of any other person. It offends no rule of law or public policy of this state of which we are aware.

---

2. Omitted portions of the section provide requirements for the filing of a copy of the agreement in the principal Delaware office of the corporation for the issuance of certificates of stock to the voting trustees, for the voting of stock where there are more than one voting trustee, and for the extension of the agreement for additional periods, not exceeding ten years each.

. . . Accordingly, the failure of Mrs. Haley to exercise her voting rights in accordance with [the arbitrator's] decision was a breach of her contract. It is no extenuation of the breach that her votes were cast for two of the three candidates directed by the arbitrator. His directions to her were part of a single plan or course of action for the voting of the shares of both parties to the agreement, calculated to utilize an advantage of joint action by them which would bring about the election of an additional director. The actual voting of Mrs. Haley's shares frustrates that plan to such an extent that it should not be treated as a partial performance of her contract.

Throughout their argument, defendants make much of the fact that all votes cast at the meeting were by the registered shareholders. The Court of Chancery may, in a review of an election, reject votes of a registered shareholder where his voting of them is found to be in violation of rights of another person. It seems to us that upon the application of Mrs. Ringling, the injured party, the votes representing Mrs. Haley's shares should not be counted. Since no infirmity in Mr. North's voting has been demonstrated, his right to recognition of what he did at the meeting should be considered in granting any relief to Mrs. Ringling; for her rights arose under a contract to which Mr. North was not a party. With this in mind, we have concluded that the election should not be declared invalid, but that effect should be given to a rejection of the votes representing Mrs. Haley's shares. No other relief seems appropriate in this proceeding. Mr. North's vote against the motion for adjournment was sufficient to defeat it. With respect to the election of directors, the return of the inspectors should be corrected to show a rejection of Mrs. Haley's votes, and to declare the election of the six persons for whom Mr. North and Mrs. Ringling voted.

This leaves one vacancy in the directorate. The question of what to do about such a vacancy was not considered by the court below and has not been argued here. For this reason, and because an election of directors at the 1947 annual meeting (which presumably will be held in the near future) may make a determination of the question unimportant, we shall not decide it on this appeal. If a decision of the point appears important to the parties, any of them may apply to raise it in the Court of Chancery, after the mandate of this court is received there.

An order should be entered directing a modification of the order of the Court of Chancery in accordance with this opinion.

■ Think about this:

(O) Did Mrs. Ringling improve her position by bringing this case?

(P) Suppose Mrs. Ringling and Mrs. Haley had continued to use a statutory voting trust with Mr. Loos as the trustee. Would that have changed the outcome?

(Q) Suppose Mrs. Ringling and Mrs. Haley had given Mr. Loos an irrevocable proxy to vote their shares in accordance with his own instructions. Would it really have been irrevocable? Would it have changed the outcome?

(R) Many commentators have criticized the court in *Ringling* for failing to grant specific performance of the Ringling-Haley agreement. Would that have left Mrs. Ringling better off? Consider the following provision. What might it change about the analysis and/or outcome of *Ringling*?

MODEL BUSINESS CORPORATION ACT

§7.31. Voting Agreements

(a) Two or more shareholders may provide for the manner in which they will vote their shares by signing an agreement for that purpose. A voting agreement created under this section is not subject to the provisions of section 7.30 [the provision on statutory voting trusts].

(b) A voting agreement created under this section is specifically enforceable.

 Time Out for PR

At least Mr. Loos didn't direct "the ladies" to vote for him instead of Mr. Dunn. Still, was there any problem with agreeing to represent them both or with agreeing to act as their arbitrator?

With respect to the initial representation, the place to look is American Bar Association Model Rule of Professional Conduct 1.7, which turns on the lawyer's reasonable belief that the lawyer will be able to provide competent and diligent representation to each affected client—but also requiring informed, written consent.

Acting as an arbitrator has implications for future representation. Model Rule 1.12(a) provides: ". . . a lawyer shall not represent anyone in connection with a matter in which the lawyer participated personally and substantially . . . as an arbitrator, mediator or other third-party neutral, unless all parties to the proceeding give informed consent, confirmed in writing." What would this actually prohibit, in the cast of Mr. Loos? Would it extend to others in his firm? (Yes, unless he is screened. See Model Rule 1.12(c).)

It is worth pausing for a moment to pull together a few threads having to do with shareholder agreements relating to control. Here are some questions to ask:

- Does the agreement trespass on the authority of the board?
- Does it constitute an illegal voting trust?
- Is there a reliable enforcement mechanism?
- Does it violate any fiduciary duty the parties might owe to non-party shareholders?

The fourth question is dealt with in another chapter.

D. Other Planning Possibilities

The material above covers the shareholder voting agreement and the statutory voting trust in some detail. It also touched on the creative use of classes of stock, cumulative voting, and irrevocable proxies. It did not discuss such obvious devices as quorum and voting requirements. In truth the range of possible solutions to small business governance problems probably is limited only by the business planner's imagination.

One device, however, is often particularly useful and quite simple. Since one major problem in close corporations is oppression through denial of salary and dividends, a minority shareholder seeking protection might just demand an employment contract for some fixed term. Particularly useful terms to protect the employee shareholder are (1) a salary escalator clause, which will protect against oppression through salary freeze; and (2) a liquidated damages or "golden parachute" clause, which may cause the majority group to think twice before trying any funny business.

A final thing to remember, however, is that however nifty some lawyerly solutions might seem, there really are no perfect answers to these problems. Internal governance conflicts are common and probably unavoidable in small businesses. That is why statutes provide ways to resolve deadlocks after they arise and methods for dysfunctional corporations to be dissolved. It also is why, in some jurisdictions, the law has evolved to provide that the shareholders of close corporations owed one another fiduciary duties. All these rather more last-resort alternatives are discussed in the next chapter.

Connections: Buy-Sell Agreements

There are many circumstances in which shareholders of close corporations will want to provide for terms on which they will buy shares from one another. The reasons can range from a method of dispute resolution to matters of estate planning. Frequently, too, shareholders will want to make sure that they do not wind up in what feels like an unwanted partnership with some third party to whom an initial shareholder might later sell. There is additional material in the online Supplement relating to buy-sell agreements, but beware: These arrangements have important tax implications that are beyond the scope of this course.

Test Yourself

Assume Applicability of the Most Current Version of the Model Business Corporation Act

1. Joe, John, and Jim are three shareholders of XYZ, Inc., and together they own 45 percent of its shares. They know that by voting together, they can control a large portion of the company's board of directors. They also know that Joe is brightest among them and most involved in the company's affairs, so they provide in a written agreement among them that they will each vote all of their shares at each annual shareholders' meeting exactly as Joe directs them to do. The arrangement is for an indefinite term and can be revoked only by the parties' unanimous agreement. This arrangement is legally unenforceable because:

    a. It is void as against public policy.
    b. Its term exceeds ten years.
    c. It is unsupported by consideration.
    d. There is no obvious reason on these facts that this arrangement would be legally unenforceable.

Questions 2-6 rely on the following facts:

Bernie and his twin brother Bart, now in their seventies, founded a grocery store long ago, and have operated it together ever since. Immediately upon its founding, Bernie and Bart incorporated their business and called it B&B Grocery, Inc. They have each always served as the two members of B&B Grocery's board of directors, and they each own 50 percent of the company's outstanding stock. Shortly after the company's incorporation, they executed a shareholder's agreement between them, which they intended to help them avoid problems in the management of the business.

As parties to the shareholder's agreement, Bernie and Bart agreed that they would always vote for themselves as the two members of B&B Grocery's board. They also included the following provision, under the heading "Designated Tiebreaker":

> In any case, as to a matter for which either board action or shareholder action is required, if the board or the shareholders reach unresolvable disagreement, the matter shall be referred to the Designated Tiebreaker, who shall be the person designated herein, and whose decision as to such matters shall be final.

The shareholder's agreement included another provision appointing B&B Grocery's outside attorney, Bob Shady, as the "Designated Tiebreaker." Bob has agreed so to act.

Finally, pursuant to the shareholder's agreement Bernie and Bart promised that as the company's directors, they would each always vote for an annual payment of dividends in the amount of $500 per share.

2. If Bernie chose to vote for someone other than Bart for the position of director, could Bart enforce the shareholder's agreement against him?

   a. No. Although shareholders may normally agree as to whom they will vote for, they are not permitted to make board elections a foregone conclusion.
   b. No, because proxies may not be given by shareholders in close corporations.
   c. No, because irrevocable proxies may not be given by shareholders in close corporations.
   d. None of the above.

3. If B&B Grocery, Inc. were incorporated in Delaware, would Bernie and Bart's agreement constitute an illegal voting trust?

   a. Yes, because it is irrevocable.
   b. Yes, because it separates voting from ownership.
   c. Yes, because it is for an indefinite term.
   d. Answers a, b, and c are correct.
   e. No.

4. If it were not for the "Designated Tiebreaker" provision in their shareholder's agreement, Bernie and Bart would each be at a significant risk of oppression. True or False?

   a. True. They are both effectively minority shareholders—neither holds a majority.
   b. True, if they are both dependent on their salaries and/or dividends from B&B Grocery.
   c. True. "Oppression," as a practical matter, is a risk in all closely held corporations.
   d. False, as a practical matter.

5. Which of the following best characterizes the enforceability of the provision of the shareholder's agreement concerning the payment of dividends?

   a. Enforceable, because shareholders are permitted to bind themselves as to any matter on which they are entitled to vote.
   b. Enforceable, because directors are permitted to bind themselves as to any matter on which they are entitled to vote.
   c. Unenforceable, because as a matter of statute law dividends must be approved by board vote.
   d. It is hard to say, though if B&B were publicly traded the answer would likely be that it is unenforceable.

6. What risks has Bob Shady undertaken by agreeing to act as "Designated Tiebreaker"?

    a. None.

    b. Probably none, because the nature of his duties as attorney are unlikely to conflict with his duties as Designated Tiebreaker.

    c. He may risk conflict of interest, since he also acts as the company's attorney.

    d. Probably none, since he is not an officer or director and therefore will not owe any fiduciary duties.

26

Special Considerations in the Close Corporation Context, Part II: Fiduciary Duty and Oppression

Obviously, carefully planned businesses can take preemptive steps in the design of their management to avoid or at least soften the risks of deadlock and oppression. Indeed, it is among your chief purposes as counselor to the small business client to imagine difficulties that might arise in the client's envisioned business model and think of solutions to them. Still, things go wrong. This chapter discusses some of the mechanisms the law provides to deal with problems the parties have failed to prevent. The cases presented all concern the problems inherent in holding minority positions in illiquid corporate stock.

Chapter Outline

A. Introduction

B. Unequal Access to Corporate Assets: A Different Fiduciary Standard for Close Corporations

- Recognition of the problem: the Massachusetts equal opportunity "experiment"
- Significance of an integrated close corporation statute: the Delaware rebuttal
  - No special treatment for non-electing corporations
  - Directors who are controlling shareholders simply bear the usual burden of establishing intrinsic fairness

C. Generalizing *Donahue*: The *Wilkes* Burden-Shifting Framework and the Problem of Routine Management

- Refining the *Donahue* standard with the *Wilkes* burden-shifting framework
- Business as usual in New York

Test Yourself

A. Introduction

Closely held corporations—and, indeed, all small businesses—face special problems of governance and internal dispute resolution that do not affect large businesses. One of the most acute problems is oppression. Because ownership interests in a small business are likely to be highly illiquid, a member who is frustrated for one reason or another will normally find it quite difficult to exit. Surely, a small business member could just quit and leave; the problem is that it will often be quite difficult for that person to extract the original investment put into the company. Unless there are special arrangements in place, the problem can become especially acute in closely held corporations, as opposed to other small businesses, because shareholders normally have no right to participate in management beyond the opportunity to vote for directors once per year. Accordingly, if a minority shareholder comes into disfavor, a majority shareholder or bloc of shareholders can seriously oppress that person by (1) denying employment with the company and (2) refusing to pay dividends. A minority shareholder in this position has very few options and, short of legal

Connections: Partnerships

Although close corporations frequently are treated by their shareholders as if they were partnerships, the exit rights of partners are quite different. Even where it breaches an agreement to do so, a partner may dissociate at will. What happens next can be a matter as to which the partners have provided in advance or negotiate on the spot. Failing that, there are statutory solutions. In corporations, the shareholders have no default exit rights at all.

action, has no practical means to enjoy any benefit from the investment made in the company.

This is quite different than the situation of public corporation shareholders. By definition there will be some public market in which shareholders can sell their interest. A minority shareholder unhappy with the company can merely sell out (although not necessarily at the same price originally paid).

 What does it look like?

Check the online Supplement for the following sample documents that are relevant to this chapter:

- A simple employment contract
- Articles of Incorporation for a Delaware statutory close corporation

---

B. Unequal Access to Corporate Assets: A Different Fiduciary Standard for Close Corporations

The following case, *Donahue v. Rodd Electrotype*, was a watershed, and introduced a new regime under which certain long-recognized close corporation problems would be treated with special protections that had not before existed. While it has not been followed universally—as demonstrated in the Delaware case below, *Nixon v. Blackwell*—it has been followed widely and probably states something of a majority rule for treatment of close corporation oppression problems. However, the specific language and standards suggested in *Donahue* itself would require some modification before the rule was widely disseminated. Thus, *Donahue*'s "equal opportunity" approach represents something of a high-water mark. Even the Massachusetts high court would refine the standard only a year later, in a case presented below called *Wilkes v. Springside Nursing Home*, apparently having recognized that *Donahue*'s breadth and uncompromising terms could pose serious managerial problems when applied across the range of ordinary decision making.

DONAHUE v. RODD ELECTROTYPE OF NEW ENGLAND, INC.

Supreme Judicial Court of Massachusetts
328 N.E.2d 505 (1975)

TAURO, Chief Justice.

The plaintiff, Euphemia Donahue, a minority stockholder in the Rodd Electrotype Company of New England, Inc. (Rodd Electrotype), a Massachusetts corporation, brings this suit against the directors of Rodd Electrotype, Charles H. Rodd, Frederick I. Rodd and Mr. Harold E. Magnuson, against Harry C. Rodd, a former director, officer, and controlling stockholder of Rodd Electrotype and against Rodd Electrotype (hereinafter called defendants). The plaintiff seeks to rescind Rodd Electrotype's purchase of Harry Rodd's shares in Rodd Electrotype and to compel Harry Rodd "to repay to the corporation the purchase price of said shares, $36,000, together with interest from the date of purchase." The plaintiff alleges that the defendants caused the corporation to purchase the shares in violation of their fiduciary duty to her, a minority stockholder of Rodd Electrotype.

The trial judge, after hearing oral testimony, dismissed the plaintiff's bill on the merits. He found that the purchase was without prejudice to the plaintiff and implicitly found that the transaction had been carried out in good faith and with inherent fairness. The Appeals Court affirmed with costs. . . . The case is before us on the plaintiff's application for further appellate review. . . .

The evidence may be summarized as follows: [The defendant, Harry C. Rodd, and the plaintiff's deceased husband, Joseph Donahue, had worked for the defendant corporation since 1935 and 1936, respectively. Eventually, they became the owners of 80 percent and 20 percent of the company's shares. Mr. Donahue became plant superintendent, but was not involved in managing the business. By contrast, Mr. Rodd and one of his sons, Charles, were involved in corporate management and served on the board of directors. Another of Mr. Rodd's sons, Frederick, replaced Mr. Donahue in 1965 as plant superintendent, and his son-in-law also worked for the business.]

From 1959 to 1967, Harry Rodd pursued what may fairly be termed a gift program by which he distributed the majority of his [two hundred] shares equally among his two sons and his daughter, Phyllis E. Mason. Each child received thirty-nine shares. Two shares were returned to the corporate treasury in 1966.

We come now to the events of 1970 which form the grounds for the plaintiff's complaint. In May of 1970, Harry Rodd was seventy-seven years old. The record indicates that for some time he had not enjoyed the best of health and that he had undergone a number of operations. His sons wished him to retire. Mr. Rodd was not averse to this suggestion. However, he insisted that some financial arrangements be made with respect to his remaining eighty-one shares of stock. A number of conferences ensued. Harry Rodd and Charles Rodd (representing the company) negotiated terms of purchase for forty-five shares which, Charles Rodd testified, would reflect the book value and liquidating value of the shares.

A special board meeting convened on July 13, 1970. As the first order of business, Harry Rodd resigned his directorship of Rodd Electrotype. The remaining incumbent directors, Charles Rodd and Mr. Harold E. Magnuson (clerk of the company and a defendant and defense attorney in the instant suit), elected Frederick Rodd to replace his father. The three directors then authorized Rodd Electrotype's president (Charles Rodd) to execute an agreement between Harry Rodd and the company in which the company would purchase forty-five shares for $800 a share ($36,000).

[After Harry Rodd engaged in further divestiture to his children,] the shareholdings in Rodd Electrotype were apportioned as follows: Charles Rodd, Frederick Rodd and Phyllis Mason each held fifty-one shares; the Donahues held fifty shares.

[In March 1971, the Donahues learned about the purchase of Harry Rodd's shares at a shareholders' meeting, at which the Donahues refused to ratify the transaction.]

A few weeks after the meeting, the Donahues, acting through their attorney, offered their shares to the corporation on the same terms given to Harry Rodd. Mr. Harold E. Magnuson replied by letter that the corporation would not purchase the shares and was not in a financial position to do so.[1] This suit followed.

In her argument before this court, the plaintiff has characterized the corporate purchase of Harry Rodd's shares as an unlawful distribution of corporate assets to controlling stockholders. She urges that the distribution constitutes a breach of the fiduciary duty owed by the Rodds, as controlling stockholders, to her, a minority stockholder in the enterprise, because the Rodds failed to accord her an equal opportunity to sell her shares to the corporation. The defendants reply that the stock purchase was within the powers of the corporation and met the requirements of good faith and inherent fairness imposed on a fiduciary in his dealings with the corporation. They assert that there is no right to equal opportunity in corporate stock purchases for the corporate treasury. For the reasons hereinafter noted, we agree with the plaintiff and reverse the decree of the Superior Court. However, we limit the applicability of our holding to "close corporations," as hereinafter defined. Whether the holding should apply to other corporations is left for decision in another case, on a proper record.

A. Close Corporations. In previous opinions, we have alluded to the distinctive nature of the close corporation . . . , but have never defined precisely what is meant by a close corporation. There is no single, generally accepted definition. Some commentators emphasize an "integration of ownership and management". . . . Others focus on the number of stockholders and the nature of the market for the stock. In this view, close corporations have few stockholders; there is little market for corporate stock. The Supreme Court of Illinois adopted this latter view in Galler v. Galler, 203 N.E.2d 577 (1965): "For our purposes, a close corporation is one in which the stock is held in a few hands, or in a few families, and wherein it is not at all, or only rarely, dealt in by buying or selling." *Id.* at 583. . . . We accept aspects of both definitions. We deem a close corporation to be typified by: (1) a small number of stockholders; (2) no ready market for the corporate stock; and (3) substantial majority stockholder participation in the management, direction and operations of the corporation.

As thus defined, the close corporation bears striking resemblance to a partnership. Commentators and courts have noted that the close corporation is often little more than an "incorporated" or "chartered" partnership. . . . The stockholders "clothe" their partnership "with the benefits peculiar to a corporation, limited liability, perpetuity and the like." . . . In essence, though, the enterprise remains one in which ownership is limited to the original parties or transferees of their stock to whom the other stockholders have agreed, in which ownership and management

> **Connections: Unincorporated Entities**
>
> The owners of a small business now have additional garments with which to "clothe" themselves in corporate-type benefits. These include, of course, the limited liability company and, in some jurisdictions, the limited liability partnership. Issues involving fiduciary duty also arise in those contexts.

---

1. Between 1965 and 1969, the company offered to purchase the Donahue shares for amounts between $2,000 and $10,000 ($40 to $200 a share). The Donahues rejected these offers.

are in the same hands, and in which the owners are quite dependent on one another for the success of the enterprise. Many close corporations are "really partnerships, between two or three people who contribute their capital, skills, experience and labor." . . . Just as in a partnership, the relationship among the stockholders must be one of trust, confidence and absolute loyalty if the enterprise is to succeed. Close corporations with substantial assets and with more numerous stockholders are no different from smaller close corporations in this regard. All participants rely on the fidelity and abilities of those stockholders who hold office. Disloyalty and self-seeking conduct on the part of any stockholder will engender bickering, corporate stalemates, and, perhaps, efforts to achieve dissolution. . . .

Although the corporate form provides the above-mentioned advantages for the stockholders (limited liability, perpetuity, and so forth), it also supplies an opportunity for the majority stockholders to oppress or disadvantage minority stockholders. The minority is vulnerable to a variety of oppressive devices, termed "freeze-outs," which the majority may employ. An authoritative study of such "freeze-outs" enumerates some of the possibilities: "The squeezers (those who employ the freeze-out techniques) may refuse to declare dividends; they may drain off the corporation's earnings in the form of exorbitant salaries and bonuses to the majority shareholder-officers and perhaps to their relatives, or in the form of high rent by the corporation for property leased from majority shareholders . . . ; they may deprive minority shareholders of corporate offices and of employment by the company; they may cause the corporation to sell its assets at an inadequate price to the majority shareholders. . . ." F.H. O'Neal

and J. Derwin, Expulsion or Oppression of Business Associates, 42 (1961). In particular, the power of the board of directors, controlled by the majority, to declare or withhold dividends and to deny the minority employment is easily converted to a device to disadvantage minority stockholders. . . .

The minority can, of course, initiate suit against the majority and their directors. Self-serving conduct by directors is proscribed by the director's fiduciary obligation to the corporation. However, in practice, the plaintiff will find difficulty in challenging dividend or employment policies. Such policies are considered to be within the judgment of the directors. . . .

Thus, when these types of "freeze-outs" are attempted by the majority stockholders, the minority stockholders, cut off from all corporation-related revenues, must either suffer their losses or seek a buyer for their shares. Many minority stockholders will be unwilling or unable to wait for an alteration in majority policy. Typically, the minority stockholder in a close corporation has a substantial percentage of his personal assets invested in the corporation. The stockholder may have anticipated that his salary from his position with the corporation would be his livelihood. Thus, he cannot afford to wait passively. He must liquidate his investment in the close corporation in order to reinvest the funds in income-producing enterprises.

At this point, the true plight of the minority stockholder in a close corporation becomes manifest. He cannot easily reclaim his capital. In a large public corporation, the oppressed or dissident minority stockholder could sell his stock in order to extricate some of his invested capital. By definition, this market is not available for shares in the close corporation. In a partnership, a partner who feels abused by his fellow partners may cause dissolution by his "express will . . . at any time" and recover his share of partnership assets and accumulated profits. . . . If dissolution results in a breach of the partnership articles, the culpable partner will be liable in damages. By contrast, the stockholder in the close corporation or "incorporated partnership" may achieve dissolution and recovery of his share of the enterprise assets only by compliance with the rigorous terms of the applicable chapter of the General Laws. . . . To secure dissolution of the ordinary close corporation subject to G.L. c. 156B, the stockholder, in the absence of corporate deadlock, must own at least fifty per cent of the shares or have the advantage of a favorable provision in the articles of organization. The minority stockholder, by definition lacking fifty per cent of the corporate shares, can never "authorize" the corporation to file a petition for dissolution . . . by his own vote. He will seldom have at his disposal the requisite favorable provision in the articles of organization.

Thus, in a close corporation, the minority stockholders may be trapped in a disadvantageous situation. No outsider would knowingly assume the position of the disadvantaged minority. The outsider would have the same difficulties. To cut losses, the minority stockholder may be compelled to deal with the majority. This is the capstone of the majority plan. Majority "freeze-out" schemes which withhold dividends are designed to compel the minority to relinquish stock at inadequate prices. . . . When the minority stockholder agrees to sell out at less than fair value, the majority has won.

Because of the fundamental resemblance of the close corporation to the partnership, the trust and confidence which are essential to this scale and manner of enterprise, and the inherent danger to minority interests in the close corporation, we hold that stockholders in the close corporation owe one another substantially the same fiduciary duty in the operation of the enterprise that partners owe to one another. In our previous decisions, we have defined the standard of duty owed by partners to one another as the "utmost good faith and loyalty." Stockholders in close corporations must discharge their management and stockholder responsibilities in conformity with this strict good faith standard. They may not act out of avarice, expediency or self-interest in derogation of their duty of loyalty to the other stockholders and to the corporation.

We contrast this strict good faith standard with the somewhat less stringent standard of fiduciary duty to which directors and stockholders of all corporations must adhere in the discharge of their corporate responsibilities. Corporate directors are held to a good faith and inherent fairness standard of conduct . . . and are not "permitted to serve two masters whose interests are antagonistic."

Connections: Finest Loyalty

Officers and directors are fiduciaries and owe the corporation a duty of loyalty.

Justice Cardozo

Partners also are fiduciaries and, at common law, owed a duty of the finest loyalty.

Is that a distinction without a difference? It is not unusual to see *Meinhard v. Salmon* invoked as authority in a case involving corporate officers and directors—and it usually means the defendant is going to lose.

. . . "Their paramount duty is to the corporation, and their personal pecuniary interests are subordinate to that duty."
. . .

The more rigorous duty of partners and participants in a joint adventure, here extended to stockholders in a close corporation, was described by then Chief Judge Cardozo of the New York Court of Appeals in Meinhard v. Salmon, 164 N.E. 545 (1928): "Joint adventurers, like copartners, owe to one another, while the enterprise continues, the duty of the finest loyalty. Many forms of conduct permissible in a workaday world for those acting at arm's length, are forbidden to those bound by fiduciary ties. . . . Not honesty alone, but the punctilio of an honor the most sensitive, is then the standard of behavior." *Id.* at 546. . . .

. . . In the instant case, we extend this strict duty of loyalty to all stockholders in close corporations. The circumstances which justified findings of relationships of trust and confidence in these particular cases exist universally in modified form in all close corporations. . . .

B. Equal Opportunity in a Close Corporation. Under settled Massachusetts law, a domestic corporation, unless forbidden by statute, has the power to purchase its own shares. An agreement to reacquire stock "(is) enforceable, subject, at least, to the limitations that the purchase must be made in good faith and without prejudice to creditors and stockholders." When the corporation reacquiring its own stock is a close corporation, the purchase is subject to the additional requirement, in the light of our holding in this opinion, that the stockholders, who, as directors or controlling stockholders, caused the corporation to enter into the stock purchase agreement, must have acted with the utmost good faith and loyalty to the other stockholders.

To meet this test, if the stockholder whose shares were purchased was a member of the controlling group, the controlling stockholders must cause the corporation to offer each stockholder an equal opportunity to sell a ratable number of his shares to the corporation at an identical price. Purchase by the corporation confers substantial benefits on the members of the controlling group whose shares were purchased. These benefits are not available to the minority stockholders if the corporation does not also offer them an opportunity to sell their shares. The controlling group may not, consistent with its strict duty to the minority, utilize its control of the corporation to obtain special advantages and disproportionate benefit from its share ownership. . . .

The benefits conferred by the purchase are twofold: (1) provision of a market for shares; (2) access to corporate assets for personal use. By definition, there is no ready market for shares of a close corporation. The purchase creates a market for shares which previously had been unmarketable. It transforms a previously illiquid investment into a liquid one. If the close corporation purchases shares only from a member of the controlling group, the controlling stockholder can convert his shares into cash at a time when none of the other stockholders can. Consistent with its strict fiduciary duty, the controlling group may not utilize its control of the corporation to establish an exclusive market in previously unmarketable shares from which the minority stockholders are excluded. . . .

The purchase also distributes corporate assets to the stockholder whose shares were purchased. Unless an equal opportunity is given to all stockholders, the purchase of shares from a member of the controlling group operates as a preferential distribution of assets. In exchange for his shares, he receives a percentage of the contributed capital and accumulated profits of the enterprise. The funds he so receives are available for his personal use. The other stockholders benefit from no such access to corporate property and cannot withdraw their shares of the corporate profits and capital in this manner unless the controlling group acquiesces. Although the purchase price for the controlling stockholder's shares may seem fair to the corporation and other stockholders under the tests established in the prior case law, the controlling stockholder whose stock has been purchased has still received a relative advantage over his fellow stockholders, inconsistent with his strict fiduciary duty—an opportunity to turn corporate funds to personal use.

The rule of equal opportunity in stock purchases by close corporations provides equal access to these benefits for all stockholders. We hold that, in any case in which the controlling stockholders have exercised their power over the corporation to deny the minority such equal opportunity, the minority shall be entitled to appropriate relief. . . .

C. Application of the Law to this Case. We turn now to the application of the learning set forth above to the facts of the instant case.

The strict standard of duty is plainly applicable to the stockholders in Rodd Electrotype. Rodd Electrotype is a close corporation. Members of the Rodd and Donahue families are the sole owners of the corporation's stock. In actual numbers, the corporation, immediately prior to the corporate purchase of Harry Rodd's shares, had six stockholders. The shares have not been traded, and no market for them seems to exist. Harry Rodd, Charles Rodd, Frederick Rodd, William G. Mason (Phyllis Mason's husband), and the plaintiff's husband all worked for the corporation. The Rodds have retained the paramount management positions.

Through their control of these management positions and of the majority of the Rodd Electrotype stock, the Rodds effectively controlled the corporation. In testing the stock purchase from Harry Rodd against the applicable strict fiduciary standard, we treat the Rodd family as a single controlling group. We reject the defendants' contention that the Rodd family cannot be treated as a unit for this purpose. From the evidence, it is clear that the Rodd family was a close-knit one with strong community of interest. Harry Rodd had hired his sons to work in the family business, Rodd Electrotype. As he aged, he transferred

Connections: Sale of Control to Third Parties

When a majority shareholder sells control to a third party a different body of precedents is invoked. These precedents may create an issue even in the context of a publicly held corporation.

portions of his stock holdings to his children. Charles Rodd and Frederick Rodd were given positions of responsibility in the business as he withdrew from active management. In these circumstances, it is realistic to assume that appreciation, gratitude, and filial devotion would prevent the younger Rodds from opposing a plan which would provide funds for their father's retirement.

Moreover, a strong motive of interest requires that the Rodds be considered a controlling group. When Charles Rodd and Frederick Rodd were called on to represent the corporation in its dealings with their father, they must have known that further advancement within the corporation and benefits would follow their father's retirement and the purchase of his stock. The corporate purchase would take only forty-five of Harry Rodd's eighty-one shares. The remaining thirty-six shares were to be divided among Harry Rodd's children in equal amounts by gift and sale. Receipt of their portion of the thirty-six shares and purchase by the corporation of forty-five shares would effectively transfer full control of the corporation to Frederick Rodd and Charles Rodd, if they chose to act in concert with each other or if one of them chose to ally with his sister. Moreover, Frederick Rodd was the obvious successor to his father as director and corporate treasurer when those posts became vacant after his father's retirement. Failure to complete the corporate purchase (in other words, impeding their father's retirement plan) would have delayed, and perhaps have suspended indefinitely, the transfer of these benefits to the younger Rodds. They could not be expected to oppose their father's wishes in this matter. Although the defendants are correct when they assert that no express agreement involving a quid pro quo—subsequent stock gifts for votes from the directors—was proved, no express agreement is necessary to demonstrate the identity of interest which disciplines a controlling group acting in unison. . . .

On its face, then, the purchase of Harry Rodd's shares by the corporation is a breach of the duty which the controlling stockholders, the Rodds, owed to the minority stockholders, the plaintiff and her son. The purchase distributed a portion of the corporate assets to Harry Rodd, a member of the controlling group, in exchange for his shares. The plaintiff and her son were not offered an equal opportunity to sell their shares to the corporation. In fact, their efforts to obtain an equal opportunity were rebuffed by the corporate representative. As the trial judge found, they did not, in any manner, ratify the transaction with Harry Rodd.

Because of the foregoing, we hold that the plaintiff is entitled to relief. Two forms of suitable relief are set out hereinafter. The judge below is to enter an appropriate judgment. The judgment may require Harry Rodd to remit $36,000 with interest at the legal rate from July 15, 1970, to Rodd Electrotype in exchange for forty-five shares of Rodd Electrotype treasury stock. This, in substance, is the specific relief requested in the plaintiff's bill of complaint. Interest is manifestly appropriate. A stockholder, who, in violation of his fiduciary duty to the other stockholders, has obtained assets from his corporation and has had those assets available for his own use, must pay for that use. In the alternative, the judgment may require Rodd Electrotype to purchase all of the plaintiff's shares for $36,000 without interest. In the circumstances of this case, we view this as the equal opportunity which the plaintiff should have received. Harry Rodd's retention of thirty-six shares, which were to be sold and given to his children within a year of the Rodd Electrotype purchase, cannot disguise the fact that the corporation acquired one hundred per cent of that portion of his holdings (forty-five shares) which he did not intend his children to own. The plaintiff is entitled to have one hundred per cent of her forty-five shares similarly purchased.

■ **Think about this:**

(A) The trial court implicitly found that the directors of Rodd Electrotype had discharged their duty of loyalty, and the Massachusetts Supreme Judicial Court does not seem to disagree. How about you?

(B) Is there a difference between "inherent fairness" and "finest loyalty"?

(C) As a matter of public policy, should the shareholders of close corporations be permitted to limit the fiduciary duties they owe one another?

(D) Could there ever be a legitimate business reason for the directors of a close corporation to want to purchase one shareholder's shares but not another's?

(E) Can the Massachusetts Supreme Judicial Court's alternative remedy possibly be right? If Mrs. Donahue owned only one share, should she still receive $36,000?

 Dear Prof.: What about control premiums? Didn't you say someplace else in the book that shares that carry control are more valuable?

Well, yes. Controlling shares sometimes command a price that is quite a bit higher than the price of non-controlling shares (some studies put it at 30-40 percent). Keep in mind, though, that as the court saw it in *Donahue*, control did not change hands, it just shifted from one generation to the next.

One late-twentieth-century innovation in the laws of partnership was the result of dissatisfaction in some quarters with the amorphous concept of "finest loyalty." Thus, for a time, both the Revised Uniform Partnership Act and the Uniform Limited Liability Company Act provided that the duty of loyalty was limited to the duties listed below. Both Acts now more modestly provide (both in §409(b)) that the duty of loyalty *includes* the following obligations:

Room to Argue: Limits on Loyalty

The modern trend toward limiting the duty of loyalty often is justified in terms of efficiency. There are, however, fierce proponents of the older, more robust versions. You can read more about the debate in the online Supplement.

(1) to account to the [partnership/company] and hold as trustee for it any property, profit, or benefit derived by the [partner/member]:

(A) in the conduct and winding up of the [partnership/company]'s business; or

(B) from a use by the [partner/member] of the [partnership/company]'s property; or

(C) from the appropriation of a [partnership/company] opportunity;

(2) to refrain from dealing with the [partnership/company] in the conduct or winding up of the [partnership/company] business as or on behalf of a person having an interest adverse to the [partnership/company]; and

(3) to refrain from competing with the [partnership/company] in the conduct of the [partnership/company]'s business before the dissolution of the [partnership/company].

Partners and members are not permitted to eliminate the duty of loyalty, but (under §105 of each of the two Acts) can, in the partnership or operating agreement, eliminate or alter the aspects of the duty of loyalty listed in §409(b), as well as identify specific types of activities that do not violate the duty of loyalty, both subject to a test of whether the resulting limitation is manifestly unreasonable. In addition, they can, by a method specified in the relevant agreement, authorize or ratify acts that otherwise would violate the duty of loyalty. The ability to authorize or ratify apparently is not circumscribed by the concept of "manifestly unreasonable," but the relevant decision maker(s) must be "disinterested and independent" and must act "after full disclosure of all material facts."

One would expect these developments in unincorporated entity law to have gravitational pull on the precedents relating to close corporations.

 Time Out for PR

Note the roles in *Donahue* of Attorney Harold E. Magnuson—company clerk, director, defendant, and defense attorney. He almost certainly also was general counsel to the corporation.

There are, of course, rules about both testifying and acting as an attorney at the same trial (see American Bar Association Model Rule of Professional Conduct 3.7), and against having a proprietary interest in litigation one is conducting for another (Model Rule 1.8(i)). Apart from those, might Mrs. Donahue have any reason to complain? Does a corporation's attorney represent its shareholders? The general answer is "no—unless." The creation of the attorney-client relationship is based on the reasonable understanding of the putative client, and in the close corporation context it is easy for shareholders to become confused.

The *Donahue* approach required a controlling shareholder selling shares to a close corporation to cause the corporation to give minority shareholders an "equal opportunity" to sell their shares. "Closeness" was, of course, determined as a matter of the court's own common law test.

However, a number of states have addressed close corporation problems with separate statutory regimes, frequently referred to as "integrated close corporation statutes." The idea is that, by causing the corporation to file the appropriate election, the shareholders will claim such perceived advantages as the ability to participate directly in management. There generally are stated cut-offs for the ability to maintain integrated close corporation status. In Delaware, for instance, there can be no more than 30 shareholders. The following case, among other things, addresses the effect of the availability of this special form on the shareholders' rights against one another.

NIXON v. BLACKWELL

Supreme Court of Delaware
626 A.2d 1366 (1992)

VEASEY, Chief Justice: . . .

I. FACTS . . .

Plaintiffs are 14 minority stockholders of Class B, non-voting, stock of E.C. Barton & Co. (the "Corporation"). [Each plaintiff received his or her shares by reason of gift or bequest from the founder of the Corporation, who intended that the entity be employee-controlled through the Class A stock.] The individual defendants are the members of the board of directors (the "Board" or the "directors"). The Corporation is also a defendant. Plaintiffs collectively own only Class B stock, and own no Class A stock. Their total holdings comprise approximately 25 percent of all the common stock outstanding as of the end of fiscal year 1989.

At all relevant times, the Board consisted of ten individuals who either are currently employed, or were once employed, by the Corporation. At the time this suit was filed, these directors collectively owned approximately 47.5 percent of all the outstanding Class A shares. The remaining Class A shares were held by certain other present and former employees of the Corporation. . . .

D. The Employee Stock Ownership Plan ("ESOP")

In November 1975 the Corporation established an ESOP designed to hold Class B non-voting stock for the benefit of eligible employees of the Corporation. The ESOP is a tax-qualified profit-sharing plan whereby employees of the Corporation are allocated a share of the assets held by the plan in proportion to their annual compensation, subject to certain vesting requirements. The ESOP is funded by annual cash contributions from the Corporation. Under the plan, terminating and retiring employees are entitled to receive their interest in the

ESOP by taking Class B stock or cash in lieu of stock. It appears from the record that most terminating employees and retirees elect to receive cash in lieu of stock. The Corporation commissions an annual appraisal of the Corporation to determine the value of its stock for ESOP purposes. Thus, the ESOP provides employee Class B stockholders with a substantial measure of liquidity not available to non-employee stockholders. The Corporation had the option of repurchasing Class A stock from the employees upon their retirement or death. The estates of the employee stockholders did not have a corresponding right to put the stock to the Corporation.

E. The Key Man Insurance Policies

The Corporation also purchased certain key man life insurance policies with death benefits payable to the Corporation. Several early policies insuring the lives of key executives and directors were purchased during Mr. Barton's lifetime with death benefits payable to the Corporation. In 1982 the Corporation purchased additional key man policies in connection with agreements entered into between the Corporation and nine key officers and directors. Each executive executed an agreement giving the Corporation a call option to substitute Class B non-voting stock for their Class A voting stock upon the occurrence of certain events, including death and termination of employment, so that the voting shares could be reissued to new key personnel. In return, the Board adopted a resolution creating a non-binding recommendation that a portion of the key man life insurance proceeds be used to repurchase the exchanged Class B stock from the executives' estates at a price at least equal to 80 percent of their ESOP value. . . . [T]he ultimate decision on the use of insurance proceeds for this purpose was left to the discretion of the Corporation's management or the Board. . . .

II. PROCEEDINGS IN THE COURT OF CHANCERY . . .

At trial, the plaintiffs charged the defendants with (1) attempting to force the minority stockholders to sell their shares at a discount by embarking on a scheme to pay negligible dividends, (2) breaching their fiduciary duties by authorizing excessive compensation for themselves and other employees of the Corporation, and (3) breaching their fiduciary duties by pursuing a discriminatory liquidity policy that favors employee stockholders over non-employee stockholders through the ESOP and key man life insurance policies. The plaintiffs sought money damages for past dividends, a one-time liquidity dividend, and a guarantee of future dividends at a specified rate.

The Vice Chancellor held that the Corporation's low-dividend policy was within the bounds of business judgment, that the executive compensation levels were not excessive, and ruled in favor of defendants on these issues. The Vice Chancellor further held, however, that the defendant directors had breached their fiduciary duties to the minority. The basis for this ruling was that it was "inherently unfair" for the defendants to establish the ESOP and to purchase key man life insurance to provide liquidity for themselves while providing no comparable method by which the non-employee Class B stockholders may liquidate their stock at fair value. Holding that the "needs of all stockholders must be considered and addressed when providing liquidity," the court ruled that the directors breached their fiduciary duties, and granted relief to plaintiffs. The trial court ruled against the plaintiffs on all the other issues. Since plaintiffs have not appealed those rulings, they are not before this Court. . . .

V. APPLICABLE PRINCIPLES OF SUBSTANTIVE LAW

Defendants contend that the trial court erred in not applying the business judgment rule. Since the defendants benefited from the ESOP and could have benefited from the key man life insurance beyond that which benefited other stockholders generally, the defendants are on both sides of the transaction. For that reason, we agree with the trial court that the entire fairness test applies to this aspect of the case. Accordingly, defendants have the burden of showing the entire fairness of those transactions. . . .

The trial court in this case, however, appears to have adopted the novel legal principle that Class B stockholders had a right to "liquidity" equal to that which the court found to be available to the defendants. It is well established in our jurisprudence that stockholders need not always be treated equally for all purposes. See Unocal Corp. v. Mesa Petroleum Co., Del. Supr., 493 A.2d 946, 957 (1985) ("Unocal") (discriminatory exchange offer held valid); and Cheff v. Mathes, Del. Supr., 199 A.2d 548, 554-56 (1964) (selective stock repurchase held valid). To hold that fairness necessarily requires precise equality is to beg the question:

> Many scholars, though few courts, conclude that one aspect of fiduciary duty is the equal treatment of investors. Their argument takes the following form: fiduciary principles require fair conduct; equal treatment is fair conduct; hence, fiduciary principles require equal treatment. The conclusion does not follow. The argument depends on an equivalence between *equal* and *fair* treatment. To say that fiduciary principles require equal treatment is to beg the question whether investors would contract for equal or even equivalent treatment.

Frank H. Easterbrook and Daniel R. Fischel, The Economic Structure of Corporate Law 110 (1991) (emphasis in original). This holding of the trial court overlooks the significant facts that the minority stockholders were not: (a) employees of the Corporation; (b) entitled to share in an ESOP; (c) qualified for key man insurance; or (d) protected by specific provisions in the certificate of incorporation, by-laws, or a stockholders' agreement.

There is support in this record for the fact that the ESOP is a corporate benefit and was established, at least in part, to benefit the Corporation. Generally speaking, the creation of ESOPs is a normal corporate practice and is generally thought to benefit the corporation. The same is

---

Room to Argue: The Relationship Between Fairness and Efficiency

The scholarly debate over what is fair, what is efficient, and whether they in fact converge, was somewhat feverish in the 1980s and 1990s. It is a bit quieter today, but still is alive and well. You can read more in the online Supplement.

true generally with respect to key man insurance programs. If such corporate practices were necessarily to require equal treatment for non-employee stockholders, that would be a matter for legislative determination in Delaware. There is no such legislation to that effect. If we were to adopt such a rule, our decision would border on judicial legislation.

Accordingly, we hold that the Vice Chancellor erred as a matter of law in concluding that the liquidity afforded to the employee stockholders by the ESOP and the key man insurance required substantially equal treatment for the non-employee stockholders. . . .

We hold on this record that defendants have met their burden of establishing the entire fairness of their dealings with the non-employee Class B stockholders, and are entitled to judgment. The record is sufficient to conclude that plaintiffs' claim that the defendant directors have maintained a discriminatory policy of favoring Class A employee stockholders over Class B non-employee stockholders is without merit. . . . An ESOP, for example, is normally established for employees. Accordingly, there is no inequity in limiting ESOP benefits to the employee stockholders. Indeed, it makes no sense to include non-employees in ESOP benefits. The fact that the Class B stock represented 75 percent of the Corporation's total equity is irrelevant to the issue of fair dealing. The Class B stock was given no voting rights because those stockholders were not intended to have a direct voice in the management and operation of the Corporation. They were simply passive investors—entitled to be treated fairly but not necessarily to be treated equally. The fortunes of the Corporation rested with the Class A employee stockholders and the Class B stockholders benefited from the multiple increases in value of their Class B stock. Moreover, the Board made continuing efforts to buy back the Class B stock. . . .

VI. NO SPECIAL RULES FOR A "CLOSELY-HELD CORPORATION" NOT QUALIFIED AS A "CLOSE CORPORATION" UNDER SUBCHAPTER XIV OF THE DELAWARE GENERAL CORPORATION LAW

We wish to address one further matter which was raised at oral argument before this Court: Whether there should be any special, judicially-created rules to "protect" minority stockholders of closely-held Delaware corporations.[2]

The case at bar points up the basic dilemma of minority stockholders in receiving fair value for their stock as to which there is no market and no market valuation. It is not difficult to be sympathetic, in the abstract, to a stockholder who finds himself or herself in that position. A stockholder who bargains for stock in a closely-held corporation and who pays for those shares (unlike the

---

2. Compare ROBERT B. THOMPSON, THE SHAREHOLDER'S CAUSE OF ACTION FOR OPPRESSION, 48 BUS. LAW. 699 (1993) and F. HODGE O'NEAL AND ROBERT B. THOMPSON, O'NEAL'S CLOSE CORPORATIONS: LAW AND PRACTICE, §§8.07-8.09 (3d ed. 1987) (favoring court formulation of a special rule protecting the minority from oppression) with FRANK H. EASTERBROOK AND DANIEL R. FISCHEL, THE ECONOMIC STRUCTURE OF CORPORATE LAW 228-52 (1991) (noting that "courts have found the equal opportunity rule . . . impossible to administer," *id.* at 247).

plaintiffs in this case who acquired their stock through gift) can make a business judgment whether to buy into such a minority position, and if so on what terms. One could bargain for definitive provisions of self-ordering permitted to a Delaware corporation through the certificate of incorporation or by-laws by reason of the provisions in 8 Del. C. §§102, 109, and 141(a). Moreover, in addition to such mechanisms, a stockholder intending to buy into a minority position in a Delaware corporation may enter into definitive stockholder agreements, and such agreements may provide for elaborate earnings tests, buy-out provisions, voting trusts, or other voting agreements. See, e.g., 8 Del. C. §218. . . .

The tools of good corporate practice are designed to give a purchasing minority stockholder the opportunity to bargain for protection before parting with consideration. It would do violence to normal corporate practice and our corporation law to fashion an *ad hoc* ruling which would result in a court-imposed stockholder buy-out for which the parties had not contracted.

In 1967, when the Delaware General Corporation Law was significantly revised, a new Subchapter XIV entitled "Close Corporations; Special Provisions," became a part of that law for the first time. While these provisions were patterned in theory after close corporation statutes in Florida and Maryland, "the Delaware provisions were unique and influenced the development of similar legislation in a number of other states. . . ." *See* Ernest L. Folk, III, Rodman Ward, Jr., and Edward P. Welch, 2 Folk on the Delaware General Corporation Law 404 (1988). Subchapter XIV is a narrowly constructed statute which applies only to a corporation which is designated as a "close corporation" in its certificate of incorporation, and which fulfills other requirements, including a limitation to 30 on the number of stockholders, that all classes of stock have to have at least one restriction on transfer, and that there be no "public offering." 8 Del. C. §342. Accordingly, subchapter XIV applies only to "close corporations," as defined in section 342. "Unless a corporation elects to become a close corporation under this subchapter in the manner prescribed in this subchapter, it shall be subject in all respects to this chapter, except this subchapter." 8 Del. C. §341. The corporation before the Court in this matter, is not a "close corporation." Therefore it is not governed by the provisions of Subchapter XIV.[3]

---

3. We do not intend to imply that, if the Corporation had been a close corporation under Subchapter XIV, the result in this case would have been different.

> [S]tatutory close corporations have not found particular favor with practitioners. Practitioners have for the most part viewed the complex statutory provisions underlying the purportedly simplified operational procedures for close corporations as legal quicksand of uncertain depth and have adopted the view that the objectives sought by the subchapter are achievable for their clients with considerably less uncertainty by cloaking a conventionally created corporation with the panoply of charter provisions, transfer restrictions, by-laws, stockholders' agreements, buy-sell arrangements, irrevocable proxies, voting trusts or other contractual mechanisms which were and remain the traditional method for accomplishing the goals sought by the close corporation provisions.

David A. Drexler, Lewis S. Black, Jr., and A. Gilchrist Sparks, III, Delaware Corporation Law and Practice §43.01 (1993).

One cannot read into the situation presented in the case at bar any special relief for the minority stockholders in this closely-held, but not statutory "close corporation" because the provisions of Subchapter XIV relating to close corporations and other statutory schemes preempt the field in their respective areas. It would run counter to the spirit of the doctrine of independent legal significance, and would be inappropriate judicial legislation for this Court to fashion a special judicially-created rule for minority investors when the entity does not fall within those statutes, or when there are no negotiated special provisions in the certificate of incorporation, by-laws, or stockholder agreements. The entire fairness test, correctly applied and articulated, is the proper judicial approach.

VII. CONCLUSION

We hold that the Court of Chancery correctly determined that the entire fairness test is applicable in reviewing the actions of the defendants in establishing and implementing the ESOP and the key man life insurance program. The Vice Chancellor erred, however, as a matter of law in concluding on this record that the defendants had not carried their burden of showing entire fairness. The trial court erroneously undertook to create a novel theory of corporation law and erroneously failed to set forth and apply articulable standards for determining fairness. Moreover, certain findings of fact by the trial court were not the product of an orderly and deductive reasoning process.

In a case such as this where the business judgment rule is not applicable and the entire fairness test is applicable, the imposition of the latter test is not, alone, outcome-determinative. The doctrine of entire fairness does not lend itself to bright line precision or rigid doctrine. Yet it does not necessarily require equality, it cannot be a matter of total subjectivity on the part of the trial court, and it cannot result in a random pattern of *ad hoc* determinations which could do violence to the stability of our corporation law.

Accordingly, we REVERSE the judgment of the Court of Chancery and REMAND the matter for proceedings not inconsistent with this opinion.

■ **Think about this:**

(F) As *Nixon* suggests, even in the absence of the special duty recognized in *Donahue*, Mrs. Donahue would still have had traditional fiduciary claims at her disposal, and on the facts could probably have made out loyalty breaches without too much trouble. Assume she could overcome all procedural hurdles in suing derivatively, and assume she could make her case on the merits. Would the remedy be sufficient? How would it differ from the remedy available in *Donahue*? And, ultimately, what remedy does she *really* want?

(G) The entire fairness test will require, among other things, that the interested decision maker show that the decision was fair to the

corporation. If that test were applied to the *Donahue* facts, what would you expect the result to be?

(H) If you applied the *Donahue* test to the *Nixon* facts, what would you expect the result to be?

(I) If you were counseling one of two prospective 50-percent shareholders on corporate formation matters, would you advise incorporating in Delaware? Massachusetts? Or does it just not matter?

C. Generalizing *Donahue*: The *Wilkes* Burden-Shifting Framework and the Problem of Routine Management

As mentioned, before it could really achieve wide dissemination, *Donahue* required some refinement and generalization. The *Donahue* court developed its "duty of finest loyalty" approach to close corporations in a context specifically involving what could be described as "typical" shareholder rights. The Massachusetts Supreme Judicial Court returned the year after *Donahue* to struggle with how to generalize its standard in quite a different situation—the right to remain employed. *Wilkes* is important not for its special treatment of that narrow circumstance, but for its consideration of how to generalize *Donahue* to the whole range of ordinary decision making.

WILKES v. SPRINGSIDE NURSING HOME

Supreme Judicial Court of Massachusetts
353 N.E.2d 657 (1976)

HENNESSEY, Chief Justice.

On August 5, 1971, the plaintiff (Wilkes) filed a bill in equity for declaratory judgment in the Probate Court for Berkshire County, naming as defendants T. Edward Quinn (Quinn), Leon L. Riche (Riche), the First Agricultural National Bank of Berkshire County and Frank Sutherland MacShane as executors under the will of Lawrence R. Connor (Connor), and the Springside Nursing Home, Inc. (Springside or the corporation). Wilkes alleged that he, Quinn, Riche and Dr. Hubert A. Pipkin (Pipkin[, who later transferred his interest to Connor]) entered into a partnership agreement in 1951, prior to the incorporation of Springside, which agreement was breached in 1967 when Wilkes's salary was terminated and he was voted out as an officer and director of the corporation. Wilkes sought, among other forms of relief, damages in the amount of the salary he would have received had he continued as a director and officer of Springside subsequent to March, 1967.

. . . On appeal [of the dismissal of his action], Wilkes argued in the alternative that (1) he should recover damages for breach of the alleged partnership agreement; and (2) he should recover damages because the defendants, as majority stockholders in Springside, breached their fiduciary duty to him as a minority stockholder by their action in February and March, 1967.

... [W]e reverse ... and order the entry of a judgment substantially granting the relief sought by Wilkes under the second alternative set forth above. ...

In 1951 Wilkes acquired an option to purchase a building and lot located on the corner of Springside Avenue and North Street in Pittsfield, Massachusetts, the building having previously housed the Hillcrest Hospital. Though Wilkes was principally engaged in the roofing and siding business, he had gained a reputation locally for profitable dealings in real estate. Riche, an acquaintance of Wilkes, learned of the option, and interested Quinn (who was known to Wilkes through membership on the draft board in Pittsfield) and Pipkin (an acquaintance of both Wilkes and Riche) in joining Wilkes in his investment. The four men met and decided to participate jointly in the purchase of the building and lot as a real estate investment which, they believed, had good profit potential on resale or rental.

The parties later determined that the property would have its greatest potential for profit if it were operated by them as a nursing home. Wilkes consulted his attorney, who advised him that if the four men were to operate the contemplated nursing home as planned, they would be partners and would be liable for any debts incurred by the partnership and by each other. On the attorney's suggestion, and after consultation among themselves, ownership of the property was vested in Springside, a corporation organized under Massachusetts law.

Each of the four men invested $1,000 and subscribed to ten shares of $100 par value stock in Springside[, later proportionally increased to 115 shares each]. At the time of incorporation it was understood by all of the parties that each would be a director of Springside and each would participate actively in the management and decision making involved in operating the corporation.[4] It was, further, the understanding and intention of all the parties that, corporate resources permitting, each would receive money from the corporation in equal amounts as long as each assumed an active and ongoing responsibility for carrying a portion of the burdens necessary to operate the business.

The work involved in establishing and operating a nursing home was roughly apportioned, and each of the four men undertook his respective tasks.[5] Initially, Riche was elected president of Springside, Wilkes was elected treasurer

---

4. Wilkes testified before the master that, when the corporate officers were elected, all four men "were . . . guaranteed directorships." Riche's understanding of the parties' intentions was that they all wanted to play a part in the management of the corporation and wanted to have some "say" in the risks involved; that, to this end, they all would be directors; and that "unless you (were) a director and officer you could not participate in the decisions of (the) enterprise."

5. Wilkes took charge of the repair, upkeep and maintenance of the physical plant and grounds; Riche assumed supervision over the kitchen facilities and dietary and food aspects of the home; Pipkin was to make himself available if and when medical problems arose; and Quinn dealt with the personnel and administrative aspects of the nursing home, serving informally as a managing director. Quinn further coordinated the activities of the other parties and served as a communication link among them when matters had to be discussed and decisions had to be made without a formal meeting.

[(a position he retained until 1967)], and Quinn was elected clerk. Each of the four was listed in the articles of organization as a director of the corporation.

At some time in 1952, it became apparent that the operational income and cash flow from the business were sufficient to permit the four stockholders to draw money from the corporation on a regular basis. Each of the four original parties initially received $35 a week from the corporation. As time went on the weekly return to each was increased until, in 1955, it totalled $100. . . .

In 1965 the stockholders decided to sell a portion of the corporate property to Quinn [(then president of the corporation)] who, in addition to being a stockholder in Springside, possessed an interest in another corporation which desired to operate a rest home on the property. Wilkes was successful in prevailing on the other stockholders of Springside to procure a higher sale price for the property than Quinn apparently anticipated paying or desired to pay. After the sale was consummated, the relationship between Quinn and Wilkes began to deteriorate.

The bad blood between Quinn and Wilkes affected the attitudes of both Riche and Connor. As a consequence of the strained relations among the parties, Wilkes, in January of 1967, gave notice of his intention to sell his shares for an amount based on an appraisal of their value. In February of 1967 a directors' meeting was held and the board exercised its right to establish the salaries of its officers and employees.[6] A schedule of payments was established whereby Quinn was to receive a substantial weekly increase and Riche and Connor were to continue receiving $100 a week. Wilkes, however, was left off the list of those to whom a salary was to be paid. The directors also set the annual meeting of the stockholders for March, 1967.

At the annual meeting in March, Wilkes was not reelected as a director, nor was he reelected as an officer of the corporation. He was further informed that neither his services nor his presence at the nursing home was wanted by his associates.

The meetings of the directors and stockholders in early 1967, the master found, were used as a vehicle to force Wilkes out of active participation in the management and operation of the corporation and to cut off all corporate payments to him. Though the board of directors had the power to dismiss any officers or employees for misconduct or neglect of duties, there was no indication in the minutes of the board of directors' meeting of February, 1967, that the failure to establish a salary for Wilkes was based on either ground. The severance of Wilkes from the payroll resulted not from misconduct or neglect of duties, but because of the personal desire of Quinn, Riche and Connor to prevent him from continuing to receive money from the corporation. Despite a continuing deterioration in his personal relationship with his associates, Wilkes had consistently endeavored to carry on his responsibilities to the corporation in the same satisfactory manner and with the same degree of competence he had previously shown. Wilkes was at

---

6. The by-laws of the corporation provided that the directors, subject to the approval of the stockholders, had the power to fix the salaries of all officers and employees. This power, however, up until February, 1967, had not been exercised formally; all payments made to the four participants in the venture had resulted from the informal but unanimous approval of all the parties concerned.

all times willing to carry on his responsibilities and participation if permitted so to do and provided that he receive his weekly stipend.

1. We turn to Wilkes's claim for damages based on a breach of the fiduciary duty owed to him by the other participants in this venture. In light of the theory underlying this claim, we do not consider it vital to our approach to this case whether the claim is governed by partnership law or the law applicable to business corporations. This is so because, as all the parties agree, Springside was at all times relevant to this action, a close corporation as we have recently defined such an entity in [Donahue v. Rodd Electrotype Co., 328 N.E.2d 505 (1975)]. . . .

In *Donahue*, . . . we held that "stockholders in the close corporation owe one another substantially the same fiduciary duty in the operation of the enterprise that partners owe to one another." . . . As determined in previous decisions of this court, the standard of duty owed by partners to one another is one of "utmost good faith and loyalty." . . . Thus, we concluded in *Donahue*, with regard to "their actions relative to the operations of the enterprise and the effects of that operation on the rights and investments of other stockholders," "[s]tockholders in close corporations must discharge their management and stockholder responsibilities in conformity with this strict good faith standard. They may not act out of avarice, expediency or self-interest in derogation of their duty of loyalty to the other stockholders and to the corporation." . . .

In the *Donahue* case we recognized that one peculiar aspect of close corporations was the opportunity afforded to majority stockholders to oppress, disadvantage or "freeze out" minority stockholders. In *Donahue* itself, for example, the majority refused the minority an equal opportunity to sell a ratable number of shares to the corporation at the same price available to the majority. The net result of this refusal, we said, was that the minority could be forced to "sell out at less than fair value," . . . since there is by definition no ready market for minority stock in a close corporation.

"Freeze outs," however, may be accomplished by the use of other devices. One such device which has proved to be particularly effective in accomplishing the purpose of the majority is to deprive minority stockholders of corporate offices and of employment with the corporation. . . . This "freeze-out" technique has been successful because courts fairly consistently have been disinclined to interfere in those facets of internal corporate operations, such as the selection and retention or dismissal of officers, directors and employees, which essentially involve management decisions subject to the principle of majority control. As one authoritative source has said, "(M)any courts apparently feel that there is a legitimate sphere in which the controlling (directors or) shareholders can act in their own interest even if the minority suffers." F.H. O'Neal, "Squeeze-Outs" of Minority Shareholders 59, 78-79 (1975).

The denial of employment to the minority at the hands of the majority is especially pernicious in some instances. A guaranty of employment with the corporation may have been one of the "basic reason[s] why a minority owner has invested capital in the firm." Symposium—The Close Corporation, 52 Nw. U. L. Rev. 345, 392 (1957). The

JD/MBA: Salaries vs. Dividends

Shareholders of closely held companies commonly prefer salaries to dividends as a method of reducing federal income tax burden. There is more about this subject in the online Supplement.

minority stockholder typically depends on his salary as the principal return on his investment, since the "earnings of a close corporation . . . are distributed in major part in salaries, bonuses and retirement benefits." 1 F.H. O'Neal, Close Corporations §1.07 (1971).[7] Other noneconomic interests of the minority stockholder are likewise injuriously affected by barring him from corporate office. Such action severely restricts his participation in the management of the enterprise, and he is relegated to enjoying those benefits incident to his status as a stockholder. In sum, by terminating a minority stockholder's employment or by severing him from a position as an officer or director, the majority effectively frustrate the minority stockholder's purposes in entering on the corporate venture and also deny him an equal return on his investment.

The *Donahue* decision acknowledged, as a "natural outgrowth" of the case law of this Commonwealth, a strict obligation on the part of majority stockholders in a close corporation to deal with the minority with the utmost good faith and loyalty. On its face, this strict standard is applicable in the instant case. The distinction between the majority action in *Donahue* and the majority action in this case is more one of form than of substance. Nevertheless, we are concerned that untempered application of the strict good faith standard enunciated in *Donahue* to cases such as the one before us will result in the imposition of limitations on legitimate action by the controlling group in a close corporation which will unduly hamper its effectiveness in managing the corporation in the best interests of all concerned. The majority, concededly, have certain rights to what has been termed "selfish ownership" in the corporation which should be balanced against the concept of their fiduciary obligation to the minority. . . .

Therefore, when minority stockholders in a close corporation bring suit against the majority alleging a breach of the strict good faith duty owed to them by the majority, we must carefully analyze the action taken by the controlling stockholders in the individual case. It must be asked whether the controlling group can demonstrate a legitimate business purpose for its action. In asking this question, we acknowledge the fact that the controlling group in a close corporation must have some room to maneuver in establishing the business policy of the corporation. It must have a large measure of discretion, for example, in declaring or withholding dividends, deciding whether to merge or consolidate, establishing the salaries of corporate officers, dismissing directors with

---

7. We note here that the master found that Springside never declared or paid a dividend to its stockholders.

A Shifting Burden

or without cause, and hiring and firing corporate employees.

When an asserted business purpose for their action is advanced by the majority, however, we think it is open to minority stockholders to demonstrate that the same legitimate objective could have been achieved through an alternative course of action less harmful to the minority's interest. If called on to settle a dispute, our courts must weigh the legitimate business purpose, if any, against the practicability of a less harmful alternative.

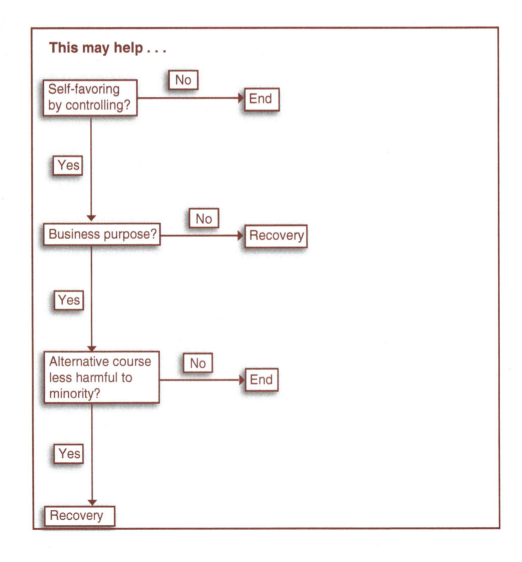

Applying this approach to the instant case it is apparent that the majority stockholders in Springside have not shown a legitimate business purpose for severing Wilkes from the payroll of the corporation or for refusing to reelect him as a salaried officer and director. The master's subsidiary findings relating to the purpose of the meetings of the directors and stockholders in February and March, 1967, are supported by the evidence. There was no showing of misconduct on Wilkes's part as a director, officer or employee of the corporation which would lead us to approve the majority action as a legitimate response to the disruptive nature of an undesirable individual bent on injuring or destroying the corporation. On the contrary, it appears that Wilkes had always accomplished his assigned share of the duties competently, and that he had never indicated an unwillingness to continue to do so.

It is an inescapable conclusion from all the evidence that the action of the majority stockholders here was a designed "freeze out" for which no legitimate business purpose has been suggested. Furthermore, we may infer that a design to pressure Wilkes into selling his shares to the corporation at a price below their value well may have been at the heart of the majority's plan.[8]

In the context of this case, several factors bear directly on the duty owed to Wilkes by his associates. At a minimum, the duty of utmost good faith and loyalty would demand that the majority consider that their action was in disregard of a long-standing policy of the stockholders that each would be a director of the corporation and that employment with the corporation would go hand in hand with stock ownership; that Wilkes was one of the four originators of the nursing home venture; and that Wilkes, like the others, had invested his capital and time for more than fifteen years with the expectation that he would continue to participate in corporate decisions. Most important is the plain fact that the cutting off of Wilkes's salary, together with the fact that the corporation never declared a dividend, assured that Wilkes would receive no return at all from the corporation.

The question of Wilkes's damages at the hands of the majority has not been thoroughly explored on the record before us. Wilkes, in his original complaint, sought damages in the amount of the $100 a week he believed he was entitled to from the time his salary was terminated up until the time this action was commenced. However, the record shows that, after Wilkes was severed from the corporate payroll, the schedule of salaries and payments made to the other stockholders varied from time to time. In addition, the duties assumed by the other stockholders after Wilkes was deprived of his share of the corporate earnings appear to have changed in significant respects.[9] Any resolution of this question must take into account whether the corporation was dissolved during the pendency of this litigation.

---

8. This inference arises from the fact that Connor, acting on behalf of the three controlling stockholders, offered to purchase Wilkes's shares for a price Connor admittedly would not have accepted for his own shares.

9. In fairness to Wilkes, who, as the master found, was at all times ready and willing to work for the corporation, it should be noted that neither the other stockholders nor their representatives may be heard to say that Wilkes's duties were performed by them and that Wilkes's damages should, for that reason, be diminished.

. . . Wilkes shall be allowed to recover from Riche, the estate of T. Edward Quinn and the estate of Lawrence R. Connor, ratably, according to the inequitable enrichment of each, the salary he would have received had he remained an officer and director of Springside. In considering the issue of damages the judge on remand shall take into account the extent to which any remaining corporate funds of Springside may be diverted to satisfy Wilkes's claim. . . .

■ **Think about this:**

(J) Why should the recovery come from the majority shareholders, rather than the corporation? Why not make the corporation pay?

(K) In arguing this case, the defendants did not know the standard that would be applied. In all future cases, won't shareholders interested in ousting other shareholders from employment be smart enough to devise a business purpose?

(L) Suppose the defendants could show that, although Wilkes was an adequate employee, another individual would be much better and would accept a lower salary. Would that mean there is a legitimate business purpose for firing Wilkes?

(M) Suppose that, although Wilkes was an adequate employee, the other shareholders could parcel out his duties among themselves without requiring more in the way of salary. Would that mean there is a legitimate business purpose for firing Wilkes?

(N) Is there any context outside of share repurchases where the equal opportunity rule would really work? How about the declaration of dividends?

(O) Does the equal opportunity doctrine still exist in Massachusetts, even in the context of share repurchases?

 Time Out for PR

Suppose that you were approached by your client, T. Edward Quinn (while he was still alive). He tells you that Wilkes is a terrific employee and a hard worker, but Quinn despises him for opposing him and wants him out. What advice would you give him on how to achieve his goals?

Suppose, instead, that you represent the corporation rather than T. Edward Quinn as an individual. You have the same conversation with T. Edward. What will you tell him? Does it make any difference whether T. Edward tells you that the corporation cannot possibly function smoothly with both he and Wilkes actively involved?

Massachusetts has been a leader in establishing a special approach for close corporations. The questions it has attempted to answer obviously come up in other states as well. The *Ingle* case, like *Wilkes*, deals with an employment dispute in the close corporation context. While *Donahue-Wilkes* can be thought of as something of a majority rule, *Ingle* is one of many examples in which states outside Massachusetts have taken their own idiosyncratic approaches.

INGLE v. GLAMORE MOTOR SALES, INC.

New York Court of Appeals
535 N.E.2d 1311 (1989)

BELLACOSA, J.

Without a contract for a definite period of employment or some other legally recognized limitation on an employer's unqualified right to discharge an at-will employee who also happens to be a minority shareholder in a close corporation, there is no insulation under the contractual and employment relationships alleged in this case from being fired or from having invoked a stock-repurchase option.

In 1964, plaintiff-appellant Ingle sought to purchase an equity interest in respondent Glamore Motor Sales, Inc. from its then sole shareholder, respondent James Glamore. Ingle was not sold an interest in the corporation initially, but he was hired as sales manager. There was no express agreement between the parties establishing either the duration or conditions of employment.

In 1966, Glamore and Ingle entered into a written shareholders' agreement which provided that Ingle would purchase 22 of Glamore's 100 shares in the corporation, that Ingle would have a five-year option to purchase an additional 18 shares, and that Glamore would nominate and vote Ingle as a director and secretary of the corporation. The agreement also gave Glamore the right to repurchase all of Ingle's stock if "Ingle shall cease to be an employee of the Corporation *for any reason*" (emphasis added). Ingle later purchased the 18 additional shares and the parties executed a new shareholders' agreement, which updated some facets and eliminated outdated ones. The repurchase provision of the 1973 agreement tracked identically the 1966 version.

On January 1, 1982, the corporation issued 60 additional shares of stock. Glamore purchased 22 shares of the new issue and his two sons (respondents William and Robert Glamore) each purchased 19 shares. The three Glamores and Ingle, the only four shareholders, entered into a third agreement reflecting the corporate relationship. The repurchase provision pertinent to this litigation is: "(b) *Termination of employment.* In the event that any Stockholder shall *cease to be an employee of the Corporation for any reason*, Glamore shall have the option, for a period of 30 days after such termination of employment, to purchase all of the shares of stock then owned by such Stockholder" (emphasis supplied).

At a special meeting of the board of directors held on May 9, 1983, Ingle was voted out of his corporate posts and fired from his employment as operating manager of the business. The termination was effective May 31, 1983. On June

1, Glamore notified Ingle that he was exercising the repurchase-upon-termination-of-employment option and in due course paid Ingle $96,000 for his 40 shares in the corporation.

Plaintiff argues that as a minority shareholder of a closely held corporation, employed without the benefit of a contract containing a durational employment protection and without any limitation on the employer's right to discharge, he is nevertheless entitled by reason of his minority shareholder status to a fiduciary-rooted protection against being fired. His theory is that his employment status should not be governed by the employment at-will doctrine but, rather, that as a minority shareholder in a close corporation he should be treated as a co-owner, equivalent to a partner, whose employment rights flow from a special duty of loyalty and good faith. He next urges that an implicit covenant of good faith and fair dealing under the shareholders' agreement precluded his termination without cause, despite the express language and nature of the agreement in that regard. He concludes that even if he is an at-will employee, an action properly lies for the respondents' breach of fiduciary duties and for wrongful interference with his employment. Ingle started two separate actions seeking

damages via seven causes of action alleging breach of fiduciary duty and of contract. Eventually all causes of action were dismissed—we believe correctly.

A minority shareholder in a close corporation, by that status alone, who contractually agrees to the repurchase of his shares upon termination of his employment for any reason, acquires no right from the corporation or majority shareholders against at-will discharge. There is nothing in law, in the agreement, or in the relationship of the parties to warrant such a contradictory and judicial alteration of the employment relationship or the express agreement. It is necessary in this case to appreciate and keep distinct the duty a corporation owes to a minority shareholder *as a shareholder* from any duty it might owe him as an employee.

Both lower courts agree, as do we, that Ingle did not sufficiently present facts raising a triable issue regarding the existence of either an oral or written employment contract fixing employment of a definite duration. Under the established common-law rule—and without any reference to the shareholders' agreement—the corporation had the right to discharge plaintiff at will.

The twist in this fact pattern is an asserted liability based on allegations that the corporate officers breached fiduciary duties of good faith and fair dealing arising from the shareholders' agreement and on tortious interference with Ingle's employment. The twist does not support a deviation from the governing principle in this case.

In Murphy v. American Home Prods. Corp. (448 N.E.2d 86), we concluded that there is no implied obligation of good faith and fair dealing in an employment at will, as that would be incongruous to the legally recognized jural relationship in that kind of employment relationship. In holding that there is no cause of action in tort for abusive or wrongful discharge of an at-will employee, we declined to allow the use of substitute nomenclature or causes, such as a prima facie tort or intentional infliction of emotional distress, to bootstrap the threshold deficiency in a wrongful discharge claim. . . .

Plaintiff confuses and tries to avoid the sequential relationship of his employment status to his shareholders' agreement by extracting an obligation from the agreement to manufacture a legally unrecognized employment security. Divestiture of his status as a shareholder, by operation of the repurchase provision, is a contractually agreed to consequence flowing directly from the firing, not vice versa. The dissent similarly confuses and inverts the Appellate Division's and our holding.

As noted, Ingle argued that the corporation discharged him because James Glamore would then have a right to repurchase his shares under the terms of the shareholders' agreement. Notably, however, Ingle never asserted that the $2,400 per share paid to him upon termination was not fairly representative of his equity interest in the corporation. He does not contend that the corporation undervalued his shares, and he accepted payment from Glamore without reservation. . . .

. . . No duty of loyalty and good faith akin to that between partners, precluding termination except for cause, arises among those operating a business in the corporate form who "have only the rights, duties and obligations of stockholders" and not those of partners (*see*, Weisman v. Awnair Corp., 3 N.Y.2d 444, 449-450).

Finally, the dissent essentially invokes an equity appeal. While we have no quarrel whatsoever with that magnificent juridical jewel applied in its proper setting, this lawsuit does not qualify. Here, fair principles of well-settled law, affecting employment and contractual relationships between private parties, govern and are entitled to respect and efficacy from this court. We cannot merely substitute our preferred notions for those of the parties themselves in such matters. . . .

Accordingly, the order of the Appellate Division should be affirmed, with costs.

HANCOCK, JR., J. (dissenting). . . .

What is remarkable about the majority opinion is that it appears to treat the employment at-will rule as a sort of categorical imperative which necessarily dictates the result in this case. There can be no question about the harshness of the outcome—assuming plaintiff's allegations to be true: the controlling shareholders are permitted to have the corporation fire plaintiff arbitrarily and in bad faith solely for the purpose of getting rid of him as a 25% stock owner.[10] . . .

---

10. The notion that plaintiff's loss must somehow be viewed as less onerous because he is not contesting the $2,400 per share cash-out price misses the point of the lawsuit. Plaintiff wants to *keep his stock*—not to sell it. The injury to plaintiff is that he is being involuntarily cashed out as a stockholder through the buy-back agreement and forced out of his investment and participation in Glamore Motor Sales, Inc. Obviously, if the buy-back agreement is held to be enforceable against plaintiff, he is precluded from complaining about the amount. He has agreed to it.

Moreover, it cannot seriously be suggested that plaintiff should be pleased with being repaid a total of $96,000 in 1983 for his $75,000 cash outlay made 17 to 15 years earlier, particularly in light of

The Appellate Division, in dismissing plaintiff's complaints, and the majority of the court, in its affirmance, have adopted defendants' literal interpretation of the phrase in paragraph 7(b) of the stockholders' agreement—"cease to be an employee of the Corporation for any reason"—as giving defendants the unfettered right to repurchase plaintiff's shares by firing him, even if arbitrarily or in bad faith. . . .

Preliminarily, it must be emphasized that the phrase "cease to be an employee of the Corporation for any reason" appears only in the stockholders' agreement and pertains exclusively to the conditions under which the *majority may exercise its right to repurchase plaintiff's stock.* . . . [T]his contractual provision clearly says nothing about the conditions under which the *corporation may terminate plaintiff's employment.*

There is no employment agreement between plaintiff and the corporation. Nothing in the original stockholders' agreement between plaintiff and James Glamore or in the subsequent agreement between plaintiff and the additional members of the Glamore family as stockholders purports to set the terms of plaintiff's relationship with the corporation or to state when or under what circumstances it may be terminated. . . . Upholding the corporation's right to discharge plaintiff here, therefore, must rest squarely on the application of the employment at-will doctrine, "that where an employment is for an indefinite term it is presumed to be a hiring at will which may be freely terminated by either party at any time for any reason or even for no reason" (Murphy v. American Home Prods. Corp., 448 N.E.2d 86). . . .

New York, like many other States, unquestionably recognizes that the status of a minority shareholder in a close corporation requires special protection from the courts. Indeed, in Matter of Kemp & Beatley (Gardstein) (64 N.Y.2d 63, 71), Chief Judge Cooke, speaking for a unanimous court stated: "'Unlike the typical shareholder in a publicly held corporation, who may be simply an investor or a speculator and cares nothing for the responsibilities of management, the shareholder in a close corporation is a co-owner of the business and wants the privileges and powers that go with ownership. His participation in that particular corporation is often his principal or sole source of income. As a matter of fact, providing employment for himself may have been the principal reason why he participated in organizing the corporation. He may or may not anticipate an ultimate profit from the sale of his interest, but he normally draws very little from the corporation as dividends. In his capacity as an officer or employee of the corporation, he looks to his salary for the principal return on his capital investment, because earnings of a close corporation, as is well known, are distributed in major part in salaries, bonuses and retirement benefits' (O'Neal,

---

the high risk he assumed in guaranteeing the corporation's loans up to $1,000,000. That he agreed to such buy-back figure, of course, supports his contention that he thought the buy-back agreement was intended to protect Glamore's control over plaintiff's stock by giving Glamore the right to repurchase the stock in the event that plaintiff died, wished to sell or transfer his shares, or voluntarily decided to quit; and that it was never in plaintiff's contemplation that the clause was to apply as the price for his shares in the event that he was involuntarily terminated.

Close Corporations [2d ed.], §1.07)." . . . The need for special protection of a minority shareholder could not be better illustrated than in the case at bar.

A person who, like plaintiff, buys a minority interest in a close corporation does so not only in the hope of enjoying an increase in value of his stake in the business but for the assurance of employment in the business in a managerial position. In addition to the security of long-term employment and the prospect of financial return in the form of salary, his expectancy includes a voice in the management and operation of the business and in the formulation of its plans for future development and growth. The anticipated rewards for his efforts differ markedly from those of the typical salaried corporate employee in a large company. . . .

Thus, the relationship of a minority shareholder to a close corporation, if fairly viewed, cannot possibly be equated with an ordinary hiring and, in the absence of a contract, regarded as nothing more than an employment at will. But this is exactly how the majority of the court has treated plaintiff's association with Glamore Motor Sales. And it has done so by not addressing the multiple relationships and the expectancies and vulnerabilities peculiar to the status of a minority shareholder in plaintiff's position—those very considerations which call for the relief that only a court of equity can give. . . .

Assuming for the moment that the case could properly be viewed merely as one at law for breach of a hiring contract, the application of the employment at-will rule in this context would still be particularly inappropriate and unfair. . . . There can be little question that the basis for the traditional employment at-will rule is in the contractual principle of mutuality of obligation, "that if the employee can quit his job at will, then so, too, must the employer have the right to terminate the relationship for any reason or no reason". . . . [T]he rationale for the employment at-will rule does not fit the situation of the typical minority shareholder-participant in a close corporation. For such participant is *not truly free* to quit at any time; and *there is consideration* which would support an implied understanding that, at least, the majority owner will not discharge him arbitrarily or in bad faith and without some legitimate business reason. . . . The same features of the minority owner-participant's status which make him particularly vulnerable to action by the majority obviously work to compel him to stay on the job. He needs to do so to protect his investment and to share in any increase in its value. . . .

■ Think about this:

(P) Notice that there was indeed planning involved at the point when plaintiff Ingle was sold shares by defendant Glamore. How could Ingle have improved his situation at the time of the purchase?

(Q) Is there any way to reconcile either the approaches or the results in *Wilkes* and *Ingle*?

Dear Prof.: I'm starting to get the impression that employment contracts are a very important part of small business planning. Is that correct?

Yes. There is a simple form of employment agreement in the online Supplement, but you should always be aware of special needs.

Test Yourself

Assume, Unless Directed to the Contrary, Applicability of the Most Current Version of the Model Business Corporation Act

1. Hypo, Inc., a closely held company, is incorporated in Massachusetts. Adam, who owns 15 of Hypo's 100 shares, was recently fired by the company and is now the only one of its shareholders not employed by it. At the same time, the company discontinued the dividend payments it traditionally had made, and reverted instead to annual employee "bonuses," based on the number of shares held by each employee. Adam likely will be entitled to a recovery from the other shareholders. True or False?

   a. True, because there probably is not a business reason for linking employee bonuses to the number of shares held.
   b. False, because dividend decisions are within the business judgment discretion of management.
   c. False, because employee termination decisions are within the business judgment discretion of management.
   d. False, because the "equal opportunity" rule no longer applies, even in Massachusetts.

2. Joe is considering taking a new job as CEO of a closely held Massachusetts corporation. Joe is unsure whether he should accept all the comforting promises concerning the job made to him by the company's chairman, Hugh Lyon. He is also annoyed by a company bylaw prohibiting company officers from owning the company's stock. Anyway, which of the following is the best reason for Joe to insist on an employment contract with employment and salary protections?

   a. The *Donahue-Wilkes* rule is not recognized in Massachusetts.
   b. The *Donahue-Wilkes* rule contains doctrinal uncertainties.
   c. *Donahue-Wilkes* protection would be unavailable to Joe.
   d. It is often uncertain when a corporation is "close" within the meaning of the *Donahue-Wilkes* rule.

Questions 3 and 4 rely on the following facts:

Ever since John and Jerry incorporated their business as a Massachusetts corporation, about eight years ago, they've managed the company's affairs together. Though they don't have official job titles, they've always paid themselves annual salaries. Until recently, they had never held either a shareholder or board meeting, and there had never been an election of directors. Strictly speaking, John has voting control of the company. Since John invested quite a bit more money, they agreed that he would take 60 percent of the shares and Jerry would take 40 percent. Several years ago, John hired two employees to work for the company, and they are still in its employ.

Last month Jerry got a letter signed by John, indicating that he was signing on behalf of the company as "controlling shareholder." The letter announced that the company would hold a shareholder meeting, the only listed agenda item being the election of a board of directors. In his own handwriting, John included the following note at the bottom of the otherwise typed letter: "Hey, bud, don't worry about this shareholder meeting business. You know we're in this together." Relying on John's words, Jerry neither attended the meeting nor gave his proxy to anyone to vote his shares.

At the meeting, John cast his entire 60 percent for himself as director. His first act as director was to hire himself as CEO. His first act as CEO was to fire Jerry as an employee and terminate any future right to salary. Jerry files suit to challenge the manner of his termination, and John immediately moves to dismiss.

3. John's actions violated his fiduciary duties as a shareholder in a closely held corporation. True or False?

  a. True, because the business has only two shareholders, is not publicly traded, and the shareholders are directly involved in management.
  b. False. John's actions could not violate any such duty because of the state in which the business is incorporated.
  c. True, if there was no valid business purpose for the termination.
  d. False. John's actions could not violate any such duty because corporate fiduciaries owe their duties to the corporation, not to individual shareholders.

4. Assuming John and Jerry incorporated their business in Delaware, rather than Massachusetts, John's actions violated his fiduciary duties as a controlling shareholder. True or False?

  a. True, because the business has only two shareholders, is not publicly traded, and the shareholders are directly involved in management.
  b. False. John's actions could not violate any such duty because of the state in which the business is incorporated.
  c. True, if there was no valid business purpose for the termination.
  d. False. John's actions could not violate any such duty because corporate fiduciaries owe their duties to the corporation, not to individual shareholders.

Questions 5-8 rely on the following facts:

Arno, Benny, and Chuck form a Massachusetts corporation that they call ABC, Inc. They themselves are the company's sole shareholders; Arno owns 10 of the company's 100 shares, and Benny and Chuck each own 45. They verbally agreed, upon formation of the corporation, that they would employ themselves in the company, and would pay themselves each a salary.

Following a recent personal disagreement, Benny and Chuck voted as two of ABC's three directors to eject Arno from the board and to fire him from his job at ABC. They then voted to discontinue ABC's traditional annual dividends.

Arno sues Benny and Chuck, alleging that his termination violated their fiduciary duties.

5. Is ABC, Inc. a "close corporation" within the meaning of *Donahue v. Rodd Electrotype*?

   a. Yes, because its shareholders are involved in its management.
   b. Yes, but only until Arno left, since at that point it was no longer true that all of its shareholders were involved in management.
   c. Yes, but only if at least some of its shareholders are related or have close personal relationships.
   d. All of the above answers are correct.
   e. Answers a and b are both correct.

6. Chuck, who happens to be an attorney, files a motion on behalf of ABC to dismiss Arno's claim, alleging that Arno does not adequately represent the other shareholders. Which of the following most likely describes how the court will rule on this motion?

   a. Grant it because Arno is now the only shareholder not employed by ABC.
   b. Grant it because Arno is the only shareholder who has suffered this particular injury.
   c. Deny it because of the nature of Arno's cause of action.
   d. Deny it for some other reason.

7. Which of the following best explains why Arno's cause of action differs from a claim for breach of the fiduciary duty of loyalty?

   a. Arno's claim is derivative in nature.
   b. Because in duty of loyalty claims the defendant normally bears the burden of proving material facts.
   c. Because of the kinds of facts that trigger the underlying duty.
   d. Because in duty of loyalty claims the basic question, in essence, is whether the challenged transaction was "legitimate" from the company's perspective.

8. How would Arno's lawsuit differ if ABC were incorporated in Delaware?

    a. It wouldn't.

    b. It would most likely be judged under the intrinsic fairness test, and it would be derivative in nature.

    c. It would most likely be judged under the business judgment rule, and it would be derivative in nature.

    d. It would most likely be judged under the business judgment rule, but it would be direct in nature since Arno challenges a personal harm.

27

Special Considerations in the Close Corporation Context, Part III: Deadlock and Dissolution

Sometimes lack of planning can lead to deadlock among shareholders and/ or directors, bringing corporate action to a halt. Ironically, sometimes it is an attempt to provide for minority protection that leads to that situation. And as we have seen at length, an acute close corporation problem can be oppression of minority shareholders. With illiquid shares, no default exit right, and little or no meaningful say in governance, a minority shareholder is vulnerable to abuse. This chapter considers a last-resort, escape-valve sort of solution reserved by corporate law to deal with both problems when they become severe: judicial dissolution.

Chapter Outline

A. Deadlock: Getting to "No"

- Deadlock of shareholders leads to the failure to elect new directors
- Deadlock of directors leads to corporate inaction

B. The Dissolution Solution

- Voluntary dissolution

- Administrative dissolution
- Judicial dissolution
    - Meaning of oppression
    - Judicial discretion

Test Yourself

A. Deadlock: Getting to "No"

Closely held corporations—and, indeed, all small businesses—face special problems of governance and internal dispute resolution that do not affect large busi-

nesses. One is the problem of oppression of minority shareholders—something that is discussed in the chapter on fiduciary duty in the close corporation context and also is addressed by one of the cases in this chapter dealing with dissolution. Another frequent and acute problem is deadlock. Deadlock is highly unlikely in the case of publicly traded corporations. Director deadlocks can be addressed simply by assuring an odd number of positions filled, and the likelihood of shareholder deadlock, when there are many thousands or millions of shares, is extremely remote. By contrast, in small businesses it is possible that either the shareholders or the board of directors will consist of an even number of people and that as to some particular issue they may be evenly divided. Indeed, if they are evenly divided, it may not even be possible to convene a quorum of the shareholders or directors.[1] Interestingly, sometimes it is an attempt at planning for corporate control that leads to deadlock. Thus, if there are high quorum or voting requirements in place to protect the minority, the minority may effectively be able to deadlock corporate decision making.

In any event, there will be situations in which a shareholder frustrated by oppression or deadlock literally has no alternative but to try to force dissolution of the company as a means to retrieve her investment. The *Hall* case set out immediately below addresses deadlock and suggests dissolution as an alternative.

---

1. Recall that in Model Act jurisdictions and most others, a quorum for shareholder meetings is a majority of those eligible to vote and for director meetings it is a majority of the authorized seats. Thus, if either group is evenly divided, one half of the group can simply refuse to attend a meeting, thereby defeating a quorum.

HALL v. HALL

Missouri Court of Appeals
506 S.W.2d 42 (1974)

DONALD B. CLARK, Special Judge.

This action involves a dispute among shareholders in a closely held corporation. The facts are not in dispute.

Respondent Musselman and Hall Contractors, Inc. (hereafter the corporation) is a Missouri corporation, the corporate stock of which was wholly owned immediately prior to September 19, 1969 in equal proportions by Edward H. Hall and respondent Harry L. Hall. On the last mentioned date, Edward H. Hall died leaving his widow, appellant surviving him. Appellant thereafter succeeded to a fifty percent stock interest in the corporation in her representative capacity as the duly appointed and acting executrix of the estate of her deceased husband and is also interested as residuary devisee of the estate.

Prior to Edward Hall's death, he and respondent Harry Hall were the only directors of the corporation. Acting to fill the vacancy created by the death of Edward, respondent Harry Hall appointed his wife, respondent Florence E. Hall, as a director of the corporation and thereafter, acting as the then board of directors, they appointed themselves as president and vice-president of the corporation. To the date of the filing of this action, no further election of directors or officers has been held and the individual respondents have continued to serve as the only directors and officers of the corporation.

Upon the failure of the individual respondents to call or convene the required annual meeting of the corporation, appellant by written and published notice called an annual meeting for the second Tuesday in May, 1970, such being the date specified in the corporate by-laws. Appellant appeared at the registered office of the corporation to participate in the business of the meeting and to vote the shares held by her in her representative capacity, but respondent Harry Hall, the only other shareholder, failed and refused to attend. The equal division of stock requires the participation of both shareholders to achieve a quorum. Being unable to transact any business without the vote of the shares of the other stockholder, appellant has subsequently adjourned the 1970 annual meeting from week to week.

Subsequent to September 19, 1969, the individual respondents have been in practical control of the corporation. As no election of directors could be held, respondents have continued in office by reason of the failure to elect or qualify any successors. At a special meeting of directors held August 6, 1970, the individual respondents by resolution directed the offering and sale of 3000 shares of the capital stock of the corporation being the balance of authorized but unissued stock. The purchase or offering price was set at $10.00 per share. Appellant indicated her desire and ability to exercise her preemptive right to purchase one-half of the additional stock so offered but

Connections: Filling Vacancies

MBCA §8.10 deals with vacancies on the board. In general, unless the Articles of Incorporation provide otherwise, a vacancy may be filled by either the shareholders or the board. If the directors remaining in office constitute less than a quorum, they nonetheless may fill the vacancy by a majority vote.

contended that the stock issue would be invalid having been approved by directors unlawfully holding office.

In her petition to the court below, appellant sought to enjoin respondent Harry Hall from refusing to attend shareholders' meetings of the corporation, to enjoin the individual respondents from establishing a terminal date for exercise of preemptive purchase rights for the new issue and from continuing to act as directors and officers of the corporation pending a meeting of shareholders. On the motion of respondents asserting failure to state a cause of action, respondents' petition was dismissed and this appeal has resulted. . . .

The substance of appellant's complaint is that her fifty percent ownership interest in the corporation has been rendered impotent by the refusal of respondent Harry Hall to attend and participate in stockholders' meetings. Of course, such is an inevitable consequence where disputes between equal shareholders occur as Section 351.265 RS Mo 1969, V.A.M.S., constitutes a quorum as the majority of outstanding shares entitled to vote and conditions valid corporate acts on the decision of majority of the quorum. Recognizing then that the owners of fifty percent or more of the corporate stock may frustrate the conduct of business at stockholder's meetings, is such inaction unlawful and if not, do remaining stockholders have a remedy?

The very nature of the corporate form is the creation by statute of an entity separate and apart from the individuals who own, manage and operate it. One who acquires corporate stock obtains an interest in the corporate assets after payment of corporate debts and a right to participate in management which he may or may not exercise. The holder of shares is under no obligation whatever to the corporation other than to make full payment of the consideration for which the shares are issued. Section 351.275 RS Mo 1969, V.A.M.S. As participation by a shareholder in management of corporate affairs is voluntary, it necessarily follows that no shareholder may be compelled to attend or participate in shareholders' meetings. Any different rule would contradict the distinction which separates the corporate existence from the identity of its shareholders and which vests management responsibilities in the directors.

Conceding that the failure of respondent Harry Hall to attend stockholders' meetings has injured appellant in preventing her from participating in the management of the corporation, if respondent is under no legal duty to participate, how may a court of equity compel him by injunction to attend and vote at a stockholders' meeting? No maxim of equity may be invoked to destroy an existing legal right nor may equity create a right at law which does not exist. . . .

No allegation was made by appellant of any contractual obligation on the part of respondent Harry Hall to attend and participate in stockholders meetings and none exists by statute or rule of law. It therefore follows of necessity that a court of equity may not by injunction compel that for which no legal duty lies. The trial court was correct in refusing to grant the mandatory injunction requested.

Although appellant's petition alleged oppression by respondent Harry Hall in the matter of salary payments from corporate funds to the individual respondents and further alleged dilution, wasting and diversion of corporate assets, no suggestion is made as to why appellant may not move to dissolve the corporation under Section 351.485 RSMo 1969, V.A.M.S., or, as the trial court suggested, try by *quo warranto* the right of the individual respondents to continue in the offices of directors and corporate officers when the statutory requirements for annual stockholders' meetings have been subverted. As is noted in Fletcher-Cyclopedia Corporations, Vol. 5, Chapter 13, p. 22, although *quo warranto* as a remedy to oust one from an office illegally held would not produce a judgment requiring an election of officers, it might produce a vacancy necessitating one. Alternative methods whereby appellant may obtain redress do not require ruling on this appeal. . . .

> ### Connections: Cumulative Voting
>
> Cumulative voting permits shareholders to multiply the number of their shares times the number of vacancies to be filled, and to cast their votes for fewer than the number of directors to be elected.

The *Hall* case involves a deadlock of shareholders. In contrast, consider Gearing v. Kelly, 182 N.E.2d 391 (N.Y. Ct. App. 1962). There, a director stayed away from a meeting to prevent the formation of a quorum that could lawfully act to fill vacancies on the board. The other directors acted nonetheless. When the shareholder who controlled the truant director sued to set aside the election as illegal, the court held that the controlled director's conduct estopped the shareholder from complaining. MBCA §8.10(a)(3) was designed to defeat this result, stating that unless the articles provide otherwise, if the directors remaining in office constitute fewer than a quorum, they nonetheless may fill the vacancy by a majority vote.

■ **Think about this:**

(A) Why did Harry Hall refuse to go to meetings? What would have happened if he had gone? Does it make any difference whether voting for directors was straight or cumulative?

(B) Why might a director's refusal to attend a meeting present any different considerations from a shareholder's refusal to attend?

(C) How does MBCA §8.10(a)(3) defeat the outcome in *Gearing v. Kelly*?

(D) Is the outcome in *Hall* consistent with the idea that the shareholders of a closely held corporation owe fiduciary duties to one another?

(E) Does it seem to you that it would be permissible for Harry Hall and his wife to cause the corporation to sell them enough shares to break the deadlock?

(F) What would you suggest the plaintiff try next?

B. The Dissolution Solution

 What does it look like?

Check the online Supplement for the following sample documents that are relevant to this chapter:

- Articles of dissolution for a voluntary dissolution

There are times when a minority shareholder in a closely held corporation will be disadvantaged for one reason or another, and will have very literally no option except to try to force the dissolution of the company. The procedures for voluntary dissolution resemble those for other fundamental transactions such as amendment of the articles, merger, and sale of substantially all the assets. The directors must propose dissolution and the shareholders must approve it. Then, articles of dissolution must be filed with the state. Statutes typically provide methods for dissolving corporations to give notice to creditors and establish cut-offs for claims. MBCA Subchapter 14A also addresses such matters as revocation of dissolution, establishing security for contingent claims, and the duties of the directors during the dissolution process. MBCA Subchapter 14B deals with administrative dissolution for failure to pay franchise taxes or failure to file required reports, for example. Subchapter 14C, on judicial dissolutions, begins with the following section.

REVISED MODEL BUSINESS CORPORATION ACT CHAPTER 14: DISSOLUTION

Subchapter C: Judicial Dissolution

§14.30 Grounds for Judicial Dissolution

The [court] may dissolve a corporation:

(a)(1) in a proceeding by the attorney general if it is established that:

(i) the corporation obtained its articles of incorporation through fraud; or

(ii) the corporation has continued to exceed or abuse the authority conferred upon it by law;

(2) in a proceeding by a shareholder if it is established that:

(i) the directors are deadlocked in the management of the corporate affairs, the shareholders are unable to break the deadlock, and irreparable injury to the corporation is threatened or being suffered, or the business and affairs of the corporation can no longer be conducted to the advantage of the shareholders generally, because of the deadlock;

(ii) the directors or those in control of the corporation have acted, are acting, or will act in a manner that is illegal, oppressive, or fraudulent;

(iii) the shareholders are deadlocked in voting power and have failed, for a period that includes at least two consecutive annual meeting dates, to elect successors to directors whose terms have expired; or

(iv) the corporate assets are being misapplied or wasted;

(3) in a proceeding by a creditor if it is established that:

(i) the creditor's claim has been reduced to judgment, the execution on the judgment returned unsatisfied, and the corporation is insolvent; or

(ii) the corporation has admitted in writing that the creditor's claim is due and owing and the corporation is insolvent; or

(4) in a proceeding by the corporation to have its voluntary dissolution continued under court supervision; or

(5) in a proceeding by a shareholder if the corporation has abandoned its business and has failed within a reasonable time to liquidate and distribute its assets and dissolve. . . .

[In part (b), §14.30 goes on to provide that sub-section (a)(2) does not apply to publicly held companies.]

There is an important pressure valve appearing later in the same Subchapter:

§14.34 Election to Purchase in Lieu of Dissolution

(a) In a proceeding under section 14.30(2) to dissolve a corporation, the corporation may elect or, if it fails to elect, one or more shareholders may elect to purchase all shares owned by the petitioning shareholder at the fair value of the shares. . . .

Obviously, the existence of a statute does not resolve all possible questions. For instance, judicial dissolution under the Model Act and in many other jurisdictions is permitted in cases of "oppression." This term of art is often not defined by the statute invoking it; rather, it is explored in cases like the one below. Notice that New York's dissolution statute is quite similar though not identical to MBCA 14.30(2)(ii).

IN RE KEMP & BEATLEY, INC.

New York Court of Appeals
473 N.E.2d 1173 (1984)

COOKE, Chief Judge. . . .

I

The business concern of Kemp & Beatley, incorporated under the laws of New York, designs and manufactures table linens and sundry tabletop items. The company's stock consists of 1,500 outstanding shares held by eight shareholders. Petitioner Dissin had been employed by the company for 42 years when, in

June 1979, he resigned. Prior to resignation, Dissin served as vice-president and a director of Kemp & Beatley. Over the course of his employment, Dissin had acquired stock in the company and currently owns 200 shares.

Petitioner Gardstein, like Dissin, had been a long-time employee of the company. Hired in 1944, Gardstein was for the next 35 years involved in various aspects of the business including material procurement, product design, and plant management. His employment was terminated by the company in December 1980. He currently owns 105 shares of Kemp & Beatley stock.

Apparent unhappiness surrounded petitioners' leaving the employ of the company. Of particular concern was that they no longer received any distribution of the company's earnings. Petitioners considered themselves to be "frozen out" of the company; whereas it had been their experience when with the company to receive a distribution of the company's earnings according to their stock-holdings, in the form of either dividends or extra compensation, that distribution was no longer forthcoming.

Gardstein and Dissin, together holding 20.33% of the company's outstanding stock, commenced the instant proceeding in June 1981, seeking dissolution of Kemp & Beatley pursuant to section 1104-a of the Business Corporation Law. Their petition alleged "fraudulent and oppressive" conduct by the company's board of directors such as to render petitioners' stock "a virtually worthless asset." . . .

The involuntary-dissolution statute (Business Corporation Law, §1104-a) permits dissolution when a corporation's controlling faction is found guilty of "oppressive action" toward the complaining shareholders. The referee considered oppression to arise when "those in control" of the corporation "have acted in such a manner as to defeat those expectations of the minority stockholders which formed the basis of [their] participation in the venture." The expectations of petitioners that they would not be arbitrarily excluded from gaining a return on their investment and that their stock would be purchased by the corporation upon termination of employment, were deemed defeated by prevailing corporate policies. Dissolution was recommended in the referee's report, subject to giving respondent corporation an opportunity to purchase petitioners' stock.

JD/MBA: Salary vs. Dividends

Close corporation shareholders commonly prefer salaries to dividends as a method of reducing their federal income tax burden. There is more about this subject in the online Supplement.

The Supreme Court confirmed the referee's report. It, too, concluded that due to the corporation's new dividend policy petitioners had been prevented from receiving any return on their investments. Liquidation of the corporate assets was found the only means by which petitioners would receive a fair return. The court considered judicial dissolution of a corporation to be "a serious and severe remedy." Consequently, the order of dissolution was conditioned upon the corporation's being permitted to purchase petitioners' stock. The Appellate Division affirmed, without opinion. . . .

At issue in this appeal is the scope of section 1104-a of the Business Corporation Law. Specifically, this court must determine whether the provision for involuntary dissolution when the "directors or those in control of the corporation have been guilty of . . . oppressive actions toward the complaining shareholders" was properly applied in the circumstances of this case. We hold that it was, and therefore affirm.

II

Judicially ordered dissolution of a corporation at the behest of minority interests is a remedy of relatively recent vintage in New York. Historically, this State's courts were considered divested of equity jurisdiction to order dissolution, as statutory prescriptions were deemed exclusive. Statutes permitting judicial dissolution of corporations either limited the types of corporations under their purview or restricted the parties who could petition for dissolution to the Attorney-General, or the directors, trustees, or majority shareholders of the corporation.

Minority shareholders were granted standing in the absence of statutory authority to seek dissolution of corporations when controlling shareholders engaged in certain egregious conduct. Predicated on the majority shareholders' fiduciary obligation to treat all shareholders fairly and equally, to preserve corporate assets, and to fulfill their responsibilities of corporate management with "scrupulous good faith," the courts' equitable power can be invoked when "it appears that the directors and majority shareholders 'have so palpably breached the fiduciary duty they owe to the minority shareholders that they are disqualified from exercising the exclusive discretion and the dissolution power given to them by statute.'" (Leibert v. Clapp, 196 N.E.2d 540, quoting Hoffman, New Horizons for the Close Corporation, 28 Brooklyn L. Rev. 1, 14.) True to the ancient principle that equity jurisdiction will not lie when there exists a remedy at law, the courts have not entertained a minority's petition in equity when their rights and interests could be adequately protected in a legal action, such as by a shareholder's derivative suit.

Supplementing this principle of judicially ordered equitable dissolution of a corporation, the Legislature has shown a special solicitude toward the rights of minority shareholders of closely held corporations by enacting section 1104-a of the Business Corporation Law. That statute provides a mechanism for the holders of at least 20% of the outstanding shares of a corporation whose stock is not traded on a securities market to petition for its dissolution "under special circumstances" (see Business Corporation Law, §1104-a, subd. [a]). The circumstances that give rise to dissolution fall into two general classifications: mistreatment of complaining shareholders (subd. [a], par. [1]), or misappropriation of corporate assets (subd. [a], par. [2]) by controlling shareholders, directors or officers.

Section 1104-a (subd. [a], par. [1]) describes three types of proscribed activity: "illegal," "fraudulent," and "oppressive" conduct. The first two terms are familiar words that are commonly understood at law. The last, however, does not enjoy the same certainty gained through long usage. As no definition is provided by the statute, it falls upon the courts to provide guidance. . . .

The statutory concept of "oppressive actions" can, perhaps, best be understood by examining the characteristics of close corporations and the Legislature's general purpose in creating this involuntary-dissolution statute. It is widely understood that, in addition to supplying capital to a contemplated or ongoing enterprise and expecting a fair and equal return, parties comprising the ownership of a close corporation may expect to be actively involved in its management and operation. . . .

As a leading commentator in the field has observed: "Unlike the typical shareholder in a publicly held corporation, who may be simply an investor or a speculator and cares nothing for the responsibilities of management, the shareholder in a close corporation is a co-owner of the business and wants the privileges and powers that go with ownership. His participation in that particular corporation is often his principal or sole source of income. As a matter of fact, providing employment for himself may have been the principal reason why he participated in organizing the corporation. He may or may not anticipate an ultimate profit from the sale of his interest, but he normally draws very little from the corporation as dividends. In his capacity as an officer or employee of the corporation, he looks to his salary for the principal return on his capital investment, because earnings of a close corporation, as is well known, are distributed in major part in salaries, bonuses and retirement benefits." (O'Neal, Close Corporations [2d ed.], §1.07, at pp. 21-22 [n. omitted].)

Shareholders enjoy flexibility in memorializing these expectations through agreements setting forth each party's rights and obligations in corporate governance. In the absence of such an agreement, however, ultimate decision-making power respecting corporate policy will be reposed in the holders of a majority interest in the corporation. A wielding of this power by any group controlling a corporation may serve to destroy a stockholder's vital interests and expectations.

As the stock of closely held corporations generally is not readily salable, a minority shareholder at odds with management policies may be without either a voice in protecting his or her interests or any reasonable means of withdrawing his or her investment. This predicament may fairly be considered the legislative concern underlying the provision at issue in this case; inclusion of the criteria that the corporation's stock not be traded on securities markets and that the complaining shareholder be subject to oppressive actions supports this conclusion.

Defining oppressive conduct as distinct from illegality in the present context has been considered in other forums. The question has been resolved by considering oppressive actions to refer to conduct that substantially defeats the

"reasonable expectations" held by minority shareholders in committing their capital to the particular enterprise. . . . This concept is consistent
with the apparent purpose underlying the provision under review. A shareholder who reasonably
expected that ownership in the corporation would
entitle him or her to a job, a share of corporate
earnings, a place in corporate management, or
some other form of security, would be oppressed
in a very real sense when others in the corporation
seek to defeat those expectations and there exists
no effective means of salvaging the investment.

Given the nature of close corporations and the
remedial purpose of the statute, this court holds
that utilizing a complaining shareholder's "reasonable expectations" as a means of identifying and
measuring conduct alleged to be oppressive is appropriate. A court considering a petition alleging oppressive conduct must investigate what the majority
shareholders knew, or should have known, to be the petitioner's expectations
in entering the particular enterprise. Majority conduct should not be deemed
oppressive simply because the petitioner's subjective hopes and desires in joining the venture are not fulfilled. Disappointment alone should not necessarily
be equated with oppression.

Rather, oppression should be deemed to arise only when the majority conduct substantially defeats expectations that, objectively viewed, were both reasonable under the circumstances and were central to the petitioner's decision to
join the venture. It would be inappropriate, however, for us in this case to delineate the contours of the courts' consideration in determining whether directors
have been guilty of oppressive conduct. As in other areas of the law, much will
depend on the circumstances in the individual case.

The appropriateness of an order of dissolution is in every case vested in
the sound discretion of the court considering the application (see Business
Corporation Law, §1111, subd. [a]). Under the terms of this statute, courts are
instructed to consider both whether "liquidation of the corporation is the only
feasible means" to protect the complaining shareholder's expectation of a fair
return on his or her investment and whether dissolution "is reasonably necessary" to protect "the rights or interests of any substantial number of shareholders" not limited to those complaining (Business Corporation Law, §1104-a,
subd. [b], pars. [1], [2]). Implicit in this direction is that once oppressive conduct
is found, consideration must be given to the totality of circumstances surrounding the current state of corporate affairs and relations to determine whether
some remedy short of or other than dissolution constitutes a feasible means of
satisfying both the petitioner's expectations and the rights and interests of any
other substantial group of shareholders (see, also, Business Corporation Law,
§1111, subd. [b], par. [1]).

By invoking the statute, a petitioner has manifested his or her belief that dissolution may be the only appropriate remedy. Assuming the petitioner has set

forth a *prima facie* case of oppressive conduct, it should be incumbent upon the parties seeking to forestall dissolution to demonstrate to the court the existence of an adequate, alternative remedy. A court has broad latitude in fashioning alternative relief, but when fulfillment of the oppressed petitioner's expectations by these means is doubtful, such as when there has been a complete deterioration of relations between the parties, a court should not hesitate to order dissolution. Every order of dissolution, however, must be conditioned upon permitting any shareholder of the corporation to elect to purchase the complaining shareholder's stock at fair value (see Business Corporation Law, §1118).

One further observation is in order. The purpose of this involuntary dissolution statute is to provide protection to the minority shareholder whose reasonable expectations in undertaking the venture have been frustrated and who has no adequate means of recovering his or her investment. It would be contrary to this remedial purpose to permit its use by minority shareholders as merely a coercive tool. Therefore, the minority shareholder whose own acts, made in bad faith and undertaken with a view toward forcing an involuntary dissolution, give rise to the complained-of oppression should be given no quarter in the statutory protection.

III

There was sufficient evidence presented at the hearing to support the conclusion that Kemp & Beatley had a long-standing policy of awarding de facto dividends based on stock ownership in the form of "extra compensation bonuses." Petitioners, both of whom had extensive experience in the management of the company, testified to this effect. Moreover, both related that receipt of this compensation, whether as true dividends or disguised as "extra compensation," was a known incident to ownership of the company's stock understood by all of the company's principals. Finally, there was uncontroverted proof that this policy was changed either shortly before or shortly after petitioners' employment ended. Extra compensation was still awarded by the company. The only difference was that stock ownership was no longer a basis for the payments; it was asserted that the basis became services rendered to the corporation. It was not unreasonable for the fact finder to have determined that this change in policy amounted to nothing less than an attempt to exclude petitioners from gaining any return on their investment through the mere recharacterization of distributions of corporate income. Under the circumstances of this case, there was no error in determining that this conduct constituted oppressive action within the meaning of section 1104-a of the Business Corporation Law.

Nor may it be said that Supreme Court abused its discretion in ordering Kemp & Beatley's dissolution, subject to an opportunity for a buy-out of petitioners' shares. After the referee had found that the controlling faction of the company was, in effect, attempting to "squeeze-out" petitioners by offering them no return on their investment and increasing other executive compensation, respondents, in opposing the report's confirmation, attempted only to controvert the factual basis of the report. They suggested no feasible, alternative remedy to the forced dissolution. In light of an apparent deterioration in relations between petitioners and the governing shareholders of Kemp & Beatley, it was not unreasonable for the court to have determined that a forced buy-out of petitioners' shares or liquidation of the corporation's assets was the only means by which petitioners could be guaranteed a fair return on their investments.

Accordingly, the order of the Appellate Division should be modified, with costs to petitioners-respondents, by affirming the substantive determination of that court but extending the time for exercising the option to purchase petitioners-respondents' shares to 30 days following this court's determination.

■ **Think about this:**

(G) The court refers to "the majority shareholders' fiduciary obligation to treat all shareholders fairly and equally, to preserve corporate assets, and to fulfill their responsibilities of corporate management with 'scrupulous good faith.'" Does this mean the minority shareholders have a right to sue the majority as an alternative to seeking dissolution?

(H) The plaintiffs in this case had, between them, 20.33 percent of the shares of Kemp & Beatley. What would have happened if they had only 19 percent? What does that suggest as a planning matter?

Note that in the *Kemp & Beatley* matter, the court refers to the trial court's discretion in ordering dissolution. Note, too, that MBCA §14.30 says that a court *may* dissolve a corporation on certain grounds, not that it must do so. The case below casts light on one of the considerations a court might take into account.

IN THE MATTER OF RADOM & NEIDORFF, INC.

New York Court of Appeals
307 N.Y. 1 (1954)

DESMOND, J.

Radom & Neidorff, Inc., the proposed dissolution of which is before us here, is a domestic corporation which has, for many years, conducted, with great success, the business of lithographing or printing musical compositions. For some thirty years prior to February 18, 1950, Henry Neidorff, now deceased, husband of respondent Anna Neidorff, and David Radom, brother-in-law of Neidorff and brother of Mrs. Neidorff, were the sole stockholders, each holding eighty shares. Henry Neidorff's will made his wife his executrix and bequeathed her the stock, so that, ever since his death, petitioner-appellant David Radom and Anna Neidorff, brother and sister, have been the sole and equal stockholders. Although brother and sister, they were unfriendly before Neidorff's death and their estrangement continues. On July 17, 1950, five months after Neidorff's death, Radom brought this proceeding, praying that the corporation be dissolved under section 103 of the General Corporation Law, the applicable part of which is as follows:

> §103. *Petition in case of deadlock.* Unless otherwise provided in the certificate of incorporation, if a corporation has an even number of directors who are equally divided respecting the management of its affairs, or if the votes of its stockholders are so divided that they cannot elect a board of directors, the holders of one-half of the stock entitled to vote at an election of directors may present a verified petition for dissolution of the corporation as prescribed in this article.

That statute, like others in article 9 of the General Corporation Law, describes the situations in which dissolution may be petitioned for, but, as we shall show later, it does not mandate the granting of the relief in every such case.

The petition here stated to the court that the corporation is solvent and its operations successful, but that, since Henry Neidorff's death, his widow (respondent here) has refused to co-operate with petitioner as president, and that she refuses to sign his salary checks, leaving him without salary, although he has the sole burden of running the business. It was alleged, too, that, because of "unresolved disagreements" between petitioner and respondent, election of any directors, at a stockholders' meeting held for that purpose in June, 1950, had proved impossible. A schedule attached to the petition showed corporate assets consisting of machinery and supplies worth about $9,500, cash about $82,000, and no indebtedness except about $17,000 owed to petitioner (plus his salary claim). Mrs. Neidorff's answering papers alleged that, while her husband was alive, the two owners had each drawn about $25,000 per year from the corporation, that, shortly after her husband's death, petitioner had asked her to allow him alone to sign all checks, which request she refused, that he had then offered her $75,000 for her stock, and, on her rejection thereof, had threatened to have the corporation dissolved and to buy it in at a low price or, if she should be the purchaser, that he would start a competing business. She further alleged that she has not, since her husband's death, interfered with Radom's conduct of the business and has signed all corporate checks sent her by him except checks for his own salary which, she says, she declined to sign because of a stockholder's derivative suit brought by her against Radom, and still pending, charging him with enriching himself at this corporation's expense.

Because of other litigation now concluded (see *Matter of Radom*, 305 N.Y. 679 (1953)[, a matter pitting Mr. Radom against his children]) to which Mrs. Neidorff was not a party, but which had to do with a contest as to the ownership of the Radom stock, respondent's answering papers in this dissolution proceeding were not filed until three years after the petition was entered. From the answering papers it appears, without dispute, that for those three years, the corporation's profits before taxes had totaled about $242,000, or an annual average of about $71,000, on a gross annual business of about $250,000, and that the corporation had, in 1953, about $300,000 on deposit in banks. There are many other accusations and counteraccusations in these wordy papers, but the only material facts are undisputed: first, that these two equal stockholders dislike and distrust each other; second, that, despite the feuding and backbiting, there is no stalemate or impasse as to corporate policies; third, that the corporation is not sick but flourishing; fourth, that dissolution is not necessary for the corporation or for either stockholder; and, fifth, that petitioner, though he is in an uncomfortable and disagreeable situation for which he may or may not be at fault, has no grievance cognizable by a court except as to the nonpayment of his salary, hardly a ground for dissolving the corporation.

Doing the Numbers: Fair Price

Was Mr. Radom offering his sister a fair price?

$75,000 was three times the amount each of the owners had been receiving per year before Mr. Neidorff died. Is that good or bad?

One way to look at it:

Check out the scheduled assets at the time the petition for dissolution was filed (a mere five months after Mr. Neidorff's death): $9,500 + $82,000 = $91,500 in assets. Debts include $17,000 admittedly owed to Mr. Radom. The most the balance sheet could possibly show (assuming nothing for Mr. Radom's salary claim) would be a net equity figure of $91,500 − $17,000 = $74,500. Half of that would be $37,250. Was Mrs. Neidorff being a grasping piggy to refuse her brother's princely offer of $75,000?

Another way to look at it:

Fifty percent of the $71,000 per year the corporation was earning while the matter was pending was $35,500. That is a return on the investment of $37,250 (the amount calculated above) of over 95 percent. Where else is Mrs. Neidorff going to be able to get a return like that? If she had taken the $75,000 offered, would she have been able to invest it in something that would return $35,000, or close to 50 percent, annually?

Special Term held that these papers showed a basic and irreconcilable conflict between the two stockholders requiring dissolution, for the protection of both of them, if the petition's allegations should be proven. An order for a reference was, accordingly, made, but respondent appealed therefrom, and no hearings were held by the Referee. The Appellate Division reversed the order and dismissed the petition, pointing out, among other things, that not only have the corporation's activities not been paralyzed but that its profits have increased and its assets trebled during the pendency of this proceeding, that the failure of petitioner to receive his salary did not frustrate the corporate business and was remediable by means other than dissolution. The dismissal of the proceeding was "without prejudice, however, to the bringing of another proceeding should deadlock in fact arise in the selection of a board of directors, at a meeting of stockholders to be duly called or if other deadlock should occur threatening impairment or in fact impairing the economic operations of the corporation." (282 App. Div. 854.) Petitioner then appealed to this court.

It is worthy of passing mention, at least, that respondent has, in her papers, formally offered, and repeated the offer on the argument of the appeal before us, "to have the third director named by the American Arbitration Association, any Bar Association or any recognized and respected public body."

Clearly, the dismissal of this petition was within the discretion of the Appellate Division. There is no absolute right to dissolution under such circumstances. Even when majority stockholders file a petition because of internal corporate conflicts, the order is granted only when the competing interests "are so discordant as to prevent efficient management" and the "object of its corporate existence cannot be attained." The prime inquiry is, always, as to necessity for dissolution, that is, whether judicially-imposed death "will be beneficial to the stockholders or members and not injurious to the public" (General Corporation Law, §117). Taking everything in the petition as true, this was not such a case, and so there was no need for a reference, or for the taking of proof, under sections 106 and 113 of the General Corporation Law.

The order should be affirmed, with costs.

FULD, J. (dissenting). . . .

For upwards of thirty years, petitioner Radom and Henry Neidorff, respondent's husband, shared equally in the ownership and management of Radom & Neidorff, Inc. Through all that time, their relationship was harmonious as well as profitable. Neidorff died in 1950, at which time respondent, through inheritance, acquired her present 50% stock interest in the business. Since then, all has been discord and conflict. The parties, brother and sister, are at complete loggerheads; they have been unable to elect a board of directors; dividends have neither been declared nor distributed, although the corporation has earned profits; debts of the corporation have gone unpaid, although the corporation is solvent; petitioner, who since Neidorff's death has been the sole manager of the business, has not received a penny of his salary—amounting to $25,000 a year—because respondent has refused to sign any corporate check to his order. More, petitioner's business judgment and integrity, never before questioned, have been directly attacked in the stockholder's derivative suit, instituted by respondent, charging that he has falsified the corporation's records, converted its assets and otherwise enriched himself at its expense. Negotiations looking to the purchase by one stockholder of the other's interest were begun—in an effort to end the impasse—but they, too, have failed. . . .

. . . As the high court of New Jersey recently declared, in applying to somewhat comparable facts a statute similar to section 103 of our General Corporation Law (Matter of Collins-Doan Co., 3 N.J. 382, 396), "In the case at hand, *there is a want of that community of interest essential to corporate operation. Dissolution will serve the interests of the shareholders as well as public policy.* . . . And, if the statutory authority be deemed discretionary in essence, there is no ground for withholding its affirmative exercise here, *for there is no alternative corrective remedy. . . .* The dissension is such as to defeat the end for which the corporation was organized." (Emphasis supplied.)

Here, too, the asserted dissension, the court could find, permits of no real or effective remedy but a section 103 dissolution. And that is confirmed by a consideration of the alternatives seemingly open to petitioner. He could remain as president and manager of the corporation, without compensation, completely at odds with his embittered sister—certainly neither a natural nor a satisfying way in which to conduct a business. Or he could carry out his present plan to quit the enterprise—and thereby risk a loss, to corporation and stockholders, far greater than that involved in terminating the business. Or he could, without quitting, set up a competing enterprise—and thereby expose himself to suit for breach of fiduciary duty to the corporation. It is difficult to believe that the legislature could have intended to put one in petitioner's position to such a choice. Reason plainly indicates, and the law allows, the reasonable course of orderly dissolution pursuant to section 103.

Doing the Numbers II: Distributions in Dissolution

If the corporation were dissolved, what would Mrs. Neidorff receive?

Let's say that it would be half of approximately $220,000, calculated by adding cash of $300,000 plus estimated machinery and supplies of perhaps $10,000 and subtracting liabilities estimated at around $90,000 (composed of $17,000 plus $75,000 for three years of salary claims, rounded down). Would she be able to invest that $110,000 in something that reliably returns $35,500, or over 30 percent? What does that tell you about whether dissolution would be beneficial to the shareholders?

On the other hand, is Mrs. Neidorff being greedy after all because Mr. Radom is doing all the work?

AND why can the company make so much money with so little tied up in machinery and supplies? "Goodwill" that is "earned" by a corporation is not something that shows up as an asset on its own balance sheet, but it is something for which third parties are willing to pay. Presumably, Mr. Neidorff (who appears to be the only person who ever got along with Mr. Radom) contributed to the accumulation of that goodwill during the 30 years that he and his brother-in-law labored cheek by cheek.

If the business is sold at a fair price as a going concern, the amount available for distribution should be much more than if the assets are piecemeally liquidated.

Respondent, however, suggests that, in view of the fact that petitioner is managing the business profitably, he should continue to do so, defend against the stockholder's suit which she brought attacking his honor and integrity and himself start an action for the compensation denied him for more than three years. But, it seems self-evident, more and further litigation would only aggravate,

Connections: The Purpose of the Corporation

According to some authorities (such as the court in the august case of *Dodge v. Ford*), the purpose of the corporation is to make money for its shareholders. How does this square with the majority and dissent in *Radom & Neidorff*?

not cure, the underlying deadlock of which petitioner complains. And, if he were to bring the suggested suit for salary due him, the question arises, whom should he sue, and who is to defend?[2] The mere proposal that petitioner embark on a series of actions against the corporation, of which he is president and half owner, indicates the extent of the present impasse, as well as the futility of perpetuating it. The same is true of the other alternative suggested by respondent, namely, that the third of the three directors, required by section 5 of the Stock Corporation Law, be appointed by an impartial party. The deadlock of which petitioner complains is between the stockholders, not the directors, and, when stockholders are deadlocked, section 103 calls for dissolution, not arbitration. Beyond that, and even if the offer to elect an impartial director were relevant, it would still be necessary to inquire when it was made and under what circumstances. It does not justify, alone or in conjunction with the other facts, a summary dismissal of the proceeding without a hearing. . . .

■ **Think about this:**

(I) If you were Mr. Radom's attorney, what would you suggest he do next (other than attend family counseling)?

 Dear Prof.: I seem to notice that a fair number of deadlock and dissolution cases involve widows. I guess there's a question in there somewhere.

Planning for "succession" is a critical part of small business planning. Mentioning to a business's founders that one of them well may be hit by a bus is actually a decent strategy to get them to focus on the fact that even though everything may be sunshine and lollipops at the outset, it is important to contemplate worst-case scenarios.

---

2. In this connection, it is, perhaps, of some moment that, according to petitioner, he is the sole officer and director of the corporation.

Test Yourself

Assume, Unless Directed to the Contrary, Applicability of the Most Current Version of the Model Business Corporation Act

1. Nellie owns 50 percent of the shares of the N&N Corporation. Nancy owns the other 50 percent. Nancy is the president and the sole officer of the corporation; Nellie is not employed by N&N. Nancy has refused to attend shareholders meetings for some years, and therefore Nellie has been unable to vote to replace Nancy as a director, a great desire for Nellie because the company has also refused to pay any dividends, thus rendering Nellie's shares largely without value to her. Nellie's best remedy is probably:

   a. To sell her shares.
   b. An action for a writ *quo warranto* removing Nancy as an illegal hold-over director.
   c. An action for an injunction ordering a new shareholders' meeting.
   d. As a practical matter, none of the above will be effective remedies.

2. Hypo, Inc., is a closely held corporation. Adam, who owns 15 of Hypo's 100 shares, was recently fired by the company and is now the only one of its shareholders not employed by it. At the same time, the company discontinued the dividend payments it traditionally had made, and reverted instead to annual employee "bonuses," based on the number of shares held by each employee. Adam likely could seek judicial dissolution of ABC. True or False?

   a. True.
   b. False, because dividend decisions are within the business judgment discretion of management, and are unlikely to constitute "oppression."
   c. False, because employee termination decisions are within the business judgment discretion of management, and are unlikely to constitute "oppression."
   d. False, because he does not own at least 20 percent of ABC's stock.
   e. False, because there is no evidence of fraud or other misconduct.

3. Arno, Benny, and Chuck form a New York corporation that they call ABC, Inc. They themselves are the company's sole shareholders; Arno owns 30 of the company's 100 shares, and Benny and Chuck each own 35. They orally agreed, upon formation of the corporation, that they would employ themselves in the company, and would pay themselves each a salary.

   Following a recent personal disagreement, Benny and Chuck voted as two of ABC's three directors to eject Arno from the board and to fire him from his job at ABC. They then voted to discontinue ABC's traditional annual dividends, even though the company is very profitable. Arno seeks judicial dissolution on the grounds of oppression. Which of the following is most true?

a. Arno does not own sufficient shares to have standing.
b. Arno cannot obtain dissolution because the corporation is making money.
c. Arno cannot make out grounds for oppression.
d. The most likely outcome is a buyout of Arno's shares.

4. [Short Answer] Assume that the two 50 percent shareholders of a corporation are deadlocked and unable to elect directors. Under what circumstances would you expect a judge to grant a petition for dissolution?

5. Fill in the Blank: One test for whether a shareholder is being oppressed is whether her _____ are being defeated.

Part 7

The Federal Law of Securities Regulation: A Brief Introduction for the General Practitioner

28

Introduction to Federal Securities Regulation: The Statutory Framework, the Definition of a "Security," Registration Requirements, and Exemptions from Registration

Securities law is difficult—especially the Securities Act of 1933. That Act is so difficult, in fact, that a student or lawyer probably cannot learn it on his or her own. In at least one notable case, some very bright Supreme Court Justices and their equally intelligent clerks attempted to figure out the Securities Act on their own and failed miserably. Fortunately, though, the introduction for generalists that makes sense in a course like this one is fairly straightforward, and we're here to help you get through it. From the standpoint of the general business practitioner, the most important task is to recognize when a transaction involves a "security," so that specialized advice can be sought. The second most important task is to learn how to structure transactions to minimize the impact of the securities laws when they do apply. Those two topics will be the focus of this chapter. We will work through a few other basic topics in the chapters to follow—proxy regulation, securities fraud, insider trading, and short-swing sales.

Chapter Outline

A. Introduction and Statutory Framework

- The Securities Act of 1933: regulation of capital formation
- The Securities Exchange Act of 1934: regulation of the after-market
- Private vs. public revisited
- Disclosure vs. merit regulation
- Federal regulation vs. Blue Sky laws

B. What Is a "Security"?

- Specific and easily recognizable
  - Stock
  - Bond
  - Debenture
- General catch-alls
  - Investment contract
  - Note

C. Two Completely Separate—But Integrated—Registration Schemes

D. The Securities Act of 1933

1. The Registration and Prospectus Requirements

2. The All-Important Exemptions from the '33 Act
   - Introduction
     - Exempt securities vs. exempt transactions
     - The §4(a)(1) exemption for "other than" an issuer, underwriter, or dealer
   - The "intrastate" exemption
     - The statutory exemption of §3(a)(11)
     - The safe harbors of Rules 147 and 147A
   - The "private offering" exemption
     - The statutory exemption of §4(a)(2)
     - The safe harbor of Rule 506
   - The "limited offering" exemptions: Regulation D
     - Rule 504
     - Rule 506 (expanded)

E. The Securities Exchange Act of 1934

- Periodic reporting
- Proxy solicitation rules
- §16 insider trading
- Tender offer regulation
- Foreign Corrupt Practices Act
- Sarbanes-Oxley requirements

F. The Advantages and Disadvantages of "Going Public"

1. Advantages

2. Disadvantages

Test Yourself

 What does it look like?

Check the online Supplement for the following sample documents that are relevant to this chapter:

- Registration statement under the Securities Act of 1933
- Prospectus for use in a public offering
- Registration statement under the Securities Exchange Act of 1934
- Annual report on Form 10-K
- Quarterly report on Form 10-Q
- Report on Form 8-K

A. Introduction and Statutory Framework

All businesses must raise money in one way or another. They need money to buy materials, to buy equipment, to pay their bills, and to pay their employees. They can try to get this money in all kinds of ways. Obviously, they can attempt to raise it by selling goods or services. But they also will need to get money in other ways if they have no current revenue or if they are just beginning operation.[1] For instance, they might get loans—from friends, relatives, the principals themselves, banks, or a government small business agency. In addition, a company may raise money by seeking investment by some pool of investors. For example, a business might form itself as a partnership, to be financed by the initial contributions of the partners. A corporation will issue shares to some number of investors, and may sell bonds, which are a form of long-term secured debt.

When companies raise capital, the investors risk losing their investments. The basic purpose of the federal securities laws is said to be making sure that investors have adequate information to assess that risk. In some cases, the costs

---

1. As a matter of fact, there are other reasons to finance a business by borrowing or seeking investors, even when the firm is making profits. It can be good strategy to do so, and many profitable businesses fund their operations through debt and other investment. Matters such as these are explored in more detail in the online Supplement, as well as in courses on Securities Regulation and Corporate Finance.

of compliance with all aspects of the federal securities laws are deemed too onerous for the benefits obtained and, therefore, exemptions are provided. (There is, however, no exemption from the federal statutes that govern fraud and misleading conduct.) A basic fact to remember is that transactional practice today involves a lot of attorney time and effort spent trying to structure financial transactions in such a way as to come within these exemptions. Therefore, an important skill for every business lawyer, and especially those who counsel smaller businesses, is the ability to structure fund-raising transactions in ways that will not trigger federal securities law requirements.

 Time Out for PR

There are different ways to feel about the emphasis on avoiding application of the federal securities laws. On the one hand, federal securities laws were designed to protect investors from nefarious wrongdoing, and one might be troubled by being paid to help companies avoid well-intended consumer protection legislation. On the other hand, (1) these laws contain statutory exemptions, which were also well intended and were designed to protect small businesses, and (2) it would be bad for any lawyer's career if this or any other costly and onerous regulatory compliance obligation unnecessarily attached to a particular client, even though the client wanted to avoid it.

Thus, the securities laws do not apply every time a company tries to raise money. First of all, they apply only when a company sells *securities*. Therefore, they do not apply to such things as bank loans. Second, even when securities are involved, some purchasers may not require the full protection of the laws. Generally speaking, it is the purpose of the laws to govern sales of securities to the public. Therefore, they normally will not apply where, for example, a closely held corporation issues shares to a close circle of friends or family—provided that is where the securities will stay. But the market for those securities can become "public," and trigger federal securities rules, where investors buy them from issuers and later sell them to third parties, who in turn sell them to yet other parties, all on the speculative hope that they will go up in value.

In this book, we have often used the terms "closely held corporation" and "publicly traded corporation," but the distinction is not a bright line. To be "closely held" does not always mean "small." Often it does, but there are any number of large businesses in the world that remain closely held. Likewise, to be "public" does not necessarily mean that a company's securities are traded on a national securities exchange. Some securities are said to be traded "over the counter" (OTC). That is, members of the public can buy them, but they must buy them from broker-dealers who are not executing trades through any securities exchange. Networks of such bro-ker-dealers simply keep in touch with one another and keep track of the price at which the securities are selling.

Many "public" companies, however, are traded on a national securities exchange. A "securities exchange" is in some important sense simply a place where transactions of a certain type occur. Let's consider the most famous—the New York Stock Exchange (NYSE). The NYSE has a grand building on Wall Street near the southern tip of Manhattan. In the public eye, this building consists mainly of one great big, open room, called the "exchange floor." This is what you see on the news and in the movies with a lot of men, and sometimes a few women, shouting and waving their arms trying to buy stocks. The NYSE itself is a corporation that owns the building and manages all of the operations related to it. What happens on the exchange floor can very usefully be thought of as simply a large number of continuous, ongoing auctions for securities. As it happens, however, "floor" trading is now just the tip of the iceberg—much more trading takes place electronically.

In any event, the federal government got involved in the regulation of securities transactions only in the wake of the great stock market crash of 1929, amid a widespread public sentiment that the crash and the ensuing Depression were to be blamed on unscrupulous securities speculators. For our purposes, and those of general business planners, there are two major federal securities statutes, both adopted as part of Roosevelt's "New Deal." These are the Securities Act of 1933, 15 U.S.C. §§77a-77z-3 ('33 Act or Securities Act), and the Securities Exchange Act of 1934, 15 U.S.C. §§78a-78mm ('34 Act or Exchange Act).[2] Again very generally speaking, the '33 Act primarily regulates issuances by issuers—the essential business of capital formation. The '34 Act is intended to protect traders in the after-market, engaging in transactions from which no capital flows to the issuer. Both require registration of securities, but the registrations have different triggers and different consequences. One consequence they share is that once a company has registered under either Act, it usually will be described as "publicly held."

SECURITIES ACT OF 1933	SECURITIES EXCHANGE ACT OF 1934
Issuers' Capital Formation	Trading in the After-market

Although it is the New Deal securities acts that are of central importance, you may be aware of several pieces of securities legislation passed in the

---

2. As is the case with a number of other statutes, practitioners tend to refer to individual sections in the statutes as they appear in the Public Laws as passed by Congress, rather than the separate numbering in the codified versions in the U.S. Code. Thus, for example, 15 U.S.C. §78j(b) is much more commonly known as "§10(b) of the '34 Act."

twenty-first century. The Enron, WorldCom, and other scandals spawned the Sarbanes-Oxley Act of 2002. The financial panic in 2008 gave rise to the Dodd-Frank Act of 2010. The recession lingering after the panic prompted the Jump-Start Our Business Start-Ups (JOBS) Act of 2012, and public sentiment at the same time led to the adoption of the Stop Trading on Congressional Knowledge (STOCK) Act.[3] Each of these Acts, at the time of its adoption, was billed as "the most sweeping change in financial regulation since the Great Depression." In the case of the Dodd-Frank and JOBS Acts, most of the securities law changes (as opposed to their changes to other types of financial regulation, like Dodd-Frank's banking reforms) were amendments to portions of the '33 and '34 Acts.

The federal securities laws are administered by an agency called the Securities and Exchange Commission (SEC). The SEC receives all registration and disclosure documents that must be filed under the securities laws, and it also maintains a large enforcement staff that investigates non-compliance with the rules and violations of the law's several anti-fraud provisions. The SEC may bring civil suit against violations, and the Justice Department may bring criminal prosecution against those violations that are willful.

It is popularly said that federal securities law is "disclosure" regulation, not "merit" regulation. That is, it regulates what securities issuers must tell people to whom they offer securities, but it does not regulate the content or the riskiness of the investments themselves. Congress has long believed that it is an appropriate government role to ensure that investors have information, but not to protect them from their own choices. Therefore, while the SEC can insist on compliance with procedural guidelines, it cannot prohibit the sale of a security simply because the agency thinks the security is a bad investment.

By the time Congress passed the Securities Act, most states had been in the business of securities regulation for many years. The New Deal securities statutes preserved the ability of the states to engage in securities regulation, and they continued vigorous activity in this area. The result was fairly comprehensive, albeit widely divergent, state regulatory schemes, known as "Blue Sky" laws. In 1996, however, Congress amended federal law to reduce state jurisdiction substantially. Preemption is particularly important, as a practical matter, when considering exempt sales of securities under the Securities Act, since the use of certain federal exemptions preempts state regulation of an offering. Nonetheless, it still is not unusual for a state to exercise jurisdiction in many of the major areas covered by the Securities Act and the Exchange Act. Thus, like the Securities Act (but subject to its preemption for several kinds of issuers and transactions), the typical state statute requires that securities be registered before sale, unless an exemption is available. The typical state statute also prohibits various kinds of fraud, which is also proscribed by both the federal Securities Act and Exchange Act. In addition, in some states, where not preempted, the statute empowers state securities authorities to reject a security on quality-related grounds. In sum, the various Blue Sky laws are often complex

---

3. Cf. Chris Sagers, *A Statute by Any Other (Non-Acronomial) Name Might Smell Less Like S.P.A.M., or, the Congress of the United States Grows Increasingly D.U.M.B.*, 103 GEO. L.J. 1307 (2015).

and impose sometimes conflicting requirements, and they can be the bane of securities practitioners.

B. What Is a "Security"?

Both the Securities Act and the Exchange Act have precise definitions of the "securities" to which they apply, and, for most intents and purposes, the definitions are identical. This is helpful, but the statutory definition is both detailed and notoriously nebulous in application. The definition contained in the Securities Act, as it now exists, is as follows:

Section 2(a). Definitions. When used in this title, unless the context otherwise requires:

(1) the term "security" means any note, stock, treasury stock, security future, security-based swap, bond, debenture, evidence of indebtedness, certificate of interest or participation in any profit-sharing agreement, collateral-trust certificate, preorganization certificate or subscription, transferable share, investment contract, voting trust certificate, certificate of deposit for a security, fractional undivided interest in oil, gas, or other mineral rights, any put, call, straddle, option, or privilege on any security, certificate of deposit, or group or index of securities (including any interest therein or based on the value thereof), or any put, call, straddle, option, or privilege entered into on a national securities exchange relating to foreign currency, or, in general, any interest or instrument commonly known as a "security," or any certificate of interest or participation in, temporary or interim certificate for, receipt for, guarantee of, or warrant or right to subscribe to or purchase, any of the foregoing.

The problem is that the range of possible investment arrangements that are actually used in the world is limited only by the imaginations of businesspeople and their advisors. This problem can be simplified a great deal by recognizing that, almost without exception, "security" includes the following:

1. any share of stock in a corporation—including common and preferred stock, and
2. any bond issued by a corporation or by any other private entity.

That said, courts have found that any number of investment schemes, including some relating to earthworms, chinchillas, and payphones, also fall within the definition. In fact, there are well over a thousand cases on the subject—but this chapter presents only two. Both interpret the meaning of "investment contract," which has turned out to be the most comprehensively used term included in the statute.

More to the Story: Other Broad Terms

Although the lion's share of litigants' time has gone to the term "investment contract," as used in the definition of "security," it is not the only broad term in the definition. Consider, for instance, "evidence of indebtedness."

S.E.C. V. W.J. HOWEY CO.

Supreme Court of the United States
328 U.S. 293 (1946)

Mr. Justice MURPHY delivered the opinion of the Court.

This case involves the application of §2[(a)](1) of the Securities Act of 1933 to an offering of units of a citrus grove development coupled with a contract for cultivating, marketing and remitting the net proceeds to the investor.

The Securities and Exchange Commission instituted this action to restrain the respondents from using the mails and instrumentalities of interstate commerce in the offer and sale of unregistered and non-exempt securities in violation of §5(a) of the Act. The District Court denied the injunction, and the Fifth Circuit Court of Appeals affirmed the judgment. . . .

Most of the facts are stipulated. The respondents, W.J. Howey Company and Howey-in-the-Hills Service, Inc., are Florida corporations under direct common control and management. The Howey Company owns large tracts of citrus acreage in Lake County, Florida. During the past several years it has planted about 500 acres annually, keeping half of the groves itself and offering the other half to the public "to help us finance additional development." Howey-in-the-Hills Service, Inc., is a service company engaged in cultivating and developing many of these groves, including the harvesting and marketing of the crops.

Each prospective customer is offered both a land sales contract and a service contract, after having been told that it is not feasible to invest in a grove unless service arrangements are made. While the purchaser is free to make arrangements with other service companies, the superiority of Howey-in-the-Hills Service, Inc., is stressed. Indeed, 85% of the acreage sold during the 3-year period ending May 31, 1943, was covered by service contracts with Howey-in-the-Hills Service, Inc.

. . . Upon full payment of the purchase price the land is conveyed to the purchaser by warranty deed. Purchases are usually made in narrow strips of land arranged so that an acre consists of a row of 48 trees. . . .

The service contract, generally of a 10-year duration without option of cancellation, gives Howey-in-the-Hills Service, Inc., a leasehold interest and "full and complete" possession of the acreage. For a specified fee plus the cost of

labor and materials, the company is given full discretion and authority over the cultivation of the groves and the harvest and marketing of the crops. The company is well established in the citrus business and maintains a large force of skilled personnel and a great deal of equipment, including 75 tractors, sprayer wagons, fertilizer trucks and the like. Without the consent of the company, the land owner or purchaser has no right of entry to market the crop; thus there is ordinarily no right to specific fruit. The company is accountable only for an allocation of the net profits based upon a check made at the time of picking. All the produce is pooled by the respondent companies, which do business under their own names.

The purchasers for the most part are non-residents of Florida. They are predominantly business and professional people who lack the knowledge, skill and equipment necessary for the care and cultivation of citrus trees. They are attracted by the expectation of substantial profits. It was represented, for example, that profits during the 1943-1944 season amounted to 20% and that even greater profits might be expected during the 1944-1945 season, although only a 10% annual return was to be expected over a 10-year period. . . .

. . . The legal issue in this case turns upon a determination of whether, under the circumstances, the land sales contract, the warranty deed and the service contract together constitute an "investment contract" within the meaning of §[2(a)(1)]. . . .

The term "investment contract" is undefined by the Securities Act or by relevant legislative reports. But the term was common in many state "blue sky" laws in existence prior to the adoption of the federal statute and, although the term was also undefined by the state laws, it had been broadly construed by state courts so as to afford the investing public a full measure of protection. Form was disregarded for substance and emphasis was placed upon economic reality. An investment contract thus came to mean a contract or scheme for "the placing of capital or laying out of money in a way intended to secure income or profit from its employment." State v. Gopher Tire & Rubber Co., 177 N.W. 937, 938. This definition was uniformly applied by state courts to a variety of situations where individuals were led to invest money in a common enterprise with the expectation that they would earn a profit solely through the efforts of the promoter or of some one other than themselves.

By including an investment contract within the scope of §[2(a)(1)] of the Securities Act, Congress was using a term the meaning of which had been crystallized by this prior judicial interpretation. It is therefore reasonable to attach that meaning to the term as used by Congress, especially since such a definition is consistent with the statutory aims. In other words, an investment contract for purposes of the Securities Act means a contract, transaction or scheme whereby a person invests his money in a common enterprise and is led to expect profits solely from the efforts of the promoter or a third party, it being immaterial whether the shares in the enterprise are evidenced by formal certificates or by nominal interests in the physical assets employed in the enterprise. . . .

The transactions in this case clearly involve investment contracts as so defined. The respondent companies are offering something more than fee simple interests in land, something different from a farm or orchard coupled with management services. They are offering an opportunity to contribute money and to share in the profits of a large citrus fruit enterprise managed and partly owned by respondents. They are offering this opportunity to persons who reside in distant localities and who lack the equipment and experience requisite to the cultivation, harvesting and marketing of the citrus products. Such persons have no desire to occupy the land or to develop it themselves; they are attracted solely by the prospects of a return on their investment. Indeed, individual development of the plots of land that are offered and sold would seldom be economically feasible due to their small size. Such tracts gain utility as citrus groves only when cultivated and developed as component parts of a larger area. A common enterprise managed by respondents or third parties with adequate personnel and equipment is therefore essential if the investors are to achieve their paramount aim of a return on their investments. Their respective shares in this enterprise are evidenced by land sales contracts and warranty deeds, which serve as a convenient method of determining the investors' allocable shares of the profits. The resulting transfer of rights in land is purely incidental.

Thus all the elements of a profit-seeking business venture are present here. The investors provide the capital and share in the earnings and profits; the promoters manage, control and operate the enterprise. It follows that the arrangements whereby the investors' interests are made manifest involve investment contracts, regardless of the legal terminology in which such contracts are clothed. The investment contracts in this instance take the form of land sales contracts, warranty deeds and service contracts which respondents offer to prospective investors. . . .

This conclusion is unaffected by the fact that some purchasers choose not to accept the full offer of an investment contract by declining to enter into a service contract with the respondents. The Securities Act prohibits the offer as well as the sale of unregistered, non-exempt securities. Hence it is enough that the respondents merely offer the essential ingredients of an investment contract.

After more than a half century, *Howey* still states the test for determining the existence of an investment contract. In the intervening years, litigation has not focused on the correctness of the test, but rather on the precise meaning of one or more of its parts. For purposes of study, it is helpful to break the test down into these elements:

- investment of money;
- common enterprise;
- expectation of profits; and
- solely from the efforts of others.

The following element-by-element discussion provides a flavor of the interpretive problems inherent in the *Howey* test.

Investment of Money. The meaning of "money" can be disposed of easily. The Securities Act covers all offers and sales of securities, regardless of the form of consideration to be exchanged in the bargain. The consideration does not actually have to be money. For an "investment" to exist, one must put out consideration with the hope of a financial return.

Common Enterprise. Two clearly different formulations of a "common enterprise" requirement have emerged in the courts of appeals. One (the more common) is horizontal commonality, which concentrates on the interrelated interests of the various investors in a particular scheme. The other is vertical commonality, which focuses on the community of interest of an individual investor and the manager of the enterprise. One formulation of vertical commonality was stated in SEC v. Koscot Interplanetary, Inc., 497 F.2d 473 (5th Cir. 1974), and SEC v. Glenn W. Turner Enterprises, Inc., 474 F.2d 476 (9th Cir. 1973), each of which involved a pyramid scheme run by affiliated companies. "A common enterprise is one in which the fortunes of the investor are interwoven with and dependent upon the efforts and success of those seeking the investment or of third parties." Note that, under this formulation, there may be a common enterprise involving only one promoter and one offeree.

Expectation of Profits. One of the important cases on the *Howey* "expectation of profit" element is International Brotherhood of Teamsters v. Daniel, 439 U.S. 551 (1979). *Daniel* involved contributions by employers into a pension plan maintained for their employees. The managers invested the contributed funds to earn profits, which ultimately were to flow through to the employees as benefits. The Supreme Court found the "expectation of profit" element missing, however, focusing on what it viewed as the relatively small percentage of the plan's assets derived from earnings compared to employer contributions. United Housing Foundation, Inc. v. Forman, 421 U.S. 837 (1975), also is helpful. In that case, the purchasers of interests in a cooperative housing project received financial benefit from their ownership, primarily because the cost was subsidized. In addition, although no profit on a resale of the interests was possible, the project leased commercial space to third parties, with any income derived to be used to further reduce the rent on the housing units. The Court drew a distinction between a motive to "use or consume" and a motive to "profit" and found that the purchasers primarily sought a place to live. The prospect of income from the commercial space was, according to the Court, "far too speculative and insubstantial to bring the entire transaction within the Securities Acts."

Solely from the Efforts of Others. The "solely from the efforts of others" element of the *Howey* test is quite interesting, with one question being whether to apply the test literally. The Ninth and Fifth Circuits dealt with this question in *Glenn W. Turner* and *Koscot*. Both of those cases involved pyramid schemes in which the investors were not passive. Once brought into the scheme themselves, it was the investors' job to find new prospects and bring them to sales meetings run by the promoting companies. Those sales meetings were, the court said in *Glenn W. Turner*, "like an old time revival meeting, but directed toward the joys of making easy money rather than salvation." Both courts chose not to read "solely" literally, pointing out that "it would be easy to evade the test by adding a requirement that the buyer contribute a modicum of effort." The test those courts adopted, and which generally is followed, actually went far beyond that required to avoid the modicum of effort problem and entailed an inquiry into "whether the efforts made by those other than the investor are

the undeniably significant ones, those essential managerial efforts which affect the failure or success of the enterprise."

■ **Think about this:**

(A) Suppose that Arya owns 100 percent of the stock of A Corp. and wishes to sell his entire holdings. Anselm wishes to buy it. Is Arya offering an investment contract? Is he otherwise offering a security?

(B) Bo owns a cattle-feeding operation and does not have enough barn space to house the livestock. He negotiates with his neighbor, Briana, to use some of her barn space for his overflow. In return, he agrees to give Briana 5 percent of his net profits. Has Bo sold an investment contract?

(C) Fast-talking Celina offers Mr. and Mrs. Chance an opportunity to become part of the burgeoning earthworm industry. She sells them a very big bag of worms, with directions (place in soil and add water, but not too much). She explains that she will line up contracts with end users such as dogfood and shampoo manufacturers and promises to return to purchase as many worms as the Chances can produce, all at a premium price. Have the Chances purchased an investment contract?

(D) DaJuan is the founder and general partner of D, L.P., a limited partnership. He has sold interests to 12 limited partners. Are these interests likely to be investment contracts?

(E) Ephraim is the founder and general partner of E, L.L.L.P., a limited liability limited partnership. He has sold interests to five limited partners. Are these interests likely to be investment contracts?

Limited liability companies (like general partnerships) present interesting questions having to do with the amount of effort permitted or required, as opposed to the amount of efforts realistically expected, of investors. These questions are addressed in the following case.

UNITED STATES V. LEONARD

United States Court of Appeals for the Second Circuit
529 F.3d 83 (2008)

KATZMANN, Circuit Judge.

... Appellants Dickau and Silverstein were two of twenty-five individuals indicted for criminal fraud for their role in marketing investment interests in film companies. Following a jury trial, they were each convicted of securities fraud and conspiracy to commit securities and mail fraud. On appeal, they challenge their convictions, claiming, *inter alia*, that insufficient evidence supported the determination that the interests at issue were securities. . . . We find [this objection] to the conviction to be without merit. . . .

Carlo's Wake was a black comedy released in 1999.

BACKGROUND

Appellants Paul C. Dickau and Nanci Silverstein each operated an independent sales office ("ISO") selling interests in companies formed to finance the production and distribution of motion pictures. Dickau's ISO sold interests in Little Giant. LLC, an entity created to produce the film *Carlo's Wake*. Both appellants' ISOs sold interests in Heritage Film Group, LLC, which was established to produce the film *The Amati Girls*. As their names suggest, Little Giant and Heritage are limited liability companies ("LLCs"), and the interests in the companies took the form of investment "units," priced at $10,000 each. . . .

The government charged Dickau with four counts: one count of conspiracy to commit securities and mail fraud in relation to each of Little Giant and Heritage, and one count of securities fraud in relation to each of Little Giant and Heritage. The government charged Silverstein with one conspiracy count and one fraud count in relation to Heritage. All counts centered around the failure to disclose accurately the sales commission that the ISOs would be taking on the investment units. Following a trial in the Eastern District of New York, the jury returned a verdict of guilty on all counts against Dickau and Silverstein. Judge Wexler sentenced Dickau to forty-three months' imprisonment and ordered him to pay $499,989.64 in restitution. Judge Wexler sentenced Silverstein to six months' imprisonment, ordering her to pay $14,490 in restitution.

DISCUSSION . . .

I. Whether Sufficient Evidence Supported the Finding That the Units Were Securities

Although federal statutes enumerate many different instruments that fit the definition of security, the parties agree that the only category that potentially applies to this case is "investment contract." In the seminal case, SEC v. W.J. Howey Co., 328 U.S. 293 (1946), the Supreme Court provided the following definition of investment contract:

> an investment contract for purposes of the Securities Act means a contract, transaction or scheme whereby a person invests his money in a common enterprise and is led to expect profits solely from the efforts of the promoter or a third party, it being immaterial whether the shares in the enterprise are evidenced by formal certificates or by nominal interests in the physical assets employed in the enterprise.

Id. at 298-99. Appellants suggest that the Little Giant and Heritage units cannot constitute securities because investors never expected profits "solely from the efforts" of the promoters or others.

The Amati Girls, starring Mark Harmon, was released in 2000.

Following the Ninth Circuit's lead, *see* SEC v. Glenn W. Turner Enterprises, 474 F.2d 476, 482 (9th Cir. 1973), we have held that the word "solely" should not be construed as a literal limitation; rather, we "consider whether, under all the circumstances, the scheme was being promoted primarily as an investment or as a means whereby participants could pool their own activities, their money and the promoter's contribution in a meaningful way." SEC v. Aqua-Sonic Prods. Corp., 687 F.2d 577, 582 (2d Cir. 1982). Thus, in *Aqua-Sonic* we distinguished between companies that seek the "passive investor" and situations where there is a "reasonable expectation . . . of significant investor control." *Id.* at 585. It is the passive investor "for whose benefit the securities laws were enacted"; where there is a reasonable expectation of significant investor control, "the protection of the 1933 and 1934 Acts would be unnecessary." *Id.*

Our consideration of whether the investors in Little Giant and Heritage viewed the units primarily as a passive investment is complicated by the fact that Little Giant and Heritage were each structured as an LLC—a relatively new, hybrid vehicle that combines elements of the traditional corporation with elements of the general partnership while retaining flexibility for federal tax purposes. . . . [A]lthough "common stock is the quintessence of a security," Reves v. Ernst & Young, 494 U.S. 56, 62 (1990) (citing Landreth Timber Co. v. Landreth, 471 U.S. 681, 693 (1985)), and "[n]ormally, a general partnership interest is not considered a 'security,'" Odom v. Slavik, 703 F.2d 212, 215 (6th Cir. 1983), because of the sheer diversity of LLCs, membership interests therein resist categorical classification. Thus, an interest in an LLC is the sort of instrument that requires "case-by-case analysis" into the "economic realities" of the underlying transaction, *Reves*, 494 U.S. at 62.

One of the original promoters of Little Giant and Heritage, Russell Finnegan, testified at trial that the LLCs were structured so as to minimize the possibility that the investment units would constitute securities—"to get into . . . the gray areas of the securities law." Indeed, were we to confine ourselves to a review of the organizational documents, we would likely conclude that the interests in Little Giant and Heritage could not constitute securities because the documents would lead us to believe that members were expected to play an active role in the management of the companies.

For example, the sheet titled "Summary of Business Opportunity: Heritage Film Group, LLC" explains:

> Each Member is required to participate in the management of the Company retaining one (1) vote for each Unit acquired. Each important decision relating to the business of the Company must be submitted to a vote of the Members.
>
> The purchase of interests in the Company is not a passive investment. While specific knowledge and expertise in the day to day operation of a film producing and distributing company is not required, Members should have such knowledge and experience in general business, investment and/or financial affairs as to intelligently exercise their management and voting rights. . . . Further, each Member is required to participate in the management of the Company by serving on one or more committees established by the Members.

The summary further states that a manager may be chosen to perform certain "ministerial functions," such as keeping books and records, keeping the members informed, and circulating ballots to members, but the members retain the right to replace the manager and appoint his successor upon majority vote. Likewise, the operating agreement for Heritage provides that the "Company shall be managed by the Members. . . . [E]ach Member shall have the right to act for and bind the Company in the ordinary course of its business." . . .

In actuality, however, the Little Giant and Heritage members played an extremely passive role in the management and operation of the companies. At trial, members testified that they voted, at most, "a couple of times." Although the organizational documents provided for the formation of a number of committees, only two committees were formed for each of Heritage and Little Giant—a financial committee and a management committee. Of the 250-300 investors in Little Giant, five served on the management committee and seven served on the financial committee. Of the 350-400 investors in Heritage, ten served on the management committee and seven served on the financial committee. Thus, the vast majority of investors in both companies did not actively participate in the venture, exercising almost no control.

Record evidence allowed the jury to conclude that—notwithstanding the language in the organizational documents suggesting otherwise—from the start there could be no "reasonable expectation" of investor control, *Aqua-Sonic Prods. Corp.*, 687 F.2d at 585. . . .

For one, under the organizational documents, the members' managerial rights and obligations did not accrue until the LLCs were "fully organized." As promoter James Alex testified, so-called "interim managers" initially held legal control rights, and they decided almost every significant issue prior to the completion of fundraising: "The script, the director, the cast, the crew, scoring of it, editing. The entire picture was pretty well preproduced. . . ." Thus, the jury could reasonably have found the managerial rights contained in the organizational documents were hollow and illusory.

The jury was also entitled to consider the fact that the members appear not to have negotiated any terms of the LLC agreements. Rather, they were presented with the subscription agreements on a take-it-or-leave-it basis. That they played no role in shaping the organizational agreements themselves raises doubts as to whether the members were expected to have significant control over the enterprise.

Moreover, the members had no particular experience in film or entertainment and therefore would have had difficulty exercising their formal right to take over management of the companies after they were fully organized. *Cf. Aqua-Sonic Prods. Corp.*, 687 F.2d at 583-84 (noting that investors had no experience in selling dental products and therefore would be unlikely to feel capable of undertaking distribution themselves); Bailey v. J.W.K. Props., Inc., 904 F.2d 918, 923-24 (4th Cir. 1990) (finding that investors had "little to no control over the ultimate success or failure" of their cattle breeding investments where they had the contractual authority to direct the breeding but no expertise in selecting embryos or cross-breeding). And their number and geographic dispersion left investors particularly dependent on centralized management. We echo the

Fifth Circuit in finding that investors may be so lacking in requisite expertise, so numerous, or so dispersed that they become utterly dependent on centralized management, counteracting a legal right of control. *See* Williamson v. Tucker, 645 F.2d 404, 423-24 (5th Cir. 1981). . . .

For an even more modern twist, consider the following excerpt from a report of the Securities and Exchange Commission issued in 2017.

SECURITIES EXCHANGE ACT RELEASE NO. 81207

Securities and Exchange Commission, July 25, 2017

REPORT OF INVESTIGATION PURSUANT TO SECTION 21(a) OF THE SECURITIES EXCHANGE ACT OF 1934: THE DAO

I. Introduction and Summary

The United States Securities and Exchange Commission's ("Commission") Division of Enforcement ("Division") has investigated whether The DAO, an unincorporated organization; Slock.it UG ("Slock.it"), a German corporation; Slock.it's co-founders; and intermediaries may have violated the federal securities laws. . . .

As described more fully below, The DAO is one example of a Decentralized Autonomous Organization, which is a term used to describe a "virtual" organization embodied in computer code and executed on a distributed ledger or blockchain. The DAO was created by Slock.it and Slock.it's co-founders, with the objective of operating as a for-profit entity that would create and hold a corpus of assets through the sale of DAO Tokens to investors, which assets would then be used to fund "projects." The holders of DAO Tokens stood to share in the anticipated earnings from these projects as a return on their investment in DAO Tokens. In addition, DAO Token holders could monetize their investments in DAO Tokens by re-selling DAO Tokens on a number of web-based platforms ("Platforms") that supported secondary trading in the DAO Tokens.

After DAO Tokens were sold, but before The DAO was able to commence funding projects, an attacker used a flaw in The DAO's code to steal approximately one-third of The DAO's assets. Slock.it's co-founders and others responded by creating a work-around whereby DAO Token holders could opt to have their investment returned to them, as described in more detail below.

The investigation raised questions regarding the application of the U.S. federal securities laws to the offer and sale of DAO Tokens, including the threshold question whether DAO Tokens are securities. Based on the investigation, and under the facts presented, the Commission has determined that DAO Tokens are securities under the Securities Act of 1933 ("Securities Act") and the Securities Exchange Act of 1934 ("Exchange Act").

The Commission deems it appropriate and in the public interest to issue this report of investigation ("Report") pursuant to Section 21(a) of the Exchange Act to advise those who would use a Decentralized Autonomous Organization

("DAO Entity"), or other distributed ledger or blockchain-enabled means for capital raising, to take appropriate steps to ensure compliance with the U.S. federal securities laws. All securities offered and sold in the United States must be registered with the Commission or must qualify for an exemption from the registration requirements. In addition, any entity or person engaging in the activities of an exchange must register as a national securities exchange or operate pursuant to an exemption from such registration.

This Report reiterates these fundamental principles of the U.S. federal securities laws and describes their applicability to a new paradigm—virtual organizations or capital raising entities that use distributed ledger or blockchain technology to facilitate capital raising and/or investment and the related offer and sale of securities. The automation of certain functions through this technology, "smart contracts," or computer code, does not remove conduct from the purview of the U.S. federal securities laws. This Report also serves to stress the obligation to comply with the registration provisions of the federal securities laws with respect to products and platforms involving emerging technologies and new investor interfaces.

■ Think about this:

(F) Francisco wants to purchase a Flamed Food franchise, but doesn't have the time or money to run the business by himself. He asks Fouad to join him as a general partner. They shake hands on the deal. Does the formation of the partnership involve the sale of an investment contract?

(G) Gretel wants to start a business manufacturing a new type of grill that she has designed but doesn't have the money to do it by herself. She does, however, have plenty of time and a pronounced independent streak. She asks Guillermo to join her as a general partner. The general partnership agreement specifies that management of the business will be entirely in Gretel's hands. Does the formation of the partnership involve the sale of an investment contract?

(H) Haochen and Hannah have entered into a written general partnership agreement pursuant to which they will open a deep-fried hotdog stand. There are no special terms concerning management, which means, under prevailing law, that the general partners have equal rights to manage. They decide they need more capital, so Haochen contacts his aunt, who lives on the other side of the continent. He offers her a one-third partnership interest in exchange for $50,000. The aunt accepts, but cautions that she knows nothing about deep-fried hot dogs. Has Haochen's aunt purchased an investment contract?

Family Resemblance

Promissory notes also present interesting questions for securities lawyers. The term "note" is the first item mentioned in the definition of "security" in both the Securities Act and the Exchange Act. Complicating the matter somewhat, each Act then excludes certain notes, basically those having an original maturity not exceeding nine months, at least from certain provisions of the Act. In *Reves v. Ernst & Young* (cited in *Leonard*), the Supreme Court had to decide whether promissory notes issued by the Farmer's Cooperative of Arkansas and Oklahoma were securities. The notes were payable on demand, were uncollateralized and uninsured, and paid a variable interest rate. "While common stock is the quintessence of a security," said the Court, "the same simply cannot be said of notes, which are used in a variety of settings, not all of which involve investments." In analyzing the economic reality underlying the notes in the case before it, the *Reves* Court adopted a "family resemblance" test for determining whether a note is a security. The starting point is that a note is presumed to be a security. That presumption may be rebutted only by a showing that the note in question bears a strong resemblance, in terms of four factors, to instruments already identified as not being securities. If the note is not sufficiently similar to an item on the list, the decision whether another category should be added is to be made by examining the same factors.

The categories of instrument recognized by the Supreme Court as being notes that are not securities are the following:

> [T]he note delivered in consumer financing, the note secured by a mortgage on a home, the short term note secured by a lien on a small business or some of its assets, the note evidencing a "character" loan to a bank customer, short term notes secured by an assignment of accounts receivable, or a note which simply formalizes an open account debt incurred in the ordinary course of business (particularly if, as in the case of the customer of a broker, it is collateralized).

The four factors to be used in considering family resemblance were described in *Reves* in the following terms:

> First, we examine the transaction to assess the motivations that would prompt a reasonable seller and buyer to enter into it. [For example, is the seller's purpose the raising of money and is the buyer primarily interested in making a profit on the note or, on the other hand, is the note being used to facilitate the purchase and sale of a minor asset or consumer good?]
>
> Second, we examine the "plan of distribution" of the instrument . . . to determine whether it is an instrument in which there is "common trading for speculation or investment." [The Court noted, however, that "common trading" does not require actual trading in the financial markets.]
>
> Third, we examine the reasonable expectations of the investing public: The Court will consider instruments to be "securities" on the basis of such public expec-

tations, even where an economic analysis . . . might suggest that the instruments are not "securities" as used in that transaction. [In other words, advertising notes as securities helps to make them securities.]

Finally, we examine whether some factor such as the existence of another regulatory scheme significantly reduces the risk of the instrument, thereby rendering application of the Securities Acts unnecessary.

After applying the four-factor test to the Farmer's Cooperative notes, the Court found them to be securities since they did not bear a sufficient family resemblance to the notes the Court had previously determined not to be securities.

■ **Think about this:**

(I) Isobel wants to skip school this afternoon to go shopping. Isobel's friend, Ivan, is an excellent forger. She offers him $5 to forge a note from Isobel's mother excusing her from school for a dental appointment. If Ivan accepts, is he selling a security?

(J) Jammy Corp. retains Jill as an independent management consultant. She negotiates a contract with the company that is a very good deal for her, but her price is so high that Jammy cannot pay it right away. The president of Jammy reasons, however, that the company will be so profitable with Jill's advice that she is worth it. Jill agrees to take 50 percent of her fee in the form of a note payable out of Jammy's future profits. Has Jammy sold Jill a security?

C. Two Completely Separate—But Integrated—Registration Schemes

One confusing thing about federal securities law is that there are two statutes that greatly matter and they each require registration in some circumstances. The problem is that the two statutes have completely different tests for "registrability." The fact that a company is required to "register" a particular issuance of securities under the '33 Act does not necessarily mean that the company must also register under the '34 Act, and vice versa. The two registration requirements are as follows:

1. *'33 Act Registrability*: Under the '33 Act, unless one of the Act's exemptions is available (see below), then every offer to sell and every sale of a "security" is subject to the '33 Act. *See* '33 Act §5, 15 U.S.C. §77e.[4]

---

4. Although the '33 Act is intended primarily to regulate capital formation by the issuers of securities, some resales of previously purchased unregistered securities are also subject to the Act. Luckily, it contains a very broad exemption that covers sales by most individuals. As discussed below, §4(a)(1) of the '33 Act, 15 U.S.C. §77d(a)(1), provides that the Act's registration and disclosure requirements do not apply to "transactions by any person other than the issuer, underwriter, or dealer."

More to the Story: §12(g)

The 500-person trigger is a good rule of thumb, but the number can be increased in some cases. The actual language of '34 Act §§12(a) and (g) appears in the online Supplement.

2. *'34 Act Registrability*: The '34 Act only requires registration if one of the following situations applies:
   (a) the company has assets of more than $10 million, and it has some class of equity security held by 500 persons or more, or
   (b) the security is listed on a national securities exchange.
   See '34 Act §§12(a), (g), 15 U.S.C. §§78l(a), (g).

As a technical matter, what is registered under the '33 Act is specific securities, while under the '34 Act, it is a specific class of securities. The issuer itself is not registered under either Act.

Although the triggers are different, Securities Act and Exchange Act registration forms actually have much in common because the required general disclosures are quite similar. Adding to the confusion is the fact that issuers often are permitted to incorporate information from their '34 Act filings by reference in their '33 Act forms. The Acts intersect in other ways, as well. For instance, some exemptions from '33 Act registration are available only to companies that have not registered under the '34 Act.

A separate issue concerning applicability is that, strictly speaking, both statutes apply only to issuances of securities when the U.S. mail or some other "interstate commerce instrumentally of" is used. However, applicability of the statutes is very difficult to avoid on this ground alone. Virtually every securities transaction will involve the use of the mail, a telephone call, or some other communication that meets the very minimal modern test of "interstate commerce."

D. The Securities Act of 1933

1. The Registration and Prospectus Requirements

In convoluted terms, the '33 Act provides that unless some exemption applies, every offer to sell and every sale of securities triggers two obligations: (1) the filing of a registration statement, and (2) certain prospectus delivery requirements. The '33 Act "registration statement" is a long and complex document describing the company and the investment instrument at issue. The '33 Act "prospectus" is a document to be given to persons to whom the securities are offered, summarizing the investment and its risks, and is supposed to be the primary tool used to market the securities. It is filed as part of the registration statement. Criminal penalties are imposed for willful violations of these requirements and the SEC can bring civil actions even for unintended violations. Notably, there also are express private rights of action available to purchasers to the shares. These rights generally are regarded as quite plaintiff friendly—risking them is one of the primary "costs" of registration.

A registered public offering has a number of other major costs. Of the direct expenses, the highest is the compensation to the securities firms that sell the securities. For an offering of common stock of a few million dollars, the compensation typically is approximately 10 percent of the public offering price, or about $1 million for a $10 million offering. For larger offerings, especially for those involving debt rather than equity, the percentage compensation is lower, finally diminishing to less than 1 percent for the largest offerings of bonds. The next highest costs are legal, accounting, and printing expenses. For an initial public offering, those items easily can total $500,000; they can be much higher when complications are encountered. Filing fees, usually totaling a few thousand dollars, must also be paid. Miscellaneous expenses, including fees for a transfer agent and registrar of the securities, total another few thousand dollars.

A prospective issuer must also consider that direct expenses are just the starting point in a registered offering. Indirect expenses are substantial, especially so because they continue indefinitely. Once a company registers securities under the Securities Act, it becomes subject to the reporting requirements of the Exchange Act for at least a year. This means that annual and other reports, containing specially prepared financial statements and detailed information about a wide range of subjects, must be prepared and filed with the SEC. Except in rare cases, after a Securities Act registration, the company also meets the requirements for registration of its securities under the Exchange Act and must satisfy the reporting and other requirements of the Exchange Act even after the initial year has passed. That registration subjects it to additional continuing expenses, primarily for complying with the Commission's proxy rules at least annually. In total, Exchange Act compliance costs a company at least a few tens of thousands of dollars annually in legal, accounting, and printing costs. Beyond those expenses, a publicly held company has the annual fees of a transfer agent and registrar and the costs involved with continued dealings with securities analysts and shareholders.

2. The All-Important Exemptions from the '33 Act

Exemptions from the Securities Act's registration requirements are found in §§3 and 4, and §28 gives the Commission broad powers to create other exemptions. Section 4 is entitled "Exempted Transactions," which provides an accurate description of its coverage. Happily (and powerfully), §4(a)(1) of the '33 Act exempts transactions by "other than an issuer, underwriter, or dealer." Section 4 also provides exemptions for a number of issuer transactions. When one of these exemptions applies to a particular offering of securities, no '33 Act registration or disclosure requirement applies to that particular transaction. The title of §3, "Exempted Securities," is, however, something of a misnomer, because in addition to its list of securities that are exempt in all circumstances, it also includes a few exemptions that are specific to transactions. Examples of completely exempt securities are those issued by governments (§3(a)(2)) and those issued by religious, educational, charitable, and other such organizations (§3(a)(4)). Those securities never have to be registered under the Securities Act. Section 3 also includes,

> **More to the Story: Don't Try This at Home**
>
> There are a number of exemptions that should be attempted only with the advice of an attorney specializing in securities regulation. For the foreseeable future, these include issuances under what is fondly known as "Reg A," as well as "crowd-funding."

however, a few exemptions specific to transactions, including, in §3(a)(11), one for transactions that are completely "intrastate" in nature. This is one of the more useful exemptions for general business planners. The others are the "private offering" exemptions and certain "limited offering" exemptions.

We will discuss each of these exemptions in the sections to follow, but before we get to them, here are two important concepts involved in establishing each of them. The first is "coming to rest," and the second is "integration." "Coming to rest" deals with the issue of when a particular offering is over. The Commission considers the offering to continue until the offered securities have "come to rest" in the hands of persons who are not "merely conduits for a wider distribution." "Integration" is the question whether what purports to be a single offering should be combined with one or more other purportedly separate offerings. When offerings are integrated in that way, the larger offering, viewed as a whole, must meet the requirements of an exemption or all the securities must be registered. In Securities Act Release No. 4552, the Commission gave the following list of factors relevant to the question of integration. The Commission looks at whether

- the different offerings are part of a single plan of financing;
- the offerings involve the issuance of the same class of security;
- the offerings are made at or about the same time;
- the same type of consideration is to be received; and
- the offerings are made for the same general purpose.

(a) The Intrastate Offering Exemption

Securities Act §3(a)(11) exempts from the registration requirements of the Act

> [a]ny security which is a part of an issue offered and sold only to persons resident within a single State or Territory, where the issuer of such security is a person resident and doing business within, or, if a corporation, incorporated by and doing business within, such State or Territory.

The Commission has adopted a safe-harbor rule, Rule 147, that issuers may use to secure a §3(a)(11) exemption. A careful planner will follow the Rule. It usually is not satisfied by chance, and lawyers giving after-the-fact advice concerning the availability of the intrastate exemption typically will find themselves making arguments based on the statutory language.

 Dear Prof.: What's a "safe harbor"?

When the requirements of some part of the securities statutes are not entirely clear, the SEC frequently will assist planners by adopting a clarifying rule describing a set of circumstances that the agency believes satisfy the statute. The idea is that one can either choose to duplicate those circumstances (that is, navigate into the safe harbor), or take the far riskier course and "go naked under the statute"—clearly the raciest thing any securities lawyer ever does.

Rule 147 goes through the elements of §3(a)(11) step by step and adds a note of certainty at each point. For example, it establishes that sales efforts that are made more than six months apart typically will be treated as different issuances. In securities lingo, this means that the efforts will not be "integrated" with one another. For the purposes of the Rule, "principal residence" satisfies the residence requirement of individuals. In addition, the Rule provides objective tests for determining the residence of corporations, partnerships, and other types of business organizations. The Rule also sets objective tests for the "doing business" requirement, basically pitched at the 80 percent level for assets located in, gross revenues derived from, and proceeds to be used in the state in which the offering is made. If any *one* of the three is satisfied, the issuer will be regarded as doing business in the relevant state. In the alternative, the issuer will be regarded as doing business in any state in which a majority of its employees are located. The Rule also deals with the possibility that issuers might sell securities to residents of the same state knowing they will immediately resell them by prohibiting out-of-state resales for six months after the issuer's last sale. The Rule also contains technical requirements for precautions against interstate offers and sales of securities that are not likely to be satisfied by chance, such as placing legends on stock certificates, issuing stop-transfer instructions to transfer agents, obtaining written representations from purchaser as to residence, and disclosing the resale limitations in writing.

 Dear Prof.: By "legend" I know you don't mean anything as interesting as Beowulf or Zorro, so . . .

Short, conspicuous notices printed on stock certificates or securities marketing documents or the like are referred to as "legends." They frequently are used to warn the purchasers of shares of restrictions associated with ownership, such as "buy-sell" agreements to which they are subject. In the case of the '33 Act, the usual legend notifies purchasers that the shares cannot be resold unless the issuer receives a satisfactory opinion of counsel that the resale will not destroy the issuer's initial exemption.

In late 2016, the SEC relied on a different statutory provision in adding a second intrastate offering exemption. Section 28 allows the Commission to add exemptions it deems to be in the public interest, and it was on this authority that it adopted new Rule 147A. That rule parallels Rule 147 but specifies that issuers need not be incorporated in the state in which they seek to make the relevant offering. It also permits widespread offers to be made (including over the internet) if they bear appropriate legends and the only purchasers are residents of the state in question. These modifications would not be permitted under §3(a)(11).

(b) The Private Offering Exemption of §4(a)(2)

Section 4(a)(2) provides that the registration requirements of the '33 Act do not apply to "transactions by an issuer not involving any public offering." Transactions that can be made to fit within §4(a)(2) are called private placements, private offerings, or non-public offerings. Since the definition of "issuer" in the Act is straightforward, the only thing necessary to understand the legal requirements for a private placement is knowing what constitutes a "public offering." Regrettably, that term is not defined in the statute. The basic contours of a public offering, however, are well established in case law and in pronouncements by the Commission.

The most important Commission action on §4(a)(2) has been the adoption of Rule 506. The Rule is part of Regulation D, which is a collection of rules that governs the limited offer and sale of securities without Securities Act registration. Rule 506 is a safe-harbor rule under §4(a)(2). The overall "private placement" exemption under §4(a)(2) and the "limited offering" exemption under Rule 506 tend as a practical matter to be regarded as separate exemptions. We first discuss the statutory exemption and then examine Rule 506 later in the chapter along with the rest of Regulation D.

 Dear Prof.: What's the difference between a rule and a regulation?

Many people use the terms interchangeably and as a synonym for law. Others reserve them for laws adopted by agencies. The SEC's convention is to group discrete but related "rules" in one place and to give them the title "regulation." Thus, Rules 501 through 508 collectively are referred to as Regulation—or "Reg"—D.

For a number of reasons, the private placement exemption of §4(a)(2) traditionally has been the most important registration exemption available to issuers, and it retains major importance even though there is a distinct, freestanding safe harbor for limited offerings in Rule 506. First, the importance of having a fallback exemption, available for use when a Rule 506 limited offering or some other exemption fails, should not be underestimated. Second, in some types of transactions there is no doubt about the private nature of the transaction, and no safe-harbor rule is needed to help secure the §4(a)(2) exemption. Third, the requirements of §4(a)(2) can more easily be satisfied by chance than most other exemptions, some of which contain filing or other requirements that require advance planning. In cases when a lawyer is called in after-the-fact—after it has been found that an issuer issued securities without '33 Act registration, and the SEC or a private party has challenged the issuance—the private placement exemption may be the only exemption available to save a client from civil and criminal liability.

The leading case concerning the private placement exemption is SEC v. Ralston Purina Co., 346 U.S. 119 (1953), in which the issuer sold unregistered stock to a wide variety of non-management employees. Focusing on the legislative history of §4(a)(2), the Court found it to have been included because it was thought to describe transactions "where there is no practical need for [the Act's] application." Thus, the Court said, the applicability of the exemption "should turn on whether the particular class of persons affected needs the protection of the Act." In defining that class, the Court set forth a general criterion of "those who are shown to be able to fend for themselves" and then discussed the satisfaction of that requirement in terms of access to information on the part of the offerees. The exemption was not available to Ralston Purina, the Court determined, because the employees "were not shown to have access to the kind of information which registration would disclose."

Three aspects of the Supreme Court's handling of the issue have particular continuing interest. First, the Court spoke of the requirement that offerees "be shown" to meet the test. It is critical that the burden of proof is on the person who wants the protection of an exemption. Second, the general requirement that an offeree be able to fend for himself has given the Commission and lower courts substantial leeway in establishing specific criteria for meeting the general requirement. Third, the requirement that offerees have access to "the kind of information which registration would disclose" is somewhat flexible. The Court did not require that an offeree have access to "the" information that would be available in a registered offering, but only that he or she have access to the "kind" of information that would be available.

Offeree qualification—showing that the offeree is the kind of person who doesn't need the protections of '33 Act disclosures—is a complex factor. Every securities lawyer would agree that offers in private placements may be made only to qualified offerees. The problem is in deciding what is required for qualification. The general consensus is that an offeree may qualify on the basis of a combination of factors, including (1) risk-bearing ability, (2) degrees of sophistication with respect to business and finance, (3) the offeree representative principle (the idea that the sophistication of an agent can be imputed to an offeree), (4) the manner of disclosure (the theory being that the clearer and more detailed the disclosure, the less sophistication is required of offerees), and (5) economic bargaining power (a concept that essentially is a shorthand for describing institutional and some other types of professional investors).

(c) The Limited Offering Exemptions: Regulation D

Regulation D is an interesting amalgam. Of its two exempting rules, Rule 504 is a rule under §3(b)(1), and Rule 506 is a rule under §4(a)(2), discussed above. Thus, Rule 506 really is a private offering exemption, while Rule 504 is referred

More to the Story: *Do* Try This at Home

Reg D is set out in the online Supplement. It is a bit tough to read, but the information in this chapter should help with decoding it. Reg D frequently is used by general business planners, so taking the time to become familiar with it can be a good investment.

to as a "small" or "limited" offering exemption. It is an exercise of the SEC's ability to structure exemptions, and, although recently increased in amount, it has been in existence since the early 1980s. There are a number of other limited exemptions that are either more specialized (such as one for employee benefit plans) or more complicated, and thus not as useful to a general business planner.

The following table shows the most basic requirements and limitations on offerings under Rules 504 and 506. Note that when the dollar limit is relatively low ($5 million under Rule 504), the requirements and limitations are few. The requirements and limitations rise (under Rule 506) when the dollar limit is lifted entirely. It is important to note, however, that there are a few additional requirements that are not shown, such as the need, in some circumstances, to avoid general solicitation and impose restrictions on resale. These additional requirements are apparent upon examination of Regulation D itself.

REGULATION D EXEMPTIONS

	Rule 504	*Rule 506*
Aggregate Offering Price Limitation	$5 million (12 mos.)	Unlimited
Number of Investors	Unlimited	35 plus unlimited accredited investors
Investor Qualifications	None required	Accredited investor *or* purchaser must be sophisticated (alone or with representative)
Type of Issuer	No Exchange Act companies, investment companies, "blank check" companies, or "bad actors"	No "bad actors"

"Blank check" companies essentially are those with no known business plan. "Bad actors" are those companies who previously have run afoul of certain specified laws.

■ **Think about this:**

(K) Khalid, as 100 percent owner, has successfully operated K Corp., which is incorporated in Virginia, for some time. All of K Corp.'s past business activity has been in Virginia, but Khalid believes it is time to "take it to the next level" by expanding to Maryland and the District of Columbia. To do so will require additional investors. He intends to cause K Corp. to offer $2 million of common stock to the following: K

Corp.'s current vice president, the bank with which K Corp. has done past business, and three of Khalid's own siblings, all of whom own successful businesses worth in the millions. Can he do so without registering under the Securities Act?

(L) Continue the assumptions of Problem K, but add an additional 34 investors with no particular attributes—what might be thought of as "Joes and Janes off the street." Can Securities Act registration be avoided?

E. The Securities Exchange Act of 1934

The point of '33 Act registration is to force preparation and filing of a registration statement and distribution of the prospectus contained therein. While the '34 Act also requires an initial filing by companies to which it applies, that registration statement is only a subsidiary purpose of the '34 Act. More importantly, the filing marks the point at which most of the other legal requirements of the '34 Act apply. The only important exception for purposes of this book is §10(b), which is a broad anti-fraud provision that applies to any purchase or sale of any security, not just those registered under the '34 Act.

Once the §12 registration obligation is triggered, the '34 Act imposes six particularly significant subsidiary legal obligations:

Connections

Section 10(b), along with Rule 10b-5, prohibits fraud in all shapes and sizes, including, in some circumstances, trading while in possession of material, non-public information— commonly referred to as "insider trading." These subjects are discussed at length in Chapters 30 and 31.

Periodic Reporting. First, once a company registers securities under §12, it must comply with a series of ongoing disclosure requirements. Every registered company must prepare a series of reports, some of them annually, some of them quarterly, and others only to reflect unusual events or to update previous reports that otherwise would be misleading. Thus, firms with registered securities must submit the annual 10-K and the quarterly 10-Q, plus the 8-K for extraordinary events. This is what they mean on the news, for example, when they refer to a "quarterly earnings report" or the like. Generally speaking, companies would prefer to avoid this obligation. For one thing, SEC filings provide a great source of dirt for plaintiffs, and may harm the firm's position in capital markets. Another very interesting problem is that public reporting leads to a problem that we might call the tax/finance dilemma. Namely, every company would like its securities filings to paint the company in as positive a light as possible—because investors, banks, regulators, and other important persons read them carefully. But in accounting materials submitted to the Internal Revenue Service with a company's tax return, the company will desire to represent itself as poorly as possible. Generally, companies pay taxes only when they have profits, and therefore they will try to tell the IRS that their profits were as low as they can legitimately make them look. This tax/finance dilemma often results in very tortured use of accounting rules and is the source of a fair bit of controversy.

Proxy Solicitation Rules. Whenever any proxy is solicited from a class of securities registered under §12, the person making the solicitation must comply with the SEC's proxy rules. Such solicitations must be pre-filed with the SEC and they must follow the form prescribed in SEC rules. They are also subject to a special anti-fraud rule applicable to covered proxy solicitations, contained in '34 Act §14(a). Proxy solicitation is the subject of its own chapter in this book.

Section 16 Insider Trading. Also as detailed in a subsequent chapter, directors, officers, and holders of more than 10 percent of any class of securities registered under the '34 Act are subject to certain rules on trading in any equity securities of the company, most importantly that they are normally not allowed to capture any profit on the purchase and sale, or sale and purchase, of the company's equity securities within a six-month period. These persons must also file certain reports with the SEC describing their holdings in the company's securities.

Tender Offer Regulation. The '34 Act provides that if, following '34 Act registration, any person or group acting together becomes the owner of more than 5 percent of the securities in the registered class of securities, or makes a "tender offer" that would result in such an ownership, then the person or group must make certain disclosures to the SEC, the company, and, sometimes, the company's shareholders.

Foreign Corrupt Practices Act. All §12 companies become subject to the Foreign Corrupt Practices Act (FCPA). In essence, the FCPA prohibits such companies or their agents from bribing foreign officials. The statute was the result of certain widely publicized scandals in the 1970s.

Sarbanes-Oxley Act. Finally, the Sarbanes-Oxley Act imposed a number of requirements on §12 companies. These include special audit opinions and officer certifications, disclosures with respect to ethics codes and independent directors, and the prohibition of loaning money or extending credit to officers and directors. Some of these requirements have been suspended in this case of "emerging growth companies" (basically, those within five years of their initial public offering of securities, provided they have less than $1 billion in annual gross revenue).

 Dear Prof.: Was that a typo? One billion dollars?

Indeed, it was not a typo. Moreover, emerging growth company status (which was invented in the Jump-Start Our Business Start-Ups (JOBS) Act of 2012) confers a number of short-cuts and special privileges under the Securities Act, as well as those under the Exchange Act. The majority of companies filing under the Securities Act claim this status.

F. The Advantages and Disadvantages of "Going Public"

In summary: As a practical matter, with properly structured transactions, the only federal securities law provision that most small companies need really worry about is §10(b) of the '34 Act. Most small businesses can raise the money they need either through some form of direct loan or through offerings of securities that are small enough to come within '33 Act exemptions. Likewise, because most '34 Act obligations apply only to §12 companies, and because §12 normally applies only to quite large businesses, most '34 Act obligations will not apply.

That said, the proprietors of many companies will contemplate the pros and cons of going public, and will want advice from their lawyers about those, as well as about the legal niceties. The following (adapted from Theresa A. Gabaldon & Larry D. Soderquist, Securities Law (5th ed. 2014)) may be useful background.

1. Advantages

Cashing In. One reason the owners of a privately held company take it public is to "cash in" by selling some of their stock. Not uncommonly, entrepreneurs who start and build successful companies leave most of the company's profits in the company so as to help it grow—or better yet, spend the company's cash on expansion of the company before the cash can become taxable income. During this period, the entrepreneur may be living on little income, even though the company is worth a great deal of money. By selling some of his or her stock to the public, such an entrepreneur can raise a large amount of cash while still retaining enough stock to control the company.

Economy. Though for a number of reasons a registered public offering is a very expensive transaction, it may actually be the most economical way to raise money in a given circumstance. Bank borrowings may or may not be possible in a given situation, and, in any case, the cost may be exorbitant. In addition, the longest term available for borrowing from a bank is usually five years. Many times a company has the alternative of raising the money it needs by selling securities under one of the registration exemptions. Although an exempt offering is likely to be much cheaper than a registered offering, that is not always so. Selling in an exempt offering often means dealing with venture capitalists, who are professional investors who drive hard bargains in negotiation. The company might save a great deal of money by avoiding those negotiations.

Control. Companies may choose to sell securities publicly to retain some degree of control. For example, when a privately owned company sells common stock to venture capitalists, the purchasers likely will require great say in future decisions. In a public offering, that can be avoided. Also, when a publicly held company sells securities to the public rather than, say, to a group of institutional investors in an exempt offering, it avoids the restrictions on its activities that the buyers may demand in negotiations.

Creation of Liquidity. Creating a public market for a company's shares provides its owners with liquidity. Once sold, they will immediately begin to trade in the public markets. The old shareholders will then be able to sell their shares in the trading market, as long as certain conditions are met. Often a company wishes to raise new capital by selling stock itself (which is called a primary offering), and one or more major shareholders want to generate cash by selling shares themselves (called a secondary offering). It is common for both types of offerings to be made simultaneously.

Prestige. Never underestimate the pull of emotional factors. Such an emotional pull may occur when owners of a private company consider taking it public. The prestige of becoming a major shareholder, director, and officer of a publicly held company holds a special allure for some.

Valuation and Estate Planning. Valuation of stock in a privately held company is problematical, but it is relatively straightforward in one that is publicly held. The liquidity of stock in a publicly held company can be helpful when ownership passes at the time of death. In a privately owned company, the heirs of a sole or major shareholder sometimes find themselves in a bad bargaining position if they need to find a buyer quickly.

Executive Recruiting and Retention. In certain situations, being a publicly held company can aid in executive recruiting and retention, because the company can provide relatively liquid stock as compensation. Also, the decision to "give" stock to executives in a publicly held company is a much easier decision to make than to "give" them stock in a privately held company. Taking on a few more public shareholders is of no real consequence to the company or its managers. However, taking on minority shareholders in a privately held company is a much more serious matter—in doing so the managers may take on a whole new set of fiduciary obligations.

Acquisitions. A publicly held company is in a much better situation than a privately owned one in terms of acquisitions. When its stock is desirable, a publicly held company can acquire other companies by using newly issued, liquid stock rather than cash as consideration. Obviously, that use of stock is possible also in a private company, but it raises the issue discussed in the preceding paragraph.

2. Disadvantages

Expense. There are, of course, out-of-pocket expenses for filing registration statements under the '33 and '34 Acts, as well as for preparing '34 Act reports. The Sarbanes-Oxley Act of 2002 imposed costly certification and other requirements on companies reporting under the Exchange Act (although the JOBS Act of 2012 ameliorated those requirements for many issuers during the first five years after their initial registration under the Securities Act).

Disclosure of Information. Much of the information that must be disclosed under either or both of the Acts concerns topics the company would rather keep private. As one entrepreneur who took his company public has said, "Much of what goes on in the bedroom is visible to those who sit in the parlor."

Freedom of Action. The owners of privately held companies often are used to making decisions as they please, and formalities of decision making are often minimal. The decision-making process must change after stock is sold to the public. The greatest change stems from the legal imposition upon major owners, directors, and officers of companies of fiduciary obligations to the new shareholders. Those obligations, the proxy rules, and the flood-light of disclosure encourage greater formality and less flexibility in decision making.

Income Expectations. One objective in a private company is usually to minimize current income so as also to minimize the company's income tax. That goal is accomplished by spending cash, before it can be realized as income at the end of the year, in ways that are designed to help the company grow and prosper in the future. The managers of a company that has recently gone public must execute an immediate about face in terms of income strategy. Even though a prosperous future and a minimization of taxes are in all the shareholders' long-term interest, public shareholders have an insatiable appetite for current earnings. The reason for that attitude, of course, is that the average shareholder has no particular long-term interest in the company. Shareholders want a steep, quick rise in the stock's price that allows them to sell and take their profits. This puts heavy pressure on the managers of a publicly held company to use every means to boost current earnings, and to do so on a quarterly basis. One simple way to increase current earnings is to cut development expenses for future products or services. Often managers see the long-term dangers of doing that, but the pressures are hard to resist. And resisted or not, those pressures constitute one of the greatest disadvantages of being publicly held.

■ **Think about this:**

(M) Suppose Mia, the owner of Mia's Mince, Inc., is thinking about trying to raise $2 million to expand her business. She does not believe she can borrow any more from banks than she already has. She is thinking about trying to sell stock in the company either to private investors or in a public offering. What is your advice?

(N) Would the advice you gave in Problem M change if the amount involved were $12 million?

Time Out for PR

It is perfectly acceptable for lawyers to give advice on non-legal considerations, and it arguably would be ineffective assistance to fail to do so if one
knows a client is failing to consider an important extralegal matter.
American Bar Association Rule 1.5 (Advisor) provides:

> In representing a client, a lawyer shall exercise independent professional
> judgment and render candid advice. In rendering advice, a lawyer may
> refer not only to law but to other considerations such as moral, economic,
> social and political factors, that may be relevant to the client's situation.

Test Yourself

1. Think for a moment about what the word "security" means for purposes
   of the Securities Act of 1933.

   Which of the following is most true?

   a. A limited partner's limited partnership interest is always a security.
   b. A limited partner's limited partnership interest is never a security.
   c. A limited partner's limited partnership interest is usually a security.

2. The promoter of a viatical settlement fund collects money from investors
   and uses it to purchase from persons diagnosed as terminally ill ("investees") the right to be named beneficiary of the investees' life insurance
   contracts. Thinking, again, about what the word "security" means for purposes of the Securities Act of 1933, which of the following is most true?

   a. The arrangement described is not likely to be deemed an investment
      contract because the significant efforts are those of the investees.
   b. The arrangement is not likely to be deemed an investment contract
      because life insurance policies are not securities.
   c. The arrangement is not likely to be deemed an investment contract
      because it is not what someone commonly would think of as a security.
   d. The arrangement is likely to be deemed an investment contract.

3. Thinking yet again about what the word "security" means for purposes of
   the Securities Act of 1933, which of the following is most true?

   a. The interest of a member of a limited liability company is not a security.
   b. The interest of a member of a limited liability company is a security.

c. More information would be required before a determination could be made whether the interest of a member in a particular limited liability company is a security.

d. The only information required before one could determine whether the interest of a member in a particular limited liability company is a security is the state in which it is formed.

4. New Company's shares of common stock are closely held. It proposes to conduct an initial public offering, as the result of which it will (for the first time) have in excess of $10 million of assets and more than 500 holders of its common shares. It expects that these shares will not be traded on a registered stock exchange but will be thinly traded over the counter. It also has a class of preferred shares outstanding in the hands of 50 holders. No shares of preferred will be issued in the proposed offering.

With respect to the preferred shares, which of the following is most true?

a. There is no reason to think that the preferred shares must be registered under the Securities Exchange Act of 1934.

b. If the common shares are registered under the Securities Exchange Act of 1934, so must the preferred shares.

c. Registering the common shares will automatically register the preferred shares.

d. It is not classes of shares but the issuer itself that is registered under the Securities Exchange Act of 1934 once a triggering event has occurred.

5. Referring again to the facts of Question 4, which of the following is most true?

a. There is enough information to determine whether registration under the Securities Exchange Act of 1934 must occur.

b. There is not enough information to determine whether the common shares must be registered under the Securities Exchange Act of 1934.

c. There is not enough information to determine whether the shares of either class must be registered under the Securities Exchange Act of 1934.

d. There is enough information to determine whether the preferred shares must be registered under the Securities Exchange Act of 1934.

Proxy Regulation 29

The solicitation of proxies is one of a handful of matters of internal corporate governance largely governed by federal law. Proxies are not much regulated by state law. MBCA §7.22, for example, imposes virtually no limits on them except to require that they be in writing, that they expire after 11 months unless otherwise provided, and that they are revocable unless otherwise provided. State fiduciary law imposes some constraints, in that corporate fiduciaries owe a basic duty of "disclosure" requiring them to avoid material misstatements or omissions in any proxy solicitation. However, because federal proxy regulation tends to be preferable to plaintiffs for a variety of reasons, this state duty of disclosure is largely subsumed by federal securities law.

Chapter Outline

A. Introduction

- Proxies revisited
- The federal government effectively has preempted the field

B. Exchange Act §14(a) and the Proxy Rules

1. Exchange Act §14(a)

2. How the Proxy System Works
   - Rule 14a-101 details the disclosure requirements
   - Rule 14a-6 is a filing requirement
   - Proxy rules apply to everyone, not just management
   - Exclusions and exemptions from coverage exist in some circumstances
   - §14A requires advisory votes on compensation

3. Proposals of Security Holders
   - Under Rule 14a-7, shareholders may choose to handle their own solicitations, in which case management must (at its election) provide a list of holders or mail the shareholders' materials at the solicitors' expense

> ■ Under Rule 14a-8, shareholders meeting certain requirements may have their proposals included in management's solicitation materials

4. False or Misleading Statements
   > ■ Rule 14a-9, which prohibits false or misleading statements in a solicitation subject to regulation, may be enforced by the Securities Exchange Commission, the Department of Justice (if the violation is willful), and by private parties

C. The Private Right for Materially Misleading Communications

1. Material Fact
   > ■ The test for materiality
   > ■ What is a "fact"?

2. Causation/"Essential Link"

3. Degree of Fault Required

D. Shareholder Access to Management's Proxy

> ■ Straightforward technical limits
> ■ Somewhat amorphous substantive grounds for exclusion

Test Yourself

 What does it look like?

Check the online Supplement for the following sample documents that are relevant to this chapter:

■ Proxy statement
■ Form of proxy
■ Shareholder proposal

A. Introduction

A proxy may be thought of as an agreement by a shareholder that allows some other person to vote the shareholder's shares. Proxy voting by shareholders is a necessity for most publicly held corporations. State corporation laws require annual meetings, and typically public corporations cannot satisfy quorum requirements unless most shareholders are represented by proxy holders. Shareholders in public companies are usually passive investors only, who care primarily about their shares' immediate financial returns, and so they would have little interest in physically appearing at a shareholders' meeting. For that reason, management usually solicits proxies from a corporation's shareholders at least annually, and more often when a special shareholders' meeting is needed. In addition to that ordinary use of proxies, those attempting to take over the management of a corporation sometimes solicit proxies from shareholders to gather enough votes to oust the incumbent board. Once that solicitation begins, management intensifies its proxy solicitation efforts, and a proxy contest develops.

> **Connections: Control Transactions**
>
> It is not unusual for someone wishing to acquire control of a company to conduct a proxy solicitation on the heels of a tender offer (also regulated by federal law) or other acquisition of shares.

The federal statutory scheme for regulating proxy solicitation essentially is a gap-filler. That is, it deals only with certain narrow matters connected with shareholder voting that were thought to have been inadequately controlled by state corporate law and other federal rules. The thrust of the federal system is the mandate of full disclosure in connection with shareholders' meetings. The meetings themselves are primarily governed by state corporation law, but state laws were thought ineffective to ensure really full disclosure in proxy communications. Typically, the only regulation of such disclosure is provided by the availability, in very limited circumstances, of actions for common law fraud or breach of fiduciary duty. Those are of limited help to a shareholder whose proxy is solicited on the basis of little or no disclosure. In a more perfect world, proxy regulation probably would be handled in state corporation statutes, and, ironically, although states now might consider it, they would likely find themselves at least partially preempted by federal law.

B. Exchange Act §14(a) and the Proxy Rules

1. Exchange Act §14(a)

At the heart of the Exchange Act's scheme for the regulation of proxy solicitations is §14(a):

> It shall be unlawful for any person, by the use of the mails or by any means or instrumentality of interstate commerce or of any facility of a national securities exchange or otherwise, in contravention of such rules and regulations as the Commission may prescribe as necessary or appropriate in the public interest or for the protection of investors, to solicit or to permit the use of his name to solicit any proxy or consent or authorization in respect of any security (other than an exempted security) registered pursuant to §12 of this title.

Section 14(a) itself states no substantive rule but simply gives the Securities and Exchange Commission (SEC or Commission) the power to pass rules that have the force of law. The reach of these rules can be quite broad, since they can apply to solicitations through the mails, by any means or instrumentality of interstate commerce, through stock exchange facilities, "or otherwise." They must, however, relate to solicitations of proxies, consents, or authorizations in respect to securities that are registered under the '34 Act. The concept of "solicitation" has been defined quite broadly in case law; as discussed below, the Commission has done a great deal to cut back on it.

■ **Think about this:**

(A) If the SEC had not adopted any rules under §14(a), what would the effect of that section be?

---

2. How the Proxy System Works

Regulation 14A gives effect to §14(a). The rules making up that regulation apply broadly, though with important exceptions. On the one hand, proxy statements are not the only communications governed by the proxy rules. The proxy form itself is covered, as is, with some exceptions, any "other communication to security holders under circumstances reasonably calculated to result in the procurement, withholding or revocation of a proxy." The scope of that last provision is very broad.

But not every solicitation that could meet the broad definition is covered. First, to allow shareholders to discuss corporate matters among themselves and make public statements about them, without triggering the proxy rules, Rule 14a-1 excludes most public statements of shareholders' own voting intentions. Rule 14a-2 also largely exempts solicitations in which the shareholders or other people involved (1) are not affiliated with management, (2) do not have an individual interest in the proposal to which the solicitation relates, and (3) do not seek proxy authority or provide to anyone proxy or other forms, such as consents, relating to voting. Another useful exemption permits non-management solicitation of up to ten persons. And finally, both shareholders and management may participate in electronic shareholder forums, provided that such participation occurs more than 60 days prior to the date announced for an annual or special meeting of the shareholders of the relevant company.

When the rules apply, they minutely govern the preparation, filing, and delivery to security holders of proxy materials. The formal disclosure document that must be filed with the SEC and given to security holders is called a proxy statement. Rule 14a-101 details the information that must be included in that statement. The

---

More to the Story: Shareholder Activism

The exemptions from proxy regulation that are described here are credited with breathing life into shareholder activism. That is, flexibility exists in the rules to allow certain kinds of advocacy by shareholders without triggering the sometimes onerous obligations of proxy rules, and it is thought to have been important in shareholder governance efforts. This activism has been directed both toward improving corporate profitability and toward a variety of social causes.

Rule is voluminous and the resulting statement has much in common with the registration statements required by the '33 and '34 Acts. Rule 14a-6 requires filing with the Commission of definitive copies of the proxy statement and form of proxy no later than the date they are first used, and in some cases they must be filed with the Commission ten days in advance.

Although everyone who seeks proxy authority is subject to the proxy rules, the rules are different for solicitations conducted by management than for other solicitations. The greatest difference is that proxy statements sent by management in connection with a typical annual meeting must be accompanied or preceded by an annual report that meets detailed requirements (or specified financial statements, in the case of certain small business issuers). The annual report, together with the proxy statement, provides the security holders with basic information concerning the issuer and its recent financial history, along with specific information on matters to be voted on at the annual meeting. One of the most important matters at the annual meeting is the election of directors, and a substantial portion of the proxy statement consists of information concerning management's candidates for election to the board. For many years, extensive disclosures regarding management compensation have been required, even though this is not a matter on which shareholders have the ability to vote under state law.

Exchange Act §14A provides that the proxy statements of companies registered under the Act must include a resolution providing for an advisory vote by shareholders on the executive compensation of certain named executive officers. This vote generally is referred to as "say on pay." A separate resolution must address the frequency with which say on pay must occur, with the permissible variation between one and three years (this is known as "say on frequency"). A separate advisory resolution (known as "say on parachutes") is called for in the event that special severance compensation—so-called golden parachute compensation—is to be granted in connection with a merger or similar transaction and has not already been included in a say on pay vote. The Jump-Start Our Business Start-Ups Act of 2012, however, provided that "emerging growth companies" (essentially those with less than $1 billion in revenue and within five years of their first offering registered under the '33 Act) need not comply with these requirements, and also limited the disclosures those companies must make with respect to executive compensation.

> ## More to the Story: Executive Compensation
>
> According to the Economic Policy Institute, the CEOs of the 350 largest American companies earned an average of $15.6 million in 2016 — 271 times the pay of the average worker.
>
> SEC rules require, as of 2018, that companies reporting under the '34 Act (with some exceptions) disclose the relationship between CEO compensation and the median worker's pay. Honeywell, Inc., reported a relationship of 333 (excluding, as permitted by the rules, workers in countries such as Slovakia, Brazil, and Indonesia, totaling no more than 5 percent of total workers).

■ **Think about this:**

(B) Why would Congress have limited shareholders to an advisory role, rather than giving them genuine "say on pay"?

3. Proposals of Security Holders

A security holder may solicit proxies from fellow security holders. Rule 14a-7 provides that management must either (at its option) provide a list of the other security holders or mail the soliciting shareholder's solicitational materials, at the solicitor's expense. Either way, compliance with the general regulatory scheme is required. The cost of compliance, however, could be prohibitive. In light of that, the SEC also adopted Rule 14a-8, which requires management to include in its proxy statement proposals made by security holders, along with supporting statements (up to 500 words, including the proposal itself), when certain conditions are met. Those conditions cover such things as timeliness (not less than 120 days before the proxy statement is to be released), amount of securities held (currently $2,000 in market value or 1 percent of the shares to be voted), length of holding period (one year) and, most important, the subject of the proposal. An issuer may refuse to include a proposal on a number of grounds. Some of those grounds are that the proposal (1) under the laws of the registrant's state of incorporation is not a proper subject for action by security holders, (2) relates to an election to office, (3) relates to a matter that is *de minimis* in light of the company's assets, earnings, and sales and is not otherwise significantly related to the company's business, or (4) deals with a matter relating to the conduct of the ordinary business operations of the registrant. When a proxy statement includes a proposal of a security holder, the proxy form must provide security holders with a mechanism for telling the proxy holder how to vote on the proposal. If management wishes to exclude a security holder's proposal, it must make a filing with the Commission in which, among other things, it states its reasons. If the Commission disapproves, it would be rare for management to proceed with the exclusion; if it did, it would risk enforcement action.

■ **Think about this:**

(C) Why would the SEC have thought that proposals relating to the listed matters should be subject to exclusion?

(D) What things would you recommend be added to the list?

4. False or Misleading Statements

Most litigation in the proxy area has involved Rule 14a-9(a), which states Regulation 14A's anti-fraud prohibitions:

> No solicitation subject to this regulation shall be made by means of any proxy statement, form of proxy, notice of meeting or other communication, written or oral, containing any statement which, at the time and in the light of the circumstances under which it is made, is false or misleading

with respect to any material fact, or which omits to state any material fact necessary in order to make the statements therein not false or misleading or necessary to correct any statement in any earlier communication with respect to the solicitation of a proxy for the same meeting or subject matter which has become false or misleading.

The Commission can enforce this provision by civil action, and the Department of Justice can prosecute willful violations criminally. In addition, in 1964 the Supreme Court held, using an expansive approach from which it has retreated in other contexts, that an implied private right of action exists for violations of Rule 14a-9. J.I. Case Co. v. Borak, 377 U.S. 426 (1964). Since that time, many interesting cases involving the Rule have been brought by private plaintiffs. A discussion of some of them follows.

> ■ **Think about this:**
>
> *(E)* What is the difference between "false" and "misleading"?

C. The Private Right for Materially Misleading Communications

A private plaintiff suing under Rule 14a-9 must show that:

- A non-exempt "proxy solicitation" was made, within the definition of SEC Rule 14a-1,
- that contained a misleading statement or omission,
- relating to a "material fact,"
- in circumstances where the shareholder's vote was an "essential link" to accomplishing the transaction complained of, and
- the defendant acted with the requisite culpability.

Some of these elements are amplified below.

1. Material Fact

Under Rule 14a-9, and, in fact, under all other anti-fraud rules under the federal securities laws, a misstatement or omission must be material before it gives rise to a cause of action. The current standard of materiality, used in all securities law contexts, was set forth by the Supreme Court in a Rule 14a-9 case, TSC Industries, Inc. v. Northway, Inc., 426 U.S. 438, 449 (1976): "An omitted fact is material if there is a substantial likelihood that a reasonable shareholder would consider it important in deciding how to vote." Elaborating on the standard, the Court indicated that the standard contemplates a showing of a substantial likelihood that, under all the circumstances, the omitted fact would have assumed actual significance in the deliberations of the reasonable shareholder. Understanding the substantial-likelihood standard itself is relatively easy. It is sometimes difficult, however, to predict what misstatement or omission a court will determine fits under the standard. A very interesting Supreme Court rumination on what a material *fact* can be appears in Virginia Bankshares, Inc. v. Sandberg, 501 U.S. 1083 (1991), which also features an important discussion of causation. *Virginia Bankshares* appears below, following the *Mills* case.

■ **Think about this:**

(F) Would you say that a reasonable shareholder would consider it important in deciding how to vote to know that a proposed director is a child pornographer? A felon convicted of embezzlement?

(G) Is an estimate a fact? How about an opinion?

---

2. Causation/"Essential Link"

The Supreme Court also has declared that causation is a required element in private right of action cases under Rule 14a-9. The interesting question is how to prove it. The seminal case on the subject is *Mills v. Electric Auto-Lite Co.*

MILLS v. ELECTRIC AUTO-LITE CO.

Supreme Court of the United States
396 U.S. 375 (1970)

Mr. Justice HARLAN delivered the opinion of the Court.

This case requires us to consider a basic aspect of the implied private right of action for violation of §14(a) of the Securities Exchange Act of 1934, recognized by this Court in J. I. Case Co. v. Borak, 377 U.S. 426 (1964). As in *Borak* the asserted wrong is that a corporate merger was accomplished through the use of a proxy statement that was materially false or misleading. The question with which we deal is what causal relationship must be shown between such a statement and the merger to establish a cause of action based on the violation of the Act.

Petitioners were shareholders of the Electric Auto-Lite Company until 1963, when it was merged into Mergenthaler Linotype Company. They brought suit on the day before the shareholders' meeting at which the vote was to take place on the merger against Auto-Lite, Mergenthaler, and a third company, American

Manufacturing Company, Inc. The complaint sought an injunction against the voting by Auto-Lite's management of all proxies obtained by means of an allegedly misleading proxy solicitation; however, it did not seek a temporary restraining order, and the voting went ahead as scheduled the following day. Several months later petitioners filed an amended complaint, seeking to have the merger set aside and to obtain such other relief as might be proper.

In Count II of the amended complaint, which is the only count before us, petitioners . . . alleged that the proxy statement sent out by the Auto-Lite management to solicit shareholders' votes in favor of the merger was misleading, in violation of §14(a) of the Act and SEC Rule 14a-9 thereunder. (17 CFR §240.14a-9.) Petitioners recited that before the merger Mergenthaler owned over 50% of the outstanding shares of Auto-Lite common stock, and had been in control of Auto-Lite for two years. American Manufacturing in turn owned about one-third of the outstanding shares of Mergenthaler, and for two years had been in voting control of Mergenthaler and, through it, of Auto-Lite. Petitioners charged that in light of these circumstances the proxy statement was misleading in that it told Auto-Lite shareholders that their board of directors recommended approval of the merger without also informing them that all 11 of Auto-Lite's directors were nominees of Mergenthaler and were under the "control and domination of Mergenthaler." Petitioners asserted the right to complain of this alleged violation both derivatively on behalf of Auto-Lite and as representatives of the class of all its minority shareholders.

On petitioners' motion for summary judgment with respect to Count II, the District Court for the Northern District of Illinois ruled as a matter of law that the claimed defect in the proxy statement was, in light of the circumstances in which the statement was made, a material omission. The District Court concluded, from its reading of the *Borak* opinion, that it had to hold a hearing on the issue whether there was "a causal connection between the finding that there has been a violation of the disclosure requirements of §14(a) and the alleged injury to the plaintiffs" before it could consider what remedies would be appropriate.

After holding such a hearing, the court found that under the terms of the merger agreement, an affirmative vote of two-thirds of the Auto-Lite shares was required for approval of the merger, and that the respondent companies owned and controlled about 54% of the outstanding shares. Therefore, to obtain authorization of the merger, respondents had to secure the approval of a substantial number of the minority shareholders. At the stockholders' meeting, approximately 950,000 shares, out of 1,160,000 shares outstanding, were voted in favor of the merger. This included 317,000 votes obtained by proxy from the minority shareholders, votes that were "necessary and

More to the Story: Causation

It seems natural that a causal link between the defendant's wrong and the plaintiff's injury should be required—but why? And what happens when an injunction is sought, rather than damages or rescission?

In fact, when Congress has created express causes of action under the federal securities laws, it sometimes has dispensed with any causation requirement.

indispensable to the approval of the merger." The District Court concluded that a causal relationship had thus been shown, and it granted an interlocutory judgment in favor of petitioners on the issue of liability, referring the case to a master for consideration of appropriate relief. . . . [The Seventh Circuit] affirmed the District Court's conclusion that the proxy statement was materially deficient, but reversed on the question of causation. The court acknowledged that, if an injunction had been sought a sufficient time before the stockholders' meeting, "corrective measures would have been appropriate." However, since this suit was brought too late for preventive action, the courts had to determine "whether the misleading statement and omission caused the submission of sufficient proxies," as a prerequisite to a determination of liability under the Act. If the respondents could show, "by a preponderance of probabilities, that the merger would have received a sufficient vote even if the proxy statement had not been misleading in the respect found," petitioners would be entitled to no relief of any kind.

The Court of Appeals acknowledged that this test corresponds to the common-law fraud test of whether the injured party relied on the misrepresentation. However, rightly concluding that "(r)eliance by thousands of individuals, as here, can scarcely be inquired into," the court ruled that the issue was to be determined by proof of the fairness of the terms of the merger. If respondents could show that the merger had merit and was fair to the minority shareholders, the trial court would be justified in concluding that a sufficient number of shareholders would have approved the merger had there been no deficiency in the proxy statement. In that case respondents would be entitled to a judgment in their favor.

Claiming that the Court of Appeals has construed this Court's decision in *Borak* in a manner that frustrates the statute's policy of enforcement through private litigation, the petitioners then sought review in this Court. We granted certiorari, believing that resolution of this basic issue should be made at this stage of the litigation and not postponed until after a trial under the Court of Appeals' decision.

II

As we stressed in *Borak*, §14(a) stemmed from a congressional belief that "[f]air corporate suffrage is an important right that should attach to every equity security bought on a public exchange." H.R. Rep. No. 1383, 73d Cong., 2d Sess., 13. The provision was intended to promote "the free exercise of the voting rights of stockholders" by ensuring that proxies would be solicited with "explanation to the stockholder of the real nature of the questions for which authority to cast his vote is sought." *Id.* at 14; S. Rep. No. 792, 73d Cong., 2d Sess., 12. The decision below, by permitting all liability to be foreclosed on the basis of a finding that the merger was fair, would allow the stockholders to be by-passed, at least where the only legal challenge to the merger is a suit for retrospective relief after the meeting has been held. A judicial appraisal of the merger's merits could be substituted for the actual and informed vote of the stockholders.

The result would be to insulate from private redress an entire category of proxy violations—those relating to matters other than the terms of the merger. Even outrageous misrepresentations in a proxy solicitation, if they did not relate to the terms of the transaction, would give rise to no cause of action under §14(a). Particularly if carried over to enforcement actions by the Securities and Exchange Commission itself, such a result would subvert the congressional purpose of ensuring full and fair disclosure to shareholders.

Further, recognition of the fairness of the merger as a complete defense would confront small shareholders with an additional obstacle to making a successful challenge to a proposal recommended through a defective proxy statement. The risk that they would be unable to rebut the corporation's evidence of the fairness of the proposal, and thus to establish their cause of action, would be bound to discourage such shareholders from the private enforcement of the proxy rules that "provides a necessary supplement to Commission action." J.I. Case Co. v. Borak, 377 U.S., at 432.[1]

Such a frustration of the congressional policy is not required by anything in the wording of the statute or in our opinion in the *Borak* case. Section 14(a) declares it "unlawful" to solicit proxies in contravention of Commission rules, and SEC Rule 14a-9 prohibits solicitations "containing any statement which . . . is false or misleading with respect to any material fact, or which omits to state any material fact necessary in order to make the statements therein not false or misleading. . . ." Use of a solicitation that is materially misleading is itself a violation of law, as the Court of Appeals recognized in stating that injunctive relief would be available to remedy such a defect if sought prior to the stockholders' meeting. In *Borak*, which came to this Court on a dismissal of the complaint, the Court limited its inquiry to whether a violation of §14(a) gives rise to "a federal cause of action for rescission or damages," 377 U.S., at 428. Referring to the argument made by petitioners there "that the merger can be dissolved only if it was fraudulent or non-beneficial, issues upon which the proxy material would not bear," the Court stated: "But the causal relationship of the proxy material and the merger are questions of fact to be resolved at trial, not here. We therefore do not discuss this point further." *Id.*, at 431. In the present case there has been a hearing specifically directed to the causation problem. The question before the Court is whether the facts found on the basis of that hearing are sufficient in law to establish petitioners' cause of action, and we conclude that they are.

Where the misstatement or omission in a proxy statement has been shown to be "material," as it was found to be here, that determination itself indubitably embodies a conclusion that the defect was of such a character that it might have been considered important by a reasonable shareholder who was in the process

---

1. The Court of Appeals' ruling that "causation" may be negated by proof of the fairness of the merger also rests on a dubious behavioral assumption. There is no justification for presuming that the shareholders of every corporation are willing to accept any and every fair merger offer put before them; yet such a presumption is implicit in the opinion of the Court of Appeals. . . . In practice . . . the objective fairness of the proposal would seemingly be determinative of liability [under the Seventh Circuit approach]. But, in view of the many other factors that might lead shareholders to prefer their current position to that of owners of a larger, combined enterprise, it is pure conjecture to assume that the fairness of the proposal will always be determinative of their vote. . . .

of deciding how to vote. This requirement that the defect have a significant propensity to affect the voting process is found in the express terms of Rule 14a-9, and it adequately serves the purpose of ensuring that a cause of action cannot be established by proof of a defect so trivial, or so unrelated to the transaction for which approval is sought, that correction of the defect or imposition of liability would not further the interests protected by §14(a).

Essential Link?

There is no need to supplement this requirement, as did the Court of Appeals, with a requirement of proof of whether the defect actually had a decisive effect on the voting. Where there has been a finding of materiality, a shareholder has made a sufficient showing of causal relationship between the violation and the injury for which he seeks redress if, as here, he proves that the proxy solicitation itself, rather than the particular defect in the solicitation materials, was an essential link in the accomplishment of the transaction. This objective test will avoid the impracticalities of determining how many votes were affected, and, by resolving doubts in favor of those the statute is designed to protect, will effectuate the congressional policy of ensuring that the shareholders are able to make an informed choice when they are consulted on corporate transactions. . . .

III

Our conclusion that petitioners have established their case by showing that proxies necessary to approval of the merger were obtained by means of a materially misleading solicitation implies nothing about the form of relief to which they may be entitled. We held in *Borak* that upon finding a violation the courts were "to be alert to provide such remedies as are necessary to make effective the congressional purpose," noting specifically that such remedies are not to be limited to prospective relief. 377 U.S., at 433. In devising retrospective relief for violation of the proxy rules, the federal courts should consider the same factors that would govern the relief granted for any similar illegality or fraud. One important factor may be the fairness of the terms of the merger. Possible forms of relief will include setting aside the merger or granting other equitable relief, but, as the Court of Appeals below noted, nothing in the statutory policy "requires the court to unscramble a corporate transaction merely because a violation occurred." 403 F.2d, at 436. In selecting a remedy the lower courts should exercise "the sound discretion which guides the determinations of courts of equity," keeping in mind the role of equity as "the instrument for nice adjustment and reconciliation between the public interest and private needs as well as between competing private claims." . . .

Monetary relief will, of course, also be a possibility. Where the defect in the proxy solicitation relates to the specific terms of the merger, the district court might appropriately order an accounting to ensure that the shareholders receive the value that was represented as coming to them. On the other hand, where, as here, the misleading aspect of the solicitation did not relate to terms of the merger, monetary relief might be afforded to the shareholders only if the merger resulted in a reduction of the earnings or earnings potential of their holdings. In short, damages should be recoverable only to the extent that they can be shown. If commingling of the assets and operations of the merged companies makes it impossible to establish direct injury from the merger, relief might be predicated on a determination of the fairness of the terms of the merger at the time it was approved. These questions, of course, are for decision in the first instance by the District Court on remand, and our singling out of some of the possibilities is not intended to exclude others. . . .

For the foregoing reasons we conclude that the judgment of the Court of Appeals should be vacated and the case remanded to that court for further proceedings consistent with this opinion.

■ Think about this:

(H) Will the test adopted in *Mills* work for both actions for injunctions before-the-fact and actions for damages or rescission after-the-fact?

(I) What would you tell the plaintiffs in *Mills* they will have to show with respect to damages? What do you think they are most likely to receive?

Actually, the reliance of shareholders in *Mills* probably could have been examined by having a research firm survey a random sample of shareholders. There is no doubt about what such a survey would have shown: A majority of non-institutional shareholders voted for the merger without reading the proxy statement. Thus, the merger would have gone through virtually regardless of what the statement had said. Should that have made a difference in the Court's reasoning? If not, what is the primary purpose of requiring proxy disclosure?

When the Supreme Court got its first post-*Mills* chance to speak to the issue of what it takes to form an "essential link" in the accomplishment of a transaction, it showed an inclination not to be expansive. The case was *Virginia Bankshares, Inc. v. Sandberg* (which also has something to say about material facts).

Connections: Intrinsic Fairness

When a transaction involves self-interest on the part of a majority shareholder, it is not unusual to seek approval by the disinterested minority in an attempt to establish intrinsic fairness. This step is only useful, of course, where the minority is fully informed.

VIRGINIA BANKSHARES, INC. v. SANDBERG

Supreme Court of the United States
501 U.S. 1083 (1991)

Justice SOUTER delivered the opinion of the Court. . . .

The questions before us are whether a statement couched in conclusory or qualitative terms purporting to explain directors' reasons for recommending certain corporate action can be materially misleading within the meaning of Rule 14a-9, and whether causation of damages compensable under §14(a) can be shown by a member of a class of minority shareholders whose votes are not required by law or corporate bylaw to authorize the corporate action subject to the proxy solicitation. We hold that knowingly false statements of reasons may be actionable even though conclusory in form, but that respondents have failed to demonstrate the equitable basis required to extend the §14(a) private action to such shareholders when any indication of congressional intent to do so is lacking.

I

In December 1986, First American Bankshares, Inc. (FABI), a bank holding company, began a "freeze-out" merger, in which the First American Bank of Virginia (Bank) eventually merged into Virginia Bankshares, Inc. (VBI), a wholly owned subsidiary of FABI. VBI owned 85% of the Bank's shares, the remaining 15% being in the hands of some 2,000 minority shareholders. FABI hired the investment banking firm of Keefe, Bruyette & Woods (KBW) to give an opinion on the appropriate price for shares of the minority holders, who would lose their interests in the Bank as a result of the merger. Based on market quotations and unverified information from FABI, KBW gave the Bank's executive committee an opinion that $42 a share would be a fair price for the minority stock. The executive committee approved the merger proposal at that price, and the full board followed suit.

Although Virginia law required only that such a merger proposal be submitted to a vote at a shareholders' meeting, and that the meeting be preceded by circulation of a statement of information to the shareholders, the directors nevertheless solicited proxies for voting on the proposal at the annual meeting set for April 21, 1987. In their solicitation, the directors urged the proposal's adoption and stated they had approved the plan because of its opportunity for the minority shareholders to achieve a "high" value, which they elsewhere described as a "fair" price, for their stock.

Although most minority shareholders gave the proxies requested, respondent Sandberg did not, and after approval of the merger she sought damages in the United States District Court for the Eastern District of Virginia from VBI, FABI, and the directors of the Bank. She pleaded two counts, one for soliciting proxies in violation of §14(a) and Rule 14a-9, and the other for breaching fiduciary duties owed to the minority shareholders under state law. Under the first count, Sandberg alleged, among other things, that the directors had not believed that the price offered was high or that the terms of the merger were fair, but had recommended the merger only because they believed they had no alternative if they wished to remain on the board. At trial, Sandberg invoked language from this Court's opinion in Mills v. Electric Auto-Lite Co., 396 U.S. 375, 385 (1970), to obtain an instruction that the jury could find for her without a showing of her own reliance on the alleged misstatements, so long as they were material and the proxy solicitation was an "essential link" in the merger process.

The jury's verdicts were for Sandberg on both counts, after finding violations of Rule 14a-9 by all defendants and a breach of fiduciary duties by the Bank's directors. The jury awarded Sandberg $18 a share, having found that she would have received $60 if her stock had been valued adequately. . . .

On appeal, the United States Court of Appeals for the Fourth Circuit affirmed the judgments, holding that certain statements in the proxy solicitation were materially misleading for purposes of the Rule, and that respondents could maintain their action even though their votes had not been needed to effectuate the merger. . . .

II

The Court of Appeals affirmed petitioners' liability for two statements found to have been materially misleading in violation of §14(a) of the Act, one of which was that "The Plan of Merger has been approved by the Board of Directors because it provides an opportunity for the Bank's public shareholders to achieve a high value for their shares." Petitioners argue that statements of opinion or belief incorporating indefinite and unverifiable expressions cannot be actionable as misstatements of material fact within the meaning of Rule 14a-9, and that such a declaration of opinion or belief should never be actionable when placed in a proxy solicitation incorporating statements of fact sufficient to enable readers to draw their own, independent conclusions.

A

We consider first the actionability *per se* of statements of reasons, opinion, or belief. Because such a statement by definition purports to express what is consciously on the speaker's mind, we interpret the jury verdict as finding that the directors' statements of belief and opinion were made with knowledge that the directors did not hold the beliefs or opinions expressed, and we confine our discussion to statements so made. That such statements may be materially significant raises no serious question. . . . Shareholders know that directors usually have knowledge and expertness far exceeding the normal investor's resources, and the directors' perceived superiority is magnified even further by the common knowledge that state law customarily

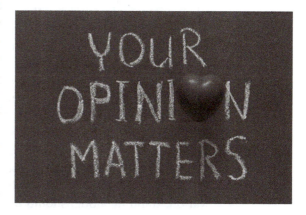

obliges them to exercise their judgment in the shareholders' interest. Naturally, then, the shareowner faced with a proxy request will think it important to know the directors' beliefs about the course they recommend and their specific reasons for urging the stockholders to embrace it.

B

1

But, assuming materiality, the question remains whether statements of reasons, opinions, or beliefs are statements "with respect to . . . material fact[s]" so as to fall within the strictures of the Rule. . . .

. . . Such statements are factual in two senses: as statements that the directors do act for the reasons given or hold the belief stated and as statements about the subject matter of the reason or belief expressed. . . . Reasons for directors' recommendations or statements of belief are . . . characteristically matters of corporate record subject to documentation, to be supported or attacked by evidence of historical fact outside a plaintiff's control. Such evidence would include not only corporate minutes and other statements of the directors themselves, but circumstantial evidence bearing on the facts that would reasonably underlie the reasons claimed and the honesty of any statement that those reasons are the basis for a recommendation or other action, a point that becomes especially clear when the reasons or beliefs go to valuations in dollars and cents.

It is no answer to argue, as petitioners do, that the quoted statement on which liability was predicated did not express a reason in dollars and cents, but focused instead on the "indefinite and unverifiable" term, "high" value, much like the similar claim that the merger's terms were "fair" to shareholders. The objection ignores the fact that such conclusory terms in a commercial context are reasonably understood to rest on a factual basis that justifies them as accurate, the absence of which renders them misleading. . . .

2

Under §14(a), then, a plaintiff is permitted to prove a specific statement of reason knowingly false or misleadingly incomplete, even when stated in conclusory terms. In reaching this conclusion we have considered statements of reasons of the sort exemplified here, which misstate the speaker's reasons and also mislead about the stated subject matter (*e.g.*, the value of the shares). A statement of belief may be open to objection only in the former respect, however, solely as a misstatement of the psychological fact of the speaker's belief in what he says. In this case, for example, the Court of Appeals alluded to just such limited falsity in observing that "the jury was certainly justified in believing that the directors did not believe a merger at $42 per share was in the minority stockholders' interest but, rather, that they voted as they did for other reasons, *e.g.*, retaining their seats on the board."

The question arises, then, whether disbelief, or undisclosed belief or motivation, standing alone, should be a sufficient basis to sustain an action under

§14(a), absent proof by the sort of objective evidence described above that the statement also expressly or impliedly asserted something false or misleading about its subject matter. We think that proof of mere disbelief or belief undisclosed should not suffice for liability under §14(a), and if nothing more had been required or proven in this case, we would reverse for that reason. . . .

This may help . . .

If you would find it useful, complete the chart to indicate when a cause of action will exist.

	Directors	Believe	Statement
Statement		Yes	No
Is	Yes		
True	No		

. . . [T]o recognize liability on mere disbelief or undisclosed motive without any demonstration that the proxy statement was false or misleading about its subject would authorize §14(a) litigation confined solely to what one skeptical court spoke of as the "impurities" of a director's "unclean heart." Stedman v. Storer, 308 F. Supp. 881, 887 (S.D.N.Y. 1969) (dealing with §10(b)). . . . While it is true that the liability, if recognized, would rest on an actual, not hypothetical, psychological fact, the temptation to rest an otherwise nonexistent §14(a) action on psychological enquiry alone would threaten . . . strike suits and attrition by discovery. . . . We therefore hold disbelief or undisclosed motivation, standing alone, insufficient to satisfy the element of fact that must be established under §14(a).

C

Petitioners' fall-back position assumes the same relationship between a conclusory judgment and its underlying facts that we described in Part II-B-1, supra. Thus, citing Radol v. Thomas, 534 F. Supp. 1302, 1315, 1316 (SD Ohio 1982), petitioners argue that even if conclusory statements of reason or belief can be actionable under §14(a), we should confine liability to instances where the proxy material fails to disclose the offending statement's factual basis. There would be no justification for holding the shareholders entitled to judicial relief, that is, when they were given evidence that a stated reason for a proxy recommendation was misleading and an opportunity to draw that conclusion themselves.

The answer to this argument rests on the difference between a merely misleading statement and one that is materially so. While a misleading statement will not always lose its deceptive edge simply by joinder with others that are true, the true statements may discredit the other one so obviously that the risk of real deception drops to nil. Since liability under §14(a) must rest not only on deceptiveness but materiality as well (*i.e.*, it has to be significant enough to be important to a reasonable investor deciding how to vote), petitioners are on perfectly firm ground insofar as they argue that publishing accurate facts in a proxy statement can render a misleading proposition too unimportant to ground liability.

But not every mixture with the true will neutralize the deceptive. If it would take a financial analyst to spot the tension between the one and the other, whatever is misleading will remain materially so, and liability should follow. . . . The point of a proxy statement, after all, should be to inform, not to challenge the reader's critical wits. Only when the inconsistency would exhaust the misleading conclusion's capacity to influence the reasonable shareholder would a §14(a) action fail on the element of materiality.

Suffice it to say that the evidence invoked by petitioners in the instant case fell short of compelling the jury to find the facial materiality of the misleading statement neutralized. . . .

III

The second issue before us, left open in *Mills v. Electric Auto-Lite Co.*, is whether causation of damages compensable through the implied private right of action under §14(a) can be demonstrated by a member of a class of minority shareholders whose votes are not required by law or corporate bylaw to authorize the transaction giving rise to the claim. . . .

Although a majority stockholder in *Mills* controlled just over half the corporation's shares, a two-thirds vote was needed to approve the merger proposal. . . . In [*Mills*] the Court found the solicitation essential, as contrasted with one addressed to a class of minority shareholders without votes required by law or by law to authorize the action proposed, and left it for another day to decide whether such a minority shareholder could demonstrate causation. . . .

In this case, respondents address *Mills'* open question by proffering two theories that the proxy solicitation addressed to them was an "essential link" under the *Mills* causation test. They argue, first, that a link existed and was essential simply because VBI and FABI would have been unwilling to proceed with the merger without the approval manifested by the minority shareholders' proxies, which would not have been obtained without the solicitation's express misstatements and misleading omissions. On this reasoning, the causal connection would depend on a desire to avoid bad shareholder or public relations, and the essential character of the causal link would stem not from the enforceable terms of the parties' corporate relationship, but from one party's apprehension of the ill will of the other.

In the alternative, respondents argue that the proxy statement was an essential link between the directors' proposal and the merger because it was the means to satisfy a state statutory requirement of minority shareholder approval, as a condition for saving the merger from voidability resulting from a conflict of interest on the part of one of the Bank's directors, Jack Beddow, who voted in favor of the merger while also serving as a director of FABI. Under the terms of Va. Code Ann. §13.1-691(A) (1989), minority approval after disclosure of the material facts about the transaction and the director's interest was one of three avenues to insulate the merger from later attack for conflict, the two others being ratification by the Bank's directors after like disclosure and proof that the merger was fair to the corporation. On this theory, causation would depend on the use of the proxy statement for the purpose of obtaining votes sufficient to bar a minority shareholder from commencing proceedings to declare the merger void.

Although respondents have proffered each of these theories as establishing a chain of causal connection in which the proxy statement is claimed to have been an "essential link," neither theory presents the proxy solicitation as essential in the sense of *Mills'* causal sequence, in which the solicitation links a directors' proposal with the votes legally required to authorize the action proposed. As a consequence, each theory would, if adopted, extend the scope of *Borak* actions beyond the ambit of *Mills* and expand the class of plaintiffs entitled to bring *Borak* actions to include shareholders whose initial authorization of the transaction prompting the proxy solicitation is unnecessary.

Assessing the legitimacy of any such extension or expansion calls for the application of some fundamental principles governing recognition of a right of action implied by a federal statute, the first of which was not, in fact, the considered focus of the *Borak* opinion. The rule that has emerged in the years since *Borak* and *Mills* came down is that recognition of any private right of action for violating a federal statute must ultimately rest on congressional intent to provide a private remedy, Touche Ross & Co. v. Redington, 442 U.S. 560, 575 (1979). From this the corollary follows that the breadth of the right once recognized should not, as a general matter, grow beyond the scope congressionally intended.

This rule and corollary present respondents with a serious obstacle, for we can find no manifestation of intent to recognize a cause of action (or class of plaintiffs) as broad as respondents' theory of causation would entail. . . .

Looking to the Act's text and legislative history . . . reveals little that would help toward understanding the intended scope of any private right. . . .

The congressional silence that is thus a serious obstacle to the expansion of cognizable *Borak* causation is not, however, a necessarily insurmountable barrier. This is not the first effort in recent years to expand the scope of an action originally inferred from the Act without "conclusive guidance" from Congress, see Blue Chip Stamps v. Manor Drug Stores, 421 U.S. [723, 737 (1975)], and we may look to that earlier case for the proper response to such a plea for expansion. There, we accepted the proposition that where a legal structure of private statutory rights has developed without clear indications of congressional intent, the contours of that structure need not be frozen absolutely when the result would be demonstrably inequitable to a class of would-be plaintiffs with claims comparable to those previously recognized. Faced in that case with such a claim for equality in rounding out the scope of an implied private statutory right of action, we looked to policy reasons for deciding where the outer limits of the right should lie. We may do no less here, in the face of respondents' pleas for a private remedy to place them on the same footing as shareholders with votes necessary for initial corporate action.

A

. . . [T]hreats of speculative claims and procedural intractability are inherent in respondents' theory of causation linked through the directors' desire for a cosmetic vote. Causation would turn on inferences about what the corporate directors would have thought and done without the minority shareholder approval unneeded to authorize action. A subsequently dissatisfied minority shareholder would have virtual license to allege that managerial timidity would have doomed corporate action but for the ostensible approval induced by a misleading statement, and opposing claims of hypothetical diffidence and hypothetical boldness on the part of directors would probably provide enough depositions in the usual case to preclude any judicial resolution short of the credibility judgments that can only come after trial. Reliable evidence would seldom exist. Directors would understand the prudence of making a few statements about plans to proceed even without minority endorsement, and discovery would be a quest for recollections of oral conversations at odds with the official pronouncements, in hopes of finding support for ex post facto guesses about how much heat the directors would have stood in the absence of minority approval. The issues would be hazy, their litigation protracted, and their resolution unreliable. Given a choice, we would reject any theory of causation that raised such prospects, and we reject this one.

B

The theory of causal necessity derived from the requirements of Virginia law dealing with postmerger ratification seeks to identify the essential character of the proxy solicitation from its function in obtaining the minority approval that would preclude a minority suit attacking the merger. Since the link is said to be a step in the process of barring a class of shareholders from resort to a state remedy otherwise available, this theory of causation rests upon the proposition of policy that §14(a) should provide a federal remedy whenever a false or misleading proxy statement results in the loss under state law of a shareholder plaintiff's state remedy for the enforcement of a state right. Respondents agree with the suggestions of counsel for the SEC and FDIC that causation be recognized, for example, when a minority shareholder has been induced by a misleading proxy statement to forfeit a state-law right to an appraisal remedy by voting to approve a transaction, or when such a shareholder has been deterred from obtaining an order enjoining a damaging transaction by a proxy solicitation that misrepresents the facts on which an injunction could properly have been issued. . . . Respondents claim that in this case a predicate for recognizing just such a causal link exists in Va. Code Ann. §13.1-691(A)(2) (1989), which sets the conditions under which the merger may be insulated from suit by a minority shareholder seeking to void it on account of Beddow's conflict.

This case does not, however, require us to decide whether §14(a) provides a cause of action for lost state remedies, since there is no indication in the law or facts before us that the proxy solicitation resulted in any such loss. The contrary appears to be the case. Assuming the soundness of respondents' characterization of the proxy statement as materially misleading, the very terms of the

Virginia statute indicate that a favorable minority vote induced by the solicitation would not suffice to render the merger invulnerable to later attack on the ground of the conflict. The statute bars a shareholder from seeking to avoid a transaction tainted by a director's conflict if, inter alia, the minority shareholders ratified the transaction following disclosure of the material facts of the transaction and the conflict. Va. Code Ann. §13.1-691(A)(2) (1989). Assuming that the material facts about the merger and Beddow's interests were not accurately disclosed, the minority votes were inadequate to ratify the merger under state law, and there was no loss of state remedy to connect the proxy solicitation with harm to minority shareholders irredressable under state law. Nor is there a claim here that the statement misled respondents into entertaining a false belief that they had no chance to upset the merger, until the time for bringing suit had run out. . . .

■ Think about this:

(J) After this case, will loss of a state remedy ever satisfy the "essential link" test? Will state remedies ever be lost if a false or misleading representation was involved?

(K) Suppose that the directors in this case had not said they were recommending the merger *because* they believed the price was high, but simply said they believed the price was high? Would that make a difference to the analysis?

(L) Suppose that a board of directors acted recklessly in forming the opinion that an offered merger price was high, stated that opinion, and turned out to be wrong. Would the directors be liable? How about if they were right?

(M) Suppose that a board of directors dishonestly and counterfactually state an opinion that the price offered in a merger is high, when in fact it is a bit lower than market price. Will liability attach?

3. Degree of Fault Required

The Supreme Court has never determined the degree of fault required to support a finding of liability under Rule 14a-9. Courts of appeals have gone both ways on the question, with the choice being between negligence and scienter (which loosely is defined as a state of mind more culpable than negligence). Negligence is the choice of the Second Circuit, which sometimes is referred to as the "mother court" of securities law. In reaching that conclusion, in Gerstle v. Gamble-Skogmo, Inc., 478 F.2d 1281 (2d Cir. 1973), the court discussed why scienter is required in a Rule 10b-5 action (because of language in §10(b) indicating a congressional intent to limit the scope of the section and its rules to actions involving fraud or deception), and then differentiated the situation under Rule 14a-9. "In contrast," said the court, "the scope of the rulemaking authority granted under §14(a) is broad, extending to all proxy regulation 'necessary or appropriate in the public interest or for the protection of investors' and not limited by any words connoting fraud or deception."

Several years after *Gerstle*, the Sixth Circuit revisited the issue in a case in which an accounting firm was sued for defects in a client's proxy statement. In Adams v. Standard Knitting Mills, Inc., 623 F.2d 422 (6th Cir. 1980), the court determined that scienter was required to support such a claim, and based its conclusion on two grounds. First, it differentiated between the accountants and their clients, making the case for differing treatment because accountants do not benefit from the proxy vote and are not in privity with the shareholders. Second, it read the legislative history of §14(a) as pointing to the requirement of scienter for such outsiders as accountants. Interestingly, the Sixth Circuit's analysis of that history would support the imposition of a scienter requirement in all Rule 14a-9 cases. Other courts subsequently have declined to extend *Adams* to issuers and corporate insiders. *See, e.g.,* Fradkin v. Ernst, 571 F. Supp. 829 (N.D. Ohio 1983).

■ **Think about this:**

(N) Suppose that the defendant is the corporate issuer and the corporate officials responsible for drafting the proxy statement were not negligent in the slightest. Nonetheless, a statement of material fact turns out to be incorrect. Will it be actionable? Is such a scenario really possible?

D. Shareholder Access to Management's Proxy

As noted, above, Rule 14a-8 requires management to include in its proxy statement proposals made by security holders when certain conditions are met. Those conditions are addressed in the Rule (which is set out in the online Supplement) in a fairly user friendly Q & A format. Matters such as timeliness, the length of the proposal, and the amount of securities that must be held by a proposing shareholder are straightforward. The proper subject matter for proposals is elusive, to say the least. The grounds on which a proposal can be excluded are quite broad. The three broadest probably are that the proposal: (1) under the laws of the registrant's state of incorporation is not a proper subject for action by security holders, (2) relates to an election to office, or (3) deals with a matter relating to the conduct of the ordinary business operations of the

Connections: The Limited Governance Role of Shareholders

Remember that, as a matter of state law, the shareholders of public corporations generally play the limited role of voting only for directors and certain fundamental changes.

registrant. In addition, there is a ground for exclusion based on lack of relevance if the proposal relates to operations which account for less than 5 percent of the company's total assets, net earnings and gross sales and is not otherwise significantly related to the company's business.

Obviously, the first ground is a matter of state law, but the Commission will assume (subject to rebuttal by management) that a proposal cast as a request or recommendation by the shareholders that the board of directors take action is proper. With respect to the next two, it is fair to say that the Commission has not been entirely consistent in its interpretation of either "related to an election to office" or "matter relating to the conduct of ordinary business operations." With respect to the former, there has been a great deal of drama and litigation, but the Rule now provides that a proposal can be excluded if it

1. would disqualify a nominee who is standing for election;
2. would remove a director from office before that director's term expired;
3. questions the competence, business judgment, or character of one or more nominees or directors;
4. seeks to include a specific individual in the company's proxy materials for election to the board of directors; or
5. otherwise could affect the outcome of the upcoming election of directors.

This obviously still leaves plenty to fight about.

■ **Think about this:**

(O) Ollie, the holder of a substantial position in Omega Corp., wants to introduce a proposal requesting the board of directors of Omega to explain why the annual fees paid each director are twice as much as what the average Omega worker makes, even though the company lost money last year. Might that be excluded on the grounds that it "relates to an election"?

(P) Why shouldn't shareholders be permitted to affect the outcome of elections and, in particular, question the competence and character of nominees?

There have been flip-flops over time in the SEC's interpretation of what constitutes the "conduct of ordinary business operations." For instance, in the 1990s it took the position that a company policy that discriminated on the basis of sexual orientation related to "rank and file" hiring and dismissal and thus was an ordinary business matter. Then, after pressure, it reverted to its prior position that the only issue with respect to a proposal related to employment was whether or not the subject matter of the proposed amendment raises a "significant social policy issue." It now tends to articulate its test in terms of whether a proposal "transcends" day-to-day business matters and raises "policy issues so significant that it would be appropriate for a shareholder vote." *See* Securities and Exchange Commission Staff Legal Bulletin No. 14H (CF) (Oct. 22, 2015).

The following case is an example of how one court looked at a related issue raised by the rule that a proposal may be excluded if it relates to operations that account for less than 5 percent of the company's total assets, net earnings, and gross sales and is not otherwise significantly related to the company's business.

LOVENHEIM v. IROQUOIS BRANDS, LTD.

United States District Court for the District of Columbia
618 F. Supp. 554 (1985)

This matter is now before the Court on plaintiff's motion for preliminary injunction.

Plaintiff Peter C. Lovenheim, owner of two hundred shares of common stock in Iroquois Brands, Ltd. (hereinafter "Iroquois/Delaware"), seeks to bar Iroquois/Delaware from excluding from the proxy materials being sent to all shareholders in preparation for an upcoming shareholder meeting information concerning a proposed resolution he intends to offer at the meeting. Mr. Lovenheim's proposed resolution relates to the procedure used to force-feed geese for production of *paté de foie gras* in France,[2] a type of *paté* imported by Iroquois/Delaware. Specifically, his resolution calls upon the Directors of Iroquois/Delaware to:

> form a committee to study the methods by which its French supplier produces *paté de foie gras*, and report to the shareholders its findings and opinions, based on expert consultation, on whether this production method causes undue distress, pain or suffering to the animals involved and, if so, whether further distribution of this product should be discontinued until a more humane production method is developed.

Mr. Lovenheim's right to compel Iroquois/Delaware to insert information concerning his proposal in the proxy materials turns on the applicability of §14(a) of the Securities Exchange Act of 1934, 15 U.S.C. §78n(a) ("the Exchange

---

2. *Paté de foie gras* is made from the liver of geese. According to Mr. Lovenheim's affidavit, force-feeding is frequently used in order to expand the liver and thereby produce a larger quantity of *paté*. Mr. Lovenheim's affidavit also contains a description of the force-feeding process:

> Force-feeding usually begins when the geese are four months old. On some farms where feeding is mechanized, the bird's body and wings are placed in a metal brace and its neck is stretched. Through a funnel inserted 10-12 inches down the throat of the goose, a machine pumps up to 400 grams of corn-based mash into its stomach. An elastic band around the goose's throat prevents regurgitation. When feeding is manual, a handler uses a funnel and stick to force the mash down.

Plaintiff contends that such force-feeding is a form of cruelty to animals.

Plaintiff has offered no evidence that force-feeding is used by Iroquois/Delaware's supplier in producing the *paté* imported by Iroquois/Delaware. However his proposal calls upon the committee he seeks to create to investigate this question.

Act"), and the shareholder proposal rule promulgated by the Securities and Exchange Commission ("SEC"), Rule 14a-8. That rule states in pertinent part:

> If any security holder of an issuer notifies the issuer of his intention to present a proposal for action at a forthcoming meeting of the issuer's security holders, the issuer shall set forth the proposal in its proxy statement and identify it in its form of proxy and provide means by which security holders [presenting a proposal may present in the proxy statement a statement of not more than 200 words in support of the proposal].*

Iroquois/Delaware has refused to allow information concerning Mr. Lovenheim's proposal to be included in proxy materials being sent in connection with the next annual shareholders meeting. In doing so, Iroquois/Delaware relies on an exception to the general requirement of Rule 14a-8, Rule 14a-8(c)(5). That exception provides that an issuer of securities "may omit a proposal and any statement in support thereof" from its proxy statement and form of proxy:

> if the proposal relates to operations which account for less than 5 percent of the issuer's total assets at the end of its most recent fiscal year, and for less than 5 percent of its net earnings and gross sales for its most recent fiscal year, and is not otherwise significantly related to the issuer's business. . . .

II. LIKELIHOOD OF PLAINTIFF PREVAILING ON MERITS . . .

Iroquois/Delaware's reliance on the argument that [the Rule 14a-8(c)(5)] exception applies is based on the following information contained in the affidavit of its president: Iroquois/Delaware has annual revenues of $141 million with $6 million in annual profits and $78 million in assets. In contrast, its *paté de foie gras* sales were just $79,000 last year, representing a net loss on *paté* sales of $3,121. Iroquois/Delaware has only $34,000 in assets related to *paté*. Thus none of the company's net earnings and less than .05 percent of its assets are implicated by plaintiff's proposal. These levels are obviously far below the five percent threshold set forth in the first portion of the exception claimed by Iroquois/Delaware.

    Plaintiff does not contest that his proposed resolution relates to a matter of little economic significance to Iroquois/Delaware. Nevertheless he contends that the Rule 14a-8(c)(5) exception is not applicable as it cannot be said that his proposal "is not otherwise significantly related to the issuer's business" as is required by the final portion

JD/MBA: Reading Financial Statements

Total Assets can be found on the left side of a balance sheet—and are just what they sound like.

Net Earnings and Gross Sales are income statement concepts.

Gross Sales is the amount received when goods are sold, before deducting their costs, and excludes revenue from other sources.

Net Earnings is the difference between revenue from all sources and all expenses.

Gross Sales can be quite high, even when Net Earnings are quite low.

---

    * *Editors' Note:* The paraphrase is in the original and reflects the Rule at the time. The Rule now allows 500 words to be allocated between the proposal and any supporting statement as the proponent sees fit.

of that exception. In other words, plaintiff's argument that Rule 14a-8 does not permit omission of his proposal rests on the assertion that the rule and statute on which it is based do not permit omission merely because a proposal is not economically significant where a proposal has "ethical or social significance."[3]

Iroquois/Delaware challenges plaintiff's view that ethical and social proposals cannot be excluded even if they do not meet the economic or five percent test. Instead, Iroquois/Delaware views the exception solely in economic terms as permitting omission of any proposals relating to a *de minimis* share of assets and profits. Iroquois/Delaware asserts that since corporations are economic entities, only an economic test is appropriate.

The Court would note that the applicability of the Rule 14a-8(c)(5) exception to Mr. Lovenheim's proposal represents a close question given the lack of clarity in the exception itself. In effect, plaintiff relies on the word "otherwise," suggesting that it indicates the drafters of the rule intended that other noneconomic tests of significance be used. Iroquois/Delaware relies on the fact that the rule examines other significance in relation to the issuer's business. Because of the apparent ambiguity of the rule, the Court considers the history of the shareholder proposal rule in determining the proper interpretation of the most recent version of that rule.

Prior to 1983, paragraph 14a-8(c)(5) excluded proposals "not significantly related to the issuer's business" but did not contain an objective economic significance test such as the five percent of sales, assets, and earnings specified in the first part of the current version. Although a series of SEC decisions through 1976 allowing issuers to exclude proposals challenging compliance with the Arab economic boycott of Israel allowed exclusion if the issuer did less than one percent of their business with Arab countries or Israel, the Commission stated later in 1976 that it did "not believe that subparagraph (c)(5) should be hinged solely on the economic relativity of a proposal." Securities Exchange Act Release No. 12,999 (1976). Thus the Commission required inclusion "in many situations in which the related business comprised less than one percent" of the company's revenues, profits or assets "where the proposal has raised policy questions important enough to be considered 'significantly related' to the issuer's business."

As indicated above, the 1983 revision adopted the five percent test of economic significance in an effort to create a more objective standard. Nevertheless, in adopting this standard, the Commission stated that proposals will be includable notwithstanding their "failure to reach the specified economic thresholds if a significant relationship to the issuer's business is demonstrated on the face of

---

3. The assertion that the proposal is significant in an ethical and social sense relies on plaintiff's argument that "the very availability of a market for products that may be obtained through the inhumane force-feeding of geese cannot help but contribute to the continuation of such treatment." Plaintiff's brief characterizes the humane treatment of animals as among the foundations of western culture and cites in support of this view the Seven Laws of Noah, an animal protection statute enacted by the Massachusetts Bay Colony in 1641, numerous federal statutes enacted since 1877, and animal protection laws existing in all fifty states and the District of Columbia. An additional indication of the significance of plaintiff's proposal is the support of such leading organizations in the field of animal care as the American Society for the Prevention of Cruelty to Animals and The Humane Society of the United States for measures aimed at discontinuing use of force-feeding.

the resolution or supporting statement." Securities Exchange Act Release No. 19,135 (1982). Thus it seems clear based on the history of the rule that "the meaning of 'significantly related' is not limited to economic significance."

The only decision in this Circuit cited by the parties relating to the scope of §14 and the shareholder proposal rule is Medical Committee for Human Rights v. SEC, 432 F.2d 659 (D.C. Cir. 1970).[4] That case concerned an effort by shareholders of Dow Chemical Company to advise other shareholders of their proposal directed at prohibiting Dow's production of napalm. Dow had relied on the counterpart of the 14a-8(c)(5) exemption then in effect[5] to exclude the proposal from proxy materials and the SEC accepted Dow's position without elaborating on its basis for doing so. In remanding the matter back to the SEC for the Commission to provide the basis for its decision, the Court noted what it termed "substantial questions" as to whether an interpretation of the shareholder proposal rule "which permitted omission of [a] proposal as one motivated primarily by *general* political or social concerns would conflict with the congressional intent underlying section 14(a) of the [Exchange] Act." 432 F.2d at 680 (emphasis in original).[6]

Iroquois/Delaware attempts to distinguish *Medical Committee for Human Rights* as a case where a company sought to exclude a proposal that, unlike Mr. Lovenheim's proposal, was economically significant merely because the motivation of the proponents was political. The argument is not without appeal given the fact that the *Medical Committee* Court was confronted with a regulation that contained no reference to economic significance. Yet the *Medical Committee* decision contains language suggesting that the Court assumed napalm was not economically significant to Dow:

> The management of Dow Chemical Company is repeatedly quoted in sources which include the company's own publications as proclaiming that the decision to continue manufacturing and marketing napalm was made not because of business considerations, *but in spite of them*; that management in essence decided to

---

4. The *Medical Committee* decision was vacated as moot by the Supreme Court after the shareholder proposal at issue failed to get support from three percent of all shareholders, thereby triggering a separate basis for exclusion, Rule 14a-8(c)(4)(i), 17 C.F.R. §240.14a-8(c)(4)(i). *See* SEC v. Medical Committee for Human Rights, 404 U.S. 403, 406 (1972).

5. Rule 14a-8(c)(2), 17 C.F.R. §240.14a-8(c)(2) (1970), permitted exclusion if a proposal was submitted "primarily for the purpose of promoting general economic, political, racial, religious, social or similar causes."

6. The Court defined the purpose of section 14(a) of assuring that shareholders exercise their right "to control the important decisions which affect them in their capacity as stockholders and owners of the corporation." 432 F.2d at 680-81.

Room to Argue: The Role of Shareholder Activism

There is a burgeoning literature on the purpose of the corporation and the role of activist shareholders. You can read more about this in the online Supplement. It is important to note that divestiture probably has a far more powerful effect than shareholder resolutions.

pursue a course of activity which generated little profit for the shareholders. . . .

Id. at 681 (emphasis in original).

This Court need not consider, as the *Medical Committee* decision implied, whether a rule allowing exclusion of all proposals not meeting specified levels of economic significance violates the scope of section 14(a) of the Exchange Act. *See* 432 F.2d at 680. Whether or not the Securities and Exchange Commission could properly adopt such a rule, the Court cannot ignore the history of the rule which reveals no decision by the Commission to limit the determination to the economic criteria relied on by Iroquois/Delaware. The Court therefore holds that in light of the ethical and social significance of plaintiff's proposal and the fact that it implicates significant levels of sales, plaintiff has shown a likelihood of prevailing on the merits with regard to the issue of whether his proposal is "otherwise significantly related" to Iroquois/Delaware's business.[7] . . .

IV. CONCLUSION

For the reasons discussed above, the Court concludes that plaintiff's motion for preliminary injunction should be granted.

■ **Think about this:**

(Q) Why is it necessary to have an exclusion for matters in the ordinary conduct of business *and* the exclusion discussed in *Lovenheim*? Will there ever be a case when a matter that is not in the ordinary course will be excluded as not otherwise significant to the business?

(R) Why did the proponent in *Lovenheim* only request that a committee be formed, rather than request the directors to cause the corporation to cease importing paté?

(S) If (and that's *if*) the purpose of the corporation is to make money for shareholders, why should they ever be permitted to express opinions about social or ethical issues?

(T) Iroquois/Delaware suggested a distinction between political and social issues that the court found it unnecessary to address. What is the distinction?

---

7. The result would, of course, be different if plaintiff's proposal was ethically significant in the abstract but had no meaningful relationship to the business of Iroquois/Delaware as Iroquois/Delaware was not engaged in the business of importing *paté de foie gras.*

Test Yourself

1. Achmed is a shareholder of Alpha Corporation. (You may assume this corporation is subject to §14 of the Securities Exchange Act of 1934.) He owns approximately 2 percent of the corporation's outstanding common stock. Achmed has learned that the management of Alpha intends to send out proxy solicitations to its shareholders for the purpose of obtaining their votes to reelect the present board of directors. Achmed makes a written demand on the board to include the following proposals in its solicitation materials: (1) that Percy be appointed president and (2) that the employee restrooms in Alpha's manufacturing facility be updated.

    Based on the foregoing, which of the following statements is most likely to be true?

    a. Management is not required to include either proposal in its solicitation materials.
    b. Management must include the first proposal (pertaining to Percy), but not the second one (pertaining to the restrooms), in its solicitation materials.
    c. Management must include both proposals in its solicitation materials if Achmed has owned his shares for at least one year.
    d. Management must include the second proposal in its solicitation materials, but not the first one.

2. Berto is a shareholder of Beta Corporation. (You may assume this corporation is subject to §14 of the Securities Exchange Act of 1934.) He owns approximately 2 percent of the corporation's outstanding common stock. Berto has learned that the management of Beta intends to send out proxy solicitations to its shareholders for the purpose of obtaining their votes to reelect the present board of directors. Berto makes a written demand on the board to include the following proposals in its solicitation materials: (1) that a woman be appointed president and (2) a recommendation that transgender employees be permitted to use the employee restrooms of their choice in Beta's manufacturing facility.

    Based on the foregoing, which of the following statements is most likely to be true?

    a. Management is not required to include either proposal in its solicitation materials.
    b. Management must include the first proposal (pertaining to appointment of a woman), but not the second one (pertaining to the use of restrooms), in its solicitation materials.
    c. Management must include both proposals in its solicitation materials if Berto has owned his shares for at least one year.
    d. Management must include the second proposal in its solicitation materials, but not the first one.

3. Chunhua is a shareholder of Gamma Corporation. (You may assume this corporation is subject to §14 of the Securities Exchange Act of 1934.) She owns stock in the corporation that has a value of $2,000, and she has been a shareholder for 14 months. Chunhua wants to submit an advisory proposal to the stockholders of Gamma, urging the corporation to expand its operations into the solar energy field. Gamma was formed for the purpose of developing energy sources, but has not previously been involved in solar power.

   Based on the foregoing, which of the following statements is most likely to be true?

   a. Management must include Chunhua's proposal in its proxy solicitation materials, because of its significance, regardless of its length.
   b. Management must include Chunhua's proposal in its proxy solicitation materials if it does not, with any supporting statement, exceed 500 words.
   c. Management must include Chunhua's statement in its proxy solicitation materials if it does not, with any supporting statement, exceed 500 words, but may charge Chunhua for the reasonable costs associated with mailing her proposal to Gamma's shareholders.
   d. Management is not required to include Chunhua's proposal in its solicitation materials, but must provide her with a mailing list of Gamma's shareholders, or else independently mail her proposal to the shareholders at Chunhua's expense.

4. Dre is a director of Delta Corporation. (You may assume this corporation is subject to §14 of the Securities Exchange Act of 1934.) The board of Delta solicited proxies for their reelection. Although other members of the board had, from time to time, heard rumors of Dre's criminal background, no conclusive proof of this background had ever been brought to their attention. However, a reasonably thorough investigation would have disclosed that, before his first election to the board, Dre had been convicted of several crimes involving breach of trust.

   The proxy solicitation failed to make mention of Dre's prior contacts with the criminal justice system, and Dre was elected. Following the election, Pru, a shareholder with less than 1 percent of Delta's stock who did not want Dre to sit on Delta's board, commenced an action to rescind the proxy votes obtained by Dre immediately before the election. (You may assume Pru gave her proxy to reelect the board and that Dre would not have been elected but for the proxies obtained via the solicitation.)

   Based on the foregoing, which of the following statements is most likely to be true?

   a. Pru should be successful.
   b. Pru's suit will not be successful because she lacks standing (i.e., she owned less than 1 percent of Delta's stock).

c. Pru is not likely to be successful because she did not commence her action until after Dre's election.

d. The omission of Dre's past criminal background was probably not material because his convictions did not involve his conduct as a director of Delta.

5. Edith is a shareholder of Epsilon, Inc. (You may assume this corporation is subject to §14 of the Securities Exchange Act of 1934.) Epsilon is in the solar energy field. The board of Epsilon solicited proxies for the approval of the merger of Epsilon into Zeta Corp., even though a single shareholder (not Zeta Corp.) owned sufficient shares to compel the merger. Zeta Corp. is in the energy field, but has concentrated on coal and gas. The directors of Epsilon expressed the opinion that the merger will "in no way change the nature of the enterprise in which our shareholders have invested." Edith does not agree and seeks to enjoin the merger, claiming that the directors' statement is false and misleading.

Based on the foregoing, which of the following statements is most likely to be true?

a. Whether Edith has standing depends on how many shares she owns.

b. The statement of the board is unlikely to be material.

c. Edith will be unable to prove that the solicitation is an essential link in accomplishing the transaction.

d. Answers b and c are both correct.

30

Fraud and Related Issues Under Rule 10b-5

Corporate stock is always a security; in many cases, interests in other limited liability entities also are securities. In fact, in the right circumstances even general partnerships may find that they have issued securities to passive partners. Debt instruments such as bonds and debentures also constitute securities. And the purchase or sale of any security—yes, *any* security—is subject to Securities Exchange Act Rule 10b-5. The Rule, in general terms, prohibits fraudulent or misleading conduct in connection with any such purchase or sale.

Chapter Outline

A. Overview of Rule 10b-5

- Relationship of §10(b) and Rule 10b-5
- Covers all securities
- Major contexts: misleading conduct and insider trading
- Different elements for government and private litigants

B. General Requirements

1. The "Manipulative or Deceptive" Requirement
   - Rule 10b-5 not available for "mere" breaches of fiduciary duty

2. The "Materiality" Requirement
   - No immateriality as a matter of law
   - The definition of materiality

3. The "In Connection With" Requirement
   - The "touch" test

4. The "Scienter" Requirement
   - State of mind more culpable than negligence

C. Additional Requirements for Private Plaintiffs

1. The "Purchaser-Seller" Requirement
   - Policies underlying requirement that plaintiff be an actual purchaser or seller

2. Reliance and Causation
   - Transaction and loss causation
   - The fraud-on-the-market theory

Test Yourself

A. Overview of Rule 10b-5

The Securities and Exchange Commission (SEC) adopted Rule 10b-5 in 1942 to close a gap in the anti-fraud provisions of the securities laws. The SEC had discovered that a corporation's president was inducing shareholders to sell their shares to him at a low price by claiming the company was doing badly, while in fact it was doing very well. The general anti-fraud provision then available, §17(a) of the Securities Act of 1933 (Securities Act), did not apply because it covers fraud only in the *sale* of securities, not in their *purchase*. To solve the problem, the SEC's staff drafted Rule 10b-5 by combining the various prohibitions of the Securities Act provision with language from §10(b) of the Securities Exchange Act of 1934 (Exchange Act). Section 10(b) states that it is unlawful to use, "in connection with the purchase or sale of any security, any manipulative or deceptive device or contrivance" in violation of any SEC rule. The staff presented the Rule to the Commissioners, who passed it in a single day without comment, except for Commissioner Sumner Pike, who said, "Well, we are against fraud, aren't we?"

 Dear Prof.: A single day? No comments? What happened to the Administrative Procedures Act? Doesn't it apply to the SEC?

Good eye. The Administrative Procedure Act does apply to the SEC, but it was not adopted until 1946, so Rule 10b-5 came in just under the wire. If Rule 10b-5 were drafted today, a notice and comment period would be necessary.

Here is the resulting rule:

RULE 10b-5. EMPLOYMENT OF MANIPULATIVE AND DECEPTIVE DEVICES

It shall be unlawful for any person, directly or indirectly, by the use of any means or instrumentality of interstate commerce, or of the mails or of any facility of any national securities exchange,

(a) To employ any device, scheme, or artifice to defraud,

(b) To make any untrue statement of a material fact or to omit to state a material fact necessary in order to make the statements made, in the light of the circumstances under which they were made, not misleading, or

(c) To engage in any act, practice, or course of business which operates or would operate as a fraud or deceit upon any person, in connection with the purchase or sale of any security.

It is crucial to note that Rule 10b-5, as it says, applies to the purchase or sale of *any* security, not just those that are registered under the Exchange Act. It thus covers the sale of shares by even the smallest of start-up companies and often may also apply to interests in partnerships and limited liability companies.

The first big event in the history of Rule 10b-5 was in 1946, when a district court found that an implied private right of action exists under the Rule.[1] Its use subsequently soared, partially as a result of the following case (which quotes from an important SEC enforcement proceeding). This case in part involves insider trading, to which the next chapter is devoted, but also deals with an issuer's duty to refrain from misstatements. In addition, it introduces many of the themes appearing in Rule 10b-5 jurisprudence.

Connections: The Definition of "Security"

As covered elsewhere in this book, "security" is broadly defined under the federal securities laws to include stock, bonds, debentures, and a number of other things, the most litigated of which is the "investment contract." An investment contract is a scheme pursuant to which there is

- an investment of money
- in a common enterprise
- in expectation of profit
- primarily from the managerial or entrepreneurial efforts of someone other than the investor.

S.E.C. V. TEXAS GULF SULPHUR CO.

United States Court of Appeals for the Second Circuit
401 F.2d 833 (1968)

WATERMAN, Circuit Judge:

This action was commenced in the United States District Court for the Southern District of New York by the Securities and Exchange Commission (the SEC) pursuant to Sec. 21(e) of the Securities Exchange Act of 1934 (the Act), 15 U.S.C. §78u(e), against Texas Gulf Sulphur Company (TGS) and several of its officers, directors and employees, to enjoin certain conduct by TGS and the individual defendants said to violate Section 10(b) of the Act, 15 U.S.C. Section 78j(b), and Rule 10b-5 (17 CFR 240.10b-5) (the Rule), promulgated thereunder, and to compel the rescission by the individual defendants of

---

1. Kardon v. National Gypsum Co., 69 F. Supp. 512 (E.D. Pa. 1946).

JD/MBA: Calls and Puts

A "call" is an option to purchase a security at a specific price on or before a certain date.

Incidentally, a different sort of option is also very common, and it is the flip side of the call—a "put" is an option to sell a security at a specific price on or before a certain date.

securities transactions assertedly conducted contrary to law. The complaint alleged (1) that defendants Fogarty, Mollison, Darke, Murray, Huntington, O'Neill, Clayton, Crawford, and Coates had either personally or through agents purchased TGS stock or calls thereon from November 12, 1963 through April 16, 1964 on the basis of material inside information concerning the results of TGS drilling in Timmins, Ontario, while such information remained undisclosed to the investing public generally or to the particular sellers; (2) that defendants Darke and Coates had divulged such information to others for use in purchasing TGS stock or calls or recommended its purchase while the information was undisclosed to the public or to the sellers; that defendants Stephens, Fogarty, Mollison, Holyk, and Kline had accepted options to purchase TGS stock on Feb. 20, 1964 without disclosing the material information as to the drilling progress to either the Stock Option Committee or the TGS Board of Directors; and (4) that TGS issued a deceptive press release on April 12, 1964. . . .

THE FACTUAL SETTING

This action derives from the exploratory activities of TGS begun in 1957 on the Canadian Shield in eastern Canada. In March of 1959, aerial geophysical surveys were conducted over more than 15,000 square miles of this area by a group led by defendant Mollison, a mining engineer and a Vice President of TGS. The group included defendant Holyk, TGS's chief geologist, defendant Clayton, an electrical engineer and geophysicist, and defendant Darke, a geologist. These operations resulted in the detection of numerous anomalies, i.e., extraordinary variations in the conductivity of rocks, one of which was on the Kidd 55 segment of land located near Timmins, Ontario.

[An exploration in the fall of 1963 yielded remarkable finds of rich mineral deposits, which convinced TGS that it was desirable to acquire the entirety of the Kidd 55 segment. In order to facilitate this acquisition TGS President Stephens instructed the exploration group to keep the results of an initial drill (K-55-1) confidential and undisclosed even as to other officers, directors, and employees of TGS. The company then deliberately conducted a drill on barren land, and then suspended drilling. By March 27, 1964, TGS decided that the land acquisition program had advanced to such a point that the company could resume drilling. It did so on March 31.]

During this period, from November 12, 1963 when K-55-1 was completed, to March 31, 1964 when drilling was resumed, certain of the individual defendants . . . and persons . . . said to have received "tips" from them, purchased TGS stock or calls thereon. Prior to these transactions these persons had owned 1135 shares of TGS stock

Connections: *Caveat Venditor*

Note that no one seems to think there is anything wrong with TGS's failure to disclose the results of its exploration to the owners of the mineral rights it is seeking to acquire. When buying or selling something other than a "security," like land, there generally is no duty to disclose absent a fiduciary duty to do so. See Chapters 12 and 20.

and possessed no calls; thereafter they owned a total of 8235 shares and possessed 12,300 calls.

On February 20, 1964, also during this period, TGS issued stock options to 26 of its officers and employees whose salaries exceeded a specified amount, five of whom were the individual defendants Stephens, Fogarty, Mollison, Holyk, and Kline. Of these, only Kline was unaware of the detailed results of K-55-1, but he, too, knew that a hole containing favorable bodies of copper and zinc ore had been drilled in Timmins. At this time, neither the TGS Stock Option Committee nor its Board of Directors had been informed of the results of K-55-1, presumably because of the pending land acquisition program which required confidentiality. All of the foregoing defendants accepted the options granted them.

[From March 31 through April 10, TGS continued to discover evidence that a body of commercially mineable ore might exist in the area. According to the calculations of the experts who testified for the SEC, TGS had, by April 10, already discovered 6.2 to 8.3 million tons of proven ore having gross assay values from $26 to $29 per ton.]

Meanwhile, rumors that a major ore strike was in the making had been circulating throughout Canada. On the morning of Saturday, April 11, Stephens at his home in Greenwich, Conn. read in the New York Herald Tribune and in the New York Times unauthorized reports of the TGS drilling which seemed to infer a rich strike from the fact that the drill cores had been flown to the United States for chemical assay. Stephens immediately contacted Fogarty at his home in Rye, N.Y., who in turn telephoned and later that day visited Mollison at Mollison's home in Greenwich to obtain a current report and evaluation of the drilling progress. The following morning, Sunday, Fogarty again telephoned Mollison, inquiring whether Mollison had any further information and told him to return to Timmins with Holyk, the TGS Chief Geologist, as soon as possible "to move things along." With the aid of one Carroll, a public relations consultant, Fogarty drafted a press release designed to quell the rumors, which release, after having been channeled through Stephens and Huntington, a TGS attorney, was issued at 3:00 P.M. on Sunday, April 12, and which appeared in the morning newspapers of general circulation on Monday, April 13. It read in pertinent part as follows:

NEW YORK, April 12—The following statement was made today by Dr. Charles F. Fogarty, executive vice president of Texas Gulf Sulphur Company, in regard to the company's drilling operations near Timmins, Ontario, Canada. Dr. Fogarty said:

"During the past few days, the exploration activities of Texas Gulf Sulphur in the area of Timmins, Ontario, have been widely reported in the press, coupled with rumors of a substantial copper discovery there. These reports exaggerate the scale of operations, and mention plans and statistics of size and grade of ore that are without factual basis and have evidently originated by speculation of people not connected with TGS. . . .

Defendant Fogarty went on to became chairman and CEO of TGS, holding those positions until 1981 when he perished in the crash of the company plane. According to his obituary, he grew up in the Mullen Home for Boys in Fort Logan, Colorado, and was survived by eight children, one of whom was a priest.

"Most of the areas drilled in Eastern Canada have revealed either barren pyrite or graphite without value; a few have resulted in discoveries of small or marginal sulphide ore bodies.

"Recent drilling on one property near Timmins has led to preliminary indications that more drilling would be required for proper evaluation of this prospect. The drilling done to date has not been conclusive, but the statements made by many outside quarters are unreliable and include information and figures that are not available to TGS.

"The work done to date has not been sufficient to reach definite conclusions and any statement as to size and grade of ore would be premature and possibly misleading. When we have progressed to the point where reasonable and logical conclusions can be made, TGS will issue a definite statement to its stockholders and to the public in order to clarify the Timmins project." . . .

The evidence as to the effect of this release on the investing public was equivocal and less than abundant. . . .

Meanwhile, drilling operations continued [to yield highly favorable results].

While drilling activity ensued to completion, TGC officials were taking steps toward ultimate disclosure of the discovery. On April 13, a previously-invited reporter for The Northern Miner, a Canadian mining industry journal, visited the drillsite, interviewed Mollison, Holyk and Darke, and prepared an article which confirmed a 10 million ton ore strike. This report, after having been submitted to Mollison and returned to the reporter unamended on April 15, was published in the April 16 issue. A statement relative to the extent of the discovery, in substantial

Ticker tape machines became obsolete in the 1960s, but were the first digital method for transmitting stock prices and other financial information. Based on telegraph technology, the machines made a ticking noise as they printed.

part drafted by Mollison, was given to the Ontario Minister of Mines for release to the Canadian media. Mollison and Holyk expected it to be released over the airways at 11 P.M. on April 15th, but, for undisclosed reasons, it was not released until 9:40 A.M. on the 16th. An official detailed statement, announcing a strike of at least 25 million tons of ore, based on the drilling data set forth above, was read to representatives of American financial media from 10:00 A.M. to 10:10 or 10:15 A.M. on April 16, and appeared over Merrill Lynch's private wire at 10:29 A.M. and, somewhat later than expected, over the Dow Jones ticker tape at 10:54 A.M.

Between the time the first press release was issued on April 12 and the dissemination of the TGS official announcement on the morning of April 16, the only defendants before us on appeal who engaged in market activity were Clayton and Crawford and TGS director Coates. Clayton ordered 200 shares of TGS stock through his Canadian broker on April 15 and the order was executed that day over the Midwest Stock Exchange. Crawford ordered 300 shares at midnight on the 15th and another 300 shares at 8:30 A.M. the next day, and these orders were executed over the Midwest Exchange in Chicago at its opening on April 16. Coates left the TGS press conference and called his broker son-in-law Haemisegger shortly before 10:20 A.M. on the 16th and ordered 2,000 shares of TGS for family trust accounts of which Coates was a trustee but not a beneficiary; Haemisegger executed this order over the

New York and Midwest Exchanges, and he and his customers purchased 1500 additional shares.

During the period of drilling in Timmins, the market price of TGS stock fluctuated but steadily gained overall. On Friday, November 8, when the drilling began, the stock closed at 17 3/8. . . . By May 15, TGS stock was selling at 58 1/4.

I. THE INDIVIDUAL DEFENDANTS

A. Introductory . . .

. . . The essence of [Rule 10b-5] is that anyone who, trading for his own account in the securities of a corporation has "access, directly or indirectly, to information intended to be available only for a corporate purpose and not for the personal benefit of anyone" may not take "advantage of such information knowing it is unavailable to those with whom he is dealing," i.e., the investing public. Matter of Cady, Roberts & Co., 40 SEC 907, 912 (1961). Insiders, as directors or management officers are, of course, by this Rule, precluded from so unfairly dealing, but the Rule is also applicable to one possessing the information who may not be strictly termed an "insider" within the meaning of Sec. 16(b) of the Act. *Cady, Roberts, supra.* Thus, anyone in possession of material inside information must either disclose it to the investing public, or, if he is disabled from disclosing it in order to protect a corporate confidence, or he chooses not to do so, must abstain from trading in or recommending the securities concerned while such inside information remains undisclosed. So, it is here no justification for insider activity that disclosure was forbidden by the legitimate corporate objective of acquiring options to purchase the land surrounding the exploration site; if the information was, as the SEC contends, material,[2] its possessors should have kept out of the market until disclosure was accomplished. *Cady, Roberts, supra* at 911. . . .

B. Material Inside Information

An insider is not, of course, always foreclosed from investing in his own company merely because he may be more familiar with company operations than are outside investors. An insider's duty to disclose information or his duty to abstain from dealing in his company's securities arises only in "those situations which are essentially extraordinary in nature and which are reasonably certain to have a substantial effect on the market price of the security if (the extraordinary situation is) disclosed." Fleischer, *Securities Trading and Corporate Information Practices: The Implications of the* Texas *Gulf Sulphur Proceeding*, 51 Va. L. Rev. 1271, 1289.

> **Connections: Short-Swing Trading**
>
> Section 16(b) of the Exchange Act, discussed at length elsewhere in this book, requires the officers and directors of Exchange Act reporting companies, as well as the holders of more than 10 percent of a class of shares registered under the Act, to disgorge any profits made by buying and selling, or selling and buying, the issuer's securities within anything less than six months.

---

2. Congress intended by the Exchange Act to eliminate the idea that the use of inside information for personal advantage was a normal emolument of corporate office. . . .

More to the Story: Materiality

The test for materiality stated in this case is close to the one the Supreme Court ultimately endorsed in *Basic v. Levinson* (below) for all of federal securities law: A fact is material if there is a substantial likelihood that a reasonable investor would consider it important. Put another way, in the context of an omitted fact, there must be a substantial likelihood that the disclosure of the omitted fact would have been viewed by the reasonable investor as having significantly altered the "total mix" of information made available.

Materiality is, of course, a concept that also is important in tort and contract law.

Nor is an insider obligated to confer upon outside investors the benefit of his superior financial or other expert analysis by disclosing his educated guesses or predictions.... The only regulatory objective is that access to material information be enjoyed equally, but this objective requires nothing more than the disclosure of basic facts so that outsiders may draw upon their own evaluative expertise in reaching their own investment decisions with knowledge equal to that of the insiders.

This is not to suggest, however, as did the trial court, that "the test of materiality must necessarily be a conservative one, particularly since many actions under Section 10(b) are brought on the basis of hindsight," 258 F. Supp. 262 at 280, in the sense that the materiality of facts is to be assessed solely by measuring the effect the knowledge of the facts would have upon prudent or conservative investors. As we stated in List v. Fashion Park, Inc., 340 F.2d 457, 462, "The basic test of materiality . . . is whether a reasonable man would attach importance . . . in determining his choice of action in the transaction in question. Restatement, Torts §538(2)(a); accord Prosser, Torts 554-55; I Harper & James, Torts 565-66." This, of course, encompasses any fact ". . . which in reasonable and objective contemplation might affect the value of the corporation's stock or securities. . . ." List v. Fashion Park, Inc., *supra* at 462, quoting from Kohler v. Kohler Co., 319 F.2d 634, 642 (7th Cir. 1963). Such a fact is a material fact and must be effectively disclosed to the investing public prior to the commencement of insider trading in the corporation's securities. The speculators and chartists of Wall and Bay Streets are also "reasonable" investors entitled to the same legal protection afforded conservative traders. Thus, material facts include not only information disclosing the earnings and distributions of a company but also those facts which affect the probable future of the company and those which may affect the desire of investors to buy, sell, or hold the company's securities.

In each case, then, whether facts are material within Rule 10b-5 when the facts relate to a particular event and are undisclosed by those persons who are knowledgeable thereof will depend at any given time upon a balancing of both the indicated probability that the event will occur and the anticipated magnitude of the event in light of the totality of the company activity. Here, . . . knowledge of the possibility, which surely was more than marginal, of the existence of a mine of the vast magnitude indicated by the remarkably rich drill core located rather close to the surface (suggesting mineability by the less

Open pit mining generally is much less expensive than extractive methods requiring tunneling.

expensive open pit method) within the confines of a large anomaly (suggesting an extensive region of mineralization) might well have affected the price of TGS stock and would certainly have been an important fact to a reasonable, if speculative, investor in deciding whether he should buy, sell, or hold. After all, this first drill core was "unusually good and . . . excited the interest and speculation of those who knew about it." 258 F. Supp. at 282.

. . . Our survey of the facts found below conclusively establishes that knowledge of the results of the discovery hole, K-55-1, would have been important to a reasonable investor and might have affected the price of the stock.[3] On April 16, The Northern Miner, a trade publication in wide circulation among mining stock specialists, called K-55-1, the discovery hole, "one of the most impressive drill holes completed in modern times." Roche, a Canadian broker whose firm specialized in mining securities, characterized the importance to investors of the results of K-55-1. He stated that the completion of "the first drill hole" with "a 600 foot drill core is very very significant . . . anything over 200 feet is considered very significant and 600 feet is just beyond your wildest imagination." . . .

Finally, a major factor in determining whether the K-55-1 discovery was a material fact is the importance attached to the drilling results by those who knew about it. In view of other unrelated recent developments favorably affecting TGS, participation by an informed person in a regular stock-purchase program, or even sporadic trading by an informed person, might lend only nominal support to the inference of the materiality of the K-55-1 discovery; nevertheless, the timing by those who knew of it of their stock purchases and their purchases of *short-term* calls—purchases in some cases by individuals who had never before purchased calls or even TGS stock—virtually compels the inference that the insiders were influenced by the drilling results. . . . No reason appears why outside investors, perhaps better acquainted with speculative modes of investment and with, in many cases, perhaps more capital at their disposal for intelligent speculation, would have been less influenced, and would not have been similarly motivated to invest if they had known what the insider investors knew about the K-55-1 discovery. . . .

The core of Rule 10b-5 is the implementation of the Congressional purpose that all investors should have equal access to the rewards of participation in securities transactions. It was the intent of Congress that all members of the investing public should be subject to identical market risks, which market risks include, of course the

---

Room to Argue: Is Insider Trading Good or Bad?

Some academics argue that insider trading is beneficial both because it is an efficient form of compensation and because it is a method of disseminating information that makes financial markets more efficient. Readings on this subject may be found in the online Supplement.

---

3. We do not suggest that material facts must be disclosed immediately; the timing of disclosure is a matter for the business judgment of the corporate officers entrusted with the management of the corporation within the affirmative disclosure requirements promulgated by the exchanges and by the SEC. Here, a valuable corporate purpose was served by delaying the publication of the K-55-1 discovery. We do intend to convey, however, that where a corporate purpose is thus served by withholding the news of a material fact, those persons who are thus quite properly true to their corporate trust must not during the period of non-disclosure deal personally in the corporation's securities or give to outsiders confidential information not generally available to all the corporations' stockholders and to the public at large.

risk that one's evaluative capacity or one's capital available to put at risk may exceed another's capacity or capital. The insiders here were not trading on an equal footing with the outside investors. They alone were in a position to evaluate the probability and magnitude of what seemed from the outset to be a major ore strike; they alone could invest safely, secure in the expectation that the price of TGS stock would rise substantially in the event such a major strike should materialize, but would decline little, if at all, in the event of failure. . . . Such inequities based upon unequal access to knowledge should not be shrugged off as inevitable in our way of life, or, in view of the congressional concern in the area, remain uncorrected.

We hold, therefore, that all transactions in TGS stock or calls by individuals apprised of the drilling results of K-55-1 were made in violation of Rule 10b-5. . . .

C. When May Insiders Act?

Appellant Crawford, who ordered the purchase of TGS stock shortly before the TGS April 16 official announcement, and defendant Coates, who placed orders with and communicated the news to his broker immediately after the official announcement was read at the TGS-called press conference, concede that they were in possession of material information. They contend, however, that their purchases were not proscribed purchases for the news had already been effectively disclosed. We disagree.

Crawford telephoned his orders to his Chicago broker about midnight on April 15 and again at 8:30 in the morning of the 16th, with instructions to buy at the opening of the Midwest Stock Exchange that morning. The trial court's finding that "he sought to, and did, 'beat the news,'" 258 F. Supp. at 287, is well documented by the record. . . .

. . . The reading of a news release, which prompted Coates into action, is merely the first step in the process of dissemination required for compliance with the regulatory objective of providing all investors with an equal opportunity to make informed investment judgments. Assuming that the contents of the official release could instantaneously be acted upon, at the minimum Coates should have waited until the news could reasonably have been expected to appear over the media of widest circulation, the Dow Jones broad tape, rather than hastening to insure an advantage to himself and his broker son-in-law. . . .

JD/MBA: Stock Options

Stock options are a common form of employee compensation intended to provide incentive to work hard to improve a corporation's profitability. Basically, they give the employee the right to purchase the corporation's stock at a future date at a price higher than the market price on the date of the grant. Then, if the market price on the exercise date exceeds the option price, the employee has an instant gain.

There are many who argue, however, that stock options encourage too much focus on short-term profitability rather than long-term planning.

E. May Insiders Accept Stock Options Without Disclosing Material Information to the Issuer?

On February 20, 1964, defendants Stephens, Fogarty, Mollison, Holyk and Kline accepted stock options issued to them and a number of other top officers of TGS, although not one of them had informed the Stock Option Committee of the Board of Directors or the Board of the results of K-55-1, which information we have held was then material. [The court proceeded to find receipt of the options to violate Rule 10b-5 with respect to all defendants other than Holyk and Mollison, whom the lower court had found could reasonably assume that their superiors would report the results and as to whom the SEC had not appealed.]

II. THE CORPORATE DEFENDANT

A. Introductory

At 3:00 P.M. on April 12, 1964, evidently believing it desirable to comment upon the rumors concerning the Timmins project, TGS issued the press release quoted [above]. The SEC argued below and maintains on this appeal that this release painted a misleading and deceptive picture of the drilling progress at the time of its issuance, and hence violated Rule 10b-5(2). TGS relies on the holding of the court below that "the issuance of the release produced no unusual market action" and "in the absence of a showing that the purpose of the April 12 press release was to affect the market price of TGS stock to the advantage of TGS or its insiders, the issuance of the press release did not constitute a violation of Section 10(b) or Rule 10b-5 since it was not issued 'in connection with the purchase or sale of any security'" and, alternatively, "even if it had been established that the April 12 release was issued in connection with the purchase or sale of any security, the Commission has failed to demonstrate that it was false, misleading or deceptive." 258 F. Supp. at 294. . . .

B. The "In Connection With . . ." Requirement . . .

. . . [I]t seems clear from the legislative purpose Congress expressed in the Act, and the legislative history of Section 10(b) that Congress when it used the phrase "in connection with the purchase or sale of any security" intended only that the device employed, whatever it might be, be of a sort that would cause reasonable investors to rely thereon, and, in connection therewith, so relying, cause them to purchase or sell a corporation's securities. There is no indication that Congress intended that the corporations or persons responsible for the issuance of a misleading statement would not violate the section unless they engaged in related securities transactions. . . .

C. Did the Issuance of the April 12 Release Violate Rule 10b-5?

Turning first to the question of whether the release was misleading, i.e., whether it conveyed to the public a false impression of the drilling situation at the time of its issuance, we note initially that the trial court did not actually decide this question. . . .

The choice of an ambiguous general statement rather than a summary of the specific facts cannot reasonably be justified by any claimed urgency. The avoidance of liability for misrepresentation in the event that the Timmins project failed, a highly unlikely event as of April 12 or April 13, did not forbid the accurate and truthful divulgence of detailed results which need not, of course, have been accompanied by conclusory assertions of success. Nor is it any justification that such an explicit disclosure of the truth might have "encouraged the rumor mill which they were seeking to allay." 258 F. Supp. at 296.

We conclude, then, that, having established that the release was issued in a manner reasonably calculated to affect the market price of TGS stock and to influence the investing public, we must remand to the district court to decide whether the release was misleading to the reasonable investor and if found to be misleading, whether the court in its discretion should issue the injunction the SEC seeks. . . .

■ Think about this:

(A) Just how were the shareholders who sold their shares to the individual defendants injured by the defendants' non-disclosure? Wouldn't they just have sold to someone else at the same price?

(B) Is it clear that the conduct of TGS injured anyone?

The increased use of Rule 10b-5 was aided by expansive judicial interpretations between 1968 and 1975. The Rule's history since then is characterized by refinements that generally make the Rule less useful to private plaintiffs. Still, Rule 10b-5 clearly occupies the preeminent position among the anti-fraud provisions in the securities laws. The best known use of the Rule has been in insider trading cases, typically those in which an officer, director, or other person who has a fiduciary relationship with a corporation buys or sells the company's securities when in the possession of material, non-public information. But the Rule also has been used in at least five other situations:

- when a corporation issues misleading information to the public, or keeps silent when it has a duty to disclose;
- when an insider selectively discloses material, non-public information to another party, who then trades securities based on the information (generally called "tipping");
- when a person mismanages a corporation in ways that are connected with the purchase or sale of securities;
- when a securities firm or another person manipulates the market for a security traded in the over the counter market; and
- when a securities firm or securities professional engages in certain other forms of conduct connected with the purchase or sale of securities.

More to the Story: SOX

With the passage of the Sarbanes-Oxley Act of 2002 (SOX), Rule 10b-5 gained company. SOX amended title 18 of the United States Code to add a new section, 1348, prohibiting fraud in connection with the purchase or sale of securities of Exchange Act reporting companies. Since Rule 10b-5 sweeps more broadly, one wonders why the new section was necessary—but it does carry a longer potential prison sentence (25 years as opposed to 20).

The last two uses are quite specialized and are beyond the scope of this text. Insider trading and tipping will be discussed in the next chapter. The rest of the material in this chapter relates generally to litigation under Rule 10b-5.

Government	Private Plaintiff
Manipulation or Deception	Manipulation or Deception
Materiality	Materiality
In Connection With	In Connection With
Scienter	Scienter
	Purchaser or Seller
	Causation

In reading a case interpreting Rule 10b-5 it usually is helpful to ask oneself whether the case was brought by the government or by private plaintiffs. This distinction is significant because private plaintiffs must make showings not required of the SEC or the Department of Justice. Coverage in this chapter therefore separates discussion of those showings generally required from discussion of those showings required only of private plaintiffs.

B. General Requirements

There are certain elements that must be addressed in all Rule 10b-5 litigation. These include:

- the "manipulative or deceptive" requirement
- the "materiality" requirement
- the "in connection with" requirement
- the "scienter" requirement

This section describes these general requirements. The following section deals with the additional elements that must be shown by private plaintiffs.

1. The "Manipulative or Deceptive" Requirement

As demonstrated in the following case, Rule 10b-5 always must be understood in light of its enabling statutory provision, Exchange Act §10(b), which speaks of manipulative or deceptive devices and contrivances.

More to the Story

Secondary Liability. This chapter deals with primary violators of Rule 10b-5. There is more in the online supplement on the subject of secondary liability.

SANTA FE INDUSTRIES, INC. V. GREEN

Supreme Court of the United States
430 U.S. 462 (1977)

Mr. Justice WHITE delivered the opinion of the Court.

The issue in this case involves the reach and coverage of §10(b) of the Securities Exchange Act of 1934 and Rule 10b-5 thereunder in the context of a Delaware short-form merger transaction used by the majority stockholder of a corporation to eliminate the minority interest.

I

In 1936, petitioner Santa Fe Industries, Inc. (Santa Fe), acquired control of 60% of the stock of Kirby Lumber Corp. (Kirby), a Delaware corporation. Through a series of purchases over the succeeding years, Santa Fe increased its control of Kirby's stock to 95%; the purchase prices during the period 1968-1973 ranged from $65 to $92.50 per share. In 1974, wishing to acquire 100% ownership of Kirby, Santa Fe availed itself of §253 of the Delaware Corporation Law, known as the "short-form merger" statute. Section 253 permits a parent corporation owning at least 90% of the stock of a subsidiary to merge with that subsidiary, upon approval by the parent's board of directors, and to make payment in cash for the shares of the minority stockholders. The statute does not require the consent of, or advance notice to, the minority stockholders. However, notice of the merger must be given within 10 days after its effective date, and any stockholder who is dissatisfied with the terms of the merger may petition the Delaware Court of Chancery for a decree ordering the surviving corporation to pay him the fair value of the shares, as determined by a court-appointed appraiser subject to review by the court.

Santa Fe obtained independent appraisals of the physical assets of Kirby—land, timber, buildings, and machinery—and of Kirby's oil, gas, and mineral interests. These appraisals, together with other financial information, were submitted to Morgan Stanley & Co. (Morgan Stanley), an investment banking firm retained to appraise the fair market value of Kirby stock. Kirby's physical assets were appraised at $320 million (amounting to $640 for each of the 500,000 shares); Kirby's stock was valued by Morgan Stanley at $125 per share. Under the terms of the merger, minority stockholders were offered $150 per share. . . .

Respondents, minority stockholders of Kirby, objected to the terms of the merger, but did not pursue their appraisal remedy in the Delaware Court of Chancery. Instead, they brought this action in federal court on behalf of the corporation and other minority stockholders, seeking to set aside the merger or to recover what they claimed to be the fair value of their shares. The amended complaint asserted that, based on the fair market value

Connections: M&A

Corporate acquisitions are dealt with at length elsewhere in this book. "Short-form" provisions permitting a parent corporation's board of directors to approve a merger unilaterally, without approval by the subsidiary's outside shareholders, are quite common. *See, e.g.,* MBCA §11.05.

of Kirby's physical assets as revealed by the appraisal included in the information statement sent to minority shareholders, Kirby's stock was worth at least $772 per share. The complaint alleged further that the merger took place without prior notice to minority stockholders; that the purpose of the merger was to appropriate the difference between the "conceded pro rata value of the physical assets" and the offer of $150 per share—to "freez[e] out the minority stockholders at a wholly inadequate price"; and that Santa Fe, knowing the appraised value of the physical assets, obtained a "fraudulent appraisal" of the stock from Morgan Stanley and offered $25 above that appraisal "in order to lull the minority stockholders into erroneously believing that [Santa Fe was] generous." This course of conduct was alleged to be "a violation of Rule 10b-5 because defendants employed a 'device, scheme, or artifice to defraud' and engaged in an 'act, practice or course of business which operates or would operate as a fraud or deceit upon any person, in connection with the purchase or sale of any security.'" . . .

The District Court dismissed the complaint for failure to state a claim upon which relief could be granted. . . .

A divided Court of Appeals for the Second Circuit reversed. . . .

II

. . . [T]he Court of Appeals' approach to the interpretation of Rule 10b-5 is inconsistent with that taken by the Court last Term in Ernst & Ernst v. Hochfelder, 425 U.S. 185 (1976).

Ernst & Ernst makes clear that in deciding whether a complaint states a cause of action for "fraud" under Rule 10b-5, "we turn first to the language of §10(b), for '[t]he starting point in every case involving construction of a statute is the language itself.'" . . .

. . . [A]s the Court [held in *Ernst & Ernst*], the language of the statute must control the interpretation of the Rule: Rule 10b-5 was adopted pursuant to authority granted the [Securities and Exchange] Commission under §10(b). The rulemaking power granted to an administrative agency charged with the administration of a federal statute is not the power to make law. Rather, it is "'the power to adopt regulations to carry into effect the will of Congress as expressed by the statute.'" . . . [The scope of the Rule] cannot exceed the power granted the Commission by Congress under §10(b).

The language of §10(b) gives no indication that Congress meant to prohibit any conduct not involving manipulation or deception. Nor have we been cited to any evidence in the legislative history that would support a departure from the language of the statute. . . . [T]hus the claim of fraud and fiduciary breach in this complaint states a cause of action under any part of Rule 10b-5 only if the conduct alleged can be fairly viewed as "manipulative or deceptive" within the meaning of the statute.

III

It is our judgment that the transaction, if carried out as alleged in the complaint, was neither deceptive nor manipulative and therefore did not violate either §10(b) of the Act or Rule 10b-5.

As we have indicated, the case comes to us on the premise that the complaint failed to allege a material misrepresentation or material failure to disclose. The finding of the District Court, undisturbed by the Court of Appeals, was that there was no "omission" or "misstatement" in the information statement accompanying the notice of merger. On the basis of the information provided, minority shareholders could either accept the price offered or reject it and seek an appraisal in the Delaware Court of Chancery. Their choice was fairly presented, and they were furnished with all relevant information on which to base their decision.

We therefore find inapposite the cases relied upon by respondents and the court below, in which the breaches of fiduciary duty held violative of Rule 10b-5 included some element of deception. Those cases forcefully reflect the principle that "[§]10(b) must be read flexibly, not technically and restrictively" and that the statute provides a cause of action for any plaintiff who "suffer[s] an injury as a result of deceptive practices touching its sale [or purchase] of securities. . . ." Superintendent of Insurance v. Bankers Life & Cas. Co., 404 U.S. 6, 12-13 (1971). But the cases do not support the proposition . . . that a breach of fiduciary duty by majority stockholders, without any deception, misrepresentation, or nondisclosure, violates the statute and the Rule.

It is also readily apparent that the conduct alleged in the complaint was not "manipulative" within the meaning of the statute. "Manipulation" is "virtually a term of art when used in connection with securities markets." *Ernst & Ernst*, 425 U.S., at 199. The term refers generally to practices, such as wash sales, matched orders, or rigged prices, that are intended to mislead investors by artificially affecting market activity. . . .

Connections: Appraisal

As described elsewhere in this book, shareholders frequently have the right to receive the appraised cash value of their shares if they dissent from, or have no right to vote on, certain transactions such as mergers and share exchanges. These rights are not limitless. For instance, under MBCA §13.02(b), there generally are no appraisal rights for the holders of publicly traded shares.

IV . . .

We thus adhere to the position that "Congress by §10(b) did not seek to regulate transactions which constitute no more than internal corporate mismanagement." Superintendent of Insurance v. Bankers Life & Cas. Co., 404 U.S., at 12. There may well be a need for uniform federal fiduciary standards to govern mergers such as that challenged in this complaint. But those standards should not be supplied by judicial extension of §10(b) and Rule 10b-5 to "cover the corporate universe." . . .

■ **Think about this:**

(C) Suppose there was no appraisal remedy available as a matter of state law. Would—or should—that have made a difference to the Court?

(D) Suppose the notice sent to the shareholders had not contained an appraisal of Kirby's physical assets. Would—or should—that have made a difference to the Court?

(E) Was the conduct of the individual defendants in *Texas Gulf Sulphur* manipulative or deceptive, or just a breach of fiduciary duty?

2. The "Materiality" Requirement

Only the second clause of Rule 10b-5 specifically uses the word "material," but there never has been any doubt that materiality must be shown for any violation of the Rule. Materiality is regarded as having the same definition throughout the federal securities laws, so discussions of materiality set out in the Rule 10b-5 context, including in *Texas Gulf Sulphur*, inform understanding of the concept under other provisions of the Securities and Exchange Acts. The next case is an important Supreme Court opinion under Rule 10b-5 that addresses materiality.

BASIC INC. V. LEVINSON

Supreme Court of the United States
485 U.S. 224 (1988)

Justice BLACKMUN delivered the opinion of the Court.

This case requires us to apply the materiality requirement of section 10(b) of the Securities Exchange Act of 1934 (1934 Act) and the Securities and Exchange Commission's Rule 10b-5, promulgated thereunder, in the context of preliminary corporate merger discussions. We must also determine whether a person who traded a corporation's shares on a securities exchange after the issuance of a materially misleading statement by the corporation may invoke a rebuttable presumption that, in trading, he relied on the integrity of the price set by the market. [Portions of the case relating to the latter issue appear later in this chapter.]

I

Prior to December 20, 1978, Basic Incorporated was a publicly traded company primarily engaged in the business of manufacturing chemical refractors for the steel industry. As early as 1965 or 1966, Combustion Engineering, Inc., a company producing mostly alumina-based refractors, expressed some interest in acquiring Basic, but was deterred from pursuing this inclination seriously because of antitrust concerns it then entertained. In 1976, however, regulatory action opened the way to a renewal of Combustion's interest. The "Strategic Plan," dated October 25, 1976, for Combustion's Industrial Products Group included the objective: "Acquire Basic Inc. $30 million."

Beginning in September 1976, Combustion representatives had meetings and telephone conversations with Basic officers and directors, including petitioners here, concerning the possibility of a merger. During 1977 and 1978, Basic made three public statements denying that it was engaged in merger negotiations. On December 18, 1978, Basic asked the New York Stock Exchange to suspend trading in its shares and issued a release stating that it had been "approached" by another company concerning a merger. On December 19, Basic's board endorsed Combustion's offer of $46 per share for its common stock, and on the following day publicly announced its approval of Combustion's tender offer for all outstanding shares.

Respondents are former Basic shareholders who sold their stock after Basic's first public statement of October 21, 1977, and before the suspension of trading in December 1978. Respondents brought a class action against Basic and its directors, asserting that the defendants issued three false or misleading public statements and thereby were in violation of section 10(b) of the 1934 Act and of Rule 10b-5. Respondents alleged that they were injured by selling Basic shares at artificially depressed prices in a market affected by petitioners' misleading statements and in reliance thereon.

. . . [T]he District Court granted summary judgment for the defendants. It held that, as a matter of law, any misstatements were immaterial: there were no negotiations ongoing at the time of the first statement, and although negotiations were taking place when the second and third statements were issued, those negotiations were not "destined, with reasonable certainty, to become a merger agreement in principle." The United States Court of Appeals for the Sixth Circuit . . . reversed the District Court's summary judgment, and remanded the case. . . .

II

The 1934 Act was designed to protect investors against manipulation of stock prices. Underlying the adoption of extensive disclosure requirements was a legislative philosophy: "There cannot be honest markets without honest publicity. Manipulation and dishonest practices of the market place thrive upon mystery and secrecy." H.R. Rep. No. 1383, 73d Cong., 2d Sess., 11 (1934). This Court "repeatedly has described the 'fundamental purpose' of the Act as implementing a 'philosophy of full disclosure.'" Santa Fe Industries, Inc. v. Green, 430 U.S. 462, 477-478 (1977), quoting SEC v. Capital Gains Research Bureau, Inc., 375 U.S. 180, 186 (1963). . . .

. . . [T]he Court . . . explicitly has defined a standard of materiality under the securities laws, see TSC Industries, Inc. v. Northway, Inc., 426 U.S. 438 (1976), concluding in the proxy-solicitation context that "an omitted fact is material if there is a substantial likelihood that a reasonable shareholder would consider it important in deciding how to vote." Id., at 449. Acknowledging that certain information concerning corporate developments could well be of "dubious significance," the Court was careful not to set too low a standard of materiality; it was concerned that a minimal standard might bring an overabundance of information within its reach, and lead management "simply to bury the shareholders in an avalanche of trivial information—a result that is hardly conducive to informed decisionmaking." It further explained that to fulfill the materiality requirement "there must be a substantial likelihood that the disclosure of the omitted fact would have been viewed by the reasonable investor as having significantly altered the 'total mix' of information made available." We now expressly adopt the *TSC Industries* standard of materiality for the section 10(b) and Rule 10b-5 context.

III

The application of this materiality standard to preliminary merger discussions is not self-evident. Where the impact of the corporate development on the target's fortune is certain and clear, the *TSC Industries* materiality definition admits straightforward application. Where, on the other hand, the event is contingent or speculative in nature, it is difficult to ascertain whether the "reasonable investor" would have considered the omitted information significant at the time. Merger negotiations, because of the ever-present possibility that the contemplated transaction will not be effectuated, fall into the latter category.

A

Petitioners urge upon us a Third Circuit test for resolving this difficulty. Under this approach, preliminary merger discussions do not become material until "agreement-in-principle" as to the price and structure of the transaction has been reached between the would-be merger partners. By definition, then, information concerning any negotiations not yet at the agreement-in-principle stage could be withheld or even misrepresented without a violation of Rule 10b-5.

Three rationales have been offered in support of the "agreement-in-principle" test. The first derives from the concern expressed in *TSC Industries* that an investor not be overwhelmed by excessively detailed and trivial information, and focuses on the substantial risk that preliminary merger discussions may collapse because such discussions are inherently tentative, disclosure of their existence itself could mislead investors and foster false optimism. The other two justifications for the agreement-in-principle standard are based on management concerns: because the requirement of "agreement-in-principle" limits the scope of disclosure obligations, it helps preserve the confidentiality of merger discussions where earlier disclosure might prejudice the negotiations; and the test also provides a usable, bright-line rule for determining when disclosure must be made.

None of these policy-based rationales, however, purports to explain why drawing the line at agreement-in-principle reflects the significance of the information upon the investor's decision. The first rationale, and the only one connected to the concerns expressed in *TSC Industries*, stands soundly rejected, even by a Court of Appeals that otherwise has accepted the wisdom of the agreement-in-principle test. "It assumes that investors are nitwits, unable to appreciate—even when told—that mergers are risky propositions up until the closing." Flamm v. Eberstadt, 814 F.2d [1169, 1175 (7th Cir. 1987)]. Disclosure, and not paternalistic withholding of accurate information, is the policy chosen and expressed by Congress. We have recognized time and again, a "fundamental purpose" of the various securities acts, "was to substitute a philosophy of full disclosure for the philosophy of caveat emptor and thus to achieve a high standard of business ethics in the securities industry." SEC v. Capital Gains Research Bureau, Inc., 375 U.S. 180, 186 (1963). The role of the materiality requirement is not to "attribute to investors a child-like simplicity, an inability to grasp the probabilistic significance of negotiations," Flamm v. Eberstadt, 814 F.2d, at 1175, but to filter out essentially useless information that a reasonable investor would not consider significant, even as part of a larger "mix" of factors to consider in making his investment decision.

The second rationale, the importance of secrecy during the early stages of merger discussions, also seems irrelevant to an assessment whether their existence is significant to the trading decision of a reasonable investor. To avoid a "bidding war" over its target, an acquiring firm often will insist that negotiations remain confidential, and at least one Court of Appeals has stated that "silence pending settlement of the price and structure of a deal is beneficial to most investors, most of the time." Flamm v. Eberstadt, 814 F.2d at 1177.

Room to Argue: Bidding Wars

There is indeed a healthy amount of dispute as to whether acquisitions involving multiple possible acquirers generate more shareholder wealth than acquisitions "privately" negotiated by management with a single suitor. Is this something courts really should figure out before deciding issues such as the one presented in this case?

We need not ascertain, however, whether secrecy necessarily maximizes shareholder wealth—although we note that the proposition is at least disputed as a matter of theory and empirical research—for this case does not concern the TIMING of a disclosure; it concerns only its accuracy and completeness. We face here the narrow question whether information concerning the existence and status of preliminary merger discussions is significant to the reasonable investor's trading decision. Arguments based on the premise that some disclosure would be "premature" in a sense are more properly considered under the rubric of an issuer's duty to disclose. The "secrecy" rationale is simply inapposite to the definition of materiality.

The final justification offered in support of the agreement-in-principle test seems to be directed solely at the comfort of corporate managers. A bright-line rule indeed is easier to follow than a standard that requires the exercise of judgment in the light of all the circumstances. But ease of application alone is not an excuse for ignoring the purposes of the securities acts and Congress' policy decisions. Any approach that designates a single fact or occurrence as always determinative of an inherently fact-specific finding such as materiality, must necessarily be over- or under-inclusive. . . .

C

Even before this Court's decision in *TSC Industries*, the Second Circuit had explained the role of the materiality requirement of Rule 10b-5, with respect to contingent or speculative information or events, in a manner that gave that term meaning that is independent of the other provisions of the Rule. Under such circumstances, materiality "will depend at any given time upon a balancing of both the indicated probability that the event will occur and the anticipated magnitude of the event in light of the totality of the company activity." SEC v. Texas Gulf Sulphur Co., 401 F.2d, at 849. Interestingly, neither the Third Circuit decision adopting the agreement-in-principle test nor petitioners here take issue with this general standard. Rather, they suggest that with respect to preliminary merger discussions, there are good reasons to draw a line at agreement on price and structure.

> **Doing the Numbers: Magnitude and Probability**
>
> $100 \times 100\% = \$100$
>
> $10{,}000 \times 1\% = \$100$

In a subsequent decision, the late Judge Friendly, writing for a Second Circuit panel, applied the *Texas Gulf Sulphur* probability/magnitude approach in the specific context of preliminary merger negotiations. After acknowledging that materiality is something to be determined on the basis of the particular facts of each case, he stated:

> Since a merger in which it is bought out is the most important event that can occur in a small corporation's life, to wit, its death, we think that inside information, as regards a merger of this sort, can become material at an earlier stage than would be the case as regards lesser transactions—and this even though the mortality rate of mergers in such formative stages is doubtless high. SEC v. Geon Industries, Inc., 531 F.2d 39, 47-48 (C.A.2 1976).

We agree with that analysis. Whether merger discussions in any particular case are material therefore depends on the facts. Generally, in order to assess the probability that the event will occur, a factfinder will need to look to indicia of interest in the transaction at the highest corporate levels. Without attempting to catalog all such possible factors, we note by way of example that board resolutions, instructions to investment bankers, and actual negotiations between principals or their intermediaries may serve as indicia of interest. To assess the magnitude of the transaction to the issuer of the securities allegedly manipulated, a factfinder will need to consider such facts as the size of the two corporate entities and of the potential premiums over market value. No particular event or factor short of closing the transaction need be either necessary or sufficient by itself to render merger discussions material. . . .

■ **Think about this:**

(F) Suppose that a pharmaceutical company has received reports of adverse events (to be non-euphemistic, deaths) associated with its products. There are not, however, enough reports to establish a statistically significant risk that the product is in fact causing the events. Are the reports material?

3. The "In Connection With" Requirement

To be subject to Rule 10b-5, the conduct prohibited by the Rule must be "in connection with the purchase or sale of [a] security." In cases involving public dissemination of false or misleading information "in a medium upon which an investor would presumably rely," courts have tended to find that the "in connection with" requirement may be satisfied by a showing of materiality. Under the "means of dissemination plus materiality" standard, ". . . it is irrelevant that the misrepresentations were not made for the purpose or the object of influencing the investment decision of market participants."

In cases not involving public dissemination, the "in connection with" requirement has presented some real challenges. The leading case in that area is Superintendent of Insurance of New York v. Bankers Life & Casualty Co., 404 U.S. 6 (1971). The facts and allegations in that case are complex. Briefly stated, the board of directors of a corporation allegedly was deceived into authorizing the sale of bonds by a misrepresentation involving what would happen to the cash from the sale (essentially, it was embezzled). With very little discussion, the Supreme Court found that the complaint stated a cause of action under the Rule. Although the Court noted that "Congress by §10(b) did not seek to regulate transactions which constitute no more than internal corporate mismanagement," it found the fraudulent conduct to be "in connection with" the sale of bonds, saying that the corporation allegedly "suffered an injury as a result of deceptive practices touching its sale of securities. . . ." This is known as the "touch" test.

In 2002, the Court returned to the "in connection with" requirement in SEC v. Zandford, 535 U.S. 813 (2002). Zandford, a securities salesperson, convinced an elderly man, in poor health, to open a brokerage account for himself and his disabled daughter. Zandford sold securities he had bought for the account and then stole most of the proceeds. The Fourth Circuit reasoned that Zandford's sales of securities were incidental to his scheme to defraud, and therefore not in connection with the sale of securities. The Supreme Court reversed, saying, "[I]t is enough that the scheme to defraud and the sale of securities coincide." The Court distinguished cases in which a thief simply invested the proceeds of a routine conversion in the stock market.

4. The "Scienter" Requirement

Any violation of a provision of the Exchange Act that is willful can, under §32, be criminally prosecuted by the Department of Justice. Otherwise, liability under Rule 10b-5 is premised on a state of mind that is more culpable than negligence. The following case presents the reasoning in the context of a private right of action.

ERNST & ERNST V. HOCHFELDER

Supreme Court of the United States
425 U.S. 185 (1976)

Mr. Justice POWELL delivered the opinion of the Court.

The issue in this case is whether an action for civil damages may lie under §10(b) of the Securities Exchange Act of 1934 (1934 Act), and Securities and

Exchange Commission Rule 10b-5, in the absence of an allegation of intent to deceive, manipulate, or defraud on the part of the defendant.

I

Petitioner, Ernst & Ernst, is an accounting firm. From 1946 through 1967 it was retained by First Securities Company of Chicago (First Securities), a small brokerage firm and member of the Midwest Stock Exchange and of the National Association of Securities Dealers, to perform periodic audits of the firm's books and records. In connection with these audits Ernst & Ernst prepared for filing with the Securities and Exchange Commission (Commission) the annual reports required of First Securities under §17(a) of the 1934 Act. . . .

Respondents were customers of First Securities who invested in a fraudulent securities scheme perpetrated by Leston B. Nay, president of the firm and owner of 92% of its stock. Nay induced the respondents to invest funds in "escrow" accounts that he represented would yield a high rate of return. Respondents did so from 1942 through 1966, with the majority of the transactions occurring in the 1950's. In fact, there were no escrow accounts as Nay converted respondents' funds to his own use immediately upon receipt. . . .

This fraud came to light in 1968 when Nay committed suicide, leaving a note that described First Securities as bankrupt and the escrow accounts as "spurious." Respondents subsequently filed this action for damages against Ernst & Ernst in the United States District Court for the Northern District of Illinois under §10(b) of the 1934 Act. The complaint charged that Nay's escrow scheme violated §10(b) and Commission Rule 10b-5, and that Ernst & Ernst had "aided and abetted" Nay's violations by its "failure" to conduct proper audits of First Securities. As revealed through discovery, respondents' cause of action rested on a theory of negligent nonfeasance. The premise was that Ernst & Ernst had failed to utilize "appropriate auditing procedures" in its audits of First Securities, thereby failing to discover internal practices of the firm said to prevent an effective audit. The practice principally relied on was Nay's rule that only he could open mail addressed to him at First Securities or addressed to First Securities to his attention, even if it arrived in his absence. Respondents contended that if Ernst & Ernst had conducted a proper audit, it would have discovered this "mail rule." The existence of the rule then would have been disclosed in reports to the Exchange and to the Commission by Ernst & Ernst as an irregular procedure that prevented an effective audit. This would have led to an investigation of Nay that would have revealed the fraudulent scheme. Respondents specifically disclaimed the existence of fraud or intentional misconduct on the part of Ernst & Ernst.

After extensive discovery the District Court granted Ernst & Ernst's motion for summary judgment and dismissed the action. . . .

The Court of Appeals for the Seventh Circuit reversed. . . .

We granted certiorari to resolve the question whether a private cause of action for damages will lie under §10(b)

Connections: Aiding and Abetting

Note that in this case no one questioned whether aiding-and-abetting liability existed under Rule 10b-5. The Supreme Court subsequently decided that it did not, at least in the context of private litigation.

and Rule 10b-5 in the absence of any allegation of "scienter"—intent to deceive, manipulate, or defraud. We conclude that it will not and therefore we reverse.

II . . .

. . . [D]uring the 30-year period since a private cause of action was first implied under §10(b) and Rule 10b-5, a substantial body of case law and commentary has developed as to its elements. Courts and commentators long have differed with regard to whether scienter is a necessary element of such a cause of action, or whether negligent conduct alone is sufficient. . . .

A

Section 10(b) makes unlawful the use or employment of "any manipulative or deceptive device or contrivance" in contravention of Commission rules. The words "manipulative or deceptive" used in conjunction with "device or contrivance" strongly suggest that §10(b) was intended to proscribe knowing or intentional misconduct.

In its amicus curiae brief, however, the Commission contends that nothing in the language "manipulative or deceptive device or contrivance" limits its operation to knowing or intentional practices. In support of its view, the Commission cites the overall congressional purpose in the 1933 and 1934 Acts to protect investors against false and deceptive practices that might injure them. The Commission then reasons that since the "effect" upon investors of given conduct is the same regardless of whether the conduct is negligent or intentional, Congress must have intended to bar all such practices and not just those done knowingly or intentionally. The logic of this effect-oriented approach would impose liability for wholly faultless conduct where such conduct results in harm to investors, a result the Commission would be unlikely to support. But apart from where its logic might lead, the Commission would add a gloss to the operative language of the statute quite different from its commonly accepted meaning. The argument simply ignores the use of the words "manipulative," "device," and "contrivance"—terms that make unmistakable a congressional intent to proscribe a type of conduct quite different from negligence. Use of the word "manipulative" is especially significant. It is and was virtually a term of art when used in connection with securities markets. It connotes intentional or willful conduct designed to deceive or defraud investors by controlling or artificially affecting the price of securities. . . .

. . . Congress fashioned standards of fault in the express civil remedies in the 1933 and 1934 Acts on a particularized basis. Ascertainment of congressional intent with respect to the standard of liability created by a particular section of the Acts must therefore rest primarily on the language of that section. Where, as here, we deal with a judicially implied liability, the statutory language certainly is no less important. In view of the language of §10(b), which so clearly connotes intentional misconduct, and mindful that the language of a statute controls when sufficiently clear in its context, further inquiry may be unnecessary. We turn now, nevertheless, to the legislative history of the 1934 Act to ascertain whether there is support for the meaning attributed to §10(b) by the Commission and respondents.

B . . .

Neither the intended scope of §10(b) nor the reasons for the changes in its operative language are revealed explicitly in the legislative history of the 1934 Act, which deals primarily with other aspects of the legislation. There is no indication, however, that §10(b) was intended to proscribe conduct not involving scienter. The extensive hearings that preceded passage of the 1934 Act touched only briefly on §10, and most of the discussion was devoted to the enumerated devices that the Commission is empowered to proscribe under §10(a). The most relevant exposition of the provision that was to become §10(b) was by Thomas G. Corcoran, a spokesman for the drafters. Corcoran indicated: "Subsection (c) [§10(b)] says, 'Thou shalt not devise any other cunning devices.' . . . Of course subsection (c) is a catch-all clause to prevent manipulative devices. I do not think there is any objection to that kind of clause. The Commission should have the authority to deal with new manipulative devices."

This brief explanation of §10(b) by a spokesman for its drafters is significant. The section was described rightly as a "catchall" clause to enable the Commission "to deal with new manipulative [or cunning] devices." It is difficult to believe that any lawyer, legislative draftsman, or legislator would use these words if the intent was to create liability for merely negligent acts or omissions. Neither the legislative history nor the briefs supporting respondents identify any usage or authority for construing "manipulative [or cunning] devices" to include negligence. . . .

The Supreme Court in *Hochfelder* specifically left open two questions. The first is whether scienter is required to be proved in an enforcement action by the Commission. The second is whether recklessness is sufficient by itself to constitute scienter. The first of these questions was answered affirmatively in Aaron v. SEC, 446 U.S. 680 (1980). Virtually all courts that have addressed the second question have found that recklessness in some form constitutes scienter.

> ### ■ Think about this:
>
> **(G)** Is it possible to recklessly deceive or manipulate someone?
>
> **(H)** Is there any public policy reason to permit reckless deception?

C. Additional Requirements for Private Plaintiffs

As noted above, some elements must be addressed in Rule 10b-5 litigation, no matter who is suing—the Justice Department, the SEC, or a private plaintiff. Private plaintiffs, however, must also address the matters described in this section:

- the "purchaser-seller" requirement
- the "reliance and causation" requirement

More to the Story: Attempts to Purchase

In a later case, Wharf (Holdings) Ltd. v. United International Holdings, Inc., 532 U.S. 588 (2001), the Court made quick work of disposing of an argument that oral contracts for the sale of securities may not serve as the basis for "purchaser" status if the prospective seller has no intent to perform. The case was considered significant for its change of tone from *Blue Chip*.

1. The "Purchaser-Seller" Requirement

Early in the life of Rule 10b-5, the Second Circuit's opinion in Birnbaum v. Newport Steel Corp., 193 F.2d 461 (2d Cir. 1952), established the requirement that a private plaintiff had to be a purchaser or seller of securities to have standing to sue under the Rule. Over two decades later, the Supreme Court agreed. In Blue Chip Stamps v. Manor Drug Stores, 421 U.S. 723 (1975), offerees in a Securities Act registered offering sued under Rule 10b-5 alleging that the prospectus through which they were offered shares "was materially misleading in its overly pessimistic appraisal of Blue Chip's status and future prospects." (The alleged facts made sense only because Blue Chip had been required under an anti-trust consent decree to make the offering of its stock at a favorable price to persons allegedly injured by anti-competitive activities.) The Court discussed at length the evils that would arise in the absence of the "purchaser-seller" requirement, such as the chance for "vexatious litigation" in which questions such as whether a plaintiff would have purchased or sold securities, and the amount the plaintiff would have purchased or sold, are answerable only in a trial on the basis of oral testimony about state of mind.

Room to Argue: What's So Great About Cause?

You probably spent some time on this question in Torts class: Why do we generally require the plaintiff to show a causal link between his injury and the defendant's wrong-doing?

Professor Butts and the Self-Operating Napkin Rube Goldberg, 1931

2. Reliance and Causation

In thinking about reliance and causation, cases involving non-disclosure must be distinguished from those involving misstatements; non-disclosure is considered in Chapter 31 on insider trading. This section deals with the requirement that a private plaintiff show that the defendant's affirmative material misrepresentations caused the plaintiff's injury. This generally requires the plaintiff to establish reliance on the misrepresentation in question. This requirement is not always what it may seem, however, for the courts have adopted an interesting theory of causation known as the "fraud-on-the-market" theory. The following case gives the Supreme Court's initial take on the matter.

BASIC INC. V. LEVINSON

Supreme Court of the United States
485 U.S. 224 (1988)

Justice BLACKMUN delivered the opinion of the Court....

I

Prior to December 20, 1978, Basic Incorporated was a publicly traded company primarily engaged in the business of manufacturing chemical refractors for the steel industry. . . .

Beginning in September 1976, Combustion [Engineering, Inc.] representatives had meetings and telephone conversations with Basic officers and directors, including petitioners here, concerning the possibility of a merger. During 1977 and 1978, Basic made three public statements denying that it was engaged in merger negotiations. On December 18, 1978, Basic asked the New York Stock Exchange to suspend trading in its shares and issued a release stating that it had been "approached" by another company concerning a merger. On December 19, Basic's board endorsed Combustion's offer of $46 per share for its common stock, and on the following day publicly announced its approval of Combustion's tender offer for all outstanding shares.

Respondents are former Basic shareholders who sold their stock after Basic's first public statement of October 21, 1977, and before the suspension of trading in December 1978. Respondents brought a class action against Basic and its directors, asserting that the defendants issued three false or misleading public statements and thereby were in violation of section 10(b) of the 1934 Act and of Rule 10b-5. Respondents alleged that they were injured by selling Basic shares at artificially depressed prices in a market affected by petitioners' misleading statements and in reliance thereon.

The District Court adopted a presumption of reliance by members of the plaintiff class upon petitioners' public statements that enabled the court to conclude that common questions of fact or law predominated over particular questions pertaining to individual plaintiffs. The District Court therefore certified respondents' class. On the merits, however, the District Court granted summary judgment for the defendants. . . .

The United States Court of Appeals for the Sixth Circuit affirmed the class certification, but reversed the District Court's summary judgment, and remanded the case. . . .

> **More to the Story: Transaction vs. Loss Causation**
>
> The type of causation discussed in this case is called transaction causation. In addition to transaction causation, courts have required proof of loss causation—essentially, proof that the matter misrepresented was what gave rise to the loss of value about which the plaintiff complains. Congress eventually codified the loss causation requirement in Exchange Act §21D(b)(4).

The Court of Appeals joined a number of other circuits in accepting the "fraud-on-the-market theory" to create a rebuttable presumption that respondents relied on petitioners' material misrepresentations, noting that without the presumption it would be impractical to certify a class under Fed. Rule Civ. Proc. 23(b)(3). . . .

IV

A

. . . [S]uccinctly put:

> The fraud on the market theory is based on the hypothesis that, in an open and developed securities market, the price of a company's stock is determined by the available material information regarding the company and its business. . . . [M]isleading statements will therefore defraud purchasers of stock even if the purchasers do not directly rely on the misstatements. . . . [T]he causal connection between the defendants' fraud and the plaintiffs' purchase of stock in such a case is no less significant than in a case of direct reliance on misrepresentations. Peil v. Speiser, 806 F.2d 1154, 1160-1161 (C.A.3 1986).

Room to Argue: The ECMH

One version of what is known as the "efficient capital markets hypothesis" contends that, in an efficient market, all publicly known information is quickly impounded in the price of securities. This and other forms of the hypothesis are discussed in the online Supplement.

It is important to note, however, that not everyone believes in the hypothesis and that there is more evidence against it now than there was in 1988.

Our task, of course, is not to assess the general validity of the theory, but to consider whether it was proper for the courts below to apply a rebuttable presumption of reliance, supported in part by the fraud-on-the-market theory.

. . . [I]n their amended complaint, the named plaintiffs alleged that in reliance on Basic's statements they sold their shares of Basic stock in the depressed market created by petitioners. Requiring proof of individualized reliance from each member of the proposed plaintiff class effectively would have prevented respondents from proceeding with a class action, since individual issues then would have overwhelmed the common ones. The District Court found that the presumption of reliance created by the fraud-on-the-market theory provided "a practical resolution to the problem of balancing the substantive requirement, of proof of reliance in securities cases against the procedural requisites of Fed. Rule Civ. Proc. 23." The District Court thus concluded that with reference to each public statement and its impact upon the open market for Basic shares, common questions predominated over individual questions, as required by Fed. Rule Civ. Proc. 23(a)(2) and (b)(3).

Petitioners and their amici complain that the fraud-on-the-market theory effectively eliminates the requirement that a plaintiff asserting a claim under Rule 10b-5 prove reliance. They note that reliance is, and long has been, an element of common-law fraud. . . .

We agree that reliance is an element of a Rule 10b-5 cause of action. Reliance provides the requisite causal connection between a defendant's misrepresentation and a plaintiff's injury. There is, however, more than one way to demonstrate the causal connection. Indeed, we previously have dispensed with a requirement of positive proof of reliance, where a duty to disclose material information had been breached, concluding that the necessary nexus between the plaintiff's injury and the defendant's wrongful conduct had been established. See Affiliated Ute Citizens v. United States, 406 U.S. [128, 153-154 (1972)]. Similarly, we did not require proof that material omissions or misstatements in a proxy statement decisively affected voting, because the proxy solicitation itself, rather than the defect in the solicitation materials, served as an essential link in the transaction. See Mills v. Electric Auto-Lite Co., 396 U.S. 375, 384-385 (1970).

The modern securities markets, literally millions of shares changing hands daily, differ from the face-to-face transactions contemplated by early fraud cases, and our understanding of Rule 10b-5's reliance requirement must encompass these differences.

In face-to-face transactions, the inquiry into an investor's reliance upon information is into the subjective pricing of that information by that investor. With the presence of a market, the market is interposed between seller and buyer and, ideally, transmits information to the investor in the processed form of a market price. Thus the market is performing a substantial part of the valuation process performed by the investor in a face-to-face transaction. The market is acting as the unpaid agent of the investor, informing him that given all the information available to it, the value of the stock is worth the market price. In re LTV Securities Litigation, 88 F.R.D. 134, 143 (N.D. Tex. 1980).

The sacrifice of Odin (1895) by Lorenz Frølich

B

Presumptions typically serve to assist courts in managing circumstances in which direct proof, for one reason or another, is rendered difficult. The courts below accepted a presumption, created by the fraud-on-the-market theory and subject to rebuttal by petitioners, that persons who had traded Basic shares had done so in reliance on the integrity of the price set by the market, but because of petitioners' material misrepresentations that price had been fraudulently depressed. Requiring a plaintiff to show a speculative state of facts, i.e., how he would have acted if omitted material information had been disclosed, or if the misrepresentation had not been made, would place an unnecessarily unrealistic evidentiary burden on the Rule 10b-5 plaintiff who has traded on an impersonal market.

Arising out of considerations of fairness, public policy, and probability, as well as judicial economy, presumptions are also useful devices for allocating the burdens of proof between parties. The presumption of reliance employed in this case is consistent with, and, by facilitating Rule 10b-5 litigation, supports, the congressional policy embodied in the 1934 Act. In drafting that Act, Congress expressly relied on the premise that securities markets are affected by information, and enacted legislation to facilitate an investor's reliance on the integrity of those markets:

> No investor, no speculator, can safely buy and sell securities upon the exchanges without having an intelligent basis for

Don't Mess with Odin

The common law requirement of cause has been traced to ancient Germanic vengeance customs. Obviously, if an injury were attributable to the will of a god, rather than the act of an individual, wreaking vengeance would be highly disrespectful.

forming his judgment as to the value of the securities he buys or sells. The idea of a free and open public market is built upon the theory that competing judgments of buyers and sellers as to the fair price of a security brings about a situation where the market price reflects as nearly as possible a just price. Just as artificial manipulation tends to upset the true function of an open market, so the hiding and secreting of important information obstructs the operation of the markets as indices of real value.

H.R. Rep. No. 1383, supra, at 11.

The presumption is also supported by common sense and probability. Recent empirical studies have tended to confirm Congress' premise that the market price of shares traded on well-developed markets reflects all publicly available information, and, hence, any material misrepresentations. It has been noted that "it is hard to imagine that there ever is a buyer or seller who does not rely on market integrity. Who would knowingly roll the dice in a crooked crap game?" Schlanger v. Four-Phase Systems Inc., 555 F. Supp. 535, 538 (S.D.N.Y. 1982). Indeed, nearly every court that has considered the proposition has concluded that where materially misleading statements have been disseminated into an impersonal, well-developed market for securities, the reliance of individual plaintiffs on the integrity of the market price may be presumed. Commentators generally have applauded the adoption of one variation or another of the fraud-on-the-market theory. An investor who buys or sells stock at the price set by the market does so in reliance on the integrity of that price. Because most publicly available information is reflected in market price, an investor's reliance on any public material misrepresentations, therefore, may be presumed for purposes of a Rule 10b-5 action.

C

The Court of Appeals found that petitioners "made public, material misrepresentations and respondents sold Basic stock in an impersonal, efficient market. Thus the class, as defined by the district court, has established the threshold facts for proving their loss." The court acknowledged that petitioners may rebut proof of the elements giving rise to the presumption, or show that the misrepresentation in fact did not lead to a distortion of price or that an individual plaintiff traded or would have traded despite his knowing the statement was false.

Any showing that severs the link between the alleged misrepresentation and either the price received (or paid) by the plaintiff, or his decision to trade at a fair market price, will be sufficient to rebut the presumption of reliance. For example, if petitioners could show that the "market makers" were privy to the truth about the merger discussions here with Combustion, and thus that the market price would not have been affected by their misrepresentations, the causal connection could be broken: the basis for finding that the fraud had been transmitted through market price would be gone. Similarly, if, despite petitioners' allegedly fraudulent attempt to manipulate market price, news of the merger discussions credibly entered the market and dissipated the effects of the misstatements, those who traded Basic shares after the corrective statements would have no direct or indirect connection with the fraud. Petitioners also could rebut the presumption of reliance as to plaintiffs who would have divested themselves of their Basic shares without relying on the integrity of the market. For example, a plaintiff who believed that Basic's statements were false and that Basic was indeed engaged in merger discussions, and who consequently believed that Basic stock was artificially underpriced, but sold his shares nevertheless because of other unrelated concerns, e.g., potential antitrust problems, or political pressures to divest from shares of certain businesses, could not be said to have relied on the integrity of a price he knew had been manipulated. . . .

━━━━━━━━━

In Haliburton Co. v. Erica P. John Fund, Inc., 573 U.S. ___ (2014), the Court confirmed it was not error to apply the fraud on the market theory and clarified that the defendant could attempt to show lack of price impact at the class certification stage.

■ **Think about this:**

(I) Is transaction causation the same thing as proximate cause?

(J) Was the Court really treating the issue as one of loss causation rather than transaction causation?

(K) Suppose Priscilla purchases 1,000 shares of Drugs, Inc. for $50 per share. She would not have bought them if she had known that the Food and Drug Administration was on the verge of denying permission to Drugs, Inc. to sell a much-touted new drug. Spokespersons on behalf of Drugs, Inc. had recently been claiming approval was near even though they had very good reason to know that was not true. Still, before the denial takes place, Drugs, Inc's only research and manufacturing facility is destroyed by a meteor, resulting in a decline in the price of its stock to ten cents per share. After the denial is announced, the stock price does not budge. What can Priscilla recover from Drugs, Inc.?

 Time Out for PR

Regardless of any liability a lawyer might—or might not—incur under federal securities law, there may be a professional obligation to take action in light of a client's misrepresentation. There is a great deal of variety from state to state, but American Bar Association Model Rules 1.6 and 4.1 provide a good starting point.

Rule 1.6 Confidentiality of Information

(a) A lawyer shall not reveal information relating to the representation of a client unless the client gives informed consent, the disclosure is impliedly authorized in order to carry out the representation or the disclosure is permitted by paragraph (b).

(b) A lawyer may reveal information relating to the representation of a client to the extent the lawyer reasonably believes necessary: . . .

(2) to prevent the client from committing a crime or fraud that is reasonably certain to result in substantial injury to the financial interests or property of another and in furtherance of which the client has used or is using the lawyer's services;

(3) to prevent, mitigate or rectify substantial injury to the financial interests or property of another that is reasonably certain to result or has resulted from the client's commission of a crime or fraud in furtherance of which the client has used the lawyer's services;

Rule 4.1 Truthfulness in Statements to Others

In the course of representing a client a lawyer shall not knowingly:

(a) make a false statement of material fact or law to a third person; or

(b) fail to disclose a material fact to a third person when disclosure is necessary to avoid assisting a criminal or fraudulent act by a client, unless disclosure is prohibited by Rule 1.6.

Test Yourself

Dora is the president of El Dorado, Inc., a mining company. She is told by Edgar, an engineer for the company, that he has located a major ore strike. Unfortunately, it is on land that El Dorado does not own. He suggests that Dora attempt to acquire the land without disclosing to anyone, including El Dorado's board, the extent of the strike. Dora comes up with the idea of telling the board that the land simply will be a good real estate investment. The board balks at paying cash, but authorizes Dora to negotiate to acquire the land in exchange for shares of the company.

Unfortunately, Edgar has a drinking problem, and talks freely about the strike at a local bar. Word begins to spread and Paul, the owner of the land for which Dora is negotiating, gets wind of it. He asks if the rumor is true, but Dora denies it. As a result, he accepts shares worth $100,000, which is what he believes to be the fair market value of the land. After the strike subsequently is announced, his shares double in value.

1. Is Edgar liable under Rule 10b-5?

   a. No, because he is not a purchaser or seller of El Dorado shares.
   b. No, because he is not an officer of El Dorado.
   c. No, because no misrepresentation is attributed to him.
   d. Probably so because he intentionally participated in Dora's scheme.

2. Is Dora liable under Rule 10b-5?

   a. No, because she was acting on behalf of El Dorado.
   b. No, because she was under no obligation to tell Paul anything about the value of his own land.
   c. Not unless El Dorado has registered shares under the Exchange Act.
   d. Probably so because she engaged in intentional misrepresentation in connection with the sale of a security.

3. Is El Dorado liable under Rule 10b-5?

   a. No, because the board did not know about the ore strike.
   b. Not unless it has registered shares under the Exchange Act.
   c. Probably so because Dora's misrepresentation may be attributed to it.
   d. No, because Paul's shares increased in value.

4. Assuming, for purposes of this question, that Dora is liable under Rule 10b-5, which of the following best describes the parties who might successfully sue her?

   a. Only the SEC.
   b. Both the SEC and the Department of Justice.
   c. The SEC, the Department of Justice, and Paul.
   d. Only Paul.

5. Assuming, for purposes of this question, that El Dorado is liable under Rule 10b-5, which of the following best describes the parties who might successfully sue it?

   a. Only the SEC.
   b. Both the SEC and the Department of Justice.
   c. The SEC, the Department of Justice, and Paul.
   d. Only Paul.

6. If you were advising Paul on the likelihood that he would prevail in a suit against Dora, you would say:

   a. He would satisfy the purchaser or seller requirement.
   b. He would satisfy the requirement that he prove reliance.

c. Answers a and b are both correct.

d. Neither answer a nor answer b is correct.

7. If you were advising Paul on the likelihood that he would prevail in a suit against Dora, you would say:

a. It appears that proof of scienter would be the greatest impediment.

b. It appears that proof of materiality would be the greatest impediment.

c. It appears that satisfaction of the "in connection with" requirement would be the greatest impediment.

d. It appears that satisfaction of the requirement that he prove loss causation would be the greatest impediment.

31

Trading by Insiders: Rule 10b-5

Rule 10b-5 under the Securities Exchange Act of 1934 has been applied in many contexts, notably including "inside trading." The term is somewhat misleading as some people not traditionally thought of as insiders may find themselves in trouble for trading while in possession of material non-public information. On the other hand, the Rule is not so broad as to pick up all cases of informational asymmetry. The primary task of this chapter is to clarify when Rule 10b-5 applies. It also describes the elements that must be shown by litigants seeking to impose 10b-5 liability in insider trading cases.

Chapter Outline

A. Overview: Use of Rule 10b-5 in the Context of Insider Trading

- Elements to be shown in any action
- Additional elements to be shown by a private plaintiff

B. Persons Subject to Trading Constraints

- Traditional insiders
- Temporary insiders
- Misappropriators
- Tippees
- Persons with non-public information relating to tender offers
- Employees of the federal government

C. Reliance and Causation in the Context of Insider Trading

- Trading face to face
- Open market trading
- Contemporaneous traders and §20A

Test Yourself

A. Overview: Use of Rule 10b-5 in the Context of Insider Trading

As explored in more depth elsewhere in this text, Rule 10b-5 under the Securities Exchange Act of 1934 (Exchange Act) is the most general anti-fraud provision under the federal securities laws. It applies to the purchase of sale of *any* security, not just those that are registered under the Exchange Act. The general elements of a violation of Rule 10b-5 are:

- The "manipulative or deceptive" requirement: The conduct complained of must involve fraud or misleading of some sort.
- The "materiality" requirement: There must be a substantial likelihood that the information that is false or undisclosed would be considered important by a reasonable investor.
- The "in connection with" requirement: The fraud or misleading must occur in the context of a transaction that "touches" the purchase or sale of a security.
- The "scienter" requirement: The defendant must have acted with a state of mind that is more culpable than negligence.

There are additional showings that must be made by private plaintiffs seeking to recover under the now-well-established implied private right under Rule 10b-5:

- the "purchaser or seller" requirement
- the "reliance/causation" requirement

One of the most frequent invocations of Rule 10b-5 is in the context of what is known as "insider trading." The biggest issue in this context involves the "manipulative or deceptive" requirement, since whether conduct is fraudulent or misleading sometimes can depend on the role of the actor.

Rule 10b-5. Employment of Manipulative and Deceptive Devices

It shall be unlawful for any person, directly or indirectly, by the use of any means or instrumentality of interstate commerce, or of the mails or of any facility of any national securities exchange,

   (a) To employ any device, scheme, or artifice to defraud,
   (b) To make any untrue statement of a material fact or to omit to state a material fact necessary in order to make the statements made, in the light of the circumstances under which they were made, not misleading, or
   (c) To engage in any act, practice, or course of business which operates or would operate as a fraud or deceit upon any person,

in connection with the purchase or sale of any security.

B. Persons Subject to Trading Constraints

Everyone has a duty to refrain from making material *affirmative* misrepresentations in connection with the purchase or sale of a security. However, not everyone has a duty to *disclose* material information before making such a purchase or sale. That is, not everyone can violate Rule 10b-5 through their *omissions*. The question of who is subject to the trading constraints of Rule 10b-5 has become one of the most interesting aspects of the Rule. The following Securities and Exchange Commission (SEC or Commission) enforcement proceeding is the seminal authority on the subject.

IN RE CADY, ROBERTS & CO.

Securities and Exchange Commission
40 S.E.C. 907 (1961)

By Cary, Chairman:

This is a case of first impression and one of signal importance in our administration of the Federal securities acts. It involves a selling broker who executes a solicited order and sells for discretionary accounts (including that of his wife) upon an exchange. The crucial question is what are the duties of such a broker after receiving non-public information as to a company's dividend action from a director who is employed by the same brokerage firm.

These proceedings were instituted to determine whether Cady, Roberts & Co. ("registrant") and Robert M. Gintel ("Gintel"), the selling broker and a partner of the registrant, willfully violated the "anti-fraud" provisions of Section 10(b) of the Securities Exchange Act of 1934 ("Exchange Act"), Rule 10b-5 issued under that Act and Section 17(a) of the Securities Act of 1933 ("Securities Act") and, if so, whether any disciplinary action is necessary or appropriate in the public interest. The respondents have submitted an offer of settlement which essentially provides that the facts stipulated by respondents shall constitute the record in these proceedings for the purposes of determining the occurrence of a willful violation of the designated anti-fraud provisions and the entering of an appropriate order, on the condition that no sanction may be entered in excess of a suspension of Gintel for 20 days from the New York Stock Exchange.

The facts are as follows:

Early in November 1959, Roy T. Hurley, then President and Chairman of the Board of Curtiss-Wright Corporation, invited 2,000 representatives of the press, the military and the financial and business communities to a public unveiling on November 23, of a new type of internal combustion engine being developed by the company. On November 24, 1959, press announcements concerning the

Connections: Declaration of Dividends

As discussed in Chapter 15, there is no entitlement to dividends. Payment of dividends is up to the discretion of the directors, subject to statutory limitations designed for the protection of creditors.

new engine appeared in certain newspapers. On that day Curtiss-Wright stock was one of the most active issues on the New York Stock Exchange, closing at 35¼, up 3¼ on a volume of 88,700 shares. From November 6, through November 23, Gintel had purchased approximately 11,000 shares of Curtiss-Wright stock for about 30 discretionary accounts of customers of registrant. With the rise in the price on November 24, he began selling Curtiss-Wright shares for these accounts and sold on that day a total of 2,200 shares on the Exchange.

The activity in Curtiss-Wright stock on the Exchange continued the next morning, November 25, and the price rose to 40¾, a new high for the year. Gintel continued sales for the discretionary accounts and, between the opening of the market and about 11:00 A.M., he sold 4,300 shares.

On the morning of November 25, the Curtiss-Wright directors, including J. Cheever Cowdin ("Cowdin"), then a registered representative of registrant, met to consider, among other things, the declaration of a quarterly dividend. The company had paid a dividend, although not earned, of $.625 per share for each of the first three quarters of 1959. The Curtiss-Wright board, over the objections of Hurley, who favored declaration of a dividend at the same rate as in the prior quarters, approved a dividend for the fourth quarter at the reduced rate of $.375 per share. At approximately 11:00 A.M., the board authorized transmission of information of this action by telegram to the New York Stock Exchange. The Secretary of Curtiss-Wright immediately left the meeting room to arrange for this communication. There was a short delay in the transmission of the telegram because of a typing problem and the telegram, although transmitted to Western Union at 11:12 A.M., was not delivered to the Exchange until 12:29 P.M. It had been customary for the company also to advise the Dow Jones News Ticker Service of any dividend action. However, apparently through some mistake or inadvertence, the Wall Street Journal was not given the news until approximately 11:45 A.M. and the announcement did not appear on the Dow Jones ticker tape until 11:48 A.M.

Sometime after the dividend decision, there was a recess of the Curtiss-Wright directors' meeting, during which Cowdin telephoned registrant's office and left a message for Gintel that the dividend had been cut. Upon receiving this information, Gintel entered two sell orders for execution on the Exchange, one to sell 2,000 shares of Curtiss-Wright stock for 10 accounts, and the other to sell short 5,000 shares for 11 accounts. Four hundred of the 5,000 shares were sold for three of Cowdin's customers. According to Cowdin, pursuant to directions from his clients, he had given instructions to Gintel to take profits on these 400 shares if the stock took a "run-up." These orders were executed at 11:15 and 11:18 A.M. at 40¼ and 40⅜, respectively.

JD/MBA: Selling Short

"Selling short" means agreeing to sell shares that you don't own. It is a strategy employed if you are betting that the price is going to go down, permitting you to purchase the shares at the new, lower, price in order to satisfy your sale obligation.

When the dividend announcement appeared on the Dow Jones tape at 11:48 A.M., the Exchange was compelled to suspend trading in Curtiss-Wright because of the large number of sell orders. Trading in Curtiss-Wright stock was resumed at 1:59 P.M. at $36\frac{1}{2}$[,] ranged during the balance of the day between $34\frac{1}{4}$ and 37, and closed at $34\frac{7}{8}$.

VIOLATION OF ANTI-FRAUD PROVISIONS

So many times that citation is unnecessary, we have indicated that the purchase and sale of securities is a field in special need of regulation for the protection of investors. To this end one of the major purposes of the securities acts is the prevention of fraud, manipulation or deception in connection with securities transactions. Consistent with this objective, Section 17(a) of the Securities Act, Section 10(b) of the Exchange Act and Rule 10b-5, issued under that Section, are broad remedial provisions aimed at reaching misleading or deceptive activities, whether or not they are precisely and technically sufficient to sustain a common law action for fraud and deceit. Indeed, despite the decline in importance of a "Federal rule" in the light of *Erie R. Co. v. Tompkins*, the securities acts may be said to have generated a wholly new and far-reaching body of Federal corporation law. . . .

Section 17 and Rule 10b-5 apply to securities transactions by "any person." Misrepresentations will lie within their ambit, no matter who the speaker may be. An affirmative duty to disclose material information has been traditionally imposed on corporate "insiders," particularly officers, directors, or controlling stockholders. We, and the courts have consistently held that insiders must disclose material facts which are known to them by virtue of their position but which are not known to persons with whom they deal and which, if known, would affect their investment judgment. Failure to make disclosure in these circumstances constitutes a violation of the anti-fraud provisions. If, on the other hand, disclosure prior to effecting a purchase or sale would be improper or unrealistic under the circumstances, we believe the alternative is to forego the transaction.

The ingredients are here and we accordingly find that Gintel willfully violated Sections 17(a) and 10(b) and Rule 10b-5. We also find a similar violation by the registrant, since the actions of Gintel, a member of registrant, in the course of his employment are to be regarded as actions of registrant itself. It was obvious that a reduction in the quarterly dividend by the Board of Directors was a material fact which could be expected to have an adverse impact on the market price of the company's stock. The rapidity with which Gintel acted upon receipt of the information confirms his own recognition of that conclusion.

We have already noted that the anti-fraud provisions are phrased in terms of "any person" and that a special obligation has been traditionally required

Doing the Numbers

The previous dividend rate of $.625 gave an annualized rate of $2.50, for a return of almost 8 percent on shares selling at approximately $32 (their price on November 23, 1959).

This is calculated as follows:

$2.50 is x% of $32.
Thus, $2.50 = x32$
$2.50/32 = x32/32$
$.078 = x$

The new dividend rate of $.375 gave an annualized rate of $1.50, for a return of just over 4 percent on shares selling at around $35 (their price on November 25, 1959).

$1.50 = x% of $35
$1.50 = x35$
$1.50/35 = x35/35$
$.0428 = x$

Room to Argue: Is Inside Trading Good or Bad?

Not everyone agrees that it is inherently unfair for insiders to trade on "informational asymmetry." In fact, there are those who believe that permitting such trading is both an effective way to compensate managers and a way to improve market efficiency. As to the latter, insider trades might help disseminate information that an issuer may not be ready to publicly announce. Permitting trades on asymmetric information also might compensate the investment in generating information, and therefore incentivize the investment in the first place, and some argue that that preserving that incentive is ultimately best for everyone. There is more about this subject in the online Supplement.

of corporate insiders, e.g., officers, directors and controlling stockholders. These three groups, however, do not exhaust the classes of persons upon whom there is such an obligation. Analytically, the obligation rests on two principal elements; first, the existence of a relationship giving access, directly or indirectly, to information intended to be available only for a corporate purpose and not for the personal benefit of anyone, and second, the inherent unfairness involved where a party takes advantage of such information knowing it is unavailable to those with whom he is dealing. In considering these elements under the broad language of the anti-fraud provisions we are not to be circumscribed by fine distinctions and rigid classifications. Thus our task here is to identify those persons who are in a special relationship with a company and privy to its internal affairs, and thereby suffer correlative duties in trading in its securities. Intimacy demands restraint lest the uninformed be exploited.

The facts here impose on Gintel the responsibilities of those commonly referred to as "insiders." He received the information prior to its public release from a director of Curtiss-Wright, Cowdin, who was associated with the registrant. Cowdin's relationship to the company clearly prohibited him from selling the securities affected by the information without disclosure. By logical sequence, it should prohibit Gintel, a partner of registrant. This prohibition extends not only over his own account, but to selling for discretionary accounts and soliciting and executing other orders. In somewhat analogous circumstances, we have charged a broker-dealer who effects securities transactions for an insider and who knows that the insider possesses non-public material information with the affirmative duty to make appropriate disclosures or disassociate himself from the transaction.

We cannot accept respondents' contention that an insider's responsibility is limited to existing stockholders and that he has no special duties when sales of securities are made to non-stockholders. This approach is too narrow. It ignores the plight of the buying public—wholly unprotected from the misuse of special information. . . .

■ **Think about this:**

(A) Do you think there was anything suspicious about Gintel's conduct in the days before November 24 or on November 24?

> *(B)* The SEC identified a source of Gintel's duty to disclose the information he knew or abstain from selling. Did the Commission find it in some person's fiduciary duty or something else? And if the basis was in some fiduciary duty, to whom was the duty owed?

The Commission began its analysis in *Cady, Roberts* with a focus on the fact that the prohibitions of the Rule were phrased in terms of their applicability to "any person." Although the Commission then laid an analytical base for determining who has obligations under the Rule, this base was virtually lost in the period of the Rule's growth. In the influential case of SEC v. Texas Gulf Sulphur Co., 401 F.2d 833 (2d Cir. 1968), for example, the Second Circuit at

Connections

The *Texas Gulf Sulphur* case is set out in Chapter 30, illustrating many of the themes of litigation under Rule 10b-5.

one point baldly stated that "*anyone* in possession of material inside information must either disclose it to the investing public, or [refrain from trading]." [Emphasis added.]

In the years following *Texas Gulf Sulphur*, securities lawyers and courts tended to view the trading constraints of Rule 10b-5 as broadly as the Second Circuit did in that case. Then, however, the Supreme Court decided *Chiarella v. United States*.

CHIARELLA V. UNITED STATES

Supreme Court of the United States
445 U.S. 222 (1980)

Mr. Justice POWELL delivered the opinion of the Court.

The question in this case is whether a person who learns from the confidential documents of one corporation that it is planning an attempt to secure control of a second corporation violates §10(b) of the Securities Exchange Act of 1934 if he fails to disclose the impending takeover before trading in the target company's securities.

I

Petitioner is a printer by trade. In 1975 and 1976, he worked as a "markup man" in the New York composing room of Pandick Press, a financial printer. Among documents that petitioner handled were five announcements of corporate takeover bids. When these documents were delivered to the printer, the identities of the acquiring and target corporations were concealed by blank spaces or false names. The true names were sent to the printer on the night of the final printing.

Connections: Tender Offers

One method of acquiring control of a corporation is simply to buy the necessary shares on the public markets. When an attempt at this is made by publicly offering to pay a premium price, it is known as a "tender offer," discussed elsewhere in this text.

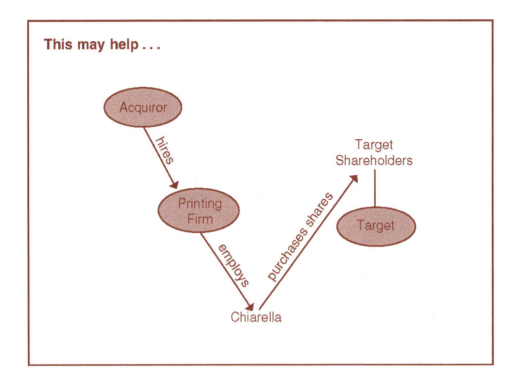

The petitioner, however, was able to deduce the names of the target companies before the final printing from other information contained in the documents. Without disclosing his knowledge, petitioner purchased stock in the target companies and sold the shares immediately after the takeover attempts were made public. By this method, petitioner realized a gain of slightly more than $30,000 in the course of 14 months. Subsequently, the Securities and Exchange Commission (Commission or SEC) began an investigation of his trading activities. In May 1977, petitioner entered into a consent decree with the Commission in which he agreed to return his profits to the sellers of the shares. On the same day, he was discharged by Pandick Press.

In January 1978, petitioner was indicted on 17 counts of violating §10(b) of the Securities Exchange Act of 1934 (1934 Act) and SEC Rule 10b-5. After petitioner unsuccessfully moved to dismiss the indictment, he was brought to trial and convicted on all counts.

The Court of Appeals for the Second Circuit affirmed petitioner's conviction. We granted certiorari, and we now reverse.

II . . .

This case concerns the legal effect of the petitioner's silence. The District Court's charge permitted the jury to convict the petitioner if it found that he willfully failed to inform sellers of target company securities that he knew of a forthcoming takeover bid that would make their shares more valuable. . . .

. . . [B]ut one who fails to disclose material information prior to the consummation of a transaction commits fraud only when he is under a duty to do so. And the duty to disclose arises when one party has information "that the other [party] is entitled to know because of a fiduciary or similar relation of trust and confidence between them."[1] . . .

III

In this case, the petitioner was convicted of violating §10(b) although he was not a corporate insider and he received no confidential information from the target company. Moreover, the "market information" upon which he relied did not concern the earning power or operations of the target company, but only the plans of the acquiring company. Petitioner's use of that information was not a fraud under §10(b) unless he was subject to an affirmative duty to disclose it before trading. In this case, the jury instructions failed to specify any such duty. In effect, the trial court instructed the jury that petitioner owed a duty to everyone; to all sellers, indeed, to the market as a whole. The jury simply was told to decide whether petitioner used material, non-public information at a time when "he knew other people trading in the securities market did not have access to the same information." . . .

We cannot affirm petitioner's conviction without recognizing a general duty between all participants in market transactions to forgo actions based on material, non-public information. Formulation of such a broad duty, which departs radically from the established doctrine that duty arises from a specific relationship between two parties, should not be undertaken absent some explicit evidence of congressional intent.

. . . [N]o such evidence emerges from the language or legislative history of §10(b). . . .

. . . We hold that a duty to disclose under §10(b) does not arise from the mere possession of non-public market information. . . .

IV

In its brief to this Court, the United States offers an alternative theory to support petitioner's conviction. It argues that petitioner breached a duty to the acquiring corporation when he acted upon information that he obtained by virtue of his position as an employee of a printer employed by the corporation. The breach of this duty is said to support a conviction under §10(b) for fraud perpetrated upon both the acquiring corporation and the sellers.

We need not decide whether this theory has merit for it was not submitted to the jury. . . .

---

1. Restatement of the Law 2d, Torts §551(2)(a) (1976).

■ **Think about this:**

(C) Suppose Chiarella had worked for a printer employed by one of the targets of the acquisitions described. Would or should that have made a difference?

More to the Story: And More Than One Way to Peel an Orange

Under §14(a) of the Exchange Act, the SEC is authorized to regulate non-deceptive acts relating to tender offers if that regulation is a "reasonably designed" method of *preventing* fraud or manipulation (rather than *defining* it, as is the case under §10(b)). In the wake of disappointment over the outcome in *Chiarella*, it quickly adopted *Rule 14e-3*. This Rule generally makes it illegal to purchase or sell, or cause to be purchased or sold, securities that are or are to be the subject of a tender offer (or certain related securities) when a person "is in possession of material information relating to such tender offer which information he knows or has reason to know is nonpublic and which he knows or has reason to know has been acquired" from the tender offeror or the target, or from someone connected with either. The Rule also makes it illegal for insiders to tip others with material information about tender offers. Rule 14e-3 may be violated without the existence of a related violation of a fiduciary or other such duty, as is required in a Rule 10b-5 case. Had Rule 14e-3 been in effect at the time of *Chiarella*, it presumably would have resolved the case, and not in Mr. Chiarella's favor. It was invoked, and its application upheld, in the *O'Hagan* case set out below.

Lawyers trying Rule 10b-5 cases after *Chiarella* tended to plead their cases using the alternative theory that had been argued to the Supreme Court but that had not been submitted to the *Chiarella* jury. This became known as the "misappropriation theory." The theory returned to the Court in Carpenter v. United States, 484 U.S. 19 (1987). The Court split evenly on the applicability of the theory to the tippees of a reporter who traded on the basis of stock recommendations to be published by his employer, the *Wall Street Journal*. It did, however, find that the conduct in that case constituted a violation of federal mail and wire fraud statutes (18 U.S.C. §§1341 and 1343).

 Dear Prof.: If mail and wire fraud statutes are available to prosecute inside traders like Carpenter, why should anyone care whether Rule 10b-5 does too?

Only the Department of Justice can invoke the mail and wire fraud statutes. The SEC and private parties cannot. In addition, although scienter is a

> requirement of Rule 10b-5 liability, this is simply a state of mind more culpable than negligence, whereas liability for mail and wire fraud requires intent.

Finally, in 1997, the Court endorsed the misappropriation theory in *United States v. O'Hagan*, which appears below.

UNITED STATES V. O'HAGAN

Supreme Court of the United States
521 U.S. 642 (1997)

Justice GINSBURG delivered the opinion of the Court.

This case concerns the interpretation and enforcement of §10(b) . . . of the Securities Exchange Act of 1934, and [Rule 10b-5] made by the Securities and Exchange Commission. . . . [I]n particular, we address and resolve this [issue:] Is a person who trades in securities for personal profit, using confidential information misappropriated in breach of a fiduciary duty to the source of the information, guilty of violating §10(b) and Rule 10b-5? . . .

I

Respondent James Herman O'Hagan was a partner in the law firm of Dorsey & Whitney in Minneapolis, Minnesota. In July 1988, Grand Metropolitan PLC (Grand Met), a company based in London, England, retained Dorsey & Whitney as local counsel to represent Grand Met regarding a potential tender offer for the common stock of the Pillsbury Company, headquartered in Minneapolis. Both Grand Met and Dorsey & Whitney took precautions to protect the confidentiality of Grand Met's tender offer plans. O'Hagan did no work on the Grand Met representation. [O]n October 4, 1988, Grand Met publicly announced its tender offer for Pillsbury stock.

On August 18, 1988, . . . O'Hagan began purchasing call options for Pillsbury stock. Each option gave him the right to purchase 100 shares of Pillsbury stock by a specified date in September 1988. Later in August and in September, O'Hagan made additional purchases of Pillsbury call options. By the end of September, he owned 2,500 unexpired Pillsbury options, apparently more than any other individual investor. O'Hagan also purchased, in September 1988, some 5,000 shares of Pillsbury common stock, at a price just under $39 per share. When Grand Met announced its tender offer in October, the price of Pillsbury stock rose to nearly $60 per share. O'Hagan then sold his Pillsbury call options and common stock, making a profit of more than $4.3 million.

Thank You, Captain Obvious

The SEC has a number of methods—some non-public—of detecting suspicious trading patterns. This one probably was not very difficult to identify.

JD/MBA: Calls

As the text of the case makes reasonably clear, a call is an option permitting the holder to purchase a security at a given price on or before a particular date. Purchase of calls is a strategy employed when one is predicting an increase in price.

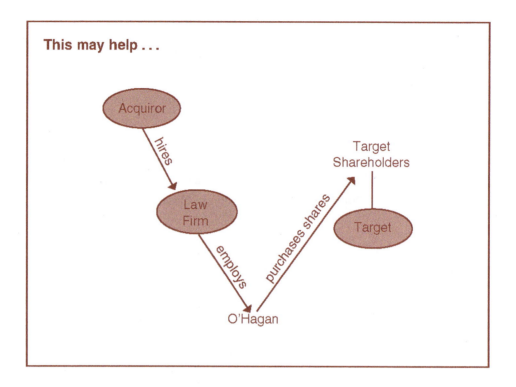

The Securities and Exchange Commission (SEC or Commission) initiated an investigation into O'Hagan's transactions, culminating in [an] indictment. The indictment alleged that O'Hagan defrauded his law firm and its client, Grand Met, by using for his own trading purposes material, nonpublic information regarding Grand Met's planned tender offer. According to the indictment, O'Hagan used the profits he gained through this trading to conceal his previous embezzlement and conversion of unrelated client trust funds. A jury convicted O'Hagan on all . . . counts, and he was sentenced to a 41-month term of imprisonment.

A divided panel of the Court of Appeals for the Eighth Circuit reversed all of O'Hagan's convictions. Liability under §10(b) and Rule 10b-5, the Eighth Circuit held, may not be grounded on the "misappropriation theory" of securities fraud on which the prosecution relied. . . .

Decisions of the Courts of Appeals are in conflict on the propriety of the misappropriation theory under §10(b) and Rule 10b-5. . . . We granted certiorari, and now reverse the Eighth Circuit's judgment.

II . . .

A . . .

Under the "traditional" or "classical theory" of insider trading liability, §10(b) and Rule 10b-5 are violated when a corporate insider trades in the securities of his corporation on the basis of material, nonpublic information. Trading on such information qualifies as a "deceptive device" under §10(b), we have affirmed, because "a relationship of trust and confidence [exists] between the shareholders of a corporation and those insiders who have obtained confidential information by reason of their position with that corporation." Chiarella v. United States, 445 U.S. 222, 228 (1980). That relationship, we recognized, "gives rise to a duty to disclose [or to abstain from trading] because of the 'necessity of preventing a corporate insider from . . . taking unfair advantage of . . . uninformed . . . stockholders.'" The classical theory applies not only to officers, directors, and other permanent insiders of a corporation, but also to attorneys, accountants, consultants, and others who temporarily become fiduciaries of a corporation.

> ### More to the Story: Temporary Insiders
>
> The Court is referring to attorneys, consultants, and others who are temporarily fiduciaries of an issuer and who trade in that issuer's securities. Members of this group generally are referred to as "temporary insiders."

The "misappropriation theory" holds that a person commits fraud "in connection with" a securities transaction, and thereby violates §10(b) and Rule 10b-5, when he misappropriates confidential information for securities trading purposes, in breach of a duty owed to the source of the information. Under this theory, a fiduciary's undisclosed, self-serving use of a principal's information to purchase or sell securities, in breach of a duty of loyalty and confidentiality, defrauds the principal of the exclusive use of that information. In lieu of premising liability on a fiduciary relationship between company insider and purchaser or seller of the company's stock, the misappropriation theory premises liability on a fiduciary-turned-trader's deception of those who entrusted him with access to confidential information.

The two theories are complementary, each addressing efforts to capitalize on nonpublic information through the purchase or sale of securities. The classical theory targets a corporate insider's breach of duty to shareholders with whom the insider transacts; the misappropriation theory outlaws trading on the basis of nonpublic information by a corporate "outsider" in breach of a duty owed not to a trading party, but to the source of the information. The misappropriation theory is thus designed to "protect the integrity of the securities markets against abuses by 'outsiders' to a corporation who have access to confidential information that will affect the corporation's security price when revealed, but who owe no fiduciary or other duty to that corporation's shareholders." [Brief for United States.]

In this case, the indictment alleged that O'Hagan, in breach of a duty of trust and confidence he owed to his law firm, Dorsey & Whitney, and to its client, Grand Met, traded on the basis of nonpublic information regarding Grand Met's planned tender offer for Pillsbury common stock. This conduct, the Government charged, constituted a fraudulent device in connection with the purchase and sale of securities.

B

We agree with the Government that misappropriation, as just defined, satisfies §10(b)'s requirement that chargeable conduct involve a "deceptive device or contrivance" used "in connection with" the purchase or sale of securities. We

observe, first, that misappropriators, as the Government describes them, deal in deception. A fiduciary who "[pretends] loyalty to the principal while secretly converting the principal's information for personal gain," Brief for United States 17, "dupes" or defrauds the principal. . . .

. . . Deception through nondisclosure is central to the theory of liability for which the Government seeks recognition. As counsel for the Government stated in explanation of the theory at oral argument: "To satisfy the common law rule that a trustee may not use the property that [has] been entrusted [to] him, there would have to be consent. To satisfy the requirement of the Securities Act that there be no deception, there would only have to be disclosure."

The misappropriation theory advanced by the Government is consistent with Santa Fe Industries, Inc. v. Green, 430 U.S. 462 (1977), a decision underscoring that §10(b) is not an all-purpose breach of fiduciary duty ban; rather, it trains on conduct involving manipulation or deception. In contrast to the Government's allegations in this case, in *Santa Fe Industries*, all pertinent facts were disclosed by the persons charged with violating §10(b) and Rule 10b-5, therefore, there was no deception through nondisclosure to which liability under those provisions could attach. Similarly, full disclosure forecloses liability under the misappropriation theory: Because the deception essential to the misappropriation theory involves feigning fidelity to the source of information, if the fiduciary discloses to the source that he plans to trade on the nonpublic information, there is no "deceptive device" and thus no §10(b) violation—although the fiduciary-turned-trader may remain liable under state law for breach of a duty of loyalty.

We turn next to the §10(b) requirement that the misappropriator's deceptive use of information be "in connection with the purchase or sale of [a] security." This element is satisfied because the fiduciary's fraud is consummated, not when the fiduciary gains the confidential information, but when, without disclosure to his principal, he uses the information to purchase or sell securities. The securities transaction and the breach of duty thus coincide. This is so even though the person or entity defrauded is not the other party to the trade, but is, instead, the source of the nonpublic information. A misappropriator who trades on the basis of material, nonpublic information, in short, gains his advantageous market position through deception; he deceives the source of the information and simultaneously harms members of the investing public.

The misappropriation theory targets information of a sort that misappropriators ordinarily capitalize upon to gain no-risk profits through the purchase or sale of securities. Should a misappropriator put such information to other use, the statute's prohibition would not be implicated. The theory does not catch all conceivable forms of fraud involving confidential information; rather, it catches fraudulent means of capitalizing on such information through securities transactions.

The Government notes another limitation on the forms of fraud §10(b) reaches: "The misappropriation theory would not . . . apply to a case in which a person defrauded a bank into giving him a loan or embezzled cash from another, and then used the proceeds of the misdeed to purchase securities." In such a case, the Government states, "the proceeds would have value to the malefactor apart from their use in a securities transaction, and the fraud would be complete as soon as the money was obtained." In other words, money can buy, if not anything, then at least many things; its misappropriation may thus be viewed as sufficiently detached from a subsequent securities transaction that §10(b)'s "in connection with" requirement would not be met.

> **This may help . . .**
>
> Elements of misappropriation:
>
> - fiduciary or similar duty?
> - undisclosed breach?
> - in connection with the purchase or sale of a security?

The dissent's charge that the misappropriation theory is incoherent because information, like funds, can be put to multiple uses, misses the point. The Exchange Act was enacted in part "to insure the maintenance of fair and honest markets," 15 U.S.C. §78(b), and there is no question that fraudulent uses of confidential information fall within §10(b)'s prohibition if the fraud is "in connection with" a securities transaction. It is hardly remarkable that a rule suitably applied to the fraudulent uses of certain kinds of information would be stretched beyond reason were it applied to the fraudulent use of money. . . .

The misappropriation theory comports with §10(b)'s language, which requires deception "in connection with the purchase or sale of any security," not deception of an identifiable purchaser or seller. The theory is also well-tuned to an animating purpose of the Exchange Act: to insure honest securities markets and thereby promote investor confidence. Although informational disparity is inevitable in the securities markets, investors likely would hesitate to venture their capital in a market where trading based on misappropriated nonpublic information is unchecked by law. An investor's informational disadvantage vis-a-vis a misappropriator with material, nonpublic information stems from contrivance, not luck; it is a disadvantage that cannot be overcome with research or skill.

In sum, considering the inhibiting impact on market participation of trading on misappropriated information, and the congressional purposes underlying §10(b), it makes scant sense to hold a lawyer like O'Hagan a §10(b) violator if he works for a law firm representing the target of a tender offer, but not if he works for a law firm representing the bidder. The text of the statute requires no such result. The misappropriation at issue here was properly made the subject of a §10(b) charge because it meets the statutory requirement that there be "deceptive" conduct "in connection with" securities transactions. . . .

More to the Story: Trading by Federal Employees

One issue that had percolated for years is whether Rule 10b-5 trading constraints properly apply to the securities transactions of government employees in possession of non-public information, acquired in their official capacities. In 2012, the Stop Trading on Congressional Knowledge (STOCK) Act became law. The STOCK Act is intended, in part, to make it clear that Rule 10b-5 prohibits members and employees of Congress, as well as employees of the executive and judicial branches of government, from engaging in securities transactions while aware of material non-public information derived from federal employment. This was accomplished by an amendment to §21A (which otherwise deals with civil penalties for insider trading). The amendment provides that, for purposes of §10 and Rule 10b-5, federal government employees are in a position of trust and confidence owed to the government and the citizens of the United States with respect to all information they acquire in their official capacities.

Rule 10b5-2 addresses the circumstances in which there is a duty based on a "relationship of trust and confidence" sufficient to find liability under the "misappropriation" theory approved by *O'Hagan*. According to the Rule, such a duty exists if (1) "a person agrees to maintain information in confidence"; (2) the person communicating the material non-public information and the recipient "have a history, pattern, or practice of sharing confidences" resulting in a reasonable expectation of confidentiality; or (3) the person communicating the material non-public information and the recipient are spouses, parents, or siblings. Family members may, however, prove that because of the particular facts and circumstances of their relationship, no duty of trust and confidence existed.

There have been a number of interesting cases involving applications of the misappropriation theory. One such case, SEC v. Rocklage, 470 F.3d 1 (1st Cir. 2006), dealt with *O'Hagan*'s deception requirement in a family context. There, the court held that the SEC had stated a claim against a wife who told her husband that she was going to pass his confidential information to her brother. The rationale was that the requisite deception had occurred when she initially permitted him to reveal the information while intending to leak it.

 Time Out for PR

O'Hagan's conduct presumably would have been a concern for the bar authorities, as well as for the federal government. Consider the following excerpts from the American Bar Association's Model Rules of Professional Conduct:

Rule 1.8 Conflict of Interest: Current Clients: Specific Rules

. . .

(b) A lawyer shall not use information relating to representation of a client to the disadvantage of the client unless the client gives informed consent, except as permitted or required by these Rules. . . .

Rule 8.4 Misconduct

It is professional misconduct for a lawyer to:

(b) commit a criminal act that reflects adversely on the lawyer's honesty, trustworthiness or fitness as a lawyer in other respects;

(c) engage in conduct involving dishonesty, fraud, deceit or misrepresentation. . . .

■ Think about this:

(D) Howard, a stealthy and talented hacker, gains remote access to top-secret computer files belonging to Discovery, Inc. The files indicate that Discovery has discovered a new process that, when announced, will surely drive up the price of its stock dramatically. Howard, who previously had no relationship with Discovery, purchases a large number of its shares. Is he liable under Rule 10b-5? Might he otherwise be liable under any other obviously applicable legal theory?

(E) Allie, an attorney at a law firm representing Acquisico, learns that Acquisico plans to make a tender offer for the shares of Targuette, Inc., the price of which recently has declined from $40 to $36 per share. The day before, Allie had asked her broker to buy her 1,000 shares of Targuette stock as soon as its price declined to $35 per share. What should Allie do?

(F) Raul, a reporter for the *Wall Street Journal*, writes a column recommending the purchase or sale of various securities. His opinion has the power to move the market. He is fed up with the job, however, and decides to make a market killing on the way out. He writes a column recommending the sale of Dumpit, Inc. He then sells 100,000 Dumpit shares short. After it is too late to prevent the story from appearing, he sends an email to his superior at the *Wall Street Journal* advising that he is quitting and disclosing what he has done. Is he liable under Rule 10b-5?

(G) Same facts as Problem F except that Raul emails his superior before his short sale, at a time when it is too late to stop the story, but again advising that he is quitting and disclosing his intent to sell his Dumpit

shares short. If he follows through with his plan, will he be liable under Rule 10b-5?

(H) Same facts as Problem F except that Raul's email is sent while there is still time to kill the column. The superior has always liked Raul and sends him back an email that says: "May the Force be with you." If Raul follows through with his plan, will he be liable under Rule 10b-5?

The question whether computer hackers and their tippees could be liable under the misappropriation theory was raised in SEC v. Dorozhko, 574 F.3d 42 (2d Cir. 2009). The Second Circuit held that the answer was "no," but did invite prosecution of hackers under an affirmative deception theory, saying that "misrepresenting one's identity in order to gain access to information that otherwise is off limits and then stealing that information is plainly 'deceptive.'"

The Supreme Court has decided another case addressing who is subject to the trading constraints of Rule 10b-5. This case, *Dirks v. SEC*, concerns the circumstances under which tippee liability exists.

DIRKS V. SEC

Supreme Court of the United States
463 U.S. 646 (1983)

Justice POWELL delivered the opinion of the Court.

Petitioner Raymond Dirks received material non-public information from "insiders" of a corporation with which he had no connection. He disclosed this information to investors who relied on it in trading in the shares of the corporation. The question is whether Dirks violated the anti-fraud provisions of the federal securities laws by this disclosure.

I

In 1973, Dirks was an officer of a New York broker-dealer firm who specialized in providing investment analysis of insurance company securities to institutional investors. On March 6, Dirks received information from Ronald Secrist, a former officer of Equity Funding of America. Secrist alleged that the assets of Equity Funding, a diversified corporation primarily engaged in selling life insurance and mutual funds, were vastly overstated as the result of fraudulent corporate practices. Secrist also stated that various regulatory agencies had failed to act on similar charges made by Equity Funding employees. He urged Dirks to verify the fraud and disclose it publicly.

Dirks decided to investigate the allegations. He visited Equity Funding's headquarters in Los Angeles and

The Billion Dollar Bubble is a 1976 film about the insurance embezzlement scheme at Equity Funding Corporation of America. James Woods stars in the role of an actuary. At least two books have been written about the scandal, including one co-authored by Raymond Dirks.

interviewed several officers and employees of the corporation. The senior management denied any wrongdoing, but certain corporation employees corroborated the charges of fraud. Neither Dirks nor his firm owned or traded any Equity Funding stock, but throughout his investigation he openly discussed the information he had obtained with a number of clients and investors. Some of these persons sold their holdings of Equity Funding securities, including five investment advisers who liquidated holdings of more than $16 million.

While Dirks was in Los Angeles, he was in touch regularly with William Blundell, the *Wall Street Journal*'s Los Angeles bureau chief. Dirks urged Blundell to write a story on the fraud allegations. Blundell did not believe, however, that such a massive fraud could go undetected and declined to write the story. He feared that publishing such damaging hearsay might be libelous.

During the two-week period in which Dirks pursued his investigation and spread word of Secrist's charges, the price of Equity Funding stock fell from $26 per share to less than $15 per share. This led the New York Stock Exchange to halt trading on March 27. Shortly thereafter California insurance authorities impounded Equity Funding's records and uncovered evidence of the fraud. Only then did the Securities and Exchange Commission (SEC) file a complaint against Equity Funding and only then, on April 2, did the *Wall Street Journal* publish a front-page story based largely on information assembled by Dirks. Equity Funding immediately went into receivership.

The SEC began an investigation into Dirks' role in the exposure of the fraud. After a hearing by an administrative law judge, the SEC found that Dirks had aided and abetted violations of . . . §10(b) of the Securities Exchange Act of 1934, and SEC Rule 10b-5, by repeating the allegations of fraud to members of the investment community who later sold their Equity Funding stock. The SEC concluded: "Where 'tippees'—regardless of their motivation or occupation—come into possession of material 'information that they know is confidential and know or should know came from a corporate insider,' they must either publicly disclose that information or refrain from trading." 21 S.E.C. Docket 1401, 1407 (1981) (footnote omitted) (quoting Chiarella v. United States, 445 U.S. 222, 230 n. 12 (1980)). Recognizing, however, that Dirks "played an important role in bringing [Equity Funding's] massive fraud to light," the SEC only censured him.

Dirks sought review in the Court of Appeals for the District of Columbia Circuit. The court entered judgment against Dirks. . . .

III

We were explicit in *Chiarella* in saying that there can be no duty to disclose where the person who has traded on inside information "was not [the corporation's] agent, . . . was not a fiduciary, [or] was not a person in whom the sellers [of the securities] had placed their trust and confidence." Not to require such a fiduciary relationship, we recognized, would "depar[t] radically from the established doctrine that duty arises from a specific relationship between two parties" and would amount to "rec-

Connections: The "Misappropriation Theory"

Dirks was decided before the Supreme Court had acknowledged the "misappropriation theory" of insider trading, discussed above.

ognizing a general duty between all participants in market transactions to forgo actions based on material, non-public information." This requirement of a specific relationship between the shareholders and the individual trading on inside information has created analytical difficulties for the SEC and courts in policing tippees who trade on inside information. Unlike insiders who have independent fiduciary duties to both the corporation and its shareholders, the typical tippee has no such relationships. In view of this absence, it has been unclear how a tippee acquires the . . . duty to refrain from trading on inside information. . . .

A

. . . Here, the SEC maintains that anyone who knowingly receives nonpublic material information from an insider has a fiduciary duty to disclose before trading.

In effect, the SEC's theory of tippee liability . . . appears rooted in the idea that the antifraud provisions require equal information among all traders. This conflicts with the principle set forth in *Chiarella* that only some persons, under some circumstances, will be barred from trading while in possession of material nonpublic information. Judge Wright correctly read our opinion in *Chiarella* as repudiating any notion that all traders must enjoy equal information before trading: "[T]he 'information' theory is rejected. Because the disclose-or-refrain duty is extraordinary, it attaches only when a party has legal obligations other than a mere duty to comply with the general antifraud proscriptions in the federal securities laws." 220 U.S. App. D. C., at 322, 681 F.2d, at 837. See *Chiarella*, 445 U.S., at 235, n. 20. We reaffirm today that "[a] duty [to disclose] arises from the relationship between parties . . . and not merely from one's ability to acquire information because of his position in the market." *Id.*, at 231-232, n. 14.

Imposing a duty to disclose or abstain solely because a person knowingly receives material nonpublic information from an insider and trades on it could have an inhibiting influence on the role of market analysts, which the SEC itself recognizes is necessary to the preservation of a healthy market. It is commonplace for analysts to "ferret out and analyze information," 21 S.E.C. Docket, at 1406, and this often is done by meeting with and questioning corporate officers and others who are insiders. And information that the analysts obtain normally may be the basis for judgments as to the market worth of a corporation's securities. The analyst's judgment in this respect is made available in market letters or otherwise to clients of the firm. It is the nature of this type of information, and indeed of the markets themselves, that such information cannot be made simultaneously available to all of the corporation's stockholders or the public generally.

More to the Story: Regulation FD

The Court's admiring tone with respect to the important role of financial analysts is distinctly ironic, given later developments.

In 2000, the SEC adopted Regulation FD in order to prevent companies from favoring financial analysts and certain others with non-public information. Basically, it requires that information intentionally disclosed to market professionals and existing shareholders, who might trade on the information, must be simultaneously disclosed to the public. If disclosure is unintentionally made to a market professional or existing shareholder, public disclosure must take place "promptly" after a senior officer learns what has happened.

B

The conclusion that recipients of inside information do not invariably acquire a duty to disclose or abstain does not mean that such tippees always are free to trade on the information. The need for a ban on some tippee trading is clear. Not only are insiders forbidden by their fiduciary relationship from personally using undisclosed corporate information to their advantage, but they also may not give such information to an outsider for the same improper purpose of exploiting the information for their personal gain. See 15 U.S.C. §78t(b) (making it unlawful to do indirectly "by means of any other person" any act made unlawful by the federal securities laws). Similarly, the transactions of those who knowingly participate with the fiduciary in such a breach are "as forbidden" as transactions "on behalf of the trustee himself." Mosser v. Darrow, 341 U.S. 267, 272 (1951). . . . Thus, the tippee's duty to disclose or abstain is derivative from that of the insider's duty. See Tr. of Oral Arg. 38. Cf. *Chiarella*, 445 U.S., at 246, n. 1 (Blackmun, J., dissenting). As we noted in *Chiarella*, "[t]he tippee's obligation has been viewed as arising from his role as a participant after the fact in the insider's breach of a fiduciary duty." *Id.*, at 230, n. 12.

Thus, some tippees must assume an insider's duty to the shareholders not because they receive inside information, but rather because it has been made available to them *improperly*. And for Rule 10b-5 purposes, the insider's disclosure is improper only where it would violate his *Cady, Roberts* duty. Thus, a tippee assumes a fiduciary duty to the shareholders of a corporation not to trade on material nonpublic information only when the insider has breached his fiduciary duty to the shareholders by disclosing the information to the tippee and the tippee knows or should know that there has been a breach. . . . Tipping thus properly is viewed only as a means of indirectly violating the *Cady, Roberts* disclose-or-abstain rule.

C

In determining whether a tippee is under an obligation to disclose or abstain, it . . . is necessary to determine whether the insider's "tip" constituted a breach of the insider's fiduciary duty. All disclosures of confidential corporate information are not inconsistent with the duty insiders owe to shareholders. In contrast to the extraordinary facts of this case, the more typical situation in which there will be a question whether disclosure violates the insider's . . . duty is when insiders disclose information to analysts. In some situations, the insider will act consistently with his fiduciary duty to shareholders, and yet release of the information may affect the market. For example, it may not be clear either to the corporate insider or to the recipient analyst [] whether the information will be viewed as material non-public information. Corporate officials may mistakenly think the information already has been disclosed or that it is not material enough to affect the market. Whether disclosure is a breach of duty therefore depends in large part on the purpose of the disclosure. This standard was identified by the SEC itself in [In re Cady, Roberts & Co., 40 S.E.C. 907 (1961)]: a purpose of the securities laws was to eliminate "use of inside information for personal advantage." Thus, the test is whether the insider personally will benefit, directly or indirectly, from his disclosure. Absent some personal gain, there has been no breach of duty to stockholders. And absent a breach by the insider, there is no derivative breach. . . .

. . . [T]his requires courts to focus on objective criteria, *i.e.*, whether the insider receives a direct or indirect personal benefit from the disclosure, such as a pecuniary gain or a reputational benefit that will translate into future earnings. There are objective facts and circumstances that often justify such an inference. For example, there may be a relationship between the insider and the recipient that suggests a *quid pro quo* from the latter, or an intention to benefit the particular recipient. The elements of fiduciary duty and exploitation of non-public information also exist when an insider makes a gift of confidential information to a trading relative or friend. The tip and trade resemble trading by the insider himself followed by a gift of the profits to the recipient. . . .

IV

Under the inside-trading and tipping rules set forth above, we find that there was no actionable violation by Dirks. It is undisputed that Dirks himself was a stranger to Equity Funding, with no pre-existing fiduciary duty to its shareholders. He took no action, directly or indirectly, that induced the shareholders or officers of Equity Funding to repose trust or confidence in him. There was no expectation by Dirks' sources that he would keep their information in confidence. Nor did Dirks misappropriate or illegally obtain the information about Equity Funding. Unless the insiders breached their *Cady, Roberts* duty to shareholders in disclosing the non-public information to Dirks, he breached no duty when he passed it on to investors as well as to the *Wall Street Journal.*

It is clear that neither Secrist nor the other Equity Funding employees violated their *Cady, Roberts* duty to the corporation's shareholders by providing information to Dirks. The tippers received no monetary or personal benefit for revealing Equity Funding's secrets, nor was their purpose to make a gift of valuable information to Dirks. As the facts of this case clearly indicate, the tippers were motivated by a desire to expose the fraud. In the absence of a breach of duty to shareholders by the insiders, there was no derivative breach by Dirks. Dirks therefore could not have been "a participant after the fact in [an] insider's breach of a fiduciary duty." *Chiarella,* 445 U.S., at 230, n. 12. . . .

More to the Story: Exception

Rule 10b5-1, which provides that the duty to disclose is triggered once the defendant is aware of material inside information, contains limited exceptions. One of them allows trading in accordance with a predetermined plan. The SEC now questions whether the exception is being abused.

Naturally, there are still questions to be resolved, among them the following:

• Must a tipper intend to benefit personally from a tip in all types of insider trading cases? *Dirks* involved a so-called classical insider owing a duty to the company whose stock was traded. In a case involving tipping by a misappropriating employee of Citibank, the litigants and the Supreme Court all assumed that the *Dirks* personal-benefit framework applied in that context as well. Salman v. United States, 580 U.S. ___ (2016).

- Is it necessary that the tipper know that his or her disclosure was improper? In United States v. Evans, 486 F.3d 315 (7th Cir. 2007), the Seventh Circuit answered "no."
- Is an insider — and his or her illicit tippee — precluded from trading without disclosing the non-public information in question once he or she possesses it, or must he or she intend to "use" the information? Under Rule 10b5-1, it is enough to show that a defendant was aware of material inside information when trading.

■ **Think about this:**

(1) Felecia is a first-class passenger on a flight from New York City to San Francisco. Dipping her hand into the seat pocket, she discovers a thumb drive. Curious, she checks its contents. The files she reads clearly indicate that the drive is the property of Pharmco, Inc., a large pharmaceutical company, and that Pharmco is on the verge of announcing a tremendous new breakthrough that surely will result in an increase in the price of the stock. Felecia, who has no relationship with Pharmco or anyone who works there, assumes that the thumb drive was negligently left behind by a corporate officer. May Felecia buy Pharmco stock before the breakthrough is announced?

In summary, here is a list of those who are subject to a duty to disclose or abstain from trading:

- "classical" or "traditional" insiders;
- temporary insiders;
- misappropriators;
- certain persons with material non-public information about tender offers;
- federal employees;
- tippees.

C. Reliance and Causation in the Context of Insider Trading

More to the Story: Suits by the Suits

Because of the difficulties associated with private litigation, most of the enforcement burden has fallen on the government. Section 32 of the Exchange

Act authorizes criminal prosecution for willful violations. In addition, Exchange Act §21A allows the SEC to seek civil penalties, both on inside traders and on persons who control inside traders and knowingly or recklessly fail to take appropriate steps to prevent the inside trading. The penalty is in the discretion of the court, but may be as high as three times the profit gained, or loss avoided, as a result of insider trading, except in the case of controlling persons, whose penalties can be as high as $1,425,000. Section 21A also provides for the payment of bounties of up to 10 percent of the penalty to persons who provide information that leads to the imposition of a penalty.

Ordinarily, a private plaintiff suing for a violation of Rule 10b-5 is required to demonstrate both reliance and causation. Reliance and causation involving non-disclosure (which of course is the whole point of insider trading) are complex subjects. The starting point is Affiliated Ute Citizens v. United States, 406 U.S. 128 (1972). There, the Court struggled with reliance and causation in the context of face-to-face dealings between officers of a bank who engaged in stock transactions with members of the Ute tribe. The major allegations were the failure of the bank officers to disclose material information. The Court found that "[u]nder the circumstances of this case, involving primarily a failure to disclose, positive proof of reliance is not a prerequisite to recovery. All that is necessary is that the facts withheld be material. . . . This obligation to disclose and this withholding of a material fact establish the requisite element of causation in fact." Lower courts generally have read the case as establishing a rebuttable presumption of reliance on the non-existence of the withheld facts in the context of face-to-face trading.

Connections: The Purchaser or Seller Requirement

Private plaintiffs in insider trading cases, like any private plaintiff under Rule 10b-5, also are required to show that they are actual purchasers or sellers of the stock that is the subject of the complaint.

Complaints based on open market trading in violation of the duty to disclose or refrain from trading have not been greeted as enthusiastically. The courts have noted, among other things, that the number of possible plaintiffs could be so numerous that some traditional damage measures might result in liability hugely disproportionate to the defendants' profit. Those courts resolving the causation issue in a plaintiff's favor have tended toward a disgorgement measure—which greatly diminished the enthusiasm of the plaintiffs' bar.

■ **Think about this:**

(J)   Oscar is an open-market trader who sold shares of Breakthrough, Inc., the day before a big breakthrough is announced. He would not have sold if he had known about the breakthrough. What additional facts would Oscar need to prove in order to recover from Isaac, an insider who, on the same day that Oscar sold, bought the same number of Breakthrough, Inc.'s shares that Oscar sold?

More to the Story: And More Than One Way to Peel an Orange

Exchange Act §20A presents an interesting, if not particularly useful, approach to insider trading. Notably, it does *not* say that purchasing or selling a security while in possession of material non-public information violates the Exchange Act. Instead, it says in effect that *if* such a purchase or sale violates the Exchange Act, §20A consequences attach. This piggy-back approach means that a complete analysis of whether a violation of some other provision (such as Rule 10b-5) logically must precede application of §20A. Disgorgement is the measure of damages, which must be shared by those trading "contemporaneously" in the same class of shares traded by the violator. This could encompass such a large group as to leave little incentive for any plaintiff to initiate litigation. As a result, §20A has never had much impact.

On October 16, 2009, former hedge fund manager and billionaire Raj Rajaratnam was arrested for insider trading resulting in illicit profits of $63.8 million. In 2011, he was sentenced to 11 years in prison and fines of over $150 million. His story is the subject of the movie *Billion Dollar Raja*, in which he is portrayed by the actor Mohanlal (pictured).

Here is the address of a link to a 17-minute wiretap used to convict him: https://commons.wikimedia.org/wiki/File:GalleonWiretap_RajatGupta-Raj Rajaratnam.ogg.

Test Yourself

Questions 1-4 are objective questions:

1. Section 10(b) of the Exchange Act:

   a. is relevant only with respect to purchases or sales of securities traded on a national securities exchange.

   b. is relevant only with respect to purchases or sales of securities registered under the Exchange Act.

c. is relevant with respect to purchases or sales of any security.

d. is relevant only with respect to purchases or sales of securities registered under either the Securities Act or the Exchange Act.

2. P is the president of Testex, Inc., which manufactures a variety of products out of Flarp. Testex does not make Flarp itself; rather, it purchases Flarp from whichever of the three Flarp manufacturers is offering it at the best price. P has, for some time, owned a significant number of the shares of each of the three Flarp manufacturers. Testex scientists have now determined that Gloop, rather than Flarp, could be used to manufacture all Testex products. Gloop is cheaper and more resilient than Flarp, and is produced by different companies than those that produce Flarp. These findings have not been publicly announced. P suspects that once they are, other companies relying on Flarp will quickly come to similar conclusions. P immediately sells all of his shares of the Flarp manufacturers. Which of the following positions is most likely to be taken by the SEC with respect to P's activities?

   a. P has violated his duty to disclose or abstain from trading under §10(b) and Rule 10b-5 of the Exchange Act because he is a "traditional" insider of Testex.

   b. P has violated his duty to disclose or abstain from trading under §10(b) and Rule 10b-5 of the Exchange Act because he is a tippee of information relating to the Flarp manufacturers.

   c. P has engaged in deceitful conduct in violation of §10(b) and Rule 10b-5 of the Exchange Act because he has misappropriated proprietary information belonging to Testex.

   d. P has not violated §10(b) and Rule 10b-5 of the Exchange Act.

3. Continuing the factual assumptions of Question 2, which of the following is most true?

   a. Persons purchasing Flarp shares on the days P sold his shares will be able to recover only if they can establish a causal connection between their purchase and his sale.

   b. Persons purchasing Flarp shares on the days P sold his shares will not be able to recover, even if P violated a duty to disclose or refrain from trading.

   c. Persons purchasing Flarp shares on the days P sold his shares will be able to recover, assuming he violated a duty to disclose or refrain from trading.

   d. Persons purchasing Flarp shares on the days P sold his shares will be able to recover.

4. The liability of a tippee under §10(b) and Rule 10b-5 is:

   a. dependent on whether the tipper was a traditional insider or a misappropriator.
   b. dependent on whether the tipper breached a duty in making the tip.
   c. dependent on whether the tippee conferred a benefit on the tipper in exchange for the tip.
   d. none of the above.

Question 5 is an essay question:

5. Jetco, a corporation whose stock is traded on a national stock exchange, has 200,000 shares of $25 par value common stock outstanding. Dan, who owns 100 shares of Jetco stock, is a director of Jetco. Five months ago, Dan learned that Jetco had developed a secret new invention to convert organic waste to commercial fuel and that a public announcement of the invention was soon to be made. Dan immediately emailed three of Jetco's shareholders who, Dan knew, had previously announced their willingness to sell their shares for $22 per share, a price that was $3 a share above book value. Dan offered them $25 per share. They accepted his offer and sold a total of 4,200 shares to Dan. At this time, Dan also accepted, and immediately exercised, stock option rights to purchase 1,000 authorized, but previously unissued, shares from Jetco, for which he paid the option price of $21 per share. A week later, the invention was announced, and the market value of Jetco stock rose substantially. A few days ago, Dan sold, for $50 per share, the 4,200 shares he had acquired from the three dissatisfied shareholders. Please devote approximately 15 minutes to discussing Dan's potential liabilities, and to whom, as a result of the above transactions.[2]

---

2. This question is based on one originally appearing in *Siegel's Corporations and Other Business Entities* (Theresa Gabaldon, ed., 5th ed. 2012).

32

Trading by Insiders: Short-Swing Trading Under §16(b)

Rule 10b-5 under the Securities Exchange Act of 1934 is a broad anti-fraud provision that has been applied in many contexts, notably including "inside trading." It was not, however, part of Congress's original plan for dealing with informational asymmetry. That honor belongs to §16(b), which is a prophylactic device intended to prevent insiders from profiting on trades likely to be based on non-public information. The actions described in §16(b) are not illegal; they simply are pointless from the standpoint of making a profit.

Chapter Outline

A. Statutory Scheme

- §16(a) reporting
- §16(b) disgorgement

B. Persons Liable

- Officers and directors
  - Titles and deputization
- Greater than 10 percent beneficial holders
  - Attribution

C. What Constitutes a Purchase or Sale?

D. Timing of Purchases and Sales

- Greater than 10 percent beneficial owners at time of both purchase and sale
- Different rule for officers and directors

E. Standing to Sue
- The corporation
- Any shareholder

F. Calculation of Profits
- Highest sales price and lowest purchase price within a less than six-month period

---

Test Yourself

 What does it look like?

Check the online Supplement for the following sample documents that are relevant to this chapter:

- Exchange Act Forms 3, 4, and 5 for reporting share ownership under §16(a)

A. Statutory Scheme

Exchange Act §16(b) is designed to minimize the unfair use of inside information. Under that section, profits made by insiders from transactions involving equity securities of publicly held companies, when a purchase and a sale are made less than six months apart, must be disgorged and paid to the issuer.

Before examining §16(b), it is helpful to contemplate §16(a). That section requires beneficial owners of more than 10 percent of a class of equity security that is registered under the Exchange Act, and officers and directors of issuers of such securities, to file reports with the SEC and relevant securities exchanges concerning their holdings of all equity securities of such issuers. Section 16(a) sets the filing periods for initial reports to be filed upon becoming subject to the section (basically, at the same time a company registers an equity security under the Exchange Act or within ten days of becoming a person listed in the section, unless the SEC provides for a shorter period). It also establishes the filing period for reports of changes in ownership—which now stands at within two business days after the change. Rule 16a-3 details the reporting requirements, providing for the use of relatively short, fill-in-the-blanks forms that must be posted on the issuer's website not later than the end of the next business day after the report is filed.

Why §16(a)?

- To inform the market;
- To aid enforcement of §16(b).

Section 16(b) provides that:

1. Any *profit*;
2. by any person *subject to the reporting requirements of §16(a)*;
3. realized on any *purchase and sale*, or *sale and purchase*;
4. within any period of *less than six months*;
5. of any non-exempt *equity* security of an issuer that has an *equity security registered under the Exchange Act*, or of any security-based swap agreement involving any such equity security

"shall inure to and be recoverable by the issuer." Under §16(b), an issuer may sue to recover these so-called short-swing profits. Moreover, any security holder of the issuer may sue derivatively to recover the profits when, after request, the issuer fails to bring suit within 60 days or when it fails diligently to prosecute a claim once filed.

Many questions concerning §16 are answered by the SEC's highly detailed rules. One thing to note is that the grant of a derivative security, such as a stock option, is deemed to be a purchase of the underlying equity security, thus triggering (unless there is an applicable exemption) §16(b) short-swing trading liability if the purchase can be matched with an appropriate sale within less than six months either way.

Most general questions that arise under §16(b) can be grouped under one of five topics:

- persons liable,
- what constitutes a purchase or sale,
- timing of purchases and sales,
- who has standing to sue, and
- calculation of profits.

Interestingly, unlike most provisions in the Exchange Act, §16(b) is not a criminal provision. It does not make short-swing trading illegal. Instead, the section merely provides that the profits from certain trades essentially belong to the issuer.

B. Persons Liable

On the question of persons subject to §16(b), the statute speaks in terms of officers, directors, and greater than 10 percent beneficial owners. Intricacies are buried beneath the surface. This section deals with the significance of title, as opposed to function, and the concept that

Connections: Derivative Litigation

There are, as discussed elsewhere in this book, many requirements ordinarily associated with bringing derivative litigation. They do **not** apply to litigation under §16(b).

"deputization" imposes liability on the "sheriff." It also will describe the problems created by beneficial ownership of shares.

Titles. One interesting issue relates to titles. For most purposes, of course, a person's status as an officer or director of a corporation depends on whether he or she has been elected an officer or director in accordance with the requirements of state corporation law and the corporation's by-laws. Things are not so simple under §16(b). Two special definitions create complications:

> **Section 3(a)(7).** The term "director" means any director of a corporation or any person performing similar functions with respect to any organization, whether incorporated or unincorporated.

> **Rule 16a-1(f).** The term "officer" shall mean an issuer's president, principal financial officer, principal accounting officer (or, if there is no such accounting officer, the controller), any vice-president of the issuer in charge of a principal business unit, division or function (such as sales, administration, or finance), any other officer who performs a policy-making function, or any other person who performs similar policy-making functions for the issuer. Officers of the issuer's parent(s) or subsidiaries shall be deemed officers of the issuer if they perform such policy-making functions for the issuer. . . .

Thus, it is clear that title alone does not determine who is subject to short-swing trading limits.

Deputization. Under the "deputization" theory, §16(b) can apply to a person or entity who, although not otherwise subject to the rule, is represented by a person who sits on the corporation's board of directors. Perhaps the most important case on deputization is Feder v. Martin Marietta Corp., 406 F.2d 260 (2d Cir. 1969). There, the president of Martin Marietta served as a director of Sperry Rand Corp. during a period when Martin Marietta was purchasing large amounts of Sperry stock, which it sold shortly after the president resigned his directorship. The Second Circuit found Martin Marietta to be Sperry's "director" under §16(b), emphasizing that the president was ultimately responsible for Martin Marietta's operations, including its investments.

Beneficial Ownership. Under §16(b), an insider must disgorge "profits realized *by him*" (emphasis added). Though usually straightforward, this requirement can pose problems. For example, when shares are traded by a director's spouse or by an officer for the account of a minor child, are the profits realized "by" the insider?

Rule 16a-1(a)(2) indicates that for such determinations:

> [T]he term "beneficial owner" shall mean any person who, directly or indirectly, through any contract, arrangement, understanding, relationship or

otherwise, has or shares a direct or indirect pecuniary interest in the equity securities, subject to the following. . . .

The Rule then provides that a pecuniary interest means "the opportunity, directly or indirectly, to profit or share in any profit derived from a transaction in the subject securities." It also presumes "indirect pecuniary interest" to include securities held by immediate family members who share the same home, though "the presumption . . . may be rebutted. . . ."

Another interesting beneficial ownership issue arises under §16 when two or more people agree to act together in buying, holding, voting, or selling securities. The question is whether the group is considered the beneficial owner of the relevant securities held by members of the group. In short, the answer under Rule 16a-1(a)(1) is "yes."

> **Connections: Record vs. Beneficial Owners**
>
> As discussed elsewhere in this book, corporate law distinguishes "record owners," who, as far as the corporation is concerned, are entitled to vote and receive distributions, from "beneficial owners," whose rights depend on their arrangements with the record owners.

C. What Constitutes a Purchase or Sale?

Determining what constitutes a purchase or sale is easy in the usual context, but can be difficult when unorthodox transactions are involved. The most important case is Kern County Land Co. v. Occidental Petroleum Corp., 411 U.S. 582 (1973). There, the Supreme Court evaluated a complex series of transactions involving a shareholder's frustrated takeover attempt. The deal resulted in the sale of its shares, not of the acquisition target, but of a separate company with which the target had merged. The Court found no opportunity for speculative abuse and thus no "sale" for §16(b) purposes.

The SEC, keying off the concept of lack of opportunity for speculative abuse, has adopted a number of rules excluding transactions from the coverage of §16(b). These include (unsurprisingly) gifts and transfers of shares in and out of voting trusts. Also excluded are acquisitions pursuant to dividend reinvestment programs, stock splits, and stock dividends, as well as transactions pursuant to a "qualifying" employee stock ownership plan. On the other hand, establishing a "call" (the right to buy at a stated price) position on an equity security generally is deemed a purchase of that security and establishing a "put" (the right to sell at a stated price) position generally is deemed a sale of the underlying security. The exercise of the call or put is disregarded for §16(b) purposes, although it must be reported under §16(a).

> **More to the Story: Selling Short**
>
> It probably is worth noting that those who are subject to §16(a) and (b) are flatly prohibited by §16(c) from "selling short" — that is, entering into an agreement to sell the relevant issuer's equity securities without owning them.

D. Timing of Purchases and Sales

Section 16(b) contains the following provision on the issue of timing: "This subsection shall not be construed to cover any transaction where [a] beneficial owner [with 10 percent or more] was not such both at the time of the purchase and sale, or the sale and purchase." In general, this provision is clear enough. Still, the Supreme Court has been called on to decide two cases that deal with subtleties.

RELIANCE ELECTRIC CO. v. EMERSON ELECTRIC CO.

Supreme Court of the United States
404 U.S. 418 (1972)

Mr. Justice STEWART delivered the opinion of the Court.

Section 16(b) of the Securities Exchange Act of 1934 provides, among other things, that a corporation may recover for itself the profits realized by an owner of more than 10% of its shares from a purchase and sale of its stock within any six-month period, provided that the owner held more than 10% "both at the time of the purchase and sale." In this case, the respondent, the owner of 13.2% of a corporation's shares, disposed of its entire holdings in two sales, both of them within six months of purchase. The first sale reduced the respondent's holdings to 9.96%, and the second disposed of the remainder. The question presented is whether the profits derived from the second sale are recoverable by the Corporation under §16(b). We hold that they are not.

I

On June 16, 1967, the respondent, Emerson Electric Co., acquired 13.2% of the outstanding common stock of Dodge Manufacturing Co., pursuant to a tender offer made in an unsuccessful attempt to take over Dodge. The purchase price for this stock was $63 per share. Shortly thereafter, the shareholders of Dodge approved a merger with the petitioner, Reliance Electric Co. Faced with the certain failure of any further attempt to take over Dodge, and with the prospect of being forced to exchange its Dodge shares for stock in the merged corporation in the near future, Emerson, following a plan outlined by its general counsel, decided to dispose of enough shares to bring its holdings below 10%, in order to immunize the disposal of the remainder of its shares from liability under §16(b).

Pursuant to counsel's recommendation, Emerson on August 28 sold 37,000 shares of Dodge common stock to a brokerage house at $68 per share. This sale reduced Emerson's holdings in Dodge to 9.96% of the outstanding common stock. The remaining shares were then sold to Dodge at $69 per share on September 11.

After a demand on it by Reliance for the profits realized on both sales, Emerson filed this action seeking a declaratory judgment as to its liability under §16(b). . . .

. . . [T]he District Court held Emerson liable for the entire amount of its profits. The court found that Emerson's sales of Dodge stock were "effected pursuant to a single predetermined plan of disposition with the

---

This may help . . .

Reliance Electric Co. v. Emerson Electric Co. Timeline

6/16/67
13.2% Purchase @ $63

8/28/67
3.24% Sale @ $68

9/11/67
9.96% Sale @ $69

overall intent and purpose of avoiding Section 16(b) liability," and construed the term "time of . . . sale" to include "the entire period during which a series of related transactions take place pursuant to a plan by which a 10% beneficial owner disposes of his stock holdings."

On an interlocutory appeal . . . the Court of Appeals upheld the finding that Emerson "split" its sale of Dodge stock simply in order to avoid most of its potential liability under §16(b), but it held this fact irrelevant under the statute so long as the two sales are "not legally tied to each other and [are] made at different times to different buyers. . . ." Accordingly, the Court of Appeals reversed the District Court's judgment as to Emerson's liability for its profits on the September 11 sale, and remanded for a determination of the amount of Emerson's liability on the August 28 sale. . . .

II . . .

Among the "objective standards" contained in §16(b) is the requirement that a 10% owner be such "both at the time of the purchase and sale . . . of the security involved." Read literally, this language clearly contemplates that a statutory insider might sell enough shares to bring his holdings below 10%, and later—but still within six months—sell additional shares free from liability under the statute. Indeed, commentators on the securities laws have recommended this exact procedure for a 10% owner who, like Emerson, wishes to dispose of his holdings within six months of their purchase.

Under the approach urged by Reliance, and adopted by the District Court, the apparent immunity of profits derived from Emerson's second sale is lost where the two sales, though independent in every other respect, are "interrelated parts of a single plan." But a "plan" to sell that is conceived within six months of purchase clearly would not fall within §16(b) if the sale were made after the six months had expired, and we see no basis in the statute for a different result where the 10% requirement is involved rather than the six-month limitation.

■ Think about this:

(A) Can you see a policy reason to distinguish "a 'plan' to sell that is conceived within six months of purchase" from what went on in *Reliance Electric*?

The *Reliance Electric* holding has found its way into Rule 16a-2(c). Still, it should not be taken too far. For instance, in Reece Corp. v. Walco National Corp., 565 F. Supp. 158 (S.D.N.Y. 1983), the seller and the purchaser arranged to structure a bifurcated sales transaction to avoid §16(b) liability, obviously relying on *Reliance Electric*. The total shares to be sold amounted to 14.48 percent of an issuer's outstanding common stock. The parties entered into two separate sales agreements, signing and performing under the first agreement on one day and doing the same with the other agreement the next day. Partially to minimize

profits on the first sale, which would inarguably come under §16(b), the parties set the price in this sale much lower than the average price for which the stock was to be sold in both transactions. Accordingly, they set the price for the shares involved in the second sale at higher than the average price. Although, as a legal matter, neither the purchaser nor the seller had to sign the second sales agreement after the completion of the first sale, the business realities were such that both parties wanted the second sale to follow the first as planned. In the resultant §16(b) litigation, the district court refused to find that *Reliance Electric* protected the seller from disgorging profits on the second sale. After determining that the *Reliance Electric* holding "should be restricted closely to its facts," the court decided that "[t]he attempt to divide [the transaction] into two 'sales' was wholly artificial and contrived" and that there was, in substance, only one sale.

In the following case, the Court answered the question whether a person purchasing securities that put his holdings above the 10 percent level is a beneficial owner at the time of the purchase.

FOREMOST-MCKESSON, INC. v. PROVIDENT SECURITIES CO.

Supreme Court of the United States
423 U.S. 232 (1976)

Mr. Justice POWELL delivered the opinion of the Court.

This case presents an unresolved issue under §16(b) of the Securities Exchange Act of 1934 (Act). . . . [T]he question presented here is whether a person purchasing securities that put his holdings above the 10% level is a beneficial owner "at the time of the purchase" so that he must account for profits realized on a sale of those securities within six months. The United States Court of Appeals for the Ninth Circuit answered this question in the negative. We affirm.

I

Respondent, Provident Securities Co., was a personal holding company. In 1968 Provident decided tentatively to liquidate and dissolve, and it engaged an agent to find a purchaser for its assets. Petitioner, Foremost-McKesson, Inc., emerged as a potential purchaser. . . .

. . . Provident and Foremost executed a purchase agreement . . . on September 25, 1969. The agreement provided that Foremost would buy two-thirds of Provident's assets for $4.25 million in cash and $49.75 million in Foremost convertible subordinated debentures. The agreement further provided that Foremost would register under the Securities Act of 1933 $25 million in principal amount of the debentures and would participate in an underwriting agreement by which those debentures would be sold to the public. At the closing on October 15, 1969, Foremost delivered to Provident the cash and a $40 million debenture which was subsequently exchanged for two debentures in the principal amounts of $25 million and $15 million. Foremost also delivered a $2.5 million debenture to an escrow agent on the closing date. On October 20 Foremost delivered to Provident a $7.25 million debenture representing the balance of the purchase price. These debentures were immediately convertible into more than 10% of Foremost's outstanding common stock.

On October 21 Provident, Foremost, and a group of underwriters executed an underwriting agreement to be closed on October 28. The agreement provided for sale to the underwriters of the $25 million debenture. On October 24 Provident distributed the $15 million and $7.25 million debentures to its stockholders, reducing the amount of Foremost common into which the company's holdings were convertible to less than 10%. On October 28 the closing under the underwriting agreement was accomplished. Provident thereafter distributed the cash proceeds of the debenture sale to its stockholders and dissolved.

Provident's holdings in Foremost debentures as of October 20 were large enough to make it a beneficial owner of Foremost within the meaning of §16. Having acquired and disposed of these securities within six months, Provident faced the prospect of a suit by Foremost to recover any profits realized on the sale of the debenture to the underwriters. Provident therefore sued for a declaration that it was not liable to Foremost under §16(b). The District Court granted summary judgment for Provident, and the Court of Appeals affirmed. . . .

This may help . . .

Foremost-McKesson, Inc. v. Provident Securities Co. Timeline

9/25/69
Purchase of Debentures Convertible into > 10% Common

10/24/69
Distribution of Sufficient Debentures to Reduce to < 10%

10/28/69
Sale of Remaining Debentures

II

The meaning of the exemptive provision has been disputed since §16(b) was first enacted. The discussion has focused on the application of the provision to a purchase-sale sequence, the principal disagreement being whether "at the time of the purchase" means "before the purchase" or "immediately after the purchase." The difference in construction is determinative of a beneficial owner's liability in cases such as Provident's where such owner sells within six months of purchase the securities the acquisition of which made him a beneficial owner. The commentators divided immediately over which construction Congress intended, and they remain divided. The Courts of Appeals also are in disagreement over the issue. . . .

III . . .

B

The exemptive provision, which applies only to beneficial owners and not to other statutory insiders, must have been included in §16(b) for a purpose.

Although the extensive legislative history of the Act is bereft of any explicit explanation of Congress' intent, the evolution of §16(b) from its initial proposal through passage does shed significant light on the purpose of the exemptive provision. . . .

Thomas G. Corcoran, a spokesman for S. 2693's drafters, explained §[16(b)] as forbidding an insider "to carry on any short-term specu[la]tions in the stock. He cannot, with his inside information get in and out of stock within six months." Hearings on H.R. 7852 and H.R. 8720 before the House Committee on Interstate and Foreign Commerce, 73d Cong., 2d Sess., 133 (1934). The Court of Appeals concluded that §[16(b)] of S. 2693 would have applied only to a beneficial owner who had that status before a purchase-sale sequence was initiated, and we agree. Foremost appears not to contest this point. The question thus becomes whether H.R. 8720's change in the language imposing liability and its addition of the exemptive provision were intended to change S. 2693's result in a purchase-sale sequence by a beneficial owner. We think the legislative history shows no such intent. . . .

. . . [W]e hold that, in a purchase-sale sequence, a beneficial owner must account for profits only if he was a beneficial owner "before the purchase." . . .

The holding in *Foremost-McKesson* has now been incorporated into SEC Rule 16a-2(c).

■ **Think about this:**

(B) Why was Foremost suing McKesson? Doesn't it seem obvious that Foremost had consented to McKesson's transactions?

■ **And this:**

(C) If *Foremost-McKesson* had been decided before *Reliance Electric*, would the litigation in *Reliance Electric* have been necessary?

The resolution of timing issues is somewhat different for officers and directors than for beneficial owners. Section 16(b) provides that it does not "cover any transaction where [a 10 percent plus] beneficial owner was not such both at the time of the purchase and sale, or the sale and purchase," but the statute is silent on timing issues in the case of officers and directors. The SEC has filled the gap, however. Rule 16a-2(a) provides that transactions occurring before a person becomes an officer or director are not subject to §16 (except when an officer or director becomes subject to the section solely because his or her corporation has registered a class of equity securities under the Exchange Act). The story is different for transactions occurring after the termination of officer or director status. All such transactions are, under Rule 16a-2(b), subject to §16 if they can be matched, within the required six-month period, with a purchase or sale that occurred when the person was an officer or director.

E. Standing to Sue

Section 16(b) provides that a plaintiff must be the "owner of [a] security of the issuer" at the time suit is "instituted." The courts have construed this quite literally, easily finding that individuals who have purchased shares after short-swing trading has occurred have standing to sue, even if it appears that their purchases were motivated by the prospect of bringing the litigation. In Gollust v. Mendell, 501 U.S. 115 (1991), the Supreme Court also took a literal approach in deciding that a shareholder who has properly begun a §16 action can maintain it after the shareholder's stock has been exchanged for stock in the parent corporation as a result of a merger.

Time Out for PR

Why might someone acquire a share simply to bring a suit the proceeds of which will go to the issuer, rather than the shareholder bringing the suit? The answer is attorney's fees, which are regularly awarded out of the amount the defendant is required to disgorge. Thus, attorneys who peruse §16(a) filings to find §16(b) profits arrange for clients to purchase the share(s) necessary to give standing. In thinking about the propriety of this conduct, consider American Bar Association Model Rule 7.3.

Rule 7.3 Solicitation of Clients

(a) A lawyer shall not by in-person, live telephone or real-time electronic contact solicit professional employment when a significant motive for the lawyer's doing so is the lawyer's pecuniary gain, unless the person contacted:

    (1) is a lawyer; or

    (2) has a family, close personal, or prior professional relationship with the lawyer.

F. Calculation of Profits

Section 16(b) provides no guidance on how to calculate profits, and the method developed by the courts is, perhaps, less than intuitively obvious. Theoretically, there are a number of possibilities. For example, one could take a six-month period and subtract total sales prices from total purchase prices to arrive at total profits. Alternatively, one could calculate profits by matching purchases and sales by stock certificate numbers when possible and, when that technique is impossible, use the "first in-first out" approach. Courts rejected those alternatives early on, however, in favor of an approach that sharpens the teeth of §16(b).

The approach they adopted and its supporting rationale were spelled out in a 1943 Second Circuit case, Smolowe v. Delendo Corp., 136 F.2d 231, 239 (2d Cir. 1943):

> We must suppose that the statute was intended to be thoroughgoing, to squeeze all possible profits out of stock transactions, and thus to establish a standard so high as to prevent any conflict between the selfish interest of a fiduciary officer, director, or stockholder and the faithful performance of his duty. The only rule whereby all possible profits can be surely recovered is that of lowest price in, highest price out within six months. . . .

Note in the example that transactions are broken down into whatever components are necessary to effect a match that maximizes profits (share by share if necessary). For example, one purchase of 100 shares will be matched with 100 sales of one share each if that leads to the greatest profits.

Note, too, that the matches for a multi-share transaction that is broken into components can cover a period of just short of one year, not slightly less than six months. The only requirement is that, in each individual match, the purchase and sale must be within six months of each other. For example, as indicated above, in the case of a 500-share sale on July 1, 200 shares involved in the match were purchased on February 1 and 100 on November 1, even though February and November are more than six months apart.

Doing the Numbers: Section 16(b)

The following hypothetical purchases and sales illustrate how the method described above works:

January 1	100 shares purchased at $10
February 1	200 shares purchased at $10
March 1	100 shares purchased at $11
April 1	100 shares purchased at $11
May 1	100 shares purchased at $12
June 1	100 shares purchased at $12
July 1	500 shares sold at $12
August 1	200 shares sold at $10
September 1	100 shares purchased at $7
October 1	100 shares purchased at $7
November 1	100 shares purchased at $7
December 1	100 shares sold at $8

Profits are calculated by matching the highest sales price (500 shares sold at $12 on July 1) with the lowest purchase prices for a total of 500 shares (100 shares purchased on September 1, October 1, and November 1 at $7, and 200 shares purchased on February 1 at $10).

The total sales price was, then, $6,000 (500 × $12) and the total purchase price $4,100 (300 × $7 = $2,100, plus 200 × $10 = $2,000), leading to a profit of $1,900.

Once those matches are made, there are no other purchases and sales that can be matched to find a profit, and so all other transactions are ignored.

■ Think about this:

(D) Assume that Victor, a vice president of Delendo, Inc., engages in the following series of transactions. What is his §16(b) profit?

Date	Transaction
February 1	200 shares purchased at $10
April 1	50 shares sold at $20
June 1	50 shares sold at $25
August 1	50 shares purchased at $15

(E) Now assume that Victor did not attain his position until March 1. Does that change the calculation?

(F) Assume, instead, that Victor was a vice president before February 1, but resigned on July 1. Does that change the calculation?

(G) Assume that Irina is an investor who has no shares of Delendo, Inc., before engaging in the following transactions. Assume, too, that Delendo has 1 million outstanding shares. What is Irina's §16(b) profit?

Date	Transaction
February 1	50,000 shares purchased at $20
April 1	10,000 shares sold at $15
June 1	70,000 shares purchased at $25
August 1	10,000 shares sold at $30
September 1	5,000 shares sold at $15
October 1	40,000 shares purchased at $10

Test Yourself

1. Short-swing trading under §16(b) is:

a. Criminal.
b. Criminal only if it is willful.
c. Only a civil violation of the Exchange Act.
d. Not a violation of the Exchange Act.

2. Trades that must be reported under §16(a):

a. Include only trades of the equity securities of an issuer that has registered a class of equity securities under the Exchange Act.
b. Include only trades of the securities of an issuer that has registered a class of securities under the Exchange Act.
c. Include only trades of the equity securities of an issuer that has registered a class of any securities under the Exchange Act.
d. Include only trades of the securities of an issuer that has registered a class of equity securities under the Exchange Act.

3. For purposes of §16:

a. "Equity security" includes an instrument convertible into an equity security.
b. "Equity security" includes an option to acquire an equity security.
c. Both answer a and answer b are correct.
d. Neither answer a nor answer b is correct.

4. If a trade is reported under §16(a):

a. It is exempt from matching for §16(b) purposes.
b. It will result in the disgorgement of profit for §16(b) purposes.
c. It is eligible for matching under §16(b).
d. It is not necessarily eligible for matching under §16(b).

5. Quizco, Inc., owns 9 percent of the common stock of Exam Corp. The class is registered under the Exchange Act. Veronica, one of Quizco's vice presidents, sits on the board of directors of Exam Corp. Which of the following is most true?

a. Quizco does not have to file reports under §16(a).
b. Quizco does have to file reports under §16(a).
c. Whether Quizco has to file reports depends on whether Veronica owns at least 1 percent of Exam Corp.'s common stock.
d. Whether Quizco has to file reports depends on whether Veronica is representing its interests when she sits on Exam Corp.'s board.

6. On January 2, 2018, Priscilla purchased 5 percent of the shares of Hypoxico. The shares are part of a class registered under the Exchange Act. On February 1, 2018, Priscilla, who previously had no position with Hypoxico, is elected as its president. On March 1, 2018, she purchases an additional 6 percent of Hypoxico's shares. On April 1, she sells 2 percent. On May 1, she is fired. On June 1, she sells all of her remaining Hypoxico shares. Which of her transactions are subject to matching under §16(b)?

   a. All of them.
   b. None of them.
   c. All transactions after she became president of Hypoxico.
   d. All transactions while she was president of Hypoxico.

7. Which of the following best describes the rule for when a shareholder may sue under §16(b)?

   a. She must have been a shareholder at the time the transactions giving rise to §16(b) liability occurred.
   b. She must have been a shareholder at the time at least one of the transactions giving rise to §16(b) liability occurred.
   c. She must have been a shareholder at the time at least one of the transactions giving rise to §16(b) liability occurred and at the time her lawsuit is filed.
   d. She must be a shareholder at the time the lawsuit is filed.

8. Which of the following best describes the method for calculating the amount of §16(b) profit a defendant has earned within a less than six-month period?

   a. Whichever method results in the highest figure.
   b. Matching the lowest purchase price with the highest sales price until all available matches are made.
   c. Matching actual shares when possible, then matching the lowest purchase price with the highest sales price until all available matches are made.
   d. Calculating the total sales price for the period and deducting the total purchase price for the period.

Glossary

Terms printed in SMALL CAPITALS are defined elsewhere in the Glossary.

These definitions are intended to be helpful to students using this book. In some cases we omit details or technical qualifications, and in many cases further depth can be found in more technical dictionaries or encyclopedias.

1933 Act *or* '33 Act   *See* SECURITIES ACT OF 1933.

1934 Act *or* '34 Act   *See* SECURITIES AND EXCHANGE ACT OF 1934.

[1]**Accounting**   A professional discipline devoted to measuring the value and performance of business firms. Of key importance in the law of business organizations, accountants periodically produce FINANCIAL STATEMENTS for firms they serve and, in the case of publicly traded firms, they are produced for inclusion in public filings with the SECURITIES AND EXCHANGE COMMISSION.

[2]**Accounting**   A judicial remedy under which partners in GENERAL PARTNERSHIPS and some other UNINCORPORATED ENTITIES may resolve disputes among themselves related to the firm's affairs. Because the accounting is a plenary resolution of all disputes among members, it ordinarily entails a valuation of the firm and each member's interest in it.

Accounting Rule   A now disfavored and largely defunct rule under which courts once required disputes among partners, of any nature, ordinarily to be resolved only through the judicial remedy of ACCOUNTING. Because the accounting remedy is time-consuming and expensive, it often made the resolution of minor disputes prohibitive. Though the accounting rule itself has been almost universally rejected, all jurisdictions still recognize the accounting as a remedy available to partners, which often may be demanded by individual partners as of right.

Actual Authority   AUTHORITY that an AGENT reasonably believes that he or she holds based on MANIFESTATIONS of the PRINCIPAL. It has two chief distinctions from APPARENT AUTHORITY. First, it depends on the *agent's* reasonable belief of the principal's intent, based on the principal's objective manifestations (whereas apparent authority depends on the reasonable belief of the third party with whom the agent deals). Second, actually authorized actions do not in themselves violate the agent's fiduciary duty or otherwise invite legal sanction, whereas actions only apparently authorized ordinarily do breach fiduciary duty.

Adoption   An act by which a person takes on liability under a contract that otherwise would not have bound the person. By contrast to RATIFICATION, adoption is not retroactive. That is, the adopted act becomes binding on the adopter as of the day of the adoption, but legal consequences that would have been binding on the adopter arising before the date of the adoption do not bind the adopter. Strictly speaking, this is because, unlike ratification, adoption is actually the creation of a new contract as of the date of adoption. Ratification is taking on liability under existing contract terms that otherwise would not be binding.

Agency   The legal relationship between AGENT and PRINCIPAL.

Agency Cost   A loss or disappointment of expectations on the part of a person who employs someone else to perform a task. The disappointment is caused by the tendency of persons and those who perform functions for them to have differing incentives. As a common example, employees working in a restaurant or store may lack incentive to work harder or better than necessary to meet minimum expectations, and will not personally internalize any concern for the firm's performance. Another example commonly discussed in the law of business organizations is that in most larger firms, of a necessity, the investments of some pool of more or less PASSIVE INVESTORS will be under the control of a centralized management, and that management may not fully incorporate the investors' interests. For example, corporate officers may prefer more pay or perquisites, less demanding workloads, or less risky business strategies than would optimize shareholders' interests.

Agent   One who acts on behalf of another (known as the agent's principal) in the context of relationship of agency, and subject to the other's control.

ALI   *See* AMERICAN LAW INSTITUTE.

American Law Institute (ALI)   A private, not-for-profit entity founded in 1923 by William Howard Taft and other prominent legal figures, and now comprised about 4,000 judges, lawyers, and academics. The ALI exists to study, criticize, and improve American law, particularly its common law. It is best known for producing the RESTATEMENTS OF LAW, which purport to codify common law topics as best they can be synthesized on a national level. In this book we rely at some length on the Restatement (Third) of the Law of Agency. The ALI has produced a number of other works as well, including model codes to govern areas usually governed by state or federal statutory law. In this book we lay some emphasis on one such work, the AMERICAN LAW INSTITUTE PRINCIPLES OF CORPORATE GOVERNANCE.

American Law Institute Principles of Corporate Governance   A model code of corporation law, produced in part as an alternative to the widely adopted MODEL BUSINESS CORPORATION ACT, a code produced by the American Bar Association. The *Principles* have never been adopted in whole in any jurisdiction, but individual sections have been influential in specific cases.

Articles of Incorporation   The constitutive document of a corporation. In order to create the firm, the articles must be filed with the SECRETARY OF STATE or equivalent state official. They set out the firm's basic governance and capital structure, at a minimum, and can also include other provisions, including special governance rules or limitations on the firm's longevity, purposes, or powers.

Assent   Agreement to something, as in agreement to creation of an AGENCY relationship or a GENERAL PARTNERSHIP. MANIFESTATIONS of assent play a significant role in the laws of AGENCY and UNINCORPORATED ENTITIES, where creation of the relationships themselves and the creation of AUTHORITY within them depend on objectively manifested assent. Because manifestations are almost always judged objectively, they are frequently found to have been made in cases that might be contrary to a party's subjective intent. Also for this reason, and because neither agency nor general partnership requires the filing of any government formalities for their creation, those relationships can be created by accident.

Apparent Authority   AUTHORITY that a third party with whom an AGENT deals reasonably believes the agent to hold based on MANIFESTATIONS of the PRINCIPAL. It has two chief distinctions from ACTUAL AUTHORITY. First, it depends on the reasonable belief of the third party with whom an agent deals as to the principal's intent, based on the principal's objective manifestations (whereas actual authority depends on the *agent's* reasonable belief). Second, actually authorized actions do not in themselves violate the agent's fiduciary duty or otherwise invite legal sanction, whereas actions only apparently authorized ordinarily do breach fiduciary duty.

Appraisal   A remedy for SHAREHOLDERS disappointed with the consideration imposed on them in a change-in-control transaction, such as a MERGER or SHARE EXCHANGE. The appraisal remedy entitles a shareholder to a judicial valuation of the shareholder's shares, and if the result is a value higher than the consideration offered in the transaction, the shareholder is entitled to recover the difference. Jurisdictions vary as to whether appraisal rights are available to shareholders whose firm agrees to a DISPOSITION OF ASSETS. Where they are available, appraisal rights are usually the shareholder's exclusive remedy.

Authority   The power of a person to bind another person to contracts or liabilities or otherwise alter their legal relations. AGENTS, including management officials of corporations or other business entities, ordinarily have some power to bind their PRINCIPALS, partners have power to bind their PARTNERSHIPS, and members in MEMBER-MANAGED LIMITED LIABILITY COMPANIES do as well.

Balance Sheet   A FINANCIAL STATEMENT that lists all assets, liabilities, and owners' equity interests of a firm at a given time, using the equation assets = liabilities + owners' equity.

Blue Sky Law   A body of state statutory securities regulations that govern the issuance of securities within a given state. Whether or not a given securities issuance is subject to federal regulatory obligations, it must also comply with the Blue Sky law (or establish an exemption from compliance) in every state in which the securities will be marketed or sold.

Board of Directors   A body within a CORPORATION in which is vested the ultimate decision-making authority for the affairs of the company. Board members (known as DIRECTORS) must be elected by holders of voting shares, and corporations must hold at least one general shareholder meeting annually for the purpose of electing directors. The board elects and oversees the firm's officers, and it sets broad policy for the firm. Certain functions must be performed by the board, including authorization of DIVIDENDS or issuances of new stock, proposals for amendments to the ARTICLES OF INCORPORATION, and proposals for MERGER or other change in control transactions.

Bond   A DEBT SECURITY, and more specifically a secured one. The term is often used loosely to refer to both secured and unsecured debt securities, though an unsecured debt security is more properly known as a DEBENTURE.

[1]Book Value   The value of an asset as recorded on a firm's BALANCE SHEET. Because under GENERALLY ACCEPTED ACCOUNTING PRINCIPLES most assets are accounted for at their purchase price (under the so-called HISTORICAL COST rule), and because those rules also require that many assets be DEPRECIATED according to assumed rates of depreciation, an asset's book value at any given time generally will be the price a firm paid for it minus an assumed amount of depreciation.

[2]Book Value   The total value of the equity interests of a firm, as shown on its balance sheet as the difference between assets and liabilities.

Break-up Fee   A term in an agreement for a change in control transaction requiring the target firm to pay a fixed penalty if the transaction fails to be consummated. Often the penalty must be paid only if the failure is caused by specifically listed events, like the acquirer's failure to secure financing or regulatory approvals. Break-up fees are often said merely to compensate the acquiring firm for its time and expenses in pursuing a failed deal, but they often also serve other strategic purposes. Most importantly they are widely used to discourage competing HOSTILE TAKEOVER efforts by third parties while the deal is pending. Thus, one reason the break-up fee is ordinarily to be paid by the target firm is that if the deal is threatened by a competing TENDER OFFER by some third-party buyer, the obligation to pay the break-up fee would make completion of the tender offer less attractive. *Cf.* REVERSE BREAK-UP FEE.

Broker   A person or firm that buys and sells securities on behalf of clients. *Cf.* BROKER-DEALER and DEALER.

Broker-Dealer   A person or firm that buys and sells securities both on behalf of clients and on its own account. *Cf.* BROKER and DEALER.

Business Judgment Rule   A rule within the law of FIDUCIARY DUTY governing the standard of liability by which some fiduciaries are judged when accused of breaching the DUTY OF CARE. The business judgment rule applies to the conscious business decisions (as opposed to nonfeasance or failures to act) of corporate fiduciaries, including DIRECTORS, OFFICERS, and CONTROLLING SHAREHOLDERS, and is also usually held to apply to the conscious business decisions of managers within UNINCORPORATED ENTITIES. The rule is phrased in varying ways in differing jurisdictions. Generally speaking, though, when a defendant subject to the rule makes a conscious business decision, the decision does not violate the defendant's duty of care so long as it was not self-interested, was reasonably informed, and was rationally related to the best interests of the firm.

There has been academic dispute and some uncertainty in the case law over whether the business judgment rule is a substantive standard of liability or is merely a presumption or a standard of review or some other purely procedural rule. In this book we generally treat the rule as a substantive standard of liability. *Cf.* GROSS NEGLIGENCE.

Business Opportunity Doctrine   A rule of FIDUCIARY DUTY requiring that a fiduciary ordinarily may not invest in an opportunity that would be desirable to the beneficiary without first offering the opportunity to the beneficiary. Strictly speaking, the rule is a special application of the DUTY OF LOYALTY.

Buy-Back   *See* STOCK BUY-BACK.

C Corporation   A corporation taxed under Subchapter C of the Internal Revenue Code, the salient feature of which is that it imposes DOUBLE TAXATION on the corporation and its shareholders.

Call   An OPTION that entitles the holder to buy some security or commodity at a specified price on or before a specified date.

Capital   Money or other resources invested in a firm for the purpose of producing the firm's product or service.

[1]**Capitalization**   The sum of wealth invested in a firm, as measured by the total of shareholder's EQUITY (including COMMON STOCK, PREFERRED STOCK, and RETAINED EARNINGS) and long-term debt. (Long-term debt is included because the money borrowed or the resources purchased with it represent a part of the firm's ongoing stock of working resources.) "Capitalization" should not be confused with MARKET CAPITALIZATION.

[2]**Capitalization**   In ACCOUNTING, treating the purchase price of something as creating an asset rather than an expense. "Capitalization" should not be confused with MARKET CAPITALIZATION.

Capital Appreciation   An increase in value of any asset. Capital appreciation can be entirely passive, without the investor taking action to make the asset more valuable, simply because supply and demand conditions for it change. Investors can generate capital appreciation much more actively, however, as by working to grow a business and make it profitable. Capital appreciation will ordinarily not be captured in the FINANCIAL STATEMENTS generated in ACCOUNTING, because they ordinarily record the value of assets at their HISTORICAL COST and subject them to assumed DEPRECIATION, and also because they do not reflect the value of a firm's GOODWILL.

Capital Structure   The mix of different kinds of investments made in a firm. In general terms, a firm's capital structure will be some combination of DEBT and EQUITY. Since debt is generally more risky from the firm's perspective—because it contractually obligates the firm to repay principal and interest whether or not the firm is earning sufficient revenue to cover it—a firm with more debt vis-à-vis equity is usually said to be more risky than a firm with less.

***Caremark* Duty**   *See* DUTY TO MONITOR.

Cash Flow Statement   A standard FINANCIAL STATEMENT that summarizes cash receipts and payments for the relevant period. An important purpose of the cash flow statement is to estimate a firm's short-term viability and credit-worthiness, as it reflects the firm's ability to pay its obligations as they come due.

CEO   *See* CHIEF EXECUTIVE OFFICER.

Certificate of Incorporation   *See* ARTICLES OF INCORPORATION.

CFO   *See* CHIEF FINANCIAL OFFICER.

Charter   *See* ARTICLES OF INCORPORATION.

Chief Executive Officer (CEO)   Generally, the highest-ranking executive within a business. Most large corporations appoint at least one officer with this title, and occasionally firms have two or more such persons, typically identifying them as "co-CEOs."

Chief Financial Officer (CFO)   A firm's highest-ranking officer with primarily financial responsibilities. The duties assigned to the CFO are typically broad, and usually include management of the firm's financial planning, financial risk, and financial recordkeeping.

Closely Held Corporation   A corporation that is not PUBLICLY TRADED. As with the latter term, closely held corporation has no precise definition and is not a legal term of art. Generally speaking, it implies a firm with a small number of shareholders and no ready market for its shares. A chief feature of close corporations is that because their shares tend to be highly illiquid, and because corporation statutes do not permit unilateral dissolution by shareholders or other tools for forced liquidity, minority shareholders face substantial risk of OPPRESSION.

Common Stock   Corporate EQUITY STOCK typically having rights to vote in BOARD OF DIRECTORS elections and other matters on which shareholders are entitled to vote, but enjoying no preference for dividends or payment on dissolution. *Cf.* PREFERRED STOCK.

Conflict of Interest   A situation in which one owes a duty to one party that conflicts either with one's own personal interests or with one's countervailing duties to another party. For example, it is a conflict of interest for a corporate FIDUCIARY to cause the corporation to enter into a transaction in which the fiduciary also has a personal pecuniary interest, as for example when the fiduciary agrees to sell his or her own property to the corporation. Likewise, it is a conflict of interest for the fiduciary to act on behalf of the corporation in a transaction in which the fiduciary also owes fiduciary duties to an opposing party in the transaction, as might occur when an officer of one corporation negotiates the purchase of property from another corporation on whose board of directors the officer also sits. Action under conflict of interest is not necessarily a breach of duty, but may subject a fiduciary to risk of liability for breach of the DUTY OF LOYALTY.

Consolidation   A MERGER following which both merging firms will cease their independent existence, and will continue as a wholly new firm combining the assets of both. *Cf.* TRUE MERGER.

Controlling Shareholder   A person who, usually by virtue of owning either a statistical majority of a corporation's voting shares or a large minority of them along with other indicia of influence, controls the corporation, generally because of the ability to elect its BOARD OF DIRECTORS. The chief legal consequence of being held a controlling shareholder is that persons of that description owe certain fiduciary duties to their corporations.

Corporate Seal   A physical device by which documents may be stamped with an official symbol indicating that they are authentic. The seal is often entrusted to the corporate SECRETARY, an officer who by custom holds authority to attest to the authenticity of corporate documents. The significance of the seal largely has been abolished.

Corporation   As used in this book, a private, for-profit entity formed under the corporation statute of a given state.

Corporation by Estoppel   An equitable doctrine under which courts may recognize the existence of a corporation that has not been properly formed in order to protect the interests of one or more persons who have changed position in reliance on the belief in corporate existence. The doctrine may be applied in a variety of contexts.

Corporation De Facto   An equitable doctrine under which courts may recognize the existence of a corporation and protect its shareholders with limited liability even though at the time they incurred liability, the corporation had not come into existence. Courts are likely to apply the doctrine only where the failure to incorporate was inadvertent and the PROMOTERS believed it had properly been formed.

Crown Jewels   A TAKEOVER DEFENSE under which a target corporation agrees to sell some valuable asset at a loss to a third party, in the event that a takeover proponent acquires some stated percentage of the firm's stock.

Cumulative Voting   A system of shareholder voting meant to assist minority shareholders in securing representation on their boards of directors. In a cumulative voting system, shareholders may apportion the total number of votes they would be entitled to cast for all open board seats to fewer than all races. As a practical example, imagine you own 100 shares of voting stock in a corporation, and that five vacancies on the board are slated for election at the annual shareholders' meeting. Under either cumulative or traditional, non-cumulative voting, you will be entitled to cast a total of 500 votes—one vote per share in each race. But under the two systems you can apportion them differently. Under traditional voting, you could only cast one vote per share for each vacancy—and so, you could cast 100 votes in each race. But under cumulative voting, you could apportion all of the total votes to which you are entitled to one race, casting 500 total votes for one candidate, or 250 votes each for two candidates, or any other combination you choose.

Deadlock   A situation in which the voting members of some decision-making body within a business entity are evenly split. Since decision usually requires at least a simple majority, an evenly divided body cannot make decisions. This can happen in corporations with even-numbered boards of directors or boards in which only an even number of seats are currently filled, and it can happen among shareholders when opposing factions hold equal numbers of shares. (As a practical matter, a shareholder deadlock can only happen in CLOSELY HELD firms.)

Dealer   A firm that buys and sells securities on its own account. *Cf.* BROKER and BROKER-DEALER.

Debenture   An unsecured DEBT SECURITY. *Cf.* BOND.

Debt   An amount the repayment of which is owed or due. The concept typically is used in opposition to EQUITY. *Cf.* DEBT SECURITY.

Debt Security   A SECURITY that represents a loan of money from the investor to the ISSUER, which must be repaid, usually with interest, within a specified time period. Unlike an EQUITY security, debt securities do not represent any ownership interest in the firm and generally confer no governance rights on the investor. Variations are many. Two major categories are BONDS, which (with the exception of federal government bonds) ordinarily are secured by collateral, and DEBENTURES, which are not.

De Facto Corporation   See CORPORATION DE FACTO.

Delaware Court of Chancery   One of the two major trial court systems of the state of Delaware. Because Delaware is one of the few American states to have preserved the distinction between law and equity, it maintains two separate trial court systems. Most corporate law matters in Delaware are within the purview of the Court of Chancery.

[1]**Depreciation**   A decline in the value of an asset.

[2]**Depreciation**   In ACCOUNTING, an assumed (and often artificial) rate by which the value of an asset will be reduced each year on a firm's FINANCIAL STATEMENTS.

Derivative   A contract that derives its value from the value of some other asset. For example, an OPTION is a simple derivative instrument. An option is a contract giving its buyer the right to purchase some asset from the seller of the option, at a specified price, on or before a particular date. The value of the option to both its buyer and seller depends on the value of the underlying security—if the value of the security goes above the specified purchase price during the relevant period, then the option pays off for the buyer but not the seller, and vice versa. Derivative investments are often explained as HEDGING devices, in that they can be used by an investor to offset the risk of some corresponding investment. For example, an airline must purchase large amounts of jet fuel and is exposed to risk because of changing fuel prices. The firm might hedge against that risk by entering into derivative contracts under which the airline will receive a specified payment if the price of jet fuel exceeds a certain amount. To that extent, derivatives often resemble simple insurance contracts. However, derivatives serve other purposes, including sheer speculation.

Director   A member of a corporation's BOARD OF DIRECTORS.

Disposition of Assets   A change-in-control transaction in which one firm agrees to sell all or substantially all of its assets to another firm or buyer. Jurisdictions vary as to whether shareholders in the selling firm are entitled to voting and appraisal rights (as they would be in other change-in-control transactions having the same substantive consequences, like MERGER or SHARE EXCHANGE).

Dissociation   Under many UNINCORPORATED ENTITY statutes, an act causing the separation of one member from the firm, an event that typically ends the member's ability to bind the firm to liabilities and, in GENERAL PARTNERSHIPS, ends the partner's risk of most firm liabilities going forward. Dissociation itself is to be distinguished from DISSOLUTION, which is the formal end of the business as a going entity and requires WINDING DOWN of its affairs and liquidation of its assets. Whether dissociation triggers dissolution depends on the circumstances of the dissociation and also varies by statute. For example, many LIMITED LIABILITY COMPANY statutes contain HOTEL CALIFORNIA provisions, providing that voluntary dissociation does not cause dissolution.

Dissolution   In many UNINCORPORATED ENTITY statutes, a special concept specifically distinguished from DISSOCIATION. In those statutes, dissociation is merely an act that separates a member from the firm, and it may or may not trigger dissolution. When events triggering dissolution do occur, the firm must then discontinue operations as a going entity, WIND DOWN its affairs, and liquidate its assets.

Distribution   Any distribution of cash or property to a corporation's shareholders. Distributions of retained earning also are known as DIVIDENDS. Noncash DIVIDENDS are often known as IN-KIND DIVIDENDS.

Diversification of Risk   The spreading of one's investments in relatively small amounts across many different investment opportunities, the risks of which are not closely correlated, rather than investing large amounts in a few opportunities. Where the individual investment's risks are not correlated—that is, they will not all likely fail at the same time, as might be the case if all the investments are in the same industry—then the damage from failure of any one investment is minimized.

Dividend   A distribution of cash to a corporation's shareholders representing a sharing of profits. *Cf.* DISTRIBUTION.

Division of Labor   The breaking down of some task into sub-tasks, which is generally thought to make the performance of the overall task better or more efficient.

***Donahue-Wilkes* Duty**   A fiduciary duty that some jurisdictions impose on shareholders of CLOSELY HELD CORPORATIONS. The duty is owed by each shareholder to all others (by contrast to the traditional corporate fiduciary duties, owed only by OFFICERS, DIRECTORS, and CONTROLLING SHAREHOLDERS, and owed by them only to the corporation itself). The duty was most famously recognized by the courts of Massachusetts in Donahue v. Rodd Electrotype Co.

of New England, Inc., 328 N.E.2d 505 (Mass. 1975), and Wilkes v. Springside Nursing Home, Inc., 353 N.E.2d 657 (Mass. 1976).

Double Taxation The tax imposed on corporations taxed under Subchapter C of the Internal Revenue Code, under which the corporation must first pay income tax on its earnings, like any individual taxpayer. Then, any distribution of profit to shareholders is taxed again to the shareholders who receive it. Each dollar of profit earned by such a corporation is therefore taxed twice, to the extent that it is distributed to shareholders.

Duty of Care One of the two traditional FIDUCIARY DUTIES (the other being the DUTY OF LOYALTY), the duty of care requires a fiduciary to exercise some degree of skill, diligence, and prudence in the performance of tasks on behalf of the beneficiary. Corporate fiduciaries and managers of UNINCORPORATED ENTITIES owe the duty of care, but, insofar as prudence is concerned, their liability under it is usually judged under the deferential BUSINESS JUDGMENT RULE.

Duty of Disclosure A FIDUCIARY DUTY sometimes described as existing independently of the traditional DUTY OF CARE and DUTY OF LOYALTY, the duty of disclosure would require a fiduciary to provide the beneficiary with certain facts under appropriate circumstances. This book takes the view that the duty of disclosure is better thought of not as a freestanding, independent duty, but a reflection of the duties of care and loyalty, depending on the facts. For example, where a fiduciary acts under CONFLICT OF INTEREST, the duty of loyalty will require the fiduciary to disclose to the beneficiary the fact of the conflict and any facts material to the transaction in question. But if there is no conflict of interest, the fiduciary will owe obligations to disclose only where it would violate the duty of care to fail to do so.

Duty of Loyalty One of the two traditional FIDUCIARY DUTIES (the other being the DUTY OF CARE), the duty of loyalty provides that where a fiduciary acts under CONFLICT OF INTEREST the underlying transaction can be challenged and set aside, sometimes under special rules like the BUSINESS OPPORTUNITY DOCTRINE, depending on the circumstances, but often under the more generic INTRINSIC FAIRNESS TEST.

Duty to Monitor A FIDUCIARY DUTY of corporate directors to establish systems of information reporting to detect internal wrongdoing where failure to do so would be so grotesque as to violate their obligation of GOOD FAITH. The duty was recognized in In re Caremark International Inc. Derivative Litigation, 698 A.2d 959 (Del. Ch. 1996), and it is frequently known as the *Caremark* duty, though it was significantly elaborated in later Delaware Supreme Court authority. Boards had long had an obligation to investigate risks of wrongdoing wherever "red flags" appeared to indicate they might exist, but *Caremark* added that such a duty could exist in some circumstances even without a red flag. Specifically, if harm befell a company from internal wrongdoing that the board failed to discover through some "utter," "sustained and systematic failure to exercise oversight," then it could constitute a breach of the directors' duties. This standard received a significant theoretical elaboration in Stone v. Ritter, 911 A.2d 362 (Del. 2006). *Stone* held that a failure to monitor would be actionable only if it constituted a breach of the obligation of good faith as defined in In re The Walt Disney Co. Derivative Litigation, 906 A.2d 27 (Del. 2006). *Disney* held that action in bad faith is conduct intentionally harmful to the company or an intentional dereliction or conscious disregard of one's responsibilities. In addition to holding that a failure to monitor must meet this standard to be actionable, *Stone* established that, in Delaware, good faith is not an independent fiduciary duty separate from the DUTY OF CARE and DUTY OF LOYALTY, but is simply a component of the duty of loyalty.

Edwards-Gingrich Loophole   A common strategy for tax-avoidance that seems to explain the otherwise unlikely ubiquity of the S Corporation. Because Medicare and Medicaid taxes are calculated on the total of employee salaries, businesses in which equity owners (like lawyers or other professionals) would ordinarily receive large distributions of salary are formed as S CORPORATIONS that pay the principals minimal salary and distribute the rest of the firm's profits as dividends. The dividends are taxable, but only single-taxed, since the firm is an S Corporation, and the minimization of salary reduces Medicare and Medicaid taxes.

Entire Fairness Test   *see* INTRINSIC FAIRNESS TEST.

[1]**Equity** The value of one's ownership in a firm or other asset.

[2]**Equity** An ownership interest in a firm, such as a share of STOCK in a corporation, a partnership interest in a GENERAL PARTNERSHIP, or a membership in a LIMITED LIABILITY COMPANY.

Exchange   *see* SECURITIES EXCHANGE.

Exculpatory Clause   In corporation law, the phrase usually refers to a provision in the ARTICLES OF INCORPORATION excusing directors for monetary liability for breaches of the DUTY OF CARE. In many jurisdictions they are authorized by statute, as in the widely adopted Delaware General Corporation Law §102(b)(7) and the very similar MODEL BUSINESS CORPORATION ACT §2.02(b)(4). Under such laws directors still face injunctive liability for all fiduciary breaches and full monetary liability for acts in bad faith or in breach of the DUTY OF LOYALTY. Exculpatory clauses also are known as "RAINCOAT PROVISIONS."

Expense   The cost of carrying out a firm's ongoing major activities.

Fair Accounting Standards Board (FASB)   A private, non-profit entity established by the U.S. accounting profession to develop standards for proper accounting. Specifically, FASB develops and maintains GENERALLY ACCEPTED ACCOUNTING STANDARDS, which the SECURITIES AND EXCHANGE COMMISSION requires be used in preparing FINANCIAL STATEMENTS filed under the federal securities laws.

Fiduciary   A person who has both the power and the obligation to act on behalf of another and who therefore owes FIDUCIARY DUTIES. All AGENTS are fiduciaries with respect to their PRINCIPALS.

Fiduciary Duty   A legal obligation owed by a FIDUCIARY by reason of that status. Various classes of persons throughout American law may owe fiduciary duties. Within the law of business organizations, fiduciaries include AGENTS, PARTNERS, general partners in LIMITED PARTNERSHIPS, members in MEMBER-MANAGED LIMITED LIABILITY COMPANIES, managers in MANAGER-MANAGED LIMITED LIABILITY COMPANIES, and, in some jurisdictions, shareholders in CLOSELY HELD CORPORATIONS (where the *DONAHUE-WILKES* DUTY or its equivalent is recognized). It is often said that the common law traditionally recognized two main fiduciary duties, the DUTY OF CARE and DUTY OF LOYALTY. In recent decades courts have identified specific applications in particular contexts, including, in the HOSTILE TAKEOVER context, the *UNOCAL* DUTY and the *REVLON* DUTY.

Fiduciary Out Clause   A term in an agreement for a change-in-control transaction permitting the target corporation to rescind its recommendation to shareholders to approve the transaction. Usually the change in recommendation is permitted only if the target receives a superior offer or if some other intervening event causes the board to believe the deal is no longer in the firm's best interests. The clause is called a "fiduciary out" clause because it is said to be needed for the target board to comply with its fiduciary obligation to secure the best acquisition price for the firm's shareholders. There is uncertainty, however, whether any limits on the target board's freedom to change recommendation are enforceable in light of the board's fiduciary obligation to shareholders, particularly where the REVLON DUTY has attached.

Financial Statement   Documents periodically produced by accountants to measure the value and performance of firms. The basic financial statements are the BALANCE SHEET, the INCOME STATEMENT, and the CASH FLOW STATEMENT.

Firm   A business entity. In this book we follow the convention of business and economists and use "firm" broadly to mean any business entity, rather than the habit of lawyers to use "firm" to refer only to "law firms."

Front-Loaded Tender Offer   A TWO-TIERED TENDER OFFER in which the consideration to be paid shareholders in the initial tender offer phase is more desirable (often much more so) than that to be paid when the remaining minority is merged out in the second, merger phase. The goal is to pressure shareholders into selling in the initial phase, perhaps at a lower price than they might otherwise demand.

General Counsel   A company's chief legal officer. In large corporations the general counsel is ordinarily an employee of the corporation and holds the office of vice president or equivalent status. Not uncommonly, smaller corporations engage outside counsel and employ them as general counsel, directing to them oversight of the company's legal affairs.

General Partnership   An association of two or more persons to carry on as co-owners a business for profit that has not been formed under a statute conferring some other status. Its chief attributes are that, by default statutory rules, each member has full, unlimited personal liability for the firm's debts, equal say in management, and an equal share in the firm's profits and losses.

Generally Accepted Accounting Principles (GAAP)   A set of rules maintained by the FAIR ACCOUNTING STANDARDS BOARD that govern ACCOUNTING and the preparation of FINANCIAL STATEMENTS.

Golden Parachute   A term in an employment contract providing for liquidated damages on the employee's termination. To describe such a term as a "golden" parachute usually connotes that the benefits to be paid are very generous, and generally such terms are reserved for high-ranking officers. Can be used as a TAKEOVER DEFENSE.

Good Faith   In general terms, "good faith" is a loosely defined concept used in many areas of law, and connotes action without bad intentions. While the term is frequently used in business entity law, and is frequently said to be an obligation of corporate and other business entity fiduciaries, it is often used without clear definition and in many jurisdictions it has no clear meaning or limits. That said, the concept has a number of significant specific consequences because, among other things, action in bad faith cannot enjoy the protection of the BUSINESS JUDGMENT RULE, a fiduciary's liability for it cannot be INDEMNIFIED, and corporate fiduciaries cannot be shielded for acts in bad faith under EXCULPATORY CLAUSES. Moreover, the courts of one jurisdiction—Delaware—have struggled to clarify the concept. In In re The Walt Disney Co. Derivative Litigation, 906 A.2d 27 (Del. 2006), the court held that action in bad faith can constitute either action with the deliberate intent to harm the beneficiary or intentional dereliction or conscious disregard of one's responsibilities. Mere negligent inaction is not enough, even where it might constitute a breach of the DUTY OF CARE. Another decision, Stone v. Ritter, 911 A.2d 362 (Del. 2006), clarified that in Delaware, good faith is not an independent fiduciary duty separate from the duty of care and DUTY OF LOYALTY. It is simply a component of the duty of loyalty.

Goodwill   The value of a firm as a going entity over and above the liquidation value of its assets; the amount a purchaser of the firm would pay in excess of the value of the firm's assets. Goodwill reflects the firm's expectation of future revenues.

Go-Shop Clause   A term in an agreement for a change-in-control transaction permitting the target firm to seek superior offers from third parties during a specified period. The usual rationale is to ensure that target firm shareholders receive an adequate price. *Cf.* NO-SHOP CLAUSE.

Greenmail   A coercive strategy under which the greenmailer acquires a significant minority percentage of a company's stock and threatens to take control in order to pressure the company to repurchase the stock at a premium price.

Gross Negligence   In Delaware law, the standard of liability under which a corporate fiduciary can be found to have breached the DUTY OF CARE.

Hedge   To make one investment that offsets the risk of another. Hedging can be accomplished simply through DIVERSIFICATION. By investing in different companies in different industries and different circumstances—which reduces the risk that the different investments would rise or fall together—the risk of any one of the investments failing will be offset by the likelihood that most of the rest will succeed. Hedging can also be accomplished with DERIVATIVES. For example, say you buy 10 shares of stock in XYZ, Inc. at $5 per share. You might be concerned about the risk of the trading price of the stock falling too low. You could hedge against that risk by buying a PUT OPTION from another investor, giving you the right to sell that investor your 10 shares within a given period at a price of $3. You might still lose money, but the put option avoids loss of your entire investment during the specified period.

Hedge Fund   A fund that employs a proprietary strategy for investing pooled capital. Hedge funds generally require very large investments from each participant, and require the investments to be kept in the fund for a specified period. They are designed to avoid most regulation; as part of that strategy their investors must satisfy certain wealth and/or sophistication tests. The name is a historical accident, since today most hedge funds are not primarily concerned with HEDGING against risk (the original hedge funds were focused on hedging risk).

Historical Cost   The price at which an asset was acquired. In ACCOUNTING, assets are ordinarily accounted for at their historical cost on FINANCIAL STATE-MENTS, and are then DEPRECIATED according to assumed rates. This "historical cost rule" is sometimes artificial, in that it may report a relatively low value for an asset that has in fact appreciated.

Hostile Takeover   A change-in-control transaction effected over the opposition of the target company's board of directors. As a practical matter, a hostile takeover generally takes the form of a TENDER OFFER because, unlike the other possible change-in-control transactions—the MERGER, the SHARE EXCHANGE, or the DISPOSITION OF ASSETS—a tender offer does not require acquiescence of the target firm's board.

Hotel California Provision   A provision in a state LIMITED LIABILITY COM-PANY STATUTE providing that voluntary withdrawal does not cause DISSOCIA-TION or DISSOLUTION. The practical effect is that a member may leave the firm and no longer participate in its affairs, but the member also has no means to force a withdrawal of his or her investment in the firm. The name alludes to the lyrics of the famous song: one can check out, but never leave.

Income Statement   A FINANCIAL STATEMENT reporting the revenues, expenses and profits or losses of a business firm for a given period. Unlike the BALANCE SHEET, the income statement is a moving picture of the firm's financial state over time.

Incorporation   The act of causing a corporation to come in to being. In most jurisdictions, incorporation is accomplished simply by delivering the ARTICLES OF INCORPORATION to the SECRETARY OF STATE for filing.

Incorporator   A person who causes ARTICLES OF INCORPORATION to be filed on behalf of a corporation.

Indemnification   Reimbursement by one person of expenses incurred by another. Agents enjoy certain rights of indemnification as a matter of agency law and corporate officers and directors and the managers of UNINCORPO-RATED ENTITIES enjoy some mandatory indemnification rights as well.

Indenture   *See* TRUST INDENTURE.

Indenture Trustee   The party appointed to act as trustee administering the TRUST INDENTURE governing an issuance of DEBT SECURITIES. The trustee must be appointed by the issuer and is required to represent the interests of the investors. The trustee is typically a commercial bank or trust company. The trustee's appointment is ordinarily required in most public debt issuances by the Trust Indenture Act of 1939.

Index Fund   A mutual fund with a portfolio designed to match the performance of some stock market index. An "index" is simply some set of stocks or other securities chosen as representative of the market or some part of it, like the familiar Dow Jones Industrial Average or the S&P 500.

Initial Public Offering (IPO)   A company's first sale of SECURITIES to the public. An IPO can be of EQUITY or DEBT securities. IPO transactions are heavily regulated and expensive affairs, and generally are administered with the aid of an INVESTMENT BANK acting as UNDERWRITER.

In-Kind Dividend   A pro rata distribution of profits to shareholders in the form of anything of value, other than cash. In principle the property distributed could be anything, but often it will consist of the firm's own stock or the securities of some other firm. *Cf.* DISTRIBUTION.

Insolvency   Often defined as either the inability to pay debts as they come due or the state in which the firm's assets are worth less than its liabilities. Insolvency is colloquially known as "being in the red" (as opposed to "being in the black," both references to the one-time accounting practice of writing positive values in black and negative ones in red).

Inspector of Election   A person appointed to administer voting at corporate shareholder meetings. The inspector need not be an officer of the corporation or otherwise affiliated with it, and can be a third party hired for the purpose. The inspector plays certain key statutory roles, including determining the shares entitled to vote and resolving disputes over the validity of proxies.

Institutional Investor   An investor that is a firm rather than an individual, and typically a financially sophisticated firm, like a bank, investment firm, MUTUAL FUND, insurance company, or pension fund.

Interest   A payment required of a borrower, over and above repayment of the PRINCIPAL amount, to compensate the lender for use of its funds. Interest on debt sometimes is calculated at a fixed rate, but it need not be. For example, interest is sometimes paid as a percentage of profits, up to some specified total.

Intrinsic Fairness Test   The standard of liability under which fiduciaries are ordinarily judged when they have acted under CONFLICT OF INTEREST, and accordingly are challenged for breach of the DUTY OF LOYALTY. In some circumstances a more specialized test such as the BUSINESS OPPORTUNITY DOCTRINE will apply.

Investment Advisor   A person or firm that makes investment recommendations for a fee, whether through direct investment management or publications. Unless exempt, investment advisors are subject to the Investment Advisors Act of 1940, which requires registration with the SECURITIES AND EXCHANGE COMMISSION and compliance with certain other requirements.

Investment Bank   A financial firm that assists in funding and executing financial transactions. Among their major functions is acting as UNDERWRITER for PUBLIC OFFERINGS of EQUITY and DEBT SECURITIES. They also act as financial advisors to corporate clients in MERGERS and other major transactions, and many of them serve as BROKERS to institutional clients. Most investment banks also have proprietary trading operations in which the firm trades in securities on its own account, earning its return on its trading profits.

Investment Company   A company that (in exchange for its shares) pools the funds of large numbers of investors and invests them collectively. Though there are other categories, the most familiar kind of investment company is the MUTUAL FUND. Investment companies are ordinarily regulated by the SECURITIES AND EXCHANGE COMMISSION under the Investment Company Act of 1940.

Investment Contract   One of the many terms contained in the statutory definitions of "security" in both the SECURITIES ACT OF 1933 and the SECURITIES AND EXCHANGE ACT OF 1934, which courts have treated as something of a catch-all. Under the leading construction of the term, it is a scheme pursuant to which "a person invests his money in a common enterprise and is led to expect profits solely from the efforts of the promoter or a third party. . . ." SEC v. W. J. Howey Co, 328 U.S. 293, 299 (1946).

IPO   *see* INITIAL PUBLIC OFFERING.

Issuer   A firm that issues a SECURITY.

Joint Venture   An endeavor in which two separate firms cooperate. The term is not a legal term of art and it has no precise meaning, although it is often used to refer to a general partnership formed for a specific, limited-term purpose. Typically, a joint venture is formed either by the contribution of resources by both firms subject to agreement governing rights and management, which creates a GENERAL PARTNERSHIP, or by the creation of a new, freestanding entity jointly owned by the members.

Leverage   The degree to which a firm has financed its operations with debt. A firm that has borrowed more to fund itself is said to be more heavily leveraged. Leverage poses strategic issues for both borrowers and investors. On the one hand, borrowing is riskier to the borrower than taking EQUITY investments. In the former, the borrower must repay PRINCIPAL and INTEREST timely or face legal liability, regardless whether the borrower is earning sufficient revenue to cover those obligations.

In the latter, the firm ordinarily has no obligation to distribute profits or make other payments, and so takes no risk of obligations to its owners in times when there are insufficient revenues. But on the other hand, from the borrower's perspective, leverage has advantages. First, payments of interest are tax-deductible to the borrower, whereas distributions of profit to equity investors are not. Second, leverage can make investments highly profitable to the borrower. Say you invest $100 of your own money in an investment, with a return of $10. The return on your investment would be 10 percent. But if you can borrow $90 of the required $100 at an interest rate of 5 percent ($4.50), then the $5.50 you keep represents a return of 55 percent.

Limited Liability   Protection for equity owners in a limited liability entity, such as a CORPORATION, a LIMITED LIABILITY COMPANY, a LIMITED LIABILITY PARTNERSHIP, or the like, from personal liability for the firm's own obligations. In practical effect limited liability means that if the firm becomes insolvent or is unable to satisfy claims against it, its creditors cannot then execute their claims against the firm's owners.

Limited Liability Company   An entity formed under a state limited liability company statute. Its chief attributes are that members enjoy LIMITED LIABILITY, the firm can enjoy PASS-THROUGH TAXATION, and its governance rules generally can be tailored as the participants desire.

Limited Liability Limited Partnership   A LIMITED PARTNERSHIP formed under a statute that permits a LIMITED LIABILITY election, under which even the firm's general partners enjoy limited liability.

Limited Liability Partnership   A GENERAL PARTNERSHIP formed under a statute that permits a LIMITED LIABILITY election, under which the partners enjoy complete or (in some states) partial limited liability.

Limited Partnership   A firm created under a state limited partnership statute. Its chief attribute is that it consists of two classes of partners, whose roles and liability differ. First, there must be at least one general partner. The default rule is that the general partners hold managerial power for the firm, but, unless the LIMITED LIABILITY LIMITED PARTNERSHIP form is available, also have full UNLIMITED LIABILITY for the partnership's obligations. Second, there can be any number of limited partners. The limited partners enjoy LIMITED LIABILITY, though historically they were required to avoid interference in management to preserve that privilege.

Liquidity   The ease with which the value of an asset can be extracted from it and spent. Cash is the most liquid of all assets, as it can always be spent for its full value immediately.

Lock-up Clause   A loose term connoting any sort of clause in an agreement for a change-in-control transaction requiring some penalty to dissuade the target firm from abandoning the deal. Lock-up clauses may include a BREAK-UP FEE, a CROWN JEWELS clause, or a STOCK OPTION pursuant to which the disappointed buyer may purchase target-firm stock at a discount.

Manager-Managed Limited Liability Company   A LIMITED LIABILITY COMPANY in which the members have elected not to manage the firm themselves, and rather to appoint managers (who may or may not themselves be members) to manage the firm. The chief consequence is that, unlike the case of a MEMBER-MANAGED LIMITED LIABILITY COMPANY, the members have no fiduciary duties to the firm and lack authority to bind it.

Manifestation   In the law of AGENCY and some UNINCORPORATED ENTITIES, an outward indication of one's intent. Usually manifestations may be written, spoken, or non-verbal.

Market   In economics, the collection of possible buyers and sellers for some good or service. Markets are thought to have essentially self-regulatory properties, in that when they are healthy and properly functioning, they tend to push price downward and require efficient production of the sellers' output.

Market Capitalization   The total dollar value of a firm's outstanding shares. In publicly traded firms, market capitalization can be calculated by multiplying the firm's total outstanding shares by their current trading price.

Market Maker   A BROKER-DEALER that holds itself out as available to buy and sell large quantities of a given SECURITY at specified prices. Market makers are essential to the operation of SECURITIES markets, as they provide the liquidity essential to active trading. Market makers earn a return on the activity by maintaining a small difference or "spread" between the price at which they are willing to buy and the price at which they are willing to sell the security.

Master Limited Partnership (MLP)   A LIMITED PARTNERSHIP that is publicly traded on a SECURITIES EXCHANGE. As a practical matter, MLPs operate in certain narrow lines of business (mostly involving mineral exploration) because except in those areas federal tax laws treat any publicly traded limited partnership as an entity subject to DOUBLE TAXATION.

Member-Managed Limited Liability Company   A LIMITED LIABILITY COMPANY that the members have chosen to manage themselves. The chief consequence is that, unlike the case of a MANAGER-MANAGED LIMITED LIABILITY COMPANY, the members owe fiduciary duties to the firm and they have authority to bind it.

Merger   A change-in-control transaction, authorized by statute, in which two firms are combined into one. Merger usually requires approval of both the BOARD OF DIRECTORS and SHAREHOLDERS of the target firm, the approval of the board of directors of the acquiring firm, and often the approval of the shareholders of the acquiring firm as well. The legal consequence of merger is that the firms cease separate legal existence, and that the assets and liabilities of the acquired firm become those of the acquiring firm. *See* CONSOLIDATION; TRUE MERGER.

Model Business Corporation Act   A model statute produced by the American Bar Association's Section of Business Law and adopted by a majority of the states. The Act was first promulgated in 1950 and has been revised many times. The last major substantive revision was in 1984, and that code, with its many, rather less ambitious refinements since, generally is still known as the Revised Model Business Corporation Act.

Model Rules of Professional Conduct   A model code of professional conduct for lawyers, produced by the American Bar Association and now substantially followed by most states. In this book, all materials concerning ethical conduct in business contexts are keyed to these Model Rules.

Mutual Fund   An entity that, in exchange for its shares, pools investors' funds for reinvestment in other securities. Mutual funds are administered by professional investment managers.

No-Shop Clause   A term in an agreement for a change-in-control transaction prohibiting the target firm from soliciting other bids for purchase of the company.

Officer   An employee of a corporation with relatively high managerial responsibility. Officers commonly include the CHIEF EXECUTIVE OFFICER, PRESIDENT, CHIEF FINANCIAL OFFICER, TREASURER, and SECRETARY, but may include any number of other high-ranking employees with a range of responsibilities.

Oppression   Conduct within a closely held firm in which a controlling shareholder or group denies a minority shareholder or group access to financial returns from the company and participation in management. Oppression takes its force from the fact that minority shareholders in closely held firms will by definition have highly illiquid stock. Since corporate shareholders have no default right of unilateral dissolution or other means to force a cashing-out of their investment, they will be dependent on the controlling group for access to any return on that investment.

Option   A contract under which one party may buy a SECURITY from the other at a specified price, typically within some specified time period.

Outstanding Shares   Shares of STOCK that have been issued by a corporation and that it has not reacquired or redeemed.

Over-the-Counter (OTC) Security   A security traded in some manner other than on a formal SECURITIES EXCHANGE. Frequently, OTC securities are traded through networks of DEALERS.

Pac Man Defense   A TAKEOVER DEFENSE in which a target firm facing a HOSTILE TAKEOVER attempts to acquire the takeover proponent instead.

Partnership   *See* GENERAL PARTNERSHIP. Note that while the term "partnership" often colloquially stands for "general partnership," several other business entities are also forms of partnership, including the LIMITED PARTNERSHIP, the LIMITED LIABILITY PARTNERSHIP, and the LIMITED LIABILITY LIMITED PARTNERSHIP.

Passive Investor   An investor who takes no role in a firm's management. Corporate shareholders are frequently passive, especially in PUBLICLY TRADED companies, though they need not be. LIMITED PARTNERS are at least nominally passive, and members in MANAGER-MANAGED LIMITED LIABILITY COMPANIES are passive.

Piercing the Corporate Veil   An equitable doctrine under which a court may permit a corporation's creditors to execute their claims against the personal assets of the company's shareholders or other controlling figures.

Poison Pill   Any of a range of TAKEOVER DEFENSES in which the acquisition by a person of some specified number of a firm's shares will trigger some legal consequence making the target firm much more expensive or difficult to buy. For example, a corporation might adopt a plan under which if any person acquires 20 percent of its outstanding stock, the firm would repurchase some substantial number of the remaining outstanding shares either at a high price or in exchange for debt securities paying a high rate of interest. The effect would be to decrease the value of the firm to the acquiring party. Variations are many, and poison pills range from relatively simple plans to extremely complex ones.

Preferred Stock   Corporate EQUITY STOCK typically having no voting rights, but enjoying a preference to receive some fixed amount of dividends before any dividends are paid to holders of COMMON STOCK. Preferred stock also often enjoys a preference to receive a fixed payment on dissolution before common stock holders receive any.

Pre-Incorporation Liability   Liability incurred by a PROMOTER purporting to act on behalf of a corporation before it has come into existence. Because LIMITED LIABILITY does not attach until a corporation is formed, actions by PROMOTERS are their own actions, though they may purportedly be on behalf of the firm. Moreover, where two or more promoters act on behalf of the same firm (in which case they are often known as co-promoters), they frequently are jointly and severally liable for all obligations incurred by any of them.

President   A high-ranking officer who may or may not be a firm's CHIEF EXECUTIVE OFFICER. In some firms one person holds both titles; in other firms there may be a CEO and a president.

¹**Principal**   A party to an AGENCY relationship upon whose behalf the other (known as the AGENT) acts, subject to the principal's control.

²**Principal**   The base amount that is borrowed by a borrower from a lender, and which must be repaid, not including any INTEREST.

Private Placement   An issuance of securities designed to qualify for an exemption from registration under the SECURITIES ACT OF 1933 by reason of the relative wealth, sophistication, and/or access to information of the investors.

Profit   For accounting purposes, the difference between a firm's REVENUE and its EXPENSES. Profit can be defined in different ways and in particular it is defined very differently by economists, but in any context, it connotes the firm's overall revenue minus some measure of its costs.

Promoter   A person who acts on behalf of a business firm before it has been formally organized.

Prospectus   Although for purposes of the federal securities law the term has a highly specialized meaning, in common parlance it generally refers to a formal document describing the attributes of a SECURITY to be issued and its issuer. Unless an issuance of securities is exempt from the SECURITIES ACT OF 1933, the issuer must file a prospectus with the SECURITIES AND EXCHANGE

COMMISSION and make a copy available to those persons to whom the security is marketed or sold.

Proxy   The term can have different meanings, and is used differently under different corporation statutes, but it relates to situations in which the owner of a voting corporate security authorizes another person to cast that share's vote. Typically, the term means the document by which a shareholder authorizes another to cast their vote, but it may also refer to the person to whom the authorization is given.

Proxy Regulation   Rules under the Securities Exchange Act of 1934 governing PROXY SOLICITATIONS to shareholders in PUBLICLY TRADED firms. Where the proxy rules apply, the person making the solicitation must make a filing in advance with the SECURITIES AND EXCHANGE COMMISSION and must comply with certain disclosure requirements.

Proxy Solicitation   This is a term that is the subject of both case law and specific regulations of the SECURITIES AND EXCHANGE COMMISSION, but generally may be used to describe any communication directed to a corporate shareholder requesting the shareholder's PROXY.

Publicly Traded Corporation   Like CLOSELY HELD CORPORATION, this term is not a legal term of art and has no precise definition. Generally speaking, a firm is publicly held where it has issued a large number of shares to a large number of passive investors not otherwise involved in the company, and where there is some ready, reasonably liquid market for SECONDARY TRADING in its shares.

Put   An OPTION that permits the purchaser to sell a SECURITY or some other underlying asset at a specified price on or before a given date. The purpose of a put option is usually to HEDGE against falling prices in the underlying asset.

Raincoat Provision   *See* EXCULPATORY CLAUSE.

[1]**Ratification**   An act by which a person or firm makes itself subject to a liability purportedly made on its behalf, but which would not otherwise be binding. Unlike ADOPTION, ratification is retroactive.

[2]**Ratification**   A vote of approval of an already binding liability. For example, a corporate officer might execute a contract with a third party as to which the officer has sufficient authority to bind the firm, but nevertheless submit it to a vote of ratification by the company's BOARD OF DIRECTORS or SHAREHOLDERS. The purpose of this sort of ratification is generally to alleviate concerns that the person who incurred the liability has violated a FIDUCIARY DUTY.

Registration Statement   A filing made by a securities-issuing firm with the SECURITIES AND EXCHANGE COMMISSION under the SECURITIES ACT OF 1933. Although issuers also register classes of securities under the SECURITIES AND EXCHANGE ACT OF 1934, the filing is not usually referred to as a registration statement.

Restatement of Law   Any one of a series of codifications of common law doctrine promulgated by the AMERICAN LAW INSTITUTE. In this book we rely at some length on the Restatement (Third) of the Law of Agency.

Retained Earnings   PROFIT accumulated by a firm over time and not yet distributed to owners. Retained earnings may be held in the form of cash or other liquid investments, or they may be reinvested in the firm's operations.

Reverse Break-up Fee   A term in a change in control agreement similar to a BREAK-UP FEE, except that the penalty is to be paid by the acquiring firm rather than the target.

Reverse Stock Split   An act by which a corporation causes the number of its OUTSTANDING SHARES to be proportionally reduced. The split ostensibly affects shareholders equally, so, for example, in a 2-to-1 split, every shareholder's holdings of the company's stock are cut exactly in half. Because the split affects every shareholder equally, it should have no effect on any shareholder's percentage voting rights or the total value of any shareholder's shares. The split does, however, increase the trading price of the stock, since there are fewer shares in number even though the company has the same value. One purpose of a reverse stock split is to raise the price of a stock that is thought to have fallen too low. This may have very practical consequences, since many INSTITUTIONAL INVESTORS have rules against investing in stock whose price is too low, and STOCK EXCHANGE listing requirements may mandate a minimum price. *Cf.* STOCK SPLIT. Another objective may be to force minority shareholders to accept cash in exchange for their shares, if the split ratio is set so as to preclude the minority holders from receiving entire shares.

Revenue   The total amount earned by a firm in a given period for its major, ongoing activities, without deducting EXPENSES. *cf.* PROFIT.

Revised Uniform Limited Partnership Act (RULPA)   A model code promulgated by the UNIFORM LAW COMMISSION to govern LIMITED PARTNERSHIPS. ULC had issued a prior statute in 1916 that was widely adopted, but since its promulgation in 1976, RULPA has replaced its predecessor in many states. ULC also issued a substantial revision to RULPA in 2001, but it has not been widely followed.

Revised Uniform Partnership Act   A model code promulgated by the UNIFORM LAW COMMISSION to govern GENERAL PARTNERSHIPS. The revised Act, first issued in 1992 and substantially revised in 1997, replaced the original UNIFORM PARTNERSHIP ACT of 1914 and has now been adopted in a majority of states.

***Revlon* Duty**   A fiduciary duty of outside directors triggered in some cases of HOSTILE TAKEOVER or other change-in-control transaction, first recognized in Revlon Inc. v. MacAndrews & Forbes Holdings, Inc., 506 A.2d 173 (Del. 1985). Without suggesting that there are definite parameters, it is fair to say that the duty is triggered where break-up of the company or a substantial change in the nature of control of the company is imminent (as for example where a publicly traded company is to be acquired by a party that will become its controlling shareholder). Where the duty is triggered, it requires the outside directors to cease efforts to thwart takeover or otherwise preserve their control over the long-term policy of the firm, and instead seek to auction the company to the highest bidder. *Cf. UNOCAL* DUTY.

S Corporation   A corporation taxed under Subchapter S of the Internal Revenue Code. Unlike the C CORPORATION, an S Corporation is subject only to single and not DOUBLE TAXATION.

Seal   *see* CORPORATE SEAL.

Secondary Trading   Sales of securities not from the issuer to an initial buyer but between a shareholder and subsequent, third-party buyers. For example, most trading on SECURITIES EXCHANGES is secondary trading.

Secretary   A corporate officer whose primary duties traditionally included authenticating official company documents and registration and recordkeeping concerning shareholders. Today corporate secretaries also typically undertake significant legal and regulatory compliance duties.

Secretary of State   A state government official in most states who oversees an agency typically known as the department of state. The secretary of state plays a role in business organization law, as most business entities must be formed by the filing of documents with the department of state in the state of formation.

Securities Act of 1933   15 U.S.C. §§77a-77aa. A statute adopted in 1933 to require that in all nonexempt issuances of securities, the issuer provide certain minimal information concerning the security to the persons to whom the securities are marketed or sold.

Securities and Exchange Act of 1934   15 U.S.C. §§78a-78pp. A statute adopted in 1934 to create the SECURITIES AND EXCHANGE COMMISSION and provide a panoply of regulations relating primarily to secondary market trading and/or the issuers and holders of securities subject to such trading. *Cf.* SECONDARY TRADING.

Securities and Exchange Commission (SEC)   A federal agency created by the SECURITIES AND EXCHANGE ACT OF 1934 and charged with administering that statute, the SECURITIES ACT OF 1933, and several other statutes.

Securities Exchange   Although this is a term with a specialized definition which, when satisfied, requires registration with the SECURITIES AND EXCHANGE COMMISSION, it generally is used to refer to a place or system pursuant to which shares are actively traded, or to an organization formed for the purpose of maintaining such a place or system.

Security   An instrument representing an investment in a business firm or other endeavor. Colloquially the term connotes at a minimum any corporate STOCK or DEBT SECURITY, but many other instruments might qualify. Within the federal law of securities regulation under the SECURITIES ACT OF 1933 and the SECURITIES AND EXCHANGE ACT OF 1934, the term is defined very broadly, and can include virtually any scheme pursuant to which a person invests money expecting a return to be generated primarily by the efforts of others.

Share   One unit of EQUITY in a business firm. Although a share could include a unit of corporate STOCK, a membership interest in a LIMITED LIABILITY

COMPANY, or an ownership unit in a GENERAL PARTNERSHIP, the term most often is used in the corporate context.

Share Exchange   A change-in-control transaction in which, following approval by the target corporation's board and shareholders, all shares in the target corporation are acquired in exchange for consideration paid by the acquiring corporation, which may consist of cash, securities, or some other thing of value. Following the transaction, the target firm continues as the acquiring firm's wholly owned subsidiary.

Shareholder   A person who owns a share or shares of corporate STOCK.

Shark Repellant   A TAKEOVER DEFENSE.

Short Sale   A sale of a SECURITY that the seller does not actually own, but rather has borrowed, with the expectation that the price of the security will go down. If it does, the short seller will then be able to procure shares on the market at the lower price to return them to the party that originally leant the shares. The result is a profit—the difference between the higher price at which the short seller originally sold the borrowed shares and the lower price at which he later buys replacement shares. Of course, there is also the risk that the price will go up in the interim, causing the short seller a loss. Also, the lender of the original shares, which usually will be the short seller's broker or some other institution, usually charges a fee for the service.

Sole Proprietorship   A business firm owned entirely by one person, as to which no steps have been taken to incorporate or organize in any other form.

Stock   An EQUITY security issued by a corporation.

Stock Buy-Back   A repurchase by a corporation of its own OUTSTANDING SHARES from SHAREHOLDERS who currently own them. Because a stock buy-back that is proportional across all shareholders does not affect any shareholder's percentage voting rights, the only practical effect of such a buy-back is to distribute profits to shareholders. And indeed, stock buy-backs are generally treated in the law like DIVIDENDS. For example, as with dividends, a stock buy-back cannot be performed if it would cause the firm to become insolvent.

Stockholder   *See* SHAREHOLDER.

Stock Option   *See* OPTION.

Stock Split   An issuance of new stock to existing shareholders in proportion to their current holdings. The effect is simply to increase the number of OUT-STANDING SHARES. It has no effect on the total value of a current shareholder's interest or on their percentage voting power. The usual purpose of a stock split is to reduce the trading price of stock that is thought to have risen too high, to make it seem more affordable. *Cf.* REVERSE STOCK SPLIT.

Takeover   The acquisition of a controlling interest in one firm by another firm or investor. Generally, "takeover" connotes HOSTILE TAKEOVER, and therefore a TENDER OFFER.

Takeover Defense   Any maneuver by which a company makes itself less vulnerable to HOSTILE TAKEOVER. *See* CROWN JEWELS; PAC MAN DEFENSE; POISON PILL; WHITE KNIGHT.

Target Company   The firm to be acquired in a change-in-control transaction, such as a MERGER, SHARE EXCHANGE, or TENDER OFFER.

Tender Offer   Although this term has a specific legal meaning, it generally refers to an offer on the open market to purchase shares of a publicly traded firm, usually at a premium, with the goal of acquiring a controlling percentage of its voting stock. Because the offer is made directly to the shareholders, there is no need for acquiescence by the target firm's board, and for this reason the term tender offer is largely synonymous with HOSTILE TAKEOVER. In that respect it differs from all other change-in-control transactions, which essentially always require cooperation of the target firm's board.

Treasurer   A corporate officer, typically acting as or reporting to the CHIEF FINANCIAL OFFICER, who runs a corporation's treasury department. In effect, the treasurer is a financial risk manager, with responsibility to ensure that the corporation has sufficient liquid assets with which to pay its obligations as they come due.

True Merger   A MERGER following which one of the merging firms (usually referred to as the "target firm" or "acquired firm") will cease to have independent existence. The other firm (the "acquiring firm") will continue as the survivor. *Cf.* CONSOLIDATION.

Trust Indenture   A special subsidiary agreement required in most public issuances of DEBT SECURITIES, under which the issuer appoints a third-party INDENTURE TRUSTEE to act as a fiduciary who represents the interests of the investors. Trust indentures are governed by the Trust Indenture Act of 1939, and generally are required when debt securities are publicly issued.

Two-Tier Taxation   *see* DOUBLE TAXATION.

Two-Tier Tender Offer   A TENDER OFFER in which acquisition of the target firm's shares will occur in two phases. Strictly speaking, the second phase is ordinarily not a tender offer at all. Rather, the acquirer will secure a majority of the company's voting stock in the first phase, and then in the second phase use that voting majority to approve a merger of the target firm into the acquiring firm. The terms of the merger may require the remaining minority shareholders to accept cash or other consideration in exchange for their shares. *Cf.* FRONT-LOADED TENDER OFFER.

Underwriter   Colloquially, a firm, which ordinarily is an investment bank, that manages a PUBLIC OFFERING of some SECURITY on behalf of the issuer, which is the underwriter's client. There is also a much more specialized meaning under the federal securities laws.

Uniform Law Commission (ULC)   Formerly known as the National Conference of Commissioners on Uniform State Laws, the ULC is a non-profit association formed in 1892 to produce model codes to improve and harmonize state law. It is comprised of commissioners formally appointed by each state government.

Uniform Limited Liability Company Act (ULLCA)   A model code promulgated by the UNIFORM LAW COMMISSION to govern LIMITED LIABILITY COMPANIES. ULLCA was first adopted in 1995 and substantially revised in 2006. It has not yet been widely adopted, presumably because of its promulgation subsequent to the adoption of LLC-enabling legislation by all 50 states.

Uniform Partnership Act   A model code promulgated by the UNIFORM LAW COMMISSION (then known as the National Conference of Commissioners on Uniform State Laws) in 1914, to govern GENERAL PARTNERSHIPS. In its day it was adopted by every state but Louisiana, but it has been superseded by the REVISED UNIFORM PARTNERSHIP ACT of 1997 in a majority of states.

Unincorporated Entity   A business entity that is not incorporated under a state corporation statute. Unincorporated entities include GENERAL PARTNERSHIPS, LIMITED PARTNERSHIPS, LIMITED LIABILITY PARTNERSHIPS, LIMITED LIABILITY LIMITED PARTNERSHIPS, and LIMITED LIABILITY COMPANIES.

Unlimited Liability   The legal status under which a participant in a firm bears personal responsibility for the firm's debts. In practical effect, if the firm becomes insolvent or is unable to pay claims against it, creditors may then execute their claims against the personal assets of a participant with unlimited liability. Unlimited liability has become comparatively unusual in American law, because it is now so easily avoided without adverse tax consequences or loss of managerial participation by LIMITED LIABILITY participants.

Unocal Duty   A FIDUCIARY DUTY of outside directors in cases of threatened HOSTILE TAKEOVER, first recognized in Unocal Corp. v. Mesa Petroleum Co., 493 A.2d 946 (Del. 1985). In effect, wherever a corporation takes any step meant to thwart hostile takeover, an outside director must be able to demonstrate that it was based on reasonable investigation into threat to corporate policy and effectiveness, and must be reasonably balanced in relation to the threat posed. *Cf.* REVLON DUTY.

Watered Stock   Stock for which the agreed-upon consideration is invalid or has not been paid by the purchaser of the stock. If a corporation becomes insolvent or unable to pay claims against it, and its stock is watered, creditors may execute their claims against shareholders who have not paid full and valid consideration, up to the amount of the unpaid consideration.

White Knight   A TAKEOVER DEFENSE in which the target firm in a HOSTILE TAKEOVER engages some third-party firm to acquire it, as a buyer preferable to the takeover proponent.

Williams Act   A statute adopted in 1969 as an amendment to the SECURITIES AND EXCHANGE ACT OF 1934 and now appearing as provisions of 15 U.S.C. §§78m, 78n. Among other things, the Williams Act requires that when any person seeks to acquire more than 5 percent of a class of securities registered under the '34 Act by TENDER OFFER, the person must make certain filings with the SECURITIES AND EXCHANGE COMMISSION, and must make disclosures to target firm shareholders.

Winding Down　　A process required following DISSOLUTION of a firm, in which its business affairs are ended, its assets liquidated, liabilities resolved, and any residue distributed to the EQUITY owners. The term "winding up" sometimes is used to refer to the same process.

Table of Cases

Principal cases are italicized.

Index